D1258071

FEMINIST JURISPRUDENCE
CASES AND MATERIALS

Fourth Edition

▪ ▪ ▪

By

Cynthia Grant Bowman
Dorothea S. Clarke Professor of Law
Cornell Law School

Laura A. Rosenbury
Professor of Law
Washington University Law School

Deborah Tuerkheimer
Professor of Law
DePaul University College of Law

Kimberly A. Yuracko
Professor of Law
Northwestern University School of Law

AMERICAN CASEBOOK SERIES®

WEST®
A Thomson Reuters business

Mat #41029307

610 Opperman Drive
St. Paul, MN 55123
1–800–313–9378

Printed in the United States of America

ISBN: 978–0–314–26463–3

To Ben, Michael, and David
from C.G.B.

To Nalini and Michele
from L.R.

To Max and Leo
from D.T.

To Michael and Sacha
from K.Y.

Preface to the Fourth Edition

The first edition of this book was the product of the collaboration of three women—Mary Becker, Cynthia Grant Bowman, and N. Morrison Torrey—who taught law and were committed to the participation of women as genuine equals in our society, in our educational, legal and political institutions, in the world of work, and in the family. We included a variety of materials, drawn both from standard legal sources, like cases and statutes, and from less typical sources from other disciplines, in order to raise central questions about the progress women have made toward these goals, the destinations that might be desirable, and the routes from here to there. Our goal was also to introduce the reader to the world of current feminist scholarship and activism. The presentation was thus grounded in feminism, although one pervasive theme was that there are many types of feminism, which may often lead to different conclusions on important issues. We also sought to include the perspectives of women of different races, classes, and sexual orientations, while knowing that our capacity to realize this goal was necessarily limited. We nonetheless endeavored to include readings from multiple perspectives and to raise questions from a variety of viewpoints.

Since publication of the first edition, there have been many new developments in the law concerning issues of vital importance to women. Writing on feminism and feminist topics has flourished, including new work in areas such as critical race feminism, queer theory, and post-modern feminist theory. This fourth edition continues the commitments of the original book but attempts to do much more. We continue to present a diversity of feminist perspectives on issues affecting women's lives and to broaden our presentation of those perspectives by being both more multicultural and international than the previous editions. As a result, new depth has been added to the many questions of gender and equality discussed throughout the book. Viewing them from many differing perspectives, we gain opportunities for insights that were less accessible in prior editions. Our goal remains the same: to invite controversy and discussion about all of the issues and perspectives included and to lead us all to a more profound and inclusive understanding of the conditions of equality.

This new edition marks the retirement of two authors, Mary Becker and Victoria Nourse, and the addition of two new authors, who bring to it their substantial expertise in the areas of women and violence (Deborah Tuerkheimer) and of feminist theory and family law (Laura Rosenbury); their new insights inform the pages that follow.

For research and other assistance on this new edition, Cynthia Grant Bowman thanks Gina Jackson, her assistant, Natanya DeWeese, her research assistant, and Jean Callihan and Amy Emerson at the Cornell Law School

Library. Laura Rosenbury is grateful to Susan Appleton, Adrienne Davis, Tracy Higgins, Martha Minow, and Marc Spindelman, as well as to research assistants Caitlin Argyros, Elizabeth Chen, Chelsea Duncan, Shay Hinton, Jane Louise Moore–Maley, and Krysten Skogstad. Deborah Tuerkheimer is grateful to her research assistants, Amanda Graham, Stella Kestell, Alex Lubyansky, Elizabeth Lyons, and Justin Whitesides, as well as Lawrence Arendt, Walter Baumann, and Jody Raphael at DePaul University College of Law. Kimberly Yuracko thanks Michael Sobczak, her assistant, Libby Weiss, her research assistant, and Marcia Lehr, her library liaison.

Research support was provided to Cynthia Grant Bowman by Cornell Law School; to Laura Rosenbury by Washington University School of Law; to Deborah Tuerkheimer by DePaul University College of Law; and to Kimberly Yuracko from the Northwestern University School of Law Summer Faculty Research Program.

Finally, for purposes of clarity, the reader should know that citations, footnotes, concurring and dissenting opinions have been omitted from the cases and other materials included in this book without specifically noting that omissions have been made; footnotes remaining in excerpted materials retain their original numbers. Any footnotes added by the authors of this book are indicated by the use of small-case letters.

CYNTHIA GRANT BOWMAN
LAURA A. ROSENBURY
DEBORAH TUERKHEIMER
KIMBERLY A. YURACKO

July 2010

Copyright Acknowledgements and Reprint Permissions

We gratefully acknowledge the following authors and publishers who have allowed us to reprint excerpts from copyrighted materials:

Chapter 2:

Excerpts from "Conservative Free Speech and the Uneasy Case for Judicial Review" by Mary Becker, Copyright © 1993 by University of Colorado Law Review. Reprinted with permission of the University of Colorado Law Review and of the author.

Chapter 3:

Excerpts from "Consciousness Raising" by Catharine A. MacKinnon reprinted by permission from TOWARD A FEMINIST THEORY OF THE STATE by Catharine A. MacKinnon, Cambridge, Mass.: Harvard University Press, Copyright © 1989 by Catharine A. MacKinnon.

Excerpts from IN A DIFFERENT VOICE: PSYCHOLOGICAL THEORY AND WOMEN'S DEVELOPMENT by Carol Gilligan, pp. 25–29, Cambridge, Mass.: Harvard University Press, Copyright © 1982, 1993 by Carol Gilligan. Reprinted by permission of Harvard University Press and of the author.

Excerpts from Zillah Eisenstein, "Constructing a Theory of Capitalist Patriarchy and Socialist Feminism," originally published in Critical Sociology, Volume 25, Number 2/3, pp. 196–217 (1999). Copyright © 1999 by Sage Publications Ltd. Reprinted with permission of Sage Publications Ltd. and of the author.

Excerpts from "No Male or Female" by Mary Anne Case reprinted by permission from TRANSCENDING THE BOUNDARIES OF LAW: GENERATIONS OF FEMINISM AND LEGAL THEORY, edited by Martha Albertson Fineman. Copyright © 2010 by Routledge–Cavendish. Reproduced by permission of Routledge–Cavendish/Taylor & Francis Books UK and of the author.

Exerpts from "Sex Inequality" by Catharine A. MacKinnon reprinted by permission from SEXUAL HARASSMENT OF WORKING WOMEN by Catharine A. MacKinnon, Copyright © 1979 by Yale University, reprinted by permission of Yale University Press.

Excerpts from "Sexuality" by Catharine A. MacKinnon reprinted by permission from FEMINISM UNMODIFIED: DISCOURSES ON LIFE AND LAW by Catharine A. MacKinnon, Cambridge, Mass.: Harvard University Press, Copyright © 1987 by the President and Fellows of Harvard College.

Excerpts from "Difference and Dominance" by Catharine A. MacKinnon reprinted by permission from FEMINISM UNMODIFIED: DISCOURSES ON LIFE AND LAW by Catharine A. MacKinnon, Cambridge, Mass.: Harvard University Press, Copyright © 1987 by the President and Fellows of Harvard College.

Excerpts from "The Problem of Marxism and Feminism" by Catharine A. MacKinnon reprinted by permission from TOWARD A FEMINIST THEORY OF THE STATE by Catharine A. MacKinnon, Cambridge, Mass.: Harvard University Press, Copyright © 1989 by Catharine A. MacKinnon.

Excerpts from "The Difference in Women's Hedonic Lives: A Phenomenological Critique of Feminist Legal Theory" by Robin L. West, Copyright © 1987 by Wisconsin Women's Law Journal. Reproduced with permission of Wisconsin Women's Law Journal and of the author.

Excerpts from CARING FOR JUSTICE by Robin L. West, Copyright © 1997, 1999 by New York University Press. Reprinted with permission of New York University Press and of the author.

Excerpts from "Towards a Substantive Feminism" by Mary Becker. Copyright © 1999 by the University of Chicago. Reproduced with permission of the University of Chicago Legal Forum and of the author.

Excerpts from "Feminist Jurisprudence: Grounding the Theories" by Patricia A. Cain, Copyright © 1989 by The Regents of the University of California. Reprinted from the Berkeley Women's Law Journal Vol. 4, No. 2, pp: 191, 201–03, 205–07, 209, 210, 212–14 by permission of the Regents of the University of California and of the author.

Excerpts from Trina Grillo, "Anti–Essentialism and Intersectionality: Tools to Dismantle the Master's House," Copyright © 1995 by The Regents of the University of California. Reprinted from the Berkeley Women's Law Journal, Vol. 10, No. 1, pp: 17–22, 24–30 by permission of the Regents of the University of California and of Stephanie Wildman as representative of Catherine Grillo, Trustee of the Estate of Trina Grillo.

Excerpts from "Las Olvidadas—Gendered In Justice/Gendered Injustice: Latinas, Fronteras and The Law" by Berta Esperanza Hernandez–Truyol, Copyright © 1998 by University of Iowa Law School Journal of Gender, Race, & Justice. Reprinted by permission of University of Iowa Law School Journal of Gender, Race, & Justice and of the author.

Excerpts from "We The People: Jurisprudence In Color" from WHERE IS YOUR BODY? by Mari J. Matsuda. Copyright © 1996 by Mari J. Matsuda. Reprinted by permission of Beacon Press, Boston and of the author.

Excerpts from "A Postmodern Feminist Legal Manifesto (An Unfinished Draft)" by Mary Joe Frug, Copyright © 1992 by Harvard Law Review. Reprinted by permission of Harvard Law Review and of Gerald Frug, as representative of the Estate of Mary Joe Frug.

Excerpts from " 'By Reason of Their Sex': Feminist Theory, Postmodernism, and Justice" by Tracy E. Higgins, Copyright © 1995 by Cornell Law Review. Reprinted by permission of Cornell Law Review and of the author.

Excerpts from "Refashioning the Unfashionable: Claiming Lesbian Identities in the Legal Context" by Diana Majury in Canadian Journal of Women & Law, Vol. 7, Copyright © 1994 University of Toronto Press Incorporated. Reprinted by permission of University of Toronto Press Incorporated (www.utpjournals.com) and of the author.

Excerpts from SPLIT DECISIONS: HOW AND WHY TO TAKE A BREAK FROM FEMINISM by Janet Halley, published by Princeton University Press, Copyright © 2006 by Janet Halley. Reprinted by permission of the author.

Excerpts from Margaret Jane Radin, "The Pragmatist and the Feminist," in Southern California Law Review, Vol. 63. Copyright © 1990 Southern California Law Review. Reprinted with the permission of Southern California Law Review and of the author.

Chapter 4:

Excerpts from "Rape" by Susan Estrich, Copyright © 1986 by Yale University, reprinted with permission of The Yale Law Journal Company, Inc., from *The Yale Law Journal*, Vol. 95, pp. 1087, and of the author.

Excerpts from "Demarginalizing the Intersection of Race and Sex: A Black Feminist Critique of Antidiscrimination Doctrine, Feminist Theory and Antiracist Politics" by Kimberlé Crenshaw, Copyright © 1989 by the University of Chicago, reprinted with permission of the University of Chicago Legal Forum and of the author.

Excerpts from BATTERED WOMEN AS SURVIVORS: AN ALTERNATIVE TO TREATING LEARNED HELPLESSNESS by Edward W. Gondolf with Ellen R. Fisher, Copyright © 1988 by Lexington Books, reprinted with permission of Edward W. Gondolf and of Rowman & Littlefield Publishing Group.

Excerpts from "Domestic Violence: Differentation Among Different Types of Intimate Partner Violence: Research Update and Implications for Interventions" by Joan B. Kelly and Michael P. Johnson. Originally published in Family Court Review, Copyright © 2008 by John Wiley & Sons, reprinted with permission of John Wiley & Sons and of the authors.

Excerpts from "Domestic Violence: The Case for Aggressive Prosecution" by Donna Wills, reprinted with permission of the author. Originally published in UCLA Women's Law Journal, Copyright © 1997, by The Regents of the University of California.

Excerpts from "Killing Her Softly: Intimate Abuse and the Violence of State Intervention" by Linda G. Mills, Professor, Social Work, Public Policy, and Law, New York University, Copyright © 1999 by The Harvard Law Review Association, reprinted with permission of the Harvard Law Review and of the author.

Excerpts from "Rape, Resurrection, and the Quest for Truth: The Law and Science of Rape Trauma Syndrome in Constitutional Balance with the Rights of the Accused" by Kathryn M. Davis, Copyright © 1998 Hastings Law

Review, reprinted with permission of O'Brien Center for Scholarly Publications, University of California, Hastings College of the Law, and of the author.

Excerpts from "The Protection Racket: Rape Trauma Syndrome, Psychiatric Labeling, and Law" by Susan Stefan, Copyright © 1994 by Northwestern University School of Law, *Northwestern University Law Review*, reprinted with permission of the Northwestern University Law Review.

Excerpts from "Prostitution: A Contemporary Form of Slavery" by Dorchen Leidholdt, Copyright © 1998 by Dorchen Leidholdt, reprinted with permission of the author.

Excerpts from THE INDUSTRIAL VAGINA: THE POLITICAL ECONOMY OF THE SEX TRADE by Sheila Jeffreys, Routledge/Taylor & Francis Group, LLC, Copyright © 2009 Sheila Jeffreys, reprinted with permission of the author.

Excerpts from "The Feminist Debate over Prostitution Reform: Prostitutes' Rights Groups, Radical Feminists and the (Im)possibility of Consent" by Jody Freeman, Copyright © 1990 by The Regents of the University of California, reprinted from the Berkeley Women's Law Journal Vol. 5, pp: 75–79, 81–88, 90, 92–94, 102, 105–08 (1989–90) with permission of the Regents of the University of California and the author.

Excerpts from "Sex Trafficking and Criminalization: In Defense of Feminist Abolitionism" by Michelle Madden Dempsey, to be published in 2010 by the University of Pennsylvania Law Review, reprinted with permission of the author.

Excerpts from "From the International to the Local in Feminist Legal Responses to Rape, Prostitution/Sex Work, and Sex Trafficking: Four Studies in Contemporary Governance Feminism" by Janet Halley, Prabha Kotiswaran, Hila Shamir & Chantal Thomas, Copyright © 2006 Harvard Journal of Law and Gender, reprinted with permission of the Harvard Journal of Law and Gender and of Chantal Thomas.

Excerpts from "Francis Biddle's Sister: Pornography, Civil Rights, and Speech" by Catharine A. MacKinnon, reprinted by permission from FEMINISM UNMODIFIED: DISCOURSES ON LIFE AND LAW by Catharine A. MacKinnon, Cambridge, Mass.: Harvard University Press, Copyright © 1987 by the President and Fellows of Harvard College.

Excerpts from "Cruel to be Hard: Men and Pornography" by Robert Jensen, Copyright © 2004 by Civic Research Insitutute, Sexual Assault Report, Vol. 7, No. 3, www.civicresearchinstitute.com/sar.html, reprinted with permission of the Civic Research Institute and of the author.

Excerpts from "Pornography and Civil Rights: A New Day for Women's Equality" reprinted by permission from ORGANIZING AGAINST PORNOGRAPHY, 1988. ©1988 by Catharine MacKinnon and Andrea Dworkin.

Excerpts from "All Porn All the Time" by Amy Adler, Copyright © 2007 by New York University Review of Law & Social Change, reprinted with permission of the New York University Review of Law & Social Change and of the author.

Excerpts from Feminism and Pornography in the Twenty–First Century: The Internet's Impact on the Feminist Pornography Debate" by Courtney W. Daum, Copyright © 2009 by Women's Rights Law Reporter, reprinted with permission of Women's Rights Law Reporter and of the author.

Chapter 5:

Excerpts from THE MORAL PROPERTY OF WOMEN (Revised Edition 2002) by Linda Gordon, Copyright © 1974, 1976, 1990, 2002 by Linda Gordon, reprinted by permission of the author.

Excerpts from ABORTION AND WOMAN'S CHOICE: THE STATE, SEXUALITY, AND REPRODUCTIVE FREEDOM (Revised Edition) by Rosalind Pollack Petchesky, Copyright ©1984, 1990 by Northeastern University Press, reprinted with the permission of the University Press of New England and of the author.

Excerpts from Judith Jarvis Thomson, A DEFENSE OF ABORTION. Copyright © 1971 by Princeton University Press. Reprinted by permission of Princeton University Press.

Excerpts from FEMINISM WITHOUT ILLUSIONS: A CRITIQUE OF INDIVIDUALISM by Elizabeth Fox–Genovese. Copyright © 1991 by The University of North Carolina Press. Used by permission of the publisher, www.uncpress.unc.edu.

Excerpts from ABORTION AND THE POLITICS OF MOTHERHOOD by Kristin Luker, Copyright © 1984 by the Regents of the University of California, reprinted with the permission of the University of California Press and of the author.

Excerpts from "The Creation of Fetal Rights: Conflicts with Women's Constitutional Rights to Liberty, Privacy, and Equal Protection" by Dawn E. Johnsen, Copyright © 1991 by The Yale Law Journal Company, Inc., reprinted by permission of the Yale Law Journal Company from The Yale Law Journal, Vol. 95, pages 599–625, and of the author.

Excerpts from "Punishing Drug Addicts Who Have Babies: Women of Color, Equality, and the Right of Privacy" by Dorothy E. Roberts, Copyright © 1991 by the Harvard Law Review Association. Reprinted by permission of the Harvard Law Review Association from *The Harvard Law Review*, Vol. 104, pages 1419–1481, and of the author.

Chapter 6:

Excerpts from BEYOND (STRAIGHT AND GAY) MARRIAGE: VALUING ALL FAMILIES UNDER THE LAW by Nancy Polikoff, Copyright © 2008 by Beacon Press. Reprinted by permission of Beacon Press and of the author.

Excerpts from THE SEXUAL CONTRACT by Carole Pateman, published by Stanford University Press, Copyright © Carole Pateman. All rights reserved. Used with the permission of Stanford University Press (www.sup.org) and of the author.

Excerpts from JUSTICE, GENDER, AND THE FAMILY by Susan Moller Okin, Copyright © 1989 Basic Books/Perseus Books Group. Reprinted by permission of Basic Books/Perseus Books Group.

Excerpts from MARRIAGE, SEXUALITY, AND GENDER by Robin West, Copyright © 2007 Paradigm Publishers. Reprinted by permission of Paradigm Publishers and of the author.

Excerpts from THE NEUTERED MOTHER, THE SEXUAL FAMILY AND OTHER TWENTIETH CENTURY TRAGEDIES by Martha Albertson Fineman, Copyright © 1995 by Martha Albertson Fineman, reproduced by permission of Routledge/Taylor & Francis Group, LLC and of the author.

Excerpts from "Legal Treatment of Cohabitation in the United States" by Cynthia Grant Bowman, Copyright © 2004 by John Wiley and Sons, reprinted with permission of John Wiley and Sons and of the author.

Excerpts from "Friends with Benefits?" by Laura A. Rosenbury, Copyright © by Laura A. Rosenbury, reprinted with permission of the Michigan Law Review and of the author.

Chapter 7:

Excerpts from "Transgressive Caregiving" by Laura T. Kessler, Copyright © 2005 by Florida State University Law Review, reprinted with permission of the Florida State University Law Review and of the author.

Excerpts from "Theorizing Yes: An Essay on Feminism, Law, and Desire" by Katherine M. Franke, Copyright © 2001 by Columbia Law Review, reprinted with permission of the Columbia Law Review and of the author.

Excerpts from "Family Law and Gay and Lesbian Family Issues in the Twentieth Century" by David L. Chambers and Nancy D. Polikoff, published in Family Law Quarterly, Volume 33, No. 3, Fall 1999. Copyright © 1999 by the American Bar Association. Reprinted with permission of the American Bar Association and of the authors.

Excerpts from "A Defense of Paid Family Leave" by Gillian Lester, Copyright © 2005 by the President and Fellows of Harvard College, reprinted with permission of the Harvard Journal of Law and Gender and of the author.

Excerpts from "Are Gender Stereotypes Bad for Women? Rethinking AntiDiscrimination Law and Work–Family Conflict" by Julie Suk, Copyright © 2010 Columbia Law Review, reprinted with permission of the Columbia Law Review and of the author.

Excerpts from THE SECOND SHIFT by Arlie Hochschild and Ann Machung, Copyright © 1989, 2003 by Arlie Hochschild. Used by permission of Viking Penguin, a division of Penguin Group (USA) Inc. and of the authors.

Excerpts from "Why Men Don't Rear Children: A Power Analysis" by M. Rivka Polatnick, Copyright © 1973, 1982 by M. Rivka Polatnick, reprinted with permission of Rowman & Littlefield Publishers, Inc. and of the author.

Excerpts from WOMEN AND CHILDREN LAST: THE PLIGHT OF POOR WOMEN IN AFFLUENT AMERICA by Ruth Sidel, Copyright © 1986 by Ruth Sidel. Used by permission of Viking Penguin, a division of Penguin Group (USA) Inc. and of the author.

Excerpts from MAID IN THE U.S.A. by Mary Romero, Copyright © 1992 by Routledge, Inc. Reproduced by permission of Routledge/Taylor & Francis Group, LLC and of the author.

Excerpts from "The Value of Black Mothers' Work" by Dorothy E. Roberts, Copyright © 1994 by the Connecticut Law Review, reprinted with permission of the Connecticut Law Review and of the author.

Excerpts from "Child Custody in the 21st Century: How the American Law Institute Proposes to Achieve Predictability and Still Protect the Individual Child's Best Interests" by Katharine T. Bartlett, Copyright © 1999 by Willamette Law Review, reprinted with permission of the Willamette Law Review and of the author.

Excerpts from "The Economics of Divorce: Social and Economic Consequences of Property, Alimony, and Child Support Awards" by Lenore Weitzman, originally published in 28 UCLA L. Rev. 1181, Copyright © 1981 by Lenore Weitzman. Reprinted with permission of the the author.

Excerpts from "Multiple Families, Multiple Goals, Multiple Failures: The Need for "Limited Equalization as a Theory of Child Support" by Adrienne Jennings Lockie, Copyright © 2009 by the President and Fellows of Harvard College, reprinted with permission of the Harvard Journal of Law and Gender and of the author.

Chapter 8:

Excerpts from "Portia Denied: Unmasking Gender Bias on the LSAT and its Relationship to Racial Diversity in Legal Education" by William C. Kidder, Copyright © 2000 by Yale Journal of Law and Feminism. Reprinted with permission of the Yale Journal of Law and Feminism from *The Yale Journal of Law and Feminism*, Vol. 12, pp. 1–42 (2000).

Excerpts from "The Future of Affirmative Action: Reclaiming the Innovative Ideal" by Susan Sturm and Lani Guinier, originally published in 84 California Law Review 953 (1996), Copyright (c) 1996 by Susan Sturm and Lani Guinier, reprinted with permission of the authors.

Excerpts from *Power at Play* by Michael A. Messner, Copyright © 1992 by Michael A. Messner, reprinted by permission of the publisher, Beacon Press, Boston, and with permission of the author.

Excerpts from FEMINIST ACCUSED OF SEXUAL HARRASMENT by Jane Gallop, Copyright © 1997 by Duke University Press, reprinted by permission of Duke University Press and of the author.

Excerpts from "If He Hollers Let Him Go: Regulating Racist Speech on Campus" by Charles R. Lawrence, III, Copyright © 1990 by Duke Law Journal, reprinted with permission of the Duke Law Journal and of the author.

Excerpts from "The Difference in Women's Hedonic Lives: A Phenomenological Critique of Feminist Legal Theory" by Robin L. West, Copyright © 1987 by Wisconsin Journal of Law, Gender and Society, reprinted with the permission of the Wisconsin Journal of Law, Gender and Society and of the author.

Chapter 9:

Excerpts from "The New Jurisprudence of Sexual Harassment" by Kathryn Abrams, Copyright © 1998 by Cornell Law Review, reprinted with permission of the Cornell Law Review and of the author.

Excerpts from "A Hair Piece: Perspectives on the Intersection of Race and Gender" by Paulette M. Caldwell, originally published in Duke Law Journal, Vol. 1991, reprinted in CRITICAL RACE FEMINISM: A READER, edited by Adrien Wing. Copyright © 1991 by Paulette M. Caldwell. Reprinted with permission of the Duke Law Journal, Paulette M. Caldwell and Adrien Wing.

Excerpts from "The Central Mistake of Sex Discrimination Law: The Disaggregation of Sex from Gender" by Katherine Franke, Copyright © 1995 by University of Pennsylvania Law Review, reprinted with permission of the University of Pennsylvania Law Review and of the author.

Excerpts from "The Proximate Causes of Employment Discrimination" by Barbara F. Reskin, originally published in Contemporary Sociology, Vol. 29, No. 2, pp. 319, 322–323. Copyright © 2000 by American Sociological Association, reprinted with permission of the American Sociological Association and of the author.

Excerpts from "What's Wrong with Sexual Harassment?" by Katherine M. Franke, Copyright © 1997 by Stanford Law Review, reprinted with permission of the Stanford Law Review and of the author.

Chapter 10:

Excerpts from "Becoming Gentlemen: Women's Experiences at One Ivy League Law School" by Lani Guinier, Michelle Fine, and Jane Balin, with Ann Bartow and Deborah Lee Stachel, Copyright © 1994 by the Trustees of the University of Pennsylvania, reprinted with the permission of the University of Pennsylvania Law Review and William S. Hein & Company, Inc. and of Lani Guinier.

Excerpts from "Feminist Legal Theory, Feminist Lawmaking, and the Legal Profession" by Cynthia Grant Bowman and Elizabeth M. Schneider, Copyright © 1998 by Fordham Law Review, reprinted with the permission of the Fordham Law Review and the authors.

Excerpts from "Sex Discrimination or Gender Inequality?" by Leslie Bender, Copyright © 1989 by Leslie Bender and the Fordham Law Review, reprinted with the permission of the Fordham Law Review and the author.

Excerpts from "Portia in a Different Voice: Speculations on a Women's Lawyering Process" by Carrie Menkel–Meadow, Copyright © 1985 by the Regents of the University of California. Reprinted from the Berkeley Women's Law Journal Vol. 1, No. 1, by permission of the Regents of the University of California and of the author.

Excerpts from "The Mediation Alternative: Process Dangers for Women" by Trina Grillo, Copyright © 1991 by Trina Grillo, reprinted by permission of

The Yale Law Journal Company from The Yale Law Journal, Vol. 100, pages 1545–1610 and of Stephanie Wildman as representative of Catherine Grillo, Trustee of the Estate of Trina Grillo.

Excerpts from "Notes from the Field: A Reply to Professor Colker" by Sarah H. Burns, Copyright © 1990 by the President and Fellows of Harvard College and the Harvard Women's Law Journal, reprinted with the permission of the Harvard Women's Law Journal and the author.

Chapter 11:

Excerpts from Barbara R. Bergmann. In *Saving Our Children from Poverty: What the United States Can Learn from France.* Copyright © 1996 Russell Sage Foundation, 112 East 64th Street, New York, NY 10021. Reprinted with permission of Russell Sage Foundation and of the author.

Excerpts from *Love's Labors: Essays on Women, Equality and Dependency* by Eva Kittay, Copyright © 1999 by Eva Kittay, reprinted by permission of the publisher, Routledge, and of the author.

Excerpts from *Care and Equality: Inventing a New Family Politics* by Mona Harrington, Copyright © 2000 by Mona Harrington, reprinted by permission of the publisher, Routledge, and of the author.

Summary of Contents

TABLE OF CONTENTS

TABLE OF CASES

The principal cases are in bold type. Cases cited or discussed in the text are in roman type. References are to pages. Cases cited in principal cases and within other quoted materials are not included.

FEMINIST JURISPRUDENCE
CASES AND MATERIALS

Fourth Edition

CHAPTER 1

THE HISTORICAL BACKGROUND OF FEMINIST LEGAL THEORY

■ ■ ■

The history of the women's movement in the United States can be divided into at least two periods. One runs from the Seneca Falls Convention in 1848 to passage of the Nineteenth Amendment granting women the right to vote in 1920. Then, after a period of relative inactivity, the movement for the equality of women revived with a fury in the 1960s. It is sometimes assumed that the first period was confined to the suffrage movement. In fact, however, later activists inherited from those earlier feminists a rich history of struggles—intellectual, legal, and political—during which women emphasized many themes in addition to political rights. These included the right to economic independence and equality, access to education, the right to control their own sexual and reproductive lives, rights to their children and property both within marriage and upon divorce, and the right to safety in the workplace, at home, and in public places. In this chapter we briefly describe the 19th and early 20th-century women's movement in the United States and show the broad-based and radical critique of gender and society that is part of its legacy to modern feminists.

A. THE WOMAN MOVEMENT: 1840–1870

The 19th–century "woman movement"[1] in the United States was ignited at the 1840 Anti–Slavery Convention in London, during which Lucretia Mott and Elizabeth Cady Stanton were denied delegate status and consigned to the balcony, leading them to launch a women's rights campaign when they returned home.[2] While this description is clearly

1. Nineteenth-century women used the term "woman movement" to refer both to the suffrage movement and to other struggles for social, legal, and political reform; the use of the singular form, "woman," reflected the presumed unity of interests among women. The term "feminism" came into use in the 1910's, to denote a movement that was narrower in membership than the suffrage movement but broader in its intent to revolutionize many aspects of the relations between men and women. Nancy F. Cott, The Grounding of Modern Feminism 3 (1987).

2. See Eleanor Flexner, Century of Struggle: The Woman's Rights Movement in the United States 71 (rev. ed. 1975; orig. pub. 1959).

Resolved, That it is the duty of the women of this country to secure to themselves their sacred right to the elective franchise.

Resolved, That the equality of human rights results necessarily from the fact of the identity of the race in capabilities and responsibilities.

Resolved, therefore, That, being invested by the Creator with the same capabilities, and the same consciousness of responsibility for their exercise, it is demonstrably the right and duty of woman, equally with man, to promote every righteous cause by every righteous means; and especially in regard to the great subjects of morals and religion, it is self-evidently her right to participate with her brother in teaching them, both in private and in public, by writing and by speaking, by any instrumentalities proper to be used, and in any assemblies proper to be held; and this being a self-evident truth growing out of the divinely implanted principles of human nature, any custom or authority adverse to it, whether modern or wearing the hoary sanction of antiquity, is to be regarded as a self-evident falsehood, and at war with mankind.

[At the last session Lucretia Mott offered and spoke to the following resolution:]

Resolved, That the speedy success of our cause depends upon the zealous and untiring efforts of both men and women, for the overthrow of the monopoly of the pulpit, and for the securing to woman an equal participation with men in the various trades, professions, and commerce.

As the Declaration of Sentiments so aptly put it, married women were "civilly dead" in the first half of the 19th century, for the common law doctrine of coverture treated them as one being with their husbands, who exercised all rights on behalf of the unit. Thus married women could not own property in their own names, enter into contracts, hold property in their own earnings, hold title to the property they inherited or bequeath property, or gain guardianship or custody of their children in case of legal separation.[8] In the face of these laws, Lucy Stone and Henry Blackwell entered into marriage in 1855 "under protest," reading and signing at their wedding a document explicitly protesting the legal rights given to the husband over his wife.[9]

At the time of the Seneca Falls Convention in 1848, the focus of the woman movement was upon these legal rights and on other social and economic issues, including the right to divorce and to a more equal relationship within marriage, educational opportunity and employment, and the concept of female inferiority enshrined in organized religion and politics. The legislatures in state after state ultimately passed Married

8. See Norma Basch, In the Eyes of the Law: Women, Marriage, and Property in Nineteenth-Century New York 42–69 (1982).

9. For the text of the Stone–Blackwell protest, see Feminism: The Essential Historical Writings 103–05 (Miriam Schneir, ed. 1972).

CHAPTER 1

THE HISTORICAL BACKGROUND OF FEMINIST LEGAL THEORY

■ ■ ■

The history of the women's movement in the United States can be divided into at least two periods. One runs from the Seneca Falls Convention in 1848 to passage of the Nineteenth Amendment granting women the right to vote in 1920. Then, after a period of relative inactivity, the movement for the equality of women revived with a fury in the 1960s. It is sometimes assumed that the first period was confined to the suffrage movement. In fact, however, later activists inherited from those earlier feminists a rich history of struggles—intellectual, legal, and political—during which women emphasized many themes in addition to political rights. These included the right to economic independence and equality, access to education, the right to control their own sexual and reproductive lives, rights to their children and property both within marriage and upon divorce, and the right to safety in the workplace, at home, and in public places. In this chapter we briefly describe the 19th and early 20th-century women's movement in the United States and show the broad-based and radical critique of gender and society that is part of its legacy to modern feminists.

A. THE WOMAN MOVEMENT: 1840–1870

The 19th–century "woman movement"[1] in the United States was ignited at the 1840 Anti–Slavery Convention in London, during which Lucretia Mott and Elizabeth Cady Stanton were denied delegate status and consigned to the balcony, leading them to launch a women's rights campaign when they returned home.[2] While this description is clearly

---

1. Nineteenth-century women used the term "woman movement" to refer both to the suffrage movement and to other struggles for social, legal, and political reform; the use of the singular form, "woman," reflected the presumed unity of interests among women. The term "feminism" came into use in the 1910's, to denote a movement that was narrower in membership than the suffrage movement but broader in its intent to revolutionize many aspects of the relations between men and women. Nancy F. Cott, The Grounding of Modern Feminism 3 (1987).

2. See Eleanor Flexner, Century of Struggle: The Woman's Rights Movement in the United States 71 (rev. ed. 1975; orig. pub. 1959).

oversimplified, it points to a number of important characteristics of the early woman movement. Many of its leaders, like Mott, Stanton, and the Grimké sisters, gained their initial political experience in the abolitionist movement, which offered them an egalitarian ideology and theory of social change.[3] Many of these women were among the first generation of women in the United States to receive a formal education, and they found a sense of purpose in abolitionism in a society where most forms of political and economic activity were closed to them. Because custom prohibited women from speaking in public to mixed assemblies of men and women, they quickly learned that, in order to further the anti-slavery cause, they must press for their own rights as well.[4] Abolitionism also gave these early feminists male allies like Frederick Douglass, Henry Blackwell (husband of Lucy Stone), and William Lloyd Garrison.

On July 19 and 20, 1848, the first Women's Rights Convention in the United States took place at Seneca Falls, New York, where Elizabeth Cady Stanton then lived. Approximately 250 women and 40 men attended in response to an advertisement placed in the local newspaper. The abolitionist leaders Lucretia Mott and Frederick Douglass were present. Stanton, Mott, Martha C. Wright, and Mary Ann McClintock drafted the Declaration of Sentiments and resolutions presented at the convention, modeling them on the Declaration of Independence.[5] Elizabeth Cady Stanton argued strongly for the inclusion of a resolution demanding the right to vote; this was the only resolution that did not pass unanimously, carrying only by a small margin.[6] Ironically, suffrage was to become almost the exclusive goal of one branch of the woman movement in the late 19th and early 20th centuries. Only one woman present at Seneca Falls lived to vote in the 1920 presidential election, the first one after ratification of the Nineteenth Amendment.[7]

The Seneca Falls Declaration, which appears below, is the central document of this period of activism by American women, when their efforts were concentrated primarily upon reform at the state level to improve the legal status of women. Note, however, that the list of grievances in the Declaration contains not only an attack on various discriminatory statutes but also a statement of fundamental feminist principles, attacking the "supremacy of man," the unequal allocation of power in family, state and church, and the different moral codes applied to men and women—an agenda shared by modern feminist theory.

---

3. See, e.g., Paula Giddings, When and Where I Enter: The Impact of Black Women on Race and Sex in America 55 (1984). Something similar happened in the 1960's, when white women joined the civil rights struggle and then formed their own groups in reaction to the unequal treatment they received within the Left. See, e.g., Sara Evans, Personal Politics: The Roots of Women's Liberation in the Civil Rights Movement and the New Left 23 (1979).

4. Flexner, above note 2, at 44–50.

5. Id. at 74–75.

6. Id. at 77.

7. Id.

THE DECLARATION OF SENTIMENTS

Seneca Falls, New York, July 19–20, 1848.

When, in the course of human events, it becomes necessary for one portion of the family of man to assume among the people of the earth a position different from that which they have hitherto occupied, but one to which the laws of nature and of nature's God entitle them, a decent respect to the opinions of mankind requires that they should declare the causes that impel them to such a course.

We hold these truths to be self-evident: that all men and women are created equal; they are endowed by their Creator with certain inalienable rights; that among these are life, liberty, and the pursuit of happiness; that to secure these rights governments are instituted, deriving their just powers from the consent of the governed. Whenever any form of government becomes destructive of these ends, it is the right of those who suffer from it to refuse allegiance to it, and to insist upon the institution of a new government, laying its foundation on such principles, and organizing its powers in such form, as to them shall seem most likely to effect their safety and happiness. Prudence, indeed, will dictate that governments long established should not be changed for light and transient causes; and accordingly all experience hath shown that mankind are more disposed to suffer, while evils are sufferable, than to right themselves by abolishing the forms to which they were accustomed. But when a long train of abuses and usurpations, pursuing invariably the same object evinces a design to reduce them under absolute despotism, it is their duty to throw off such government, and to provide new guards for their future security. Such has been the patient sufferance of the women under this government, and such is now the necessity which constrains them to demand the equal station to which they are entitled.

The history of mankind is a history of repeated injuries and usurpations on the part of man toward woman, having in direct object the establishment of an absolute tyranny over her. To prove this, let facts be submitted to a candid world.

He has never permitted her to exercise her inalienable right to the elective franchise.

He has compelled her to submit to laws, in the formation of which she had no voice.

He has withheld from her rights which are given to the most ignorant and degraded men—both natives and foreigners.

Having deprived her of this first right of a citizen, the elective franchise, thereby leaving her without representation in the halls of legislation, he has oppressed her on all sides.

He has made her, if married, in the eye of the law, civilly dead.

He has taken from her all right in property, even to the wages she earns.

He has made her, morally, an irresponsible being, as she can commit many crimes with impunity, provided they be done in the presence of her husband. In the covenant of marriage, she is compelled to promise obedience to her husband, he becoming, to all intents and purposes, her master—the law giving him power to deprive her of her liberty, and to administer chastisement.

He has so framed the laws of divorce, as to what shall be the proper causes, and in case of separation, to whom the guardianship of the children shall be given, as to be wholly regardless of the happiness of women—the law, in all cases, going upon a false supposition of the supremacy of man, and giving all power into his hands.

After depriving her of all rights as a married woman, if single, and the owner of property, he has taxed her to support a government which recognizes her only when her property can be made profitable to it.

He has monopolized nearly all the profitable employments, and from those she is permitted to follow, she receives but a scanty remuneration. He closes against her all the avenues to wealth and distinction which he considers most honorable to himself. As a teacher of theology, medicine, or law, she is not known.

He has denied her the facilities for obtaining a thorough education, all colleges being closed against her.

He allows her in Church, as well as State, but a subordinate position, claiming Apostolic authority for her exclusion from the ministry, and, with some exceptions, from any public participation in the affairs of the Church.

He has created a false public sentiment by giving to the world a different code of morals for men and women, by which moral delinquencies which exclude women from society, are not only tolerated, but deemed of little account in man.

He has usurped the prerogative of Jehovah himself, claiming it as his right to assign for her a sphere of action, when that belongs to her conscience and to her God.

He has endeavored, in every way that he could, to destroy her confidence in her own powers, to lessen her self-respect, and to make her willing to lead a dependent and abject life.

Now, in view of this entire disfranchisement of one-half the people of this country, their social and religious degradation—in view of the unjust laws above mentioned, and because women do feel themselves aggrieved, oppressed, and fraudulently deprived of their most sacred rights, we insist that they have immediate admission to all the rights and privileges which belong to them as citizens of the United States.

In entering upon the great work before us, we anticipate no small amount of misconception, misrepresentation, and ridicule; but we shall use every instrumentality within our power to effect our object. We shall employ agents, circulate tracts, petition the State and National legislatures, and endeavor to enlist the pulpit and the press in our behalf. We hope this Convention will be followed by a series of Conventions embracing every part of the country.

Resolutions

WHEREAS, The great precept of nature is conceded to be, that "man shall pursue his own true and substantial happiness." Blackstone in his Commentaries remarks, that this law of Nature being coeval with mankind, and dictated by God himself, is of course superior in obligation to any other. It is binding over all the globe, in all countries and at all times; no human laws are of any validity if contrary to this, and such of them as are valid, derive all their force, and all their validity, and all their authority, mediately and immediately, from this original; therefore,

Resolved, That such laws as conflict, in any way, with the true and substantial happiness of woman, are contrary to the great precept of nature and of no validity, for this is "superior in obligation to any other."

Resolved, That all laws which prevent woman from occupying such a station in society as her conscience shall dictate, or which place her in a position inferior to that of man, are contrary to the great precept of nature, and therefore of no force or authority.

Resolved, That woman is man's equal—was intended to be so by the Creator, and the highest good of the race demands that she should be recognized as such.

Resolved, That the women of this country ought to be enlightened in regard to the laws under which they live, that they may no longer publish their degradation by declaring themselves satisfied with their present position, nor their ignorance, by asserting that they have all the rights they want.

Resolved, That inasmuch as man, while claiming for himself intellectual superiority, does accord to woman moral superiority, it is pre-eminently his duty to encourage her to speak and teach, as she has an opportunity, in all religious assemblies.

Resolved, That the same amount of virtue, delicacy, and refinement of behavior that is required of woman in the social state, should also be required of man, and the same transgressions should be visited with equal severity on both man and woman.

Resolved, That the objection of indelicacy and impropriety, which is so often brought against woman when she addresses a public audience, comes with a very ill-grace from those who encourage, by their attendance, her appearance on the stage, in the concert, or in feats of the circus.

Resolved, That woman has too long rested satisfied in the circumscribed limits which corrupt citizens and a perverted application of the Scriptures have marked out for her, and that it is time she should move in the enlarged sphere which her great Creator has assigned her.

Resolved, That it is the duty of the women of this country to secure to themselves their sacred right to the elective franchise.

Resolved, That the equality of human rights results necessarily from the fact of the identity of the race in capabilities and responsibilities.

Resolved, therefore, That, being invested by the Creator with the same capabilities, and the same consciousness of responsibility for their exercise, it is demonstrably the right and duty of woman, equally with man, to promote every righteous cause by every righteous means; and especially in regard to the great subjects of morals and religion, it is self-evidently her right to participate with her brother in teaching them, both in private and in public, by writing and by speaking, by any instrumentalities proper to be used, and in any assemblies proper to be held; and this being a self-evident truth growing out of the divinely implanted principles of human nature, any custom or authority adverse to it, whether modern or wearing the hoary sanction of antiquity, is to be regarded as a self-evident falsehood, and at war with mankind.

[At the last session Lucretia Mott offered and spoke to the following resolution:]

Resolved, That the speedy success of our cause depends upon the zealous and untiring efforts of both men and women, for the overthrow of the monopoly of the pulpit, and for the securing to woman an equal participation with men in the various trades, professions, and commerce.

As the Declaration of Sentiments so aptly put it, married women were "civilly dead" in the first half of the 19th century, for the common law doctrine of coverture treated them as one being with their husbands, who exercised all rights on behalf of the unit. Thus married women could not own property in their own names, enter into contracts, hold property in their own earnings, hold title to the property they inherited or bequeath property, or gain guardianship or custody of their children in case of legal separation.[8] In the face of these laws, Lucy Stone and Henry Blackwell entered into marriage in 1855 "under protest," reading and signing at their wedding a document explicitly protesting the legal rights given to the husband over his wife.[9]

At the time of the Seneca Falls Convention in 1848, the focus of the woman movement was upon these legal rights and on other social and economic issues, including the right to divorce and to a more equal relationship within marriage, educational opportunity and employment, and the concept of female inferiority enshrined in organized religion and politics. The legislatures in state after state ultimately passed Married

8. See Norma Basch, In the Eyes of the Law: Women, Marriage, and Property in Nineteenth–Century New York 42–69 (1982).

9. For the text of the Stone–Blackwell protest, see Feminism: The Essential Historical Writings 103–05 (Miriam Schneir, ed. 1972).

Women's Property Acts to remedy the common law coverture restrictions. In some states, their passage resulted from determined political campaigns, during which women who had never been politically active previously went from door to door obtaining signatures on petitions for legislative change.[10] One of the first of these acts, passed in New York in 1848, appears below.

MARRIED WOMEN'S PROPERTY ACT

Laws of New York, ch. 200 (1848).

§ 1. The real and personal property of any female who may hereafter marry, and which she shall own at the time of marriage, and the rents, issues and profits thereof shall not be subject to the disposal of her husband, nor be liable for his debts, and shall continue her sole and separate property, as if she were a single female.

§ 2. The real and personal property, and the rents, issues and profits thereof of any female now married shall not be subject to the disposal of her husband; but shall be her sole and separate property as if she were a single female except so far as the same may be liable for the debts of her husband heretofore contracted.

§ 3. It shall be lawful for any married female to receive, by gift, grant, devise or bequest, from any person other than her husband and hold to her sole and separate use, as if she were a single female, real and personal property, and the rents, issues and profits thereof, and the same shall not be subject to the disposal of her husband, nor be liable for his debts.

§ 4. All contracts made between persons in contemplation of marriage shall remain in full force after such marriage takes place.

Although the Married Women's Property Acts were intended to be a remedy for the civil death of women under coverture, the concern of many legislators (who were, of course, all male) was to insulate the estates of their married daughters from spendthrift sons-in-law and their creditors and to clarify the legal situation for those creditors in a time of economic upheaval.[11] In the South, their concern was also to protect their daughters' inheritance of slaves.[12] After the laws were passed, the courts frequently interpreted them so narrowly that the rights contemplated in the text of a statute were not extended to women in fact.[13] The New York legislature, for example, passed another Married Women's Property Act in

10. Flexner, above note 2, at 86–89.

11. Basch, above note 8, at 124–26.

12. See Women's America: Refocusing the Past 532 (Linda K. Kerber & Jane Sherron De Hart, eds. 3d ed. 1991).

13. See Basch, above note 8, at 200–32. For the texts of the 1848 and 1860 New York Married Women's Property Acts, see id. at 233–35.

1860. The 1860 statute was much broader in its protections than that passed in 1848, making mothers joint guardians of their children, equal in powers, rights, and duties with their husbands. The 1860 Act also, explicitly and in greater detail than the 1848 statute, gave women the right to own property, collect their own wages, sue in court, and have property rights upon their husbands' deaths. Yet again, the judicial interpretation of the 1860 statute was so narrow that it was necessary to pass yet another law in 1884, explicitly giving married women the right, among other things, to enter into contracts as if they were single persons, even though full contractual capacity was implied by the wording of the 1860 Act.[14] Thus, women's rights activists had to return to the state legislatures repeatedly or, believing that an inequity had been remedied, they turned their attention to other things, while each legislative advance was gutted by judicial interpretation.

In addition to legislative campaigns, after 1850 women's rights conventions and numerous local meetings took place on an annual basis in the northern states. One of these women's rights conventions, in Akron, Ohio in 1851, was the occasion for the famous "Ain't I A Woman?" speech by Sojourner Truth, an African American woman who was a former slave. Hostile men had been repeatedly disrupting the meeting when Truth took the podium to confront their anti-women's rights arguments.[15] Her powerful speech not only quieted the crowd but also presented a graphic reminder of the important issues of race and class that divided women at that time. The contents of her speech, emphasizing qualities of strength, starkly contrasted with the ideology of "true womanhood" in the 19th century—a pervasive stereotype in fiction and advice literature for women, encouraging them to cultivate the virtues of domesticity, purity, and submissiveness and to remain in the private sphere of family while the world of work increasingly moved out of the home.[16]

Sojourner Truth's speech appears below to illustrate the dynamic interrelationship of the women's movement throughout its history with issues of race and class—through analogies, often-precarious alliances, and the continuing debate within feminist theory about the similarities and differences of interest between women of different races and classes.[17]

---

14. Id. at 224.

15. See Flexner, above note 2, at 90–91.

16. Barbara Welter, The Cult of True Womanhood: 1820–1860, 18 Am. Q. 151–52 (1966). The image of "true womanhood" never corresponded to reality for most women. See, e.g., Jeanne Boydston, The Pastoralization of Housework, in Kerber & De Hart, above note 12, at 148 (the ideology of gender spheres in fact obscured the value of labor women performed in the household and marginalized working-class women who did not remain in the home).

17. For historically influential analogies between race and sex, see, e.g., Gunnar Myrdal, An American Dilemma: The Negro Problem and Modern Democracy 1073–78 (1962; orig. pub. 1944); Helen Mayer Hacker, Women as a Minority Group, 30 Social Forces 60 (1951). See also discussion of essentialism in Chapter 3, below. But see Reva B. Siegel, She The People: The Nineteenth Amendment, Sex Equality, Federalism, and the Family, 115 Harv. L. Rev. 947, 953–63 (2002) (arguing that building the 20th-century litigation campaign for women's equality on the analogy to race in fact hindered the development of sex discrimination doctrine). See also Serena Mayeri, "A Common Fate of Discrimination": Race–Gender Analogies in Legal and Historical Perspective,

SOJOURNER TRUTH, "AIN'T I A WOMAN?" (1851)

In Feminism: The Essential Historical Writings 94–95 (Miriam Schneir, ed. 1972).

Well, children, where there is so much racket there must be something out of kilter. I think that "twixt the negroes of the South and the women at the North, all talking about rights, the white men will be in a fix pretty soon. But what's all this here talking about?

That man over there says that women need to be helped into carriages, and lifted over ditches, and to have the best place everywhere. Nobody ever helps me into carriages, or over mud-puddles, or gives me any best place! And ain't I a woman? Look at me! Look at my arm! I have ploughed and planted, and gathered into barns, and no man could head me! And ain't I a woman? I could work as much and eat as much as a man—when I could get it—and bear the lash as well! And ain't I a woman? I have borne thirteen children, and seen them most all sold off to slavery, and when I cried out with my mother's grief, none but Jesus heard me! And ain't I a woman?

Then they talk about this thing in the head; what's this they call it? [Intellect, someone whispers.] That's it, honey. What's that got to do with women's rights or negro's rights? If my cup won't hold but a pint, and yours holds a quart, wouldn't you be mean not to let me have my little half-measure full?

Then that little man in black there, he says women can't have as much rights as men, 'cause Christ wasn't a woman! Where did your Christ come from? Where did your Christ come from? From God and a woman! Man had nothing to do with Him.

If the first woman God ever made was strong enough to turn the world upside down all alone, these women together ought to be able to turn it back, and get it right side up again! And now they is asking to do it, the men better let them.

Obliged to you for hearing me, and now old Sojourner ain't got nothing more to say.

In 1860, women's rights activists postponed their demand for equal rights in deference to the Civil War; but they assumed that, after supporting the war effort, women would receive the vote along with the freed slaves.[18] Instead, the word "male" entered the Constitution for the first time in the text of the Fourteenth Amendment. Furthermore, women's former abolitionist allies did not support inclusion of sex in the Fifteenth Amendment as one of the grounds upon which suffrage could not be

110 Yale L.J. 1045 (2001) (emphasizing the limitations imposed by the race-sex analogy upon the development of sex discrimination law).

18. Flexner, above note 2, at 81, 109.

abridged, because they feared that this would endanger extension of the vote to Black males.[19] The debate over the Fifteenth Amendment and these bitter disappointments for women's rights activists led to the rupture of their alliance with the larger equal rights movement and to a split within the woman movement itself.

In 1869, women representatives to the American Equal Rights Association formed the National Woman Suffrage Association (NWSA), led by Elizabeth Cady Stanton and Susan B. Anthony, with the objective of securing the passage of a constitutional amendment to enfranchise women. This group, under Stanton's leadership, also continued the wide agenda embodied in the Declaration of Sentiments, including severe criticism of contemporary marriage and divorce law, a critique of religion, and a cultural critique of the many ways women were socialized to think of themselves as inferior.[20] Others, led by Lucy Stone and Henry Blackwell, split off to found the more cautious American Woman Suffrage Association (AWSA) and mounted campaigns for suffrage on a state-by-state basis. Unlike NWSA, AWSA avoided issues of divorce, religion, and the rights of working women, for fear of alienating other sections of the community from AWSA's single-minded quest for the vote.[21]

B. THE SUFFRAGE MOVEMENT: 1870–1920

Among its initial strategies, NWSA mounted a legal campaign to obtain the ballot. Susan B. Anthony registered to vote in 1872 in Rochester, New York, and she and 14 other women actually cast ballots. They were charged with violating a provision of the 1870 Civil Rights Act designed to prevent white men from canceling out Black male votes by casting more than one ballot.[22] Although Anthony was denied the right to testify on her own behalf in court, she made numerous public speeches before the trial in an attempt to influence prospective jurors; in these speeches she argued, among other things, that she was entitled to vote as one of the privileges and immunities guaranteed to citizens under the Fourteenth Amendment, that the condition of women was one of servitude, and that she was being denied a jury of her peers.[23] The case never made it to the jurors, however, as the judge directed a verdict of guilty on the criminal charges; but Anthony was not sentenced to jail and never paid the $100 fine.[24] At her sentencing, before the judge could silence her, Susan B. Anthony denounced the all-male legal system that had convicted her.[25]

---

19. Joan Hoff, Law, Gender, and Injustice: A Legal History of U.S. Women 146–49 (1991). Political self-interest was also a motivating factor, as the Northern-based Republicans did not want to endanger the political potential of attracting the Black male vote by introducing the woman question. Id. at 149.

20. Flexner, above note 2, at 155–56.

21. Id.

22. Hoff, above note 19, at 153.

23. Id. at 153–57.

24. Id. at 157–60.

25. For the text of Susan B. Anthony's speech in United States v. Susan B. Anthony, see Schneir, ed., above note 9, at 134–36.

Although other women also attempted to vote in the 1870's, only one case made it to the Supreme Court—that brought by Virginia Minor, who sued her local registrar of voting in Missouri.[26] Minor argued that the right to vote was one of the privileges and immunities of citizenship under the Fourteenth Amendment and that, if women were denied that right, the United States was not a republic but a despotism.[27] Rejecting this argument, the Court unanimously held that, although women were citizens, the Framers had never intended to enfranchise them.

After these failures in the courts, the suffrage movement turned to the political arena. A suffrage amendment was introduced into Congress in 1868; and a later version referred to as the Anthony Amendment was introduced in 1878 and every subsequent year until 1896, when it disappeared from the congressional agenda until 1913.[28]

As the struggle for suffrage grew more protracted, the movement became increasingly focused upon that one goal. Demands concerning divorce, trade unionism, and prostitution were dropped, as were attacks upon organized religion and the earlier leaders' radical critique of marriage as an institution. Moreover, its proponents recharacterized the demand for suffrage, originally based on natural law, as merited by women's traditional role as mothers and as critical to their ability to bring special insight and morality into political life.[29] Many activists in the suffrage movement either emerged from or allied themselves with the temperance movement, aiming to protect women whose husbands' drinking dissipated their family income or resulted in domestic violence; but this alliance evoked opposition from brewing interests which proceeded to fund anti-suffrage campaigns.[30]

At the same time, the suffrage movement became increasingly and overtly racist and nativist. In the hope of attracting support from conservatives and southerners, suffragists emphasized the value of granting the vote to women in order to counterbalance the votes of Black men and male immigrants and even suggested educational requirements to vote that would in effect have limited suffrage to middle-class white native-born citizens.[31] In the name of tactical expediency, the suffrage movement, reunited in 1890 into the National American Woman Suffrage Association (NAWSA), refused membership to the Black women's clubs, refused to support Black women's demands, and even segregated public functions of

---

26. Minor v. Happersett, 88 U.S. (21 Wall.) 162 (1874).

27. Hoff, above note 19, at 171.

28. Flexner, above note 2, at 176–78.

29. See generally Aileen S. Kraditor, The Ideas of the Woman Suffrage Movement, 1890–1920 (1965).

30. See, e.g., Flexner, above note 2, at 185–89, 305.

31. Giddings, above note 3, at 124.

their own in deference to southern "sensitivities."[32] In 1913, for example, the leaders of the Washington suffrage march asked the intrepid Black journalist, organizer, and international anti-lynching advocate Ida B. Wells to join the segregated section of the march rather than to walk with the Illinois delegation; Wells slipped out of the segregated group and asserted her place with the women from Illinois nonetheless.[33]

The southern states opposed women's suffrage to the end,[34] so the suffragists' expedient racism turned out to be both tragic and fruitless; and it divided them from their natural allies. Black women consistently supported universal suffrage after the debate over the Civil War amendments; and at the end of Reconstruction they began to create organizations and institutions to assert equal rights, including suffrage, as well as to press their claims to education, entry into the professions, and other aspects of economic and social equality.[35] Educated and middle-class Black women formed clubs that pressed for a variety of social reforms, such as child care and improvements in the status of working women.[36] Much of their attention, however, focused of necessity upon the deprivation and violence visited upon Black men and women alike.

A stark example is the anti-lynching movement organized by Ida B. Wells in reaction to the rash of lynchings during this period.[37] Women—southern women in particular—were slow to perceive the fundamentally feminist nature of the anti-lynching movement. Lynching was typically a response to allegations that a Black man had raped or sexually insulted a white woman in some fashion (often very minor).[38] Allegations of rape and the fear generated by the terrorism of barbaric public lynchings were used as an excuse for subordinating Blacks. But it was only in the lynching epidemic of the 1920's that southern white women began to confront the sexism implicit in the lynching mentality, to see chivalry as a means of controlling women, and to connect it with lynching.[39] As one historian put it, "pursuit of the black rapist represented a trade-off[;] * * * the right of the southern lady to protection presupposed her obligation to obey."[40]

Throughout this period, Black women confronted sexual harassment by their employers and an increase in domestic violence—problems they

32. The African American women's federation of clubs was rejected for membership in NAWSA for fear it would lead to defeat of the suffrage amendment in the South, and in 1899 NAWSA refused to endorse a resolution brought by certain Black women against segregated accommodations in railroad carriages. Angela Y. Davis, Women, Race, and Class 144, 118 (1981).

33. Giddings, above note 3, at 127–28.

34. Flexner, above note 2, at 337.

35. Giddings, above note 3, at 75, 119.

36. Id. at 95–101.

37. See id. at 17–31, 89–92.

38. The irony of the lynching scenario, as Wells pointed out, was that while Black men were being falsely accused of raping white women, Black women were raped by white men repeatedly with impunity, both during slavery and as domestic servants. Id. at 31.

39. Id. at 206–07.

40. Jacquelyn Dowd Hall, Revolt Against Chivalry: Jessie Daniel Ames and the Women's Campaign Against Lynching 151 (1979).

shared with white women.[41] Yet in other ways the experience of Black women differed from that of the white suffragists. Never considered the delicate flowers celebrated by the 19th-century cult of true womanhood,[42] Black women had worked in large numbers, as slaves and after abolition often as domestic servants or, if they were fortunate enough to gain an education, teaching in African American schools.[43] Thus, when Black women organized women's groups or clubs, their attention immediately turned to issues central to the welfare of working women and their children.[44] By contrast, the clubs formed by middle-class white women tended to emphasize (although not exclusively) issues of more direct interest to them, such as establishing libraries and hospitals to benefit their communities and the provision of services to children.[45]

A substantial number of educated women did become involved in movements for social reform during the Progressive era. Some, like Jane Addams, Lillian Wald, and Florence Kelley, founded settlement houses, providing direct services to residents of lower-income and immigrant neighborhoods. These reformers fought for political and economic reforms, such as safer conditions in factories and neighborhoods, and for minimum wage and maximum hour legislation, some of which applied only to women and children.[46] Others worked within the National Consumers League to support the needs of working class women, and working women and their allies struggled for better conditions through the Women's Trade Union League.[47]

At the end of the 19th century, there was still one issue upon which women's groups all agreed: extension of the suffrage to women. Although it took 50 years after passage of the Fifteenth Amendment, this goal was finally achieved in 1920, when the last state necessary ratified the Nineteenth Amendment. Some attribute this final victory to the importation of militant tactics from the British suffrage movement by Alice Paul and her Woman's Party.[48] The last years before suffrage were marked by mass marches, picketing, imprisonment of picketers, hunger strikes, and radical tactics not characteristic of the suffrage movement in the United States until that time. The long, slow process of lobbying on the national level continued as well, including several campaigns to target and defeat senators who had voted against the suffrage amendment in 1918.[49] Per-

41. Giddings, above note 3, at 64, 101.

42. See note 16, above.

43. Giddings, above note 3, at 63, 77–78. Industrial opportunities were largely closed to Black women. Id. at 78.

44. Id. at 96–101.

45. Flexner, above note 2, at 182–84; Giddings, above note 3, at 97.

46. Flexner, above note 2, at 208–21.

47. William L. O'Neill, Everyone Was Brave: The Rise and Fall of Feminism in America 95–102 (1969).

48. Flexner, above note 2, at 259, 272–79. Women's suffrage was attained in Great Britain in 1918 for freeholders, wives of freeholders, and women over 30 and extended to all women in 1928. Id. at 321, 390 n. 6.

49. Id. at 319–37.

haps most important, the numerous campaigns from 1890 to 1920 to win suffrage on the state level finally bore fruit on the national level: the number of votes for suffrage in Congress reflected the female suffrage that had been achieved in the states and thus the accountability of national representatives to an electorate that included women.[50] As a result of all these efforts, the Nineteenth Amendment became part of the United States Constitution on August 26, 1920.

C. FEMINISM AFTER THE NINETEENTH AMENDMENT

After the lengthy struggle for suffrage, the coalition that achieved it collapsed, some say of sheer exhaustion.[51] Others attribute this collapse to the suffragists' concentration upon one political goal, to the exclusion of social and economic issues. Once that goal—the vote—did not turn out to be a panacea for the ills affecting women, interest in further activism was bound to wane.[52] A related explanation sees the conservatism and tactical expediency of the second and third generations of women's leaders as having separated the movement from the earlier and broader critique of woman's place in marriage and the economy, thereby losing the grounding for a more long-lasting movement for change.[53]

The suffragists had indeed oversold the vote as an instrument through which newly enfranchised women would transform the values of the nation. Women did not turn out to vote in a massive and powerful bloc after 1920, and the differences of race and class that had been submerged in their unified demand for suffrage reemerged.[54] Moreover, NAWSA itself, after requiring decades of political activity, experience, and organizational skill of its supporters, designated as its successor organization the newly formed League of Women Voters (LWV), which decided to remain strictly non-partisan.[55] The LWV also did not explicitly define itself as a feminist group, although its members pressed for many of the social programs supported by the women reformers of the Progressive era.[56] The National Woman's Party, on the other hand, defined itself as a feminist but single-issue group; its program was to strike a blow at the hundreds of discriminatory laws throughout the country by the passage of an Equal Rights Amendment (ERA) banning discrimination on the basis of sex.[57] The campaign for the ERA, described in more detail in Chapter Two,

---

50. See Anne F. Scott & Andrew M. Scott, One Half the People: The Fight for Woman Suffrage 161–62, 166–68 (1975).

51. See, e.g., Judith Hole & Ellen Levine, The Rebirth of Feminism 14 (1971).

52. William H. Chafe, The Paradox of Change: American Women in the 20th Century 32 (1991).

53. O'Neill, above note 47, at 273–74.

54. Chafe, above note 52, at 30.

55. Id. at 23–24.

56. Cott, above note 1, at 86.

57. Chafe, above note 52, at 48–49.

resulted in a serious split in the women's movement, as social reformers and trade union activists opposed the ERA for fear of its impact upon the sex-specific protective legislation they had worked so long to pass.

Though feminists were no longer unified in a mass movement after suffrage was achieved, in the 1920's women activists and social reformers continued their activity on a variety of issues critical to the welfare of women and children—federally supported infant and maternal health education, citizenship rights for wives of aliens, and child labor laws, for example.[58] Many of the women reformers involved in these struggles were instrumental in laying the groundwork for the New Deal and, indeed, performed important functions in the New Deal itself.[59] Eleanor Roosevelt played a central role in connecting the persons, programs, and ideas of the progressive social reformers with the Democratic Party during the 1920's and 30's.[60]

Most women who entered the workplace for the first time, as many white, middle-class women did during the Depression and the labor shortage of the Second World War, confronted severe discrimination. They worked in sex-segregated jobs and were paid much less for their work than men. During the 1920's and 30's, over 40% of all women in manufacturing worked in the textile industry, and more than 75% of women professionals were either teachers or nurses.[61] Many industries simply did not hire women—at least until their labor was required to replace the men who were drafted into the armed forces after the Japanese attack on Pearl Harbor. When the veterans returned, however, they replaced women in these positions, although most women remained in the workforce in other, less well-paid, jobs.[62] Throughout this period, Black and immigrant women were largely confined to the most marginal jobs.[63] Moreover, even during the years when women's labor was actively solicited for defense industries, the community services and child care that would have helped them combine their economic role with their roles within the family were not widely available.[64] Thus, the economic independence touted by earlier reformers as a result of employment outside the home turned out, for many women, to be a new form of exploitation.

---

58. Cott, above note 1, at 97–98.

59. Chafe, above note 52, at 34–41; J. Stanley Lemons, The Woman Citizen: Social Feminism in the 1920s 228, 243–44 (1973).

60. See, e.g., Blanche Wiesen Cook, Eleanor Roosevelt, Vol. I: 1884–1933 288–301, 319–79 (1992).

61. Chafe, above note 52, at 73.

62. Id. at 122–23, 159–60.

63. Giddings, above note 3, at 232–36.

64. See Chafe, above note 52, at 141–51. In wartime England, by contrast, "Central Kitchens" prepared meals for women factory workers to carry home to their families. Id. at 143. A few workplaces in the United States did provide federally subsidized child care during the war, notably the center at the Kaiser shipbuilding plant in Portland, Oregon, which was open 24 hours a day and provided sick-child care, shopping services, and low-cost carry-out dinners. See Ruth Sidel, Women and Children Last 119–20 (1986).

For the mass of women, the interwar era was a confusing period. On the one hand, a revolution in dress and sexual mores produced the "flapper," the sexually liberated woman who drank and smoked and wore short dresses; on the other hand, this liberation from the customs of their mothers was accompanied by continuing fidelity to the goals of a traditional marriage, home, and family. More women married, and they married at a younger age; and for the first time, the number of women obtaining graduate degrees, entering professions, or aspiring to make use of their college degrees declined.[65] A new cult of domesticity, linked with psychoanalytic notions about the nature of women and media promotion of consumption aimed at housewives, reinforced the traditional ideology of home and motherhood as woman's sphere, at least for white, middle-class women.[66]

This "feminine mystique" was described by Betty Friedan in her 1963 book of that name, from which some date the beginning of the renewed women's movement in the United States.[67] There were, however, strong connections to the earlier women's movement. While the women's liberation movement of the 1960's resulted in part from the mobilization of middle-class educated women by Friedan and others and from the politicization of women in the civil rights movement, it was also linked to earlier generations of women activists and social reformers through the involvement of older women like Eleanor Roosevelt, whom President Kennedy appointed to chair the President's Commission on the Status of Women in 1960.[68] The resurgent movement, described in the next chapter, renewed not only the critique of the social, legal, and economic status of women raised in the mid–19th century, but also the early reformers' cultural critique of women's lives.

---

65. Cott, above note 1, at 147; Chafe, above note 52, at 111–18.

66. Chafe, above note 52, at 104–116; Cott, above note 1, at 147–74.

67. Flexner, above note 2, at 344. A more nuanced account of the origins of the renewed women's movement is provided in Chapter 2.

68. See, e.g., Jane Sherron De Hart, The New Feminism and the Dynamics of Social Change, in Kerber & De Hart, eds., above note 12, at 502–12.

CHAPTER 2

CONSTITUTIONAL "EQUALITY"

■ ■ ■

A. HISTORICAL INTRODUCTION

After suffrage, Alice Paul and the National Woman's Party supported the first equal rights amendment for women (ERA). This version was first introduced into Congress in 1923:

> Men and women shall have equal rights throughout the United States and in every place subject to its jurisdiction. Congress shall have power to enforce this article by appropriate legislation.

Supporters argued that this amendment would eliminate the many distinctions between women and men in laws regulating employment, families, citizenship, competency, crimes, and criminal sentences.[1]

A few examples from each area give a sense of the breadth of sex-specific regulation in effect at the time.[2] State laws often specified maximum hours or minimum wages for women workers in general or in certain industries, or banned women from bartending or working in factories at night, whereas state legislatures assumed that men needed no protection in the workplace. Family law was almost entirely sex-specific, with a strong presumption that mothers should serve as sole custodians of young children after a divorce. The husband was head of the household with a minimal obligation to support his wife and children and the right to determine the domicile of the family. His wife was obligated to provide homemaking and caretaking services in accordance with her husband's desires. In many states married women were still denied full rights to contract and to own property, despite the passage of the Married Women's Property Acts described in Chapter 1.

---

1. Nancy F. Cott, The Grounding of Modern Feminism 115–42 (1987); Sara M. Evans, Born of Liberty: A History of Women in America 187, 193 (1989).

2. The discussion in text relies on the thorough descriptions of sex-specific laws in Leo Kanowitz, Women and the Law: The Unfinished Revolution (1969); Barbara A. Brown, Thomas I. Emerson, Gail Falk & Ann E. Freedman, The Equal Rights Amendment: A Constitutional Basis for Equal Rights for Women, 80 Yale L.J. 871 (1971) (one of the main sources upon which Congress relied during its consideration of the ERA in the 1970s); John D. Johnston, Jr. & Charles L. Knapp, Sex Discrimination by Law: A Study in Judicial Perspective, 46 N.Y.U. L. Rev. 675 (1971).

Men were subject to the draft, while women could not serve as members of the armed forces prior to World War II (with the exception of the Navy during World War I). Yet veterans often received powerful preferences for government employment. Many states denied women the ability to serve on juries under the same rules as men. The legal age of majority tended to be lower for women than men, and women were allowed to marry at younger ages. Criminal law routinely distinguished between women and men in statutes defining rape, statutory rape, and prostitution. Some statutes imposed harsher criminal penalties on women than men. Laws governing places of public accommodation or entertainment often banned women from bars, wrestling matches, and other public events.

ERA supporters wanted to eradicate these and other discriminatory laws in a single blow. Throughout the 1920s and for decades to come, however, the vast majority of women's rights activists opposed the ERA. They worried about the consequences of eliminating sex-specific family laws as well as laws "protecting" women workers because of their special needs and responsibilities. Although this position strikes some today as conservative, at the time the anti-ERA position was associated with progressives. The ERA position, in contrast, was generally supported by economic conservatives opposed to all government regulation of employment. Indeed, Woman's Party "[m]embers were conservative on most social issues and some were racist."[3]

The progressive anti-ERA position had its roots in opposition to 19th century labor practices. Appalled by the sweat shop conditions under which many immigrants and other workers, male and female, labored for low wages in American workplaces, reformers pushed for various protections. Protectionist legislation varied from state to state and took many forms, including maximum hours, minimum wages, mandatory time off for lunch and breaks, and weight-lifting limits. States often applied these laws only to women, however, and some statutes barred women from holding certain jobs at all, such as working at night in factories.[4] Progressive ERA opponents wanted similar protections to be extended to all workers and viewed women-specific legislation as an important first step in that strategy. More fundamentally, to progressives as well as socialists, "the ERA was an individualistic approach inconsistent with their basic frames of reference and their analysis of the social causes" of inequalities.[5]

---

3. Flora Davis, Moving the Mountain: The Women's Movement in America Since 1960 34 (1991); see also Katherine Pollak Ellickson, The President's Commission on the Status of Women: Its Formation, Functioning and Contribution 6 (1976); Judith Paterson, Be Somebody: A Biography of Marguerite Rawalt 140 (1986).

4. For a survey and discussion of protectionist labor legislation, see Judith A. Baer, The Chains of Protection (1978).

5. Mary Becker, The Sixties Shift to Formal Equality and the Courts: An Argument for Pragmatism and Politics, 40 Wm. & Mary L. Rev. 209, 214 (1998). Much of the text preceding this footnote is also drawn from Becker's article.

Protectionist legislation both helped and hurt women. Progressive reformers saw women-specific legislation as important because—then as now—women working for wages often worked a second shift at home, and because some women-specific laws served as proxies for anti-discrimination laws. For example, laws protected women from requirements beyond the strength of many women, such as lifting extremely heavy objects. Laws limiting women's hours in certain industries—such as maximum hours limits on women employed in laundries—also helped women find time for domestic duties and childcare. At the same time, laws banning women from certain kinds of employment—such as working in factories at night—doubtless hurt women, limiting them to a smaller subset of lower paying jobs. And protectionist legislation reinforced stereotypes that women were weaker and therefore less desirable employees than men.

Between the passage of the suffrage amendment in 1920 and the beginning of the revived women's movement in the early sixties, feminist activists remained divided into two camps, one supporting the early ERA and one opposed. Between 1923 and 1969, this ERA was introduced yearly in Congress. From 1940 on, the Republican party endorsed the ERA because it would eliminate protectionist legislation disliked by business. Democrats tended to oppose the ERA because the party was closely aligned with organized labor, a powerful advocate of protectionist legislation for workers male and female. Throughout this period, the ERA was defeated by a coalition of social conservatives, who were opposed to changing the status of women, and Democrats and progressives, like Eleanor Roosevelt, who feared that the ERA would invalidate sex-specific protective legislation as well as sex-specific family laws protecting women and children at divorce.[6]

The PCSW Compromise

In 1962, President Kennedy established the President's Commission on the Status of Women (PCSW) with Eleanor Roosevelt as its chair, just as the feminist movement was once again becoming more visible. Women were living longer and had greater control over reproduction. More women, whether married or single, were working for wages outside the home. Many younger women—like their foremothers in the 19th century—became involved in the struggle for racial and economic justice; many of these women objected to their subordinate and supportive positions within the civil rights, antiwar, and other "left" movements and were inspired by these movements to protest their own mistreatment.[7]

6. See Ellickson, above note 3, at 6; Blanche Linden–Ward & Carol Hurd Green, American Women in the 1960s: Changing the Future 2–3 (1993); Jane Mansbridge, Why We Lost the ERA 8–9 (1986).

7. Jane Sherron De Hart, The New Feminism and the Dynamics of Social Change, in Women's America: Refocusing the Past 589 (Linda K. Kerber & Jane Sherron De Hart eds., 5th ed. 2000); Sarah Evans, Personal Politics: The Roots of Women's Liberation in the Civil Rights Movement and the New Left 74–89, 102–25, 201–11 (1979).

Most, but not all, of the members of the PCSW were ERA opponents. Pauli Murray,[8] a member of the PCSW's Committee on Civil and Political Rights, suggested a compromise that finally broke the gridlock over the ERA. Murray was a longtime activist in the labor movement, the NAACP, and other civil rights organizations. She recommended that women seek equality through the courts under the Fourteenth Amendment, as civil rights activists had done in seeking equality for Blacks. Murray suggested that under such an approach, the courts could uphold sex-specific legislation that was good for women and strike sex-specific legislation that was bad for women. In its final report, the PCSW recommended going to the courts with the argument that the Equal Protection Clause banned discrimination against women. If that strategy failed, the PCSW stated that it *might* be appropriate to seek an ERA.

The PCSW compromise on the ERA was an important breakthrough. Virtually all activists committed to improving the status of women now agreed on a short-term strategy. Equally important, the PCSW brought together women leaders from all over the country and created forward momentum on women's issues just as the renewed women's movement began. Betty Friedan's book, *The Feminine Mystique*, was also published in 1963, leading to many discussions among educated women about their domestic roles. Reminiscent of the earlier woman's movement, more women began to embrace the word "feminist."[9] Many states formed commissions to investigate women's status, and soon every state would have such a commission.

Title VII and Support for a New ERA

In 1964, in the wake of the assassination of President Kennedy and in response to the civil rights movement that he supported, Congress enacted the Civil Rights Act of 1964, which banned race discrimination in many settings, including education (Title IX of the Act) and private employment (Title VII). Title VII of the Act also eliminated one of the major barriers to an ERA by including sex as one of the prohibited bases for adverse employment actions, alongside race, color, religion, and national origin.

The conventional wisdom is that "sex" was added as a floor amendment to Title VII in an attempt to derail the bill by adding what many saw as an obviously ludicrous provision, but the story is far more complicated. In fact, many women and men worked for and supported the inclusion of "sex."[10] The ban on sex discrimination was added in the House of Representatives by a conservative southerner who opposed Title VII's ban

8. For information on Murray, see Pauli Murray, The Autobiography of a Black Activist, Feminist, Lawyer, Priest and Poet (1987). For a detailed history of the PCSW compromise and Murray's key strategic role, see Serena Mayeri, Constitutional Choices: Legal Feminism and the Historical Dynamics of Change, 92 Cal. L. Rev. 755, 763–801 (2004).

9. Paterson, above note 3, at 152.

10. Jo Freeman, How "Sex" Got into Title VII: Persistent Opportunism as a Maker of Public Policy, 9 Law & Inequality 163, 176–78, 182 (1991); Robert C. Bird, More Than a Congressional Joke: A Fresh Look at the Legislative History of Sex Discrimination of the 1964 Civil Rights Act, 3 Wm. & Mary J. Women & L. 137, 138, 157–61 (1997).

on race discrimination, and he hoped that the addition of "sex" would derail the bill, but if the bill were to pass he wanted it to cover sex discrimination. On July 2, 1964, Title VII was enacted *with* the provision banning sex discrimination in private and public employment in the United States. By 1970, courts were interpreting Title VII as banning protective labor legislation. Thus, within a few years of its passage, Title VII eliminated one of the strongest reasons for feminist and progressive opposition to an ERA.[11]

The drive for an ERA gained momentum throughout the 1960s as more and more mainstream women leaders became supporters. There was now new wording for the Amendment:

> Section 1. Equality of rights under the law shall not be denied or abridged by the United States or by any State on account of sex.
>
> Section 2. The Congress shall have the power to enforce, by appropriate legislation, the provisions of this article.

In May 1970, Senator Birch Bayh, a Democrat from Indiana and chairman of the Senate Judiciary Committee's Subcommittee on Constitutional Amendments, held hearings on the ERA—the first action in Congress in almost ten years. Later that year, the UAW became the first union to endorse the ERA. In May 1971, the Senate Judiciary Committee held hearings, and testimony overwhelmingly ran in support of the amendment. In June of 1971, the Labor Department reversed its long-standing opposition and endorsed the ERA. The ERA then passed the House in August 1971 and the Senate in February 1972. On that same day, the Hawaii legislature ratified the amendment and five more states did so over the next two days. By the end of 1973, thirty states had ratified the ERA, putting the amendment seven states away from becoming part of the United States Constitution. But opposition began building at this point, and only five more states had ratified the amendment by 1977, for a total of thirty-five. No state ratified the amendment after 1977, and in 1982 the period of ratification expired despite enormous efforts by feminists in state after state.

Backlash

The final opposition to the ERA mounted for two reasons, both connected to the Supreme Court. Most important was the Supreme Court's 1973 decision in Roe v. Wade, 410 U.S. 113 (1973), which invalidated criminal bans on abortion on the grounds that the constitutional right to privacy encompassed the decision to have an abortion during the early stages of pregnancy. Abortion opponents immediately began to mobilize and tended generally to oppose changes in the legal treatment of women, including the ERA.[12]

11. For a more thorough discussion of the shift in opinion on an ERA in the 1960's, see Becker, above note 5.

12. See Elizabeth Pleck, Failed Strategies, Renewed Hope, in Rights of Passage: The Past and Future of the ERA 106, 110 (Joan Hoff-Wilson ed., 1986).

The other reason was the success of Pauli Murray's idea: going to the courts for equality on the basis of sex under the Fourteenth Amendment to the Constitution. Murray had suggested litigation by a group focused on sex discrimination (patterned after the NAACP with its focus on race discrimination). The New York office of the American Civil Liberties Union organized a Women's Rights Project headed by Ruth Bader Ginsburg with precisely this goal. In 1971, the first of its cases was decided by the Supreme Court: Reed v. Reed, 404 U.S. 71 (1971). The Court held unconstitutional under the Fourteenth Amendment a state statute preferring men over women as executors of the estates of deceased relatives. The Court decided another such case in 1973, two more in 1974, four in 1975, and so on, all of which are described later in this chapter. As the Supreme Court expanded the reach of the Fourteenth Amendment, ERA opponents were increasingly successful in arguing that the ERA would make no difference to the Constitution apart from mandating co-ed bathrooms and requiring women to fight in combat, both of which were controversial.

Differences Among Activists

Both approaches widely accepted by feminists in the early seventies—fighting for the ERA and seeking sex equality under the Fourteenth Amendment—were liberal approaches. Both sought to maximize women's choices by giving women rights to be treated like other individuals irrespective of sex. But not all feminists at this time were liberals. There were at least two other identifiable kinds of feminists: socialist feminists and radical feminists.

Liberal feminists regarded men as important allies who were also oppressed by rigid sex roles that denied them individual choice. Using a standard modeled on the standard developed in race cases made sense: government should treat all similarly situated individuals similarly regardless of sex (or race). Following the NAACP's example, these feminists worked within the system to achieve change by focusing on "gaining equal opportunity for women as individuals * * * consistent with the 'American Creed.' "[13] Liberal feminists stressed the similarities, rather than the differences, between individual women and men, as well as the need to increase freedom for all people by eliminating sex-based roles and stereotypes. Liberal feminists focused at an early date on the legal system and on using the courts as instruments of change.

In contrast, socialist and radical feminists sought to change existing structures of society instead of working within them; they were not especially interested in working for incremental change, lest their energy be dissipated in easy but small victories. In many ways, socialist and radical feminists were similar, given their backgrounds in the Left and civil rights movements. Both groups of feminists stressed the needs, interests, and rights of groups (capital versus labor, women versus men)

13. William H. Chafe, The Paradox of Change: American Women in the 20th Century 237 (1991). See also Cary Franklin, The Anti-Stereotyping Principle in Constitutional Sex Discrimination Law, 85 N.Y.U. L. Rev. 83, 101 (2010).

more than those of individuals, as well as the connections between various forms of oppression, such as racism and classism. They also each developed what has become the preeminent feminist method: consciousness raising. The method borrowed from a technique used to organize poor workers by encouraging them to talk about their problems with each other in small groups in order to see the systemic social causes of their oppression and the need for political solutions. Women in the socialist or Marxist movement, dissatisfied with their relegation to support positions such as secretaries, typists, coffee makers, and lovers of movement men, began to use the technique themselves. Radical feminists also used the technique to help women, many of whom shared similar problems, realize the systemic and political nature of the problems they faced. The technique as applied to women soon became known as consciousness raising, and it became "both a method for developing theory and a strategy for building up the new movement."[14] Soon even liberal feminists, and women who did not embrace the term feminist, were using the method to emphasize that the personal is political.

Socialist and radical feminists differed, however, in their views of the societal structures requiring change. Socialist feminists located the sources of women's oppression in the structure of capitalism and focused on uniting with other oppressed groups in fighting all forms of oppression, rather than organizing or struggling separately to advance the interests of women. Radical feminists identified men as the oppressors and, unlike liberal or socialist feminists, did not support building coalitions with men. Instead, radical feminists stressed that women and men have conflicting interests, and thus they tended to favor separatism and the development of a women's culture. Because of this focus, "radical" feminism came to mean feminists who were "woman-identified"[15] and who analyzed oppression primarily in terms of sex, although radical feminists also focused on other groups as well, such as people of color and workers, rather than the individuals central to liberal feminism.

Many radical feminists were lesbians, as were many women involved in the feminist movement throughout the 1960s and '70s. Within radical feminism, however, lesbian feminism became an identifiable intellectual approach and a political strategy. Many radical feminists regarded "heterosexuality as the cornerstone of male supremacy and lesbianism as the 'greatest threat' to its continued existence."[16] As such, some regarded sexual partnerships with other women as essential for feminists, while others argued that sexual behavior was less important than being woman-identified.

Throughout the fight for suffrage and the decades that followed, activists found themselves in many bitter battles over homophobia within campaigns for women's equality. Before suffrage, "sexologists" and other

14. Evans, above note 7, at 214; see also id. at 134–37, 215–25.

15. Chafe, above note 13, at 207.

16. De Hart, above note 7, at 512.

"experts," who had recently discovered "female sexual inverts," warned that these "inverts" were responsible for demands for increased independence and freedom for women.[17] Lesbian-baiting was thus used to frighten women away from the early woman movement. This pattern was repeated in the 1960s and early 1970s, with many heterosexual feminists hostile to lesbians, afraid that identification of themselves or of their organizations with lesbians would marginalize them, their groups, and their cause. Many lesbians responded by becoming more, rather than less, visible and vocal, demanding recognition of the problems with heterosexuality and challenging women who assumed that they were heterosexual to analyze the connections between heterosexuality and their oppression.

Similarly, racism was rampant within the fight for suffrage and continued to infect the women's movement after suffrage. Since the revival of the women's movement, Black feminist leaders have played important roles,[18] and Black women generally have been more supportive than white women of specific policy issues such as equal pay and government-supported child care. But many Black women and other women of color regard feminism in all its forms as a *white* women's movement. And, in fact, women in organized feminist groups, at both leadership and membership levels, have been disproportionately white.

These white women often ignored, and continue to ignore, the ways that prioritizing the elimination of sexual oppression abstracted from racial oppression is a product of white privilege. Many women of color in turn have been reluctant to give top priority to an agenda that overlooks the ways that sex is always also raced (and race is similarly always also sexed). White feminists' focus on sex as a "lowest common denominator" renders invisible the ways the experiences of women of color are shaped by a complicated combination of racism and sexism. For example, for some Latina women, problems caused by immigration rules and related social practices are far greater than, and often exacerbate, the problems prioritized by white activists. The solutions sought by these activists therefore can have little relevance for Latina women: effective police response to domestic violence, for instance, is meaningless if one cannot call the police because of one's status as an illegal alien. Similarly, Black women may be reluctant to call police to enforce protective orders given the disproportionately high arrest rates of Black men.[19] Finally, the emphasis on liberal approaches to change through law has had the effect of doing the most for those women most like men in power: elite white women. Seeking high-profile victories, the feminist agenda has thus often consisted of issues of

17. See Cott, above note 1, at 159–62; see also Havelock Ellis, Sexual Inversion (3d ed. 1915).

18. For example, Pauli Murray, Shirley Chisholm, Barbara Jordan, and Eleanor Holmes Norton.

19. For more examples, see Kimberlé Crenshaw, Mapping the Margins: Intersectionality, Identity Politics and Violence Against Women of Color, 43 Stan. L. Rev. 1241 (1991). See also Luke Charles Harris, The Challenge and Possibility for Black Males to Embrace Feminism, in Black Men on Race, Gender, and Sexuality 383, 383–86 (Devon W. Carbado ed., 1999).

little interest to other women, such as the entrance of elite women into professions.[20]

The Dominance of Liberal Feminism

Liberal feminism came to dominate understandings of sexual equality in law and throughout society. This happened in part because of the media's presentation of radical and socialist feminism as "ludicrous" and "beyond the pale" of acceptable discourse or protest.[21] Liberalism, with its use of widely accepted cultural norms such as individualism and its commitment to incremental change within the existing order, has been less threatening and in some ways more effective than radical or socialist feminism. By the mid 1970s, radical feminism had "dissipated" as an identifiable branch of the women's movement,[22] and by 1977, socialist feminist groups had disintegrated as a result of disputes over whether sex or class analysis should take precedence.

As a result, lawyers and nonlawyers alike tend to think of sexual equality as the right of an individual not to be treated differently from another individual because of sex. It is a right that men as well as women can invoke to avoid being treated based on their sex rather than as individuals. For liberals, equality is achieved when individuals face the same choices regardless of sex, thus enabling each individual to maximize her or his own self-interest. Other conceptions of equality and feminism remain influential in the academy, however, as will be seen in the feminist theories discussed in Chapter 3.

Feminists had an opportunity to move away from liberal feminism when the ERA was reintroduced into Congress in 1983. In contrast to the earlier campaigns for the ERA, feminists arranged for testimony at Congressional hearings that emphasized the limits of the liberal approach to gender equality embraced by the Supreme Court, as described in the rest of this chapter. In particular, feminists argued that the ERA could address laws that did not distinguish between men and women on their face, but nevertheless disproportionately harmed women.[23] Congress narrowly rejected the 1983 ERA; although the ERA continues to be introduced into Congress even today, there has not been another sustained effort to move beyond liberal feminism.

B. THE DEVELOPMENT OF A CONSTITUTIONAL STANDARD FOR SEX EQUALITY

By 1971, when the Supreme Court handed down Reed v. Reed, 404 U.S. 71 (1971), it had already established a special constitutional standard

20. Jo Freeman, The Politics of Women's Liberation 38–43 (1975).

21. Chafe, above note 13, at 235.

22. Alice Echols, Daring to Be Bad: Radical Feminism in America 1967–1975 287 (1989).

23. Serena Mayeri, A New E.R.A. or a New Era? Amendment Advocacy and the Reconstitution of Feminism, 103 Nw. U. L. Rev. 1223, 1249–1262 (2009).

for race discrimination. In other cases and in general, the Court requires that legislation have only a rational basis to be found constitutional; that is, that there be a plausible relationship between a statute and a legitimate governmental interest. Legislation scrutinized under this standard almost always survives. A heightened standard applies to legislation involving certain constitutional rights, such as the First Amendment guarantees of free speech and religious freedom or the Fourteenth Amendment guarantee of equal protection for certain "suspect" or vulnerable groups.

The NAACP argued that race was such a suspect class in its challenge to Jim Crow segregation, the legally mandated separation of the races in schools, seating on buses, restaurants, hotels and motels, washrooms, swimming pools, and even drinking fountains. The Supreme Court eventually agreed, holding that when a statute classifies individuals on the basis of race, the most searching level of review—strict scrutiny—must be used. Under this heightened standard, legislation is consistent with the Equal Protection Clause of the Fourteenth Amendment only if the suspect classification is necessary to achieve some "legitimate overriding purpose independent of invidious racial discrimination."[24] Under this standard, all explicit racial classifications were held unconstitutional from 1945 through 1971, when the Supreme Court began to consider what standard might be appropriate in cases involving sex classifications. At that point, the racial classifications struck had always been harmful to racial minorities, the prototype being racial segregation; the first affirmative action case was decided only in 1978.[25]

To this day, the level of scrutiny used to evaluate the constitutionality of sex classifications is a variation on the standard used in race cases. Liberal feminists generally accepted this standard until the end of the seventies, at which point many began to question the nature of the standard articulated by the Supreme Court. We turn now to examine the development of that standard.

1. THE FIRST CASE

All sex-specific laws became subject to constitutional challenge with the Supreme Court's decision in Reed v. Reed, 404 U.S. 71 (1971). The Idaho statute at issue in *Reed* identified various categories of people who qualified for appointment as administrator of an estate. In the event there were two people of different sexes who were equally qualified in terms of their relationship to the decedent, the statute preferred the man as executor. Idaho justified the preference as a reasonable way to avoid a tie (without wasting state resources in a court hearing) by selecting the person more likely to have experience with business affairs.

---

24. Loving v. Virginia, 388 U.S. 1 (1967).

25. Regents of the Univ. of Cal. v. Bakke, 438 U.S. 265 (1978).

The *Reed* case arose as a dispute between two separated parents. Their son, Skip, was reluctant to visit his father, a man described as "difficult" by his mother. When Skip was a teenager, his father requested a week-long visit. Skip did not want to go and, after two or three days, called his mother and asked if he could come home. His mother urged him to stay because "his father had visiting rights."[26] Skip committed suicide on Wednesday of that week, shooting himself with one of his father's guns, and both parents wanted to administer his estate.[27] The Idaho courts named the father as administrator, consistent with the terms of the Idaho statute. The mother was represented on appeal to the United States Supreme Court by the Women's Rights Project (WRP) of the ACLU. Ruth Bader Ginsburg and the other attorneys involved in this appeal argued that the strict scrutiny standard developed for racial classifications should also apply to classifications based on sex.

The Supreme Court recognized the legitimacy of the state's interest in minimizing courts' workloads. But the Court nevertheless regarded the preference for men as inconsistent with the Equal Protection Clause, stating its reason and describing the new standard in a single conclusory sentence:

> To give a mandatory preference to members of either sex over members of the other, merely to accomplish the elimination of hearings on the merits, is to make the very kind of arbitrary legislative choice forbidden by the Equal Protection Clause of the Fourteenth Amendment; and whatever may be said as to the positive values of avoiding intrafamily controversy, the choice in this context may not lawfully be mandated solely on the basis of sex.[28]

In doing so, the Court acknowledged that it was applying more than rational basis review, because "the objective of reducing the workload on probate courts by eliminating one class of contests is not without some legitimacy,"[29] but the Court did not apply strict scrutiny. The Court provided no explanation or guidance about the heightened level of scrutiny it employed between those poles. On remand, the parents were named joint administrators of the estate of their deceased son.

NOTES ON REED

1. Is the standard for race discrimination, developed to deal with Jim Crow segregation, an appropriate model for sex discrimination? How are relationships between the races similar to relationships between the sexes, and in what ways are they different? Are laws explicitly classifying on the basis of sex as likely to hurt women as those explicitly discriminating on the

---

26. Supreme Court Decisions and Women's Rights: Milestones to Equality 40 (Claire Cushman ed., 2001).

27. Id. For more background on *Reed*, see Fred Strebeigh, Equal: Women Reshape American Law 28–47 (2009).

28. 404 U.S. at 76–77.

29. Id. at 76.

basis of race? When we compare race and sex discrimination, do we miss the discrimination women of color face? Does the analogy of race discrimination to sex discrimination give white women the false sense that they understand the experiences of women of color? See Trina Grillo & Stephanie Wildman, Obscuring the Importance of Race: The Implication of Making Comparisons Between Racism and Sexism (or Other–Isms), in Stephanie Wildman, Privilege Revealed: How Invisible Preference Undermines America 85 (1996).

2. What sorts of laws and governmental practices will be perceived as sex discrimination under a standard banning explicit classifications by sex? Will such an approach threaten desirable rules? Reva B. Siegel argues that the development of the law of sex discrimination based on the analogy to race has resulted in a body of law with serious shortcomings. In her view, the Court in sex discrimination cases should have read the Fourteenth Amendment in light of the constitutional history of the Nineteenth Amendment, with its broad-based attack on the position of women within the family. The result, in her opinion, would have been to incorporate an emphasis upon full citizenship for women, requiring both changes in the private sphere and federal intervention, thus leading to substantially different outcomes in modern litigation (e.g., upholding the civil rights remedy in the Violence Against Women Act, which was struck down on federalism grounds (discussed in Chapter 4, Section D(5), below)). Siegel, She The People: The Nineteenth Amendment, Sex Equality, Federalism, and The Family, 115 Harv. L. Rev. 947 (2002). What do you think of this argument? How do you think the Court might have interpreted the Fourteenth Amendment differently?

3. Do you think that racial inequality is best addressed by a constitutional standard banning classifications based on race, particularly now that Jim Crow segregation has been dismantled and some race-specific rules (such as affirmative action) may actually benefit racial minorities? The Supreme Court has become increasingly hostile to race-based affirmative action. Compare Regents of the University of California v. Bakke, 438 U.S. 265 (1978) (upholding state university admission policy under which applicant's race was *one* factor to be taken into account and *not* a quota) with City of Richmond v. J.A. Croson Co., 488 U.S. 469 (1989) (striking city program setting aside 30% of city contracts for minority contractors in city with a 50% black population and a history of awarding 99.33% of contracts to nonminority businesses). Serena Mayeri chronicles a history of feminist attempts to apply sex equality doctrine to race in order to show that this "reverse analogy" could be useful even if the race to sex equality analogy is not. Starting in the mid-1970s, feminist lawyers, including Ginsburg, argued that the lower level of scrutiny applied to sex classifications, particularly the standard's deference to classifications designed to address societal discrimination, should be applied to the context of race-based affirmative action. Although these arguments have generally been unsuccessful, remnants continue to be found in now-Justice Ginsburg's opinions in affirmative action cases. Mayeri, Reconstructing the Race-Sex Analogy, 49 Wm. & Mary L. Rev. 1789, 1839–57 (2008). What are the advantages and disadvantages of such an approach? What might be some other instances of "mutually beneficial reciprocity," id. at 1856, between sex and race discrimination laws?

4. Defenders of both race and sex classifications have long invoked "mutual benefits" arguments to maintain that everyone, including women and people of color, benefit from the limits the law places upon them. Although such arguments were eventually rejected in contexts such as slavery, protectionist labor legislation, and marital rape, Jill Elaine Hasday illustrates the ways the arguments still surface today. For example, the Supreme Court has held that women benefit from certain restrictions on abortion, and the Court has restricted affirmative action programs because it believes such programs both constitute reverse racism and stigmatize people of color. Hasday argues that the validity of current iterations of mutual benefits arguments should be analyzed according to the following criteria: (1) whether advocates asserting that rights and opportunities will injure women or people of color are consistent in their arguments, (2) whether they present evidence of actual harm, (3) whether they rely on narrow assumptions about how women or people of color should behave, and (4) whether they engage with counterarguments and opposing viewpoints. Hasday, Protecting Them From Themselves: The Persistence of Mutual Benefits Arguments For Sex and Race Inequality, 84 N.Y.U. L. Rev. 1464, 1528–39 (2009). How would you apply Hasday's framework to challenges to race-based affirmative action? What might Siegel's or Mayeri's analysis, above notes 2 and 3, add to your approach? In what instances might departures from formal race or sex equality actually benefit women and people of color today?

2. FOUR VOTES FOR STRICT SCRUTINY

The ACLU WRP under Ruth Bader Ginsburg was amicus curiae for the plaintiff in the next sex discrimination case decided on equal protection grounds, Frontiero v. Richardson, 411 U.S. 677 (1973).[30] The plaintiff, a married woman who was an officer in the Air Force, argued that she was denied equal protection by laws automatically giving spousal benefits to married men but denying them to married women absent a showing that the wife provided more than half the husband's support. As in *Reed*, the WRP argued that the strict scrutiny standard developed for racial classifications should also apply to classifications based on sex. This time, four Justices agreed, but a majority of the court could not agree on the standard to be applied.

Eight of the nine justices—all but Justice Rehnquist—agreed that the Air Force policy unconstitutionally discriminated on the basis of sex. Justice Brennan, writing for four members of the Court, used strict scrutiny to strike the statute. He referred to "our Nation's * * * long and unfortunate history of sex discrimination," 411 U.S. at 684, and also noted that sex, like race, is an immutable but highly visible characteristic bearing no relation to ability to contribute to society, id. at 686. Finally, he explained that Congress had shown "an increasing sensitivity to sex-based classifications" over the previous decade by enacting the Equal Pay

30. For extensive discussions of the litigation history of *Frontiero*, see Serena Mayeri, "When the Trouble Started": The Story of *Frontiero v. Richardson*, in Women and the Law Stories (Elizabeth M. Schneider & Stephanie M. Wildman eds., 2010); Strebeigh, above note 27, at 48–64.

Act and Title VII and passing the ERA. Id. Congressional concern was particularly relevant because of Congress' power to enforce the Equal Protection Clause under Section 5 of the Fourteenth Amendment. Once Justice Brennan had adopted strict scrutiny as the appropriate standard, it was easy to strike the statute in *Frontiero* since administrative convenience was the sole justification for differential treatment of women and men in the Air Force. The other four justices agreed that the Air Force policy at issue in *Frontiero* was unconstitutional, but they applied the *Reed* standard rather than adopting strict scrutiny in light of the then-pending ERA. The four justices provided no more guidance about the nature of the *Reed* standard.

NOTES ON FRONTIERO

1. Once they realized that the Supreme Court would not extend strict scrutiny to sex, Ruth Bader Ginsburg and the WRP shifted their strategy, concentrating "on chipping away at sexual stereotyping through cases that demonstrated the inequities that may result to *males* from an unthinking application of generalizations about the sexes." Margaret A. Berger, Litigation on Behalf of Women: A Review for the Ford Foundation 18–19 (1980) (emphasis added). But they lost the first of these cases, Kahn v. Shevin, 416 U.S. 351 (1974). The plaintiff was a widower challenging Florida's property tax exemption of $500 per year for widows. In a six-three decision (Brennan, Marshall, and White dissenting), the Court upheld the classification. The Court began by noting that women working full time tended to earn less than 60 cents for every dollar earned by men and that the death of a spouse would often force into this inhospitable market a widow who previously had depended on her spouse. In light of these realities, the Court upheld the classification as a reasonable measure "designed to further the state policy of cushioning the financial impact of spousal loss upon the sex for which that loss imposes a disproportionately heavy burden." Id. at 355. Would you have argued against the exemption for widows in *Kahn*? What are the strongest arguments for upholding the exemption? Is the holding in *Kahn* necessarily inconsistent with a liberal approach to sexual equality? Why or why not?

2. The Women's Rights Project also lost the next case in which it filed an amicus brief, though it was brought by a woman and involved a particularly important issue: whether discrimination on the basis of pregnancy is permissible. The case is reprinted below. How would you formulate an argument that pregnancy discrimination is sex discrimination?

3. PREGNANCY DISCRIMINATION

GEDULDIG v. AIELLO

Supreme Court of the United States, 1974.
417 U.S. 484, 94 S.Ct. 2485, 41 L.Ed.2d 256.

MR. JUSTICE STEWART delivered the opinion of the Court.

We cannot agree that the exclusion of [pregnancy] from coverage [under California's disability insurance program] amounts to invidious discrimination under the Equal Protection Clause. * * * Although California has created a program to insure most risks of employment disability, it has not chosen to insure all such risks, and this decision is reflected in the level of annual contributions exacted from participating employees. This Court has held that, consistently with the Equal Protection Clause, a State "may take one step at a time, addressing itself to the phase of the problem which seems most acute to the legislative mind...." Particularly with respect to social welfare programs, so long as the line drawn by the State is rationally supportable, the courts will not interpose their judgment as to the appropriate stopping point. "(T)he Equal Protection Clause does not require that a State must choose between attacking every aspect of a problem or not attacking the problem at all."

* * *

The State has a legitimate interest in maintaining the self-supporting nature of its insurance program. Similarly, it has an interest in distributing the available resources in such a way as to keep benefit payments at an adequate level for disabilities that are covered, rather than to cover all disabilities inadequately. Finally, California has a legitimate concern in maintaining the contribution rate at a level that will not unduly burden participating employees, particularly low-income employees who may be most in need of the disability insurance.

These policies provide an objective and wholly noninvidious basis for the State's decision not to create a more comprehensive insurance program than it has. There is no evidence in the record that the selection of the risks insured by the program worked to discriminate against any definable group or class in terms of the aggregate risk protection derived by that group or class from the program.[20] There is no risk from which men are protected and women are not. Likewise, there is no risk from which women are protected and men are not.[21]

The appellee simply contends that, although she has received insurance protection equivalent to that provided all other participating employees, she has suffered discrimination because she encountered a risk that

---

20. The dissenting opinion to the contrary, this case is thus a far cry from cases involving discrimination based upon gender as such. The California insurance program does not exclude anyone from benefit eligibility because of gender but merely removes one physical condition—pregnancy—from the list of compensable disabilities. While it is true that only women can become pregnant it does not follow that every legislative classification concerning pregnancy is a sex-based classification * * *. Absent a showing that distinctions involving pregnancy are mere pretexts designed to effect an invidious discrimination against the members of one sex or the other, lawmakers are constitutionally free to include or exclude pregnancy from the coverage of legislation such as this on any reasonable basis, just as with respect to any other physical condition. The lack of identity between the excluded disability and gender as such under this insurance program becomes clear upon the most cursory analysis. The program divides potential recipients into two groups—pregnant women and nonpregnant persons. While the first group is exclusively female, the second includes members of both sexes. * * *

21. Indeed, the appellant submitted to the District Court data that indicated that both the annual claim rate and the annual claim cost are greater for women than for men. As the District Court acknowledged, "women contribute about 28% of the total disability insurance fund and receive back about 38% of the fund in benefits." Several amici curiae have represented to the Court that they have had a similar experience under private disability insurance programs.

was outside the program's protection. For the reasons we have stated, we hold that this contention is not a valid one under the Equal Protection Clause of the Fourteenth Amendment.

* * *

MR. JUSTICE BRENNAN, with whom MR. JUSTICE DOUGLAS and MR. JUSTICE MARSHALL join, dissenting.

* * *

California's disability insurance program was enacted to supplement the State's unemployment insurance and workmen's compensation programs by providing benefits to wage earners to cushion the economic effects of income loss and medical expenses resulting from sickness or injury. * * *

To achieve the Act's broad humanitarian goals, the legislature fashioned a pooled-risk disability fund covering all employees at the same rate of contribution, regardless of individual risk.[2] The only requirement that must be satisfied before an employee becomes eligible to receive disability benefits is that the employee must have contributed 1% of a minimum income of $300 during a one-year base period. * * * Benefits are payable for a maximum of 26 weeks, but may not exceed one-half of the employee's total base-period earnings. Finally, compensation is paid for virtually all disabling conditions without regard to cost, voluntariness, uniqueness, predictability, or "normalcy" of the disability. Thus, for example, workers are compensated for costly disabilities such as heart attacks, voluntary disabilities such as cosmetic surgery or sterilization, disabilities unique to sex or race such as prostatectomies or sickle-cell anemia, pre-existing conditions inevitably resulting in disability such as degenerative arthritis or cataracts, and "normal" disabilities such as removal of irritating wisdom teeth or other orthodontia.

Despite the Code's broad goals and scope of coverage, compensation is denied for disabilities suffered in connection with a "normal" pregnancy—disabilities suffered only by women. Disabilities caused by pregnancy, however, like other physically disabling conditions covered by the Code, require medical care, often include hospitalization, anesthesia and surgical procedures, and may involve genuine risk to life. Moreover, the economic effects caused by pregnancy-related disabilities are functionally indistinguishable from the effects caused by any other disability: wages are lost due to a physical inability to work, and medical expenses are incurred for the delivery of the child and for postpartum care.[5] In my view, by singling out for less favorable treatment a gender-linked disability peculiar to

2. California deliberately decided not to classify employees on the basis of actuarial data. Thus, the contribution rate for a particular group of employees is not tied to that group's predicted rate of disability claims.

5. Nearly two-thirds of all women who work do so of necessity: either they are unmarried or their husbands earn less than $7,000 per year. * * * "[I]n 1972, a woman working full time had a median income which was only 57.9% of the median for males—a figure actually six points lower than had been achieved in 1955."

women, the State has created a double standard for disability compensation: a limitation is imposed upon the disabilities for which women workers may recover, while men receive full compensation for all disabilities suffered, including those that affect only or primarily their sex, such as prostatectomies, circumcision, hemophilia, and gout. In effect, one set of rules is applied to females and another to males. Such dissimilar treatment of men and women, on the basis of physical characteristics inextricably linked to one sex, inevitably constitutes sex discrimination.

* * *

California's legitimate interest in fiscal integrity could easily have been achieved through a variety of less drastic, sexually neutral means. As the District Court observed:

> Even using (the State's) estimate of the cost of expanding the program to include pregnancy-related disabilities, however, it is clear that including these disabilities would not destroy the program. The increased costs could be accommodated quite easily by making reasonable changes in the contribution rate, the maximum benefits allowable, and the other variables affecting the solvency of the program. For example, the entire cost increase estimated by defendant could be met by requiring workers to contribute an additional amount of approximately .364% of their salary and increasing the maximum annual contribution to about $119.

TEXT NOTE: DISPARATE TREATMENT AND DISPARATE IMPACT

Title VII of the Civil Rights Act of 1964, whose passage is described earlier in this chapter, was enacted before the Supreme Court recognized the Equal Protection Clause of the Fourteenth Amendment as relevant to any discrimination on the basis of sex. Courts recognize two kinds of employment discrimination claims under Title VII: disparate treatment and disparate impact.

A disparate treatment claim alleges that similarly-situated women and men have been treated differently. Such claims can be broken down into two types: allegations of facial (open, overt) disparate treatment and allegations of subtle disparate treatment. Facial disparate treatment occurs when a rule or policy openly, on its face, by its very terms, treats women one way and men another. Thus, for example, a rule that excludes all women from night work in factories (as some protectionist legislation did) discriminates overtly—on its face—on the basis of sex. If a rule or policy explicitly discriminates on the basis of sex, there is no *additional* requirement of any particular intent. The intent to treat individuals differently because of their sex is demonstrated by the terms of the discriminatory policy itself. Since the passage of Title VII, overt discrimination has become increasingly rare.

The other form of disparate treatment is subtle and common even today. For example, a lawyer believes that her firm imposes a higher standard on women than men for promotion to partnership. The law firm has, of course, no policy *overtly* requiring women to be more productive workers, but there are no objective measures of productivity, nor any objective and reliable predictors of future value as a partner. If that lawyer sues, the ultimate question is whether the employer in fact treated men and women differently. The employer will argue that more men than women were promoted to partner not because they were men, but because they were more valuable employees or displayed more of the traits which the firm associates with future success as a partner. Part of the plaintiff's case might be evidence that the employer routinely treats women in stereotypical ways, as demonstrated, for example, by some partners routinely referring to some of the young female associates as "chicks" or "girls," or asking them (but not the male associates) to babysit. Here, circumstantial evidence revealing the intent of the employer—the intent to discriminate against women rather than merely select the most valuable partners—becomes a critical part of the plaintiff's demonstration that in fact women were treated differently than men.

In contrast, a disparate impact claim alleges that a gender-neutral rule or policy has a disparate impact on women. For example, a facially gender-neutral requirement that employees be 5′ 10″ tall or taller and weigh at least 220 pounds has a disparate impact on women, who will disproportionately (relative to men) fail to meet this qualification. Here, there is a clear standard or baseline for comparison: the proportion of men who meet this standard (say 20%) can be compared with the proportion of women who meet this standard (say 3%). In light of this difference, the requirement obviously has a disparate impact on women.

Although disparate impact claims have been recognized under Title VII (subject to a defense of business necessity), such claims have never been recognized in constitutional cases. Disparate impact claims are not even recognized under the strict scrutiny standard applicable to constitutional cases involving racial discrimination. The Court's concern seems to be that disparate impact would not be workable as a constitutional standard because legislation routinely has all sorts of disparate impacts on all sorts of groups. For constitutional cases, disparate treatment must be shown, though unconstitutional disparate treatment can be either overt or subtle. If subtle, the plaintiff must establish an intent to discriminate on an impermissible basis.

NOTES ON GEDULDIG

1. As discussed earlier, the first cases applying the Equal Protection Clause to sex-based discrimination—*Reed*, *Frontiero*, and *Kahn*—all involved *facially* discriminatory rules treating all women one way and all men another. The *Reed* statute gave a preference to male over female relatives in selecting executors of estates. In *Frontiero*, the Air Force automatically gave spousal benefits to wives of Air Force personnel, but gave such benefits to husbands only when an individual husband was dependent on his wife for more than half his support. In *Kahn,* a Florida statute that gave a $500 property tax exemption to widows but not to widowers was upheld as constitutional, despite discrimination on the basis of sex, because it furthered a legitimate state policy, cushioning the loss of a spouse for the more economically vulnerable survivor.

Geduldig was the first case to reach the Court in which the challenged rule arguably did not discriminate on its face between women and men. Women were in both categories: "pregnant women and nonpregnant persons" (to quote the language used by the Court in footnote 20). Because the classification was based not on "gender" but on pregnancy, the Court did not view it as overt discrimination on the basis of sex, i.e., as distinguishing on its face between women and men. Because there was no overt sex discrimination (according to the Court's analysis), the distinction is not disparate treatment on the basis of sex unless the employer adopted it in order to treat women one way and men another. Do you agree with the Court that the statute does not discriminate on its face on the basis of sex? How would you frame a disparate treatment argument for the plaintiffs in *Geduldig* given the classification between "pregnant women and nonpregnant persons"?

2. In her brief for the plaintiffs, Wendy Williams (and co-counsel) argued:

> Classifications based upon physical characteristics unique to one sex are sex-based classifications. Sex unique characteristics, particularly the capacity to become pregnant, are what define a person as a man or a woman, and the legal benefits or burdens which are based on such characteristics are burdens or benefits conferred because of a person's gender-identity. * * * Whether differential treatment on the basis of pregnancy is justified must depend upon the purpose of legislation and whether the differences between that "unique" characteristic and other characteristics are relevant to that purpose.

Appellee's Brief in Geduldig v. Aiello, No. 73–640, at 24–25 (Oct. Term 1973). In an amicus brief filed by the Women's Rights Project, Ginsburg also argued that the California plan at issue in *Geduldig* was *overt* discrimination on the basis of sex:

> [T]he state applies a double standard. It allows men to recover for any condition which affects them, including conditions which affect only men. But it denies benefits to women disabled by pregnancy, a condition that affects only women. A policy of this kind is overt sex discrimination. * * *
>
> Pregnancy is a uniquely female condition. * * * The [lower court] noted at the outset that discrimination of this kind, since it is based on a sex-linked characteristic, is sex discrimination.

Amicus Brief of ACLU in Geduldig v. Aiello, No. 73–640, at 18–19 (Oct. Term 1973); see also the discussion of the plaintiff's litigation strategy in Strebeigh, above footnote 27, at 90–103. What features of the Court's approach made it easy to reject these arguments? Can you think of other arguments that might have persuaded the Supreme Court?

3. The discrimination standard developed by the Supreme Court is often described as "formal equality." Under this approach, similarly situated individuals must be treated similarly regardless of sex (or race or other protected characteristics). The Court could have fashioned a formal equality standard (requiring that similarly situated individuals be treated similarly) that would encompass pregnancy discrimination as Wendy Williams argued in her brief. Williams has suggested that the Court reached its "cultural limits" on this

issue, unable to move beyond the ways society subsumes women within motherhood to see that distinctions based on motherhood could be sex discrimination. Wendy W. Williams, The Equality Crisis: Some Reflections on Culture, Courts, and Feminism, 7 Women's Rts. L. Rep. 175 (1983). Do you agree? To the extent true, could you use this point to argue against a formal equality approach? For general critiques of formal equality, see Patricia J. Williams, The Alchemy of Race and Rights 104–10 (1991) (criticizing formal equality under conditions of substantive inequality and likening the Court's equality standard to a machine that makes sausage no matter what you throw into it); Linda S. Greene, Race in the 21st Century: Equality Through Law?, 64 Tul. L. Rev. 1515 (1990) (discussing problems with formalism and equality).

Is Wendy Williams suggesting that both the state of California and the Supreme Court were blinded by stereotypes about women's roles? Ginsburg also argued in her brief that California's approach had "all the earmarks of [a] self-fulfilling prophecy. If women are treated by the state * * * as detached from the work force when pregnancy disables them, * * * it is not surprising that some succumb to the disincentives barring the way to return, and to appellant's stereotyped vision of women's place post-birth." Amicus Brief of ACLU, above note 2, at 17. Cary Franklin argues that this argument and similar ones went well beyond a formal equality approach, instead calling for the application of an anti-stereotyping doctrine in sex discrimination cases. Franklin, The Anti-Stereotyping Principle in Constitutional Sex Discrimination Law, 85 N.Y.U. L. Rev. 83, 120–28 (2010). How might an anti-stereotyping approach operate differently than a formal equality approach? How might the two approaches collapse into one another?

4. Covering all of male workers' disabilities was an important goal of the fund. Why wasn't it equally important to cover all of female workers' disabilities? If you think that there was sex discrimination in the design of the plan in *Geduldig*, how would you describe it? Was it based on animus, an intent to discriminate *against* women? Do you agree with the Court that there was no sex discrimination because California did not discriminate on the basis of sex *per se* (in and of itself) but rather on the basis of pregnancy in light of women's relative contributions and draw from the fund?

Does this analysis suggest that the formal equality standard applied in *Geduldig* is actually androcentric (male-centered) because it entitles women only to equal treatment under rules and practices developed by and for men? See Catharine A. MacKinnon, Feminism Unmodified 36–37 (1987). *Geduldig* seems to suggest that a woman must look and behave like a man to be protected by the constitutional sex equality standard because as soon as she is perceived as different (pregnant, for example), differential treatment is justified. Is this a problem? If so, could it be avoided by a different constitutional standard?

5. How would you address the fact that women received proportionately more in annual benefits than their share of contributions (see footnote 21 of the majority opinion)? Ginsburg argued that California *intended* to discriminate on the basis of sex:

> Indeed, the conclusion that California's disability scheme discriminates on the basis of sex is inescapable, for appellant admits to a discriminatory motive. Throughout this litigation, California has contended that, in its view, women already receive a disproportionately high share of benefits because they contribute 28% to the funds and receive 38% of the benefits. Hence, the state legislature, to prevent an even greater distortion between male and female claimants, may exclude disabilities due to pregnancy. Appellant [the State of California] ignores the fact that women constitute 40% of the workforce. Their contribution of only 28% of the fund is reflective of the typically low wages received by women. Women in fact receive less in benefits than their percentage in the work force would lead one to expect. However, even if they did use the fund disproportionately, that would not justify an exclusion directed solely at women. One may wonder if disproportionate use of the fund by blacks or Catholics would be thought by appellant to be sufficient justification for limiting access of those groups to the fund. While appellant's argument is clearly without merit, the fact that it is pressed insistently leaves no doubt on the point considered here: exclusion from eligibility for benefits of women disabled due to pregnancy is expressly designed to discriminate against women as a class. The presence of a discriminatory motive should be taken into consideration by the Court in its analysis of whether the classification is constitutionally infirm.

Amicus Brief of ACLU, above note 2, at 23–24. Why did this argument fail? How did the Court turn Ginsburg's argument into an explanation about why the plan did *not* discriminate on the basis of sex?

Recall, as Justice Brennan describes in his dissent, that employees paid 1% of their wages (up to a certain specified amount) into the fund. Although women constituted 40% of the workforce, they contributed only 28% of the fund because of their lower pay. Why, as Ginsburg's brief asks, didn't the fund's designers check to see whether members of religious or racial minorities or other identifiable groups were drawing more than their share? Given the contribution structure, low-wage workers in general were surely drawing more than their share of benefits. Why wasn't this seen as a problem and claims limited for all low-wage workers, not just women? Why did those in control of the plan only worry about *women* drawing more than their share?

6. The majority in *Geduldig* described the state's legitimate interest as "distributing the available resources in such a way as to keep benefit payments at an adequate level for disabilities that are covered, rather than to cover all disabilities inadequately." What does this mean exactly? Why might a state reasonably decide to cover disabilities associated with elective surgery, including cosmetic surgery, but not disabilities associated with pregnancy, given the information included in footnote 5 of Justice Brennan's dissent? Even if the state was concerned that women were drawing more than their share of benefits, why not begin by cutting cosmetic and all other elective surgery for women to reduce women's draw? What assumptions about pregnant women could make rational a policy providing insurance for disabilities caused by cosmetic surgery or skiing accidents but denying it for pregnancy-related disabilities? In light of such assumptions, do you agree with the Court that there is "an objective and wholly noninvidious basis [i.e., no discrimina-

tory intent] for the State's decision" to cover all disabilities but those related to pregnancy?

7. As described in the text note before these questions, disparate impact analysis looks to see whether a facially neutral rule or policy has a disparate impact on certain groups relative to other groups. Did the California plan have a disparate impact on women? All of men's disabilities were covered, but not all of women's. On the other hand, women drew more in benefits than men relative to their contributions (even without coverage of pregnancy-related disabilities). Is there a problem picking the appropriate baseline (i.e., selecting the appropriate standard for comparison)? In considering whether the plan has a disparate impact on women, wouldn't one have to identify a single appropriate alternative for comparison so that one could consider whether the California plan at issue in *Geduldig* had a disparate impact on women relative to the alternative? Given that alternatives in this context could be structured many ways (some better, some worse for women), is this an insurmountable hurdle for the use of disparate impact in many constitutional cases? Why doesn't this problem occur in the employment context when, for example, a plaintiff challenges a height or weight requirement?

8. In an article written after *Geduldig* was decided, Wendy Williams argued "that laws and rules which do not overtly classify on the basis of sex, but which have a disproportionately negative effect upon one sex, warrant, under appropriate circumstances, placing a burden of justification upon the party defending the law or rule in court." Wendy W. Williams, Equality's Riddle: Pregnancy and the Equal Treatment-Special Treatment Debate, 13 N.Y.U. Rev. L. & Soc. Change 325, 330 (1984–85). Can you fashion a workable disparate impact standard for constitutional cases? How would you define "appropriate circumstances"?

9. The same question—whether discrimination on the basis of pregnancy is sex discrimination—arises under Title VII. Although the meaning of discrimination under this statute (as described in the text note above on disparate treatment and disparate impact) is not always identical to its meaning under the Constitution, the Supreme Court interpreted Title VII consistently with *Geduldig* in the context of pregnancy discrimination. In General Electric Co. v. Gilbert, 429 U.S. 125 (1976), the Supreme Court held that an employer did not discriminate on the basis of sex under Title VII when medical benefits did not include costs associated with pregnancy. After pressure from women's groups, Congress overturned *Gilbert* with the Pregnancy Discrimination Act of 1978 (PDA), 42 U.S.C. § 2000e(k). The PDA defines sex discrimination to include distinctions based on pregnancy, childbirth, or related medical conditions.

Geduldig's holding that discrimination on the basis of pregnancy is not overt sex discrimination under the Constitution was affirmed by the Court in Bray v. Alexandria Women's Health Clinic, 506 U.S. 263 (1993). The issue in *Bray* was whether one of the civil rights statutes (42 U.S.C. § 1985(c), providing a private federal cause of action for private conspiracy to, among other things, deprive "any person or class of persons of the equal protection of the laws") allowed the plaintiffs to sue protesters obstructing access to abortion clinics. The Court held that the cause of action was available against members of a private conspiracy only if the conspirators had discriminated against women as a class. But since discrimination on the basis of pregnancy (or its termination) was not discrimination on the basis of sex under *Geduldig*, the § 1985(c) cause of action was unavailable.

10. Ten years after *Bray*, in Nevada Department of Human Resources v. Hibbs, 538 U.S. 721 (2003), the Supreme Court, in an opinion authored by then Chief Justice Rehnquist, upheld the Family and Medical Leave Act, finding that the act was appropriate legislation to enforce the Equal Protection Clause. (The FMLA is discussed in more detail in Chapter 7.) Reva Siegel emphasizes the ways that *Hibbs* reframed earlier pregnancy discrimination cases by holding that state action based upon judgments about "mothers and mothers-to-be" denies women equal citizenship. Siegel, You've Come a Long Way, Baby: Rehnquist's New Approach to Pregnancy Discrimination in *Hibbs*, 58 Stan. L. Rev. 1871, 1882–86 (2006) (quoting *Hibbs*, 538 U.S. at 736). Indeed, *Hibbs* indicated that legislation offering extended pregnancy leave, in excess of the amount of time medically indicated, to women but not men violated the Equal Protection Clause because it reinforced stereotypes about the appropriate roles of fathers and mothers. "Where Rehnquist once saw questions of women's bodies, he now saw questions of women's roles," says Siegel. Id. at 1897.

Siegel concludes that pregnancy classifications are now impermissible if they rest on sex-role stereotypes and are "not solely attributable to physical differences between the sexes." Id. at 1891–94 & n. 104. See also Neil S. Siegel & Reva B. Siegel, *Struck* by Stereotype: Ruth Bader Ginsburg on Pregnancy Discrimination as Sex Discrimination, 59 Duke L.J. 771, 792–96 (2010); Siegel & Siegel, Pregnancy and Sex Role Stereotyping: From *Struck* to *Carhart*, 70 Ohio St. L.J. 1095, 1111–13 (2009). How is this argument similar to and different from the arguments made by Williams and Ginsburg in the *Geduldig* litigation? How might the new test identified by Siegel have helped the plaintiffs in *Geduldig*? How might the Court reach the same outcome in *Geduldig* even after *Hibbs*? What does such an analysis reveal about the potential limits of an anti-stereotyping approach? For an application of a similar anti-stereotyping approach to child abuse laws that prosecute pregnant women based solely on their drug use, see Julie B. Ehrlich, Breaking the Law by Giving Birth: The War on Drugs, The War on Reproductive Rights, and the War on Women, 32 N.Y.U. Rev. L. & Soc. Change 381, 406–15 (2008).

11. Kim Shayo Buchanan argues that the Court's subsequent decision in Lawrence v. Texas, 539 U.S. 558 (2003), also provides a basis for rejecting the legacy of *Geduldig* and *Bray*. *Lawrence* invalidated a criminal prohibition on same-sex sodomy because "our laws and tradition afford constitutional protection to personal decisions relating to marriage, procreation, contraception, family relationships, child rearing, and education." Id. at 574. Reading *Lawrence* in combination with *Hibbs*, Buchanan contends that there is now an "equal sexual liberty approach to the gendered regulation of sex" that "reveals the unconstitutional gender stereotypes that inform the simultaneous legal entrenchment of heterosexual pleasure as a male entitlement and of pregnancy as a punishment for women's participation in disfavored heterosex." Buchanan, *Lawrence v. Geduldig*, Regulating Women's Sexuality, 56 Emory L.J. 1235, 1296 (2007). Such stereotypes include "that women alone

should bear responsibility for birth control, pregnancy, and children" and "that a woman's only proper role is as wife and mother." Id. at 1297. In Buchanan's view, pregnancy classifications should now be "viewed as red flags that can alert the court to the risk of gender stereotyping." Id. at 1300. How is this argument similar to and different from Siegel's, as set forth in note 10? What could it add to the litigation strategy of the *Geduldig* plaintiffs? How do you think the Court would respond?

4. SETTLING ON AN INTERMEDIATE STANDARD

CRAIG v. BOREN

Supreme Court of the United States, 1976.
429 U.S. 190, 97 S.Ct. 451, 50 L.Ed.2d 397.

MR. JUSTICE BRENNAN delivered the opinion of the Court.

The interaction of two sections of an Oklahoma statute prohibits the sale of "nonintoxicating" 3.2% beer to males under the age of 21 and to females under the age of 18. The question to be decided is whether such a gender-based differential constitutes a denial to males 18–20 years of age of the equal protection of the laws in violation of the Fourteenth Amendment.

* * *

Analysis may appropriately begin with the reminder that *Reed* emphasized that statutory classifications that distinguish between males and females are "subject to scrutiny under the Equal Protection Clause." To withstand constitutional challenge, previous cases establish that classifications by gender must serve important governmental objectives and must be substantially related to achievement of those objectives. Thus, in Reed, the objectives of "reducing the workload on probate courts," and "avoiding intrafamily controversy," were deemed of insufficient importance to sustain use of an overt gender criterion in the appointment of administrators of intestate decedents' estates. Decisions following Reed similarly have rejected administrative ease and convenience as sufficiently important objectives to justify gender-based classifications.

* * *

We accept for purposes of discussion the District Court's identification of the objective underlying [the statute] as the enhancement of traffic safety. Clearly, the protection of public health and safety represents an important function of state and local governments. However, appellees' statistics in our view cannot support the conclusion that the gender-based distinction closely serves to achieve that objective and therefore the distinction cannot under Reed withstand equal protection challenge.

The appellees introduced a variety of statistical surveys. * * *

The most focused and relevant of the statistical surveys, arrests of 18–20-year-olds for alcohol-related driving offenses, exemplifies the ultimate unpersuasiveness of this evidentiary record. Viewed in terms of the correlation between sex and the actual activity that Oklahoma seeks to regulate—driving while under the influence of alcohol—the statistics broadly establish that .18% of females and 2% of males in that age group were arrested for that offense. While such a disparity is not trivial in a statistical sense, it hardly can form the basis for employment of a gender line as a classifying device. Certainly if maleness is to serve as a proxy for drinking and driving, a correlation of 2% must be considered an unduly tenuous "fit." Indeed, prior cases have consistently rejected the use of sex as a decisionmaking factor even though the statutes in question certainly rested on far more predictive empirical relationships than this.

* * *

* * * [T]he showing offered by the appellees does not satisfy us that sex represents a legitimate, accurate proxy for the regulation of drinking and driving. In fact, when it is further recognized that Oklahoma's statute prohibits only the selling of 3.2% beer to young males and not their drinking the beverage once acquired (even after purchase by their 18–20-year-old female companions), the relationship between gender and traffic safety becomes far too tenuous to satisfy *Reed*'s requirement that the gender-based difference be substantially related to achievement of the statutory objective.

We hold, therefore, that under *Reed,* Oklahoma's 3.2% beer statute invidiously discriminates against males 18–20 years of age.

* * *

[Concurring opinions by Justices Powell, Blackmun, and Stewart and a dissenting opinion by Chief Justice Burger have been omitted.]

MR. JUSTICE STEVENS, concurring.

* * *

In this case, the classification is not as obnoxious as some the Court has condemned, nor as inoffensive as some the Court has accepted. It is objectionable because it is based on an accident of birth, because it is a mere remnant of the now almost universally rejected tradition of discriminating against males in this age bracket, and because, to the extent it reflects any physical difference between males and females, it is actually perverse. The question then is whether the traffic safety justification put forward by the State is sufficient to make an otherwise offensive classification acceptable.

The classification is not totally irrational. For the evidence does indicate that there are more males than females in this age bracket who drive and also more who drink. Nevertheless, there are several reasons why I regard the justification as unacceptable. It is difficult to believe that the statute was actually intended to cope with the problem of traffic safety, since it has only a minimal effect on access to a not very intoxicating beverage and does not prohibit its consumption. Moreover, the empirical data submitted by the State accentuate the unfairness of treating all 18–21-year-old males as inferior to their female counterparts. The legislation imposes a restraint on 100% of the males in the class allegedly because about 2% of them have probably violated one or more laws relating to the consumption of alcoholic beverages. It is unlikely that this law will have a significant deterrent effect either on that 2% or on the law-abiding 98%. But even assuming some such slight benefit, it does not seem to me that an insult to all of the young men of the State can be justified by visiting the sins of the 2% on the 98%.

* * *

MR. JUSTICE REHNQUIST, dissenting.

The Court's disposition of this case is objectionable on two grounds. First is its conclusion that men challenging a gender-based statute which treats them less favorably than women may invoke a more stringent standard of judicial review than pertains to most other types of classifications. Second is the Court's enunciation of this standard, without citation to any source, as being that "classifications by gender must serve important governmental objectives and must be substantially related to achievement of those objectives." The only redeeming feature of the Court's opinion, to my mind, is that it apparently signals a retreat by those who joined the plurality opinion in Frontiero v. Richardson, from their view that sex is a "suspect" classification for purposes of equal protection analysis. I think the Oklahoma statute challenged here need pass only the "rational basis" equal protection analysis and I believe that it is constitutional under that analysis.

* * *

* * * [T]he question [is] whether the incidence of drunk driving among young men is sufficiently greater than among young women to justify differential treatment. Notwithstanding the Court's critique of the statistical evidence, that evidence suggests clear differences between the drinking and driving habits of young men and women. Those differences are grounds enough for the State reasonably to conclude that young males pose by far the greater drunk-driving hazard, both in terms of sheer numbers and in terms of hazard on a per-driver basis. The gender-based difference in treatment in this case is therefore not irrational.

The Court's argument that a 2% correlation between maleness and drunk driving is constitutionally insufficient therefore does not pose an equal protection issue concerning discrimination between males and females. The clearest demonstration of this is the fact that the precise argument made by the Court would be equally applicable to a flat bar on such purchases by anyone, male or female, in the 18–20 age group; in fact it would apply a fortiori in that case given the even more "tenuous 'fit' " between drunk-driving arrests and femaleness. * * *

The Oklahoma Legislature could have believed that 18–20-year-old males drive substantially more, and tend more often to be intoxicated than their female counterparts; that they prefer beer and admit to drinking and driving at a higher rate than females; and that they suffer traffic injuries out of proportion to the part they make up of the population. * * * There being no violation of either equal protection or due process, the statute should accordingly be upheld.

NOTES ON CRAIG

1. *Craig* is widely understood as establishing an intermediate standard of review for legislation classifying by sex: sex-based classifications must "serve important governmental objectives and must be substantially related to the achievement of these objectives." As such, the standard in cases involving sex discrimination is a weakened version of the strict scrutiny standard applied to racial classifications. Is this difference appropriate? Is it adequate in light of the potential problems of using race discrimination doctrine as a model for sex discrimination doctrine?

2. Do you agree with Justice Stevens that the Oklahoma statute was objectionable because it was a "remnant of the now almost universally rejected tradition of discriminating against males in this age bracket"? Do you think the statute insults and discriminates against young men? What might "discriminates *against*" mean in this context? Are rules against liquor sales to minors based on dislike of young people? What do you think were the real reasons for the differential treatment of young men and young women? What assumptions about young people and their relationships might explain this differential treatment? Could you argue that the Oklahoma statute actually discriminates against young women? How? Is discrimination with respect to the ability to buy alcohol an important aspect of the systemic subordination of women?

3. Which approach in *Craig*—Justice Brennan's, Justice Stevens's, or Justice Rehnquist's—do you find most compelling? Which has the potential to do the most for women in the short run? In the long run?

4. In a speech made while Reed v. Reed was pending before the Supreme Court but before the decision was handed down, Ruth Bader Ginsburg discussed whether there would be any need for the ERA if she was successful in *Reed*. She stated that:

> [I]t is at least arguable that the right of men to equal protection will be better secured by the equal rights amendment than it is under the existing equal protection of the laws guarantee. Supporters of the amendment maintain that it declares sex a prohibited classification, not merely a suspect classification. With few exceptions relating to personal privacy and physical characteristics unique to one sex, the constitutional mandate would be absolute if the amendment is adopted. Suspect classification, on the other hand, relates to the group that has borne the stigma of inferiority or second class treatment; it has not been used to shield the culture's dominant group from discrimination. Accordingly, the female sex could be aided by the suspect classification doctrine, while non-suspect status would be the lot of men. Thus laws discriminating against

women might be subject to rigid scrutiny, while a disadvantage imposed by law on men would pass muster if supportable on any rational ground.

Ginsburg, Sex and Unequal Protection: Men and Women as Victims, 11 J. Fam. L. 347, 361–62 (1971). Was it a mistake for the Court to allow men to sue for sex discrimination (and whites to sue for race discrimination) under the Equal Protection Clause? What are the differences between a standard enforceable only by women and racial minorities and one enforceable by all? Which standard will better protect the interests of women and racial minorities? Why?

In 1979, the Supreme Court ruled for the husband in a divorce case involving a sex-specific alimony rule. Orr v. Orr, 440 U.S. 268 (1979). The Court held that a statute authorizing judicial awards of alimony from men to women after divorce but not from women to men was unconstitutional because homemakers could be protected by gender-neutral rules that would not reinforce stereotypes of women as destined only for a dependent role. In fact, judges interpreting gender-neutral statutes have become less likely to give homemakers long-term awards; today even long-term homemakers receive in most cases only short-term "rehabilitative" awards for four years or so. For an early discussion of the dangers of a formal equality approach in family law, see Martha A. Fineman, Implementing Equality: Ideology, Contradiction and Social Change, 1983 Wis. L. Rev. 789. For a discussion of how Fineman's views have developed, see Fineman, Equality: Still Illusive After All These Years, in Gender Equality: Dimensions of Women's Equal Citizenship 251, 253–66 (Linda C. McClain & Joanna L. Grossman eds., 2009). Does this illustrate some of the potential harms of formal equality for women? Or might gender-neutral rules ultimately encourage men and women to eschew traditional gender roles, like that of the housewife and male breadwinner?

5. In a 1975 speech published in 1976, Ruth Bader Ginsburg suggested that the use of the word "sex" (as in "sex discrimination") might be evocative of sexuality, whereas gender "by contrast, has a neutral, clinical tone that may ward off distracting associations." She therefore recommended using "gender" instead of "sex." Ginsburg, Gender and the Constitution, 44 U. Cin. L. Rev. 1, 1 (1976). At this time and, we suspect, not coincidentally, the terminology used by the Supreme Court changed. Prior to *Craig*, decided in 1976, the Court occasionally used "gender" rather than "sex," but was more likely to use "sex." See, for example, the pre-*Craig* cases in this chapter, in which "sex" is routinely used; "gender" is used only once by Justice Brennan in his dissent in *Geduldig*, where he refers to "a gender-linked disability peculiar to women." *Craig* marks a decided shift from "sex" to "gender." In *Craig*, the majority uses "gender" six times in the short excerpt above; in the excerpt of his dissent, Rehnquist uses "gender" three times.

What are the possible meanings of sex and gender? Are these terms interchangeable? Sex is sometimes used to refer to physical sex (whether one was born a female or a male in terms of physical characteristics), while gender is sometimes used to refer to the cultural construct built on that perceived physical reality (masculinity and femininity). Indeed, Justice Scalia adopted such a definition in his dissent in J.E.B. v. Alabama, an excerpt from which appears below. 511 U.S. at 157, n.1. Are there other differences in the usage of these terms? Are there substantive consequences to assuming their equivalence for purposes of identifying discrimination? What are the possible differences between the meaning of sex discrimination and the meaning of gender discrimination?

6. Some feminists object to the sex-gender distinction on the following ground:

> [S]ex, gender and sexuality are inextricably linked and cannot be disentangled from each other. This is the case both for those who see femininity and masculinity as culturally constructed and for those who assume that some essential difference exists prior to cultural influences. Feminists interested in asserting women's "difference" * * * often object to the sex-gender distinction because they see it as denying the specificity of women's bodily experience.

Stevi Jackson, Gender and Heterosexuality: A Materialist Feminist Analysis, in (Hetero)sexual Politics 11, 11 (Mary Maynard & June Purvis eds., 1995). What is the point Jackson makes here about the use of "gender" being a denial of "women's bodily experiences"? Do you agree with Jackson? Note that the Supreme Court started consistently using the term "gender" only after it considered the pregnancy classification at issue in *Geduldig*. How might this support Jackson's argument?

7. Does physical "sex" have a "natural" referent, a meaning independent of culture and women's subordinate status? Postmodern feminists argue that our existing categories of women and men and even of sex are entirely the product of gender construction and hierarchy, with no pre-existing meaning. For example, Monique Wittig, a French postmodern feminist, posits: " 'It is oppression that creates sex and not the contrary.' " Jackson, above note 6, at 16 (quoting Wittig, The Straight Mind and Other Essays 2 (1992)). Similarly, Judith Butler writes that "gender is not to culture as sex is to nature; gender is also the discursive/cultural means by which 'sexed nature' or a 'natural sex' is produced and established as 'prediscursive,' prior to culture, a politically neutral surface *on which* culture acts." As such, sex is constructed as "the radically unconstructed." Butler, Gender Trouble 7 (1990) (emphasis in original). What does it mean to say that sex has no meaning independent of gender? Do you agree? How might Jackson respond? What term(s) do you think the Supreme Court should use?

C. THE STANDARD IN ACTION

1. THE MILITARY

PERSONNEL ADMINISTRATOR OF MASSACHUSETTS v. FEENEY

Supreme Court of the United States, 1979.
442 U.S. 256, 99 S.Ct. 2282, 60 L.Ed.2d 870.

MR. JUSTICE STEWART delivered the opinion of the Court.

This case presents a challenge to the constitutionality of the Massachusetts veterans' preference statute on the ground that it discriminates against women in violation of the Equal Protection Clause of the Fourteenth Amendment. * * * [A]ll veterans who qualify for state civil service positions must be considered for appointment ahead of any qualifying nonveterans. The preference operates overwhelmingly to the advantage of males.

The appellee Helen B. Feeney is not a veteran. She brought this action * * * alleging that the absolute preference formula * * * inevitably operates to exclude women from consideration for the best Massachusetts civil service jobs and thus unconstitutionally denies them the equal protection of the laws. * * *

The District Court found that the absolute preference afforded by Massachusetts to veterans has a devastating impact upon the employment opportunities of women. * * *

The Federal Government and virtually all of the States grant some sort of hiring preference to veterans. The Massachusetts preference, which is loosely termed an "absolute lifetime" preference, is among the most generous. * * *

The veterans' hiring preference in Massachusetts, as in other jurisdictions, has traditionally been justified as a measure designed to reward veterans for the sacrifice of military service, to ease the transition from military to civilian life, to encourage patriotic service, and to attract loyal and well-disciplined people to civil service occupations. * * * The Massachusetts law dates back to 1884, when the State, as part of its first civil service legislation, gave a statutory preference to civil service applicants who were Civil War veterans if their qualifications were equal to those of nonveterans. * * *

Notwithstanding the apparent attempts by Massachusetts to include as many military women as possible within the scope of the preference, the statute today benefits an overwhelmingly male class. This is attributable in some measure to the variety of federal statutes, regulations, and policies that have restricted the number of women who could enlist in the United States Armed Forces, and largely to the simple fact that women have never been subjected to a military draft.

When this litigation was commenced, then, over 98% of the veterans in Massachusetts were male; only 1.8% were female. And over one-quarter of the Massachusetts population were veterans. During the decade between 1963 and 1973 when the appellee was actively participating in the State's merit selection system, 47,005 new permanent appointments were made in the classified official service. 43% of those hired were women, and 57% were men. Of the women appointed, 1.8% were veterans, while 54% of the men had veteran status. A large unspecified percentage of the female appointees were serving in lower paying positions for which males traditionally had not applied.[22] * * *

22. The former exemption for "women's requisitions," * * * may have operated in the 20th century to protect these types of jobs from the impact of the preference. However, the statutory history indicates that this was not its purpose. The provision dates back to the 1896 veterans'

The sole question for decision on this appeal is whether Massachusetts, in granting an absolute lifetime preference to veterans, has discriminated against women in violation of the Equal Protection Clause of the Fourteenth Amendment.

* * *

When a statute gender-neutral on its face is challenged on the ground that its effects upon women are disproportionately adverse, a twofold inquiry is * * * appropriate. The first question is whether the statutory classification is indeed neutral in the sense that it is not gender-based. If the classification itself, covert or overt, is not based upon gender, the second question is whether the adverse effect reflects invidious gender-based discrimination. * * *

If the impact of this statute could not be plausibly explained on a neutral ground, impact itself would signal that the real classification made by the law was in fact not neutral. But there can be but one answer to the question whether this veteran preference excludes significant numbers of women from preferred state jobs because they are women or because they are nonveterans. Apart from the facts that the definition of "veterans" in the statute has always been neutral as to gender and that Massachusetts has consistently defined veteran status in a way that has been inclusive of women who have served in the military, this is not a law that can plausibly be explained only as a gender-based classification. Indeed, it is not a law that can rationally be explained on that ground. Veteran status is not uniquely male. Although few women benefit from the preference the nonveteran class is not substantially all female. To the contrary, significant numbers of nonveterans are men, and all nonveterans—male as well as female—are placed at a disadvantage. Too many men are affected by [the preference] to permit the inference that the statute is but a pretext for preferring men over women.

* * * The distinction made by [the preference] is, as it seems to be, quite simply between veterans and nonveterans, not between men and women.

The dispositive question, then, is whether the appellee has shown that a gender-based discriminatory purpose has, at least in some measure, shaped the Massachusetts veterans' preference legislation. * * * [S]he points to two basic factors. * * * The first is the nature of the preference, which is said to be demonstrably gender-biased in the sense that it favors a status reserved under federal military policy primarily to men. The second concerns the impact of the absolute lifetime preference upon the employment opportunities of women, an impact claimed to be too inevit-

---

preference law and was retained in the law substantially unchanged until it was eliminated in 1971. * * * Since veterans in 1896 were a small but an exclusively male class, such a provision was apparently included to ensure that the statute would not be construed to outlaw a pre-existing practice of single-sex hiring explicitly authorized under the 1884 Civil Service statute. The veterans' preference statute at no point endorsed this practice. Historical materials indicate, however, that the early preference law may have operated to encourage the employment of women in positions from which they previously had been excluded.

able to have been unintended. The appellee contends that these factors, coupled with the fact that the preference itself has little if any relevance to actual job performance, more than suffice to prove the discriminatory intent required to establish a constitutional violation.

* * *

The appellee's ultimate argument rests upon the presumption, common to the criminal and civil law, that a person intends the natural and foreseeable consequences of his voluntary actions. Her position was well stated in the concurring opinion in the District Court: "Conceding . . . that the goal here was to benefit the veteran, there is no reason to absolve the legislature from awareness that the means chosen to achieve this goal would freeze women out of all those state jobs actively sought by men. To be sure, the legislature did not wish to harm women. But the cutting-off of women's opportunities was an inevitable concomitant of the chosen scheme—as inevitable as the proposition that if tails is up, heads must be down. Where a law's consequences are that inevitable, can they meaningfully be described as unintended?"

* * *

"Discriminatory purpose," however, implies more than intent as volition or intent as awareness of consequences. It implies that the decisionmaker, in this case a state legislature, selected or reaffirmed a particular course of action at least in part "because of," not merely "in spite of," its adverse effects upon an identifiable group. Yet, nothing in the record demonstrates that this preference for veterans was originally devised or subsequently re-enacted because it would accomplish the collateral goal of keeping women in a stereotypic and predefined place in the Massachusetts Civil Service.

To the contrary, the statutory history shows that the benefit of the preference was consistently offered to "any person" who was a veteran. That benefit has been extended to women under a very broad statutory definition of the term veteran. The preference formula itself, which is the focal point of this challenge, was first adopted—so it appears from this record—out of a perceived need to help a small group of older Civil War veterans. It has since been reaffirmed and extended only to cover new veterans. When the totality of legislative actions establishing and extending the Massachusetts veterans' preference are considered, the law remains what it purports to be: a preference for veterans of either sex over nonveterans of either sex, not for men over women.

[The concurrence of JUSTICES STEVENS and WHITE is omitted.]

MR. JUSTICE MARSHALL, with whom MR. JUSTICE BRENNAN joins, dissenting.

* * * In my judgment, Massachusetts' choice of an absolute veterans' preference system evinces purposeful gender-based discrimination. And because the statutory scheme bears no substantial relationship to a

legitimate governmental objective, it cannot withstand scrutiny under the Equal Protection Clause.

* * *

That a legislature seeks to advantage one group does not, as a matter of logic or of common sense, exclude the possibility that it also intends to disadvantage another. Individuals in general and lawmakers in particular frequently act for a variety of reasons. As this Court [has] recognized, "[r]arely can it be said that a legislature or administrative body operating under a broad mandate made a decision motivated solely by a single concern." Absent an omniscience not commonly attributed to the judiciary, it will often be impossible to ascertain the sole or even dominant purpose of a given statute. Thus, the critical constitutional inquiry is not whether an illicit consideration was the primary or but-for cause of a decision, but rather whether it had an appreciable role in shaping a given legislative enactment. Where there is "proof that a discriminatory purpose has been a motivating factor in the decision, . . . judicial deference is no longer justified."

Moreover, since reliable evidence of subjective intentions is seldom obtainable, resort to inference based on objective factors is generally unavoidable. To discern the purposes underlying facially neutral policies, this Court has therefore considered the degree, inevitability, and foreseeability of any disproportionate impact as well as the alternatives reasonably available.

In the instant case, the impact of the Massachusetts statute on women is undisputed. Any veteran with a passing grade on the civil service exam must be placed ahead of a nonveteran, regardless of their respective scores. The District Court found that, as a practical matter, this preference supplants test results as the determinant of upper level civil service appointments. Because less than 2% of the women in Massachusetts are veterans, the absolute-preference formula has rendered desirable state civil service employment an almost exclusively male prerogative.

As the District Court recognized, this consequence follows foreseeably, indeed inexorably, from the long history of policies severely limiting women's participation in the military. Although neutral in form, the statute is anything but neutral in application. It inescapably reserves a major sector of public employment to "an already established class which, as a matter of historical fact, is 98% male." * * * Where the foreseeable impact of a facially neutral policy is so disproportionate, the burden should rest on the State to establish that sex-based considerations played no part in the choice of the particular legislative scheme.

Clearly, that burden was not sustained here. The legislative history of the statute reflects the Commonwealth's patent appreciation of the impact the preference system would have on women, and an equally evident desire to mitigate that impact only with respect to certain traditionally female occupations. Until 1971, the statute and implementing civil service regulations exempted from operation of the preference any job requisitions "especially calling for women." In practice, this exemption, coupled with the absolute preference for veterans, has created a gender-based civil service hierarchy, with women occupying low-grade clerical and secretarial jobs and men holding more responsible and remunerative positions.

> [Justice Marshall concluded that the Massachusetts preference could not survive intermediate scrutiny under *Craig* once it was seen as a form of sex discrimination.]

NOTES ON FEENEY

1. Do you agree that rules favoring soldiers and disfavoring motherhood, such as those at issue in *Feeney* and *Geduldig*, do not constitute discrimination on the basis of sex? How does discrimination on the basis of sex operate? The Court in *Feeney* seems to assume that discrimination against women is motivated by some sort of conscious animus or ill will. Why does the Court focus so much on the consciousness and motives of the discriminator in this case? Why in *Feeney*, as in *Geduldig*, is discriminatory intent necessary? Can you provide examples from your own life of sex discrimination or sexism based on the unconscious and inadvertent actions of others?

Does the requirement of intent in this kind of case serve male interests by being conservative and non-threatening? How does it preserve the important sex-related privileges enjoyed by the men who had adopted the policy? Does the requirement of intent focus on the mindset of powerful men instead of the harm discrimination causes women? See Alan David Freeman, Legitimizing Racial Discrimination Through Antidiscrimination Law: A Critical Review of Supreme Court Doctrine, 62 Minn. L. Rev. 1049 (1978) (responding to similar questions in the context of race discrimination).

2. If the Court were to adopt the standard suggested by David Strauss in his article, Discriminatory Intent and the Taming of *Brown,* 56 U. Chi. L. Rev. 935 (1989), the key question would be whether the legislature would have enacted the same statute were the groups reversed. This, Strauss argues, should be the key question: would the mostly male Massachusetts legislature have passed the veterans' preference statute had the vast majority of veterans been women? If not, then sex discrimination should be regarded as the but-for cause of the statute. Is this a workable alternative to the Court's standard? How does the Court's standard differ from the reversing-the-groups standard? Which standard is more likely to capture discrimination on the basis of sex? What are the advantages and disadvantages of these two approaches? If you were to apply the reversing-the-groups test to the classification at issue in *Feeney,* would you conclude that the statute discriminated on the basis of sex?

3. In his article, David Strauss suggests that motherhood is much like military service: mothers, like soldiers, make important contributions to society, risking physical hazards and disruptions of careers. Strauss, above note 2, at 1001. Christine Littleton made a similar point in an earlier article, Reconstructing Sexual Equality, 75 Calif. L. Rev. 1279, 1329–30 (1987), when she suggested that government should give soldiers and mothers the same benefits. Do you agree? Do you think that the failure of states to enact

maternal preference statutes for state employment reveals sex discrimination? What problems do you see in attempting to improve the status of mothers by valuing mothering according to the value of soldiering? Are soldiering and mothering equally valuable? What about those women who do not become mothers? What about men who engage in "mothering"?

4. Virtually all states as well as the federal government give preferences to veterans for government employment. Are these veterans' preferences in government employment equivalent to wages or other benefits for soldiers and veterans, such as those provided in the GI Bill? Are there reasons to see the employment-preference benefit as more problematic than other veterans' benefits? Should veterans' dominance in government be regarded as consistent with (a) democracy, (b) the "Republican Form of Government" guaranteed by section four of Article IV of the United States Constitution, or (c) sex equality?

ROSTKER v. GOLDBERG

Supreme Court of the United States, 1981.
453 U.S. 57, 101 S.Ct. 2646, 69 L.Ed.2d 478.

JUSTICE REHNQUIST delivered the opinion of the Court.

The question presented is whether the Military Selective Service Act violates the Fifth Amendment to the United States Constitution in authorizing the President to require the registration of males and not females.

[Registration for the draft ended in 1975, but in 1980, in response to the Soviet invasion of Afghanistan, President Carter decided to reinstitute registration. In seeking funds for this purpose from Congress, he asked Congress to amend the Act to allow the registration and eventual conscription of women. Congress agreed to allocate the necessary funds but declined to amend the Act to include women. As a result, the statute at issue in this case, the Military Selective Service Act (MSSA), gave the President the power to register only men 18 to 26 years of age. The sole purpose of such registration was for use in a subsequent draft, though congressional action would be necessary to draft.

The case itself began in 1971 as part of the opposition to the Vietnam war. Eventually, one of the claims was that the Vietnam registration and draft of men was impermissible sex-based discrimination. After a number of years during which nothing happened, in 1980 the District Court for the Eastern District of Pennsylvania found that the Act, recently given new vitality by President Carter, impermissibly discriminated on the basis of sex, in violation of the Due Process Clause of the Fifth Amendment (incorporating the Equal Protection Clause of the Fourteenth Amendment), which forbids such discrimination by the federal government under the standard articulated in Craig v. Boren, discussed above. The District Court concluded that no "important government interest" supported registration of only men. The court did not reach the issue of women in combat, since registration of women would not necessarily require their deployment in combat.]

* * *

This is not * * * merely a case involving the customary deference accorded congressional decisions. The case arises in the context of Congress' authority over national defense and military affairs, and perhaps in no other area has the Court accorded Congress greater deference. * * *

Not only is the scope of Congress' constitutional power in this area broad, but the lack of competence on the part of the courts is marked. * * *

This case is quite different from several of the gender-based discrimination cases we have considered in that, despite appellees' assertions, Congress did not act "unthinkingly" or "reflexively and not for any considered reason." The question of registering women for the draft not only received considerable national attention and was the subject of wide-ranging public debate, but also was extensively considered by Congress in hearings, floor debate, and in committee. Hearings held by both Houses of Congress in response to the President's request for authorization to register women adduced extensive testimony and evidence concerning the issue.

* * *

* * * [T]he decision to exempt women from registration was not the " 'accidental by-product of a traditional way of thinking about females.' " In *Michael M.* [v. Sonoma County Superior Court, 450 U.S. 464 (1981) (upholding sex-discriminatory statutory rape law); excerpt in Chapter 4], we rejected a similar argument because of action by the California Legislature considering and rejecting proposals to make a statute challenged on discrimination grounds gender-neutral. The cause for rejecting the argument is considerably stronger here. The issue was considered at great length, and Congress clearly expressed its purpose and intent.

* * *

Congress determined that any future draft, which would be facilitated by the registration scheme, would be characterized by a need for combat troops. The Senate Report explained, in a specific finding later adopted by both Houses, that "[i]f mobilization were to be ordered in a wartime scenario, the primary manpower need would be for combat replacements." * * *

Women as a group, however, unlike men as a group, are not eligible for combat. The restrictions on the participation of women in combat in the Navy and Air Force are statutory. * * * The Army and Marine Corps preclude the use of women in combat as a matter of established policy. Congress specifically recognized and endorsed the exclusion of women from combat in exempting women from registration. * * *

This is not a case of Congress arbitrarily choosing to burden one of two similarly situated groups, such as would be the case with an all-black or all-white, or an all-Catholic or all-Lutheran, or an all-Republican or all-Democratic registration. Men and women, because of the combat restrictions on women, are simply not similarly situated for purposes of a draft or registration for a draft.

Congress' decision to authorize the registration of only men, therefore, does not violate the Due Process Clause. The exemption of women from registration is not only sufficiently but also closely related to Congress' purpose in authorizing registration. The fact that Congress and the Executive have decided that women should not serve in combat fully justifies Congress in not authorizing their registration, since the purpose of registration is to develop a pool of potential combat troops. As was the case in *Schlesinger v. Ballard* [419 U.S. 498 (1975) (holding that the Navy can give women two extra years under an up-or-out promotion policy)], "the gender classification is not invidious, but rather realistically reflects the fact that the sexes are not similarly situated" in this case. The Constitution requires that Congress treat similarly situated persons similarly, not that it engage in gestures of superficial equality.

* * *

[A]ssuming that a small number of women could be drafted for noncombat roles, Congress simply did not consider it worth the added burdens of including women in draft and registration plans. * * *

Congress also concluded that whatever the need for women for noncombat roles during mobilization, whether 80,000 or less, it could be met by volunteers. * * *

Most significantly, Congress determined that staffing noncombat positions with women during a mobilization would be positively detrimental to the important goal of military flexibility. * * *

In light of the foregoing, we conclude that Congress acted well within its constitutional authority when it authorized the registration of men, and not women, under the Military Selective Service Act. The decision of the District Court holding otherwise is accordingly

Reversed.

JUSTICE WHITE, with whom JUSTICE BRENNAN joins, dissenting.

* * *

As I understand the record, * * * in order to secure the personnel it needs during mobilization, the Government cannot rely on volunteers and must register and draft not only to fill combat positions and those noncombat positions that must be filled by combat-trained men, but also to secure the personnel needed for jobs that can be performed by persons ineligible for combat without diminishing military effectiveness. The claim is that in providing for the latter category of positions, Congress is free to register and draft only men. I discern no adequate justification for this kind of discrimination between men and women. Accordingly, with all due respect, I dissent.

JUSTICE MARSHALL, with whom JUSTICE BRENNAN joins, dissenting.

The Court today places its imprimatur on one of the most potent remaining public expressions of "ancient canards about the proper role of women." It upholds a statute that requires males but not females to register for the draft, and which thereby categorically excludes women from a fundamental civic obligation. Because I believe the Court's decision is inconsistent with the Constitution's guarantee of equal protection of the laws, I dissent.

* * *

* * * The Court * * * reasons that since women are not eligible for assignment to combat, Congress' decision to exclude them from registration is not unconstitutional discrimination inasmuch as "[m]en and women, because of the combat restrictions on women, are simply not similarly situated for purposes of a draft or registration for a draft." * * *

* * * [A]lthough the Court purports to apply the *Craig v. Boren* test, the "similarly situated" analysis the Court employs is in fact significantly different from the *Craig v. Boren* approach. The Court essentially reasons that the gender classification employed by the MSSA is constitutionally permissible because nondiscrimination is not necessary to achieve the purpose of registration to prepare for a draft of combat troops. In other words, the majority concludes that women may be excluded from registration because they will not be needed in the event of a draft.

This analysis, however, focuses on the wrong question. The relevant inquiry under the *Craig v. Boren* test is not whether a *gender-neutral* classification would substantially advance important governmental interests. Rather, the question is whether the gender-based classification is itself substantially related to the achievement of the asserted governmental interest. Thus, the Government's task in this case is to demonstrate that excluding women from registration substantially furthers the goal of preparing for a draft of combat troops. Or to put it another way, the Government must show that registering women would substantially impede its efforts to prepare for such a draft. Under our precedents, the Government cannot meet this burden without showing that a gender-neutral statute would be a less effective means of attaining this end. As the Court explained in *Orr v. Orr,* 440 U.S. [268], 283 [(1979) (holding unconstitutional state divorce law providing for alimony payments by men only)]:

> Where, as here, the [Government's] . . . purposes are as well served by a gender-neutral classification as one that gender classifies and therefore carries with it the baggage of sexual stereotypes, the [Government] cannot be permitted to classify on the basis of sex.

In this case, the Government makes no claim that preparing for a draft of combat troops cannot be accomplished just as effectively by *registering* both men and women but *drafting* only men if only men turn out to be needed. Nor can the Government argue that this alternative entails the additional cost and administrative inconvenience of registering women. This Court has repeatedly stated that the administrative convenience of employing a gender classification is not an adequate constitutional justification under the *Craig v. Boren* test.

NOTES ON ROSTKER

1. When is a statute distinguishing between women and men nevertheless constitutional under the standard articulated in Craig v. Boren? How would you apply this standard to the male-only registration for military service at issue in *Rostker*? Who has the stronger analytical position on this question: the majority or Justice Marshall in dissent?

2. Do all the justices assume that it would be constitutional to send only men into combat? Wouldn't such a policy inevitably reinforce traditional sex roles? How might the Court justify upholding the constitutionality of such a policy despite this effect and its facial discrimination on the basis of sex? What significant governmental interest is served by the only-men-in-combat rule? How would you assess that interest? Are there alternative ways to serve that interest? Why isn't that interest weighed against women's interest in equality? How would the Court respond to the assertion that one of the interests served by the men-only combat rule is keeping women subordinate to men despite their majority status in a democracy? Why does this consideration—the political effects on women as citizens—disappear from the calculus in thinking about the issue under the Court's equal protection jurisprudence?

3. The *Rostker* majority relies on the fact that the policy registering only men was adopted after Congress thought about the issue. The Court concludes that the policy was therefore not an " 'accidental by-product of a traditional way of thinking about females.' " Why does the Court ignore the possibility that it was the *deliberate* by-product of such thinking? Shouldn't the fact that the policy was adopted after deliberation count *against* it if based on traditional ways of thinking about women? As the Court itself considered the matter, Congress decided not to register women because it was unwilling to draft women for combat. Isn't it possible, perhaps likely, that the no-combat policy was based in part on traditional sex roles and stereotypes?

4. Women made up 14.5 percent of the United States armed forces, and ten percent of the deployed forces, as of 2009. Between 2001 and 2009, 218,000 female troops were deployed in military campaigns in Afghanistan and Iraq. Department of Defense, Report to the White House Council on Women and Girls 20 (2009). Although the Department of Defense (DOD) continues to prohibit the assignment of female troops to brigades that engage in "direct ground combat," the DOD acknowledges that "women may still find themselves in a situation that may necessitate combat action, such as defending them or their units from attack." Therefore, "service members regardless of gender are equipped, trained and prepared to defend the United States." Id. at 3. Moreover, female troops have played a crucial role in Afghanistan, performing many essential tasks that men cannot perform

because of cultural restrictions. For example, U.S. military women search Afghan women for improvised explosive devices and reach out to the community as part of "female engagement teams" designed to win over Afghan women. Elizabeth Bumiller, In Camouflage or Veil, a Fragile Bond, N.Y. Times, May 29, 2010, at A1. As of July 3, 2010, female troops accounted for 129 of the 6,545 troops killed in Iraq and Afghanistan. For a continuously updated compilation of war casualties, see http://siadapp.dmdc.osd.mil/personnel/CASUALTY/castop.htm.

Jill Elaine Hasday has analyzed the ways that women's legal status in the military has changed since *Rostker* without intervention from the courts—for example, Congress has repealed all statutory combat exclusions—concluding that "extrajudicial transformation in women's military status has * * * seriously undermined *Rostker's* foundation because *Rostker's* reasoning, premises, and expectations do not match how the nation has evolved." Hasday, Fighting Women: The Military, Sex, and Extrajudicial Constitutional Change, 93 Minn. L. Rev. 96, 151 (2008). What might be some of the advantages and disadvantages of this "extrajudicial transformation"? In contrast, what might be some of the advantages and disadvantages of the sort of top-down change the Supreme Court can force? What strategy is preferable to integrate women into military power? What is left of *Rostker* after the transformation identified by Hasday? Does the transformation eradicate the effect of the stereotypes embedded in the no-combat policy? Why does such a policy remain, at least formally? For a critique of the no-combat policy on military effectiveness grounds, see Martha McSally, Women in Combat: Is the Current Policy Obsolete?, 14 Duke J. Gender L. & Pol'y 1011, 1016–17 (2007).

5. In light of the Supreme Court's decision in District of Columbia v. Heller, ___ U.S. ___, 128 S.Ct. 2783 (2008), holding that a D.C. gun control statute violated the Second Amendment, could you frame an argument that the Second Amendment prohibits the exclusion of women from combat? The Second Amendment provides that "A well regulated Militia, being necessary to the security of a free State, the right of the people to keep and bear Arms, shall not be infringed." Given the Second Amendment, Congress could not pass a statute allowing only non-citizen mercenaries from other countries to bear arms in American military units. Why is it permissible to keep women, a majority of the citizenry, from carrying arms in the military? How do you think the Supreme Court would respond to an argument that women cannot be deprived of the right to bear arms in the military? See Akhil Reed Amar, *Heller*, HLR, and Holistic Legal Reasoning, 122 Harv. L. Rev. 145, 188–89 (2008); Elizabeth L. Hillman, *Heller*, Citizenship and the Right to Serve in the Military, 60 Hastings L.J. 1269 (2009).

6. What are the reasons women might want to be included in the military and in combat? Are there, for example, consequences in terms of women's power in politics and in the military? Think of a woman running against a veteran for public office or applying for a job in government. What are the chances of a woman with no combat experience attaining high military rank, such as becoming Joint Chief of Staff? Why doesn't the Court even mention the *Feeney* problem in *Rostker,* i.e., that women are frozen out of many powerful political positions by the combination of differential participation rates of women and men in the modern military (differences required

by Congress and based on women's ineligibility for combat) and veterans' preferences for state employment? Should it matter that different governmental bodies set these policies, that is, that the federal government limits women's military participation, and states then award positions in state government to veterans? How does the promotion in 2008 of General Ann E. Dunwoody to four star general (the highest rank attainable short of General of the Army) change your thoughts on *Feeney*'s relevance in this respect, if at all? Dunwoody attained that rank without "official" ground combat experience.

7. In what other ways does the military, as currently structured, contribute to women's inequality? Consider, for example, the military's super-masculine culture, with its emphasis on training boys to be "real" men and the routine disparagement of girls and women during basic training. Or consider that the military teaches men to use violence. What are the likely results of such policies on the intimate relations of men and women and on their relative power in the private spheres? How might this difference affect domestic violence, stranger rape, date rape, and marital rape? See Chapter 4 for more on the prevalence of rape in the United States. Does the no-combat rule reflect and reinforce a taboo against women using violence in our culture? What is the potential relation between that taboo and the high levels of male-on-female violence, as described in Chapter 4?

8. Male-on-female violence is also prevalent within the military. In 2008, approximately 1,500 female troops made "unrestricted reports" of sexual assault and approximately 700 female troops made "restricted reports." DOD Report, above note 4, at 24. As is also the case outside of the military, the rate of assault is likely much higher than that reported. See Jodie Friedman, Reporting Sexual Assault of Women in the Military, 14 Cardozo J.L. & Gender 375 (2008). What might the military do to reduce instances of sexual assault? Or is some degree of sexual assault inevitable so long as military culture remains male-dominated? See Jessica L. Cornett, The U.S. Military Responds to Rape: Will Recent Changes be Enough?, 29 Women's Rts. L. Rep. 99 (2008); Jamie R. Abrams, The Collateral Consequences of Masculinizing Violence, 16 Wm. & Mary J. Women & L. 703, 715–22, 736–45 (2010). In contrast to sexual assault rates, the overall rate of sexual harassment in the military declined from 1988 to 2002. Deborah J. Bostock & James G. Daley, Lifetime and Current Sexual Assault and Harassment Victimization Rates of Active-Duty United States Air Force Women, 13 Violence Against Women 927, 928–29 (2007). What might account for the difference?

9. What is the relationship between sexism and homophobia in the military? For example, is there a connection between the no-women-in-combat rule and the military ban on "out" lesbians and gay men? In what ways does military culture, with its glorification of "real" male warriors and denigration of the feminine, rest on the subordination of lesbians and gay men? Why are military women in nontraditional jobs, or those who file reports of sexual assault or harassment, especially likely to be accused of being lesbian? See Michelle M. Benecke & Kirstin S. Dodge, Military Women in Nontraditional Job Fields: Casualties of the Armed Forces' War on Homosexuals, 13 Harv. Women's L.J. 215 (1990); Servicemembers Legal Defense Network, 2009 Annual Report, at 2. Are lesbians especially threatening to military norms and

values? Although women make up only 14.5 percent of the military, they comprise about 43 percent of the lesbian, gay and bisexual troops serving on active duty. Gary J. Gates, Lesbian, Gay and Bisexual Men and Women in the US Military: Updated Estimates 1–2 (Williams Institute 2010).

10. One of President Clinton's first actions after becoming president in 1993 was to attempt to end the military's ban on lesbian and gay soldiers. When that became politically impossible because of vehement opposition from many in the military and elsewhere, he compromised on a new policy of "don't ask, don't tell," which was supposed to be more accepting than the traditional ban. Under "don't ask, don't tell," soldiers were free to be gay or lesbian in their private lives; the military was not to ask about sexual orientation; and as long as gay and lesbian soldiers didn't tell people about their sexual orientation, they were free to serve in the military.

In September 2010, the United States District Court for the Central District of California declared the policy unconstitutional, finding it violated troops' substantive due process rights under the Fifth Amendment as well as troops' First Amendment free speech rights. Memorandum Opinion, Log Cabin Republicans v. United States, No. CV 04-08425-VAP (C.D. Cal. Sept. 9, 2010). Relying on the right to intimate conduct articulated in Lawrence v. Texas, 539 U.S. 558 (2003) and First Amendment doctrine tailored for the military context, the court applied heightened scrutiny when evaluating both claims. In finding that the policy failed to survive such scrutiny because it does not further an important governmental interest, the court relied on a number of statistics, including the fact that between 1994 and 2009, 13,023 servicemembers were discharged under the act. *Log Cabin Republicans*, at 57–58. Based on a decline in discharges under the act after 2001, however, the court found that "during wartime the military retains servicemembers known to be homosexual, despite the Don't Ask, Don't Tell Act requiring discharge, because of the heightened need for troops." Id. at 59. President Obama has also vowed to end the policy, and in early 2010, the House of Representatives adopted an amendment to the National Defense Authorization Act that could lead to the repeal of the policy in early 2011. David M. Herszenhorn & Carl Hulse, House Votes to Allow 'Don't Ask, Don't Tell' Repeal, N.Y. Times, May 27, 2010, at A1. A Senate vote was pending as of the time of the district court's opinion.

"Don't ask, don't tell" specifically regulates homosexual acts, statements, and same-sex marriage. Because the policy has such a large focus on sexual acts, Zachary A. Kramer suggests that the policy is part of a larger military policy of regulating sex, including the extensive regulation of heterosexual sex acts, although the court in *Log Cabin Republicans* emphasized that heterosexual troops are free to talk about their intimate lives whereas homosexual and bisexual troops are not. Kramer ultimately argues that the military should stop regulating any form of consensual sex. For further discussion, see Kramer, Heterosexuality and Military Service, 104 Nw. U. L. Rev. Colloquy 341 (2010). What justifications might the military have for regulating consensual sex acts between same-sex or different-sex partners? How might such regulation prevent sexual assault and harassment? How might it not?

11. As of 2009, twenty-five countries allowed gay and lesbian service members to serve openly in their armed services. UCSB's Palm Center, Countries That Allow Military Service by Openly Gay People 1 (2009). Studies reveal that many, if not all, of these countries managed the transition to open service smoothly. Columbia Law School Sexuality & Gender Law Clinic, A Report on The Inclusion of Openly Gay and Lesbian Servicemembers in U.S. Allies' Armed Forces (2010). Other countries have also long permitted women to serve in combat roles. McSally, above note 4, at 1057–58. Why has the United States been resistant to changes adopted by so many other countries?

12. What are the strongest arguments that can be made *against* drafting women into the military or combat today, given differences in the way girls and boys are socialized and macho military culture? If women may be more pacifist than men, would that argue for or against their inclusion in the military in equal numbers? Can women's activities as pacifists ever be as effective as men's while they are excluded from the draft and combat? Think, for example, of women who opposed the Vietnam War and had no draft cards to burn. What are the strongest arguments for requiring women to serve in equal numbers and in equal capacities, despite the many differences in what such service might mean for women?

2. JURIES

In the federal judicial system and most state systems, statutes or rules allow litigants to exclude a certain number of jurors in both civil and criminal trials by the use of "peremptory challenges," challenges which need not specify a reason for eliminating the prospective juror. Jurors can also be challenged for cause, but such challenges must be supported by a reason for thinking the individual juror is likely to be biased in the case at bar. Peremptory and for-cause challenges are made after the jurors have filled out qualification forms providing a great deal of information about themselves and after voir dire, in which the lawyers or the judge question jurors about relevant experiences, attitudes, and possible biases. The issue in the next case is whether the constitutional decisions banning race-based peremptory challenges should be extended to sex-based peremptory challenges.

J.E.B. v. ALABAMA

Supreme Court of the United States, 1994.
511 U.S. 127, 114 S.Ct. 1419, 128 L.Ed.2d 89.

JUSTICE BLACKMUN delivered the opinion of the Court.

* * *

On behalf of * * * T.B., the mother of a minor child, respondent State of Alabama filed a complaint for paternity and child support against petitioner J.E.B. * * * The trial court assembled a panel of 36 potential jurors, 12 males and 24 females. After the court excused three jurors for cause, only 10 of the remaining 33 jurors were male. The State then used

9 of its 10 peremptory strikes to remove male jurors; petitioner used all but one of his strikes to remove female jurors. As a result, all the selected jurors were female. [The jury found that the defendant was the father of the minor child after hearing scientific evidence demonstrating a 99.92% probability that he had fathered the child.]

* * *

We granted certiorari * * * to resolve * * * whether the Equal Protection Clause forbids peremptory challenges on the basis of gender as well as on the basis of race. Today we reaffirm what, by now, should be axiomatic: Intentional discrimination on the basis of gender by state actors violates the Equal Protection Clause, particularly where, as here, the discrimination serves to ratify and perpetuate invidious, archaic, and overbroad stereotypes about the relative abilities of men and women.

> [The common law traditionally excluded women from juries to shield them from ugliness in light of their fragility and innocence. In 1975, the Supreme Court held that women were constitutionally entitled to be on lists of potential jurors on the same terms as men. Taylor v. Louisiana, 419 U.S. 522 (1975). Thereafter, however, prosecutors and defendants remained free to strike jurors from a particular jury on the basis of their sex by the use of peremptory challenges, though race was held an impermissible basis for a peremptory strike in a criminal case in Batson v. Kentucky, 476 U.S. 79 (1986).]

* * *

* * * [W]e do not weigh the value of peremptory challenges as an institution against our asserted commitment to eradicate invidious discrimination from the courtroom. Instead, we consider whether peremptory challenges based on gender stereotypes provide substantial aid to a litigant's effort to secure a fair and impartial jury. * * *

Far from proffering an exceptionally persuasive justification for its gender-based peremptory challenges, respondent maintains that its decision to strike virtually all the males from the jury in this case "may reasonably have been based upon the perception, supported by history, that men otherwise totally qualified to serve upon a jury might be more sympathetic and receptive to the arguments of a man alleged in a paternity action to be the father of an out-of-wedlock child, while women equally qualified to serve upon a jury might be more sympathetic and receptive to the arguments of the complaining witness who bore the child."[9]

---

9. Respondent cites one study in support of its quasi-empirical claim that women and men may have different attitudes about certain issues justifying the use of gender as a proxy for bias. See R. Hastie, S. Penrod and N. Pennington, Inside the Jury 140 (1983). The authors conclude: "Neither student nor citizen judgments for typical criminal case material have revealed differences between male and female verdict preferences. ...The picture differs [only] for rape cases, where female jurors appear to be somewhat more conviction-prone than male jurors". The majority of studies suggest that gender plays no identifiable role in jurors' attitudes. * * *

We shall not accept as a defense to gender-based peremptory challenges "the very stereotype the law condemns." Respondent's rationale, not unlike those regularly expressed for gender-based strikes, is reminiscent of the arguments advanced to justify the total exclusion of women from juries. Respondent offers virtually no support for the conclusion that gender alone is an accurate predictor of juror's attitudes; yet it urges this Court to condone the same stereotypes that justified the wholesale exclusion of women from juries and the ballot box.[11] * * *

Discrimination in jury selection, whether based on race or on gender, causes harm to the litigants, the community, and the individual jurors who are wrongfully excluded from participation in the judicial process. The litigants are harmed by the risk that the prejudice which motivated the discriminatory selection of the jury will infect the entire proceedings. The community is harmed by the State's participation in the perpetuation of invidious group stereotypes and the inevitable loss of confidence in our judicial system that state-sanctioned discrimination in the courtroom engenders.

* * *

Our conclusion that litigants may not strike potential jurors solely on the basis of gender does not imply the elimination of all peremptory challenges. * * * Parties still may remove jurors whom they feel might be less acceptable than others on the panel; gender simply may not serve as a proxy for bias. * * * Even strikes based on characteristics that are disproportionately associated with one gender could be appropriate, absent a showing of pretext.[16]

If conducted properly, voir dire can inform litigants about potential jurors, making reliance upon stereotypical and pejorative notions about a particular gender or race both unnecessary and unwise. Voir dire provides a means of discovering actual or implied bias and a firmer basis upon which the parties may exercise their peremptory challenges intelligently.

* * *

Failing to provide jurors the same protection against gender discrimination as race discrimination could frustrate the purpose of *Batson* itself.

---

11. Even if a measure of truth can be found in some of the gender stereotypes used to justify gender-based peremptory challenges, that fact alone cannot support discrimination on the basis of gender in jury selection. We have made abundantly clear in past cases that gender classifications that rest on impermissible stereotypes violate the Equal Protection Clause, even when some statistical support can be conjured up for the generalization. * * * The generalization advanced by Alabama in support of its asserted right to discriminate on the basis of gender is, at the least, overbroad, and serves only to perpetuate the same "outmoded notions of the relative capabilities of men and women," * * * that we have invalidated in other contexts. * * * The Equal Protection Clause, as interpreted by decisions of this Court, acknowledges that a shred of truth may be contained in some stereotypes, but requires that state actors look beyond the surface before making judgments about people that are likely to stigmatize as well as to perpetuate historical patterns of discrimination.

16. For example, challenging all persons who have had military experience would disproportionately affect men at this time, while challenging all persons employed as nurses would disproportionately affect women. Without a showing of pretext, however, these challenges may well not be unconstitutional, since they are not gender or race based.

Because gender and race are overlapping categories, gender can be used as a pretext for racial discrimination.[18] Allowing parties to remove racial minorities from the jury not because of their race, but because of their gender, contravenes well-established equal protection principles and could insulate effectively racial discrimination from judicial scrutiny.

Equal opportunity * * * reaffirms the promise of equality under the law—that all citizens, regardless of race, ethnicity, or gender, have the chance to take part directly in our democracy. * * * When persons are excluded from participation in our democratic processes solely because of race or gender, this promise of equality dims, and the integrity of our judicial system is jeopardized.

* * *

The judgment of the Court of Civil Appeals of Alabama is reversed and the case is remanded to that court for further proceedings not inconsistent with this opinion.

CHIEF JUSTICE REHNQUIST, dissenting.

I agree with the dissent of Justice Scalia, which I have joined. I add these words in support of its conclusion. Accepting Batson v. Kentucky as correctly decided, there are sufficient differences between race and gender discrimination such that the principle of *Batson* should not be extended to peremptory challenges to potential jurors based on sex.

That race and sex discrimination are different is acknowledged by our equal protection jurisprudence, which accords different levels of protection to the two groups. Classifications based on race are inherently suspect, triggering "strict scrutiny," while gender-based classifications are judged under a heightened, but less searching, standard of review. Racial groups comprise numerical minorities in our society, warranting in some situations a greater need for protection, whereas the population is divided almost equally between men and women. Furthermore, while substantial discrimination against both groups still lingers in our society, racial equality has proved a more challenging goal to achieve on many fronts than gender equality.

* * * *Batson* is best understood as a recognition that race lies at the core of the commands of the Fourteenth Amendment. Not surprisingly, all of our post-*Batson* cases have dealt with the use of peremptory strikes to remove black or racially identified venirepersons, and all have described *Batson* as fashioning a rule aimed at preventing purposeful discrimination against a cognizable racial group. * * * *Batson* does not apply "[o]utside the uniquely sensitive area of race."

Under the Equal Protection Clause, these differences mean that the balance should tilt in favor of peremptory challenges when sex, not race, is

18. The temptation to use gender as a pretext for racial discrimination may explain why the majority of the lower court decisions extending *Batson* to gender involve the use of peremptory challenges to remove minority women. All four of the gender-based peremptory cases to reach the federal courts of appeals involved the striking of minority women.

the issue. Unlike the Court, I think the State has shown that jury strikes on the basis of gender "substantially further" the State's legitimate interest in achieving a fair and impartial trial through the venerable practice of peremptory challenges. The two sexes differ, both biologically and, to a diminishing extent, in experience. It is not merely "stereotyping" to say that these differences may produce a difference in outlook which is brought to the jury room. Accordingly, use of peremptory challenges on the basis of sex is generally not the sort of derogatory and invidious act which peremptory challenges directed at black jurors may be.

Justice O'Connor's concurring opinion recognizes several of the costs associated with extending Batson to gender-based peremptory challenges—lengthier trials, an increase in the number and complexity of appeals addressing jury selection, and a "diminished . . . ability of litigants to act on sometimes accurate gender-based assumptions about juror attitudes." These costs are, in my view, needlessly imposed by the Court's opinion, because the Constitution simply does not require the result that it reaches.

JUSTICE SCALIA, with whom THE CHIEF JUSTICE and JUSTICE THOMAS join, dissenting.

Today's opinion is an inspiring demonstration of how thoroughly up-to-date and right-thinking we Justices are in matters pertaining to the sexes (or as the Court would have it, the genders), and how sternly we disapprove the male chauvinist attitudes of our predecessors. The price to be paid for this display—a modest price, surely—is that most of the opinion is quite irrelevant to the case at hand. The hasty reader will be surprised to learn, for example, that this lawsuit involves a complaint about the use of peremptory challenges to exclude *men* from a petit jury. To be sure, petitioner, a man, used all but one of *his* peremptory strikes to remove *women* from the jury (he used his last challenge to strike the sole remaining male from the pool), but the validity of *his* strikes is not before us. * * *

The Court also spends time establishing that the use of sex as a proxy for particular views or sympathies is unwise and perhaps irrational. The opinion stresses the lack of statistical evidence to support the widely held belief that, at least in certain types of cases, a juror's sex has some statistically significant predictive value as to how the juror will behave. This assertion seems to place the Court in opposition to its earlier Sixth Amendment "fair cross-section" cases. But times and trends do change, and unisex is unquestionably in fashion. Personally, I am less inclined to demand statistics, and more inclined to credit the perceptions of experienced litigators who have had money on the line. But it does not matter. * * * Even if sex was a remarkably good predictor in certain cases, the Court would find its use in peremptories unconstitutional.

Of course the relationship of sex to partiality *would have been* relevant if the Court had demanded in this case what it ordinarily demands: that the complaining party have suffered some injury. * * * But if men and women jurors are (as the Court thinks) fungible, then the only arguable injury from the prosecutor's "impermissible" use of male sex as the basis for his peremptories is injury to the stricken juror, not to the defendant. Indeed, far from having suffered harm, petitioner, a state actor under our precedents * * * has himself actually *inflicted* harm on female jurors. * * * Not only has petitioner, by implication of the Court's own reasoning, suffered no harm, but the scientific evidence presented at trial established petitioner's paternity with 99.92% accuracy. Insofar as petitioner is concerned, this is a case of harmless error if there ever was one; a retrial will do nothing but divert the State's judicial and prosecutorial resources, allowing either petitioner or some other malefactor to go free.

* * *

The irrationality of today's strike-by-strike approach to equal protection is evident from the consequences of extending it to its logical conclusion. If * * * sex-based [trial] stratagems do not survive heightened scrutiny—then the prosecutor presumably violates the Constitution when he selects a male or female police officer to testify because he believes one or the other sex might be more convincing in the context of the particular case, or because he believes one or the other might be more appealing to a predominantly male or female jury. A decision to stress one line of argument or present certain witnesses before a mostly female jury—for example, to stress that the defendant victimized women—becomes, under the Court's reasoning, intentional discrimination by a state actor on the basis of gender.

In order, it seems to me, not to eliminate any real denial of equal protection, but simply to pay conspicuous obeisance to the equality of the sexes, the Court imperils a practice that has been considered an essential part of fair jury trial since the dawn of the common law. The Constitution of the United States neither requires nor permits this vandalizing of our people's traditions.

For these reasons, I dissent.

NOTES ON J.E.B.

1. In *J.E.B.*, the Court describes the issue as "whether peremptory challenges based on gender stereotypes provide substantial aid to a litigant's effort to secure a fair and impartial jury." How does the whole peremptory challenge jury-selection system relate to the goal of a fair and impartial jury? Parties use their peremptory challenges to produce the jury most likely to find in their favor (and, when they can afford it, do so after very expensive consultants have tested for characteristics likely to be associated with a finding in favor of the person who has hired them). If one wanted a fair jury, is this the system one would design? For example, Maureen Howard argues that in criminal cases, prosecutors should voluntarily waive peremptory challenges in order to preserve justice and fairness. Howard, Taking the High Road: Why Prosecutors Should Voluntarily Waive Peremptory Challenges, 23

Geo. J. Legal Ethics 369 (2010). Is this a realistic approach, given that securing a jury via peremptory challenges likely increases a litigant's chances of winning a case?

2. Justice O'Connor, in her concurrence with the majority, discussed some of the costs of expanding *Batson* to include exclusions based on gender. "In extending *Batson* to gender we have added an additional burden to the state and federal trial process, taken a step closer to eliminating the peremptory challenge, and diminished the ability of litigants to act on sometimes accurate gender-based assumptions about juror attitudes." 511 U.S. at 149–50. In order to combat these costs, O'Connor suggests that only the government should be prohibited from using gender-based peremptory challenges. However, several courts have expressly refused to follow O'Connor's suggestion. See State v. George, 910 A.2d 931 (Conn. 2006); Wiley v. Commonwealth, 978 S.W.2d 333 (Ky. Ct. App. 1998). What else could help mitigate the costs O'Connor mentions?

3. If men and women do have differing attitudes on some questions, should the legal system necessarily ignore those differences to ensure fair outcomes? Is the majority inconsistent in asserting both that the sex of jurors makes no difference and that the decision below should be reversed? The majority doubts that male and female jurors would react differently, but states in footnote 11 that even if there were a correlation between sex and juror attitudes, jurors could not be stricken on peremptory challenges because of their sex. Is the court implicitly employing an anti-stereotyping rationale, like that discussed above in the notes to *Geduldig*? Why didn't the Court instead focus on whether one group was more likely to reach *accurate* conclusions? For example, if male jurors decide in favor of defendants in paternity actions when there is conclusive evidence of paternity (such as the evidence in this case, indicating with a 99.92% level of certainty that the defendant was the father), isn't there a serious problem if any man is on the jury? Is ignoring the problem a solution?

According to Lorrie Luellig, there are a number of areas in which women generally have different attitudes than men. She reports that "empirical studies illustrate that female jurors are more likely than male jurors to convict rape defendants." Luellig, Why *J.E.B. v. T.B.* Will Fail to Advance Equality: A Call for Discrimination in Jury Selection, 10 Wis. Women's L.J. 403, 421 (1995). Women are also *less* "influenced than their male counterparts by the rape victim's virginity, her social status, or society's myths about rape." Id. These differences are exacerbated by the reality that rape law "has itself traditionally adopted a male viewpoint." Id. at 422. Luellig suggests that sexist attitudes, which generally are higher among men than among women, id. at 435–36, may also prejudice outcomes in other cases, such as those in which battered women have killed abusive partners. She concludes that "[i]n rape and battered women cases, the presence of women on a jury makes the jury less sexist—it makes the trial more impartial, not more biased." Id. at 428. Assuming that Luellig is right about the empirical evidence, do you agree with her conclusion? How would you decide *J.E.B.* if you were a justice convinced of the accuracy of such evidence?

4. Between the 1994 decision of the Court in *J.E.B.* and the publication of Luellig's article in 1995, there were sixty-eight appellate cases raising the issue of sex-based juror exclusion. Only three were civil. Luellig, above note 3, at 448–49. Of the sixty-five criminal appellate cases, fifty-seven were brought by male criminal defendants seeking reversal of their convictions. In 91% of those, men were objecting to the exclusion of men (i.e., the inclusion of women). Forty-seven percent of them had been convicted of male-on-female crimes. Id. at 449–50. Should the Supreme Court have considered the interests of female victims of crime in a just verdict? Does the result in *J.E.B.* actually promote *women's* equality, given that its major effect seems to be giving male criminal defendants (almost half of whom have harmed a female victim) an argument for reversing convictions by juries with "too many" women, though the evidence suggests that women may be fairer than men in at least some of these cases?

5. In the text and footnote 16, the *J.E.B.* majority states that peremptory challenges can be based on factors that result disproportionately in the exclusion of one sex or the other (such as being a veteran) as long as there is no showing of pretext, i.e., that the factor was really chosen *in order* to exclude women as such or men as such. Is it easy or difficult for lawyers to explain sex-based exclusions in neutral terms? How would you do so if you were arguing for such exclusions?

6. Under *J.E.B.*, would the Constitution be violated by the prosecutor's choosing, as Justice Scalia suggests, a female police officer to testify (rather than a male police officer) before a predominantly female jury? Can you distinguish this hypo from *J.E.B.*? Is it unconstitutional for the state to use a female attorney to defend itself against a charge that it discriminated against women in employment?

7. In his dissent, Chief Justice Rehnquist maintains that *J.E.B.* is wrongly decided because "[i]t is not merely 'stereotyping' to say that [women's and men's biological differences and, to a diminishing extent, differences in experience] may produce a difference in outlook which is brought to the jury room." Are differences in experiences of, for example, Black and white citizens such that they too might bring "a difference in outlook" to the jury room? Why does Rehnquist think that such differences in outlook would justify sex-based but not race-based peremptories? How does this view relate to Justice Rehnquist's later approach in *Hibbs*, discussed above in the notes to *Geduldig*?

8. In *J.E.B.*, the Supreme Court justifies its holding on the ground that the purpose of *Batson* (banning race discrimination in peremptories) will be frustrated unless there is a parallel ban on "gender discrimination": "[B]ecause gender and race are overlapping categories, gender can [otherwise] be used as a pretext for racial discrimination." And in footnote 18, the Court indicates that most of the "lower court decisions extending *Batson* to gender involve the use of peremptory challenges to remove minority women." This is the Court's first use of intersectionality analysis, i.e., reasoning premised on the need to recognize that women of color experience intersecting forms of discrimination. Does the Court's substantive point—that the rule with respect to sex must parallel that with respect to race if minority women are to be

protected—suggest that all solutions to discrimination must be parallel for sex and race? Do you agree? How does this relate to the arguments made by Reva Siegel and Serena Mayeri, discussed above in the notes to *Reed*?

The D.C. Court of Appeals dealt with intersectionality in a slightly different context when considering a case involving the exclusion of prospective jurors because they were both black *and* female. Robinson v. United States, 878 A.2d 1273 (D.C. 2005). Although the trial court had ruled that race and gender combinations were not protected under *Batson* or *J.E.B.*, the appellate court declared that such exclusions were discriminatory on account of both race *and* gender. What do you think would happen, however, if the intersection occurred between a suspect category, like race or gender, and a non-suspect category, such as work experience or hairstyle? Would the non-suspect category be seen as a legitimate reason to exclude the juror, or would reliance on race or gender make the exclusion improper? What does this reveal about some of the difficulties of proving that exclusions were in fact based on race or gender?

9. Prior to *J.E.B.*, the Court considered a case in which the prosecutor used peremptory challenges to exclude two Latino jurors from a jury on the ground that they were bilingual and there was to be testimony in Spanish. Because they were bilingual, their understanding of the testimony would not depend entirely on the official English translation, which is all that the judge and other jurors would understand. Although a majority of Latinos are bilingual, the Court held that the exclusion on the basis of bilingualism when the bilingual juror honestly states that she or he might not be able to disregard the original Spanish testimony was not racial discrimination. Hernandez v. New York, 500 U.S. 352 (1991). Juan F. Perea has pointed out that courts assume that all racism operates in the way white racism against Blacks has operated, i.e., in terms of a black-white paradigm. Minorities for whom discrimination operates in other ways are even less likely than Blacks to have their experiences of discrimination recognized as such by the courts. Perea, Ethnicity and the Constitution: Beyond the Black and White Binary Constitution, 36 Wm. & Mary L. Rev. 571, 594–603 (1995). Do you agree? How would you change the concept of race discrimination to avoid this problem? How might Perea's analysis also apply to gender discrimination?

10. How would a fair system for selecting a jury work? Should peremptory challenges be eliminated entirely? Just as sex can be used to exclude Black women from juries in the absence of a ban on sex-based peremptories, so too other factors can be used as pretexts for the exclusion of racial minorities and women from juries in a system that allows peremptories. Nancy Marder advocates the elimination of peremptories (and a slight expansion of for-cause exclusions) in order to better serve the functions of the jury: to include a range of values and perspectives in public decisionmaking, to render accurate verdicts, and to ensure fairness. Marder, Beyond Gender: Peremptory Challenges and the Roles of the Jury, 73 Tex. L. Rev. 1041 (1995); see also Roger Ford, Modeling the Effects of Peremptory Challenges on Jury Selection and Jury Verdicts, 17 Geo. Mason L. Rev. 377 (2010) (illustrating how peremptory challenges potentially lead to biased juries, as well as juries unrepresentative of the community).

D. BACK TOWARDS STRICT SCRUTINY?

UNITED STATES v. VIRGINIA

Supreme Court of the United States, 1996.
518 U.S. 515, 116 S.Ct. 2264, 135 L.Ed.2d 735.

[Justice Thomas took no part in the proceedings because his son was a student at the Citadel, which prior to 1995 was also a public all-male military college much like VMI.]

JUSTICE GINSBURG delivered the opinion of the Court.

Virginia's public institutions of higher learning include an incomparable military college, Virginia Military Institute (VMI). The United States maintains that the Constitution's equal protection guarantee precludes Virginia from reserving exclusively to men the unique educational opportunities VMI affords. We agree. * * *

VMI produces its "citizen-soldiers" through "an adversative, or doubting, model of education" which features "[p]hysical rigor, mental stress, absolute equality of treatment, absence of privacy, minute regulation of behavior, and indoctrination in desirable values." As one Commandant of Cadets described it, the adversative method "dissects the young student," and makes him aware of his "limits and capabilities," so that he knows "how far he can go with his anger, ... how much he can take under stress, ... exactly what he can do when he is physically exhausted."

VMI cadets live in spartan barracks where surveillance is constant and privacy nonexistent; they wear uniforms, eat together in the mess hall, and regularly participate in drills. Entering students are incessantly exposed to the rat line, "an extreme form of the adversative model," comparable in intensity to Marine Corps boot camp. Tormenting and punishing, the rat line bonds new cadets to their fellow sufferers and, when they have completed the 7–month experience, to their former tormentors.

VMI's "adversative model" is further characterized by a hierarchical "class system" of privileges and responsibilities, a "dyke system" for assigning a senior class mentor to each entering class "rat," and a stringently enforced "honor code," which prescribes that a cadet " 'does not lie, cheat, steal nor tolerate those who do.' " * * *

In the two years preceding the lawsuit, the District Court noted, VMI had received inquiries from 347 women, but had responded to none of them. "[S]ome women, at least," the court said, "would want to attend the school if they had the opportunity." The court further recognized that, with recruitment, VMI could "achieve at least 10% female enrollment"—"a sufficient 'critical mass' to provide the female cadets with a positive educational experience." And it was also established that "some women are capable of all the individual activities required of VMI cadets." * * *

The District Court [ruled in favor of VMI, reasoning] that education in "a single-gender environment, be it male or female," yields substantial benefits. VMI's school for men brought diversity to an otherwise coeducational Virginia system, and that diversity was "enhanced by VMI's unique method of instruction." If single-gender education for males ranks as an important governmental objective, it becomes obvious, the District Court concluded, that the only means of achieving the objective "is to exclude women from the all-male institution—VMI." * * *

The [Court of Appeals for the Fourth Circuit] greeted with skepticism Virginia's assertion that it offers single-sex education at VMI as a facet of the Commonwealth's overarching and undisputed policy to advance "autonomy and diversity." The court [explained that] "[a] policy of diversity which aims to provide an array of educational opportunities, including single-gender institutions, must do more than favor one gender." * * *

Remanding the case, the appeals court assigned to Virginia, in the first instance, responsibility for selecting a remedial course. * * * The court suggested these options for the Commonwealth: Admit women to VMI; establish parallel institutions or programs; or abandon state support, leaving VMI free to pursue its policies as a private institution. * * *

In response to the Fourth Circuit's ruling, Virginia proposed a parallel program for women: Virginia Women's Institute for Leadership (VWIL). The 4-year, state-sponsored undergraduate program would be located at Mary Baldwin College, a private liberal arts school for women, and would be open, initially, to about 25 to 30 students. Although VWIL would share VMI's mission—to produce "citizen-soldiers"—the VWIL program would differ, as does Mary Baldwin College, from VMI in academic offerings, methods of education, and financial resources.

* * *

Virginia returned to the District Court seeking approval of its proposed remedial plan, and the court decided the plan met the requirements of the Equal Protection Clause [as did a divided Court of Appeals for the Fourth Circuit.] * * *

The cross-petitions in this case present two ultimate issues. First, does Virginia's exclusion of women from the educational opportunities provided by VMI—extraordinary opportunities for military training and civilian leadership development—deny to women "capable of all of the individual activities required of VMI cadets" the equal protection of the laws guaranteed by the Fourteenth Amendment? Second, if VMI's "unique" situation as Virginia's sole single-sex public institution of higher education offends the Constitution's equal protection principle, what is the remedial requirement?

* * *

Without equating gender classifications, for all purposes, to classifications based on race or national origin,[6] the Court, in [decisions beginning with *Reed v. Reed* in 1971], has carefully inspected official action that closes a door or denies opportunity to women (or to men). * * * [T]he reviewing court must determine whether the proffered justification is "exceedingly persuasive." The burden of justification is demanding and it rests entirely on the State. The State must show "at least that the [challenged] classification serves 'important governmental objectives and that the discriminatory means employed' are 'substantially related to the achievement of those objectives.' " The justification must be genuine, not hypothesized or invented *post hoc* in response to litigation. And it must not rely on overbroad generalizations about the different talents, capacities, or preferences of males and females.

The heightened review standard our precedent establishes does not make sex a proscribed classification. Supposed "inherent differences" are no longer accepted as a ground for race or national origin classifications. Physical differences between men and women, however, are enduring: "[T]he two sexes are not fungible; a community made up exclusively of one [sex] is different from a community composed of both."

"Inherent differences" between men and women, we have come to appreciate, remain cause for celebration, but not for denigration of the members of either sex or for artificial constraints on an individual's opportunity. Sex classifications may be used to compensate women "for particular economic disabilities [they have] suffered," to "promot[e] equal employment opportunity, to advance full development of the talent and capacities of our Nation's people."[7] But such classifications may not be used, as they once were, to create or perpetuate the legal, social, and economic inferiority of women. * * *

Virginia * * * asserts two justifications in defense of VMI's exclusion of women. First, * * * "single-sex education provides important educational benefits," and the option of single-sex education contributes to "diversity in educational approaches." Second, * * * "the unique VMI method of character development and leadership training," the school's adversative approach, would have to be modified were VMI to admit women. We consider these two justifications in turn.

Single-sex education affords pedagogical benefits to at least some students, Virginia emphasizes, and that reality is uncontested in this litigation.[8] Similarly, it is not disputed that diversity among public edu-

---

6. The Court has thus far reserved most stringent judicial scrutiny for classifications based on race or national origin, but last Term observed that strict scrutiny of such classifications is not inevitably "fatal in fact." Adarand Constructors, Inc. v. Pena, 515 U.S. 200, 237 (1995).

7. Several amici have urged that diversity in educational opportunities is an altogether appropriate governmental pursuit and that single-sex schools can contribute importantly to such diversity. Indeed, it is the mission of some single-sex schools "to dissipate, rather than perpetuate, traditional gender classifications." We do not question the State's prerogative evenhandedly to support diverse educational opportunities. We address specifically and only an educational opportunity recognized by the District Court and the Court of Appeals as "unique," an opportunity available only at Virginia's premier military institute, the State's sole single-sex public university or college.

8. On this point, the dissent sees fire where there is no flame. "Both men and women can benefit from a single-sex education," the District Court recognized, although "the beneficial

cational institutions can serve the public good. But Virginia has not shown that VMI was established, or has been maintained, with a view to diversifying, by its categorical exclusion of women, educational opportunities within the State. In cases of this genre, our precedent instructs that "benign" justifications proffered in defense of categorical exclusions will not be accepted automatically; a tenable justification must describe actual state purposes, not rationalizations for actions in fact differently grounded.

* * *

* * * A purpose genuinely to advance an array of educational options, as the Court of Appeals recognized, is not served by VMI's historic and constant plan—a plan to "afford a unique educational benefit only to males." However "liberally" this plan serves the State's sons, it makes no provision whatever for her daughters. That is not equal protection.

Virginia next argues that VMI's adversative method of training provides educational benefits that cannot be made available, unmodified, to women. * * *

The District Court forecast from expert witness testimony, and the Court of Appeals accepted, that coeducation would materially affect "at least these three aspects of VMI's program—physical training, the absence of privacy, and the adversative approach." And it is uncontested that women's admission would require accommodations, primarily in arranging housing assignments and physical training programs for female cadets. It is also undisputed, however, that "the VMI methodology could be used to educate women." The District Court even allowed that some women may prefer it to the methodology a women's college might pursue. * * * The parties, furthermore, agree that "*some* women can meet the physical standards [VMI] now impose[s] on men." In sum, "neither the goal of producing citizen soldiers," VMI's *raison d'etre*, "nor VMI's implementing methodology is inherently unsuitable to women." * * *

It may be assumed, for purposes of this decision, that most women would not choose VMI's adversative method. [But] it is also probable that "many men would not want to be educated in such an environment." * * * [T]he question is whether the Commonwealth can constitutionally deny to women who have the will and capacity, the training and attendant opportunities that VMI uniquely affords.

The notion that admission of women would downgrade VMI's stature, destroy the adversative system and, with it, even the school,[11] is a

---

effects" of such education, the court added, apparently "are stronger among women than among men." The United States does not challenge that recognition. Cf. C. Jencks and D. Riesman, The Academic Revolution 297–298 (1968):

> The pluralistic argument for preserving all-male colleges is uncomfortably similar to the pluralistic argument for preserving all-white colleges.... The all-male college would be relatively easy to defend if it emerged from a world in which women were established as fully equal to men. But it does not. It is therefore likely to be a witting or unwitting device for preserving tacit assumptions of male superiority—assumptions for which women must eventually pay.

11. * * * Forecasts of the same kind were made regarding admission of women to the federal military academies.

judgment hardly proved, a prediction hardly different from other "self-fulfilling prophec[ies]" once routinely used to deny rights or opportunities. When women first sought admission to the bar and access to legal education, concerns of the same order were expressed. * * *

Women's successful entry into the federal military academies, and their participation in the Nation's military forces, indicate that Virginia's fears for the future of VMI may not be solidly grounded.[15] * * *.

Virginia and VMI trained their argument on "means" rather than "end," and thus misperceived our precedent. Single-sex education at VMI serves an "important governmental objective," they maintained, and exclusion of women is not only "substantially related," it is essential to that objective. By this notably circular argument, the "straightforward" test *Mississippi Univ. for Women* described [excerpt in Chapter 8] was bent and bowed.

[Virginia's] misunderstanding and, in turn, the District Court's, is apparent from VMI's mission: to produce "citizen-soldiers," individuals " 'imbued with love of learning, confident in the functions and attitudes of leadership, possessing a high sense of public service, advocates of the American democracy and free enterprise system, and ready . . . to defend their country in time of national peril.' " Surely that goal is great enough to accommodate women, who today count as citizens in our American democracy equal in stature to men. Just as surely, the State's great goal is not substantially advanced by women's categorical exclusion, in total disregard of their individual merit, from the State's premier "citizen-soldier" corps. Virginia, in sum, "has fallen far short of establishing the 'exceedingly persuasive justification,' " that must be the solid base for any gender-defined classification.

* * *

[The Court turns to the second issue: the constitutionality of Virginia's remedy.] Virginia chose not to eliminate, but to leave untouched, VMI's exclusionary policy. For women only, however, Virginia proposed a separate program, different in kind from VMI and unequal in tangible and intangible facilities. Having violated the Constitution's equal protection requirement, Virginia was obliged to show that its remedial proposal "directly address[ed] and relate[d] to" the violation, i.e., the equal protection denied to women ready, willing, and able to benefit from educational opportunities of the kind VMI offers. * * *

VWIL students participate in ROTC and a "largely ceremonial" Virginia Corps of Cadets, but Virginia deliberately did not make VWIL a military institute. The VWIL House is not a military-style residence and VWIL students need not live together throughout the 4–year program, eat meals together, or wear uniforms during the school day. VWIL students

15. Inclusion of women in settings where, traditionally, they were not wanted inevitably entails a period of adjustment. As one West Point cadet squad leader recounted: "[T]he classes of '78 and '79 see the women as women, but the classes of '80 and '81 see them as classmates." U.S. Military Academy, A. Vitters, Report of Admission of Women.

thus do not experience the "barracks" life "crucial to the VMI experience," the spartan living arrangements designed to foster an "egalitarian ethic." "[T]he most important aspects of the VMI educational experience occur in the barracks," the District Court found, yet Virginia deemed that core experience nonessential, indeed inappropriate, for training its female citizen-soldiers.

VWIL students receive their "leadership training" in seminars, externships, and speaker series, episodes and encounters lacking the "[p]hysical rigor, mental stress, ... minute regulation of behavior, and indoctrination in desirable values" made hallmarks of VMI's citizen-soldier training. Kept away from the pressures, hazards, and psychological bonding characteristic of VMI's adversative training, VWIL students will not know the "feeling of tremendous accomplishment" commonly experienced by VMI's successful cadets.

Virginia maintains that these methodological differences are "justified pedagogically," based on "important differences between men and women in learning and developmental needs," "psychological and sociological differences" Virginia describes as "real" and "not stereotypes." The Task Force charged with developing the leadership program for women, drawn from the staff and faculty at Mary Baldwin College, "determined that a military model and, especially VMI's adversative method, would be wholly inappropriate for educating and training *most women*." The Commonwealth embraced the Task Force view, as did expert witnesses who testified for Virginia.

As earlier stated, generalizations about "the way women are," estimates of what is appropriate for *most women*, no longer justify denying opportunity to women whose talent and capacity place them outside the average description. Notably, Virginia never asserted that VMI's method of education suits *most men*. It is also revealing that Virginia accounted for its failure to make the VWIL experience "the entirely militaristic experience of VMI" on the ground that VWIL "is planned for women who do not necessarily expect to pursue military careers." By that reasoning, VMI's "entirely militaristic" program would be inappropriate for men in general or as a group, for "[o]nly about 15% of VMI cadets enter career military service."

In contrast to the generalizations about women on which Virginia rests, we note again these dispositive realities: VMI's "implementing methodology" is not "inherently unsuitable to women," "some women ... do well under [the] adversative model," "some women, at least, would want to attend [VMI] if they had the opportunity," "some women are capable of all of the individual activities required of VMI cadets," and "can meet the physical standards [VMI] now impose[s] on men." It is on behalf of these women that the United States has instituted this suit, and it is for them that a remedy must be crafted,[19] a remedy that will end

19. Admitting women to VMI would undoubtedly require alterations necessary to afford members of each sex privacy from the other sex in living arrangements, and to adjust aspects of the physical training programs. * * *

their exclusion from a state-supplied educational opportunity for which they are fit, a decree that will "bar like discrimination in the future."

In myriad respects other than military training, VWIL does not qualify as VMI's equal. VWIL's student body, faculty, course offerings, and facilities hardly match VMI's. Nor can the VWIL graduate anticipate the benefits associated with VMI's 157-year history, the school's prestige, and its influential alumni network. * * *

For the reasons stated, the initial judgment of the Court of Appeals is affirmed, the final judgment of the Court of Appeals is reversed, and the case is remanded for further proceedings consistent with this opinion.

CHIEF JUSTICE REHNQUIST, concurring in judgment.

[While Chief Justice Rehnquist agreed with the outcome of the case, he disagreed with the rationale the Court used, which, to him, suggested the possibility of applying a new constitutional standard in sex-discrimination cases.] * * *

In the end, the women's institution Virginia proposes, VWIL, fails as a remedy, because it is distinctly inferior to the existing men's institution and will continue to be for the foreseeable future. * * *

JUSTICE SCALIA, dissenting.

* * * [I]t is my view that, whatever abstract tests we may choose to devise, they cannot supersede—and indeed ought to be crafted *so as to reflect*—those constant and unbroken national traditions that embody the people's understanding of ambiguous constitutional texts. More specifically, it is my view that "when a practice not expressly prohibited by the text of the Bill of Rights bears the endorsement of a long tradition of open, widespread, and unchallenged use that dates back to the beginning of the Republic, we have no proper basis for striking it down."

The all-male constitution of VMI comes squarely within such a governing tradition. Founded by the Commonwealth of Virginia in 1839 and continuously maintained by it since, VMI has always admitted only men. And in that regard it has not been unusual. For almost all of VMI's more than a century and a half of existence, its single-sex status reflected the uniform practice for government-supported military colleges. * * * The people may decide to change the one tradition, like the other, through democratic processes; but the assertion that either tradition has been unconstitutional through the centuries is not law, but politics-smuggled-into-law.

And the same applies, more broadly, to single-sex education in general, which, as I shall discuss, is threatened by today's decision with the cut-off of all state and federal support. Government-run *non*military educational institutions for the two sexes have until very recently also been part of our national tradition. * * *

* * *

Although the Court in two places recites the test as stated in *Hogan*, which asks whether the State has demonstrated "that the classification serves important governmental objectives and that the discriminatory means employed are substantially related to the achievement of those objectives," the Court never answers the question presented in anything resembling that form. When it engages in analysis, the Court instead prefers the phrase "exceedingly persuasive justification" from *Hogan*. The Court's nine invocations of that phrase, and even its fanciful description of that imponderable as "the core instruction" of [earlier] decisions would be unobjectionable if the Court acknowledged that *whether* a "justification" is "exceedingly persuasive" must be assessed by asking "[whether] the classification serves important governmental objectives and [whether] the discriminatory means employed are substantially related to the achievement of those objectives." Instead, however, the Court proceeds to interpret "exceedingly persuasive justification" in a fashion that contradicts the reasoning of *Hogan* and our other precedents.

* * *

* * * Intermediate scrutiny has never required a least-restrictive-means analysis, but only a "substantial relation" between the classification and the state interests that it serves. Thus, in Califano v. Webster, 430 U.S. 313 (1977), we upheld a congressional statute that provided higher Social Security benefits for women than for men. We reasoned that "women . . . as such have been unfairly hindered from earning as much as men," but we did not require proof that each woman so benefited had suffered discrimination or that each disadvantaged man had not; it was sufficient that even under the former congressional scheme "women *on the average* received lower retirement benefits than men." The reasoning in our other intermediate-scrutiny cases has similarly required only a substantial relation between end and means, not a perfect fit. * * * There is simply no support in our cases for the notion that a sex-based classification is invalid unless it relates to characteristics that hold true in every instance.

Not content to execute a *de facto* abandonment of the intermediate scrutiny that has been our standard for sex-based classifications for some two decades, the Court purports to reserve the question whether, even in principle, a higher standard (i.e., strict scrutiny) should apply. * * * [This is] misleading, insofar as [it] suggests that we have not already categorically *held* strict scrutiny to be inapplicable to sex-based classifications. And [it is] * * * irresponsible, insofar as [it] destabilize[s] current law. Our task is to clarify the law—not to muddy the waters, and not to exact over-compliance by intimidation. * * *

The Court's intimations are particularly out of place because it is perfectly clear that, if the question of the applicable standard of review for sex-based classifications were to be regarded as an appropriate subject for reconsideration, the stronger argument would be not for elevating the standard to strict scrutiny, but for reducing it to rational-basis review.

* * * [N]ormal, rational-basis review of sex-based classifications would be much more in accord with the genesis of heightened standards of judicial review, the famous footnote in *United States v. Carolene Products Co.*, 304 U.S. 144 (1938), which said (intimatingly) that we did not have to inquire in the case at hand "whether prejudice against discrete and insular minorities may be a special condition, which tends seriously to curtail the operation of those political processes ordinarily to be relied upon to protect minorities, and which may call for a correspondingly more searching judicial inquiry." It is hard to consider women a "discrete and insular minority" unable to employ the "political processes ordinarily to be relied upon," when they constitute a majority of the electorate. And the suggestion that they are incapable of exerting that political power smacks of the same paternalism that the Court so roundly condemns. Moreover, a long list of legislation proves the proposition false.

* * *

The only hope for state-assisted single-sex private schools is that the Court will not apply in the future the principles of law it has applied today. That is a substantial hope, I am happy and ashamed to say. After all, did not the Court today abandon the principles of law it has applied in our earlier sex-classification cases? And does not the Court positively invite private colleges to rely upon our ad-hocery by assuring them this case is "unique"? * * *

* * *

In an odd sort of way, it is precisely VMI's attachment to such old-fashioned concepts as manly "honor" that has made it, and the system it represents, the target of those who today succeed in abolishing public single-sex education. The record contains a booklet that all first-year VMI students (the so-called "rats") were required to keep in their possession at all times. Near the end there appears the following period-piece, entitled "The Code of a Gentleman":

> Without a strict observance of the fundamental Code of Honor, no man, no matter how "polished," can be considered a gentleman. * * * He is the descendant of the knight, the crusader; he is the defender of the defenseless and the champion of justice . . . or he is not a Gentleman. A gentleman * * * Does not lose his temper; nor exhibit anger, fear, hate, embarrassment, ardor or hilarity in public. Does not hail a lady from a club window. A gentleman never discusses the merits or demerits of a lady. Does not mention names exactly as he avoids the mention of what things cost. Does not borrow money from a friend, except in dire need. Money borrowed is a debt of honor, and must be repaid as promptly as possible. * * *. He treats people with courtesy, no matter what their social position may be. Does not slap strangers on the back nor so much as lay a finger on a lady. Does not "lick the boots of those above" nor "kick the face of those below him

on the social ladder.'' Does not take advantage of another's helplessness or ignorance[.] * * *

I do not know whether the men of VMI lived by this Code; perhaps not. But it is powerfully impressive that a public institution of higher education still in existence sought to have them do so. I do not think any of us, women included, will be better off for its destruction.

NOTES ON VMI

1. As discussed earlier in this chapter, Ginsburg, on behalf of the WRP, argued unsuccessfully in *Frontiero* that the Court should employ a strict scrutiny standard when considering the constitutionality of sex-based classifications. In *VMI,* does Ginsburg finally succeed in establishing strict scrutiny as the constitutional standard? What, if any, is the difference between the standard in *VMI* and that in Craig v. Boren (''classification by gender must serve important governmental objectives and must be substantially related to achievement of those objectives'')? What difference does Scalia see?

2. Ginsburg states: '' 'Inherent differences' between men and women, we have come to appreciate, remain cause for celebration but not for denigration of members of either sex or for artificial constraints on an individual's opportunity.'' Does this suggest that the Court should recognize all classifications based on inherent differences (such as pregnancy, physical size, upper-body strength, etc.) as sex discrimination, or do so at least when the classifications place ''artificial constraints on an individual's opportunity''? If so, what are the implications for *Geduldig* and *Bray*, in which, as discussed above, the Court held that pregnancy discrimination is not sex discrimination in constitutional cases?

Cary Franklin argues that VMI ''makes clear that anti-stereotyping doctrine governs all instances of sex-based state action, whether or not 'real' differences are involved.'' Franklin, The Anti-Stereotyping Principle in Constitutional Sex Discrimination Law, 85 N.Y.U. L. Rev. 83, 163 (2010). How does this triumph promote women's interests? How might it hurt women's interests? See Valorie K. Vojdik, Beyond Stereotyping in Equal Protection Doctrine: Reframing the Exclusion of Women from Combat, 57 Ala. L. Rev. 303, 307–22 (2005) (arguing that the anti-stereotyping approach should be enriched by an anti-subordination approach and that VMI supports such a path). Why hasn't the Court also extended an anti-stereotyping doctrine to race discrimination cases? See Neomi Rao, Gender, Race, and Individual Dignity: Evaluating Justice Ginsburg's Equality Jurisprudence, 70 Ohio St. L.J. 1053, 1080–84 (2009) (arguing that the Court should).

3. The VWIL continues to exist, despite the holding in *VMI*, declaring on its website that it provides ''the only all-female Corps of Cadets in the world.'' http://www.mbc.edu/vwil/ (last visited July 12, 2010). In a comparison of VMI and VWIL, Mary Anne Case reports: ''Most cadets at VMI strive for excellence neither with respect to their shoes nor their grades. Rather, they learn what they can get away with, in matters military as well as academic.'' Case, Two Cheers for Cheerleading: The Noisy Integration of VMI and the Quiet Success of Virginia Women in Leadership, 1999 U. Chi. Legal F. 347, 371. They also

learn to survive ritual humiliation and debasement and, as they become more senior in the Cadet corps, to humiliate and debase others. For example, "breakout" at VMI is the last event before the end of the probationary period for new cadets. As the final step of breakout, rats (first-year cadets) must climb to the top of a muddy hill despite the interference of upper classmen. Case describes breakout the first year after the admission of women:

> The final step of breakout began at the foot of a muddy field, artificially muddied by the hoses of the local fire department because, despite fears of hypothermia on an abnormally cold March day, the upperclassmen threatened not to participate unless there was "more water" to maximize the rats' suffering. The rats had been up since before dawn, they were exhausted; led in a semi-daze to the foot of the hill, they were then flung on their faces into the mud by upperclassmen, who mingled taunts with cautionary admonitions to shield one's eyes from the mud. Some rats hurled themselves into the mud. Is the lesson they have learned to abase themselves rather than waiting to be abased? Surrounded by upperclassmen shouting abuse and impeding their path, the rats crawled on their faces across the field to the base of the hill. There, as they began to climb, apparently helpful upperclass hands reached down to pull them upwards. But, just as a rat reached the crest of the hill, the once helping hand let go, and worse, pushed him or her back down. Is the lesson here you never know whom to trust—although you can't refuse help, you can't rely on it either? Gradually, over the bodies of their classmates below, the rats pushed toward the summit. Is the lesson here that the only way to the top is to step on people? It is not, as I had expected, a lesson of conscious cooperative strategizing. The rats seemed lost in the isolated world of their own struggles, oblivious to those around them, grabbing each other's legs as if they were tree trunks—just something to hang onto.

Id. at 372–73. In contrast, at VWIL, the nULLS (first-year students, equivalent to "rats" at VMI) marked the end of the probationary period by working together cooperatively in solving logic problems and forming a human pyramid. After a 14–mile march they walk "through an arch of sabers held by upperclassmen to be welcomed into the corps." Id. at 372. According to VWIL's website, the "rite" at the end of the nULLS period is now a "secret," but it remains a "long day filled with challenge, determination and celebration of your achievements." http://www.mbc.edu/vwil/traditions.php (last visited July 12, 2010).

Given these differences, are you surprised by the fact that VWIL cadets have outperformed VMI in ROTC and AMSC (American Association of Military Schools and Colleges) drill competitions? Case, above, at 377. Case suggests that this may be because many of the women at VWIL—including the woman who scored as top cadet in the competitions with VMI—have been cheerleaders, and cheerleading is great preparation for military drill. Id. at 377. How might Case's point about cheerleaders reinforce stereotypes? What else does it do?

4. VWIL cadets have another advantage—besides the cheerleading backgrounds of many—over VMI cadets in drill competitions: the more supportive atmosphere of VWIL appears to be far more effective in training cadets in

drill. Case reports that "[a]t the end of their first day training, the rats * * * at VMI were a sorry lot—terrified, sweating, shaking, and exhausted, they were unable to tell their left feet from their right. A day of drilling has many of them still tripping over their own feet and none of them smiling." Case, above note 3, at 378. In contrast, at the end of their first day, the women at VWIL "seemed to be having a good time" and had mastered an amazing amount of skill in military drill in one day. Id. at 379. Do you think that VMI has a positive impact on the men enrolled there? In addition to being less effective in drill competitions, how might the men at VMI be harmed by the VMI culture?

Indeed, the educational experts at the *VMI* trial testified that there is no evidence that VMI's adversative method is good for anyone. Case, above note 3, at 363–64. Case concludes that Virginia was "more interested in preserving a masculine standard at all costs than in training the best possible citizen-soldiers by the most suitable methods." Id. at 364. Despite the lack of evidence on the effectiveness of the "adversative method," does Ginsburg accept its superiority to the VWIL approach? See id. at 367 ("Kept away from the pressures, hazards, and psychological bonding characteristic of VMI's adversative training, VWIL students will not know the 'feeling of tremendous accomplishment' commonly experienced by VMI's successful cadets.") (quoting Ginsburg).

Yet, reports Case, "the VWIL program, which arguably is the greater success of the two, has far less funding, far less attention and a far more uncertain future." Id. at 350. What explains the greater likelihood of survival for VMI though VWIL may well be superior educationally (for men as well as women)? Why isn't this difference seen as an aspect of sex discrimination?

5. Does the manly code of honor quoted by Justice Scalia in his dissenting opinion seem consistent with real life at VMI? Do upperclassmen treat rats with "courtesy" and refuse to "kick the face of those below * * * on the social ladder"? Are they defenders of the defenseless and the champions of justice? Are there parts of the code of honor that are troubling? What is wrong with showing feelings in public?

6. Is the preservation of an institution of super-masculine culture a legitimate governmental objective? Isn't it likely that admission of women to VMI *will* "destroy" the institution as it was prior to the Supreme Court's decision? Is the availability of diverse educational institutions (including single-sex educational institutions) a legitimate governmental objective? Does Ginsburg accept educational diversity (including single-sex institutions) as a legitimate governmental purpose (though she does not find it credible as Virginia's purpose in *VMI*)? Under what circumstances, if any, might she uphold a single-sex public educational institution? See also the discussion of single-sex education in Chapter 8.

7. In his dissent, Scalia notes that most legislation is constitutional as long as it passes rational basis review. Heightened review for legislation treating differently members of different groups—as in strict scrutiny for racial classifications—is justified by the need to protect "discrete and insular minorities" who cannot protect their own interests through ordinary politics. Women are actually a *majority* of the population. What arguments might

justify heightened scrutiny for sex-based classifications despite women's majority status? On the other hand, might heightened scrutiny pose problems for women? Might there be advantages for women in relying on legislative change instead of the courts? Why does Ginsburg seem to want an even higher standard of review (strict scrutiny) rather than a return to rational basis?

8. What does Ginsburg see as the problem with *VMI* from the perspective of women and equality between the sexes? Can you see other problems with *VMI* from the perspective of women? Was sexism at VMI limited to the exclusion of women? What was the connection between VMI's exclusion of women and its glorification of super-masculinity? Why doesn't Ginsburg mention any of these other problems?

9. Whose standard is better for women, Ginsburg's or Scalia's? Which women would do better under Ginsburg's standard and which women would do better under Scalia's standard? Similarly, which women would be hurt by each Justice's respective standard?

10. The first women admitted to the Citadel, the only other all-male public military university, reported horrific levels of harassment and assault. The Citadel's policy was to treat the women the same as the men; the women were to look like men, act like men, and accept discipline like men. But during their first year, two of the four women reported being sprayed with flammable liquid and having their clothes set on fire, being harassed sexually, physically, and verbally, and forced to drink alcohol. Although these incidents were alleged to be part of the ritual hazing suffered by all new students, the women claimed that they were particular targets. Valorie K. Vojdik, Gender Outlaws: Challenging Masculinity in Traditionally Male Environments, 17 Berkeley Women's L.J. 68 (2002). Susan Faludi gives a fascinating description of the Citadel's dysfunctional super-masculine culture in Stiffed: The Betrayal of the American Man 114–21, 123–32, 136–40, 143–51 (1999). In contrast, the women at VMI report being treated no worse than "the guys." Case, above note 3, at 375. See also Catherine S. Manegold, In Glory's Shadow: Shannon Faulkner, The Citadel, and a Changing America (2000); Laura Fairchild Brodie, Breaking Out: VMI and the Coming of Women (2000).

Would you be interested in attending VMI, the Citadel, or VWIL? Why or why not?

E. TWENTIETH CENTURY EQUAL PROTECTION SEX DISCRIMINATION CASES 1971–2000[31]

CASE and TYPE	OUTCOME	RATIONALE	NOTES
Reed v. Reed, 404 U.S. 71 (1971). Overt disparate treatment.	Female pltf wins; Ct strikes statute creating preference for male estate executors.	This is the very sort of arbitrary classification forbidden by EPC; administrative expenses cannot justify sex-based preference.	Ginsburg litigates first-successful sex-based equal protection challenge as part of the WRP.
Frontiero v. Richardson, 411 U.S. 677 (1973). Overt disparate treatment.	Female pltf wins; Ct strikes rule giving benefits to all spouses of men but only to economically dependent spouses of women in the Air Force.	Four votes for striking classification under strict scrutiny. Four for striking it under standard of *Reed*.	Ginsburg and the WRP argue for strict scrutiny in amicus brief.
Kahn v. Shevin, 416 U.S. 351 (1974). Overt disparate treatment.	Male pltf loses; Ct upholds property tax exemption of $500 a year for widows.	Reasonable measure to cushion effect of death of spouse for sex (women) "for which that loss imposes a disproportionately heavy burden."	Ginsburg and the WRP decide to bring cases with male pltfs after losing on strict scrutiny, hoping that the harm of stereotypes will be more visible.
Geduldig v. Aiello, 417 U.S. 484 (1974). Ct sees neither disparate treatment nor disparate impact.	Female pltf loses; Ct upholds state disability plan covering all but pregnancy-related disabilities.	Ct explains that this is not sex discrimination but discrimination between "pregnant women and nonpregnant persons."	Ginsburg and WRP file amicus brief arguing that the state's plan is *overt* sex discrimination and that the state *intended* to treat women and men differently.
Schlesinger v. Ballard, 419 U.S. 498 (1975). Overt disparate treatment.	Male pltf loses; Ct upholds rule giving female officers two more years in rank under military up-or-out policy.	Distinction "reflects, not archaic and overbroad generalizations, but, instead, the demonstrable fact that male and female line officers in the Navy are not similarly situated with respect to opportunities for professional service."	This policy was developed in response to the military's ban on women in combat.
Taylor v. Louisiana, 419 U.S. 522 (1975). Overt disparate treatment.	Male deft in prosecution for kidnapping and rape wins challenge to exclusion of most women from juror rolls.	"Louisiana's special exemption for women operates to exclude them from petit juries, which in our view is contrary to the command of the Sixth and Fourteenth Amendments."	Overruling Hoyt v. Florida, 368 U.S. 57 (1961) (upholding Fla. rule excluding women from jury service in case in which wife was on trial for killing her abusive and unfaithful husband).

31. This table summarizes all the Supreme Court cases interpreting sex discrimination under the Equal Protection Clause of the Fourteenth Amendment from the first case holding that the Equal Protection Clause prohibits discrimination on the basis of sex (Reed v. Reed) through the end of the twentieth century. In this chart, "pltf" is used for plaintiff, "deft" is used for defendant, "Ct" is used for Court, "EPC" is used for Equal Protection Clause, "WRP" is used for Women's Rights Project (of the ACLU), and "SS" is used for Social Security.

CASE and TYPE	OUTCOME	RATIONALE	NOTES
Weinberger v. Wiesenfeld, 420 U.S. 636 (1975). Overt disparate treatment.	Male pltf wins; Ct holds that widower must be given SS benefits available to widows.	The generalization "that men are more likely than women to be the primary supporters of their spouses and children is not entirely without empirical support. But such a gender-based generalization cannot suffice to justify the denigration of the efforts of women who do work and whose earnings contribute significantly to their families' support."	Main problem with SS from the perspective of women are distinctions between breadwinners and caretakers, not those between women and men.
Stanton v. Stanton, 421 U.S. 7 (1975). Overt disparate treatment.	Female pltf wins; Ct strikes statute creating different ages of majority for young women (18) and men (21) (and hence giving more years of parental support to young men).	"[W]e perceive nothing rational in" this legislation, "which, when related to the divorce decree, results in the appellee's liability for support for [a daughter] only to age 18 but for [a son] to age 21."	
Craig v. Boren, 429 U.S. 190 (1976). Overt disparate treatment.	Male pltf wins; Ct holds unconstitutional different rules on ability of young people to buy 3.2% beer.	Although females in this age group are less likely than males to drink and drive, a correlation of only 2% between being male and driving after drinking is too "tenuous a 'fit.' "	Ct shifts from "sex" to "gender" and settles on "intermediate" level of scrutiny: "classifications by gender must serve important governmental objectives and must be substantially related to achievement of those objectives."
Califano v. Goldfarb, 430 U.S. 199 (1977). Overt disparate treatment.	Male pltf wins; Ct strikes SS provision automatically giving benefits to widows by requiring that widowers show dependence on wife for at least 50% of support.	This statute "deprive[s] women of protection for their families which men receive as a result of their employment." It is unconstitutional "when supported by no more substantial justification than 'archaic and overbroad generalizations,' or 'old notions,' such as 'assumptions as to dependency.' "	Ginsburg litigates, as part of the WRP, arguing that sex-classifications in the employment context should be per se invalid.
Califano v. Webster, 430 U.S. 313 (1977). Overt disparate treatment.	Male pltf loses; Ct upholds temporary provision giving women advantage of being able to exclude two more low-earning years than men in calculating average monthly wage (resulting in higher SS draws after retirement).	"The more favorable treatment of the female wage earner enacted here was not the result of 'archaic and overbroad generalizations' about women." Rather, it "operated directly to compensate women for past economic discrimination."	In *Goldfarb* the differential SS provision "penalized women wage earners," whereas the one in *Webster* redresses " 'disparate treatment of women.' "

CASE and TYPE	OUTCOME	RATIONALE	NOTES
Fiallo v. Bell, 430 U.S. 787 (1977). Overt disparate treatment.	Male pltf loses; Ct upholds immigration rules giving mothers and their illegitimate children a more privileged status than fathers and their illegitimate children.	"Policies pertaining to the entry of aliens and their right to remain here are peculiarly concerned with the political conduct of government. * * * [T]he formulation of these policies is entrusted exclusively to Congress."	Much of the decision rests on federalism grounds.
Orr v. Orr, 440 U.S. 268 (1979). Overt disparate treatment.	Male pltf wins; Ct strikes alimony statute imposing obligation only on husbands to support wives.	Unnecessary for state to use sex as a proxy for need, since statute already provides for "individualized hearings at which the parties' relative financial circumstances are considered."	Many feminists have questioned the benefit of this gender-neutral rule.
Parham v. Hughes, 441 U.S. 347 (1979). Overt disparate treatment.	Male pltf loses; Ct upholds statute precluding father from suing for wrongful death of child if paternity had not been established prior to child's death.	State law need not afford unwed fathers all rights of unwed mothers because not similarly situated. Only paternity is uncertain at birth, and the father is less likely than the mother to establish a relationship with the child.	
Caban v. Mohammed, 441 U.S. 380 (1979). Overt disparate treatment.	Male pltf wins; Ct strikes state statute giving only unwed mothers right to consent to (or veto) adoption of child.	"In those cases where the father has never come forward to participate in the rearing of his child, nothing in the EPC precludes the State from withholding from him the privilege of vetoing the adoption of that child."	
Davis v. Passman, 442 U.S. 228 (1979). Overt disparate treatment.	Female pltf wins; Ct holds that Congressman who refuses to hire women for staff positions unconstitutionally discriminates on the basis of sex.	Plaintiff "has a federal constitutional right to be free from gender discrimination."	Focus of decision is on whether pltf has standing to bring an action for damages directly under the Constitution and without any statutory authorization.
Personnel Administrator of Massachusetts v. Feeney, 442 U.S. 256 (1979). Ct sees only disparate impact.	Female pltf loses; Ct holds preference for veterans in state employment is not sex discrimination, though under the preference 98% of state's civil servants at upper levels are male.	This statute reflects only "a preference for veterans." There is nothing suggesting that it was enacted to "accomplish the collateral goal of keeping women in a stereotypic and predefined place in the Massachusetts Civil Service."	Women were excluded from the military prior to WWII (except for WWI women in the Navy) and ever since then Congress has by statute authorized far fewer women than men in uniform.

CASE and TYPE	OUTCOME	RATIONALE	NOTES
Great American Federal Savings & Loan v. Novotny, 442 U.S. 366 (1979). Ct does not reach the merits of the discrimination claim.	Male pltf loses attempt to bring sex-discrimination claim—that he had been fired for supporting female co-workers—under § 1985(3), which redresses private conspiracies to deprive someone of their constitutional right to equal protection.	Court holds that rights enforceable by Title VII cannot be asserted under § 1985(3), a less specific statute.	
Califano v. Westcott, 443 U.S. 76(1979). Overt disparate treatment.	Female pltf wins; Ct strikes statute-giving aid to low-income two-parent families when the father, but not the mother, was unemployed.	"For mothers who are primary providers for their families and who are unemployed, [the statute] is obviously gender based, for it deprives them and their families of benefits solely on the basis of sex."	The Court therefore finds the traditional "family-wage system" violates equal protection.
Wengler v. Druggists Mutual Insurance Company, 446 U.S. 142 (1980). Overt disparate treatment.	Male pltf wins; Ct strikes worker's compensation law requiring widower, but not widow, to show incapacitation or dependence in order to receive death benefits.	"The Missouri law indisputably mandates gender-based discrimination * * * against both men and women. The provision discriminates against a woman since, in the case of her death, benefits are payable to her spouse only if he is * * * dependent on her."	
Michael M. v. Superior Ct. of Sonoma County, 450 U.S. 464 (1981). Overt disparate treatment.	Male criminal deft loses. Ct upholds statutory rape law criminalizing "an act of sexual intercourse accomplished with a female not the wife of the perpetrator, where the female is under the age of 18 years."	Women and men are not similarly situated with respect to pregnancy and the "physical, emotional, and psychological consequences of sexual activity." The section protects "women from sexual intercourse at an age when those consequences are particularly severe."	The young woman was 16.5 years old, the young man 17.5 years. She told him to stop, but he hit her "back down on the bench." Ct views these latter facts as irrelevant to its analysis.
Kirchberg v. Feenstra, 450 U.S. 455 (1981). Overt disparate treatment.	Female pltf wins; Ct strikes down community property law giving husband unilateral control of jointly owned marital property.	"By granting the husband exclusive control over the disposition of community property, [the statute] clearly embodies the type of express gender-based discrimination that we have held unconstitutional."	
Rostker v. Goldberg, 453 U.S. 57 (1981). Overt disparate treatment.	Male pltf loses; Ct upholds selective service registration limited to males.	Since "[w]omen as a group" are not eligible for combat, they need not be registered.	Ct stresses that the decision to exempt women from registration for a possible draft was not an " 'accidental by-product of a traditional way of thinking about females,' " but made by Congress after hearings and debate on the issue.

CASE and TYPE	OUTCOME	RATIONALE	NOTES
Mississippi University for Women v. Hogan, 458 U.S. 718 (1982). Overt disparate treatment.	Male pltf wins; Ct holds that Mississippi cannot operate a nursing school for women only.	Ct rejects argument that this is affirmative action (compensation for discrimination) because there is no evidence women lack nursing opportunities; policy perpetuates stereotypes of nursing as women's work.	In her majority opinion, Sandra Day O'Connor uses the term "exceedingly persuasive" twice.
Heckler v. Mathews, 465 U.S. 728 (1984). Overt disparate treatment.	Male pltf loses; Ct upholds gender-based pension offset exception to SS survivor benefits as a temporary transitional measure to protect reliance on old rules in shift from system in which only widows were automatically entitled to survivors' benefits to gender-neutral system.	"Although the offset exception temporarily revives the gender-based eligibility requirement invalidated in *Goldfarb*, Congress's purpose" is not to provide for females who are assumed to be economically dependent on the earnings of their spouses (as was true in *Goldfarb*).	The court emphasized that the provision was adopted "in order to protect the expectations of persons, both men and women, who had planned their retirements based on" law that pre-dated *Goldfarb.*
Bray v. Alexandria Women's Health Clinic, 506 U.S. 263 (1993). Ct sees only disparate impact.	Female pltf loses; Ct holds that obstruction of abortion facilities by protesters is not sex discrimination and not, therefore, actionable under § 1985(3), which allows suits against private actors who have conspired to deprive any one of equal protection of the laws.	Actions directed at women seeking abortions are not sex discrimination because not directed at "women *by reason of their sex.*"	Ct affirms *Geduldig* in constitutional cases.
J.E.B. v. Alabama ex rel. T.B., 511 U.S. 127 (1994). Overt disparate treatment.	Male deft wins claim that the state discriminated on the basis of sex when it used peremptory challenges to exclude men from jury. (The deft used all but one of his challenges to strike women from the jury in this paternity action.)	This intentional discrimination by state actors ratifies and perpetuates invidious, archaic, and overbroad stereotypes about the relative abilities of women and men.	Blackmun, writing for majority, uses "exceedingly persuasive" twice, and O'Connor uses it twice in her concurrence.
U.S. v. Virginia, 518 U.S. 515 (1996). Overt disparate treatment.	Female pltf wins; Ct holds that Virginia Military Institute cannot exclude women from admissions.	"[N]o persuasive evidence that VMI's male-only admission policy 'is in furtherance of a state policy of' 'diversity.' " Ct holds that the notion that women would "destroy the adversative system" was an unproven prediction, "no different from other 'self-fulfilling prophec[ies]'."	Ginsburg, who litigated *Reed* and argued for strict scrutiny in *Frontiero*, writes the opinion of the Ct using "exceedingly persuasive" nine times. In footnote 6, Ginsburg states that "thus far" the Ct has reserved strict scrutiny for race cases.

CASE and TYPE	OUTCOME	RATIONALE	NOTES
Miller v. Albright, 523 U.S. 420 (1998). Overt disparate treatment.	Pltf is the daughter of a male citizen. Six justices uphold denial of citizenship although, had her mother been the U.S. citizen, she would have qualified for citizenship.	Of the six justices voting to dismiss, two held no standing, two held that the Ct lacked the power to grant relief, and two held discrimination permissible as serving important governmental interests.	Plurality opinion gave no clear ruling on the INS statute at issue.
	WHO WON?	**WHO LOST?**	**WHO SUED**
Women pltfs	won 7	lost 4	11 cases with women as pltfs
Men pltfs[32]	won 9	lost 9	18 cases with men as pltfs
TOTAL CASES	16 wins	13 losses	29 TOTAL CASES

NOTES ON TWENTIETH CENTURY EQUAL PROTECTION CASES

1. The first case of the 21st century provoked a great deal of controversy. In Nguyen v. INS, 533 U.S. 53 (2001), the Supreme Court answered the question left open in Miller v. Albright and upheld in a five-to-four decision an immigration statute giving automatic citizenship to children born to unmarried citizen mothers and noncitizen fathers but requiring children born to unmarried citizen fathers and noncitizen mothers to prove paternity before the age of 18. The plaintiffs were both Nguyen and his citizen father, who had raised him. The Court held that the statute's overt sex distinction did not violate the Equal Protection Clause because of the biological difference between mothers and fathers at the time of birth. Can you understand why commentators (and the dissenting justices) saw a stark contrast between this decision and the level of scrutiny applied in United States v. Virginia (excerpt above)? See, e.g., Serena Mayeri, Constitutional Choices: Legal Feminism and the Historical Dynamics of Change, 92 Calif. L. Rev. 755, 826–32 (2004) (arguing that *Nguyen* "illustrated the limitations of intermediate scrutiny as a reliable guarantor of sex-based equal protection"); William N. Eskridge, Jr., Some Effects of Identity-Based Social Movements on Constitutional Law in the Twentieth Century, 100 Mich. L. Rev. 2062, 2259 (2002) (arguing that the *Nguyen* result would undoubtedly have been different if the distinction between his parents was based on race rather than sex). Based on the evidence of the thirty cases discussed above (the twenty-nine in the table above plus *Nguyen*), do you think you can predict the outcomes of future equal protection cases?

In 2010, the Supreme Court granted certiorari to a 9th Circuit case involving a defendant, Ruben Flores-Villar, with a citizen father and a noncitizen mother, in which the defendant claimed citizenship as a defense to

32. This category includes Miller v. Albright in which the daughter of a male American citizen argued that the statute giving automatic citizenship to children of female American citizens (but not to the children of males) discriminates on the basis of sex, and Taylor v. Louisiana, case 6, in which a male plaintiff successfully challenged exclusion of women from the jury pool, a decision which may benefit women although the plaintiff was male.

a deportation charge. United States v. Flores-Villar, 536 F.3d 990 (9th Cir. 2008), cert. granted sub. nom, Flores-Villar v. United States, ___ U.S. ___, 130 S. Ct. 1878 (2010). Under the immigration statute at issue, a child born outside of the United States to a citizen father can become a citizen if the father has lived in the United States for at least five years after the age of 14. In contrast, a similarly situated child born to a citizen mother can become a citizen if the mother has lived in the United States for at least one year after the age of 14. Flores-Villar argues that the statute's differential requirements for mothers and fathers is impermissible sex discrimination. The 9th Circuit rejected this argument, finding the statute constitutional based on the intermediate scrutiny standard used in *Nguyen*. How do you think the Supreme Court will rule? What else would you want to know in order to make a prediction? Does it matter who is on the Court?

2. Should one be troubled by the fact that so many of the sex equality cases have been brought by men? Beginning with Reed v. Reed in 1971 through the end of 2000, the Court decided twenty-nine constitutional sex discrimination cases. Men brought eigthteen of these cases, women eleven. Of the sixteen cases in which a sex-based equal protection argument won, the person making the argument was a man in the majority of cases (nine). Are there any substantive consequences to these numbers? Would it have been better to limit the equal protection challenges to suits brought by women and members of minority groups?

Recall Ginsburg's 1971 speech, quoted earlier in this chapter, in which she discussed what difference the ERA might make. She suggested that if the courts extended the Equal Protection Clause to sex discrimination, it would be doubtful that men could sue for discrimination absent an ERA. Should the Court have drawn the line suggested by Ginsburg in that speech and allowed only women (and racial minorities) to sue for discrimination under the Equal Protection Clause? For a defense of Ginburg's strategy on anti-stereotyping grounds, see Cary Franklin, The Anti-Stereotyping Principle in Constitutional Sex Discrimination Law, 85 N.Y.U. L. Rev. 83, 120–28 (2010).

3. How do the cases in which the Supreme Court has found sex discrimination relate to the problems of sexual inequality in our society? How important are they relative to *Geduldig*, *Feeney*, and *Rostker*, cases in which the Supreme Court was refused to find sex discrimination? If you conclude that women have "won" only the relatively unimportant cases, why do you think that has happened? Could this result have been avoided? How?

4. Has the Court's standard changed over time? If a legislative classification explicitly discriminates between women and men, is it as likely to be sustained today, even though such a classification might have been upheld in the past? For example, how do you think today's Supreme Court would come out in Kahn v. Shevin (1974)? The Court also upheld a sex-based classification that arguably favored women in Califano v. Webster (1977). In your opinion, would today's Court uphold the constitutionality of such provisions were they still in existence? Would the Court be more or less likely to uphold such classifications under a strict scrutiny standard?

5. Would you support an explicit constitutional standard of strict scrutiny for laws treating women one way and men another? Would an ERA require

such a standard? What difference, if any, might such a standard make in light of the VMI decision discussed earlier in this chapter? Under typical formulations of strict scrutiny, a rule that discriminates on an impermissible basis such as race is constitutional only if it serves a "compelling governmental interest." Historically, race-based classifications have fallen unless the measure challenged was regarded as a form of affirmative action designed to redress past discrimination. Compare Shelley v. Kraemer, 334 U.S. 1 (1948) (holding unconstitutional racially restrictive covenants forbidding racial minorities from owning land) with Regents of the University of California v. Bakke, 438 U.S. 265 (1978) (upholding affirmative action plan for educational program where race was one factor taken into account). In recent years, the Supreme Court has increasingly struck down race-based affirmative action plans as unconstitutional. See, e.g., City of Richmond v. J.A. Croson Co., 488 U.S. 469 (1989) (holding unconstitutional a city's affirmative action plan to set aside a portion of city contracts for minority contractors); Adarand Constructors, Inc. v. Pena, 515 U.S. 200 (1995) (holding unconstitutional Small Business Administration regulations creating a financial incentive for contractors to hire minority subcontractors); Gratz v. Bollinger, 539 U.S. 244 (2003) (holding unconstitutional an affirmative action program for undergraduates at a state university); but see Grutter v. Bollinger, 539 U.S. 306 (2003) (upholding an affirmative action program at a state law school, at least for the next twenty-five years).

6. Perhaps strict scrutiny would make the most difference in the cases in which the Court upheld as constitutional a classification explicitly treating women and men differently: Kahn v. Shevin; Schlesinger v. Ballard; Califano v. Webster; Fiallo v. Bell; Parham v. Hughes; Michael M. v. Superior Court of Sonoma County; Rostker v. Goldberg; Heckler v. Mathews; and the cases about acquiring citizenship through male or female parents. Would any or all of these cases come out differently under strict scrutiny? Can you think of other cases that might come out differently depending on which standard the Court uses? How do you think Ginsburg, Scalia, and the other members of today's Court would answer these questions?

7. As the chart above illustrates, the Court has *only* found sex discrimination in constitutional cases involving overt disparate treatment, i.e., rules or policies explicitly treating women one way and men another. As noted earlier in this chapter (in the text note on disparate treatment and disparate impact), under the Court's standard it is *possible* to find unconstitutional sex discrimination in cases without facial discrimination. Theoretically, a plaintiff can show that, though no formal rule or policy required differential treatment of women and men, women and men were in fact treated differently. Intent is a critical element in such cases, as illustrated by *Geduldig* and *Feeney*; the plaintiff must show that, rather than discriminating on the basis of pregnancy or veteran status, the state actor *intended* to treat women and men differently. But, as illustrated by *Geduldig* and *Feeney*, no woman has ever won with such an argument in a constitutional case. It is now relatively rare for a state or state actor *explicitly* to discriminate between women and men. What problems may result from the difficulty of establishing a constitutional violation in the absence of an explicit sex-based classification? What are some solutions?

8. Not surprisingly, the number of cases brought under the formal equality standard applicable in sex cases—which has thus far recognized sex discrimination only when overt—has declined over time. States and governmental entities no longer adopt policies and rules which discriminate facially on the basis of sex. Can you think of cases that might still be brought, instances in which governmental units do engage in overt sex discrimination? Think of three major factors contributing to women's inequality, factors as to which government has some influence. Would it be possible to bring a sex discrimination claim to challenge any of the items on your list? Even if it was a good idea to have the Supreme Court strike as unconstitutional statutes discriminating on the basis of sex in the past, is it a good idea for the future?

F. JUDICIAL REVIEW

MARY BECKER, CONSERVATIVE FREE SPEECH AND THE UNEASY CASE FOR JUDICIAL REVIEW

64 U. Colo. L. Rev. 975, 986–99, 1002–06, 1008–11 (1993).

In our democracy, the legislative and executive branches consist of, or are controlled by, people who are elected and accountable for their actions to the voters. Indeed, the legitimacy of our government is understood as based thereon. Yet federal judges limit the ability of the majority to govern. Federal judges are not elected, but appointed for life by the President with the advice and consent of the Senate. Their interpretations of the Constitution are final and binding on the other branches of government. Thus, a politically-insulated group often sets final and binding limits on what the other branches of government—and ultimately, "we the people"—can do. In so doing, binding judicial review degrades democratic deliberations. * * *

Judicial Bias

* * *

There are a number of ways in which judicial bias can be a problem for women. One obvious way is that the all-male Supreme Court which developed the discretionary intermediate standard for sex equality cases in the 1970s had an incentive to pick an approach that would maximize men's interests (in breaking rigid sex roles that sometimes hurt men) without requiring significant change in relationships between the sexes, since real change would often be detrimental to men. The current constitutional standard does, I believe, reflect and serve these needs and ends.

Judicial bias is often a very subtle, not easily perceived, problem. It need not be that judges hate women or even believe unconsciously that men are innately superior human beings to women. Bias will occur when judges look at the world from a perspective held by men more than women. The result of even so-subtle a bias will be legal rules better adapted to the needs of men than those of women. Consider, for example, the pregnancy discrimination cases in the 1970s, in which the Supreme

Court (all men) held that sex discrimination (for both constitutional and Title VII purposes) does not include pregnancy discrimination: such discrimination is discrimination between pregnant and non-pregnant persons rather than discrimination on the basis of sex. * * *

An even more subtle form of judicial bias is the Court's primary commitment to its own legitimacy (or to the perception of its legitimacy). The Court's concern for its own legitimacy naturally results in decisions based on its own needs rather than on a commitment to equality between the sexes. I am fairly certain, for example, that the Court would be loath to require women to be treated exactly like men for all military purposes, including draft and combat, because its action would be seen as illegitimate by many Americans (though the Court's own approach to sex equality would seem to require such a result). Yet women can never be men's political equals while denied full military participation.

Given judicial interests conflicting with women's, it is not surprising that, in considering claims other than sex-discrimination, such as free speech or religion, the Justices have narrowed their consideration of what is relevant, excluding harms to women[47] rather than balancing the First Amendment's requirement of free speech against the Fourteenth Amendment's commitment to equality. In this fashion, negative rights that on their face have nothing to do with gender can serve to perpetuate the second class status of a majority of the population even if a commitment to equality between the sexes supposedly exists elsewhere in the Constitution. * * *

Although legislators are mostly male and many are no less biased than judges, they are subject to direct pressure from female constituents and do not operate within a system bounded by precedent. As women's political power continues to grow, this difference may become more important. Binding judicial review insulates decisions harmful to women—the commitment to formal equality, the refusal to consider harms to women in assessing free speech claims, the perception that sex discrimination and pregnancy discrimination are different things—from correction through women's participation in and pressure on the legislative process, where women can exercise significant power in light of their majority status. For example, the Title VII pregnancy discrimination case was overruled by Congress (so that sex discrimination in employment includes discrimination on the basis of pregnancy), though the Supreme Court recently affirmed the constitutional case. As this example also suggests, a top-down judicially-enforced approach to equality may also be inconsistent with the kind of experimentation necessary if we are ever to figure out either what equality between the sexes might look like or how to get there.

47. American Booksellers Assoc. v. Hudnut, 771 F.2d 323 (7th Cir. 1985); R.A.V. v. City of St. Paul, [505 U.S. 377] (1992); Penelope Steator, Judicial Indifference to Pornography's Harm: American Booksellers v. Hudnut, 17 Golden Gate U. L. Rev. 297 (1987).

Experimentation

* * *

A pragmatist, like myself, considers it unlikely that human beings can divine the best solutions to complex issues in the abstract, using top-down theories, rather than through experimentation. A related problem is that not all approaches work as judicial standards. If the best approaches do not work as judicial standards, then binding judicial review will preclude them. * * *

The need for experimentation is particularly high in an area like equality between the sexes in which there is no consensus about what a world with sexual equality would look like let alone agreement on the means to get there. When the Court closes off certain approaches as unconstitutional, it may make exceedingly difficult or preclude the development of appropriate solutions. * * * There might also be more than one form of equality between the sexes, and the differences between various forms might be important. The Supreme Court, by taking the only approach it could apparently imagine in the 1970s, may rule out of bounds certain forms of equality superior to the one it picked. Perhaps also, different approaches may be appropriate at various times as well as in various contexts. * * * A decentralized approach would allow experimentation to see what sorts of rules work best, and work best at various times as well as various contexts, in seeking equality between the sexes.

* * *

Democratic Deliberations

There are a number of ways in which binding judicial review can interfere with political movements and impede quality in democratic deliberations. This point is especially important since women are a majority group; to the extent that binding judicial review is a barrier to women's successful use of their political power as a majority group, it is illegitimate. In the discussion that follows, I note three major problems: legitimizing the status quo; keeping important controversies off the agenda of ordinary politics while obscuring their difficulty; and interfering with political movements.

1. Legitimating the status quo.

An ineffective equality standard, such as that arguably adopted by the Court * * * legitimates and stabilizes the status quo, keeping men in control of what equality between the sexes means without effecting real change. If the Supreme Court requires equality between the sexes, what exists must be equality. If women complain thereafter, their whining cannot deserve serious consideration.

There exists a more insidious form of this problem. We revere our Constitution. To the extent that injuries to women are someone else's constitutional right (in the sense that effective remedies are unconstitutional), women are less likely even to see their injuries as such or as an appropriate point for political organization and protest. As Robin West has noted: "The tendency of all subordinated persons toward self-belittlement by trivializing the nature of their injuries is geometrically enhanced by the self-perception that their injuries do not exist because their infliction is constitutionally protected."[61] There can be no more effective way to deter effective political action by a majority group than to turn their injuries into the constitutional rights of others so effectively that the injuries become invisible as such, though not unfelt. Free speech often functions in this manner; take, for example, the question of regulation of pornography.

2. Keeping important controversies off the ordinary democratic agenda and obscuring their difficulty.

* * *

When constitutional issues are regarded as beyond the scope of ordinary politics, the public is deprived of the opportunity to learn through discussions about constitutional problems. Indeed, the language of our Supreme Court tends to mask, rather than illuminate, the complexity of constitutional questions, supporting its own legitimacy by making decisions seem inevitable. This tendency serves to hide the real issues and their complexity from the public.

* * *

Perhaps most troubling is the tendency of judicial review, by taking items off the ordinary political agenda and obscuring their difficulty, to impede or even preclude the development of a new consensus through the resolution of the issue in electoral politics. It seems quite likely that binding judicial review has made it difficult to work out any new consensus on * * * equality between the sexes. I discuss this point in more detail below.

* * *

3. Interference with political movements.

* * *

Binding judicial review can impede political movements even when the Supreme Court does not actually block success. The relegation of high matters, such as sexual equality, to the courts saps political movements of their strength, particularly after ineffective victories. At the same time, judicial review can mobilize the opposition, and the Court itself will be influenced by the resulting political climate, a climate it has helped create.

When ineffective judicial victories weaken a movement, there may be less grass-roots pressure for change. Yet, real change in the relationship between the sexes is unlikely without change at the grass-roots level. Decisions from on high are unlikely to transform intimate relationships.

---

61. Robin West, Constitutional Skepticism, 72 B.U. L. Rev. 765 (1992).

Judicial victories protecting one or some outsider groups, but not all such groups, also interfere with the development of effective coalitions. This may be most harmful to the most [politically] vulnerable groups, such as lesbians, bisexuals, and gay men. Real or perceived judicial protection of less marginal groups, such as straight women or racial minorities, may mean that these groups are less likely to form effective coalitions with the more marginal groups. Judicial review is, therefore, a "divide and conquer" strategy.

In thinking about the effect of binding judicial review on outsiders' political movements, the appropriate baseline is how these movements would operate were there no such review. Had women focused all the time, energy, and money spent in the 1970s on a direct and single-minded focus on legislatures and legislative reform (including reform of abortion laws and of sex-specific legislation), rather than seeking binding judicial review in one form or another, women might well have ended the decade with more political experience and power. Women would have been different themselves and would have ended up in different places within important institutions. Women's consciousness would have been transformed by their experiences fighting for appropriate reforms. Instead, large amounts of time, energy, money, and commitment were spent on litigation campaigns and the drive for the ERA in the hope that male judges, operating within a tradition-bound system, would give women equality. Women are more likely to achieve real social equality as a result of a million and one piecemeal legislative changes than as a result of an abstract judicial standard.

The institution of binding judicial review has encouraged women, a majority group, to rely on mostly-male elite judges for equality rather than on their own political power, thus draining the strength from women's political movement for direct political power. This is dangerous for women. It becomes even more dangerous when one considers that it is futile to look to judges for much in the way of real social change * * *.

NOTES ON JUDICIAL REVIEW

1. Compare and contrast Becker's critique of binding judicial review in sex equality cases and the argument made by Justice Scalia in his dissent in *VMI* for an end to heightened scrutiny for sex-based classifications. What is similar? Different?

2. Becker states that "judicial review can impede political movements." In what ways did judicial review contribute to the defeat of the ERA drive, as discussed earlier in this chapter? Do you favor continued judicial review in gender cases? Why or why not? Might judicial review be less necessary now than in the past? See Rosalind Dixon, Female Justices, Feminism, and the Politics of Judicial Appointment, 21 Yale J.L. & Feminism 297, 336–38 (2010) ("For gender equality to be realized, it may no longer be necessary for the Supreme Court to play as active a role at a jurisprudential level as it did in earlier decades. Between the Court and Congress, legal changes have been

introduced in the United States over the last three decades which have largely eliminated ongoing formal barriers to women's equal opportunity and dignity.").

3. Would there be political benefits to women were a legislature, in a system without judicial review, to enact a law explicitly treating women and men differently in a way harmful to women? How might women react? Might they be likely to mobilize politically, push for more women in office, and make their voices heard in other ways? (Recall that the number of women in the Senate increased from three to six after the Senate confirmed Clarence Thomas's appointment to the Supreme Court despite Anita Hill's testimony about his sexual harassment of her. The Senate Judiciary Committee was all male and treated Hill in ways that angered many women, as did Thomas's confirmation. For further analysis on the hearings from a variety of perspectives, see Race-ing Justice En-gendering Power: Essays on Anita Hill, Clarence Thomas, and the Construction of Social Reality (Toni Morrison ed., 1992)). How do you think women in your state would react if the state legislature passed a statute today banning (as some protectionist legislation did in the past) all women from working at night in factories?

4. Becker's focus is on women, not racial minorities or other outsider groups. She suggests, however, that racial minorities might also be better off without binding judicial review:

> Binding judicial review of fundamental rights, such as speech, is likely to hurt minorities as well as women as it develops into a[n increasingly] conservative right. And, just as many feminists have been critical of the Court's approach to sexual inequality under the Fourteenth Amendment, many critical race scholars have been critical of the Court's decisions prohibiting racial classifications, as accomplishing too little while legitimating the status quo as "equality," thus weakening the political struggle for real social equality. Perhaps the Supreme Court's conservative approach to racial equality is becoming a barrier to further progress in a world without Jim Crow. The Court certainly seems eager to deny continuing problems in the relationship between the races as well as that between the sexes.

64 U. Colo. L. Rev. at 983. Do you think that binding judicial review is a valuable protection needed by members of vulnerable minority groups in a democracy? Or is it a conservative influence, tending to sap the strength of movements for social change while adopting a conservative notion of racial equality? Apart from cases involving voting, the Court has also found race discrimination in constitutional cases *only* when it is overt. As with sex discrimination, overt discrimination on the basis of race is rare today outside the context of affirmative action. And increasingly, the court holds race-based affirmative action unconstitutional, as discussed in the previous section. The case for judicial review of racial classifications is, therefore, becoming increasingly weak.

Another problem is that for many Asian and Latina/o Americans, ethnic identity involves a variable set of traits "including nationality, race, language, and cultural heritage and [physical] features, among other traits." Juan F. Perea, Ethnicity and the Constitution: Beyond the Black and White Binary

Constitution, 36 Wm. & Mary L. Rev. 571, 577 (1995). But even overt discrimination on the basis of these traits does not necessarily violate the Constitution. See the discussion of Hernandez v. New York, 500 U.S. 352 (1991), above in the notes after *J.E.B.* In light of these problems, do you favor continued judicial review in race cases?

5. When imagining a world in which the races are equal, white Americans often seem to imagine one in which racial differences have disappeared because other races have been assimilated into white culture. But meaningful racial equality is likely to be more complicated. Indeed, more than one kind of racial equality might be possible. Imagine a world of racial equality in which there is respect for, and appreciation of, a diversity of cultures, ethnic groups, and races. When you imagine other worlds of racial equality, what do you envision? How does it differ from the Supreme Court's vision? Which one would you prefer? Does the Supreme Court's increasingly colorblind approach make some forms of racial equality more difficult to envision, let alone achieve?

How does your thinking differ when considering gender equality, if at all? Do you think the Court will ever move toward a gender-blind approach? What would such an approach look like? What are some other visions for a world in which women and men are equal? For a discussion of what equality might look like if a "hypothetical set of feminist drafters * * * were to constitutionalize women's equality from scratch," see Kathleen M. Sullivan, Constitutionalizing Women's Equality, 90 Calif. L. Rev. 735, 747–61 (2002). See also Mary Anne Case, Reflections on Constitutionalizing Women's Equality, 90 Calif. L. Rev. 765, 782 (2003) (commenting on Sullivan's article and critiquing her title because "it is not enough to get for women what men have").

6. Why might binding judicial review be even more problematic for women than for racial minorities given women's majority status? Is it relevant that women and men live together in families, whereas members of other subordinate groups are considerably less likely to live in family units with members of the dominant group? Do women of all colors tend to view their experiences of inequality in their own homes and intimate relationships as personal rather than political? Are members of racial minorities more likely to see their experiences of race-linked problems as political?

If women do tend to view the inequality they experience as personal, does it follow that anything tending to dampen women's political struggles is especially dangerous, particularly in light of women's majority status and the biases of mostly-male judges? How might aspects of the Constitution beyond judicial review also thwart women's political success? See Paula Monopoli, Gender and Constitutional Design, 115 Yale L.J. 2643, 2644 (2006) (arguing that "the Hamiltonian vision of an expansive executive with plenary power is the model least likely to result in women's ascending to executive office"). See also Helen Irving, Where Have All the Women Gone? Gender and the Literature on Constitutional Design, available at http://ssrn.com/abstract=1604889 (May 2010).

CHAPTER 3

FEMINIST LEGAL THEORY

■ ■ ■

A. INTRODUCTION

During the 1970's, feminist legal scholars tended to assume that the liberal approach to sexual inequality—the approach adopted by the Supreme Court in the cases we considered in Chapter 2—was the appropriate legal tactic. There was little "feminist theory" in the legal academy beyond the important insight that sex-specific laws perpetuate rigid sex roles.

Feminist theory exploded in the 1980's, not only in law but in other disciplines as well. In the legal literature, the first sign of this development was the 1979 publication of Catharine A. MacKinnon's first book, Sexual Harassment of Working Women. This important work, as well as two articles MacKinnon published in the early 1980's in the women's studies journal Signs, included a biting critique of liberal equality doctrine and argued that inequality could be better understood and redressed under what she referred to as the dominance theory. Under this approach, MacKinnon emphasized that sex-specific laws do more than promote sex-role stereotyping or arbitrary differentiation between the sexes; instead, such laws contribute to the hierarchy of men over women and permit men to continue to exert power over women. In subsequent work, MacKinnon developed an even more sophisticated theory of how sex discrimination operates, in large part by deploying her dominance theory to reveal how gender and sex hierarchy is constructed and perpetuated through men's appropriation of women's bodies. MacKinnon's approach was reminiscent of some earlier radical and socialist approaches, in that she argued that equality could not be achieved within existing structures, including a legal system that embraced liberal equality theory. Her approach differed, however, in her focus on sexual penetration as the primary source of male hierarchy.

Other feminists focused on difference rather than dominance during the 1980's. These feminists generally followed one of two major strands of difference theory, both rooted in earlier movement politics. One strand, which we refer to as the relational feminist strand, focused on differences between women and men. Some radical feminists, often lesbian and uniformly critical of patriarchal culture, had argued for separatism and the development of an alternative women's culture, which its proponents believed would be superior to the dominant (male) culture. In the academy, some theorists similarly valorized those attributes associated with women but did not call for separatism, an approach like that taken by cultural feminists in the past; other theorists argued such valorization was dangerous because any differences between women and men resulted from socialization in a male-dominated society. Much of this debate focused on psychologist Carol Gilligan's influential book, In a Different Voice, published in 1982. The other major strand of difference theory, with roots in other aspects of socialist and radical feminism of the 1970s, considered differences among women of different races, classes, and sexual orientations. This strand, which we will call anti-essentialist feminism, often focused on uncovering the hidden biases and assumptions within the various approaches to feminism, particularly white privilege and compulsory heterosexuality.

This chapter begins with a brief discussion of consciousness raising, *the* feminist method that played a large role in reviving the women's movement beginning in the 1960s, and a discussion of theories outside of the law that influenced legal feminists as they extended their analyses beyond formal equality theory. We next present a variety of feminist theoretical approaches to inequality, beginning with MacKinnon's dominance theory, moving to difference theories, and then analyzing other strands of feminist theory as they developed in the final decades of the 20th century and the beginning of the 21st.

B. FEMINIST METHODOLOGY

CATHARINE A. MACKINNON, CONSCIOUSNESS RAISING

In Toward a Feminist Theory of the State 83, 86–88, 93–95, 99–104 (1989).

* * * What brings people to be conscious of their oppression as common rather than remaining on the level of bad feelings, to see their group identity as a systematic necessity that benefits another group, is the first question of organizing. The fact that consciousness-raising groups were there presupposes the discovery that they were there to make. But what may have begun as a working assumption becomes a working discovery: women are a group, in the sense that a shared reality of treatment exists sufficient to provide a basis for identification—at least enough to begin talking about it in a group of women. This often pre-articulate consensus shapes a procedure, the purpose of which becomes to unpack the concrete moment-to-moment meaning of being a woman in a society that men dominate, by looking at how women see their everyday experience in it. Women's lives are discussed in all their momentous triviality, that is, as they are lived through. The technique explores the social world each woman inhabits through her speaking of it, through

comparison with other women's experiences, and through women's experiences of each other in the group itself. Metaphors of hearing and speaking commonly evoke the transformation women experience from silence to voice. * * *

The fact that men were not physically present was usually considered necessary to the process. Although the ways of seeing that women have learned in relation to men were very much present or there would be little to discuss, men's temporary concrete absence helped women feel more free of the immediate imperative to compete for male attention and approval, to be passive or get intimidated, or to support men's version of reality. It made speech possible. With these constraints at some remove, women often found that the group confirmed awarenesses they had hidden, including from themselves. Subjects like sexuality, family, body, money, and power could be discussed more openly. The pain of women's roles and women's stake in them could be confronted critically, without the need every minute to reassure men that these changes were not threatening to them or to defend women's breaking of roles as desirable. The all-woman context valued women to each other as sources of insight, advice, information, stimulation, and problems. By providing room for women to be close, these groups demonstrated how far women were separated and how that separation deprived women of access to the way their treatment is systematized. * * * The point of the process was not so much that hitherto-undisclosed facts were unearthed or that denied perceptions were corroborated or even that reality was tested, although all these happened. It was not only that silence was broken and that speech occurred. The point was, and is, that this process moved the reference point for truth and thereby the definition of reality as such. Consciousness raising alters the terms of validation by creating community through a process that redefines what counts as verification. This process gives both content and form to women's point of view.

Concretely, consciousness-raising groups often focused on specific incidents and internal dialogue: what happened today, how did it make you feel, why did you feel that way, how do you feel now? Extensive attention was paid to small situations and denigrated pursuits that made up the common life of women in terms of energy, time, intensity, and definition—prominently, housework and sexuality. * * *

Intercourse was interrogated: how and by whom it is initiated, its timing, woman's feelings during and after, its place in relationships, its meaning, its place in being a woman. Other subjects included interactions in routine situations like walking down the street, talking with bus drivers, interacting with cocktail waitresses. Women's stories—work and how they came to do it; children; sexual history, including history of sexual abuse—were explored. * * *

* * *

Perhaps the most pervasive realization of consciousness raising was that men as a group benefit from these same arrangements by which women are deprived. Women see that men derive many advantages from women's roles, including being served and kept in mind, supported and sustained, having their children cared for and their sexual needs catered to, and being kept from the necessity of doing jobs so menial they consider them beneath them unless there is no other job (or a woman) around. But the major advantage men derive, dubious though it may seem to some, is the process, the value, the mechanism by which their interest itself is enforced and perpetuated and sustained: power. Power in its socially male form. It is not only that men treat women badly, although often they do, but that it is their choice whether or not to do so. This understanding of power is one of the key comprehensions of feminism. The reality it points to, because it is everywhere and relatively invariant, appears to be nowhere separable from the whole, from the totality it defines.

* * *

These discussions explored the functioning of sex roles in even one's closest "personal" relations, where it was thought women were most "ourselves," hence most free. Indeed, the reverse often seemed to be the case. The measure of closeness often seemed to be the measure of the oppression. When shared with other women, one's most private events often came to look the most stereotypical, the most for the public. Each woman, in her own particular, even chosen, way reproduces in her most private relations a structure of dominance and submission which characterizes the entire public order. * * *

The analysis that the personal is the political came out of consciousness raising. It has four interconnected facets. First, women as a group are dominated by men as a group, and therefore as individuals. Second, women are subordinated in society, not by personal nature or by biology. Third, the gender division, which includes the sex division of labor which keeps women in high-heeled low-status jobs, pervades and determines even women's personal feelings in relationships. Fourth, since a woman's problems are not hers individually but those of women as a whole, they cannot be addressed except as a whole. In this analysis of gender as a nonnatural characteristic of a division of power in society, the personal becomes the political.

* * *

Consciousness raising discovered that one form of the social existence of male power is inside women. In this form, male power becomes self-enforcing. Women become "thingified in the head." Once incarnated, male superiority tends to be reaffirmed and reinforced in what can be seen as well as in what can be done. So male power both is and is not illusory. As it justifies itself, namely as natural, universal, unchangeable, given, and morally correct, it is illusory; but the fact that it is powerful is no illusion. Power is a social relation. * * *

* * *

As a way of knowing about social conditions, consciousness raising * * * shows women their situation in a way that affirms they can act to change it. Consciousness raising socializes women's knowing. It produces an analysis of woman's world which is not objective in the positivistic sense of being a perfect reflection of reality conceived as abstract object; it is certainly not distanced or aperspectival. It is collective and critical. * * *

* * *

Feminism locates the relation of woman's consciousness to her life situation in the relation of two moments: being shaped in the image of one's oppression, yet struggling against it. In so doing, women struggle against the world in themselves as well as toward a future. The real question, both for explanation and for organizing, is what is the relation between the first process, woman becoming her role, and the second, her rejection of it?

* * *

Feminism, through consciousness raising, has grasped the completeness of the incursion into who one really becomes through growing up female in a male-dominated society. This effect can be understood as a distortion of self. It is not only one's current self one is understanding, but the self that understands what one has become as a distortion. On one level, this is exactly right. On another level, it exposes a dilemma: understanding women's conditions leads to the conclusion that women are damaged. If the reality of this damage is accepted, women are in fact not full people in the sense that men are allowed to become. So on what basis can a demand for equal treatment be grounded? If women are what they are made, are determined, women must create new conditions, take control of their determinants. But how does one come to know this? On the other hand, if women go beyond the prescribed limitations on the basis (presumably) of something outside their conditions, such as being able to see the injustice or damage of inequality, what is the damage of inequality? * * *

* * *

Consciousness raising has revealed that male power is real. It is just not the only reality, as it claims to be. Male power is a myth that makes itself true. To raise consciousness is to confront male power in its duality: as at once total on one side and a delusion on the other. In consciousness raising, women learn they have learned that men are everything, women their negation, but the sexes are equal. The content of the message is revealed as true and false at the same time; in fact, each part reflects the other transvalued. If "Men are all, women their negation" is taken as social criticism rather than as simple description, it becomes clear for the first time that women are men's equals, everywhere in chains. The chains become visible, the civil inferiority—the inequality—the product of subjection and a mode of its enforcement. Reciprocally, the moment it is seen that this life as we know it is not equality, that the sexes are not socially equal, womanhood can no longer be defined in terms of lack of maleness, as negativity. For the first time, the question of what a woman is seeks its ground in and of a world understood as neither of its making nor in its own image, and finds, within a critical embrace of woman's fractured and alien image, the shadow world women have made and a vision of the possibility of equality. * * *

NOTES ON FEMINIST METHODOLOGY

1. If sexual inequality is socially constructed, how is it possible to step out of that socialization, even temporarily, to see oppression and privilege? What are the limits on our ability to understand inequality in our own society? Why, how, and when are any of us able to criticize our own culture?

How does MacKinnon deal with the tension between women's internalization of male power and women's ability to critique male power? If male power constructs reality, how does MacKinnon think it ever becomes possible for any woman to critique that reality? Does MacKinnon's valorization of consciousness raising implicitly rely on the existence of women who can escape male power and develop some independence from men, either through education or other class privilege, before assisting other women in consciousness-raising groups?

2. MacKinnon states that "understanding women's conditions leads to the conclusion that women are damaged. If the reality of this damage is accepted, women are in fact not full people in the sense that men are allowed to become." What does "full people" mean in this context? Is MacKinnon adopting a male standard or suggesting that there can be some objective standard of personhood outside of gender construction? Either way, how might MacKinnon fall into some of the same traps that limit liberal equality theory?

Can you describe ways in which men as well as women are damaged by living in a culture in which women are to be feminine (supportive, nurturing, emotional, dependent) and men are to be masculine (powerful, fearless, successful and bread-winning, competitive, and, of course, nonemotional)? Are there ways in which women are hurt more than men and ways in which men are hurt more than women? Are there ways in which men are not full people in the sense that women are allowed to become? Why does MacKinnon mention only the ways women are damaged and less than full people?

3. MacKinnon states: "In consciousness raising, women learn they have learned that men are everything, women their negation, but the sexes are equal." Are girls and women bombarded with messages insisting both that (1) boys and men are superior to, more important than, girls and women; *and* (2) that women and men are equal? How might those contradictory messages be even more prevalent today than in the 1970s or 1980s? How might the contradiction be less apparent given the development of the equal protection law discussed in the previous chapter? How did you respond to these messages at different stages in your life? How do you respond now?

4. MacKinnon never uses the term "false consciousness," but many commentators use that term to explicate or critique MacKinnon's approach. False consciousness generally means that women might sometimes act against their own self-interest because they have internalized male norms and standards as part of their consciousness. For example, one might regard a woman who chooses to have breast implants, despite having healthy breasts, as doing so because of "false" consciousness. Despite MacKinnon's silence, is a notion of something like false consciousness implicit in her analysis? If one's consciousness has been "raised," does it follow that one had a "false" or inadequate consciousness prior to its being raised? Given social construction, is it ever possible to have "true consciousness"?

5. What might be considered modern versions of consciousness-raising groups? Book clubs? Feminist blogs? Discussions among friends of reality TV shows? What opportunities for consciousness raising currently exist at your law school? What other opportunities could you create?

6. In addition to consciousness raising, Katharine T. Bartlett identified two other feminist legal methods "grounded in women's experiences of exclusion": "asking the woman question" and feminist practical reasoning. Bartlett, Feminist Legal Methods, 103 Harv. L. Rev. 829 (1990). She writes:

> The woman question asks about the gender implications of a social practice or rule: have women been left out of consideration? If so, in what way; how might that omission be corrected? What difference would it make to do so? In law, asking the woman question means examining how the law fails to take into account the experiences and values that seem more typical of women than of men, for whatever reason, or how existing legal standards and concepts might disadvantage women. The question assumes that some features of the law may be not only nonneutral in a general sense, but also "male" in a specific sense. The purpose of the woman question is to expose those features and how they operate, and to suggest how they might be corrected.
>
> * * *
>
> As a form of legal reasoning, practical reasoning has many meanings invoked in many contexts for many different purposes. I present a version of practical reasoning in this section that I call "feminist practical reasoning." This version combines some aspects of a classic Aristotelian model of practical deliberation with a feminist focus on identifying and taking into account the perspectives of the excluded. Although this form of reasoning may not always provide clear decision methods for resolving every legal dispute, it builds upon the "practical" in its focus on the specific, real-life dilemmas posed by human conflict-dilemmas that more abstract forms of legal reasoning often tend to gloss over. In focusing on the "real" rather than the abstract, practical reasoning has some kinship to legal realism and critical legal studies, but there are important differences.

Id. at 837, 850. Do these additional methods alleviate some of the potential shortcomings of consciousness raising? How might they benefit the feminist project? How might they harm the feminist project?

C. SOME INFLUENTIAL FEMINIST THEORIES OUTSIDE OF LAW

Consciousness raising spurred the development of new feminist theories in multiple disciplines. Some of these sought to explore the ways women were different than men. Others proposed more systemic change of societal structures thought to perpetuate both gender hierarchy and other forms of oppression. We present two such theories here before turning to feminist legal theory.

CAROL GILLIGAN, IN A DIFFERENT VOICE: PSYCHOLOGICAL THEORY AND WOMEN'S DEVELOPMENT

25–29 (1982).

[Psychologists had developed, prior to Gilligan's work, theoretical frameworks and scales for evaluating moral development. In this passage, Gilligan critiques Lawrence Kohlberg's scale as applied to two adolescents, one a girl and the other a boy, on the ground that Kohlberg rates as more mature the boy's approach because it is based on the "logic" of rules and is hence superior to the more relational approach of the girl. The thesis of Gilligan's book is that psychologists have ignored or undervalued the relational, caring voice when considering moral problems, preferring a voice that speaks of abstract rules.]

* * * While current theory brightly illuminates the line and the logic of the boy's thought, it casts scant light on that of the girl. The choice of a girl whose moral judgments elude existing categories of developmental assessment is meant to highlight the issue of interpretation rather than to exemplify sex differences per se. Adding a new line of interpretation, based on the imagery of the girl's thought, makes it possible not only to see development where previously development was not discerned but also to consider differences in the understanding of relationships without scaling these differences from better to worse.

The two children were in the same sixth-grade class at school and were participants in the rights and responsibilities study, designed to explore different conceptions of morality and self. The sample selected for this study was chosen to focus the variables of gender and age while maximizing developmental potential by holding constant, at a high level, the factors of intelligence, education, and social class that have been associated with moral development, at least as measured by existing scales. The two children in question, Amy and Jake, were both bright and articulate and, at least in their eleven-year-old aspirations, resisted easy categories of sex-role stereotyping, since Amy aspired to become a scientist while Jake preferred English to math. Yet their moral judgments seem initially to confirm familiar notions about differences between the sexes, suggesting that the edge girls have on moral development during the early school years gives way at puberty with the ascendance of formal logical thought in boys.

The dilemma that these eleven-year-olds were asked to resolve was one in the series devised by Kohlberg to measure moral development in adolescence by presenting a conflict between moral norms and exploring the logic of its resolution. In this particular dilemma, a man named Heinz considers whether or not to steal a drug which he cannot afford to buy in order to save the life of his wife. In the standard format of Kohlberg's interviewing procedure, the description of the dilemma itself—Heinz's predicament, the wife's disease, the druggist's refusal to lower his price—is followed by the question, "Should Heinz steal the drug?" The reasons for and against stealing are then explored through a series of questions that vary and extend the parameters of the dilemma in a way designed to reveal the underlying structure of moral thought.

Jake, at eleven, is clear from the outset that Heinz should steal the drug. Constructing the dilemma, as Kohlberg did, as a conflict between the values of property and life, he discerns the logical priority of life and uses that logic to justify his choice:

> For one thing, a human life is worth more than money, and if the druggist only makes $1,000, he is still going to live, but if Heinz doesn't steal the drug, his wife is going to die. (*Why is life worth more than money?*) Because the druggist can get a thousand dollars later from rich people with cancer, but Heinz can't get his wife again. (*Why not?*) Because people are all different and so you couldn't get Heinz's wife again.

Asked whether Heinz should steal the drug if he does not love his wife, Jake replies that he should, saying that not only is there "a difference between hating and killing," but also, if Heinz were caught, "the judge would probably think it was the right thing to do." Asked about the fact that, in stealing, Heinz would be breaking the law, he says that "the laws have mistakes, and you can't go writing up a law for everything that you can imagine."

Thus, while taking the law into account and recognizing its function in maintaining social order (the judge, Jake says, "should give Heinz the lightest possible sentence"), he also sees the law as man-made and therefore subject to error and change. Yet his judgment that Heinz should steal the drug, like his view of the law as having mistakes, rests on the assumption of agreement, a societal consensus around moral values that allows one to know and expect others to recognize what is "the right thing to do."

Fascinated by the power of logic, this eleven-year-old boy locates truth in math, which, he says, is "the only thing that is totally logical." Considering the moral dilemma to be "sort of like a math problem with humans," he sets it up as an equation and proceeds to work out the solution. Since his solution is rationally derived, he assumes that anyone following reason would arrive at the same conclusion and thus that a judge would also consider stealing to be the right thing for Heinz to do. * * *

* * *

In contrast, Amy's response to the dilemma conveys a very different impression, an image of development stunted by a failure of logic, an inability to think for herself. Asked if Heinz should steal the drug, she replies in a way that seems evasive and unsure:

> Well, I don't think so. I think there might be other ways besides stealing it, like if he could borrow the money or make a loan or something, but he really shouldn't steal the drug—but his wife shouldn't die either.

Asked why he should not steal the drug, she considers neither property nor law but rather the effect that theft could have on the relationship between Heinz and his wife:

> If he stole the drug, he might save his wife then, but if he did, he might have to go to jail, and then his wife might get sicker again, and he couldn't get more of the drug, and it might not be good. So, they should really just talk it out and find some other way to make the money.

Seeing in the dilemma not a math problem with humans but a narrative of relationships that extends over time, Amy envisions the wife's continuing need for her husband and the husband's continuing concern for his wife and seeks to respond to the druggist's need in a way that would sustain rather than sever connection. Just as she ties the wife's survival to the preservation of relationships, so she considers the value of the wife's life in a context of relationships, saying that it would be wrong to let her die because, "if she died, it hurts a lot of people and it hurts her." Since Amy's moral judgment is grounded in the belief that, "if somebody has something that would keep somebody alive, then it's not right not to give it to them," she considers the problem in the dilemma to arise not from the druggist's assertion of rights but from his failure of response.

As the interviewer proceeds with the series of questions that follow from Kohlberg's construction of the dilemma, Amy's answers remain essentially unchanged, the various probes serving neither to elucidate nor to modify her initial response. Whether or not Heinz loves his wife, he still shouldn't steal or let her die; if it were a stranger dying instead, Amy says that "if the stranger didn't have anybody near or anyone she knew," then Heinz should try to save her life, but he should not steal the drug. But as the interviewer conveys through the repetition of questions that the answers she gave were not heard or not right, Amy's confidence begins to diminish, and her replies become more constrained and unsure. Asked again why Heinz should not steal the drug, she simply repeats, "Because it's not right." Asked again to explain why, she states again that theft would not be a good solution, adding lamely, "if he took it, he might not know how to give it to his wife, and so his wife might still die." Failing to see the dilemma as a self-contained problem in moral logic, she does not discern the internal structure of its resolution; as she constructs the problem differently herself, Kohlberg's conception completely evades her.

Instead, seeing a world comprised of relationships rather than of people standing alone, a world that coheres through human connection rather than through systems of rules, she finds the puzzle in the dilemma to lie in the failure of the druggist to respond to the wife. Saying that "it is not right for someone to die when their life could be saved," she assumes that if the druggist were to see the consequences of his refusal to lower his price, he would realize that "he should just give it to the wife and then have the husband pay back the money later." Thus she considers the solution to the dilemma to lie in making the wife's condition more salient to the druggist or, that failing, in appealing to others who are in a position to help.

Just as Jake is confident the judge would agree that stealing is the right thing for Heinz to do, so Amy is confident that, "if Heinz and the druggist had talked it out long enough, they could reach something besides stealing." As he considers the law to "have mistakes," so she sees this drama as a mistake, believing that "the world should just share things more and then people wouldn't have to steal." Both children thus recognize the need for agreement but see it as mediated in different ways—he impersonally through systems of logic and law, she personally through communication in relationship. Just as he relies on the conventions of logic to deduce the solution to this dilemma, assuming these conventions to be shared, so she relies on a process of communication, assuming connection and believing that her voice will be heard. Yet while his assumptions about agreement are confirmed by the convergence in logic between his answers and the questions posed, her assumptions are belied by the failure of communication, the interviewer's inability to understand her response.

ZILLAH EISENSTEIN, CONSTRUCTING A THEORY OF CAPITALIST PATRIARCHY AND SOCIALIST FEMINISM

In Women, Class, and the Feminist Imagination 114, 114–15, 129, 135–40 (Karen V. Hansen & Ilene J. Philipson eds., 1990).

Although there are socialist women who are committed to understanding and changing the system of capitalism, socialist feminists are committed to understanding the system of power deriving from capitalist patriarchy. I choose this phrase, capitalist patriarchy, to emphasize the existing mutual dependence of the capitalist class structure and male supremacy. Understanding the interdependence of patriarchy and capitalism is essential to the political analysis of socialist feminism. It becomes necessary to understand that patriarchy (as male supremacy) existed before capitalism and continues in postcapitalist societies. And yet to say that, within the present system of power, either patriarchy or capitalism causes the other is to fail to understand their present mutually reinforcing system and dialectical relationship, a relationship that must be understood if the structure of oppression is to be changed. Socialist feminism in this sense moves beyond singular Marxist analysis and isolated radical feminist theory. The capitalist class structure and the hierarchical sexual structuring of society are the problem.

Power is dealt with in a dichotomous way by socialist women and radical feminists. In these analyses, they see power as deriving from either one's sex or one's economic class position. The critique of power as it is rooted in the male/female distinction focuses most often on patriarchy. The critique of power as it is rooted in the bourgeoisie/proletariat distinction focuses on capitalism. One studies *either* the social relations of production *or* the social relations of reproduction, domestic *or* wage labor, the private *or* the public realms, the family *or* the economy, ideology *or* material conditions, the sexual division of labor *or* capitalist class relations, as oppressive. Even though almost all women are implicated in both sides of these activities, "woman" is dealt with as though she were not. Such a conceptual picture of woman hampers one's understanding of the complexity of her oppression. Dichotomy wins out over reality. * * *

* * *

Marxist analysis seeks a historical explanation of existing power relationships in terms of economic class relations, and radical feminism deals with the biological reality of power. Socialist feminism, on the other hand, analyzes power in terms of its class origins as well as its patriarchal roots. In such an analysis capitalism and patriarchy are not simply autonomous systems, but neither are they one and the same thing. They are, in present form, mutually dependent.

* * *

Although the sexual division of labor and society antedates capitalism, it has come to be further institutionalized and specifically defined through the nuclear family in terms of the needs of advanced capitalism. It now has much more form and structure than it did in precapitalist societies. In precapitalist society the home was defined as the producing economic unit. Men, women, and children worked together in the home or on the farm to produce the goods necessary for their lives. Women still were procreators and child raisers, but the necessities and organization of work *limited the impact* of the sexual role distinction. This is not to say that sexual equality existed but rather to point to the importance of understanding the specific structure and use of the sexual division of labor today.

With the rise of industrial capitalism, men were brought out of the home into the wage-labor economy, disrupting the earlier organization of labor. Women became relegated to the home, considered nonproductive, and viewed *solely* in terms of the previous loosely defined sex roles.

Although women were "mothers" before industrial capitalism, this was not an exclusive role, whereas with industrial capitalism women became "housewives." "The housewife emerged, alongside the proletariat—the two characteristic laborers of developed capitalist society."[45] The work that women continued to perform in the home was not conceived of as work. Productive labor was now defined as wage labor, labor that produces surplus profit—capital. "In sheer quantity, household labor, including child care, constitutes a huge amount of socially necessary production. Nevertheless, in a society based on commodity production, it is not usually considered 'real work' since it is outside of trade and the market place."[46]

* * *

All the processes involved in domestic work help in the perpetuation of the existing society. (1) Women stabilize patriarchal structures (the family, housewife, mother) by fulfilling these very roles. (2) Simultaneously, women are reproducing new workers, for both the paid and the unpaid labor force; they "care for" the men and children of the society. (3) They work in the labor force as well, for lesser wages. (4) They stabilize the economy through their role as consumers. And this role is perpetuated very specifically through patriarchal institutions and ideology. If the other side of production is consumption, the other side of capitalism is patriarchy.

It is important to note the discrepancy between patriarchal ideology and the material reality of women's lives [given the numbers of women working in the wage economy today.] * * * Because women are not defined as workers within the ruling ideology, however, they are not paid for their labor, or are paid less than men. The sexual definition of woman as mother keeps her in the home doing unpaid labor and/or enables her to be hired at a lower wage because of her sexual definition of inferiority. During periods of high unemployment women either do not find jobs or are paid at an even lower rate. The sexual division of labor and society remains intact even with women in the paid economy. Ideology adjusts to this by defining women as working mothers. And the two jobs get done for less than the price of one.

The bourgeoisie profits from the basic arrangement of women's work, as do all individual men who benefit from labor done for them in the home. All men, regardless of class, benefit, although differentially, from the system of privileges they acquire within patriarchal society. This system could not be organized as such if the ideology and structures of sex roles were not basic to the society. * * *

---

45. [See Eli] Zaretsky, "Capitalism, [the Family, and Personal Life]" [pts. 1–2, *Socialist Revolution* Nos. 13–14 (January–April 1973):] 114.

46. Margaret Benston, "The Political Economy of Women's Liberation," Free Press pamphlet, at 15.

* * * Once the sexual division of labor is challenged, particularly in terms of its connection to the capitalist order, one of the basic forms of the organization of work—especially affecting the home but with wide ramifications for the entire society—will be challenged. This challenge endangers a free labor pool (which infiltrates almost all aspects of living) and a cheap labor pool, and also endangers the fundamental social and political organization of the society, which is sexual hierarchy itself. The very order and control that derive from the arrangements of power implied in the sexual organization of society will be destroyed.

If we realize that there are basically two kinds of work in capitalist society, wage labor and domestic labor, we realize that we must alter the way we think about workers. What is really needed at this point is further work on what class analysis specifically means for women. The assignment of class for a woman is often done in terms of her husband's class standing. That is, class categories are primarily male-defined categories; woman is not viewed as an autonomous being; the categories become confused. According to what criteria is a woman termed middle-class?

* * *

What does it mean to say that a middle-class woman's life is different and easier than a working-class woman's life when her status as such is significantly different from that of her middle-class male "equivalent"? What of the woman who earns no money at all (as houseworker) and is termed middle class because her husband is? Does she have the same freedom, autonomy, or control over her life as the middle-class man who earns his own way? How does her position compare to that of a single woman with a poorly paid job?

* * *

A feminist class analysis must begin with distinctions drawn among women in terms of the work they do within the political economy as a whole (the family and the paid labor force). This would involve making distinctions among (1) working women outside the home, distinguishing professional from nonprofessional; (2) houseworkers, distinguishing housewives from wealthy women who do not work; (3) women who are houseworkers (housewives) and also work outside the home; (4) welfare women; and (5) unemployed women. Whether a woman is (a) married, (b) single, or (c) divorced is also important in analyzing how her work defines her class position. These class distinctions need to be further defined in terms of the issue of race.

We then need to study how women within these categories relate to the major activities of women in terms of the shared experience of women (rather than in terms of the class differentiations among them)—reproduction, child rearing, sexuality, consumption, maintenance of home. What we will discover in this exploratory feminist class analysis, then, is a complicated and varied pattern whose multigridded conceptualization mirrors the complexity of sex and class differentials in the reality of women's life and experience.

The model with which we would be working would direct attention to class differences within the context of the basic relationship between the sexual hierarchy of society and capitalism. Such an analysis of socialist feminism could continue to explore the relationships between these systems, which in essence are not separate systems and hence need to be dealt with in their internal web. Also, such an examination should serve one overriding objective of the liberation of woman. It should seek to realize her potential for living in social community rather than in isolated homes; her potential for creative work rather than alienating or mindless work; her potential for critical consciousness as opposed to false consciousness; and her potential for uninhibited sexuality arising from new conceptions of sexuality.

* * *

The importance of socialist feminist strategy, to the extent that it exists, is that it grows out of women's struggle with their daily existence—production, reproduction, children, consumption, jobs. The potential for revolutionary consciousness derives from the fact that women's lives under capitalist patriarchy are being squeezed, from the most intimate levels—such as how they feed their children—to the more public levels of their monotonous, tiring, low-skill, sex-defined, low-wage jobs. Women are working in the labor force, and for less, and they are maintaining the family system, having less to make do with. This is the base from which consciousness can develop. We need to try organizing political action and developing political consciousness about our oppression within the hierarchical sexual division of society and from an understanding of how this connects to the capitalist division of labor. * * *

NOTES ON DIFFERENCE THEORY AND SOCIALIST FEMINISM

1. How do each of the theories above seek to alter women's positions within society? What conceptions of women's realities do the theories share? Where do the theories diverge? Could both theories be used to promote societal change, or do feminists have to choose between one theory or the other? How do you see each theory potentially intersecting with law?

2. Modern relational, or cultural, feminism is often traced to Gilligan's book, In a Different Voice. In the nineteenth and early twentieth centuries, women also emphasized the value of traditionally feminine qualities and activities, such as caretaking and relationships, and argued that these values should occupy just as important a place in society and law as so-called male values of breadwinning, abstract thinking, and individual preferences. How does Gilligan build upon such arguments?

Cultural feminism is often critiqued as claiming that women's values are superior to men's and that women are innately superior to men. Is Gilligan also vulnerable to that critique? What are the potential harms of emphasizing women's differences from men? Conversely, what are the potential dangers of pushing *only* for equality without increasing our valuation of caretaking? Feminist legal theorists, such as Robin West, discussed below, embrace relational feminism as a way to transcend the limits of liberal equality theory in legal analysis. What do you think of such an approach? For a critique of extending relational feminism to law, see Pamela S. Karlan & Daniel R. Ortiz, In a Diffident Voice: Relational Feminism, Abortion Rights, and the Feminist Legal Agenda, 87 Nw. U. L. Rev. 858 (1993).

3. There is some ambiguity in Gilligan's work with respect to whether the different voice she identifies, the relational caring voice, is *women's*. Do you think we can validly make such a generalization? Are Jake's responses devoid of attention to relationships and care? How would you respond to Heinz's dilemma? Is your response consistent with Gilligan's findings? See generally Isabel Marcus, Paul J. Spiegelman, Ellen C. DuBois, Mary C. Dunlap, Carol J. Gilligan, Carrie J. Menkel–Meadow & Catharine A. MacKinnon, Feminist Discourse, Moral Values, and the Law—A Conversation, 34 Buff. L. Rev. 11 (1985).

Soon after Gilligan's book was published, a number of criticisms were aimed at Gilligan's methods in general and also at her analysis of the various interviews described in her book. See, e.g., Linda K. Kerber, Catherine G. Greeno, Eleanor E. Maccoby, Zella Luria, Carol B. Stack & Carol Gilligan, On *In a Different Voice:* An Interdisciplinary Forum, 11 Signs 304 (1986); Judy Auerbach, Linda Blum, Vicki Smith & Christine Williams, Commentary, On Gilligan's *In a Different Voice,* 11 Feminist St. 149 (1985); Debra Nails, Social–Scientific Sexism: Gilligan's Mismeasure of Man, 50 Soc. Res. 643 (1983); John M. Broughton, Women's Rationality and Men's Virtues: A Critique of Gender Dualism in Gilligan's Theory of Moral Development, 50 Soc. Res. 597 (1983).

Experimental studies to determine whether women and men approach moral issues in different voices were also conducted, with mixed results. Compare, e.g., William J. Friedman, Amy B. Robinson & Britt L. Friedman, Sex Differences in Moral Judgments? A Test of Gilligan's Theory, 11 Psych. Women Q. 37 (1987) (finding no significant differences between women and men college students in responses to four hypothetical moral issues), with Mary K. Rothbart, Dean Hanley & Marc Albert, Gender Differences in Moral Reasoning, 15 Sex Roles 645 (1986) (finding that although both men and women college students used both moral orientations widely in response to hypothetical moral dilemmas, women were somewhat more likely to respond in terms of care and men in terms of rights); Maureen Rose Ford & Carol Rotter Lower, Gender Differences in Moral Reasoning: A Comparison of the Use of Justice and Care Orientations, 50 J. Personality & Soc. Psych. 777 (1986) (finding that the ethic of care was more likely to be used by more feminine males than by less feminine males). See also the discussion about "different voice lawyering" in Chapter 10.

4. What sorts of implications might Gilligan's discussion of Amy's perspective have for various fields of law? For criminal law? For torts? For example, should tort law require individuals to act as Good Samaritans? See Leslie Bender, A Lawyer's Primer on Feminist Theory and Tort, 38 J. Legal

Educ. 3 (1988); Lucinda M. Finley, A Break in the Silence: Including Women's Issues in a Torts Class, 1 Yale J.L. & Feminism 41 (1989).

In what ways might Justice Ginsburg, the author of the *VMI* opinion discussed in Chapter 2, respond to Gilligan? How did the leadership school for women (VWIL) in that case incorporate different-voice insights? Why wasn't that approach—an approach specifically geared toward women's reasoning and learning styles—sufficient for equal protection purposes?

5. As discussed in Chapter 2, many of the feminists who came out of the civil rights and antiwar movements in the 1960s were influenced by socialism. Greatly oversimplified, the socialist tradition emphasizes that historical change is determined by economic forces, on the one hand, and the accompanying mode of economic and social organization particular to that era, on the other. In the current period of capitalism, the means of production (factories, tools, capital) are privately owned and controlled by one class (the bourgeoisie) and labor is performed by another class (the working class or proletariat) who do not own the means of production, but instead trade labor to the owners of capital in return for a wage. Each historical period is also characterized by its dominant classes, and historical change is the result of class struggle. Each economic revolution is thus accompanied by a political revolution, to establish the form of state which serves the economic purposes of the dominant class and maintains control by that class over other classes. For capitalism, the liberal democratic, or "nightwatchman," state is said to perform these functions by assuring order yet guaranteeing a large measure of freedom in the so-called private sphere. History, according to socialist theory, is a dialectical process of class struggle; that is, it proceeds by the confrontation of opposites which are then superseded by a new synthesis. For more on socialism, see The Marx–Engels Reader (Robert C. Tucker ed., 2d ed. 1978).

Within the socialist movement, women and some men had repeatedly asked what was known as "the woman question," pointing to the oppression of women during all historical periods. But the dominant presumption in traditional socialist theory was that a revolution to overthrow capitalism and establish an economy owned and controlled by all would automatically result in the equality of women as well. Socialist feminists, in contrast, point out that throughout all historical stages the division of labor particular to that economic stage is *also* accompanied by patriarchy, that is, the dominance of men over women, and by a sexual division of labor in which women—as a group, regardless of their class—perform tasks that are valued less and paid less, benefiting men as a group. Thus feminists within the socialist tradition began to ask whether another dialectic was at work, one based on gender, and to seek ways to combine this analysis with one based on class. Eisenstein's excerpt is one example of such an attempt, referred to as "dual systems theory." How does Eisenstein theorize the intersection of gender and class? Who would benefit from the systemic changes she proposes?

6. What do you see as the strengths and weaknesses of socialist feminism? Do you think that women could be a revolutionary class? How do the interests of women differ according to the economic class of the woman and/or of her husband or father? What problems are caused by the fact that the

interests of many women are so identified with those of the men with whom they share or shared a household? Why might lesbians or Black women, Latina women, or other women of color be reluctant to use their energy and political power for a revolutionary class of *women*?

7. Does women's attainment of equality in the workplace require fundamental economic changes in the organization of work? What types of changes? How would Gilligan likely answer that question? How would Eisenstein? Could domestic work be socialized? What might that mean? Would some forms of socialization be desirable and others undesirable? Would any of them benefit women exclusively? If the answer is no, is that an advantage or disadvantage of socialist feminism?

8. Socialist feminists have done important work showing the many ways in which patriarchy supports the economic system in which we live, for example, by providing marginal workers who can be drawn into the workforce as needed, who are paid less than men in the workplace, and provide domestic labor for free. See, e.g., Heidi I. Hartmann, Capitalism, Patriarchy, and Job Segregation by Sex, in Women, Class, and the Feminist Imagination 146–48, 158, 168–70 (Karen V. Hansen & Ilene J. Philipson eds., 1990). Can you think of other ways in which capitalism and patriarchy are mutually reinforcing? What are some examples based on women's status as both sexual objects for men and consumers for capitalists? What are the potential political effects of this interaction?

Does Eisenstein discuss the interaction of race and class or sex, race, and class? What are some potential ways in which racism and capitalism are mutually reinforcing? What about ways in which patriarchy, racism, and capitalism are mutually reinforcing? Does Gilligan provide any insight?

9. With the exception of MacKinnon, feminist legal theorists tend not to display their debt to Marxism openly, although many advocate changes that could be characterized as socialist, such as paid parental leave, free quality education for all children, and universal health insurance. In addition, Janet Halley has called on legal feminists to "return to a socialist feminist understanding" of women's subordination at work because "socialist feminism provides the more germane insights into women's working lives," Halley, Sexuality Harassment, in Left Legalism/Left Critique 80, 81 (Wendy Brown & Janet Halley eds., 2002). Tucker Culbertson and Jack Jackson, however, question Halley's commitment to socialism. See Culbertson & Jackson, Proper Objects, Different Subjects and Juridical Horizons in Radical Legal Critique, in Feminist and Queer Legal Theory: Intimate Encounters, Uncomfortable Conversations 135, 146–51 (Martha Albertson Fineman, Jack E. Jackson & Adam P. Romero eds., 2009). Why do you think many feminists are reluctant to identify themselves as socialists? What about practicing lawyers? Can you think of arguments or strategies you might adopt as a lawyer that would be suggested by or influenced by socialist feminism? What about arguments or strategies that would be influenced by Gilligan's findings? In which contexts might each theory assist your case and in which contexts might each theory hurt your case?

TEXT NOTE ON COMPULSORY HETEROSEXUALITY

In her path-breaking article, Compulsory Heterosexuality and Lesbian Existence, 5 Signs 631 (1980), Adrienne Rich analyzed the ways that women's relationships with other women have long been denied and stigmatized. She argued that such treatment was part of a larger system of compulsory heterosexuality in which heterosexuality has been imposed on women through violence and the constant repetition of the notion—in fairy tales, novels, movies, and academic scholarship, including feminist scholarship—that women are "naturally" heterosexual, a repetition which would be unnecessary if women were in fact heterosexual by nature.

Rich also emphasized, however, that "women have always resisted male tyranny." Rich uses the term "lesbian continuum" to refer to the fact that women depend on intimate connections with other women, whether or not those connections include genital sexual contact. The first such relationship is with one's mother. But throughout their lives, girls and women depend on other girls and women for support and the richness of shared emotional lives. Rich claims that for all women, woman-identification through these relationships with women is a source of energy, power, and strength. If we consider this wide range of women's connection to other women, then we can see that every woman lives along a lesbian continuum.

NOTES ON COMPULSORY HETEROSEXUALITY

1. Given Rich's arguments, what is the relationship between heterosexuality and women's subordination? Why might it matter—both to the individuals and to the political struggle—that a woman invests her emotional, economic, and sexual energy and resources in another woman rather than a man? Is it less legitimate in any sense for a woman to be a lesbian for political reasons than because of personal desire? Can one separate desire and politics?

2. What pressures to be heterosexual do you experience? Do you agree with Rich that it is difficult to know whether (hetero)sexuality is freely lived? If female heterosexuality is compulsory, why are so many heterosexual women so sure that they are "really" heterosexual? Can you imagine a culture and legal system in which heterosexuality is not compulsory? In that world, what would be different about the stories we tell children? How would the legal system change? The media? Social interactions?

3. In what ways does Rich challenge the immutability of sexual orientation? Drawing upon the discussion in Chapter 2 of analogies between race and sex, why might gay-rights activists want to make arguments relying on the immutability of sexual orientation? What are the advantages and disadvantages of such arguments compared to Rich's analysis?

4. Do you think that women's sexuality is often more fluid than men's? Some studies suggest that this might be true. See Lisa M. Diamond, Sexual Fluidity: Understanding Women's Love and Desire (2008); Mary Becker, Women, Morality, and Sexual Orientation, 8 UCLA Women's L.J. 165, 211 (1998). Do you think such fluidity operates in the same way for all women? Why might women experience more sexual fluidity than men?

5. Do you agree with Rich that feminists contribute to the suppression of lesbian existence? Sarah Lucia Hoagland has argued that feminist reform has been androcentric and heterocentric because it focuses on improving women's relationships with men and "sets up women to value change in men more highly than change in women," making any failure "a failure of effort on women's part, not a refusal on men's part." Hoagland, Lesbian Ethics: Toward New Value 57–58 (1988). Feminist reform "forces women to prove that men's fears are unfounded—to prove that women, or 'real' women, are not lesbians or manhaters. It forces women to appear feminine and prove they are not threatening." Id. Do you agree? Do you feel such pressure, especially (perhaps) since you've been taking this course? What is the source of the pressure?

D. FEMINIST LEGAL THEORIES

Feminist lawyers initially did not develop distinctive new theories designed to address women's treatment within the law. Instead, these lawyers embraced formal equality, the approach underlying the litigation described in Chapter 2, and did not develop theories justifying the approach at that time. Only after feminist lawyers developed alternative theories of gender equality did defenses of formal equality emerge. We begin with a brief description and defense of formal equality theory and then consider the substance of Catharine MacKinnon's dominance theory, the difference theories that challenged both dominance and liberal equality theories, and other approaches to feminist legal theory rooted in critical theories from other disciplines. We end by presenting a case study in which to apply those theories and compare them to liberal equality theory.

1. FORMAL EQUALITY THEORY

TEXT NOTE ON FORMAL EQUALITY THEORY

Most students do not need an introduction to formal equality theory; they are familiar with it already. This is essentially the liberal democratic theory of John Stuart Mill and others that animates much of the U.S. legal system. It assumes that individuals should be given as much liberty as possible without hurting others or interfering with their liberty. It is, in many ways, a basis for what we have been discussing so far in studying the development of constitutional notions of equality and equal protection.

Formal equality theory starts from the assumption that individuals are separate atoms and, for the most part, self-interested and rational; they will make the "best" choices if they are left to choose for themselves. A goal, therefore, is to maximize the choices available to each individual, regardless of gender or other aspects of identity. Individuals should not be treated according to stereotypes based upon gender, and each should be given an equal opportunity to compete in the public sphere of politics, employment, education, and the like.

The image often used to illustrate formal equality theory is that of a level playing field. Such a field is provided by taking away public-sphere obstacles to equal competition, such as gender-specific laws limiting opportunities available to women. Extra help to individuals or groups based on past legal treatment or private-sphere differences is not provided; in fact, such forms of differential treatment are viewed as "special rights" at odds with the goal of equality. In other words, under liberal equality theory, the law should not attempt to make up for the ways inequality in the private sphere may limit the capacity to compete in the public sphere. Men and women should be treated alike in the public sphere, despite whatever burdens they may bring with them from their private lives.

MARY ANNE CASE, NO MALE OR FEMALE

In Transcending the Boundaries of Law: Generations of Feminism and Legal Theory 83, 92–95 (Martha Albertson Fineman ed., 2010).

* * * [I] want to highlight my disappointment at seeing how in my lifetime, feminism and conservatism have come to be seen as antithetical by both feminists and conservatives in the United States. * * *

* * *

[Some time ago] I was invited to speak at a Federalist Society conference on feminism. This was the occasion for my meeting Martha Fineman, my fellow panelist, and the first of many occasions in which Martha and I modeled disagreement among feminists: using arguments developed in her book on divorce reform, The Illusion of Equality, she was the only participant in the conference to challenge my call for the equality of the sexes as an unproblematically shared normative goal. Like all the panels at the conference, the one to which Martha and I were assigned was structured in a way I repudiated, as a debate between the feminists and the federalists, as if the two points of view were antithetical. * * * [T]he mutually exclusive nature of feminism and conservatism may today be a political reality but it is not an inevitable truth. * * *

Over the course of the last decade, therefore, I had gradually been resigning myself to the fact that the idea of a feminist conservative was off the table—until, of course, 2008, when Katie Couric asked staunchly conservative Republican Vice-Presidential candidate and Alaska governor Sarah Palin the following questions, and Palin responded with the most coherent answers she gave to any questions asked of her in the course of the 2008 Presidential campaign:

> Couric: Do you consider yourself a feminist?
>
> Palin: I do. I'm a feminist who believes in equal rights and I believe that women certainly today have every opportunity that a man has to succeed and to try to do it all anyway. And I'm very, very thankful that I've been brought up in a family where gender hasn't been an issue. You know, I've been expected to do everything growing up that the boys were doing. We were out chopping wood and you're out hunting and fishing and filling our freezer with good wild Alaskan game to feed our family. So it kinda started with that. With just that

> expectation that the boys and the girls in my community were expected to do the same and accomplish the same. That's just been instilled in me.
>
> Couric: What is your definition of feminist?
>
> Palin: Someone who believes in equal rights. Someone who would not stand for oppression against women.

Although Palin's description of her beliefs sounds in sameness feminism, her definition is an inclusive one. It is the standard dictionary definition and one I have always personally endorsed. As I explained to the Federalist Society, attempting to persuade them that it was possible to be both a feminist and a federalist, "Dictionary definitions generally talk about a commitment to the equality of the sexes, a commitment to women's rights and the removal of restrictions that discriminate against them. I hope that there are few who, using this terminology, would not be feminists."

Unfortunately, when Brian Williams asked Palin the same question ("Governor, are you a feminist?") less than a month later, she did not give the same answer. Instead, she said,

> I'm not gonna label myself anything, Brian ... And I think that's what annoys a lot of Americans, especially in a political campaign, is to start trying to label different parts of America different, different backgrounds, different ... I'm not going to put a label on myself. But I do believe in women's rights, I believe in equal rights, and I am so thankful I was brought up in a family where really gender has never been an issue....

I realize there are many on both the left and right who might be more comfortable with Palin's second answer. On the left are many who think Palin has no right to claim the title "feminist" if she does not hold certain substantive policy positions and act on them in her political life. For some, an organization like "Feminists for Life," the anti-abortion group to which both Palin and the wife of Chief Justice John Roberts have ties, is a contradiction in terms. It seems to me, however, far preferable to have debates on such matters as abortion policy from within feminism than to seek to enforce a monolithic feminist orthodoxy and excommunicate from the feminist fold those who disagree. * * *

I certainly don't want to endorse Palin. I would no more support her simply because she claims to be a feminist than I would support her, as some argued that I should, simply because she is a woman. I also agree with Palin's critics that it is important to highlight any hypocrisy or inconsistency in her politics on women's issues and to prevent her from cynically exploiting a feminist label. I don't want to get involved in labeling Palin or anyone else, but I do want to start a conversation on feminism that does not preclude any view on any other matters unrelated to sex and gender, the equality of the sexes and the oppression of women, and I hope that this will once again be possible. As my own Catholic girlhood demonstrates, inspiration for commitment to the cause of feminism can spring from the most unpredictable of sources, and, if even one young girl growing up in a conservative family can feel more comfortable calling herself a feminist because Sarah Palin has done so too, I am left more hopeful for future generations making it beyond the boundaries of the law.

NOTES ON FORMAL EQUALITY FEMINISM

1. What are your reactions to Case's approach? Do you share Case's views of Sarah Palin, the Republican Vice-Presidential candidate in 2008?

2. How are Case's views similar to those embraced by liberal equality theorists, such as Justice Ginsburg? In 1989, Ginsburg wrote:

> The 1970s cases in which I participated under ACLU auspices all rested on the same fundamental premise: that the law's differential treatment of men and women, typically rationalized as reflecting "natural" differences between the sexes, historically had tended to contribute to women's subordination—their confined "place" in man's world—even when conceived as protective of the fairer, but weaker and dependent-prone sex. The arguments addressed to the courts were designed to reveal and to challenge the assumptions underpinning traditional sex-specific rules, and to move the Supreme Court in the direction of a constitutional principle that would provide for heightened, thoughtful review of gender classifications. * * *
>
> The ACLU Women's Rights Project in the 1970s was hardly so bold or so prescient as to essay articulation of a comprehensive theoretical vision of a world in which men did not define women's place. The endeavor was less lofty, more immediately and practically oriented; it was, as I earlier stated, to pursue a series of cases that might illuminate the most common instances of gender distinctions in the law, and thereby provide a basis for the evolution of constitutional doctrine and attendant legislative change. * * *
>
> * * *
>
> Some observers have portrayed the 1970s litigation as assimilationist in outlook, insistent on formal equality, opening doors only to comfortably situated women willing to accept men's rules and be treated like men, even a misguided effort that harmed more women than it helped. These critics question the advocacy of strict scrutiny for gender classifications as in *Reed* and *Frontiero*, the representation furnished male plaintiffs as in *Wiesenfeld*, and the heavy focus on classifications that could be characterized as burdening both men and women.
>
> Such comment seems to me not fair. The litigation of the 1970s helped unsettle previously accepted conceptions of men's and women's separate spheres, and thereby added impetus to efforts ongoing in the political arena to advance women's opportunities and stature. An appeal to courts at that time could not have been expected to do much more.

Ruth Bader Ginsburg & Barbara Flagg, Some Reflections on the Feminist Legal Thought of the 1970s, 1989 U. Chi. Legal F. 9, 11, 14–15, 17. Would Ginsburg agree with Case? Does Ginsburg see any downside to formal equality? Or does she see it as the necessary first step to gender equality, a step that has done no harm? Do you agree? Even if formal equality was a necessary first step, how might it have advantaged some women more than others and hurt at least some women in some situations? How should feminists respond to such effects of liberal equality theory?

3. What legislative solutions to women's inequality might be precluded by Case's sameness approach or the current formal equality standard discussed in Chapter 2? Has the Supreme Court's narrow notion of equality come to dominate equality's meaning in the culture at large, making effective legislation less likely?

2. DOMINANCE FEMINISM

In her first book, Catharine MacKinnon referred to her theory as the "inequality approach," in order to contrast it with the liberal equality approach adopted by the Supreme Court in the 1970s. In the brief excerpt from that book immediately below, you will see MacKinnon use that term while also referring to the dominance that would later take center stage in her work. In the excerpts that follow, from books published eight and ten years after her first, you will see MacKinnon's full embrace of the dominance approach, an embrace which began in the early 1980s in two articles MacKinnon published in the women's studies journal Signs.

CATHARINE A. MACKINNON, SEX INEQUALITY

In Sexual Harassment of Working Women 117–18 (1979).

A rule or practice is discriminatory, in the inequality approach, if it participates in the systemic social deprivation of one sex because of sex. The only question for litigation is whether the policy or practice in question integrally contributes to the maintenance of an underclass or a deprived position because of gender status. The disadvantage which constitutes the injury of discrimination is not the failure to be treated "without regard to" one's sex; that is the injury of arbitrary differentiation. The unfairness lies in being deprived *because* of being a woman or a man, a deprivation given meaning in the social context of the dominance or preference of one sex over the other. The social problem addressed is not the failure to ignore woman's essential sameness with man, but the recognition of womanhood to women's comparative disadvantage. In this approach, few reasons, not even biological ones, can justify the institutionalized disadvantage of women. Comparability of sex characteristics is not required because policies are proscribed which transform women's sex-based differences from men into social and economic deprivations. All that is required are comparatively unequal results.

Under the inequality approach, variables as to which women and men are not comparable, such as pregnancy or sexuality, would be among the *first* to trigger suspicion and scrutiny, rather than the last; they would not be exceptions to the rule. From the inequality perspective the question on the *Gilbert*[a] facts would be: is not the structure of the job market, which accommodates the physical needs, life cycle, and family expectations of men but not of women, integral to women's inferior employment status? What can then justify a policy that makes pregnancy, a condition unique and common to women as a gender, into a disadvantage in employment? The affirmative form of the argument is that the health needs of women workers should be accommodated equally with those of men.

CATHARINE A. MACKINNON, SEXUALITY

In Feminism Unmodified 5–8 (1987).

Since 1970, feminists have uncovered a vast amount of sexual abuse of women by men. Rape, battery, sexual harassment, sexual abuse of children, prostitution, and pornography, seen for the first time in their true scope and interconnectedness, form a distinctive pattern: the power of men over women in society. These abuses are as allowed de facto as they are prohibited de jure. Formal prohibition has done little to alter their frequency; it has helped make it hard to believe that they are so common. The reports that are believed are treated as if the events and their victims are statistically deviant, because the events they report have been branded as morally and legally deviant. In fact, it is the woman who has not been sexually abused who deviates.

The reason feminism uncovered this reality, its methodological secret, is that feminism is built on believing women's accounts of sexual use and abuse by men. The pervasiveness of male sexual violence against women is therefore not denied, minimized, trivialized, eroticized, or excepted as marginal or episodic or placed to one side while more important matters are discussed. The fact that only 7.8 percent of women in the United States have not been sexually assaulted or harassed in their lifetime is not considered inconsequential or isolated. The fact that sexual violation is a sexual practice is faced. A new paradigm begins here, one that fits the reality of the experience to be explained. All the ways in which women are suppressed and subjected—restricted, intruded on, violated, objectified—are recognized as what sex is for women and as the meaning and content of femininity.

If this is done, sexuality itself is no longer unimplicated in women's second-class status. Sexual violence can no longer be categorized away as violence not sex. Women do not thrive on violation, whether or not it is done through sex. But our rapists, serial murderers ("I killed my mother for the same reason I've killed all those other women. The reason was sex."), and child molesters ("It's as natural for me to have sex with

---

a. General Electric Co. v. Gilbert, 429 U.S. 125 (1976). The issue in *Gilbert* was whether an employer violated Title VII's ban on sex discrimination by treating pregnancy-related expenses differently than other expenses under its health insurance plan. The Court held that sex discrimination under Title VII did not include pregnancy discrimination. Congress subsequently amended Title VII with the Pregnancy Discrimination Act and overruled *Gilbert*. The reasoning of *Gilbert* was much like that in *Geduldig*, the constitutional sex-equality pregnancy case discussed in Chapter 2.

children the way it's natural for some people to have sex with women.") enjoy their acts sexually and as men, to be redundant. It is sex *for them.* What is sex except that which is felt as sexual? When acts of dominance and submission, up to and including acts of violence, are experienced as sexually arousing, as sex itself, that is what they are. The mutual exclusivity of sex and violence is preserved in the face of this evidence by immunizing as "sex" whatever causes a sexual response and by stigmatizing questioning it as repressive, knowing that what is thereby exempted includes humiliation and brutality and molestation and murder as well as rape by any definition. Violence is sex when it is practiced as sex. If violation of the powerless is part of what is sexy about sex, as well as central in the meaning of male and female, the place of sexuality in gender and the place of gender in sexuality need to be looked at together.

When this is done, sexuality appears as the interactive dynamic of gender as an inequality. Stopped as an attribute of a person, sex inequality takes the form of gender; moving as a relation between people, it takes the form of sexuality. Gender emerges as the congealed form of the sexualization of inequality between men and women. So long as this is socially the case, the feelings or acts or desires of particular individuals notwithstanding, gender inequality will divide their society into two communities of interest. The male centrally features hierarchy of control. Aggression against those with less power is experienced as sexual pleasure, an entitlement of masculinity. For the female, subordination is sexualized, in the way that dominance is for the male, as pleasure as well as gender identity, as femininity. Dominance, principally by men, and submission, principally by women, will be the ruling code through which sexual pleasure is experienced. Sexism will be a political inequality that is sexually enjoyed, if unequally so.

Sexual abuse works as a form of terror in creating and maintaining this arrangement. It is a terror so perfectly motivated and systematically concerted that it never need be intentionally organized—an arrangement that, as long as it lasted, would seal the immortality of any totalitarianism. I have come to think that the unique effectiveness of terrorism, like that against Jews in Argentina, is that it is at once absolutely systematic and absolutely random: systematic because one group is its target and lives knowing it; random because there is no way of telling who is next on the list. Just to get through another day, women must spend an incredible amount of time, life, and energy cowed, fearful, and colonized, trying to figure out how not to be next on the list. Learning by osmosis what men want in a woman and trying to give it to them, women hope that being the wanted image will alter their odds. Paying attention to every detail of every incident of a woman's violation they can get their hands on, women attempt not to be her. The problem is, combining even a few circumstances, descriptions, conditions, and details of acts of sexual abuse reveals that no woman has a chance. To be about to be raped is to be gender female in the process of going about life as usual. Some things do increase the odds, like being Black. One cannot live one's life attempting not to be a Black woman. As Black women well know, one cannot save it that way, either.

Because the inequality of the sexes is socially defined as the enjoyment of sexuality itself, gender inequality appears consensual. This helps explain the peculiar durability of male supremacy as a system of hegemony as well as its imperviousness to change once it exists. It also helps explain some of the otherwise more bewildering modes of female collaboration. The belief that whatever is sexually arousing is, ipso facto, empowering for women is revealed as a strategy in male rule. It may be worth considering that heterosexuality, the predominant social arrangement that fuses this sexuality of abuse and objectification with gender in intercourse, with attendant trauma, torture, and dehumanization, organizes women's pleasure so as to give us a stake in our own subordination. It may even be that to be "anti-sex," to be against this sex that is sex, is to refuse to affirm loyalty to this political system of inequality whose dynamic is male control and use and access to women—which would account for the stigma of the epithet.

CATHARINE A. MACKINNON, DIFFERENCE AND DOMINANCE

In Feminism Unmodified 32–45 (1987).

What is a gender question a question of? What is an inequality question a question of? These two questions underlie applications of the equality principle to issues of gender, but they are seldom explicitly asked. I think it speaks to the way gender has structured thought and perception that mainstream legal and moral theory tacitly gives the same answer to them both: these are questions of sameness and difference. The mainstream doctrine of the law of sex discrimination that results is, in my view, largely responsible for the fact that sex equality law has been so utterly ineffective at getting women what we need and are socially prevented from having on the basis of a condition of birth: a chance at productive lives of reasonable physical security, self-expression, individuation, and minimal respect and dignity. Here I expose the sameness/difference theory of sex equality, briefly show how it dominates sex discrimination law and policy and underlies its discontents, and propose an alternative that might do something.

According to the approach to sex equality that has dominated politics, law, and social perception, equality is an equivalence, not a distinction, and sex is a distinction. The legal mandate of equal treatment—which is both a systemic norm and a specific legal doctrine—becomes a matter of treating likes alike and unlikes unlike; and the sexes are defined as such by their mutual unlikeness. Put another way, gender is socially constructed as difference epistemologically; sex discrimination law bounds gender equality by difference doctrinally. A built-in tension exists between this concept of equality, which presupposes sameness, and this concept of sex, which presupposes difference. Sex equality thus becomes a contradiction in terms, something of an oxymoron, which may suggest why we are having such a difficult time getting it.

Upon further scrutiny, two alternate paths to equality for women emerge within this dominant approach, paths that roughly follow the lines of this tension. The leading one is: be the same as men. This path is termed gender neutrality doctrinally and the single standard philosophically. It is testimony to how substance gets itself up as form in law that this rule is considered formal equality. Because this approach mirrors the ideology of the social world, it is considered abstract, meaning transparent of substance; also for this reason it is considered not only to be *the* standard, but *a* standard at all. It is so far the leading rule that the words "equal to" are code for, equivalent to, the words "the same as"—referent for both unspecified.

To women who want equality yet find that you are different, the doctrine provides an alternative route: be different from men. This equal recognition of difference is termed the special benefit rule or special protection rule legally, the double standard philosophically. It is in rather bad odor. Like pregnancy, which always calls it up, it is something of a doctrinal embarrassment. Considered an exception to true equality and not really a rule of law at all, this is the one place where the law of sex discrimination admits it is recognizing something substantive. * * *

The philosophy underlying the difference approach is that sex *is* a difference, a division, a distinction, beneath which lies a stratum of human commonality, sameness. The moral thrust of the sameness branch of the doctrine is to make normative rules conform to this empirical reality by granting women access to what men have access to: to the extent that women are no different from men, we deserve what they have. The differences branch, which is generally seen as patronizing but necessary to avoid absurdity, exists to value or compensate women for what we are or have become distinctively as women (by which is meant, unlike men) under existing conditions.

My concern is not with which of these paths to sex equality is preferable in the long run or more appropriate to any particular issue, although most discourse on sex discrimination revolves about these questions as if that were all there is. My point is logically prior: to treat issues of sex equality as issues of sameness and difference *is to take a particular approach.* I call this the difference approach because it is obsessed with the sex difference. The main theme in the fugue is "we're the same, we're the same, we're the same." The counterpoint theme (in a higher register) is "but we're different, but we're different, but we're different." Its underlying story is: on the first day, difference was; on the second day, a division was created upon it; on the third day, irrational instances of dominance arose. Division may be rational or irrational. Dominance either seems or is justified. Difference *is*.

There is a politics to this. Concealed is the substantive way in which man has become the measure of all things. Under the sameness standard, women are measured according to our correspondence with man, our equality judged by our proximity to his measure. Under the difference standard, we are measured according to our lack of correspondence with him, our womanhood judged by our distance from his measure. Gender neutrality is thus simply the male standard, and the special protection rule is simply the female standard, but do not be deceived: masculinity, or maleness, is the referent for both. Think about it like those anatomy models in medical school. A male body is the human body; all those extra things women have are studied in ob/gyn. It truly is a situation in which more is less. Approaching sex discrimination in this way—as if sex questions are difference questions and equality questions are sameness questions—provides two ways for the law to hold women to a male standard and call that sex equality.

Having been very hard on the difference answer to sex equality questions, I should say that it takes up a very important problem: how to get women access to everything we have been excluded from, while also valuing everything that women are or have been allowed to become or have developed as a consequence of our struggle either not to be excluded from most of life's pursuits or to be taken seriously under the terms that have been permitted to be our terms. It negotiates what we have managed in relation to men. Legally articulated as the need to conform normative standards to existing reality, the strongest doctrinal expression of its sameness idea would prohibit taking gender into account in any way.

Its guiding impulse is: we're as good as you. Anything you can do, we can do. Just get out of the way. I have to confess a sincere affection for this approach. It has gotten women some access to employment and education, the public pursuits, including academic, professional, and blue-collar work; the military; and more than nominal access to athletics. It has moved to change the dead ends that were all we were seen as good for and has altered what passed for women's lack of physical training, which was really serious training in passivity and enforced weakness. * * *

* * *

Feminists have this nasty habit of counting bodies and refusing not to notice their gender. As applied, the sameness standard has mostly gotten men the benefit of those few things women have historically had—for all the good they did us. Almost every sex discrimination case that has been won at the Supreme Court level has been brought by a man. * * * The equality principle in this guise mobilizes the idea that the way to get things for women is to get them for men. Men have gotten them. Have women? We still have not got equal pay, or equal work, far less equal pay for equal work, and we are close to losing separate enclaves like women's schools through this approach.

Here is why. In reality, which this approach is not long on because it is liberal idealism talking to itself, virtually every quality that distinguishes men from women is already affirmatively compensated in this society. Men's physiology defines most sports, their needs define auto and health insurance coverage, their socially designed biographies define work-place expectations and successful career patterns, their perspectives and concerns define quality in scholarship, their experiences and obsessions define merit, their objectification of life defines art, their military service defines citizenship, their presence defines family, their inability to get along with each other—their wars and rulerships—defines history, their image defines god, and their genitals define sex. For each of their differences from women, what amounts to an affirmative action plan is in effect, otherwise known as the structure and values of American society. But whenever women are, by this standard, "different" from men and insist on not having it held against us, whenever a difference is used to keep us second class and we refuse to smile about it, equality law has a paradigm trauma and it's crisis time for the doctrine.

What this doctrine has apparently meant by sex inequality is not what happens to us. The law of sex discrimination that has resulted seems to be looking only for those ways women are kept down that have *not* wrapped themselves up as a difference—whether original, imposed, or imagined. Start with original: what to do about the fact that women actually have an ability men still lack, gestating children in utero. Pregnancy therefore is a difference. Difference doctrine says it is sex discrimination to give women what we need, because only women need it. It is not sex discrimination not to give women what we need because then only women will not get what we need. Move into imposed: what to do about the fact that most women are segregated into low-paying jobs where there are no men. Suspecting that the structure of the marketplace will be entirely subverted if comparable worth is put into effect, difference doctrine says that because there is no man to set a standard from which women's treatment is a deviation, there is no sex discrimination here, only sex difference. Never mind that there is no man to compare with because no man would do that job if he had a choice, and of course he has because he is a man, so he won't.

Now move into the so-called subtle reaches of the imposed category, the de facto area. Most jobs in fact require that the person, gender neutral, who is qualified for them will be someone who is not the primary caretaker of a preschool child. Pointing out that this raises a concern of sex in a society in which women are expected to care for the children is taken as day one of taking gender into account in the structuring of jobs. To do that would violate the rule against not noticing situated differences based on gender, so it never emerges that day one of taking gender into account was the day the job was structured with the expectation that its occupant would have no child care responsibilities. Imaginary sex differences—such as between male and female applicants to administer estates or between males aging and dying and females aging and dying—I will concede, the doctrine can handle.

I will also concede that there are many differences between women and men. I mean, can you imagine elevating one half of a population and denigrating the other half and producing a population in which everyone is the same? What the sameness standard fails to notice is that men's differences from women are equal to women's differences from men. There is an *equality* there. Yet the sexes are not socially equal. The difference approach misses the fact that hierarchy of power produces real as well as fantasized differences, differences that are also inequalities. What is missing in the difference approach is what Aristotle missed in his empiricist notion that equality means treating likes alike and unlikes unlike, and nobody has questioned it since. Why should you have to be the same as a man to get what a man gets simply because he is one? Why does maleness provide an original entitlement, not questioned on the basis of *its* gender, so that is it women—women who want to make a case of unequal treatment in a world men have made in their image (this is really the part Aristotle missed)—who have to show in effect that they are men in every relevant respect, unfortunately mistaken for women on the basis of an accident of birth?

The women that gender neutrality benefits, and there are some, show the suppositions of this approach in highest relief. They are mostly women who have been able to construct a biography that somewhat approximates the male norm, at least on paper. They are the qualified, the least of sex discrimination's victims. When they are denied a man's chance, it looks the most like sex bias. The more unequal society gets, the fewer such women are permitted to exist. Therefore, the more unequal society gets, the *less* likely the difference doctrine is to be able to do anything about it, because unequal power creates both the appearance and the reality of sex differences along the same lines as it creates its sex inequalities.

The special benefits side of the difference approach has not compensated for the differential of being second class. The special benefits rule is the only place in mainstream equality doctrine where you get to identify as a woman and not have that mean giving up all claim to equal treatment—but it comes close. Under its double standard, women who stand to inherit something when their husbands die have gotten the exclusion of a small percentage of the inheritance tax, to the tune of Justice Douglas waxing eloquent about the difficulties of all women's economic situation.[22] If we're going to be stigmatized as different, it would be nice if the compensation would fit the disparity. * * *

The double standard of these rules doesn't give women the dignity of the single standard; it also does not (as the differences standard does) suppress the gender of its referent, which is, of course, the female gender. I must also confess some affection for this standard. The work of Carol Gilligan on gender differences in moral reasoning gives it a lot of dignity, more than it has ever had, more, frankly, than I thought it ever could have. But she achieves for moral reasoning what the special protection rule achieves in law: the affirmative rather than the negative valuation of that which has accurately distinguished women from men, by making it seem as though those attributes, with their consequences, really are

22. Kahn v. Shevin, 416 U.S. 351, 353 (1974).

somehow ours, rather than what male supremacy has attributed to us for its own use. For women to affirm difference, when difference means dominance, as it does with gender, means to affirm the qualities and characteristics of powerlessness.

* * *

* * * I do not think that the way women reason morally is morality "in a different voice." I think it is morality in a higher register, in the feminine voice. Women value care because men have valued us according to the care we give them, and we could probably use some. Women think in relational terms because our existence is defined in relation to men. Further, when you are powerless, you don't just speak differently. A lot, you don't speak. Your speech is not just differently articulated, it is silenced. Eliminated, gone. You aren't just deprived of a language with which to articulate your distinctiveness, although you are; you are deprived of a life out of which articulation might come. Not being heard is not just a function of lack of recognition, not just that no one knows how to listen to you, although it is that; it is also silence of the deep kind, the silence of being prevented from having anything to say. Sometimes it is permanent. All I am saying is that the damage of sexism is real, and reifying that into differences is an insult to our possibilities.

* * *

There is an alternative approach * * *. In this approach, an equality question is a question of the distribution of power. Gender is also a question of power, specifically of male supremacy and female subordination. The question of equality, from the standpoint of what it is going to take to get it, is at root a question of hierarchy, which—as power succeeds in constructing social perception and social reality—derivatively becomes a categorical distinction, a difference. Here, on the first day that matters, dominance was achieved, probably by force. By the second day, division along the same lines had to be relatively firmly in place. On the third day, if not sooner, differences were demarcated, together with social systems to exaggerate them in perception and in fact, *because* the systematically differential delivery of benefits and deprivations required making no mistake about who was who. Comparatively speaking, man has been resting ever since. Gender might not even code as difference, might not mean distinction epistemologically, were it not for its consequences for social power.

I call this the dominance approach, and it is the ground I have been standing on in criticizing mainstream law. The goal of this dissident approach is not to make legal categories trace and trap the way things are. It is not to make rules that fit reality. It is critical of reality. Its task is not to formulate abstract standards that will produce determinate outcomes in particular cases. Its project is more substantive, more jurisprudential than formulaic, which is why it is difficult for the mainstream discourse to dignify it as an approach to doctrine or to imagine it as a rule of law at all.

It proposes to expose that which women have had little choice but to be confined to, in order to change it.

The dominance approach centers on the most sex-differential abuses of women as a gender, abuses that sex equality law in its difference garb could not confront. It is based on a reality about which little of a systematic nature was known before 1970, a reality that calls for a new conception of the problem of sex inequality. This new information includes not only the extent and intractability of sex segregation into poverty, which has been known before, but the range of issues termed violence against women, which has not been. It combines women's material desperation, through being relegated to categories of jobs that pay nil, with the massive amount of rape and attempted rape—44% of all women—about which virtually nothing is done; the sexual assault of children—38% of girls and 10% of boys—which is apparently endemic to the patriarchal family; the battery of women that is systematic in one quarter to one third of our homes; prostitution, women's fundamental economic condition, what we do when all else fails, and for many women in this country, all else fails often; and pornography, an industry that traffics in female flesh, making sex inequality into sex to the tune of eight billion dollars a year in profits largely to organized crime.

These experiences have been silenced out of the difference definition of sex equality largely because they happen almost exclusively to women. Understand: for this reason, they are considered *not* to raise sex equality issues. Because this treatment is done almost uniquely to women, it is implicitly treated as a difference, the sex difference, when in fact it is the socially situated subjection of women. The whole point of women's social relegation to inferiority as a gender is that for the most part these things aren't done to men. Men are not paid half of what women are paid for doing the same work on the basis of their equal difference. * * *

* * *

Looking at the difference approach and the dominance approach from each other's point of view clarifies some otherwise confusing tensions in sex equality debates. From the point of view of the dominance approach, it becomes clear that the difference approach adopts the point of view of male supremacy on the status of the sexes. Simply by treating the status quo as "the standard," it invisibly and uncritically accepts the arrangements under male supremacy. In this sense, the difference approach is masculinist, although it can be expressed in a female voice. The dominance approach, in that it sees the inequalities of the social world from the standpoint of the subordination of women to men, is feminist.

* * *

I say, give women equal power in social life. Let what we say matter, then we will discourse on questions of morality. Take your foot off our necks, then we will hear in what tongue women speak. So long as sex equality is limited by sex difference, whether you like it or don't like it, whether you value it or seek to negate it, whether you stake it out as a grounds for feminism or occupy it as the terrain of misogyny, women will be born, degraded, and die. We would settle for that equal protection of the laws under which one would be born, live, and die, in a country where protection is not a dirty word and equality is not a special privilege.

CATHARINE A. MACKINNON, THE PROBLEM OF MARXISM AND FEMINISM

In Toward a Feminist Theory of the State 3–4 (1989).

Sexuality is to feminism what work is to marxism: that which is most one's own, yet most taken away. Marxist theory argues that society is fundamentally constructed of the relations people form as they do and make things needed to survive humanly. Work is the social process of shaping and transforming the material and social worlds, creating people as social beings as they create value. It is that activity by which people become who they are. Class is its structure, production its consequence, capital a congealed form, and control its issue.

Implicit in feminist theory is a parallel argument: the molding, direction, and expression of sexuality organizes society into two sexes: women and men. This division underlies the totality of social relations. Sexuality is the social process through which social relations of gender are created, organized, expressed, and directed, creating the social beings we know as women and men, as their relations create society. As work is to marxism, sexuality to feminism is socially constructed yet constructing, universal as activity yet historically specific, jointly comprised of matter and mind. As the organized expropriation of the work of some for the benefit of others defines a class, workers, the organized expropriation of the sexuality of some for the use of others defines the sex, woman. Heterosexuality is its social structure, desire its internal dynamic, gender and family its congealed forms, sex roles its qualities generalized to social persona, reproduction a consequence, and control its issue.

Marxism and feminism provide accounts of the way social arrangements of patterned and cumulative disparity can be internally rational and systematic yet unjust. Both are theories of power, its social derivations and its maldistribution. Both are theories of social inequality. In unequal societies, gender and with it sexual desire and kinship structures, like value and with it acquisitiveness and the forms of property ownership, are considered presocial, part of the natural world, primordial or magical or aboriginal. As marxism exposes value as a social creation, feminism exposes desire as socially relational, internally necessary to unequal social orders but historically contingent.

NOTES ON DOMINANCE FEMINISM

1. What are the key ways that MacKinnon's theory differs from liberal equality theory? What does MacKinnon mean when she says that the liberal

equality standard adopted by the Supreme Court is a male standard, under which "man has become the measure of all things"? If government must treat women and men the same, under the same rules and standards, how is this approach "male"?

According to the formal equality approach, inequality consists of treating similarly situated women and men differently. According to MacKinnon, most inequality results from treating differences differently, meaning the systematic valuation of those traits and experiences associated with men and devaluation of those associated with women. Which definition encompasses more gender inequality? Which standard would work better in the hands of judges? Might your answer depend on who the judges are?

How would MacKinnon analyze the issue in *VMI*, the last case excerpted in Chapter 2 involving the all-male military academy? What would she see as the core problem in that case? Compare MacKinnon's identification of the problem with that of Justice Ginsburg in her opinion in *VMI*. Which view do you find more compelling?

2. In what ways is MacKinnon responding to Gilligan? What is the nature of MacKinnon's disagreement with Gilligan's focus on women's differences? What does MacKinnon mean when she claims "the difference approach is masculinist, although it can be expressed in a female voice"? Do you agree that "[t]he dominance approach, in that it sees the inequalities of the social world from the standpoint of the subordination of women to men, is feminist"? Does this mean that MacKinnon believes there is only one feminist approach for all women?

Why is MacKinnon reluctant to identify the relational caring voice with women? Do you agree with her? If MacKinnon is right that this is the voice of women because "men have valued us according to the care we give them," what follows? Are there reasons, apart from male insistence, why women might want to embrace this voice? What might be the advantages generally, and for women specifically, of valuing relationships and care in our society? How would MacKinnon respond?

3. Martha Mahoney states:

> [M]otherhood is not easily incorporated into MacKinnon's vision because it is in some tension with her emphasis on what is done to women. Pregnancy, in contrast, is consistent with her emphasis on women as the objects of male domination, in part because it is a consequence of sexual intercourse with a man, and fits with a vision of women's-body-done-to-by-a-man. But raising children is both creative and oppressed. Understanding motherhood therefore requires a vision of women as actors in the world—shaping children's lives, struggling to meet the tasks society hands them with the resources available—as well as trapped with children in a system of male domination.

Mahoney, Whiteness and Women, In Practice and Theory: A Reply to Catharine MacKinnon, 5 Yale J.L. & Feminism 217, 237–38 (1993). Do you agree that MacKinnon fails to incorporate mothering? Or is MacKinnon emphasizing that dominant structures do not incorporate mothering? What dangers does MacKinnon see in valuing positively the care and nurturing women provide? How would Mahoney likely respond?

4. MacKinnon emphasizes that men exert power over women through sexuality. What does MacKinnon mean by "sexuality"? Do you think she is referring to sex acts? If so, which ones? How, in MacKinnon's view, is "sexuality" different from "heterosexuality"? How is "sexuality" different from "acts of dominance and submission"? Why might MacKinnon want to emphasize that such differences are minimal or nonexistent? What might be some of the harms of that approach?

What forms of power might MacKinnon be ignoring? What forms of power might women exert in various situations?

5. What, in MacKinnon's view, is the connection between gender and sexuality or "sexual desire"? MacKinnon writes above: "Gender emerges as the congealed form of the sexualization of inequality between men and women." Does this mean that certain sex acts create gender? If so, what creates the "inequality between men and women"? Is it the same thing for all men and women?

In her earlier Signs articles, MacKinnon emphasized that "[s]exual objectification is the primary process of the subjection of women. It unites act with word, construction with expression, perception with enforcement, myth with reality. Man fucks woman; subject verb object"; and "[t]o be rap*able*, a position which is social, not biological, defines what a woman *is*." MacKinnon, Feminism, Marxism, Method, and the State: An Agenda for Theory, 7 Signs 515, 541 (1982); MacKinnon, Feminism, Marxism, Method, and the State: Toward a Feminist Jurisprudence, 8 Signs 635, 651 (1983). Under MacKinnon's theory, can women desire or enjoy sexual intercourse with men without perpetuating the inequality of the sexes? Or is such enjoyment always a form of "female collaboration"? What about women having sex with other women or men having sex with other men? Do same-sex sexual relations escape the dynamics MacKinnon identifies? How might MacKinnon's theory be read to suggest that women who refrain from sexual intercourse with men, and men who refrain from sexual intercourse with women, are gender-free? How might MacKinnon respond?

6. How would MacKinnon assess whether we have reached equality? According to MacKinnon, what should be the primary goal of feminist activists? Given MacKinnon's invocation of marxism, how does MacKinnon's approach differ from Eisenstein's?

Many people read MacKinnon as arguing that women must obtain sufficient power to transform existing social institutions, including the male-dominated institution of heterosexuality. Do you agree that this is the appropriate goal, short- or long-term? How might such an approach achieve equality and how might it not? In contrast, Nancy Fraser argues that MacKinnon sees dominance and subordination in terms of individual relationships rather than in terms of groups and social structures. MacKinnon sees male dominance "as a dyadic power relation in which a male superordinate commands a female subordinate. It is a master/subject relation." Fraser, Justice Interruptus: Critical Reflections on the "Postsocialist" Condition 225 (1997). Is this a more accurate description of MacKinnon's focus? If so, how does this affect your understanding of MacKinnon's goal? How might individual change lead to systemic change? How might it not?

7. Should obtaining power on any level be feminists' primary objective? How has power been defined in our culture? Who has defined it? In a 1983 essay, Marilyn Frye described power and oppression as follows:

> The experience of oppressed people is that the living of one's life is confined and shaped by forces and barriers which are not accidental or occasional and hence avoidable, but are systematically related to each other in such a way as to catch one between and among them and restrict or penalize motion in any direction. It is the experience of being caged in: all avenues, in every direction, are blocked or booby trapped.
>
> Cages. Consider a bird cage. If you look very closely at just one wire in the cage, you cannot see the other wires.

Frye, Oppression in The Politics of Reality: Essays in Feminist Theory 1, 4 (1983). Frye points out that those on each side of a barrier face it, but they do not necessarily face similar barriers. Do you think MacKinnon would agree with Frye's description? Can such oppression be alleviated without the oppressed exercising power themselves? How might such an exercise of power itself be oppressive? Is there a sense in which MacKinnon's approach is androcentric, meaning that it embraces a male-centered standard? Can you think of circumstances in which a goal other than obtaining power might be more important for a woman or women as a group?

8. MacKinnon states that the women who benefit from liberal equality theory are those whose biographies are most like men's. Do you agree? Are all law students among "the qualified, the least of sex discrimination's victims"? How should feminist lawyers and law students judge an equality standard? How would an agenda designed for the most vulnerable women differ from the agenda of feminist litigators pushing for formal equality in the 1970s? How might MacKinnon's theory help the most vulnerable women and how might it not?

9. If women are shaped by social circumstances and experiences in a male-dominated world, aren't men also shaped by social circumstances and experiences? Does MacKinnon assume that men's voice is authentically male though she denies that women's voice is authentically female? Does she seem to suggest that men have an essential unchanging domineering nature?

3. RELATIONAL FEMINISM

As MacKinnon urged legal feminists to adopt a dominance approach to gender inequality, Robin West began to develop an alternative critique of liberal equality theory, one that focused on women's connectedness rather than their autonomy or oppression. Drawing upon the work of Carol Gilligan, West urged legal feminists to consider ways the law could embrace traditionally female values and qualities just as it embraces traditionally male values and qualities. The excerpts below elucidate

West's theory of relational feminism and its potential use in law reform efforts.

ROBIN L. WEST, THE DIFFERENCE IN WOMEN'S HEDONIC LIVES: A PHENOMENOLOGICAL CRITIQUE OF FEMINIST LEGAL THEORY

3 Wis. Women's L.J. 81, 81–83, 85–90, 93–94, 98, 101–02, 104, 111–13, 116–17, 129, 139–42 (1987).

Women's subjective, hedonic lives are different from men's. The quality of our suffering is different from that of men's, as is the nature of our joy. Furthermore, and of more direct concern to feminist lawyers, the quantity of pain and pleasure enjoyed or suffered by the two genders is different: women suffer more than men. The two points are related. One reason that women suffer more than men is that women often find painful the same objective event or condition that men find pleasurable. The introduction of oxymorons in our vocabulary, wrought by feminist victories, evidences this difference in women's and men's hedonic lives. The phrases "date-rape," for example, and "sexual harassment," capture these different subjective experiences of shared social realities. * * *

* * *

* * * Just as women's work is not recognized or compensated by the market culture, women's injuries are often not recognized or compensated *as injuries* by the legal culture. The dismissal of women's gender-specific suffering comes in various forms, but the outcome is always the same: women's suffering for one reason or another is outside the scope of legal redress. Thus, women's distinctive, gender-specific injuries are now or have in the recent past been variously dismissed as trivial (sexual harassment on the street); consensual (sexual harassment on the job); humorous (non-violent marital rape); participatory, subconsciously wanted, or self-induced (father/daughter incest); natural or biological, and therefore inevitable (childbirth); sporadic, and conceptually continuous with gender-neutral pain (rape, viewed as a crime of violence); deserved or private (domestic violence); non-existent (pornography); incomprehensible (unpleasant and unwanted consensual sex) or legally predetermined (marital rape, in states with the marital exemption).

It is not so clear, though, *why* women's suffering is so pervasively dismissed or trivialized by legal culture, or more importantly what to do about it. * * *

* * *

[I suggest that the] blanket dismissal of women's gender-specific suffering by the legal culture may be (partly) a reflection of the extent to which the pain women feel is *not understood,* and *that* it is not understood may be because it is itself different, and not just a product of our difference. Thus, it may be that women suffer more because we suffer differently. * * * If the pain women feel is different—not shared by men—then it is not surprising that men cannot readily empathize with women who suffer, much less share in the effort to resist the source of their injuries. The strategic inference I draw is this: if we want to enlist the aid of the larger legal culture, the feel of our gender-specific pain must be described before we can ever hope to communicate its magnitude.

Focus on the "difference" of our hedonic lives also suggests a different way to address the related problem of "false consciousness." As feminists know all too well, it is not just the legal culture which trivializes women's suffering, women do so also. Again, if we focus on the distinctiveness of our pain, this becomes less surprising. An injury uniquely sustained by a disempowered group will lack a name, a history, and in general a linguistic reality. Consequently, the victim as well as the perpetrator will transform the pain into *something else,* such as, for example, punishment, or flattery, or transcendence, or unconscious pleasure. A victim's response to an injury which is perceived by the victim as deservedly punitive, consensual, natural, subconsciously desired, legally inevitable, or trivial will be very different from a response to an injury which is perceived as simply *painful.* We change our behavior in response to the threat of what we perceive as punishment; we diminish ourselves in response to injuries we perceive as trivial; we reconstruct our pasts in response to injuries we perceive as subconsciously desired; we negate our inner selves in response to injuries we perceive as consensual and we constrain our potentiality in response to injuries we perceive as inevitable. We respond to pain, on the other hand, by resisting the source of the pain. The strategic inference should be clear: we must give voice to the hurting self, even when that hurting self sounds like a child rather than an adult; even when that hurting self voices "trivial" complaints; even when the hurting self is ambivalent toward the harm and even when (especially when) the hurting self is talking a language not heard in public discourse. * * *

[I can think of four possible reasons for feminist legal theorists' failure to provide] rich descriptions of women's subjective, hedonic lives, particularly the pain in those lives * * *.

The first reason is linguistic. It is *hard* to talk about our pain and pleasure * * * because they are different. Our language is inadequate to the task. * * * The second reason is psychological. Before we can convince others of the seriousness of the injuries we sustain, we must first convince ourselves, and so long as others are unconvinced, to some extent, we will be as well. * * * The third and underlying problem is political. The inadequacy of language and the problem of "false consciousness" are but reflections of what is surely the core obstacle to the development of feminist discourse on the nature of gender-specific pain, which is an unwilling and resisting audience. * * *

However, at least one reason—and perhaps the main reason—that feminist legal theorists have neglected the hedonic dimension of our difference * * * is * * * the emerging logic of feminist legal theory itself. By virtue of the models of legal criticism that feminist legal theorists have embraced, we've literally defined the subjective, hedonic aspect of our differences out of existence. * * *

[L]iberal-legal feminist theorists—true to their liberalism—want women to have more choices, and * * * *radical-legal* feminist theorists—true to their radicalism—want women to have more power. Both models direct our critical attention *outward*—liberalism to the number of choices we have, radicalism to the amount of power. * * * Neither model directs our critical attention *inward*. Consequently, and unsurprisingly, neither liberal nor radical feminist legal critics have committed themselves to the task of determining the measure of women's happiness or suffering.

Which is not to say that liberal and radical feminist legal theorists are unconcerned about women's subjective well-being. Rather, each group dismisses the normative significance of women's pain and suffering because of the essentially strategic choices made by the underlying (nonfeminist) politics embraced by that group, and the depictions of human nature those choices entail. That is, radicals, liberals, and feminists all have great concern for people's subjective happiness. But neither radical nor liberal legalism—nor their feminist derivatives—aim for happiness or well-being *directly*. * * *

The cost *to women* of feminist legal theorists' endorsement of the anti-phenomenological methodology and anti-hedonic norms of the models they endorse is very high. It renders liberal and radical feminist legal theorists peculiarly uncritical—*as feminists*—of the visions of the human and thus of the normative assumptions of the models for legal criticism which they have respectively embraced. * * *

* * *

I. Liberal Feminism: Consent, Autonomy and the Giving Self

Perhaps the most widely held normative commitment of mainstream liberal legal theorists is that individuals should be free to choose their own style of life, and to exercise that freedom of choice in as many spheres as possible—economic, political and personal. * * *

* * *

I want to suggest * * * that many women, much of the time, consent to transactions, changes, or situations in the world so as to satisfy not their own desires or to maximize their own pleasure, as liberal legalism and liberal legal feminism both presume, but to maximize the pleasure and satiate the desires of others, and that they do so by virtue of conditions which only women experience. I will sometimes call the cluster of "other-regarding," other-pleasing motivations that rule these women's actions the "giving self," so as to distinguish it from the "liberal self": the cluster of self-regarding "rational" motivations presumed by liberal legalism. * * *

I believe that women become giving rather than liberal selves for a range of reasons—including our (biological) pregnability and our (social) training for our role as primary caretakers[.] * * * [In addition, a] fully justified fear of acquisitive and violent male sexuality * * * permeates many women's—perhaps all women's—sexual and emotional self-definition. Women respond to this fear by *re-constituting* themselves in a way that controls the danger and suppresses the fear. Thus: women define themselves as "giving selves" so as to obviate the threat, the danger, the pain, and the fear of being self-regarding selves from whom their sexuality is taken.

* * *

How do women respond to the total fear that accompanies the daily violence that characterizes an abusive domestic relationship? What does such fear *teach* you? A woman cannot live in a state of terror *every day* and what a battered woman learns in an abusive marriage is how to define herself in such a way that she can on occasion suppress the fear. Thus, what a violent intimate relationship taught me was to live *for the other.* * * *

* * *

Many more women * * * know the fear and the threat of violence implicit in promiscuous heterosexuality. A "date" with a man who is utterly—aggressively—uninterested in your subjective well-being, and at the same time, utterly consumed by his expectation and his felt compulsion to *have you* is a frightening encounter. * * *

* * *

One way (there are others) that a young girl can respond to the "rising panic" she feels on a date is by defining herself as "giving." A straightforward, sensible, protective reaction to someone who is indifferent to your subjectivity, and at the same time must have you as an object, is to hide your subjective self and objectify and then give your sexual self for his pleasure and your safety. * * *

* * *

One way that (some) women respond to the pervasive, silent, unspoken and invisible fear of rape in their lives is by giving their (sexual) selves to a consensual, protective, and monogamous relationship. This is widely denied—but it may be widely denied because it is so widely presumed. It is, after all, precisely what we are supposed to do. * * *

* * *

II. Radical Feminism and the Ethical Primacy of Power and Equality

Radical feminist legal theory begins with a description of women which is diametrically opposed to that embraced by liberal feminists. Liberal feminists assume a definitional *equality*—a "sameness"—between the female and male experience of consensual choice, and then argue that the legal system should respect that fundamental, empirical equality. In sharp contrast, radical feminists assume a definitional *in*equality of women—women are *definitionally* the disempowered group—and urge the legal system to eradicate that disempowerment and thereby make women what they presently are not, and that is equal. Radical feminism thus begins with a denial of the liberal feminist's starting assumption. Women and men are *not* equally autonomous individuals. Women, unlike men, live in a world with two sovereigns—the state, and men—and this is true not just some of the time but all of the time. Women, unlike men, are definitionally submissive twice over; once vis-a-vis the state, and once vis-a-vis the superior power of men. A legal regime which ignores this central reality will simply perpetuate the fundamental, underlying inequality.

The cause of women's disempowerment, as well as its effect, is the expropriation of our sexuality. Women are the group, in Catharine MacKinnon's phrase, "from whom sexuality is expropriated," in the same sense that workers are, definitionally, the group from whom labor is expropriated. Women are the gender from whom sex is *taken*. * * *

This much, radical feminist legal theory shares with radical feminism, and with this much I am in full agreement. Where radical feminist legal theory has departed from radical feminism, I believe, is in the normative argument it draws from the insight that women are, definitionally, the group from whom sexuality is expropriated. * * *

First, radical feminist legal theory, like radical legalism, begins with a highly particularized although largely implicit description of the human being. People are, in short, assumed to be such that there exists a correlation between objectively equal distributions of power—including sexual power—and subjectively happy and good lives. Domination makes us evil and submission makes us miserable; substantive equality will make us both moral and happy; and both claims are true because of, and by reference to, this conception of our essential human nature. Radical legal theorists, including radical feminist legal theorists, are as committed to the equation of objective, substantive equality and subjective well being, and the view of our nature on which it rests, as the liberal legal theorist is committed to the equation of objective consent and subjective happiness.

Second, both radical legalism and radical feminist legalism draw from this depiction of the human being the normative inference that it is the imbalance of power which facilitates expropriation (of work for the radical legalist, of sex for the radical feminist legalist), rather than the expropriation itself, which is *definitionally* bad, and then the further inference that it is definitionally bad *whether* or *not the expropriation it facilitates is experientially felt as painful*. The strategic consequence immediately follows: radical legal reform should aim to eradicate hierarchy and thereby attain a substantively equal social world. Thus we should oppose not what makes us miserable—the violent expropriation of our work or our sexuality—but the hierarchy of power which facilitates it, for by doing so we will better target the true cause of our misery. We should support not what makes us happy, but what makes us substantively equal, because by doing so we will invariably further our true interest, even if not our felt pleasure. * * *

* * *

Radical feminist legal theorists' failure to credit phenomenological reports of conflict between egalitarian ideals and women's subjective, hedonic, felt pleasures is generally benign, for one simple reason. The area of conflict is not great. Women want the fruits of substantive equality[.] * * * Over vast areas of our lives, there is no conflict between our desires, our felt pleasures, and radical feminist ideals.

In one area of our lives, however,—namely our erotic lives—there has emerged a conflict between the radical feminist legal theorists' conception of an equalitarian ideal and women's subjective desire. The radical feminist's commitment to equality, and identification of the expropriation of our sexuality as the consequence of our relative disempowerment entails the normative conclusion that sexual inequality *itself* is what is politically undesirable. Thus, male dominance and female submission in sexuality *is* the evil: they express as well as *are* women's substantive inequality. But women report—with increasing frequency and as often as not in consciousness-raising sessions—that equality *in sexuality* is not what we find pleasurable or desirable. Rather, the experience of dominance and submission that go with the controlled, but fantastic, "expropriation" of our sexuality is precisely what *is* sexually desirable, exciting and pleasurable—in fantasy for many; in reality for some. This creates a conflict between theory and method as well as between stated ideal and felt pleasure: what should we *do* when the consciousness that is raised in consciousness-raising finds pleasure in what is definitionally regarded as substantively undesirable—sexual submission, domination and erotic inequality? * * *

* * *

I believe that sexual submission has erotic *appeal* and *value* when it is an expression of *trust;* is damaging, injurious and painful when it is an expression of *fear;* and is *dangerous* because of its ambiguity: both others and we ourselves have difficulty in disentangling the two. * * *

* * *

Conclusion: Women's Difference, and an Alternative Standard for a Feminist Critique of Law

* * * Both liberal and radical legalism share a vision of the human being—and therefore of our subjective well-being—as "autonomous." The liberal insists that choice is necessary for the "true" exercise of that autonomy—and thus is an adequate proxy for subjective well-being—while the radical insists the same for power. But this strategic difference should not blind us to their commonality. Both the liberal and the radical legalist have accepted the Kantian assumption that *to be human* is to be in some sense autonomous—meaning, minimally, to be differentiated, or individuated, from the rest of social life.

Underlying and underscoring the poor fit between the proxies for subjective well-being endorsed by liberals and radicals—choice and power—and women's subjective, hedonic lives is the simple fact that women's lives—*because of our biological, reproductive role*—are drastically at odds with this fundamental vision of human life. Women's lives are *not* autonomous, they are profoundly relational. This is at least the biological reflection, if not the biological cause, of virtually all aspects, hedonic and otherwise, of our "difference." Women, and *only* women, and *most* women, transcend *physically* the differentiation or individuation of biological self from the rest of human life trumpeted as the norm by the entire Kantian tradition. When a woman is pregnant her biological life embraces the embryonic life of another. When she later nurtures children, her needs will embrace their needs. The experience of being human, for women, differentially from men, includes the counter-autonomous experience of a shared physical identity between woman and fetus, as well as the counter-autonomous experience of the emotional and psychological bond between mother and infant.[89]

Our reproductive role renders us non-autonomous in a second, less obvious, but ultimately more far-reaching sense. Emotionally and morally women may benefit from the dependency of the fetus and the infant upon us. But *materially* we are more often burdened than enriched by that dependency. And because we are burdened, we differentially depend more heavily upon others, both for our own survival, and for the survival of the children who are part of us. Women, more than men, depend upon relationships with others, because the weakest of human beings—infants—depend upon us.

Thus, motherhood leaves us vulnerable: a woman giving birth is unable to defend herself against aggression; a woman nursing an infant is physically exposed; a woman nurturing and feeding the young is less able to feed herself. Motherhood leaves us unequal: because of her distinctive nurturing role, a mother is either stronger or weaker than those to whom she is closest. She is stronger than the infant, and because of her nurturing response to that fact she is weaker than her autonomous brother. Most assuredly, then, a mother is not *autonomous*; she is both depended upon and thereby dependent on others—she depends upon others who are stronger than she, as others who are weaker depend upon her. To the considerable degree that our potentiality for motherhood defines ourselves, women's lives are relational, not autonomous. As mothers we nurture the weak and we depend upon the strong. More than do men, we live in an interdependent and hierarchical natural web with others of varying degrees of strength.

---

89. I am describing the way women's lives *are*, not the way they should be or have to be, and I therefore see no reason to distinguish biological from social causes of our counter-autonomous lives. If men became more nurturant of children, they too would become less "autonomous." My general point is that whatever subclass of adult human beings nurtures the young will be relatively less autonomous than the subclass that does not.

* * * If women's "difference" lies in the fact that our lives are relational rather than autonomous, and if autonomy is a necessary attribute of a human being, then women's difference rather abruptly implies that women are not human beings. Politics that are designed to benefit human beings—including liberal and radical legalism—will leave women out in the cold.

This is not a novel insight: that women are not human as human is now conceived has in a sense always been the dominant problem for feminism. But the two characteristic ways in which modern feminist legal theorists have responded to this dilemma are both, I think, flawed. The liberal feminist's solution is to deny it. The fact that women become pregnant, give birth, and nurse infants is a difference that *does not count.* It does not make us any less "autonomous" than men. For reasons which by now should be familiar, this response does not work: if the last century has taught us anything at all, it is that this liberal strategy of denial is a disservice. If we embrace a false conception of our nature we can be sure of only one thing, and that is that legal reform based on such a conception will only occasionally—and then only incidentally—benefit real instead of hypothetical women.

The radical feminist's proposal is that we seek to *become* autonomous creatures. We are indeed not "autonomous," but what that reflects is our lack of power—our social, political and legal victimization—not our essential nature. To the extent that we become autonomous by gaining power, we will *become* the beneficiaries of the legal system designed to promote the well-being of just such people. This radical vision is at root deeply assimilationist—by gaining power, we become equal, as we become equal we become less "relational"—meaning less victimized—as we become less relational we become more autonomous, and as we become more autonomous we become more like "human beings"—more like men. Radical assimilation, though, has costs no less weighty (and no less familiar) than liberal denial. There is no guarantee that women can become autonomous "human beings," no guarantee that women want to, and at heart, no persuasive argument that women should.

A very new and third response, which does not fit easily (or at all) within the liberal and radical models described above, and which I think has great promise, is that feminists should insist on women's humanity—and thus on our entitlements—and on the wrongness of the dominant conception of what it means to be a "human being." We should insist * * * [on] an equal "acceptance of our difference." This third course is surely more promising—it has truth and candor on its side—but without hedonistic criticism it is insufficient: *which* differences are to be accepted? The root of our difference may be that our lives are relational rather than autonomous, which is reflected in our needs and has its roots in our reproductive role. But even thus defined, our "difference" has many dimensions. If "difference" includes our differential suffering, or our differential vulnerability to sexual assault, or our differential endurance of pain, or our differentially negative self-esteem, then "acceptance" of those differences will backfire. We need more than just acceptance of our differences; we need a vocabulary in which to articulate and then evaluate them, as well as the power to reject or affirm them.

ROBIN WEST, CARING FOR JUSTICE

36–38, 79, 81–83 (1997).

A number of liberal, radical and postmodern feminists (and some nonfeminists) have noted the critical point made here, to wit that the cultural feminist valorization of the ethic of care leaves us with a moral world in which care and justice, although no longer viewed hierarchically, are instead viewed as complementary checks on each other, albeit checks originating from different spheres: one public and one private; one masculine, one feminine; one governing the relations of citizens, the other governing the relations of friends or intimates. They then go on, however, to make the *political*, or strategic, objection that the political *benefits* of this valorization, for women, will be minimal, and indeed may be outweighed by the costs. The work women perform, even if acknowledged as morally significant, will continue to be undercompensated and undervalued as it remains exclusively or predominantly female. Furthermore, the valorization of the ethic of care runs the risk of further stereotyping women as the "caring sex," and the attendant political risk of continuing the "gilded cage" phenomenon. In essence, the critics claim, all the injurious consequences, and particularly for women, of the traditional opposition between these two virtues will remain, even assuming that the hierarchy traditionally established between them vanishes. * * *

I think this objection to the relational-feminist project—which, again, has come for the most part from other feminists—albeit an important one, is misguided. Rather, *if the relational-feminist project is successful*, the societal valuation of care as moral work which would follow the philosophical and political work summarized above, would have real-world consequences that would help alleviate, rather than aggravate, women's subordination. If we, societally, truly valued caring work, that value would be *evidenced* in a wide array of social and political transformations, ranging from reforms in family law, social security law, and employment law, to more "macro" changes in the structure of family, wage labor, and market life. Should these transformations occur, it really wouldn't be as important as it seems to be now whether or not women are more "naturally" suited for these tasks. If there were not such a heavy economic and social penalty attached to their performance, presumably both women and men would be more inclined to engage in them. But more importantly, if we "valued" care the way we value justice, we would value, and compensate, to say nothing of ritualistically "honoring," the work of mothering equally with the work of judging. If we did so, it would matter less than it does now whether women or men tended to do the bulk of mothering work.

* * *

* * * The relational-feminist account places the circles [of care and justice] on an equal, nonhierarchal level, but still generally, not touching each other. Imagine instead that the circles of care and justice are *overlapping*—not concentric, not independent, and not hierarchally positioned, but overlapping. My contention is that *only in the area of overlap* will one find *either* true justice *or* true care. Another way to put it is simply that each is a necessary condition of the other. In the nonoverlapping areas of the circles, one finds, respectively, only a self-righteous smugness where one would hope to find justice, and a tribal or animalistic partiality where one would hope to find care.

* * *

Just as nurturance is not in the end very caring if it is not tempered by the justice-based demand for consistency, so compassion is more lacking than exemplary of an ethic of care if not tempered by personal integrity. Although there is much to admire in those individuals among us who are so genuinely giving and compassionate as to be in some sense "selfless," there is also good reason to be wary of a quite different kind of "selflessness," often coupled with shows of compassion. That is a selflessness rooted not in a genuinely empathic regard for the other, but rather in a harmful and injurious lack of regard for oneself: a sense of self-loathing, a lack of self-esteem or self-respect, and at root a failure to give oneself one's "due": a quite general, massive denial of the importance, equality, and dignity of oneself. The self-loathing individual often appears to be what might be called a "giving self," but she is giving for the self-denying, rather than other-affirming, reason that she defines herself by giving herself away. Such a self is, quintessentially, a self that lacks integrity. Because she lacks integrity, she is also a self that cannot truly be compassionate. It is hard to "give" when one defines oneself as by nature "giving," and given.

* * *

Relationships of care, untempered by the demands of justice, resulting in the creation of injured, harmed, exhausted, compromised, and self-loathing "giving selves," rather than in genuinely compassionate and giving individuals, are ubiquitous in this society, and it is far more often women than men who are injured by them. There are two major reasons for the disproportionate impact. The first is simply that by upbringing, girls, far more than boys, are taught through the medium of parental love—that all—powerful creator of the sense of self—that at least in the domestic realm it is self-sacrifice that will be rewarded (or will be rewarded above all else) with the bestowal of parental approval. The girl who learns that self-sacrifice in the home is rewarded with parental love, or attention, or praise, may well become a compassionate person, but the compassion is rooted in a deep need for acceptance which is itself tied to sacrifice. The result may be a good deal of "caring" for others: women, far more than men, perform the overwhelming number of utterly *un*compensated domestic tasks—from the emotional labor of maintaining adult intimate relationships to the time-consuming, repetitive, physically exhausting and emotionally demanding work involved in raising children and running a home—which are needed to keep this society functioning. And they do so, for the most part, within "relationships of care" within which their self-sacrifice is assumed both by the participants in the relationship and by the outside society as exemplary of virtue. That "virtue," however, comes with a high psychic price as well as the self-evidently high economic price, and that is the damage done to the woman's own sense of personal integrity, and even sense of selfhood: the caring is for approval, and the self who seeks approval is a self who must deny her own interests, ambitions, projects and independence. More concretely, to perform daily, time-consuming, difficult tasks for no compensation and with no recognition of the toll taken on one's own individuated life projects is to undertake work which can only be understood, much less accomplished, through a process of self-belittlement and even self-betrayal. A caring relationship that disproportionately shifts the great bulk of this work on one member but not the other is exemplary of injustice, whether or not the unjustly burdened partner views herself and her work as embodying an ethic of care.

The second reason that women, more than men, may be "giving" for less than laudatory reasons has to do with the prevalence of sexual violence directed against women, far more than against men, in this culture. Because of that violence, women live with a source of fear that must somehow be *managed* if one is to navigate adulthood. And one way to manage fear is to "give oneself" to marriage, or to a long-term relationship with a man, which the woman perceives either rightly or wrongly will stave off the danger, and hence the fear, of sexual assault by other men. Many of these relationships may no doubt be joyous, but it is not unreasonable to assume that many of them are quite the opposite: that on a very deep emotional level, they are joy-deadening pacts of protection in which the woman has traded away, in a sense, her right to bodily pleasure, full autonomy, and sensual integrity in exchange for a measure of safety. This "trade," far from rational, may be unacknowledged, and when it is so, the result will often be a giving self of the sort that concerns us here—a self who learns to give not out of an admirable compassionate impulse, but because of a fear that should she not, she will be *taken*, and perhaps in violent and life-threatening ways. * * *

More simply, the reason for women's disproportionate embrace of the giving self, and the psychic cost to personal integrity that self entails, might simply be women's political subordination to men—it would surely not be the only example of a subordinated class coming to accept its own subordination by accepting a dwindled-down self image. But whatever its causes, the giving self to which I'm referring reflects a trait of personhood—a very real human potential—which is far better characterized as an injury than as a virtue. The many women and the occasional man who define themselves as not-selves suffer a decreased sense of personal autonomy, of independence, of individuation, and of integrity. There is no reason to celebrate these stunted selves whose very existence is dramatic evidence of massive social injustice, by misconstruing the selflessness they exemplify as the virtue of compassion.

MARY BECKER, TOWARDS A SUBSTANTIVE FEMINISM

[An earlier version of this essay appeared as parts of Patriarchy and Inequality: Towards a Substantive Feminism, 1999 U. Chi. Legal F. 21, 48, 50–51, 81.]

Neither of the two dominant strands of feminism in the United States today can challenge patriarchy, with its glorification of masculinity defined in terms of power and control. Formal equality cannot do so because it is empty of values: it gives women only the right to what men are entitled to under the rules and values worked out by and for men. Dominance feminism, with its focus on power as it is defined in our society, does have a value (power), but it is a patriarchal value. And it is quite possible to give power to *some* women, women who share patriarchal values and attitudes (or who pretend they do), without threatening patriarchy as a social system. In this essay, I describe a Relational Feminism, with roots in cultural feminism, but building on the work of West and [Allan] Johnson. Unlike formal equality and dominance feminism, relational feminism does have the potential to challenge patriarchy because it emphasizes values inconsistent with patriarchal values: caretaking and relationships.

RELATIONAL FEMINISM

* * *

The goal of relational feminism is a society in which all human beings, women as well as men, can find human fulfillment and happiness. We need, therefore to target *both* the cultural *over*valuation of masculine qualities and the cultural *under*valuation of feminine qualities; the cultural focus on men and their needs and the concomitant tendency to see women as less than fully human and their injuries or needs as the result of their own (unfortunate) choices. We must also target the cultural insistence that women and men are essentially different. In the ideal world of relational feminists, women and men would have access to the support and opportunities necessary for human fulfillment and happiness; valuable traits would be valued whether masculine or feminine and whether displayed by women or men. Relational feminism stresses the need to value community, relationships, and traditional feminine qualities because these valuable qualities have been so undervalued in our overly individualistic and masculinist culture.

Relational feminism does not reject as always inappropriate either the equal treatment of similarly-situated women and men (formal equality's focus) or more power as it is currently defined (dominance feminism's focus). But relational equality has a different focus: working for human happiness and fulfillment for women (and men). Often, similar treatment of similarly-situated women and men will be appropriate from a relational feminist perspective. And often, giving more power, as it is currently described, to women will be appropriate. All else being equal, it is good (conducive to human happiness and fulfillment) for similar individuals to be treated similarly regardless of sex and good for women to have as much power, as it is currently described, as men. Sometimes, however, all is not otherwise equal, and other goods may be more important for women than either of these. More importantly, one's focus determines one's agenda and priorities. Relational feminism's focus will produce a quite different agenda with quite different priorities from either a formal equality or dominance focus.

Values and Perspectives

1. *Commit to care and nurture others and to value the relationships and caretaking of others.* Allan Johnson characterizes our culture's insistence that people are separate and autonomous rather than fundamentally relational as patriarchy's "Great Lie." To counter this lie, we must insist on the value of just and caring relationships and of caretaking, with particular emphasis on the need to ensure the economic well-being of dependents' caretakers.

2. *Recognize that women and men sometimes have conflicting interests, and value policies serving women's needs when different from men's.* Because a patriarchal society is male-centered and male-identified, men's needs tend to dominate the agenda. In addition, patriarchy denies any conflicts of interest between women and men. An explicit focus on women's needs and how to meet them is necessary because a patriarchal culture's consideration of human needs will inevitably and even unintentionally focus on male needs and perspectives. A woman-centered focus will threaten patriarchy because it places women's needs at the center, an activity inconsistent with patriarchy's androcentrism.

3. *Value female sexual agency.* Patriarchy denies that women can be sexual agents making moral decisions in light of their own sexual desires. Patriarchy teaches that a woman should agree to sex with "her" man when he desires it regardless of whether she desires it or is likely to find it pleasurable. As beings with their own ends and purposes, women should be encouraged to develop as sexual agents, capable of saying "no" to sex they do not desire and of seeking their own sexual pleasures.

4. *Value qualities that are valuable regardless of whether they are displayed by a woman or a man.* Because patriarchy rests on the belief that women and men are essentially different, patriarchy values and rewards women and men for conforming to gender stereotypes. For example, in custody disputes, many courts consider economic stability as a reason for awarding custody to the father, who has been the primary breadwinner throughout the marriage. In contrast, mothers who have worked for wages throughout the marriage, most of whom have also been primary caretakers of the children, often lose

custody because they work outside the home. It is important to break the link between sex and valuation.

CONSTITUTIONAL STANDARDS AND COURT ENFORCEMENT

Patriarchy is far too malleable and flexible to be "caught" by any standard capable of being administered by courts. One could ask courts to determine whether a challenged rule or policy contributes to inequality between women and men under a relational feminist analysis, just as MacKinnon asks judges to determine whether a rule or policy contributes to the inequitable distribution of power between women and men. But neither standard would be judicially manageable. The problem is never one rule or practice in isolation, but how it works and what it means within its surrounding social structures. In addition, the answer depends on what alternative will ultimately replace the challenged rule, a matter beyond the control, and often beyond the knowledge, of courts.

Nor is any judicially-manageable standard consistent with the experimentation needed to discover what a world of equality between women and men might look like and what sorts of policies and approaches are appropriate in moving towards that world. We don't—and can't—know what is the ideal approach to inequality between all women and men in all variations of class, race, and culture in the United States.

Given the difficulty of figuring out the proper approach to a particular issue in this very complicated world, any approach to eliminating oppressions of race, class, sex, and sexual orientation must necessarily be experimental and tentative.

NOTES ON RELATIONAL FEMINISM

1. In general, what does West see as similar between liberal equality theory ("liberal feminism") and dominance theory ("radical feminism")? What does she see as different? How does she critique each? How would Case likely respond? How would MacKinnon likely respond? Why does West believe her theory is more compelling than either approach? Are there inherent dangers in focusing on women's pleasures and pains? Why does Becker believe West's approach is superior to either liberal equality theory or dominance theory?

2. Do you think West overgeneralizes? Is West saying that all women are different from all men and that these differences are based on their reproductive capacities? Or is she saying that women today, as a group, tend to be different from men as a group, though of course there will be overlap between women and men and variation among women and among men? Either way, do you agree with West that women feel or tend to feel less separate than men because of their experiences of pregnancy, childbirth, and breastfeeding? Is it the actual experiences that count, or women's ability to engage in such activities? In your experience, how do women and men differ in interactions with others, if at all? When you refer to differences between women and men, do you mean that all men are one way and all women another?

3. What, in West's view, would make the relational-feminist project "successful"? What would it mean to "truly" value care work? Do you agree with West's conception of feminist success? Which women would benefit the most from West's approach? Which women would benefit the least, or even be harmed? How would men be helped or hurt? Would there be identifiable differences between the sexes in West's successful world?

Do any women or men currently possess "true care," or will it come into being only after the success of the relational-feminist project? What is the opposite of "true care"? Is West claiming that some women engage in "false" care or are otherwise falsely conscious? How might critics of MacKinnon also criticize West on this point?

In what ways is Becker more optimistic about relational, or cultural, feminism than West? In what ways is Becker more wary? How do you think Becker would envision the success of the relational-feminist account? How would that vision of success differ from West's, if at all? How do you think MacKinnon would respond to West or Becker?

4. How is West's analysis similar to Gilligan's, and how does it differ? Do you think West would claim that Amy, the girl in Gilligan's study, is engaging in "true care"? How might Amy's answers instead reveal that she has learned "that self-sacrifice in the home is rewarded with parental love, or attention, or praise," and thus her "compassion is rooted in a deep need for acceptance which is itself tied to sacrifice"?

5. Do you know individuals whose care is rooted "in a harmful and injurious lack of regard for oneself"? If so, do these individuals tend to be women more often than men, as West claims? Do you agree with the reasons West offers for why such individuals tend to be women? What might be some other reasons? Is West overly critical of these individuals? How might West be adopting an androcentric standard or a standard similar to that embraced by liberal equality theory?

6. West says that "women are not human as human is now conceived." This is reminiscent of MacKinnon's statement in the first excerpt in this chapter, Consciousness Raising, that women are "damaged" and "are in fact not full people in the sense that men are allowed to become." What problem is West identifying? Is it the same problem MacKinnon is identifying? What solution is each suggesting? Which solution do you find more appealing?

What other aspects of West's analysis might be considered similar to MacKinnon's? How are women's experiences of pregnancy, child birth, and breastfeeding similar to or different from the experiences emphasized by MacKinnon? How might West, like MacKinnon, be criticized for adopting an androcentric approach? Do you find their distinctions based on women's unique physical experiences persuasive?

7. Is West's analysis heterocentric? What of a lesbian who has never been pregnant or experienced heterosexual intercourse (or experienced it only a few times); is she not a woman? Would she be lacking the "essential" experiences and psychological feelings of women? Might this woman nevertheless see and feel herself as more connected to others and less individuated than men? Why?

Jennifer Nedelsky engages in an analysis similar to West's in Reconceiving Autonomy: Sources, Thoughts, and Possibilities, 1 Yale J.L. & Feminism 7 (1989). According to Nedelsky, the "autonomous individual" of liberalism is a being unconnected to others. Property is "the central symbol for this vision of autonomy, for it can both literally and figuratively provide the necessary walls. The most perfectly autonomous man is thus the most perfectly isolated." Id. at 12. Nedelsky points to the need to develop a more accurate concept of autonomy, one recognizing that:

> what actually enables people to be autonomous * * * is not isolation, but relationships—with parents, teachers, friends, loved ones—that provide the support and guidance necessary for the development and experience of autonomy. I think, therefore, that the most promising model, symbol, or metaphor for autonomy is not property, but child-rearing.

Id. Do you agree that childrearing could be a metaphor for autonomy? Or do you find West's argument that "motherhood leaves us vulnerable" more compelling? Are women more likely to see people in terms of relationships—even when discussing autonomy—than men? How might this be true even for lesbians who have not given birth or raised children, or women who otherwise choose not to give birth or to prioritize childrearing in their lives? How might it not? What about men who prioritize childrearing in their lives? See also Jennifer Nedelsky, Law, Boundaries, and the Bounded Self, 30 Representations 162 (1990).

8. Does West's characterization of women as vulnerable and dependent and men as autonomous reinforce patriarchy? How might theories like West's reinforce constructions of gender instead of challenging them?

9. In addition to drawing upon West's work, Becker discusses the work of Allan Johnson. Johnson writes:

> Patriarchy is grounded in a Great Lie that the answer to life's needs is disconnection, competition, and control rather than connection, sharing, and cooperation. The Great Lie separates men from what they need most by encouraging them to be autonomous and disconnected when in fact human existence is fundamentally relational. * * * Who are we if not our ties to other people—"I *am* ... a father, a husband, a worker, a friend, a son, a brother"? But patriarchal culture turns the truth inside out, and "self-made man" goes from oxymoron to cultural ideal. And somewhere between the need for human connection and the imperative to control, the two merge, and a sense of control becomes the closest many men ever come to feeling connected with anything, including themselves.
>
> * * * [T]he cycle of control and fear that drives patriarchy has more to do with relations among men than with women, for it is men who control men's standing *as men*. With few exceptions, men look to other men—not women—to affirm their manhood, whether as coaches, friends, teammates, co-workers, sports figures, fathers, or mentors.
>
> * * *
>
> In more subtle ways, misogyny arises out of a system that offers women to men as a form of compensation. Because patriarchy limits men's emotional and spiritual lives, and because men rarely risk being

> vulnerable with other men, they often look to women as a way to ease the resulting sense of emptiness, meaninglessness, and disconnection. However, the patriarchal expectation that "real men" are autonomous and independent sets men up to both want and resent women at the same time. This is made all the worse by the fact that women can't possibly give men what they want, since autonomy and independence are illusions. Caught in this bind, men could face the truth of the system that put them there in the first place. They could look at patriarchy and how their position in it creates this dilemma. The path of least resistance, however, is to resent and blame women for what men lack, by accusing women of not being loving or sexual enough, of being manipulative, withholding, selfish bitches who deserve to be punished.

Allan Johnson, The Gender Knot: Unraveling Our Patriarchal Legacy 53, 56, 65 (revd. ed. 2005). What connections does Becker make between the work of West and Johnson? In your view, how is Johnson's analysis similar to that embraced by West and how is it different? Is Johnson claiming that men are injured in much the same way that West believes some caring women are injured? How might Johnson's analysis also be similar to MacKinnon's approach? Why do you think Becker invokes Johnson to support West's approach but not MacKinnon's?

10. What does Becker believe is the driving force behind the maintenance of patriarchy? How does that view differ from the views articulated by West, Johnson, MacKinnon, or your own views? What are the potential relationships between patriarchy and women's subordination? How does relational feminism attempt to disrupt those relationships? How does that approach differ from approaches potentially adopted by Johnson or MacKinnon?

11. What kinds of policies would foster the female sexual agency that Becker desires? What would female sexual agency look like? How would it differ from female sexuality in the United States today? How do you think West would answer these questions? How would MacKinnon? In a world which recognized, respected, supported, and fostered female sexual agency, would women who did not want to become pregnant engage in uncontracepted intercourse with men? Would women consent to unwanted sex with anyone? When would women engage in sexual activities? Might the meaning of "sex" change? How is "sex" currently defined in our culture? If someone asked you how many times you had sex last month, what would you count and not count?

12. West suggests that, apart from the erotic, there are few conflicts between women's pleasures and pains and substantive equality. Do you agree? Can you think of other conflicts? What about potential conflicts posed by mothering and caretaking? Or in a world of inequality, in which women are socialized differently from men, might men and women view success in the workplace differently? Is there a conflict between short-term comfort with a "feminine" role and long-term frustration with that role?

13. Which view of feminism discussed so far—liberal equality, dominance, or relational—do you find most compelling? Might women of various classes, races, and sexual orientations answer that question differently? Which theory might be strategically better for various groups of women? Is it

possible to talk about a material basis for differences between the sexes without thinking that all women and men are "essentially" and "biologically" different and, hence, that all women are the same?

4. ANTI-ESSENTIALISM

As MacKinnon and West compared and contrasted their theories, other feminists began to critique both of those approaches to feminism. These feminists did not revert to liberal equality theory, however. Instead, they criticized all three approaches to women's equality by focusing on the ways those approaches ignored differences *among* women. Within the legal academy, Kimberlé Crenshaw was one of the first theorists to engage in this anti-essentialist approach by calling on judges, feminists, and antiracist activists to examine the intersections between race and gender:

> One of the very few Black women's studies books is entitled *All the Women are White, All the Blacks Are Men, But Some of Us Are Brave.* I have chosen this title as a point of departure in my efforts to develop a Black feminist criticism because it sets forth a problematic consequence of the tendency to treat race and gender as mutually exclusive categories of experience and analysis. * * * I want to examine how this tendency is perpetuated by a single-axis framework that is dominant in antidiscrimination law and that is also reflected in feminist theory and antiracist politics.
>
> * * * In other words, in race discrimination cases, discrimination tends to be viewed in terms of sex- or class-privileged Blacks; in sex discrimination cases, the focus is on race- and class-privileged women.
>
> * * *
>
> The value of feminist theory to Black women is diminished because it evolves from a white racial context that is seldom acknowledged. Not only are women of color in fact overlooked, but their exclusion is reinforced when *white* women speak for and as *women*. The authoritative universal voice—usually white male subjectivity masquerading as non-racial, non-gendered objectivity—is merely transferred to those who, but for gender, share many of the same cultural, economic and social characteristics. When feminist theory attempts to describe women's experiences through analyzing patriarchy, sexuality, or separate spheres ideology, it often overlooks the role of race. Feminists thus ignore how their own race functions to mitigate some aspects of sexism and, moreover, how it often privileges them over and contributes to the domination of other women. * * *[1]

This section first explores various anti-essentialist critiques of feminism and then considers theories moving toward a critical race feminism.

1. Kimberlé Crenshaw, Demarginalizing the Intersection of Race and Sex: A Black Feminist Critique of Antidiscrimination Doctrine, Feminist Theory and Antiracist Politics, 1989 U. Chi. Legal F. 139, 139–40, 154.

a. Essentialist Critiques of Feminism

PATRICIA A. CAIN, FEMINIST JURISPRUDENCE: GROUNDING THE THEORIES

4 Berkeley Women's L.J. 191, 191, 201–03, 205, 207, 209–10, 212–14 (1989).

* * * [F]eminist legal theorists often ignore, or at best marginalize, lesbian experience. I call this the problem of the invisible lesbian. It is a problem that has serious consequences for the building of feminist legal theory.

* * *

One might expect cultural feminists and dominance theorists who engage in legal scholarship (such as Gilligan and MacKinnon, respectively) to acknowledge the relevance of lesbian experience in their writings. It is particularly surprising to discover the invisible lesbian problem in the work of cultural feminists. In disciplines other than law, feminist theorists working to reclaim women's culture and its values have often focused on lesbian community. But in legal scholarship, discussions of female value focus on "woman as mother."

* * *

Dominance theorists also tend to ignore lesbian experience. Catharine MacKinnon, for example, has argued that women are constantly and always subordinated to men. In MacKinnon's view, any special abilities for caring and connection come, not from the positive aspects of motherhood, but from the negative effects of subordination. Women build webs of connection to survive the subordination. "Women value care because men have valued us according to the care we give them...."

To the claim that lesbian experience is different, that lesbians are not subordinate to men, that their care is not male-directed, MacKinnon appears to have two different responses. Her first response is that exceptions do not matter. MacKinnon's intent is to offer a critique of the structural condition of women as sexual subordinates and not to make existential claims about all women. It does not affect her theory that *all* women are not always subordinated to men. Thus, for MacKinnon, lesbian experience of non-subordination is simply irrelevant.

Her second response is more troubling. It goes beyond the assertion that lesbian experience is irrelevant; it denies the claim that lesbian experience is free from male domination.

> Some have argued that lesbian sexuality—meaning here simply women having sex with women, not with men—solves the problem of gender by eliminating men from women's voluntary sexual encounters. Yet women's sexuality remains constructed under conditions of male supremacy; women remain socially defined as women in relation to men; the definition of women as men's inferiors remains sexual even if not heterosexual, whether men are present at the time or not.

I find this passage objectionable for several reasons. My primary objection is that MacKinnon has defined lesbian sexuality to suit her purposes ("*simply* women having sex with women"—i.e., with nothing else changed except that a woman replaces a man). Although I do not dispute that lesbian couples can sometimes ape their heterosexual counterparts, I am infuriated by MacKinnon's silencing of the rest of lesbian experience. Where is MacKinnon's feminist method? To whom does she choose to listen? Would it not enrich her theory to recognize the reality of non-subordination that some lesbians claim as their experiential reality and ask about its relevance to her underlying theory? And yet, because her theory is premised on a single commonality among women, sexual subordination, MacKinnon fails to see the relevance of the lesbian claim to non-domination, even when it stands * * * in front of her.

* * *

I believe that current feminist legal theory is deficient and impoverished because it has not paid sufficient attention to the real life experiences of women who do not speak the "dominant discourse." Elsewhere I have urged that feminist law teaching ought to include "listening to difference" and "making connections." Here I urge the same for feminist legal scholarship.

* * *

I ask those of you in the audience who are heterosexual to focus on an important love relationship in your life. This could be a present relationship or a past one, or even the relationship you hope to have. I ask you: how would you feel about this relationship if it had to be kept utterly secret? Would you feel "at one with the world" if a slight mistake in language ("we" instead of "I") could lead to alienation from your friends and family, loss of your job? Would you feel at one with your lover if the only time you could touch or look into each other's eyes was in your own home—with the curtains drawn? What would such self-consciousness do to your relationship?

* * *

* * * The invisibility of lesbian existence * * * removes the lesbian possibility from view. If there are no lesbians, the only possibility is heterosexuality. Men will assume all women are equally available as sex partners. Women will choose men and never question that choice.

If the choice is never questioned, can it be an authentic choice? Do heterosexual women really choose men or are they victims of false consciousness? And if they are victims of false consciousness, then how do we know that most women are heterosexual? Might they not choose otherwise if they were truly free to choose?

Marilyn Frye offers a challenge to feminist academics and I want to echo her in repeating it here for feminist legal theorists:

I want to ask heterosexual academic feminists to do some hard analytical and reflective work. To begin with, I want to say to them:

> I wish you would notice that you are heterosexual.
>
> I wish you would grow to the understanding that you choose heterosexuality.
>
> I would like you to rise each morning and know that you are heterosexual and that you choose to be heterosexual—that you are and choose to be a member of a privileged and dominant class, one of your privileges being not to notice.
>
> I wish you would stop and seriously consider, as a broad and longterm feminist political strategy, the conversion of women to a woman-identified and woman-directed sexuality. . . .[107]

Frye reports that a typical response by heterosexual women to such inquiries is that, although they may understand what she is saying, they cannot just up and decide to be lesbian. I, too, have women colleagues and friends who similarly respond, with a shake of the head, that they are hopelessly heterosexual, that they just are not sexually attracted to women.

Frye says that she wants to ask such women (and so do I), "Why not? Why don't women turn you on? Why aren't you attracted to women?" These are serious questions. Frye encourages heterosexual women to consider the origins of their sexual orientation:

> The suppression of lesbian feeling, sensibility, and response has been so thorough and so brutal for such a long time, that if there were not a strong and widespread inclination to lesbianism, it would have been erased from human life. There is so much pressure on women to be heterosexual, and this pressure is both so pervasive and so completely denied, that I think heterosexuality cannot come naturally to many women; I think that widespread heterosexuality among women is a highly artificial product of the patriarchy. . . . I want heterosexual women to do intense and serious consciousness-raising and exploration of their own personal histories and to find out how and when in their own development the separation of women from the erotic came about for them. I would like heterosexual women to be as actively curious about how and why and when they became heterosexual as I have been about how and why and when I became lesbian.[110]

* * *

* * * I, and other lesbians who live our private lives removed from the intimate presence of men do indeed experience time free from male domination. When we leave the male-dominated public sphere, we come home to a woman-identified private sphere. That does not mean that the patriarchy as an institution does not exist for us or that the patriarchy

---

107. Frye, *A Lesbian Perspective on Women's Studies* 194, 196 (M. Cruikshank ed., 1982).

110. Id. at 196–97.

does not exist during the time that we experience freedom from male domination. It means simply that we experience significant periods of nonsubordination, during which we, as women, are free to develop a sense of self that is our own and not a mere construct of the patriarchy.

* * *

The problem with current feminist theory is that the more abstract and universal it is, the more it fails to relate to the lived reality of many women. One problem with much feminist legal theory is that it has abstracted and universalized from the experience of heterosexual women. Consider again Marilyn Frye's challenge to heterosexual academic feminists: "I wish you would notice that you are heterosexual. I wish you would grow to the understanding that you choose heterosexuality . . . that you are and choose to be a member of a privileged and dominant class, one of your privileges being not to notice."

* * *

My "lesbian standpoint" enables me to see two versions of reality. The dominant reality, which I experience as "theirs," includes the following: lesbians are not mothers, all women are dominated by men, male relationships are valuable and female relationships are not, lesbian is a dirty word, lesbians are sick, women who live alone desire men, women who live together desire men, no one knows a lesbian, lesbians don't have families, all feminist legal theorists are heterosexual, all women in this room are heterosexual, lesbians are sex, most women are heterosexual and not lesbian.

By contrast, the reality that I live, the reality I call "mine," includes the following: some mothers are lesbian, many women are lesbian, many lesbian women are not dominated by men, many women do not desire men, lesbian is a beautiful word, lesbians are love, love is intimacy, the heterosexual/lesbian dichotomy is false, all lesbians are born into families, lesbians are family, some feminist legal theorists are lesbian, lesbians are brave.

Why is the lesbian so invisible in feminist legal theory? Why is "my reality" so different from "their reality?" And which reality is true? For the postmodernist, the last question is meaningless. But the first two are not.

TRINA GRILLO, ANTI-ESSENTIALISM AND INTERSECTIONALITY: TOOLS TO DISMANTLE THE MASTER'S HOUSE

10 Berkeley Women's L.J. 16, 17–22, 24–25, 27–30 (1995).

The basis of intersectionality and anti-essentialism is this:

Each of us in the world sits at the intersection of many categories: She is Latina, woman, short, mother, lesbian, daughter, brown-eyed, long-haired, quick-witted, short-tempered, worker, stubborn. At any one moment in time and in space, some of these categories are central to her being and her ability to act in the world. Others matter not at all. Some categories, such as race, gender, class, and sexual orientation, are important most of the time. Others are rarely important. When something or someone highlights one of her categories and brings it to the fore, she may be a dominant person, an oppressor of others. Other times, even most of the time, she may be oppressed herself. * * *

I am going to talk now about intersectionality and anti-essentialism and will begin by talking about them separately. I believe these two concepts embody what is essentially the same critique, but made from two different starting points. For simplicity's sake, as I continue I am often going to talk about them together.

Intersectionality

Above, I described a single, whole woman. Yet if we turn the traditional tools of legal analysis upon this woman, we find she is someone entirely different. She is fragmented, capable of being only one thing at a time. For example, under a traditional legal approach, when her situation is analyzed as a woman, it is not analyzed as a Latina. She is a mother or a worker, but never both at the same time. Her characteristics are not connected one to the other; instead, they exist separately, suspended in time and space. This fragmenting of identity by legal analysis, a fragmenting entirely at odds with the concrete life of this woman, is the subject of the intersectionality critique.

* * * Kimberlé Crenshaw explodes the discussion of race and gender discrimination in her work on intersectionality. She notes that women of color stand at the intersection of the categories of race and gender, and that their experiences are not simply that of racial oppression plus gender oppression. One case she uses for her analysis says it all: When a group of Black women faced discrimination, they were held to have no legal cause of action because neither white women nor Black men were discriminated against in the same way. Therefore, they were recognized as victims of neither race nor gender discrimination. Makes perfect sense. And, of course, you have all seen the many newspaper articles talking about the progress of "women and Blacks"; Black women are completely lost in this description.

* * *

The intersectionality critique has been extended by both Stephanie Wildman and Elvia Arriola.[10] Both note that while Professor Crenshaw discusses a woman standing at the single intersection of race and gender, in fact we all stand at multiple intersections of our fragmented legal

10. Stephanie Wildman, Language and Silence: Making Systems of Privilege and Subordination Visible, in Critical Race Theory: The Cutting Edge (Richard Delgado ed., 1995); Elvia Arriola, Gendered Inequality: Lesbians, Gays and Feminist Legal Theory, 9 Berkeley Women's L.J. 103 (1994).

selves. Professor Arriola notes that a single discriminatory act can be based on many characteristics of the victim and calls for a radical dismantling of the traditional analytical framework. Professor Wildman supplies the necessary element for this dismantling. She explains why the "woman" experience of, for example, a woman of color is different from that of a white woman. In every set of categories there is not only subordination, but also its counterpart, privilege.

* * *

To look at white, middle-class women as subordinated *as women* is accurate as far as it goes, but their experience of oppression is not interchangeable with the oppression of non-white, non-middle-class women. The whiteness and middle-class status supply privilege even as the femaleness conveys oppression.

Anti–Essentialism

Essentialism is the notion that there is a single woman's, or Black person's, or any other group's, experience that can be described independently from other aspects of the person—that there is an "essence" to that experience. An essentialist outlook assumes that the experience of being a member of the group under discussion is a stable one, one with a clear meaning, a meaning constant through time, space, and different historical, social, political, and personal contexts.

The perceived need to define what "women's" experience is and what oppression "as women" means has prompted some feminists to analyze the situation of woman by stripping away race and class. To be able to separate out the oppressions of race and class (as well as sexual orientation and other bases of oppressions), the theory goes, we must look at someone who is not experiencing those oppressions and then we will see what oppression on the basis of gender alone looks like. This approach, however, assumes that the strands of identity are separable, that the experience of a white woman dealing with a white man, or raising a white child, is the same experience that a Black woman has dealing with a Black man, or raising a Black child. But as the intersectionality critique has taught us, they are different and not just additively.

Race and class can never be just "subtracted" because they are in ways inextricable from gender. The attempt to subtract race and class elevates white, middle-class experience into the norm, making it the prototypical experience. * * *

For a Black woman, race and gender are not separate, but neither are they for white women. White women often think of themselves as "without a race" rather than as white. Thus, exploring white women's experiences, although a worthy task, does not produce a picture of a raceless "essential woman." * * *

* * *

In a thoughtful and at times devastating critique, Angela Harris has shown how essentialism in feminist legal theory has betrayed feminism's promise to listen to the experiences of real women.[20] Her suggestion is that we focus on the notion of multiple consciousness as an appropriate way "to describe a world in which people are not oppressed only or primarily on the basis of gender, but also on the bases of race, class, sexual orientation and other categories in inextricable webs." Those of us who are outsiders or who do not fit neatly within standard categories have various voices within ourselves. We speak partly with one voice and partly with another, going back and forth, a process that Mari Matsuda has said can lead to genius or madness or both.[22]

But remember, we speak with multiple voices only because we have categories that describe these voices as separate from one another. Let's think for a minute about something that is in truth impossible to imagine—that the Latina mother I first described was the definer of categories. She would not have to speak with multiple voices, because once she said she was, for example, Latina (or lesbian, or a woman), we would automatically know she was these other things. In fact, a whole different set of categories would exist. We cannot even begin to speculate what these categories might be because we are all still ordering our world by the categories given us by the dominant culture. We have no words and perhaps no circuits in our brains for thinking about these other categories. But suppose my Latina mother (by this shorthand, I identify what are for me her most salient qualities) was the definer. We could then leave it to those whose wholeness was not included in her described categories to say, "Wait, I need to add my voice to this. When you talk about women, why are you automatically assuming they are Latinas, lesbian, and working class? Why does woman, unmodified, have to mean that? Don't make me fragment parts of my identity by talking about women and whites as if they were mutually exclusive categories; after all, it *is* possible to be a woman and be white at the same time." And then the Latina mother could say, "Well, I appreciate what you're saying and I think we need to take into account your differences. Perhaps we can give you ten minutes at the end of the program. And next time we'll make sure we have a white face on the panel. But, we're all in this together, and by putting forth your separate identity you're making it hard for us to fight the patriarchy."

Some have described the anti-essentialism and intersectionality critiques as dangerous in that, if carried to their furthest conclusions, they make it impossible to talk of any oppression. If each woman, if each Black, has a different experience, how can one say that women as women, or Blacks as Blacks, are oppressed? How can we use the feminist method of paying attention to our experience, without being essentialist ourselves?

---

20. Angela P. Harris, Race and Essentialism in Feminist Legal Theory, 42 Stan. L. Rev. 581, 587 (1990).

22. Mari Matsuda, When the First Quail Calls: Multiple Consciousness as Jurisprudential Method, 11 Women's Rts. L. Rep. 7, 8 (1989).

* * * If we emphasize our differences, then do we not risk losing all credence *as women*? * * *

I think it is important to emphasize that essentialism is not always a bad thing; however, unconscious, self-protective, self-advancing essentialism is. The question is whether the essentialism, which is sometimes unavoidable, is explicit, is considered temporary, and is contingent.

* * *

Lessons To Be Learned From the Anti-Essentialism and Intersectionality Critiques

Now that I have summarized the anti-essentialism and intersectionality critiques of feminist legal theory, I want to talk about at least three lessons they bring to our own work.

Lesson One

The anti-essentialism and intersectionality critiques teach us to look carefully at what is in front of our faces. When things are being described in ways contrary to our sensory experiences, we must pay particular attention. * * *

* * *

* * * [R]ace is not a biological concept, but a social and historical construct. The reason that I grew up considering myself, as we then said, Negro, is that a racist system described me in that way. Most Blacks in the United States are persons of "mixed blood," if such a thing can be said to exist, and have both white and Black ancestors. If there were such a thing as a biological white, I would be at least half that, and so would many other Blacks. However, the fact that race is an historical and social construct certainly does not mean that it does not exist. Experiences, histories, and communities have all developed around this concept; so if we abandon race, we abandon communities that may have been initially formed as a result of racism but have become something else entirely.

* * *

If we accept the definition of Black which we have been given—a definition which historically defined anyone with "one drop of Black blood" as Black—we ignore the existence of multiracial people. We ignore people whose experiences may be different from those experiences which have been defined as constituting the Black experience—that is, the "essentialized" Black experience. By so essentializing, we assume that the taxonomy of race proposed by nineteenth-century white supremacists—that human beings can be classified into four races and everyone fits neatly into one slot—is a valid one. On the other hand, if we do classify multiracial people as Black, the potential for group solidarity is much greater. "We are all Black," we say. "You cannot divide us."

* * *

Lesson Two

Another way that anti-essentialism and intersectionality critiques help us is by keeping us from being diverted by what Regina Austin calls "the running of the oppression sweepstakes."[39]

* * * The lessons of anti-essentialism and intersectionality are that the oppressions cannot be dismantled separately because they mutually reinforce each other. Racism uses sexism as its enforcer. Homophobia enforces sexism by making people pay a heavy price for departing from socialized gender roles. And those of us who are middle-class, or members of otherwise privileged elites, can be used as unwitting perpetuators of the subordination of others.

We have spent a lot of time arguing over whose pain is greater. That time would be better used trying to understand the complex ways that race, gender, sexual orientation, and class (among other things) are related.

A note: To say that the oppressions are related does not mean that they are the same. It is dangerous at the least to expect that experiencing one oppression means that one understands the others. In fact, to expect so is disrespectful in that it wipes out the true, lived experience of that group in exchange for one's own, self-serving fantasy.

Lesson Three

We all have the impulse to essentialize. It is built into our brains. This means it is important to remember who we are. Even though we may be "underrepresented" persons in many ways, many of us are living in this very master's house that we are hoping to help dismantle. We may be living in the basement, and the others in the house are not always particularly nice to us, but our view is still shaped by where we are situated.

* * *

What this means in terms of process is that we should not deny this distance, but, as Regina Austin has advised, acknowledge it and attempt to bridge it.[43] What this means is that although our own experience is our touchstone, we must be careful about generalizing from that experience. In other words, we must be careful about essentializing the experiences of persons in the group to which we belong. I certainly cannot speak for all Black persons, Latinas, or women. What I can do is to pay careful attention to the lives and material conditions of women who are underrepresented in the law and to believe that their struggles have meaning and have much to teach me and the world. What I can also do is help their voices be heard, not by presuming to speak for them, but rather by doing

39. Regina Austin, Sapphire Bound!, 1989 Wis. L. Rev. 539, 546.

43. Austin, supra note 39, at 545.

what I can to put a microphone in front of them. What I can do is to work where I am today to make these changes.

* * *

Then we have the problem of determining which voices we need to help bring forward. When I told you about the Latina mother, I told you that in some situations she was dominant, privileged; in others, perhaps most, she was subordinated. The dangerous thing for her would be to go through life as if she were always subordinated, because she then might not notice situations in which she was ignoring someone else's voice. We need to notice the areas in which we are privileged, and in those areas we need to be careful to listen to the concrete, lived experiences of those who are less privileged. Although I am always willing to talk to the very privileged, I generally assume, I think rightly, that I have heard their story.

Anti-essentialism and intersectionality are checks on us; they help us make sure that we do not speak for those we cannot speak for or ask others to share our agenda while they patiently wait for their own. * * *

Those of us who are part-time residents in the master's house have much to gain by taking this approach, which recognizes privilege. For our view may be in some ways more obstructed than the view of people who are comparatively less privileged. * * * Of course, it is easy to romanticize the vision of the outsiders. Some acts labelled resistant actually reproduce and support the status quo. Still, I think it is important to accept what I view as fact: That each of us has a limited view of the world, that we have a better chance of forming a vision of a post-patriarchal, post-racist society both by trusting in our own experiences and by seeking out voices that are drowned out by essentialism in all its forms.

NOTES ON ESSENTIALIST CRITIQUES OF FEMINISM

1. Angela P. Harris describes a personal story in which Cain and Grillo, at a 1988 meeting of the West Coast "fem-crits," "asked all the women present to pick out two or three words to describe who they were." Harris recounts: "None of the white women mentioned their race; all of the women of color did." Harris, Race and Essentialism in Feminist Legal Theory, 42 Stan. L. Rev. 581, 604 (1990). How do you tend to describe yourself? Do you identify your sex, race, sexual orientation, nationality, marital status, parenting status, educational background, religion, or other factors? Do you think it is still likely that only members of racial minorities include race or ethnicity? What about sex? Do all women tend to include "woman," "mother," or some other gendered term? Or are some women, particularly women in some or all minority groups, less likely to include a gendered term than are white women? What about men? Are white men more likely to include a gendered term than a racial term? Do you think it is likely that only lesbians and gay men identify their sexual orientation?

Which aspects of your identity are foremost for you? Do those aspects change from time to time? What circumstances determine which is foremost?

2. Do you agree with Crenshaw, Cain, and Grillo that feminist legal theorists should avoid analyzing sex inequality on its own, without also considering race, sexual orientation, or other aspects of identity? Is it ever possible to address sex inequality on its own? Are Crenshaw and Grillo arguing that race has been missing from feminist legal theory or that only one race has been included? Does silence about race always support white privilege? Does sex always have a race? How is Cain's approach similar yet different? Does sex always have a sexual orientation?

Similarly, does sex always have a socioeconomic class or educational background? Are many or even most of the differences between white and Black or Latina women based entirely on race, or are they associated also with class differences? Has the feminist agenda been skewed with respect to class as well as race and sexual orientation? How does anti-essentialist theory relate to the argument made by MacKinnon that liberal equality theory tends to benefit women who are already privileged?

3. Angela P. Harris describes Robin West's relational theory as essentialist by definition because West describes women as "ontologically distinct from men." Harris, above note 1, at 602. Do you agree with Harris that West's bracketing of issues of race leads "to the installation of white women on the throne of essential womanhood"? Id. at 603. How does this happen? What are some of the consequences? Is West's theory also essentialist with regard to lesbian women?

Harris also analyzes MacKinnon's dominance theory, expressing concern that MacKinnon often relegates Black women to footnotes or describes their experiences as just like white women's "only more so." Id. at 595, 601. How might such a deployment of race support white privilege? How can white feminist theorists acknowledge and resist that privilege?

4. Do you think that feminists can talk about women without committing the cognitive error of essentializing "women" or "woman"? How? Identify commonalities and differences between women across various forms of difference. Are these commonalities and differences based on stereotypes, personal experience, or empirical data? Why is it important sometimes to see commonalities among women? How can it be dangerous?

Think of the major items on the feminist agenda over the last thirty years or so. Even issues important to all women, such as domestic violence, often have in fact been addressed only in the context of the needs of heterosexual, white, middle-class women. For example, many domestic violence statutes do not cover domestic violence when women are domestic partners, as discussed in Chapter 4. Why do you think that feminist activists failed to include lesbians within the focus of many legal reforms?

5. What other subsets of women do feminist theories often fail to address? Beverly Encarguez Perez notes that while feminist theories have come to consider Black and Latina women, they still tend to overlook Asian American women. Perez, Woman Warrior Meets Mail-Order Bride: Finding an Asian American Voice in the Women's Movement, 18 Berkeley Women's L.J. 211, 211–14 (2003). Perez argues that stereotypes of Asians as "model minorities" who have achieved some measure of success have led feminists to believe that Asian American women "do not need the help of white America."

Id. at 14. How might Asian American women experience the intersection between race and gender differently than Black and Latina women? Why do you think there is so little analysis about their unique subordination? Must there be a critical mass of vocal individuals within nonmajority groups for feminist theory to begin to address them? Should feminist theory strive to cover as many women as possible while acknowledging that some may be left out, or might it be better to develop theories explicitly focused on certain groups of women?

6. How should conflicts of interest between and among women be resolved? For example, some white women may resist affirmative action that would benefit many women because it may also disadvantage white men. Are these women choosing solidarity with their white brothers, fathers, and husbands over solidarity with other women? Are they protecting their white privilege at the expense of achieving gender equality? See Sumi Cho, Commentary: Understanding White Women's Ambivalence Towards Affirmative Action: Theorizing Political Accountability In Coalitions, 71 UMKC L. Rev. 399, 404–07 (2002); Sylvia A. Law, White Privilege and Affirmative Action, 32 Akron L. Rev. 603, 618–28 (1999).

What about white women who remain silent about racial issues? Do they believe they are deferring to the views of women of color, or are they merely uncomfortable confronting white privilege? Janis L. McDonald discusses the "polite white" feminist, who graciously remains quiet and listens when confronted with questions about the essentializing aspects of her theories and then responds to such concerns with silence and absentmindedness. See McDonald, Why Do We Eat Our Young?: Journals As a Feminist Battleground: Looking in the Honest Mirror of Privilege: "Polite White" Reflections, 12 Colum. J. Gender & L. 650, 653–59 (2003). Might similar arguments be made about heterosexual women who remain silent about lesbian issues?

7. Though acknowledging the attractions of essentialism (intellectual ease, emotional safety, preservation of the power of a dominant group, and cognitive simplification), Angela Harris argues that "there are at least three major contributions that black women have to offer post-essentialist feminist theory: the recognition of a self that is multiplicitous, not unitary; the recognition that differences are always relational rather than inherent; and the recognition that wholeness and commonality are acts of will and creativity, rather than passive discovery." Harris, above note 1, at 605–08. What does she mean? Do you agree?

8. Compare racism within feminism with sexism within the civil rights movement. Do you agree with Crenshaw that both are obstacles to the advancement of Black women and to the development of policies and laws meeting their needs? How have the agendas of both the feminist and civil rights movements been skewed by sexism and racism, obscuring discrimination against Black women and impeding needed reforms? How can these problems be addressed?

Luke Charles Harris suggests that incorporating feminism within Black communities can help break down the patriarchal constructs that reinforce racism:

> We must confront the reality that patriarchal political visions are dangerous; among other things, they obscure concerns that should be at the heart of our political agenda. A feminist perspective affords us the opportunity to identify and take account of the ways in which race, class, gender, and sexual orientation intersect to shape the problems and interests of our entire community. Embracing feminism would require us to acknowledge that the racist stereotypes on which criminal justice policies are founded result from white supremacist views about Black men's maleness, as well as their Blackness.

Harris, The Challenge and Possibility for Black Males to Embrace Feminism, in Black Men on Race, Gender, and Sexuality 383, 383 (Devon W. Carbado ed., 1999). Do you agree? What aspects of patriarchy is Harris discussing? Is Harris suggesting that patriarchy, like sex, is always raced?

9. Derrick A. Bell has described ways in which racism has complicated relationships between Black women and men. Due to incarceration rates, for example, there is a shortage of young Black men in the Black community. In addition, Bell points to:

> The continuing powerlessness of black men[, which] affects black women as well, particularly strong black women. * * * Her strength makes her intolerant of weakness, particularly in those whose weakness threatens her survival. Thus, even though she may love a man, her contempt for weakness will come out. And if her man is black, you can believe that in this society there will be many opportunities for that weakness to be all too obvious—no matter how successful he is and how strong he tries to be. No matter how hard she tries to accept him as he is, her true estimate of his strength comes out in ways that her man reads as a lack of respect—and resents precisely because he knows damn well that because of this society's racism he can never earn the respect his woman wants to give, and cannot.

Bell, And We Are Not Saved: The Elusive Quest for Racial Justice 209–10 (1987). Bell describes how, for a Black man, resisting racism and sexism at the same time is therefore extraordinarily difficult. Do you agree? Is there a higher expectation for Black men to resist sexism because of their own struggles with racism? How might resisting racism and sexism at the same time also be difficult for Black women? How are the women Bell describes potentially engaging in sexism and/or racism? Is resistance to racism and sexism less complicated for white men or white women? Or for other men and women of color?

10. Are women in other subordinated groups likely to feel, as Black women often do, that they should keep quiet about gender inequities rather than publicly protest in ways that may undermine the solidarity of their group? How are such conflicts likely to be experienced by Latina women? Asian American women? Other nonwhite women? What about lesbians in the larger gay and lesbian movement? What about religious women?

11. Catharine MacKinnon and Robin West have each responded to anti-essentialist critiques of their work. MacKinnon resists "the notion that there is no such thing as the oppression of women as such":

> If white women's oppression is an illusion of privilege and a rip-off and reduction of the civil rights movement, we are being told that there is no such thing as a woman, that our practice produces no theory, and that there is no such thing as discrimination on the basis of sex.

MacKinnon, From Practice to Theory, or What is a White Woman Anyway?, 4 Yale J.L. & Feminism 13, 20 (1991). West describes the intersection of race and sex as raising "the most challenging set of problems facing feminism," but emphasizes "that the problem it highlights is *racism*, and specifically white racism, not essentialism." West, Caring for Justice 14–15 (1997). West goes on to argue:

> There are at least two pragmatic reasons to resist—or at least remain uncommitted toward—the seductive anti-essentialist premise that there are no necessary attributes which women share, and hence no "essence" that can inform either our political strategy or our moral discourse. The first is purely political: if one is concerned about furthering women's well-being, it won't do to deny the existence of women. The second, though, has less to do with the politics of women's equality and more to do with the quality of our public conversations. There is a real danger of cutting off fruitful inquiry if we cut off inquiry into sex and gender differences solely out of worries over stereotyping.

Id. at 19. What do you think of these responses? How might dominance and relational feminism recognize and incorporate the different experiences and interests of women of different colors and sexual orientations? In what ways are both theories grounded on an assumption that women's experiences are universal? Is it possible to talk about differences between women and men if women do not share an essential nature? Take a specific experience of many women, such as motherhood, and compare it across race, sexual orientation, and class. In what ways is it the same? In what ways is it different? Do dominance and relational feminists demand a commonality not to be found in the real world?

12. MacKinnon asks: "What is being a woman if it does not include being oppressed as one?" MacKinnon, above note 11, at 20. Similarly, West writes: "All women in this society, to take just one example, are vulnerable to rape and to a higher risk of serious injury from domestic violence than are men." West, above note 11, at 15. Does male violence, more than motherhood, unify women across race, sexual orientation, and class? Cain resists that idea in her excerpt above. Angela Harris writes that "the notion that women's commonality lies in their shared victimization by men 'directly reflects male supremacist thinking. Sexist ideology teaches women that to be female is to be a victim.' " Harris, above note 1, at 613 (quoting bell hooks). How might the identification of women as victims be inherent in any critical analysis of women's social status, and thus inherent in any form of feminism?

What are the dangers of defining women as victims of male violence? According to Allan Johnson:

> [T]he "victim feminism" criticism works because it draws attention away from men as victimizers and focuses instead on women who are victimized. In one sense, critics are correct that focusing on women as victims is counterproductive, but not because we should instead ignore victimiza-

tion altogether. The real reason to avoid an exclusive focus on women as victims is to free us to concentrate on the compelling fact that men are the ones who victimize, and such behavior and the patriarchal system that encourages it are the problem. Otherwise we might find ourselves concentrating on male victimization of women as something that happens to women without being done by men.

The shift in focus can be as simple as the difference between saying "Each year 100,000 women are sexually assaulted" and "Each year men sexually assault 100,000 women." * * *

Johnson, The Gender Knot, at 111 (emphasis in original). Would an anti-essentialist theorist agree with Johnson's assessment of the problem? With Johnson's assessment of the solution? Is defining women as victims equally dangerous for all women? Or is such a definition likely to miss both many of the positive aspects of women's lives as well as the ways in which women oppress other women? What about the ways women, or feminists, may oppress men? See the discussion of Janet Halley later in this chapter.

b. Toward a Critical Race Feminism

BERTA ESPERANZA HERNÁNDEZ-TRUYOL, LAS OLVIDADAS—GENDERED IN JUSTICE/GENDERED INJUSTICE: LATINAS, FRONTER AS AND THE LAW

1 J. Gender Race & Just. 353, 355–61, 368–71, 379 (1998).

The dearth of information on Latinas, regardless of the fields one researches, ranging from law to psychology and from education to poverty, is evidence that Latinas are *olvidadas* [the forgotten ones, feminine]. The Latina consistently is lost in the statistical reporting maze. She either falls under the general category of Latino, the male-gendered ethnic descriptive, or in the catch-all of "minority" women where the Latina is undifferentiated from the Black, Asian, American Indian, and other women of color. Yet, as this piece will show, some aspects of Latinas' lives such as language, family and culture are not shared with all other women of color. These differences merit disaggregated consideration, evaluation, and reporting on Latinas to permit an understanding of Latinas' particular needs, conditions and positions.

* * *

Demographics: *Las Olvidadas—Quienes Somos*

* * * Although Latinas/os share some aspects of culture and language, Latinas/os in the United States are a very diverse peoples of all colors and races, ethnicities, national origins, ancestries, religions, cultures and sexualities. Thus, despite the homogenizing effect of the single term Latina/o to describe a group, it is important to bear in mind the great heterogeneity of the individuals comprising the group. Indeed,

Latinas'/os' panethnicity raises questions about the ability, viability or practicality of studying Latinas/os *qua* Latinas/os.

Latinas themselves are a heterogeneous group. Some are citizens, and some not; some are recent arrivals and some have been here for generations; some speak Spanish, some English, some both. Depending on the country of origin/ancestry, colloquialisms in the Spanish language differ. Yet notwithstanding these differences, their burdens are similar: Latinas face major obstacles in every road of life due to the experience of multilayered discrimination. For Latinas, universal gender concerns are exacerbated and compounded by discrimination based on national origin, ethnicity, language, culture and race. In addition to the same challenges women face globally, Latinas also confront distinct issues, including an increased likelihood of raising children alone, rising poverty, poor educational status and a disproportionate threat from domestic violence and the AIDS virus. These multiple boundaries erect formidable obstacles to Latinas' attainment of justice.

Latinas are at the bottom of the pile regardless of what demographic factor one analyzes: education, work or income. Latinas/os are the least educated of all ethnic and racial groups in the United States. Significantly, the denial to Latinas of access to justice in education is particularly harmful as data suggests that the "biggest barrier for [Latinas' progress in society] is education."

In addition to the injustice confronted in the area of education, Latinas do not enjoy economic justice. Marginalized in the labor market, regardless of job distribution—whether we have glass-ceiling or sticky floor jobs—Latinas consistently are the lowest wage earners among all workers, including Non–Latina White Women (NLaW) and Black women. While in the 1980s the wages of women of color as a whole rose relative to the income of NLaW, Latinas' wages *declined*. Today, Latinas are twice as likely as NLaW to be in the lowest paying jobs.

Although the feminization of poverty phenomenon is global, it disproportionately affects women of color and, in particular, Latinas. Latinas, heads of households in 23% of families as compared with only 16% of non-Latina/o families, have the lowest median income of any group. Predictably, therefore, Latinas are also the least likely of all workers to have pension or health benefits. * * *

Even when employed outside of the home for pay, over a quarter of working Latinas are employed in the service industry. Of these jobs, one is prone to find Latinas working as maids, private household cleaners and servants, janitors, nursing aids and orderlies, cooks and child care takers—all very low paying jobs with little, if any, hope for advancement. Conversely, few Latinas hold managerial and professional positions. * * *

Sadly for Latinas, working full time does not ensure a "living wage" or even a non-poverty level wage. The latest figures available establish that a Latina earns $.54 for each dollar a NLaW earns. This 30–40% gap can be attributed to the multiple employment discriminations Latinas encounter as sex, race and ethnic "others." Adding insult to injury, a Latina with a college degree earns less than a NLaW with only a high school diploma.

Thus, as the previous discussion shows, regardless of classification, ranging from education to employment, from poverty to management, Latinas are truly *mujeres marginadas*—outsiders who define the margins. The following section explores structural bases of Latina marginalization.

Injustice—*Fronteras*/External Barriers: Social, Economic and Legal

Rights are meaningless to the population that cannot exercise them. Women's exclusion from participation in the public (indeed even the private) sphere:

> is a direct result of their systematic exclusion, by custom and by law, from access to key elements of empowerment: education, physical and social freedom of movement, and mentorship by those already in power. It is evidence of structural inequality that cannot be addressed effectively by refinement of theoretical concepts or discourse on rights.
>
> Structural inequality results in the perpetuation of injustice and ignorance despite all efforts to enact and enforce legal rights. The term "structural inequality" refers to the essential power imbalance between women and men, in which men have held most of the power to make decisions that affect women, families, and society. This imbalance results in fundamental injustice.

Significantly, the same "imbalance" is true in this country on the basis of race/ethnicity. Latinas have a third degree of subordination because of their culture. This triple crown of gendered, racialized/ethnicized, and cultured injustice requires a total re/construction to integrate the faces of Latinas in justice.

That discrimination against Latinas exists in all aspects of life resulting in the marginalization of Latinas in public discourse is patent. One simply needs to point to the lack of data on Latinas to confirm that they have not been the objects or subjects of social scientific concern. Latinas' plight is compounded by their multiple differences from the *normativo*. One major factor for Latinas' invisibility lies in the nature of the system.

In general, external barriers to women's advancement include elements of "organizational culture" as well as factors of "organizational structure." * * *

* * *

Fronteras in the Law

Legal Paradigms—The Conflation of Race, Ethnicity and Nationality

It is no surprise that in the justice system, structural barriers for Latinas exist, both in its theoretical foundation and in its practical, tangible manifestations. The normative legal paradigm in the United States presents an omnibus barrier for Latinas as many-layered others. For example, the system was created in the image of the founding fathers. Consequently, the system's image of what is normal is the white, Anglo/Western European, Judeo/Christian, English-speaking, educated, moneyed, propertied, heterosexual, physically and mentally able man—the quintessential "reasonable man." Pursuant to this structure, Latinas are a very different "other." Gender, race and ethnicity are three deviations from the norm all Latinas share. In addition, in light of the demographic information provided above, religion, class, language, culture, education and propertied status often add to the Latinas' differences from what has been constituted as normative.

In the United States, the dominant legal construct is ruled by a dichotomous black/white racial paradigm into which Latinas/os simply do not fit neatly. In this country, the rule of hypodescent, the so-called one-drop rule, defines as "Black" anyone who has one drop of Black blood, regardless of phenotype. Moreover, the construction of race in the United States conflates race with ethnicity. Indeed Latinas/os in this country are considered not white and also not black *because* they are Latinas/os—regardless of phenotype or taxonomy. To be sure, this presents an absurd conflict as race and ethnicity are different categories.

This paradigm is in sharp contrast with Latinas/os' (at least caribeñas/os') perspectives on race. While in the United States the one-drop rule operates to render Black anyone who has one drop of Black blood, the obverse is true in the Caribbean. There, the rule is *blanqueamiento* ("whitening") where one drop of white blood starts you en route to desirable whiteness. No doubt, both cultures (structures) favor the "white" (colonizer's) *tez* (complexion), but the approaches are dramatically different.

Thus, the result of the foundational black-white paradigm is to racialize ethnicity (and ethnicize race) with sometimes interesting, ironic, incoherent results. Existing race/ethnic categories of "white, not of Hispanic origin," "black, not of Hispanic origin," Hispanic, Asian, and American Indian are both under- and over-inclusive because, as they are race and ethnic categories, the de-racialization of ethnicity and the de-ethnicizing of race is wholly inappropriate. For example, an Afro-Cuban is both Black and Cuban, meaning s/he is *both* Black *and* of Hispanic origin, a dual classification that results in bias in both worlds. Interestingly, more recent categories' specific notations that Hispanics can be of any race still fail to recognize the realities and possibilities of the multiple discriminations to which Latinas/os are subjected on a daily basis.

These varied perspectives of race and the conflation/confusion of race and ethnicity, which also often become interchangeable and confused with national origin, stand in the way of Latinas' attaining justice and generate nativistic feelings. One manifestation is the rendering of all Latinas/os within the United States, regardless of citizenship, as "alien"—outsiders, others, different looking—a status that is compounded by the otherness effected by Spanish speaking and Spanish names.

The overarching racist/nativistic impetus behind recent immigration reform resulting from the confusion of the varied categories of race, ethnicity and nationality has even affected puertorriqueñas/os who are U.S. citizens by birth. Data show that even though the Immigration Reform and Control Act of 1986 (IRCA) does not apply to native-born citizens, IRCA's employer sanction provisions have had a negative impact on puertorriqueñas/os simply because they are *perceived* to be foreign because they "look" or "sound" different. One reported egregious rejection of a citizen's application (for an unskilled watch packer job) entailed a company's refusing the applicant's offer of a Puerto Rican birth certificate, social security card, and voter registration card as evidence of legal status and instead insisting on a "green card." The company lost the case, of course, and was chastised by the court for requesting from a citizen a document—the green card—that only foreigners can obtain. Nonetheless, this occurrence reveals the consequence of the dominant paradigm's conflation of race, ethnicity and nationality.

* * *

Fronteras in the Justice System

Beyond its theoretical underpinnings, other structural aspects of the justice system interfere with Latinas' attainment of justice. Latinas/os in the justice system who either provide or use services list the courts, police, social service agencies, governmental and welfare centers and the English-language media as discriminators.

[In this section, Hernández-Truyol describes the justice system experienced by Latinas in the United States, including crumbling, dirty facilities, language problems when negotiating courthouses and courtrooms, and the underrepresentation of Latinas/os on juries.]

* * *

The Role of Language

One perpetrator of Latinas' marginalization at myriad dimensions is language. For example, the gendered nature of Spanish, where the male gender is the norm in both the spoken and written forms, renders Latinas non-existent, foreign, alien, non-belonging in their own tongue. This characteristic of Spanish-speak facilitates the male norm's obliteration of Latinas in their own *ambiente*—home, work and church—and is Latinas' ghost wherever they travel.

Similarly, Spanish-accented English speech, unlike most other accented versions, be it Midwestern, Southern or Northeastern, results in a qualitative judgment about the speaker. The Latina is unintelligent, uneducated and illiterate. Spanish-accented English becomes code for the negative, undesirable other and not for the exotic other that an Australian or French accent would invoke.

In addition, a Latina is affected by language if she does not speak English. Lack of English language skills immediately renders Latinas foreign, though we may be native-born citizens whose jurisdiction has Spanish as the native, official tongue. For example, anyone born in Puerto Rico is a native-born, Spanish-speaking citizen. * * * Yet one's birthright citizenship is questioned because of speaking a language that is seen as a foreign tongue. All of these realities combine to marginalize, exclude and silence Latinas in virtually every aspect of their lives.

MARI J. MATSUDA, WE THE PEOPLE: JURISPRUDENCE IN COLOR

In Where Is Your Body? 21–27 (1996).

What is the jurisprudential tradition that sets apart the emerging view of law developed by people of color? It encompasses several key elements: historical memory, duality, criticism, race consciousness, pragmatism, and utopianism. The methodology of this jurisprudence is grounded in the particulars of social reality and the experience of people of color. This method is consciously historical and revisionist, attempting to know history from the bottom—from the fear and namelessness of the slave, from the broken treaties of the indigenous Americans, and from the daily experience of racial hierarchy. Understanding history from the bottom has forced these scholars to sources often ignored: journals, poems, the records of practitioners, the rhetoric of intellectuals of color, oral histories, the writers' own experience of life in a hierarchically arranged world, and even to the dreams they dream at night in their sleep.

This methodology, which rejects presentist, eurocentric descriptions of social phenomena, offers a unique description of law. The description is realist. It accepts the standard teaching of street wisdom: law is essentially political. It accepts as well the pragmatic use of law as a tool for social change and the aspirational core of law as the human dream of peaceable existence. If these views seem contradictory, that is consistent with another component of outsider jurisprudence—it is jurisprudence recognizing, struggling within, and utilizing contradiction, dualism and ambiguity.

The world described by legal scholars of color is one infused with racism. This description ties law to racism, showing that law is both a product and a promoter of racism. Like the feminists who have shown that patriarchy has had its own march through history, related to but distinct from the march of class struggle, scholars of color have also shown how racism must be understood as a distinct phenomenon.

The hopeful part of the description offered by outsider theorists is the recognition of the vulnerability of racist structures. The few who have managed to subject the many to conditions of degradation have used a variety of devices, from genocide to liberal doublespeak, that reveal the deep contradictions and instability inherent in any racist organization of social life. All the sorrow songs of outsider jurisprudence are thus tempered by an underlying descriptive message of the possibility of human social progress.

This progress can lead to a just world free of existing conditions of domination. The prescriptive message of this jurisprudence offers signposts to guide our way there—the focus on effects. The need to attack the effects of racism in order to attack its deep, hidden, tangled roots characterizes outsider thinking about law. Outsiders thus search for * * * legal tools that have a progressive effect, defying the habit of neutral principles to disappoint. They have proposed rachetlike measures—including affirmative action, reparations, and the criminalization of racist propaganda—to eliminate existing effects of oppression. These exciting doctrinal moves had their genesis in communities of people of color. Such measures are best implemented through formal rules, formal procedures, and formal concepts of rights because informality and oppression are frequent fellow travelers.

This identifies another tendency in jurisprudence by people of color: pragmatism and bottom-line instrumentalism in the use of law to achieve social change. Recall the litigants and lawyers of color bringing case after case challenging manifestations of racism throughout the history of this country. We have the famous cases—*Plessy, Brown, Korematsu, Lau*[4]—and the unknown cases that pepper the reporters of every state in this nation: cases of ordinary people who suffered some racist affront—lying landlord, a surly theater usher, a biased employer—and chose to fight back. One of my fantasies is that someday we will put up bronze plaques in all the theaters, train stations, schools, factories, and offices where these people, with their lovely cacophony of African–American, Asian, Latino, and Native–American surnames, fought their legal fights.

Bringing these elements together offers a challenge to classical and critical jurisprudence and a vision of law unlike any other. The historical memory and consciousness of race allies us with realist, critical legal theorists, and legal historians of the instrumentalist and law-and-society schools. Frederick Douglass, as we know, was a legal realist before Oliver Wendell Holmes.

What sets the jurisprudence of color apart, however, from the various modernist and postmodernist schools is the pragmatism rooted in concrete political organizing. In this sense, the jurisprudence of color forms an uneasy alliance with neoformalists, liberal reformists, and civil libertari-

4. *Plessy v. Ferguson*, 163 U.S. 537 (1896) (upholding a law requiring separate railway accommodations for whites and Blacks); *Brown v. Board of Education*, 347 U.S. 483 (1954) (holding that "[s]eparate educational facilities are inherently unequal" and that laws requiring or permitting racial segregation of schools violate equal protection); *Korematsu v. United States*, 323 U.S. 214 (1944) (upholding the internment of Japanese Americans during World War II on the ground of military necessity); and *Lau v. Nichols*, 414 U.S. 563 (1974) (holding that the school system's failure to provide English instruction to Chinese–American students with limited English proficiency violated equal protection).

ans in commitment to the use of the rule of law to fight racism and in an unwillingness to stand naked in the face of oppression without a sword, a shield, or at least a legal precedent in our hands. Scholars of color have attempted to articulate a theoretical basis for using law while remaining deeply critical of it.

As Jose Bracamonte pointed out in his foreword to the *Harvard Civil Rights—Civil Liberties* Minority Critique of Critical Legal Studies,[5] people of color cannot afford to indulge in deconstruction for its own sake. Our critique is goal oriented. The work produced by scholars of color ties pragmatic law reform to criticism and radical theory in a way no one on the jurisprudential scene, except for our feminist sisters, is doing.

Our alliance with feminism will be, I believe, most fruitful for us. Martha Minow's * * * foreword to the Supreme Court edition of the *Harvard Law Review* * * * grapples with the ideas of difference, duality, and the tantalizing promise of law.[6] Out of the struggle to understand the ways in which mainstream legal consciousness is white, male, Christian, able-bodied, economically privileged, and heterosexual will come a legal theory more profound than any other we have seen emanating from Anglo–American law schools. I speak of nothing less than transcendence of the self-declared bankruptcy of modernist thought and of something as dear as peace, freedom, and justice—words our poets, organizers, and legal scholars have never been too shy to speak.

To close, let me offer a road map of the work we are doing and suggestions for what we need to do to develop the jurisprudence of color.

First, description tells the untold stories of experiences of people of color under law and documents the facts of both our contributions and our exclusion. Using lawyerly expertise in reading legal documents, we should mine the primary sources to describe the role of race in American legal history.

Next, doctrinal development and critique has a long history in the experience of people of color. This is the work that stretches and shapes legal categories and advocates particular legal results. We should resist the trap of downgrading descriptive and doctrinal work. This trap is particularly prevalent at elite law schools. Descriptive and doctrinal work is not second-class work. It is work that in itself presents a sophisticated theoretical position, namely, that a legal response to the immediate needs of oppressed communities is a valuable method for deriving a theory of law and justice.

That brings us to the final category: theory. As phase one of the theoretical project, we need to critique the texts of law cases, casebooks, law review articles, and jurisprudence monographs—to show how mainstream writers fail to account for racism and the experience of outsiders. You no doubt have a favorite article in the critique genre, and I want to

5. Jose Bracamonte, Foreword, "Minority Critiques of the Critical Legal Studies Movement," *Harvard Civil Rights–Civil Liberties Law Review* 22 (1982): 297.

6. [Martha] Minow, "Justice Engendered," *Harvard Law Review* 101 (1987): 10.

beg for more. Where are our critiques, for example, of the standard textbooks used in the law schools?

The second stage of our theoretical work—theory building—will follow from critique. From identifying what is missing from standard jurisprudence it follows that we have ideas about what to fill in. We are here in the particular physical sense of our personal genealogies because we are the children of survivors, of people who judged correctly which fights to fight, when to lay low, and when to assert personhood. We are the children of generations before us who refused to accept the message of racial inferiority. Now I come dangerously close to privileging our experience in a way that is false. There are mistakes and villains in our histories. What I intend to suggest is only that there is something about life on this side of the color line that has theory-building potential. There is a reason that Justice Thurgood Marshall understands things not only about people of color but also about women, poor people, homosexuals, the physically disabled, and other outsiders that his colleagues in all their intelligence often fail to understand. It is not that being Black is a prerequisite to this understanding, as Justice Brennan demonstrates; rather, I want to identify and tap the source of Justice Marshall's vision that is related to his experience as a Black person.

Tapping that source is what jurisprudence is all about: the search for justice. The search for justice in the nuclear age carries an urgency previously unknown to humankind. As lawyers and theorists, let us go swiftly to our own histories and bring back to the law schools the truths we find there.

NOTES ON TOWARD A CRITICAL RACE FEMINISM

1. Hernández-Truyol argues that theories of inequality, including feminist legal theory, have failed to address the particular challenges facing Latina women. She therefore begins to articulate a feminist theory built around Latinas' interests and needs. Matsuda offers a pragmatic approach for addressing racial exclusions within feminism, calling for a dynamic use of feminist methods to theorize racism. How do the two approaches intersect? Do you think Matsuda offers Hernández-Truyol tools for continuing the development of her feminist theory built around Latinas' interests and needs? How might Hernández-Truyol use the increased description and story-telling urged by Matsuda to combat marginalization? Do you think it is possible to create a feminist theory that does not ignore or marginalize the very real differences among women of all colors?

2. Somewhat paradoxically, Matsuda also calls for more doctrinal work in legal education and scholarship, noting that it is currently denigrated at elite law schools, but people of color can benefit from renewed emphasis upon "formal rules, formal procedures, and formal concepts of rights." Have you experienced either of Matsuda's suggested approaches in your own law school classes? Have your professors infused doctrinal courses with issues of gender, race, class, and sexual orientation? Did you find those courses more effective? Why or why not?

3. When you think about "race," do you automatically think "black/white"? How does discrimination against Latinas/os operate? How is it similar to and how is it different from discrimination against Blacks? From discrimination against Asian Americans?

Scholars of color have criticized Black writers for analyzing racism in terms of a black-white paradigm which "distorts history and contributes to the marginalization of non-Black peoples of color." See, e.g., Juan F. Perea, The Black/White Binary Paradigm of Race: The Normal Science of American Racial Thought, 85 Calif. L. Rev. 1213, 1213 (1997); Eduardo Luna, How the Black/White Paradigm Renders Mexicans/Mexican Americans and Discrimination Against Them Invisible, 14 Berkeley La Raza L.J. 225 (2003). For responses to such criticisms, see Leslie Espinoza & Angela P. Harris, Afterword: Embracing the Tar-Baby—LatCrit Theory and the Sticky Mess, 10 La Raza L.J. 499 (1998); Athena D. Mutua, Shifting Bottoms and Rotating Centers: Reflections on LatCrit III and the Black/White Paradigm, 53 U. Miami L. Rev. 1177 (1999).

What about multi- or bi-racial women and men? Is it assumed that they will choose to identify with one race? Does feminism pressure women to make such a choice? See Carrie Lynn H. Okizaki, Comment, "What Are You?": Hapa-Girl and Multiracial Identity, 71 U. Colo. L. Rev. 463, 484–86 (2000).

4. The Supreme Court subjects classifications based on race and national origin to strict scrutiny. But distinctions based on language, culture, ethnicity, and immigration status are not subject to any scrutiny. For Latinas, can race and national origin be disentangled from language, culture, ethnicity, and immigration status? What are the consequences of the fact that, in reality, discrimination on the basis of race and national origin (constitutionally suspect) is entangled with discrimination on the basis of language, culture, ethnicity, and immigration status (not constitutionally suspect)? Is the black/white paradigm in American culture and constitutional law part of the problem?

Are culture and language intertwined with race discrimination for many Blacks as well? Under the black/white paradigm, does the Constitution reach, for example, discrimination on the basis of linguistic or cultural differences even for Blacks?

5. In what ways can feminist legal theorists address the problems that undocumented women face? How would most NLaW women in the United States answer that question?

Immigration status causes many problems for immigrant women, particularly when their partners are violent and abusive. A woman who is here illegally will be extremely reluctant to call the police or use the legal system to protect herself and her children from harm. For more thorough discussions of the many problems faced by immigrant women in abusive relationships, see, e.g., Cecelia M. Espenoza, No Relief For The Weary: VAWA Relief Denied For Battered Immigrants Lost In The Intersections, 83 Marq. L. Rev. 163 (1999); Linda Kelly, Stories From The Front: Seeking Refuge For Battered Immigrants In The Violence Against Women Act, 92 Nw. U. L. Rev. 665 (1998); Lee J. Teran, Barriers To Protection At Home And Abroad: Mexican Victims Of Domestic Violence And The Violence Against Women Act, 17 B.U. Int'l L.J. 1

(1999); Karin Wang, Battered Asian American Women: Community Responses from the Battered Women's Movement and the Asian American Community, 3 Asian L.J. 151 (1996).

What position should feminists take on immigration? Should feminists support open borders? Is any other position compatible with the needs of *all* women as women?

6. According to Matsuda, Justice Thurgood Marshall understood "things not only about people of color but also about women, poor people, homosexuals, the physically disabled, and other outsiders that his colleagues in all their intelligence often fail to understand." She also notes that Justice Brennan's similar ability to understand indicates that "being Black is [not] a prerequisite to this understanding." But she nevertheless sees "Justice Marshall's vision [as] related to his experience as a Black person." For examples of Justices Marshall's and Brennan's insight into cases involving sex discrimination, see the three important cases in Chapter 2 in which the Court failed to see sex discrimination: *Geduldig* (Marshall joins Brennan's dissent), *Feeney* (Brennan joins Marshall's dissent); and *Rostker* (Brennan joins Marshall's dissent). Do you agree with Matsuda that there is a connection between Justice Marshall's experiences as a Black person and his ability to see discrimination invisible to most of the Justices on the Court? If you answered yes, do you believe that this would be true of any justice of color, such as Justice Thomas or Justice Sotomayor? Is Matsuda making an essentialist claim? What exactly is the connection she sees?

7. Are female justices more likely, because of their experiences as women, to see important aspects about the realities of not just women, but also of poor people, people of color, homosexuals, and people with disabilities? Rosalind Dixon believes that Justice Ginsburg and former Justice O'Connor were better able to understand sex discrimination based on their own life experiences. Dixon hypothesizes that younger justices, such as Sonia Sotomayor and Elena Kagan, will be less likely to engage in feminist judging because they lack a consistent experience with sex discrimination. See Dixon, Female Justices, Feminism and the Politics of Judicial Appointment: A Re–Examination, 21 Yale J.L. & Feminism 297 (2010) (also detailing empirical evidence that there is little correlation between gender and feminist judging among female court of appeals judges).

8. During her confirmation hearings, now-Supreme Court Justice Sonia Sotomayor was questioned about a previous speech in which she stated: "I would hope that a wise Latina woman with the richness of her experiences would more often than not reach a better conclusion than a white male who hasn't lived that life." Sotomayor, A Latina Judge's Voice, 13 Berkeley La Raza L.J. 87, 92 (2002). What were your views of that statement before this class? How have your views changed, if at all?

How did Sotomayor's gender and race influence her confirmation hearings? At one point during the hearings, Senator Tom Coburn asked Sotomayor whether she thought individuals possessed an individual right to self-defense in their homes when under attack. After much back and forth, Sotomayor made a distinction based on the imminence of the threat, emphasizing that if, for instance, "the threat was in this room * * * and I go home

* * * get a gun, come back and shoot you, that may not be legal under New York law." Senator Coburn replied: "You'll have lots of explaining to do," borrowing one of Desi Arnaz's lines from "I Love Lucy." Sheryl Gay Stolberg & Neil A. Lewis, Sotomayor Fends Off Republican Queries on Abortion and Guns, N.Y. Times, July 16, 2009, at A18. Would such remarks ever be targeted toward a white man? Or even a Latino man? Or a white woman?

9. Are there dangers to analogizing between "ism's"? Trina Grillo and Stephanie Wildman have described a phenomenon they had observed at racially mixed academic meetings when analogies between race and sex were used:

> When a speaker compared sexism and racism, the significance of race was marginalized and obscured, and the different role that race plays in the lives of people of color and of whites was overlooked. The concerns of whites became the focus of discussion, even when the conversation had supposedly centered on race discrimination. Essentialist presumptions became implicit in the discussion: it would be assumed, for example, that "women" referred to white women and "Blacks" meant African American men. Finally, people with little experience in thinking about racism/white supremacy, but who had a hard-won understanding of the allegedly analogous oppression (sexism or some other ism), assumed that they comprehended the experience of people of color and thus had standing to speak on their behalf.
>
> * * *
>
> * * * We concluded that these phenomena have much to do with the dangers inherent in what had previously seemed to us to be a creative and solidarity-producing process—analogizing sex discrimination to race discrimination. These dangers were obscured by the promise that to discuss and compare oppressions might lead to coalition building and understanding. On an individual psychological level, we empathize with and understand others by comparing their situations with some aspects of our own. * * *
>
> * * *
>
> Comparing sexism to racism perpetuates patterns of racial domination by minimizing the impact of racism, rendering it an insignificant phenomenon—one of a laundry list of isms or oppressions that society must suffer. * * *

Grillo & Wildman, Obscuring the Importance of Race: The Implications of Making Comparisons between Racism and Sexism (Or Other Isms), in Stephanie Wildman, Privilege Revealed: How Invisible Preference Undermines America 85, 88–90 (1996). Have you seen the phenomena described by Grillo and Wildman? Did they occur in your classroom discussions of the similarities and differences between sex and race? Did you notice it? Are there ways this could have been avoided or minimized? How?

10. How would a critical race feminist agenda differ from a formal equality agenda? A dominance feminist agenda? A relational feminist agenda?

5. POSTMODERN FEMINISMS

Beginning in the late 1980s, feminist legal theorists began to engage with various forms of critical theory being developed and embraced by other parts of the academy. This theoretical engagement permitted feminist jurisprudence to explore new directions and new solutions to issues of women's inequality. Much of this work is difficult to categorize, but Ann Scales uses the umbrella term poststructuralism to refer to a "group of intellectual efforts" focused on "exposing and subverting supposed deep structures."[2] This section will describe legal feminists' engagement with one of those efforts, postmodernism.

MARY JOE FRUG, A POSTMODERN FEMINIST LEGAL MANIFESTO (AN UNFINISHED DRAFT[a])

105 Harv. L. Rev. 1045, 1046–52, 1055 (1992).

One "Principle"

The liberal equality doctrine is often understood as an engine of liberation with respect to sex-specific rules. This imagery suggests the repressive function of law, a function that feminists have inventively sought to appropriate and exploit through critical scholarship, litigation, and legislative campaigns. Examples of these efforts include work seeking to strengthen domestic violence statutes, to enact a model anti-pornography ordinance, and to expand sexual harassment doctrine.

The postmodern position locating human experience as inescapably within language suggests that feminists should not overlook the constructive function of legal language as a critical frontier for feminist reforms. To put this "principle" more bluntly, legal discourse should be recognized as a site of political struggle over sex differences.

This is not a proposal that we try to promote a benevolent and fixed meaning for sex differences. (See the "principle" below.) Rather, the argument is that continuous interpretive struggles over the meaning of sex differences can have an impact on patriarchal legal power.

Another "Principle"

In their most vulgar, bootlegged versions, both radical and cultural legal feminisms depict male and female sexual identities as anatomically determined and psychologically predictable. This is inconsistent with the semiotic character of sex differences and the impact that historical specificity has on any individual identity. In postmodern jargon, this treatment of sexual identity is inconsistent with a decentered, polymorphous, contingent understanding of the subject.

---

2. Scales, Poststructuralism on Trial, in Feminist and Queer Legal Theory: Intimate Encounters, Uncomfortable Conversations 395, 396 (Martha Albertson Fineman, Jack E. Jackson & Adam P. Romero eds., 2009).

a. Mary Joe Frug was murdered on April 4, 1991. She had not yet completed this article at the time of her death.

Because sex differences are semiotic—that is, constituted by a system of signs that we produce and interpret—each of us inescapably produces herself within the gender meaning system, although the meaning of gender is indeterminate or undecidable. The dilemma of difference, which the liberal equality guarantee seeks to avoid through neutrality, is unavoidable.

* * *

II. Applying Postmodern "Principles": Law and the Female Body

A. Introduction

* * *

Regardless of how commonplace the constructed character of sex differences may be, particular differences can seem quite deeply embedded within the sexes—so much so, in fact, that the social construction thesis is undermined. When applied to differences that seem especially entrenched—differences such as masculine aggression or feminine compassion, or differences related to the erotic and reproductive aspects of women's lives, social construction seems like a clichéd, improbable, and unconvincing account of experience, an explanation for sex differences that undervalues "reality." This reaction does not necessarily provoke a return to a "natural" explanation for sex differences; but it does radically stunt the liberatory potential of the social construction thesis. One's expectations for law reform projects are reduced; law might be able to mitigate the harsh impact of these embedded traits on women's lives, but law does not seem responsible for constructing them.

* * * One of my objectives is to explain and challenge the essentializing impulse that places particular sex differences outside the borders of legal responsibility. Another objective is to provide an analysis of the legal role in the production of gendered identity that will invigorate the liberatory potential of the social construction thesis.

I have chosen the relationship of law to the female body as my principal focus. I am convinced that law is more cunningly disguised but just as implicated in the production of apparently intractable sex-related traits as in those that seem more legally malleable. Since the anatomical distinctions between the sexes seem not only "natural" but fundamental to identity, proposing and describing the role of law in the production of the meaning of the female body seems like the most convincing subject with which to defend my case. * * * I will argue that legal rules—like other cultural mechanisms—encode the female body with meanings. Legal discourse then explains and rationalizes these meanings by an appeal to the "natural" differences between the sexes, differences that the rules themselves help to produce. The formal norm of legal neutrality conceals the way in which legal rules participate in the construction of those meanings.

The proliferation of women's legal rights during the past two decades has liberated women from some of the restraining meanings of femininity. This liberation has been enhanced by the emergence of different feminisms over the past decade. These feminisms have made possible a stance of opposition toward a singular feminine identity; they have demonstrated that women stand in a multitude of places, depending on time and geographical location, on race, age, sexual preference, health, class status, religion, and other factors. Despite these significant changes, there remains a common residue of meaning that seems affixed, as if by nature, to the female body. Law participates in creating that meaning.

I will argue that there are at least three general claims that can be made about the relationship between legal rules and legal discourse and the meaning of the female body:

1. Legal rules permit and sometimes mandate the terrorization of the female body. This occurs by a combination of provisions that inadequately protect women against physical abuse and that encourage women to seek refuge against insecurity. One meaning of "female body," then, is a body that is "in terror," a body that has learned to scurry, to cringe, and to submit. Legal discourse supports that meaning.

2. Legal rules permit and sometimes mandate the maternalization of the female body. This occurs with the use of provisions that reward women for singularly assuming responsibilities after childbirth and with those that penalize conduct—such as sexuality or labor market work—that conflicts with mothering. Maternalization also occurs through rules such as abortion restrictions that compel women to become mothers and by domestic relations rules that favor mothers over fathers as parents. Another meaning of "female body," then, is a body that is "for" maternity. Legal discourse supports that meaning.

3. Legal rules permit and sometimes mandate the sexualization of the female body. This occurs through provisions that criminalize individual sexual conduct, such as rules against commercial sex (prostitution) or same sex practices (homosexuality) and also through rules that legitimate and support institutions such as the pornography, advertising, and entertainment industries that eroticize the female body. Sexualization also occurs, paradoxically, in the application of rules such as rape and sexual harassment laws that are designed to protect women against sex-related injuries. These rules grant or deny women protection by interrogating their sexual promiscuity. The more sexually available or desiring a woman looks, the less protection these rules are likely to give her. Another meaning of "female body," then, is a body that is "for" sex with men, a body that is "desirable" and also rapable, that wants sex and wants raping. Legal discourse supports that meaning.

These groups of legal rules and discourse constitute a system that "constructs" or engenders the female body. The feminine figures the rules pose are naturalized within legal discourse by declaration—"women are (choose one) weak, nurturing, sexy"—and by a host of linguistic strategies that link women to particular images of the female body. By deploying these images, legal discourse rationalizes, explains, and renders authoritative the female body rule network. The impact of the rule network on women's reality in turn reacts back on the discourse, reinforcing the "truth" of these images.

Contractions of confidence in the thesis that sex differences are socially constructed have had a significant impact on women in law. Liberal jurists, for example, have been unwilling to extend the protection of the gender equality guarantee to anatomical distinctions between female and male bodies; these differences seem so basic to individual identity that law need not—or should not—be responsible for them. Feminist legal scholars have been unable to overcome this intransigence, partly because we ourselves sometimes find particular sex-related traits quite intransigent. Indeed, one way to understand the fracturing of law-related feminism into separate schools of thought over the past decade is by the sexual traits that are considered unsusceptible to legal transformation and by the criticisms these analyses have provoked within our own ranks.

The fracturing of feminist criticism has occurred partly because particular sex differences seem so powerfully fixed that feminists are as unable to resist their "naturalization" as liberal jurists. But feminists also cling to particular sex-related differences because of a strategic desire to protect the feminist legal agenda from sabotage. Many feminist critics have argued that the condition of "real" women makes it too early to be post-feminist. The social construction thesis is useful to feminists insofar as it informs and supports our efforts to improve the condition of women in law. If, or when, the social construction thesis seems about to deconstruct the basic category of woman, its usefulness to feminism is problematized. How can we build a political coalition to advance the position of women in law if the subject that drives our efforts is "indeterminate," "incoherent," or "contingent?"

I think this concern is based upon a misperception of where we are in the legal struggle against sexism. I think we are in danger of being politically immobilized by a system for the production of what sex means that makes particular sex differences seem "natural." If my assessment is right, then describing the mechanics of this system is potentially enabling rather than disempowering; it may reveal opportunities for resisting the legal role in producing the radical asymmetry between the sexes.

I also think this concern is based on a misperception about the impact of deconstruction. Skeptics tend to think, I believe, that the legal deconstruction of "woman"—in one paper or in many papers, say, written over the next decade—will entail the immediate destruction of "women" as identifiable subjects who are affected by law reform projects. Despite the healthy, self-serving respect I have for the influence of legal scholarship and for the role of law as a significant cultural factor (among many) that contributes to the production of femininity, I think "women" cannot be eliminated from our lexicon very quickly. The question this paper addresses is not whether sex differences exist—they do—or how to transcend them—we can't—but the character of their treatment in law.

* * *

[Frug then uses the example of anti-prostitution rules to discuss the ways that the regulation of prostitution, through law and "a network of cultural practices," terrorize and sexualize women. Prostitution is discussed in more detail in Chapter 4. Of particular note here are the ways such rules also relate to marriage and maternalization:]

* * * The terrorization of sex workers affects women who are not sex workers by encouraging them to do whatever they can to avoid being asked if they are "for" illegal sex. Indeed, marriage can function as one of these avoidance mechanisms, in that, conventionally, marriage signals that a woman has chosen legal sex over illegal sex.

* * * Regardless of whether a woman is terrorized or sexualized, there are social incentives to reduce the hardships of her position, either by marrying or by aligning herself with a pimp. In both cases she typically becomes emotionally, financially, physically, and sexually dependent on and subordinate to a man.

* * * I argue that the dominated female body does not fully capture the impact of anti-prostitution rules on women. This is because anti-prostitution rules also maternalize the female body, by virtue of the interrelationship between anti-prostitution rules and legal rules that encourage women to bear and rear children. The maternalized female body triangulates the relationship between law and the meanings of the female body. It proposes a choice of roles for women.

* * * The legal rules that criminalize prostitution are located in a legal system in which other legal rules legalize sex—rules, for example, that establish marriage as the legal site of sex and that link marital sex to reproduction by, for example, legitimating children born in marriage. As a result of this conjuncture, anti-prostitution rules maternalize the female body. They not only interrogate women with the question of whether they are for or against prostitution; they also raise the question of whether a woman is for illegal sex or whether she is for legal, maternalized sex.

TRACY E. HIGGINS, "BY REASON OF THEIR SEX": FEMINIST THEORY, POSTMODERNISM, AND JUSTICE

80 Cornell L. Rev. 1536, 1588–91, 1593 (1995).

[I]f we surrender the modernist conception of truth, how are we to choose among multiple and conflicting accounts? More precisely, if postmodernism requires feminists to relinquish the claim to tell truer stories of women's lives, can feminists nevertheless claim to tell better stories?

Feminists have reacted to this challenge of postmodernism in at least two ways. While conceding the contingency of any particular account of women's experience, some have attempted to preserve feminist narrative authority by privileging feminist method, particularly standpoint epistemology. Their effort rests on the assumption that women's stories that are a product of feminist methodology reflect women's experience more completely, in a form undistorted (or less distorted) by patriarchy. For example, Catharine MacKinnon, although suggesting that sexuality is a product of social construction, posits an identity of woman that has been distorted or silenced under patriarchy and that may be discoverable (albeit imperfectly) through feminist method. These accounts of women's experience are better, she suggests, not because they are truer to some ideal woman but simply because they are less constrained by the false consciousness produced by women's oppression.[242]

MacKinnon's reliance on the concept of social construction distinguishes her standpoint epistemology from more essentialist (and less postmodern) versions. She suggests that feminists should use consciousness-raising to expose the role of patriarchy in constructing women's experience and to begin to articulate a transformative vision of gender. She does not directly posit the existence of an authentic self that may be revealed through process. Nevertheless, her reliance on consciousness-raising does imply a belief in women's access to truth or at least to knowledge that may legitimately be privileged.

Other feminists have relied less on claims about women's relationship to truth than on the value of fuller process. Conceding that feminists cannot claim to know what is true, they suggest simply that more inclusive accounts or theories are better than less inclusive ones. Thus, they emphasize the inclusion of women's voices in the process, whether it be scientific or legal. For example, feminists in the natural sciences have argued that the inclusion of women as researchers and as research subjects has improved the development of scientific theory by making it more complete than it once was. In the legal realm, Mari Matsuda has argued that a concept of justice that takes into account the perspective of the subordinated can be accepted as better or more complete, even within a framework of contingent truth.[245] Similarly, Margaret Jane Radin has argued that the deliberate inclusion of marginalized groups serves as an antidote to what she terms the "bad coherence" problem that renders pragmatism (arguably) indifferent to social injustice.[246]

242. Compare MacKinnon, [Toward A Feminist Theory of the State (1990)], at 135 (rejecting women's accounts of sexual pleasure as products of sexual oppression) and MacKinnon, supra [Feminism Unmodified: Discourses on Life and Law (1987)], at 39 (criticizing analysis of sexual difference as "reaffirming what we have been") with MacKinnon, supra [Toward a Feminist Theory of the State (1990)], at 115 (explaining that "[t]reating some women's views as merely wrong, because they are unconscious conditioned reflections of oppression and thus complicitous in it, posits objective ground").

245. See, e.g., Matsuda, [Pragmatism Modified and the False Consciousness Problem, 63 S. Cal. L. Rev. 1763 (1990)], at [1]764–68; Mari J. Matsuda, Looking to the Bottom: Critical Legal Studies and Reparations, 22 Harv. C.R.-C.L. L. Rev. 323 (1987).

246. See Radin, [The Pragmatist and the Feminist, 63 S. Cal. L. Rev. 1699 (1990)], at 1705–11.

None of these efforts resolves the fundamental challenge posed by postmodernism: How do we argue effectively if we can no longer claim access to truth? Instead, these efforts attempt to replace a substantive vision of truth (a "true" definition of woman) with a non-substantive value scheme. In other words, rather than evaluate an account of gender against a particular conception of woman, these approaches encourage us to focus on whether the account is the product of a particular methodology or a sufficiently inclusive process. Of course, the privileging of such accounts simply reflects a normative decision—if not a decision about what is true, then a decision that certain methods or processes are preferred. Thus, we can accept an account of women's experience that emerges as a product of consciousness-raising as better (or truer) only to the extent that we accept the value of the methodology. A principle defined through the participation of marginalized groups is better (or truer) only to the extent that we accept broader participation as a component of what defines truth or justice or legitimacy. Feminists' reliance on method cannot, therefore, offer an exogenous basis for proving or supporting our substantive commitments any more than the Supreme Court's reliance on social science or biology. Rather, the privileging of women's voices implicit in feminist method simply reflects those commitments. Moving away from truth claims to process claims only shifts the arena of debate.

It is not surprising, then, that these approaches cannot definitively resolve conflicts among women's own accounts of their experiences. Indeed, focusing on such conflicts reveals the degree to which debates over both authority and method turn ultimately on substantive claims. * * *

* * *

Thus, rather than leading to the notion that all truths are equal, feminist antifoundationalism merely emphasizes the role of power in defining truth or in setting truth-defining rules. For example, although most feminists (though not all) would agree that reproductive control is essential to women's equality, the centrality of abortion rights is not "true" in the sense of deriving from some post-patriarchal reality. One may deem an equality-based theory of abortion that accounts for differences among women to be better than competing accounts premised on privacy or even anti-choice accounts only to the extent that it more successfully (meaning more persuasively) translates the complicated experience of abortion into the terms of legal discourse.

More generally, relinquishing a representational account of knowledge transforms feminist arguments from claims of authority to claims of advocacy. Feminism thus avoids the virtually unanswerable critique regarding the accuracy of a particular representation of women's experience. Instead, the validity of a position depends upon whether it offers a persuasive account of the connection between women's experience and substantive commitments to equality and justice. Feminism need not claim to do more than offer such an account.

NOTES ON POSTMODERN FEMINISMS

1. Based on the above excerpts, how would you define postmodernism? How would you define postmodern feminism? Jessica Knouse writes:

> Postmodern thinkers * * * view individual identity as a product of the existing socially constructed categories. The range of potential identities is limited by the scope of the available categories. Individuals cannot transcend their own perspective; they cannot think or feel without reference to externally constructed categories. * * *
>
> Because individual identity is considered to be entirely contingent upon socially constructed categories, understanding how these categories are created and manipulated is crucial. * * *
>
> * * *
>
> Postmodern feminists are concerned specifically with deconstruction of the male/female binary, because it privileges male sex roles, marginalizes female sex roles, and has the additional deleterious effect of limiting individuals to one of two potential roles, a choice predetermined by anatomical sex. The postmodern feminist goal is not simply to equalize power between the sexes or to redefine the existing sex roles. Rather, the goal is to destabilize the sex hierarchy such that the traditional categories—"man" and "woman"—are eventually rendered irrelevant to identity creation.

Knouse, Using Postmodern Feminist Legal Theory to Interrupt the Reinscription of Sex Stereotypes Through the Institution of Marriage, 16 Hastings Women's L.J. 159, 164–66 (2005). Do you think Frug and Higgins would agree with this description? How might their conceptions of postmodern feminist legal theory differ from Knouse's?

2. Writing outside of law, Judith Butler has developed a nuanced account of gender construction, an account that questions whether gender can ever be deconstructed given its role in constituting our very notions of what is human:

> Simone de Beauvoir wrote in *The Second Sex* that "one is not born a woman, but rather *becomes* one." The phrase is odd, even nonsensical, for how can one become a woman if one wasn't a woman all along? And who is this "one" who does the becoming? Is there some human who becomes its gender at some point in time? * * *
>
> * * * The mark of gender appears to "qualify" bodies as human bodies; the moment in which an infant becomes humanized is when the question, "is it a boy or girl?" is answered. Those bodily figures who do not fit into either gender fall outside the human, indeed, constitute the domain of the dehumanized and the abject against which the human itself is constituted. If gender is always there, delimiting in advance what qualifies as the human, how can we speak of a human who becomes its gender, as if gender were a postscript or a cultural afterthought?

Butler, Gender Trouble: Feminism and the Subversion of Identity 111 (1990). If gender is always present, and always will be present, what is the point of analyzing gender construction? Will feminist legal theorists actually benefit from such an analysis?

3. Butler suggests that attention to gender construction can nonetheless be productive because such analysis reveals that "genders can be neither true nor false, but are only produced as the truth effects of a discourse of primary and stable identity," including legal discourse. Butler, above note 2, at 136. Butler agrees with Frug that feminists cannot "transcend" sex differences, but argues that feminists can expose the "imitative structure of gender itself" and the ways that "gender attributes * * * are not expressive but performative." Id. at 136, 141. In doing so, Butler believes feminists might be able to engage in gender performances that "enact and reveal the performativity of gender itself in a way that destabilizes the naturalized categories of identity and desire." Id. at 139. In particular, Butler invokes the concept of drag in order "to trace the moments where the binary system of gender is disputed and challenged, where the coherence of the categories are put into question, and where the very social life of gender turns out to be malleable and transformable." Butler, Undoing Gender 216 (2004).

What do you think of these possibilities? How do you perform your gender? How could you perform your gender with a difference, so that you are simultaneously complying with and resisting gender constructions? How might Frug's discussion of motherhood as "propos[ing] a choice of roles for women" provide an example of this simultaneous compliance and resistance?

4. What are the potential advantages of postmodern approaches to feminist legal theory? How might such approaches affect legal discourse? How might that discourse lead to substantive legal change? How do you think Frug would have developed her arguments if she had not met her untimely death? How might she have built upon Higgins' ideas for legal advocacy in a postmodern world?

5. Cain also discusses postmodernism in her excerpt above. Cain suggests that postmodernism may be able to address essentialism within feminist legal theory:

> Why is the lesbian so invisible in feminist legal theory? Why is my "reality" so different from "their reality?" And which reality is true? For the postmodernist, the last question is meaningless. But the first two are not.

Cain, excerpt above, at 214. What is the relationship between postmodernism and anti-essentialism? Higgins discusses the ways essentialism has participated in the construction of gender and how postmodernism might address that essentialism:

> * * * When feminists aspire to account for women's oppression through claims of cross-cultural commonality, they construct the feminist subject through exclusions and, as Judith Butler has observed, "those excluded domains return to haunt the integrity and unity of the feminist 'we'."

* * *

> The postmodern skepticism of grand theory resonates with feminist legal theory's increasing distrust of universal claims about women. Postmodernism suggests that the problem lies not in ensuring that the representation of women's experience is accurate, but rather in the concept of representation itself. * * * In short, gender itself is a product of power and language and social institutions, including law, not a reality that preexists those structures. * * *

Higgins, above at 1568–70 (quoting Butler, Contingent Foundations: Feminism and the Question of "Postmodernism," in Feminists Theorize the Political 3, 14 (Judith Butler & Joan Scott eds., 1992)). Does postmodernism's focus on gender construction and its rejection of truth mean that it is always immune from critiques that it is essentialist? How might Frug be seen as essentializing women? See, e.g., Ruth Colker, Response, The Example of Lesbians: Posthumous Reply to Mary Joe Frug, 105 Harv. L. Rev. 1084 (1992).

6. What are the potential harms of postmodern approaches to feminist legal theory? How does Higgins address those harms? Do you find her analysis convincing? How do you predict MacKinnon or West would respond to Frug and Higgins? See MacKinnon, Points Against Postmodernism, 75 Chi.-Kent L. Rev. 687, 711 (2000) ("My feeling is, if the postmodernists took responsibility for changing even one real thing, they would learn more about theory than everything they have written to date put together."); West, Caring for Justice 259 (1997) ("I will urge that the four central ideas of postmodern social theory that have proven to be of most interest to critical legal theorists * * * will not further our understanding of patriarchy and will frustrate rather than further our attempts to end it.").

TEXT NOTE ON SEX-POSITIVE FEMINISM AND THIRD-WAVE FEMINISM

Postmodern feminism is also often assumed to embrace and promote the possibility of female sexual pleasure. By considering the ways that bodies and desire are constructed, and emphasizing that sex can never be universally experienced, postmodernists implicitly reject a conception of sex acts as inherently dominating or subordinating. Indeed, postmodernists believe that sex acts, like gender, are also constructed through discourse.[3] As such, sexuality is not a "stubborn drive" that needs to be either controlled or liberated through law.[4] Instead, the law plays a role in producing the very sexuality that it seeks to repress or liberate.

Some feminist legal theorists have asked whether feminists have also played a role in producing women's sexuality. Katherine M. Franke asks if feminist legal theorists "run any risk of constructing women as de-sexualized dependency workers" by focusing so much of their analysis on women's roles as mothers.[5] She writes:

---

3. See, e.g., 1 Michel Foucault, The History of Sexuality: An Introduction 103–14 (Robert Hurley trans., Vintage Books 1990) (1978).

4. Id. at 103.

5. Franke, Theorizing Yes: An Essay on Feminism, Law, and Desire, 101 Colum. L. Rev. 181, 204 (2001).

> Men have almost entirely colonized the domain of sexuality that is the excess over reproduction as for them and about them. Movies, advertising, and fashion are largely projections of male fantasy—what would it mean for women to appropriate some of this cultural excess? Just as we have accepted that sexual orientation is not merely a natural phenomenon, might we also want to explore the degree to which our passions, fantasies, secret and not so secret desires are products of the world we live in? * * *
>
> Surely legal feminists would want to theorize the *sexual* nature of human sexuality that is the "excess over or potential difference from the bare choreographies of procreation." Is there a reason why we have neglected to take notice of the fact that women are substantially more likely to be unhappy about their sex lives than are men? Is there something that we, as legal feminists, should be doing to address the fact that forty-three percent of women in the United States are suffering from diagnosable sexual dysfunction, symptomized by a lack of interest in sex, inability to achieve orgasm or arousal, and pain or discomfort during sex?
>
> We have done a more than adequate job of theorizing circumstances in which "no" is the right answer to a sexual encounter, but where are we on the conditions under which we would be inclined to say "yes"? * * *[6]

Sex-positive feminism also developed outside of postmodernism as a response to Catharine MacKinnon's feminist campaign against pornography, discussed in Chapter 4.[7] These feminists borrowed arguments from gay men committed to sex-liberation, among others. More recently, so called third-wave feminists have embraced sexual pleasure as a fundamental aspect of their feminist platform. Among other things, they recognize the multifaceted nature of sex work and argue that women "should take charge of their own sexual satisfaction."[8]

NOTES ON SEX-POSITIVE AND THIRD-WAVE FEMINISM

1. How are these approaches to feminism different from Mary Becker's call for feminists to develop theories that "value female sexual agency"? See Becker, Toward a Substantive Feminism, excerpted above. Is Franke correct that feminists have failed to theorize the nature of "sexuality that is the excess over reproduction"? Why might Franke believe that Becker is not committed to promoting female sexual pleasure? How might Franke and Becker have differing views on what constitutes "the excess over reproduction"? What do you imagine when you think of "sexuality that is the excess over reproduction"?

2. Do you agree that male sexual fantasies dominate popular culture? Have younger feminists begun to shift sexual pleasure from a male domain to

---

6. Id. at 205–06.

7. See, e.g., Ian Halley, Queer Theory by Men, 11 Duke J. Gender L. & Pol'y 7, 13–14 (2004).

8. Bridget J. Crawford, Toward a Third-Wave Feminist Legal Theory: Young Women, Pornography and the Praxis of Pleasure, 14 Mich. J. Gender & L. 99, 122, 152–55 (2007).

a more female-centered domain? In what ways is sexual pleasure still presumed to be a male domain? What legal strategies would you suggest for addressing many women's unhappiness with their sex lives?

3. Do you consider yourself a third-wave feminist? If so, is sexual pleasure an important part of your conception of feminism? What other issues do you care most about? How has this chapter changed your views of feminism, if at all?

6. LESBIAN AND QUEER LEGAL THEORY

At the same time that postmodernists were questioning the usefulness of identity categories, many lesbians expressed concern that the legal strategies adopted by both feminists and gay men were insufficient to address the nature of lesbian inequality. These lesbians therefore proposed a separate and unique strand of lesbian legal theory. Queer theorists, in contrast, embraced the principles of postmodernism and post-structuralism to develop a legal theory that promoted queer interests as distinct from the interests of the gay and lesbian communities. Even more than postmodernists, queer theorists reject categorization, instead focusing on the fluidity of gender, sex, and identity. Such theorists would therefore likely reject this chapter's attempts to delineate separate schools of feminist legal thought and emphasize the ways that the chapter participates in the creation of difference, as opposed to merely describing difference. We acknowledge that critique and encourage you to adopt it if, after reading this chapter, you find it to be the most convincing theoretical approach to addressing inequality.

DIANA MAJURY, REFASHIONING THE UNFASHIONABLE: CLAIMING LESBIAN IDENTITIES IN THE LEGAL CONTEXT

7 Can. J. Women & L. 286, 306–17 (1994).

Lesbians have been subject to the sexism and male dominance of gay men within joint organizations and society at large. As a result, lesbians have been assumed to be the same as gay men; they have been subjected to, and judged by, the stereotypes of gay men; they have been assumed to have the same interests, goals and needs as gay men; they have been assumed to suffer from the same forms of discrimination, and in the same ways, as gay men.

As a female in this society, a lesbian's experience of inequality is very different from that of a gay man. She is likely to be in a worse economic situation than a gay man, in terms of current finances and economic opportunities; she is likely to have more limited and less remunerative job prospects than he; she is more likely to be trying to support children, with all of the attendant problems and expenses that child care presents in the context of the paid work force. Reproduction and child custody are issues of central concern to some lesbians, while, at best, they have been seen as peripheral to gay issues. While the use of psychiatry against lesbians and the pathologization of lesbians as mentally ill have been common practices historically, they have received little attention as gay concerns. The physical and sexual violence inflicted upon lesbians is different, in terms of where it takes place, the forms it takes, and its overall impact, from the violence to which gay men are subjected. The focus and import of issues of sex, sexuality, and sexual practice are different for lesbians than they are for gay men. Lesbians, particularly outspoken lesbian-identified lesbians, are being subjected to a vicious and virulent anti-lesbian, anti-woman backlash.

The term sexual orientation seems inappropriate and inadequate to ground the specific inequalities experienced by lesbians. There is no doubt that lesbians should support gay men as an oppressed group, as we should support any oppressed group. But the question is, given all the differences between lesbians and gay men, played out as they are in the context of the power imbalance of gender, is there enough in common to warrant treatment as a single group for anti-discrimination purposes? Are the discriminations experienced by lesbians and gays sufficiently similar to be lumped together under a single ground of discrimination? Are we looking for a new gender neutral term such as, for example, "sexual identity," that might more accurately capture the meaning of being a lesbian and that is capable of being defined in law and society as including lesbians in their realities, as well as gay men in theirs? Or is the hegemony of male dominance so overpowering, are the experiences and issues for lesbians and gays so different, as to necessitate that lesbians resist the identification of lesbian inequality with gay inequality and insist on the recognition of lesbians as a distinct group, experiencing discrimination, not under some umbrella term that includes gay men, but specific to lesbians? Or is lesbian discrimination an extreme form of discrimination against women; is sex discrimination the more appropriate umbrella under which to challenge lesbian discrimination?

Lesbian Inequality as Sex Inequality

* * *

The argument that discrimination against lesbians and gays is sex discrimination has generally been articulated, where it has been argued at all, as a formal equality argument. The argument, under the formal equality model, is that it is sex discrimination to deny women the rights that men have, or to restrict women in ways that men are not restricted in the exercise of their rights, including the right to have full and committed sexual relationships with women. The argument applies, in the converse, to support gay male rights. Thus, for example, the argument in support of the right to gay marriage is that to permit a man to marry a woman but at the same time to deny him the right to marry another man is to construct an unconstitutional classification "on account of sex." This is the classic formal equality, "but for sex" argument in which sex is put forward as the sole impediment to the right, privilege or benefit being sought. In the lesbian or gay context, the argument is that "but for" my gender, or alternatively "but for" the gender of my chosen partner, I would have access to the right being denied me. While the simplicity of this "but for sex" version of a sex equality argument may make it appear attractive, it is an argument that undermines, if not contradicts, an inequality-based approach. As with all formal equality arguments, the "but for sex" argument is premised on an assertion of compliance with the dominant standard. Lesbians and gays are put forward as the same as heterosexuals, gender being cast as an insignificant difference. To the extent that lesbians and gays are able and willing to "heterosexualize" themselves, they argue that they should have access to the privileges of heterosexuality. Thus lesbian mothers have been granted custody of their children as long as they appear to be heterosexual, that is, that they are not politically or sexually active as lesbians. A successful formal equality analysis in this context would mean that the least oppressed lesbians and gays, that is, those most like the dominant group, would be granted heterosexual status. As a corollary, the most oppressed lesbians and gays would be further marginalized and subject to more extreme forms of discrimination and subordination.

The fact that gays have by and large not been successful even under the formal equality model of sex discrimination is a reflection of the depth and resistance of the hatred and fear of lesbians and gays. Even when lesbians and gays present themselves as the same as heterosexuals, they are not accepted. If lesbians and gays were "just like" heterosexuals, then the only threat that we would pose would be to the strict gender differentiation imposed by heterosexuality. The rejection of even assimilated lesbians and gays is strong testament to the commitment to retain gender difference, that is to the preservation of gender inequality. This recognition that gender and sex inequality are the underpinnings of "sexual orientation" discrimination gives rise to the more complex, inequality-based analysis of lesbian discrimination as sex discrimination. Judicial rejection of the formal sex equality analysis of discrimination against lesbians and gays is premised on an asserted difference between lesbians and gays and their relationships on the one hand and heterosexuals and heterosexual relationships on the other. This "difference" is all about gender; it is described primarily in terms of sexual intercourse and reproduction, but also in terms of gender roles and ascribed gender qualities.

Lesbians are discriminated against because they challenge dominant understandings and meanings of gender in our society. And the more, and the more overtly, we challenge gender, the more, and the more overtly, we are discriminated against. Gender differentiation, premised on the subordination of women, is as essential to heterosexualism as it is to sexism. Lesbian inequalities are sex inequalities because they are rooted in a highly circumscribed definition of gender and gender roles, according to which women are seen only in relation to men. Women who define themselves, and who, in so doing, define themselves without any reference to men, are de-sexed; either they are seen as not women or their "sex", that is their lesbianism, is denied. Either way, this is sex discrimination at its most extreme.

Sexuality is one of the defining features of gender, in terms of both reproduction and presumed male sexual access to females. Gender stereotypes and the gender hierarchy are premised on heterosexuality. Heterosexuality and the gender stereotypes and hierarchy to which it gives rise have, in the past, been assumed to be biologically based, that is, seen as essential components of one's biological sex. In this heterosexual sexual context, the male is seen as aggressive, independent, dominant; the female is seen as passive, dependent, submissive. Male sexual violence against women is a reflection of, as well as a function of, the deeply rooted connections between gender inequality, sex and sexuality. Heterosexuality becomes one of the demarcations and reinforcers of gender "difference" and of women's inequality. Heterosexuality is prescribed and promoted through law and other social institutions:

> History suggests that a primary purpose and effect of state enforcement of heterosexuality is to preserve gender differentiation and the relationships premised upon it. Thus, constitutional restraints against gender discrimination must also be applied to laws censuring homosexuality.[81]

Lesbian oppression functions to reinforce and perpetuate strict notions of gender differentiation. Lesbian inequality is the warning to girls and women not to challenge the prescribed meaning of being female in this society. Those girls and women who do start to assert their autonomy and to challenge their sexual subordination and the centrality/necessity of men in women's lives are often quickly and powerfully reminded that it could get worse. They are called "lesbian" or "dyke", not because they do, or are even thought to, have "sex" with women, but because the ostracism and increased inequality that the label "lesbian" represents are used to try to bring women back into gender line. Women and girls who do not focus their attention on men are called "man-haters", a term stereotypically understood as synonymous with lesbian, a term that is explicitly designed to re-focus attention back on men.

Discrimination against lesbians is sex discrimination, perhaps in its starkest and most overt form. It is important to argue lesbian discrimination as sex discrimination in legal fora as elsewhere, because this analysis challenges sex inequality in fundamental and radical ways. However, strategically, it is probably not advisable to leave lesbian inequalities to be addressed exclusively through the prohibition of sex discrimination. The lesbian discrimination as sex discrimination analysis requires a fairly sophisticated understanding of sex equality/inequality. As with any other uncharted equality territory, rejection of a sex equality analysis, at the first instance, is indicative neither of its validity as equality theory nor of

---

81. [Sylvia] Law, [Homosexuality and the Social Meaning of Gender, 1988 Wis. L. Rev. 187,] at 230.

its potential eventually to be integrated into our jurisprudence. It may take time for the lesbian sex discrimination analysis to be heard and understood in the courtroom, which is precisely why it is important to continue to speak it, develop it, argue its appropriateness and insist that it be heard and understood on our terms. Some of the equality arguments which now seem commonplace in our jurisprudence at first instance seemed incredibly risky and impossible to expect courts to understand.

It seems to me that there might, in most cases, be a substantial difference between arguing lesbian inequality as sex discrimination rather than as sexual orientation discrimination or even lesbian discrimination. Take, for instance, the "spousal" benefit cases. These cases have generally been presented in terms of heterosexual couples being given something that has not been given to so called "same-sex" couples. Lesbian and gay couples are seen as being denied these benefits because of their sexual orientation. A sex equality analysis of spousal benefits would more readily and clearly expose the gendered assumption of dependence, need, and obligation upon which most of these benefits are premised. Spousal benefits then perpetuate the gendered conditions which lend credence to these gendered assumptions. It is a self-perpetuating system of sexual inequality. A sex equality analysis would question the fundamental premise that benefits should necessarily or logically be disseminated through sexual relationships. A sex equality analysis would open up the larger question of why we as a society endorse such benefits and to whom, in the interests of fairness and equity, they should be allocated. If the issues are dependence, need, and obligation, why then are these not the criteria for distribution? Such an approach may provide the grounding for arguments for universalized benefits. It may be that not only the analysis, but the result, might be quite different from a sex equality perspective.

However, in the interim, as lesbian sex equality is being developed, lesbians need to be named specifically as a protected group in order to avoid lesbian claims being dismissed summarily, leaving lesbians without any legal protection against discrimination. While the sexual orientation umbrella, as it has been legally and socially constructed in the context of male supremacy, may be inappropriate, the sex umbrella, as it has been legally constructed, may, at least for the moment, be inadequate. The legal recognition of discrimination against lesbians as a prohibited ground of discrimination will provide the foot in the door that will enable the sex discrimination arguments to be made. Sex discrimination can be claimed and argued as a separate ground, in conjunction with the lesbian discrimination ground, as well as in conjunction with any other ground that may apply. While lesbian discrimination may be the ground which the court feels required to hear and consider in full, they will have to sit through, and at least give some thought to, the sex discrimination argument as well. In addition, the lesbian discrimination ground would be argued in terms of sex discrimination, that discrimination against lesbians is discrimination against women who are challenging the circumscribed meanings of gender. In Canada, sexual harassment had first to be included as a separate ground of discrimination before it was definitively recognized as a form of sex discrimination; lesbian discrimination may have to follow this same path.

Conclusion

* * *

While I feel myself on the verge of saying that discrimination against lesbians is fully understood and conceptualized as sex discrimination, I will always seem to pull back just short of that assertion. Is there something more that is discrimination against lesbians that is not captured by a sex discrimination analysis? While I have some persisting sense that there is something more and that I am missing a piece that makes lesbian inequality something separate from sex inequality, I do not know what that piece is.

Ruthann Robson argues that lesbian jurisprudence is not the same as feminist jurisprudence:

> Feminist jurisprudence is most often concerned with women *vis-à-vis* men; the difference/sameness debates on equality issues evince this preoccupation. The essential exercise is comparing women with men; the essential goal is equality with men.
>
> As I conceptualize lesbian jurisprudence, it has a different focus. If lesbians are women-identified women, then measurements are not relative to men; men's measurements are in some sense irrelevant.[90]

While I think (hope) that feminist jurisprudence is becoming less focused on women in relation to men and more on women in their own right, I would agree with Robson that lesbian jurisprudence cannot be collapsed into feminist jurisprudence. However, I do not think that the same argument applies to lesbian inequality as sex inequality. The sex inequality analysis is very much focused on lesbians as women, not in comparison to men, but in terms of challenging notions of gender. An inequality-based approach is directed toward redressing the inequalities experienced by lesbians, not to making the treatment of lesbians accord with the treatment of non-lesbians. However, Robson's rejection of attempts to collapse lesbianism into gender reinforces my concern that I am missing something unique about lesbian inequality.

* * *

This brings me back to the more fundamental question of whether all of these categories are irredeemably problematic because they are apparently mutually exclusive and negate the complexity and specificity of compound forms of discrimination. Perhaps this whole "boxed" human rights approach is so rigid and narrowly focused as to be incapable of expansion or flexibility. These same questions apply to the lesbian category, itself. But, in the face of the current very real life oppressions of

90. [Ruthann] Robson, "Lesbian Jurisprudence?," [8 Law & Ineq. 443,] at 449 [(1989–90)].

lesbians, I think it politically unwise for lesbians and their supporters to abandon the category. To me this is tantamount to abandoning each other. Instead I claim with pride, joy, and fear—my lesbian identity.

JANET HALLEY, SPLIT DECISIONS: HOW AND WHY TO TAKE A BREAK FROM FEMINISM

13–14, 20–23, 112–14, 273, 319–21, 342–43, 346 (2006).

* * * I think it is simply uncontestable that feminism itself is internally riven and has seen parts of itself break off and become—not merely diverse parts of feminism but—something else. I will argue that several of the intellectual/political projects that have resulted bring hypotheses about sexual life and power which are inconsistent with any version of feminism currently on offer. Certainly these alternative projects have constituencies that can't be described as f [Halley's shorthand for women, femininity, and/or female or feminine gender]. That is, there is a political struggle going on right now among a range of constituencies and within many of their members—elements that promote various theories of sexuality, explore various theories of power, advocate various ways of sexual life. Each would imagine and thus wield power differently; each would govern differently; each would precipitate different sexual possibilities and realities; each would distribute status and authority to different bodies, different acts, different relationships—and (let's face it) take status and authority from different bodies, acts, relationships.

Apprehending this is, it seems to me, a simple predicate of responsible power wielding. And here I come up against the profound commitment of so many participants in the politics that engage me in this book—not merely feminist ones; gay ones, queer ones, trans ones also—to an understanding of themselves as utterly without power. The intellectual, institutional, and affective trends contributing to this attitude are many: the proliferation on the left of minoritizing identity-based vocabularies in which high-priority political and moral claims can be made only by the "marginalized" and the "silenced"; the subordination-theoretical assumption that power is always bad; the fact that so many intellectually and politically productive contributors to this politics work in humanities departments, and that these departments are in a deep crisis, experienced as powerlessness, about their place in the university; the seeming inability of most participants in these politics to move beyond a certain sentimental and moralistic view of law and legal action in which nothing short of complete and total moral vindication by the Supreme Court is legal power. * * *

* * *

Governance Feminism

If you look around the United States, Canada, the European Union, the human rights establishment, even the World Bank, you see plenty of places where feminism, far from operating from underground, is running things. Sex harassment, child sexual abuse, pornography, sexual violence, antiprostitution and antitrafficking regimes, prosecutable marital rape, rape shield rules: these feminist justice projects have moved off the street and into the state. In family law alone, feminism has scored numerous victories that prefer the wife to the husband and the mother to the father: the presumption that young children must spend substantial time with their mothers, the rise of alimony, the shift in common-law-property states to equitable division of property upon divorce, the replacement of "cruelty" with "domestic violence" as a fault grounds for divorce, the revitalization of intimate torts like alienation of affections, criminal conversation, and seduction as women's lawsuits.

It would be a mistake to think that governance issues only from that combination of courts, legislatures, and police which constitutes the everyday image of "the state." Employers, schools, health care institutions, and a whole range of entities, often formally "private," govern too—and feminism has substantial parts of them under its control. Just think of the tremendous effort that U.S. employers and schools must devote to the regulation of sexual conduct at work, through sexual harassment policies that have produced a sexual harassment bureaucracy with its own cadre of professionals and its own legal character. And many feminist policy campaigns take power in the form of ideological shifts within state and nonstate entities that don't turn explicitly on m/f [Halley's shorthand for any distinction between something male or masculine and something female or feminine]. Consider, as a possible example, that one result of feminist rape activism is the elevation of child sexual abuse as a serious enforcement priority complete with "zero tolerance" enforcement attitudes; other kinds of child neglect and abuse, other kinds of adult/adult interpersonal violence, lack the charisma of the sexual offenses. They fall into the background. And this is an effect of governance feminism.

Feminists have learned how to participate in what is often called "the new governance." Ask any group of U.S. Women's Studies majors what they intend to do with their degree: many will say that they intend to "work in an NGO." Global governance and local governance are often done through informal, opaque, ideologically committed "nongovernmental organizations" that strategize hard—sometimes successfully—to become indispensable when major new fluidities in formal power emerge. A classic example is the highly effective feminist activism aimed at the ad hoc criminal courts formed by the United Nations to prosecute war crimes in Rwanda and the former Yugoslavia: feminist and legal players have written that this effort substantially changed the rules. By positing themselves as experts on women, sexuality, motherhood, and so on, feminists walk the halls of power.

And feminism exerts itself in the culture wars as a real force to be contended with. It has convinced lots of men that the "new man" must defer to feminism on questions relating to women's welfare in sex and reproduction. In the United States, the only left-of-center locales where male masculinity is worshiped anymore are gay and male. The Vatican has noticed the cultural diffusion of feminist consciousness and is worried: its Congregation for the Doctrine of the Faith, presided over by Joseph Cardinal Ratzinger (since installed as Pope Benedict XVI), has issued an important dogmatic letter specifically to refute feminism, complete with a concentrated attack on the ideas that biological sex and cultural gender are distinct and independently variable, and that foundational biological difference between m and f should not be a source of social norms. That is to say, the current pope has devoted a substantial portion of his time to refuting feminism. * * *

In some important senses, then, feminism rules. Governance feminism.

Not only that, it wants to rule. It has a will to power.

And not only that, it has a will to power—and it has actual power—that extends from the White House and the corporate boardroom through to the minute power dynamics that Foucault included in his theory of the governance of the self. Feminism may face powers greater than its own in its constant involvement with its opponents; but it deals with them in the very terms of power.

Feminism, Sexual and Reproductive

This book takes it as a fait accompli that feminists often divide their labor between sexuality, on one hand, and reproduction, on the other, as distinct domains of feminist concern.

There are important reasons not to comply with this division. Socialist feminism, for instance, when it was a very active element of U.S. feminism, persistently aimed for formulations that understood sexuality and reproduction to be profoundly linked. * * *

To justify taxonomic location of the present project, I'll just say that most feminist work over the last several decades has given great prominence to sexuality or reproduction as the key term for articulating m/f, m > f, and carrying a brief for f. * * * I make no claim that the arguments advanced here would necessarily work on the reproduction side. This book—it's about sex.

* * *

Gay Identity/Feminism/Queer Theory

Queer theory—feminist and non—has emerged as a search for ways to do work on same-sex desire and erotic life more generally, without recourse to these problematic models [of dominance and cultural feminism]. Here are some places where queer theory diverges from gay-identity politics. As they have confronted each other so far, gay-identity theories and queer theory seek the welfare of different sexual subjects. A gay-identity approach posits that some people are homosexual and that the stigma attached to this kind of person should be removed. It is receptive to claims that homosexuality is biologically caused, and frequently manifests itself in assertions that lesbians and gay men are very different. It is a minoritizing identity-based project; it sports a subordination theory; and it seeks equality. By contrast, a queer approach regards the homosexual/heterosexual distinction with skepticism and even resentment, building arguments that it is historically contingent and is itself oppressive. It regards gender with the same skepticism. Producers of queer theory tend to think they expose and erode strong identity differentiations between gay men and lesbians or between men and women generally. A gay-identity approach fosters specifically gay culture and gay ghettos, and engages in loyalty projects like "outing" and the denunciation of homosexuals who "convert" to heterosexuality. Conversely, a queer approach thinks it is fine to be "queer in the streets, straight in the sheets"; encourages contingent and alterable sexual identification along dimensions other than the sex of one's sexual object choice, such as the object's gender or particular sexual acts; and takes within its purview not only same-sex love that does not express itself in sexual acts, but also cross-sex love that does.

Thus a gay-identity analytic thinks that there are homosexuals just as women's-subordination feminisms think that there are women; they object to the social subordination of these discrete constituencies; and they at least tend to, if not need to, maintain the discreteness of the identities on whose behalf they labor in order to present themselves as coherent.

Queer work, by contrast, wants to be anti-identitarian. It tries to dissociate male bodies, masculinity, and superordination from each other, rendering sexuality a domain in which sex 1 [Halley's shorthand for the purported bodily difference between men and women], gender, and power are highly mobile. The masculinity of women * * * and the appetitive sexual abjection of men * * * could not be noticed in the vocabulary of MacKinnon's theory of gender and would be decried as morally defective by cultural feminism. Queer thinking agrees with MacKinnon and cultural feminism that sexuality is shot through with power, but it is much more open to the idea that the result is only episodically, not structurally, domination.

Oddly, though, the actual theory that people think is queer theory remains, often, homo-supremacist and gender-mobility-supremacist. The symptom of this return to feminist terms, which I will note whenever it appears, is its failure, so far anyway, to produce interesting nondismissive and normatively unfraught work on the queerness of masculine male heterosexual desire for the sexy femininity of women. And it is in love with the edge, implying contempt for the average, the everyday, the reassuringly persistent. * * * [Q]ueer theory often falls into step with the commitment to m/f, m > f, and carrying a brief for f, to the convergentism, the structuralism, the identitarianism, and the prescriptive deployment of theory that I think have so eroded feminism and gay-identity theory as seedgrounds for critical work.

* * *

My idea is that a different attitude to theory is possible. When theory is hypothetical, and also when it is critical, it is less hostile to the existence of inconsistent theories operating at top speed "over there." It is more capable of apprehending these theories as possible competitors, as producing different worlds, as articulating different social goods and bads, and as driving divergent political desires. It is more capable of splitting decisions.

* * *

Breaking with the Politics of Injury/Seeing around Corners of Our Own Construction

The objection that Taking a Break [from Feminism] discounts and even denies the harm suffered by women, dissected and reassembled, yields a triad of descriptive stakes: women are injured, they do not cause any social harm, and men, who injure women, are immune from harm—female injury + female innocence + male immunity. Feminists often produce this triad as if it were feminism; and as if the three stakes were tied so tightly together that each requires assertion of the others.

This is the crux of the contemporary politics of injury. Women's subordination has been understood as their injury; subordination is figured as injuredness. Questioning whether the woman was injured is thought to be, in itself, unfeminist and is sometimes even said to "reinjure her." * * * Moreover, the woman is "innocent" in the strict, minimal etymological sense that she "lack[s] the capacity to injure: [that she is] innocuous, harmless." Attributing to her the agency, the will, the malice—even simply the capacity—to cause harm to others also sounds unfeminist and is (oddly) understood also to constitute a denial that she was injured. And the man, the subordinator, is understood to be immune from injury. He might have to give up his ill-gotten gains, make restitution, get his foot off our necks, learn to listen to a different voice, and so forth, but describing his suffering as a wrong done by, or even as a social cost of, the assertion of women's interests produces perhaps the most acute feminist resistance.

The pattern is pretty endemic in contemporary feminism. Prostitution is understood to harm women while or by benefiting johns and pimps; pornography degrades women to produce male sexual pleasure; and so on. It seems more not feminist to suggest that men are injured by women in these practices—or even simply that they are injured—than to suggest that women may not be injured by men in them.

Of course all feminism posits that female subordination is not accidental, random, buckshot. Instead, power-feminist and cultural-feminist projects insert their articulations of trauma, torture, offended dignity, pain, suffering, agony—or disempowerment, domination, deprivation, exclusion, marginalization, invisibilization, silencing, etc.—into subordination theories: the eroticization of domination and the degradation of women's distinctive values, respectively, harm women while benefiting men.

As I've said, this idea can be a very useful hypothesis for eager justice-seekers to have on hand. But presupposing that such a theory fully describes the world—refusing to Take a Break to see whether something else might be going on as well or instead—commits feminism to being unable to see around corners of its own construction.

* * *

But do you really want to think that way? Because of course we all know that some women lie, and that others are interpellated into real experience that is not in their "real" interests; some women manage to hurt other people and social interests; some men are injured by some women. What produces the intense will to blind-spot, even to deny, these obvious facts about the social world?

* * *

Resisting Bad Faith

* * *

Of course, operating in bad faith might actually be a good thing. It's a way of tying yourself to the mast and making it more likely that you'll finish a voyage you might otherwise interrupt, possibly with disastrous consequences. But there are many, many reasons to worry about this kind of political consciousness. Not seeing the productive effects of one's purposive actions can cause one to intensify them. If, for instance, you don't think that young men approach heterosexuality with fear and trembling and suffer the inevitable failures of intimacy with deep pangs, you might end up imagining that male-disadvantaging statutory rape laws—which you might be advocating in your effort to protect adolescent girls—have no social costs at all, and so you might proceed, once you've got male-disadvantaging statutory rape laws, to intensify them through the addition of rape shield rules, shifts in the burden of proof, pro-prosecution presumptions, and so on. You could keep doing this until the tolerated residuum of abuse had shrunk to its practical minimum and the number of false-positive convictions of perfectly lovely, sexually animated young men had ballooned to what would be, even to you, intolerable levels. But you wouldn't notice.

* * *

Deconstituting Women's Suffering

* * *

While feminism is committed to affirming and identifying itself with female injury, it may thereby, unintentionally, intensify it. Oddly, representing women as end points of pain, imagining them as lacking the agency to cause harm to others and particularly to harm men, feminists refuse also to see women—even injured ones—as powerful actors. Feminism objectifies women, feminism erases their agency—could that be right? We might need to Take a Break from Feminism to notice that the crying girl is really suffering; that she really didn't have to; and that her wails may have something in them of a (possibly successful) wish for revenge.

If we are going to think that way, we are faced with a very profound problem about the relationship between power and resistance. If a social subordination exists and an antisubordination discourse—while also pursuing its antisubordination goals—ratifies it, fixes it, creates the discursive capacity for its experiential uptake by the subordinated, all the while hanging a bull's-eye on it, then where does one intervene to attack it? This is a real question, rife with real and strategic difficulties. * * *

NOTES ON LESBIAN AND QUEER LEGAL THEORY

1. How would you articulate the differences between lesbian legal theory, gay-identity theory, and queer theory? Are there any areas of overlap between the theories? How might the three theories serve similar goals and how might they not?

2. What does Majury see as the connection between discrimination against lesbians and sex discrimination? What does she see as the unique aspects of each form of discrimination? How would you make an argument in support of state benefits for same-sex couples if you wanted to eliminate discrimination on the basis of sexual orientation? How would your argument change if you wanted to eliminate sex discrimination? Which argument is more powerful? Which argument do you prefer analytically? Which is likely to be more threatening to listeners? Which would you use if arguing in a court and which would you use if arguing to a legislature?

3. Do you agree with Majury that the distribution of benefits to spouses (of employees or of workers covered by social security) is a form of sex discrimination, as well as a form of discrimination against gays and lesbians? Why or why not? Could you make an argument that spousal benefits are sex discrimination using formal equality? Dominance feminism? Relational feminism? Anti-essentialist feminism? Critical race feminism? Postmodern feminism? Which arguments do you think are strongest?

4. Majury is troubled by conceptualizing discrimination against lesbians as *only* sex discrimination and finds herself "pull[ing] back just short" of asserting that "discrimination against lesbians is fully understood and conceptualized as sex discrimination." What differences might there be between discrimination against lesbians and sex discrimination? What dangers might there be for lesbians in understanding and conceptualizing discrimination against lesbians as (only) sex discrimination? If discrimination against lesbians is to some extent something other than or different from sex discrimination, what is the difference?

Can sexism be eliminated by focusing solely on the needs of heterosexual women? Why might it be necessary to address the needs of lesbians in order to eliminate bias against straight women? Might the tendency of many heterosexual feminists to distance themselves from lesbians ultimately be self-defeating? Have you seen this tendency in groups in which you have been involved? How have you responded?

5. Halley is also concerned about legal reforms designed to address sex discrimination, proposing that readers "take a break from feminism" in order to examine the potential harms of "governance feminism." What, exactly, are these harms in Halley's view? How does Halley define "governance feminism"? Would all of the feminist legal theories described in this chapter fall within that term or only some of them? Which ones? Do you agree with Halley that feminists now wield power in a number of important arenas throughout society? In what contexts have you seen feminists wield power? In which contexts have you seen feminists wield little or no power? How do feminists wield power at your law school, if at all? Who benefits from such uses of power and who is hurt?

6. If we follow Halley's suggestion to take a break from (governance) feminism, where will we end up? Halley seems to suggest that queer theory would fill the void, although she articulates some shortcomings with that approach as well. For what purposes might queer theory be a more useful strategy than governance feminism? Who benefits from queer theory? Who is harmed?

7. How would you define queer theory? Is it even possible to define queer theory given that the theory resists categorization and attempts to defy definition? Or is that in and of itself a definition? For an attempt to define queer theory, see Laurie Rose Kepros, Queer Theory: Weed or Seed in the Garden of Legal Theory?, 9 Law & Sex. 279 (2000); but see Martha Albertson Fineman, Introduction: Feminist and Queer Legal Theory, in Feminist and Queer Legal Theory: Intimate Encounters, Uncomfortable Conversations 1, 5 (Martha Albertson Fineman, Jack E. Jackson & Adam P. Romero eds., 2009) (criticizing Kepros's definition for failing to embrace the fluidity of queerness). Halley has at times used a definition that places queer theory near sex-positive feminism:

> The queer project carries a brief for the weirdness of sex wherever it appears; it is (or should be) agnostic about where, when, and among or between whom the intensities of sex are possible. * * * [I]t would resist the redistribution of sexual intensities achieved under color of women's equality or moral virtue.

Halley, Sexuality Harassment, in Left Legalism/Left Critique 80, 98 (Wendy Brown & Janet Halley eds., 2002). What do you think of that conception of queer theory? Does it help explain why Halley wants to take a break from feminism?

8. Who does Halley believe is harmed "under color of women's equality or moral virtue"? Gay men and lesbians? Just gay men? All men? Women of all sexual orientations? For an argument that we can address Halley's concerns even within feminism, see Adam P. Romero, Methodological Descriptions: "Feminist" and "Queer" Legal Theories, in Feminist and Queer Legal Theory, above note 7, at 179.

9. After considering both Majury and Halley, which approach do you find more compelling? How might you use parts of each in developing your own theory of inequality? How might legal education be enhanced by incorporating the insights of theorists like both Majury and Halley? See Kim Brooks & Debra Parkes, Queering Legal Education: A Project of Theoretical Discovery, 27 Harv. Women's L.J. 89 (2004).

7. PRAGMATIC FEMINISM

Some approaches to feminist legal theory attempt to remain distinct whereas others overlap with one another. Pragmatic feminism explicitly borrows from multiple approaches. We describe that multiplicity here.

MARGARET JANE RADIN, THE PRAGMATIST AND THE FEMINIST

63 S. Cal. L. Rev. 1699, 1699–1701, 1704, 1706–08 (1990).

I begin at the point it became clear to me that I was combining pragmatism and feminism. That point was in my thinking about the transition problem of the double bind in the context of contested commodification of sexuality and reproductive capacity. If the social regime permits buying and selling of sexual and reproductive activities, thereby treating them as fungible market commodities given the current capitalistic understandings of monetary exchange, there is a threat to the personhood of women, who are the "owners" of these "commodities." The threat to personhood from commodification arises because essential attributes are treated as severable fungible objects, and this denies the integrity and uniqueness of the self. But if the social regime prohibits this kind of commodification, it denies women the choice to market their sexual or reproductive services, and given the current feminization of poverty and lack of avenues for free choice for women, this also poses a threat to the personhood of women. The threat from enforced noncommodification arises because narrowing women's choices is a threat to liberation, and because their choices to market sexual or reproductive services, even if nonideal, may represent the best alternatives available to those who would choose them.

Thus the double bind: both commodification and noncommodification may be harmful. Harmful, that is, under our current social conditions. Neither one need be harmful in an ideal world. The fact that money changes hands need not necessarily contaminate human interactions of sharing, nor must the fact that a social order makes nonmonetary sharing its norm necessarily deprive or subordinate anyone. That commodification now tends toward fungibility of women and noncommodification now tends toward their domination and continued subordination are artifacts of the current social hierarchy. In other words, the fact of oppression is what gives rise to the double bind.

Thus, it appears that the solution to the double bind is not to solve but to dissolve it: remove the oppressive circumstances. But in the meantime, if we are practically limited to those two choices, which are we to choose? I think that the answer must be pragmatic. We must look carefully at the nonideal circumstances in each case and decide which horn of the dilemma is better (or less bad), and we must keep re-deciding as time goes on.

To generalize a bit, it seems that there are two ways to think about justice. One is to think about justice in an ideal world, the best world that we can now conceive. The other is to think about nonideal justice: given where we now find ourselves, what is the better decision? In making this decision, we think about what actions can bring us closer to ideal justice. For example, if we allow commodification, we may push further away any ideal of a less commodified future. But if we enforce noncommodification, we may push further away any ideal of a less dominated future. In making our decisions of nonideal justice, we must also realize that these decisions will help to reconstitute our ideals. For example, if we commodify all attributes of personhood, the ideal of personhood we now know will evolve into another one that does not conceive fungibility as bad. The double bind, then, is a problem involving nonideal justice, and I think its only solution can be pragmatic. There is no general solution; there are only piecemeal, temporary solutions.

I also think of the double bind as a problem of transition, because I think of nonideal justice as the process by which we try to make progress (effect a transition) toward our vision of the good world. I think we should recognize that all decisions about justice, as opposed to theories about it, are pragmatic decisions in the transition. At the same time we should also recognize that ideal theory is also necessary, because we need to know what we are trying to achieve. In other words, our visions and nonideal decisions, our theory and practice, paradoxically constitute each other.

Having discovered the double bind in true pragmatic fashion, by working on a specific problem, I now see it everywhere. The double bind is pervasive in the issues we have thought of as "women's issues." The reason it is pervasive is to be sought in the perspective of oppression. For a group subject to structures of domination, all roads thought to be progressive can pack a backlash. * * *

* * *

Perhaps it is obvious that the reason the double bind recurs throughout feminist struggles is that it is an artifact of the dominant social conception of the meaning of gender. The double bind is a series of two-pronged dilemmas in which both prongs are, or can be, losers for the oppressed. Once we realize this, we may say it is equally obvious that the way out of the double bind is to dissolve these dilemmas by changing the framework that creates them. That is, we must dissolve the prevalent conception of gender.

Calling for dissolution of the prevalent conception of gender is the visionary half of the problem: we must create a new vision of the meaning of male and female in order to change the dominant social conception of gender and change the double bind. In order to do that, however, we need the social empowerment that the dominant social conception of gender keeps us from achieving.

Then how can we make progress? The other half of the problem is the nonideal problem of transition from the present situation toward our ideal. Here is where the pragmatist feminist comes into her own. The pragmatist solution is to confront each dilemma separately and choose the alternative that will hinder empowerment the least and further it the most. The pragmatist feminist need not seek a general solution that will dictate how to resolve all double bind issues. Appropriate solutions may all differ, depending on the current stage of women's empowerment, and how the proposed solution might move the current social conception of gender and our vision of how gender should be reconceived for the future. Indeed, the "same" double bind may demand a different solution tomorrow from the one we find best today.

* * *

The pragmatists were famous for their theory of truth without the capital T—their theory that truth is inevitably plural, concrete, and provisional. John Dewey wrote, "Truth is a collection of truths; and these constituent truths are in the keeping of the best available methods of inquiry and testing as to matters-of-fact." * * *

Pragmatism and feminism largely share, I think, the commitment to finding knowledge in the particulars of experience. It is a commitment against abstract idealism, transcendence, foundationalism, and atemporal universality; and in favor of immanence, historicity, concreteness, situatedness, contextuality, embeddedness, narrativity of meaning.

If feminists largely share the pragmatist commitment that truth is hammered out piecemeal in the crucible of life and our situatedness, they also share the pragmatist understanding that truth is provisional and everchanging. Too, they also share the pragmatist commitment to concrete particulars. Since the details of our life are connected with what we know, those details matter. Thus, the pragmatist and the feminist both arrive at an embodied perspectivist view of knowledge.

It is not surprising that pragmatists have stressed embodiment more than other philosophers, nor that feminists have stressed it even more. Once we understand that the details of our embodiment matter for what the world is for us (which in some pragmatist views is all the world is), then it must indeed be important that only one half of humans directly experience menstruation, pregnancy, birth, and lactation. So it is no wonder that feminists write about prostitution, contract motherhood, rape, child care, and the PMS defense. It is not just the fact that these are women's issues that makes these writings feminist—they are after all human issues—but specifically the instantiation of the perspective of female embodiment.

Another pragmatist commitment that is largely shared by feminists is the dissolution of traditional dichotomies. Pragmatists and feminists have rejected the dichotomy between thought and action, or between theory and practice. John Dewey especially made this his theme; and he also rejected the dichotomies of reason and feeling, mind and body, nature and nurture, connection and separation, and means and ends. In a commitment that is not, at least not yet, shared by modern pragmatists, feminists have also largely rejected the traditional dichotomy of public (man) and private (woman). For these feminists, the personal is political.

One more strong resonance between the pragmatist and the feminist is in concrete methodology. The feminist commitment to learning through consciousness raising in groups can be regarded as the culmination of the pragmatist understanding that, for consciousness to exist at all, there must be shared meaning arising out of shared interactions with the world. * * *

NOTES ON PRAGMATIC FEMINISM

1. Many of the feminist approaches described in this chapter are pragmatic. A dominance theorist would be pragmatic about how best to change the distribution of power between women and men. A formal equality feminist would be pragmatic about which gender-neutral rule to adopt, whether, for example, to adopt an unpaid parental leave policy as soon as it is politically feasible or hold out for paid parental leave. A relational feminist would stress "embodiment" like pragmatists long have and be pragmatic about how best to improve the quality of women's lives. As Tracy Higgins emphasized, a postmodern feminist would join the pragmatist in applauding "the dissolution of traditional dichotomies" and similarly resist a singular conception of truth (indeed any truth at all). Despite these similarities, what aspects of Radin's analysis make her approach unique? What are the advantages of pragmatism in and of itself? What might be the advantages of adopting a pragmatic lens to determine which feminist approach to use in particular circumstances?

Perhaps there are problems with any single approach. For example, all else being equal, which it often is not, it may be desirable to seek a gender-neutral solution while also increasing women's power, promoting women's subjective pleasure, and reducing women's subjective pain. Should feminists approach any particular issue by balancing multiple goals, with an eye towards doing what is best for women, particularly the most vulnerable women? What would be the advantages and disadvantages of such an approach?

2. Radin sees relational, or cultural, feminism as problematic:

> Among feminist scholars, there is a critique of cultural feminism going on which starts from this question: If you were lucky enough to be a dominant group and wanted to dominate society, and you had the power to fashion the language in which people could construct their own

> identity and self-conception and ways in which they relate to other people, how would you construct a perfect subordinate group? Well, I think that you would make them cooperative, empathetic, nurturing of others, self-sacrificing, noncompetitive, and nonaggressive. The critique says that these characteristics that are attached to women may have been created under domination, and may need to be criticized rather than ensconced as the essence of women and uncritically praised. Uncritical acceptance of cultural feminism may play into a form of backlash.

Margaret Jane Radin, Please Be Careful with Cultural Feminism, 45 Stan. L. Rev. 1567, 1568 (1993). Would MacKinnon agree with Radin? See MacKinnon, Difference and Dominance, excerpted above. Does Becker's articulation of relational feminism avoid this problem? Why or why not? How would you resolve it?

Might there be risks associated with *not* arguing for the need to place greater value on caretaking? Is it possible to argue that caretaking is undervalued without implying that only women should be caretakers and that women should only be caretakers? Does the need to increase our culture's valuation of (at least some) traditionally feminine traits and activities while working for equality create a double bind? If we increase the value associated with traditionally feminine roles and qualities, we encourage women to stay in such roles and, as a result, to stay subordinate since power in the current social system lies elsewhere. On the other hand, if we do not place greater value on caretaking, community, relationships, etc., but continue to push *only* for equality, we are likely to push women to compete more in the market on the terms created for workers without significant caretaking responsibilities. We may end up in a world with too little caretaking. Does Radin ignore the double bind with respect to valuation of traditionally feminine qualities and traits? Would you prefer to live in the world that exists today, in one in which women did no more caretaking than men and were as aggressive and competitive, or in neither? What if women change and men do not? What if we end up in a world with too little caretaking? Would women be happier?

3. Earlier writers discussed Radin's double bind using somewhat different terms. Marilyn Frye continued her discussion of power and oppression by emphasizing that oppression means being literally pressed in many directions:

> * * * Something pressed is something caught between or among forces and barriers which are so related to each other that jointly they restrain, restrict or prevent the thing's motion or mobility. * * *
>
> * * * One of the most characteristic and ubiquitous features of the world as experienced by oppressed people is the double bind—situations in which options are reduced to a very few and all of them expose one to penalty, censure or deprivation. * * *

Frye, Oppression, in The Politics of Reality: Essays in Feminist Theory 1, 2 (1983). As examples, Frye points to the pressures on young women to be, and not to be, sexually active and the pressures on all subordinated people to "smile and be cheerful," thus participating in the denial of their oppression, or face alternatives which can be worse, such as loss of one's livelihood for being "mean, bitter, angry, or dangerous." Id. at 2–3. Describe some of the double binds you face on a daily basis. Do you feel double binds within your law school? When interviewing with or working at law firms or at other legal organizations? How do you "choose the alternative that will hinder empowerment the least and further it the most"? Do you find that your chosen solution changes regularly?

Some of Radin's contemporaries also discussed the double bind. Christine A. Littleton called the double bind "the problem of transition." Littleton, Women's Experience and the Problem of Transition: Perspectives on Male Battering of Women, 1989 U. Chi. Legal F. 23. Littleton argued that in a world of inequality, there are no risk-free strategies for improving women's situation. Do you agree? When considering how to resolve an issue of inequality, is the double bind always present or only usually or occasionally present?

4. Mari Matsuda wrote that she would:

> bend pragmatism toward liberation in three ways: First, I would weight the pragmatic method to identify and give special credence to the perspective of the subordinated; second, I would add a first principle of anti-subordination; and third, I would claim that the use of pragmatic method with a normative first principle is not inconsistent.

Matsuda, Pragmatism Modified and The False Consciousness Problem, 63 S. Cal. L. Rev. 1763, 1764 (1990). Do you agree? What are the arguments for and against giving "special credence to the perspective of the subordinated"? How would a pragmatist approach the elimination of subordination?

5. A pragmatic feminist would see experimentation as critically important, since as humans we are unable to imagine appropriate solutions to complex social problems using only abstract reason rather than trial and error. Do we need more experimentation in approaching inequality between the sexes? What would such experimentation entail? What would a world of sex equality look like? How would one get there from here? If we are unsure of either of these points, does that suggest the need for a pragmatic approach, one which permits experimentation with respect to ends and means?

6. What do you see as the strengths and weaknesses of pragmatic feminism? How might it be applied to various issues facing women? See Deborah L. Brake, Title IX as Pragmatic Feminism, 55 Clev. St. L. Rev. 513 (2007); Mary Becker, Strength in Diversity: Feminist Theoretical Approaches to Child Custody and Same–Sex Relationships, 23 Stetson L. Rev. 701 (1994).

E. A CASE STUDY

Prepare a chart like the one that follows. Use it to identify and contrast some of the major differences among the different approaches to feminist legal theory that you have considered. In row 1, identify what a world of equality would look like under each theory. How would you know you had reached equality under each of the approaches? In row 2, identify what each theory views as the major problem(s) associated with inequality. In row 3, describe what each theory views as the deep problem, root, or mainspring of inequality. In row 4, describe the ideal world each approach envisions. In row 5, list the values underlying each theory. In row 6, describe the method used by each approach. In rows 7 and 8, describe the strengths and weaknesses of each approach. See Mary Becker, Patriarchy and Inequality: Towards a Substantive Feminism, 1999 U. Chi. Legal F. 21, 46–48.

Theory	Liberal Equality	Anti-Essentialism	Post-modernism	[Theory of your choice]
Equality Principle				
Targeted Inequalities				
Fundamental Problem				
Ideal World				
Values				
Method				
Strengths				
Weaknesses				

Once you have finished the chart, please use it to analyze the following case study.

CASE STUDY: CALIFORNIA FEDERAL SAVINGS AND LOAN ASSOCIATION V. GUERRA

In 1978, California enacted legislation requiring employers to provide unpaid leave for childbirth but not for other temporary disabilities. The case arose when Lillian Garland, a single mother, sought to return to work as a receptionist after taking a two-month leave following the birth of her daughter. Her employer told her that her former position had been filled and that there were no similar positions available. Garland was unable to find another job immediately and, because of her unemployment, lost her apartment and eventually custody of her daughter.

When Garland sought to enforce her right to maternity leave under the California statute, the legislation was challenged as inconsistent with the federal Pregnancy Discrimination Act (PDA), which mandates that pregnancy be treated the same as other temporary disabilities for all employment-related purposes. In this case, California Federal Savings and Loan (known as "Cal Fed"), the employer, argued that the California law was inconsistent with and preempted by the federal statute because the state legislation was sex-specific.

The *Cal Fed* case evoked substantial dispute among feminist activists, legal scholars, and lawyers. The American Civil Liberties Union and other groups filed an amicus brief, portions of which appear below, arguing that the California legislation was preempted by the PDA. The National Organization for Women (NOW), the NOW Legal Defense and Education Fund, and the National Women's Law Center, among others, also filed an amicus brief, arguing that the California statute should be upheld only if employers were required to provide unpaid disability leave to *all* employees. Professor Wendy Williams was of counsel to this group. A number of feminist law professors, labor unions, and other groups filed still another amicus brief arguing that the California legislation should be upheld as enacted. Professors Christine

Littleton and Judith Resnik served as counsel on this brief, portions of which also appear below.

These briefs from the *Cal Fed* case are presented to provide a concrete context for discussions of the theoretical approaches presented above. Chapter 7 contains a fuller discussion of the issues for women and society raised by parental leave policies.

AMICUS BRIEF OF THE ACLU, LEAGUE OF WOMEN VOTERS, ET AL. IN CALIFORNIA FEDERAL SAVINGS AND LOAN ASSOCIATION v. GUERRA

No. 85–494 (1985).

[Arguing that the California statute is illegitimate sex discrimination]

Do women require, or are they entitled to, special pregnancy-related job benefits which men do not receive because they cannot become pregnant? Is pregnancy so different a disability as to negate the Congressionally-mandated right to legal equality between the sexes in the workplace? Does the fact that pregnancy is a unique physical condition, often of great personal consequence to the women and men involved, necessarily imply that it cannot be compared to other physical conditions that may similarly affect an employee's ability to work?

These questions have been answered unequivocally by Congress in the Pregnancy Discrimination Act ("PDA"), an amendment to Title VII. The PDA embodies the legislative judgment that women will secure equality, equity and greater tangible benefits when legal distinctions based on sex and pregnancy are eliminated, and when the similarities in the rights and needs of both sexes are seen to override their differences. The PDA thus adopts the view that pregnancy is analogous to other temporary physical conditions that may affect an employee's ability to work.

Congress had ample reason to reject *all* pregnancy-based distinctions when it enacted the PDA. Historically, protective legislation like § 12945(b)(2), designed to compensate women for the burdens imposed by pregnancy and motherhood, reinforced the distinctions between male and female workers, with powerful adverse consequences for women workers. Protectionist laws reflect an ideology which values women most highly for their childbearing and nurturing roles. Such laws reinforce stereotypes about women's inclinations and abilities; they deter employers from hiring women of childbearing age or funnel them into less responsible positions; and they make women *appear* to be more expensive, less reliable employees. Recognizing this history and its legacy, Congress elected to make pregnancy comparable to other temporary physical conditions that may affect an employee's ability to work, so as to direct attention away from debilitating stereotypes about pregnant women and focus attention on workers' need for disability leave itself.

As Congress recognized, pregnancy is neither an appropriate nor rational proxy for the need for disability benefits. Overall disability data indicate that, even including pregnancy, women do not require significantly more disability leave than men, and that numerous factors other than pregnancy correlate better with work-related disability. Even if this were not the case, the provision of sex-specific benefits is still not justifiable, since the provision of benefits on a gender-neutral basis would serve the interests of pregnant women and the state equally well. For the same reason, the statute cannot be rationalized as affirmative action.

The task here is to recognize the real needs of pregnant workers without at the same time destroying their right to equality in the workplace and perpetuating stereotypes which have, for generations, cast women "into an apologetic place in relation to work." The provision of special benefits for pregnant workers places women perpetually outside the mainstream of the labor force, permanently marginalizing their role as workers, and is not the answer.

AMICUS BRIEF OF COALITION FOR REPRODUCTIVE EQUALITY IN THE WORKPLACE, ET AL. IN CALIFORNIA FEDERAL SAVINGS AND LOAN ASSOCIATION v. GUERRA

No. 85–494 (1985).

[Arguing that the California statute is valid]

California law makes it an unfair employment practice for an employer to refuse to grant reasonable leave to female employees temporarily disabled by pregnancy, childbirth or related medical conditions. It thus remedies a form of sex discrimination not currently addressed by federal law—the discriminatory impact that inadequate leave policies have on working women's right of procreative choice.

Both men and women have a constitutional right to procreative choice, a fundamental right that includes the choice to become a parent. *Skinner v. Oklahoma,* 316 U.S. 535 (1942); *Cleveland Board of Education v. LaFleur,* 414 U.S. 632 (1974).

Leave policies that are inadequate to the needs of temporarily disabled workers may affect the *employment* interests of both sexes, but such policies additionally place a burden on working women's exercise of a fundamental *non*-employment right—the right of procreative choice—while having no impact whatsoever on the procreative rights of working men. A female employee subject to an inadequate leave policy is forced to choose between exercising her right to procreate and keeping her job—a choice her male co-workers never face.

California Government Code § 12945(b)(2) (West 1980) reduces the discriminatory impact of inadequate leave policies on women's procreative rights, while conferring no special benefit on any group of employees and imposing no special burden on others. It simply allows both male and female employees to exercise their procreative rights without jeopardizing their jobs.

In guaranteeing equal employment rights under Title VII, Congress could not have intended to prevent states from enabling equal exercise by working women and men of fundamental rights such as procreative choice. Absent a clear and manifest intent to preempt, states are free to enact labor legislation, especially legislation that prohibits discrimination. Title VII explicitly preserves state antidiscrimination laws that cover areas broader than those covered by Title VII, and encourages the states to take additional measures against sex discrimination.

Title VII preempts only those state laws that are unlawful under, or inconsistent with the purposes of, Title VII. The California statute is neither. It provides an additional remedy against sex discrimination. There is no inconsistency between Title VII's goal of removing artificial barriers to equal employment opportunity between the sexes and the California statute's effect of equalizing male and female employees' ability to exercise procreative choice without jeopardizing their jobs. The Pregnancy Discrimination Act ("PDA") does not alter this conclusion. The California statute must therefore be upheld.

NOTES ON CAL FED

1. Although supporting opposite sides of the litigation, how could both of the briefs above be viewed as embodying liberal equality theory? In what ways could either or both of the briefs also be viewed as embodying aspects of dominance, relational, anti-essentialist feminism, or other approaches to feminist legal theory? How would the arguments differ if MacKinnon, West, Crenshaw, Cain, Grillo, Frug, or Halley, for example, had instead written the briefs? What theory or combination of theories do you think could best address the constitutionality of the California legislation? What would be the main theme of your brief in the case?

2. Which brief do you think had the more compelling argument with respect to the impact of the California legislation? Did the statute eliminate entirely "the discriminatory impact that inadequate leave policies have on working women's right of reproductive choice," as described in the Reproductive Equality in the Workplace brief? How might the impact vary for women of differing ages, races, classes, religions, and sexual orientations? Under the statute, leave was unpaid (although California is now one of only a few states to offer paid leave). Wouldn't unpaid maternity leave have a disparate impact on the reproductive freedom of *most* women workers relative to men?

Subsequent studies have found that laws mandating unpaid parental leave for both men and women to care for a new child have been relatively easy for businesses to implement, cost little, and did not reduce productivity or profit. See Sarah Fass, Nat'l Ctr. for Children in Poverty, Paid Leave in the States 5 (2009); U.S. Dep't of Labor, Balancing the Needs of Families and Employers: Family and Medical Leave Surveys: 2000 Update 6–5 tbl.6.3

(2001). For an extended discussion of both paid and unpaid parental leave, see Chapter 7.

3. Why might MacKinnon support a law requiring employers to give employees unpaid maternity leave? Would she see such policies, perhaps even *paid* maternity leave, as increasing women's power by permitting mothers to keep jobs after childbirth like fathers already do? Or would she regard such policies as decreasing women's power by reinforcing traditional stereotypes of women's and men's roles; encouraging women to be primary caretakers of children; and permitting men to have sex with women without fully paying the price?

How would West's views likely differ? How would she begin thinking about the issue? What factors would she consider? How would she reach a conclusion? What sorts of results might make her rethink her position? How might *Cal Fed* present a conflict between acknowledging women's pleasures and pains and achieving substantive equality?

4. In an article co-authored with Barbara Flagg, then-Judge Ginsburg wrote:

> The logical progression from the 1970s litigation, it seems to me, is to another arena, not to the courts with their distinctly limited capacity, but to the legislature. Once the law books have been cleared of prescriptions of the kind Sally Reed, Sharon Frontiero, and Stephen Wiesenfeld challenged, what should one strive to enact instead? If women were dominant in our legislatures, what would their program be? Would they put through laws granting leave singularly to pregnant workers, with a guaranteed right to return to the job? Or would they press instead for legislation like the Family and Medical Leave Act, a measure that takes the woman at work as a model or motivator, but spreads out to shelter others: men and women who need time off not only to care for a newborn, but to attend to a seriously ill child, spouse, elderly parent or self? We do not yet have legislation of this sort but the very idea of it is no longer an impossible dream.

Ruth Bader Ginsburg & Flagg, Some Reflections on the Feminist Legal Thought of the 1970s, 1989 U. Chi. Legal F. 9, 18. In light of that statement and her decision in *VMI*, do you think Ginsburg would strike the *Cal Fed* statute as a violation of the Equal Protection Clause? If so, which women would be hurt the most? Which women might be helped?

5. If you were a judge hearing *Cal Fed*, what other, perhaps better, outcomes might you support? If you were a state legislator, what other forms of legislation might you support to further women's equality? See Mary E. Becker, Prince Charming: Abstract Equality, 1987 Sup. Ct. Rev. 201, 229–30.

6. Is the dispute over maternity leave, as the ACLU argues, just another episode in the long saga of feminists' struggle over protective legislation, as discussed in Chapter 2? If not, how is it distinguishable?

7. The Supreme Court held that the California legislation was not preempted by the PDA, because the PDA's legislative history indicated that Congress intended to prohibit discrimination *against* pregnancy, but not preferential treatment *for* pregnant workers. Because the California statute

was not inconsistent with either the PDA or the purposes of Title VII, it was not preempted by federal law. California Fed. Sav. & Loan Ass'n v. Guerra, 479 U.S. 272 (1987). How does this analysis compare to yours? If you had the opportunity to discuss feminist legal theory with Justice Marshall, the author of the opinion, which theories would you emphasize? How would you try to inform his analysis of this and other issues of sex equality?

CHAPTER 4

VIOLENCE AGAINST WOMEN

■ ■ ■

A. INTRODUCTION

Violence against women is "severe and pervasive throughout the world."[1] On average, at least one in three women experiences physical or sexual violence at the hands of an intimate partner, and half of all murdered women are killed by a current or former intimate. For women between the ages of 15 and 44, World Bank data suggest that the risk presented by cancer, motor vehicle accidents, war and malaria is outweighed by the likelihood of rape and domestic violence. The sex trafficking industry continues to grow, along with the global market in pornography. Violence against women is, in short, a global pandemic.[2] According to United Nations Secretary–General Ban Ki-moon, "violence against women and girls continues unabated in every continent, country and culture. It takes a devastating toll on women's lives, on their families and on society as a whole. Most societies prohibit such violence—yet the reality is that too often, it is covered up or tacitly condoned."

As throughout the world, violence against women in the United States remains a widespread reality. The Department of Justice estimates that there were just under 600,000 violent crimes committed by intimate partners in 2008; intimate partners include spouses, ex-spouses, and

---

1. U. N. Dep't of Pub. Info., February 2008. Statistics cited in this paragraph are drawn from United Nations Secretary General's In–Depth Study on Violence Against Women (2006) and other United Nations sources, as well as from the World Health Organization's landmark 2005 study of over 24,000 women in ten countries. See, e.g., The Secretary General, In-depth Study on all Forms of Violence Against Women, delivered to the General Assembly, U.N. Doc. A/61/122/Add.1 (July 6, 2006), available at http://daccess-ods.un.org/access.nsf/Get?Open & DS=A/61/122/ADD.1&Lang=E; World Health Organization, Multi–Country Study on Women's Health and Domestic Violence Against Women: Summary Report of Initial Results on Prevalence, Health Outcomes and Women's Responses, (2005), available at http://www.who.int/gender/violence/who_multicountry_study/en. See also, U.N. Special Rapporteur of Violence Against Women, 15 Years of the United Nations Special Rapporteur on Violence Against Women, Its Causes and Consequences (1994–2009), (June 2009), available at http://www2.ohchr.org/english/issues/women/rapporteur/docs/15YearReviewofVAWMandate.pdf.

2. In March 2010, Secretary of State Hillary Clinton remarked to the United Nations Commission on the Status of Women, "though many countries have passed laws to deter violence against women, it remains a global pandemic." Secretary of State Hillary Rodham Clinton, Remarks at the UN Commission on the Status of Women (March 10, 2010) (transcript and video available at http://www.state.gov/secretary/rm/2010/03/138320.htm).

boyfriends or girlfriends.[3] In 2000, however, the Centers for Disease Control and the National Institute of Justice reported much higher annual estimates for intimate partner violence. According to one of the largest national surveys, nearly one-quarter of all women reported that they had been raped or assaulted by a spouse or boyfriend at some time in their life.[4] Numbers have been controversial in this field, but researchers have generated a massive amount of data since the passage of the Violence Against Women Act in 1994. Even by conservative estimates, women experience significant violence[5]—most of which they never report to the police.[6] The economic effects of violence against women are enormous: according to a CDC study commissioned by Congress to quantify these effects, the cost of intimate partner violence (including physical assault, rape and stalking) exceeds $5.8 billion each year.[7]

---

3. U.S. Dep't of Justice, Bureau of Justice Statistics, Bulletin: Criminal Victimization, 2008, [hereinafter 2008 Criminal Victimization Bulletin], Table 6 at 5 (September 2009). The 2008 Criminal Victimization Bulletin was released in 2009 but is based on data from 2008. This study is based on the National Crime Victimization Survey. For more information about the survey method, see http://bjs.ojp.usdoj.gov/index.cfm?ty=dcdetail&iid=245.

4. Nat'l Inst. of Justice and Ctrs. for Disease Control and Prevention, Extent, Nature, and Consequences of Intimate Partner Violence: Findings From the National Violence Against Women Survey, at iii (July 2000) (surveying 16,000 men and women and finding 4.8 million intimate partner physical assaults or rapes perpetrated against women and approximately 2.9 million intimate partner physical assaults perpetrated against men annually) [hereinafter 2000 NVAW Survey]. See id. (25% figure over lifetime). The Centers for Disease Control and Prevention (CDC) undertook the National Violence Against Women (NVAW) survey in 1995 and 1996, yet it is still the only one of its kind in terms of both comprehensiveness and statistical accuracy. However, starting in 2010, the CDC, along with several other agencies, began collecting data for the new National Intimate Partner and Sexual Violence Surveillance System (NISVSS). According to the CDC, NISVSS will "provide national and state-level data, producing frequent, consistent, and reliable information on the magnitude and nature of intimate partner violence, sexual violence and stalking." Daniel J. Whitaker & LeRoy Reese, Ctrs. for Disease Control and Prevention, Preventing Intimate Partner Violence & Sexual Violence: Program Activities Guide (2007), available at http://www.cdc.gov/ncipc/dvp/Preventing_IPV_SV.pdf. The CDC plans to release the findings as they become available at http://www.cdc.gov/violenceprevention/NISVSS/index.html.

5. U.S. Dep't of Justice, Bureau of Justice Statistics, Family Violence Statistics Including Statistics on Strangers and Acquaintances 1, Table 3.1 (June 2005) (showing women as 81% of spouses and 71% of dating partners victimized by fatal violence). The underlying data of the 2005 Family Violence Report also suggests that the totals may mislead. For example, it shows 1.7 million crimes against spouses and 2 million against boyfriends and girlfriends, as the latter were considered "nonfamily" crimes. Id. at 9. There is good reason to believe that the National Crime Victim Survey on which this report is based undercounts spousal violence; as the interviews that lead to this data may not be conducted in private, the survey undercounts the number of repeat incidents, and questions about domestic violence are asked in the context of a crime survey. See id., Appendix (acknowledging data discrepancies); 2000 NVAW Survey, above note 2, at 13–14, 19–23 (explaining limitations of NCVS survey).

6. According to the 2000 NVAW Survey, women reported to the police in only one-fifth of all rapes, one-quarter of all assaults, and one-half of all intimate-perpetrated stalking incidents. According to the 2008 Criminal Victimization Bulletin, above footnote 3, women reported about 50% of all violent crimes to the police, and about 41% of all rapes or sexual assaults were reported to the police, at 6 Text Table 4, 7 Table 8. The different numbers may reflect different survey methods used: the NVAW survey was an in-home computer-based survey administered by a researcher; the BJS data is based on the National Crime Victimization Survey—a phone survey. For more information on the survey methodologies see http://www.cdc.gov/ViolencePrevention/intimatepartnerviolence/datasources.html, and http://bjs.ojp.usdoj.gov/index.cfm?ty=dcdetail&iid=245.

7. Ctrs. for Disease Control and Prevention, Costs of Intimate Partner Violence Against Women in the United States (2003), available at http://www.cdc.gov/violenceprevention/pub/IPV_cost.html. The total economic cost of domestic violence consists of nearly $4.1 billion for direct

What we tend to consider criminal violence, however, may be just part of a larger system of violence against women, much of which remains trivialized by the law. One need look no farther than the street, the setting for commonplace harassment that, as Cynthia Grant Bowman suggests, "both evokes and reinforces women's legitimate fear of rape."[8] Bowman explains:

> It does so by reminding women that they are vulnerable to attack and by demonstrating that any man may choose to invade a woman's personal space, physically or psychologically, if he feels like it. Thus, street harassment forms part of a whole spectrum of means by which men objectify women and assert coercive power over them, one which is more invidious because it is so pervasive and appears, deceptively, to be trivial.[9]

Technology continues to generate different mechanisms for harassment, to much the same effect. In particular, apart from its transformation of the sex trafficking and pornography industries, the internet has enabled new forms of violence against women. Danielle Keats Citron summarizes cyber gender harassment and its impact:

> The online harassment of women exemplifies twenty-first century behavior that profoundly harms women yet too often remains overlooked and even trivialized. This harassment includes rape threats, doctored photographs portraying women being strangled, postings of women's home addresses alongside suggestions that they are interested in anonymous sex, and technological attacks that shut down blogs and websites. It impedes women's full participation in online life, often driving them offline, and undermines their autonomy, identity, dignity, and well-being.[10]

Citron's work shows how all forms of violence, no matter how "trivial," create a system of constant reminders that women are vulnerable and targets *solely* by virtue of gender. As some researchers have put it, violence is simply the "female fear."[11]

Until recently, the study of intimate violence within the law has tended to isolate as "women's issues" particular kinds of violence, such as rape, "domestic violence," and sexual harassment. In many ways this has been extraordinarily helpful—even revolutionary. It has spotlighted problems that quite literally had no names; in the late twentieth century, it is

---

medical and mental health care services, $0.9 billion in lost productivity for victims of nonfatal violence, and $0.9 billion in lifetime earnings lost by femicide victims. To be clear, the overall cost estimated by the CDC does not encompass the effects of non-intimate violence against women.

8. Cynthia Grant Bowman, Street Harassment and the Informal Ghettoization of Women, 106 Harv. L. Rev. 517, 540 (1993).

9. Id.

10. Danielle Keats Citron, Law's Expressive Value in Combating Cyber Gender Harassment, 108 Mich. L. Rev. 373 (2009).

11. See Sandra S. Tangri, Martha R. Burt & Leanor B. Johnson, Sexual Harassment at Work: Three Explanatory Models, 38 J. Soc. Issues 33, 48 (1982); Margaret T. Gordon & Stephanie Riger, The Female Fear (1989).

fair to say that feminists revealed problems hidden for decades. As Deborah Rhode writes, "[f]or most of this nation's history, most sexual abuse went unnamed, unreported, unchallenged, and unchanged. Until the last quarter century, America had no legal term or conceptual cubby-hole for sexual harassment. There also were no rape crisis policies or battered women's shelters, no studies of the frequency of acquaintance rape or spousal abuse, and no discussion of the link between pornography and sexual violence. All this has changed." [Unfortunately,] "longstanding patterns of denial remain much the same."[12]

This chapter examines how gender and, in particular, intimate relationships affect the law of violence across a wide spectrum of offenses, from murder to rape to prostitution and pornography. Although we have included numerous manifestations of violence against women within this single chapter, the effects of violence permeate all aspects of our lives, including race, culture, socioeconomic status, mothering, marriage, reproduction, work, education, and sexuality. As you read the following materials, think about how the many forms of violence against women are integrated into a single, pervasive system and the impact of that system on our lives. To what extent is violence against women a manifestation of gender hierarchy? What counts as violence? Also consider the patterns of thought and law that one finds across different forms of violence—claims of victim desert or provocation, efforts to naturalize violence (to make it part of something that cannot be "controlled"), the dichotomization of victim/agent—and whether these patterns have analogues across law's doctrinal categories. Finally, reflect on how the insights of feminism have shaped our legal response to violence against women, and how law might yet be reformed to better recognize and redress its harms.

Note: Some of the material in this chapter may be disturbing to readers. Also, while we recognize the distinction between "victim" and "survivor," we have used those terms interchangeably in this chapter without intending to imply a negative meaning to "victim." We have also used the term "domestic violence" interchangeably with the less domesticating "intimate partner violence."

B. HOMICIDE

1. MANSLAUGHTER v. MURDER: THE QUESTION OF PROVOCATION

Experts agree that homicide is a predominantly male act. Males are ten times more likely than females to commit murder.[13] Women are particularly at risk for intimate killings and sex-related homicides. In

12. Deborah L. Rhode, Speaking of Sex: The Denial of Gender Inequality 95 (1997).

13. Fed. Bureau of Investigation, 2008 Crime in the United States, Expanded Homicide Data Table 3: Murder Offenders (2008), available at http://www.fbi.gov/ucr/cius2008/offenses/expanded_information/data/shrtable_03.html. As more FBI data sets become available, the FBI posts them at: http://www.fbi.gov/ucr/ucr.htm.

2007, about 45% of female homicide victims were killed by an "intimate"—meaning a spouse, an ex-spouse, or a boyfriend; approximately 5% of males were killed by intimates.[14] While the intimate homicide rate has generally declined since 1995, "of all female murder victims, the proportion killed by an intimate has been increasing."[15]

In the past fifteen years, a number of critics have challenged the way that murder law treats intimate homicide; some, such as Victoria Nourse and Susan Estrich, have claimed it allows men to "get away with murder" by reducing premeditated murder charges to those of manslaughter. The doctrinal focus of this claim is the "provocation" or "heat of passion" defense, which does not acquit but reduces the verdict from murder to manslaughter and is frequently invoked in intimate homicide cases.[16] According to one government study, "[w]hile most persons arrested (70%) for spouse murder were charged with first-degree murder, most persons convicted (52%)" had manslaughter as their conviction offense. In some states, this mitigation factor may mean little in terms of the number of years spent in prison; in others it can be substantial. According to figures for 2003, the mean state prison sentence length for manslaughter was approximately half that of murder, and the mean time served for manslaughter was about four years (49 months).[17]

The following case has been taught in criminal law casebooks for decades on the theory that it applies a sound and compassionate "reformed" rule for intimate homicide. Do you agree?

PEOPLE v. BERRY

Supreme Court of California, 1976.
18 Cal.3d 509, 556 P.2d 777, 134 Cal.Rptr. 415.

SULLIVAN, JUSTICE.

Defendant Albert Joseph Berry was charged by indictment with one count of murder. * * * Defendant was sentenced to state prison for the term prescribed by law. He appeals from the judgment of conviction.

Defendant contends that there is sufficient evidence in the record to show that he committed the homicide while in a state of uncontrollable rage caused by provocation * * * and therefore that it was error for the

---

14. Unless otherwise indicated, the homicide figures appearing in this paragraph can be found at U.S. Dep't of Justice, Bureau of Justice Statistics, Homicide Trends in the United States (1976–2005): http://bjs.ojp.usdoj.gov/content/homicide/gender.cfm, last visited July 16, 2010 [hereinafter Homicide Trends].

15. Homicide Trends (citing FBI, Supplementary Homicide Reports, 1976–2005).

16. See, e.g., Susan Estrich, Getting Away With Murder: How Politics Is Destroying the Criminal Justice System (1998); Victoria F. Nourse, Passion's Progress: Modern Law Reform and the Provocation Defense, 106 Yale L.J. 1331 (1997); Dan M. Kahan & Martha Nussbaum, Two Conceptions of Emotion in Criminal Law, 96 Colum. L. Rev. 269 (1996); Jeremy Horder, Provocation and Responsibility (1992).

17. U.S. Dep't of Justice, Bureau of Justice Statistics, Spouse Murder Defendants in Large Urban Counties at iii (Sept. 1995) (manslaughter/murder rate (j)); State Univ. of N.Y. at Albany, Bureau of Justice Statistics, Sourcebook of Criminal Justice Statistics 2003 Table 6.44 at 511, available at www.albany.edu/sourcebook/pdf/t644.pdf (mean years of punishment).

trial court to fail to instruct the jury on voluntary manslaughter as indeed he had requested. He claims * * * that he was entitled to an instruction on voluntary manslaughter as defined by statute since the killing was done upon a sudden quarrel or heat of passion. * * *

Defendant, a cook, 46 years old, and Rachel Pessah, a 20-year-old girl from Israel, were married on May 27, 1974. Three days later Rachel went to Israel by herself, returning on July 13, 1974. On July 23, 1974, defendant choked Rachel into unconsciousness. She was treated at a hospital where she reported her strangulation by defendant to an officer of the San Francisco Police Department. On July 25, Inspector Sammon, who had been assigned to the case, met with Rachel and as a result of the interview a warrant was issued for defendant's arrest.

While Rachel was at the hospital, defendant removed his clothes from their apartment and stored them in a Greyhound Bus Depot locker. He stayed overnight at the home of a friend, Mrs. Jean Berk, admitting to her that he had choked his wife. On July 26, he telephoned Mrs. Berk and informed her that he had killed Rachel with a telephone cord on that morning at their apartment. The next day Mrs. Berk and two others telephoned the police to report a possible homicide and met Officer Kelleher at defendant's apartment. They gained entry and found Rachel on the bathroom floor. A pathologist from the coroner's office concluded that the cause of Rachel's death was strangulation. Defendant was arrested on August 1, 1974, and confessed to the killing.

At trial defendant did not deny strangling his wife, but claimed through his own testimony and the testimony of a psychiatrist, Dr. Martin Blinder, that he was provoked into killing her because of a sudden and uncontrollable rage so as to reduce the offense to one of voluntary manslaughter. He testified that upon her return from Israel, Rachel announced to him that while there she had fallen in love with another man, one Yako, and had enjoyed his sexual favors, that he was coming to this country to claim her and that she wished a divorce. Thus commenced a tormenting two weeks in which Rachel alternately taunted defendant with her involvement with Yako and at the same time sexually excited defendant, indicating her desire to remain with him.

* * *

After their marriage, Rachel lived with defendant for only three days and then left for Israel. Immediately upon her return to San Francisco she told defendant about her relationship with and love for Yako. This brought about further argument and a brawl that evening in which defendant choked Rachel and she responded by scratching him deeply many times. Nonetheless they continued to live together. Rachel kept taunting defendant with Yako and demanding a divorce. She claimed she thought she might be pregnant by Yako. She showed defendant pictures of herself with Yako. Nevertheless, during a return trip from Santa Rosa, Rachel demanded immediate sexual intercourse with defendant in the car, which was achieved; however upon reaching their apartment, she again stated that she loved Yako and that she would not have intercourse with defendant in the future.

On the evening of July 22d defendant and Rachel went to a movie where they engaged in heavy petting. When they returned home and got into bed, Rachel announced that she had intended to make love with defendant, "But I am saving myself for this man Yako, so I don't think I will." Defendant got out of bed and prepared to leave the apartment whereupon Rachel screamed and yelled at him. Defendant choked her into unconsciousness.

Two hours later defendant called a taxi for his wife to take her to the hospital. He put his clothes in the Greyhound bus station and went to the home of his friend Mrs. Berk for the night. The next day he went to Reno and returned the day after. Rachel informed him by telephone that there was a warrant for his arrest as a result of her report to the police about the choking incident. On July 25th defendant returned to the apartment to talk to Rachel, but she was out. He slept there overnight. Rachel returned around 11 a.m. the next day. Upon seeing defendant there, she said, "I suppose you have come here to kill me." Defendant responded, "yes," changed his response to "no," and then again to "yes," and finally stated "I have really come to talk to you." Rachel began screaming. Defendant grabbed her by the shoulder and tried to stop her screaming. She continued. They struggled and finally defendant strangled her with a telephone cord.

Dr. Martin Blinder, a physician and psychiatrist, called by the defense, testified that Rachel was a depressed, suicidally inclined girl and that this suicidal impulse led her to involve herself ever more deeply in a dangerous situation with defendant. She did this by sexually arousing him and taunting him into jealous rages in an unconscious desire to provoke him into killing her and thus consummating her desire for suicide. Throughout the period commencing with her return from Israel until her death, that is from July 13 to July 26, Rachel continually provoked defendant with sexual taunts and incitements, alternating acceptance and rejection of him. This conduct was accompanied by repeated references to her involvement with another man; it led defendant to choke her on two occasions, until finally she achieved her unconscious desire and was strangled. Dr. Blinder testified that as a result of this cumulative series of provocations, defendant at the time he fatally strangled Rachel, was in a state of uncontrollable rage, completely under the sway of passion.

We first take up defendant's claim that on the basis of the foregoing evidence he was entitled to an instruction on voluntary manslaughter as defined by statute which is "the unlawful killing of a human being, without malice . . . upon a sudden quarrel or heat of passion." In People v. Valentine (1946), this court, in an extensive review of the law of manslaughter, specifically approved the following quotation from People v. Logan (1917) as a correct statement of the law: "In the present condition of our law it is left to the jurors to say whether or not the facts and circumstances in evidence are sufficient to lead them to believe that the defendant did, or to create a reasonable doubt in their minds as to whether or not he did, commit his offense under a heat of passion. The jury is further to be admonished and advised by the court that this heat of passion must be such a passion as would naturally be aroused in the mind of an ordinarily reasonable person under the given facts and circumstances, and that, consequently, no defendant may set up his own standard of conduct and justify or excuse himself because in fact his passions were aroused, unless further the jury believe that the facts and circumstances were sufficient to arouse the passions of the ordinarily reasonable man.... For the fundamental of the inquiry is whether or not the defendant's reason was, at the time of his act, so disturbed or obscured by some passion—not necessarily fear and never, of course, the passion for revenge—to such an extent as would render ordinary men of average disposition liable to act rashly or without due deliberation and reflection, and from this passion rather than from judgment."

We further held in *Valentine* that there is no specific type of provocation required by section 192 and that verbal provocation may be sufficient. In People v. Borchers (1958) in the course of explaining the phrase "heat of passion" used in the statute defining manslaughter we pointed out that "passion" need not mean "rage" or "anger" but may be any "[violent], intense, high-wrought or enthusiastic emotion" and concluded there "that defendant was aroused to a heat of 'passion' by a series of events over a considerable period of time...." Accordingly we there declared that evidence of admissions of infidelity by the defendant's paramour, taunts directed to him and other conduct, "supports a finding that defendant killed in wild desperation induced by [the woman's] long continued provocatory conduct." We find this reasoning persuasive in the case now before us. Defendant's testimony chronicles a two-week period of provocatory conduct by his wife Rachel that could arouse a passion of jealousy, pain and sexual rage in an ordinary man of average disposition such as to cause him to act rashly from this passion. It is significant that both defendant and Dr. Blinder testified that the former was in the heat of passion under an uncontrollable rage when he killed Rachel.

The Attorney General contends that the killing could not have been done in the heat of passion because there was a cooling period, defendant having waited in the apartment for 20 hours. However, the long course of provocatory conduct, which had resulted in intermittent outbreaks of rage under specific provocation in the past, reached its final culmination in the apartment when Rachel began screaming. Both defendant and Dr. Blinder testified that defendant killed in a state of uncontrollable rage, of passion, and there is ample evidence in the record to support the conclusion that this passion was the result of the long course of provocatory conduct by Rachel, just as the killing emerged from such conduct in *Borchers*. * * *

[T]he court did commit error in refusing to instruct on voluntary manslaughter based on sudden quarrel or heat of passion. * * * Since this theory of provocation constituted defendant's entire defense to the first count, we have no difficulty concluding that the failure to give such instruction was prejudicial error and requires us to reverse the conviction of murder of the first degree.

NOTES ON PROVOCATION

1. Was Berry a victim of his emotions, a killer who snapped and was thus unlikely to commit other offenses? Or, by concluding that the victim, who is dead, pursued a "long course of provocatory conduct," did the court blame Rachel for her own death? What is the significance of the fact that Berry waited twenty hours to kill? What if you knew that there was evidence at trial that Berry had a conviction for stabbing and injuring another wife, his second? What if he stated when he arrived at the police station, "I deliberately waited to kill her. No pretense, no bullshi[t], no nothing." Donna Coker, Heat of Passion and Wife Killing: Men Who Batter/Men Who Kill, 2 S. Cal. Rev. L. & Women's Studies 71, 117, 121 (1992–1993). A defense lawyer will respond that if there is "some" evidence on which a reasonable jury could find "provocation" then the proper legal result is that the jury is to make the decision about provocation. And, yet, at common law, such a case would never have gone to a jury because of a rule demanding that the actor kill immediately upon seeing his wife "in flagrante delicto"; words alone were never enough. Here, those requirements were not satisfied, and so, under traditional law, the defense would not have gone to the jury. Modern law has expanded the law of provocation in large part out of compassion for defendants, but how has this reform actually affected women? For one view, see Victoria F. Nourse: Passion's Progress, Modern Law Reform and the Provocation Defense, 106 Yale L.J. 1331 (1997).

2. Was Berry a batterer? Based on a review of the trial transcript, Donna Coker argues that Berry is a classic case of a batterer. After reviewing Dr. Blinder's testimony, Coker finds that he testified not simply that it was Rachel's provocatory acts that prompted Berry's actions, but "the cumulative rage resulting from the provocation of all the women in Berry's entire life."

> In essence, Berry's defense was that he was the sort of man who abused women—but the twist was Blinder's psychiatric explanation that Berry's violence was a result of his choosing women who enraged him and provoked him to violence. The fact that Berry had a prior conviction for assaulting his ex-wife with a butcher knife, that in past relationships with other women he had destroyed their property, forcing former girlfriends to "put him out of the house, locking the door," indicated to Blinder the personality of the *women* with whom Berry involved himself, more than it demonstrated Berry's dangerous and abusive nature. * * * Blinder's testimony provides a classic portrait of an abuser. Berry was *most* dangerous when women threatened to leave him. Berry was "emotionally dependent" on wives and girlfriends; he threatened physical violence in order to control women; he destroyed women's property; and he had a history of violent relationships with wives and lovers. * * * The irony of [Dr. Blinder's] testimony is found in its confirmation that Berry had a *propensity* to assault wives and lovers under circumstances in which he claimed the woman's infidelity provoked him. Rachel, then, became the

> recipient of Berry's cumulative rage against all the past women in his life. In a tautological way, Berry's past abuse of other women was used to strengthen his claim of *Rachel's* provocative nature * * *.

Coker, above note 1, at 118–20 (emphasis in original).

3. In the area of rape law, commentators have identified for some time the notion of "rape myths." As Morrison Torrey explains, one of these myths is that women precipitate (in essence provoke) rape by their behavior. Morrison Torrey, When Will We Be Believed? Rape Myths and the Idea of a Fair Trial in Rape Prosecutions, 24 U.C. Davis L. Rev. 1013, 1025–27 (1991). So, too, there are pervasive provocation stories in cases of battering, the most prominent being that the woman provoked the violence (or at least did not prevent it) by staying. Martha R. Mahoney, Exit: Power and the Idea of Leaving in Love, Work, and the Confirmation Hearings, 65 S. Cal. L. Rev. 1283, 1285 (1992). In *Berry*, the "defense portrayed Rachel as a vindictive—albeit confused—woman who sexually used and abused Berry in order to gain her own death." Coker, above note 1, at 122. Dr. Blinder even testified that Rachel in effect wanted to die, that she was a "suicidally inclined girl" with an "unconscious desire to provoke [Berry] into killing her." People v. Berry, 556 P.2d 777, 780 (Cal. 1976). Do rape myths actually apply more broadly to other crimes, like homicide? We will explore these myths further in Section D.

4. Almost every state in the union recognizes a form of the "heat of passion" defense, even if the forms differ rather substantially from state to state. See Nourse, above note 1, at 1339–42. One exception is the state of Maryland, which amended its laws to eliminate adultery as a ground for a provocation claim after a controversial case put the defense in a bad light. Md. Code Ann., Crim. Law § 2–207(b) (West 2006).

The case that led to a change in Maryland's law occurred as follows: Kenneth Peacock returned to his house to find his wife in bed with another man. He threatened the man and his wife, then went downstairs. After drinking a gallon of wine, he returned upstairs with a shotgun and shot his wife who was in the process of packing to leave. The sentencing judge stated as follows:

> I cannot think of a circumstance whereby personal rage is uncontrollable greater than this for someone who is happily married. And that is not mere lip service, it is a fact. * * * I seriously wonder how many married men * * * would have the strength to walk away, but without inflicting some corporal punishment. * * * I shudder to think what I would do. I'm not known for having the quietest disposition * * *. So the sentence of the court is that I will impose * * * a sentence of three years * * *. I recommend work release immediately. I also will recommend * * * home detention. * * * Upon his conclusion of the eighteen months or that portion of [work release,] I'm going to place Mr. Peacock on probation for a period of one year.

Maryland v. Peacock, No. 94–CR–0943 (Balt. County Cir. Ct. Oct. 17, 1994) (Cahill, J.). Ultimately, the judge was disciplined for his behavior, and the law was changed. Why do you suppose other jurisdictions have not followed Maryland? Is it because social norms have now evolved and juries and judges do not recommend manslaughter verdicts because the provocation defense in such circumstances seems unreasonable?

5. The original justification for including "sight of adultery" cases under the provocation defense was that the defendant's property (his wife's chastity) had been wrongfully taken, and the early cases all dealt with the killing of a romantic rival (rather than the woman). The analogy was to theft. As one English court put it: "jealousy is the rage of a man, and adultery is the highest invasion of property. * * * If a thief comes to rob another, it is lawful to kill him. And if a man comes to rob a man's posterity and his family, yet to kill him is manslaughter. So is the law though it may seem hard, the killing in the one case should not be as justifiable as the other. * * * * So that a man cannot receive a higher provocation." Regina v. Mawgridge, [1707] Kel. 1, 117, in 84 Eng. Rep. 1107, 1115. Does the property rationale suggest women's sexuality is owned by men? Or is the defense a classic example of women being largely irrelevant to the claim, the principal focus being male honor vis-à-vis other males? Does the property rationale fit in a world where women, rather than men, are killed as the result of romantic rage?

6. The modern law of provocation has tended to expand the defense by focusing on the mental state of the offenders, rather than the nature of the provoking acts. This has the effect of placing norms about passion and intimate relations into the minds of the parties. Most modern jurisdictions (although not all) have rejected the notion of a limited set of provoking acts and expanded the defense to include any "reasonable" provocation. The modern theory of the defense has been that a killing in the heat of passion is not as culpable because it lacks premeditation. Do you think that if a man were to kill his boss in a heat of passion, the jury would find his passion "uncontrollable"? Why do people commonly believe that passion is uncontrollable in the context of an intimate relation when it is controllable elsewhere?

7. Criminal law scholars have generally assumed that provoked homicides can never lead to complete acquittal: the provocation defense reduces the verdict, but does not eliminate a penalty. In earlier times, however, cultural practices may have led to a very different conclusion. Historians have uncovered a good deal of evidence that an "unwritten law" once prevailed which held that men who killed to defend their honor and home could be acquitted. The legal theory of the defense was a form of insanity laced with notions of male and female honor all wrapped up in rhetoric about the "defense of the home." In the early part of the century, this "unwritten law" was referred to as "dementia Americana." There are few appellate cases on point (if it succeeded the defendants were acquitted and so would not appeal), but a wealth of historical evidence, including accounts of some of the most famous murder trials in history. See, e.g., Martha Merrill Umphrey, Media Melodrama, Sensationalism and the 1907 Trial of Harry Thaw, 43 N.Y. L. Sch. L. Rev. 715, 715 (1999); Hendrik Hartog, Lawyering, Husbands' Rights, and the "Unwritten Law" in Nineteenth Century America, 84 J. Am. Hist. 67 (1997); Robert M. Ireland, The Libertine Must Die: Sexual Dishonor and the Unwritten Law in the Nineteenth–Century United States, 23 J. Soc. Hist. 27 (1989). A few jurisdictions actually codified the unwritten law and some southern courts embraced it. See, e.g., Biggs v. Georgia, 29 Ga. 723, 728–29 (1860) ("Has an American jury ever convicted a husband or father of murder

or manslaughter, for killing the seducer of his wife or daughter?"). This claim was not limited to the nineteenth century, but lived on at least until the 1930s. See David Stannard, Honor Killing: How the Infamous 'Massie Affair' Transformed Hawai'i (2005) (recounting the history of the Massie case, a nation-stopping melodrama involving the "unwritten law" and rape); Case Comment, Recognition of the Honor Defense under the Insanity Plea, 43 Yale L. J. 809 (1934). What does this history of a form of the insanity defense say about the power of gender? What does it say about the law's vision of extreme emotion?

8. There is some evidence that provocation has been used, in modern cases, even when there is no sexual infidelity involved, but simply when the victim has left the relationship. See Nourse, above note 1, at 1342–58. For instance, in State v. Forrest, 578 A.2d 1066 (Conn. 1990), the jury was instructed on the modern provocation defense where the victim "attended a party with the defendant and thereafter 'told the defendant not to believe that they would get back together.' As they were driving home, the defendant got angry, pulled a shotgun from the trunk, and killed." Should a man who hears that his former girlfriend does not want to reunite be entitled to have a claim of provocation go to the jury? What is your assessment of cases that give a claim of provocation to the jury when a man learns that his wife has filed for divorce? See People v. Guevara, 521 N.Y.S.2d 292, 293 (N.Y. App. Div. 1987). If a woman has the right to seek divorce, why should the law benefit one who impinges on that right?

9. The killing of women, typically by an intimate, has often been referred to as "femicide." What explains why men kill their wives, girlfriends, and former intimates? Should the phenomenon be generally understood as domestic violence? Consider the following documented empirical data:

- Femicides "typically culminate a long history of domestic abuse aimed at dominating and silencing the victim." Brief for the Domestic Violence Legal Empowerment and Appeals Project (DV LEAP), California Partnership to End Domestic Violence, Legal Momentum, et al. as Amici Curiae Supporting Respondent at 32, Giles v. California, 128 S. Ct. 2678 (2008) (No. 07–6053), 2008 U.S. S. Ct. Briefs LEXIS 353 at 48–49 (citing Jacquelyn C. Campbell, Assessing Dangerousness: Violence By Batterers and Child Abusers (2d ed. 2007)).
- "The chance of murder is at its peak upon separation." Id. (citing American Psychological Association, Violence and Family: Report of the American Psychological Association Presidential Task Force on Violence and the Family 39 (1996)).
- The "single most important risk factor for gendered homicide is the level of entrapment established when physical domination through beatings and sexual assault (rape) is supported by intimidation, isolation, and control over money, food, sex, work, and access to family and friends." Brief for Battered Women's Justice Project et. al. as Amici Curiae Supporting Respondent at 7, Giles v. California, 128 S. Ct. 2678 (2008) (No. 07–6053), 2008 U.S. S. Ct. Briefs LEXIS 355 (quoting Evan Stark & Anne Flitcraft, Women at Risk: Domestic Violence and Women's Health 146 (1996)).

Does the term "control killings" aptly describe lethal domestic violence?[18] What are the advantages and disadvantages of conceptualizing intimate femicide in this manner?

2. SELF-DEFENSE: WOMEN WHO KILL

Men and women tend to kill their partners in different situations: women, not men, tend to kill in response to violence or perceived violence. As one Department of Justice study found, according to information contained in prosecutors' files, more "wife defendants (44%) than husband defendants (10%) had been assaulted by their spouse (threatened with a weapon or physically assaulted) at or around the time of the murder."[19]

Consider in this light the proper relationship between cases in which the defendant is provoked to kill by violence and cases in which the defendant is provoked to kill, as in *Berry*, by extreme emotional distress, brought on by separation or infidelity. In *Berry*, the defendant sought a manslaughter verdict based on his claim of extreme emotional distress, and his right to have the jury hear his claim was upheld on appeal; in the case below, Judy Norman was found guilty of manslaughter, though her entitlement to have the jury decide her claim was ultimately reversed on appeal. Is this the proper relation of the claims given the differences in the circumstances? Is it possible that the superficial equality of desired result (manslaughter) betrays a disparity in proper outcomes (the male defendant should be convicted of premeditated murder but the female acquitted or given a reduced sentence)? Does formal equality of rules enforce inequality?

STATE v. NORMAN

Supreme Court of North Carolina, 1989.
324 N.C. 253, 378 S.E.2d 8.

MITCHELL, JUSTICE

The defendant was tried [for] the first degree murder of her husband. The jury found the defendant guilty of voluntary manslaughter. The defendant appealed from the trial court's judgment sentencing her to six years imprisonment. The Court of Appeals granted a new trial, citing as error the trial court's refusal to submit a possible verdict of acquittal by reason of perfect self-defense. Notwithstanding the uncontroverted evidence that the defendant shot her husband three times in the back of the head as he lay sleeping in his bed, the Court of Appeals held that the defendant's evidence that she exhibited what has come to be called "the battered wife syndrome" entitled her to have the jury consider whether the homicide was an act of perfect self-defense and, thus, not a legal wrong. * * *

18. Deborah Tuerkheimer, Control Killings, 87 Tex. L. Rev. See Also 117 (2009).

19. U.S. Dep't of Justice, Bureau of Justice Statistics, Spouse Murder Defendants in Large Urban Counties at iv (Sept. 1995).

The defendant presented evidence tending to show a long history of physical and mental abuse by her husband due to his alcoholism. At the time of the killing, the thirty-nine-year-old defendant and her husband had been married almost twenty-five years and had several children. The defendant testified that her husband had started drinking and abusing her about five years after they were married. His physical abuse of her consisted of frequent assaults that included slapping, punching and kicking her, striking her with various objects, and throwing glasses, beer bottles and other objects at her. The defendant described other specific incidents of abuse, such as her husband putting her cigarettes out on her, throwing hot coffee on her, breaking glass against her face and crushing food on her face. Although the defendant did not present evidence of ever having received medical treatment for any physical injuries inflicted by her husband, she displayed several scars about her face which she attributed to her husband's assaults.

The defendant's evidence also tended to show other indignities inflicted upon her by her husband. Her evidence tended to show that her husband did not work and forced her to make money by prostitution, and that he made humor of that fact to family and friends. He would beat her if she resisted going out to prostitute herself or if he was unsatisfied with the amounts of money she made. He routinely called the defendant "dog," "bitch" and "whore," and on a few occasions made her eat pet food out of the pets' bowls and bark like a dog. He often made her sleep on the floor. At times, he deprived her of food and refused to let her get food for the family. During those years of abuse, the defendant's husband threatened numerous times to kill her and to maim her in various ways.

The defendant said her husband's abuse occurred only when he was intoxicated, but that he would not give up drinking. She said she and her husband "got along very well when he was sober," and that he was "a good guy" when he was not drunk. She had accompanied her husband to the local mental health center for sporadic counseling sessions for his problem, but he continued to drink.

In the early morning hours on the day before his death, the defendant's husband, who was intoxicated, went to a rest area off I–85 near Kings Mountain where the defendant was engaging in prostitution and assaulted her. While driving home, he was stopped by a patrolman and jailed on a charge of driving while impaired. After the defendant's mother got him out of jail at the defendant's request later that morning, he resumed his drinking and abuse of the defendant.

The defendant's evidence also tended to show that her husband seemed angrier than ever after he was released from jail and that his abuse of the defendant was more frequent. That evening, sheriff's deputies were called to the Norman residence, and the defendant complained that her husband had been beating her all day and she could not take it anymore. The defendant was advised to file a complaint, but she said she was afraid her husband would kill her if she had him arrested. The deputies told her they needed a warrant before they could arrest her husband, and they left the scene.

The deputies were called back less than an hour later after the defendant had taken a bottle of pills. The defendant's husband cursed her and called her names as she was attended by paramedics, and he told them to let her die. A sheriff's deputy finally chased him back into his house as the defendant was put into an ambulance. The defendant's stomach was pumped at the local hospital, and she was sent home with her mother.

While in the hospital, the defendant was visited by a therapist with whom she discussed filing charges against her husband and having him committed for treatment. Before the therapist left, the defendant agreed to go to the mental health center the next day to discuss those possibilities. The therapist testified at trial that the defendant seemed depressed in the hospital, and that she expressed considerable anger toward her husband. He testified that the defendant threatened a number of times that night to kill her husband and that she said she should kill him "because of the things he had done to her."

The next day, the day she shot her husband, the defendant went to the mental health center to talk about charges and possible commitment, and she confronted her husband with that possibility. She testified that she told her husband later that day: "J. T., straighten up. Quit drinking. I'm going to have you committed to help you." She said her husband then told her he would "see them coming" and would cut her throat before they got to him.

The defendant also went to the social services office that day to seek welfare benefits, but her husband followed her there, interrupted her interview and made her go home with him. He continued his abuse of her, threatening to kill and to maim her, slapping her, kicking her, and throwing objects at her. At one point, he took her cigarette and put it out on her, causing a small burn on her upper torso. He would not let her eat or bring food into the house for their children.

That evening, the defendant and her husband went into their bedroom to lie down, and he called her a "dog" and made her lie on the floor when he lay down on the bed. Their daughter brought in her baby to leave with the defendant, and the defendant's husband agreed to let her babysit. After the defendant's husband fell asleep, the baby started crying and the defendant took it to her mother's house so it would not wake up her husband. She returned shortly with the pistol and killed her husband.

The defendant testified at trial that she was too afraid of her husband to press charges against him or to leave him. She said that she had temporarily left their home on several previous occasions, but he had always found her, brought her home and beaten her. Asked why she killed her husband, the defendant replied: "Because I was scared of him and I knowed when he woke up, it was going to be the same thing, and I was scared when he took me to the truck stop that night it was going to be worse than he had ever been. I just couldn't take it no more. There ain't no way, even if it means going to prison. It's better than living in that. That's worse hell than anything."

The defendant and other witnesses testified that for years her husband had frequently threatened to kill her and to maim her. When asked if she believed those threats, the defendant replied: "Yes. I believed him; he would, he would kill me if he got a chance. If he thought he wouldn't a had to went to jail, he would a done it."

Two expert witnesses in forensic psychology and psychiatry who examined the defendant after the shooting, Dr. William Tyson and Dr. Robert Rollins, testified that the defendant fit the profile of battered wife syndrome. This condition, they testified, is characterized by such abuse and degradation that the battered wife comes to believe she is unable to help herself and cannot expect help from anyone else. She believes that she cannot escape the complete control of her husband and that he is invulnerable to law enforcement and other sources of help.

Dr. Tyson, a psychologist, was asked his opinion as to whether, on 12 June 1985, "it appeared reasonably necessary for Judy Norman to shoot J. T. Norman?" He replied: "I believe that ... Mrs. Norman believed herself to be doomed ... to a life of the worst kind of torture and abuse, degradation that she had experienced over the years in a progressive way; that it would only get worse, and that death was inevitable...." Dr. Tyson later added: "I think Judy Norman felt that she had no choice, both in the protection of herself and her family, but to engage, exhibit deadly force against Mr. Norman, and that in so doing, she was sacrificing herself, both for herself and for her family."

Dr. Rollins, who was the defendant's attending physician at Dorothea Dix Hospital when she was sent there for evaluation, testified that in his opinion the defendant was a typical abused spouse and that "[s]he saw herself as powerless to deal with the situation, that there was no alternative, no way she could escape it." Dr. Rollins was asked his opinion as to whether "on June 12th, 1985, it appeared reasonably necessary that Judy Norman would take the life of J. T. Norman?" Dr. Rollins replied that in his opinion, "that course of action did appear necessary to Mrs. Norman."

Based on the evidence that the defendant exhibited battered wife syndrome, that she believed she could not escape her husband nor expect help from others, that her husband had threatened her, and that her husband's abuse of her had worsened in the two days preceding his death, the Court of Appeals concluded that a jury reasonably could have found that her killing of her husband was justified as an act of perfect self-defense. The Court of Appeals reasoned that the nature of battered wife syndrome is such that a jury could not be precluded from finding the defendant killed her husband lawfully in perfect self-defense, even though he was asleep when she killed him. We disagree.

The right to kill in self-defense is based on the necessity, real or reasonably apparent, of killing an unlawful aggressor to save oneself from imminent death or great bodily harm at his hands. Our law has recognized that self-preservation under such circumstances springs from a primal impulse and is an inherent right of natural law.

In North Carolina, a defendant is entitled to have the jury consider acquittal by reason of perfect self-defense when the evidence, viewed in the light most favorable to the defendant, tends to show that at the time of the killing it appeared to the defendant and she believed it to be necessary to kill the decedent to save herself from imminent death or great bodily harm. That belief must be reasonable, however, in that the circumstances as they appeared to the defendant would create such a belief in the mind of a person of ordinary firmness. * * * A killing in the proper exercise of the right of perfect self-defense is always completely justified in law and constitutes no legal wrong.

Our law also recognizes an imperfect right of self-defense in certain circumstances, including, for example, when the defendant is the initial aggressor, but without intent to kill or to seriously injure the decedent, and the decedent escalates the confrontation to a point where it reasonably appears to the defendant to be necessary to kill the decedent to save herself from imminent death or great bodily harm. Although the culpability of a defendant who kills in the exercise of imperfect self-defense is reduced, such a defendant is not justified in the killing so as to be entitled to acquittal, but is guilty at least of voluntary manslaughter.

The defendant in the present case was not entitled to a jury instruction on either perfect or imperfect self-defense. * * * The killing of another human being is the most extreme recourse to our inherent right of self-preservation and can be justified in law only by the utmost real or apparent necessity brought about by the decedent. * * * Only if defendants are required to show that they killed due to a reasonable belief that death or great bodily harm was imminent can the justification for homicide remain clearly and firmly rooted in necessity. The imminence requirement ensures that deadly force will be used only where it is necessary as a last resort in the exercise of the inherent right of self-preservation. * * *

The term "imminent," as used to describe such perceived threats of death or great bodily harm as will justify a homicide by reason of perfect self-defense, has been defined as "immediate danger, such as must be instantly met, such as cannot be guarded against by calling for the assistance of others or the protection of the law." Black's Law Dictionary 676 (5th ed. 1979). Our cases have sometimes used the phrase "about to suffer" interchangeably with "imminent" to describe the immediacy of threat that is required to justify killing in self-defense.

The evidence in this case did not tend to show that the defendant reasonably believed that she was confronted by a threat of imminent death or great bodily harm. The evidence tended to show that no harm was "imminent" or about to happen to the defendant when she shot her husband. The uncontroverted evidence was that her husband had been asleep for some time when she walked to her mother's house, returned with the pistol, fixed the pistol after it jammed and then shot her husband three times in the back of the head. The defendant was not faced with an instantaneous choice between killing her husband or being killed or seriously injured. Instead, all of the evidence tended to show that the defendant had ample time and opportunity to resort to other means of preventing further abuse by her husband. There was no action underway by the decedent from which the jury could have found that the defendant had reasonable grounds to believe either that a felonious assault was imminent or that it might result in her death or great bodily injury.* * *

Additionally, the lack of any belief by the defendant—reasonable or otherwise—that she faced a threat of imminent death or great bodily harm from the drunk and sleeping victim in the present case was illustrated by the defendant and her own expert witnesses when testifying about her subjective assessment of her situation at the time of the killing. The psychologist and psychiatrist replied affirmatively when asked their opinions of whether killing her husband "appeared reasonably necessary" to the defendant at the time of the homicide. That testimony spoke of no imminent threat nor of any fear by the defendant of death or great bodily harm, imminent or otherwise. Testimony in the form of a conclusion that a killing "appeared reasonably necessary" to a defendant does not tend to show all that must be shown to establish self-defense. More specifically, for a killing to be in self-defense, the perceived necessity must arise from a reasonable fear of imminent death or great bodily harm.

Dr. Tyson additionally testified that the defendant "believed herself to be doomed ... to a life of the worst kind of torture and abuse, degradation that she had experienced over the years in a progressive way; that it would only get worse, and that death was inevitable." Such evidence of the defendant's speculative beliefs concerning her remote and indefinite future, while indicating she had felt generally threatened, did not tend to show that she killed in the belief—reasonable or otherwise—that her husband presented a threat of imminent death or great bodily harm. Under our law of self-defense, a defendant's subjective belief of what might be "inevitable" at some indefinite point in the future does not equate to what she believes to be "imminent." Dr. Tyson's opinion that the defendant believed it was necessary to kill her husband for "the protection of herself and her family" was similarly indefinite and devoid of time frame and did not tend to show a threat or fear of imminent harm.

The defendant testified that, "I knowed when he woke up, it was going to be the same thing, and I was scared when he took me to the truck stop that night it was going to be worse than he had ever been." She also testified, when asked if she believed her husband's threats: "Yes.... [H]e would kill me if he got a chance. If he thought he wouldn't a had to went to jail, he would a done it." Testimony about such indefinite fears concerning what her sleeping husband might do at some time in the future did not tend to establish a fear—reasonable or otherwise—of imminent death or great bodily harm at the time of the killing. * * *

The reasoning of our Court of Appeals in this case proposes to change the established law of self-defense by giving the term "imminent" a meaning substantially more indefinite and all-encompassing than its present meaning. This would result in a substantial relaxation of the requirement of real or apparent necessity to justify homicide. Such reasoning proposes justifying the taking of human life not upon the reasonable belief it is necessary to prevent death or great bodily harm—which the imminence requirement ensures—but upon purely subjective speculation that the decedent probably would present a threat to life at a future time and that the defendant would not be able to avoid the predicted threat.

The Court of Appeals suggests that such speculation would have been particularly reliable in the present case because the jury, based on the evidence of the decedent's intensified abuse during the thirty-six hours preceding his death, could have found that the decedent's passive state at the time of his death was "but a momentary hiatus in a continuous reign of terror by the decedent [and] the defendant merely took advantage of her first opportunity to protect herself." Requiring jury instructions on perfect self-defense in such situations, however, would still tend to make opportune homicide lawful as a result of mere subjective predictions of indefinite future assaults and circumstances. Such predictions of future assaults to justify the defendant's use of deadly force in this case would be entirely speculative, because there was no evidence that her husband had ever inflicted any harm upon her that approached life-threatening injury, even during the "reign of terror." It is far from clear in the defendant's poignant evidence that any abuse by the decedent had ever involved the degree of physical threat required to justify the defendant in using deadly force, even when those threats were imminent. The use of deadly force in self-defense to prevent harm other than death or great bodily harm is excessive as a matter of law. * * *

The relaxed requirements for perfect self-defense proposed by our Court of Appeals would tend to categorically legalize the opportune killing of abusive husbands by their wives solely on the basis of the wives' testimony concerning their subjective speculation as to the probability of future felonious assaults by their husbands. Homicidal self-help would then become a lawful solution, and perhaps the easiest and most effective solution, to this problem. * * *

In conclusion, we decline to expand our law of self-defense beyond the limits of immediacy and necessity which have heretofore provided an appropriately narrow but firm basis upon which homicide may be justified and, thus, lawful by reason of perfect self-defense or upon which a defendant's culpability may be reduced by reason of imperfect self-defense. As we have shown, the evidence in this case did not entitle the defendant to jury instructions on either perfect or imperfect self-defense.

JUSTICE MARTIN, dissenting.

Evidence presented by defendant described a twenty-year history of beatings and other dehumanizing and degrading treatment by her husband. In his expert testimony a clinical psychologist concluded that defendant fit "and exceed[ed]" the profile of an abused or battered spouse, analogizing this treatment to the dehumanization process suffered by prisoners of war under the Nazis during the Second World War and the brainwashing techniques of the Korean War. The psychologist described the defendant as a woman incarcerated by abuse, by fear, and by her conviction that her husband was invincible and inescapable:

> Mrs. Norman didn't leave because she believed, fully believed that escape was totally impossible. There was no place to go. He, she had left before; he had come and gotten her. She had gone to the Department of Social Services. He had come and gotten her. The law, she believed the law could not protect her; no one could protect her, and I must admit, looking over the records, that there was nothing done that would contradict that belief. She fully believed that he was invulnerable to the law and to all social agencies that were available; that nobody could withstand his power. As a result, there was no such thing as escape.

* * * This testimony describes defendant's perception of circumstances in which she was held hostage to her husband's abuse for two decades and which ultimately compelled her to kill him. This testimony alone is evidence amply indicating the first two elements required for entitlement to an instruction on self-defense.

In addition to the testimony of the clinical psychologist, defendant presented the testimony of witnesses who had actually seen defendant's husband abuse her. These witnesses described circumstances that caused not only defendant to believe escape was impossible, but that also convinced them of its impossibility. Defendant's isolation and helplessness were evident in testimony that her family was intimidated by her husband into acquiescing in his torture of her. Witnesses also described defendant's experience with social service agencies and the law, which had contributed to her sense of futility and abandonment through the inefficacy of their protection and the strength of her husband's wrath when they failed. Where torture appears interminable and escape impossible, the belief that only the death of the oppressor can provide relief is reasonable in the mind of a person of ordinary firmness, let alone in the mind of the defendant, who, like a prisoner of war of some years, has been deprived of her humanity and is held hostage by fear.

* * * Constant fear means a perpetual anticipation of the next blow, a perpetual expectation that the next blow will kill. "[T]he battered wife is constantly in a heightened state of terror because she is certain that one day her husband will kill her during the course of a beating. * * * Thus from the perspective of the battered wife, the danger is constantly 'immediate.' " For the battered wife, if there is no escape, if there is no window of relief or momentary sense of safety, then the next attack, which could be the fatal one, is imminent. In the context of the doctrine of self-defense, "imminent" is a term the meaning of which must be grasped from the

defendant's point of view. Properly stated, the second prong of the question is not whether the threat was in fact imminent, but whether defendant's belief in the impending nature of the threat, given the circumstances as she saw them, was reasonable in the mind of a person of ordinary firmness.

Defendant's intense fear, based on her belief that her husband intended not only to maim or deface her, as he had in the past, but to kill her, was evident in the testimony of witnesses who recounted events of the last three days of the decedent's life. This testimony could have led a juror to conclude that defendant reasonably perceived a threat to her life as "imminent," even while her husband slept. Over these three days, her husband's anger was exhibited in an unprecedented crescendo of violence. The evidence showed defendant's fear and sense of hopelessness similarly intensifying, leading to an unsuccessful attempt to escape through suicide and culminating in her belief that escape would be possible only through her husband's death.

* * *

From this evidence of the exacerbated nature of the last three days of twenty years of provocation, a juror could conclude that defendant believed that her husband's threats to her life were viable, that serious bodily harm was imminent, and that it was necessary to kill her husband to escape that harm. And from this evidence a juror could find defendant's belief in the necessity to kill her husband not merely reasonable but compelling.

NOTES ON SELF-DEFENSE

1. Four years after she was convicted and two months after she entered prison, Judy Norman had her sentence commuted by North Carolina's then-Governor Jim Martin. Governor Martin refused to discuss the reasons for the commutation, but concluded that Norman's sentence should be that of "time served." When released from prison, Norman said: "It's wrong to take a life * * *. But the laws are not hard enough on the men that batter women." She also reported that her aim was to work with battered women to see what she could do to help them leave abusive relationships. Elizabeth Leland, Abused Wife's Sentence Commuted; Woman Killed Husband In 1985, Charlotte Observer, July 8, 1989, at 1B.

2. Despite the amount of commentary it has generated among lawyers, *Norman* is not typical of cases in which battered women kill. Appellate case law, which is likely to over-represent these very difficult cases, in fact shows that most battered women's homicide cases resemble other appellate self-defense cases in the sense that the killing occurs in the midst of a violent confrontation. The cases involve a threat, a move toward a gun, a step toward a beer bottle. The law of self-defense requires an "imminent" threat of serious or deadly harm, and so the question in these cases is whether the threat was serious and timely enough to justify killing. In short, the best evidence we have is that most killings by women in the battering context are

confrontational and that the *Norman*-type situation, where a man is killed in his sleep, is unusual. Holly Maguigan, Battered Women and Self-Defense: Myths and Misconceptions in Current Reform Proposals, 140 U. Pa. L. Rev. 379 (1991); Victoria F. Nourse, Self-Defense and Subjectivity, 68 U. Chi. L. Rev. 1235 (2001).

Although the best evidence suggests *Norman* is unusual, critics repeat the contrary assumption: that battered women frequently or often kill when a husband is defenseless or sleeping. See, e.g., David L. Faigman & Amy J. Wright, The Battered Woman Syndrome in the Age of Science, 39 Ariz. L. Rev. 67, 81 (1997) ("in many cases in which women kill their batterers, the traditional criteria of self-defense are not met or are met imperfectly"). Is this an example of how false factual assumptions—stereotypes—can shift the nature of the debate on gender issues? Is this an example of a homicide myth that trades on images of the vengeful woman? Or are the facts of *Norman* not all that distinct from those involved in a more typical confrontational killing? Put differently, given the pattern of violent conduct that preceded the killing, is Judy Norman any different from a battered woman who kills when a knife is over her head?

3. Imminence is the doctrinal requirement that poses a problem in cases like Norman's. Although it is often thought that imminence is a self-evidently "temporal" requirement, it is clear that its meaning is more complex, and can change depending upon the context. If Judy Norman had been kidnapped, the imminence requirement would have been viewed quite differently: a hostage, for example, may kill at any time, and need not wait until the knife is literally over her head. In a study of the meaning of imminence, it was found that imminence can operate as a proxy for other norms, including the idea that the victim "should have left the relationship." Consider the following case:

> Barbara Watson killed her common law husband while she was struggling with him. And yet the trial court rejected her claim of self-defense on grounds of imminence. Why? Not because of time. This was not the killing of a sleeping man hours after the last bout. There was a clear confrontation—eyewitnesses testified that the victim had jumped on top of Mrs. Watson and that he had her "around the neck." The trial court based its imminence finding in part on the following: the threat was not imminent because of the *"parties' relationship involving 'a long course of physical abuse.'"* Put another way, the threat was not imminent because the victim had been battered, that is, because Mrs. Watson should have left the relationship before the final attack. Imminence represented a judgment not of fact but of norm. Mrs. Watson was found guilty of manslaughter by the trial court, a sentence the appellate court reversed on the facts.

Nourse, above note 2, at 1246–47 (discussing Commonwealth v. Watson, 431 A.2d 949 (Pa. 1981)) (emphasis added). *Watson* is clearly an egregious case: given that the victim had the defendant "around the neck," no reasonable judge should have rejected a finding of imminence. The question *Watson* raises is whether imminence is really as simple as the *Norman* court suggests. Is this another instance of a myth of violence (that victims should "leave") influencing the application of law? Is the *Norman* court using imminence to require Judy Norman to "leave" the relationship?

4. What difference should it make that Judy Norman sought help and it was denied? Should the state's failure to protect her play some role in considering whether she was "justified" in killing? Since Blackstone's day, the law of self-defense has assumed that one could be justified in killing in situations where the state could not possibly protect you—for example, when the knife was quite literally over your head. When, on the other hand, the police officer is at one's elbow, almost no defense will apply. This suggests that included in the theory of defenses is a set of assumptions about state protection. What if those assumptions are wrong? See Victoria F. Nourse, Reconceptualizing Criminal Law Defenses, 151 U. Pa. L. Rev. 1691, 1797–09 (2003). If the state has actually failed to protect, should the woman be considered in a state of nature? Does the state's failure to protect make it easier to see how a woman might be "justified" in killing and analogized to the hostage or prisoner of war?

Traditional critics of the hostage argument worry that if women in Judy Norman's situation are considered "justified" in their actions (that she did the "right" thing), then this amounts to a claim that J.T. forfeited his life by his battering (a rather unpalatable application of a non-state death penalty). The answer, Joshua Dressler asserts, is to consider Judy Norman's case not in the realm of self-defense but, instead, as a case about duress, where her failure to leave is excused because she had no "fair opportunity" to resist the violence. One problem with such a claim is that duress is typically unavailable in homicide prosecutions; however, one virtue is that it addresses overtly the "failure to leave" question which tends to bedevil debates about self-defense (even though it is not an official legal requirement of self-defense). See Joshua Dressler, Battered Women and Sleeping Abusers: Some Reflections, 3 Ohio St. J. Crim. L. 457 (2006).

Should a battered woman who kills under circumstances like Judy Norman's be exculpated? If so, why? Is it because she acted properly, given the available options (in which case, she would be "justified")? Or because, though her conduct was wrong, we nevertheless do not hold her responsible (in which case, she would be "excused")? If the latter is true, is it because the battered woman suffers from a "syndrome?" What risks are involved in pathologizing battered women in this manner? Are there other ways of understanding why a battered woman who kills in an apparently "non-confrontational" setting should be excused?

5. Within the legal and scholarly community, battered woman syndrome has been extremely controversial; indeed, at one point, it was fair to say that the battered woman was the "poster child" for claims of the "abuse excuse." See, e.g., Alan M. Dershowitz, The Abuse Excuse and Other Cop–Outs, Sob Stories, and Evasions of Responsibility (1994). After a good deal of resistance, battered woman syndrome evidence is now widely accepted in courts of law. As of 1994, one study found that "[e]xpert testimony on battering and its effects" had been held admissible, at least in part, in "each of the 50 states and the District of Columbia." Janet Parrish, Trend Analysis: Expert Testimony on Battering and Its Effects in Criminal Cases, 11 Wis. Women's L. J.

75, 83 (1996). The syndrome is based on the work of Lenore Walker, which we address more fully in Section C.

Despite the widespread admissibility of battered woman syndrome evidence, critics insist that the syndrome is politically motivated and offers women "special" advantages. See, e.g., Robert P. Mosteller, Syndromes and Politics in Criminal Trials and Evidence Law, 46 Duke L.J. 461 (1996); Faigman & Wright, above note 2, at 73. To determine whether the rule creates special advantages, one must consider the baseline from which the rule proceeds. If one assumes that the law is *ex ante* equal, then battered woman's syndrome provides a special advantage. But what if the law is not equal? What if it creates disadvantages for women? Consider the *Watson* case, described in note 3 above, where the woman was being choked, but the trial judge found the threat was "not imminent." Technically, this was an incorrect application of the law—and quite obviously so. Precisely for that reason, it shows how sex-biased norms—that she should have left—may trump the law. (There is no rule in self-defense law that a defendant loses the defense if she fails to "leave" a place, such as a bar, that she knows to be violent.) If this is right, one might argue that battered woman syndrome is a proper prophylactic measure to battle the sex bias evident in cases like *Watson*. See Nourse, above note 2, at 1288–91 (making such an argument). Rather than advocate for the admissibility of syndrome evidence, would it have been better for battered women to directly challenge on equal protection grounds the sex bias in the law of self-defense, and request jury instructions rebutting the stereotypes associated with battered women (she wants it; she should have left, etc.)? Or was it impossible to address the sex bias in law without the enunciation of a formal, scientifically authoritative, syndrome?

6. Elizabeth Schneider, an early advocate of battered women, has argued for a self-defense standard that resists sexist stereotype and one that includes the battered woman's experiences. Schneider explains:

> The crux of self-defense is the concept of reasonableness. In order for a defense lawyer to believe that a battered woman has a credible claim of self-defense, the lawyer will first have to overcome sex-based stereotypes of reasonableness, understand enough about the experiences of battered women to be able to fully consider whether the woman's actions are reasonable, and be able to listen to the woman's experiences sensitive to the problems of gender-bias. * * *
>
> The next step was to make sure that battered women's experiences were heard, first by defense lawyers in the process of representation and choice of defense, and then in the courtroom, regardless of what defense was chosen. Thus the second emphasis of this work was the crucial role of admission of evidence on battering, first from the woman and others who might have observed or known about the violence, and then from experts who might be able to explain those experiences and assist fact-finders to overcome myths and misconceptions that might impede their consideration. Admission of evidence at trial concerning battering was deemed crucial, because of the view that the social relations of domination, the history and experience of abuse, were not only relevant but essential to the determination of guilt. In short, the goal was to improve the rationali-

> ty of the fact-finding process, not to have every battered woman on trial plead self-defense. Nonetheless, the argument for the relevance of the social context of battering in order to improve the rationality of the fact-finding process has become confused with the notion of a separate defense of battering in the public mind.

Elizabeth M. Schneider, Self–Defense and Relations of Domination: Moral and Legal Perspectives on Battered Women Who Kill: Resistance to Equality, 57 U. Pitt. L. Rev. 477, 496–97 (1996). In response to arguments like those above, some jurisdictions (while retaining some element of objectivity) have adopted more subjective reasonableness standards. See State v. Thomas, 673 N.E.2d 1339 (Ohio 1997) (applying a "reasonable battered woman" standard). What are the implications of these developments? Does a "reasonable battered woman" standard mean that women are receiving special treatment? Does it undercut the notion of equality for women? Or does it properly reflect the feminist insight that the law tends to obscure women's experiences? See Victoria F. Nourse, After the Reasonable Man: Getting Over the Subjectivity/Objectivity Question, 11 New Crim. L. Rev. 33 (2008). As a practical matter, given the infrequency with which women use lethal violence and the pacifism with which women are associated, is it possible that battered women defendants are actually disadvantaged by a standard that compares their behavior to that of the "reasonable woman?"

7. Battered women who fail to conform to stereotypical images of helplessness are more likely to confront juror skepticism regarding claims of long-term abuse. Women of color may be particularly disadvantaged by this realty. How are assumptions regarding race embedded in the standard of reasonableness against which battered women defendants are evaluated? Consider the remarks of Linda Ammons:

> There may not be a one-to-one correlation between seeing a black woman as a strong matriarch; or as an alluring, provocative Jezebel; or as a punishing, provoking Sapphire; or as a welfare cheat, and seeing the defendant as violent. If one were to accept the common mythology about black males, a black female defendant on trial for murdering her partner should benefit from a juror's perception that black men are violent, assuming that the alleged aggressor was a black male. But, when a juror is trying to reconcile what he or she believes about African–American females and what is perceived as helplessness, the typical images of black women may be a barrier to seeing the defendant as not culpable (either because of her strength of character, or her suspect character) for the violent encounter(s).

Linda Ammons, Mules, Madonnas, Babies, Bathwater, Racial Imagery and Stereotypes: The African–American Woman and the Battered Woman Syndrome, 1995 Wis. L. Rev. 1003, 1076–77. Critical race critiques of "the battered woman" are further explored in Section C, below.

C. INTIMATE PARTNER VIOLENCE

Official government estimates of intimate partner violence vary enormously, ranging from approximately 650,000 all the way to 7.7 million violent crimes per year.[20] This rather large variance reflects different definitions of violence as well as different survey methodologies. For example, in 2008 the Bureau of Justice Statistics estimated that there were approximately 88,000 violent crimes committed against males by intimate partners and 500,000 violent crimes against females by intimate partners.[21] But in 2000, the Centers for Disease Control and the National Institute of Justice reported *annual* figures twice as high for intimate partner violence alone.[22] Even the most conservative figures, however, show that intimate partner violence is a major social problem[23] As one review of the literature concluded, although many would like to believe otherwise, "family violence is the most prevalent form of violence in this country."[24]

Intimate partner violence was not consistently recognized as a serious social problem until attention was focused upon it in the 1970's by the women's movement. Beating one's wife, known as the right of chastisement, was long condoned by the common law; the right was not formally repudiated in the United States until the latter part of the 19th century. Yet when the common law right of chastisement was abolished, the case law developed doctrines that continued effectively to shield domestic violence from public intervention—the doctrines of marital privacy and of inter-spousal tort immunity.[25] As a result, although battering was no longer legally approved, its victims had no effective civil or criminal remedies.

The extent of battering in the United States and the plight of the abused woman were widely studied and publicized during the 1970's.[26]

---

20. The 650,000 yearly figure appears in U.S. Dep't of Justice, Bureau of Justice Statistics, Female Victims of Violence [hereinafter 2009 Violence Report], 2 (October 2009), of which 550,000 involved female victims. The 7.7 million figure is a total from the NVAW Survey, above footnote 4, at iii (surveying 16,000 men and women and finding 4.8 million intimate partner physical assaults or rapes perpetrated against women and approximately 2.9 million intimate partner physical assaults perpetrated against men annually). See id. (25% figure over lifetime). For the government's acknowledgement of its own discrepant studies, see Bureau of Justice Statistics, Special Report: Intimate partner Violence 1, Appendix at 4. For some of the problems, see 2000 NVAW Survey, above footnote 4, available at http://bjs.ojp.usdoj.gov/index.cfm?ty=pbdetail&iid=2024.

21. U.S. Dep't of Justice, Bureau of Justice Statistics, Criminal Victimization [hereinafter 2008 Criminal Victimization Bulletin], 5 (2008). This study is based on the National Crime Victimization Survey; more information about the survey method see http://bjs.ojp.usdoj.gov/index.cfm?ty=dcdetail&iid=245.

22. 2000 NVAW Survey, above footnote 4, at iii (July 2000) (surveying 16,000 men and women and finding 4.8 million intimate partner physical assaults or rapes perpetrated against women and approximately 2.9 million intimate partner physical assaults perpetrated against men annually).

23. 2009 Violence Report, above footnote 20, at 2.

24. Patrick Tolan, Deborah Gorman–Smith & David Henry, Family Violence, 57 Ann. Rev. Psych. 557, 559 (2006).

25. See Reva B. Siegel, "The Rule of Love": Wife Beating as Prerogative and Privacy, 105 Yale L.J. 2117, 2150–70 (1996).

26. See, e.g., Lenore Walker, The Battered Woman (1979); Terry Davidson, Conjugal Crime: Understanding and Changing the Wifebeating Pattern (1978); Del Martin, Battered Wives (1976); Murray A. Straus, Richard J. Gelles & Suzanne K. Steinmetz, Behind Closed Doors: Violence in the American Family (1980).

The publicity was accompanied by efforts at civil law reform, aimed at providing more effective and easily accessible legal remedies for abused women, including temporary orders of protection that can be obtained ex parte (without notice) and grant broad relief, such as child custody, support, and exclusive possession of the marital residence, in addition to an injunction against harassment or even contact with the petitioner.[27] Today, all fifty states have some form of civil domestic violence code,[28] and about half of the states have revised their criminal codes to include one or more domestic violence offenses.[29]

Statutory reform is not effective without cooperation from law enforcement personnel, however.[30] Traditionally, domestic violence calls were either ignored by the police or treated differently from other crimes; often the police would just try to calm down the batterer and then leave without making an arrest; and sometimes police did nothing at all. In 1976, major class action lawsuits were filed on behalf of battering victims in Oakland, California and New York City. These suits resulted in settlements or consent judgments incorporating new policies on the part of police departments responding to domestic violence calls, including, among other things, pro-arrest mandates and efforts to inform victims of their right to obtain a protective order and of other available services.[31] Many more police departments reexamined their policies after a federal jury awarded one plaintiff $2.3 million in 1984 based on a failure of police officers to respond to repeated requests to protect her from an abusive husband.[32]

More recently, intimate partner violence has been defined as a subject for serious societal concern and study. Under pressure from activists, police departments have become more sensitive to the dynamics of battering, and, as we describe below, have experimented with mandatory arrest policies. Local prosecutors have added special domestic violence units, and some now pursue no-drop or mandatory prosecution policies. Additional resources also became available for law enforcement, training, and shel-

---

27. See 750 ILCS 60/101 et seq. (originally passed in 1982).

28. See Catherine F. Klein & Leslye E. Orloff, Providing Legal Protection for Battered Women: An Analysis of State Statutes and Case Law, 21 Hofstra L. Rev. 801 (1993) (providing an in-depth analysis of state civil protection order statutes).

29. See, e.g., Joan Zorza, Women Battering: High Cost and the State of the Law, 28 Clearinghouse Rev. 383, 388 (1994); 50 State Statutory Surveys, Domestic Violence, 0030 Surveys 7 (West 2009).

30. Tort actions based on domestic violence are exceedingly rare. As Jennifer Wriggins notes:

> People who commit domestic violence are, in theory, liable under intentional tort theories, in additional to whatever liability they may face under criminal law. But despite the frequency with which people are injured by 'domestic violence torts,' very few tort suits are brought to seek recovery for the harms domestic violence causes.

Jennifer Wriggins, Domestic Violence Torts, 75 S. Cal. L. Rev. 121, 123–124 (2001). For a proposal to enhance civil liability for domestic violence torts through insurance reform, see id.

31. See Joan Zorza, The Criminal Law of Misdemeanor Domestic Violence, 1970–1990, 83 J. Crim. L. & Criminology 46, 54–59 (1992).

32. Thurman v. City of Torrington, 595 F.Supp. 1521 (D.Conn.1984).

ters under the Violence Against Women Act in 1994.[33] The Act authorized expenditures to the states for partner violence prevention and prosecution, but conditioned the funds upon the recipient states giving full faith and credit to orders of protection issued by other states, providing government assistance with service of process, criminalizing violations of protective orders, and encouraging, by law or policy, the arrest of domestic violence offenders who violate the terms of a protective order.[34] VAWA also made it a federal crime to cross state lines for the purpose of abusing an intimate partner.[35] In addition, federal funding for shelters was doubled, and new grants were given to train police and prosecutors, set up special units, and track incidents.[36]

Some progress appears to have been made, but substantial problems remain, and many of the remedies and experiments generate their own problems or exacerbate others. For example, in 2008 only about half of the intimate partner violence against women was reported to police.[37] Even when a report is made and an offender arrested, he is rarely detained for more than a few hours; and the consequences of conviction are typically mild, leaving the woman who signed the complaint a target for further, retaliatory violence. Moreover, the moment when the woman attempts to end the relationship may be the most dangerous time.[38]

Overall, the criminal law's incident-based approach to defining unlawful behavior may be ill-suited to redress the ongoing, patterned nature of battering.[39] An accurate description of domestic violence is "premised on an understanding of coercive behavior and of power and control—including a continuum of sexual and verbal abuse, threats, economic coercion, stalking, and social isolation—rather than 'number of hits.' "[40] As psychologist Mary Ann Dutton explains:

> Abusive behavior does not occur as a series of discrete events. Although a set of discrete abusive incidents can typically be identified within an abusive relationship, an understanding of the dynamic of power and control within an intimate relationship goes beyond these discrete incidents. To negate the impact of the time period between discrete episodes of serious violence—a time period during which the woman may never know when the next incident will occur, and may continue to live with on-going psychological abuse—is to fail to

---

33. Title IV of the Violent Crime Control Act of 1994, 108 Stat. 1796, Pub. L. 103–322.

34. See 18 U.S.C. §§ 2265 (2000); 3796hh(c) (2000).

35. 18 U.S.C. § 2261 (2000).

36. 42 U.S.C. § 10410 (2000).

37. 2009 Violence Report, above footnote 20, at 2.

38. Martha R. Mahoney, Legal Images of Battered Women: Redefining the Issue of Separation, 90 Mich. L. Rev. 1, 64–65 (1991).

39. Deborah Tuerkheimer, Recognizing and Remedying the Harm of Battering: A Call to Criminalize Domestic Violence, 94 J. Crim. L & Criminology 959, 962–969 (2004).

40. Elizabeth Schneider, Battered Women and Feminist Lawmaking 65 (2000).

recognize what some battered woman experience as a continuing "state of siege."[41]

In this section, we examine a number of major issues that arise in a feminist analysis of intimate partner violence and appropriate remedies for it. We first discuss conflicting views of the battered woman, as victim or survivor, and how the particularities of race, culture, religion, immigration status, and sexual orientation, among others, impact the experience of abuse. Second, we explore theories of why domestic violence occurs—why men batter their intimate partners and whether there are effective legal and/or therapeutic interventions in the individual case. Third, we turn to more general questions involved in society's use of the law to intervene in situations of intimate partner abuse, including the response by police and the debate over mandatory prosecution. Finally, we examine the Violence Against Women Act, its failed civil rights remedy, and its federal law against battering. (We focus on marital rape in Section D, below.)

1. THE BATTERED WOMAN

Early research on the battered woman by pioneer Lenore Walker contributed to two basic concepts in the field—the cycle of violence and learned helplessness. Both concepts remain controversial. Walker argued, in her early work, that a "battered woman believes that if she somehow could find the right way to help this man, with whom she has a strong love bond, then the mean part of him would disappear."[42] Instead, a cycle of violence may occur:

> Many battering relationships display a cycle of violence that appears to follow behavioral reinforcement theory. The three-phase violence cycle that I used as a framework for my investigation is based on a tension-reduction hypothesis. The first phase is a period of tension building during which the woman does have some minimum control of the frequency and severity of the abusive incidents. She can slow them down by trying to give the man what he wants or speed them up by refusing to meet his (sometimes unreasonable) demands. Her efforts are more successful at the beginning of this phase than toward its end. Eventually, the couple reaches the period of inevitability, when attempts at control no longer work, and phase two—the explosion—occurs. When this acute battering incident occurs, the others, including the police, often get involved. It is the shortest of the three phases but causes the most physical harm. When medical attention is sought, which occurs in less than 50% of known cases, it follows this second phase. By the time the second phase is over, there is a physiological release of tension which is a reinforcer. Often there is a

41. Mary Ann Dutton, Understanding Women's Responses to Domestic Violence: A Redefinition of Battered Woman Syndrome, 21 Hofstra L. Rev. 1191, 1208 (1993). See generally Evan Stark, Coercive Control: How Men Entrap Women in Personal Life (2007).

42. The quote in the text is drawn from a summary of earlier work in Lenore E. A. Walker, Psychology and Violence Against Women, 44 Am. Psychologist 695, 697 (1989). For the early work, see Lenore E.A. Walker, The Battered Woman (1979).

> period of loving contrition that follows as the third phase, but in some relationships there is only a period of no tension that also serves as the reinforcer. Obviously, the apparent rewards of remaining in the relationship mostly occur in the third phase.

Lenore E. A. Walker, Psychology and Violence Against Women, 44 Am. Psychologist 695, 697 (1989).

Walker also sought to explain why women did not "leave" the relationship and posited, as a partial explanation, a phenomenon known as learned helplessness—a concept taken from experiments conducted by Martin Seligman. Seligman administered electric shocks to dogs in circumstances in which the dog had no control over the shock. Once the dogs were put in a situation where they could escape the shock, they did not. Seligman concluded that the dogs had learned to be helpless. Walker writes of her application of this theory to battered women: "Learned helplessness explains the loss of the ability to predict contingent outcomes after exposure to repeated random and variable inescapable aversive stimuli. This model helps one understand the psychological changes in battered women that partially account for their staying in abusive relationships."[43]

Since then, Walker has gone on to emphasize that battered women are not "one-size-fits-all" and that research shows that "few battered women actually fit the stereotyped model of a passive and helpless woman who never fights back to protect herself or her children."[44] Instead, Walker argues that the most unifying characteristic of battered women is the psychological phenomenon known as post-traumatic stress disorder.[45] The concepts of learned helplessness and the idea of a category known as "the battered woman" remain controversial among researchers, legal critics and feminists alike, as we see in the materials that follow.

EDWARD W. GONDOLF WITH ELLEN R. FISHER, BATTERED WOMEN AS SURVIVORS: AN ALTERNATIVE TO TREATING LEARNED HELPLESSNESS

11–12, 17–22, 24–25 (1988).

Our assertion that battered women are active survivors raises a fundamental theoretical issue. It appears to contradict the prevailing characterization that battered women suffer from learned helplessness. According to learned helplessness, battered women tend to "give up" in the course of being abused; they suffer psychological paralysis and an underlying masochism that needs to be treated by specialized therapy.

---

43. Id.

44. Lenore E. A. Walker, Current Perspectives on Men Who Batter Women—Implications for Intervention and Treatment to Stop Violence Against Women: Comment on Gottman et al. (1995), 9 J. Fam. Psych. 264, 266 (1995).

45. Lenore E. A. Walker, The Battered Woman Syndrome Is A Psychological Consequence of Abuse; Current Controversies on Family Violence 133, 138–44 (R. J. Gelles & D.R. Loseke, eds. 1993).

Our survivor hypothesis, on the other hand, suggests that women respond to abuse with helpseeking efforts that are largely unmet. What the women most need are the resources and social support that would enable them to become more independent and leave the batterer.

* * *

Toward a Survivor Theory

The Survivor Hypothesis

* * *[B]attered women remain in abusive situations not because they have been passive but because they have tried to escape with no avail. We offer, therefore, a survivor hypothesis that contradicts the assumptions of learned helplessness: Battered women increase their helpseeking in the face of increased violence, rather than decrease helpseeking as learned helplessness would suggest. More specifically, we contend that help seeking is likely to increase as wife abuse, child abuse, and the batterer's antisocial behavior (substance abuse, general violence, and arrests) increase. This helpseeking may be mediated, as current research suggests, by the resources available to the woman, her commitment to the relationship, the number of children she has, and the kinds of abuse she may have experienced as a child.

The fundamental assumption is, however, that woman [sic] seek assistance in proportion to the realization that they and their children are more and more in danger. They are attempting, in a very logical fashion, to assure themselves and their children protection and therefore survival. Their effort to survive transcends even fearsome danger, depression or guilt, and economic constraints. It supersedes the "giving up and giving in" which occurs according to learned helplessness. In this effort to survive, battered women are, in fact, heroically assertive and persistent.

* * *

The Myth of Masochism

The implications of female masochism raised with learned helplessness have been similarly challenged. As the empirical studies suggest, battered women do not appear to be "victim prone." Women contribute to the violence only in the fact that they are female. As Paula Caplan (1985) in The Myth of Female Masochism forcefully argues, too often the feminine qualities of self-denial, trustfulness, nurturing, and friendliness are reinterpreted as naïveté and vulnerability.

Furthermore, it is highly debatable that assertiveness and carefulness in themselves can lessen one's vulnerability. Numerous studies have shown that male violence is for the most part indiscriminate and unpredictable. Gloria Steinem (1983) poignantly alludes to this in reevaluating the severely abused porno star, Linda Lovelace. She likens looking for some predisposition or inclination for abuse to asking, "What in your background led you to a concentration camp?"

* * *

* * * Even in the midst of severe psychological impairment, such as depression, many battered women seek help, adapt, and push on. This is not to say that we should expect battered women, or other survivors of misfortune, to bounce back on their own. Rather, by receiving the proper supports, one's inner strength can be realized, resiliency demonstrated, and a new life made.

This process is one that must be supported by helpers rather than invoked by them. This is accomplished by what some call a reflexive approach; that is, helpers accentuate the potential for self-transcendence in others by displaying it in themselves. The challenge is, therefore, for helpers to express resiliency, determination, and optimism, rather than succumb to the learned helplessness of so many bureaucratized help sources. As a result, so-called clients are more likely to discover and express their own resiliency. This approach is not some Pollyanna or positive thinking. It is a matter of community building—that is, creating a place where positive role models promote mutual support.

Shelters have afforded one of the most promising experiments in this regard. Women and children, by virtue of their circumstances, are joined in a kind of intentional community where not only emotions and experience are shared but also the common tasks of daily life. The "muddling with the mundane" in the communal living arrangements of shelters—the negotiating and even haggling over food, shelter, and children—potentially teaches much in itself. If managed effectively, shelter life may encourage women to assert themselves in new ways, clarify issues and fears, and collaborate with other women in need. In the process, the intimidating isolation that so many battered women experience is broken and an internal fortitude released.

Redefining the Symptoms

* * *

The so-called symptoms of learned helplessness may in fact be part of the adjustment to active helpseeking. They may represent traumatic shock from the abuse, a sense of commitment to the batterer, or separation anxiety amidst an unresponsive community. All of these are quite natural and healthy responses but not entirely acceptable ones in a patriarchal (or male-dominated) society that values cool detachment. Not to respond with some doubts, anxiety, or depression would suggest emotional superficiality and denial of the real difficulties faced in helpseeking.

First, the symptoms of learned helplessness may be a temporary manifestation of traumatic shock. Many of the women arriving at shelters have suffered severe physical abuse equivalent to what one might experience in a severe auto accident. What appears as physical unresponsiveness or psychological depression may therefore be more an effort of the body and mind to heal themselves. The women, rather than being passive and withdrawn personalities, are going through a necessary healing process. They need not so much psychotherapy as time and space to recuperate.

Second, the symptoms may reflect an effort by battered women to save the relationship. Seeking help represents, in some sense, an admission of failure to fulfill the traditional female role of nurturing and domesticity. It appears to some women, too, as a breach of the marriage vow to love and honor one's spouse. As several of the interview studies show, battered women do initially blame themselves for not being nurturing, supportive, or loving enough to make the marriage work. It is important, however, to distinguish this initial sense of failure from the sense of an uncontrollable universe which underlies learned helplessness.

Third, the depression and guilt in some shelter women may be an expression of separation anxiety that understandably accompanies leaving the batterer. The women face tremendous uncertainty in separating even temporarily from the batterer. They fear reprisals for leaving, loss of custody of the children, and losing their home and financial support. The unknown of trying to survive on one's own can be as frightening as returning to a violent man. The prospects of obtaining employment sufficient to support oneself and children are minimal for most shelter women, especially considering their lack of previous experience and education. This coupled with the feminization of poverty in contemporary America makes a return to the batterer the lesser of the two evils. At least there is a faint hope that the batterer will change, whereas the prospects for change in the larger community seem less favorable.

* * *

Addressing Patriarchal Assumptions

* * *According to feminist analysis, patriarchy—a system of male dominance—underlies much of the tendency to characterize women as deficient and to respond insufficiently. But it emerges in the helpseeking of battered women not so much as a conscious conspiracy of males against females but as a style of thought and interaction that is "masculine" in its deference to hierarchy, expertise, technique, and individualism. This approach has emphasized a pathological analysis of problems, a medical model of treatment, and privitization [sic] of family life.

The first patriarchal assumption rooted deep in our society is that problems are caused by some individual pathology. Our social policies tend to address deviance and dysfunction in individuals or families rather than in the structures of society as a whole. In fact, social policy is more often used to preserve that social structure rather than change it. The result is that individuals are to be restrained or managed for the social well-being. Our social science must therefore identify what is "wrong" with individuals and find ways to "fix" them or bring them back to the norm.

Allocating resources to women in a way that would increase their social status or power is therefore resisted.

A second patriarchal assumption is that the medical model of professional expertise is the most appropriate form of treatment. The medical model has loosely been characterized as experts treating the problem "within" the person. That is, there is some dysfunction in the body or mind that is responsible for socially deviant acts. This orientation has given rise to an abundance of clinical psychologies that look for the root of our problems in the dysfunction of our thought processes and seek to right them through expert persuasion. Most of these "treatments" are technique-based; they impersonalize the helping process by slighting the emotional nurturing, mutual self-disclosure, and long-term commitment that are so fundamental to the feminine perspective.

A third patriarchal assumption at odds with the survivor notion is the continued privatization of family life. At a time of tremendous social transition and dislocation, there is a tendency to allow and expect families to fend for themselves in the name of autonomy. While families or individual family members may receive "treatment," it is increasingly difficult to obtain adequate housing, child care, income assistance, and meaningful employment. * * *

NOTES ON BATTERED WOMEN

1. What are the implications of the victim and survivor paradigms proposed by Walker and by Gondolf? Do they dictate different legal treatment of domestic violence? What if some women respond as Walker describes and others as Gondolf and Fisher posit?

2. How would the different feminist theorists discussed in Chapter Three analyze the problem of domestic violence? Would they be likely to reach different conclusions about solutions to recommend?

3. To what extent is spousal abuse a problem of male-female relations, and to what extent is it a problem of a more generalized relationship between love and violence, sexuality and power? If marriage is one of the risk factors for battering, why does violence occur in both heterosexual cohabiting relationships and in gay and lesbian relationships as well? Are we forced to conclude that domestic violence is inherent in sexually intimate relationships in general today? To the extent the institution of marriage is implicated, are there any reforms that you think would decrease the violence? If marriage were not conceived by our legal system as an irretrievably private institution, would this diminish the amount of violence? How would this shift impact upon other types of rights for women, especially reproductive rights?

4. How should we analyze the problem of women's violence against men? A persistent critique, from the right, has been the claim that feminists have failed to acknowledge that men are battered by women. In one influential article, for example, Linda Kelly complains that feminists have all but ignored the millions of men who are the victims of battering. Linda Kelly, Disabusing the Definition of Domestic Abuse: How Women Batter Men and

the Role of the Feminist State, 30 Fla. St. U. L. Rev. 791 (2003). The truth, we are told, is that "husbands and wives are roughly equal in their use of any form of physical violence." Id. at 795. This claim, although exaggerated, is not without some statistical support: the 2000 NVAW study found 4.8 million intimate partner physical assaults or rapes perpetrated against women and approximately 2.9 million intimate partner physical assaults perpetrated against men annually. 2000 NVAW Survey, above footnote 4, at iii. But this data is contradicted by other official estimates: Justice Department figures, for example, suggest that the vast majority of domestic violence is committed by men against women and girls. See 2009 Violence Report, above footnote 20, at 1 ("[T]he rate of intimate partner victimization for females was 4.3 victimizations per 1,000 females age 12 or older. The equivalent rate of intimate partner violence against males was 0.8 victimizations per 1,000 males age 12 or older.").

Most fundamentally, the type of data on which Kelly relies does not tell us the "context" in which the violence occurred. Responding in part to this problem, in 2007 the Johnson Foundation hosted a jointly sponsored conference ("The Wingspread Conference on Domestic Violence and Family Courts") to further understandings of how domestic violence should be defined and measured. The resulting Conference Report summarizes:

> There was consensus among conference participants that the impact of domestic violence depends in large part on the context in which it occurs. Identical violent acts may have different meanings depending on the impact on the victim and the intent of the perpetrator. Consider a situation where partner A slaps partner B. First imagine that when the incident takes place there is no prior history of physical violence or of other abusive behaviors between A and B. Then imagine that, although this incident is the first instance of physical violence, A has previously undermined B's efforts to seek employment, denigrated B's parenting in front of the children, and isolated B from her family and friends. Then imagine a situation where A broke B's nose the week before and A is threatening to kill B and harm their children. The act of slapping is the same in each situation but the impact and consequences are very different.

Nancy Ver Steegh & Clare Dalton, Report from the Wingspread Conference on Domestic Violence and Family Courts, 46 Fam. Ct. Rev. 454, 456–57 (2008).

5. Viewing violence in a context has important implications for evaluating existing empirical research and the controversy surrounding it. As the above-described Wingspread Conference Report explains:

> Because of contradictory research findings, researchers have historically disagreed about the extent to which males as opposed to females initiate domestic violence. Crime studies and police-call data show much higher rates of assault by men than by women. However, so-called "family conflict" studies have found nearly equal rates of assault by men and women (and also higher overall rates of assault). Both groups agree that women are more likely to be injured and suffer other repercussions as a result of the violence.

> Further investigation of patterns of domestic violence could shed light on the contradictory findings. For example, Murray Straus suggests that researchers have studied different populations experiencing different types of violence. Researcher Michael P. Johnson analyzed the data used in both types of studies and concluded that the crime and police-call data studies were measuring violence used in the exercise of coercive control, which is primarily perpetrated by men, and that the "family conflict" studies were predominantly measuring violence driven by conflict, which may be initiated equally by men and women.
>
> Many conference participants felt strongly that domestic violence is not gender neutral [and] that gender inequality underlies the violence in many families.

Id. at 459.

Do you agree that "domestic violence is not gender neutral?" If so, how should feminists make sense of data showing that men are victims of violence by women? Does the fact that women use violence against men undermine feminist theories of domestic violence? For one response, see Emily Sack, Battered Women and the State: The Struggle for the Future of Domestic Violence Policy, 2004 Wis. L. Rev. 1657, 1700–10.

6. Is "the battered woman" a helpful construct? Clare Dalton suggests the utility of recognizing that many experiences of abuse are shared, while also acknowledging the multiplicity of perspectives that characterize the lives of battered women. For instance:

> Some will have been in long-term abusive relationships, while others will have left soon after the violence started. Some will have experienced physical violence as a regular—daily, weekly or monthly—part of their relationship, while others will have suffered only occasional or even rare incidents of violence in a relationship otherwise more emotionally than physically abusive. Some will have children, which complicates their ongoing relationship with their abusers, while others will not. Some will feel that their abusers have already accepted that the relationship is over, while others will still be persecuted by abusers unwilling to give them up. Some will feel that the relationship, while unhealthy and injurious, was never life-threatening, while others may still expect to die at the hands of their abusers.

Clare Dalton, Domestic Violence, Domestic Torts and Divorce: Constraints and Possibilities, 31 New Eng. L. Rev. 319, 330–31 (1997).

Dalton concludes that "many abusive relationships have enough in common with one another that we can make useful generalizations * * * as long as those generalizations do not harden into stereotypes." Do you agree? What are the benefits and drawbacks of defining "the battered woman" and her experiences?

7. One significant critique of "the battered woman" construct comes from critical race theory. Morrison, a long time advocate of battered women, has argued that the entire notion of "the battered woman" is "racialized as white." Adele Morrison, Deconstructing the Image Repertoire of Women of Color: Changing the Domestic Violence (Dis)Course: Moving from White

Victim to Multi–Cultural Survivor, 39 U.C. Davis L. Rev. 1061, 1077 (2006). According to this critique, since all identity is constructed in terms of its opposites, women of color are viewed as "other," and thus not entitled to wear the label of the pure, white "victim" that domestic violence discourse has constructed. Morrison writes: "Because the 'battered woman' is white, those women of color who are in abusive relationships are not included in the image of the victim. Stereotypes and myths exist, such as 'Blacks just like to fight,' 'Latinas are hot blooded' and 'Asian women are trained for this sort of thing.' " Id. at 1082–83. Morrison argues that all women, white and Black, would benefit by replacing the white "cult of true victimhood" with a focus on the ways in which all victims survive and endure. Do you agree? Is this a racial critique or simply a reaffirmation of Gondolf's survivor thesis? Morrison argues that by centering women of color in the domestic violence discourse, advocates are more likely to focus on the efforts of all women to endure and escape violence. Why would this be so?

8. Like most crime, the fact is that battering is predominantly intraracial. Yet African Americans as a whole (men and women) are at far greater risk of the most serious forms of intimate partner violence. Although 12 percent of the population, African Americans are almost one quarter of spousal homicide victims and almost half (48%) of the victims of homicide by a boyfriend or girlfriend. U.S. Dep't of Justice, Bureau of Justice Statistics, Family Violence Statistics on Strangers and Acquaintances, Table 3.2 (June 2005). In 2007, African American female homicide victims were twice as likely as white female homicide victims to be killed by a spouse, and four times more likely than white females to be killed by a boyfriend or girlfriend. 2009 Violence Report, above footnote 20, at 3.

Critical race feminists sometimes attribute this violence to the legacy of slavery and racism, as well as to Eurocentric gender ideology and its notions of both Black and white masculinity: "Those Black men who wish to become 'master' by fulfilling traditional definitions of masculinity—both Eurocentric and white-defined for African–Americans—and who are blocked from doing so can become dangerous to those closest to them." Patricia Hill Collins, Black Feminist Thought: Knowledge, Consciousness, and the Politics of Empowerment 186 (1990). See also Beth Richie, Battered Black Women: A Challenge for the Black Community, The Black Scholar, Mar./Apr. 1985, at 41–42. Yet African American women may be reluctant to break silence about this problem within the Black community, lest they appear disloyal to Black men, and reluctant to enlist the help of the police for protection, when the criminal justice system has historically treated Black males so discriminatorily. See, e.g., Kimberlé Crenshaw, Mapping the Margins: Intersectionality, Identity Politics, and Violence Against Women of Color, 43 Stan. L. Rev. 1241, 1253–65 (1993). Patricia Hill Collins, among others, suggests that an Afrocentric analysis of domestic violence nonetheless "must avoid excusing abuse as an inevitable consequence of the racism Black men experience. Instead, we need a holistic analysis of how race, gender, and class oppression frame the gender ideology internalized by both African–American women and men." Collins, above, at 188. How might such an analysis contribute to the creation of effective remedies for domestic violence in communities of color? How might feminist discourse be enriched by accounting for what Kimberlé Crenshaw describes as intersectionality—the convergence of systems of race, gender and class domination?

9. Although it is sometimes simpler to speak of persons "of color" as if they constituted a single category, racial and ethnic differences among groups should not be underestimated in the context of domestic violence. Although the data are mixed on whether women in the Latino community suffer from a disproportionate share of intimate partner violence, Latinas may be particularly vulnerable to domestic violence, for reasons that may include limited English proficiency, lower levels of educational achievement, uncertain immigration status, and overrepresentation in low-paying jobs. Michelle deCasas, Protecting Hispanic Women: The Inadequacy of Domestic Violence Policy, 24 Chicano–Latino L. Rev. 56 (2003). Note: Poverty is highly correlated with intimate partner abuse: "intimate partners victimized women living in households with the lowest annual household income at a rate nearly 7 times that of women living in households with the highest annual household income." U.S. Dep't of Justice, Bureau of Justice Statistics, Special Report: Intimate Partner Violence, at 4 (2000).

Cultural norms and stereotypes, as well as patriarchal family structures, may also put Latinas at particular risk. Jenny Rivera, Domestic Violence Against Latinas by Latino Males: An Analysis of Race, National Origin, and Gender Differentials, 14 B.C. Third World L.J. 231, 237–41 (1994). Like African American women, Latinas are often suspicious of police, prosecutors and judges, who may be culturally distant from the Latino community and have acted repressively toward it in the past. Id. at 246–50. Particularly difficult problems are experienced by women who are either undocumented or immigrants with conditional status, whose rights to remain in the country depend upon remaining married to the abusive husband. See Michelle J. Anderson, A License To Abuse: The Impact of Conditional Status on Female Immigrants, 102 Yale L.J. 1401 (1993). While the Violence Against Women Act included a number of provisions aimed at easing immigration barriers for battered women, implementation of these reforms has proven problematic. See Julie Dinnerstein, Working with Immigrant Victims of Domestic Violence, in Immigration Remedies for Domestic Violence Victims: VAWA Self–Petitions and Battered Spouse Waivers, Sanctuary for Families Center for Battered Women's Legal Services (2006). Latinas are less likely to seek help when they are abused, and shelters and other social service agencies are often ill-equipped to deal with their needs. Rivera, above, at 251–55. What, if any, legal changes can address these problems? Are there extra-legal programs that might be more effective in increasing the safety of Latina women?

10. In addition to problems with language, immigration status, and mistrust of the police, Asian American women seeking remedies for domestic violence experience problems unique to their culture and community. Asian American communities are overwhelmingly immigrant and often speak a variety of languages (e.g., Lao, Hmong, languages from the Indian subcontinent) for which specialized services—police investigatory resources, counselors, and battered women's shelters, for example—are not available. Karin Wang, Battered Asian American Women: Community Responses from the Battered Women's Movement and the Asian American Community, 3 Asian L.J. 151, 162–67 (1996). Moreover, female immigrants may have come to this

country specifically for the purpose of arranged marriages and are especially vulnerable. Id. at 166–68. Traditional Asian American communities typically emphasize family unity and "keeping face" more than the rights of the individual within the family, and the role of women is subordinate to that of men. Id. at 168–71. Yet, while women are expected to stay in the home, the poverty in which many recent immigrant families find themselves requires many to find work in the paid labor market, thus transforming traditional gender roles and creating a source of threat to many men. Id. at 170–71. Asian American civil rights groups, however, have tended to ignore the problems of women, and European American domestic violence groups have tended to ignore the special needs of Asian American women. Id. at 178–81.

The plight of battered women in this community has been exacerbated by the well-publicized cases in which Asian American men have raised a "cultural defense" in trials for murdering their wives, arguing that traditional values about adultery and the role of women should provide either an excuse or mitigation for their crimes. In one such case, a Chinese immigrant who killed his wife by bludgeoning her with a claw hammer, was sentenced to manslaughter rather than murder and placed on probation after he introduced evidence that his violent response to her adultery was normal in his culture of origin. See Holly Maguigan, Cultural Evidence and Male Violence: Are Feminist and Multiculturalist Reformers on a Collision Course in Criminal Courts?, 70 N.Y.U. L. Rev. 36 (1995); Leti Volpp, (Mis)identifying Culture: Asian Women and the "Cultural Defense," 17 Harv. Women's L.J. 57 (1994). In fact, the cultural evidence introduced in this trial was highly questionable. See Volpp, above, at 70. When, if ever, should the cultural traditions of the couple involved in a violent relationship be considered by the legal system?

11. Domestic violence can also be a problem for Native American women, especially as a result of the destruction of traditional culture. For example, Navajo culture was not only gender egalitarian but also matrilocal, that is, a married couple would live with or near the wife's family, who would protect her from any abuse. See James W. Zion & Elsie B. Zion, Hozho' Sokee'—Stay Together Nicely: Domestic Violence Under Navajo Common Law, 25 Ariz. St. L.J. 407, 412–15 (1993). Forced relocation, forced livestock reduction, and the assignment of title to land, however, reduced the power of women, as men were forced into the wage economy and generally assigned the title to land and livestock; divorce, freely available under traditional law, was also prohibited. Id. at 419–20; see also Donna Coker, Enhancing Autonomy for Battered Women: Lessons from Navajo Peacemaking, 47 UCLA L. Rev. 1, 16–22 (1999). After the deaths of two women from domestic violence, in 1991 the Navajo Nation Council passed a Domestic Abuse Protection Act, which authorized tribal courts to issue protective orders but also encouraged use of the Peacemaker Courts, which were modeled upon institutions of Navajo common law. Zion & Zion, above, at 407–08; Coker, above, at 32. The Peacemaker Courts use a blend of mediation, restorative justice, therapeutic intervention, family counseling, and Navajo religious teaching and offer a broad range of remedies, including reparations in the form of money, goods, or personal services and referrals to a variety of support systems, including referring the abuser to traditional healing ceremonies. Coker, above, at 35–36, 42–46. Could similar institutions be of help in other communities? See Laurie Kohn, What's

So Funny About Peace, Love, and Understanding? Restorative Justice as A New Paradigm for Domestic Violence Reform, 40 Seton Hall L. Rev. 517 (2010). What, if any, problems do you see with applying a restorative justice model to the domestic violence realm? See Grillo, excerpted in Chapter 10, Joan B. Kelly, Michael P. Johnson, Differentiation Among Types of Intimate Partner Violence: Research Update and Implications for Interventions, 46 Fam. Ct. Rev. 476, 492–93 (2008).

12. Battered women from minority religious populations, including Muslim women, may face particular problems. Muslim activists in the United States estimate that approximately ten percent of Muslim women are abused emotionally, psychologically, sexually, and/or physically by their husbands. Nooria Faizi, Domestic Violence in the Muslim Community, 10 Tex. J. Women & L. 209, 209–10 (2001). Some argue that for every case of abuse reported, "almost fifty are unreported and that less than two percent of victims actually seek help." Id. at 210. Special problems may arise in this community because of perceived religious injunctions. As Nooria Faizi reports, "[d]eviation from Islamic teachings is believed to be one of the major causes of domestic violence in Muslim families." Id. at 211. Muslim women often believe that Muslim men use the Qur'an and Sunnah "to justify their behavior," even though the interpretations they provide of these religious documents are often tenuous or inconsistent with other religious doctrines. Id. at 211–14. Then, too, there are special problems faced by Muslim women in seeking help, including the fear that shelters will not recognize their particular religious and dietary needs. A Muslim woman might fear seeking help not only because it might violate her religious beliefs, but also because she fears that it will reenforce negative impressions of Islam by Westerners. See id. at 217–18. Azizah Y. al-Hibri posits that the impact of September 11, 2001 has compounded these challenges: "[w]here latent problems of domestic violence already existed [in the American Muslim community], the new pressures made the situation worse." Azizah Y. al-Hibri, 27 Fordham Int'l L. J. 195, 196 (2003). Is the experience of religious minorities comparable to that of ethnic or racial minorities? Does your answer depend on the particular religion involved? See Stacey A. Guthartz, Domestic Violence and the Jewish Community, 11 Mich. J. Gender & L. 27 (2004). In general, should religion be considered when designing and providing services for battered women?

13. Some feminist critics assert that the phenomenon of battering in same-sex relationships represents a fundamental critique of feminism itself: if men batter men and women batter women, then male/female relations cannot sit at the core of battering relationships. As we will see in the context of male prison rape, discussed in Section D, one's response to such a claim may depend upon disaggregating sex and gender. Just as the male victim of a rape in prison may be coded and treated as a "female," so too, it has been claimed by some that the fundamental dynamic of violence remains gendered, without regard to the biological sex of the parties:

> [I]n a patriarchal society, abusive behavior is an element of the construct "man." Patriarchal society values the norms of that construction (e.g., aggressiveness and competitiveness) so highly that any behavior that is included therein becomes something to which all people aspire, regardless of sex or gender. * * * Choosing to act out abusively toward an intimate

> partner is coded as an aspect of being a man. Being a victim of that abuse is coded as an aspect of being a woman. The individual's biological sex (or actual self-identified gender) is irrelevant. Thus same-sex domestic violence—all domestic violence—is rooted in sexism.

Adele Morrison, Queering Domestic Violence to "Straighten Out" Criminal Law: What Might Happen When Queer Theory and Practice Meet Criminal Law's Conventional Responses to Domestic Violence, 13 S. Cal. Rev. L. & Women's Stud. 81, 139 (2003). Are you convinced by this argument? Does it resolve the conceptual problem or make it much more complex?

14. Research on intimate partner violence in same-sex couples is still at an early stage of development. Many of the national studies relied upon throughout this section do not specifically count same-sex couples in their research. The NVAW survey, which does attempt to account for same-sex couples' violence, showed male-perpetrated and female-perpetrated violence occurs at roughly the same rate as in heterosexual couples. 2000 NVAW Survey, above footnote 4 at 30, Exhibit 9.

Researches have noted additional difficulties unique to lesbian, gay, bisexual and transgender (LGBT) victims. See, e.g., Michelle Aulivola, Outing Domestic Violence: Affording Appropriate Protections to Gay and Lesbian Victims, 42 Fam. Ct. Rev. 162, 164–165 (2004). In the LGBT context, the abusive same-sex partner may exercise coercion by 'outing'—threatening to expose the victim's sexuality. Isolation is a particularly powerful mechanism of control, where the victim is more likely to be estranged from family members. Yet shelters, which provide invaluable safety to victimized heterosexuals, often exclude LGBT victims. Id. Until Lawrence v. Texas, 539 U.S. 558 (2003), LGBT victims might even have been criminally prosecuted under sodomy statutes when they came forward in an attempt to get the abuse to stop. Even now, when LGBT victims do report their abuse, some states do not classify same-sex partner violence as 'domestic violence' under their criminal and civil statutes. Shannon Little, Challenging Changing Legal Definitions of Family in Same–Sex Domestic Violence, 19 Hastings Women's L.J. 259, 263–264 (2008). LGBT victims also legitimately fear that prejudice in police ranks or the justice system will cause them to be mistreated, mistaken for the abuser, or not taken seriously. Id. at 262. See also National Coalition of Anti–Violence Programs, Lesbian, Gay, Bisexual, Transgender, and Queer Domestic Violence in the United States in 2008, 26 (2009), available at http://www.avp.org/publications.htm.

How is lesbian battering similar to, and/or different from, domestic violence between heterosexual couples? How should the system respond to gay male victims? Is the experience of gay males with intimate partner violence different from that of heterosexual women? For further discussion of these issues, see Patrick Letellier, Gay and Bisexual Male Domestic Violence Victimization: Challenges to Feminist Theory and Responses to Violence, 9 Violence & Victims 95, 95–97, 98–102 (1994); Ruthann Robson, Lavender Bruises: Intra–Lesbian Violence, Law and Lesbian Legal Theory, 20 Golden Gate U. L. Rev. 567, 581–91 (1990).

2. THE BATTERER

JOAN B. KELLY, PH.D. AND MICHAEL P. JOHNSON, PH.D., DOMESTIC VIOLENCE: DIFFERENTIATION AMONG TYPES OF INTIMATE PARTNER VIOLENCE: RESEARCH UPDATE AND IMPLICATIONS FOR INTERVENTIONS

46 Fam. Ct. Rev. 476 (July, 2008)

Over the past decade, a growing body of empirical research has convincingly demonstrated the existence of different types or patterns of intimate partner violence. * * * Among women's advocates * * * there are those who recognize that long-term adherence to the conviction that all domestic violence is battering has hindered the development of more sophisticated assessment protocols and treatment programs that may identify and address problems of violence for both men and women more effectively.

* * *

The value of differentiating among types of domestic violence is that appropriate screening instruments and processes can be developed that more accurately describe the central dynamics of the partner violence, the context, and the consequences. This can lead to better decision making, appropriate sanctions, and more effective treatment programs tailored to the different characteristics of partner violence. In family court, reliable differentiation of intimate partner violence is expected to provide a firmer foundation for determining whether parent-child contact is appropriate, what safeguards are necessary, and what type of parenting plans are likely to promote healthy outcomes for children and parent-child relationships. It is possible, as well, that increased understanding and acceptance of differentiation among types of domestic violence by the broad spectrum of service providers, evaluators, academics, and policy makers will diminish the current turf and gender wars and lead to more effective partnerships and policies that share the common goal of reducing violence and its destructive effects on families. * * *

[W]hen family sociologists and/or advocates for men claim that domestic violence is perpetrated equally by men and women, referring to the data from large survey studies, they are describing Situational Couple Violence, not Coercive Controlling Violence. As will be discussed, these two types of violence differ in significant ways, including causes, participation, consequences to participants, and forms of intervention required.

Coercive Controlling Violence

Researchers identify Coercive Controlling Violence by the pattern of power and control in which it is embedded. The * * * major forms of control that constitute Coercive Controlling Violence [are:] intimidation; emotional abuse; isolation; minimizing, denying, and blaming; use of children; asserting male privilege; economic abuse; and coercion and threats. Abusers do not necessarily use all of these tactics, but they do use a combination of the ones that they feel are most likely to work for them. Because these nonviolent control tactics may be effective without the use of violence (especially if there has been a history of violence in the past), Coercive Controlling Violence does not necessarily manifest itself in high levels of violence. * * *

In heterosexual relationships, Coercive Controlling Violence is perpetrated primarily by men. For example, Johnson found that 97% of the Coercive Controlling Violence in the Pittsburgh sample was male-perpetrated. * * * Although Coercive Controlling Violence does not *always* involve frequent and/or severe violence, on average its violence is more frequent and severe than other types of intimate partner violence. The combination of these higher levels of violence with the pattern of coercive control that defines Coercive Controlling Violence produces a highly negative impact on victims.

* * *

It is not unusual for victims of Coercive Controlling Violence to report that the psychological impact of their experience is worse than the physical effects. * * *

Violent Resistance

The research on intimate partner violence has clearly indicated that many women resist Coercive Controlling Violence with violence of their own. Although in the early literature such violence was generally referred to as "self-defense," we prefer the term Violent Resistance because self-defense is a legal concept that has very specific meanings that are subject to change as the law changes and because there are varieties of violent resistance that have little to do with these legal meanings of self-defense.

Nevertheless, much Violent Resistance does meet at least the common-sense definition of self-defense * * *.

* * *

Situational Couple Violence

Situational Couple Violence is the most common type of physical aggression in the general population of married spouses and cohabiting partners, and is perpetrated by both men and women. It is not a more minor version of Coercive Controlling Violence; rather, it is a different type of intimate partner violence with different causes and consequences. Situational Couple Violence is not embedded in a relationship-wide pattern of power, coercion, and control. Generally, Situational Couple Violence results from situations or arguments between partners that escalate on occasion into physical violence. One or both partners appear to have poor ability to manage their conflicts and/or poor control of anger. Most often, Situational Couple Violence has a lower per-couple frequency of occurrence and more often involves minor forms of violence (pushing, shoving, grabbing, etc.) when compared to Coercive Controlling Violence. Fear of the partner is not characteristic of women or men in Situational Couple Violence, whether perpetrator, mutual combatant, or victim. Unlike the misogynistic attitudes toward women characteristic of men who use Coercive Controlling Violence, men who are involved in Situational Couple Violence do not differ from nonviolent men on measures of misogyny.

Some verbally aggressive behaviors (cursing, yelling, and name calling) reported in Situational Couple Violence are similar to the emotional abuse of Coercive Controlling Violence, and jealousy may also exist as a recurrent theme in Situational Couple Violence, with accusations of infidelity expressed in conflicts. However, the violence and emotional abuse of Situational Couple Violence are not accompanied by a chronic pattern of controlling, intimidating, or stalking behaviors.

Situational Couple Violence is initiated at similar rates by men and women, as measured by large survey studies and community samples. * * * Based on knowledge available, this gender symmetry is associated primarily with Situational Couple Violence and not Coercive Controlling Violence. It is hoped that future research will enable clearer distinctions between violence that arises primarily from partner conflicts in contrast to violence that is embedded in patterns of coercion and control.

Separation–Instigated Violence

Of special relevance to those working with separating and divorcing families is violence instigated by the separation where there was no prior history of violence in the intimate partner relationship or in other settings. Seen symmetrically in both men and women, these are unexpected and uncharacteristic acts of violence perpetrated by a partner with a history of civilized and contained behavior. Therefore, this is not Coercive Controlling Violence as neither partner reported being intimidated, fearful, or controlled by the other during the marriage. Separation–Instigated Violence is triggered by experiences such as a traumatic separation (e.g., the home emptied and the children taken when the parent is at work), public humiliation of a prominent professional or political figure by a process server, allegations of child or sexual abuse, or the discovery of a lover in the partner's bed. The violence represents an atypical and serious loss of psychological control (sometimes described as "just going nuts"), is typically limited to one or two episodes at the beginning of or during the separation period, and ranges from mild to more severe forms of violence.

NOTES ON MEN WHO BATTER

1. What are the implications of research differentiating among types of intimate violence? How should the legal system respond?

2. Cheryl Hanna has suggested that "[n]o evidence yet supports the proposition that there is a 'profile of a batterer.' Just as women's experiences

of violence are influenced by both internal and external factors, so too is men's behavior influenced by a number of variables that make batterers as different as they are alike. These differences partially account for the failure of treatment to deter violence in many cases." Cheryl Hanna, The Paradox of Hope: The Crime and Punishment of Domestic Violence, 39 Wm. & Mary L. Rev. 1505, 1561 (1998). Hanna further explains:

> Some of the most promising domestic violence research attempts to differentiate among batterers. Different "types" of batterers emerge from a synthesis of this research. * * * Emerging typologies among different researchers are surprisingly similar: differences lie more in terminology than in concept. Family-only batterers constitute approximately fifty percent of all batterer samples. These men tend to engage in the least severe marital violence, psychological and sexual abuse. Family-only batterers are less impulsive, less likely to use weapons, and more likely to be apologetic after abusive incidents. These men may be the most deterred by the threat of criminal sanctions and the most treatable because of their ability to function normally outside of their relationships.
>
> Borderline batterers constitute approximately twenty-five percent of batterer samples. These men tend to "engage in moderate to severe abuse, including psychological and sexual abuse." Their violence generally is confined to the family, but not always. They may evince borderline personality characteristics and may have problems associated with drugs and alcohol. Batterer treatment, as it is currently structured, is likely to be insufficient to change their behavior because many men in this group may need more intensive treatment.
>
> Generally violent or antisocial batterers engage in moderate to severe violence, including psychological and sexual abuse. Edward Gondolf terms these batterers sociopathic. It is estimated that this group constitutes twenty-five percent of batterer samples. Uniformly, studies have found that generally violent men engage in more severe family violence than family-only men. This finding challenges the myth that abusers are only violent against family members. Generally violent batterers often have extensive criminal histories, including property, drug or alcohol offenses, and violent crimes against nonfamily victims. These men are the most impulsive, the most likely to use weapons, and feel the least amount of empathy towards their victims. Batterer treatment programs for this group are inappropriate given the high degree of danger they pose. Arguably, sociopathic batterers may be untreatable, and, in many cases, ought to be incarcerated if only to protect their potential victims.

Id. at 1562–65. Is batterer "treatment" ever an appropriate judicial disposition of a domestic violence case? Does your answer depend on what treatment entails? On the proven efficacy of such programs? On whether, in any given case, the victim is expressing a desire that her abuser receive treatment?

3. Might batterer profile evidence be useful in court, both to prosecute batterers (especially in homicide cases, where the victim cannot testify) and to defend battered women who kill their abusers? Expert testimony could, for example, set the violence in context and explain to factfinders evidence that might otherwise seem confusing, such as the apparent charm of many

domestic violence defendants and their lack of any criminal record. See Myrna S. Raeder, The Better Way: The Role of Batterers' Profiles and Expert "Social Framework" Background in Cases Implicating Domestic Violence, 68 U. Colo. L. Rev. 147, 182–84 (1979). Yet profile evidence is generally inadmissible in the prosecution's case because of the ban on character and prior bad acts evidence. Id. at 160–67; see Fed. R. Evid. 404. Do you think these rules of evidence should be changed in cases involving repeated, cyclical offense? If so, how would you change them? Are there other ways in which such evidence could be admitted, so long as the expert did not testify that the defendant conformed to the profile?

4. What causes men to batter? Not surprisingly, considerable controversy surrounds this question. Several scholars point out that abusive conduct which is explained by individual psychology (or psychopathology) in the U.S. is attributed to "culture" when enacted by, for example, Asian Americans or Africans. Leti Volpp, Blaming Culture for Bad Behavior, 12 Yale J.L. & Humanities 89, 96 (2000); Cynthia Grant Bowman, Theories of Domestic Violence in the African Context, 11 Am. U. J. Gender Soc. Pol'y & L. 847, 858 (2003). What are the implications of blaming intimate partner violence on psychology, as opposed to a culture of violence?

5. Is American society characterized by a culture of violence? If so, is battering best understood as simply one manifestation of this culture? Wayne Ewing argues that male abusiveness is not simply tolerated in our society, but that "[v]iolence is taught as the normal, appropriate and necessary behavior of power and control," and can only be understood in the context of what he calls "the civic advocacy of violence":

> The teaching of violence is so pervasive, so totally a part of male experience, that I think it best to acknowledge this teaching as a *civic,* rather than as a cultural or as a social phenomenon. * * *
>
> Analyses which interweave the advocacy of male violence with "Super-Bowl Culture" have never been refuted. It is too obvious. Civic expectations—translated into professionalism, financial commitments, city planning for recreational space, the raising of male children for competitive sport, * * *—all result in the monument of the National Football League, symbol and reality at once of the advocacy of violence.

Wayne Ewing, The Civic Advocacy of Violence, in Men's Lives 301, 304–05 (Michael S. Kimmel & Michael A. Messner, eds. 1995). What do you think of this argument? If you agree, what does this say about the possibility of solving the problem of domestic violence in our society as a whole? If the attributes of batterers are simply those of "everyman," what is to be done? How can one explain the fact that some men do *not* batter their spouses and girlfriends? Moreover, even if violence is general, why are women its customary target?

6. A number of studies have found a correlation between domestic abuse and abuse in the batterer's family of origin. Research supports the proposition that men who are victimized by abuse as children, as well as men who witness abuse of their mother, are more likely to abuse their partners. See Joan B. Kelly & Michael P. Johnson, Differentiation Among Types of Intimate Partner Violence: Research Update and Implications for Interventions, 46 Fam. Ct. Rev. 476, 489–90 (2008); Neil S. Jacobson & John M. Gottman, When Men

Batter Women: New Insights Into Ending Abusive Relationships, 36–39, 43–46, 93–97 (1998). How can we attempt to interrupt this intergenerational transmission of violence? What are the implications for the legal treatment of domestic abuse?

7. Do biomedical factors help to explain male battering? From a biologist's perspective, men have an inherited tendency to secrete adrenalin when they believe themselves to be sexually threatened by other males. The label applied to this arousal, however, will be socially determined. Thus, male aggression against females is part of male reproductive strategies geared toward reproducing offspring and ensuring paternity; this sexual aggression is well-documented throughout the primate world and cross-culturally. Hanna, above note 2, at 1567; see also Molly J. Walker Wilson, An Evolutionary Perspective on Male Domestic Violence: Practical and Policy Implications, 32 Am. J. Crim. L. 291 (2005). Do you believe that evolutionary theories contribute to our understanding of domestic violence? What are the implications for our legal system if biological factors indeed play a role in battering? Should feminists be wary of evolutionary approaches to explaining domestic violence? Are such approaches biologically deterministic? If so, do they offer an excuse for battering? We will return to these questions in the context of rape, Section D, below.

8. Should sentencing policy and individual case dispositions take into account why men batter? Is the notion of treatment dependent on a particular understanding of the causes of abuse?

9. Is batterer treatment effective in changing men's behaviors? A consensus has emerged that it is not. A national study by the Center for Court Innovation summarizes existing research:

> Although batterer programs are now widespread, the rationale for using them has become a matter of growing contention. When batterer programs first originated in the late 1970s, supporters typically described them as one prong in a "coordinated community response" to domestic violence, guided by the aim of "changing the climate of tolerance for this type of violence" Initially, the purpose was to get the participants to stop their abusive behavior. Accordingly, rehabilitation has been and continues to be the focus of research. Over 35 batterer program studies have been completed since the 1980s. Recently, five key studies have emerged that employ experimental techniques, assigning offenders at random to a batterer program or a control condition in an effort to provide definitive evidence of whether or not the programs produce a reduction in re-abuse. The results suggest that they do not. Four of the five experimental trials, including all four completed over the past decade, showed no effect of batterer programs on recidivism. The most recent literature review found that batterer programs overall do not reduce re-offending, especially when measured by victim report, or at best show only marginal effects.

Melissa Labriola, Michael Rempel, Chris S. O'Sullivan, & Phyllis B. Frank, Court Responses to Batter Program Noncompliance, Center for Court Innovation Research, at iii (2007), available at http://www.ncjrs.gov/pdffiles1/nij/grants/230399.pdf.

Given that batterer programs have been proven largely ineffectual, should they be considered viable sentencing options? Why or why not? Some proponents have suggested that the programs "serve as an appropriate penalty (when jail is not an option) and monitoring mechanism, effecting offender *accountability*." Id. at 7. Are you convinced? If not, do you view incarceration as the appropriate sanction for domestic violence? See Hanna, above note 2, at 1577 ("Too few, not too many, men are incarcerated for severe and chronic violence against their intimate partners"). What are the advantages and disadvantages of greater reliance on incarceration as a default sentence in cases of battering?

10. Should batterers—either men who stand convicted of abuse, or those subject to domestic violence restraining orders—be allowed to possess firearms? For a summary and critique of existing federal law that prohibits possession under these circumstances, see Tom Lininger, A Better Way to Disarm Batterers, 54 Hastings L.J. 525 (2003). What unintended consequences might result from this statutory scheme? See Lisa D. May, The Backfiring of Domestic Violence Firearms Bans, 14 Colum. J. Gender & L. 1 (2005). Would you support passage of a state law that prevents abusers from possessing firearms? Why or why not?

3. THE CONSTITUTION AND POLICE RESPONSE TO DOMESTIC VIOLENCE

CITY OF CASTLE ROCK v. JESSICA GONZALES

United States Supreme Court June 27, 2005.
545 U.S. 748, 125 S.Ct. 2796, 162 L.Ed.2d 658.

JUSTICE SCALIA delivered the opinion of the Court.

* * *

The horrible facts of this case are contained in the complaint that respondent Jessica Gonzales filed in Federal District Court. * * * Respondent alleges that petitioner, the town of Castle Rock, Colorado, violated the Due Process Clause of the Fourteenth Amendment to the United States Constitution when its police officers, acting pursuant to official policy or custom, failed to respond properly to her repeated reports that her estranged husband was violating the terms of a restraining order.

The restraining order had been issued by a state trial court several weeks earlier in conjunction with respondent's divorce proceedings. The original form order, issued on May 21, 1999, and served on respondent's husband on June 4, 1999, commanded him not to "molest or disturb the peace of [respondent] or of any child," and to remain at least 100 yards from the family home at all times. * * * The bottom of the preprinted form noted that the reverse side contained "IMPORTANT NOTICES FOR RESTRAINED PARTIES AND LAW ENFORCEMENT OFFICIALS." *Ibid.* (emphasis deleted). The preprinted text on the back of the form included the following **"WARNING"**:

> "**A KNOWING VIOLATION OF A RESTRAINING ORDER IS A CRIME** .... A VIOLATION WILL ALSO CONSTITUTE CONTEMPT OF COURT. **YOU MAY BE ARRESTED** WITHOUT NOTICE IF A LAW ENFORCEMENT OFFICER HAS PROBABLE CAUSE TO BELIEVE THAT YOU HAVE KNOWINGLY VIOLATED THIS ORDER." *Id.*, at 1144 (emphasis in original).

The preprinted text on the back of the form also included a **"NOTICE TO LAW ENFORCEMENT OFFICIALS,"** which read in part:

> "YOU SHALL USE EVERY REASONABLE MEANS TO ENFORCE THIS RESTRAINING ORDER. YOU SHALL ARREST, OR, IF AN ARREST WOULD BE IMPRACTICAL UNDER THE CIRCUMSTANCES, SEEK A WARRANT FOR THE ARREST OF THE RESTRAINED PERSON WHEN YOU HAVE INFORMATION AMOUNTING TO PROBABLE CAUSE THAT THE RESTRAINED PERSON HAS VIOLATED OR ATTEMPTED TO VIOLATE ANY PROVISION OF THIS ORDER AND THE RESTRAINED PERSON HAS BEEN PROPERLY SERVED WITH A COPY OF THIS ORDER OR HAS RECEIVED ACTUAL NOTICE OF THE EXISTENCE OF THIS ORDER." *Ibid.* (same).

On June 4, 1999, the state trial court modified the terms of the restraining order and made it permanent. * * *

According to the complaint, at about 5 or 5:30 p.m. on Tuesday, June 22, 1999, respondent's husband took the three daughters while they were playing outside the family home. No advance arrangements had been made for him to see the daughters that evening. When respondent noticed the children were missing, she suspected her husband had taken them. At about 7:30 p.m., she called the Castle Rock Police Department, which dispatched two officers. The complaint continues: "When [the officers] arrived ..., she showed them a copy of the TRO and requested that it be enforced and the three children be returned to her immediately. [The officers] stated that there was nothing they could do about the TRO and suggested that [respondent] call the Police Department again if the three children did not return home by 10:00 p.m."

At approximately 8:30 p.m., respondent talked to her husband on his cellular telephone. He told her "he had the three children [at an] amusement park in Denver." *Ibid.* She called the police again and asked them to "have someone check for" her husband or his vehicle at the amusement park and "put out an [all points bulletin]" for her husband, but the officer with whom she spoke "refused to do so," again telling her to "wait until 10:00 p.m. and see if" her husband returned the girls.

At approximately 10:10 p.m., respondent called the police and said her children were still missing, but she was now told to wait until midnight. She called at midnight and told the dispatcher her children were still missing. She went to her husband's apartment and, finding nobody there, called the police at 12:10 a.m.; she was told to wait for an officer to arrive. When none came, she went to the police station at 12:50 a.m. and submitted an incident report. The officer who took the report "made no reasonable effort to enforce the TRO or locate the three children. Instead, he went to dinner."

At approximately 3:20 a.m., respondent's husband arrived at the police station and opened fire with a semiautomatic handgun he had purchased earlier that evening. Police shot back, killing him. Inside the cab of his pickup truck, they found the bodies of all three daughters, whom he had already murdered.

On the basis of the foregoing factual allegations, respondent brought an action under Rev. Stat. § 1979, 42 U.S.C. § 1983, claiming that the town violated the Due Process Clause because its police department had "an official policy or custom of failing to respond properly to complaints of restraining order violations" and "tolerate[d] the non-enforcement of restraining orders by its police officers."[3] The complaint also alleged that the town's actions "were taken either willfully, recklessly or with such gross negligence as to indicate wanton disregard and deliberate indifference to" respondent's civil rights.

Before answering the complaint, the defendants filed a motion to dismiss under Federal Rule of Civil Procedure 12(b)(6). The District Court granted the motion, concluding that, whether construed as making a substantive due process or procedural due process claim, respondent's complaint failed to state a claim upon which relief could be granted.

A panel of the Court of Appeals affirmed the rejection of a substantive due process claim, but found that respondent had alleged a cognizable procedural due process claim. On rehearing en banc, a divided court reached the same disposition, concluding that respondent had a "protected property interest in the enforcement of the terms of her restraining order" and that the town had deprived her of due process because "the police never 'heard' nor seriously entertained her request to enforce and protect her interests in the restraining order." We granted certiorari. * * *

II

The Fourteenth Amendment to the United States Constitution provides that a State shall not "deprive any person of life, liberty, or property, without due process of law." Amdt. 14, § 1. In 42 U.S.C. § 1983, Congress has created a federal cause of action for "the deprivation of any rights, privileges, or immunities secured by the Constitution and laws." Respondent claims the benefit of this provision on the ground that she had a property interest in police enforcement of the restraining order against her husband; and that the town deprived her of this property

3. Three officers were also named as defendants in the complaint, but the Court of Appeals concluded that they were entitled to qualified immunity. Respondent did not file a cross-petition challenging that aspect of the judgment. [Under Harlow v. Fitzgerald, 457 U.S. 800 (1982), municipal officers are immune from suit if the right allegedly violated was not "clearly established" at the time of their action.]

without due process by having a policy that tolerated nonenforcement of restraining orders.

As the Court of Appeals recognized, we left a similar question unanswered in *DeShaney v. Winnebago County Dept. of Social Servs.,* 489 U.S. 189, (1989), another case with "undeniably tragic" facts: Local child-protection officials had failed to protect a young boy from beatings by his father that left him severely brain damaged. We held that the so-called "substantive" component of the Due Process Clause does not "requir[e] the State to protect the life, liberty, and property of its citizens against invasion by private actors." We noted, however, that the petitioner had not properly preserved the argument that—and we thus "decline[d] to consider" whether—state "child protection statutes gave [him] an 'entitlement' to receive protective services in accordance with the terms of the statute, an entitlement which would enjoy due process protection."

The procedural component of the Due Process Clause does not protect everything that might be described as a "benefit": "To have a property interest in a benefit, a person clearly must have more than an abstract need or desire" and "more than a unilateral expectation of it. He must, instead, have a legitimate claim of entitlement to it." *Board of Regents of State Colleges v. Roth,* 408 U.S. 564 (1972). Such entitlements are, " 'of course, . . . not created by the Constitution. Rather, they are created and their dimensions are defined by existing rules or understandings that stem from an independent source such as state law.' "

A

Our cases recognize that a benefit is not a protected entitlement if government officials may grant or deny it in their discretion. The Court of Appeals in this case determined that Colorado law created an entitlement to enforcement of the restraining order because the "court-issued restraining order . . . specifically dictated that its terms must be enforced" and a "state statute command[ed]" enforcement of the order when certain objective conditions were met (probable cause to believe that the order had been violated and that the object of the order had received notice of its existence).

* * *

B

The critical language in the restraining order came not from any part of the order itself (which was signed by the state-court trial judge and directed to the restrained party, respondent's husband), but from the preprinted notice to law-enforcement personnel that appeared on the back of the order. That notice effectively restated the statutory provision describing "peace officers' duties" related to the crime of violation of a restraining order. At the time of the conduct at issue in this case, that provision read as follows:

* * *

"(b) *A peace officer shall arrest, or, if an arrest would be impractical under the circumstances, seek a warrant for the arrest of a restrained person* when the peace officer has information amounting to probable cause that:

"(I) The restrained person has violated or attempted to violate any provision of a restraining order; and

"(II) The restrained person has been properly served with a copy of the restraining order or the restrained person has received actual notice of the existence and substance of such order.

"(c) In making the probable cause determination described in paragraph (b) of this subsection (3), a peace officer shall assume that the information received from the registry is accurate. *A peace officer shall enforce a valid restraining order whether or not there is a record of the restraining order in the registry.*" Colo.Rev.Stat. § 18–6–803.5(3) (Lexis 1999) (emphases added).

The Court of Appeals concluded that this statutory provision—especially taken in conjunction with a statement from its legislative history, and with another statute restricting criminal and civil liability for officers making arrests[7]—established the Colorado Legislature's clear intent "to alter the fact that the police were not enforcing domestic abuse restraining orders," and thus its intent "that the recipient of a domestic abuse restraining order have an entitlement to its enforcement." Any other result, it said, "would render domestic abuse restraining orders utterly valueless."

This last statement is sheer hyperbole. Whether or not respondent had a right to enforce the restraining order, it rendered certain otherwise lawful conduct by her husband both criminal and in contempt of court. See §§ 18–6–803.5(2)(a), (7). The creation of grounds on which he could be arrested, criminally prosecuted, and held in contempt was hardly "valueless"—even if the prospect of those sanctions ultimately failed to prevent him from committing three murders and a suicide.

We do not believe that these provisions of Colorado law truly made enforcement of restraining orders *mandatory*.

* * *

[A] true mandate of police action would require some stronger indication from the Colorado Legislature * * *

* * *

Even if we were to think otherwise concerning the creation of an entitlement by Colorado, it is by no means clear that an individual entitlement to enforcement of a restraining order could constitute a

7. Under Colo.Rev.Stat. § 18–6–803.5(5) (Lexis 1999), "[a] peace officer arresting a person for violating a restraining order or otherwise enforcing a restraining order" was not to be held civilly or criminally liable unless he acted "in bad faith and with malice" or violated "rules adopted by the Colorado supreme court."

"property" interest for purposes of the Due Process Clause. Such a right would not, of course, resemble any traditional conception of property. Although that alone does not disqualify it from due process protection, as *Roth* and its progeny show, the right to have a restraining order enforced does not "have some ascertainable monetary value," as even our "*Roth*-type property-as-entitlement" cases have implicitly required. * * *

We conclude, therefore, that respondent did not, for purposes of the Due Process Clause, have a property interest in police enforcement of the restraining order against her husband. It is accordingly unnecessary to address the Court of Appeals' determination that the town's custom or policy prevented the police from giving her due process when they deprived her of that alleged interest.

In light of today's decision and that in *DeShaney,* the benefit that a third party may receive from having someone else arrested for a crime generally does not trigger protections under the Due Process Clause, neither in its procedural nor in its "substantive" manifestations.

* * *

The judgment of the Court of Appeals is

Reversed.

JUSTICE STEVENS, with whom JUSTICE GINSBURG joins, dissenting.

* * *

It is perfectly clear, on the one hand, that neither the Federal Constitution itself, nor any federal statute, granted respondent or her children any individual entitlement to police protection. See *DeShaney,* 489 U.S. 189 (1989). Nor, I assume, does any Colorado statute create any such entitlement for the ordinary citizen. On the other hand, it is equally clear that federal law imposes no impediment to the creation of such an entitlement by Colorado law. Respondent certainly could have entered into a contract with a private security firm, obligating the firm to provide protection to respondent's family; respondent's interest in such a contract would unquestionably constitute "property" within the meaning of the Due Process Clause. If a Colorado statute enacted for her benefit, or a valid order entered by a Colorado judge, created the functional equivalent of such a private contract by granting respondent an entitlement to mandatory individual protection by the local police force, that state-created right would also qualify as "property" entitled to constitutional protection.

* * *

Three flaws in the Court's rather superficial analysis of the merits highlight the unwisdom of its decision to answer the state-law question *de novo.* First, the Court places undue weight on the various statutes throughout the country that seemingly mandate police enforcement but are generally understood to preserve police discretion. As a result, the Court gives short shrift to the unique case of "mandatory arrest" statutes in the domestic violence context; States passed a wave of these statutes in the 1980's and 1990's with the unmistakable goal of eliminating police discretion in this area. Second, the Court's formalistic analysis fails to take seriously the fact that the Colorado statute at issue in this case was enacted for the benefit of the narrow class of persons who are beneficiaries of domestic restraining orders, and that the order at issue in this case was specifically intended to provide protection to respondent and her children. Finally, the Court is simply wrong to assert that a citizen's interest in the government's commitment to provide police enforcement in certain defined circumstances does not resemble any "traditional conception of property"; in fact, a citizen's property interest in such a commitment is just as concrete and worthy of protection as her interest in any other important service the government or a private firm has undertaken to provide.

* * *

Because respondent had a property interest in the enforcement of the restraining order, state officials could not deprive her of that interest without observing fair procedures. Her description of the police behavior in this case and the department's callous policy of failing to respond properly to reports of restraining order violations clearly alleges a due process violation. At the very least, due process requires that the relevant state decisionmaker *listen* to the claimant and then *apply the relevant criteria* in reaching his decision. The failure to observe these minimal procedural safeguards creates an unacceptable risk of arbitrary and "erroneous deprivation[s]." According to respondent's complaint * * * the process she was afforded by the police constituted nothing more than a " 'sham or a pretense.' "

Accordingly, I respectfully dissent.

NOTES ON CONSTITUTIONAL CLAIMS AND DOMESTIC VIOLENCE

1. What factors do you think account for the well documented reluctance of police to pursue domestic violence claims? Is the traditional split between the public and private spheres the culprit here? Is this exacerbated or amplified by the institutional incentives of police and prosecutors to refuse to pursue cases that they believe are unlikely to succeed? Who is most likely to be impacted by non-enforcement of domestic violence laws? See Meghan S. Chandek & Amanda L. Robinson, Differential Police Response to Black Battered Women, 12 Women & Crim. Just. 29, 30–31 (2000).

2. As evidenced by *Castle Rock*, constitutional claims of police "failure to protect" in domestic violence cases—whether grounded in the right to procedural due process, substantive due process, or equal protection—have been largely unsuccessful. What might account for widespread judicial unwillingness to recognize these claims?

3. *DeShaney*, cited in *Castle Rock* by both the majority and dissent for the proposition that Jessica Gonzalez's procedural due process claim was

foreclosed, rests on the assumption that the state has no affirmative duty to protect individuals who are not in state custody. The *Deshaney* Court struggled to outline the difference between what is often referred to as "negative freedom" (not preventing the individual from exercising her rights) and "positive freedom" (state action to enable the individual to exercise her rights). Where the state fails to protect its citizens from violence perpetrated against them by other citizens in the face of requests for protection, is the *DeShaney* approach in fact consistent with the basic premises of liberal democratic government? Isn't police protection under these circumstances at the core of the theoretical justification for entry into civil government, that is, the establishment of a central authority as a means of protecting individuals from the war of all against all? See Thomas Hobbes, Leviathan pt. I, ch. 13 (1651).

4. Notwithstanding some notable successes, e.g., Thurman v. City of Torrington, 595 F. Supp. 1521 (D. Conn. 1984), domestic violence victims have rarely prevailed on equal protection claims based on police inaction. These claims have been made significantly more difficult by the fact that the claim is characterized not as one about gender, but as one about "domestic violence." See, e.g., *Feeney*, excerpted in Chapter 2 (requiring a showing of discriminatory intent for laws that do not distinguish facially based on gender). Can you think of a way to re-characterize the discrimination involved in these cases as one about gender rather than domestic violence? Ruth Bader Ginsburg has always emphasized, in her equal protection opinions, the pernicious influence of gender stereotypes. See, e.g., United States v. Virginia, 518 U.S. 515 (1996). Is it possible to argue that the "discrimination" is not against a particular kind of violence (domestic or not), but that state actors (the police) refused to act because of "violence myths" about *women*—that she provoked the violence, she lied about it, or she exaggerated its significance? What kinds of proof problems would you anticipate with such claims? Stephanie Wildman argues that equal protection means "not maintaining male privilege and ensuring women can be full societal participants." Stephanie Wildman, 98 Mich L. Rev. 1797, 1816–17 (2000). Do you agree? What are the advantages and disadvantages of this formulation?

5. Does a police policy that provides less protection to victims of domestic violence than to other victims of violence constitute discrimination on the basis of sex? Why or why not? How would a plaintiff show, in order to survive summary judgment, that discrimination against women was the motivating factor in such a policy or practice? What problems would you anticipate with claims based on statistical proof of disparate arrest rates in domestic/non-domestic cases? See, e.g., Ricketts v. City of Columbia, 36 F.3d 775 (8th Cir. 1994). Would it make a difference if sex discrimination claims were subject to strict scrutiny? Or are domestic violence victims effectively deprived of a remedy by application of *Feeney*'s standard?

6. After *Castle Rock*, what is the practical import of restraining orders? If you were a state legislator committed to creating a mandatory enforcement mechanism, how would you proceed? If you represented Jessica Gonzalez, what additional avenues of relief would you pursue? See Caroline Bettinger Lopez, Jessica Gonzalez v. United States: An Emerging Model for Domestic Violence and Human Rights Advocacy in the United States, 21 Harv. Hum.

Rts. J. 183 (2008) (describing Gonzalez's petition against the United States, filed with the Inter-American Commission on Human Rights, alleging deprivation of human rights).

4. THE DEBATE OVER MANDATORY PROSECUTION

DONNA WILLS, DOMESTIC VIOLENCE: THE CASE FOR AGGRESSIVE PROSECUTION

7 UCLA Women's L.J. 173, 173–176, 179–82 (1997).

Prosecutors throughout the country, and especially in the State of California, have begun taking a more aggressive stance towards domestic violence prosecutions by instituting a "no drop" or "no dismissal" policy. Based on my experience as a veteran prosecutor who specializes in these cases, I firmly believe that this policy is the enlightened approach to domestic violence prosecutions. Fundamentally, a "no drop" policy takes the decision of whether or not to prosecute the batterer off the victim's shoulders and puts it where it belongs: in the discretion of the prosecutors whose job it is to enforce society's criminal laws and hold offenders accountable for their crimes. The prosecutor's client is the State, not the victim. Accordingly, prosecutorial agencies that have opted for aggressive prosecution have concluded that their client's interest in protecting the safety and well-being of all of its citizens overrides the individual victim's desire to dictate whether and when criminal charges are filed.

Aggressive prosecution is the appropriate response to domestic violence cases for several reasons. First, domestic violence affects more than just the individual victim; it is a public safety issue that affects all of society. Second, prosecutors cannot rely upon domestic violence victims to appropriately vindicate the State's interests in holding batterers responsible for the crimes they commit because victims often decline to press charges. Third, prosecutors must intervene to protect victims and their children and to prevent batterers from further intimidating their victims and manipulating the justice system.

II. Domestic Violence is a Public Safety Issue

Domestic violence is a societal, not merely an individual, problem; it is not just about two people in a private relationship working out their "family problems." The harm caused by this violence refuses to be neatly confined between the abuser and the victim. Rather, domestic violence impacts everyone: children, neighbors, extended family, the workplace, hospital emergency rooms, Good Samaritans who are killed while trying to intervene, and the death row inmates who cite it as a reason not to be killed. The State has a legitimate interest in maintaining public safety, especially by ensuring that domestic violence offenders are not allowed to flourish unabated.

Domestic violence advocates were correct in supporting laws that codified domestic violence as both a crime against the individual *and* a crime against the State. When prosecutors file charges, we enforce these laws and reinforce the fact that domestic violence is criminal conduct. In California, the Penal Code explains why special attention should be devoted to the prosecution of batterers: "The Legislature hereby finds that spousal abusers present a clear and present danger to the mental and physical well-being of the *citizens* of the State of California."[4] Besides being "an unacknowledged epidemic in our society," domestic violence is the leading cause of injury to women, a major factor in female homicide, a contributing factor to female suicide, a major risk for child abuse, and a major precursor for future batterers and violent youth offenders. The State cannot ignore the human tragedies that are caused by domestic violence.

The primary duty of government is to protect its citizens from assault as vigorously in the home as on the streets. The victims subject to domestic abuse are often not the only people who suffer. Most notably, children are secondary victims of violence in the home. The link between domestic violence and child abuse, both emotional and physical, cannot be ignored. Each year, between three and ten million children are forced to witness the emotional devastation of one parent abusing or killing the other. Many are injured in the "crossfire" while trying to protect the assaulted parent, or are used as pawns or shields and are harmed by blows intended for someone else. Some are born with birth defects because their mothers were battered during pregnancy. Children of domestic violence are silent victims who suffer without the options available to adults. Thus, aggressive prosecution furthers the State's goal of protecting not only the victim, but also the children in homes where domestic violence occurs.

Researchers have yet to determine the extent to which aggressive prosecution actually combats the problem of domestic violence. Although some recent studies have questioned whether mandatory arrest of batterers is beneficial in deterring domestic violence, such studies are misleading. No studies have focused on the incremental effects that aggressive prosecution has had on controlling, if not eliminating, recidivism. Nor has current research addressed the role of aggressive prosecution in decreasing the public's tolerance of domestic violence. Prosecutors realize all too well that criminal intervention alone may not be the ultimate "cure" for domestic violence any more than it is a complete solution to gang violence, carjackings, sexual assaults, child abuse, or any other kind of anti-social violence perpetrated by one human being against another. Indeed, criminal intervention does not guarantee that a batterer will forever refrain from further violence. However, failure to try to achieve this goal is not an acceptable alternative. Research notwithstanding, aggressive prosecution of batterers is a criminal justice decision predicated on what is best for the

4. Cal. Penal Code § 273.8 (West 1988) (amended 1994) (emphasis added).

common good, not a scientifically formulated antidote guaranteed to transform batterers into peaceful spouses or model partners.

* * *

IV. Batterers Must Not Be Allowed to Control Justice

Batterers are "master manipulators." They will do anything to convince their victims to get the prosecution to drop the charges. They call from jail threatening retaliation. They cajole their victim with promises of reform. They remind her that they may lose their jobs and, hence, the family income. They send love letters, pledging future bliss and happiness. They have their family members turn off the victim's electricity and threaten to kick the victim and her children out into the street. They pay for the victim to leave town so that she will not be subpoenaed. They use community property to pay for an expensive lawyer to try to convince the jury that the whole thing was the victim's fault and that she attacked him. They prey on the victim's personal weaknesses, especially drug and alcohol abuse, physical and mental disabilities, and her love for their children. They negotiate financial and property incentives that cause acute memories of terror and pain to fade dramatically. Prosecutors watch with practiced patience as these vulnerable victims succumb to their batterers' intimidation and manipulation. Then, "no drop" prosecutors try to hold the batterers responsible regardless of the victims' lack of cooperation by using creative legal maneuvering.

Supporters of "no drop" domestic violence policies realize that empowering victims by giving them the discretion to prosecute, or even to threaten to prosecute, in actuality only empowers batterers to further manipulate and endanger their victims' lives, the children's lives, and the safety and well-being of the entire community. By proceeding with the prosecution with or without victim cooperation, the prosecutor minimizes the victim's value to the batterer as an ally to defeat criminal prosecution. A "no drop" policy means prosecutors will not allow batterers to control the system of justice through their victims.

* * *

When the 911 call is made to law enforcement, the criminal justice system is triggered. When the report of violence is made, that moment signifies that the victim is *without the power to get the batterer to stop the violence*. However, the criminal justice system is not without power to encourage the batterer to cease and desist. Arrest and prosecution, however temporary, serve notice on the batterer that what he did was wrong and warrants his immediate removal from the community. It also gives the victim a breather—time and opportunity to access counseling services, to investigate alternatives to life with a violent partner, to form a plan for safety, and to have authority focused on the batterer to stop the violence.

Prosecutors are aware of complaints that "no drop" policies make battered women feel "powerless" to keep the government, specifically the courts, from "interfering" in their lives. Some object to the court "dictating" what will happen to the case and the abuser in the aftermath of reporting the abuse. However, prosecutors must seize the "window of opportunity" given to us by the report of violence to get the batterer's attention. Working closely with victim advocates, prosecutors try to convince battered women to see the wisdom of criminal justice intervention. We tell the victims that we proceed with the prosecution because we cannot allow the batterer to believe that physical abuse is acceptable. We tell them that left without intervention, the violence may increase both in frequency of occurrence and severity of injury, often leading to the tragic scenario where he kills her or she kills him while defending herself against his aggression. We tell victims that the children suffer when they see their mother hurt and that the children need their mother to stay alive and well. We try to help them form a safety plan and deal with their fear, financial concerns, and future uncertainties, *with or without the batterer*.

* * *

No humane society can allow any citizen, battered woman or otherwise, to be beaten and terrorized while being held emotionally hostage to love and fear or blackmailed by financial dependence and cultural mores. As guardians of public safety, prosecutors must proceed against domestic violence offenders *with or without victim cooperation* as long as there is legally sufficient evidence. This policy of aggressive prosecution adopts the wisdom that "[t]here is no excuse for domestic violence." * * *

LINDA G. MILLS, KILLING HER SOFTLY: INTIMATE ABUSE AND THE VIOLENCE OF STATE INTERVENTION

113 Harv. L. Rev. 550, 567–68, 576–77, 582–85, 595–97, 609–11 (1999).

I. MANDATORY POLICIES

* * * Very few studies have tested the effectiveness of mandatory prosecution policies in eliminating violence in battered women's lives. Indeed, the one randomized study specific to the topic, conducted by David Ford and Jean Regoli in 1986, suggested mixed results at best.[81] Ford and Regoli assigned batterers to one of three tracks: pre-trial diversion, prosecution and rehabilitation, or prosecution and other sanctions (such as jail time). The study found that if a battered woman files charges in a jurisdiction that permits her to drop the case and she refuses to drop it, she is at lower risk of subsequent abuse than if she had been in a jurisdiction that made that decision for her through a mandatory prosecution policy. Ford and Regoli surmised that prevention of future incidents of violence was related to the victim's "power" to drop the charges.

A recent study on the effects of prosecution on recidivism presented

81. See David A. Ford & Mary Jean Regoli, The Criminal Prosecution of Wife Assaulters: Process, Problems, and Effects, in Legal Responses to Wife Assault: Current Trends and Evaluation 127, 151–57 (N. Zoe Hilton ed., 1993).

striking results.[85] After reviewing a large sample of domestic violence misdemeanor cases (1133), the researchers found that prosecution had no effect on the likelihood of re-arrest of the batterer within a six-month period. More specifically, Robert Davis and his co-authors determined that recidivism was unaffected by whether a case was dropped, dismissed, or prosecuted. While the authors warned that their findings were tentative, they nevertheless concluded that "there is little support for the idea that law enforcement responses to domestic violence misdemeanors reduce or eliminate violence." Given these study findings, the advantages of mandatory interventions do not clearly outweigh the disadvantages, especially if these interventions protect the safety of white women at the expense of African–American women.

* * *

II. Clinical Concerns

[Mills next discusses the clinical literature on treatment of survivors of traumatic events.]

B. The Healing Process

* * *

Certain clinical rules govern a healing relationship. For example, the empowerment of the survivor is the most important goal. Empowerment provides a space for the battered woman to decide how to proceed in the healing process. This kind of empowerment does not imply that she is obligated to choose among options; rather, it suggests the need for those involved in the healing process to present options and relevant data, encouraging the survivor to choose the path with which she is most comfortable. In Herman's terms:

> [The survivor] must be the author and arbiter of her own recovery. Others may offer advice, support, assistance, affection, and care, but not cure. Many benevolent and well-intentioned attempts to assist the survivor founder because this fundamental principle of empowerment is not observed. No intervention that takes power away from the survivor can possibly foster her recovery, no matter how much it appears to be in her immediate best interest.[138]

Hence, helping victims restore power and control and diminishing their helplessness by increasing their choices can contribute significantly to reversing the negative dynamics that dominate the abusive relationship. This reversal, in turn, fosters the victim's capacity to engage in a healthy and affirming relationship. * * *

* * *

85. See [Robert C. Davis, Barbara E. Smith & Laura B. Nickles, The Deterrent Effect of Prosecuting Domestic Violence Misdemeanors, 44 Crime & Delinq. 434, 441 (1998)].

138. [Judith Lewis Herman, Trauma and Recovery 133 (1997).]

C. *Clinical Explanations for State Actors' Violence*

* * *

The view that state responsibility in domestic violence cases should be limited to the goal of protection is conceptually narrow and clinically inappropriate. This position neglects the state's collective obligation to its victimized citizenry to respond to intimate abuse in ways that reliably interrupt patterns of violence and that begin to eradicate the underlying dynamics that cause violent ruptures in the first place. * * *

Mandatory interventions, such as arrest, prosecution, and reporting, treat battered women as fragile, uncooperative, mentally ill, and/or indecisive. These reactions may, in their simplest form, be manifestations of state actors' unexpressed desire to silence or to mask their feelings of guilt, rage, and shame, which their interactions with victims of abuse so easily generate. These unexpressed feelings and counter-transference reactions are not without consequences; they infect the state's relationships with battered women and reduce the possibility of developing a healing dynamic that may actually result in transformation.

That state actors are likely to feel overwhelmed and helpless in the face of their interactions with survivors of intimate abuse is understandable. Battered women's stories are painful for anyone to hear. For state actors, who are not trained to anticipate their own reactions, victims' abuse histories can be threatening, even unbearable. I fear that, instead of working through their feelings in ways that facilitate their relationships with the battered women, state actors become infected by the violence they witness and inadvertently reproduce its most destructive forms.

* * *

III. Schematic of State Violence

* * *

B. *State Officials as Abusers*

From the accumulated evidence, a dynamic between the state and the battered woman emerges that distinctly mimics the violent dynamic in the battering relationship. Three correlative themes are the most problematic. First, mandatory interventions reinforce the battered woman's psychic injury and encourage feelings of guilt, low self-esteem, and dependency. Mandatory interventions are predicated on the assumption that state actors are incapable of distinguishing between battered women who are truly suffering from "learned helplessness" and battered women who are capable of making reasoned decisions about which healing strategies to pursue. * * *

Second, mandatory interventions may have the ironic effect of realigning the battered woman with the batterer. Some studies suggest and numerous authors have surmised that when the battered woman has a negative interaction with the state, she is less likely to rely on governmental assistance in the future. Indeed, some have argued, as I am arguing, that if a battered woman is given the choice between abuse by the batterer, which is familiar, and abuse by state actors, which is unfamiliar, she is likely to choose the abuse she knows best.

Finally, mandatory interventions deny the battered woman an important opportunity to partner with the state to help ensure her future safety. The Ford and Regoli study, along with the clinical literature discussed in Part II, clearly indicates the importance of developing new methods for encouraging battered women to engage with state actors in the development of tailored and strategic responses to the women's situations that reflect their and their children's best interests.

* * *

IV. Survivor–Centered Model

* * *

A. Elements of a Survivor–Centered Model

To counteract the destructive dynamics of the current relationship between the state and battered women described in sections II and III, I have developed a Survivor–Centered Model of state response to domestic violence. This approach assumes that the victim of domestic violence is searching for a path toward healing, that state actors should help facilitate her psychological health as well as her physical safety, and that the victim of domestic violence is in the best position to dictate the terms of her healing. In opposition to the current destructive dynamics of the state's relationship with the battered woman, I present a framework for reversing the destructive typologies of emotional abuse described earlier. I describe eight subcategories of the Survivor–Centered Model and analyze how each element can encourage state actors to relate in healthier ways toward battered women. * * *

[Here Mills describes the eight elements of her approach: acceptance, respect, reassurance, engagement, resocialization, empowerment, emotional responsiveness, and liberation.]

* * *

B. A New State Dynamic in Intimate Abuse Cases

In light of the importance of adopting a new state dynamic in intimate abuse cases, state actors should heed the clinical call to action. To engage constructively in dialogue with battered women, state actors must be more sensitive to the psychological state of the battered woman. State actors should expect that battered women will appear anxious, overwhelmed, confused, and angry, or helpless, docile, or detached. State actors should expect these distinct emotional reactions from survivors of violence, and they should identify these reactions as unique opportunities for and possible indications of healing. That agents currently view these emotions as deviant, inappropriate, or "uncooperative," rather than as indicative of the trauma that the state seeks to address, is one of the primary impediments to effective interaction with survivors of intimate abuse.

Battered women who seek the state's assistance require, first and foremost, reconnection and relationship. The few studies that have explored these issues have found that battered women feel most satisfied with state interactions when they feel heard. Even in her confusion, the battered woman is conscious and wants a response that she can control. This response may involve the survivor's need for a savior or protector, someone she initially idealizes, as she attempts to work through her trauma history. Under these circumstances, state officials can function as partners in helping her come to terms with her sense of vulnerability and helplessness. Having her story heard and her individual situation recognized may be the first step on the battered woman's path to healing and change.

Knowing that the "omnipotent savior" dynamic is likely to emerge in their relationship with the battered woman, and that the fragile reconnection the survivor seeks is likely to fail if she perceives a replication of the original abuse in the criminal justice process, state actors need to honor the long-term healing connection over a short-term solution of arresting and prosecuting the batterer. Given the scant evidence that mandatory interventions reduce violence, and the obvious fact that a battered woman's resolution to terminate the abusive relationship is the most enduring hope for her long-term safety, state actors should turn their attention toward the healing strategies that are most likely to alter permanently patterns of violence.

Acceptance, respect, reassurance, engagement, resocialization, empowerment, emotional responsiveness, and liberation represent the antithesis to abuse. Reorienting the relationship between battered women and state actors using a Survivor–Centered Model of interaction provides a critical opportunity for healing through state intervention. If the survivor desired to arrest and prosecute, especially after advocates had an opportunity to inform her of the effectiveness of these actions, then prosecutors could proceed with legal measures. If, on the other hand, the battered woman sought alternative responses, including counseling for herself or the batterer, state actors would respect those desires instead.

Karla Fischer and Mary Rose studied factors that encourage battered women to leave their abusive relationships.[264] Their provocative study tried to determine the point at which battered women decide "enough is enough." State actors can help survivors make their way toward "enough is enough" by listening closely to the battered woman's narrative and by responding in ways that reinforce healthy interaction. Forming a healthy relationship with the battered woman might be just the impetus she needs

---

264. See [Karla Fischer & Mary Rose, When "Enough Is Enough": Battered Women's Decision Making Around Court Orders of Protection, 41 Crime & Delinq. 414 (1995)].

to understand that she is entitled to a different kind of love. This realization may or may not result in leaving the abusive relationship. As I discussed earlier, leaving may not be an option for cultural, financial, or religious reasons. Consistent with the clinical literature, a Survivor–Centered Approach would help a battered woman take steps toward her own recovery, in or out of the abusive relationship, while she pursued more direct methods of treatment through therapy.

NOTES ON MANDATORY PROSECUTION AND POLICING

1. Do you think that policies like "no-drop" or mandatory prosecution, which take the decision to prosecute her abuser out of the abused woman's hands, are a good idea? What are the advantages and disadvantages of such policies? How should prosecutors balance a woman's interest against the public interest in condemning and deterring battering? If children are involved, should their interests be taken into account? Is this type of balancing best left to the discretion of individual prosecutors to perform on a case-by-case basis? Why or why not?

2. Does Mills' proposal for a survivor centered model for prosecutors in effect require law enforcement officials to act as therapists? Is this appropriate? Emily Sack has reviewed the growing divide between those who urge criminalization of domestic violence and those who argue for what might be termed a psychological or treatment model. She claims that Mills' approach does not empower women any more than do criminal justice models; it simply places a different person or group of persons (therapists) in control. She also contends that Mills' work has now become quite popular among fathers' rights groups and what she calls "pseudofeminists" who seek to return us to a world in which domestic violence is once again seen as a "family quarrel" dependent upon the participants' peculiar psychology. See Emily Sack, Battered Women and the State: The Struggle for the Future of Domestic Violence Policy, 2004 Wis. L. Rev. 1657, 1676–78 (2004). Do you agree?

3. How would the different feminist theorists discussed in Chapter 3 analyze the issue of mandatory prosecution or mandatory arrest? What would each recommend?

4. Pro-prosecution policies vary from "hard" to "soft" no-drop. The first is typified by San Diego, where every felony case is pursued, despite the victim's wishes. In jurisdictions that thus mandate victim participation, the woman may be required to sign statements, be photographed, be interviewed, provide the state with other evidence, produce her children, and appear throughout the proceedings. Cheryl Hanna, No Right To Choose: Mandated Victim Participation in Domestic Violence Prosecutions, 109 Harv. L. Rev. 1849, 1867 (1996). In some instances, domestic violence victims have even been imprisoned for failure to testify. Id. at 1894. After implementing a hard no-drop policy, homicides related to domestic violence fell in San Diego from 30 in 1985 to seven in 1994. Id. at 1862–64. Soft no-drop policies do not force victims to participate but provide them with support services and strongly encourage them to pursue the case. Id. at 1863. Studies show that assigning a domestic violence advocate to shelter clients or simply the availability of social

support from family and friends can in fact substantially decrease repeat violence and increase the woman's effectiveness in ending the relationship; one study showed that victims with interpersonal support were twice as likely to cooperate voluntarily with the prosecution. See Deborah Epstein, Effective Intervention in Domestic Violence Cases: Rethinking the Roles of Prosecutors, Judges, and the Court System, 11 Yale J.L. & Feminism 3, 19–20 (1999). How should these various statistics and studies be weighed? What if those who are especially resistant to reporting and prosecuting domestic abuse are women of color?

5. Cheryl Hanna, a former prosecutor in the Baltimore Domestic Violence Unit, believes that mandatory prosecution is a better policy choice than dismissing cases when women refuse to participate, even though the solution is imperfect and entails risks to the victim's sense of autonomy. Hanna, above note 4, at 1856. She reaches this conclusion through application of the pragmatic feminist approach described in Chapter 3, concluding that "[a]t this point in history * * * the long-term benefits of mandated participation outweigh the short-term costs * * * [and] we need to examine the influence that mandated participation has on the effectiveness of the criminal justice system as well as the impact of such a policy on individual women." Id. at 1888. What are the short-and long-term costs and benefits of mandatory prosecution in your opinion? How do you assess them? How would Linda Mills, in the excerpt above?

6. In 1996, the District of Columbia adopted a no-drop policy that was immediately followed by an enormous increase in domestic violence cases—from 40 misdemeanor cases out of 19,000 emergency domestic violence calls in 1989 to 8,000 by 1997–98—and resulted in a 69% conviction rate, which approximates that in other misdemeanor bench trials. Epstein, above note 4, at 16. In every case where it is available, prosecutors rely heavily on evidence other than victim testimony, introducing photographs, tapes of calls to the 911 emergency number, hospital records, and police testimony. In fact, the state relies *exclusively* upon this type of evidence half the time, when the victim refuses to testify; yet the conviction rate in both types of cases is identical. Id. at 18. To what would you attribute this result? Does it provide any insight into how jurors assess the credibility of domestic violence victims? What policy implications would you draw from D.C.'s example? (The D.C. changes were part of a larger reform of the domestic violence system, including the establishment of integrated domestic violence courts that handle both civil and criminal cases arising out of domestic violence, coordinate information about various incidents and claims, and offer a broad range of civil and criminal, short-and long-term remedies. See id. at 21–38.)

7. Apart from the merits of proceeding with a prosecution without the victim's participation is the question of whether a case can be proven beyond a reasonable doubt without her testimony. A trio of cases decided by the United States Supreme Court since 2004 has transformed this inquiry, dramatically impacting the prosecution of domestic violence. The cases—Crawford v. Washington, 541 U.S. 36 (2004), Davis v. Washington, 547 U.S. 813 (2006), and Giles v. California, ___ U.S. ___, 128 S.Ct. 2678 (2008)—have altered a criminal defendant's right of confrontation, overturning decades of jurisprudence that co-existed peacefully with the evolution of a practice

known as "victimless" or "evidence-based" prosecution. Consider this description of the practice and its uncertain future:

> The evidence in "evidence-based" domestic violence prosecutions may consist of medical records, photographs, police officer observations of the crime scene, incriminating statements by the defendant and, on rare occasions, ear-witness or eye-witness testimony. But because domestic violence seldom occurs in the presence of adult witnesses, a victim's statements describing the crime—statements to a 911–operator, to neighbors who provided assistance in the aftermath, to responding police officers, or to treating medical professionals—are typically essential to completing the narrative. Provided these statements fall within an exception to the rule against hearsay, they were—before Crawford—generally admissible.
>
> Until 2004, the framework for Confrontation Clause challenges allowed the introduction of out of court statements provided they were deemed "reliable." Thus, in many cases, even without the testimony of the victim, prosecutors could try and could convict defendants of domestic violence. Even more important, the ability to credibly represent that sufficient evidence existed to prove a defendant's guilt—absent victim notwithstanding—allowed for the pre-trial resolution (through plea agreements) of countless cases that would previously have been dismissed.
>
> When the Court decided Crawford, it upended this approach. * * * Abruptly, the evidence typically relied upon in evidence-based prosecutions became subject to constitutional challenge. The immediate impact on the prosecution of domestic violence was profound.

Deborah Tuerkheimer, Forfeiture After Giles: the Relevance of "Domestic Violence Context," 13 Lewis & Clark L. Rev. 711 (2009). How should domestic violence advocates respond to this Court-imposed turn away from victimless prosecution? Will prosecutors now devote more resources to securing victim cooperation in domestic violence cases? Or are other scenarios more likely? What policy or legal reforms might effectively respond to the latest jurisprudential developments? See Tom Lininger, The Sound of Silence: Holding Batterers Accountable for Silencing Their Victims, 87 Tex. L. Rev 857 (2009).

8. Mandatory arrest, like mandatory prosecution, has been the subject of enormous controversy. Early debate focused on the deterrent value of arrest in intimate partner violence. In an early experiment conducted in Minneapolis, arresting the offender was found to substantially reduce repeat violence, as compared to attempting to counsel the parties or sending the assailant away from home for several hours. Lawrence W. Sherman & Richard A. Berk, The Specific Deterrent Effects of Arrest For Domestic Assault, 49 Am. Soc. Rev. 261, 261 (1984). Other studies have had mixed results, with some showing that arrest may deter further violence by certain types of offenders—those who are employed, middle-class and white—but potentially be harmful for women who are Black and poor, by causing repeat violence in retaliation for the arrest. Lawrence W. Sherman et al., The Variable Effects of Arrest on Criminal Careers: The Milwaukee Domestic Violence Experiment, 83 J. Crim. L. & Criminology 137, 158–63 (1992). If the effects of arrest are variable according to class, race and employment status, as Sherman et al.

assert, what do you think might account for these differences? In light of the variance, what policies should be followed by police departments answering domestic violence calls?

9. Does the social science resolve the question of the value of arrest? It has become fairly standard in law reviews and social science literature to argue that further study failed to replicate the results of the original Minneapolis experiment. There are dissenters, however. See Cynthia Grant Bowman, The Arrest Experiments: A Feminist Critique, 83 J. Crim. L. & Criminology 201 (1992) (summarizing a number of theoretical problems with the studies). Joan Zorza argues that the studies actually support arrest when properly interpreted. Joan Zorza, Must We Stop Arresting Batterers?: Analysis and Policy Implications of the New Police Domestic Violence Studies, 28 New Eng. L. Rev. 929 (1994). A more recent government study appears to confirm Zorza's overall conclusion that the replication studies actually support arrest options. See Christopher D. Maxwell et al., The Effects of Arrest on Intimate Partner Violence: New Evidence from the Spouse Assault Replication Program, Nat'l Inst. Justice Research Brief 1, 4–9 (U.S. Dep't of Justice) (July 2001); see also Sack, above note 2, at 1676–78.

One major problem with the studies is their aim: to measure deterrence. As feminists have pointed out, this may not be the point of arrest policies (particularly given that it cannot be lost on perpetrators that, even if arrested, they are unlikely to be convicted or spend time in jail). If the point of pro-arrest policies is to change police attitudes, then deterrence is not the proper thing to measure; changing police attitudes is. Another goal of arrest might be to determine whether it helps or harms women, whether it increases women's sense of control of the situation or not. See Bowman, above, at 203–04. In fact, some evidence suggests that reporting violence, rather than the arrest, may have a significant deterrent effect. Richard B. Felson, Jeffrey M. Ackerman & Catherine A. Gallagher, Police Intervention and the Repeat of Domestic Assault, 43 Criminology 563 (2005).

Finally, there is a broader problem with applying research on deterrence. Social scientists' models of deterrence will yield little change in public policy if they fail to reflect the ambiguity of the idea of deterrence: in the public sphere, people seek to deter that which they perceive as bad conduct, regardless of whether the conduct is actually subject to deterrent effect. Put differently, deterrence in the public sphere is a cultural concept, not a social science algorithm. Lawrence Sherman (who authored the original domestic violence study) has found that police raids on crack houses do not effectively deter. Lawrence W. Sherman et al., Deterrent Effects of Police Raids on Crack Houses: A Randomized Controlled Experiment, 12 Justice Q. 755, 770 (Dec. 1995) ("we found quite modest deterrent effects"). Does this mean that the public is likely to give up on such policies? Why not? Might this same phenomenon help to explain why the replication studies have been widely viewed not to support arrest, when in fact they may?

10. As discussed above, problems with involving the police in domestic violence are exacerbated in communities of color, where the police are regarded with deep-seated suspicion and an arrest may lead to retaliation against the victim or even deportation both for the batterer and his victim.

However, amidst an overall trend of increased reporting of domestic violence to the police, African American women report their victimization at significantly higher rates than other groups (67% versus 50% for white women), as do Hispanic females (65% versus 52% for non-Hispanic females). Department of Justice, Bureau of Justice Statistics, Special Report: Intimate Partner Violence 7 (2000). How would you explain these trends?

11. As mentioned above, LGBT victims of domestic violence are often extremely reluctant to call the police because of well-documented homophobia among the police themselves, who rarely arrest the batterer unless the victim has sustained extremely serious injuries or, if they do, arrest the victim as well, and often submit both to degrading treatment. Patrick Letellier, Gay and Bisexual Male Domestic Violence Victimization: Challenges to Feminist Theory and Responses to Violence, 9 Violence & Victims 95, 102–03 (1994). "Mutual combat" arrests are more common because male victims, unlike females, are socially conditioned to strike back when physically attacked; their more equal physical strength also makes them more capable of self-defense and less susceptible to serious injury, although this does not, of course, lessen the culpability of the aggressor. Id. at 100–02. Moreover, reporting an attack will likely result in the victim unwillingly revealing his sexual orientation and perhaps suffering severe consequences from the community, his employer, and health insurers. Id. at 103. What can be done to encourage the law enforcement community to respond to battering in LGBT relationships in a manner that is sensitive to these substantial problems? Would legal change be effective, or is this simply a social and/or political issue?

5. LEGAL DEVELOPMENTS: THE VIOLENCE AGAINST WOMEN ACT

In 1994, President Clinton signed into law the Violence Against Women Act ("VAWA"), as part of an omnibus crime bill, the Violent Crime Control Act of 1994.[46] Women's groups lobbied hard to get Congress to pass a law creating federal protections for women on the grounds that states were not vigorously pursuing cases involving violence against women. D.C.'s delegate, Eleanor Holmes Norton, claimed at the time, "VAWA gives women what blacks have had since the Civil War—civil protection. There is still plenty of racial violence in this country, but there is less because those laws are on the books and are invoked."[47]

The Act was Congress's first comprehensive attempt to deal with violence against women. VAWA included an array of provisions on rape and battering focusing on prevention, funding, and evidentiary matters. It also included the federal government's first criminal law against battering, 18 U.S.C. § 2261 (2006). The Act's most controversial provision,

46. Pub. L. 103–322, 108 Stats. 1796, Pub. L. 103–322. For the history of the Act, see Victoria F. Nourse, Where Violence, Relationship and Equality Meet: The Violence Against Women Act's Civil Rights Remedy, 15 Wis. Women's L.J. 257 (2000). For a defense by one of the authors, see Senator Sen. Joseph R. Biden, Jr., The Civil Rights Remedy of the Violence Against Women Act: A Defense, 37 Harv. J. on Legis. 1 (2000).

47. Christy's Crusade, Ms. Magazine, Apr./May 2000, at 61.

however, was its private civil rights remedy for victims of gender-based violence, modeled on late nineteenth century laws aimed to protect African–Americans. As Catharine MacKinnon later described it, "for the first time in United States history, the VAWA established zero tolerance for sex-based violence as a matter of public policy in providing that 'all persons within the United States shall have the right to be free from crimes of violence motivated by gender.' "[48]

The civil rights remedy provided as follows:

* * *

> (c) Cause of action. A person * * * who commits a crime of violence motivated by gender * * * shall be liable to the party injured, in an action for the recovery of compensatory and punitive damages, injunctive and declaratory relief, and such other relief as a court may deem appropriate
>
> (d) Definitions. For purposes of this section—
>
> (1) the term "crime of violence motivated by gender" means a crime of violence committed because of gender or on the basis of gender, and due, at least in part, to an animus based on the victim's gender; and
>
> (2) the term "crime of violence" means—* * * an act or series of acts that would constitute a felony [as defined by federal law] * * * [and without regard] for the relationship between the person who takes such action and the individual against whom such action is taken [i.e., applies to cases of marital rape and intimate partner violence which would be excluded under state laws providing for some variation of a marital rape exemption or interspousal tort immunity].
>
> (e) Limitation and procedures.
>
> (1) Limitation. Nothing in this section entitles a person to a cause of action under subsection (c) of this section for random acts of violence unrelated to gender or for acts that cannot be demonstrated, by a preponderance of the evidence, to be motivated by gender
>
> * * *
>
> (2) No prior criminal action. Nothing in this section requires a prior criminal complaint, prosecution, or conviction to establish the elements of a cause of action * * *.

42 U.S.C.§ 13981 (enacted 1994).

Congress asserted power to pass VAWA under the Commerce Clause and the Fourteenth Amendment to the Constitution. At the time Congress wrote the law, the reigning precedent under the Commerce Clause suggested that Congress had the power to act to prevent any activities that, under a rational basis test, had a substantial effect on commerce. Congress found, for example, that violence against women costs American

48. Catharine A. MacKinnon, Disputing Male Sovereignty: On United States v. Morrison, 114 Harv. L. Rev. 135, 137 (2000).

taxpayers in the range of 3 to 5 billion dollars a year. The year after VAWA was passed, the Supreme Court narrowed the applicable test for commerce clause authority in *United States v. Lopez*,[49] striking down a gun law on the theory that the activity in question—possession of a gun—was not itself economic in nature. Five years later, in United States v. Morrison,[50] the Supreme Court struck down the civil rights remedy in VAWA on the *Lopez* theory that the crimes addressed were themselves not economic, rejecting claims of Congress's power on federalism grounds.

Critics have decried the result in *Morrison* on a number of grounds, including the fact that the Supreme Court used sexist stereotypes in its analysis, suggesting that because VAWA might cover "domestic" matters, it should not be covered by federal law.[51] Others have asserted that the concept of federalism used by the court (remitting violence against women to the states) was inconsistent with the states' own wishes (a majority of state attorneys general filed amicus briefs supporting the law) and relied upon nineteenth century cases that were thought interred in the 1960's.[52] Still others, like the dissenters, led by Justice Souter, insisted that the Congress had compiled a "mountain of data" about the discriminatory application of laws to prevent violence against women, and that the Court's proper role was to defer to Congress, not to contravene its will.[53] Finally, some have asserted that, even if federalism concerns dictate deference to the states in most matters, it is perverse to apply this rule in cases where equality is at issue. The history of race discrimination makes clear that it is far easier to perpetuate inequality in a state than a nation. Where there is documented discrimination, this is precisely where federal intervention is needed (in other words, Congress's commerce power should be at its height when combined with authority under the Fourteenth Amendment).[54]

NOTES ABOUT VAWA

1. Note that VAWA addressed violence motivated by *gender* rather than violence based on *sex*. Of course, "violence on the basis of sex" sounds bizarre in the context of rape. But recall from Chapter 2 that, since *Craig v. Boren* (1976), the Supreme Court Justices (other than Scalia) have consistently referred to "gender" rather than "sex" discrimination in applying constitutional and other anti-discrimination laws. This shift stems from Ruth Bader Ginsburg's proposal, discussed in Chapter 2, to use gender (which has a

49. 514 U.S. 549 (1995).

50. 529 U.S. 598 (2000).

51. See Judith Resnik, Categorical Federalism: Jurisdiction, Gender and the Globe, 111 Yale L.J. 619 (2001). See also Sally Goldfarb, The Supreme Court, The Violence Against Women Act, and the Use and Abuse of Federalism, 71 Fordham L.J. 57 (2002); Sally Goldfarb, Violence Against Women and the Persistence of Privacy, 61 Ohio St. L.J. 1 (2000).

52. See United States v. Morrison, 529 U.S. at 621–23 (relying on the Civil Rights Cases of 1883).

53. Id. at 628 (Souter, J. dissenting).

54. See Victoria F. Nourse, Toward a New Constitutional Anatomy, 56 Stan. L. Rev. 835, 879–882 & n.172 (2004).

"neutral, clinical tone") rather than sex (which is evocative of sexuality). Is intimate partner violence a crime of sex discrimination or a crime of gender discrimination? What is the difference? How would you prove that an act of intimate partner violence was a form of sex discrimination? How would you prove that an act of intimate partner violence was a form of gender discrimination? Are sex and gender discrimination necessarily synonymous in the context of battering? Which is more accurate? What does each leave out? Reconsider these arguments in the context of rape, below Section D.

2. In the employment context, rape by an employer may form the basis of a sex discrimination claim. Why should or should not this rationale apply outside the workplace? Is it because sexual harassment occurs in a context (work) that makes sexual activity appear anomalous, while sex in other contexts (a loving relationship) seems quite appropriate? Was the fear, then, that critics might misperceive the law as making all sex a civil rights violation? Or was it the fear that sex itself was too much of a focus, that gender inferiority was the central issue?

3. As discussed in Chapter 2, the law of gender discrimination holds that women may not be subject to systemic disadvantages on the basis of gendered stereotypes (archaic generalizations, such as claims about women's place in the home, inherent worth only as a sexual object, incapacity to perform particular kinds of jobs, myths about deserving violence, etc.). If a state denies benefits based on such generalizations, it acts unconstitutionally. So, too, as will be described more fully in Chapter 9, if an employer imposes burdens based on such generalizations, that employer violates Title VII. Why shouldn't there be a remedy if the harm is even greater—if, rather than losing benefits or a job, you are beaten because of the same generalizations or raped because of your failure to comply with these norms? Think of a batterer who prevents his wife from working outside the home or, as in the *Norman* case (above, Section B), forces his wife to prostitute herself. Think of a rapist, like the one in *Morrison*, who, after the rape, explained that he "liked" to "get girls drunk" and "f . . ." them. United States v. Morrison, 529 U.S. 598 (2000) (omitting the "f" expletive and referring readers to the briefs).

4. Why do you think Congress passed VAWA? Does the law represent a recognition that the criminal law system is unable to respond appropriately to crimes of violence against women? What are the failures of criminal justice with regards to violence against women? Should we be attempting to reform the criminal system rather than resorting to civil suits? Which is likely to be more successful from an institutional perspective? An individual perspective? Remember that, after the acquittal verdict in the O.J. Simpson case, Simpson was sued in a civil suit for the murder of his wife, and lost. Now that the VAWA civil rights remedy has been declared unconstitutional, what legislative strategy should be developed?

5. The "price" of passing VAWA was the inclusion of language in the civil rights remedy that limited it to cases of gender "animus"—a response to arguments that the law was overbroad and would cover every act of "random" violence. See Judith Resnik, The Programmatic Judiciary: Lobbying, Judging and Invalidating the Violence Against Women Act, 74 S. Cal. L. Rev.

269 (2000) (describing how federal judges appointed by Chief Justice Rehnquist lobbied for this requirement); see also Fred Strebreigh, Equal: Women Reshape American Law (2009) (explaining the role of the federal judiciary in the development of the animus requirement). Some feminists were critical of this because of Supreme Court precedents that tended to equate gender discrimination with hatred of women. See Bray v. Alexandria Women's Health Clinic, 506 U.S. 263 (1993); Jennifer Gaffney, Amending the Violence Against Women Act: Creating a Rebuttable Presumption of Gender Animus in Rape Cases, 6 J.L. & Pol'y 247 (1997). On the other hand, the legislative history of VAWA makes clear that it was to be applied in concert with precedents from Title VII, that the animus was required to exist only "in part," and that animus was defined to mean "purpose" as opposed to "hatred." See Liu v. Striuli, 36 F. Supp. 2d 452 (D.R.I. 1999) (holding requisite amount of animus can be analyzed in Title VII framework; if it satisfies Title VII, it will be satisfied in state Gender Motivated Violence Act). How would you define animus?

6. Illinois, like many other states, has enacted a Hate Crime Statute, 720 ILCS 5/12–7.1 (1993). The law provides that:

> A person commits a hate crime when, by reason of the race, color, creed, religion, ancestry, gender, sexual orientation, physical or mental disability, or national origin of another individual or group of individuals, he commits assault, battery, aggravated assault, misdemeanor theft, criminal trespass to residence, misdemeanor criminal damage to property, criminal trespass to vehicle, criminal trespass to real property, mob action or disorderly conduct. * * *

Id. at 7.1(a). To provide additional strength, the statute also creates a civil cause of action for anyone who is injured, or whose property is damaged, by a hate crime. The court may award compensatory and punitive damages, as well as attorneys' fees. Id. at 7.1(c). Does this law apply to intimate partner violence? Could you persuade a court that battering constitutes a "hate crime"? What arguments would you make? What kinds of evidence would you use to establish your claim?

6. THE FEDERAL ROLE IN BATTERING CASES

The 1994 Violence Against Women Act provided, for the first time, a federal role in the area of battering. Although the Supreme Court struck down the act's civil rights remedy on the grounds that Congress had no constitutional power to enact it, much of the Act remained in effect. For example, VAWA created a new federal cause of action where battering involved the crossing of state lines (a traditional backstop federal remedy applicable to most other crimes). In this 2005 case, notice the severity and scope of the violence, its association with other crimes, and the nature of the defendant's argument. Consider whether new developments bring with them old arguments.

UNITED STATES v. MATTHEW EVANS DOWD

United States Court of Appeals for the Ninth Circuit, 2005.
417 F.3d 1080.

FISHER, CIRCUIT JUDGE:

A jury convicted Matthew Evans Dowd of violating the federal interstate domestic violence law. He argues that the jury did not have sufficient evidence that he forced or coerced his companion, Danna Johnson, to cross state lines, as the statute requires, because she had reasonable opportunities to escape. * * *

I.

The events giving rise to Dowd's conviction occurred over an 8–month period between May and December 2002. Dowd and Johnson had met before in 1999, in Missoula, Montana, where Johnson had worked as a respiratory therapist. In August 2001, after becoming romantically involved, Dowd and Johnson moved in together, and Johnson, under Dowd's influence, began using methamphetamines. Dowd left her a few months later and shortly thereafter was indicted for distribution and possession of methamphetamine, possession of a firearm in relation to a drug-trafficking crime and being a drug user in possession of a firearm. Dowd was arrested and later pled guilty to two of the counts. He petitioned the court to attend a drug rehabilitation facility in Butte, Montana, before his sentencing. In May 2002, he was discharged and was supposed to surrender to the Missoula Detention Center within three hours of his release. Instead, he fled.

In the meantime, Johnson had lost her job, quit using drugs and moved to Colorado. After her move to Colorado, Johnson contacted Dowd's mother because Johnson knew Dowd had been in trouble. Dowd's mother told Johnson that he was on probation for six years, working in California and was clean and sober. Dowd's mother urged Johnson to speak with Dowd by phone. They did so, and when Dowd fled the rehabilitation facility in Missoula in May 2002, he headed to Colorado, where he knew Johnson was then living.

The two moved in together, but within a week Johnson realized Dowd was buying drugs. She confronted him one night about the drug purchases, prompting an altercation at a local bar. She walked out of the bar to go home, but Dowd followed her, swung at her and unsuccessfully tried to force her into the car. Johnson did not return home until many hours after the incident, thinking it was safe to go back into their apartment because Dowd did not have a key. Dowd, however, had broken in and was waiting inside when she entered the apartment. He punched, raped and tried to suffocate her. Dowd then told Johnson that they needed to leave the apartment because the neighbors could hear everything, and he no longer felt safe there. After Dowd said that he planned to leave and take her with him, Johnson tried to run out of the apartment to a local convenience store but Dowd overpowered her. Johnson testified that "he said he couldn't let me go because he was an escaped felon and I would just rat on him." Until that point, she had not known Dowd was an escaped felon.

Dowd pulled Johnson by the hair and pushed her down the street, shoving the back of her head until she got into the car's driver's seat. They stopped at a phone booth where Dowd called his mother. However, Dowd had tied a shoelace to the car key so that when they stopped, he could pull the key out of the ignition and take it with him. Without the car key, Johnson could not drive away and did not believe she could run fast enough to escape on foot.

That night, the pair stayed in a motel because Dowd did not feel it was safe to return to their apartment, and he was awaiting money from his mother. Dowd kept close tabs on Johnson at the motel, for example hovering over her as she checked into their room. Johnson said she did not try to seek help or escape at that time because she worried that there would be repercussions for her family.

The next day, they returned to the apartment to pack up their clothes, dishes and other personal items. The apartment manager testified that he saw Johnson unloading boxes from the trunk of her car and that she appeared upset. The manager also said that while Johnson was at the apartment, Dowd was at the manager's house, some two-and-a-half miles away, doing landscaping work.

After collecting their belongings, Dowd made Johnson drive straight from Colorado to Dowd's mother's home in Montana. Johnson did not scream out for help along the way because she was too afraid for the lives of her grandchildren and sister, whom Dowd had threatened to kill. On their drive, Dowd taunted Johnson by asking her: "How did it almost feel to die today?" Dowd removed the car key at every gas station or phone break. Johnson said she unsuccessfully tried to ruin the transmission of the car—hoping that would stop the progress of their trip—by throwing the car into reverse while driving at 75 miles an hour. When her plan failed, and seeing no other options for getting away from Dowd, Johnson decided during the road trip, "I'll do what he says and when we get to his mother's house, his mother will help me." But when they arrived in Montana, Dowd's mother told Johnson not to antagonize her son because that would only result in more beatings. Dowd continued to physically and sexually abuse Johnson at his mother's house, where they stayed intermittently over the following weeks. Johnson said Dowd would wrench her neck and beat her so that she was covered with bruises. "He would laugh and make fun of me, that I was walking like an old woman. And it was because I hurt so bad."

About a week and a half after arriving in Montana, Johnson drove Dowd to Utah for three to four days, so that he could purchase drugs. On a second trip to Utah, Dowd sold items at pawn shops so he could purchase drugs. On one occasion, Johnson went into a pawn shop when

Dowd was not around. But Johnson said she was too afraid for her family's well-being to run away. When in Utah, Johnson and Dowd stayed with Dowd's brother at a motel. The motel manager testified that at times Johnson would walk around the motel alone, for example going to the candy machine by herself. The manager noted that Johnson appeared to have bruises around her eyes. Johnson testified that during the trips between Montana and Utah, Dowd was beating her almost every day, and she was weak from not having eaten. Dowd also brought a gun with him on the trips to Utah, intending to pawn it while there, and would threaten Johnson with the gun in the car. The second trip to Utah lasted about a week before the pair returned to Montana.

On New Year's Eve 2002, the two went to a bar in Montana, where Dowd got drunk. Dowd insisted they leave and drove the car back to his mother's house. When they arrived, Johnson pulled the car key out of the ignition and jumped out of the car. Johnson then attempted to get into the driver's seat, but Dowd grabbed her and threw her down an embankment. He left her for dead and went into his mother's house. Johnson was able to get into the car and drive to a friend's house.

Johnson hid out with different individuals for almost a month because she heard that Dowd "was hunting me down." She eventually called the agents who had been searching for Dowd since he became a fugitive. A medical expert diagnosed Johnson with post-traumatic stress disorder. During the medical interview, Johnson spoke of being repeatedly choked and showed some signs of injury to her neck. She also had restricted movement in her jaw. * * *

The federal interstate domestic violence statute requires that the defendant cause "a spouse or intimate partner to travel in interstate or foreign commerce ... by force, coercion, duress, or fraud." 18 U.S.C. § 2261(a)(2). As the Fourth Circuit has explained, the "words 'force, coercion, or duress' necessarily require that the victim is a non-consenting participant in the interstate travel." Dowd argues that despite all the evidence of his physical and psychological abuse of Johnson, the government failed to prove that Johnson traveled with him across state lines involuntarily. In particular, he cites various opportunities she had to escape; that she stayed even when he was not around, he contends, negates any finding of force or coercion. We conclude to the contrary—the evidence supports a finding that Dowd, using both force and coercion (or duress), caused Johnson to accompany him on their interstate travels.

First, there was sufficient evidence that Dowd forced Johnson to cross state lines. The jury heard detailed testimony from Johnson that Dowd beat and raped her in Colorado just before his decision to leave for Montana. When she tried to run for the convenience store, Dowd overpowered her, dragged her by her hair to the car and made her start driving. The pair stayed that night at a motel, where Dowd kept close watch on Johnson. The next day they returned to the apartment to pick up their belongings. Dowd ordered Johnson to make sure every item of his was out of the apartment, particularly his identification. Once they began driving, Dowd "kept complete control of the car" by holding onto the key and threatening to kill Johnson and her family if she did not obey him.

These acts of physical violence and dominance before and during the drive from Colorado to Montana could permit a reasonable juror to find that Dowd caused Johnson to drive across state lines by force.

Johnson also described repeated acts of violence Dowd committed against her while at his mother's home in Montana, including in between the two trips to Utah. Although some time elapsed between the beatings and rapes and the Utah trips, the jury could have reasonably concluded that the pattern of Dowd's abuse caused Johnson to join him on these trips. That Dowd chose to threaten her with a gun reinforces that Johnson was not a volunteer.

Second, the evidence supported a finding by the jury that Dowd caused Johnson to cross state lines by coercion or duress. As to this element of the offense, the district court (without objection) instructed the jury as follows:

> The terms coercion and duress are interchangeable. Coercion or duress exists when an individual is subject to actual or threatened force of such a nature as to induce a well-founded fear of impending death or serious bodily harm from which there is no reasonable opportunity to escape.

Dowd contends that because Johnson was sometimes free from his supervision during their interstate trips and able to talk with others who could have provided help, she had a reasonable opportunity to escape, thus precluding any claim that he coerced her to cross state lines.

The district court's jury instruction, modeled after the interpretation of § 2261(a)(2) by the Fourth and Sixth Circuits, properly defined the elements of coercion or duress, which we shall refer to simply as "coercion." Applying that definition here, we hold that the jury had overwhelming evidence from which to find that Dowd coerced Johnson to travel between the three states. The jury also could have concluded that Dowd's systematic physical and psychological coercion prevented Johnson from escaping earlier than she did. For example, Johnson testified that she dared not leave Dowd because she was "too afraid for my daughter and my grandchildren and my sister's life." She said that Dowd was always telling her exactly what to do, and she knew "if I didn't do it, exactly what was going to happen." Dowd closely scripted her phone conversations with her sister, so that Johnson could do little more than ask her sister for money. Johnson added that she was concerned that she would be charged with harboring a fugitive, a fear Dowd deliberately planted in her mind. She further said that at times during their journey, she was weak from not eating and being beaten, and she did not think she could outrun Dowd even if she tried. Dowd also carried his gun on their trips to Utah, using it to threaten Johnson. Finally, Johnson discovered that neither Dowd's mother nor his brother would help her escape.

Dowd argues that Johnson had reasonable opportunities to escape when she was outside his supervision, such as when she went to retrieve their belongings from the apartment and Dowd was miles away at the apartment manager's house; during their drive from Colorado to Montana when Dowd stopped to make phone calls, when Johnson was alone in Dowd's mother's home or when she went to a pawn shop by herself in Utah.

But coercion does not mean the defendant has to maintain constant physical control or oversight of his victim. Indeed, the statute is written in the disjunctive—"force, coercion, duress, or fraud"—denoting that coercion is different from the actual use of force, and indicating that a victim's will to escape can be undermined by a variety of means not involving immediate physical force, including threats of reprisal or psychological conditioning. As the Sixth Circuit has observed, "a person who has just been beaten in the manner [the victim] had been is far less capable physically and emotionally of attempting an escape, formulating a method of escape, or eliciting aid from others."

We also draw support for our interpretation from the legislative history of the Violence Against Women Act, which contains the interstate domestic violence statute. Congress addressed the importance of recognizing the particular circumstances faced by victims of domestic violence. In enacting one measure that provided for training judges on dealing with issues of rape and domestic violence, Congress emphasized that "too often, the focus is on the woman's behavior—'Why does she stay?'—instead of an examination of why men batter and why our culture and the justice system often allow men to continue this illegal behavior." S. Rep. No. 103–138, at 46 (1993). Congress warned that such presumptions may result from a "lack [of] information about the psychological, economic, and social realities of domestic violence victims." In light of Congress' stated concerns, we believe a defendant should not avoid liability based on speculative conclusions that the victim could have escaped a violent defendant simply because he was not close at hand.

Instead, when a jury is assessing a victim's opportunity to escape, it is the victim's perspective that counts. The jury must take into account whether a reasonable person in the victim's position would believe she (or he) could effectively escape. Although we have not found cases specifically addressing the concept of escape in the context of the interstate domestic violence statute, the government analogizes to the duress defense in criminal cases. Whether an individual charged with a crime acted under duress and therefore has a valid defense depends on whether, under all of the circumstances, the defendant had a reasonable opportunity to escape rather than commit the crime. * * *

We hold that for purposes of § 2261(a)(2), whether the victim was subject to coercion or duress or had a reasonable opportunity to escape must be evaluated from the perspective of a reasonable person in the victim's position, considering all of the circumstances, including the victim's gender. Applying this standard, we conclude that the jury could have found Johnson to have been completely intimidated by Dowd's sustained actual and threatened physical, sexual and psychological abuse; his unremitting subjugation of her; his threats of retribution against her family; and her fear of being implicated in harboring a fugitive. Johnson was repeatedly beaten, raped and humiliated; she was at times weak from hunger and her injuries; she did not think she could outrun Dowd in her condition. In short, the jury easily could have determined that a woman in Johnson's position, subject to months of physical and psychological abuse at Dowd's hands, had no reasonable opportunity to escape her oppressor.

NOTES ON THE RECURRING ISSUE OF SEPARATION

1. The question of "leaving" is deeply embedded in the law surrounding intimate partner violence. It is a question asked in the cases we saw earlier in this chapter: from *Berry* (why did she come back) to *Norman* (why didn't she leave before she killed) to cases, like this one, of kidnapping and assault. Here, the "leaving" question arises in a context that is essentially "jurisdictional." The federal anti-battering law only applies when victims are transported across or caused to cross state lines. Absent that finding, there would be serious constitutional questions about whether Congress would have the power to enforce this law. Is the "leaving" question another example of a violence myth, or is the law simply encouraging women to seek help?

2. Some research suggests that women are at greatest risk when they attempt to leave the relationship. Consider in this light the argument of Martha Mahoney that the proper focus should not be on why she did not leave but upon her efforts to leave and the attack upon them—what Mahoney calls "separation assault":

> * * * The question "why didn't she leave?" shapes both social and legal inquiry on battering; much of the legal reliance on academic expertise on battered women has developed in order to address this question. At the moment of separation or attempted separation—for many women, the first encounter with the authority of law—the batterer's quest for control often becomes most acutely violent and potentially lethal. Ironically, although the proliferation of shelters and the elaboration of statutory structures facilitating the grant of protective orders vividly demonstrate both socially and legally the dangers attendant on separation, a woman's "failure" to permanently separate from a violent relationship is still widely held to be mysterious and in need of explanation, an indicator of her pathology rather than her batterer's. We have had neither cultural names nor legal doctrines specifically tailored to the particular assault on a woman's body and volition that seeks to block her from leaving, retaliate for her departure, or forcibly end the separation. I propose that we name this attack "separation assault."
>
> Separation assault is the common though invisible thread that unites the equal protection suits on enforcement of temporary restraining orders, the cases with dead women that appear in many doctrinal categories, and the cases with dead men—the self-defense cases. As with other assaults

> on women that were not cognizable until the feminist movement named and explained them, separation assault must be identified before women can recognize our own experience and before we can develop legal rules to deal with this particular sort of violence. Naming one particular aspect of the violence then illuminates the rest: for example, the very concept of "acquaintance rape" moves consciousness away from the stereotype of rape (assault by a stranger) and toward a focus on the woman's volition (violation of her will, "consent"). Similarly, by emphasizing the urgent control moves that seek to prevent the woman from ending the relationship, the concept of separation assault raises questions that inevitably focus additional attention on the ongoing struggle for power and control in the relationship.

Martha R. Mahoney, Legal Images of Battered Women: Redefining the Issue of Separation, 90 Mich. L. Rev. 1, 5–7 (1991). If one were to apply Mahoney's framework to the *Dowd* case, how would the account be written? For an overview of the many reasons women "stay" in abusive relationships, see Sarah M. Buel, Fifty Obstacles to Leaving, aka Why Abuse Victims Stay, 28 Colo. Law. 19 (Oct. 1999).

3. Deborah Tuerkheimer has argued that separation continues to arise as a legal issue because of a basic conceptual confusion: the criminal law has misconceived the very idea of battering. The law focuses too much on single-shot encounters and specific incidents of physical violence and far too little on questions of a continued pattern of control. She argues:

> Laws applied to prosecute domestic violence are generally characterized by a narrow temporal lens and a limited conception of harm. Together these paradigms obscure defining aspects of battering: ongoing patterns of power and control are not addressed; nor is the full measure of injury that these patterns inflict redressed.
>
> * * * At common law, crime was conceived as occurring at a discrete moment, and this template endures. The incident-focused criminal law contemplates "an act or omission ... taking place in an instant of time so precise that it can be associated with a particular mental state or intention." A constricted temporal frame places patterns of abuse outside of criminal law's reach: the law does not touch the pattern of conduct, for it cannot be captured by a moment in time.
>
> * * *
>
> Even where multiple episodes of physical violence are charged in a single indictment or complaint, law disregards the space between these incidents, using physicality alone to ascribe meaning. By isolating and atomizing violence in intimate relationships, law renders context meaningless. In theory and in practice this decontextualization is of critical importance. As we have seen, relationship provides the terrain on which a batterer's system of domination is enacted; relationship is essential to grasping the full measure of harm inflicted by the abuser and suffered by the victim; relationship connects and organizes what might otherwise appear to be random acts.

Deborah Tuerkheimer, Recognizing and Remedying the Harm of Battering: A Call to Criminalize Domestic Violence, 94 J. Crim. L. & Criminology 959, 972–74 (2004). One way in which to conceive Tuerkheimer's critique is to see that it aims to reverse the kind of assumptions which invite the "why didn't she leave" question; if battering is defined as a continuing course of conduct, then leaving becomes a far less insistent question. If battering were defined to cover a pattern of conduct, would it be easier or more difficult to prove at trial? Are there other reasons to reform our criminal laws to better reflect the realities of abuse? Are there alternative ways to do this?

D. RAPE

Rape, like homicide, is perpetrated primarily by males. Numbers here remain quite controversial and the government's own official estimates vary widely from 200,000 to 400,000 per year.[55] Experts argue that governmental estimates are likely to be unreliable in some cases because of the nature of survey methodologies.[56] The vast majority of sexual assaults are committed by someone known to the victim: data from the 2008 crime victim survey shows that 63% of all rapes and sexual assaults were committed by an intimate, a relative, a friend or an acquaintance.[57] The Centers for Disease Control report that "somewhere between 20 and 25% of college students report experiencing a completed or attempted rape."[58]

---

55. The 2000 National Violence Against Women Survey showed 302,091 women and 92,748 men had been raped during the prior year. U.S. Dept. of Justice, Nat'l Inst. of Justice, Full Report of the Prevalence, Incidence, and Consequences of Violence Against Women [hereinafter 2000 VAW Full Report], 13 (Nov. 2000). (We discuss the problem of male prison rape below.) In 2002, the Department of Justice reported an estimate of rapes and sexual assaults at an average of 366,460 per year from 1992 through 2000. U.S. Dep't of Justice, Bureau of Justice Statistics, Selected Findings, Rape and Sexual Assault: Reporting to Police and Medical Attention, 1992–2000, [hereinafter 2002 Rape Study], at 1 (Aug. 2002). However, for 2008, the National Crime Survey reported only 203,830 victimizations per year. U.S. Dep't of Justice, Bureau of Justice Statistics, Criminal Victimization, 2008 [hereinafter Criminal Victimization 2008], Table 1 (Sept. 2009) (see studies in footnote below, noting potential lack of privacy of interview in the national crime survey).

56. For a comparison study that aims to understand why the National Crime Survey produces low estimates compared to studies that ask more behaviorally-specific questions, see Bonnie S. Fisher, Francis T. Cullen & Michael G. Turner, The Sexual Victimization of College Women, U.S. Dep't of Justice, National Institute of Justice, Research Report (Dec. 2000). Prior to 1992, for example, National Crime Survey questioners did not even ask whether anyone in the household was subject to sexual violence but expected that this would be volunteered in response to questions on assault. See Eric P. Baumer, Richard B. Felson & Steven F. Messner, Changes in Police Notification for Rape, 1973–2000, 41 Criminology 841, 850–51 (2003) (describing the 1992 redesign).

57. Criminal Victimization 2008, above footnote 55, Table 6 (Sept. 2009).

58. Centers for Disease Control, National Center for Injury Prevention and Control, Sexual Violence: Fact Sheet, www.cdc.gov/ncipc/factsheets/svfacts.htm (citing Fisher et al., above footnote 67). Note: the Fisher et al. study reports quite low yearly rates of victimization during college. However, the same survey shows that 20% of respondents had prior to college experienced an attempted or completed forcible rape. See Fisher et al., above footnote 56, at 18 (Exhibit 7, aggregating figures for rape and attempted rape prior to college). For a 15–20% figure, see Joetta L. Carr & Karen VanDeusen, Risk Factors for Male Sexual Aggression on College Campuses, 19 J. Family Violence 279, 279 (2004).

Despite decades of reform, there remains a large gap between rapes committed according to victim surveys and rapes reported to the police. As of 2002, the Department of Justice stated that "[m]ost rapes and sexual assaults" are *not* reported to the police. According to estimates, approximately 1/3 of rapes and sexual assaults are reported to police. Low reporting rates apply to rapes committed by intimates, but also to those by strangers: "[w]hen the offender was a stranger, 54% of completed rapes, 44% of attempted rapes, and 34% of sexual assaults were not reported to the police."[59]

1. THE LAW OF RAPE

COMMONWEALTH v. BERKOWITZ

Superior Court of Pennsylvania, 1992.
415 Pa. Super. 505, 609 A.2d 1338.

PER CURIAM

In the spring of 1988, appellant and the victim were both college sophomores at East Stroudsburg State University, ages twenty and nineteen years old, respectively. They had mutual friends and acquaintances. On April nineteenth of that year, the victim went to appellant's dormitory room. What transpired in that dorm room between appellant and the victim thereafter is the subject of the instant appeal.

During a one day jury trial held on September 14, 1988, the victim gave the following account during direct examination by the Commonwealth. At roughly 2:00 on the afternoon of April 19, 1988, after attending two morning classes, the victim returned to her dormitory room. There, she drank a martini to "loosen up a little bit" before going to meet her boyfriend, with whom she had argued the night before. Roughly ten minutes later she walked to her boyfriend's dormitory lounge to meet him. He had not yet arrived.

Having nothing else to do while she waited for her boyfriend, the victim walked up to appellant's room to look for Earl Hassel, appellant's roommate. She knocked on the door several times but received no answer. She therefore wrote a note to Mr. Hassel, which read, "Hi Earl, I'm drunk. That's not why I came to see you. I haven't seen you in a while. I'll talk to you later, [victim's name]." She did so, although she had not felt any intoxicating effects from the martini, "for a laugh."

After the victim had knocked again, she tried the knob on the appellant's door. Finding it open, she walked in. She saw someone lying on the bed with a pillow over his head, whom she thought to be Earl Hassel. After lifting the pillow from his head, she realized it was appellant. She asked appellant which dresser was his roommate's. He told her, and the victim left the note.

---

59. 2002 Rape Study, above footnote 55, at 3. This may actually represent an increase from the 1970's. See Baumer et al., above footnote 56 (arguing that reporting has improved since the 1970's).

Before the victim could leave appellant's room, however, appellant asked her to stay and "hang out for a while." She complied because she "had time to kill" and because she didn't really know appellant and wanted to give him "a fair chance." Appellant asked her to give him a back rub but she declined, explaining that she did not "trust" him. Appellant then asked her to have a seat on his bed. Instead, she found a seat on the floor, and conversed for a while about a mutual friend. No physical contact between the two had, to this point, taken place.

Thereafter, however, appellant moved off the bed and down on the floor, and "kind of pushed [the victim] back with his body. It wasn't a shove, it was just kind of a leaning-type of thing." Next appellant "straddled" and started kissing the victim. The victim responded by saying, "Look, I gotta go. I'm going to meet [my boyfriend]." Then appellant lifted up her shirt and bra and began fondling her. The victim then said "no."

After roughly thirty seconds of kissing and fondling, appellant "undid his pants and he kind of moved his body up a little bit." The victim was still saying "no" but "really couldn't move because [appellant] was shifting at [her] body so he was over [her]." Appellant then tried to put his penis in her mouth. The victim did not physically resist, but rather continued to verbally protest, saying "No, I gotta go, let me go," in a "scolding" manner.

Ten or fifteen more seconds passed before the two rose to their feet. Appellant disregarded the victim's continual complaints that she "had to go," and instead walked two feet away to the door and locked it so that no one from the outside could enter.

Then, in the victim's words, "[appellant] put me down on the bed. It was kind of like—he didn't throw me on the bed. It's hard to explain. It was kind of like a push but no . . ." She did not bounce off the bed. "It wasn't slow like a romantic kind of thing, but it wasn't a fast shove either. It was kind of in the middle."

Once the victim was on the bed, appellant began "straddling" her again while he undid the knot in her sweatpants. He then removed her sweatpants and underwear from one of her legs. The victim did not physically resist in any way while on the bed because appellant was on top of her, and she "couldn't like go anywhere." She did not scream out at anytime because, "[i]t was like a dream was happening or something."

Appellant then used one of his hands to "guide" his penis into her vagina. At that point, after appellant was inside her, the victim began saying "no, no to him softly in a moaning kind of way . . . because it was just so scary." After about thirty seconds, appellant pulled out his penis and ejaculated onto the victim's stomach.

Immediately thereafter, appellant got off the victim and said, "Wow, I guess we just got carried away." To this the victim retorted, "No, we didn't get carried away, you got carried away." The victim then quickly dressed, grabbed her school books and raced downstairs to her boyfriend who was by then waiting for her in the lounge.

Once there, the victim began crying. Her boyfriend and she went up to his dorm room where, after watching the victim clean off appellant's semen from her stomach, he called the police.

Defense counsel's cross-examination elicited more details regarding the contact between appellant and the victim before the incident in question. The victim testified that roughly two weeks prior to the incident, she had attended a school seminar entitled, "Does 'no' sometimes means 'yes'?" Among other things, the lecturer at this seminar had discussed the average length and circumference of human penises. After the seminar, the victim and several of her friends had discussed the subject matter of the seminar over a speaker-telephone with appellant and his roommate Earl Hassel. The victim testified that during that telephone conversation, she had asked appellant the size of his penis. According to the victim, appellant responded by suggesting that the victim "come over and find out." She declined.

When questioned further regarding her communications with appellant prior to the April 19, 1988 incident, the victim testified that on two other occasions, she had stopped by appellant's room while intoxicated. During one of those times, she had laid [sic] down on his bed. When asked whether she had asked appellant again at that time what his penis size was, the victim testified that she did not remember.

Appellant took the stand in his own defense and offered an account of the incident and the events leading up to it which differed only as to the consent involved. According to appellant, the victim had begun communication with him after the school seminar by asking him of the size of his penis and of whether he would show it to her. Appellant had suspected that the victim wanted to pursue a sexual relationship with him because she had stopped by his room twice after the phone call while intoxicated, laying [sic] down on his bed with her legs spread and again asking to see his penis. He believed that his suspicions were confirmed when she initiated the April 19, 1988 encounter by stopping by his room (again after drinking), and waking him up.

Appellant testified that, on the day in question, he did initiate the first physical contact, but added that the victim warmly responded to his advances by passionately returning his kisses. He conceded that she was continually "whispering ... no's," but claimed that she did so while "amorously ... passionately" moaning. In effect he took such protests to be thinly veiled acts of encouragement. When asked why he locked the door, he explained that "that's not something you want somebody to just walk in on you [doing.]"

According to appellant, the two then laid [sic] down on the bed, the victim helped him take her clothing off, and he entered her. He agreed that the victim continued to say "no" while on the bed, but carefully qualified his agreement, explaining that the statements were "moaned passionately.'' According to appellant, when he saw a ''blank look on her face,'' he immediately withdrew and asked ''is anything wrong, is something the matter, is anything wrong.'' He ejaculated on her stomach thereafter because he could no longer ''control'' himself. Appellant testified that after this, the victim ''saw that it was over and then she made her move. She gets right off the bed . . . she just swings her legs over and then she puts her clothes back on.'' Then, in wholly corroborating an aspect of the victim's account, he testified that he remarked, ''Well, I guess we got carried away,'' to which she rebuked, ''No, we didn't get carried, you got carried away.''

After hearing both accounts, the jury convicted appellant of rape and indecent assault. * * * Appellant was then sentenced to serve a term of imprisonment of one to four years for rape and a concurrent term of six to twelve months for indecent assault. * * *

Appellant's argument in this regard [the sufficiency of evidence] was well summarized by appellant's counsel in his brief.

> The issues on appeal are real. At sentencing, they were recognized by the trial court as being on the cutting edge of the criminal jurisprudence of this Commonwealth:
>
> > The Court: Well, I'm comforted by the knowledge that whatever happens here today will certainly not end this case. This is going to go on and on for some time for just the very reason you suggested Mr. Mustokoff [present counsel for appellant], and that being that this case is on the cutting edge.
>
> Mr. Berkowitz prays that this Court overturns his rape conviction. He asks that this Court define the parameters between what may have been unacceptable social conduct and the criminal conduct necessary to support the charge for forcible rape.
>
> We contend that upon review, the facts show no more than what legal scholars refer to as ''reluctant submission''. The complainant herself admits that she was neither hurt nor threatened at any time during the encounter. She admits she never screamed or attempted to summon help. The incident occurred in a college dormitory in the middle of the afternoon.
>
> There has never been an affirmed conviction for forcible rape under similar circumstances. Not one factor which this Court has considered significant in prior cases, exists here. The uncontroverted evidence fails to establish forcible compulsion.

Appellant's Brief at 10.

* * *

The Commonwealth counters:

> Viewing the evidence and its inferences in the light most favorable to the Commonwealth, the jury's conclusion that the Defendant's forcible conduct overcame [the victim's] will is reasonable. The assault

> was rapid and the victim was physically overcome. Because she was acquainted with the Defendant, [the victim] had no reason to be fearful or suspicious of him and her resorting to verbal resistance only is understandable. More importantly, perhaps, it is only her lack of consent that is truly relevant. It is entirely reasonable to believe that the Defendant sat on her, pushed her on the bed and penetrated her before she had time to fully realize her plight and raise a hue and cry. If the law required active resistance, rather than the simple absence of consent, speedy penetration would immunize the most violent attacks and the goal-oriented rapist would reap an absurd reward. Certainly a victim must communicate her objections. But, contrary to the Defendant's arguments, Pennsylvania law says she can "just say no." [The victim] said "no." She said it repeatedly, clearly and sternly. She was rapidly, forcibly raped and deserves the protection of the law. * * *

Commonwealth's Brief at 6.

In Pennsylvania, the crime of rape is defined by statute as follows:

> A person commits a felony of the first degree when he engages in sexual intercourse with another person not his spouse:
>
> (1) by forcible compulsion;
>
> (2) by threat of forcible compulsion that would prevent resistance by a person of reasonable resolution;
>
> (3) who is unconscious; or
>
> (4) who is so mentally deranged or deficient that such person is incapable of consent.

18 Pa. C.S.A. § 3121. A statutory caveat to this rule may be found in section 3107 of title 18.

> Resistance Not Required
>
> The alleged victim need not resist the actor in prosecution under this chapter: Provided, however, that nothing in this section shall be construed to prohibit a defendant from introducing evidence that the alleged victim consented to the conduct in question.

The contours of Pennsylvania's rape statute, however, are not immediately apparent. As our Supreme Court explained in the landmark case, Commonwealth v. Rhodes, 510 Pa. 537, 510 A.2d 1217 (1986):

> "[F]orcible compulsion" as used in section 3121(1) includes not only physical force or violence but also moral, psychological or intellectual force used to compel a person to engage in sexual intercourse against that person's will. Closely related to section 3121(1) is section 3121(2) which applies to the situation where "forcible compulsion" is not actually used but is threatened. That section uses the phrase "by threat of forcible compulsion that would prevent resistance by a person of reasonable resolution." * * * By use of the phrase "person

> of reasonable resolution," the legislature introduced an objective standard regarding the use of threats of forcible compulsion to prevent resistance (as opposed to actual application of "forcible compulsion.")
>
> * * * Significant factors to be weighed in that determination would include the respective ages of the victim and the accused, the respective mental and physical conditions of the victim and the accused, the atmosphere and physical setting in which the incident was alleged to have taken place, the extent to which the accused may have been in a position of authority, domination or custodial control over the victim, and whether the victim was under duress. This list of possible factors is by no means exclusive.

Id., 510 Pa. at 557, 510 A.2d at 1226–27 n. 15.

* * *

Before us is not a case of mental coercion. There existed no significant disparity between the ages of appellant and the victim. They were both college sophomores at the time of the incident. Appellant was age twenty; the victim was nineteen. The record is devoid of any evidence suggesting that the physical or mental condition of one party differed from the other in any material way. Moreover, the atmosphere and physical setting in which the incident took place was in no way coercive. The victim walked freely into appellant's dorm room in the middle of the afternoon on a school day and stayed to talk of her own volition. There was no evidence to suggest that appellant was in any position of authority, domination or custodial control over the victim. Finally, no record evidence indicates that the victim was under duress. Indeed, nothing in the record manifests any intent of appellant to impose "moral, psychological or intellectual" coercion upon the victim.

Nor is this a case of a threat of forcible compulsion. When asked by defense counsel at trial whether appellant had at any point threatened her in any manner, the victim responded, "No, he didn't." Moreover, careful review of the record fails to reveal any express or even implied threat that could be viewed as one which, by the objective standard applicable herein, "would prevent resistance by a person of reasonable resolution."

Rather, the Commonwealth contends that the instant rape conviction is supported by the evidence of actual physical force used to complete the act of intercourse. Essentially, the Commonwealth maintains that, viewed in the light most favorable to it, the record establishes that the victim did not consent to engage in the intercourse, and thus, any force used to complete the act of intercourse thereafter constituted "forcible compulsion."

In response, appellant urges that the victim's testimony itself precludes a finding of "forcible compulsion." Appellant essentially argues that the indisputable lack of physical injuries and physical resistance proves that the evidence was insufficient to establish rape.

* * *

Here, the victim testified that the physical aspects of the encounter began when appellant "kind of pushed me back with his body. It wasn't a shove, it was just kind of a leaning-type thing." She did not testify that appellant "pinned" her to the floor with his hands thereafter; she testified that he "started kissing me ... [and] lift[ing] my shirt [and] bra ... straddling me kind of ... shifting at my body so that he was over me." When he attempted to have oral sex with her, appellant "knelt up straight ... [and] tried to put his penis in my mouth ... and after he obviously couldn't ... he, we got up." Although appellant then locked the door, his act cannot be seen as an attempt to imprison the victim since she knew and testified that the type of lock on the door of appellant's dorm room simply prevented those on the outside from entering but could be opened from the inside without hindrance. Appellant did not push, shove or throw the victim to his bed; he "put" her on the bed, not in a "romantic" way, but not with a "fast shove either." Once on the bed, appellant did not try to restrain the victim with his hands in any fashion. Rather, while she was "just kind of laying there," he "straddled" her, "quick[ly] undid" the knot in her sweatpants, "took off" her sweatpants and underwear, placed the "weight of his body" on top of her and "guided" his penis inside her vagina.

Even in the light most favorable to the Commonwealth, the victim's testimony as to the physical aspects of the encounter cannot serve as a basis to prove "forcible compulsion." The cold record is utterly devoid of any evidence regarding the respective sizes of either appellant or the victim. As such, we are left only to speculate as to the coercive effect of such acts as "leaning" against the victim or placing the "weight of his body" on top of her. This we may not do. Moreover, even if the record indicated some disparity in the respective weights or strength of the parties, such acts are not themselves inconsistent with consensual relations. Except for the fact that appellant was on top of the victim before and during intercourse, there is no evidence that the victim, if she had wanted to do so, could not have removed herself from appellant's bed and walked out of the room without any risk of harm or danger to herself whatsoever. These circumstances simply cannot be bootstrapped into sexual intercourse by forcible compulsion.

Similarly inconclusive is the fact that the victim testified that the act occurred in a relatively brief period of time. The short time frame might, without more, indicate that the victim desired the sexual encounter as easily as it might that she didn't, given the fact that no threats or mental coercion were alleged. At most, therefore, the physical aspects of the encounter establishes [sic] that appellant's sexual advances may have been unusually rapid, persistent and virtually uninterrupted. However inappropriate, undesirable or unacceptable such conduct may be seen to be, it does not, standing alone, prove that the victim was "forced to engage in sexual intercourse against her will."

The only evidence which remains to be considered is the fact that both the victim and appellant testified that throughout the encounter, the victim repeatedly and continually said "no." Unfortunately for the Commonwealth, under the existing statutes, this evidence alone cannot suffice to support a finding of "forcible compulsion."

Evidence of verbal resistance is unquestionably relevant in a determination of "forcible compulsion." At least twice previously this Court has given weight to the failure to heed the victim's oral admonitions. In each such case, however, evidence of verbal resistance was only found sufficient where coupled with a sufficient threat of forcible compulsion, mental coercion, or actual physical force of a type inherently inconsistent with consensual sexual intercourse. Thus, although evidence of verbal protestations may be relevant to prove that the intercourse was against the victim's will, it is not dispositive or sufficient evidence of "forcible compulsion."

If the legislature had intended to define rape, a felony of the first degree, as non-consensual intercourse, it could have done so. It did not do this. It defined rape as sexual intercourse by "forcible compulsion." If the legislature means what it said, then where as here no evidence was adduced by the Commonwealth which established either that mental coercion, or a threat, or force inherently inconsistent with consensual intercourse was used to complete the act of intercourse, the evidence is insufficient to support a rape conviction. Accordingly, we hold that the trial court erred in determining that the evidence adduced by the Commonwealth was sufficient to convict appellant of rape.

NOTES ON FORCE AND CONSENT

1. Traditionally, the law looked with particular suspicion upon the rape complaint. Lord Chief Justice Matthew Hale's now infamous seventeenth century remonstration explained: "Rape is an accusation easily to be made and hard to be proved, and harder still to be defended by the party accused, tho never so innocent," Hale, History of the Pleas of the Crown, vol. 1, 634 (R.H. Small 1847). This produced rules focused on physical resistance and prompt complaint. As one court put it: "in order to guard against false charges in cases of this kind—it has been deemed an important test of the sincerity of the woman, that while the commission of the offense was in progress, she cried aloud, struggled and complained on the first opportunity, and prosecuted the offender without delay." Stevick v. Commonwealth, 78 Pa. 460, 460 (1875). Under such a rule it was possible, as the *Berkowitz* court noted, that an appellate court could reverse a rape conviction when a victim was held down by her shoulders in a public place and multiple defendants had sex with her on the theory that the trial court did not charge on "bona fide" resistance. Commonwealth v. Moran, 97 Pa. Super. 120 (1929).

2. Most rape, according to government figures, occurs between those who know each other. Traditionally, the law has viewed this, the most prevalent form of rape, with skepticism. As Susan Estrich writes:

> * * * At one of the end of the spectrum is the "real" rape, what I will call the traditional rape: A stranger puts a gun to the head of his victim, threatens to kill her or beats her, and then engages in intercourse. In that case, the law—judges, statutes, prosecutors and all—generally acknowledge that a serious crime has been committed. But most cases deviate in one or many respects from this clear picture, making interpretation far more complex. Where less force is used or no other physical injury is inflicted, where threats are inarticulate, where the two know each other, where the setting is not an alley but a bedroom, where the initial contact was not a kidnapping but a date, where the woman says no but does not fight, the understanding is different. In such cases, the law, as reflected in the opinions of the courts, the interpretation, if not the words, of the statutes, and the decision of those within the criminal justice system, often tell us that no crime has taken place and that fault, if any is to be recognized, belongs with the woman. In concluding that such acts—what I call, for lack of a better title, "non-traditional" rapes—are not criminal, and worse, that the woman must bear any guilt, the law has reflected, legitimized and enforced a view of sex and women which celebrates male aggressiveness and punishes female passivity. And that vision, while under attack in recent years, continues to be a dominant force in our society and in the law of rape.

Susan Estrich, Rape, 95 Yale L.J. 1087, 1092 (1986).

Writing almost 20 years later, Michelle Anderson argues that this problem has not been solved by rape reform movements and that what she calls the "all-American Rape" still remains unpunished:

> Stuck as it is on the classic rape narrative, the law has fundamentally misconceived the crime. Instead of criminalizing rape, it has criminalized the extrinsic, violent assault: a bloody brawl with the goal of obtaining sex. The classic rape narrative actually involves at least two crimes: assault and rape. The all-American rape, by contrast, involves just one—the rape itself. Both historically and at present, the law has remained obsessed with criminalizing the extrinsic, violent assault and has disregarded the rape.

Michelle Anderson, All–American Rape, 79 St. John's L. Rev. 625, 627–28 (2005) (explaining that in only six states does the all-American rape constitute the highest level of offense).

3. The *Berkowitz* court concludes that no "forcible" rape has been committed. Is this consistent with recognition of the kind of "force" that is sufficient in other criminal contexts? Consider the comments of Susan Estrich:

> The requirement of force is not unique to the law of rape. But rape is different in two critical respects. First, unlike theft, if "force" is not inherent in noncriminal sex, at least physical contact is. Certainly, if a person stripped his victim, flattened that victim on the floor, lay down on top, and took the other person's wallet or jewelry, few would pause before the conclusion of a forcible robbery.

Estrich, above note 2, at 1107. If a defendant sought money and the victim said "no," would we consider the transaction a gift? Why do you think robbery is treated differently from rape?

4. What is the relationship between consent and resistance? What does a resistance requirement do for the law of rape that a non-consent requirement, alone, would not? Is victim resistance generally a requisite element of a crime? Consider again, Estrich on the unique aspects of rape law:

> * * * Mere "passive submission" or "passive assent" does not amount to consent—except in the law of rape.
>
> That the law puts a special burden on the rape victim to prove through her actions her nonconsent (or at least to account for why her actions did not demonstrate "nonconsent"), while imposing no similar burden on the victim of trespass, battery, or robbery, cannot be explained by the oft-observed fact that consensual sex is part of everyday life. Visiting (trespass with consent) is equally every day, as is philanthropy (robbery with consent), and surgery (battery with consent). Instinctively, we may think it is easier in those cases to tell the difference between consent and nonconsent. But if so, it is only because we are willing to presume that men are entitled to access to women's bodies (as opposed to their houses or their wallets), at least if they know them, and to accept male force in potentially "consensual" sexual relations.

Estrich, above note 2, at 1126. Are you persuaded by Estrich's critique? If so, what are the implications for reforming criminal law? What objections would you expect to encounter if you sought to eliminate the resistance requirement? How might these objections be answered?

5. Should a woman's statement of "no" be enough to convict a defendant of rape? Following an outcry after the *Berkowitz* case, the Pennsylvania legislature added to the statutory scheme a new crime of sexual assault, making it a second degree felony to have sexual intercourse "without the complainant's consent." 18 Pa. Cons. Stat. Ann. § 3124.1 (1998). Would this have changed the outcome of *Berkowitz*? What would happen in a case where the victim was immobilized by fear into silence?

6. Do women, especially young women, still sometimes say "no" when they mean "yes"? If so, why? Does this mean that "no" does not mean "no"? Do women sometimes give men "mixed signals" about whether they want sex or not? Would it be practical to expect the sexual initiator to *ask* his partner whether she wants to have heterosexual intercourse? Would this requirement be consistent with social norms for heterosexuals? To address these kinds of issues, Antioch College promulgated a Sexual Offense Policy stipulating that "if one person wants to initiate moving to a higher level of sexual intimacy in an interaction, that person is responsible for getting the verbal consent of the other person(s) involved before moving to that level." See Phil McCombs, Taking a Look at Love, Wash. Post, Feb. 16, 1996, at F5. While this policy was subjected to a great deal of criticism in the media (and even a Saturday Night Live skit), there is no evidence that the policy has inhibited sexual relations at Antioch. See Jason Vest, The School That's Put Sex to the Test; At Antioch, A Passionate Reaction to Consent Code, Wash. Post, Dec. 3, 1993, at G1. It appears that the policy is not stopping sex but rather forcing students to talk

about it. Do you think the policy is a good idea? What kinds of reactions would you anticipate if your school adopted a similar policy?

7. A number of jurisdictions have incorporated an understanding of consensual sex as requiring affirmative conduct on the part of the victim. For instance, consent is defined as "words or overt actions * * * indicating a freely given agreement to have sexual intercourse or sexual conduct." Wis. Stat. § 940.225(3)(2007). See also Wash. Rev. Code Ann. § 9A.44.010(7) (West 2008), Fla.Stat. § 794.011(5) (2007), State v. M.T.S., 129 N.J. 422, 609 A.2d 1266, 1277 (1992). What are the arguments for and against criminalizing sexual assault in this manner? What legal questions would you anticipate arising in a jurisdiction that adopted this approach? In your view, what statutory language best defines consent?

8. Why is the notion of consensual sex complicated in our society? What is the relationship between culture, gender socialization, and the law of rape? Is this a context in which line drawing is particularly difficult? If so, how might this challenge be most helpfully pursued? Mary I. Coombs describes the importance of exploring, through telling our stories honestly, what we consider sexual violation as opposed to sexual pleasure:

> As part of the long-term struggle for understanding and transformation, we need to examine our own experiences of sexuality and the social and psychological dynamics of those experiences. The world is not divided neatly into good sex, on the one hand, and rape and violation on the other. There are situations that fit into neither category: endured sex; "bad" sex; degrading, unpleasant, and offensive encounters; sex when one participant wants to please the other or is willing to tolerate sex for the partner's good qualities. Women need to explore the full range of arguably sexual activities and their reactions to them. For instance, a woman may say "no," but mean, "not yet; I'm not sure; let's keep talking." When sex then occurs, it is still desired despite the initial "no." Conversely, a woman may say "yes" to please a man or avoid an anticipated argument, though she did not want sex. The last category of stories in which "no" sometimes does not mean "no" can be misused or misunderstood. Although we may want to be careful where and to whom we tell these stories, we must find a place for these conversations in which we can examine our understandings of the boundaries of pleasure and danger.

Mary I. Coombs, Telling the Victim's Story, 2 Tex. J. Women & L. 277, 311–12 (1993). Is it useful for women to do what Coombs suggests? What are the risks? Is it possible to establish one standard (no may mean yes) socially and impose a different standard (no means no) legally?

9. Do most people believe that "no" means "no"? Or, consistent with the range of sexual experiences Mary Coombs discusses, do most people think "no" sometimes means "yes"? Or that a woman's behavior implies a "yes"? How do you think most young women and men view these issues? Almost one-third of college students surveyed in 1991 said that if a woman says "no" to sex, she really means "maybe" or even "yes" and that women desire and enjoy rape. Andrew E. Taslitz, Patriarchal Stories I: Cultural Rape Narratives in the Courtroom, 5 S. Cal. Rev. L. & Women's Stud. 389, 468 (1996). The

same study revealed that "almost one-quarter of the students agreed that women frequently cry rape falsely, that rape is often provoked by the victim, and that any woman can prevent rape if she really wants to do so." Id. Taslitz believes these numbers are misleadingly low "because university students are more likely to hold progressive views about rape than are the less educated, suggesting that an even larger percentage of the populace * * * is likely to admit to patriarchal views." Id.

A 2010 survey of over 1,000 Londoners found that more than half of respondents believed that a person should "take responsibility for being raped" under certain circumstances, including cases of dressing "provocatively" (28%), dancing "in a sexy way" at a night club or bar (22%) and "accepting a drink and engaging in a conversation at a bar" (13%). The youngest cohort surveyed was most likely to find that these circumstances required a rape victim to "take responsibility" for the crime. Opinion Matters, Wake Up To Rape Research Summary Report, 9–10, http://www.thehavens.co.uk/docs/Havens_Wake_Up_To_Rape_Report_Summary.pdf (2010). Do you believe that similar attitudes—and attitudes like those summarized above—pervade American society today? If so, might they impact how women's conduct is perceived? What are the implications for defining the crime of rape?

10. In one study of over 300 men, 33% self-reported that they had committed a sexual assault (8 percent of which was a rape or attempted rape, the rest for coerced sex). Antonia Abbey, Pam McAuslan, Tina Zawacki, A. Monique Clinton & Philip O. Buck, Attitudinal, Experiential, and Situational Predictors of Sexual Assault Perpetration, 16 J. Interpersonal Violence 784, 793 (2001). Of those who admitted committing a sexual assault, 78% had committed more than one. Id. at 794. These studies also show that "the more frequently that men misperceived women's sexual intentions, the more frequently they committed sexual assault." Antonia Abbey, Pam McAuslan & Lisa Thomson Ross, Sexual Assault Perpetration by College Men: The Role of Alcohol, Misperception of Sexual Intent, and Sexual Beliefs and Experiences, 17 J. Soc. & Clinical Psych. 167, 186 (1998). "College men who committed sexual assault on dates were more likely to feel that the woman had 'led them on' than men who had not engaged in this behavior." Id. at 171. Assuming this is true, how should the law address men's claims that they misperceived a woman's intentions? Does your answer change depending on what behavior(s) men relied on to conclude that they were being "led on?" Why or why not?

11. Imagine that the parties in the *Berkowitz* case were complete strangers, that she attended a different college, and that she went to his room looking for directions to a basketball game. Would this change your view of consent? If it would, consider what that does to the question of consent—does it suggest that the parties' relationship can operate as a proxy for consent? If so, how likely is it that acquaintance rape prosecutions are going to be successful, even in a jurisdiction that does not, as Pennsylvania did in *Berkowitz*, require additional force? Catharine A. MacKinnon argues that the law applies a type of sliding scale of consent, depending upon the woman's relationship to the alleged rapist:

> The law of rape divides women into spheres of consent according to indices of relationship to men. Which category of presumed consent a woman is in depends upon who she is relative to a man who wants her, not what she says or does. These categories tell men whom they can legally fuck, who is open season and who is off limits, not how to listen to women. The paradigm categories are the virginal daughter and other young girls, with whom all sex is proscribed, and the whore-like wives and prostitutes, with whom no sex is proscribed. Daughters may not consent; wives and prostitutes are assumed to, and cannot but. Actual consent or nonconsent, far less actual desire, is comparatively irrelevant. If rape laws existed to enforce women's control over access to their sexuality, as the consent defense implies, no would mean no, marital rape would not be a widespread exception, and it would not be effectively legal to rape a prostitute.

Catherine A. MacKinnon, Rape: On Coercion and Consent, in Toward a Feminist Theory of the State 171, 175 (1989). Does MacKinnon's position preclude the type of exploration urged by Mary Coombs in note 8 above? Does MacKinnon argue that "yes" often means "no"? Under what conditions would MacKinnon find "consent"?

12. Would fixing the standard of consent solve the problem of rape? For example, if one required that the defendant bear the burden of showing "affirmative consent" to the activity, what would the result be in *Berkowitz*? Is it clear? Does the very idea of consent assume *he* is the active party and *she* the passive one? If so, is this problematic? Would a singular requirement of force and/or coercion be preferable, insofar as it would maintain focus on the defendant's conduct?

13. A number of criminal law theorists have urged that rape law should be reformed by reference to traditional liberal values. Stephen J. Schulhofer, for example, has emphasized that rape should be construed as a violation of a woman's sexual autonomy. See Stephen J. Schulhofer, Unwanted Sex: The Culture of Intimidation and the Failure of Law (1998). First, what is meant by the term autonomy? Autonomy means freedom, but freedom from what? Does this concept resolve the difficult questions occurring at the boundary between what is and is not permissible sexual coercion (as in the *Berkowitz* case)? As suggested above in note 12, one critique of an emphasis on consent is that it tends to define impermissible conduct in terms of what *she* did, not what *he* did. Does a focus on "her" autonomy create a similar problem? If one's baseline assumption is that women are less credible or less deserving or likely to precipitate rape, then will an autonomy-based focus actually increase autonomy?

14. A number of other theorists have attempted to place the punishment of rape within frameworks taken from other areas of law and theory entirely, including economics. Richard A. Posner, for example, has argued that rape is a rational substitute for sex, following standard substitutability analysis within economic theory. Richard A. Posner, Sex and Reason 384–86 (1992). For Posner, a rapist is essentially a "sex thief." Robin West, Sex, Reason and a Taste for the Absurd, 81 Geo. L.J. 2413, 2430 (1993). Feminists Linda R. Hirshman and Jane A. Larson embrace the notion of sexual bargains and

attempt to use this idea for women's benefit. They analogize strong rape protections for women to those that the law provides for property: just as the market provides strong protections for property to facilitate exchange, rape law should provide strong protections for women to facilitate fair sexual bargains. They argue, for example, that a strong rape rule—one requiring affirmative consent—will facilitate sexual exchanges between men and women. Linda R. Hirshman & Jane A. Larson, Hard Bargains: The Politics of Sex 268–72 (1998). Is it wise for feminists to appropriate the assumption that sex is like property? Or are Hirshman and Larson simply trying to show that such assumptions, even if unpalatable, do not necessarily lead to the results suggested by their advocates?

2. RAPE AND RACE

KIMBERLÉ CRENSHAW, DEMARGINALIZING THE INTERSECTION OF RACE AND SEX: A BLACK FEMINIST CRITIQUE OF ANTIDISCRIMINATION DOCTRINE, FEMINIST THEORY AND ANTIRACIST POLITICS

1989 U. Chi. Legal F. 139, 157–60 (1989).

* * * A central political issue on the feminist agenda has been the pervasive problem of rape. Part of the intellectual and political effort to mobilize around this issue has involved the development of a historical critique of the role that law has played in establishing the bounds of normative sexuality and in regulating female sexual behavior. Early carnal knowledge statutes and rape laws are understood within this discourse to illustrate that the objective of rape statutes traditionally has not been to protect women from coercive intimacy but to protect and maintain a property-like interest in female chastity. Although feminists quite rightly criticize these objectives, to characterize rape law as reflecting male control over female sexuality is for Black women an oversimplified account and an ultimately inadequate account.

Rape statutes generally do not reflect *male* control over *female* sexuality, but *white* male regulation of *white* female sexuality. Historically, there has been absolutely no institutional effort to regulate Black female chastity. Courts in some states had gone so far as to instruct juries that, unlike white women, Black women were not presumed to be chaste. Also, while it was true that the attempt to regulate the sexuality of white women placed unchaste women outside the law's protection, racism restored a fallen white woman's chastity where the alleged assailant was a Black man. No such restoration was available to Black women.

The singular focus on rape as a manifestation of male power over female sexuality tends to eclipse the use of rape as a weapon of racial terror. When Black women were raped by white males, they were being raped not as women generally, but as Black women specifically: Their femaleness made them sexually vulnerable to racist domination, while their Blackness effectively denied them any protection. This white male power was reinforced by a judicial system in which the successful conviction of a white man for raping a Black woman was virtually unthinkable.

In sum, sexist expectations of chastity and racist assumptions of sexual promiscuity combined to create a distinct set of issues confronting Black women. These issues have seldom been explored in feminist literature nor are they prominent in antiracist politics. The lynching of Black males, the institutional practice that was legitimized by the regulation of white women's sexuality, has historically and contemporaneously occupied the Black agenda on sexuality and violence. Consequently, Black women are caught between a Black community that, perhaps understandably, views with suspicion attempts to litigate questions of sexual violence, and a feminist community that reinforces those suspicions by focusing on white female sexuality. The suspicion is compounded by the historical fact that the protection of white female sexuality was often the pretext for terrorizing the Black community. Even today some fear that anti-rape agendas may undermine antiracist objectives. This is the paradigmatic political and theoretical dilemma created by the intersection of race and gender: Black women are caught between ideological and political currents that combine first to create and then to bury Black women's experiences.

NOTES ON RAPE AND RACE

1. The myth that Black men rape white women has had a long, terrible history in America. In the first three decades of the twentieth century, for example, white claims of interracial rape were used to justify the lynching of Black men; in this sense, gender ideology clearly helped to create and perpetuate racism. To the extent that society still associates rape with Black men, it is a myth distinctly contrary to reality. The majority of rape is intraracial. Bureau of Justice Statistics, Criminal Victimization in the United States, Personal Crimes of Violence Statistical Tables, Table 42 (showing race of victim and perpetrator) (2007), available at http://bjs.ojp.usdoj.gov/content/pub/pdf/cvus07.pdf. How does this myth affect both white women (who are raped primarily by white men) and Black women (who live in a community in which accusations of rape have been used against Black men as a form of terrorism)?

2. Jennifer Wriggins addresses the implications of the legal system's failure to address this myth of Black on white rape:

> The legal system's treatment of rape both has furthered racism and has denied the reality of women's sexual subordination. It has disproportionately targeted Black men for punishment and made Black women both particularly vulnerable and particularly without redress. It has denied the reality of women's sexual subordination by creating a social meaning of rape which implies that the only type of sexual abuse is illegal rape and the only form of illegal rape is Black offender/white victim. Because of the interconnectedness of rape and racism, successful work against rape and other sexual coercion must deal with racism. Struggles against rape must acknowledge the differences among women and the different ways that groups other than women are disempowered. * * *

Jennifer Wriggins, Rape, Racism and the Law, 6 Harv. Women's L.J. 103, 140–41 (1983). See also Lisa A. Crooms, Speaking Partial Truths and Preserving Power: Deconstructing White Supremacy, Patriarchy, and the Rape Corroboration Rule in the Interest of Black Liberation, 40 How. L.J. 459 (1997); Elisabeth M. Iglesias, Rape, Race, and Representation: The Power of Discourse, Discourses of Power, and the Reconstruction of Heterosexuality, 49 Vand. L. Rev. 869 (1996); Darci E. Burrell, Comment, Myth, Stereotype, and the Rape of Black Women, 4 UCLA Women's L.J. 87 (1993). How should the law respond to these concerns? How can feminists effectively deal with these differences? In what ways do critical race critiques of the "battered woman," discussed in Section C, apply to the rape context?

3. IMAGES AND MYTHS OF RAPE VICTIMS

TEXT NOTE: WOMEN AS RAPE VICTIMS

Two popular books, Katie Roiphe's The Morning After: Sex, Fear, and Feminism (1994) and Naomi Wolf's Fire With Fire: The New Female Power and How to Use It (1994), are highly critical of feminist work on date rape (as well as sexual harassment and pornography), claiming that feminists have turned women into victims. Instead, according to these authors, feminists should be concentrating on women's individual agency, choice, and exercise of responsibility. According to this perspective, a feminist focus on women's victimization has reinforced stereotypical views of women as fragile and passive. In response, Elizabeth M. Schneider states that:

> their complaint of "victim feminism" and solution of "power feminism" are simplistic in failing to grapple with the systematic nature of women's subordination and women's active efforts to resist such subordination. Regretfully, they also demonstrate a lack of compassion for women, particularly women who are not in situations where they can assert "power feminism." Both books underscore the fundamental inadequacy of focusing on *either* victimization *or* agency (reconceived as "victim feminism" or "power feminism") to capture the complexity of struggle in women's lives and highlight the way this false dichotomy leads to problematic extremes.

Elizabeth M. Schneider, Feminism and the False Dichotomy of Victimization and Agency, 38 N.Y.L. Sch. L. Rev. 387, 394 (1993).

A number of sex positive feminists have articulated a somewhat different critique of rape law reform. Aya Gruber provides this overview:

> [One] critique of the criminalization of rape is that the feminist focus on the crime of rape has actually served to entrench moralistic chastity norms and foster an unhealthy female view of sex. Katherine Franke cautions feminists to be wary of pursuing policies that "nourish[] a theory of sexuality as dependency and danger at the expense of a withering positive theory of sexual possibility." "Sex-positive" theorists assert that rape reformers' emphatic insistence that women view sex nearly exclusively as a hazard emphasizes sexual passivity, decreases sexual autonomy, and has thwarted the development of theories of female

> sexuality. In addition, feminism's resolute focus on eradicating questionable (if not all) sex as if it were a virus denies women sources of pleasure. Sexual pleasure is in many ways socially constructed, and women often idealize the image of a relentless sexual pursuer singularly attuned to her secret driving passion for sex, despite her ardent protestations. Sex-positivists are rightly concerned that an overcriminalization of sexual "coercion" is difficult to distinguish from repressive chastity norms and morality policing.

Aya Gruber, Rape, Feminism and the War on Crime, 84 Wash L. Rev. 581, 611–12 (2009).

NOTES ON WOMEN AS RAPE VICTIMS

1. Which approach to rape described above do you find most compelling? Are these views mutually exclusive, or can they be reconciled? Gruber suggests that, "[l]ike agency arguments, sex-positive theories are steeped in feminist dilemma." Id. at 612. Do you agree? If so, how should this dilemma be resolved?

2. Although the myth of the Black rapist, described above, may be one of the most persistent and pernicious of rape myths, it is far from the only one. As we noted in Section B on homicide, violence myths were first noticed in the context of rape. Morrison Torrey has written about the ways in which myths about violence undermine rape law. She suggests:

> The classic rape myths can be summarized into four categories: (1) only women with 'bad' reputations are raped; (2) women are prone to sexual fantasies; (3) women precipitate rape by their appearance and behavior; and—by far the most potent myth—(4) women, motivated by revenge, blackmail, jealousy, guilt or embarrassment, falsely claim rape after consenting to sexual relations.

Morrison Torrey, When Will We Be Believed? Rape Myths and the Idea of a Fair Trial in Rape Prosecutions, 24 U.C. Davis L. Rev. 1013, 1025 (1991). Torrey argues that these myths are so pervasive, despite legal reforms, that they effectively deprive women of a "fair trial." Id. at 1016. One proposal Torrey offers to address the prejudice created by rape myths is to require all fact-finders to be "de-briefed" by expert witnesses in order to counter their belief in rape myths. Id. at 1066–71. What objections could be made to this approach? Can you think of any other ways to deal with rape myths?

3. One persistent rape myth is that women "provoke" rape by their behavior or the way that they dress. In a rape prosecution in 1989 in Florida, a woman who had worn a lace miniskirt with no underwear was slashed with a knife, hit with a rock, and raped twice. A jury of three men and three women, however, acquitted the defendant on kidnapping and rape charges. In explaining the verdict, the jury foreman said: "We felt she (the woman) asked for it the way she was dressed. The way she was dressed with that skirt, you could see everything she had. She was advertising for sex." AP, Jury: Woman in rape case "asked for it," Chi. Trib., Oct. 6, 1989, 11C. What may be most unusual about this case is the juror's express articulation of the basis for the verdict. Is there any way this bias can be remedied? The Florida legislature

acted to expand its rape shield statute to exclude "evidence presented for the purpose of showing that manner of dress of the victim at the time of the offense incited the sexual battery." Fla. Stat. Ann. § 794.022(3) (West 2007). Will this solve the problem? Does it address the fundamental problem of rape myths? In that regard, see Jennifer Temkin, Prosecuting and Defending Rape: Perspectives from the Bar, 27 J. Law & Soc'y 219, 233 (2000) (describing how woman's clothing may influence prosecutors' attitudes).

In the spring of 1999, Italy's highest appeals court overturned a rape conviction because the victim was wearing jeans at the time of the alleged rape. The court stated that "it is common knowledge that it is nearly impossible to even partially remove jeans from a person without their cooperation." The five judges who wrote the opinion were all male. Italian women, protesting the decision, wore denim to demonstrate solidarity with the victim. In fact, 60% of Italians polled about the ruling criticized it, indicating that sexual violence was a national emergency. It was predicted that the court's unpopular decision would do more than any legislation to change Italian attitudes toward sexual violence. See Greg Burke, Judged by Her Jeans: Italian Women Are Up In Arms After a Court Declares That a Woman Who is Wearing Jeans Can't Be Raped, Time Mag. Int'l ed., Mar. 1, 1999, at 51. What do you think is more effective: legislative change or public protest? How would you mobilize public protest around this issue? Since the decision in 1999, the Italian Supreme Court has issued three other opinions referencing the "jeans defense;" all three have affirmed the convictions. Benedetta Faedi, Rape, Blue Jeans, and Judicial Developments in Italy, 16 Colum. J. Eur. L. Online 13, 16–18 (2009), http://www.cjel.net/online/16_1-faedi/.

4. There is a good deal of social science evidence that young women do not, in fact, have a clear understanding of what the law deems to be rape; this is a dilemma that law and society scholars refer to as the problem of legal consciousness. Research on college campuses has yielded a remarkably consistent finding that what the law dictates as rape may not be how young women define rape. Some studies show, for example, that women do not consider it rape if they have been drinking or if there is not classic vaginal penetration. Other studies show that they tend not to consider it rape when the attacker is a boyfriend. Still others indicate that women ascribe to rape myths such as if they did not "fight back" it was not rape. See Was It Rape? The Function of Women's Rape Myth Acceptance and Definitions of Sex in Labeling Their Own Experiences, 51 Sex Roles 129 (2004) (discussing studies); Arnold S. Kahn, Jennifer Jackson, Christine Kully, Kelly Badger & Jessica Halvorsen, Calling It Rape: Differences in Experiences of Women Who Do or Do Not Label Their Sexual Assault as Rape, 27 Psych. Women Q. 233, 239–40 (2003) (same). Feminism seeks to honor women's experience. Should these personal definitions control? Should advocates stop insisting on education about the nature of rape that differs from this cultural definition? Or does this simply support those who insist that women face up to the reality of their experiences? What, in turn, does all of this say about the feminist notion of experience itself?

5. Research on criminal behavior has undermined a number of rape myths. An FBI study of serial rapists, for example, speaks to misconceptions about who rapes, and why. Robert R. Hazelwood & Janet Warren, The Serial

Rapist: His Characteristics and Victims (Part 1), 58 FBI Law Enforcement Bulletin 10 (Jan. 1989) and (Conclusion), 58 FBI Law Enforcement Bulletin 18 (Feb. 1989). "Of the 41 serial rapists interviewed, 54% had generally stable employment"; "71% had been married at least once"; "51% had served in the Armed Forces"; "52% scored above average on intelligence tests"; "54% were raised in average or above average socioeconomic environments"; "76% had been sexually abused as children"; and "36% collected pornography." Hazelwood, above at 14. The authors noted that their "findings * * * contradict popular stereotypes which characterize the serial rapist as a lonely, isolated person who lives alone and has little or no contact with his family" and that the rapists "tended to meet people easily, [and] eventually attempted to dominate the relationship." Hazelwood, above at 16, 17. When asked what factors influenced their selection of victims, 98% reported they chose victims based on availability and 95% on gender; only 39% depended on physical characteristics and 15% on the victim's clothing. Hazelwood, above at 23. What are the implications of this data for the myths described earlier?

6. Although social scientists have long studied the prevalence of rape myths (the studies are discussed in Torrey, above note 2), there remains doubt whether this research has had a significant impact on police and prosecutorial practices. One persistent feminist complaint has been of the "unfounding" of rape complaints by police and prosecutors—that is, a determination at an early stage in the proceedings, by the police or prosecutors, that there has been no crime worthy of prosecution. See Michelle Anderson, New Voices on the New Federalism: Women Do Not Report the Violence They Suffer: Violence Against Women and the State Action Doctrine, 46 Vill. L. Rev. 907, 929 (2001) (arguing that, by "unfounding and downgrading crimes involving violence against women, police departments neglect to investigate hundreds, perhaps thousands, of legitimate rape complaints every year"). Although it may be that other crimes are unfounded at greater rates, see Wayne A. Kerstetter, Criminology: Gateway to Justice: Police and Prosecutorial Response to Sexual Assaults Against Women, 81 J. Crim. L. & Criminology 267, 280 (1990), there is also evidence that police and prosecutors continue to be influenced by general social and cultural scripts discouraging arrest and prosecution in rape cases which do not satisfy the violent stranger-rape scenario. See Cassia Spohn & David Holleran, Prosecuting Sexual Assault: A Comparison of Charging Decisions in Sexual Assault Cases Involving Strangers, Acquaintances, and Intimate Partners, 18 Justice Quarterly 651, 677–78 (2001). What might account for this less-than-aggressive pursuit of acquaintance rape cases? Do police and prosecutors discount the credibility of women claiming to have been raped by their intimates? Do they credit the account but trivialize the harm done? Do they discount the likelihood of convicting a defendant at trial? Do they accurately assess these odds and proceed accordingly? Given your assessment of the most plausible explanation(s), what solutions would you propose to enhance the prosecution of acquaintance rape?

4. ATTEMPTS TO REFORM RAPE LAW

Beginning in the 1970's, the rape reform movement helped achieve a variety of changes in rape law. Most states eliminated rules requiring that the victim resist to the "utmost", file a "prompt complaint", or that her account be "corroborated." Many states redrafted their rape laws to clarify definitions of "consent" and "force."[60]

The impact of reform is difficult to measure, and research on its effects has proven inconclusive. Early empirical studies of rape reforms in Canada and selected states and urban environments in the U.S. found little or no "instrumental effect," i.e., no increase in complaints, arrests, prosecutions, and convictions.[61] More recent research finds greater reporting rates[62] and an increased likelihood that police will pursue a rape investigation.[63] Cassia Spohn and Julie Horney posit that rape law reforms have brought about a shift in institutional attitudes toward "simple" rapes (those not involving extrinsic violence, multiple assailants, or no prior relationship between the victim and offender):

> [T]he fact that the proportion of simple rape cases bound over for trial increased significantly in the post-reform period suggests that more borderline cases are being reported by victims, and accepted by police and prosecutors. It suggests that the rape law reforms have produced a climate more conducive to the full prosecution of cases of simple rape.[64]

Yet despite evidence of progress, advocates for rape victims observe that rape myths have not been eradicated. Juries are still influenced by the victim's prior behavior, clothing, lack of resistance, and failure to make a prompt complaint. As one 2005 article noted, "rape victims, especially acquaintance rape victims, continue to encounter the same hurdles that they did thirty years ago."[65]

NOTES ON RAPE REFORM

1. If legislative reform focusing on the elements necessary to prove rape is not the answer, what is the solution? The failure of legislative rape reform appears consistent with empirical data suggesting that law reform preceding social change is doomed to failure. See Gerald N. Rosenberg, The Hollow Hope: Can Courts Bring About Social Change? (1991). Can you think of any successful legal reform that preceded changed social attitudes? On the other hand, do you know of any major social reform movement whose aspirations

---

60. See Cassia Spohn, The Rape Reform Movement: The Traditional Common Law and Rape Law Reforms, 39 Jurimetrics 119, 121 (1999).

61. See Morrison Torrey, Feminist Legal Scholarship on Rape: A Maturing Look at One Form of Violence Against Women, 2 Wm. & Mary J. Women & L. 35, 45–46 (1995).

62. Eric P. Baumer, Richard B. Felson & Steven F. Messner, Changes in Police Notification for Rape, 1973–2000, 41 Criminology 841 (2003).

63. Stacy Futter & Walter R. Mebane Jr., The Effects of Rape Law Reform on Rape Case Processing, 16 Berkeley Women's L.J. 72, 73–75 (2001).

64. Cassia Spohn & Julia Horney, The Impact of Rape Law Reform on the Processing of Simple and Aggravated Rape Cases, 86 J. Crim. L. & Criminology 861, 884 (1996). See generally Cassia Spohn & Julia Horney, Rape Law Reform: A Grassroots Revolution and Its Impact (1992).

65. Ilene Seidman & Susan Vickers, The Second Wave: An Agenda for the Next Thirty Years of Rape Law Reform, 38 Suffolk U. L. Rev. 467, 468 (2005).

were not embodied in legal reform? The optimism of legal reformers and the pessimism of their critics may *both* be misplaced, according to law and society scholars who emphasize the institutional mediation of legal reform. See Lauren B. Edelman, Legal Ambiguity and Symbolic Structures: Organizational Mediation of Civil Rights Law, 97 Am. J. Soc. 1531, 1532 (1992). What kind of organizational structures do you think "mediate" rape reform in ways that interfere with its success? For instance, what institutional incentives might impact police and prosecutors?

2. Gender is a very powerful cultural phenomenon resisting reform in a wide variety of areas, not only rape law. As we have seen above, in Section B on homicide, myths such as victim provocation emerge in the application of offenses that span the criminal law. Has too much emphasis been placed on rape as opposed to other crimes? Should rape reform have focused less on "legal elements" and more on "cultural myths"? Why not spend less time on the proper definition of consent and more time on jury instructions specifically forbidding the jury from employing rape myths? Why not ask the jury to "switch" the offense to one of "money" and to ask themselves if they would come up with the same result and, if not, to explain why? Cf. Cynthia Lee, Murder and the Reasonable Man: Passion and Fear in the Criminal Courtroom 224–25 (2003) (urging an analogous form of "switching" to respond to claims of racial bias).

3. Many states have attempted to deal with repeat sexual offenders through probation, parole, and sentencing schedules. For example, Washington responded to the high rate of sex offender recidivism of sex offenders by extending their imprisonment through its "Sexually Violent Predators Act." Wash. Rev. Code Ann. § 71.09 (West 2008). The Act provides for post-sentence indefinite civil commitment for sexually violent predators, individuals convicted of, or charged with (but not tried because of incompetency) a crime of sexual violence and suffering from a mental abnormality or personality disorder which makes them likely to engage in predatory acts of sexual violence. See Lisa Taeko Greenlees, Washington State's Sexually Violent Predators Act: Model or Mistake, 29 Am. Crim. L. Rev. 107 (1991). Can you anticipate any constitutional challenges to such a law? Is this law simply a variation on general civil commitment statutes, in which anyone who is a danger to himself or others may be involuntarily committed?

In 1997, the Supreme Court upheld one of these sexually violent predator acts in Kansas v. Hendricks, 521 U.S. 346 (1997). Justice Thomas, writing for the majority, stated:

> To the extent that the civil commitment statutes we have considered set forth criteria relating to an individual's inability to control his dangerousness, the Kansas Act sets forth comparable criteria and Hendricks' condition doubtless satisfies those criteria. The mental health professionals who evaluated Hendricks diagnosed him as suffering from pedophilia, a condition the psychiatric profession itself classifies as a serious mental disorder. Hendricks even conceded that, when he becomes "stressed out," he cannot "control the urge" to molest children. This admitted lack of volitional control, coupled with a prediction of future dangerousness, adequately distinguishes Hendricks from other dangerous persons who

> are perhaps more properly dealt with exclusively through criminal proceedings. Hendricks' diagnosis as a pedophile, which qualifies as a "mental abnormality" under the Act, thus plainly suffices for due process purposes.

Id. at 360. A state's "three strikes and you're out" law (providing for extended incarceration after a violent third offense) can also prolong incarceration for repeat offenders. Would you support a sexual predator statute similar to Washington's? Why or why not?

4. Another experiment has been to require convicted sex offenders to register with the local authorities upon their release from prison. Public notice laws, such as "Megan's Law" (named for Megan Kanka after she was sexually assaulted and murdered by a released sex offender in her New Jersey neighborhood), require law enforcement agencies to notify the public when a registered sex offender moves into the community. In 2003, the Supreme Court upheld Connecticut's version of Megan's Law against a constitutional challenge. The challengers argued that the law violated their rights to procedural due process on the theory that they had no opportunity for a hearing on whether they were likely to be "currently dangerous." Connecticut Dept. of Public Safety v. Doe, 538 U.S. 1 (2003). The Supreme Court refused to address the question whether the law violated substantive due process. Do you think that public notice laws are a good policy? How do you think they will affect released sex offenders? Do you think the community has a right to know if a convicted sex offender moves in? What about the rights of a criminal defendant who has served his punishment and wants to start anew?

5. Several states have passed laws allowing, and in some cases requiring, chemical treatments of certain sex offenders, including rapists, as a condition of parole. Commonly referred to as "chemical castration," the treatment involves regular chemical injections of drugs such as Depo–Provera, which shrink the testicles, inhibit the release of testosterone and other hormones that affect the brain's tendency to sexually fantasize, and reduce sex drive in men. These effects are reversible if treatments stop, and empirical data is inconclusive with respect to whether treatment affects recidivism. See Henry T. Greely, Neuroscience and Criminal Justice: Not Responsibility But Treatment, 56 Kan. L. Rev. 1103, 1129 (2008). The state of Texas has even passed a statute authorizing, under specified conditions, surgical castration, an outpatient procedure in which the testicles are removed and permanent sterilization results. Id. at 1136. Would you expect these treatments to be effective? Should they only be imposed on rapists of a certain age? See Owen D. Jones, Sex, Culture, and the Biology of Rape: Toward Explanation and Prevention, 87 Cal. L. Rev. 827, 912–30 (1999); J. Michael Bailey & Aaron S. Greenberg, The Science and Ethics of Castration: Lessons from the *Morse* Case, 92 Nw. U. L. Rev. 1225 (1998).

6. Yet another possible institutional response to rape has been suggested by Katharine K. Baker—shaming date rapists. She notes that:

> The disregard for the question of consent on the part of men has led to a massive victimization of women. Criminally punishing nonconsensual sex has proved difficult, however, precisely because the legal proscription on nonconsensual sex competes with the masculinity norm, biological theory

> and popular belief, all of which re-enforce and legitimate the notion that men crave sex regardless of consent. Given this tension between the law and other well-established norms, it should come as little surprise that a sizable number of men have yet to internalize the moral wrong of nonconsensual sex. And even those men who have internalized the abstract wrong of non-consensual sex can have difficulty concretely identifying what nonconsensual sex is. This difficulty stems both from well established sexual behavior roles that shun explicit communication and from our continuing reluctance to explicitly discuss, both societally and individually, what consent is. Finally, the constitutional protections afforded defendants make convictions particularly difficult to secure in cases, like date rape, in which consent is the only issue.

Katherine K. Baker, Sex, Rape and Shame, 79 B.U. L. Rev. 663, 693–94 (1999). The alternative Baker proposes lies in her suggested sanction: in a closed community, such as a college, shaming the offenders. She argues that shame sanctions can subvert the linking of masculinity and sexual activity in addition to affording the victim a sense of vindication. Rather than expelling students found guilty, shaming sanctions could include being required to wear a bright orange armband; publishing the rapist's picture with the armband in the school newspaper; banning the rapist from extracurricular activities through which esteem is achieved; and listing his affiliations (such as fraternity, sports teams, etc.) so that they share his shame. Id. at 698. How do you assess the likelihood that shaming will be successful in eliminating college date rape? Can you think of other possible sanctions? What are the goals of fashioning alternative sanctions?

Note that universities, in order to be eligible for federal funds, must now collect data on campus rape and maintain sexual assault policies which provide for disciplinary procedures, usually less formal than criminal proceedings, e.g., relaxed evidentiary rules, non-unanimous convictions, less rigid standards of proof. See Higher Education Amendments of 1991 § 486(c)(1)–(2), 20 U.S.C. §§ 1092(f)(1)(F)(1994); § 1092(f)(7)(B)(i)–(B)(iii). A long-term investigation by the Center for Public Integrity (CPI) in partnership with National Public Radio concluded that, notwithstanding federal requirements, "students deemed 'responsible' for alleged sexual assaults on college campuses can face little or no consequence for their acts." Kristen Lombardi, Culture of Indifference: A Lack of Consequences for Sexual Assault, Center For Public Integrity, Feb. 24, 2010, www.publicintegrity.org/investigations/campus_assault/articles/entry/1945 (also noting that colleges expel only 10–25% of men found responsible for sexual assault.) What might account for this treatment of campus rape allegations? Do you think that the criminal justice system is better equipped to handle these cases? Why or why not? See id. ("[M]any administrators agree they would rather the criminal justice system take on cases involving campus rape allegations—if only it would. Prosecutors often shy away from such cases because they are 'he said, she said' disputes absent definitive evidence.")

7. Occasionally male defendants attempt to introduce cultural evidence to rebut the prosecution's proof of mens rea or criminal intent in crimes of violence against women. Many feminists have vigorously opposed the use of the "cultural" defense as condoning violence against women. According to

Holly Maguigan, this has created a "tension between multiculturalist and feminist values [which] is presented most clearly in cases such as Chen [in which a Chinese immigrant did not deny killing his wife, but offered evidence that he murdered her after learning of her infidelity] and Rhines [in which an African American male did not deny intercourse with an African American complainant, but contended that he made a reasonable mistake about her consent because Black people speak to each other very loudly], in which outsider men are charged with family or anti-woman violence and seek to use cultural information in their defense." Holly Maguigan, Cultural Evidence and Male Violence: Are Feminist and Multiculturalist Reformers on a Collision Course in Criminal Courts?, 70 N.Y.U. L. Rev. 36 (1995). How would you resolve this issue? Maguigan suggests that there is a middle ground; she would allow "offers of proof by defense counsel that make clear that cultural evidence is intended to prove the defendant's state of mind, not to support the assertion of a separate 'cultural defense.'" Id. at 42. Do you find this proposal an acceptable compromise? What are the dangers of allowing evidence about male-dominated cultures in criminal prosecutions? What are the dangers of excluding it? For more on the "cultural" defense and violence against women, see Leti Volpp, (Mis)Identifying Culture: Asian Women and the "Cultural Defense," 17 Harv. Women's L.J. 57 (1994); Sherene Razack, A Violent Culture or a Culturalized Violence, 3(1) Studies in Practical Philosophy 80 (2003).

5. MARITAL RAPE

The first national survey to attempt to determine the incidence and prevalence of intimate partner rape found that almost 8% of U.S. women had been raped by a partner at some time in their lifetime; independent studies of smaller samples have shown figures as high as 14% of married women.[66]

Traditionally, husbands had an absolute right to intercourse with their wives and wives were presumed to consent. Most legal commentators attribute the marital rape exemption to the seventeenth century jurist Lord Chief Justice Hale who opined that "the husband cannot be guilty of a rape committed by himself upon his lawful wife for by their mutual matrimonial consent and contract the wife hath given up herself in this kind unto her husband, which she cannot retract."[67] However, the philosophical underpinning of the marital rape exemption has been traced to an interpretation of this Biblical passage:

> The husband must give his wife what she has the right to expect, and so too the wife to the husband. The wife has no rights over her own body; it is the husband who has them. In the same way, the husband has no rights over his body; the wife has them. Do not refuse each other except by mutual consent, and then only for an agreed time, to

---

66. 2000 VAW Full Report, above footnote 55, at 25 (reporting the 8% figure); Diana Russell, Rape in Marriage 57 (1982 ed.) (reporting 14% of 644 women surveyed were the victims of at least one completed or attempted rape by their husbands or ex-husbands).

67. Matthew Hale, The History of the Pleas of the Crown (1736), ch. LVIII, at 629.

> leave yourselves free for prayer; then come together again in case Satan should take advantage of your weakness to tempt you.[68]

An understanding that this scripture made marital rape morally impossible eventually found its way into medieval Roman Catholic canon law. From canon law, the marital exemption, like most canonical regulation of sex and marriage, made its way into early English common law and, eventually, our law. The common law, at least by the nineteenth century, gave a different reason for the exemption. The "Christian" reason for the exemption was the marital debt the spouses owed each other: each had all the rights to the other's body.[69] The American version was that the wife was the husband's property; the two were one, and that one was him.

Repeal of Marital Rape Exemptions

By defining rape as intercourse with a woman "not his wife," a majority of states immunized husbands from prosecution by statute as late as 1977; other states simply relied on the common law exemption.[70] Extensive reforms in rape laws that began in the 1970's extended to the repeal, in many states, of the marital rape exemption. In part, this movement was spurred by determinations, by some courts, that the marital rape exemption violated the equal protection clause of the Fourteenth Amendment.[71]

Although no state still maintains a complete marital exemption, there remain legal distinctions in some states between rape inside and outside of marriage.[72] Some states accord a lower level of criminality to marital rapes and/or create procedural hurdles for marital rape prosecutions. For example, a search of statutes in 2010 found that marital rape may still be subject, at least in some states, to prompt complaint rules, corroboration requirements, and reduced penalties.[73]

---

68. 1 Corinthians 7:3–6 (King James Version). Michelle Anderson also notes that "[m]any rape statutes and legal interpretations of rape law have made reference to Deuteronomy, the fifth book of the Torah, for authority. Deuteronomy declared that the rape of a virgin was a civil offense but did not proscribe or punish other kinds of rape." Michelle Anderson, From Chastity Requirement to Sexuality License: Sexual Consent and a New Rape Shield Law, 70 Geo. Wash. L. Rev. 51, 61 (2002).

69. See Mary Becker, Family Law in the Secular State and Restrictions on Same–Sex Marriage: Two Are Better Than One, 2001 U. Ill. L. Rev. 1, 27–30 (2001).

70. Susan Estrich, Real Rape 73 (1988).

71. Robin L. West, Equality Theory, Marital Rape, and the Promise of the Fourteenth Amendment, 42 Fla. L. Rev. 45 (1990); see also People v. Liberta, 474 N.E.2d 567, 573 (N.Y. 1984).

72. Becker, above footnote 69, at 30. See also Victoria F. Nourse, The "Normal" Successes and Failures of Feminism and the Criminal Law, 75 Chi.–Kent L. Rev. 951 (2000).

73. See, e.g., Cal. Penal Code § 262(b) (one-year reporting requirement in marital rape cases, unless victim's allegation is corroborated by independent evidence that would be admissible at trial); S.C. Code Ann. § 16–3–658 (thirty-day reporting requirement for marital rape); Va. Code Ann. §§ 18.2–61(C), 18.2–67.1(C), 18.2–67.2(C) (permitting court, if state prosecutor and victim agree, to place marital rapist on probation pending completion of counseling or therapy; once counseling or therapy is completed, court may discharge rapist and dismiss proceedings if it "finds such action will promote maintenance of the family unit and be in the best interest of the complaining witness").

In short, reform has been difficult and yielded in many cases a rule of "separate but unequal": marital rape is dealt with under one set of rules and "real" rape under another.[74] The 1992 attempt to reform the California marital rape exemption, for example, was never able to eliminate a separate statute for marital rape or to eliminate completely a prompt complaint rule.[75] Why was the procedure so difficult? Victoria Nourse explains:

> * * * Some of the arguments legislators raised in support of separate treatment were the ones already rejected by courts (difficulties of proof, false claims, and the need to maintain marital relationships), but, in the end, the day was carried against reform not by these arguments but by their more veiled counterparts. The district attorneys' association, the criminal defense bar, and the American Civil Liberties Union all opposed various reforms of the marital rape statute and wanted to sustain its "separateness." They did not openly adhere to the discarded norms of yesteryear; instead, they claimed that the inequalities were really "better" for seemingly neutral reasons—better for defendants, better for an already overburdened criminal justice system, and, most interestingly, better for women. The complex, separate, and largely redundant statute—however it symbolized the "difference" of marital rape—made it easier for prosecutors to prosecute, they said. As one prosecutor put it, "the relationship acts as mitigation," making jurors perceive spousal rape as a crime less serious than nonspousal rape. * * *[76]

Even when marital rape is recognized as a crime, husbands are rarely prosecuted and convicted. For example, when South Carolina removed its marital exemption in 1991, one of the first rape cases prosecuted, State v. Crawford, illustrated the difficulty of convincing a jury that a husband can rape his wife. At trial, the wife testified that her husband dragged her by the throat into a bedroom, tied her hands and legs with rope and a belt, put duct tape on her eyes and mouth, and dressed her in stockings and a garter belt. He then had intercourse with her, sexually assaulted her with foreign objects, and threatened her with a knife which he ran around her breast and her stomach. The jury saw this transpire because the husband made a 30–minute videotape of the event. Her muffled screams could hardly be heard through the duct tape. At trial, the wife claimed that her cries were of pain, and that none of these activities were consensual.

When the husband testified, he claimed her cries were of pleasure during the rough sex. His defense was that when his wife said no to sex, he did not think she was serious; he knew she meant yes. He explained that they had engaged in similar sex games in the past, which he had also videotaped. The judge permitted the wife's former husband to testify that she had allowed him to tie her up many times and that she enjoyed

74. See Jill Hasday, Contest and Consent: A Legal History of Marital Rape, 88 Cal. L. Rev. 1373 (2000).

75. Cal. Penal Code § 262(b).

76. Nourse, above footnote 72, at 968–69.

violent, abusive treatment (under the marital rape law in South Carolina, the woman's past sexual history could be admitted in court). However, the judge excluded testimony from the accused's former wife that he had assaulted and raped her, too, during their marriage (the defendant's prior sexual activity was inadmissible).

Additional facts were ascertained at trial: * * * (2) before trial the defendant wrote his wife apologetic letters from prison; (3) the couple had planned to separate the night of the alleged rape; and (4) the defendant did not untie his wife when he left the house so that she had to struggle to get loose before she ran naked to a neighbor's house for help.

It took the eight-woman and four-man jury less than an hour to find the husband not guilty after a two-day trial. Jurors said there was not enough evidence to convict. The victim's response to the verdict was: "If it had been a stranger doing that to me, the whole community would have been in an uproar, a lynching party. But because it was my husband, it was OK."[77]

NOTES ON CRAWFORD AND MARITAL RAPE

1. Diana Russell concludes in her study of rape in marriage that "the social characteristics of husband-rapists may differ greatly from men who rape women other than their wives." Diana Russell, Rape in Marriage 131 (1990). What could explain this difference? What is it about marriage that encourages men who would not otherwise rape to rape their wives? Do you think the passage from Corinthians, quoted in the text note above, continues to affect the attitudes of those who believe a man cannot rape his wife?

2. Some students of marital rape assert that the interpersonal coercion husbands apply to their wives in order to obtain sex can be "humiliating, psychologically debilitating, and shattering to her sense of self-confidence and self-esteem." David Finklehor & Kersti Yllo, License to Rape: Sexual Abuse of Wives 87 (1985). Thus, in addition to the physical invasion, wives suffer in many more ways when raped by their husbands than if they were raped by a stranger. Because of these additional injuries, should marital rape be treated more harshly than stranger rape? How do you explain the fact that marital rape is not only treated less harshly, but until relatively recently was not even considered a crime?

3. In some cases, as we have seen, marital rape may be part of ongoing domestic violence. Some have argued that because battered women live under extreme oppression, they do not even recognize the coercion their husbands apply to obtain sex. Can the law remedy this situation? See Chapter 6, discussing power between husband and wife in marriage. If women, as

---

77. Facts about the *Crawford* case were compiled from: NBC Dateline, June 2, 1992 (separate interviews of Mr. and Mrs. Crawford); Larry King Live, A Controversy Over Marital Rape, CNN, May 15, 1992, Tr. #562–1 (interview with Mr. Crawford and his defense attorney); Sonya Live, Spousal Rape Laws, CNN, July 31, 1992, Tr. #105 (interview with Mrs. Crawford); Linda Goldston, California Moves to Strengthen Law for Prosecuting Spouse Rape, Houston Chronicle, Aug. 2, 1992, § A, at 13; Carolyn Pesce, Marital Rape: Verdict, USA Today, Apr. 21, 1992, § News, at 3A.

caretakers, had strong economic rights at divorce, would they say "no" to sex more often in marriage? Can you think of other ways to alter the power balance in bargaining about sex in marriage?

4. Why do you think the jury acquitted the husband in the *Crawford* case? Might showing the jury the videotape in the South Carolina case have hurt the prosecution? Why? What do we think of women when we see pictures of them naked, exposed, and being sexually used by a man? Would further changes in the South Carolina rape law have made a difference in this case? If not, what would change the outcome?

5. Early reforms aimed to protect rape victims by "shielding" the jury from evidence about their prior sexual conduct. Today, in almost every state, evidence of a victim's behavior or sexual predisposition is generally inadmissible under evidentiary rules known as "rape shield laws." See Fed. R. Evid. 412 (the federal rape shield law). These rules represent a "legislative presumption that the probative value of evidence of a complainant's prior sexual history is substantially outweighed by its potential prejudicial effect." Richard Bialczak & Dorothy Wong, Fourth Annual Review of Gender and Sexuality Law: Violence Law Chapter: Evidentiary Matters in Sexual Offense Cases, 4 Geo. J. Gender & L. 525, 539 (2002). Rape shield laws respond to the tendency of juries to acquit when a victim's sexual history is admitted in evidence, either because her testimony is discounted, or because she is viewed as unworthy of the law's protection. See Aviva Orenstein, No Bad Men! A Feminist Analysis of Character Evidence in Rape Trails, 49 Hastings L.J. 663, 684–85 (1998). These effects may be particularly pronounced where the victim is a woman of color. See Dorothy Roberts, Rape, Violence, and Women's Autonomy, 69 Chi.–Kent L. Rev. 359 (1993). Rape shield rules also seek to remove barriers to reporting rape by limiting the ability of defense counsel to cross-examine women about past sexual conduct. These laws are not absolute, however. See Fed. R. Evid. 412 (b)(1)(a)–(c). Exceptions to the general rule of exclusion are often a highly contested aspect of a rape trial. When is it appropriate for juries to learn about a woman's prior sexual conduct, with the defendant or with others? Do you think that the court in *Crawford* was right to admit Mrs. Crawford's prior history while refusing to admit testimony that Mr. Crawford had raped a former wife?

6. Traditionally, evidence law has viewed with grave suspicion the introduction of evidence of the defendant's "prior bad acts." The theory is that the jury is much more likely to convict the defendant because of his bad "character" rather than for his acts on the particular occasion charged. Some sexual offenders, including "date rapists," repeat their offenses, and rape cases typically involve unique credibility problems. To respond to this, in 1994, Congress passed new rules permitting evidence of the defendant's prior sexual misconduct to be admitted at trial. Fed. R. Evid. 413. What would have been the effect of Rule 413 in the *Crawford* prosecution? Would it have required the court to permit introduction of testimony that the defendant had raped his former wife? Many have been critical of Rule 413 on the theory that it undermines classic presumptions in favor of criminal defendants. Can you think of any other reasons that feminists might be concerned about this rule? See Orenstein, above note 5; Christina E. Wells & Erin Elliot Motley,

Reinforcing the Myth of the Crazed Rapist: A Feminist Critique of Recent Rape Legislation, 81 B.U. L. Rev. 127 (2001).

7. Would you favor a law that prohibits the media from disclosing the names of rape victims? According to the National Women's Study, 78% of rape victims and 76% of all American women surveyed favored such legislation. National Victim Center and Crime Victims Research and Treatment Center, Rape in America: A Report to the Nation 9 (Apr. 23, 1992). Over 90% of rape crisis agencies favored such laws. Id. at 11. See Deborah W. Denno, Perspectives on Disclosing Rape Victims' Names, 61 Fordham L. Rev. 1113 (1993). Would you be more likely to report a rape if you knew your name would not be published in the paper?

8. After traditional common law justifications for the marital rape exemption were rejected, new arguments sprouted up to protect husbands from criminal liability for raping their wives. For instance, in one case, in which a husband was convicted of criminal sexual assault after ramming his fist with an egg into his wife's vagina, an Illinois appellate court considered arguments that the government should not intrude into marital privacy and should promote reconciliation between spouses. People v. M.D., 595 N.E.2d 702 (Ill.App.Ct. 1992). Citing Griswold v. Connecticut, 381 U.S. 479, 85 S.Ct. 1678, 14 L.Ed.2d 510 (1965), the court, while acknowledging rights of married persons, nonetheless refused to extend the marital privacy right to nonconsensual marital relations. In doing so, the court stated that "a sexual assault perpetrated by one spouse upon the other also has a maximum destructive impact upon the marital relationship." 595 N.E.2d at 711. Recent developments in the law of liberty, see Lawrence v. Texas, 539 U.S. 558 (2003), may have created yet another round of such challenges, which have thus far proven unsuccessful. See, e.g., Muth v. Frank, 412 F.3d 808 (7th Cir. 2005) (defendant argued that incest is within constitutional protection of Lawrence); Brady v. Collins, 2010 WL 1741113 (N.D.Ohio 2010) (defendant argued that Lawrence extended constitutional protection to sex between step-parent and adult step-daughter not biologically related); State v. Van, 688 N.W.2d 600 (Neb. 2004) (defendant argued that Lawrence protected his right to engage in a nonconsensual S & M beating of a sexual partner). Can you envision other ways in which the right of privacy and/or liberty might be used to insulate men from criminal liability for acts of violence in the family?

6. RAPE TRAUMA SYNDROME AND THE EFFECTS OF SEXUAL ASSAULT

The National Institute of Mental Health has recognized that "[v]iolence poses a particular threat for women and significantly contributes to serious negative mental health consequences."[78] The consequences of both physical and sexual abuse include depression, anxiety, impaired self-esteem, post-traumatic stress disorder, and substance abuse. Does the law take this into account in the prosecution of sexual assault? Could evidentiary and other rules be developed to ameliorate these effects in the courtroom?

---

78. Women's Mental Health: Agenda for Research 11 (Anita Eichler & Delores L. Parron, eds. 1987). See also World Health Organization Report on Violence and Health 5 (2002).

A growing number of courts and legislatures have recognized that not all victims react to rape in ways that a jury readily understands. Acknowledging that actual victim responses contradict many of the commonly held misconceptions about rape, these jurisdictions allow introduction of expert testimony about Rape Trauma Syndrome (RTS). The term RTS comes from a study of 92 adult, heterogeneous female rape victims conducted by Ann Wolbert Burgess and Lynda Lytle Holmstrom.[79] They found that the rape victims they studied had a two-stage reaction to the sexual assault, with behavioral, somatic, and psychological responses at each stage. Despite concerns about the reliability of the 1970's studies, subsequent research has established that "rape victims experience more depression, anxiety, fear and social adjustment and sexual problems than women who have not been victimized."[80] That research has also shown that many rape victims experience post-traumatic stress syndrome following an assault.[81] The first excerpt below further describes what psychologists have learned about victims' response to rape. In the second, the author questions whether the focus on the victims' psychology—including rape trauma syndrome—results in the labeling of victims as "sick" and removes the issue of rape from the political sphere. In the notes that follow, we invite you to explore the question whether psychological evidence mitigates or aggravates the social problems of violence against women.

KATHRYN M. DAVIS, RAPE, RESURRECTION, AND THE QUEST FOR TRUTH: THE LAW AND SCIENCE OF RAPE TRAUMA SYNDROME IN CONSTITUTIONAL BALANCE WITH THE RIGHTS OF THE ACCUSED

49 Hastings L.J. 1511, 1516–1520 (1998).

RTS was first coined in 1974 by two psychologists to describe a two-phase model of recovery exhibited by survivors of rape. Working at a Boston hospital emergency room, Ann Burgess and Lynda Holmstrom conducted a year-long study of the physical, behavioral, and psychological responses typically displayed by women seeking treatment for rape or an attempted rape. Burgess and Holmstrom concluded that the women they examined characteristically exhibited a two-phase response to traumatic rape. According to the Burgess/Holmstrom model, a woman suffering from rape trauma syndrome initially experiences the "acute phase." This first stage of recovery occurs in the immediate hours following the attack and consists of at least two different stress reactions. According to the model, approximately half of all women victimized by rape exhibit an "expressive style" response, which is characterized by overtly emotional behavior. Women in this group may experience a range of post-rape behavioral responses including crying, sobbing, feelings of anxiety, and what may be

---

79. Ann Wolbert Burgess & Lynda Lytle Holmstrom, Rape Trauma Syndrome, 131 Am. J. Psychiatry 981, 982 (1974).

80. Patricia A. Frazier & Eugene Borgida, Rape Trauma Syndrome: A Review of Case Law and Psychological Research, 16 Law & Hum. Behav. 293, 301 (1992).

81. Id.

perceived to be "inappropriate" smiling. In contrast, other women may exhibit none of these symptoms at all, suggesting that no rape has occurred. This group exhibits a "controlled style" and is subdued, calm, and non-emotional. Physical symptoms characteristic of this first "acute phase" include soreness, bruising, headaches, sleeplessness, fatigue and genitourinary disturbance.

The second phase of recovery, called the "long-term reorganization" process, was experienced by all victims in the Burgess/Holmstrom sample and is characterized by nightmares, phobic reactions, and sexual fears. Rape survivors in this stage can manifest symptoms at various points throughout their recovery; some may not become symptomatic for months or even years after the rape Moreover, a woman could continue to exhibit symptoms that can persist for decades, and throughout her lifetime.

Since the groundbreaking Burgess/Holmstrom study, researchers have extensively documented commonly observed symptoms associated with rape trauma syndrome. While the Burgess/Holmstrom inquiry focused on describing stages of recovery, more recent research has conceptualized RTS as a range of specific symptoms characterizing a woman's physical and emotional response to forcible rape, rather than a syndrome. According to this model, women suffering from RTS may experience depression, anxiety, guilt, nightmares, fear of men, fear of indoors or outdoors (correlating to the type of environment where the rape occurred), flashbacks, and constant reliving of the traumatic event. Other indicia include withdrawal, decreased sexual desire, change in eating and sleeping habits, unease at work, and hypervigilance. Studies comparing women who have been forcibly raped with those in the general population reveal that rape victims experience these symptoms with much greater frequency than do nonvictims and victims of other traumatic events.

In addition to the two variations of RTS described above, rape is a traumatic event that can lead to the development of posttraumatic stress disorder (PTSD). PTSD was initially recognized by psychologists working with veterans of the Vietnam War and was officially defined by the American Psychiatric Association in 1980. Like other modern conceptualizations of RTS, the fourth edition of the American Psychiatric Association's Diagnostic and Statistical Manual of Mental Disorders (DSM–IV) characterizes rape-related PTSD as an identifiable set of stress-induced symptoms. However, unlike the traditional embodiment of RTS, which is premised on traumatic rape, several nonraperelated traumatic events can precipitate the onset of PTSD. Consequently, while RTS is often described as a particular type of PTSD, it is more accurate to refer to rape as a traumatic event that can result in the development of PTSD, rather than to classify RTS as a subcategory of PTSD.

According to the DSM–IV, the essential feature of PTSD is the development of characteristic symptoms resulting from exposure to an extreme traumatic stressor involving actual or threatened death or serious injury. Specifically, to be diagnosed as suffering from rape-related PTSD, the rape victim must exhibit four post-rape behavioral stress responses. First, as a general matter, the precipitating traumatic event causing the stress must be of sufficient magnitude to evoke "intense fear, helplessness, or horror" in the victim. Second, the rape victim must reexperience her trauma through flashbacks or recurrent and intrusive recollection of the rape. Dreams and nightmares are common. In particular, a survivor of rape may experience nonmastery dreams in which she is unable to successfully overpower her assailant. Third, she must present at least three avoidance and numbing symptoms. Symptoms may include avoiding activities that arouse recollection, avoiding thoughts or feelings about the trauma, numbing of responsiveness to the environment, reducing involvement with her environment, or feeling detached from others.

In order for post-rape behavior to meet the PTSD diagnostic criteria, two of the following increased arousal symptoms must be present that were not present prior to the rape: (1) difficulty falling or staying asleep; (2) irritability or outbursts of anger; (3) difficulty concentrating; (4) hypervigilance; and (5) exaggerated startle response. Although symptom duration is often not assessed in research studies, the above symptoms must be present for at least one month to qualify for a diagnosis of rape-related PTSD. And, while symptoms generally dissipate over time, they can persist for years after the victim experiences the initial trauma. Finally, the rape must have caused significant distress or impairment in social, occupational, or other important areas of a woman's functioning.

To summarize, the designation of RTS is used to refer not only to the original Burgess/Holmstrom model of recovery, but also to general post-rape behavioral responses, and the more specific symptomology associated with a diagnosis of rape-related PTSD.

SUSAN STEFAN, THE PROTECTION RACKET: RAPE TRAUMA SYNDROME, PSYCHIATRIC LABELING, AND LAW

88 Nw. U.L. Rev. 1271, 1273–76 (1994).

* * * By the late 1980s, women who acknowledged being raped were being given psychiatric diagnoses, their reactions to rape turned into pathologies and syndromes requiring treatment at the hands of professionals. The creation of these syndromes depoliticized the issue of rape by shifting attention from the prevalence of violence against women to women's reaction to violence. Contrary to popular image, far from validating women's pain, these syndromes delegitimized women's reactions to rape, isolated women as individual subjects of treatment, and turned their coping mechanisms into symptoms of disorder. Women who installed locks and purchased security devices, took self-defense classes, carried mace, changed residence, expressed anger at the criminal justice system, and "viewed the implications of being raped as extending far beyond the immediate physical and emotional trauma" were characterized as exhibiting pathological symptoms and "adjustment difficulties." By characteriz-

ing the reactions of women who had been raped as aberrational, these theories relegated each woman's experience to the realm of aberration.

Yet rape and violence, especially repeated secret sexual abuse by fathers, boyfriends, or husbands, may in fact make some women crazy. Most women do not report being raped, and they pay varying prices for their silence. An enormous proportion of women in mental institutions have suffered from sexual abuse and violence. And when women who have been raped and sexually abused are institutionalized, the "treatment" they receive fails to address the connection between past sexual abuse and present behavior such as anorexia, self-mutilation, severe depression, and attempts at suicide. Instead, institutional conditions and treatment replicate and exacerbate the pain of the original assaults and abuse, often leaving women patients in a condition that fulfills the prophecy of their pathology.

Thus, on one hand, rape trauma syndrome labels women's rational attempts to struggle through and survive the pain of sexual assault and to adapt to a violent world as symptoms of a disorder from which they should recover. On the other hand, when rape has actually caused craziness and emotional disintegration, the connection between sexual violence inflicted on women and their symptoms is erased and the treatment they receive often discourages recovery. In both instances, women are ultimately disempowered: their own accounts of their experiences are discredited or unheard, their anger is labeled inappropriate, and the status quo is preserved and solidified.

This ironic inverse is replicated in the legal system. Many courts have readily admitted rape trauma syndrome testimony in rape trials. Focusing on rape trauma syndrome in a criminal trial shifts attention from the defendant's actions to the victim's reactions. The use of rape trauma syndrome to explain "counterintuitive" reactions—such as a woman's delay in reporting rape—in terms of her pathology, precludes explaining these reactions as sensible behavior in the context of endemic male violence against women. The use of rape trauma syndrome evidence also threatens to reintroduce the parade of horribles women worked so hard to eliminate for the last twenty years: psychiatric examination of the rape victim, defendants' access to the woman's medical and psychiatric records, admission of evidence of the victim's past sexual behavior, and even corroboration requirements. It is understandable that prosecutors use rape trauma syndrome evidence in court because it may increase the chance of conviction, but its use is no feminist victory.

The mental health system's failure to connect sexual violence and the treatment of institutionalized women has been mirrored, rather than critiqued, by lawyers involved in civil rights cases on behalf of institutionalized persons. Although a long history of rape and sexual abuse may be relevant to forced medication, seclusion and restraint, and adequate treatment, no case dealing with these issues has ever addressed rape and sexual abuse.

* * *[T]he mental health profession and legal doctrine interact to construct an image of sexually abused women in research and law. This image distorts the reality of women's experience. While research on women's reactions to rape and prosecutors' use of rape trauma syndrome has been conducted in good faith to try to validate women's pain and to convict rapists, its consequences for women, both individually and collectively, are far reaching and negative.

The medicalization of women's reactions to male violence has explicitly supported social assumptions that such violence is aberrational and has served to obscure the fact that violence against women is the norm in this society. Women who report being raped are encouraged to think of the pain they suffer as their own problem, rather than to examine the social context which helps to create the pain and exacerbates it. This pain is then defined by "experts" as the problem to be overcome, and the goal is each woman's "readjustment" and "recovery" from rape.

The literature and the law on rape trauma syndrome construct rape survivors as passive, disordered victims. Yet much of the behavior that serves as the basis for labels of disorder is the product of strength, struggle, and survival. The reasons that women behave the way they do become obscured in research literature, where a woman's anger means that her symptoms remain unresolved, or in a courtroom, where only her pathology is admissible.

Some women's anger simply results in forced medication or restraint. Both research and law emphatically divide sexually violated women into previously "normal" women who have been raped and now suffer from rape trauma syndrome, from which they can recover with appropriate treatment, and "others," who are not studied, whose rapists are not prosecuted, and whose actions are never connected with sexual abuse. They are given neither therapeutic nor legal remedy for their pain. Neither researchers nor rape scholars take note of women in institutions, who are far more likely to have been raped and to continue being raped, than the women who exhibit "symptoms" like changing jobs, moving, and taking self-defense courses.

* * * Sexual assault is commonplace and * * * women's fear of it is rational, and yet * * * powerful social forces prevent this reality from being articulated. The silencing of this reality makes women who act in response to it look crazy. Some women who remain silent while enduring continual sexual assault actually do become crazy. * * * [T]he evidence [shows that there is a] * * * staggeringly high percentage of institutionalized women who have been assaulted or sexually abused * * *.

NOTES ON PSYCHOLOGY AND RAPE

1. What is your reaction to what Susan Stefan refers to as the "medicalization of women's reactions to trauma?" Does a diagnosis of RTS help or hurt a rape victim? What are the implications (social and legal) for a rape

victim who is not given this diagnosis? How does your response to RTS compare to your evaluation of BWS? Is science being used in similar ways to characterize women who are battered and women who are raped? Are you concerned with the pathologizing effects of a psychiatric diagnosis? Why or why not? Do your answers to these questions impact your assessment of whether women who are raped should be viewed as victims or as agents?

2. Should one worry, like Stefan, about using "science" as a means to transform rape law? The eminent anthropologist Mary Douglas has argued that every society, including modern technological societies, imports within its ideas of "nature" its most important social commitments. Mary Douglas, Natural Symbols: Explorations in Cosmology 74 (1996 ed.); see also generally Douglas, Purity and Danger (1966). If this is right, then, one can predict, contrary to what one might assume, that scientific solutions will not be as stable or enduring as might be expected. Indeed, if the claims of science are likely to mirror culture, then cultural conflict will find its way into science. We saw this in the context of battered woman syndrome. Consider in this light the treatment of rape trauma syndrome described in the following notes. Do these developments confirm or refute Douglas's prediction?

3. Very soon after courts began to admit expert evidence on behalf of rape victims, defense attorneys sought to appropriate it to aid defendants, using RTS expert testimony to show that the victim's behavior was *inconsistent* with that of a rape victim suffering from RTS. See Henson v. State, 535 N.E.2d 1189, 1192–93 (Ind. 1989). Can you anticipate other problems that may arise from the admission of expert testimony on RTS? Should a defendant be entitled to have his psychiatric expert examine the complaining witness if the prosecutor intends to present evidence from an examining expert that the victim of a sexual assault suffers from RTS? See People v. Wheeler, 602 N.E.2d 826, 833 (Ill. 1992) ("[W]here the victim exercises his or her right to refuse an examination, the State may not introduce evidence of rape trauma syndrome through the testimony of an examining expert"). For an overview of these problems, see Davis excerpt above.

4. After early controversy about its reliability, RTS came to be easily accepted in courts. See, e.g., Patricia A. Frazier & Eugene Borgida, Rape Trauma Syndrome: A Review of Case Law and Psychological Research, 16 Law & Hum. Behav. 293, 299–303 (1992); People v. Bledsoe, 681 P.2d 291 (Cal. 1984) (one of the early cases admitting the evidence for limited purposes). More recently, however, controversy about RTS has reemerged in a new form—the definition of "scientific" evidence. In 1993, the Supreme Court overruled 70 years of evidentiary law and created new standards for assessing the admissibility of scientific evidence. Daubert v. Merrell Dow Pharmaceuticals, 509 U.S. 579, 113 S.Ct. 2786, 125 L.Ed.2d 469 (1993). One of the criteria for admission of evidence after *Daubert* is scientific reliability, which in turn is defined by falsifiability, error rates, and peer review. These standards now apply not only to what we might call "hard science" (such as physics), but also social scientific evidence as well.

Evidentiary experts have questioned whether syndrome evidence can possibly meet *Daubert*'s standards. For example, in a journal published in 2005 by the American Psychological Association, a team of psychologists reported that "the derivation of some syndromes and profiles appears political in nature" and that their scientific basis is "questionable." See Veronica B. Dahir, James T. Richardson, Gerald P. Ginsburg, Sophia I. Gatowski, Shirley A. Dobbin & Mara L. Merlino 11 Psych. Pub. Pol'y & L. 62, 63 (2005) (discussing a broad array of syndrome evidence including RTS and battered woman syndrome). At the same time, they found that state court judges have tended to ignore *Daubert* and continued to accept syndrome testimony. Id. at 77. Was it error for women to rely upon RTS, not because it suggested they were "ill," but because relying on social science may be too weak a foundation for their claims? What happens if the science changes? One of the principal bases on which RTS has been admitted into evidence is not to prove that a rape occurred, but to rebut myths and misconceptions (such as the failure to provide a "prompt complaint")? What if the myths and misconceptions change?

5. The medical mislabeling of violence against women, as Stefan indicates, has a long history. Consider, in this light, the case of Carrie Buck, the object of one of the twentieth century's most infamous constitutional cases, Buck v. Bell, 274 U.S. 200 (1927). In an opinion by Justice Holmes, the Supreme Court upheld sterilization of asylum inmates on the theory that "three generations of imbeciles" were enough. Id. at 207. Decades later, Stephen Jay Gould discovered that Carrie Buck was not "feebleminded" and that there were no "three generations of imbeciles." Carrie was sent to the asylum because she was an unwed mother. In fact, Carrie was raped by one of her relatives. See Paul A. Lombardo, Three Generations, No Imbeciles: New Light on Buck v. Bell, 60 N.Y.U. L. Rev. 30, 54 (1985). Although the extent of the practice is never likely to be known, we do know that, during the 1920's and 1930's, those we would today term "bad girls" (girls who were believed to have violated sexual or social norms whether by their choice or not) were regularly sent to asylums, diagnosed as mentally retarded or insane, and then sterilized. See Victoria F. Nourse, In Reckless Hands: Skinner v. Oklahoma and the Near–Triumph of American Eugenics (2008). Why do you think that "bad girls"—girls who violated gender norms—were considered "mad girls"? Why were they "punished" by losing their reproductive capacities? Sterilization was sometimes referred to at the time as "legal lynching." Was the injury inflicted—sterilization—a symbol, like the castration which often accompanied lynching, of the utter powerlessness of its victims?

7. WHY MEN RAPE

TEXT NOTE: WHY MEN RAPE

One of the persistent questions raised by feminist critiques of rape law is whether rape is motivated by sex or by power. Dominance feminists have often emphasized the terroristic qualities of rape, how it influences the behavior of all women by the fear that it engenders. Andrea Dworkin has likened rape to torture and tyranny: "you can't have equality or tenderness or intimacy as long as there is rape, because rape means terror. It means that part of the population lives in a state of terror and pretends—to please and pacify you—that it doesn't."[82]

Critics insist that the equation of rape with power, rather than sex, is exaggerated and unhelpful. Some scholars of law and history suggest that rape is as much targeted at honor among men as it is at the subordination of women. Scholars from other disciplines emphasize the sexual nature of rape. Evolutionary psychologists, for example, posit that rape is biologically determined and sexually driven. Still others assert that the problem cannot be solved as stated, that sex and power are linked in ways that makes the very question unhelpful. In a world in which women are persistently devalued and subordinated, it may not be possible for women (or men) to tell the difference between power and sex. And, finally, some researchers, particularly criminologists, conclude that the question is irrelevant since rapists are "just like" other criminals.

In the notes that follow, we invite you to explore this multifaceted debate. Consider whether the question of why men rape can be answered in ways that avoid "essentializing" the rapist. Would typologies like those that have emerged to explain why men batter be useful in this context, as well? Are men who rape their wives different from men who rape their acquaintances; and are men who rape strangers different from men who know their victims? If so, how are these differences important to understanding rape? Will an emphasis on difference tend to obscure the ways in which rape is the same across contexts? Are there ways to negotiate these tensions? In general, how can an accurate understanding of why men rape advance an agenda for social and legal reform?

NOTES ON MEN AND RAPE

1. Is rape a question of honor among men or power over women? Historians have begun to unearth evidence that early American ideals of rape were largely male-male matters and that the "dominant trend in the public presentation of rape was the displacement of women from the narrative, making rape an occasion for men to speak to other men about a range of male prerogatives." Sharon Block, Rape Without Women: Print Culture and the Politicization of Rape, 1765–1815, 89 J. Am. Hist. 849, 850 (2002).

Consider in this light, the modern claim of Katharine K. Baker, who argues that many young male date rapists seek sex for the sake of impressing other men, not because their primary motive is to harm women:

> Date rapists rape to gain, or at least not lose, the esteem of others. Demonstrating one's masculinity, "being a man," is the abstract, internalized norm that gives meaning to the act of having sex. * * * [F]or many men in contemporary social settings, particularly men in overwhelmingly young male environments, to have sex, consensual or not, is to prove one's masculinity.
>
> * * *
>
> The man who remains a virgin or does not join his gang's "train" or frequently goes home alone when everyone else "scores" is somehow seen

82. See Catharine A. MacKinnon, Sex Equality 871 (2001) (quoting Dworkin).

> as a "wimp." He is not proving himself to be a man. * * * In a world in which the masculine is given more esteem than the feminine, men are likely to have more need to prove their gender, lest they be mistaken for someone less worthy of esteem or power. Such male insecurity about gender will be at its greatest in highly competitive environments in which one's masculinity is subject to challenge. Not surprisingly, this is precisely the kind of environment in which we find date rapists. They belong to all male groups that make a point of competing with each other and demonstrating their masculinity * * * [I]t is a sense of relative inferiority—a desire to prove themselves to their male peers—that drives date rapists to have such a desire for sex.

Katherine K. Baker, Sex, Rape and Shame, 79 B.U. L. Rev. 663, 673–77 (1999). Does the "disappearance" of women from the rape narrative aggravate or mitigate male responsibility for rape? Is a focus on contemporary masculine culture a helpful way of understanding rape? How is it similar to, and how is it different from, Wayne Ewing's critique of the "civic advocacy of violence," above Section C?

2. Andrew Taslitz theorizes that "date rapists" engage in "self-deception," a phenomenon which implicates both psychological processes and—as Katharine Baker discusses above—cultural forces. Taslitz explains:

> Much research suggests that most date rapists view their actions instrumentally, that is, as ways to obtain sex rather than to express hostility or to degrade another human being. * * * [T]hese men are aware that they are using force, the necessity of their doing so arising from their observations of signs of the woman's resistance, but at least some of them dismiss from their conscious minds any worry that they woman is not consenting. They prefer to presume consent or ignore it in their narrow quest for one thing: the esteem they derive from frequent sex.

Andrew E. Taslitz, Willfully Blinded: On Date Rape and Self–Deception, 28 Harv. J.L. & Gender 381, 408–10 (2005). Do you believe that this is an accurate explanation for "date rape?" If so, what are the implications for criminal law? Are men who engage in self-deception morally culpable actors? Can they be reformed? Should they be punished? Are your answers influenced by the fact that most men—even those embedded in cultures of masculinity—do not rape?

3. Are rapists invariably sexists? If so, does this mean that they are necessarily hostile to women? Psychological research on the nature of sexism posits a more complex model than one based simply on hostility. Psychologists have identified an ambivalent sexism which may mask sexism in positive feelings. Sexist attitudes may take the form, not simply of a unitary hostility to women, but of subjectively positive feelings that are based on sexist stereotypes. These researchers have focused on putatively "benevolent" sexism in which individuals believe that women are pure and special and should be protected, but which carries with it the idea that women must behave in ways that deserve protection. According to these studies, it is benevolent sexism, not hostile sexism or even rape myth acceptance, that best predicts attitudes toward acquaintance rape. Persons high in benevolent sexism were quick to blame the victim in acquaintance rape situations (presumably be-

cause the victim violated appropriate gender norms) but were unlikely to be rapists themselves; those high in hostile sexism were those more likely to actually engage in rape behavior. Dominic Abrams, G. Tendayi Viki, Gerd Bohner & Barbara Masser, Perceptions of Stranger and Acquaintance Rape: The Role of Benevolent and Hostile Sexism in Victim Blame and Rape Proclivity, 84 J. Personality & Soc. Psych. 111, 121–122 (2003); see also G. Tendayi Viki, Dominic Abrams & Barbara Masser, Evaluating Stranger and Acquaintance Rape: The Role of Benevolent Sexism in Perpetrator Blame and Recommended Sentence Length, 28 Law & Hum. Behavior 295 (2004); Peter Glick, et al., Beyond Prejudice As Simple Antipathy: Hostile and Benevolent Sexism Across Cultures, 79 J. Personality & Soc. Psych. 763 (2000). Does this research help explain why acquaintance rape is so difficult to eradicate? Why so much attention is paid to victim "provocation"? Why it is not enough to focus on men who show overt hostility toward women? What does this say about the Supreme Court's insistence that "animus" or "intent" must be shown to establish sex discrimination?

4. Reconsider the case of Morrison v. United States, which, as described above in Section C, struck down VAWA's civil rights remedy. The facts are recounted most fully by the Fourth Circuit opinion:

> Christy Brzonkala entered Virginia Polytechnic Institute ("Virginia Tech") as a freshman in the fall of 1994. On the evening of September 21, 1994, Brzonkala and another female student met two men who Brzonkala knew only by their first names and their status as members of the Virginia Tech football team. Within thirty minutes of first meeting Brzonkala, these two men, later identified as Antonio Morrison and James Crawford, raped her.
>
> Brzonkala and her friend met Morrison and Crawford on the third floor of the dormitory where Brzonkala lived. All four students talked for approximately fifteen minutes in a student dormitory room. Brzonkala's friend and Crawford then left the room.
>
> Morrison immediately asked Brzonkala if she would have sexual intercourse with him. She twice told Morrison "no," but Morrison was not deterred. As Brzonkala got up to leave the room Morrison grabbed her, and threw her, face-up, on a bed. He pushed her down by the shoulders and disrobed her. Morrison turned off the lights, used his arms to pin down her elbows and pressed his knees against her legs. Brzonkala struggled and attempted to push Morrison off, but to no avail. Without using a condom, Morrison forcibly raped her.
>
> Before Brzonkala could recover, Crawford came into the room and exchanged places with Morrison. Crawford also raped Brzonkala by holding down her arms and using his knees to pin her legs open. He, too, used no condom. When Crawford was finished, Morrison raped her for a third time, again holding her down and again without a condom.
>
> When Morrison had finished with Brzonkala, he warned her "You better not have any fucking diseases." In the months following the rape, Morrison announced publicly in the dormitory's dining room that he "like[d] to get girls drunk and fuck the shit out of them."

Brzonkala v. Virginia Polytechnic Institute and State University, 132 F.3d 949, 953 (4th Cir. 1997). For a detailed account of Morrison and efforts to enact and defend VAWA, see Fred Strebreigh, Equal: Women Reshape American Law 309–448 (2009).

Had Brzonkala been allowed to go forward with her claim, do you think she would have been able to prove that her rape was "motivated by gender," defined "as based, in part, on animus toward gender?" The Fourth Circuit concluded that "[v]irtually all of the earmarks of 'hate crimes' are asserted here: an unprovoked, severe attack, triggered by no other motive, and accompanied by language clearly stating bias." 132 F.3d at 964. Is this reasoning sound? Again, assuming the VAWA claim had been permitted, how would the civil suit have likely been defended? Does the Morrison case provide insight into why men rape? Into the underlying causes and effects of rape? As Michelle Anderson notes,

> [a]fter being raped, Brzonkala dropped out of school, suffered from depression and attempted suicide. * * * Brzonkala received no legal or quasi-legal vindication against her rapists. She lodged a complaint under Virginia Tech's Sexual Assault Policy. Two university hearings ended with no conviction for Crawford and a conviction of 'using abusive language' for Morrison. The punishment imposed on Morrison was a one-hour educational session.

Id. at 955. What lessons can be drawn from this case?

5. Is the dichotomy between sex and violence false? There is a good deal of evidence in the social science literature that sex and power are disproportionately linked in the eyes of men but not women. See Eileen L. Zurbriggen, Social Motives and Cognitive Power–Sex Associations: Predictors of Aggressive Sexual Behavior, 78 J. Personality & Soc. Psych. 559 (2000). In one study, in three different countries (England, Germany, and Zimbabwe), researchers asked participants whether certain rape scenarios made the respondents more aroused (a measure of sexuality), whether they would repeat the behavior (a measure of proclivity), and how much they enjoyed "getting their way" (a measure of dominance). Patrick Chiroro, Gerd Bohner, G. Tendayi Viki & Christopher I. Jarvis, Rape Myth Acceptance and Rape Proclivity: Expected Dominance Versus Expected Arousal as Mediators in Acquaintance–Rape Situations, 19 J. Interpersonal Violence 427, 431 (2004). The result of this cross-cultural study was that dominance was significantly related to rape proclivity, and that "anticipated enjoyment of sexual dominance mediates the relationship between [rape myth acceptance] and [rape proclivity], whereas anticipated sexual arousal does not." Id. at 436. The authors concluded that this supported "the feminist argument that rape functions as an expression of male dominance over women * * * and provides little backing for evolutionary and other theories that highlight sexual motives for rape." Id. at 436–37. At the same time, the authors note that arousal and dominance were significantly related, showing that for men, "the motives of domination and sexual stimulation may be strongly associated." Id. at 437. What are the implications of this study for feminist debate over whether rape is sex or dominance?

6. The sex/violence dichotomy is further challenged by the notion that, in a world where women are subordinated, it may be very difficult for them to tell when they have been injured. As Robin West points out in the excerpt included in Chapter 3, if an injury is "normal," then it may not be identified as injury. In this light, consider the words of a Mauritanian woman who was born into slavery and was then emancipated:

> Ask her whether she and the girls she grew up with . . . were ever raped, and her features harden in puzzlement. She listens intently as the question is framed and reframed. Finally, she replies matter-of-factly, "Of course they would come in the night when they needed to breed us. Is that what you mean by rape?"

Elinor Burkett, "God Created Me to Be a Slave," N.Y. Times, Oct. 12, 1997, § Magazine, at 56 (quoting Fatma Mint Mamadou), quoted in Catharine A. MacKinnon, Sex Equality 870 (2001). Is it possible to redress an unknown injury? Is rape reform impossible?

7. Some criminologists assert that the choice between sex and power is a false one in a different sense. In a one study, Canadian criminologists found, for example, that approximately 50 percent of adult sex offenders had a history of "nonsexual delinquent behavior, mostly for property crimes." They also noted another longitudinal study showing that 10 percent of their youthful cohorts were responsible for 62 percent of convictions of sexual and physical violence against women. Patrick Lussier, Jean Proulx & Marc Le-Blanc, Criminal Propensity, Deviant Sexual Interests and Criminal Activity of Sexual Aggressors Against Women: A Comparison of Explanatory Models, 43 Criminology 249, 251 (2005). Lussier, et al., argue that rapists are in essence like other criminals and that the best model to explain sexual deviance is the general model that describes chronic offending—lack of self-control. Id. at 269–70. These authors argue that this detracts from the standard view of specialized sexual aggression or hostility toward women. Do you think this supports or detracts from the feminist view? What exactly do you think these authors mean by "self-control"? Recall the discussion of homicide in Section B, in which it was claimed that men who lose their "self-control" should receive a mitigated homicide sentence in adultery-type situations. Does lack of self-control explain or simply rationalize violence? If members of the public saw rapists as "regular criminals," would that help or hurt the fight to stop rape?

8. Is rape biologically driven? Recent entrants into the debate about why men rape are evolutionary biologists and psychologists. According to this perspective:

> Evolutionary explanations of rape focus on the evolved differences in male and female sexuality. * * * However, the mechanisms motivating the actual rape behavior are those involved in male sexual arousal. These mechanisms include beauty detection, desire for impersonal sex, desire for partner variety, visual arousal patterns, and perhaps mechanisms designed to adjust these sexual responses to the specific act of rape. The evolutionary approach to rape sits upon the bedrock theories of sexual selection and parental involvement. These theories explain why human males have this specific set of sexual desires and arousal patterns, and

> not others, and why these desires and patterns often differ so profoundly from the evolved sexual desires and arousal patterns of human females.

Craig T. Palmer, David N. DiBari & Scott A. Wright, "Is It Sex Yet?": Theoretical and Practical Implications of the Debate Over Rapists' Motives, 39 Jurimetrics J. 271, 272–73 (1999). This position has sometimes been interpreted as biologically deterministic, impervious to cultural, social, or individual influences. As a result, many feminists are concerned that the evolutionary explanation will offer a defense to rapists. Evolutionists respond that they are simply describing "how the world is," and that feminists' focus on power and control will not be able to change the world if rape is driven by sex, not power. With which approach do you agree, and why? Notwithstanding abundant scientific critique, evolutionary theories of violence remain popular and persistent. Why might this be so? Recall that in the notes on rape and psychology, we asked whether science inevitably reflected culture, as some anthropologists and historians argue. Is an evolutionary science of violence subject to this critique?

9. In 2010, the Bureau of Justice Statistics issued a groundbreaking study of sexual abuse in juvenile detention facilities nationwide. It found that 12.1 percent, or nearly one in eight, of juveniles had been sexually abused during the preceding year. Allen J. Beck, Paige M. Harrison, & Paul Guerino, U.S. Dep't of Justice, Bureau of Justice Statistics, Sexual Victimization in State and Federal Prisons Reported by Youth, 2008–09, 3 Table 1 (Jan. 2009), available at http://bjs.ojp.usdoj.gov/content/pub/pdf/svjfry09.pdf. Because the survey did not reach the large number of children detained temporarily, its figures—staggering as they are—may represent only a "small fraction" of the problem. Lovisa Stannow & David Kaiser, The Rape of American Prisoners, The New York Review of Books, March 11, 2010. Large-scale studies of rape in adult prisons and jails also report surprisingly high numbers of victims and instances of serial assaults. Allen J. Beck & Paige M. Harrison, Bureau of Justice Statistics, Sexual Victimization in State and Federal Prisons Reported by Inmates, 2007, 7, Table 8 (2008), available at http://www.justdetention.org/pdf/svljri07.pdf. According to one expert reviewing the latest research, "it seems likely, on balance, that the studies underestimate the incidence of prisoner rape. But even taken at face value, they reveal much more systemic abuse than has been generally recognized or admitted." Stannow and Kaiser, Prisoners, above. Overall, research suggests a widespread crisis in jails, prisons and juvenile detention centers—a situation referred to as "one of this country's most widespread human rights problems, and arguably its most neglected." Id.; see also Beck, Harrison and Guerino, above; Beck and Harrison, above; National Prison Rape Elimination Commission, National Prison Rape Elimination Commission Report, (2009), available at http://www.cybercemetery.unt.edu/archive/nprec/20090820155502/http://nprec.us/files/pdfs/NPREC_FinalReport.PDF. How does recognition of the widespread nature of this problem advance our understanding of what motivates rape? Should rape law reform specifically account for prison rape? How would you begin to construct an agenda for social and legal change?

8. STATUTORY RAPE

MICHAEL M. v. SUPERIOR COURT OF SONOMA COUNTY

Supreme Court of the United States, 1981.
450 U.S. 464, 101 S.Ct. 1200, 67 L.Ed.2d 437.

JUSTICE REHNQUIST announced the judgment of the Court and delivered an opinion, in which THE CHIEF JUSTICE, JUSTICE STEWART, and JUSTICE POWELL joined.

The question presented in this case is whether California's "statutory rape" law, § 261.5 of the [California Code] violates the Equal Protection Clause of the Fourteenth Amendment. Section 261.5 defines unlawful sexual intercourse as "an act of sexual intercourse accomplished with a female not the wife of the perpetrator, where the female is under the age of 18 years." The statute thus makes men alone criminally liable for the act of sexual intercourse.

In July 1978, a complaint was filed in the Municipal Court of Sonoma County, Cal., alleging that petitioner, then a 17 1/2–year–old male, had had unlawful sexual intercourse with a female under the age of 18, in violation of § 261.5. The evidence adduced at a preliminary hearing showed that at approximately midnight on June 3, 1978, petitioner and two friends approached Sharon, a 16 1/2–year–old female, and her sister as they waited at a bus stop. Petitioner and Sharon, who had already been drinking, moved away from the others and began to kiss. After being struck in the face for rebuffing petitioner's initial advances, Sharon submitted to sexual intercourse with petitioner. Prior to trial, petitioner sought to set aside the information on both state and federal constitutional grounds, asserting that § 261.5 unlawfully discriminated on the basis of gender. The trial court and the California Court of Appeal denied petitioner's request for relief and [the Supreme Court of California affirmed the denial].

* * *

* * * Our cases have held * * * that the traditional minimum rationality test takes on a somewhat "sharper focus" when gender-based classifications are challenged. * * *

Underlying these decisions is the principle that a legislature may not "make overbroad generalizations based on sex which are entirely unrelated to any differences between men and women or which demean the ability or social status of the affected class." * * * But * * * this Court has consistently upheld statutes where the gender classification is not invidious, but rather realistically reflects the fact that the sexes are not similarly situated in certain circumstances. * * *

Applying those principles to this case, the fact that the California Legislature criminalized the act of illicit sexual intercourse with a minor female is a sure indication of its intent or purpose to discourage that conduct. Precisely why the legislature desired that result is of course somewhat less clear. This Court has long recognized that "[i]nquiries into congressional motives or purposes are a hazardous matter," and the search for the "actual" or "primary" purpose of a statute is likely to be elusive. * * *

The justification for the statute offered by the State * * * is that the legislature sought to prevent illegitimate teenage pregnancies. * * *

We need not be medical doctors to discern that young men and young women are not similarly situated with respect to the problems and the risks of sexual intercourse. Only women may become pregnant, and they suffer disproportionately the profound physical, emotional, and psychological consequences of sexual activity. The statute at issue here protects women from sexual intercourse at an age when those consequences are particularly severe.

The question thus boils down to whether a State may attack the problem of sexual intercourse and teenage pregnancy directly by prohibiting a male from having sexual intercourse with a minor female. We hold that such a statute is sufficiently related to the State's objectives to pass constitutional muster.

Because virtually all of the significant harmful and inescapably identifiable consequences of teenage pregnancy fall on the young female, a legislature acts well within its authority when it elects to punish only the participant who, by nature, suffers few of the consequences of his conduct. It is hardly unreasonable for a legislature acting to protect minor females to exclude them from punishment. Moreover, the risk of pregnancy itself constitutes a substantial deterrence to young females. No similar natural sanctions deter males. A criminal sanction imposed solely on males thus serves to roughly "equalize" the deterrents on the sexes.

We are unable to accept petitioner's contention that the statute is impermissibly underinclusive and must, in order to pass judicial scrutiny, be broadened so as to hold the female as criminally liable as the male. It is argued that this statute is not *necessary* to deter teenage pregnancy because a gender-neutral statute, where both male and female would be subject to prosecution, would serve that goal equally well. The relevant inquiry, however, is not whether the statute is drawn as precisely as it might have been, but whether the line chosen by the California Legislature is within constitutional limitations.

In any event, we cannot say that a gender-neutral statute would be as effective as the statute California has chosen to enact. The State persuasively contends that a gender-neutral statute would frustrate its interest in effective enforcement. Its view is that a female is surely less likely to report violations of the statute if she herself would be subject to criminal prosecution. In an area already fraught with prosecutorial difficulties, we decline to hold that the Equal Protection Clause requires a legislature to enact a statute so broad that it may well be incapable of enforcement.

* * *

In upholding the California statute we also recognize that this is not a case where a statute is being challenged on the grounds that it "invidiously discriminates" against females. To the contrary, the statute places a burden on males which is not shared by females. But we find nothing to suggest that men, because of past discrimination or peculiar disadvantages, are in need of the special solicitude of the courts. * * * As we have held, the statute instead reasonably reflects the fact that the consequences of sexual intercourse and pregnancy fall more heavily on the female than on the male.

Accordingly the judgment of the California Supreme Court is *Affirmed.*

* * *

JUSTICE BLACKMUN, concurring in the judgment.

It is gratifying that the plurality recognizes that "[a]t the risk of stating the obvious, teenage pregnancies ... have increased dramatically over the last two decades" and "have significant social, medical, and economic consequences for both the mother and her child, and the State." There have been times when I have wondered whether the Court was capable of this perception, particularly when it has struggled with the different but not unrelated problems that attend abortion issues.

* * *

I think, too, that it is only fair, with respect to this particular petitioner, to point out that his partner, Sharon, appears not to have been an unwilling participant in at least the initial stages of the intimacies that took place the night of June 3, 1978.* Petitioner's and Sharon's nonac-

* Sharon at the preliminary hearing testified as follows:

"Q. [by the Deputy District Attorney]. * * * Would you briefly describe what happened that night? Did you see the defendant that night in Rohnert Park?" 'A. Yes.' 'Q. Where did you first meet him?' 'A. At a bus stop.' 'Q. Was anyone with you?' 'A. My sister.' 'Q. Was anyone with the defendant?' 'A. Yes.' 'Q. How many people were with the defendant?' 'A. Two.' 'Q. Now, after you met the defendant, what happened?' 'A. We walked down to the railroad tracks.' 'Q. What happened at the railroad tracks?' 'A. We were drinking at the railroad tracks and we walked over to this bush and he started kissing me and stuff, and I was kissing him back, too, at first. Then, I was telling him to stop' 'Q. Yes.' 'A.—and I was telling him to slow down and stop.' He said, 'Okay, okay.' But then he just kept doing it. He just kept doing it * * *. We was laying there and we were kissing each other, and then he asked me if I wanted to walk him over to the park; so we walked over to the park and we sat down on a bench and then he started kissing me again and we were laying on the bench. And he told me to take my pants off. I said, 'No,' and I was trying to get up and he hit me back down on the bench and then I just said to myself, 'Forget it,' and I let him do what he wanted to do and he took my pants off and he was telling me to put my legs around him and stuff—"

* * *

"Q. Did you have sexual intercourse with the defendant?" "A. Yeah." "Q. He did put his penis into your vagina?" "A. Yes." "Q. You said that he hit you?" "A. Yeah." "Q. How did he hit you?" "A. He slugged me in the face." "Q. With what did he slug you?" "A. His fist." "Q. Where abouts

quaintance of with each other before the incident; their drinking; their withdrawal from the others of the group; their foreplay, in which she willingly participated and seems to have encouraged; and the closeness of their ages (a difference of only one year and 18 days) are factors that should make this case an unattractive one to prosecute at all, and especially to prosecute as a felony, rather than as a misdemeanor chargeable under § 261.5. But the State has chosen to prosecute in that manner, and the facts, I reluctantly conclude, may fit the crime.

JUSTICE BRENNAN, with whom JUSTICES WHITE and MARSHALL join, dissenting.

* * *

Until recently, no California court or commentator had suggested that the purpose of California's statutory rape law was to protect young women from the risk of pregnancy. Indeed, the historical development of § 261.5 demonstrates that the law was initially enacted on the premise that young women, in contrast to young men, were to be deemed legally incapable of consenting to an act of sexual intercourse. Because their chastity was considered particularly precious, those young women were felt to be uniquely in need of the State's protection. In contrast, young men were assumed to be capable of making such decisions for themselves; the law therefore did not offer them any special protection.

It is perhaps because the gender classification in California's statutory rape law was initially designed to further these outmoded sexual stereotypes, rather than to reduce the incidence of teenage pregnancies, that the State has been unable to demonstrate a substantial relationship between the classification and its newly asserted goal. But whatever the reason, the State has not shown that Cal. Penal Code § 261.5 is any more effective than a gender-neutral law would be in determining minor females from engaging in sexual intercourse. It has therefore not met its burden of proving that the statutory classification is substantially related to the achievement of its asserted goal.

* * *

JUSTICE STEVENS, dissenting.

* * *

In this case, the fact that a female confronts a greater risk of harm than a male is a reason for applying the prohibition to her—not a reason for granting her a license to use her own judgment on whether or not to assume the risk. * * * And, if we view the government's interest as that

---

in the face?" "A. On my chin." "Q. As a result of that, did you have any bruises or any kind of an injury?" "A. Yeah." "Q. What happened?" "A. I had bruises." "The Court: Did he hit you one time or did he hit you more than once?" "The Witness: He hit me about two or three times." * * *

"Q. Now, you said you had been drinking, is that correct?" "A. Yes." "Q. Would you describe your condition as a result of the drinking?" "A. I was a little drunk."

* * *

of a *parens patriae* seeking to protect its subjects from harming themselves, the discrimination is actually perverse. Would a rational parent making rules for the conduct of twin children of opposite sex simultaneously forbid the son and authorize the daughter to engage in conduct that is especially harmful to the daughter? That is the effect of this statutory classification.

* * *

The fact that the California Legislature has decided to apply its prohibition only to the male may reflect a legislative judgment that in the typical case the male is actually the more guilty party. Any such judgment must, in turn, assume that the decision to engage in the risk-creating conduct is always—or at least typically—a male decision. If that assumption is valid, the statutory classification should also be valid. But what is the support for the assumption? It is not contained in the record of this case or in any legislative history or scholarly study that has been called to our attention. I think it is supported to some extent by traditional attitudes toward male-female relationships. But the possibility that such a habitual attitude may reflect nothing more than an irrational prejudice makes it an insufficient justification for discriminatory treatment that is otherwise blatantly unfair.

NOTES ON STATUTORY RAPE

1. Why does Justice Blackmun regard this case as an unattractive one for prosecution? Do you agree with his statement that Michael's "partner" Sharon was *not* an "unwilling participant"? What would make the case more attractive to Justice Blackmun? Frances Olsen has suggested that the "explanation for Blackmun's distaste for the prosecution seems to be that Sharon did not fit the 'chaste and naive' image associated with statutory rape victims. In other words, Blackmun endorsed the double standard of sexual morality, under which men may aggress sexually against one class of females, but must leave the 'higher' class chaste." Frances Olsen, Statutory Rape: A Feminist Critique of Rights Analysis, 63 Tex. L. Rev. 387, 417 (1984). Do you agree with this assessment? Why do you think Sharon did not fight back; why did she lie there?

2. Is California correct that men are more willing to risk pregnancy during sexual intercourse? Do you need social science data to support this assumption? Is it appropriate to take judicial notice of this fact?

3. The defense in *Michael M.* contended that the statute at issue should be gender neutral, i.e., hold the female criminally liable also. However, the Court was persuaded by the State's argument that under a gender-neutral statute females would be less likely to report violations because they, too, would be subject to criminal prosecution. Are there benefits of a gender-neutral statutory rape law? What are they? What are the "outmoded sexual stereotypes" that concerned Justice Brennan? Do they continue to operate today? Have others taken their place? Do sex-specific statutory rape laws perpetuate sexual stereotypes?

4. Catharine MacKinnon notes that sex is proscribed with the "virginal daughter and other young girls." Catherine A. MacKinnon, Toward a Feminist Theory of the State 175–76 (1989). Is that what statutory rape laws are all about? Does it make sense that the day before she turns eighteen a young girl cannot say yes, and the next day she can? Is MacKinnon correct when she states that the legal age of consent "defines those above the age line as powerful whether they actually have power to consent or not. The vulnerability girls share with boys—age—dissipates with time. The vulnerability girls share with women—gender—does not." Id.

5. In light of the historical reasons for enacting sex-specific statutory rape laws, described by Justice Brennan in his dissent, what are the strongest arguments for striking a sex-specific statutory rape law? Do you agree with the majority that California's statute does not invidiously discriminate against females? What are the strongest arguments for upholding a statutory rape law like California's?

6. Why was this case prosecuted? Why didn't the prosecution charge Michael M. with rape? Was this rape? Would it be rape if no meant no? Would this be an easy case for the prosecution to win under a no-means-no standard? What problems would remain?

7. Does the question posed in *Michael M.*, whether to strike a sex-specific statutory rape law, present a "double bind"? (A double bind is created when both solutions, e.g., legalizing prostitution or eliminating prostitution, result in adverse effects for the oppressed group.) See also Olsen, above note 1 (discussing advantages and disadvantages of sex-specific statutory rape laws).

8. Most states that have eliminated sex-specific legislation like that at issue in *Michael M.* now have sex-neutral rules which require an age gap of two to five years for statutory rape, as well as a "victim" under a specified age, e.g., it would be unlawful for a twenty-year-old person to have sex with a fifteen-year-old person. What are the advantages and disadvantages of these two alternatives, i.e., the statutory rape law in California in *Michael M.*, or a neutral rule requiring an age gap? Would the neutral rule have "protected" Sharon? What sorts of girls might tend to need the sex-specific rule most, "good" girls or "bad" girls? How might class and race be relevant to this question? None of the opinions in *Michael M.* seem to illuminate this very real conflict; rather, the majority and dissenters all ignore it. Why?

9. As Michelle Oberman writes, "by age sixteen, 50% of U.S. teenagers have had sexual intercourse." Given that the age of consent to sex is set at sixteen, it follows that each one of these acts, technically, constitutes a crime. She estimates that, if one were to count them all, there would be "7.5 million incidents of statutory rape per year." Michelle Oberman, Regulating Consensual Sex With Minors: Defining A Role for Statutory Rape, 48 Buff. L. Rev. 703, 703–04 (2000). What are the risks of criminalizing conduct that is so prevalent as to be an everyday affair? See William D. Mosher, Anjani Chandra & Jo Jones, Center for Disease Control, Advance Data from Vital and Health Statistics, no. 362, Sexual Behavior and Selected Health Measures: Men and Women 15–44 Years of Age, United States (2002), available at http://www.cdc.gov/nchs/data/ad/ad362.pdf (finding 40% of 15– to 17–year–old boys and 38% of 15– to 17–year–old girls have engaged in oral sex, and 36% of boys and 39%

of girls in same age group have engaged in vaginal sex). Are statutory rape prosecutions substitutes for more difficult to prove cases, such as simple rapes? Oberman cites data showing that 29.2% of babies born to girls under sixteen were fathered by men over twenty-one and that the younger the girls, the "older the average age of the father." Id. at 705. Are statutory rape laws a crude form of reproductive control, or are they aimed at child sex abuse?

10. Given the prevalence of teenage sexual activity, the criminalization and prosecution of statutory rape often raises particularly acute line-drawing dilemmas. Consider the case where a seventeen-year-old male was sentenced to serve ten years in prison for an act involving "the [female] victim willingly performing oral sex." Humphrey v. Wilson, 652 S.E.2d 501, 521 (Ga. 2007). Is your sense that this outcome is just? The Georgia Supreme Court concluded that it constituted cruel and unusual punishment, and (based in part on a post-conviction change in state law) granted the defendant's claim for habeas relief. Id. at 542. The same court, however, affirmed the ten-year prison sentence of a defendant who "pursued the victim and got her to agree to have [oral and vaginal] sex with him and another male friend at the same time, despite the fact that the victim's parents previously told him that she was only 14 years old." Widner v. State, 631 S.E.2d 675, 676 (Ga. 2006). Can the disparate judicial treatment of these cases be rationalized? Do you find the facts of Widner more egregious than those of Wilson? If so, why? As a prosecutor, what factors would you consider when deciding whether to pursue statutory rape charges? As a legislator, how would you define the age parameters of lawful sexual activity? Are there better ways of criminalizing harmful sexual conduct?

11. According to Heidi Kitrosser, "per se age restrictions are well out of step with public, legislative, and judicial thinking." Heidi Kitrosser, Meaningful Consent: Toward a New Generation of Statutory Rape Laws, 4 Va. J. Soc. Pol'y & Law 287, 327 (1997). She proposes a new approach which would include: (1) abolishing the force requirement; (2) defining consent progressively, i.e., to be proven as either an affirmative defense or as an element of the crime, it must have some manifestation in either words or actions indicating freely-given agreement to engage in sex; (3) a combination of status and age provisions that make sexual relations between minors below a certain age and adults in particular positions of authority, trust, or supervision over them criminal as a matter of law; (4) gender neutrality; and (5) abrogating chastity and promiscuity provisions. Id. at 328–337. Kitrosser believes her proposal "more closely fits the notion of adolescent sexual autonomy, with a focus on meaningful consent as opposed to coerced submission or acquiescence." Id. at 321. Do you agree? Can you identify other possible reforms which would provide protection to minors while acknowledging their sexual autonomy? See Michelle Oberman, Turning Girls into Women: Re–Evaluating Modern Statutory Rape Law, 85 J. Crim. L. & Criminology 15 (1994).

12. Would protections for young women or men under age eighteen be needed in a world in which there was real equality between the sexes? Might different rules be appropriate in a world in which women and men are not equal?

13. In State of Florida v. Rodriguez, No. 92–47–CF–JL (July 21, 1992), a circuit court struck the Florida statutory rape statute criminalizing sexual relations between someone over 18 and someone under sixteen, as a violation of the fourteen-year-old girl's right to privacy. The minor's mother appears to have been the complaining witness who convinced the prosecutor to bring criminal charges against her pregnant daughter's nineteen-year-old boyfriend. The judge did not discuss why the Florida statute might be desirable policy. Instead, he explained that he was "inescapably compelled" by the "logic" of the Florida constitution's privacy provision and an earlier Florida case in a very different context (parental notification of abortion statute struck down as a violation of a minor's privacy right). What, if any, are the dangers of this approach? How can minors be protected from sexual abuse if they have a privacy interest in sexual relations with older people? Can you suggest a statutory solution?

14. How would the various feminist theorists discussed in Chapter 3 respond to the question of whether statutory rape laws are discriminatory against (a) men or (b) women? How would these theorists analyze whether the sexual activities of minors should be regulated?

E. PROSTITUTION

1. THE PRACTICE OF PROSTITUTION

FRANCIS T. MIKO, TRAFFICKING IN WOMEN AND CHILDREN: THE U.S. AND INTERNATIONAL RESPONSE

Congressional Research Service, Report for Congress, 1–3 (2004).

Scope of the Problem Worldwide

Trafficking in people, especially women and children, for prostitution and forced labor is one of the fastest growing areas of international criminal activity and one that is of increasing concern to the U.S. Administration, Congress, and the international community. Although men are also victimized, the overwhelming majority of those trafficked are women and children. According to the latest U.S. Government estimates, some 800,000 to 900,000 people are trafficked across borders each year worldwide for forced labor, domestic servitude, or sexual exploitation.[83] Trafficking is considered one of the largest sources of profits for organized crime, generating seven to ten billion dollars annually according to United Nations estimates.[84]

Trafficking is a problem that affects virtually every country in the world. Generally, the flow of trafficking is from less developed countries to industrialized nations, including the United States, or toward neighboring countries with marginally higher standards of living. Since trafficking is

83. U.S. Department of State, Trafficking in Persons Report, 2003, available at http://www.state.gov/g/tip/rls/tiprpt/2003. These figures do not include the large number of victims who are trafficked within borders.

84. Id.

an underground criminal enterprise, there are no precise statistics on the extent of the problem and all estimates are unreliable. The largest number of victims trafficked internationally are still believed to come from South and Southeast Asia. The former Soviet Union may be the largest new source of trafficking for prostitution and the sex industry. Many people are also trafficked to Eastern Europe. Other main source regions include Latin America and the Caribbean, and Africa. Most of the victims are sent to Asia, the Middle East, Western Europe and North America. They usually end up in large cities, vacation and tourist areas, or near military bases, where the demand is highest.

Causes of Rise in Trafficking

The reasons for the increase in trafficking are many. In general, the criminal business feeds on poverty, despair, war, crisis, and ignorance. The globalization of the world economy has increased the movement of people across borders, legally and illegally, especially from poorer to wealthier countries. International organized crime has taken advantage of the freer flow of people, money, goods and services to extend its own international reach.

Other contributing factors include:

- the continuing subordination of women in many societies, as reflected in economic, educational, and work opportunity disparities between men and women. Many societies still favor sons and view girls as an economic burden. Desperate families in some of the most impoverished countries sell their daughters to brothels or traffickers for the immediate payoff and to avoid having to pay the dowery to marry off daughters;
- the hardship and economic dislocations caused by the transition following the collapse of Communism in the former Soviet Union and Eastern Europe, as well as the wars in the former Yugoslavia. The lack of opportunity and the eagerness for a better life abroad have made many women and girls especially vulnerable to entrapment by traffickers. With the weakening of law enforcement in post-Communist societies, criminal organizations have grown and established themselves in the lucrative business of international trafficking;
- the high demand, worldwide, for trafficked women and children as sex workers, cheap sweatshop labor, and domestic workers. Traffickers are encouraged by large tax-free profits and continuing income from the same victims, until recently at very low risk;
- The inadequacy of laws and law enforcement in most origin, transit, and destination countries hampers efforts to fight trafficking. Even in the United States, more effective legal remedies are only now being implemented. Prostitution is legal or tolerated in many countries, and widespread in most. When authorities do crack down, it is usually against prostitutes, themselves. Penalties for trafficking humans for

sexual exploitation are often relatively minor compared with those for other criminal activities like drug and gun trafficking;

- The priority placed on stemming illegal immigration in many countries, including the United States, has resulted in treatment of trafficking cases as a problem of illegal immigration, thus treating victims as criminals. When police raid brothels, women are often detained and punished, subjected to human rights abuses in jail, and swiftly deported. Few steps have been taken to provide support, health care, and access to justice. Few victims dare testify against the traffickers or those who hold them, fearing retribution for themselves and their families since most governments do not offer stays of deportation or adequate protection for witnesses;
- The disinterest and in some cases even complicity of governments is another big problem. Many law-enforcement agencies and governments ignore the plight of trafficking victims and downplay the scope of the trafficking problem.

TEXT NOTE: DICHOTOMIES IN PROSTITUTION DISCOURSE

As the excerpt above illustrates, the discourse surrounding prostitution is characterized by a number of dichotomies that are often implicit, and subject to challenge. Prostituted women are often deemed either trafficked or agentic. Within the realm of recognized trafficking, consideration is largely confined to the crossing of international borders. Child prostitution is viewed as a different, and unequivocally harmful, practice as compared to the prostitution of adult women. As Sheila Jeffreys concludes, significant commentary "is based upon the premise that it is possible, or even desirable, to make distinctions between various forms of the sex industry; between child and adult prostitution, between trafficking and prostitution, between forced and free prostitution, between legal and illegal sectors, between prostitution in the west and prostitution in the non-west. The creation of distinctions legitimizes forms of prostitution by criticizing some and not others." Sheila Jeffreys, The Industrial Vagina: The Political Economy of the Global Sex Trade, 9 (2009).

Like Jeffreys, Dorchen Leidholdt has instead urged that all facets of prostitution be understood as an interconnected system of sexual violence and exploitation, which is defined as "the sexual violation of a person's human dignity, equality, and physical or mental integrity and as a practice by which some people (primarily men) achieve power and domination over others (primarily women and children) for the purposes of sexual gratification, financial gain, and/or advancement." See Dorchen Leidholdt, Prostitution: A Contemporary Form of Slavery, Speech to United Nations Working Group on Contemporary Forms of Slavery. Geneva, Switzerland, May 21, 1998. Leidholdt expands on this analytic framework:

> The fact is that sex trafficking and organized prostitution are inextricably connected and share fundamental characteristics. The victims who are targeted are the same—poor, minority, or so-called Third World women and children, frequently with histories of physical and sexual abuse. The customers are the same—men with disposable income who achieve sexual

gratification by purchasing and invading the body of a woman or child. The dynamics of power and control employed by the sex industry profiteers are the same, whether they take the form of violence and threats of violence, debt bondage, torture, imprisonment, and/or brainwashing. The harm to the victims is the same—trauma, sexually transmitted diseases, drug and alcohol addiction, the physical toll of repeated beatings by customers and pimps, the psychological and physical toll of repeated and unwanted sex, and the destruction of the sense of self, identity, and sexuality. The harm to society is the same—the reification of sex-and race-based hierarchies. Whether they purchase women who are trafficked or those who are otherwise prostituted, sex industry consumers move from the brothel into the world, that experience coloring their relations to women and girls in the rest of society. Some American men stationed in South East Asia during the Vietnam War have talked about how their immersion in military prostitution profoundly damaged their ability to relate to women and girls back home. A few former sex industry consumers, who have become leaders in the movement against sexual exploitation, have discussed similar effects of participating as customers of the sex trade. Certainly, the injuries to their sense of self and sexuality are mild compared to those of the young women who are reduced to sexual merchandise by the industry. Nevertheless, we must acknowledge that the sex industry also harms men, impairing their ability to experience sexual relations that are premised on mutual respect and equality.

The second distinction that is frequently made, to the detriment of victims and the benefit of the sex industry, is that between the sexual exploitation of children and of adults. The problem with this position is that by failing to criticize the sexual exploitation of adults, it legitimizes it. For example, to decry the prostitution of a fifteen-year-old girl but to fail to speak out against the prostitution of her seventeen-year-old sister is to tacitly sanction the sexual exploitation of the older girl. Many organizations have organized to end the sexual exploitation of children, a laudable goal, but have failed to see that the sexual exploitation of children is inextricably connected to that of adults. Studies show that in the West, at least 70 percent of the adults exploited by the sex industry were sexually abused as children. They also show that the average age of entry into prostitution is 16 or younger. It is clear that the sexually exploited children of today are the prostituted adults of tomorrow, and, as the French abolitionist organization, Le Nid, declares, "In every whore, there is a little girl murdered." Although some sex industry consumers are fixated on sex with young children, many sexually exploit young girls and young women interchangeably. We will not be able to end the sexual exploitation of children until we take a stand and develop strategies against sexual exploitation of all human beings.

The third and most problematic distinction that has recently emerged is that between so-called forced and so-called voluntary prostitution. By limiting the pool of people who can be identified as victims while simultaneously protecting large segments of the sex industry, this is the best gift that pimps and traffickers could have received. This distinction creates a vision of prostitution that is freely chosen; a vision that can be

> maintained only by ignoring all of the social conditions that force women and girls into conditions of sexual exploitation. The proponents of this distinction are sending the following message: "Don't pay attention to the poverty, the familial pressure, the incest she survived, the battering by her boyfriend, the lack of employment options available to her. Just ask whether there is a gun pointed at her head or whether she is being overtly deceived. No gun, no deceit; then no problem; not only is she voluntarily in the sex industry, she is a 'sex worker.'

Id. As you reflect on the materials that follow, try to identify the disparate conceptual treatment of various types of prostitution. Consider, as well, what ends are served by these different approaches.

SHEILA JEFFREYS, THE INDUSTRIAL VAGINA: THE POLITICAL ECONOMY OF THE GLOBAL SEX TRADE

3, 6–7 (2009).

[I]n recent decades, prostitution has been industrialized and globalized * * * [and] transformed from an illegal, small-scale, largely local and socially despised form of abuse of women into a hugely profitable and either legal or tolerated international industry. * * *

* * *

New technologies such as air travel have facilitated movement of prostituted women and girls and of the buyers and thus increased the scale and international scope of the industry. Similarly the Internet has enabled sex tourism, the mail order bride business and other forms of prostitution to expand and interrelate. New electronic technologies from the videotape to the Internet have enabled the development of a massively profitable industry with a global reach, in which women in poor countries can be delivered in film or in real time to perform sex acts for men in the west. Though the technologies which enable women's bodies to be delivered to men's bodies change and develop, the vagina and the other parts of women's bodies which form the raw material of prostitution remain resolutely "old technology" and impervious to change. The vagina becomes the centre of a business organized on an industrial scale though the vagina itself is still subject to the problems inevitably associated with the use of the interior of a woman's body in this way, in the form of pain, bleeding and abrasion, pregnancy and sexually transmitted disease, and the associated psychological harms that result from the bodies of live women being used as instruments of men's pleasure.

NOTES ON THE PRACTICE OF PROSTITUTION

1. Jeffreys cites new electronic technologies as integral to the emergence of prostitution as a global industry. In particular, the internet has significantly transformed the practice of domestic and international trafficking (including the delivery of "Mail Order Brides") and sex tourism. The "adult

services" ads on Craigslist.org alone are estimated to produce $80 million in annual profits. Erin I. Kunze, Sex Trafficking Via the Internet: How International Agreements Address the Problem and Fail to Go Far Enough, J. High Tech. L. 241, 244 (2010). See also Donna M. Hughes, The Internet and Sex Industries: Partners in Global Sexual Exploitation, 19 Tech. & Soc'y Mag. 35 (2000). Are the underlying dynamics of prostitution changed when sex is sold on-line? What challenges to legal regulation are posed by web-based prostitution in all its dimensions?

2. As a general proposition, trafficking commentary has focused on the problem of international border crossing. Largely obscured is the practice of domestic trafficking within the United States. See, e.g., U.S. Department of State, Trafficking in Persons Report (2003), available at http://www.state.gov/g/tip/rls/tiprpt/2003 (acknowledging that reported figures do not include victims who are trafficked within borders); Sara Ann Friedman, Who Is There to Help Us? How the System Fails Sexually Exploited Girls in the United States, ECPAT–USA, Inc. (2005). For an exceptional examination of the domestic trafficking problem, see Jody Raphael and Jessica Ashley, Domestic Sex Trafficking of Chicago Women and Girls (May 2008), available at http://www.icjia.state.il.us/public/pdf/ResearchReports/Sex% 20Trafficking% 20Report% 20May% 202008.pdf. What factors might explain the relative invisibility of domestic trafficking victims in both prostitution discourse and policy?

3. Central to feminist debates about prostitution is the question of agency: can/do women choose to sell sex, or is every act of prostitution necessarily coerced? Even apart from claims that gender hierarchy itself (and on its own) precludes this possibility, a considerable body of research on the lives of prostituted girls and women tends to undermine the notion of "choice" as applied to commercial sex. Especially salient in these accounts are the effects of drug addiction. In one study, "virtually all of the women encountered ... indicated that prostitution is not a chosen career. Rather, for most it is *survival sex*, and for almost all it is the result of a drug habit combined with the lack of other skills or resources. Or as one sex worker indicated: "When you need *the cracks* [crack cocaine] and you need money for other things 'cause your rent money *went on the boards* [was used to buy crack], you got to survive, and you know, to do that, the pussy works!" Hillary L. Surratt et al., Sex Work and Drug Use In a Subculture of Violence, 50 Crime & Delinq. 43, 55 (2004). See also Kimberly Tyler and Katherine Johnson, Trading Sex: Voluntary or Coerced? The Experiences of Homeless Youth, 43(3) J. Sex. Res. 208 (Aug. 2006). Prostituted women very often enter the realm of "sex work" as prostituted girls; girls who are typically sexual abuse victims, runaways, or "throwaways" when they begin selling their bodies for sex. See Jody Raphael & Deborah L. Shapiro, Violence in Indoor and Outdoor Prostitution Venues, 10 Violence Against Women 126 (2004); Jennifer K. Wesley, "Mom said we had a money maker": Sexualization and Survival Contexts among Homeless Women, 32 Symbolic Interaction 91 (2009); Eloise Dunlap et al., Girls' Sexual Development in the Inner City: From Compelled Childhood Sexual Contact to Sex-for-Things Exchanges, 12 J. Child Sexual Abuse 73 (2003); Kaethe Morris Hoffer, A Response to Sex Trafficking Chicago Style: Follow the Sisters, Speak Out, 158 U. Pa. L. Rev.

101 (2010). Given the context within which so many women are prostituted, is the construct of choice a meaningful one?

4. Violence as it implicates the meaning of "choice" merits particular attention, given the enormity of its impact on the lives of prostituted women.

> Prostituted women suffer two forms of violence, unpaid violence, which includes rape, beatings and murder from male buyers, pimps, traffickers and passers-by that is not remunerated, as well as the ordinary everyday violence of unwanted and often painful penetration that is paid for. There is a great deal of evidence from numerous well researched studies of the severe unpaid harms that women suffer in the form of psychological harms, broken bones, head injuries, sexual violence, imprisonment. Though these harms are usually understood to be particularly severe in street prostitution, there are studies to show that escort prostitution in which women visit male buyers in hotel rooms or their homes involves similar risks. * * * Prostitutors use verbal violence such as saying to a woman 'on your knees, bitch,' language which is run of the mill in the pornography from which male buyers learn the practice of prostituting women. They grab women's bodies in degrading and painful ways during bookings, such as twisting nipples, and thrusting fingers into the woman's anus to show they want anal sex. * * * The psychological harms that result from the continual disassociation of mind and body needed to survive prostitution, and the routine dehumanization integral to the practice, commonly bear all the characteristics of post-traumatic stress disorder.

Jeffreys, text note above, at 186–87.

Whether on the street or indoors, prostitution is embedded in what one researcher describes as a "subculture of violence" See Surratt et al., above note 3; Raphael and Shapiro, above note 3; Stephanie Church et al., Violence by Clients Toward Female Prostitutes in Different Work Settings: Questionnaire Survey, 332 Brit. Med. J. 524 (2001). Although efforts to generalize from the populations studied have been challenged, e.g., Ronald Weitzer, Movement to Criminalize Sex Work in the United States, 37 J.L. & Soc'y 61 (2010), even critics must concede that the accounts of prostituted women are replete with references to the physical violence they endure.

Consider the following study of such women:

> As explained by one participant, "There were times when the only way out of a situation was by the grace of God." Another reported, "Once you hit the streets, there's no guarantee you'll come back." * * * One participant's teeth had been knocked out by her boyfriend; she had also been raped at knifepoint by a trick. When asked to explain how she returned to the streets after being raped, she explained, "I just looked at it as not getting paid." Her response likely indicates a coping mechanism that apparently allowed her to return to the dangerous street environment without paralyzing fear and perhaps also with some level of personal dignity intact. When asked to describe her feelings of being beaten with a tire iron and left for dead, Sam responded, "I didn't care. I didn't think about it. I got 150 stitches and was back on the streets that same day." Another explained her attitude toward the potential for personal harm by

> saying, "You just give them what they want and pray they don't kill you." Participants rarely reported crimes of victimization to authorities. One explained, "Society and law enforcement consider a prostitute getting raped or beat as something she deserves. It goes along with the lifestyle. There's nothing that you can do."

Rochelle L. Dalla, Yan Xia & Heather Kennedy, "You Just Give them what they Want and Pray they don't Kill You": Street–Level Sex Workers' Reports of Victimization, Personal Resources, and Copying Strategies, 9 Violence Against Women 1367, 1380–81 (2003).

In the words of another prostituted woman: "alls we know is violence, alls we know is violent men." Surratt et al., above note 3, at 53.

5. Prostituted women are frequently battered in their intimate relationships. Dalla et al., above note 4, at 1382 ("despite being subjected to multiple forms of bodily injury by clients (tricks/johns), intimate partners were the source of the majority and most severe forms of abuse reported").

There is yet another way in which violence in prostitution falls within the rubric of domestic violence: researchers have found that a woman's "pimp" is often an abusive boyfriend. See, e.g., Raphael and Ashley, above note 2, at 20 (44% of women interviewed characterized their relationship to their pimp as "boyfriend" or "my man"). Yet even women who distinguish their partners from pimps describe "the behaviors of both * * * as frighteningly similar." Dalla et al., above note 4, at 1389.

> Williamson and Cluse–Tolar (2002) drew parallels between pimp-controlled prostituted women and women experiencing domestic violence by intimates. Both types of relationships are ultimately based on power and control, and more importantly, both types of relationships provide the women with certain "needs," which may include a sense of love and belonging. When a prostituted woman's primary source of support is her partner or pimp, who benefits greatly from her prostitution activities, the challenges for leaving prostitution rise exponentially. Women who have experienced an entire life of victimization are most at risk for remaining with abusive men and least likely to expect otherwise.

Id.

Evelina Giobbe offers this account of the similarities between battering and pimping:

> An examination of the power dynamics between pimp and prostitute clearly illustrates how the tactics of power and control he uses to recruit and keep a woman trapped in prostitution closely parallel those used by batterers to ensure the compliance of their wives or intimate partners. * * * These tactics include isolation of the woman; minimization and denial of the abuse; exertion of male privilege; threats and intimidation; and emotional, sexual, and physical abuse. * * * The batterer and the pimp not only use similar tactics of power and control over "their women," but share similar motives. According to Ellen Pence, of the Domestic Abuse Intervention Project in Duluth, Minnesota: "The abuser employs tactics not only to gain his partner's submission to a specific demand, but also to establish a relationship that he can rely upon in the

> future. These tactics appear to be random and inexplainable, but in the context of attempting to establish power in a relationship, random acts of violence are fully explainable." * * * The name of the game here—for "love" or money—is patriarchal power over women.

Evelina Giobbe, An Analysis of Individual, Institutional, and Cultural Pimping, 1 Mich. J. Gender & L. 33, 45–46, 50 (1993).

What policy implications flow from the multidimensional overlap between prostitution and domestic violence? In response, what legal or extra-legal reforms might you suggest? See, e.g., Raphael & Ashley, above note 2, at 42–44.

6. Sheila Jeffreys asserts that, "the sex industry undermines the equality of girls and women both in the private sphere of their relationships, families and sex lives and in the public sphere of business and the professions." Jeffreys, text note above, at 195. Does the impact of prostitution encompass group-based harm? One view is that prostitution not only reflects, but perpetuates, the subordination of women as a collective. Michelle Madden Dempsey offers this description:

> [A] world in which women are not valued as human beings tends to be a world in which harms to prostituted people will be common; a world in which such harms are common tends to be one in which women are not valued as human beings. Understood accordingly, part of the wrongfulness of the harms suffered by prostituted people is the tendency of these harms to sustain and perpetuate sexism. * * *
>
> Unlike sex discrimination and sexism, both of which involve the failure to provide women with valuable options either through ignorance or apathy, misogyny entails maliciously choosing to inflict harm based on a hatred of women. The harms often suffered by prostituted women illustrate all too well the extent to which misogyny often motivates this violence; at the same time, these harms have a tendency to sustain and perpetuate misogyny. Again, the feedback loop between these harms and patriarchal structural inequality informs a proper understanding of the wrongfulness of the harm, insofar as part of the wrongness of the harms lies in their tendency to sustain and perpetuate misogyny.
>
> The point of this analysis is simply to explain the sense in which the harms at issue * * * are not adequately understood as merely physical or even psychological harms to the individual prostituted women themselves. * * * My point is not to deny the seriousness of these harms to individual bodies or minds. Rather, my point is that these harms are not best understood from an individualistic point of view: they are best, or at least better, understood from a *feminist* point of view—one that takes into account the tendency of these harms to sustain and perpetuate patriarchal structural inequality, which subordinates women as a group.

Michelle Madden Dempsey, Sex Trafficking and Criminalization: In Defense of Feminist Abolitionism, 158 U. Pa. L. Rev. 1729, 1737–39 (2010).

Is this focus on group-based harm a helpful one? Are you persuaded that women—whether or not they themselves are prostituted—are subordinated by the practice of prostitution? If so, in what ways might this dynamic be manifested? Can group-based impacts like those posited by Jeffreys and Dempsey be measured? If not, can this theory of gender subordination nevertheless be defended?

7. With the development of the internet, recent decades have witnessed significant growth in the Mail Order Bride industry, which allows men to pay an agency for the bodies of women, mostly from poor countries. In 2007, the United Nations Trafficking Rapporteur's report noted that "an unequal balance of power * * * puts women at special risk of violence and abuse," and that women become trapped in the marriages for which they were purchased "because of immigration status, isolation, economic dependence and fear of husbands." U.N. Commission on Hum. Rts., Report of the Special Rapporteur on the Human Rights Aspects of the Victims of Trafficking in Persons, Especially Women and Children, ¶ 57–58, Doc. E/CN.4/2006/62 (February 20, 2006) (prepared by Sigma Huda), available at http://www.unhcr.org/refworld/docid/48abd53dd.html. To some feminists, "the relationship with prostitution is clear, as impoverished women from poor countries give unknown men in whom they have no affectional interest and for whom they have no desire their domestic and reproductive labour and sexual access to their bodies in order to escape from dire economic circumstances." Jeffreys, text note above, at 48. A competing feminist account views "mail order brides" as "free agents, voluntary actors, highly adventurous, courageous, strong-willed and resourceful individuals," rather than "pawns, victims or prostitutes." Nora V. Demleitner, In Good Times and Bad: The Obligation to Protect "Mail–Order Brides," 2 Women & Int'l Hum. Rts. L. 613, 626 (Kelly D. Askin & Dorean M. Koenig). Which perspective do you find more compelling? Are the two mutually exclusive, or might each reflect and inform reality?

8. Even outside the Mail Order Bride context, is the marriage/prostitution divide yet another false dichotomy? How are the two practices different? How are they the same? See generally Carole Pateman, The Sexual Contract (1988). For feminists committed to advancing the rights and well being of women, what are the benefits and drawbacks of drawing this comparison?

9. Should "exotic dancing," "lap dancing," "topless dancing," "stripping," and other such work in clubs be considered prostitution? What are the arguments for and against this designation? See Eleanor Matricka–Tyndale, et al., Exotic Dancing and Health, 31 Women and Health 87 (2000). A separate, but related, concern is that women performing as strippers may have been trafficked into the country. Should "exotic dancer" visas be issued by the state to facilitate the supply of strippers? See Audrey Macklin, Dancing Across Borders: 'Exotic Dancers,' Trafficking, and Canadian Immigration Policy, 37 Int'l Migration Rev. 464 (2006) (describing Canada's experience with an immigration policy that required women to provide "soft-porn" pictures to authorities in order to obtain stripper visas).

10. Is the commercialization of sex financially beneficial to women? Sheila Jeffreys suggests that "[t]hough prostitution forms an increasingly profitable global economic sector, the profits are largely going to those who control the business rather than to the individual prostituted women themselves." Jeffreys, text note above, at 28. Who is making money from the sex trade? See id. at 71–73, 91–92 (describing role of organized crime role in

industry); U.S. Department of State, Trafficking in Persons Report (June 2006), available at http://www.state.gov/g/tip/rls/tiprpt/2006/ (providing FBI Estimate that trafficking generates approximately $9.5 billion annually for organized crime); Miko, Trafficking in Women and Children, above. Does the answer to this question alter in any way your analysis of prostitution or its harms? How should the legal system respond to the economic realities of commercial sex?

2. SEX WORK OR SEXUAL SUBORDINATION?

JODY FREEMAN, THE FEMINIST DEBATE OVER PROSTITUTION REFORM: PROSTITUTES' RIGHTS GROUPS, RADICAL FEMINISTS AND THE (IM)POSSIBILITY OF CONSENT

5 Berkeley Women's L.J. 75, 75–79, 81–88, 90, 92–94, 102, 105–08 (1989–90).

Women who have been, or are presently, in the sex trade disagree over many contentious issues: whether their work is chosen, whether they participate in their own oppression, and whether their economic self interest should outweigh the concern that prostitution contributes to women's subordination. Prostitutes' rights groups, such as Cast Off Your Old Tired Ethics (COYOTE) and the Canadian Organization for the Rights of Prostitutes (CORP), demand that prostitution be decriminalized because it is dignified, respectable work. CORP's leadership says prostitutes should be entitled to organize, advertise, pay taxes, and receive unemployment insurance. * * *

CORP actually views prostitution as superior to many other jobs since it has distinct advantages: women set their hours and wages, work where they want to, and service only customers they choose. Prostitutes' rights groups say prostitution empowers women because it enables them to earn a living in an environment they control, or would control but for state interference. Margo St. James [who has never worked as a prostitute], of COYOTE, objects to the double standard inherent in the criminalization of prostitution: "The state's idea is that these are deviant women and normal men. But they are doing the same thing; they're engaging in the same act." CORP's spokesperson, Valerie Scott, makes prostitution sound as mundane as anything else: "Ever since I was five, I dreamed of getting into the sex industry."

The National Task Force on Prostitution (NTFP), an American organization promoting prostitutes' rights, argues that despite some exceptions, prostitution amounts to a voluntary exchange of sexual services for money. The NTFP seeks to empower prostitutes to bargain with employers and improve their working conditions. The NTFP is similar to COYOTE and CORP in support of prostitution as legitimate work, as is the English Collective of Prostitutes, which argues that "for some women to get paid for what all women are expected to do for free is a source of power for all women to refuse any free sex."

* * *

Delores French, another outspoken representative of prostitutes' rights, says that she loves being a prostitute and that "[i]t's the most honest, rewarding work I've ever done." She recounts how she became a prostitute shortly after a life threatening experience made her regret "all the things I hadn't done." She decided to "grab every appealing opportunity that came along and to experience as much about living as possible." Her husband, the vice president of the Georgia Civil Liberties Union, understands her job. He says, "[O]ur jobs are quite similar: We both free lance, we both get paid in advance, we both try to get our clients off." * * *

Before accepting the CORP * * * position as the definitive word on what prostitutes think, one should consider that women in the industry have not yet reached a consensus on whether prostitution is empowering for women. Some align themselves with * * * French: the money is attractive and their husbands support their decision to work as prostitutes. * * *

However, others testify to the harmful aspects of the trade. They recall emerging from years of denial or guilt and finally realizing that they had been oppressed by prostitution. For example, Judy Helfand says that she used to think turning men on sexually was an affirmation of her sexual power, but later changed her mind:

> What I never saw was that in basing my self-worth on men's desire I was far from developing a true sense of worth based on self love.
>
> I see this false sense of power as one way internalized oppression keeps us down.... I see that wanting men to want you sexually is what men want.
>
> In an exchange at a conference on prostitution and pornography, one participant asked, "What's so terrible about fucking for a living? I like it, I can live out my fantasies." Another replied,
>
> I don't know how you can possibly say, as busy as you are as a lady of the evening, that you like every sexual act, that you work out your fantasies! Come on, get serious! ... Can you count how many tricks you've had? You mean you have that many fantasies? Isn't it about having money to survive? ... Can't we teach women some skills so they can survive? I know that's your opinion, you like it, but prostitution to me was degrading. I grew to hate it. If I had had to fuck one more of them—boy, I would have killed him!

There are also organizations that work in direct opposition to CORP, COYOTE and the NTPF. Sarah Wynter, founder and editor of Women Hurt in Systems of Prostitution Engaged in Revolt (WHISPER), argues:

> There has been a deliberate attempt to validate men's perceived need, and self proclaimed right, to buy and sell women's bodies for sexual use. This has been accomplished, in part, by euphemizing prostitution as an occupation. Men have promoted the cultural myth that women actively seek out prostitution as a pleasurable economic alternative to

low paying, low skilled, monotonous labor, conveniently ignoring the conditions that insure women's inequality and the preconditions which make women vulnerable to prostitution.

Wynter maintains that prostitution is not a "valid," freely chosen occupation. She wants us "to stop defining prostitution as a victimless crime, and acknowledge it for what it is—a crime committed against women by men."

Despite their disagreement over whether prostitution is a legitimate occupation, virtually all those with experience inside the industry agree that the current conditions under which prostitutes must work are intolerable.

* * *

The assumptions about consent and coercion that inform the prostitutes' rights groups' position can be traced to traditional liberal theory, which is committed to autonomy, individualism, and minimal state interference in private choice. Liberal theory is premised on an assumption that individuals are atomistic, pre social beings who exist independent of their community. The justification for state power in the liberal paradigm is the notion of implied consent: individuals surrender a certain amount of authority to the state in order to protect the autonomy of everyone.

Feminist and critical legal studies have attempted to expose the inability of liberal theory to account for our connections to others, or our "social constitutiveness." The central features of liberalism—the public/private distinction, a highly individualistic conception of rights—are commonly attacked as inappropriate for, and unresponsive to, feminist demands for equality and freedom.

* * *

CORP and COYOTE's essentially liberal argument is that women and men should be permitted to use their bodies and express their sexuality as they see fit. Underlying this position is an assumption that choice is possible and that prostitutes are entitled to determine for themselves whether selling sex is harmful. They encourage prostitution as sexual expression, even if it is considered "deviant," because it is private, freely chosen, and harmless to those not involved in the transaction. Harm is defined restrictively so that contributing to the subordination of women as a class does not count.

* * *

CORP does not seem concerned with the extent to which authentic choice depends on the context in which it is exercised. CORP's leadership argues that decriminalizing and legitimizing prostitution promotes autonomy and is also the only effective way of minimizing the coercion present in "exceptional" cases. If prostitutes are permitted to organize, form support groups, and run self help networks, they will then be able to exert some control over the coercive elements of the sex trade. Putting power into the hands of the women in the industry will enable them to prevent the worst abuses of the system. Obviously, the "consent is possible" approach is fuelled by the claim that prostitutes make free choices. Many feminists have challenged that claim by questioning the accuracy of the liberal version of freedom. Radical feminists have directed their attention, instead, to coercion.

* * *

Contrary to liberal feminism, radical feminism focuses on sexuality as the mechanism of women's oppression. * * * Radical feminists reject the notion that women are empowered by fulfilling male desire, and they see the desire for prostitution as male.* * * Radical feminists say that prostitution is not a harmless, "private" transaction but a powerful means of creating, reinforcing, and perpetuating the objectification of women through sexuality. They do not take the criminalization of prostitution to mean that society is committed to undoing the subordination of women. Rather, it serves as proof that female sexuality is not only manufactured by men, but also legally controlled through the exercise of authority in order to keep women isolated and powerless. Society's acceptance of the persistent male demand for prostitutes only reminds us that all women are thought to be accessible (for a price) and that their commodification is natural.

* * *

Radical feminism understands prostitution to be a microcosm of gender hierarchy. It not only encapsulates but reinforces the objectification of women. Even an argument that prostitution has "therapeutic" potential for providing sex to those who are socially or sexually dysfunctional cannot, to the radical feminist, redeem an institution that is so central to male dominance.

NOTES ON THE HARM OF PROSTITUTION

1. Can selling sex *ever* be a genuinely consensual, truly agentic experience? If you believe it cannot, how do you make sense of the accounts of prostituted women who celebrate the "sex work" they claim to have freely chosen? See, e.g., Sex Work: Writings by Women in the Sex Industry (Priscilla Alexander & Frederique Delacoste, eds. 1987). Is refusal to accept these accounts on their face a form of paternalism? If we instead acknowledge the validity of these "pro-sex work" reports, what are the implications for feminist theory and for law?

2. Should individual choices that contribute to the maintenance of group subordination be permitted? How would the theoretical approaches described in Chapter 3 resolve these questions?

3. PROSTITUTION AND THE LAW

MICHELLE MADDEN DEMPSEY, SEX TRAFFICKING AND CRIMINALIZATION: IN DEFENSE OF FEMINIST ABOLITIONISM

158 U. Pa. L. Rev. 1729, 1730–32 (2010).

In debates regarding what sort of policy and legal responses are most appropriate in addressing the problem of sex trafficking, it is possible to identify two sides: abolitionists and nonabolitionists. Abolitionists seek to end both sex trafficking and prostitution generally, while nonabolitionists seek to end sex trafficking while allowing prostitution to continue.[1] The motivational grounding of the abolitionist movement is diverse: some people support abolitionist reforms based on conservative or reactionary political commitments, while others support abolitionism from a feminist point of view. An approach to sex trafficking that seeks to abolish both sex trafficking and prostitution generally, as part of a larger set of feminist commitments and goals, is typically referred to (and will be referred to below) as "feminist abolitionism."

Broadly speaking, feminist abolitionism tends to favor developing policy and legal responses to sex trafficking that implement what has been coined the "Swedish model."[2] This model includes social-welfare policies that assist people in exiting and avoiding prostitution; public education campaigns to raise awareness of the harms experienced by prostituted people and to change social norms that support sex trafficking and prostitution; and criminal law reforms that penalize trafficking, pimping, and the purchase of sex, while decriminalizing the sale of sex.[4]

In general, feminist abolitionism's recommendations with respect to social-welfare provision, education, and criminalizing both trafficking and

---

1. Segregating the two sides into respective camps in these terms is, admittedly, somewhat of an oversimplification. There are, of course, many areas of both actual and potential agreement between the sides, and it is possible to develop a more nuanced approach that blends aspects of each. * * *

2. For a helpful overview of the Swedish model, see Gunilla Ekberg, The Swedish Law That Prohibits the Purchase of Sexual Services: Best Practices for Prevention of Prostitution and Trafficking in Human Beings, 10 Violence Against Women 1187 (2004).

4. As its name suggests, the Swedish model was first implemented in Sweden, see Lag om förbud mot köp av sexuella tjänster (Svensk författningssamling [SFS] 1998:408) (Swed.) [Act Prohibiting the Purchase of Sexual Services] (criminalizing users of people who sell sex), although more recently the model has been adopted in Norway. See Ulrikke Moustgaard, Prostitution Legislation at a Turning Point: Will They Go the Same Way?, Nikk Magasin, 1.2009, at 24, http://www.nikk.uio.no/?module=Articles;action=Article.publicShow;ID=891 (last visited July 24, 2010) (discussing the criminalization of prostitution in Nordic countries, including Norway's decision to ban the purchase of sexual services beginning in 2009). South Korea moved toward adopting the Swedish model with two acts passed in 2004. *See* Act on the Prevention of Prostitution and Protection of Victims Thereof, Statutes of South Korea, Act No. 7212 (Mar. 22, 2004); Act on the Punishment of Procuring Prostitution and Associated Acts, Statutes of South Korea, Act No. 7196 (Mar. 22, 2004). Finland prohibits the purchase of sex from victims of human trafficking and pandering (i.e., pimping). Rikoslaki [Penal Code], 20:8 (Fin.). As discussed further below, England and Wales have recently prohibited "[p]aying for sexual services of a prostitute subjected to force, threats . . . or any other form of coercion, or . . . deception." Sexual Offences Act, 2003, c. 42, § 53A (Eng.) (as amended by Policing and Crime Act, 2009, c. 26, § 14 (Eng.)). A similar model is presently being advocated in Illinois by the Chicago Alliance Against Sexual

pimping have been largely uncontroversial. Similarly, the call to decriminalize the sale of sex is relatively uncontroversial, at least among feminist reformers.[5] However, the abolitionist recommendation to criminalize the *purchase* of sex has been a source of considerable controversy.

CHANTAL THOMAS, FROM THE INTERNATIONAL TO THE LOCAL IN FEMINIST LEGAL RESPONSES TO RAPE, PROSTITUTION/SEX WORK, AND SEX TRAFFICKING: FOUR STUDIES IN CONTEMPORARY GOVERNANCE FEMINISM

29 Harv. J.L. & Gender 335, 348–51 (2006)

Both domestically and internationally, many feminist organizations have devoted extraordinary effort toward shaping the text and the enforcement of international law criminalizing trafficking in persons in general and sex trafficking in particular.

With respect to sex trafficking, the central definitional question is the relationship between prostitution and trafficking, and the relative significance of consent versus coercion in determining a woman's participation in prostitution. Is all prostitution necessarily coercive and a form of trafficking, or is it possible for a woman to meaningfully consent to being a prostitute?

In the debate and discourse on sex trafficking, contenders for influence fall into two broad "camps" in their approaches to understanding the problem of sex trafficking and to defining the legal response to it.

"*Structuralist*" NGOs argued that prostitution necessarily constitutes a form of trafficking because it necessarily reproduces and enforces subordination of women by men. Women's engagement in prostitution manifests this dynamic of sexual subordination at its very core, reflecting and reproducing underlying larger conditions of domination.

These NGOs drew mainly from "radical" or "dominance" feminist theory pioneered by Catharine A. MacKinnon, Andrea Dworkin, and Kathleen Barry. Indeed, Barry co-founded one of the most influential NGOs at the Protocol negotiations, the Coalition Against Trafficking of Women (CATW).

In *Prostitution and Civil Rights*, MacKinnon developed this argument to show that prostitution was a stark manifestation, and one culmination, of a structure that bends women at every turn toward and into sexual subservience:

> Women are prostituted precisely in order to be degraded and subjected to cruel and brutal treatment without human limits; it is the

Exploitation. See End Demand Illinois, http://www.enddemandillinois.org (last visited Apr. 15, 2010) (focusing on the harm inflicted on the "women and girls in the sex trade").

5. Clearly this reform proposal remains controversial among conservative and reactionary abolitionists who view selling sex as immoral and would prefer to penalize both buyers *and* sellers. * * *

> opportunity to do this that is exchanged when women are bought and sold for sex.... [L]iberty for men ... includes liberal access to women, including prostituted ones. So while, for men, liberty entails that women be prostituted, for women, prostitution entails loss of all that liberty means.

In her 1979 book *Female Sexual Slavery*, Kathleen Barry did much to carry this view to the international plane, to raise international awareness of the harmful effects of prostitution, and to revive the conception of it, popular in earlier eras, as a form of slavery. Barry documented physical and psychological abuse, domination and deception of prostituted women and girls in a series of countries in Latin America and Africa, showing how many of these situations "fit the most rudimentary definition of slavery." Barry, like many others working in this area, saw her task as naming and exposing the pervasive and fundamental nature of female domination, and thereby striking the first blow toward freedom.

"Individualist" NGOs were unified by a concern that the approach to trafficking preserve the visibility of the person as an individual. An emphasis on the primacy and importance of the individual translated into a call for an establishment of a framework of individual rights of trafficked persons. Accordingly, human rights organizations formed a central voice in the individualist camp. * * *

In addition to calling for recognition of human rights, the individualist camp strongly opposed a definition of trafficking that failed to recognize the possibility of individual choice. To fail to recognize choice would be to obscure the primacy of the individual behind larger, structural concerns—an untenable position from the human rights perspective. The individualist NGOs were able to form coalitions with the participating governments that did not, within their own territories, aim for complete criminalization or abolition of prostitution.

Somewhat less visible and influential at the level of the negotiations, but still very much visible in the larger discourse around trafficking, was the "pro-work" view. This view proceeded from a view that prostitution, far from being the endpoint of a structure of degradation of women, was simply a form of wage labor. One justification for this view is the notion that anti-prostitution feminists simply "re-inscribe" the victimization of women by "buying into" the idea of prostitution as a form of degradation. Rather than seeing it this way, the pro-work view would seek to dismantle all the ways in which women are placed apart from men, by resisting the impulse to see kinds of work in which women are predominant as special for that reason. By seeing prostitution as simply another form of work, this view sought to emphasize the agency of the individual prostitute as someone who could choose to enter into this form of work, and for whom this work was not horribly degrading. Some within this "pro-work" camp would even see prostitution as a potentially liberating act, in which the woman casts off the shackles of patriarchy that would see prostitution as degrading, and finally takes control of her own body. Within the larger discourse, the pro-work view drives the call for decriminalization of prostitution.

NOTES ON THE CRIMINALIZATION OF PROSTITUTION

1. As Michelle Dempsey observes, feminist calls to criminalize—or, in many jurisdictions, to simply maintain criminal laws against—commercial sex have met with resistance. For a global overview of prostitution policies, see Dempsey, above, at 1731. On what bases might feminist objections be grounded?

One commonly invoked rationale has been articulated by Julia O'Connell Davidson:

> Whether or not we accept the idea that prostitution *should be* regarded as a form of labour like any other, the fact is that vast numbers of people do currently work in prostitution. Even where governments aim to reduce these numbers by providing realistic economic alternatives for women and girls, this is necessarily a long-term objective. In the meantime, it is vital to consider harm-reduction measures to protect those most vulnerable within the sex industry. In many contexts, one such measure would be to encourage clients to recognise prostitutes as workers with rights, including the right to refuse requests for services they do not wish to provide; to freely retract from contracts with clients; to be protected from abusive and slavery-like employment practices, and so on. Campaigns to destigmatise prostitution and recognise it as a form of work may thus, in some settings, represent a vital part of protecting women within prostitution, and it is not at all clear that this objective is compatible with calls for the universal penalisation of clients.

Julia O'Connell Davidson, 'Sleeping with the Enemy'? Some Problems with Feminist Abolitionist Calls to Penalise those who Buy Commercial Sex, 2 Soc. Pol'y & Soc'y 55, 61–62 (2003).

Are you convinced by this argument? Why or why not? For a claim that campaigns to end violence against women promote women as victim subjects and thus reinforce gender essentialism, see Ratna Kapur, The Tragedy of Victimization Rhetoric: Resurrecting the "Native" Subject in International/Post–Colonial Feminist Legal Politics, 15 Harv. Hum. Rts. J. 1 (2002).

2. Would decriminalizing prostitution lessen its stigmatizing effects? If so, should this be considered a positive move?

Martha Nussbaum offers this provocative commentary:

> All of us, with the exception of the independently wealthy and the unemployed, take money for the use of our body. Professors, factory workers, opera singers, sex workers, doctors, legislators—all do things with parts of their bodies for which others offer them a fee. Some people get good wages and some do not; some have a relatively high degree of control over their working conditions and some have little control; some have many employment options and some have very few. And some are socially stigmatized and some are not. However, the difference between the sex worker and the professor—who takes money for the use of a

particularly intimate part of her body, namely her mind—is not the difference between a "good woman" and a "bad woman." It is, usually, the difference between a prosperous well-educated woman and a poor woman with few employment options.

Martha Nussbaum, Trading on America's Puritanical Streak, Atlanta Journal–Constitution (March 14, 2008), available at http://www.ajc.com/search/content/opinion/2008/03/13/spitzered_0314.html.

Do you agree? How does your reaction to Nussbaum's remarks impact your response to the decriminalization question? For an argument that there are important differences between sex work and other work performed mostly by women, see Christine Overall, What's Wrong with Prostitution? Evaluating Sex Work, 17 J. Women & Culture in Soc'y 705 (1992).

3. If you believe that prostitution should be criminalized, do you also support a policy of prosecuting prostituted women? If not, on what basis can you argue that sex purchasers should be punished, but sex sellers should not? In reality, the law generally represents an inversion of this perspective. "Most U.S. states impose more serious penalties on people who sell sex than on those who buy. A few jurisdictions impose no criminal sanctions on the men who buy. More commonly, states following the Model Penal Code classify prostitution as a misdemeanor, but patronizing a prostitute as merely an infraction." Sylvia A. Law, Commercial Sex: Beyond Decriminalization, 73 S. Cal. L. Rev. 523, 565 (2000). Even where there is formal equality, law enforcement falls heavily on women. For example, "[a]fter Massachusetts amended its law in 1983 to make buyers and sellers equally guilty, 263 women, and not a single man, were arraigned on charges of prostitution in Boston in 1990." Id. A study in New York found that only one percent of those arrested for prostitution were johns. JoAnn L. Miller, Prostitution in Contemporary American Society, in Sexual Coercion 45, 53 (Elizabeth Grauerholz & Mary A. Koralweski, eds. 1991). According to statistics from the Bureau of Justice Statistics, in 2004, arrests for "prostitution and commercialized vice" were predominantly of women. Of approximately 20,000 arrests reported, 69.2% were of women, 30.8% of men. Sourcebook of Criminal Justice Statistics Online, Arrests by Offense Charged and Sex, United States, 2004, www.albany.edu/sourcebook/pdf/t482004.pdf (last visited July 16, 2010).

4. According to Sylvia Law, prostitution is criminalized in ways with serious racial impact: "fifty-five percent of all women arrested for prostitution, and eighty-five percent of those sentenced to jail, are women of color." Law, above note 3, at 529 (citing Tracy M. Clements, Prostitution and the American Health Care System: Denying Access to a Group of Women in Need, 11 Berkeley Women's L.J. 49, 52–53 (1996)). Is this yet another example in which a gendered system helps to perpetuate racism? What part does racism play in perpetuating prostitution? What factors might contribute to the trafficking of women of color?

5. In In re Nicolette, 779 N.Y.S.2d 487 (N.Y. App. Div.2004), a New York appellate court affirmed the delinquency order entered against a twelve-year-old girl found to have engaged in prostitution despite the fact that, based on her age, she was legally incapable of consenting to any sexual act of a noncommercial nature. Why does the law recognize victimization in one

context (sexual assault based on incapacity to consent), but not the other (prostitution)? Should minors be prosecuted for prostitution? If not, how might the law be reformed to address the problem of prostituted children? For one state's response, see New York Safe Harbor Act, N.Y. Soc. Serv. Law § 447 (McKinney 2008). See also Toolsi Gowin Meisner, Shifting the Paradigm from Prosecution to Protection of Child Victims of Prostitution, 21 Update 1 (2009). Should distinctions between the two populations (prostituted children/prostituted women) be recognized by law? Why or why not?

UNITED STATES v. FRANK

U.S. Court of Appeals, Eleventh Circuit, 2010.
599 F.3d 1221.

WILSON, CIRCUIT JUDGE

Kent Frank was convicted of traveling and engaging in illicit sexual conduct with three minor girls in Cambodia, of traveling with the intent to engage in illicit sexual conduct, and of purchasing the girls in order to produce sexually explicit visual depictions of them, in violation of 18 U.S.C. §§ 2423(b), (c) and 2251A(b)(2)(A) [parts of the PROTECT Act and Child Protection and Obscenity Enforcement Act]. * * * [W]e affirm Frank's convictions.

I. BACKGROUND

In January 2004, Frank, a United States citizen and resident, was detained in Cambodia by the Cambodian National Police ("CNP") based on a tip that Deputy Chief Keo Thea of the CNP Anti–Human Trafficking and Juvenile Protection Office received concerning unusual activities in Frank's room at the Golden Bridge Hotel. Four girls exited the hotel, and Keo detained them for questioning. Keo suspected that the girls were between fourteen to seventeen years old from their appearance and stated astrological signs. Based upon the information he learned from the girls, Keo went to Frank's hotel room, searched it, and seized various items.[3]

Keo then took Frank to the Cambodian police station, suspecting him of violating Cambodian laws. That night, Frank was not placed in a jail cell but was permitted to sleep on a cot in Keo's office. The next morning, Seng Leena, an interpreter, was brought in, and Frank was interviewed. Frank admitted that he had engaged in sexual conduct with and had taken sexually explicit photographs of Minors A, B, C, and D on multiple occasions. He confessed to paying the girls $15 or $25 to either photograph them or have sex with them.

* * *

3. Items that were found include a digital camera, a laptop, microdrives, pornographic DVDs, HIV/AIDS test kits, various lubricants, condoms, Viagra medication, an address book containing a listing for a mama-san (prostitute broker), an address of a brothel, children's video games (including one entitled "Little Mermaid II: Pinball"), Miracle Bubbles, and female children's clothing including "Looney Tunes" and "Powerpuff Girls" tops, underwear, and stockings.

At trial, the government introduced evidence that during two trips in late 2003, Frank paid the minor girls listed in the indictment to engage in sexual acts with Frank and to take sexually explicit pictures of him. From the first trip, 506 photographs were retrieved, of which 322 were not deleted. From the second trip, which culminated in Frank's arrest by Cambodian officials, law enforcement found 1,134 pictures, of which 96 were not deleted. Among other things, the pictures depicted Frank engaging in sexual conduct with Minor A, Minor B holding an OraQuick HIV test and posing in a sexually explicit manner on Christmas Day, and Minors C and D dressed in various outfits on New Year's Eve. On New Year's day, Frank took the four girls to a swimming pool and then back to his hotel to have sex with them or to take sexually explicit pictures of them.

The government also presented expert witnesses to testify as to the age of the girls. One expert witness testified that Minor B was fifteen to seventeen years old, that Minors A and C were fourteen or fifteen years old, and that Minor D was eleven or twelve years old. Another expert witness testified that the girls were under sixteen years of age. Frank's defense at trial was that he reasonably believed the girls to be eighteen years or older at the time of the offense, that he did not purchase the girls, and that he traveled to Cambodia for business and not to engage in illicit sexual conduct. * * *

* * *

As a matter of first impression, we must determine whether paying a minor directly for sex constitutes a "purchase[ ] . . . of a minor," as that term is used in 18 U.S.C. § 2251A(b)(2). The jury was instructed that to "purchase" is "to buy or to obtain or acquire in exchange for money or its equivalent, or by paying a price." Frank argues that there was insufficient evidence that he "purchas[ed] . . . a mi-nor," * * * because (1) the term "purchase" requires that a defendant purchase a minor from a third party, rather than from the minor herself; and (2) the phrase "purchase[ ] or otherwise obtain[ ] custody or control" requires that purchase must be a form of control, which Frank argues is only achieved through "sexual slavery," such as forced prostitution or captivity for the purpose of producing child pornography. We disagree.

* * *

Section 2251A(b)(2)(A) punishes "[w]hoever purchases or otherwise obtains custody or control of a minor . . . with intent to promote . . . the engaging in of sexually explicit conduct by such minor for the purpose of producing any visual depiction of such con-duct." "Purchase," as used in 18 U.S.C. § 2251A(b), is not defined. Therefore, we must construe the term in accordance with its ordinary meaning. The dictionary defines "purchase" as "to get into one's pos-session" or "to obtain (something desired) by an out-lay." Webster's Third New International Dictionary 1844 (Philip Babcock Gove et. al. eds., 1981). "Obtain" is defined as "to gain or attain possession or disposal" or "hold, keep, possess, occupy." "Possession" is defined as "the act or condition of having in or taking into one's control or holding at one's disposal." By contrast, the word "hire" is defined as "to engage the personal services of for a fixed sum." A fashion designer, therefore, would not say that she "purchased" a clothing model for a photo shoot because that relationship lacks the requisite element of "taking into one's control." Rather, the designer would say that she "hired" a clothing model because the relationship is contractual, not possessive.

The phrase "purchase a woman," however, can be used synonymously with prostitution. See, e.g., Teela Sanders, Maggie O'Neill, Jane Pitcher, Prostitution: Sex Work, Policy & Politics 85 (Sage Publications Ltd. 2009); Janice G. Raymond, Legitimating Prostitution as Sex Work: UN Labour Organization (ILO) Calls for Recognition of the Sex Industry (Part One) 2003, available at http://sisyphe.org/spip.php?article689 (last visited Mar. 11, 2010); Stefan Zweig, The World of Yester-day 83 (University of Nebraska Press 1964) (1943). This use of the word "purchase" is indicative of the complicated nature of prostitution, an act that some argue blurs the very line between possession and free will. See Dorchen A. Leidholt, Co–Executive Dir., Coal. Against Trafficking in Women, Sex Trafficking is Contemporary Slavery: Statement Presented to the United Nations General Assembly (Dec. 6, 1996), available at http://cpcabrisbane.org/Kasama/1997/V11n2/SexTrafficking.htm (last viewed Mar. 11, 2010). For this reason, it has been suggested that selling onself [sic] for money is a form of temporary enslavement. An understanding of the phrase "purchases ... a minor" to include paying a minor for sex, therefore, is acceptable under 18 U.S.C. § 2251A(b), despite the word "purchase" not generally being associated with payment for services in other contexts. For this reason, we find Frank's narrow interpretation of "purchase," which would only apply to situations where a third party sells a minor against her will to the defendant, to be at odds with its plain meaning and the context of 18 U.S.C. § 2251A.

"Purchase" does not require the sale of a minor from a third party to the defendant. In the context of child prostitution, the minor herself is turned into an object or commodity, by selling her body to be used by the defendant for a certain purpose. A minor cannot separate her services from herself because she lacks the capacity to do so. Congress used the term "purchase" alone, rather than "purchase from the minor herself," "purchase a minor's services," or "purchase from another," to encompass situations where money is paid to a third party and where money is paid directly to the minor. If Congress intended to use a narrower construction, it could have expressed that intent in the language. However, it did not, and we will not impose an additional requirement that a middleman be involved. * * *

[P]aying a minor money in exchange for sex constitutes the "purchase[ ] ... of a minor." It is the purchase itself, the paying of money to obtain or acquire the minor's body, that is the means of control.

* * * Frank's confession states that he paid young girls to have sex or take nude pictures and that he knew Minors A, C, and D because they had gone to his hotel room "for the pictures and to have sex together." Thus, a jury could have rationally found that Frank paid the minors to engage in sex and to take sexually explicit pictures. As such, the jury reasonably found that Frank "purchased" the minor girls when he paid them money to return to his hotel in order to engage in sexual relations.

* * *

Accordingly, we affirm Frank's convictions and sentences.

NOTES ON PROSECUTING SEX TRAFFICKERS, SEX TOURISTS AND "JOHNS"

1. Sex tourism has become the object of increasing public and governmental interest. In general, the flow of sex tourists is from economically developed countries to the poorer countries of South East Asia, Africa, Latin America, the Caribbean, and Eastern Europe. Sheila Jeffreys argues that

> sex tourism outsources women's subordination, allowing tourists and businessmen from rich countries to access the greater desperation and degradation that can be bought in poor countries. * * * It enables men in countries in which women are making advances towards equality, one aspect of which is the ability to deny men absolute sexual access, to buy women's sexual subordination elsewhere through their greater spending power.

Jeffreys, text note above, at 130. As Julia O'Connell Davidson notes,

> [a]n analysis of sex tourism which fails to consider its economics is doomed to provide only a partial explanation of the phenomenon, for without the obscene disparity in average per capita incomes between the countries which host sex tourists and those which supply them, sex tourism would be a marginal activity of a very different character. * * * In Thailand, a prostitute can be rented for almost twenty-four hours for * * * a sum of money that would barely secure a man a ten-minute blow job in Britain.

O'Connell Davidson, British Sex Tourists in Thailand, in (Hetero)sexual Politics 42–65 (Mary Maynard & June Purvis, eds. 1995). Do economically developed nations have a responsibility to address the problem of sex tourism? If so, what interventions are most likely to be effective?

2. Some commentators have criticized the treatment of sex tourism and prostitution as "first and foremost an expression of male patriarchal power and female powerlessness." Jacqueline Sanchez Taylor, Dollars are a Girls Best Friend? Female Tourists' Sexual Behaviour in the Caribbean, 35 (3) Sociology 749–64 (2001). Citing the practice of western women buying sex from Caribbean men, Sanchez Taylor argues that sex tourism is best understood as a manifestation of race and class privilege, as opposed to gender hierarchy. Are you persuaded that gender should be deemphasized in the analysis of sex tourism and even, perhaps, prostitution?

3. There is evidence that sex tourism cases are quite difficult to prosecute, requiring enormous amounts of international cooperation. The arrest of Michael Lewis Clark, the first man charged under the new sex tourism law, "was the result of cooperation between many groups, including the U.S. Attorney's Office, U.S. Customs in Thailand, the Cambodian National Police Commissioner General, the Prime Minister of Cambodia, the Regional Security Office of the American Embassy in Phnom Phen, the Australian Federal Police, the Joint Transnational Crime Investigation Team, and two NGOs." Karen D. Breckenridge, Justice Beyond Borders: A Comparison of Australian and U.S. Child Sex Tourism Laws, 13 Pac. Rim L. & Pol'y J. 405, 435 (2004). Clark pled guilty, but had he gone to trial, there would have been issues about obtaining testimony from foreign sources and the admissibility of anything other than live in-person testimony by the victim. The statute raises important constitutional questions as well, including whether Congress has the constitutional power under the Commerce Clause to enact the law. See United States v. Clark, 435 F.3d 1100 (9th Cir. 2006) (considering this among other questions raised by Clark on appeal). Is all this effort likely to reduce the demand for sex tourism? Given the effort required to put one sex tourist in jail, would prosecutorial resources be better directed elsewhere? Some have suggested, for example, that efforts should be made to attack the promoters of sex tours rather than individual tourists. What other kinds of strategies do you think could work?

4. Like sex tourism, sex trafficking—particularly its international dimensions—has also become an area of growing interest and concern. Here, too, difficult questions of resource allocation arise. The State Department reports that every year 600,000 to 800,000 persons are trafficked across international borders and that of those trafficked 80% are women and up to 50% are minors. U.S. Department of State Trafficking In Persons Report, 6 (2006), available at http://www.state.gov/documents/organization/66086.pdf. Within the United States, however, there remain disputes about how many victims of sex trafficking are actually imported into the United States. Early estimates suggested that this number is as high as 50,000 women and children. Liana Sun Wyler & Alison Siskin, Trafficking in Persons: U.S. Policy and Issues for Congress, Congressional Research Service, 19 (2010) (citing Amy O'Neill Richard, International Trafficking in Women to the United States: A Contemporary Manifestation of Slavery and Organized Crime, Center for the Study of Intelligence (1999)). Today, estimates appear to be somewhere between 14,500 and 17,500, although the Justice Department adds that such figures "may be overstated." See Wyler & Sisken, above, at 19. In short, "the number of U.S. citizen trafficking victims in the United States is unknown. In addition, there does not seem to be a definition of what it means to be a U.S. citizen trafficked within the United States. For example, some would argue that all prostitutes who have pimps are victims of trafficking." Id. The U.S. Attorney General reports that in 2008, the U.S. Department of Justice obtained 50 sex trafficking convictions. (These figures do not include Child Exploitation and Obscenity Enforcement Act prosecutions of child trafficking and child sex tourism.) Attorney General's Annual Report to Congress and Assessment of U.S. Government Activities to Combat Trafficking in Persons Fiscal Year 2008, 44 (2009), available at http://www.state.gov/

documents/organization/125840.pdf. Does the incidence of trafficking warrant the resources currently devoted to it? Should even more resources be expended in this effort? Or are you concerned that the attention given international sex trafficking detracts from a focus on more prevalent and more pervasive violence to women at home? How should feminists balance the demands of advocacy on behalf of different victim populations?

5. Federal efforts to address sex trafficking reflect recognition that the problem has both international and domestic dimensions; that it is inexorably linked to the immigration status of trafficking victims; and that it demands an aggressive law enforcement response. Kathleen Kim provides this overview of the evolution of federal legislation to date:

> The Trafficking Victims Protection Act of 2000 ("TVPA") was enacted to comprehensively combat human trafficking in the United States by strengthening criminal laws against the traffickers, establishing immigration relief for certain trafficking victims in the United States, and requiring the U.S. Department of State to study the global problem of trafficking and issue its findings in an annual report on the status of other states regarding their anti-trafficking efforts. * * * The TVPA was reauthorized and amended in 2003, 2005, and 2008. In addition to appropriating funding for continued anti-trafficking efforts, the 2003 amendments included a private right of action. The 2005 amendments included provisions to increase research and prevention efforts. The 2008 reauthorization greatly expanded the TVPA to reach a wider range of prohibited conduct and to confer additional civil rights to trafficked persons. Most significantly, the 2008 amendments specifically grant immigration status to trafficked persons who sue their traffickers in civil court.

Kathleen Kim, The Trafficked Worker as Private Attorney General: A Model For Enforcing the Civil Rights of Undocumented Workers, 1 U. Chi. Legal F. 247, 279–80 (2009). See generally Wyler & Siskin, above note 4.

"Severe forms of human trafficking" are defined by the TVPA as "sex trafficking in which a commercial sex act is induced by force, fraud, or coercion, or in which the person induced to perform such act has not attained 18 years of age; or * * * the recruitment, harboring, transportation, provision, or obtaining of a person for labor or services, through the use of force, fraud, coercion for the purpose of subjection to involuntary servitude, peonage, debt bondage, or slavery." Victims of Trafficking and Violence Protection Act, Pub. L. No. 106–386, § 103(8) (2000). What understandings of prostitution, of sex trafficking, and of trafficking generally, are incorporated into this definition? In your view, does it adequately describe the problem? Why or why not?

Is the TVPA's treatment of sex trafficking consistent with state and local approaches to prostitution? Moira Heiges argues that "[w]ithout acknowledging the ways in which the dominant prostitution enforcement paradigm obstructs anti-trafficking policies, it is unlikely that the U.S. will achieve significant success in reducing sex trafficking either in this country or abroad." Moira Heiges, From the Inside Out: Reforming State and Local Prostitution Enforcement to Combat Sex Trafficking in the United States and

Abroad, 94 Minn. L. Rev. 428, 430 (2009). Why might this be true? Are you persuaded?

6. The TVPA's immigration-related provisions authorize the issuance of relief on a number of grounds. In concept and in application, these provisions have proven controversial:

> Advocates and scholars have scrutinized the low number of T visas [which grant immigration relief to trafficking victims under specified conditions] awarded. Many have critiqued the government's general anti-trafficking strategy, which places primary emphasis on the criminal prosecution of traffickers as the reason for the low numbers. Some commentators have argued that the link between T visa eligibility and cooperation with law enforcement in the investigation and prosecution of the trafficking is too onerous, subjecting trafficking victims to further trauma if they must ultimately participate in criminal proceedings against their traffickers. Others contend that the government's focus on criminal enforcement makes protection measures for trafficked individuals contingent upon federal law enforcement choosing to investigate and prosecute trafficking violations. The inherent selectivity in the prosecutorial process and its utilization of trafficking victims as witnesses for the criminal process leave many trafficked persons excluded from protection benefits and ultimately from full access to justice.

Kim, above note 5, at 285–86.

What is your reaction to a policy of conditioning immigration relief on cooperation with prosecutorial efforts? (It may help to know that since passage of the TVPA approximately 200 cases have been prosecuted, about two-thirds of which have involved sex trafficking. Id. at 224.)

7. Liberal feminists have raised concerns about the growing interest of government officials in sex trafficking, charging that it has been embraced as a moral crusade by conservative women's groups and the Christian right as part of a larger project to support sexual abstinence and traditional sex roles for women. Is it possible that a focus on sex trafficking will actually undermine feminist goals? Do you agree that an anti-sex trafficking agenda risks driving the debate into questions about proper sexual behavior rather than violence and exploitation? Should feminists reject the support of those whose views they would otherwise reject, or encourage the possibility of common ground? For two views on this dilemma, see Julia O'Connell Davidson, 'Sleeping with the Enemy'? Some Problems with Feminist Abolitionist Calls to Penalise those who Buy Commercial Sex, 2 Soc. Pol'y & Soc'y 55, 61 (2003); Dempsey, excerpted above, at 1739 (responding to the "strange bedfellows" argument).

8. In 2009, a broad-based coalition of formerly prostituted women and activists successfully introduced the "End Demand Illinois" Campaign, which Kaethe Morris Hoffer, a key player in this movement, describes as

> a policy and legislative campaign directed at increasing the ability of the criminal justice system to punish demand for prostitution, while simultaneously increasing services for girls and women at risk for, suffering in, or attempting to escape prostitution. Ultimately, the End Demand Cam-

> paign seeks to decriminalize sex acts by girls and women (and sometimes boys and men) who are purchased for sex, while also "recriminalizing" all forms of purchasing and pimping.

Kaethe Morris Hoffer, A Response to Sex Trafficking Chicago Style: Follow the Sisters, Speak Out, 158 U. Pa. L. Rev. 101, 115 (2010). How should the criminal justice system address the demand side of the market for sex? If "recriminalization" is the appropriate response, should enforcement of existing laws against soliciting prostitution be given greater priority to increase the likelihood of arrest? Is this an area where shaming sanctions (e.g., showing men arrested for solicitation on local cable television, or "John TV") might be successfully employed? What is the role of civil forfeiture? Is mandatory education ("John School") likely to be effective? See Michael Shivley et al., Final Report on the Evaluation of the First Offender Prostitution Program: Report Summary (2008). Or should traditional criminal penalties—in particular, incarceration—be enhanced for the purchase of sex? Can you think of other appropriate sanctions?

DART v. CRAIGSLIST, INC.

U.S. District Court, N.D. Illinois, 2009.
665 F. Supp. 2d 961

JOHN F. GRADY, DISTRICT JUDGE.

In this diversity action Plaintiff Thomas Dart, the Sheriff of Cook County, Illinois, alleges that the "erotic" (now "adult") services section of Craigslist's popular Internet classifieds service facilitates prostitution and constitutes a public nuisance. Craigslist's users create and post "over thirty million new classified advertisements each month" for, among other things, "jobs, housing, dating, used items, and community information." Craigslist's website, which displays the ads, is viewed over nine billion times each month. The webpage located at "chicago.craigslist.org," one of many region-specific webpages on Craigslist's website, displays Chicago-related listings arranged by categories (e.g., "for sale" and "services") and subcategories (e.g., "antiques" and "computer"). Craigslist created the categories, but its users create the content of the ads and select which categories their ads will appear in. Users posting ads on the website agree to abide by Craigslist's "Terms of Use," which prohibit posting unlawful content. Users browsing the "erotic" subcategory—which is (or was) the website's most popular destination—-receive an additional "warning & disclaimer" stating that users entering that section agree to "flag 'prohibited' " any content that violates Craigslist's Terms of Use including "offers for or the solicitation of prostitution." Below the warning is a general "erotic services" link, and links to further subcategories (e.g., "w4m" (women for men)). Craigslist also gives users the option to search through ads using a word-search function.

Sheriff Dart alleges that, notwithstanding Craigslist's warnings, users routinely post advertisements in the erotic-services category "openly promis[ing] sex for money." Based on the samples that he cites in his complaint most of the ads are veiled (sometimes very thinly) using code words. He alleges, for example, that "roses" mean dollars and "greek" refers to anal sex. One advertisement states: "15 Min $50 Roses ... 1 hour $150 Roses"-so much for the code-and "How About A G–R–E–E–K Lesson I'm A Great Student!!"[2] Other sample advertisements are more ambiguous. (Pl.'s Resp. at Ex. 2 ("HELLO GENTELMEN NOW YOU MEET JADE AND TIPHANY WE DO TWO GIRL SHOWS AND INDIVISUAL CALLS!! WE GARAUNTEE THE TIME OF YOUR LIFE!!!") (spelling errors in the original).) Many of the ads include nude or nearly-nude pictures, ostensibly of the person posting the ad or offering his or her services. Sheriff Dart cites the advocacy group "The Polaris Project" for the proposition that "Craigslist is now the single largest source for prostitution, including child exploitation, in the country." Law enforcement officials (including plaintiff) regularly conduct prostitution stings using information culled from advertisements in Craigslist's erotic-services category.[3] By his own count plaintiff has arrested over 200 people through Craigslist since January of 2007. Some of those arrested were charged with pimping minors. He estimates that between January and November 2008 his department devoted 3,120 man-hours and approximately $105,081.00 to make 156 arrests.

* * *

* * * Sheriff Dart's complaint alleges that Craigslist's erotic-services category constitutes a public nuisance. See Restatement (Second) of Torts § 821B(1) ("A public nuisance is an unreasonable interference with a right common to the general public."). As "evidence" of the public nuisance he alleges that Craigslist violates federal, state, and local prostitution laws. He contends that Craigslist "solicits for a prostitute" within the meaning of [the Illinois Criminal Code] by "arrang[ing]" meetings of persons for purposes of prostitution and "direct[ing]" persons to places of prostitution. He also alleges more generally that Craigslist makes it easier for prostitutes, pimps, and patrons to conduct business. (Craigslist "streamlines the prostitution process"); * * * He seeks to recoup the money his department has spent policing Craigslist-related prostitution, compensatory damages, and punitive damages * * * [and] he requests an injunction requiring Craigslist to desist "engaging in the conduct complained of herein." * * *

Craigslist contends that it is immune from liability pursuant to Section 230(c) of the Communications Decency Act. That provision provides as follows:

> (c) Protection for "Good Samaritan" blocking and screening of offensive material
>
> (1) Treatment of publisher or speaker

---

2. Spelling variations, like the hyphens in "G–R–E–E–K," are apparently used to avoid detection by automated screening programs. This subterfuge, and the use of sexual code words generally, is specifically prohibited by Craigslist's "Erotic Services Posting Guidelines."

3. Perhaps reflecting the problem of ambiguous posts, Sheriff Dart alleges that in a typical sting an arrest is made only after the person identified in the ad offers an undercover officer sex for money.* * *

No provider or user of an interactive computer service shall be treated as the publisher or speaker of any information provided by another information content provider

* * *

Craigslist contends that § 230(c)(1) "broadly immunizes providers of interactive computer services from liability for the dissemination of third-party content." That appears to be the majority view [which this court applies to the facts of this case].* * *

D. Applying § 230(c)(1) to Plaintiff's Public–Nuisance Claim

Sheriff Dart alleges that Craigslist itself violates criminal laws prohibiting prostitution and related offenses. He alleges for example that Craigslist knowingly "arranges" meetings for the purpose of prostitution and "directs" people to places of prostitution. But these allegations strain the ordinary meaning of the terms "arrange" and "direct" unless Craigslist itself created the offending ads.[8] There is no such allegation, and given § 230(c)(1), we cannot treat Craigslist as if it did create those ads. The same goes for plaintiff's allegation that Craigslist "provid[es] the contact information of prostitutes and brothels." Craigslist does not "provide" that information, its users do. "Facilitating" and "assisting" encompass a broader range of conduct, so broad in fact that they include the services provided by intermediaries like phone companies, ISPs, and computer manufacturers. Intermediaries are not culpable for "aiding and abetting" their customers who misuse their services to commit unlawful acts.

* * *

Sheriff Dart insists * * * that Craigslist plays a more active role than an intermediary or a traditional publisher. He claims that Craigslist causes or induces its users to post unlawful ads—by having an "adult services" category with subsections like "w4m" and by permitting its users to search through the ads "based on their preferences." "A website operator can be both a service provider and a content provider: If it passively displays content that is created entirely by third parties, then it is only a service provider with respect to that content. But as to content that it creates itself, or is 'responsible, in whole or in part' for creating or developing, the website is also a content provider." * * *

We disagree with plaintiff that the "adult services" section is a special case [falling outside the immunity provisions of § 230(c)(1)]. The phrase "adult," even in conjunction with "services," is not unlawful in itself nor does it necessarily call for unlawful content. * * * A woman advertising erotic dancing for male clients ("w4m") is offering an "adult service," yet this is not prostitution. *See* [Illinois Criminal Code] (defining prostitution as "sexual penetration" or "any touching or fondling of the sex organs of

8. Webster's Third New International Dictionary 120 (Philip G. Gove et al., eds., 1970) (arrange: "to effect usu. by consulting: come to an agreement or understand about: SETTLE"); id. at 640 (direct: "to show or point out the way for").

one person by another person ... for the purpose of sexual arousal or gratification" in exchange for something of value). It may even be entitled to some limited protection under the First Amendment. Plaintiff's argument that Craigslist causes or induces illegal content is further undercut by the fact that Craigslist repeatedly warns users not to post such content. While we accept as true for the purposes of this motion plaintiff's allegation that users routinely flout Craigslist's guidelines, it is not because Craigslist has caused them to do so. Or if it has, it is only "in the sense that no one could post [unlawful content] if craigslist did not offer a forum." Section 230(c)(1) would serve little if any purpose if companies like Craigslist were found liable under state law for "causing" or "inducing" users to post unlawful content in this fashion. The fact that Craigslist also provides a wordsearch function does not change the analysis. The word-search function is a "neutral tool" that permits users to search for terms that they select in ads created by other users. It does not cause or induce anyone to create, post, or search for illegal content.

* * * Sheriff Dart may continue to use Craiglist's website to identify and pursue individuals who post allegedly unlawful content. But he cannot sue Craigslist for their conduct.[10]

CONCLUSION

Defendant's motion for judgment on the pleadings is granted.

NOTES ON PROSTITUTION AND THE INTERNET

1. Based on the facts alleged in Sheriff Dart's complaint, was Craigslist essentially acting as an internet-based pimp? See Jeff McDonald, The Oldest Profession Finds a New Medium: Craigslist and the Sex Industry, 15 Pub. Int. L. Rep. 42 (2009). What is your estimation of the legal theory of the case?

On September 15, 2010, Craigslist announced that it had closed the section of its site containing advertising for sex-related services in the U.S., while "defend[ing] its rights to carry such advertisements." Claire Cain Miller, Craigslist Says It Has Shut Its Section for Sex Ads, New York Times, Sept. 16, 2010. The company had been under increasing pressure from state attorneys general across the country to remove the advertisements. Id. Other sites posting such ads are apparently "maneuvering to get a bigger share of the business now that Craigslist is out of the game." Id.

2. The immunity provisions of the Communications Decency Act have been criticized by commentators concerned about sex trafficking and pornography. See Communications Decency Act of 1996, 47 U.S.C.A. § 230(c)(1) (West 1998); Rachel Seaton, All Claims are Not Created Equal: Challenging

10. We do not reach Craigslist's alternative argument that the requested injunction would violate the First Amendment. * * *

the Breadth of Immunity Granted by the Communication Decency Act, 6 Seton Hall Circuit Rev. 355, 365 (2010); McDonald, above note 1, at 44. Given that the internet is increasingly used to facilitate the exchange of sex, should legal actions against web sites advertising prostitution be permitted? Does your answer change depending on whether a site promotes sex tours, mail-order bride sales, child prostitution, or adult "escort" services? Why or why not?

3. Assuming that the internet will continue to shape the global sex industry and that "ending demand" is an important component of the fight against trafficking, how should the law be employed in this effort? Should extra-legal reforms also be considered?

F. PORNOGRAPHY

1. PORNOGRAPHY AS SEXUAL SUBORDINATION?

CATHARINE A. MACKINNON, FRANCIS BIDDLE'S SISTER: PORNOGRAPHY, CIVIL RIGHTS, AND SPEECH

In Feminism Unmodified: Discourses on Life and Law 163, 171–75 (1987).

In pornography, there it is, in one place, all of the abuses that women had to struggle so long even to begin to articulate, all the *unspeakable* abuse: the rape, the battery, the sexual harassment, the prostitution, and the sexual abuse of children. Only in the pornography it is called something else: sex, sex, sex, sex, and sex, respectively. Pornography sexualizes rape, battery, sexual harassment, prostitution, and child sexual abuse; it thereby celebrates, promotes, authorizes, and legitimizes them. More generally, it eroticizes the dominance and submission that is the dynamic common to them all. It makes hierarchy sexy and calls that "the truth about sex" or just a mirror of reality. Through this process pornography constructs what a woman is as what men want from sex. This is what the pornography means.

Pornography constructs what a woman is in terms of its view of what men want sexually, such that acts of rape, battery, sexual harassment, prostitution, and sexual abuse of children become acts of sexual equality. Pornography's world of equality is a harmonious and balanced place. Men and women are perfectly complementary and perfectly bipolar. Women's desire to be fucked by men is equal to men's desire to fuck women. All the ways men love to take and violate women, women love to be taken and violated. The women who most love this are most men's equals, the most liberated; the most participatory child is the most grown-up, the most equal to an adult. Their consent merely expresses or ratifies these preexisting facts.

The content of pornography is one thing. There, women substantively desire dispossession and cruelty. We desperately want to be bound, battered, tortured, humiliated, and killed. Or, to be fair to the soft core, merely taken and used. This is erotic to the male point of view. Subjection itself, with self-determination ecstatically relinquished, is the content of women's sexual desire and desirability. * * *

What pornography *does* goes beyond its content: it eroticizes hierarchy, it sexualizes inequality. It makes dominance and submission into sex. Inequality is its central dynamic; the illusion of freedom coming together with the reality of force is central to its working. Perhaps because this is a bourgeois culture, the victim must look free, appear to be freely acting. Choice is how she got there. Willing is what she is when she is being equal. It seems equally important that then and there she actually be forced and that forcing be communicated on some level, even if only through still photos of her in postures of receptivity and access, available for penetration. Pornography in this view is a form of forced sex, a practice of sexual politics, an institution of gender inequality.

* * *

In Andrea Dworkin's definitive work, *Pornography: Men Possessing Women,* sexuality itself is a social construct gendered to the ground. Male dominance here is not an artificial overlay upon an underlying inalterable substratum of uncorrupted essential sexual being. Dworkin presents a sexual theory of gender inequality of which pornography is a constitutive practice. The way pornography produces its meaning constructs and defines men and women as such. Gender has no basis in anything other than the social reality its hegemony constructs. Gender is what gender means. The process that gives sexuality its male supremacist meaning is the same process through which gender inequality becomes socially real.

In this approach, the experience of the (overwhelmingly) male audiences who consume pornography is therefore not fantasy or simulation or catharsis but sexual reality, the level of reality on which sex itself largely operates. Understanding this dimension of the problem does not require noticing that pornography models are real women to whom, in most cases, something real is being done; nor does it even require inquiring into the systematic infliction of pornography and its sexuality upon women, although it helps. What matters is the way in which the pornography itself provides what those who consume it want. Pornography *participates* in its audience's eroticism through creating an accessible sexual object, the possession and consumption of which *is* male sexuality, as socially constructed; to be consumed and possessed as which, *is* female sexuality, as socially constructed; pornography is a process that constructs it that way.

The object world is constructed according to how it looks with respect to its possible uses. Pornography defines women by how we look according to how we can be sexually used. Pornography codes how to look at women, so you know what you can do with one when you see one. Gender is an assignment made visually, both originally and in everyday life. A sex object is defined on the basis of its looks, in terms of its usability for sexual pleasure, such that both the looking—the quality of the gaze, including its point of view—and the definition according to use become eroticized as part of the sex itself. This is what the feminist concept "sex object" means. In this sense, sex in life is no less mediated than it is in art. Men have sex with their image of a woman. It is not that life and art imitate each other; in this sexuality, they *are* each other.

* * *

Obscenity law provides a very different analysis and conception of the problem of pornography. In 1973 the legal definition of obscenity became that which the average person, applying contemporary community standards, would find that, taken as a whole, appeals to the prurient interest; that which depicts or describes in a patently offensive way—you feel like you're a cop reading someone's *Miranda* rights—sexual conduct specifically defined by the applicable state law; and that which, taken as a whole, lacks serious literary, artistic, political or scientific value.[36] Feminism doubts whether the average person gender-neutral exists; has more questions about the content and process of defining what community standards are than it does about deviations from them; wonders why prurience counts but powerlessness does not and why sensibilities are better protected from offense than women are from exploitation; defines sexuality, and thus its violation and expropriation, more broadly than does state law; and questions why a body of law that has not in practice been able to tell rape from intercourse should, without further guidance, be entrusted with telling pornography from anything less. Taking the work "as a whole" ignores that which the victims of pornography have long known: legitimate settings diminish the perception of injury done to those whose trivialization and objectification they contextualize. Besides, and this is a heavy one, if a woman is subjected, why should it matter that the work has other value? Maybe what redeems the work's value is what enhances its injury to women, not to mention that existing standards of literature, art, science, and politics, examined in a feminist light, are remarkably consonant with pornography's mode, meaning, and message. And finally—first and foremost, actually—although the subject of these materials is overwhelmingly women, their contents almost entirely made up of women's bodies, our invisibility has been such, our equation as a sex *with* sex has been such, that the law of obscenity has never even considered pornography a women's issue.

Obscenity, in this light, is a moral idea, an idea about judgments of good and bad. Pornography, by contrast, is a political practice, a practice of power and powerlessness. Obscenity is ideational and abstract; pornography is concrete and substantive. The two concepts represent two entirely different things. Nudity, excess of candor, arousal or excitement, prurient appeal, illegality of the acts depicted, and unnaturalness or perversion are all qualities that bother obscenity law when sex is depicted

36. Miller v. California, 413 U.S. 15, 24 (1973).

or portrayed. Sex forced on real women so that it can be sold at a profit and forced on other real women; women's bodies trussed and maimed and raped and made into things to be hurt and obtained and accessed, and this presented as the nature of women in a way that is acted on and acted out, over and over; the coercion that is visible and the coercion that has become invisible—this and more bothers feminists about pornography. Obscenity as such probably does little harm. Pornography is integral to attitudes and behaviors of violence and discrimination that define the treatment and status of half the population.

TEXT NOTE: THE PORNOGRAPHY DEBATE

Catharine MacKinnon's understanding of pornography transformed the parameters of debate about how women are harmed by the production and consumption of pornographic materials. Starting in the 1980's, MacKinnon was variously celebrated and condemned for advancing what became known as "anti-pornography feminism," and for proposing, along with Andrea Dworkin, a Model Anti–Pornography Ordinance importing this perspective into civil law.[85] Much "second wave" feminist writing opposing the basic premises of anti-pornography feminism is dominated by reference to free speech norms, particularly in relation to the promotion of women's equality. Nadine Strossen's critique reflects this perspective:

> Encouraged by oversimplified, extremist, divisive pronouncements by feminist pro-censorship leaders, there is a widespread misperception that if you are a feminist—or a woman—you must view "pornography" as misogynistic and "detrimental" to women. And you must favor censoring it. * * *
>
> Vague censorship laws always rebound against the groups that hope to be "protected" by them. This is because such laws are enforced by the very power structure against which the disempowered censorship advocates seek protection. Given that the laws' vague and open-ended terms require the enforcing authorities to make subjective, discretionary judgments, it should not be surprising that these judgments are unsympathetic to the disempowered and marginalized.
>
> As Feminists for Free Expression stated in its letter to the Senate Judiciary Committee opposing the Pornography Victims' Compensation Act:
>
> > It is no goal of feminism to restrict individual choices or stamp out sexual imagery. Though some women and men may have this on their platform, they represent only themselves. Women are as varied as any citizens of a democracy; there is no agreement or feminist code as to what images are distasteful or even sexist. It is the right and responsibility of each woman to read, view or produce the sexual material she chooses without the intervention of the state "for her own good." We believe genuine feminism encourages individuals to

85. The ordinance and its legal treatment are discussed below.

> make these choices for themselves. This is the great benefit of being feminists in a free society.[86]

Strossen's argument illustrates one of two very different feminist conceptions of the utility of "speech" for defining and regulating pornography. For anti-censorship feminists like Strossen, women have a particular stake in a discourse around sexuality—"pornographic" or not—and its protection requires special vigilance. In stark contrast, for anti-pornography feminists, pornography is a quintessential violation on the basis of gender—it is violence and discrimination, not speech. As MacKinnon puts it, "pornography makes women into objects. Objects do not speak." MacKinnon, above, at 182.

With the emergence of new communication technologies, the ways in which pornography is produced, consumed, and studied have changed dramatically. Sex positive or "pro-pornography" feminists have entered the conversation, urging that pornography is not inherently, and therefore inevitably, harmful to women. These commentators emphasize pornography's potential for advancing the cause of women's sexual liberation, but not simply (or even mostly) because it counts as "speech." Rather, pornography is viewed as enabling the re-envisioning of women's sexuality in a manner that defies traditional patriarchal constructions. Critique is thus aimed, not at pornography itself, but at the conditions under which mainstream versions of it are produced. Also subject to challenge is the dominance of male-oriented (phallocentered) depictions of sex. Both limitations are thought to be capable of redress; in the interim, categories of woman-produced and woman-consumed pornography are embraced as mechanisms for sexual empowerment.

One proponent of this position is Drucilla Cornell, who urges that "feminism must struggle to clear the space for, rather than create new barriers to, women's exploration of their sexuality." Drucilla Cornell, The Imaginary Domain: Abortion, Pornography, and Sexual Harassment 99 (1995). Part of this effort requires greater attention to the ways in which pornography—in both its mainstream and its alternative forms—currently depicts and constructs female desire, race, and sexual gratification. See, e.g., Katherine M. Franke, Theorizing Yes: An Essay on Feminism, Law, and Desire, 101 Colum. L. Rev. 181 (2001); Jennifer C. Nash, Bearing Witness to Ghosts: Notes on Theorizing Pornography, Race, and Law, Wis. Women's L.J. 47 (2006); Carlin Meyer, Reclaiming Sex from the Pornographers: Cybersexual Possibilities, 83 Geo. L.J. 1969 (1995). The field of "porn studies" examines these intersections, resulting in growing literature that has the potential to greatly enrich feminist legal theory. See, e.g., Bridget J. Crawford, Toward a Third-Wave Feminist Legal Theory: Young Women, Pornography and the Praxis of Pleasure, 14 Mich. J. Gender & L. 99 (2007); Courtenay W. Daum, Feminism and Pornography in the Twenty-First Century: The Internet's Impact on the Feminist Pornography Debate, 30 Women's Rts. L. Rep. 543 (2009).

In what may fairly be called a new era of pornography, much that underlies its proliferation has stayed the same. Catherine MacKinnon sug-

86. Nadine Strossen, A Feminist Critique of "The" Feminist Critique of Pornography, 79 Va. L. Rev. 1099, 1107, 1143–1145 (1993) (citing Letter from the Ad Hoc Committee of Feminists for Free Expression to the Members of the Senate Judiciary Committee, Feb. 14, 1992).

gests that "[p]ornography in cyberspace is pornography in society—just broader, deeper, worse, and more of it. Pornography is a technologically sophisticated traffic in women; electronically communicated pornography traffics women in a yet more sophisticated form." Catherine A. MacKinnon, Vindication and Resistance: A Response to the Carnegie Mellon Study of Pornography in Cyberspace, 83 Geo. L.J. 1959, 1959 (1995). Yet, even for MacKinnon, the shifted terrain is significant: "[A]s new technologies open new avenues for exploitation, they can also open new avenues for resistance. As pornography comes ever more into the open, crossing new boundaries, opening new markets and pioneering new harms, it also opens itself to new scrutiny." Id. While the meaning of pornography remains deeply contested, feminists on all sides of this debate share a commitment to understanding how pornography constructs sexuality while structuring relations between and among women and men.

NOTES ON THE HARM OF PORNOGRAPHY

1. How is the harm of pornography best conceptualized? Are you persuaded that pornography furthers women's subordination? If so, do you agree with Catharine MacKinnon that the subordinating effects of pornography are what define it? Or are you convinced by the anti-censorship argument that "there is no agreement or feminist code as to what images are distasteful or even sexist?" Strossen, above, at 1144. Which of the feminist theories described in Chapter Three informs each position?

2. How do you respond to the sex positive feminist embrace of pornography's emancipatory potential? How are new technologies altering the ways in which women are disempowered and/or empowered by pornography? Notwithstanding considerable debate about the answer to this question, it is uncontroversial to assert that the internet has transformed the production and consumption of pornography. "Indeed, it is often claimed that porn drives technology and that sex has shaped the internet as it currently exists." David Slayden, Debbie Does Dallas Again and Again: Pornography, Technology, and Market Innovation, in Porn.com: Making Sense of Online Pornography 58 (Feona Attwood ed., 2010). Academic commentators are just beginning to address the implications of these developments. See generally Attwood, Porn.com, above. Fiona Attwood provides this overview of contemporary scholarship on sex and media:

> One [area of interest] is the emergence of new "savvy media practitioners," particularly those involved in the production of independent and alternative pornographies, often with a subcultural, countercultural, or queer focus. Another is the development of new porn styles that attempt to speak more effectively to new audiences—particularly women and the sexual subcultures and communities who congregate around sexual display in specific kink cultures or as part of a broader interest in culture and lifestyle issues. Women's involvement in producing online pornographies is another area of study, and the trend toward DIY porn in which rawer and rougher styles of representation dominate has also attracted attention.

> Of course, the question of porn's dangerousness has not gone away. Since the 1990s, this has largely been articulated around cyberporn and cybersex addition, or child pornography and the use of the internet by pedophiles to groom their victims. * * *
>
> More recently, porn has attracted attention in discussions about "war porn" or "atrocity porn"—real life images of torture, combat and execution circulated online—and about "shock" imagery that often represents the body in excessive and grotesque ways—leaky, uncivilized, hurt, or ruptured.

Feona Attwood, Porn Studies: From Social Problem to Cultural Practice, in Porn.com, above, at 9–10.

Will this growing body of research be helpful to answering the question of pornography's harms? To informing policy approaches? Can you identify any limitations of a research agenda that seeks to study "practices and cultures of porn that are emerging online?" Attwood, above, at 243.

3. A number of commentators have posited a relationship between our increasingly "pornified" culture and the growing sexualization of girls in this country. See, e.g., Stephen Hinshaw with Rachel Kranz, The Triple Bind: Saving Our Teenage Girls from Today's Pressures (2009); Mary Pipher, Reviving Ophelia: Saving the Selves of Adolescent Girls (1994). Have you seen evidence of this trend? For one illustration of what Peggy Orenstein calls a "12–car pileup of early sexualization," eight-year-old girls in a national dance contest evocatively performed Beyoncé's "Single Ladies (Put a Ring on It)" before a cheering crowd. Peggy Orenstein, Playing at Sexy: Will Today's Gyrating Girls Become Sexting Young Women?, New York Times Magazine, June 13, 2010, at MM11. If girls are learning at a young age that female sexuality is performative, is pornography partly causal in this development? Is the rise of "sexting" yet another manifestation of this same phenomenon? See National Campaign to Prevent Teen and Unplanned Pregnancy, Sex and Tech: Results from a Survey of Teens and Young Adults 1 (2008), available at http://www.thenationalcampaign.org/sextech/PDF/SexTech_Summary.pdf (almost one quarter of teenage girls have electronically sent or posted nude or seminude photos of themselves). What is the appropriate legal response, if any? See Catherine Arcabascio, Sexting and Teenagers: OMG R U Going 2 Jail???, 16 Rich. J.L. & Tech. 10 (2010).

4. How is male sexuality constructed by pornography? Robert Jensen offers this description:

> We live in a culture in which rape and battery continue at epidemic levels. And in this culture, men are masturbating to orgasm in front of television and computer screens that present them sex with increasing levels of callousness and cruelty toward women. And no one seems terribly concerned about this. * * * The struggle for men of conscience is to define ourselves and our sexuality differently, outside (to the degree possible) the domination/submission dynamic. It is not an easy task; like everyone, we are products of our culture and have to struggle against it. * * * This all would be easier if we could pretend that these images are consumed by some small subset of deviant men—if we could answer the question "what kind of men like those things" by pointing to emotionally

> disturbed men, or pathological men who have some problem that could explain this. Then we could identify and isolate those bad men, maybe repair them. But the answer to the questions is: Men like me. Men like all of us. Men who can't get a date and men who have all the dates they could want. Men who live alone and men who are married. Men who grew up in liberal homes in which pornography was never a big deal and men who grew up in strict religious homes in which no talk of sex was allowed. White and black and brown and any-other-color-you-can-imagine men. Rich men and poor men. And all the king's men.
>
> I am not suggesting that all men use pornography, or that all men who use pornography want material in which women are hurt and humiliated, or that all men who use pornography are bound to then want to hurt and humiliate women. I am simply saying that much of the pornography in the United States records scenes of women being hurt and humiliated; that men masturbate to orgasm to those images; and that those men are not deviants but are acting on cultural norms that are widely taught. And I am suggesting that these facts should matter to us; they should scare us. * * * In a society in which so many men are watching so much pornography that is rooted in the pain and humiliation of women, it is not difficult to understand why so many can't bear to confront it: Pornography forces men to face up to how we learned to be sexual. And pornography forces women to face up to how men see them.

Robert Jensen, Cruel to be Hard: Men and Pornography, Sexual Assault Report, January/February 2004, at 33–34, 45–48, available at http://uts.cc.utexas.edu/?rjensen/articles_2004.html.

Is an account of how men are impacted by pornography integral to a feminist understanding of its harms? Jensen observes that, "as a man, I have considerable control over the conditions in which I live and the situations I am in. Women do not have that control." Id. Is this characterization significant to your evaluation of how pornography harms men? Why have we heard so little about pornography's harms to men in the ongoing discussion about its regulation? In what ways should a feminist reform project deliberately attend to pornography's impact on men? Should we be concerned about the extent to which pornography may be sex education for many adolescent boys, especially with the now-widespread availability of pornography on the internet? See Michele L. Ybarra and Kimberly J. Mitchell, Exposure to Internet Pornography among Children and Adolescents: A National Survey, 8 CyberPsychology & Behavior 5 (2005) (reporting that 87% of males between the ages of 14 and 17 surveyed were exposed to online pornography).

5. Diana E. H. Russell, in Pornography and Rape: A Causal Model, 9 Pol. Psych. 41 (1988), has suggested that pornography might be causally related to violence and abuse in a number of ways:

> In order for rape to occur, a man must not only be predisposed to rape, but his internal and social inhibitions against acting out rape desires must be undermined. My theory in a nutshell is that pornography (1) predisposes some men to want to rape women or intensifies the predisposition in other men already so predisposed; (2) undermines some men's

internal inhibitions against acting out their rape desires; and (3) undermines some men's social inhibitions against the acting out.

Does Russell's theory strike you as sound? How else might pornography be causally related to violence and abuse?

Extensive empirical research on the relationship between pornography and violence against women has not definitively resolved the debate about whether pornography causes sexual aggression. Obviously, while one cannot expose subjects to pornography and then follow them to see if they are violent toward women, some studies have exposed male subjects to pornography and then (1) solicited self-reported responses about subsequent actual aggression against women or (2) watched subjects deliver what they believed to be electric shocks to women. See generally Diana E.H. Russell, Against Pornography: The Evidence of Harm, 142–48 (1993).

As one large-scale study conducted in 2000 concluded: "Anyone reading some of the recent reviews of the literature on the effects of sexually explicit media would have to be perplexed. On the one hand, some researchers have concluded that certain reliable effects have been demonstrated * * * whereas others strongly dismiss the existence of any reliable effects." Neil M. Malamuth, Tamara Addison, & Mary Koss, Pornography and Sexual Aggression: Are There Reliable Effects and Can We Understand Them?, 11 Ann. Rev. Sex Res. 26, 26 (2000); see also Drew A. Kingston, Neil M. Malamuth, Paul Fedoroff & William L. Marshall, The Importance of Individual Differences in Pornography Use: Theoretical Perspectives and Implications for Treating Sexual Offenders, 46(2/3) J. Sex. Res. 216 (2009). After analyzing the critiques and conducting a meta-analysis, and yet another survey, the authors concluded that their analysis showed "reliable associations between frequent pornography use and sexually aggressive behaviors, particularly for violent pornography and/or for men at high risk for sexual aggression." Malamuth et al., Pornography and Sexual Aggression, above, at 26. Of course, critics continue to challenge the existence of a link between sexual violence and pornography, and the empirical contest will wage on. In assessing the harm of pornography, how significant is empirical documentation of a tangible causal connection between consumption and violence? How should a body of equivocal quantitative evidence be evaluated? Are there other ways of measuring pornography's effects?

6. Are women who make pornography harmed by its production? Surely, as even pro-pornography commentators admit, horrible abuses are inflicted on porn sets. See, e.g., Drucilla Cornell, The Imaginary Domain 96, 99, 102, 116 (1995); Courtenay W. Daum, Feminism and Pornography in the Twenty–First Century: The Internet's Impact on the Feminist Pornography Debate, 30 Women's Rts. L. Rep. 543, 547–48, 558 (2009); Carlin Meyer, Reclaiming Sex From the Pornographers: Cybersexual Possibilities, 83 Geo. L.J. 1969, 2001 (1995). For some, this reality should be addressed by reforms like unionization and workplace regulation. See, e.g., Cornell, above, at 96–97, 115–19; Candida Royalle, Porn in the USA, in Feminism and Pornography 542–43 (Drucilla Cornell ed, 2000). For others, even under "optimal" conditions, women's "consent" to their objectification via pornography is not, and cannot possibly be, meaningful. How should the recurring question of agency be

resolved in this context? Consider one woman's story, as told and interpreted by Drucilla Cornell:

> Who becomes a porn star and why does she do so? The first answer, according to porn star Ona Zee, is money. A top porn star can make $2500 a day. The money is an economic reality, but, in the case of porn workers who have endured abusive childhoods, money can also have a symbolic and psychoanalytic function. It can serve the purpose of paying the woman back for what was brutally taken from her for free. Her "sex" is no longer ripped off. The men must pay. Does a woman simply choose to be a porn star? Does the temptation of money give us a full explanation? Ona Zee recalls that in her own experience, all porn workers are products of dysfunctional families. As she states: No little girl wakes up one morning and decides she is going to have sex for money. In psychoanalytic terms, their "choice" to become a porn star is inseparable, in many cases, from the temptation to return to the traumatic scene, to replay the trauma of some form of childhood abuse. As Ona Zee's life demonstrates, however, this replaying need not just be a repetition of the initial abuse. It can also be reparative. * * * The objection that many porn activists have to a certain feminist mentality that insists that they are "victims" is that these feminists represent a class elitism that refuses to take them seriously. For these porn workers, the scene on a pornography set can best be changed by them. As in any effort at self-organization, the emphasis is on their own ability to fight back and not on those outside the porn industry coming to their rescue. This counters the established view that porn workers are helpless victims, imprisoned in a history of abuse from which they cannot escape.

Cornell, The Imaginary Domain, above, at 116–117.

How do you make sense of Ona Zee's account? To what extent should "porn workers" be considered agents, who have chosen their work?

7. "[B]ecause what uniquely characterizes pornography is that the sex acts are not 'simulated' but 'real,' the connection between prostitution and porn work is inevitable." Cornell, The Imaginary Domain, above note 6, at 119. How does your view of "porn work" compare to your evaluation of "sex work"? More broadly, is your response to the pornography debate consistent with your understanding of the harm of prostitution? What are the similarities and differences between pornography and prostitution? Catherine MacKinnon notes that, "something is done when women are used to make pornography." Catherine A. MacKinnon, Vindication and Resistance: A Response to the Carnegie Mellon Study of Pornography in Cyberspace, 83 Geo. L.J. 1959, 1960 (1995). Does the act of filming what is done change its meaning?

8. Race is an integral component of how mainstream pornography represents sex:

> African–American women were not included in pornography as an afterthought but instead form a key pillar on which contemporary pornography itself rests. As Alice Walker points out, "The more ancient roots of modern pornography are to be found in the almost always pornographic treatment of black women who, from the moment they entered slavery

> ... were subjected to rape as the 'logical' convergence of sex and violence. Conquest, in short."

Patricia Hill Collins, Black Feminist Thought 136 (2d ed., 2000) (quoting Alice Walker, Coming Apart, in You Can't Keep a Good Woman Down 42 (1981)). That "pornography produces raced meanings" can hardly be disputed; still, "the intersection of race and pornography remains underanalyzed." Jennifer C. Nash, Bearing Witness to Ghosts: Notes on Theorizing Pornography, Race, and Law, 21 Wis. Women's L.J. 47, 50, 52 (2006). As Jennifer Nash describes:

> [r]ace is hyper-visible in pornographic works, yet race remains invisible in feminist analyses of pornography, as gender is foregrounded as the sole vector of power worthy of feminist analysis. In rendering racialized representations in pornography absent from feminist discourse, feminists have failed to generate a theory that attends to pornography's complexity, multiplicity of meanings, or connections to the maintenance (and possible disruption) of both white supremacy and patriarchy.

Id. at 71. Celine Parreñas Shimizu makes a similar observation:

> Located between the anti-pornography and sex-positive camps, racialized sexuality in pornography remains a problem that needs a more serious and more direct approach. Racialized analyses of pornography demonstrate how the simplifications of sexuality, production, consumption, and fantasy, as well as the rhetoric of gender victimization, register within the context of the lives of women of color.

Celine Parreñas Shimizu, Queens of Anal, Double, Triple, and the Gang Bang: Producing Asian/American Feminism in Pornography, 18 Yale J.L. & Feminism 235, 238 (2006).

Nash's examination of pornographic depictions of black women and Shimuzu's account of Asian/American women in pornography begin to fill the theoretical void that each scholar identifies and critiques. For an empirical treatment of how race and sexuality are portrayed on the internet, see Shoshana Magnet, Feminist Sexualities, Race and the Internet: an Investigation of suicidegirls.com, 9 New Media & Society 577 (2007).

2. PORNOGRAPHY AND THE LAW

MODEL ANTI-PORNOGRAPHY CIVIL RIGHTS ORDINANCE

Andrea Dworkin and Catharine A. MacKinnon, Pornography & Civil Rights: A New Day for Women's Equality, Appendix D (1988).

[In 1983, Minneapolis was the first city to consider a form of the Model Antipornography Civil Rights Ordinance, drafted by Andrea Dworkin and Catharine MacKinnon. After two days of public hearings, the Minneapolis City Council found that pornography violated women's civil rights and adopted a version of the Ordinance as law on December 30, 1983. After the mayor vetoed the law on January 5, 1984, it was reenacted in amended form on July 13, 1984, and vetoed once again by the mayor on the same day. Subsequently, a similar Ordinance was enacted by the

Indianapolis City Council in 1984, but later was declared unconstitutional in American Booksellers Association, Inc. v. Hudnut, which is excerpted below. On November 8, 1988, 62% of the voters in Bellingham, Washington, affirmed a referendum adopting a similar antipornography law. This Ordinance later was declared unconstitutional in Village Books v. City of Bellingham, No. 88–1470 (W.D. Wash. Feb. 9, 1989). The Ordinance has been considered for adoption in Cambridge, Massachusetts; Los Angeles, California; Madison, Wisconsin; the Commonwealth of Massachusetts; Sweden; Germany; New Zealand; and the Philippines.[a]]

Section 2. DEFINITIONS

1. "Pornography" means the graphic sexually explicit subordination of women through pictures and/or words that also includes one or more of the following:

a. women are presented dehumanized as sexual objects, things or commodities; or

b. women are presented as sexual objects who enjoy humiliation or pain; or

c. women are presented as sexual objects experiencing sexual pleasure in rape, incest, or other sexual assault; or

d. women are presented as sexual objects tied up or cut up or mutilated or bruised or physically hurt; or

e. women are presented in postures or positions of sexual submission, servility, or display; or

f. women's body parts—including but not limited to vaginas, breasts, or buttocks—are exhibited such that women are reduced to those parts; or

g. women are presented being penetrated by objects or animals; or

h. women are presented in scenarios of degradation, humiliation, injury, torture, shown as filthy or inferior, bleeding, bruised or hurt in a context that makes these conditions sexual.

2. The use of men, children, or transsexuals in the place of women in (1) of this definition is also pornography for purposes of this law.

* * *

Section 3. CAUSES OF ACTION

1. *Coercion into pornography.* It is sex discrimination to coerce, intimidate, or fraudulently induce (hereafter, "coerce") any person into performing for pornography, which injury may date from any appearance or sale of any product(s) of such performance(s). The maker(s), seller(s),

a. See generally, Margaret A. Baldwin, Pornography and the Traffic in Women: Brief on Behalf of Trudee Able Peterson, et al., Amici Curiae in Support of Defendant and Intervenor Defendants, *Village Books v. City of Bellingham,* 1 Yale J.L. & Feminism 111 (1989); James Lindgren, Defining Pornography, 141 U. Pa. L. Rev. 1153, 1157 (1993).

exhibitor(s) and/or distributor(s) of said pornography may be sued for damages and for an injunction, including to eliminate the product(s) of the performance(s) from the public view.

Proof of one or more of the following facts or conditions shall not, without more, preclude a finding of coercion:

a. that the person is a woman; or

b. that the person is or has been a prostitute; or

c. that the person has attained the age of majority; or

d. that the person is connected by blood or marriage to anyone involved in or related to the making of the pornography; or

e. that the person has previously had, or been thought to have had, sexual relations with anyone, including anyone involved in or related to the making of the pornography; or

f. that the person has previously posed for sexually explicit pictures with or for anyone, including anyone involved in or related to the making of the pornography; or

g. that anyone else, including a spouse or other relative, has given permission on the person's behalf; or

h. that the person actually consented to a use of a performance that is then changed into pornography; or

i. that the person knew that the purpose of the acts or events in question was to make pornography; or

j. that the person showed no resistance or appeared to cooperate actively in the photographic sessions or events that produced the pornography; or

k. that the person signed a contract, or made statements affirming a willingness to cooperate in the production of the pornography; or

l. that no physical force, threats, or weapons were used in the making of the pornography; or

m. that the person was paid or otherwise compensated.

2. *Forcing pornography on a person.* It is sex discrimination to force pornography on a person in any place of employment, education, home, or any public place. Complaints may be brought only against the perpetrator of the force and/or the entity or institution responsible for the force.

3. *Assault or physical attack due to pornography.* It is sex discrimination to assault, physically attack, or injure any person in a way that is directly caused by specific pornography. Complaints may be brought against the perpetrator of the assault or attack, and/or against the maker(s), distributor(s), seller(s), and/or exhibitor(s) of the specific pornography.

4. *Defamation through pornography.* It is sex discrimination to defame any person through the unauthorized use in pornography of their

proper name, image, and/or recognizable personal likeness. For purposes of this section, public figures shall be treated as private persons. Authorization once given can be revoked in writing any time prior to any publication.

5. *Trafficking in pornography.* It is sex discrimination to produce, sell, exhibit, or distribute pornography, including through private clubs.

a. Municipal, state, and federally funded public libraries or private and public university and college libraries in which pornography is available for study, including on open shelves but excluding special display presentations, shall not be construed to be trafficking in pornography.

b. Isolated passages or isolated parts shall not be the sole basis for complaints under this section.

c. Any woman may bring a complaint hereunder as a woman acting against the subordination of women. Any man, child, or transsexual who alleges injury by pornography in the way women are injured by it may also complain.

* * *

Section 4. ENFORCEMENT

1. *Civil Action.* Any person who has a cause of action under this law may complain directly to a court of competent jurisdiction for relief.

2. *Damages.*

a. Any person who has a cause of action under this law, or their estate, may seek nominal, compensatory, and/or punitive damages without limitation, including for loss, pain, suffering, reduced enjoyment of life, and special damages, as well as for reasonable costs, including attorneys' fees and costs of investigation.

b. In claims under Sec. 3(5), or other than against the perpetrator of the assault or attack under Sec. 3(3), no damages or compensation for losses shall be recoverable against maker(s) for pornography made, against distributor(s) for pornography distributed, against seller(s) for pornography sold, or against exhibitor(s) for pornography exhibited, prior to the effective date of this law.

3. *Injunctions.* Any person who violates this law may be enjoined except that:

a. In actions under Sec. 3(5), and other than against the perpetrator of the assault or attack under Sec. 3(3), no temporary or permanent injunction shall issue prior to a final judicial determination that the challenged activities constitute a violation of this law.

b. No temporary or permanent injunction shall extend beyond such pornography that, having been described with reasonable specificity by said order(s), is determined to be validly proscribed under this law.

AMERICAN BOOKSELLERS ASSOCIATION, INC. v. HUDNUT

United States Court of Appeals, Seventh Circuit, 1985.
771 F.2d 323, aff'd mem., 475 U.S. 1001, 106 S.Ct. 1172, 89 L.Ed.2d 291 (1986).

EASTERBROOK, CIRCUIT JUDGE

[The statutory material at issue in *Hudnut* were sections of Chapter 16 of the Code of Indianapolis and Marion County that addressed pornography as sex discrimination. Those provisions varied in several ways from the Model Ordinance, including limiting the trafficking cause of action to pornography that shows violence.]

Indianapolis enacted an ordinance defining "pornography" as a practice that discriminates against women. "Pornography" is to be redressed through the administrative and judicial methods used for other discrimination. The City's definition of "pornography" is considerably different from "obscenity," which the Supreme Court has held is not protected by the First Amendment.

To be "obscene" under *Miller v. California,* 413 U.S. 15 (1973), "a publication must, taken as a whole, appeal to the prurient interest, must contain patently offensive depictions or descriptions of specified sexual conduct, and on the whole have no serious literary, artistic, political, or scientific value."

Offensiveness must be assessed under the standards of the community. Both offensiveness and an appeal to something other than "normal, healthy sexual desires" are essential elements of "obscenity."

* * *

The Indianapolis ordinance does not refer to the prurient interest, to offensiveness, or to the standards of the community. It demands attention to particular depictions, not to the work judged as a whole. It is irrelevant under the ordinance whether the work has literary, artistic, political, or scientific value. The City and many amici point to these omissions as virtues. They maintain that pornography influences attitudes, and the statute is a way to alter the socialization of men and women rather than to vindicate community standards of offensiveness. And as one of the principal drafters of the ordinance has asserted, "if a woman is subjected, why should it matter that the work has other value?" Catharine A. MacKinnon, *Pornography, Civil Rights, and Speech,* 20 Harv. Civ. Rts.-Civ. Lib. L. Rev. 1, 21 (1985).

Civil rights groups and feminists have entered this case as amici on both sides. Those supporting the ordinance say that it will play an important role in reducing the tendency of men to view women as sexual objects, a tendency that leads to both unacceptable attitudes and discrimination in the workplace and violence away from it. Those opposing the ordinance point out that much radical feminist literature is explicit and depicts women in ways forbidden by the ordinance and that the ordinance would reopen old battles. It is unclear how Indianapolis would treat works from James Joyce's *Ulysses* to Homer's *Iliad;* both depict women as submissive objects for conquest and domination.

We do not try to balance the arguments for and against an ordinance such as this. The ordinance discriminates on the ground of the content of the speech. Speech treating women in the approved way—in sexual encounters "premised on equality"—is lawful no matter how sexually explicit. Speech treating women in the disapproved way—as submissive in matters sexual or as enjoying humiliation—is unlawful no matter how significant the literary, artistic, or political qualities of the work taken as a whole. The state may not ordain preferred viewpoints in this way. The Constitution forbids the state to declare one perspective right and silence opponents.

* * *

"If there is any fixed star in our constitutional constellation, it is that no official, high or petty, can prescribe what shall be orthodox in politics, nationalism, religion, or other matters of opinion or force citizens to confess by word or act their faith therein." West Virginia State Board of Education v. Barnette, 319 U.S. 624, 642 (1943). Under the First Amendment the government must leave to the people the evaluation of ideas. Bald or subtle, an idea is as powerful as the audience allows it to be. A belief may be pernicious—the beliefs of Nazis led to the death of millions, those of the Klan to the repression of millions. A pernicious belief may prevail. Totalitarian governments today rule much of the planet, practicing suppression of billions and spreading dogma that may enslave others. One of the things that separates our society from theirs is our absolute right to propagate opinions that the government finds wrong or even hateful.

* * *

Under the ordinance graphic sexually explicit speech is "pornography" or not depending on the perspective the author adopts. Speech that "subordinates" women and also, for example, presents women as enjoying pain, humiliation, or rape, or even simply presents women in "positions of servility or submission or display" is forbidden, no matter how great the literary or political value of the work taken as a whole. Speech that portrays women in positions of equality is lawful, no matter how graphic the sexual content. This is thought control. It establishes an "approved" view of women, of how they may react to sexual encounters, of how the sexes may relate to each other. Those who espouse the approved view may use sexual images; those who do not, may not.

Indianapolis justifies the ordinance on the ground that pornography affects thoughts. Men who see women depicted as subordinate are more likely to treat them so. Pornography is an aspect of dominance. It does not persuade people so much as change them. It works by socializing, by establishing the expected and the permissible. In this view pornography is not an idea; pornography is the injury.

There is much to this perspective. Beliefs are also facts. People often act in accordance with the images and patterns they find around them. People raised in a religion tend to accept the tenets of that religion, often without independent examination. People taught from birth that black people are fit only for slavery rarely rebelled against that creed; beliefs coupled with the self-interest of the masters established a social structure that inflicted great harm while enduring for centuries. Words and images act at the level of the subconscious before they persuade at the level of the conscious. Even the truth has little chance unless a statement fits within the framework of beliefs that may never have been subjected to rational study.

Therefore we accept the premises of this legislation. Depictions of subordination tend to perpetuate subordination. The subordinate status of women in turn leads to affront and lower pay at work, insult and injury at home, battery and rape on the streets. In the language of the legislature, "[p]ornography is central in creating and maintaining sex as a basis of discrimination. Pornography is a systematic practice of exploitation and subordination based on sex which differentially harms women. The bigotry and contempt it produces, with the acts of aggression it fosters, harm women's opportunities for equality and rights [of all kinds]."

Yet this simply demonstrates the power of pornography as speech. All of these unhappy effects depend on mental intermediation. Pornography affects how people see the world, their fellows, and social relations. If pornography is what pornography does, so is other speech. * * * Seditious libel is protected speech unless the danger is not only grave but also imminent.

Racial bigotry, anti-semitism, violence on television, reporters' biases—these and many more influence the culture and shape our socialization. None is directly answerable by more speech, unless that speech too finds its place in the popular culture. Yet all is protected as speech, however insidious. Any other answer leaves the government in control of all of the institutions of culture, the great censor and director of which thoughts are good for us.

Sexual responses often are unthinking responses, and the association of sexual arousal with the subordination of women therefore may have a substantial effect. But almost all cultural stimuli provoke unconscious responses. Religious ceremonies condition their participants. Teachers convey messages by selecting what not to cover; the implicit message about what is off limits or unthinkable may be more powerful than the messages for which they present rational argument. Television scripts contain unarticulated assumptions. People may be conditioned in subtle ways. If the fact that speech plays a role in a process of conditioning were enough to permit governmental regulation, that would be the end of freedom of speech.

It is possible to interpret the claim that pornography is the harm in a different way. Indianapolis emphasizes the injury that models in pornographic films and pictures may suffer. The record contains materials depicting sexual torture, penetration of women by red-hot irons and the like. These concerns have nothing to do with written materials subject to the statute, and physical injury can occur with or without the "subordination" of women. As we discuss * * *, a state may make injury in the course of producing a film unlawful independent of the viewpoint expressed in the film.

The more immediate point, however, is that the image of pain is not necessarily pain. In Body Double, a suspense film directed by Brian DePalma, a woman who has disrobed and presented a sexually explicit display is murdered by an intruder with a drill. The drill runs through the woman's body. The film is sexually explicit and a murder occurs—yet no one believes that the actress suffered pain or died. * * * Depictions may affect slavery, war, or sexual roles, but a book about slavery is not itself slavery, or a book about death by poison a murder.

Much of Indianapolis's argument rests on the belief that when speech is "unanswerable," and the metaphor that there is a "marketplace of ideas" does not apply, the First Amendment does not apply either. The metaphor is honored; Milton's *Aeropagitica* and John Stewart Mill's *On Liberty* defend freedom of speech on the ground that the truth will prevail, and many of the most important cases under the First Amendment recite this position. The Framers undoubtedly believed it. As a general matter it is true. But the Constitution does not make the dominance of truth a necessary condition of freedom of speech. To say that it does would be to confuse an outcome of free speech with a necessary condition for the application of the amendment.

* * *

We come, finally, to the argument that pornography is "low value" speech, that it is enough like obscenity that Indianapolis may prohibit it. Some cases hold that speech far removed from politics and other subjects at the core of the Framers' concerns may be subjected to special regulation. These cases do not sustain statutes that select among viewpoints, however. * * *

At all events, "pornography" is not low value speech within the meaning of these cases. Indianapolis seeks to prohibit certain speech because it believes this speech influences social relations and politics on a grand scale, that it controls attitudes at home and in the legislature. This precludes a characterization of the speech as low value. True, pornography and obscenity have sex in common. But Indianapolis left out of its definition any reference to literary, artistic, political, or scientific value. The ordinance applies to graphic sexually explicit subordination in works great and small. The Court sometimes balances the value of speech against the costs of its restriction, but it does this by category of speech and not by the content of particular works. Indianapolis has created an approved point of view and so loses the support of these cases.

Any rationale we could imagine in support of this ordinance could not be limited to sex discrimination. Free speech has been on balance an ally of those seeking change. Governments that want stasis start by restricting speech. Culture is a powerful force of continuity; Indianapolis paints pornography as part of the culture of power. Change in any complex system ultimately depends on the ability of outsiders to challenge accepted views and the reigning institutions. Without a strong guarantee of freedom of speech, there is no effective right to challenge what is.

The definition of "pornography" is unconstitutional. No construction or excision of particular terms could save it. * * * The district court came to the same conclusion. Its judgment is therefore AFFIRMED.

NOTES ON HUDNUT

1. Even though the *Hudnut* court accepts the premises of the Ordinance, i.e., that depictions of subordination lead to employment discrimination, battery, rape, and "harm women's opportunities for equality," it nonetheless finds the First Amendment superior to the Ordinance's attempt to obtain equality for women. When the Fourteenth Amendment's equal protection guarantee seems undermined by the First Amendment's protection of speech, how should this tension be resolved? Do you agree with how the *Hudnut* court answered this question? For discussions of other ways to do so, see Akhil Reed Amar, The Supreme Court, 1991 Term; The Case of the Missing Amendments: *R.A.V. v. City of St. Paul,* 106 Harv. L. Rev. 124 (1992); Akhil Reed Amar, The Bill of Rights and the Fourteenth Amendment, 101 Yale L.J. 1193 (1992); Morrison Torrey, Thoughts About Why the First Amendment Operates to Stifle the Freedom and Equality of a Subordinated Majority, 21 Women's Rts. L. Rep. 25 (1999).

2. Are all content-based laws unconstitutional? For instance, bribes, threats, fighting words, defamation, misleading commercial speech, TV and radio advertisements for cigarettes and casinos, advocating the violent overthrow of the government, obscenity, child pornography, and certain forms of labor speech are all subjected to some form of government regulation. See Cass R. Sunstein, Pornography and the First Amendment, 4 Duke L.J. 589, 613–15 (1986). In addition, employment discrimination law prohibits speech that is part of a harassing environment. How can you distinguish those restrictions from the civil action proposed in the Ordinance? How would the *Hudnut* court?

3. Does the court give appropriate weight to the fact that pornography is more likely to cause sexual arousal than is racist or anti-semitic speech, i.e., orgasm is a powerful reinforcement? Are there other ways to distinguish the examples of "speech" in above note 2, from pornography?

4. Does the *Hudnut* opinion suggest that some aspects of the Ordinance might pass constitutional muster? Which ones? Could you revise the Ordinance to satisfy the court?

5. Feminists were deeply divided over the merits of the Ordinance in its various incarnations. What are the arguments for and against adopting a civil rights approach to creating a cause of action for women harmed by pornography? Compare Catharine A. MacKinnon, Francis Biddle's Sister: Pornography, Civil Rights, and Speech, In Feminism Unmodified: Discourses on Life and Law 163 (1987), and Andrea Dworkin, Pornography: Men Possessing Women (1981), with Lisa Duggan, Nan D. Hunter & Carole S. Vance, False Promises: Feminist Anti–Pornography Legislation, 38 N.Y.L. Sch. L. Rev. 133 (1993). See also Nan D. Hunter & Sylvia A. Law, Brief Amici Curiae of Feminist Anti–Censorship Taskforce, et al., in American Booksellers Association, v. Hudnut, 21 U. Mich. J.L. Reform 69 (1987–88); Thomas I. Emerson, Pornography and the First Amendment: A Reply to Professor MacKinnon, 3 Yale L. & Pol'y Rev. 130 (1984–85) (article written in response to an earlier article by Catharine MacKinnon, Not a Moral Issue, 2 Yale L. & Pol'y Rev. 321 (1983–84)). Which theoretical frameworks provide support for these various perspectives? How does the growth of the internet and other new technologies impact the relevance of the Ordinance as a regulatory model? Are there ways that it might be adapted to better suit today's realities? Should other legal avenues instead be pursued?

3. REGULATING ONLINE PORNOGRAPHY

AMY ADLER, ALL PORN ALL THE TIME

31 N.Y.U. Rev. L. & Soc. Change 695, 695–700, 706–10 (2006–07).

In the escalating war against pornography, pornography has already won. I make this claim not to take a side in the porn wars, but rather to observe, bluntly, the new world in which we live.

Because of shifts in our culture and, most prominently, shifts in technology[,] * * * pornography has been transformed. Once a widespread but sequestered industry, pornography is now ubiquitous in our society in a way that would have been unimaginable twenty years ago. * * * So changed are our cultural standards governing display that much of what we take for granted on television or in advertisements would have been considered pornographic just two decades ago. Pornography is so commonplace that for many it is merely an annoyance—more spam to clear out of our email inboxes each morning. Porn, at least soft-core porn, is arguably now at the heart of mainstream culture. These changes are so dramatic that I would argue the war on pornography has come to resemble the war on drugs, a war that (at least for now) seems as if it cannot be won.

Why has pornography become so central to our culture? * * * There are a number of significant factors, including changes in social norms governing sexuality, and the saturation of mass media, advertising, and communications with photographic images. Yet it seems arguable that the most prominent factor driving this shift toward the mainstreaming of porn has been technological innovation. The rise of the internet and the development of other new technologies, such as digital cameras, internet relay chats, and peer-to-peer networking, have changed the playing field.

These innovations have dramatically lowered the cost of production and distribution for pornography while, at the same time, making it easier for producers and distributors to avoid detection. Pornography has the force of technology on its side.

I think it is time to reassess pornography in light of its newfound cultural dominance. * * * What does this change in the cultural landscape mean for legal regulation?

* * *

Congress has been attempting to regulate online pornography based on [its effects on children] for the last ten years, but has been repeatedly thwarted by the Supreme Court over concerns about the threat that such regulation poses to protected speech. In 1996, Congress passed the Communications Decency Act (CDA), which criminalized indecent and patently offensive online communications; the Court struck down the CDA's major provisions on constitutional grounds in 1997. In response to this defeat, Congress in 1998 passed the Child Online Protection Act (COPA). COPA was premised on the notion that some speech, even if it is constitutionally acceptable for adults to view, may be regulated because it is "harmful to minors." COPA's constitutionality was the subject of litigation for almost nine years. The Supreme Court evaluated it twice. In Ashcroft v. ACLU I, the Court issued a narrow ruling: although it rejected the Third Circuit's holding that COPA was overbroad because it relied on "contemporary community standards" in evaluating speech, the Supreme Court nonetheless remanded the case for further assessment of COPA's First Amendment validity. Two years later, in Ashcroft v. ACLU II, the Court found that private filtering technology might more effectively protect minors than Congress's proposed regulatory scheme would, and with less threat to free speech. The district court, on remand, finally issued a permanent injunction against COPA [in 2007].

The second weapon in the government's arsenal is the law of child pornography. Though extremely powerful and extremely focused, this weapon is limited in at least two important ways. First, it criminalizes only those pornographic visual images made using actual children; Congress had tried to go further, criminalizing under the rubric of child pornography wholly virtual images depicting child sexual conduct, but the Supreme Court rejected that legislation in 2002. Second, child pornography law is limited in the sense that it now fights on a vastly changed battlefield. Developed prior to the digital revolution, child pornography law is now arguably outmatched by the new ease of pornographic production and distribution brought about by technological innovation.

* * *

Finally, there is obscenity law, [which] represents the oldest of the three weapons in the government's arsenal. Although federal obscenity law dates to the mid-nineteenth century, it wasn't until 1957 that the Supreme Court first held that a category of expression called "obscenity" lacked First Amendment protection. Over the following sixteen years, the Court fought bitterly about obscenity doctrine. In 1973, over vigorous dissent, five members of the Court finally arrived at a standard definition of the term "obscene" that has remained consistent to this day.[25] Although the doctrine is settled, obscenity law has continued to provoke scathing criticism from legal scholars.

* * *

In spite of the changed cultural landscape in which we live, legal actors have fallen back on the most dated and problematic of their weapons to fight this new war. They have turned to obscenity law, a doctrine so old and creaky that it had slipped into relative disuse.

The mystery of obscenity law's revival only deepens when we consider another factor. The doctrine seems disconnected from the primary justification usually invoked in calls for censorship: the protection of children. Indeed, the rhetoric surrounding censorship proposals these days focuses insistently on pornography's threat to children—through either children's access to materials in the online environment, or the direct abuse of children in the production of child pornography. The "harmful to minors" doctrine used by Congress in COPA, for example, seems a far more straightforward way to get at the problem than obscenity law is. Child pornography law also addresses these concerns directly.

In short, given all that's wrong with obscenity law, its resurgence is quite puzzling, particularly when looked at in doctrinal isolation. I submit that the revival of obscenity law becomes much more understandable when viewed in the context of * * * child pornography law and the doctrine of "harmful to minors"—and against the backdrop that I sketched of a porn-saturated society.

* * *

[O]ne way to understand the revival of obscenity law is that it is being redeployed to make up for limitations and defeats in the realms of child pornography law and the doctrine of "harmful to minors." The story of the "Protect Act" (Prosecutorial Remedies and Other Tools to End the Exploitation of Children Today Act of 2003) provides one salient example of this theme. In 2002, the Supreme Court struck down the Child Pornography Prevention Act of 1996 (CPPA), Congress's attempt to ban "virtual" child pornography under the rubric of child pornography law. Once Congress lost its bid to use child pornography law to criminalize virtual images of child sexual conduct, what was left? Obscenity law. Thus

---

25. Miller v. California, 413 U.S. 15 (1973). By the time of the Miller decision, the Court was bitterly divided. See id. at 37–47 (Douglas, J., dissenting). Nonetheless, the Miller majority set forth a three-part test for determining whether a given work should be labeled "obscene": (a) whether the average person, applying contemporary community standards would find that the work, taken as a whole, appeals to the prurient interest; (b) whether the work depicts or describes, in a patently offensive way, sexual conduct specifically defined by the applicable state law; and (c) whether the work, taken as a whole, lacks serious literary, artistic, political, or scientific value. Id. at 24 (citations omitted). In Pope v. Illinois, 481 U.S. 497 (1987), the Court clarified that Miller's third prong should be evaluated by a reasonable person standard. Id. at 501.

the PROTECT Act explicitly invoked obscenity law as the method to restrict virtual child pornography in the wake of the Court's decision. In this way, the First Amendment victory over the attempt to expand child pornography laws became less clear cut; it simply led to an alternate approach to the problem through obscenity law.

* * *

Obscenity law also compensates for failures in the other front against pornography: the attempt to shield minors from online pornography. Reconsider the narrative I told earlier about Congress's struggles with the Court in this area. In response to mounting pressure to do something about children's easy access to online pornography, Congress has passed two major statutes, the CDA and COPA. Yet, as described above, the Court has repeatedly stood in Congress's way. Justice Breyer has described COPA, recently invalidated by a district court, as the culmination of "eight years of legislative effort, two statutes, and three Supreme Court cases."[77] In dissent in Ashcroft v. ACLU II, Breyer warned that the Court's decision "remove[d] an important weapon from the prosecutorial arsenal"; in his view, the Court left prosecutors no choice but to revert to the "all-or-nothing" method of obscenity law as a way to fight online pornography.

In this sense, the three doctrinal areas under consideration today function as parts of an interlocking hydraulic system. Each one is exquisitely sensitive to changes in the other. As child pornography and "harmful to minors" proposals face limitations, obscenity law becomes the part that bears the pressure.

NOTES ON OBSCENITY LAW

1. How are legislative and prosecutorial efforts to protect children from online pornography related to feminist concerns about pornography's effects on women? Even historically, the two domains have been afforded disparate treatment. In *Ferber*, the Supreme Court upheld the criminalization of child pornography, concluding that the "prevention of sexual exploitation and abuse of children constitutes a government objective of surpassing importance." New York v. Ferber, 458 U.S. 747, 757 (1982). Is the key distinction between children and adult women the possibility of "consent" to participate in both the production and consumption of pornography? Do the reasons for criminalizing child pornography and regulating minor's access to pornographic materials extend to women as well? How would sex positive feminists answer this question? How would you respond?

2. If Amy Adler is correct that the "war" on child pornography has led to the resurgence of obscenity law, is this development to be celebrated or condemned by feminists? Does your answer depend on how the concept of obscenity is defined? The U.S. Supreme Court has announced its understanding in Miller, cited in the excerpt above. This understanding may be contrast-

---

77. Ashcroft v. ACLU II, 542 U.S. 656, 689 (2004) (Breyer, J., dissenting). * * *

ed with how the construct is treated in Canada, where "any publication a dominant character of which is the undue exploitation of sex, or of sex and any one or more of the following subjects, namely, crime, horror, cruelty and violence, shall be deemed to be obscene." Butler v. Regina [1992] 1 S.C.R. 452 (Can.). In 1992 the Canadian Supreme Court in Butler v. Regina, unanimously upheld the criminal obscenity law. Justice Sopinka wrote:

> [I]f true equality between male and female persons is to be achieved, we cannot ignore the threat to equality resulting from exposure to audiences of certain types of violent and degrading material. Materials portraying women as a class as objects for sexual exploitation and abuse have a negative impact on "the individual's sense of self-worth and acceptance."

Id. Sopinka further clarified the law by stressing that sexually explicit erotica without violence that is not degrading or dehumanizing would not be prohibited under the law; neither would sexually explicit material which has scientific, artistic or literary merit. In its opinion, the court recognized that the obscenity law limits freedom of expression but found this limitation justified because prevention of the harms associated with the dissemination of pornography was a pressing and substantial concern warranting such a restriction.

Is this interpretation of "obscenity" consistent with the definition of pornography under Catharine MacKinnon's Model Ordinance? Do you think such a reconsideration of how we define "obscenity" under constitutional law is possible in the United States? Why or why not? Which understanding is preferable? Regardless of how obscenity is formally defined, are you troubled by the vast discretion inherent in application?

In *Butler*'s immediate aftermath,

> [o]ne of the first targets of the new law was a lesbian and gay bookstore, Glad Day Bookstore, and a magazine produced by lesbians for lesbians. Not surprisingly, the police, prosecutors, and other government officials viewed this lesbian imagery as degrading. They did not so view violent, misogynistic imagery. Other actions on the part of Canadian authorities that hold censorship power reflect similar attitudes. * * * Pursuant to their new-found authority to interdict at the border material that is "degrading" or "dehumanizing" to women, Canadian customs officials * * * confiscated several feminist works that Canadian bookstores sought to import from the United States, including two books that were written by Andrea Dworkin herself!

Nadine Strossen, A Feminist Critique of "The" Feminist Critique of Pornography, 79 Va. L. Rev. 1099, 1145–46 (1993). Are there ways to define obscenity that minimize the risks of unjust governmental enforcement? If you are skeptical of an obscenity-based prosecutorial approach, can you think of other ways in which the law could be used to address feminist concerns about pornography, both in traditional forms and online?

COURTENAY W. DAUM, FEMINISM AND PORNOGRAPHY IN THE TWENTY-FIRST CENTURY: THE INTERNET'S IMPACT ON THE FEMINIST PORNOGRAPHY DEBATE

30 Women's Rts. L. Rep. 543, 545–548 (2009).

The advent of the Internet has dramatically changed the pornography industry as well as the substance of the pornographic materials that are produced. The Internet is a unique medium that has removed the nearly exclusive control of the means of production of pornography from a few elite media conglomerates and shared it with the masses. Print pornography has long been dominated by a few elite enterprises such as Hugh Hefner's Playboy, Larry Flynt's Hustler, and until recently, Bob Guccione's Penthouse. Similarly, large commercial distributors such as Hustler Video and Vivid Entertainment Group have dominated the video and DVD pornography market as well. The Internet and its unique communicative capabilities, however, have the potential to change pornography by enabling new producers and engaging a larger audience across geographical boundaries. In much the same way that the VCR simplified the recording and viewing of pornographic videos in one's home, the Internet simplifies the production and dissemination of pornographic videos and photographs to a vast audience because the Internet enables anyone to create and maintain his or her own pornographic web sites. Thus, the Internet gives amateur pornographers access to a market that was previously the domain of elite media enterprises. In addition, just as the VCR enabled individuals who would not view pornographic films in a theater to do so in the privacy of their homes, the Internet provides a new medium for the dissemination and consumption of pornography that is even more anonymous and potentially more revolutionary.

These developments are significant because those who control the means of production—historically white males—are able to determine the type of pornographic material that will be released to the public. It has been suggested that media content is often a function of ideological position, and it has "the ability to shape perceptions that make the existing order appear natural and unchanging, with alternatives that are hard to imagine." In this way, media may work to maintain the status quo, and in the case of contemporary American society the status quo remains a patriarchal system. Due to the fact that pornography producers are able to significantly influence content, they may seek to produce pornography that affirms their own white male perspective on sex (and position in society) at the expense of the viewpoints and experiences of women, racial and ethnic minorities, and the LGBT community. If, however, white men no longer monopolize control over the means of production of pornography it is possible that the content of the pornography that is produced will be modified to represent numerous perspectives on sex and sexuality embodied by the new producers. For example, women, African–Americans, Hispanics, Asians, gays, lesbians and transsexuals are now capable of producing their own pornography for consumption by members of their respective groups and the masses or for their own exhibitionist pleasure. These developments may challenge the public's traditional understanding of pornography as well as individuals' perceptions of those portrayed in pornography. As Zillah Eisenstein explains:

> [On the Internet s]exual opportunities expand, anonymous experimentation seems easy, and curiosity is piqued. The subversive potential of the net, where sex and freedom can meet, undermines the hierarchy of patriarchal families and censorious civil society. Sex and gender order the power-effect of culture as a whole. When gender boundaries defining masculinity and femininity begin to loosen, even in virtual space[ ], they unsettle patriarchal heterosexual traditions.

As a result, it is possible to argue that a positive development associated with the Internet—and largely absent from the liberal and conservative arguments that dominate the Internet pornography debate—is the opportunity this medium presents to any and all adults interested in producing and viewing pornographic web sites either for profit or pleasure. From a feminist perspective, this development may provide women with an opportunity to express their sexual desires free from patriarchal constraints. The Internet may prove to be a sexually liberating medium for women, and subsequently become a mechanism to broadly disseminate female-centered and/or female-created pornography that depicts women's sexuality from a feminist perspective. These depictions may undermine the use of sex, as defined by men and portrayed in pornography, as a tool of patriarchy that perpetuates the empowerment of men and the victimization of and discrimination against women. The Internet may provide women with the opportunity to define sex in their own terms, thereby changing the tool of "sex" as presented in pornography so that it is not a patriarchal tool to be used against women but a feminist tool to be used to advance the interests of women.

At the same time, however, the Internet raises new concerns. The borderless nature of cyberspace allows for the broad dissemination of pornographic materials across state and national borders and increases the likelihood that illegal pornographic materials, as defined by existing obscenity laws, will be available on the Internet. The Internet aids in the dissemination of child pornography and photos and films in which individuals (adults and children) are physically and sexually abused. The proliferation of obscene materials on the Internet is of particular concern because of the real harm to individuals that occurs in the "production" of these photographs and videos. Similarly, the anonymity associated with both producing and purchasing sexually explicit depictions on the Internet may contribute to the growth of the "market" and increased demand for these images thereby increasing the risks to women, men and children who are coerced or forced into producing these materials. Finally, the ease of producing and disseminating pornography on the Internet enables the broad diffusion of pornographic images that are sexist, racist and homophobic. As a result, the patriarchal hetero-sexist pornography that dominates the existing print and video markets will continue to thrive on the Internet. Thus, it is important not to downplay the dangers or risks associated with the ease of disseminating sex on the Internet.

These are the types of developments that feminist legal scholars should be addressing in the context of the pornography debate because they have major implications for women's rights and interests and raise new questions about power and equality. For example, it may be argued that the ease of creating, disseminating, accessing and viewing pornography on the Internet has great potential benefit for women—it enables women to define their sexuality and gain access to sexually explicit depictions and educational materials—or poses a real threat to women-it increases the likelihood that women and others will be harmed in the production of pornography or as a result of the broad dissemination of pornography. Thus, one of the Internet's defining features—the democratic nature of the medium—appears to change the terms of the feminist pornography debate, but feminist legal theorists have not adequately addressed this development to date.

NOTES ON EMERGING FEMINIST APPROACHES TO PORNOGRAPHY

1. What might account for the "lag" in feminist legal discourse described by Daum? In answering this question, consider Bridget Crawford's observation, even apart from developments in the pornography sphere, that "legal scholars have been slow to notice" the insights of "third wave" feminists. Bridget J. Crawford, Toward a Third–Wave Feminist Legal Theory: Young Women, Pornography and the Praxis of Pleasure, 14 Mich. J. Gender & L. 99, 101–102 (2007). In part, incorporation of "third wave" feminist thought may be complicated by its "absence of meaningful consideration of law," which can in turn be attributed to a general philosophical orientation toward extra-legal methodologies. Id. at 105; see also id. at 162 ("Although third-wave feminists may appear to ignore the law, reject its methods or reject its accomplishments, they are very much engaged in a transformative project.").

2. With the proliferation of online pornography, many sex positive feminists have emphasized the ways in which women's sexuality can be liberated by pornography consumption, and even by its production. Commentators point to ways in which internet pornography has seemed to "democratize" pornography. As Fiona Attwood describes:

> [b]oth amateur and professional forms of new porn production have been associated with queer and female authorship and the challenge this offers to existing porn norms of sex and gender. * * * Women's involvement in porn is often seen as "helping shape and change society's views on sexuality," associated with the growing visibility of women's perspectives on sexually explicit representation and with the articulation of female desire in cultural forms.

Feona Attwood, Younger, Paler, Decidedly Less Straight": The New Porn Professionals, in Porn.com: Making Sense of Online Pornography 93–94

(Feona Attwood ed., 2010). Widely heralded are the internet's "wider possibilities for reformation and reconstruction of human sexuality.' Carlin Meyer, Reclaiming Sex From the Pornographers: Cybersexual Possibilities, 83 Geo. L.J. 1969, 1976 (1995). From this vantage, "cybersex offers [feminists] a chance to oust the dominant masculinist and misogynistic pornographers from their control over sexual territory and to begin reclaiming * * * sexuality in the relative safety of cyberspace." Id. at 1979. Accordingly, more pornography—not less—will advance the cause of sexual freedom and equality. Are you persuaded by this argument? If not, what are your points of disagreement?

3. Does the participation of women in pornography's production change the experience of: (i) women on the set; and (ii) women consumers? One woman to form her own pornography production company is Candida Royalle, who did so "to show that it was possible to produce explicit porn that had integrity, * * * to show that porn could be nonsexist, and * * * to show that porn could be life-enriching." Candida Royalle, Porn in the USA, in Feminism and Pornography 540 (Drucilla Cornell ed, 2000). In noted departures from industry norms, Royalle requires that men wear condoms, and maintains a "tremendous sense of compassion and respect" for the women working for her, which translates into limiting the number of sex scenes and hours worked per day. Id. at 548. Are improved workplace conditions the "solution" to problems facing women used to produce pornography? See Drucilla Cornell, Pornography's Temptation, in Feminism and Pornography, above, at 551. Royalle characterizes her films as "focus[ing] on sensuality, tenderness, and mutual respect—a holistic approach, instead of a collection of body parts." Royalle, above, at 549. Should pornography of this ilk be viewed as "a form of feminist practice?" Cornell, above, at 564. More generally, is Royalle's account, and her example, helpful to your assessment of whether, and how, law should be used to regulate pornography? Would you want to know more about women as producers and consumers of pornography? See Clay Calvert and Robert D. Richards, Porn in Their Words: Female Leaders in the Adult Entertainment Industry Address Free Speech, Censorship, Feminism, Culture and the Mainstreaming of Adult Content, 9 Vand. J. Ent. & Tech. L. 255 (2006). Are you concerned about the economics of the pornography industry—in particular, whether women are financially profiting? Or are these considerations irrelevant to the proper function of law in this domain?

4. On June 25, 2010, ICANN (Internet Corporation for Assigned Names and Numbers) gave provisional approval to establish a pornography-only internet domain, where addresses will have the suffix .xxx. ICANN's Press Release is available at http://www.icann.org/en/news/releases/release–25jun10–en.pdf.

Perhaps this development can best be understood as a way of zoning cyberspace. See Lawrence Lessig, Reading the Constitution in Cyberspace, 45 Emory L.J. 869, 883–895 (1996). What are the merits of this approach? Drucilla Cornell argues that:

> [n]o woman should be forced to view her own body as it is fantasized as a dismembered, castrated other, found in bits and pieces. She should also not be forced to see her "sex" as it is stereotypically presented in

> hardcore porn through explicit depiction of sex acts. * * * [N]o one should be an enforced viewer to the degree that these images do infringe on some women's imaginary domain. * * * The purpose of zoning is precisely to keep pornography safely resting in its jackets, out of the view of those who seek to inhabit or construct an imaginary domain independent of the one it offers. If we are to value the proliferation of imaginaries, we must protect the psychic space for their creation and expression.

Drucilla Cornell, The Imaginary Domain: Abortion, Pornography and Sexual Harassment 103–104 (1995). Is Cornell's understanding of the value of zoning consistent with your own? In Catherine MacKinnon's view, why would this solution be wholly inadequate? See Catherina A. MacKinnon, Only Words 15 (1993). If the .xxx domain becomes a reality, over industry objections (one executive cited the potential for "devastating" effects "in terms of cost, stigma, and the potential for additional regulation of this name space," E-mail from David McKay, President & CEO of Studio 2000, to ICANN (February 27, 2010, 15:28:58), available at http://forum.icann.org/lists/xxx-icm-agreement/msg01065.html), what will be the effect on the production and consumption of pornography? Would this be a positive development? Can you anticipate its limitations? Should zoning of this nature function as part of a more global legal response? Should it be rejected altogether?

5. Carlin Meyer, along with many others, has suggested the futility of efforts to censor cyberspace. Meyer, above note 2, at 1979–80 (citing technological and constitutional reasons for this conclusion). If she is correct, does this mean that feminists must construct a new legal framework for mitigating pornography's harmful effects? Or that the law has no place in this realm? Drucilla Cornell poses these questions:

> How can a feminist approach to pornography that challenges rather than replicates gender stereotypes be developed? How can we both recognize the nitty-gritty reality of the industry and the suffering it can impose upon its workers at the same time that we affirm the need for women to freely explore their own sexuality?

Cornell, The Imaginary Domain, above note 4, at 95–96. Is this a helpful framework for feminist discourse? Does it accept as a given the potential value of pornography for promoting women's full equality? If so, do you agree with this premise?

6. Should the law be reformed to advance women's sexual well-being? If so, how should feminists engage with this a project? Katherine Franke suggests:

> Given the well known dangers that lie in the substantive legal regulation of sexual pleasure, it may be that the best we can aspire to, as feminist legal theorists, is a set of legal analyses, frames, and supports that erect the enabling conditions for sexual pleasure. If that modest work is the best we can expect from law, that still leaves us much work to be done.

Katherine M. Franke, Theorizing Yes: An Essay on Feminism, Law, and Desire, 101 Colum. L. Rev. 181, 208 (2001). Is this an overly ambitious assessment? Regardless, do you agree that sexual pleasure is an appropriate concern of feminist legal theorists? Should a feminist law reform project encompass the goal of maximizing women's sexual pleasure?

CHAPTER 5

WOMEN AND REPRODUCTION

■ ■ ■

A. INTRODUCTION

Whether to become pregnant, and when, are important decisions in many women's lives. For women who have sexual intercourse with men, the ability to plan pregnancies is critical to equality in the workplace, educational plans, political participation—indeed, to control over the way in which their lives are spent in general. For these reasons, the availability, effectiveness, and accessibility of birth control has played an important role in the history of the women's movement, culminating in the struggle over abortion that has dominated the debate in recent decades. This history is the subject of the first part of this chapter, along with the analysis of feminist scholars and lawyers who have played a part in the movement for reproductive rights.

Women's relationship to their reproductive capacity presents some of the most difficult problems for the law to resolve—or even to conceptualize adequately. The entity represented by the symbiotic unity of a woman and her fetus has been envisaged repeatedly as a relationship between two separate persons with conflicting rights. Hence the legal system has attempted to "save" babies from their mothers, for example, by imprisoning pregnant women who take cocaine and compelling women to submit to caesarean sections against their will, with profound race and class implications. Feminist lawyers and legal scholars have become involved in all of these debates and have played central roles in litigation and legislation necessary to protect women's autonomy and bodily integrity.

Further, while new technology has permitted women to become pregnant without having sexual intercourse with men and has otherwise increased women's control over their bodies, it has also presented serious dangers of controlling women instead. Whether new forms of reproductive technology will be used by women or against them, and whether and to what extent women should be free to choose what to do with their own bodies, including offering to bear children as surrogates for others, are questions that have provoked a substantial amount of debate in the feminist community. The final sections of this chapter present portions of that debate, in a form that invites us to draw connections between the issues involved and the larger struggle over a feminist vision of humanity and equality.

B. BIRTH CONTROL AND STERILIZATION

LINDA GORDON, THE MORAL PROPERTY OF WOMEN: A HISTORY OF BIRTH CONTROL POLITICS IN AMERICA

13–14, 3–4, 295–97, 340–42 (rev'd ed. 2002).

Differences in birth control methods have social significance, in part because some techniques are more amenable to being used independently and even secretly by women, some give full control to men, while others are more likely to be used cooperatively. A list of birth control methods might look like this: infanticide; abortion; sterilization; withdrawal by the male (*coitus interruptus*); suppositories designed to form an impenetrable coating over the cervix; diaphragms, caps, or other devices which are inserted into the vagina over the cervix and withdrawn after intercourse; intrauterine devices; internal medicines—potions or pills; douching and other forms of action after intercourse designed to kill or drive out the sperm; condoms; and varieties of the rhythm methods, based on calculating the woman's fertile period and abstaining from intercourse during it. All these techniques were practiced in the ancient world and in modern preindustrial societies. Indeed, until modern hormonal chemicals there were no essentially new birth control devices, only improvements of the old.

People have been designing homemade contraceptive formulas and performing homemade abortions for years. These folk techniques cannot compete with today's methods for effectiveness and safety, but when they were developed they were extraordinary achievements. On a societal level, even a small percentage of effectiveness produces an impact on the birth rate. Today women want 100 per cent certainty that their pregnancies will be voluntary, a reasonable and practicable desire. But the development of that desire was itself produced by its historic possibility. Lacking that kind of effective contraception, women in preindustrial societies did not form such high expectations.

* * *

The birth-control movement passed through four distinct stages, each characterized by a different slogan for reproduction control. The first was "voluntary motherhood," a slogan advanced by feminists in the second half of the nineteenth century. It expressed exactly the emphasis on choice, freedom, and autonomy for women around which the women's rights movement was unified. Voluntary motherhood became a basic plank in the feminist platform, more universally endorsed than woman suffrage and, arguably, reaching farther to describe and change the plight of women than any other single issue. Stage two, approximately 1910–1920, produced the term "birth control." It represented not only a new concept but a new organizational phase, with separate birth control leagues initially created by feminists who were influenced by the large socialist movement of the time. It stood not only for women's autonomy but for transforming the gender and class order through empowering the powerless, primarily identified as the poor and the female sex. (Although "birth control" was originally associated with this specific, radical movement, it has since become the accepted generic term for reproductive control * * *.)

From 1920 through approximately 1970, the movement evolved away from the radicalism of its second stage into a liberal reform movement. This third stage produced a new slogan, "planned parenthood," in the 1940s, though the new content had been developed in the 1930s. With the revival of feminism in the late 1960s, a fourth stage began, associated first with the concept "reproductive rights." * * *

* * *

Reproductive rights struggles of the late twentieth century consumed more of the energies of the new women's movements than voluntary motherhood had in the 1870s or birth control in 1910–20. And reproductive rights struggles of the late twentieth century had a greater impact on the entire U.S. political context. Never before in the history of the birth control movement—not in its free-love associations, not in the race-suicide debates, not in the civil disobedience of the early twentieth-century campaign for the legalization of contraception—had birth control ever been so controversial. The major reason for the heightened passion about reproduction issues is precisely that they seemed to express the core aims of the women's liberation movement and thus became the major focus of the backlash against feminism. Birth control politics has become an arena for conflict between liberal and conservative ideas about family, personal freedom, state intervention, religion in politics, sexual morality, and social welfare.

* * *

The call for women's control of their reproduction, signaled by the slogan "control over our own bodies," once again identified a claim for reproductive rights that rested on a critique of male domination and a demand for women's liberation, and once again it differentiated this claim from family planning, population control, or eugenic motives. This wave of birth control agitation rested on a more grassroots and comprehensive feminist program than had the previous wave. It invented a new word—"sexism"—which condemned practices once not even reprehensible, and invented an analysis that challenged not only sexual inequality but gender itself, including the view that motherhood had to be women's primary identity.

A conservative response identified abortion and unlimited access to contraception with sexual permissiveness and subversion of tradition, the family, morality, and the word of God. Like previous antifeminist reactions, this one was by no means simply a men's movement but equally a movement of women who did not see their own interests in the dominant feminist imagery, who even saw feminism as antagonistic to women's interests. In the 1970s a new conservatism focused far more on these social/sexual issues and less on economic ones than had earlier conservative responses, and it made birth control issues, particularly abortion, far more prominent in the conservative political agenda. This new conservatism was deeply shaped by fundamentalist Christianity.

In response to the conservative attacks and the (inevitable) weakening of the feminist movement in the 1980s, the campaign for reproductive rights once again lost its exclusively feminist identity. But this loss was in part a gain, as it brought together a broad liberal coalition of feminist, mainstream birth control and population control organizations in favor of abortion and contraceptive rights. However, this retreat from a key slogan of the previous decade—"abortion on demand"—and reliance on a right to privacy and "choice" came at the cost of arguing for abortion rights as a *social* good, part of a larger group of reproductive rights that helped to create equality for women and social responsibility for children. * * *

* * *

* * * [T]he range of contraceptive choices is no greater now than it was forty years ago. Some blame feminists and consumer groups, accusing them of overreacting and causing panic about the dangers of the most "effective" contraceptives. In fact, the only case that might qualify as an example of overreaction to the fear of health hazard—the withdrawal of IUDs from the market * * * —was not a product of consumer pressure but of other market and legal forces. Others blamed government (i.e., FDA) overregulation, while still others pointed to inadequate research funds or insufficient economic incentives for drug companies. * * *

The first explanations to come from the women's movement for this lack of progress blamed a rather simply conceived sexism, expressed in research priorities: Why weren't the experts developing a male contraceptive? Why wasn't there adequate safety testing? Wouldn't the safety of a product aimed at men have been more carefully policed? * * *

* * *

But the feminist questions go deeper, to an examination of the goals of contraceptive developers and the preconditions of contraceptive use. This also requires a self-critique, since many birth control advocates and users, including feminists, had vicariously joined the scientists' search for a "magic bullet"—a contraceptive that is 100 percent effective, safe, and comfortable: perfect control in one package. * * *

* * * Like legal rights, effective contraception relies on preconditions that include not only motivation and access but also the expectation of being able to reap rewards from controlling one's destiny. In some respects recent patterns of contraceptive development actually discouraged

the taking of personal responsibility—another drawback of "magic-bullet" thinking. The orientation toward a technological solution de-emphasized the reforms needed to create the economic and social preconditions for contraceptive use, reforms designed to ameliorate poverty, reduce power differentials between men and women, provide women with more educational and work opportunities, and lessen sexual shame. In recreating contraception not as a human action but as a commodity, the "magic bullet" approach also discouraged personal responsibility and led contraceptive users to think of themselves as consumers waiting for the perfect product. The mid-twentieth-century gangbusters approach to technological development, driven in the case of drugs by the scramble of multinational pharmaceutical companies for the huge markets that make their expensive research labs profitable, provided no incentive to consider the long-term health consequences and/or discomforts of new chemicals and devices, and these dangers in turn further discouraged active contracepting. Finally, the female-only focus of high-tech contraception reinforced the view of birth control as women's responsibility and avoided the discussion and sharing of sexual as well as birth-control planning that barrier methods encourage.

NOTES ON BIRTH CONTROL

1. As Gordon notes, medical research has traditionally assumed that contraception was a matter for women, not men. Research into male contraceptives—both those involving hormonal injections to reduce sperm to low levels and others to decrease their ability to swim—has begun only recently. It is more complicated to suppress male fertility (millions of sperm versus one egg per month), and substantial side effects result from methods involving male sex hormones, which also control libido and musculature (among other things). One recently-publicized Chinese study found that monthly injections of testosterone provided safe, effective, reversible, and reliable contraception by suppressing the production of sperm. Yiqun Gu et al., Multicenter Contraceptive Efficacy Trial of Injectable Testosterone Undecanoate in Chinese Men, 94 J. Clin. Endocrinol. Metab. 1910 (2009). British researchers are also developing a hormone-free pill that men could take on a daily or "as-needed" basis that prevents the ejaculation of sperm without affecting the intensity of orgasm. Fiona Macrae, The Instant Male Pill: Scientists Unveil Contraceptive A Man Can Take Before Sex . . . While Hours Later His Fertility Returns to Normal, Daily Mail (London), Nov. 27, 2006, at 1. A good deal of the delay in research and development has been due to reluctance by drug companies to invest in male contraceptives, out of their belief that men would not use the products. Ironically, the open discussion of men's sexuality in connection with marketing Viagra and other remedies for erectile dysfunction and their immense profitability has led to a reevaluation by the companies. Studies carried out in Europe revealing that men would in fact use male contraceptives have also been a factor in persuading the pharmaceutical industry to engage in research into male contraceptives. See Nelly Oudshoorn, The Male Pill: A Biography of a Technology in the Making (2003). Moreover, one survey of 1500 American men indicated that half would be willing to try the new

method. Amir Efrati, The "Male Pill" Gets Closer to Reality, Wall St. J., Aug. 3, 2004, at D1. Several non-technological problems remain. First, the use of male contraceptives other than condoms increases the chance of HIV/AIDS for both partners. Second, do you think women will trust men who say they have taken a pill or have had an injection, given how much more women have at stake in preventing conception? Should they?

2. The lack of funding of contraception research was one aspect of a more general lack of attention to research on women's health issues and the underlying male model of health and the body. In recent years the disparity in research on women's health has received more attention, leading to revelations that no female subjects were used in a variety of major longitudinal studies. For example, research on the protective qualities of aspirin against heart attacks was performed on 22,071 men and no women. See Michelle Oberman & Margie Schaps, Women's Health and Managed Care, 65 Tenn. L. Rev. 555, 578 (1998); Leonard Abramson, Uncaring Women's Health Care, N.Y. Times, May 14, 1990, at A17. To redress these disparities, several Congresswomen introduced a bill to require gender equity in funding medical research, which resulted in the creation of an Office of Research on Women's Health within the National Institutes of Health and the funding of the Women's Health Initiative, a 15–year, $725 million study of more than 161,000 women, on the causes and treatment of diseases such as breast cancer, heart disease, and osteoporosis. Before the end of the study, results showed that hormone replacement therapy (HRT), long prescribed routinely to post-menopausal women because it was thought to prevent, among other things, bone loss and heart attacks, in fact *increased* the risk of heart disease, stroke, blood clots, breast cancer, and dementia. Nancy McVicar, Largest Health Study Changes Medical Thinking on Genders, Chi. Tribune, Mar. 2, 2005, Woman News §, at 2. More recent results show that rates of breast cancer have decreased since the use of HRT has fallen sharply in the United States. For this and other results of Women's Health Initiative studies, see http://www.whi.org/findings.

3. Historically, African Americans have been suspicious about birth control as a form of "genocide," both because of the movement's early ties to eugenics and because the call to control population growth has typically focused upon controlling the birth rates of non-white women. See, e.g., Dorothy Roberts, Killing The Black Body 56–103 (1997); Angela Y. Davis, Women Race & Class 202–15 (1981). This suspicion was exacerbated in the 1990's by the introduction of Norplant, a hormonal contraceptive that was implanted under the skin in a woman's upper arm and effectively prevented pregnancy for up to five years, yet was entirely reversible when removed. However, there were potential side effects, especially for women who have heart problems, high blood pressure, or diabetes, as many African American women do; and while Medicaid covered the cost of implanting Norplant, women experienced difficulty getting it removed. Roberts, above, at 108, 122–33. Nonetheless bills were introduced in several states mandating insertion of Norplant in cases where a woman had been convicted of child abuse; judges made insertion of Norplant a condition of probation in child abuse cases; and other proposals offered incentives to women on welfare to use Norplant. See, e.g., Stacey L. Arthur, The Norplant Prescription: Birth Control, Woman

Control, or Crime Control?, 40 U.C.L.A. L. Rev. 1 (1992); Roberts, above, at 109–10; see also Catherine Albiston, The Social Meaning of the Norplant Condition: Constitutional Considerations of Race, Class, and Gender, 9 Berkeley Women's L.J. 9 (1994) (examining the constitutionality of conditioning probation upon implantation of Norplant).

Problems with Norplant led to a decline in its use in the U.S. and a focus upon injectable contraceptives such as Depo–Provera, which prevents pregnancy for three months. Dorothy Roberts points out that both injections and Norplant are long-acting and not controlled by the user after the initial decision, reflecting an assumption that poor Black women and women in Third World countries (where both Norplant and injections were pushed by drug companies and "population control" groups) are incapable of taking responsibility for their own sexuality and reproduction. Roberts, above, at 136–48. Norplant was withdrawn from the market in 1999 due to its side effects, but courts have continued to condition probation in cases of child abuse or neglect, specifically when a woman has repeatedly given birth to drug-addicted babies, upon not becoming pregnant, leaving it to the woman to choose the means of contraception. See, e.g., In re Bobbijean P., 2 Misc.3d 1011 (N.Y. Fam. Ct. Monroe Cty 2004). What do you think of giving a woman a choice between prison, on the one hand, and abstinence or birth control, on the other?

4. Another form of contraception widely used in other parts of the world is the intrauterine device, or IUD. An early IUD, the Dalkon Shield, caused infections, miscarriages, and some deaths, leading to widespread products liability litigation, and was banned in 1975. A new generation of IUD's are being used safely and with apparent satisfaction by many women in Europe. A hormone-releasing IUD is available in the United States and is 99.7% effective and completely reversible, but fewer than 1% of American women use them. Jane E. Brody, New Devices and Effective Options in Contraception, N.Y. Times, Oct. 17, 2006, at F7. Vaginal contraceptive rings and transdermal patches are also available, although these newer forms of contraception are often not covered by insurance (only about 40% of the time, according to a 2004 study). Sharon Miller Cindrich, The Birth Control Maze, Milwaukee Journal Sentinel, Mar. 6, 2005, Lifestyle §, at 1.

5. The interaction between politics and technology in the area of birth control is complex. An example is the debate that took place over approval of the so-called "morning-after" pill. This pill, currently marketed as "Plan B," is a form of emergency contraception that can be taken up to at least 72 hours after intercourse. Plan B consists of a high dose of the hormone used in some birth control pills and is substantially cheaper than an abortion. The medical profession, scientific studies, and, initially, the FDA all concluded that the pill was a contraceptive because it apparently works by preventing ovulation early in the menstrual cycle and preventing implantation of the fertilized egg later in the cycle; unlike the so-called abortion pill, RU–486 (discussed later in the chapter), Plan B will not work if taken after implantation of the embryo, which is the ordinary definition of pregnancy. See Marcia M. Boumil & Dana Sussman, Emergency Contraception: Law, Policy and Practice, 7 Conn. Pub. Int. L.J. 157, 158–59, 173–74 (2008). Anti-abortion activists argue nonetheless that it is an abortifacient. Plan B has been available for some time in other

countries without a prescription, but the Bush Administration FDA initially refused to approve it as an over-the-counter drug, for fear that it would encourage promiscuous behavior among teenagers. Gardiner Harris, Report Details F.D.A. Rejection of Next–Day Pill, N.Y. Times, Nov. 15, 2005, at A1. (Conservatives also make this argument against vaccinating girls with the new HPV vaccine, Gardasil, although HPV triggers a deadly cervical cancer and nearly half of all sexually transmitted diseases occur among 15 to 24–year–olds. Micah Globerson, Protecting Women: A Feminist Legal Analysis of the HPV Vaccine, Gardasil, 17 Tex. J. Women & Law 67, 69–72, 75 (2007); Guttmacher Institute, Facts on American Teens' Sexual and Reproductive Health, Jan. 2010.) In July 2006, after intense protest and pressure, including the resignation of Dr. Susan Wood from her position as Assistant Commissioner for Women's Health and Director of the Office of Women's Health at the FDA and a lawsuit filed by the Center for Reproductive Rights, the FDA approved Plan B to be sold as an over-the-counter medication for women aged 18 and older but only by prescription to those younger than 18. After the election of President Obama in 2008, the FDA then reduced the over-the-counter age to 17. Guttmacher Institute, State Policies in Brief: Emergency Contraception, June 1, 2010. As of June 2010, however, two states excluded emergency contraception from their insurance coverage mandate and four states explicitly allowed pharmacists to refuse to dispense it. Id. The Obama Administration FDA may also face a similar fight over approval of an emergency contraceptive marketed in Europe as "ellaOne," which prevents conception for up to 120 hours after unprotected intercourse but is closer chemically to RU–486 than is Plan B. In June 2010, the FDA's panel of reproductive health experts recommended that the FDA approve the pill for prescription use, but the FDA is not required to follow the panel's advice and abortion opponents have vowed to fight the pill's approval. Susan Heavey, FDA Advisers Back 5–Day "Morning After" Pill, Reuters, June 17, 2010.

The necessity for prompt treatment with Plan B or other emergency contraception arises not only in cases of unprotected consensual sex but also in cases of sexual assault, which often result in the victim going to an emergency room. Catholic hospitals are reluctant to offer emergency contraception to rape victims. See, e.g., Catholics for a Free Choice, Second Chance Denied: Emergency Contraception in Catholic Hospital Emergency Rooms (reporting the results of a 2002 survey of all Catholic hospital emergency rooms). As of 2008, nine states had enacted "EC in the ER" laws requiring emergency rooms to offer emergency contraception to victims of sexual assault; three more had laws requiring that the hospital at least give information about it. Boumil & Sussman, above, at 158. Although the FDA approved the drug as a prescription contraceptive in 1999, some pharmacists have also refused to dispense it, causing some states to pass "duty-to-dispense" laws and others to pass "conscience clauses" permitting pharmacists not to follow the doctor's order to fill the prescription. Can you think of any cause of action a woman refused emergency contraception might bring against the hospital or pharmacist that failed to give it to her in a timely fashion? See, e.g., Heather A. Weisser, Abolishing the Pharmacist's Veto: An Argument in Support of a Wrongful Conception Cause of Action Against Pharmacists Who Refuse to Provide Emergency Contraception, 80 S. Cal. L. Rev. 865 (2007); Kristen

Marttila Gast, Cold Comfort Pharmacy: Pharmacist Tort Liability for Conscientious Refusals to Dispense Emergency Contraception, 16 Tex. J. Women & L. 149 (2007).

So-called conscience clauses, or religious exemptions, can present major problems for women seeking access to birth control, sterilization, and abortion. One scholar has suggested that the appropriate public policy is to balance the rights involved by ensuring that individual doctors or pharmacists may refuse but that pharmacies may not refuse to stock contraceptives as a general matter; if these drugs are not regularly stocked for other reasons (e.g., the pharmacy serves a largely elderly community), the store will be required to ensure that the patient is provided information about an alternate and timely source of emergency contraception. See Robin Fretwell Wilson, Essay: The Limits of Conscience: Moral Clashes Over Deeply Divisive Healthcare Procedures, 34 Am. J. L. & Med. 41 (2008). Do you think this is an adequate balance of the rights involved? What policy would you suggest?

At the very end of the Bush Administration, new "Provider Conscience Regulations" were rushed through the Department of Health and Human Services, going into effect on the day Obama was inaugurated; the regulations potentially allow a larger number of individuals and institutions to refuse to participate in a variety of healthcare activities on religious or moral grounds. Kim Worobec et al., HHS' New Provider Conscience Regulations, 21 The Health Lawyer 35 (2009). The Obama Administration HHS then proposed to rescind the new regulations, but this had not been accomplished by August 2010. On May 13, 2010, a bill was introduced into the Senate to impose a duty upon pharmacies to provide FDA-approved contraceptives. Access to Birth Control Act, S.3357, 111th Cong. 2d Sess. (2010). Is there any way to depoliticize these decisions? To stop the drastic policy swings regarding these health-related issues?

6. Many medical insurers initially failed to cover the costs of most forms of reversible contraception, including birth control pills, despite the fact that the costs of unintended pregnancy and/or abortion are far higher, raising issues of sex discrimination under the Pregnancy Discrimination Act. See Sylvia A. Law, Sex Discrimination and Insurance for Contraception, 73 Wash. L. Rev. 363 (1998). Some courts have held, based on theories set forth in Sylvia Law's article, that Title VII requires contraceptives to be covered by insurance policies that offer a full range of drug coverage for men. See, e.g., Erickson v. Bartell Drug Co., 141 F.Supp.2d 1266 (W.D. Wash. 2001); contra, In re Union Pacific R.R. Employment Practices Litigation, 479 F.3d 936 (8th Cir. 2007) (holding that the exclusion of contraceptives from health insurance coverage did not violate Title VII or the PDA); see also Stephen F. Befort & Elizabeth C. Borer, Equitable Prescription Drug Coverage: Preventing Sex Discrimination in Employer–Provided Health Plans, 70 La. L. Rev. 205 (2009). By 2010, 27 states had passed "contraceptive equity acts," mandating coverage of contraception under insurance policies that cover prescription drugs more generally; but 20 states allowed religious employers and insurers to refuse to comply with the state mandate. Guttmacher Institute, State Policies in Brief: Insurance Coverage of Contraceptives, June 1, 2010. The scope of the state mandates is now being tested by cases concerning whether a variety of religious organizations should be exempted from the mandate. See, e.g.,

Catholic Charities of Sacramento, Inc. v. Superior Court, 85 P.3d 67 (Cal. 2004) (holding that Catholic Charities did not qualify for the religious exemption); Catholic Charities v. Serio, 859 N.E.2d 459 (N.Y. 2006) (same). A bill to extend a federal mandate, the Equity in Prescription Insurance and Contraceptive Coverage Act, is pending in Congress, but has not been able to make it out of committee. Title II of the Prevention First Act, S.21, 11th Cong., 1st Sess. (2009). See also Jennifer Shaw, The Prevention First Act Examined: An Overview of the State of Contraception Laws As Viewed Through the Lens of Federal Legislation, 30 Women's Rts. L. Rep. 700 (2009). The new health care reform act passed in March 2010 permits but does not require qualified health plans to include family planning and contraception; the expansion of Medicaid to cover many more people will, however, result in increased access to family planning services, which are a core benefit within Medicaid. See Summary of Provisions Related to Teen and Unplanned Pregnancy in H.R. 3590: Patient Protection and Affordable Care Act, available at http://www.thenationalcampaign.org/policymakers/PDF/SummaryProvisions_TUO_HealthReform.pdf.

7. The United States has the highest rate of teen pregnancy in the industrialized world; levels of sexually transmitted diseases among American teenagers are also much higher than those in other countries. Jacqueline E. Darroch et al., Differences in Teenage Pregnancy Rates Among Five Developed Countries: The Roles of Sexual Activity and Contraceptive Use, 33 Family Planning Perspectives 244 (2001). In 2006, birth rates to girls aged 15 to 19 in the U.S. (births to 4.19% of girls in that age group) were almost twice those in the U.K. (the next highest country, with births to 2.67% of teens in that age group), and seven times the rate in Sweden (where the comparable rate was only .59%). United Nations Statistics Division, Teen Birth Rates: How Does the United States Compare?, Demographic Yearbook 2006. The percentages of teens having sexual intercourse are comparable among these countries, thus the variance in teen pregnancy and STD's can only be explained by use or non-use of contraception. Darroch et al., above.

From 1990 to 2005, the teen pregnancy rate in the U.S., though still much higher than in other developed countries, declined 41%; but it began to increase in 2005–2006. In 2006, 7.15% of all pregnancies in the U.S. were to 15–19–year–olds; about 60% of those resulted in births and 27% in abortion. Alan Guttmacher Institute, Facts on American Teens' Sexual and Reproductive Health, Jan. 2010. The birth rate for teenagers aged 15 to 17 rose 3% in 2006, from 21.4% in 2005 to 22%; the birth rate for teenagers aged 18 to 19 rose 4% in the same year, from 6.99% in 2005 to 7.3% in 2006. Center for Disease Control, Nat'l Center for Health Statistics, Joyce A. Martin et al., Births: Final Data for 2006, National Vital Statistics Reports 57:5 (Jan. 7, 2009). Although proportionally more of these births are to African American and Hispanic teenagers, patterns of sexual activity are in fact converging among teenagers of all races. Luker, Dubious Conceptions: The Politics of Teenage Pregnancy 91 (1996).

One student of teen sexuality has noted that characterizing the social problem as one of teen pregnancy, rather than one of abortion or premarital sex or out-of-wedlock births (2/3 of which are in fact to women aged 20 and older), blends two types of public concerns: the *reproductive* behavior of poor and African American teenagers and the *sexual* behavior of affluent white girls. Constance Nathanson, Dangerous Passage: The Social Control of Sexuality in Women's Adolescence 32–36, 45 (1991). In other words, middle-class white girls shouldn't be having sex, and poor girls of color shouldn't be creating social problems by having babies. Yet the problems of poor teenage mothers, such as medical problems during pregnancy, low-birthweight babies, and school drop-out rates, appear to have much more to do with their poverty than with their pregnancy. Luker, above, at 109–28. Should feminists be concerned about the teen birth rate? For what reasons? Do those reasons have to do with the welfare of the mothers? Of the babies? How? What are appropriate social programs to address the problems you identify? Might there be reasons teenage girls get pregnant, other than lack of education about birth control or unwillingness to use it, such as wanting to have a child to love and to give them a sense of purpose and identity? See, e.g., Constance Willard Williams, Black Teenage Mothers: Pregnancy and Child Rearing from Their Perspective (1991).

8. The public policy adopted by the Bush Administration to address teen pregnancy and childbirth was to fund "abstinence-only-until-marriage" sex education in the schools through a series of grants to the states accompanied by conditions: recipients of the money could not include information about contraception in their sex education programs. This type of sex education deprives students of the information they need to protect their health not only from the perils of too-early pregnancy but also from sexually transmitted diseases, including HIV/AIDS. James McGrath, Abstinence–Only Adolescent Education: Ineffective, Unpopular, and Unconstitutional, 38 U.S.F. L. Rev. 665, 666 (2004). This abstinence-only approach was continued despite a congressional review of abstinence-only curricula that found they included basic scientific errors, distorted information about contraceptives, and reinforced gender stereotypes. See Michelle Fine & Sara I. McClelland, The Politics of Teen Women's Sexuality: Public Policy and the Adolescent Female Body, 56 Emory L.J. 993, 1006–07 (2007). Indeed, the federal guidelines were tightened in early 2006 to prohibit funding any programs that mentioned non-intercourse sexual behaviors as part of an effort to remain abstinent. Id. at 1005–06. Although the content of these programs coincides with the beliefs of certain religious groups (and indeed some abstinence-only programs are even run by religious groups), they have been upheld against the challenge that this constitutes excessive entanglement of state and church forbidden by the Establishment Clause of the First Amendment. Bowen v. Kendrick, 487 U.S. 589 (1988).

The Obama administration eliminated more than $170 million in annual funding of abstinence-only programs and replaced it with a $114 million pregnancy prevention initiative to fund only programs demonstrated scientifically to be effective. Rob Stein, Abstinence-only Programs Might Work, Study Says, Wash. Post, Feb. 2, 2010, at A1. Studies show that some but not all types of formal sex education prior to first intercourse can be effective in reducing sexually risky behaviors by adolescents. Trisha E. Mueller, Lorrie Gavin & Aniket Kulkarni, The Association Between Sex Education and Youth's Engagement in Sexual Intercourse, Age at First Intercourse, and Birth Control Use at First Sex, 42 J. Adolescent Health 89 (2008). Indeed, one study showed that even some types of abstinence-only education may be effective if offered to students in grades 6 and 7 with a mean age of 12.2 years, if it addressed the context of sexual activity in the specific population (which was, in this study, inner-city African American boys and girls). The abstinence-only curriculum found to be effective, however, unlike those funded in the Bush Administration, was not moralistic in tone, did not criticize the use of condoms, and advocated delaying sex rather than complete abstinence outside of marriage; its authors opined that it would not work with older youth and persons in committed relationships, who need more comprehensive sex education aimed at safe sexual practices. John B. Jemmott III, et al., Efficacy of a Theory–Based Abstinence–Only Intervention Over 24 Months, 164 Arch. Pediatr. Adolesc. Med. 152, 157–58 (2010). What do you think should be included in the education schools give adolescents on this subject? For one feminist legal scholar's answer to that question, see Linda C. McClain, Some ABCs of Feminist Sex Education (in Light of the Sexuality Critique of Legal Feminism), 15 Colum. J. Gender & L. 63 (2006).

Sex education has been compulsory in Swedish schools, beginning in preschool, since 1955, with an emphasis on discussion and dialogue. After an initial focus on abstinence, the approach shifted to provision of information "on sexuality as tools [sic] for promoting a responsible behavior and enhance [sic] sexual life as a source of joy and happiness." Students are given extensive information about contraceptive methods, and most of those in the 15– to 16–year–old groups visit the local youth reproductive clinic to learn about the services that are available, including both contraception and abortion. Maria Danielsson, Christina Rogala & Kajsa Sundström, Teenage Sexual and Reproductive Behavior in Developed Countries: Country Report for Sweden 22–26 (2001). After sex education programs were cut back to some extent as a result of budget cuts in Sweden during the 1990's, both teen abortion rates and STD's increased steeply. K. Edgardh, Adolescent Sexual Health in Sweden, 78 Sexually Transmitted Infections 352 (2002).

ROSALIND POLLACK PETCHESKY, ABORTION AND WOMAN'S CHOICE: THE STATE, SEXUALITY, & REPRODUCTIVE FREEDOM

178–82 (rev. ed. 1990; orig. pub. 1984).

By the late 1970s in the United States, surgical sterilization had become the most prevalent form of contraception among women over the age of twenty-five.[a] * * * Its virtual irreversibility puts sterilization into a different category of fertility control from abortion or nonpermanent contraception. The great majority of women getting sterilized for contraceptive purposes are different from most women getting abortions. Women

a. After dramatic increases between 1965 and 1982 (from 16% to 42%), the prevalence of surgical sterilization of either husband or wife reported by women between 15 and 44 years old stabilized at approximately 40% of women who were or ever had been married. Nat'l Center for Health Statistics, Surgical Sterilization in the United States: Prevalence and Characteristics, 1965–95 1, 10–11 (1998). In 2002, 17% of women 15 to 44 used sterilization, and it was the leading birth control method for women 35 and older (50% of women 40–44 years old who used contraception relied on sterilization). Nat'l Center for Health Statistics, Use of Contraception and Use of Family Planning Services in the United States: 1982–2002 7, 9 (2004).

who seek sterilization are married at the time of being sterilized (87 percent), and their peak ages are around 30–34 (as opposed to 18–19 among women getting abortions). They do not want or expect to have any more children (unless they have been sterilized involuntarily or have not been informed that the operation is irreversible). Since most of the women who get abortions are unmarried, have had no children, and are under twenty-five, one would assume that for them, sterilization is not an acceptable alternative to abortion.

* * *

Moreover, while sterilization and abortion rates rose along a similar curve during the 1970s, and reflect a similarly complex weave of economic, medical, and social conditions, they are nonetheless clearly distinct phenomena. For one thing, the medical histories of sterilization and abortion are extremely different. Sterilization was always an alternative initiated through institutionalized medical means. Today it is an increasingly technical and complicated procedure, administered necessarily in a medical setting and requiring specialized surgical skill. Abortion was traditionally a procedure that remained in women's and lay practitioners' hands and only belatedly was incorporated—and then halfheartedly—into regular medical practice. Although technically defined as surgery, abortion in the early stages of pregnancy is a relatively simple procedure that could be performed adequately by trained nurse-midwives working under sanitary conditions with good hospital backup in case of complications. * * * The shift in sterilization trends and policies, however—from a cautious, restrictive policy twenty years ago to one of strong advocacy beginning in 1970—was largely *initiated* by physicians and family planners. This shift directly reflects adverse reports and women's own fears about the health hazards of the pill, particularly for older women, and the search by clinicians for a medically controlled substitute. Thus, while they represent parallel trends, the recent increases in sterilization and abortion really grow out of different dynamics in the political dialectic of reproductive control.

An important part of the history of sterilization that sets it apart from abortion is the incidence of coercive sterilization and sterilization abuse among mainly poor, immigrant, and minority women in the United States. While instances of coercion or pressure on women to get an abortion surely occur, they have nothing of the systematic, state-sanctioned character of involuntary sterilization, as a look at public policy immediately makes clear. Legislative proposals to allow the involuntary sterilization of certain groups on eugenic grounds have a long history, linked to private upper-class organizations promoting "racial betterment and WASP purity." Today sterilization programs are more subtle but nonetheless motivated by population control objectives aimed at particular groups—the "surplus" poor. A deliberate policy of manipulation if not coercion is involved when medical associations and family planning agencies advocate sterilization as a preferred form of birth control, particularly to low-income women and women of color, while withholding or minimizing information about other methods of fertility control. Such a policy is evident in the continued reimbursement by Medicaid, along with most commercial and employment-related health insurance, of 90 percent of the costs of contraceptive sterilization, while funds for abortion are cut off in most states. Practices such as the failure to inform patients adequately, in their own language, that sterilization is irreversible; the failure to provide full information about nonpermanent alternatives (including abortion); the threat of withholding welfare or Medicaid benefits to a woman or her children if she refuses "consent" in sterilization; making permanent sterilization the condition of a voluntarily sought abortion (the notorious "package deal"); using hysterectomy—with its enormously increased risks and drastic consequences—as a form of sterilization; or sterilizing minors or the mentally incompetent are all forms of sterilization abuse prohibited by the 1978 Federal Sterilization Regulations. Yet auditors' reports on federally funded sterilizations in a number of states suggest that such abuses continue in many hospitals that service the poor, largely because of the lack of effective government enforcement machinery.

Nearly all of the documented or court-adjudicated instances of sterilization abuse during the 1970s involved women who were poor and either black, Mexican–American, Puerto Rican, or Native American, or women who were incarcerated or mentally incompetent. Neo-eugenic policies and abusive practices may have played a part in effecting class and race differences in sterilization rates. National survey data from 1975–76 indicate that low-income women and women with little education (high school or lower) have significantly higher rates of sterilization than their middle-class counterparts. Moreover, among low-income, black, and Hispanic groups, it is much more likely to be women rather than men who become sterilized, for reasons that have to do with ethnic culture and history as well as clinical practices; vasectomies occur primarily among white middle-class married men. A recent report by researchers with the federal Health Care Financing Administration shows that female Medicaid recipients are between *two and four times more likely* (depending on geographical region) to be sterilized than are women not dependent on Medicaid; and nearly all Medicaid sterilizations are performed on women.

Abortion rates too tend to be higher among Medicaid-dependent and minority women than among white middle-class women. How, then, can we argue that these differentials indicate women's self-determination in the one case and abuse or nonchoice in the other? Surely the higher rates of sterilization among poor women reflect some of the same social and economic constraints and class divisions within the medical care system that structure the abortion decision among poor women (who are disproportionately women of color). In both cases, the decision is more often than not the product of a conscious, rational determination by poor women to deal with the situation at hand, rather than of manipulations or lies by doctors. In some cases sterilization may be viewed by a woman as a definite relief, a solution to her birth control problems that eliminates fear of pregnancy and hassles with men.

Generally speaking, it is not the technology of a birth control method that makes it abusive or malevolent, but the social arrangements in which that technique is embedded—the degree to which those arrangements allow for the user's conscious participation and control and respond to her personal and biological needs. Sterilization or even hysterectomy may satisfy these criteria in particular cases, depending on the situation. The same may be said for abortion. Yet, recognizing this, we also have to recognize that sterilization has been and remains distinct from abortion both in its historical uses and its practical consequences for women. In the case of sterilization, it is possible to imagine, as some demographers do, that logically, because the method is permanent, its use *always* connotes voluntary choice to terminate childbearing. In reality, we have to deal with a well-documented history in which surgical sterilization has been imposed on women without their knowledge or consent, or without their understanding that the procedure was permanent. This has not occurred with abortion, at least not in the United States or Western Europe. Involuntary sterilization, not involuntary abortion, has been the nucleus of state-sponsored eugenic and neo-eugenic population control policies precisely because it is medically controlled and is permanent. It eliminates a potential "breeder," not just a potential child; and it does not have a long-standing tradition of popular practice behind it. From the point of view of a neo-eugenicist public policy the coincidence of antiabortion and prosterilization programs is not contradictory but rather class and race specific.

Given recurrent patterns of abuse and worsening economic conditions for poor women in the United States, it seems reasonable to expect that denial of abortion funding and further restriction of legal abortions will result in higher rates of sterilization among poor women; abortion cutbacks and sterilization abuse are in this sense "opposite sides of a coin." Yet, * * * Medicaid-dependent women denied abortion funds do not seem to have turned to sterilization as an alternative. Rather, they continue to seek abortions using any means they can. This indicates that sterilization is not an adequate substitute for abortion for most women, in most circumstances; its irreversibility entirely transforms the meaning of "costs" and "risks," putting not a pregnancy but a woman's whole reproductive capacity on the line. It also indicates that political struggles over sterilization abuse by feminists and Third World groups apparently have had an impact on women's consciousness.

NOTES ON STERILIZATION AND STERILIZATION ABUSE

1. The abuses described in the Petchesky excerpt actually happened to large numbers of women and were stopped only after lawsuits and political outcry, confirming the fears of women of color about genocide. One suit, Madrigal v. Quilligan, was a class action concerning sterilizations performed

upon numerous poor and Latina women at the Los Angeles County Hospital during the 1970's without their informed consent, and sometimes even without their knowledge, when they went to the hospital to give birth. See Claudia Dreifus, Sterilizing the Poor, in Feminist Frameworks: Alternative Theoretical Accounts of the Relations Between Women and Men 58–66 (2d ed., Alison M. Jaggar & Paula S. Rothenberg, eds. 1984). In another case, the Relf sisters, aged 12 and 14, were sterilized after welfare officials asked their mother to take them to the hospital for immunizations and then had her sign a consent form for sterilization, although she was illiterate and they did not explain to her what she was signing. Relf v. Weinberger, 372 F.Supp. 1196 (D.D.C.1974). Compulsory sterilization was particularly widespread in U.S. teaching hospitals and was often required as a condition of obtaining an abortion in them. Thomas Shapiro, Sterilization Abuse and Patterns of Female Sterilization, in Population Control Politics 87, 92 (1985). Publicity about these and other cases, as well as substantial pressure and input from feminists involved in the reproductive rights movement, ultimately resulted in the issuance of guidelines by the Department of Health, Education and Welfare to assure informed consent. See, e.g., Linda Gordon, The Moral Property of Women: A History of Birth Control Politics in America 345 (rev'd ed. 2002). Although there is general agreement that the regulations are not typically observed, the problem of coerced sterilization also appears to have diminished since that time. Id. at 345–46. What does this say about whether the law is an effective instrument of social change for women? Might the class action suits be seen as another form of publicity and political pressure?

2. Sterilization abuse is often equated with the science of eugenics, a now reviled version of genetics. Eugenics was a nineteenth century science with an active life in the first three decades of the twentieth century. Supported by the claims of geneticists, sterilization abuse was promoted by doctors and heads of asylums and reached its height during the Great Depression in the 1930's. Daniel J. Kevles, In the Name of Eugenics: Genetics and the Uses of Human Heredity 114–16 (1985); see also Diane B. Paul, Controlling Human Heredity: 1865 to the Present (1995).

We will never know the precise number of persons sterilized during this period, although there is fairly reliable data that at least 40,000 people were sterilized prior to World War II. Jonas Robitscher, Eugenic Sterilization, App. 1 (1973). Some of the people sterilized during this period were labeled mentally ill, others retarded, but many would not qualify under today's definitions as having a mental illness or intellectual disability. See Stephen Jay Gould, The Mismeasure of Man, Chapter 5 (2d ed. 1996). Although it remains unclear whether women were disproportionately victims of sterilization, there is good evidence that ideas about gender had an influence on who was targeted for sterilization: men who were considered effeminate, or failing in manly virtues (including homosexuals), as well as women who failed to meet the expectations of gender roles, were often the targets of sterilization. Victoria Nourse, In Reckless Hands 196–97 n.17 (2008) (discussing the relation of gender to eugenics).

While the association of eugenics and sterilization is well known, what is less well known is that eugenics was as likely to be accepted by progressives, and even feminists, as by conservatives. For example, Margaret Sanger, the great birth control reformer, was a fairly enthusiastic supporter of eugenics. Donald Pickens, Eugenics and the Progressives 80–85 (1968); Ellen Chesler, Woman of Valor: Margaret Sanger and the Birth Control Movement in America, 195–96, 216–17 (1992). In this she was not alone: during the late 1920's and early 1930's, progressives and social reformers not only in the United States but around the world—particularly in liberal social democracies such as Sweden and Denmark—supported active sterilization programs. Paul, above, at 87–89; see also Eugenics and the Welfare State: Sterilization Policy in Denmark, Sweden, Norway, and Finland (Gunnar Broberg & Nils Roll–Hansen, eds. 2d ed. 2005). If early feminists like Sanger supported eugenics, should today's feminists be particularly vigilant in questioning their own ethical assumptions? Anti-abortion forces sometimes claim that abortion is the new eugenics. Do you think that is a fair comparison?

3. Draft a consent form that a woman who was unrepresented by counsel could sign to indicate her informed consent to sterilization. What rules would you want to impose about the conditions under which it could be executed?

4. The types of lawsuits that may be brought to challenge coercive sterilization practices include federal civil rights suits and state law claims based on negligence or battery. See Dick Grosboll, Sterilization Abuse: Current State of the Law and Remedies for Abuse, 10 Golden Gate U.L. Rev. 1147, 1163–87 (1980). Can you think of others (apart from the informed consent litigation described in note 1, above)?

5. What do you see as similarities and differences between forced sterilization and compelled implantation of Norplant (described in Section B, note 3, above)?

6. Tubal ligation, the procedure required to sterilize a woman, can be a desirable form of contraception for some groups of women. It is most commonly relied on by women who are 36 or older, women who have been married, women with two or more children, women below 150% of the federal poverty level, and women with less than a college education. It is the most common method of contraception among Black and Hispanic women. Facts on Contraceptive Use in the United States, June 2010, available at www.guttmacher.org/pubs/fb_contr_use.html (citing W.D. Mosher & J. Jones, Use of Contraception in the United States: 1982–2008, Vital and Health Statistics, 2010, Series 23, No. 29). The most common reason women report for having a tubal ligation is that they did not want more children (71 percent). Nat'l Center for Health Statistics, Dep't of Health and Human Services, Surgical Sterilization in the United States: Prevalence and Characteristics, 1965–1995 8 (1998). In 1995, 24% of married women reported having had a tubal ligation, while only 15% reported that their husbands had had a vasectomy. Id. at 1. Yet tubal ligation is many times more expensive than vasectomy and requires general anesthesia, with its attendant risks. Why do you think so many more women are sterilized than men, given the comparative ease of vasectomy versus the invasive, costly, and riskier nature of tubal ligation?

7. Women who desire sterilization may have a difficult time obtaining it. Sterilization services, like abortions and other reproductive services, including emergency contraception, are not provided at Roman Catholic health facilities,

despite the fact that they may be the only birthing facility in an area. This can pose a particular problem, for example, when a Catholic hospital and a non-Catholic hospital merge in a rural area. See Keri Tonn, Fraud on Your Conscience: Refusal to Offer Postpartum Sterilization and Its Consequences, 11 Mich. St. U. J. Med. & L. 203, 206–11 (2007). Medical experts agree that the safest time to perform a sterilization is at the time of childbirth, yet if a woman gives birth in a Catholic hospital, she will be subjected to the risks and expense of a second surgery at another facility. Susan Berke Fogel & Lourdes A. Rivera, Saving *Roe* Is Not Enough: When Religion Controls Healthcare, 31 Fordham Urb. L.J. 725, 727, 735 (2004).

8. What do you think of Petchesky's conclusion that methods of birth control are not driven by technology but by the social relations in which the technology is embedded? Can you think of other examples of technology being driven by social relations? The Petchesky excerpt is a good illustration of socialist feminist analysis. What might other feminists be likely to say about the relationship between technology and the availability of different methods of birth control?

9. For excellent historical accounts of the experience of poor women with birth control, sterilization, and abortion in the United States, see Johanna Schoen, Choice & Coercion: Birth Control, Sterilization, and Abortion in Public Health and Welfare (2005); Rickie Solinger, Pregnancy and Power: A Short History of Reproductive Politics in America (2005).

GRISWOLD v. CONNECTICUT

Supreme Court of the United States, 1965.
381 U.S. 479, 85 S.Ct. 1678, 14 L.Ed.2d 510.

MR. JUSTICE DOUGLAS delivered the opinion of the Court.

Appellant Griswold is Executive Director of the Planned Parenthood League of Connecticut. Appellant Buxton is a licensed physician and a professor at the Yale Medical School who served as Medical Director for the League at its Center in New Haven—a center open and operating from November 1 to November 10, 1961, when appellants were arrested.

They gave information, instruction, and medical advice to married persons as to the means of preventing conception. They examined the wife and prescribed the best contraceptive device or material for her use. Fees were usually charged, although some couples were serviced free.

The statutes whose constitutionality is involved in this appeal are §§ 53–32 and 54–196 of the General Statutes of Connecticut (1958 rev.). The former provides: "Any person who uses any drug, medicinal article or instrument for the purpose of preventing conception shall be fined not less than fifty dollars or imprisoned not less than sixty days nor more than one year or be both fined and imprisoned."

Section 54–196 provides: "Any person who assists, abets, counsels, causes, hires or commands another to commit any offense may be prosecuted and punished as if he were the principal offender."

The appellants were found guilty as accessories and fined $100 each * * *.

* * *

[S]pecific guarantees in the Bill of Rights have penumbras, formed by emanations from those guarantees that help give them life and substance. Various guarantees create zones of privacy. The right of association contained in the penumbra of the First Amendment is one * * *. The Third Amendment in its prohibition against the quartering of soldiers "in any house" in time of peace without the consent of the owner is another facet of that privacy. The Fourth Amendment explicitly affirms the "right of the people to be secure in their persons, houses, papers, and effects, against unreasonable searches and seizures." The Fifth Amendment in its Self–Incrimination Clause enables the citizen to create a zone of privacy which government may not force him to surrender to his detriment. The Ninth Amendment provides: "The enumeration in the Constitution, of certain rights, shall not be construed to deny or disparage others retained by the people."

* * *

The present case, then, concerns a relationship lying within the zone of privacy created by several fundamental constitutional guarantees. And it concerns a law which, in forbidding the use of contraceptives rather than regulating their manufacture or sale, seeks to achieve its goals by means having a maximum destructive impact upon that relationship. * * * Would we allow the police to search the sacred precincts of marital bedrooms for telltale signs of the use of contraceptives? The very idea is repulsive to the notions of privacy surrounding the marriage relationship.

We deal with a right of privacy older than the Bill of Rights—older than our political parties, older than our school system. Marriage is a coming together for better or for worse, hopefully enduring, and intimate to the degree of being sacred. It is an association that promotes a way of life, not causes; a harmony in living, not political faiths; a bilateral loyalty, not commercial or social projects. Yet it is an association for as noble a purpose as any involved in our prior decisions.

Reversed.

MR. JUSTICE GOLDBERG, whom THE CHIEF JUSTICE and MR. JUSTICE BRENNAN join, concurring.

* * *

* * * The language and history of the Ninth Amendment reveal that the Framers of the Constitution believed that there are additional fundamental rights, protected from governmental infringement, which exist alongside those fundamental rights specifically mentioned in the first eight constitutional amendments.

* * *

* * * To hold that a right so basic and fundamental and so deep-rooted in our society as the right of privacy in marriage may be infringed because that right is not guaranteed in so many words by the first eight amendments to the Constitution is to ignore the Ninth Amendment and to give it no effect whatsoever. Moreover, a judicial construction that this fundamental right is not protected by the Constitution because it is not mentioned in explicit terms by one of the first eight amendments or elsewhere in the Constitution would violate the Ninth Amendment, which specifically states that "(t)he enumeration in the Constitution, of certain rights shall not be construed to deny or disparage others retained by the people."

* * *

I agree with Mr. Justice Harlan's statement in his dissenting opinion in Poe v. Ullman, 367 U.S. 497, 551–552, 81 S.Ct. 1752, 1781: "Certainly the safeguarding of the home does not follow merely from the sanctity of property rights. The home derives its pre-eminence as the seat of family life. And the integrity of that life is something so fundamental that it has been found to draw to its protection the principles of more than one explicitly granted Constitutional right. * * * Of this whole 'private realm of family life' it is difficult to imagine what is more private or more intimate than a husband and wife's marital relations."

The entire fabric of the Constitution and the purposes that clearly underlie its specific guarantees demonstrate that the rights to marital privacy and to marry and raise a family are of similar order and magnitude as the fundamental rights specifically protected.

* * *

* * * Surely the Government, absent a showing of a compelling subordinating state interest, could not decree that all husbands and wives must be sterilized after two children have been born to them. Yet by their reasoning such an invasion of marital privacy would not be subject to constitutional challenge because, while it might be "silly," no provision of the Constitution specifically prevents the Government from curtailing the marital right to bear children and raise a family. * * * [I]f upon a showing of a slender basis of rationality, a law outlawing voluntary birth control by married persons is valid, then, by the same reasoning, a law requiring compulsory birth control also would seem to be valid. In my view, however, both types of law would unjustifiably intrude upon rights of marital privacy which are constitutionally protected.

* * *

Finally, it should be said of the Court's holding today that it in no way interferes with a State's proper regulation of sexual promiscuity or misconduct. As my Brother Harlan so well stated in his dissenting opinion in Poe v. Ullman, supra, 367 U.S. at 553, 81 S.Ct. at 1782:

"Adultery, homosexuality and the like are sexual intimacies which the State forbids * * * but the intimacy of husband and wife is necessarily an essential and accepted feature of the institution of marriage, an institution which the State not only must allow, but which always and in every age it has fostered and protected. It is one thing when the State exerts its power either to forbid extra-marital sexuality * * * or to say who may marry, but it is quite another when, having acknowledged a marriage and the intimacies inherent in it, it undertakes to regulate by means of the criminal law the details of that intimacy."

NOTES ON GRISWOLD

1. Both Justice Douglas and Justice Goldberg had to reach behind the language and history of the Constitution in order to find a right of privacy that included the right to contraception, which they located, respectively, in "penumbras, formed by emanations" from the Bill of Rights and in the "forgotten" Ninth Amendment. Does the result they reached strike you as appropriate as a matter of constitutional interpretation? Which route do you prefer? Is there a better route, in your opinion? What are the pro's and con's of having located the right of reproductive control in an individual right to privacy? Does this further insulate "family" matters from state review and intervention? Can you think of alternative arguments that might have been effective in striking down the Connecticut law prohibiting use of contraceptives? Justice Harlan, in his concurring opinion, argued that "the proper constitutional inquiry in this case is whether this Connecticut statute infringes the Due Process Clause of the Fourteenth Amendment because the enactment violates basic values 'implicit in the concept of ordered liberty'." 381 U.S. at 500. His analysis, later embraced by the Court in *Casey* and *Gonzalez,* which are discussed below, rests upon liberty and a substantive due process analysis under the Fourteenth Amendment rather than upon the more amorphous concept of privacy. Would arguments based on the Fourteenth Amendment's guarantee of equal protection be more useful? How? How would adherents of the differing feminist perspectives described in Chapter 3 articulate a constitutional basis for reproductive autonomy?

2. Although both the opinion of the Court in *Griswold* and the concurrence emphasized the connection between the right of reproductive privacy and the marital relationship, the Court subsequently held, on equal protection grounds, that this right extended to single persons, stating that "the marital couple is not an independent entity with a mind and heart of its own, but an association of two individuals each with a separate intellectual and emotional makeup. If the right of privacy means anything, it is the right of the *individual,* married or single, to be free from unwarranted governmental intrusion into matters so fundamentally affecting a person as the decision whether to bear or beget a child." Eisenstadt v. Baird, 405 U.S. 438, 453 (1972) (emphasis in original). Can you articulate any other bases for extending this constitutional right to individuals? (In 1977, the Court held that even unmarried minors could not be denied over-the-counter contraceptives. Carey v. Population Services Int'l, 431 U.S. 678 (1977)). Does *Eisenstadt* support a woman's right to abortion? What arguments would you make in this respect?

3. Who is likely to be protected by a notion of privacy grounded in tradition? All citizens? Or only those involved in relationships that have traditionally been accepted, or engaged in, by the majority? In *Eisenstadt*, the Supreme Court had the opportunity to protect all private, consensual sexual activity between adults, but it bypassed that question by grounding its holding in equal protection instead of liberty or privacy principles. In Bowers v. Hardwick, 478 U.S. 186, 194–96 (1986), the Supreme Court subsequently upheld a state statute criminalizing homosexual sodomy, even when consensual and conducted in the privacy of one's home. What does that case reveal about the problems a privacy standard grounded in tradition poses for lesbians and gay men? For women in general? In 2003, the Supreme Court overruled *Bowers*, holding in Lawrence v. Texas that same-sex couples possess a liberty right to engage in sodomy because, among other things, "sex can be but one element in a personal bond that is more enduring." 539 U.S. 558, 567 (2003). Does such an approach address all of the problems you identified? For a feminist analysis of the limits of *Lawrence*, see Laura A. Rosenbury & Jennifer E. Rothman, Sex In and Out of Intimacy, 59 Emory L.J. 809 (2010).

4. Would it have been better had *Griswold* come out the other way? What would the likely consequences of such a decision have been—would states have continued to ban birth control? Or would changing social mores have led to the repeal or non-enforcement of restrictions in any case?

C. ABORTION

A note about sources: To a large extent, the sources in this section have been drawn from materials created in the course of actual litigation. We have chosen to do so, despite the obvious dangers of bias introduced by using documents designed for advocacy, to show how theories developed by feminist lawyers and law professors have in fact influenced the law on this issue and to give a lively sense of the passion involved in the debate over abortion in the United States. In short, this is a very good example of how theory may inform and in fact transform practice.

1. ABORTION AND AMERICAN HISTORY

AMICUS BRIEF OF 250 AMERICAN HISTORIANS IN *PLANNED PARENTHOOD OF SOUTHEASTERN PENNSYLVANIA v. CASEY*

Nos. 91–744 and 91–902 (1992).

[This amicus brief was written by law professors Sylvia Law, Jane E. Larson, and Clyde Spillenger. The issues litigated in *Casey* are summarized in Section C2, below.]

* * *

II. AT THE TIME THE FEDERAL CONSTITUTION WAS ADOPTED, ABORTION WAS KNOWN AND NOT ILLEGAL.

* * * Through the nineteenth century, American common law decisions uniformly reaffirmed that women committed no offense in seeking

abortions. Both common law and popular American understanding drew distinctions depending upon whether the fetus was "quick," i.e. whether the woman perceived signs of independent life. There was some dispute whether a common law misdemeanor occurred when a third party destroyed a fetus, after quickening, without the woman's consent. But early common law recognition of this crime against a pregnant woman did not diminish the woman's liberty to end a pregnancy herself in its early stages.

Abortion was not a pressing social issue in colonial America, but as a social practice, it was far from unknown. Herbal abortifacients were widely known, and cookbooks and women's diaries of the era contained recipes for such medicines. Recent studies of the work of midwives in the 1700s report cases in which the midwives appeared to have provided women abortifacient compounds. Such treatments do not appear to have been regarded as extraordinary or illicit by those administering them.

* * *

In the late eighteenth century, strictures on sexual behavior loosened considerably. The incidence of premarital pregnancy rose sharply; by the late eighteenth century, one third of all New England brides were pregnant when they married, compared to less than ten percent in the seventeenth century. Falling birth rates in the 1780s suggest that, at the time of the drafting of the Constitution, the use of birth control and abortion was increasing.

III. THROUGH THE NINETEENTH CENTURY, ABORTION BECAME EVEN MORE WIDELY ACCEPTED AND HIGHLY VISIBLE.

Through the nineteenth century and well into the twentieth, abortion remained a widely accepted practice, despite growing efforts after 1860 to prohibit it. * * *

Urban couples limited family size for economic reasons: working-class married women, faced with the material difficulty of managing a family budget on a single male wage, resorted to abortion as the most effective available means of "conscious fertility control."

* * * The most common methods of abortion in the nineteenth century involved self administered herbs and devices available from pharmacists. Nonetheless, women also relied on professional abortionists: in 1871, New York City, with a population of less than one million, supported two hundred full-time abortionists, not including doctors who also sometimes performed abortions.

For most of the nineteenth century, abortion was a visible as well as common practice. "Beginning in the early 1840s abortion became, for all intents and purposes, a business, a service openly traded in the free market.... [Pervasive advertising told Americans] not only that many practitioners would provide abortion services, but that some practitioners had made the abortion business their chief livelihood. Indeed, abortions became one of the first specialties in American medical history."[26]

IV. NINETEENTH-CENTURY ABORTION RESTRICTIONS SOUGHT TO PROMOTE OBJECTIVES THAT ARE TODAY EITHER PLAINLY INAPPLICABLE OR CONSTITUTIONALLY IMPERMISSIBLE.

[B]etween 1850 and 1880, the newly formed American Medical Association, through some of its active members, became the "single most important factor in altering the legal policies toward abortion in this country."[27]

The doctors found an audience for their effort to restrict abortion because they appealed to specific social concerns and anxieties: maternal health, consumer protection, discriminatory ideas about the properly subordinate status of women, and racist/nativist fears generated by the fact that elite Protestant women often sought abortions. Some of those doctors also sought to attribute moral status to the fetus.

A. From 1820–1860, Abortion Regulation in the States Rejected Broader English Restrictions and Sought to Protect Women from Particularly Dangerous Forms of Abortion.

In 1803, English law made all forms of abortion criminal. Despite this model, for two decades, no American state restricted access to abortion. In 1821, when one state, Connecticut, acted, it prohibited only the administration of a "deadly poison, or other noxious and destructive substance" as a means of bringing about an abortion. Moreover, the act applied only after quickening, and punished only the person who administered the poison, not the woman who consumed it. * * *

In 1830, Connecticut became the first state to punish abortion after quickening. In the same year, New York, also animated by a concern for patient safety, considered a law to prohibit any surgery, unless two physicians approved it as essential. Before scientific understanding of germ theory and antisepsis, any surgical intervention was likely to be fatal. The New York act finally adopted applied only to surgical abortion and included the first "therapeutic" exception, approving abortion where two physicians agreed that it was "necessary." As the Court recognized in Roe v. Wade, until the twentieth century, abortion, particularly when done through surgical intervention, remained significantly more dangerous to the woman than childbirth. Because these early abortion laws were drafted and justified to protect women, they did not punish women as parties to an abortion.

None of these early laws, restricting forms of abortion thought to be particularly unsafe, were enforced. That absence itself speaks powerfully, particularly because abortion was a prevalent practice in this era. Despite legislative action and medical opposition, the common and openly tolerat-

26. J. Mohr, Abortion in America: The Origins and Evolution of National Policy 47 (1978).

27. J. Mohr, supra, at 157.

ed practice suggests that many Americans did not perceive abortion as morally wrong.

B. A Central Purpose of Abortion Regulation in the Nineteenth Century Was to Define Who Should Be Allowed to Control Medical Practice.

Physicians were the principal nineteenth-century proponents of laws to restrict abortion. A core purpose of the nineteenth-century laws, and of doctors in supporting them, was to control medical practice in the interest of public safety. * * *

The nineteenth century movement to regulate abortions was one chapter in a campaign by doctors that reflected a professional conflict between "regulars" (those who ultimately became the practitioners and proponents of scientific medicine) and "irregulars." As James Mohr explains:

> If a regular doctor refused to perform an abortion he knew the woman could go to one of several types of irregulars and probably receive one.... As more and more irregulars began to advertise abortion services openly, especially after 1840, regular physicians grew more and more nervous about losing their practices to healers who would provide a service that more and more American women after 1840 began to want. * * * The best way out of these dilemmas was to persuade state legislators to make abortion a criminal offense. Anti-abortion laws would weaken the appeal of the competition and take the pressure off the more marginal members of the regulars' own sect.[42]

* * *

C. Enforcement of Sharply Differentiated Concepts of the Roles and Choices of Men and Women Underlay Regulation of Abortion and Contraception in the Nineteenth Century.

* * * In addition, physicians persuaded political leaders (who were, of course, uniformly male) that "abortion constituted a threat to social order and to male authority.[44] Since the 1840s, a growing movement for women's suffrage and equality had generated popular fears that women were departing from a purely maternal role—fears fueled by the decline in family size during the nineteenth century. A central rhetorical focus of the woman's movement was framed by a new perception of women as the rightful possessors of their own bodies.

In 1871, the American Medical Association's Committee on Criminal Abortion described the woman who sought an abortion:

42. J. Mohr, supra, at 37. [The doctors were scornful of the midwives' "folklore" about the importance of quickening as well, maintaining the superiority of their own "scientific" knowledge as to when life began. Presumably their desire to put the midwives out of practice through the criminalization of abortion took precedence over an obvious competing motivation—to perform the abortion and collect the fee themselves.]

44. C. Smith-Rosenberg, Disorderly Conduct 235 (1985).

She becomes unmindful of the course marked out for her by Providence, she overlooks the duties imposed on her by the marriage contract. She yields to the pleasures—but shrinks from the pains and responsibilities of maternity; and, destitute of all delicacy and refinements, resigns herself, body and soul, into the hands of unscrupulous and wicked men.[47]

* * *

Against what they saw as an inequitable vision of gender relations, the women's movement of the nineteenth century affirmed that women—even married women—should have basic rights of self-governance, including the right to decide whether to bear a child. Early feminists sought to enhance women's control of reproduction through a campaign for "voluntary motherhood," ideally to be achieved through periodic abstinence from sexual relations. They attempted, with limited success, to analogize women's control over reproduction to the structure of rights that had overturned chattel slavery. * * *

Opposition to abortion and contraception were closely linked, and can only be understood as a reaction to the uncertainties generated by changes in family function and anxieties created by women's challenges to their historic roles of silence and subservience. These challenges were critical factors motivating the all-male state legislatures that adopted restraints on women, including restrictions on abortion. In opposition to the feminist demand for control of reproduction, the federal government in 1873 took the lead in banning access to information about both contraception and abortion [with the Comstock Act]. * * *

D. Nineteenth-Century Contraception and Abortion Regulation Also Reflected Ethnocentric Fears About the Relative Birthrates of Immigrants and White Protestants.

* * *

Beginning in the 1890s, and continuing through the first decades of the twentieth century, * * * nativist fears coalesced into a drive against what was then called "race suicide." The "race suicide" alarmists worried that women of "good stock"—prosperous, white, and Protestant—were not having enough children to maintain the political and social supremacy of their group. Anxiety over the falling birth rates of Protestant whites in comparison with other groups helped shape policy governing both birth control and abortion. As James Mohr points out, "The doctors both used and were influenced by blatant nativism.... There can be little doubt that Protestants' fears about not keeping up with the reproductive rates of Catholic immigrants played a greater role in the drive for anti-abortion laws in nineteenth-century America than Catholic opposition to abortion did."[64]

---

47. Atlee & O'Donnell, Report of the Committee on Criminal Abortion, 22 Transactions of the American Medical Association 241 (1871), quoted in C. Smith-Rosenberg, supra, at 236–37.

64. See J. Mohr, supra note 26, at 167. Horatio Robinson Storer, who spearheaded the American Medical Association's mid-nineteenth century antiabortion campaign, frequently re-

V. ENFORCEMENT OF ABORTION RESTRICTIONS IN THE FIRST HALF OF THE TWENTIETH CENTURY FOLLOWED ENTRENCHED ETHNIC AND CLASS DIFFERENTIATIONS, AFFIRMED TRADITIONAL CONCERNS ABOUT ENFORCING GENDER ROLES, AND IMPOSED ENORMOUS COSTS UPON WOMEN.

The statutory restrictions on abortion remained virtually unchanged from the early twentieth century until the 1960s. Physicians were allowed to perform abortions only "to preserve the mother's life." Nonetheless, the incidence of abortion remained high, ranging from one pregnancy in seven at the turn of the century, to one in three in 1936. Most abortions were performed illegally. Legal restrictions did not stop abortion, but made it humiliating and dangerous.

AMICUS BRIEF OF FEMINISTS FOR LIFE IN *BRAY v. ALEXANDRIA WOMEN'S HEALTH CLINIC*

No. 90–985 (1991).

[This amicus brief was written by Mary Krane Derr, a graduate student at the University of Chicago. The *Bray* case was an unsuccessful attempt to establish that anti-abortion protesters blocking access to abortion clinics were violating the civil rights of women seeking abortions.]

A. *The Early Feminists, Although Critical of Prevailing Cultural Attitudes Regarding Sexuality and the Role of Women in Marriage, Were Resolutely Opposed to Abortion.*

Feminism as a social movement has existed throughout most of American history, and the issue of abortion has been closely tied to feminist criticism of the social oppression and disenfranchisement of women. Contrary to prevailing assumptions, * * * feminists have not traditionally argued for the moral and legal acceptability of abortion. The nineteenth century founding mothers of the women's movement did not view legalized abortion as a solution to, but rather, as an abhorrent consequence of, the oppressions and disenfranchisement of women.

The testimony of these women—including Elizabeth Cady Stanton, Victoria Woodhull, and Matilda Gage—reveal a radical stance against the mistreatment of women inside and outside of marriage, a frank understanding and acceptance of female sexuality, and an uncompromising view that abortion is "ante-natal murder," "child-murder," or "ante-natal infanticide." The early feminists did not oppose abortion out of adherence to social norms. As will be seen below, they were not timid in challenging prevailing and fundamental notions of the marriage relationship, some of which prevail to this day.

Early feminist opposition to abortion was deep-seated, and addressed the causes of abortion, not just the practice. In this way, it was distin-

ferred to racial themes. Id. at 180–90; H. Storer, Why Not? A Book for Every Woman 85 (1866) ("[S]hall the great territories of the Far West be filled by our children or by those of aliens?").

guished from other anti-abortion efforts including those of the American Medical Association. Feminists documented that abortion was caused by, among other things, culturally enforced ignorance about sexual and reproductive physiology, especially family planning and fetal development; cultural construction of pregnancy as a pathological condition; a sexual double standard which permitted men to be sexually and parentally irresponsible; the social valuing of "legitimacy" over children's lives and women's well-being; and lack of social and economic support for mothers, especially single ones. Two overriding principles emerge from this early feminist literature: a condemnation of abortion as the murder of children; and the conviction that marital, social, and economic liberation of women would bolster, and not undermine, protection for the unborn.

B. The Early Feminists Considered Abortion to Be the Killing of Children.

The nineteenth-century feminists * * * understood that life begins at conception, and thus, induced abortion is the killing of that young life. * * * Historian Carl Degler has noted that this valuation of fetal life at all stages "was in line with a number of movements to reduce cruelty and to expand the concept of the sanctity of life ... the elimination of the death penalty, the peace movement, the abolition of torture and whipping in connection with crimes"—all movements which feminists supported. "The prohibiting of abortion was but the most recent effort in that larger concern." C. Degler, At Odds: Women and Family in America From the Revolution to the Present, 247 (1980).

* * *

D. Early Feminist Opposition to Abortion Was Joined to Condemnation of Male Sexual Irresponsibility and Coercion, and the Lack of Economic and Social Support for Pregnant Women Abandoned by the Fathers of Their Children.

1. The early feminists called for prevention of the circumstances giving rise to abortion. Their concern for the lives of unborn children did not preclude, but was interwoven with, a broader concern for women with crisis pregnancies, children already born, and their mothers. Susan B. Anthony expressed the holistic nature of the feminist attitude in an 1869 editorial:

> Much as I deplore the horrible crime of child-murder, earnestly as I desire its suppression, I cannot believe ... that such a law [prohibiting abortion] would have the desired effect. It seems to me to be the only moving off the top of the noxious weed, while the root remains. We want prevention, not merely punishment. We must reach the root of the evil, and destroy it.
>
> To my certain knowledge this crime is not confined to those whose love of ease, amusement and fashionable life leads them to desire immunity from the cares of children: but is practiced by those whose

inmost souls revolt from the dreadful deed, and in whose hearts the maternal feeling is pure and undying. What, then has driven these women to the desperation necessary to force them to commit such a deed? This question being answered, I believe, we shall have such an insight into the matter as to be able to talk more clearly of a remedy.

Anthony, Marriage and Maternity, The Revolution, 9(1):4 (July 8, 1869).

* * *

2. The early feminists condemned social attitudes, especially sexual double standards, which contributed to an increasing incidence of abortion. General social attitudes likewise played a role in the promotion and tolerance of abortion. Sarah F. Norton, itinerant lecturer and author, noted that "[s]ociety has come to believe it an impertinence in children to be born at all . . . [T]he single fact that child murderers practice their profession without let or hindrance, and open infant butcheries unquestioned, establishing themselves with an impunity that is not allowed to the slaughterers of cattle is, of itself, sufficient to prove that society makes a demand which they alone can supply." Tragedy, Social and Domestic, Woodhull & Claflin's Weekly, Nov. 19, 1870.

At the root of this demand were social attitudes regarding sexual behavior, illegitimacy, and the nature of pregnancy itself. The sexual "double standard"—which permitted men to behave in an irresponsible fashion, but punished the women being victimized—was universally condemned. * * *

3. The early feminists believed that the liberation of women from positions of social inequality and sexual dominance would lead to increased protection for the unborn. Since the early feminists viewed abortion as a byproduct of sexual domination by men, and the unequal position of women in society, it is not surprising that they saw equality between the sexes as a necessary prerequisite to the eradication of abortion, and an end to sexual double standards, as addressing the root cause of abortion, and eradicating it.

* * *

4. In condemning "forced maternity," the early feminists did not support abortion, but rather, opposed the cultural and sexual mores which compelled many women to become pregnant against their will. * * *

"Forced maternity" did not mean restricted access to abortion. To the early feminists, a woman was a mother once she became pregnant, and the fact that the pregnancy was unwanted in no way justified the "revolting outrage" of abortion. They also believed, however, that women had the right, within marriage, to refrain from sexual intercourse when they did not consider themselves able to bear or rear a child. Abortion resulted from the denial of the woman's "right to herself," as Matilda Gage termed it, not from the exercise of that right. * * *

NOTES ON THE USES OF HISTORY IN ABORTION LITIGATION

1. The history of abortion in the United States has been an important source of constitutional interpretation on this issue. Why should what has been done in the past be such an important source? Whose actions should we look to? The "new history" would look to those of ordinary people (for example, the abortifacient recipes in women's cookbooks described in the Historians' Brief, above), rather than to the pronouncements of legislators and doctors. If abortion was in fact a misdemeanor but laws against it were not enforced, what conclusions should we draw? On the other hand, if one believes that abortion is morally wrong, like slavery was, why should the history of its practice offer us guidance for the future?

2. Do the Historians' Brief and the Feminists for Life Brief meet head on? Are their versions of history consistent? In what ways?

3. The excerpt from the AMA's 1871 committee report included above gives some flavor of the extent to which the historical debate over abortion has been a debate about woman's proper role; the report reflects the image of an aborting woman as selfish and therefore immoral. One modern commentator believes that the rhetoric of choice in the continuing debate over the right of abortion, which emphasizes autonomous individuals with rights, making choices in pursuit of their own self-interest, exacerbates the fears of anti-abortion advocates by awakening fears of selfish mothers; moreover, this model of individual choice does not accurately describe how women make decisions about abortion and, indeed, about their lives in general. Joan Williams, Gender Wars: Selfless Women in the Republic of Choice, 66 N.Y.U. L. Rev. 1559 (1991). How do you think this rhetoric of individual freedom and choice could, or should, be altered? Would the rhetoric you envisage fit into legal theories upon which the abortion right could be defended? How?

4. The Historians' Brief describes the connection between abortion regulation and racism in the past. Do racism and anti-immigrant feelings continue to play into the abortion debate today? Is it possible that some of the opinions that make up the pro-choice majority are actually expressing hostility to women of color and their children, making abortion a form of eugenics? Might the history of racism, eugenics, and sterilization abuse cause African American women to have more complicated attitudes toward abortion than women who do not share this history of abuse? See, e.g., Angela Y. Davis, Women Race & Class 202–15 (1981).

5. It is important to set the opposition of 19th-century feminists to abortion in the context of their opposition to birth control as well. Linda Gordon points out that this opposition was grounded in attitudes central to the welfare of women: fear that the sexual freedom and promiscuity that contraception made possible would lead to greater infidelity by husbands and economic instability for wives as marriages broke up, on the one hand, and a preference for more natural methods of birth control, including abstinence and the right of a wife unilaterally to refuse sex, on the other. The latter was important to 19th-century women, not only because they had been socialized to regard sex as simply their "wifely duty," but also out of realistic fears of

the physical dangers—pregnancy, childbirth, and venereal diseases—potentially resulting from intercourse. Moreover, by joining their call for voluntary motherhood with a demand for the right to unilateral abstinence, many women directly expressed their understandable hostility to the traditional form of intercourse, defined by male desires with little regard to women's sexual pleasure. Gordon, The Moral Property of Women: A History of Birth Control Politics in America 57–67 (rev'd ed. 2002).

2. FROM ROE v. WADE TO *CASEY*

ROE v. WADE

Supreme Court of the United States, 1973.
410 U.S. 113, 93 S.Ct. 705, 35 L.Ed.2d 147.

MR. JUSTICE BLACKMUN delivered the opinion of the Court.

Jane Roe, a single woman who was residing in Dallas County, Texas, instituted this federal action in March 1970 against the District Attorney of the county. She sought a declaratory judgment that the Texas criminal abortion statutes were unconstitutional on their face, and an injunction restraining the defendant from enforcing the statutes.

Roe alleged that she was unmarried and pregnant; that she wished to terminate her pregnancy by an abortion "performed by a competent, licensed physician, under safe, clinical conditions"; that she was unable to get a "legal" abortion in Texas because her life did not appear to be threatened by the continuation of her pregnancy; and that she could not afford to travel to another jurisdiction in order to secure a legal abortion under safe conditions. * * *

It perhaps is not generally appreciated that the restrictive criminal abortion laws in effect in a majority of States today are of relatively recent vintage. Those laws, generally proscribing abortion or its attempt at any time during pregnancy except when necessary to preserve the pregnant woman's life, are not of ancient or even of common-law origin. Instead, they derive from statutory changes effected, for the most part, in the latter half of the 19th century.

* * *

3. The common law. It is undisputed that at common law, abortion performed before "quickening"—the first recognizable movement of the fetus in utero, appearing usually from the 16th to the 18th week of pregnancy—was not an indictable offense. The absence of a common-law crime for pre-quickening abortion appears to have developed from a confluence of earlier philosophical, theological, and civil and canon law concepts of when life begins. These disciplines variously approached the question in terms of the point at which the embryo or fetus became "formed" or recognizably human, or in terms of when a "person" came into being, that is, infused with a "soul" or "animated." A loose consensus evolved in early English law that these events occurred at some point

between conception and live birth. This was "mediate animation." Although Christian theology and the canon law came to fix the point of animation at 40 days for a male and 80 days for a female, a view that persisted until the 19th century, there was otherwise little agreement about the precise time of formation or animation. There was agreement, however, that prior to this point the fetus was to be regarded as part of the mother, and its destruction, therefore, was not homicide. * * *

Whether abortion of a quick fetus was a felony at common law, or even a lesser crime, is still disputed. * * * [M]ost American courts ruled, in holding or dictum, that abortion of an unquickened fetus was not criminal under their received common law, others followed Coke in stating that abortion of a quick fetus was a "misprision," a term they translated to mean "misdemeanor." * * * In 1828, New York enacted legislation that, in two respects, was to serve as a model for early anti-abortion statutes. First, while barring destruction of an unquickened fetus as well as a quick fetus, it made the former only a misdemeanor, but the latter second-degree manslaughter. Second, it incorporated a concept of therapeutic abortion by providing that an abortion was excused if it "shall have been necessary to preserve the life of such mother, or shall have been advised by two physicians to be necessary for such purpose." By 1840, when Texas had received the common law, only eight American States had statutes dealing with abortion. It was not until after the War Between the States that legislation began generally to replace the common law. Most of these initial statutes dealt severely with abortion after quickening but were lenient with it before quickening. * * *

Gradually, in the middle and late 19th century the quickening distinction disappeared from the statutory law of most States and the degree of the offense and the penalties were increased. By the end of the 1950's a large majority of the jurisdictions banned abortion, however and whenever performed, unless done to save or preserve the life of the mother. * * * In the past several years, however, a trend toward liberalization of abortion statutes has resulted in adoption, by about one-third of the States, of less stringent laws * * *.

It is thus apparent that at common law, at the time of the adoption of our Constitution, and throughout the major portion of the 19th century, abortion was viewed with less disfavor than under most American statutes currently in effect. Phrasing it another way, a woman enjoyed a substantially broader right to terminate a pregnancy than she does in most States today. At least with respect to the early stage of pregnancy, and very possibly without such a limitation, the opportunity to make this choice was present in this country well into the 19th century. Even later, the law continued for some time to treat less punitively an abortion procured in early pregnancy.

* * *

Th[e] right of privacy, whether it be founded in the Fourteenth Amendment's concept of personal liberty and restrictions upon state action, as we feel it is, or, as the District Court determined, in the Ninth Amendment's reservation of rights to the people, is broad enough to encompass a woman's decision whether or not to terminate her pregnancy. The detriment that the State would impose upon the pregnant woman by denying this choice altogether is apparent. Specific and direct harm medically diagnosable even in early pregnancy may be involved. Maternity, or additional offspring, may force upon the woman a distressful life and future. Psychological harm may be imminent. Mental and physical health may be taxed by child care. There is also the distress, for all concerned, associated with the unwanted child, and there is the problem of bringing a child into a family already unable, psychologically and otherwise, to care for it. In other cases, as in this one, the additional difficulties and continuing stigma of unwed motherhood may be involved. All these are factors the woman and her responsible physician necessarily will consider in consultation.

* * *

The Constitution does not define "person" in so many words. Section 1 of the Fourteenth Amendment contains three references to "person." The first, in defining "citizens," speaks of "persons born or naturalized in the United States." The word also appears both in the Due Process Clause and in the Equal Protection Clause. "Person" is used in other places in the Constitution * * *. But in nearly all these instances, the use of the word is such that it has application only postnatally. None indicates, with any assurance, that it has any possible prenatal application.

All this, together with our observation that throughout the major portion of the 19th century prevailing legal abortion practices were far freer than they are today, persuades us that the word "person," as used in the Fourteenth Amendment, does not include the unborn. * * *

The pregnant woman cannot be isolated in her privacy. She carries an embryo and, later, a fetus, if one accepts the medical definitions of the developing young in the human uterus. The situation therefore is inherently different from marital intimacy, or bedroom possession of obscene material, or marriage, or procreation, or education * * *.

* * * We need not resolve the difficult question of when life begins. When those trained in the respective disciplines of medicine, philosophy, and theology are unable to arrive at any consensus, the judiciary, at this point in the development of man's knowledge, is not in a position to speculate as to the answer.

It should be sufficient to note briefly the wide divergence of thinking on this most sensitive and difficult question. There has always been strong support for the view that life does not begin until live birth. This was the belief of the Stoics. It appears to be the predominant, though not the unanimous, attitude of the Jewish faith. It may be taken to represent also the position of a large segment of the Protestant community, insofar as that can be ascertained; organized groups that have taken a formal position on the abortion issue have generally regarded abortion as a matter for the conscience of the individual and her family. As we have noted, the common law found greater significance in quickening. Physicians and their scientific colleagues have regarded that event with less interest and have tended to focus either upon conception, upon live birth, or upon the interim point at which the fetus becomes "viable," that is, potentially able to live outside the mother's womb, albeit with artificial aid. Viability is usually placed at about seven months (28 weeks) but may occur earlier, even at 24 weeks. The Aristotelian theory of "mediate animation," that held sway throughout the Middle Ages and the Renaissance in Europe, continued to be official Roman Catholic dogma until the 19th century, despite opposition to this "ensoulment" theory from those in the Church who would recognize the existence of life from the moment of conception. The latter is now, of course, the official belief of the Catholic Church. * * * Substantial problems for precise definition of this view are posed, however, by new embryological data that purport to indicate that conception is a "process" over time, rather than an event, and by new medical techniques such as menstrual extraction, the "morning-after" pill, implantation of embryos, artificial insemination, and even artificial wombs.

In areas other than criminal abortion, the law has been reluctant to endorse any theory that life, as we recognize it, begins before live birth or to accord legal rights to the unborn except in narrowly defined situations and except when the rights are contingent upon live birth. * * * In short, the unborn have never been recognized in the law as persons in the whole sense.

In view of all this, we do not agree that, by adopting one theory of life, Texas may override the rights of the pregnant woman that are at stake. We repeat, however, that the State does have an important and legitimate interest in preserving and protecting the health of the pregnant woman, whether she be a resident of the State or a non-resident who seeks medical consultation and treatment there, and that it has still another important and legitimate interest in protecting the potentiality of human life. These interests are separate and distinct. Each grows in substantiality as the woman approaches term and, at a point during pregnancy, each becomes "compelling."

With respect to the State's important and legitimate interest in the health of the mother, the "compelling" point, in the light of present medical knowledge, is at approximately the end of the first trimester. This is so because of the now-established medical fact * * * that until the end of the first trimester mortality in abortion may be less than mortality in normal childbirth. It follows that, from and after this point, a State may regulate the abortion procedure to the extent that the regulation reasonably relates to the preservation and protection of maternal health. Examples of permissible state regulation in this area are requirements as to the qualifications of the person who is to perform the abortion; as to the licensure of that person; as to the facility in which the procedure is to be performed, that is, whether it must be a hospital or may be a clinic or some other place of less-than-hospital status; as to the licensing of the facility; and the like.

This means, on the other hand, that, for the period of pregnancy prior to this "compelling" point, the attending physician, in consultation with his patient, is free to determine, without regulation by the State, that, in his medical judgment, the patient's pregnancy should be terminated. If that decision is reached, the judgment may be effectuated by an abortion free of interference by the State.

With respect to the State's important and legitimate interest in potential life, the "compelling" point is at viability. This is so because the fetus then presumably has the capability of meaningful life outside the mother's womb. State regulation protective of fetal life after viability thus has both logical and biological justifications. If the State is interested in protecting fetal life after viability, it may go so far as to proscribe abortion during that period, except when it is necessary to preserve the life or health of the mother.

HARRIS v. McRAE

Supreme Court of the United States, 1980.
448 U.S. 297, 100 S.Ct. 2671, 65 L.Ed.2d 784.

MR. JUSTICE STEWART delivered the opinion of the Court.

This case presents statutory and constitutional questions concerning the public funding of abortions under Title XIX of the Social Security Act, commonly known as the "Medicaid" Act, and recent annual Appropriations Acts containing the so-called "Hyde Amendment." * * * The constitutional question * * * is whether the Hyde Amendment, by denying public funding for certain medically necessary abortions, contravenes the liberty or equal protection guarantees of the Due Process Clause of the Fifth Amendment, or either of the Religion Clauses of the First Amendment.

* * *

In Maher v. Roe, 432 U.S. 464 [1977], the Court was presented with the question whether the scope of personal constitutional freedom recognized in Roe v. Wade included an entitlement to Medicaid payments for abortions that are not medically necessary. At issue in *Maher* was a Connecticut welfare regulation under which Medicaid recipients received payments for medical services incident to childbirth, but not for medical services incident to nontherapeutic abortions.

It was the view of this Court that "the District Court misconceived the nature and scope of the fundamental right recognized in *Roe*." The doctrine of Roe v. Wade, the Court held in *Maher*, "protects the woman from unduly burdensome interference with her freedom to decide whether to terminate her pregnancy," such as the severe criminal sanctions at issue in Roe v. Wade, or the absolute requirement of spousal consent for an abortion challenged in Planned Parenthood of Central Missouri v. Danforth, 428 U.S. 52 [1976].

But the constitutional freedom recognized in *Wade* and its progeny, the *Maher* Court explained, did not prevent Connecticut from making "a value judgment favoring childbirth over abortion, and ... implement[ing] that judgment by the allocation of public funds."

* * *

The Hyde Amendment, like the Connecticut welfare regulation at issue in *Maher,* places no governmental obstacle in the path of a woman who chooses to terminate her pregnancy, but rather, by means of unequal subsidization of abortion and other medical services, encourages alternative activity deemed in the public interest. The present case does differ factually from *Maher* insofar as that case involved a failure to fund nontherapeutic abortions, whereas the Hyde Amendment withholds funding of certain medically necessary abortions.

* * * [A]lthough government may not place obstacles in the path of a woman's exercise of her freedom of choice, it need not remove those not of its own creation. Indigency falls in the latter category. The financial constraints that restrict an indigent woman's ability to enjoy the full range of constitutionally protected freedom of choice are the product not of governmental restrictions on access to abortions, but rather of her indigency. Although Congress has opted to subsidize medically necessary services generally, but not certain medically necessary abortions, the fact remains that the Hyde Amendment leaves an indigent woman with at least the same range of choice in deciding whether to obtain a medically necessary abortion as she would have had if Congress had chosen to subsidize no health care costs at all. We are thus not persuaded that the Hyde Amendment impinges on the constitutionally protected freedom of choice recognized in *Wade.*

NOTES ON ROE *AND* HARRIS

1. The opinion in Roe v. Wade agrees with the Historians' Brief's conclusions about abortion in American history, yet the story ends differently: the Historians' Brief with the tragedy of dangerous and illegal abortions, and the *Roe* Court's account with the trend toward liberalization of abortion laws in the late 1960's. Would it have been better to have allowed this process of state-by-state liberalization to run its course? What factors would you take into account in making your counter-historical assessment on this question? Mary Ann Glendon points out that most Western European nations eased access to abortion in the 1970's and that abortion is much less controversial in those countries than it is in the United States today; she argues that the debate here has been so passionate and divisive at least in part because it has been carried out in the language of individual rights, rather than of communal responsibilities and relationships, a fact which may be attributable to the judicial forum. Glendon, Abortion and Divorce in Western Law 10–62 (1987).

Gerald N. Rosenberg also notes that limits on Medicaid funding and the violent and harassing tactics used by anti-abortion protesters at abortion clinics arose only after Roe v. Wade, although the right to abortion was becoming established in most states prior to the *Roe* decision. Rosenberg, The Hollow Hope: Can Courts Bring About Social Change? 185–89 (2d ed. 2008). But see Robert Post & Reva Siegel, *Roe* Rage: Democratic Constitutionalism and Backlash, 42 Harv. C.R.–C.L. L. Rev. 373, 377 (2007) (arguing that what some see as backlash to Roe v. Wade in fact preceded the decision and was "a broad-based social movement hostile to legal efforts to secure the equality of women and the separation of church and state").

Is it possible that women would have been better off as a class and the right to abortion safer today if it had been won in legislatures rather than in the courts?

2. The woman and her life are almost absent from the discussion of abortion in Roe v. Wade, which becomes instead the story of the fetus and the doctor. Reva Siegel sees this as resulting from the fact that the Court typically reasons about reproductive regulation in physiological paradigms, seeing regulation as state action that concerns women's bodies rather than women's roles, despite the fact that the social role of women was clearly the central concern in the historical debate about abortion. Siegel, Reasoning from the Body: A Historical Perspective on Abortion Regulation and Questions of Equal Protection, 44 Stan. L. Rev. 261 (1992). Is this a necessary result of grounding the right to abortion on the right to privacy? What other theories can you think of which might have been used to argue Roe v. Wade? Were they available when it was argued? See What Roe v. Wade Should Have Said: the Nation's Top Legal Experts Rewrite America's Most Controversial Decision (Jack M. Balkin, ed. 2005) (including a variety of alternative arguments, available at the time, that might have been used in Roe v. Wade). For an account by the attorney who litigated on behalf of Jane Roe, see Sarah Weddington, A Question of Choice (1992). Later sections of this chapter present a number of alternative theories upon which the abortion right might be grounded.

3. What is the importance of the many references in *Roe* to religious beliefs about abortion and the beginning of life? Do they raise any First Amendment concerns? In Webster v. Reproductive Health Services, 492 U.S. 490 (1989), a large number of religious groups submitted an amicus brief arguing that restrictions on the right of procreative freedom invade the religious freedoms protected by the Free Exercise Clause of the First Amendment. Because of the diversity of views on abortion among religious groups, they argued, state regulation of this area will necessarily clash with the strongly-held religious beliefs of some groups and individuals, dictating that the issue should be left to the private sphere. Brief Amicus Curiae for American Jewish Congress, et al., in Webster v. Reproductive Health Services, No. 88–605 (1989) (written by law professors Martha Minow and Aviam Soifer). What do you think of this argument? What if state regulation is *essential* to the religious beliefs of some groups, because they believe abortion is murder and thus cannot be permitted by our society? Can you think of other areas in which constitutional decisions have been founded upon religion?

4. After *Harris,* the ability of an indigent woman to obtain an abortion was severely restricted. Even if the abortion is deemed medically necessary, states are not required to pay for it under the Medicaid program, although Medicaid does pay for other types of health services for indigent women. As of 2009, 33 states did not provide funding for medically necessary abortions. Guttmacher Institute: State Policies in Brief, State Funding of Abortion Under Medicaid (2009). Moreover, President Obama traded a promise to confirm and to expand the restriction on federal funding of abortions in return for the votes to pass the new health care bill in March, 2010. Under the new Patient Protection and Affordable Care Act (Pub. L. No. 111–148), Medicaid is expanded to cover many more adults but not their abortions; and in the new private insurance exchanges, the law requires that, if a plan covers abortion, the premiums to finance it must be segregated from the funds provided as federal subsidies. An Executive Order signed by the president affirmed all these restrictions, as well as barring new community health centers funded by the Act from providing abortion services. Exec. Order No. 13,535, 75 Fed. Reg. 15599 (Mar. 24, 2010). Is it constitutional for the federal government to treat pregnancy differently from other types of medical conditions? See discussion of *Geduldig* case in Chapter 2, above. Do rules developed in other contexts logically extend to abortion? Why or why not? Is it possible to attack the holding in *Harris* solely on the basis of formal equality? How? See Jennifer Keighley, Health Care Reform and Reproductive Rights: Sex Equality Arguments for Abortion Coverage in a National Plan, 33 Harv. J.L. & Gender 357 (2010). Does it make any difference that Medicaid does pay for sterilization as well as for childbirth, and that women on welfare have at times been *encouraged* to seek sterilization?

5. The Supreme Court cases, with their narrow focus on the right to be left alone by government (i.e., we are all equally free to have *and* to pay for an abortion), seem to protect relatively well-off adult white women the most and ignore the primary reproductive issues for poor women, especially poor women of color. This bias goes beyond their ability to have access to abortion and safe and effective contraception. Indeed, for many of these women, the top priority may not be the ability to *avoid* having children but rather the ability to have them under conditions of reasonable economic, physical, and emotional security. See, e.g., Angela Hooton, A Broader Vision of the Reproductive Rights Movement: Fusing Mainstream and Latina Feminism, 13 Am. U. J. Gender Soc. Pol'y & L. 59 (2005) (discussing Latinas' need for health insurance, prenatal care, preventive screenings, information about birth control, and the like). Can these types of reproductive issues be addressed by the courts? In what ways?

6. In 1989 the Supreme court decided Webster v. Reproductive Health Services, 492 U.S. 490 (1989). *Webster* was a broad-based challenge to a restrictive Missouri statute that included, among other things, viability-testing requirements prior to abortion and extensive bans on the use of public funds and facilities in abortions or abortion counseling; all of the restrictions were essentially upheld. The most notable aspect of the decision was that the Court revealed deep splits as to whether Roe v. Wade should be overruled, with four justices clearly favoring such a move. Only Justice O'Connor's argument that the validity of the Missouri statute did not turn on the

constitutionality of Roe v. Wade avoided such a result, leaving Justice Blackmun, the author of *Roe*, to voice his fears for the future of the right to an abortion in his dissent and supporters of reproductive rights to dread what might happen in the next case to come before the Court. That next case was Planned Parenthood of Southeastern Pennsylvania v. Casey, below, in 1992.

PLANNED PARENTHOOD OF SOUTHEASTERN PENNSYLVANIA v. CASEY

Supreme Court of the United States, 1992.
505 U.S. 833, 112 S.Ct. 2791, 120 L.Ed.2d 674.

[At issue in this case were the provisions of the Pennsylvania Abortion Control Act of 1982 (1) requiring informed consent before an abortion and specifying that certain information must be provided at least 24 hours before the abortion; (2) requiring consent of one of the parents of a minor seeking an abortion with the option of judicial bypass in certain circumstances; (3) requiring spousal notification by married women seeking abortions; (4) defining "medical emergency" as a condition that necessitates an abortion to avoid death or serious, irreversible harm to the mother and exempting women in that condition from the above requirements; and (5) imposing various reporting requirements on facilities that perform abortions.

Justices O'Connor, Kennedy, and Souter, writing for the plurality, reaffirmed the essential holding of Roe v. Wade—a woman's right to an abortion before fetal viability—but rejected its trimester framework. The medical emergency definition and exemption, informed consent requirement, parental consent requirement (with judicial bypass), and record-keeping provisions were upheld using an "undue burden" standard, described in the excerpt below. The spousal notification requirement and the reporting requirements pertaining to it were held unconstitutional, because they imposed an undue burden on women who fear abuse from their husbands.]

JUSTICES O'CONNOR, KENNEDY, and SOUTER announced the judgment of the Court.

I

Liberty finds no refuge in a jurisprudence of doubt. Yet 19 years after our holding that the Constitution protects a woman's right to terminate her pregnancy in its early stages, *Roe v. Wade*, 410 U.S. 113, 35 L. Ed. 2d 147, 93 S. Ct. 705 (1973), that definition of liberty is still questioned. * * *

* * *

* * * State and federal courts as well as legislatures throughout the Union must have guidance as they seek to address this subject in conformance with the Constitution. Given these premises, we find it imperative to review once more the principles that define the rights of the woman and

the legitimate authority of the State respecting the termination of pregnancies by abortion procedures.

After considering the fundamental constitutional questions resolved by *Roe,* principles of institutional integrity, and the rule of stare decisis, we are led to conclude this: the essential holding of Roe v. Wade should be retained and once again reaffirmed.

It must be stated at the outset and with clarity that Roe's essential holding, the holding we reaffirm, has three parts. First is a recognition of the right of the woman to choose to have an abortion before viability and to obtain it without undue interference from the State. Before viability, the State's interests are not strong enough to support a prohibition of abortion or the imposition of a substantial obstacle to the woman's effective right to elect the procedure. Second is a confirmation of the State's power to restrict abortions after fetal viability if the law contains exceptions for pregnancies which endanger the woman's life or health. And third is the principle that the State has legitimate interests from the outset of the pregnancy in protecting the health of the woman and the life of the fetus that may become a child. * * *

II

* * *

At the heart of liberty is the right to define one's own concept of existence, of meaning, of the universe, and of the mystery of human life. Beliefs about these matters could not define the attributes of personhood were they formed under compulsion of the State.

These considerations begin our analysis of the woman's interest in terminating her pregnancy but cannot end it, for this reason: though the abortion decision may originate within the zone of conscience and belief, it is more than a philosophic exercise. Abortion is a unique act. It is an act fraught with consequences for others * * *. Though abortion is conduct, it does not follow that the State is entitled to proscribe it in all instances. That is because the liberty of the woman is at stake in a sense unique to the human condition and so unique to the law. The mother who carries a child to full term is subject to anxieties, to physical constraints, to pain that only she must bear. * * * The destiny of the woman must be shaped to a large extent on her own conception of her spiritual imperatives and her place in society.

* * *

III

A

The obligation to follow precedent begins with necessity, and a contrary necessity marks its outer limit. * * *

* * *

[I]n this case we may inquire whether *Roe*'s central rule has been found unworkable; whether the rule's limitation on state power could be removed without serious inequity to those who have relied upon it or significant damage to the stability of the society governed by it; whether the law's growth in the intervening years has left *Roe*'s central rule a doctrinal anachronism discounted by society; and whether *Roe*'s premises of fact have so far changed in the ensuing two decades as to render its central holding somehow irrelevant or unjustifiable in dealing with the issue it addressed.

* * *

The inquiry into reliance counts the cost of a rule's repudiation as it would fall on those who have relied reasonably on the rule's continued application. * * *

* * * Abortion is customarily chosen as an unplanned response to the consequence of unplanned activity or to the failure of conventional birth control, and except on the assumption that no intercourse would have occurred but for *Roe*'s holding, such behavior may appear to justify no reliance claim. Even if reliance could be claimed on that unrealistic assumption, the argument might run, any reliance interest would be *de minimis*. * * *

To eliminate the issue of reliance that easily, however, one would need to limit cognizable reliance to specific instances of sexual activity. But to do this would be simply to refuse to face the fact that for two decades of economic and social developments, people have organized intimate relationships and made choices that define their views of themselves and their places in society, in reliance on the availability of abortion in the event that contraception should fail. The ability of women to participate equally in the economic and social life of the Nation has been facilitated by their ability to control their reproductive lives. See, e.g., R. Petchesky, Abortion and Woman's Choice 109, 133, n. 7 (rev. ed. 1990). The Constitution serves human values, and while the effect of reliance on *Roe* cannot be exactly measured, neither can the certain cost of overruling *Roe* for people who have ordered their thinking and living around that case be dismissed.

* * *

IV

* * * We conclude that the basic decision in *Roe* was based on a constitutional analysis which we cannot now repudiate. The woman's liberty is not so unlimited, however, that from the outset the State cannot show its concern for the life of the unborn, and at a later point in fetal development the State's interest in life has sufficient force so that the right of the woman to terminate the pregnancy can be restricted.

That brings us, of course, to the point where much criticism has been directed at *Roe,* a criticism that always inheres when the Court draws a specific rule from what in the Constitution is but a general standard. We conclude, however, that the urgent claims of the woman to retain the ultimate control over her destiny and her body, claims implicit in the meaning of liberty, require us to perform that function. Liberty must not be extinguished for want of a line that is clear. And it falls to us to give some real substance to the woman's liberty to determine whether to carry her pregnancy to full term.

We conclude the line should be drawn at viability, so that before that time the woman has a right to choose to terminate her pregnancy. * * *

* * * The viability line also has, as a practical matter, an element of fairness. In some broad sense it might be said that a woman who fails to act before viability has consented to the State's intervention on behalf of the developing child.

The woman's right to terminate her pregnancy before viability is the most central principle of *Roe v. Wade*. It is a rule of law and a component of liberty we cannot renounce.

On the other side of the equation is the interest of the State in the protection of potential life.* * *

* * *

Though the woman has a right to choose to terminate or continue her pregnancy before viability, it does not at all follow that the State is prohibited from taking steps to ensure that this choice is thoughtful and informed. * * *

We reject the trimester framework, which we do not consider to be part of the essential holding of *Roe*. * * * A logical reading of the central holding in *Roe* itself, and a necessary reconciliation of the liberty of the woman and the interest of the State in promoting prenatal life, require, in our view, that we abandon the trimester framework as a rigid prohibition on all previability regulation aimed at the protection of fetal life. * * *

* * *

* * * The fact that a law which serves a valid purpose, one not designed to strike at the right itself, has the incidental effect of making it more difficult or more expensive to procure an abortion cannot be enough to invalidate it. Only where state regulation imposes an undue burden on a woman's ability to make this decision does the power of the State reach into the heart of the liberty protected by the Due Process Clause.

* * *

A finding of an undue burden is a shorthand for the conclusion that a state regulation has the purpose or effect of placing a substantial obstacle in the path of a woman seeking an abortion of a nonviable fetus. A statute with this purpose is invalid because the means chosen by the State to further the interest in potential life must be calculated to inform the woman's free choice, not hinder it. And a statute which, while furthering the interest in potential life or some other valid state interest, has the effect of placing a substantial obstacle in the path of a woman's choice cannot be considered a permissible means of serving its legitimate ends. * * *

* * *

[The Court held that the statute's definition of "medical emergency" and requirement of informed consent did not place an undue burden on the abortion right.]

[*Spousal notification*]

Section 3209 of Pennsylvania's abortion law provides, except in cases of medical emergency, that no physician shall perform an abortion on a married woman without receiving a signed statement from the woman that she has notified her spouse that she is about to undergo an abortion. * * *

The District Court heard the testimony of numerous expert witnesses, and made detailed findings of fact regarding the effect of this statute. * * *

These findings are supported by studies of domestic violence. The American Medical Association (AMA) has published a summary of the recent research in this field, which indicates that in an average 12-month period in this country, approximately two million women are the victims of severe assaults by their male partners. In a 1985 survey, women reported that nearly one of every eight husbands had assaulted their wives during the past year. The AMA views these figures as "marked underestimates," because the nature of these incidents discourages women from reporting them, and because surveys typically exclude the very poor, those who do not speak English well, and women who are homeless or in institutions or hospitals when the survey is conducted. * * *

* * * Many victims of domestic violence remain with their abusers, perhaps because they perceive no superior alternative. Many abused women who find temporary refuge in shelters return to their husbands, in large part because they have no other source of income. Returning to one's abuser can be dangerous. Recent Federal Bureau of Investigation statistics disclose that 8.8% of all homicide victims in the United States are killed by their spouse. Thirty percent of female homicide victims are killed by their male partners.

* * * In well-functioning marriages, spouses discuss important intimate decisions such as whether to bear a child. But there are millions of women in this country who are the victims of regular physical and psychological abuse at the hands of their husbands. Should these women become pregnant, they may have very good reasons for not wishing to inform their husbands of their decision to obtain an abortion. Many may have justifiable fears of physical abuse, but may be no less fearful of the consequences of reporting prior abuse to the Commonwealth of Pennsylvania. Many may have a reasonable fear that notifying their husbands will

provoke further instances of child abuse * * *. Many may fear devastating forms of psychological abuse from their husbands, including verbal harassment, threats of future violence, the destruction of possessions, physical confinement to the home, the withdrawal of financial support, or the disclosure of the abortion to family and friends. These methods of psychological abuse may act as even more of a deterrent to notification than the possibility of physical violence * * *. And many women who are pregnant as a result of sexual assaults by their husbands will be unable to avail themselves of the exception for spousal sexual assault, because the exception requires that the woman have notified law enforcement authorities within 90 days of the assault, and her husband will be notified of her report once an investigation begins. * * *

The spousal notification requirement is thus likely to prevent a significant number of women from obtaining an abortion. It does not merely make abortions a little more difficult or expensive to obtain; for many women, it will impose a substantial obstacle. We must not blind ourselves to the fact that the significant number of women who fear for their safety and the safety of their children are likely to be deterred from procuring an abortion as surely as if the Commonwealth had outlawed abortion in all cases.

* * *

* * * If these cases concerned a State's ability to require the mother to notify the father before taking some action with respect to a living child raised by both, therefore, it would be reasonable to conclude as a general matter that the father's interest in the welfare of the child and the mother's interest are equal.

Before birth, however, the issue takes on a very different cast. It is an inescapable biological fact that state regulation with respect to the child a woman is carrying will have a far greater impact on the mother's liberty than on the father's. The effect of state regulation on a woman's protected liberty is doubly deserving of scrutiny in such a case, as the State has touched not only upon the private sphere of the family but upon the very bodily integrity of the pregnant woman. * * *

Section 3209 embodies a view of marriage consonant with the common-law status of married women but repugnant to our present understanding of marriage and of the nature of the rights secured by the Constitution. Women do not lose their constitutionally protected liberty when they marry. * * *

* * *

> [Justice Stevens agreed with the majority, but would have retained the trimester framework and have struck down the informed consent requirement as imposing an undue burden on a woman seeking an abortion. Justice Blackmun dissented from much of the majority opinion, in favor of retaining the trimester framework and fundamental interest standard of Roe v. Wade; he would have also invalidated

the counseling and 24–hour delay, parental consent, and reporting requirements.]

CHIEF JUSTICE REHNQUIST, with whom JUSTICE WHITE, JUSTICE SCALIA, and JUSTICE THOMAS join, concurring in the judgment in part and dissenting in part.

* * *

The joint opinion * * * points to the reliance interests involved in this context in its effort to explain why precedent must be followed for precedent's sake. Certainly it is true that where reliance is truly at issue, as in the case of judicial decisions that have formed the basis for private decisions, "[c]onsiderations in favor of stare decisis are at their acme." But * * * any traditional notion of reliance is not applicable here. The Court today cuts back on the protection afforded by *Roe,* and no one claims that this action defeats any reliance interest in the disavowed trimester framework. Similarly, reliance interests would not be diminished were the Court to go further and acknowledge the full error of *Roe,* as "reproductive planning could take virtually immediate account of" this action.

The joint opinion thus turns to what can only be described as an unconventional—and unconvincing—notion of reliance, a view based on the surmise that the availability of abortion since *Roe* has led to "two decades of economic and social developments" that would be undercut if the error of *Roe* were recognized. The joint opinion's assertion of this fact is undeveloped and totally conclusory. In fact, one can not be sure to what economic and social developments the opinion is referring. Surely it is dubious to suggest that women have reached their "places in society" in reliance upon *Roe,* rather than as a result of their determination to obtain higher education and compete with men in the job market, and of society's increasing recognition of their ability to fill positions that were previously thought to be reserved only for men.

In the end, having failed to put forth any evidence to prove any true reliance, the joint opinion's argument is based solely on generalized assertions about the national psyche, on a belief that the people of this country have grown accustomed to the *Roe* decision over the last 19 years and have "ordered their thinking and living around" it. As an initial matter, one might inquire how the joint opinion can view the "central holding" of *Roe* as so deeply rooted in our constitutional culture, when it so casually uproots and disposes of that same decision's trimester framework. Furthermore, at various points in the past, the same could have been said about this Court's erroneous decisions that the Constitution allowed "separate but equal" treatment of minorities, see Plessy v. Ferguson, 163 U.S. 537, 16 S.Ct. 1138, 41 L.Ed. 256 (1896) * * *. The "separate but equal" doctrine lasted 58 years after *Plessy* * * *. However, the simple fact that a generation or more had grown used to these major decisions did not prevent the Court from correcting its errors in those cases, nor should it prevent us from correctly interpreting the Constitution here.

[Justices Rehnquist, White, Scalia, and Thomas concurred in most of the majority opinion but would have overruled Roe v. Wade and thus would have upheld even the spousal notification requirement using a rational relationship standard, rather than the undue burden test.]

NOTES ON CASEY

1. After *Webster,* when only the vote of Justice O'Connor prevented Roe v. Wade from being overruled, proponents of the right of abortion feared the worst. Instead, the *Casey* Court not only refused to overturn *Roe* but also, unlike previous opinions, included feminist arguments and research in its analysis. The woman's presence, her life and her concerns, moved to center stage in sections of the joint opinion. At the same time, the Court upheld almost every restriction the state had placed upon abortion, including, for example, a 24–hour waiting period in the face of district court findings that requiring two separate visits to the clinic could delay abortions up to two weeks, thus making the procedure more dangerous medically. *Casey,* 744 F.Supp. 1323, 1351–52 (E.D. Pa. 1990). The *Casey* opinion also overturned the *Roe* framework, replacing it with the vague and undefined "undue burden" test. One observer pointed out that the *Casey* opinion virtually invited the states to test whether one after another abortion-restrictive law constituted an "undue burden" and noted that while its language lulled pro-choice advocates into complacency, more than 300 anti-choice measures were adopted by the states between 1995 and 2002. Elizabeth A. Cavendish, *Casey* Reflections, 10 J. Gender, Social Policy & Law 305, 309–10 (2002).

One difference between *Casey*'s undue burden test and the *Roe* trimester structure is that the state's interest in the health of both mother and fetus is extended into the pre-viability stage, thus allowing "pre-viability restrictions having nothing to do with women's health, restrictions that would have been invalid under *Roe.*" Caitlin E. Borgmann, Winter Count: Taking Stock of Abortion Rights after *Casey* and *Carhart,* 31 Fordham Urban L.J. 675, 681 (2004). What are the implications of this difference? Are there other differences between *Casey*'s undue burden test and the *Roe* trimester structure?

2. Who has the better of the argument over reliance: the joint opinion or the dissent? Is the discussion of reliance in *Casey* just the standard way a court considers whether to overrule its own prior opinions? Or does the joint opinion mean something more by its discussion of reliance? Have you or women and men in your generation relied on the right to abortion? How? Would this reliance disappear if the Court gave women a 90–day warning that the right was to be taken away? A reliance argument is most effectively used by defenders of the status quo. Can you distinguish reliance on Roe v. Wade from reliance on the "separate but equal" doctrine, an analogy suggested by Justice Rehnquist's dissent in *Casey*?

There is another kind of reliance the Court does not mention in *Casey*—that of pro-choice activists, who did not continue to press for legislative liberalization on abortion in the 1970's in reliance on Roe v. Wade. Why doesn't the majority mention this kind of reliance? Should this type of reliance be protected more, or less, than the reliance of women and men as individuals in making choices and forming goals, values, and self images? What differences are there between the Court's reliance argument and political reliance on the availability of abortion rights? Could some of the points in the reliance discussion be made without reference to reliance as such?

3. In situations not involving domestic violence, what, if any, rights do you think fathers should have in relation to the decision to abort? Compare the discussion of this issue in *Casey* with that in Planned Parenthood of Central Missouri v. Danforth, 428 U.S. 52, 67–71 (1976). See also Andrea M. Sharrin, Potential Fathers and Abortion: A Woman's Womb Is Not A Man's Castle, 55 Brook. L.Rev. 1359 (1990). Does it make any difference that men are still obligated to support children they would have preferred to abort? Should unwilling fathers be obligated to pay child support? See Sally Sheldon, Unwilling Fathers and Abortion: Terminating Men's Child Support Obligations, 66 Mod. L. Rev. 175 (2003); Ethan J. Leib, A Man's Right to Choose: Men Deserve Voice in Abortion Decision, 28 Legal Times 60 (2005).

4. Another main issue in *Casey* was the requirement of parental notification and consent prior to a minor's obtaining an abortion. The Pennsylvania statute provided that an unemancipated young woman under 18 could not obtain an abortion without the consent of one of her parents or a guardian except in an emergency; if no parental consent were given, however, a court could nonetheless authorize the abortion if it determined that she was mature enough to give informed consent or that an abortion was in her best interest ("judicial bypass") in accordance with past Supreme Court holdings. *Casey,* 505 U.S. at 899. The *Casey* Court upheld the one-parent consent requirement, provided that there was an adequate procedure for judicial bypass. By 2009, 34 states had statutes that required either parental consent or notification. Carol Sanger, Decisional Dignity: Teenage Abortion, Bypass Hearings, and The Misuse of Law, 18 Colum. J. Gender & L. 409, 421 (2009). An empirical study of the operation of judicial bypass procedures in Alabama, Pennsylvania, and Tennessee reported that the courts are poorly prepared to handle inquiries from teenagers about judicial bypass procedures, that they turn away inquiries, fail to instruct teenagers about their rights under the state statute, and give out either inadequate or inaccurate information. Helena Silverstein, Girls on the Stand: How Courts Fail Pregnant Minors 52–71 (2007). In addition, many judges refuse to hear bypass petitions, causing additional delay, procedural hassles, and travel to another jurisdiction, a problem that is exacerbated in areas where judges run for election on an anti-abortion platform. Sanger, above, at 493–97. Although the overwhelming majority of requests for judicial bypass are granted, the judicial process requires the teenage girl to reveal very private information to an authoritative adult and appears calculated to either deter abortion or to punish those who seek it. Id. at 436, 444–54, 471–79.

Studies of minors who are unwilling to notify their parents show that this decision is only partly associated with fear of parental disagreement about the choice of abortion; other reasons for not notifying parents include multiple concurrent family stresses, an absent father (in states requiring two-parent consent), family violence, parental substance abuse, and a feeling of having "betrayed" the family by becoming pregnant. See Robert W. Blum, Michael D. Resnick & Trisha Stark, Factors Associated with the Use of Court Bypass by Minors to Obtain Abortions, 22 Family Planning Perspectives 158, 160 (July–Aug. 1990). What are the pro's and con's of the different possible approaches to minors' obtaining abortions? Should they be able to do so without parental consent? At what age? Under what conditions? Do you think a judge should be involved in this decision? Are judges (who are still primarily male) satisfactory substitutes for parents? Do you think most teenagers are capable of making this decision on their own? Of approaching a court on their own? If teenage girls are deterred from seeking a legal abortion, what is the likely consequence? Is a girl not mature enough to make the abortion decision mature enough to have a child? Should there be an exception to parental notice requirements for victims of incest?

One empirical study of teens seeking abortions without involving their parents shows that they had, for the most part, very good reasons not to involve their parents, and that most of them did in fact involve some adult in their decision, often a professional adviser or (especially in the case of African Americans) an extended family member. The author suggests that consulting another responsible adult should be made an alternative to the current requirement of either parental consent or court involvement, which is often very traumatic for these young women. J. Shoshanna Ehrlich, Grounded in the Reality of Their Lives: Listening to Teens Who Make the Abortion Decision Without Involving Their Parents, 18 Berkeley Women's L.J. 61 (2003). Ehrlich argued in another article that "despite consistent judicial language to the contrary, parental involvement laws have more to do with limiting abortion rights than with promoting family communication and prudent teenage decision-making." Journey Through the Courts: Minors, Abortion and the Quest for Reproductive Fairness, 10 Yale J. Law & Feminism 1, 2 (1998). See also J. Shoshanna Ehrlich, Who Decides? The Abortion Rights of Teens (2006).

5. How do spousal notification and parental notification requirements differ, apart from the age of the pregnant woman? What is the significance of age? Which do you think constitutes more of an "undue burden" upon the right to an abortion?

6. In light of the regulations upheld and those struck down in *Casey*, how does the *Casey* Court define what is an "undue burden"? Must it be absolutely prohibitive of abortion? If a regulation may pose some incremental risk to the mother, is it an undue burden? If each regulation challenged is individually not a total obstruction, what of their cumulative effect? If abortion is made more costly and risky by waiting periods and the necessity to notify a parent, is it genuinely available to young or poor pregnant women?

TEXT NOTE: THE BATTLE OVER ABORTION AFTER CASEY

The battle over abortion has taken place in the streets as well as the courts. After *Roe*, anti-abortion forces were initially led by Roman Catholics, many of whom had emerged from the anti-war and civil rights movement and coalesced into the Pro–Life Action Network led by Joseph Scheidler. By the late 1980's, however, a younger, fundamentalist Protestant leadership had come to the fore, organized into Operation Rescue, whose tactics became increasingly extreme.[1] Street protests became efforts to block access to clinics where abortions were performed. In response, feminist groups filed suits to enjoin or restrain such conduct by imposing buffer zones to prevent Operation Rescue's supporters from harassing patients walking to and from abortion clinics. In a series of cases, the Supreme Court laid down guidelines for accommodating the free speech rights of the protesters, on the one hand, and the interests in public safety, protection of property rights, and protection of a woman's freedom to seek pregnancy-related services, on the other.[2]

More violent anti-abortion protests erupted in the 1990's, including arson and bombing of clinics as well as the murder of doctors who performed abortions.[3] In 1995, a break-away group from Operation Rescue produced a "Deadly Dozen" list containing the names of abortion providers, which was subsequently published on the Internet; by January 1996 five of those on the list had been shot or subjected to other forms of violence.[4] One doctor, David Gunn, and the doctor who replaced him, along with an escort, were murdered at a clinic in Pensacola, Florida in 1993 and 1994.[5] Another abortion opponent entered two abortion clinics in Boston in 1994, shooting and killing two receptionists and injuring others.[6] And in October 1998, Dr. Barnett Slepian, an abortion provider in Buffalo, was murdered by a gunman shooting through a window of the doctor's home.[7]

The first shootings were followed by passage of the Freedom of Access to Clinic Entrances Act (FACE) in May 1994, which made it a federal crime to block access to clinics or to commit acts aimed at denying a woman access to an abortion.[8] A federal court also issued a permanent injunction under FACE against groups' disseminating the "Deadly Dozen" list and poster and a list of names and information about abortion providers (known as the "Nuremberg Files") on the Internet.[9] Ultimately, damage awards against the anti-abortion groups and individuals were upheld on remand, in the amount of $526,336

1. See generally James Risen & Judy L. Thomas, Wrath of Angels: The American Abortion War (1998). See also Alesha E. Doan, Opposition & Intimidation: The Abortion Wars & Strategies of Political Harassment (2007).

2. Madsen v. Women's Health Center, Inc., 512 U.S. 753 (1994) (upholding a 36–foot buffer zone protecting entrances to a clinic and its parking lot); Schenck v. Pro–Choice Network of Western New York, 519 U.S. 357 (1997) (upholding a 15–foot fixed buffer zone around clinic doorways, driveways, and parking lot entrances, while striking down a 15–foot "floating" buffer that prohibited demonstrating within 15 feet of any person entering or leaving the clinic); Hill v. Colorado, 530 U.S. 703 (2000) (upholding a Colorado criminal statute prohibiting protesters from knowingly approaching within eight feet of an individual who is within 100 feet of a health care facility entrance without that individual's consent).

3. See Risen & Thomas, above note 1, at 339–71; Karen O'Connor, No Neutral Ground? Abortion Politics in an Age of Absolutes 162–64 (Tables 7.2 & 7.3) (1996).

4. O'Connor, above note 3, at 172.

5. Risen & Thomas, above note 1, at 339–49, 361–65.

6. Id. at 367–68. For a chronological account of attacks on abortion providers, see Patricia Baird–Windle & Eleanor J. Bader, Targets of Hatred: Anti–Abortion Terrorism 61–250 (2001).

7. Jim Yardley & David Rohde, Abortion Doctor in Buffalo Slain; Sniper Attack Fits Violent Pattern, N.Y.Times, Oct. 25, 1998, at A1.

8. 18 U.S.C.A. § 248.

9. Planned Parenthood of the Columbia/Willamette, Inc., et al. v. American Coalition of Life Activists, et al., 290 F.3d 1058 (9th Cir. 2002) (en banc), cert. denied, 539 U.S. 958 (2003).

compensatory damages, for which the defendants were jointly and severally liable, and punitive damages ranging from $3.5 to $8 million against each individual defendant and $16,750,000 against each of the defendant groups.[10] The court held that such high punitive damage awards were necessary because the defendants were apparently undeterrable by other means, having repeatedly violated injunctions.

Pro-choice lawyers have sought damage remedies against the groups seeking to blockade abortion clinics in hopes that the accumulating damages would take a severe toll on the major anti-abortion groups, which were also split by interpersonal quarrels and disagreements over the use of violence.[11] For a variety of reasons, including the damage awards, enforcement of FACE, cases upholding "buffer zones," and the apprehension and punishment (capital punishment in one case) of persons responsible for murdering doctors and others at abortion clinics, violence has declined, but it has not disappeared. On May 31, 2009, Dr. George Tiller, one of the few doctors to perform late-term abortions, was shot to death while handing out bulletins at the door of his church on Sunday morning; his clinic subsequently closed.[12]

Abortion opponents have continued their activity through the courts and legislatures, passing state and federal statutes that chip away at the scope of the right to abortion. The numerous state statutes regulating abortion, most of them transparent attempts to make the process virtually impossible to negotiate and to drive providers out of business, have become known as TRAP (Targeted Regulations of Abortion Providers) laws.[13] Onerous licensing and reporting requirements have been upheld by the courts. For example, the Supreme Court has upheld under the undue burden standard a statute restricting abortions to licensed physicians in a state (Montana) where providers were few, a restriction transparently aimed at one of the most active providers, who was a physician's assistant.[14] Another TRAP tactic has been to pass a statute, as some states have done, that makes the provision of an abortion a strict liability tort with no cap on the amount of damages, making doctors unwilling to risk liability. Such statutes operate effectively to ban constitutionally protected conduct but have evaded preenforcement review by the courts on grounds of legislative immunity and lack of standing.[15]

Abortion has also been a central issue in national elections and has contributed to a gender gap in voting patterns for President and in Congressional races.[16] As a result, a number of federal policies have flip-flopped with a change of Administration. When Bill Clinton was elected President in 1992,

---

10. Planned Parenthood of the Columbia/Willamette, Inc., et al. v. American Coalition of Life Activists, et al., 300 F.Supp.2d 1055, 1064–65 (D.Or. 2004).

11. See Risen & Thomas, above note 1, at 295–314.

12. Joe Stumpe & Monica Davey, Abortion Doctor Shot to Death in Kansas Church, N.Y. Times, June 1, 2009, at A1; Monica Davey, Kansas Abortion Clinic Operated by Doctor Who Was Killed Closes Permanently, N.Y. Times, June 10, 2009, at A16.

13. See, e.g., Dawn Johnsen, "TRAP"ing *Roe* in Indiana and a Common–Ground Alternative, 118 Yale L.J. 1356 (2009).

14. Mazurek v. Armstrong, 520 U.S. 968 (1997).

15. See Maya Manian, Privatizing Bans on Abortion: Eviscerating Constitutional Rights Through Tort Remedies, 80 Temple L. Rev. 123 (2007).

16. See O'Connor, above note 3, at 115–53.

owing a good deal to support from pro-choice women, he immediately issued a number of executive orders reversing the so-called "gag rule" against abortion counseling in federally funded programs, directing the Secretary of Health and Human Services to review the ban on importation of RU 486, and cancelling the prohibition of U.S. aid to international programs that include abortion counseling.[17] After the 2000 election, President George W. Bush reversed almost every one of these actions and extended some of them. The so-called "global gag rule" under Bush prohibited funding any international family planning groups that included abortion, abortion counseling, or advocacy of abortion among their services (which often also include HIV/AIDS counseling and prevention).[18] The results of this policy were especially dangerous for the health of women in developing countries.[19] Upon the election of President Obama, funding was promptly restored to international health groups that perform, promote, or counsel about abortion.[20]

NOTES ON ABORTION AFTER CASEY

1. The violent responses of anti-abortion militants has played a role in decreasing the numbers of doctors willing to perform abortions, and medical residency programs providing routine training in first-semester abortions also declined from 23% in 1985 to 12% in 1991. James Risen & Judy L. Thomas, Wrath of Angels: The American Abortion War 376 (1998). The number of facilities providing abortions declined by 14% between 1992 and 1996, by 11% from 1996 to 2000, and an additional 2% between 2000 and 2005. More than three decades after Roe v. Wade, abortions were unavailable in 87% of U.S. counties, affecting 35% of American women, especially in rural areas, the South, and the Midwest, causing many women to travel long distances to obtain an abortion. Rachel K. Jones, Mia Zolna, Stanley K. Henshaw & Lawrence B. Finer, Abortion in the United States: Incidence and Access to Services, 2005, 40 Perspectives on Sexual & Reproductive Health 6, 10–12, 14 (2008). See also Carole Joffe, Dispatches From the Abortion Wars: The Costs of Fanaticism to Doctors, Patients, and the Rest of Us 21–45 (2009) (describing the challenges that face doctors who consider becoming abortion providers).

Rates of abortion have also fallen. After an initial rise from 21.7 per 1,000 women in 1975 to a high of 29.3 per 1,000 in 1980–1981, the rate of abortion in the U.S. fell to 19.4 per 1,000 by 2005. U.S. Census Bureau, Statistical Abstract of the United States 2010, Table 100. Abortions by Selected Characteristics: 1990 to 2005. This was the lowest rate of abortions since 1974. Jones, Zolna, Henshaw & Finer, above, at 9. The use of emergency contraception accounted for almost half the decrease between 1994 and 2000. Beth A. Burkstrand–Reid, The Invisible Woman: Availability and Culpability in Repro-

---

17. Id. at 151.

18. See, e.g., Kaci Bishop, Politics Before Policy: The Bush Administration, International Family Planning, and Foreign Policy, 29 N.C.J. Int'l L. & Com. Reg. 521 (2004).

19. See, e.g., E. Dana Neacsu, Imposing Sexual Restraint Abroad, 2002 L. Rev. M.S.U.–D.C.L. 885, 892 (reporting that when a similar gag order was in effect during the Reagan Administration the abortion rate grew in affected countries, where abortion is often illegal and very dangerous).

20. Rob Stein & Michael Shear, Funding Restored to Groups That Perform Abortions, Other Care, Washington Post, Jan. 24, 2009.

ductive Health Jurisprudence, 81 U. Colo. L. Rev. 97, 115 (2010). The rate among white non-Hispanic women in the U.S. (10.5 per 1,000 in 2005) is comparable to that in some other developed countries, though still higher than that in most of Western Europe; the rate among poor women and women of color is twice as high, however. Census Bureau, Table 100, above. Nonetheless, the abortion rate for African American women in the United States has declined sharply, from 63.9 per 1,000 in 1990 to 49.3 per 1,000 in 2005. Id. What do you think accounts for these differences, both internationally and among groups based on income and race? Abortion rates appear to be comparable in countries where abortion is legal and where it is illegal, but the number of women dying in abortions is sharply higher in the latter. Elisabeth Rosenthal, Legal or Not, Abortion Rates Compare, N.Y. Times, Oct. 12, 2007, at A8.

2. Abortion remains available legally but in practice may be difficult to obtain, even in extreme cases. Consider the case of a 26–year–old mother of two who was denied an abortion at a Louisiana public hospital, despite the fact that she suffered from a serious heart disease and was on the list for a heart transplant when she became pregnant. Her heart condition qualified her for disability benefits, including Medicaid; but the abortion was denied under Louisiana law, which allows abortions in public institutions only when the mother's life is endangered or in cases of rape or incest. When a panel of doctors concluded that her chance of dying was 50% or less, the state university medical center refused the abortion, which was subsequently performed in Texas after abortion rights organizations mobilized to pay for the procedure. Ruth Sorelle, Louisiana Woman Gets Abortion Here; Heart Defect Spurs Procedure in Texas, Houston Chronicle, Oct. 21, 1998, at 29. In short, although the right to abortion may exist, its availability may be extremely limited for a variety of reasons. Given such limitations, is it accurate to characterize the current legal regime as one of a "right" to abortion? See Robin West, From Choice to Reproductive Justice: De–Constitutionalizing Abortion Rights, 118 Yale L.J. 1394, 1403 (2009) ("what the Court created in *Roe v. Wade* is *not* a right to legal abortion; it is a negative right against the criminalization of abortion in some circumstances").

3. What, if any, lessons do you think can be drawn from this account of the decreased availability of abortion about the relationship of law to social change in an area where public opinion is sharply divided?

4. The First Amendment played an important role in abortion-related litigation in the 1990's. It was raised with some success on behalf of the anti-abortion protesters in the clinic access cases described above, in opposing overly broad or floating buffer zones. Moreover, in 1991, the Supreme Court upheld the so-called "gag rule," which prohibited doctors and clinics receiving federal funds from counseling about abortion or providing referrals for that purpose, in the face of First Amendment arguments, on the grounds that the government was simply choosing, as in Harris v. McRae, to subsidize family planning services that lead to conception and childbirth and declining to promote abortion. Rust v. Sullivan, 500 U.S. 173 (1991). The dissent pointed out that the Court was thereby upholding viewpoint-based suppression of speech. Dorothy Roberts adds that the decision did particular violence to women of color, because it "upheld regulations that deliberately withheld

from women in these communities knowledge critical to their reproductive health and autonomy." Roberts, *Rust v. Sullivan* and the Control of Knowledge, 61 Geo. Wash. L. Rev. 587, 590 (1993). How can you reconcile the decisions in these cases, protecting the speech of clinic protesters but suppressing that of doctors and other medical personnel?

5. Many pro-choice activists had great hopes that RU 486, the so-called "abortion pill," would allow women to avoid abortion clinics and picket lines. The pills, prescribed by a doctor, are effective in terminating a pregnancy during the first seven weeks of pregnancy. The woman can take them in the privacy of her home but must return to the doctor for a follow-up visit. RU 486, or medical (as opposed to surgical) abortion, has only been available in the United States since September 2000. Anti-abortion politics explain the long unavailability of RU 486, which was developed in 1980 and used extensively in France, Britain, Sweden, and China. After protests and boycott threats by "right-to-life" groups, the initial manufacturer dropped the drug, but was subsequently ordered to market it by the French government, which declared that RU 486 was the "moral property of women, not just the drug company." Etienne–Emile Baulieu, The "Abortion Pill" 49 (1991) (written by the scientist who developed the drug). The combination of anti-abortion protests, which played a role in the Food and Drug Administration's barring importation of the drug, and the drug company's fear of a boycott of its other products prevented the introduction of RU 486 into the United States, even as a treatment for other medical conditions. See, e.g., Lawrence Lader, RU 486 106–08 (1991). Although the FDA found, after clinical trials, that RU 486 was both safe and effective in September 1996, it was not finally approved for marketing until September 28, 2000. Gina Kolata, U.S. Approves Abortion Pill, N.Y. Times, Sept. 29, 2000, at A1.

Anti-abortion forces continued their struggle against RU 486 even after its approval, threatening to picket or boycott private practitioners who prescribed it and pressuring the Bush Administration FDA to withdraw its approval. Nonetheless, after a slow start, the use of RU 486 had risen sharply by 2005, when it accounted for 13% of all abortions, and 22% of those before the ninth week. Jones, Zolna, Henshaw & Finer, note 1 above, at 13. Experience in Europe has shown that the shift to RU 486 was not associated with any increase in the overall abortion rate. Rachel K. Jones & Stanley K. Henshaw, Mifepristone for Early Medical Abortion: Experiences in France, Great Britain and Sweden, 34 Perspectives on Sexual & Reproductive Health 154 (2002).

6. Unsurprisingly, the definition of undue burden has been litigated in case after case since the Supreme Court's decision in *Casey*. One heavily-litigated area has involved late-term (second and third trimester) abortions by a procedure involving destruction of the fetus in the birth canal rather than in the uterus; these so-called "partial birth abortion" cases constitute a relatively small proportion of all abortions but have been seized upon as a way to highlight the grisly nature of the procedure. This method of abortion is sometimes used in pregnancies of 12 to 24 weeks duration (about 90% of all abortions performed in the U.S. take place before 12 weeks). Given that amniocentesis, the main test for serious birth defects, cannot be performed until the second trimester and results are not known for several weeks, use of

this method can be necessary in cases where the test reveals substantial birth defects, including those in which the child will die soon after birth or its birth may seriously threaten the mother's health. Suzanne E. Skov, Abortion: Stenberg v. Carhart: The Abortion Debate Goes Technical, 14 J. Contemp. Legal Issues 235 (2004). In Stenberg v. Carhart, 530 U.S. 914 (2000), the Supreme Court held, by a five to four vote, that a Nebraska statute banning the procedure was unconstitutional because it placed a substantial obstacle in the path of a woman seeking to abort a nonviable fetus and thus was an undue burden upon the right to an abortion. The Court found that the statute was also unconstitutional because it did not contain an exception for maternal health, although a substantial number of doctors believe that the challenged method is less risky for many women, and because the ban could also be interpreted to cover other procedures commonly performed in the first trimester.

After *Stenberg*, the U.S. Congress passed a Partial–Birth Abortion Ban Act virtually identical to the Nebraska statute struck down in that case, including in it "medical findings" that this procedure is *never* necessary for the health of the mother and may be harmful to her. 18 U.S.C. § 1531 (2003). Cases challenging the constitutionality of the federal act in two federal circuits were consolidated into the case that appears below. In both of the cases, the federal district and appellate courts had all found the Partial Birth Abortion Act unconstitutional under *Stenberg*. Why do you think anti-abortion groups challenge procedures that are used in such a small percentage of all abortions?

GONZALES v. CARHART

Supreme Court of the United States, 2007.
550 U.S. 124, 127 S.Ct. 1610, 167 L.Ed.2d 480

JUSTICE KENNEDY delivered the opinion of the Court.

These cases require us to consider the validity of the Partial–Birth Abortion Ban Act of 2003 (Act), a federal statute regulating abortion procedures. * * *

* * *

Abortion methods vary depending to some extent on the preferences of the physician and, of course, on the term of the pregnancy and the resulting stage of the unborn child's development. Between 85 and 90 percent of the approximately 1.3 million abortions performed each year in the United States take place in the first three months of pregnancy, which is to say in the first trimester. * * *

Of the remaining abortions that take place each year, most occur in the second trimester. The surgical procedure referred to as "dilation and evacuation" or "D & E" is the usual abortion method in this trimester.

[The court here describes the second trimester methods in detail, both D & E and "intact D & E." The difference between the two is that the fetus is dismembered in the first and delivered intact in the second.]

* * * By the time of the Stenberg decision, about 30 States had enacted bans designed to prohibit the procedure. * * * In 2003, after this Court's decision in Stenberg, Congress passed the Act at issue here. On November 5, 2003, President Bush signed the Act into law. * * *

The Act responded to Stenberg in two ways. First, Congress made factual findings. * * * Congress found, among other things, that "[a] moral, medical, and ethical consensus exists that the practice of performing a partial-birth abortion ... is a gruesome and inhumane procedure that is never medically necessary and should be prohibited."

* * *

Under the principles accepted as controlling here, the Act, as we have interpreted it, would be unconstitutional "if its purpose or effect is to place a substantial obstacle in the path of a woman seeking an abortion before the fetus attains viability." Casey, 505 U. S., at 878. The abortions affected by the Act's regulations take place both previability and postviability; so the quoted language and the undue burden analysis it relies upon are applicable. The question is whether the Act, measured by its text in this facial attack, imposes a substantial obstacle to late-term, but previability, abortions. * * *

* * * The Act proscribes a method of abortion in which a fetus is killed just inches before completion of the birth process. Congress stated as follows: "Implicitly approving such a brutal and inhumane procedure by choosing not to prohibit it will further coarsen society to the humanity of not only newborns, but all vulnerable and innocent human life, making it increasingly difficult to protect such life." The Act expresses respect for the dignity of human life.

Congress was concerned, furthermore, with the effects on the medical community and on its reputation caused by the practice of partial-birth abortion. * * *

Casey reaffirmed these governmental objectives. The government may use its voice and its regulatory authority to show its profound respect for the life within the woman. * * * Where it has a rational basis to act, and it does not impose an undue burden, the State may use its regulatory power to bar certain procedures and substitute others, all in furtherance of its legitimate interests in regulating the medical profession in order to promote respect for life, including life of the unborn.

The Act's ban on abortions that involve partial delivery of a living fetus furthers the Government's objectives. No one would dispute that, for many, D & E is a procedure itself laden with the power to devalue human life. * * * Congress determined that the abortion methods it proscribed had a "disturbing similarity to the killing of a newborn infant," and thus it was concerned with "draw[ing] a bright line that clearly distinguishes abortion and infanticide." The Court has in the past confirmed the validity of drawing boundaries to prevent certain practices that extinguish life and are close to actions that are condemned. Glucksberg found reasonable the State's "fear that permitting assisted suicide will start it down the path to voluntary and perhaps even involuntary euthanasia."

Respect for human life finds an ultimate expression in the bond of love the mother has for her child. The Act recognizes this reality as well. Whether to have an abortion requires a difficult and painful moral decision. While we find no reliable data to measure the phenomenon, it seems unexceptionable to conclude some women come to regret their choice to abort the infant life they once created and sustained. See Brief for Sandra Cano et al. as Amici Curiae * * *. Severe depression and loss of esteem can follow.

In a decision so fraught with emotional consequence some doctors may prefer not to disclose precise details of the means that will be used, confining themselves to the required statement of risks the procedure entails. From one standpoint this ought not to be surprising. Any number of patients facing imminent surgical procedures would prefer not to hear all details, lest the usual anxiety preceding invasive medical procedures become the more intense. This is likely the case with the abortion procedures here in issue.

It is, however, precisely this lack of information concerning the way in which the fetus will be killed that is of legitimate concern to the State. The State has an interest in ensuring so grave a choice is well informed. It is self-evident that a mother who comes to regret her choice to abort must struggle with grief more anguished and sorrow more profound when she learns, only after the event, what she once did not know: that she allowed a doctor to pierce the skull and vacuum the fast-developing brain of her unborn child, a child assuming the human form.

It is a reasonable inference that a necessary effect of the regulation and the knowledge it conveys will be to encourage some women to carry the infant to full term, thus reducing the absolute number of late-term abortions. The medical profession, furthermore, may find different and less shocking methods to abort the fetus in the second trimester, thereby accommodating legislative demand. * * *

* * *

The Act's furtherance of legitimate government interests bears upon, but does not resolve, the next question: whether the Act has the effect of imposing an unconstitutional burden on the abortion right because it does not allow use of the barred procedure where " 'necessary, in appropriate medical judgment, for [the] preservation of the ... health of the mother.' " The prohibition in the Act would be unconstitutional, under precedents we here assume to be controlling, if it "subject[ed] [women] to significant health risks." In Ayotte the parties agreed a health exception to the challenged parental-involvement statute was necessary "to avert serious and often irreversible damage to [a pregnant minor's] health." Here, by contrast, whether the Act creates significant health risks for women has been a contested factual question. The evidence presented in the trial courts and before Congress demonstrates both sides have medical support for their position.

* * *

Medical uncertainty does not foreclose the exercise of legislative power in the abortion context any more than it does in other contexts. The medical uncertainty over whether the Act's prohibition creates significant health risks provides a sufficient basis to conclude in this facial attack that the Act does not impose an undue burden.

The conclusion that the Act does not impose an undue burden is supported by other considerations. Alternatives are available to the prohibited procedure. As we have noted, the Act does not proscribe D & E. * * *

* * * The Act is not invalid on its face where there is uncertainty over whether the barred procedure is ever necessary to preserve a woman's health, given the availability of other abortion procedures that are considered to be safe alternatives.

JUSTICE GINSBURG, with whom JUSTICE STEVENS, JUSTICE SOUTER, AND JUSTICE BREYER join, dissenting.

* * * Today's decision is alarming. It refuses to take Casey and Stenberg seriously. It tolerates, indeed applauds, federal intervention to ban nationwide a procedure found necessary and proper in certain cases by the American College of Obstetricians and Gynecologists (ACOG). It blurs the line, firmly drawn in Casey, between previability and postviability abortions. And, for the first time since Roe, the Court blesses a prohibition with no exception safeguarding a woman's health.

I dissent from the Court's disposition. Retreating from prior rulings that abortion restrictions cannot be imposed absent an exception safeguarding a woman's health, the Court upholds an Act that surely would not survive under the close scrutiny that previously attended state-decreed limitations on a woman's reproductive choices.

* * *

Ultimately, the Court admits that "moral concerns" are at work, concerns that could yield prohibitions on any abortion. Notably, the concerns expressed are untethered to any ground genuinely serving the Government's interest in preserving life. By allowing such concerns to carry the day and case, overriding fundamental rights, the Court dishonors our precedent.

Revealing in this regard, the Court invokes an antiabortion shibboleth for which it concededly has no reliable evidence: Women who have abortions come to regret their choices, and consequently suffer from "[s]evere depression and loss of esteem." Because of women's fragile emotional state and because of the "bond of love the mother has for her child," the Court worries, doctors may withhold information about the nature of the intact D & E procedure. The solution the Court approves, then, is *not* to require doctors to inform women, accurately and adequately, of the different procedures and their attendant risks. Instead, the Court deprives women of the right to make an autonomous choice, even at the expense of their safety.

This way of thinking reflects ancient notions about women's place in the family and under the Constitution-ideas that have long since been discredited.

[The dissent then cites, for purposes of comparison, Muller v. Oregon and Bradwell v. State, on the one hand, and United States v. Virginia and Califano v. Goldfarb, on the other, both of the latter cases rejecting "overbroad generalizations" about women.]

* * *

Though today's opinion does not go so far as to discard Roe or Casey, the Court, differently composed than it was when we last considered a restrictive abortion regulation, is hardly faithful to our earlier invocations of "the rule of law" and the "principles of stare decisis." Congress imposed a ban despite our clear prior holdings that the State cannot proscribe an abortion procedure when its use is necessary to protect a woman's health. Although Congress' findings could not withstand the crucible of trial, the Court defers to the legislative override of our Constitution-based rulings. A decision so at odds with our jurisprudence should not have staying power.

In sum, the notion that the Partial–Birth Abortion Ban Act furthers any legitimate governmental interest is, quite simply, irrational. The Court's defense of the statute provides no saving explanation. In candor, the Act, and the Court's defense of it, cannot be understood as anything other than an effort to chip away at a right declared again and again by this Court—and with increasing comprehension of its centrality to women's lives. * * *

NOTES ON GONZALEZ V. CARHART

1. Justice Ginsburg took the unusual step of reading her dissent in open court. Do you agree with her pessimism about the status of the right to abortion after *Gonzalez*? One scholar believes that *Gonzalez* "accomplished little more than validating a politically popular abortion restriction that was symbolically important, but of little practical consequence." Neal Devins, How *Planned Parenthood v. Casey* (Pretty Much) Settled the Abortion Wars, 118 Yale L.J. 1318, 1345 (2009). He believes that public and judicial opinion had settled around the compromise worked out in *Casey*. Also, the Court did interpret the Partial Birth Abortion statute to ban only intact D & E and not the other D & E procedure, which is followed in the vast majority of second-trimester abortions, and also allowed for the possibility of an as-applied challenge to the prohibition of intact D & E. Reva Siegel sees Justice Kennedy as essentially applying the reasoning of *Casey* in this and other respects. Reva B. Siegel, Dignity and the Politics of Protection: Abortion Restrictions Under

Casey/Carhart, 117 Yale. L. J. 1694, 1770 (2008) (hereafter "Siegel, Yale 2008"). Or is *Gonzalez* just one more step in the incrementalist strategy to overturn Roe v. Wade when the time—and composition of the Supreme Court—is right?

2. The Supreme Court distinguished *Gonzalez* from *Stenberg,* which was a challenge to a substantially identical statute, on the grounds that the federal statute included Congressional findings to the effect that "[a] moral, medical, and ethical consensus exists that the practice of performing a partial-birth abortion . . . is a gruesome and inhumane procedure that is never medically necessary and should be prohibited." Thus, the Court held, the federal statute was constitutionally valid even though it lacked an exception for the health of the mother. What type of findings are these, and to what deference are they entitled? Should courts give different levels of deference to findings that purport to be scientific facts and those that are expressions of moral opinion? Courts deciding abortion cases prior to this have generally not deferred to legislative factfinding but have independently reviewed the relevant evidence. See Caitlin E. Borgmann, Judicial Evasion and Disingenuous Legislative Appeals to Science in the Abortion Controversy, 17 J. L. & Pol'y 15, 22–28 (2008–09). Borgmann sees the Supreme Court in this case, like the Eighth Circuit in the South Dakota case described below (see note 4), as feeling "compelled to disguise these moral viewpoints as scientific fact." Id. at 16. In addition, the *Gonzalez* Court seems to have reversed the ordinary burden of proof about whether a regulation poses a risk to women's health when there is acknowledged medical disagreement on the issue: in *Stenberg*, it had concluded that the burden lay with the government to show that a health exception was never necessary, but in *Gonzalez*, the risk of uncertainty falls on the plaintiff. Priscilla J. Smith, Responsibility for Life: How Abortion Serves Women's Interests in Motherhood, 17 J.L. & Pol'y 97, 141 (2008–09).

Moreover, Justice Kennedy concluded in *Gonzalez* that women were likely to have regrets about abortion without citing any scientific evidence in support of this conclusion and in the face of substantial evidence to the contrary. See *Gonzalez*, 550 U.S. at 183 n.7 (Ginsburg, J., dissenting) (listing studies in peer-reviewed journals finding to the contrary); Reva B. Siegel, The Right's Reasons: Constitutional Conflict and the Spread of Woman–Protective Antiabortion Argument, 57 Duke L.J. 1641, 1653–54 n.44 (2008) (hereafter "Siegel, Duke 2008") (describing numerous scholarly and scientific reports to the contrary). Instead, Justice Kennedy cited to the Amicus Brief filed for Sandra Cano et al. The support referred to in that brief is a series of quotes from affidavits gathered by an anti-abortion project called Operation Outcry from women who claim to have been harmed by abortion. The affidavits were gathered for a lawsuit by the plaintiffs in Roe v. Wade and Doe v. Bolton as new evidence which they argued was a basis to reopen their cases. Siegel, Duke 2008, at 1644. What, if any, weight should be given to these affidavits, in light of the conflicting statements contained in another amicus brief submitted in *Gonzalez* by women who had chosen second-trimester abortions (see Siegel, Yale 2008, at 1732) and the Voices Brief, excerpts from which are contained in the next section? And what is the significance of the fact that Congress focused on fetal protection when passing the Partial Birth Abortion Act, not upon harms to women?

3. Reva Siegel has traced the development of a new strategy on the part of the anti-abortion movement, one that has broken into Supreme Court case law for the first time in *Gonzalez*. This strategy has been to shift from the earlier emphasis on fetal protection to an emphasis on protection of women, infusing some of the rhetoric of feminism into the new argument. This new type of woman-protective, or gender paternalist, argument began to develop as a strain within the anti-abortion movement with references to so-called Post Abortion Syndrome by crisis pregnancy counselors during the Reagan Administration to assert that women who had abortions suffered significant psychological trauma as a result. Reagan's own anti-abortion Surgeon General, C. Everett Koop, concluded that there was not enough scientific evidence to draw such a conclusion about the impact of abortion on women. See Siegel, Duke 2008, at 1651–61, 1663. The new strategy, which ultimately won the day within the anti-abortion movement, is particularly well adapted to an era of public dismay at the clinic violence that resulted from the drive to protect fetuses. Id. at 1664.

A key stage in the development of the woman-protective strategy was the unsuccessful campaign for an abortion ban in South Dakota, where a task force of the state legislature issued a report emphasizing, contrary to the findings of various scientific studies, the psychological and physical harms resulting to women who have abortions and the need to protect them from alleged misrepresentations, coercion, and societal pressures that drive them to make a decision that so contradicts their fundamental nature as mothers. See Reva B. Siegel, The New Politics of Abortion: An Equality Analysis of Woman–Protective Abortion Restrictions, 2007 U. Ill. L. Rev. 991, 1007–13 (2007). The task force found that it was inconceivable that "a pregnant mother [was] capable of being involved in the termination of the life of her own child without risk of suffering significant psychological trauma and distress. To do so is beyond the normal, natural, and healthy capability of a woman whose natural instincts are to protect and nurture her child." Id. at 1012. What echoes of this strategy do you see in the text of *Gonzalez* in the excerpt above? Are these the "ancient notions about women's place in the family and under the Constitution ... that have long since been discarded" about which Justice Ginsburg speaks in her dissent? The one advantage of this new strategy from the perspective of pro-choice advocates, according to Siegel, is that the new argument is susceptible to attack under the Equal Protection Clause because it is patently based on constitutionally prohibited stereotypes about women's roles. Id. at 1029–53; see also Siegel, Yale 2008, above, at 1777–79, 1792. How would you go about structuring such an argument?

4. One strange aspect of the *Gonzalez* opinion is that it reads as though it were a case about informed consent to a medical procedure rather than a total ban on a particular procedure for second-trimester abortions. That is, the Court decided to ban intact D & E in order to protect women from the consequences of deciding to undergo such a procedure, opining that their decisions to do so must be uninformed, coerced, based on misrepresentation, and the like. As a number of legal scholars have pointed out, this is a substantial deviation from the law of informed consent. The common law doctrine of informed consent requires that a patient deciding about a medical

procedure be informed about the procedure, its benefits and its risks, and those of alternatives to it; the standard for the information to be given is typically measured by what a reasonable patient would want to know, and the facts to be disclosed must be accepted by a reasonable section of the medical community. Rebecca Dresser, From Double Standard to Double Bind: Informed Choice in Abortion Law, 76 Geo. Wash. L. Rev. 1599, 1603–94 (2008). The Supreme Court held to this standard in abortion cases until *Casey*, when it upheld a statute aimed at influencing women to carry pregnancies to term by requiring doctors to provide women with information that basically communicated a community judgment disfavoring abortion, rather than simply giving information needed to make an autonomous decision. Siegel, Yale 2008, at 1757–58. *Casey* nonetheless required that the information to be disclosed be truthful and non-misleading. As of 2008, it was estimated that 29 states had informed consent statutes aimed at discouraging abortion. Dresser, above at 1609. That passed by the state of South Dakota is the most extreme, requiring that the woman be warned of risks such as psychological distress and suicide and given a written statement by the doctor that the abortion "will terminate the life of a whole, separate, unique, living human being" and her own existing and protected relationship to it. Id. at 1612. The statute was challenged under *Casey*'s undue burden standard and also as compelled speech violating the First Amendment rights of the doctor; the federal district court initially enjoined the law and was affirmed by the Court of Appeals but was ultimately reversed by the Eight Circuit Court of Appeals en banc, which found that the provisions set forth permissible biological information, not impermissible ideological information. Planned Parenthood v. Rounds, 530 F.3d 724, 737 (8th Cir. 2008) (en banc). By 2008, 14 states had passed laws mandating that a woman seeking an abortion have either seen or been offered the opportunity to see an ultrasound image of the fetus, and 14 more states had introduced bills to that effect. Carol Sanger, Seeing and Believing: Mandatory Ultrasound and the Path to a Protected Choice, 56 UCLA L. Rev. 351, 375–76 n.112 (2008). See also Guttmacher Institute, State Policies in Brief, Requirements for Ultrasound, June 1, 2010 (also containing a table of ultrasound requirements on a state-by-state basis).

Courts' approval of special informed consent standards in the abortion context brings women's capacity for autonomous healthcare decisionmaking into question. In the words of one commentator, the *Casey and Gonzalez* standards see women "as incapable decision-makers in need of the State's 'protection' provided through biased information disguised as 'informed consent' legislation." Maya Manian, The Irrational Woman: Informed Consent and Abortion Decision–Making, 16 Duke J. Gender L. & Pol'y 223, 226 (2009). That same suspicion runs through Gonzalez v. Carhart, where women are seen as unable to make informed decisions about intact D & E. Instead of just trying to dissuade them, or make them feel guilty about their decisions, however, the Court outright prohibited the procedure on the grounds that they might become upset and regret it later. Could one not also say that the information provided is inaccurate, by providing only one point of view on the nature of the fetus and not balancing it with other points of view?

5. The *Gonzalez* Court also concluded that intact D & E should be prohibited in order to protect the medical profession and the community from

approving a procedure that was similar to "the killing of a newborn infant," analogizing its decision in this respect to its prohibition of assisted suicide in the *Glucksberg* case. Washington v. Glucksberg, 521 U.S. 702 (1997). How might you distinguish the situation of abortion versus infanticide from the right to die versus assisted suicide?

3. ALTERNATIVE THEORIES SUPPORTING THE RIGHT TO ABORTION

As should be obvious from the amicus briefs in the previous section, feminist lawyers and law professors have played a central role in the struggle over legal regulation of abortion. In this section we present another way in which academics have attempted to further this debate, by developing alternative theories upon which the right to abortion might be based, instead of upon the right to privacy embraced in Roe v. Wade or the liberty interests articulated by the joint opinion in *Casey*. The excerpts and notes below present examples of arguments based upon women's experiences of abortion, a variety of arguments based upon self-defense, an approach grounded in equal protection, and a relational feminist perspective.

a. Arguments Based on Women's Experiences

BRIEF FOR THE AMICI CURIAE WOMEN WHO HAVE HAD ABORTIONS, IN *WEBSTER v. REPRODUCTIVE HEALTH SERVICES*

No. 88–605 (1989).

[This brief, known as the "Voices Brief," relies upon letters from some 2,887 women who have had abortions and 627 friends of women who have had abortions, describing their abortion decisions and their experiences both before and after Roe v. Wade.]

The conditions under which illegal abortions were performed were bad. It was estimated that "as many as 5,000 American women die[d] each year as a direct result of criminal abortion. The figure of 5,000 may be a minimum estimate, inasmuch as such deaths are mislabeled or unreported." R. Schwarz, Septic Abortion 7 (1968). * * *

A large number of illegal abortions were self-induced or performed by unskilled and untrained personnel working under dangerous septic conditions, unaccountable to professional guidelines and safeguards and unreached by ordinary government licensing procedures or other safeguards. Medical procedures, record-keeping and referral techniques were guided by concerns about detection, not best medical judgment.

The women received treatment which was often delayed under conditions of severe physical and emotional stress. The process was degrading. Follow up care was entirely lacking or inadequate. These dangerous and humiliating conditions existed precisely because abortions were illegal; they are graphically described by some amici:

* * *

> I am a 60 year old woman deeply troubled by the possibility that women's constitutional right to determine their own reproductive rights is being threatened and may be taken away....
>
> When I was in my twenties I had an illegal abortion. There were no other options that I saw at that time. Because of the illegality, it was extremely difficult to find someone who would discuss how to find someone to help me. People were afraid. As a consequence, when I finally found a source I had gone beyond the time of a safe procedure. I lied to the "doctor" because I knew he wouldn't do it if I told him how far along I was.... He insisted I come by myself which I did. Is there any way I can describe my fear. He was unclean, he joked a lot, his hands were rough, his breath was bad. He forcefully approached me to have sex with him because "what harm would there be under the circumstance?" That, of course, explained his reason for insisting that I come alone. So, on top of the fear for my physical safety in that situation, the agony of decision about what I was doing, the need to keep this secret away from everyone I knew and face it alone, there was the disgust, repulsion and deep fear that if I didn't do what he wanted he would send me away....
>
> I never want another woman to have to experience what I went through. My plea is that simple.

* * *

In deciding whether to bear a child or have an abortion, a woman thoughtfully considers the realities of motherhood, her obligations to herself and her family, and the social and economic injustices which she (and her offspring) must face. Her assessment is highly contextual and personal. Furthermore, it is moral—deriving from her diverse duties and her ability to fulfill them, which only she can evaluate.

* * *

Women express a variety of concerns in assessing their responsibilities including competing demands within the family, lack of adequate financial resources, and existing health problems incompatible with pregnancy and childbirth. Usually more than one factor is important.

Women weigh these concerns, as well as the highly demanding responsibilities that accompany motherhood. Most of the women who have abortions choose at some time to become mothers, but they choose to do so at times when they are financially, physically and emotionally prepared properly to care for a child. * * *

* * *

> I have personally had an abortion.... I was twenty-five years old at the time, divorced with two small children, ages five and seven, and a senior in college.... I was putting myself through college with the help of my family, raising my children as a single parent with very little emotional or financial support from my extremely immature ex-husband; I was making grades good enough to consistently keep me on the dean's honor roll and contemplating going to graduate school.
>
> When I became pregnant I was terrified at the prospect of bringing another child into the world, knowing that I was already strained to the limit, both financially and emotionally with the two children I had. I felt certain that bearing this child would be a disaster for me, my educational plans, my children and possibly for the relationship with the father. After an incredible amount of soul-searching discussions with the father and with doctors and counselors ... I decided to have an abortion.
>
> * * *
>
> I am a divorced professional woman, who is raising three children alone. I barely make it from paycheck to paycheck. My children are very healthy, happy and loved....
>
> I have yet to receive any assistance of any kind in raising my children.
>
> Most times, I feel like I am at the end of the ropes, juggling a career (I am forced to work 2 jobs to support my children, but one of them is a career), finances which are barely met, childraising alone....
>
> I chose abortion. I chose to limit myself to dealing with the too much responsibility I have now. All women should have the right to choose how much responsibility they feel they are able to handle. Especially since she is the only one she knows she can count on.
>
> * * *

Some women facing unplanned pregnancies are already dealing with troubled families, abusive spouses and extreme emotional distress. Some of these women decide that they should not bring a child (or another child) into such an environment:

> In 1984 I became pregnant by accident. I was married to a man who had become a physically abusive alcoholic. We had one child, age 3, at the time. I didn't see any way out of the relationship for myself.... My husband was not then working.... I was the sole support for my family at this time and had virtually no help from my husband in any area of responsibility. I was emotionally distraught much of the time because I felt I was not providing the material or emotional environment that my child deserved, and because of the constant pressures of physical and emotional abuse.... I knew I could not add the work of caring for another child to my burden, it would have broken me....

> With no joy in my heart but with the knowledge that I was certainly making the right choice I had an abortion.

* * *

Some women are struggling with alcohol or drug abuse that they are unable to overcome at the time of pregnancy.

> I was 38 years old, married with two children. We were and are still a typical suburban family—as far as the outside world can see. But life was not ordinary for us in 1982. I was (I am) chemically addicted to the drug alcohol. Beginning in October, 1981 I made my first feeble attempts at recovery from alcoholism.... I wandered in and out of AA meetings....
>
> In the midst of this rollercoaster ride of addiction—in February, 1982, I realized I could be pregnant.... I was frantic, frightened, drained physically, emotionally, spiritually from my alcoholism. I could not manage my own life. The prospect of a baby was overwhelming!.... I chose to have an abortion....
>
> I continued efforts toward recovery, and with the help of support of AA, I have not had a drink since April 13, 1982.

* * *

Many women have faced the revelation that the fetus may be born with serious disabilities. Here again, the woman must decide, ideally with the best available and least biased information and support, whether she can meet existing responsibilities and provide for the expected new responsibility. In addition, some women decide that they cannot give birth to a child who they know would live a lifetime of tragic pain.

> I would never, never, never, in a million years, deliberately and knowingly bring another Tay–Sachs child into the world. The knowledge that I have the ability to spare another child the degradation that my cherished daughter is going through means everything to me. It would be a crime to put another child through the humiliation and pain that this cruel disease inflicts.
>
> At the same time, the hope of someday having a healthy child, and the knowledge that it can happen if we will only have the strength to keep trying, is one of the few things that is helping to keep me sane through the anguish of watching my child slowly die. If abortion were to be made illegal, I would have to give up that hope, as I would never take the risk of conceiving and having to bear another child with Tay–Sachs.[37]

AMICUS BRIEF OF THE NATIONAL COUNCIL OF

37. Tay–Sachs is a genetic disease occurring in infants and children. Children afflicted with Tay–Sachs disease, or one of the similar allied diseases, suffer slow degeneration, severe mental and physical impairment, resulting in their deaths in infancy or very early childhood.

NEGRO WOMEN, ET AL., IN *WEBSTER v. REPRODUCTIVE HEALTH SERVICES*

No. 88–605 (1989).

[This brief was filed on behalf of a number of organizations representing African American, Asian American, Latina and Native American women.]

While Roe v. Wade benefited women of all classes, races and ages, its effect on the health and mortality of poor women, particularly women of color, was, and still is, especially significant. * * *

Laws restricting access to abortion * * * did not prevent women from seeking abortions. While a small number of upper and middle class women had access to safe, sanitary abortions in private hospitals and doctors' offices, and some others were able to afford travel to safer illegal providers, poor women, unable to afford the cost of either long distant trips or private doctors, were forced to resort to illegal abortions under the most frightening, unhygienic and often life-threatening conditions. Permanent loss of reproductive capacity or death were not uncommon. Because of the generally poor quality of health care available in their communities, women of color were disproportionately represented among those who died or were left sterile by illegal abortions. One study estimated that mishandled criminal abortions were the principal cause of maternal death in the United States, in the 1960's, killing 5,000 women a year. However, women of color risked their lives at much higher rates than did white women if they chose not to continue their pregnancy.

In 1965, in New York, for example, although there were 4 abortion deaths for every 100,000 live births for white women; for non-white women there were 56 abortion deaths per 100,000; for Puerto Rican women, there were 61.

* * *

Between 1967–1969 when abortions were not legal in New York, and 1970–1972 when they were legal, the average annual rate of abortion-related death fell by 51% in New York State. In the 19 comparative states the decline was substantially less—29%.

After legalization [nation-wide, by Roe v. Wade], the change nationally was similar. Despite the drop in the overall number of maternal deaths after *Roe,* however, a greater percentage of women of color than white women continued to die from illegal abortions. Between 1975 and 1979, several years after abortion was legalized, 82% of the women who died after illegal abortions were African–American and Latina.

[The authors then discuss the impact upon women of color of the regulations and restrictions challenged in *Webster.*]

1. Laws Requiring That All Abortions Be Performed in Hospitals Would Effectively Preclude Abortions for Poor Women and Women of Color.

* * *

To require that abortions be performed in hospitals will place an added burden on the already inadequate delivery of health care to the poor. For general health care, poor families are dependent on public hospitals which are severely overcrowded and understaffed.

Even though hospitals are the ordinary source of medical care for the poor, access to abortions in hospitals is limited and in most communities unavailable. In 1979–1980 only 17% of all public hospitals in the United States reported doing at least one abortion and only 22% of all abortions took place in hospitals, with a mere 32% of those hospitals providing abortions after 14 weeks of pregnancy. For Native American women who live on reservations,[35] and African–American women in the rural South, there has been even less access. To require that all abortions be performed at hospitals would severely restrict the numbers of abortion providers. Additionally, it would render abortion inaccessible to women in most communities in the country.

* * *

If states are permitted to require hospitalization for abortion throughout pregnancy, the cost of an abortion will increase artificially. The cost of abortions in hospitals is at least five times greater than the cost of clinic abortions. Although a first-trimester abortion in a clinic costs $200–300, the same abortion in a hospital costs $1200–1300. The cost for women who require second-trimester hospital abortions is even greater.

The cost of an in-hospital first-trimester abortion would be almost four times the average monthly AFDC payment ($375) for a family of three. Medicaid-eligible women who receive an average of $375 per month for themselves and their children cannot afford $200–$300 for a first-trimester clinic abortion. Yet many women, living in states which do not fund abortions, have managed to pay this sum by using all or part of their meager grants for daily living expenses. Increasing the cost to $1200 or $1300 will foreclose that option, making illegal abortion, once again, the only choice for poor women.

* * *

The increased cost of abortion is only part of the financial burden created by a hospitalization requirement. The cost of travel, of overnight stays, of childcare and of lost time from employment need to be factored in. The impact of a hospitalization requirement would fall especially heavily upon teenagers from poor families or those with no independent access to resources.

---

35. Almost half a million Native Americans live on reservations and in historic trust areas. Yet no Indian Health Service clinic or hospital were [sic] permitted to perform abortions even when there was private payment until 1982. Then federal regulations permitted abortions at Indian Health Service facilities, but only when the woman's life is endangered.

BRIEF OF SANDRA CANO, AND 180 WOMEN INJURED BY ABORTION IN *GONZALES v. CARHART*

No. 05–380 (2006)

[What follows are excerpts from the 178 affidavits originally filed in the United States District Court for the Northern District of Georgia in 2003 in Doe v. Bolton, in an unsuccessful attempt to reopen that 1973 case. These are the first 10 affidavits that appear in Appendix B to the Cano brief in *Gonzalez*, upon which Justice Kennedy relied in his decision excerpted in the previous section. We have omitted the names of the affiants, which were given in the Appendix to the brief.]

The State of Tennessee

* * *

How has abortion affected you? It has completely messed up my life. It was not the best way to start out in marriage. I was depressed, didn't want my husband to touch me, felt guilty, had suicidal thoughts, cried a lot, *terribly* depressed!

The State of Tennessee

* * *

How has abortion affected you? Too many ways to write!—It ended, or attributed [sic] to my divorce from the father. I'm overly concerned and worried about my living children. I've had nightmares for years. I'm worried that I may develop breast cancer. The loss of relationship with my aborted child can never be replaced. I've had problems with eating disorders and depression. It took me 18 years to reconcile my relationship with God which had previously been very important to me. It forever altered my life.

The State of Florida

* * *

How has abortion affected you? Deep regret—initially I was suicidal—as the years have progressed I have developed a heightened level of bitterness and anger and self-hate. I feared God, have not been able to attend church because of my fear of God, unforgiveness, shame, guilt, condemnation, inability to bond and fit in with other women, inability to be intimate. The deep emotional scars were a large contributing factor in my divorce—a very, very catastrophic choice! Great sense of loss and grief.

The State of Georgia

* * *

HOW HAS ABORTION AFFECTED YOU? YES. I FEEL EMOTIONALLY SCARRED. YEARS WENT BY OF HIDING IT. THEN SOMETHING STARTED TRIGGERING FLASHBACKS. CHILDREN'S BIRTHDAYS BRING ON EXTREME SADNESS. CHRISTMAS TIME BRINGS ON TIMES OF DEPRESSION, REGRET, AND WONDERING WHAT WOULD MY CHILDREN HAVE BEEN LIKE. COULD THEY HAVE

MADE A DIFFERENCE IN THE WORLD. WHY COULDN'T I HAVE GIVEN THEM A CHANCE AT LIFE LIKE MY MOTHER GAVE ME! NO ONE EVER SHOWED ME THE STAGES OF PREGNANCY. IF SOMEONE HAD, I WOULDN'T HAVE WENT THROUGH IT. IF I WOULD HAVE KNOWN THE EMOTIONAL EFFECTS THAT WAS YEARS LATER, I WOULD HAVE RECONSIDERED.

The State of Utah

* * *

How has abortion affected you? Depression, low-self esteem, guilt, condemnation, and shame, sleepless nights, nightmares and torment, thoughts of self-hate and suicide, lost, confused, destroyed relationships throughout my life, unloved, unlovable, unable to trust God or anyone. Only God can heal this! Post-abortion ectopic pregnancy, fear of not being able to conceive and birth healthy babies, pain, unable to receive love and healing from God and others, worthlessness, strive and drive to perform to be loved and accepted, isolation—emotionally. Lost, confused, needy—shunned by others. I reach out to [sic] for help. In a state where I could not forgive myself. Psychologically damaged for the rest of your life (until God heals). I have regretted my choices the rest of my life. Grief, anxiety, regret, morbid obesity and health problems, scar tissue, blood clots. Damaged marriage. Abortion hurts women.

The State of Texas

* * *

How has abortion affected you? 11 years later I am obviously still affected. Initially, I suffered from depression, alcohol use increased, increased promiscuity, due to my lowered self-esteem. My grades suffered in college. Relationships were difficult. I had nightmares, flashbacks, and grief. Now with a 6 year old son, I am overly protective to a fault. His relationship with his father is damaged because of my own fears of losing my son. I feel God could still punish me by taking this child away. It's mired my motivation and hindered my career (ironically since my reasoning in part to have an abortion was so my career wouldn't be hindered.) It has cut the soul out of my entire life.

The State of Arkansas

* * *

How has abortion affected you? In the beginning I thought I was doing the right thing. Only afterwards did I realize the TRUTH! My conscience was seared, my heart was broken. I lived in a state of depression looking at drugs as the answer to my problem. And the problem—I had killed my child? See you don't realize what happens to yourself until it's too late, you've already done it and there's no turning back. I can't turn back time—if I could—I WOULDN'T HAVE AN ABORTION!! I was emotionally torn apart. I didn't know what happiness was, confusion, my best friend! I built a wall around myself with bricks of denial. Shutting EVERYONE out!! I hated myself. Thinking of suicide MANY, MANY times, I could not live with myself.

The State of Florida

* * *

How has abortion affected you? For twenty-eight years, I have mourned, gone thru depression around Victoria's birthdate, became angry as the years passed. My sleep pattern changed. I'm up and down all night. I became promiscuous, in and out of relationships, choosing men beneath my standards to make myself feel better, though I love people, over the years I became more anti-social as I felt I wasn't good enough to be around others, I would start educational classes and never completed them. I felt like people were trying to get too close to my personal life . . .

The State of Georgia

* * *

How has abortion affected you? My abortion devastated me. I lost respect for my boyfriend, respect for myself. I became an alcoholic, dabbled in drugs to forget what I had done! I had relationships with men who disrespected me because I felt I didn't deserve better. I had nightmares, night sweats, and even now go through periods of depression and crying.

The State of Florida

* * *

How has abortion affected you? It devastated my life. Immediately after abortion 1–2 days after hemorrhaging to death requiring emergency D & C, mental health problems/nervous breakdown/psychosis/suicidal/low-self esteem/difficulty parenting child. I did have alcoholism/faith damage/social damage changing my views of society as hate-filled cold, and uncaring/loss of my child's life/bitter heartbreak to not be able to undo the effects of abortion.

NOTES ON WOMEN'S EXPERIENCE OF ABORTION

1. Recent studies of why women have abortions confirm the reasons given in the Voices Brief, above. Women cite economic reasons (73%), relationship problems (48%), having completed childbearing (40%), unreadiness to have a child (33%), and concerns about the health of the fetus (13%) or of the woman herself (12%). A common theme is inability to nurture a child both financially and emotionally. Priscilla J. Smith, Responsibility for Life: How Abortion Serves Women's Interests in Motherhood, 17 J.L. & Pol'y 97, 106–09 (2008–09).

2. The Voices Brief represents a very different type of legal document, emerging from the stories women told of their own life experience, recounted

in their own terms and not in the language of abstract legal doctrine. What do you think of breaking the bounds of accepted legal discourse in this fashion? Under what circumstances do you think it is or is not a good idea? One feminist legal scholar has argued that the only genuinely authentic form of feminist litigation is a dialogue based upon an understanding of the impact of abortion regulation upon women's well-being and of the interests at stake on each side of the issue. Ruth Colker, Feminist Litigation: An Oxymoron?—A Study of the Briefs Filed in *William L. Webster v. Reproductive Health Services,* 13 Harv.Women's L.J. 137 (1990). Could one effectively brief a case based on such a dialogue? How?

3. The Women of Color Brief also juxtaposes "real world" experience to abstract discussion of legal doctrine—in this case to the doctrine of "undue burden." This type of argument, demonstrating that a regulation like the requirement that abortions take place in the hospital, which may not seem burdensome unless viewed in context (real lack of access to hospitals by women living in rural areas or on Indian reservations), is a much more familiar type of legal argumentation, in the style of a "Brandeis brief" (so called after the brief filed by (later Supreme Court justice) Louis D. Brandeis in Muller v. Oregon, 208 U.S. 412 (1908), using statistical and sociological data to support upholding legislation limiting hours of women working in laundries by detailing the effects of working long hours on women and their families). Is this type of argument, about actual access to abortion services, likely to succeed in light of Harris v. McRae? In light of current legal interpretations of undue burden?

4. What are the common themes that appear in the excerpt above from the affidavits attached to the amicus brief in *Gonzalez*? Similar themes appear throughout the appendix to the Cano brief. (Sandra Cano herself did not in fact have an abortion but gave her baby up for adoption.) What are those common themes? Note that most of the women are religious and from Southern states. Misspellings and grammatical errors, along with the repeated use of capital letters and exclamation points, also seem to indicate that these women have different class and educational backgrounds than many of the women quoted in the Voices Brief. It seems clear that different women have different reactions to the experience of abortion; how should we as feminists address that fact? Should the regrets experienced by one group deprive others of access to abortion?

5. Might some of the concerns expressed by the women in the affidavits submitted in the *Gonzalez* case have been addressed by effective professional counseling in advance of the abortion? Would you support a law mandating such counseling? How might you use the affidavits to support or challenge the informed consent laws currently enacted in many states?

6. Would any of the Cano affidavits have been admissible in the *Gonzalez* case at a trial? Is the evidence given in them relevant, considering that none of the affiants appears to have had the D & E procedure at issue in *Gonzalez* and none of the affidavits address the risk-related health concerns that were at issue in the case? If it would not have been admitted at trial, should this evidence have been considered on appeal? How much weight should be given to it?

7. In her dissent, Justice Ginsburg calls abortion regret an "anti-abortion shibboleth" and cites many peer-reviewed scientific studies finding no link between abortion and subsequent depression or other psychiatric disorders. How should feminists respond when scientific studies refute the lived experiences of some women? What if the scientific studies came out the other way? How do you predict Justice Ginsburg would have responded to such studies? How would you?

8. As discussed in Chapter 4, some feminists point to the depression and drug and alcohol use of women engaged in sex work as one of the reasons to criminalize prostitution and to create civil liability for the production of pornography and operation of strip clubs. How, if at all, are those arguments different from the arguments adopted by Justice Kennedy in *Gonzalez*? Can you articulate a rationale for relying on such evidence in the context of sex work but not in the context of abortion?

9. Does the opinion for the *Casey* plurality appreciate the importance of the conditions under which women have sex? Catharine MacKinnon emphasizes the need to see abortion in the context of women's lack of control over sex:

> * * * [W]omen often do not use birth control because of its social meaning, a meaning we did not create. Using contraception means acknowledging and planning the possibility of intercourse, accepting one's sexual availability, and appearing nonspontaneous. It means appearing available to male incursions. * * * I wonder if a woman can be presumed to control access to her sexuality if she feels unable to interrupt intercourse to insert a diaphragm; or worse, cannot even want to, aware that she risks a pregnancy she knows she does not want. * * * Sex doesn't look a whole lot like freedom when it appears normatively less costly for women to risk an undesired, often painful, traumatic, dangerous, sometimes illegal, and potentially life-threatening procedure than to protect themselves in advance. Yet abortion policy has never been explicitly approached in the context of how women get pregnant, that is, as a consequence of intercourse under conditions of gender inequality; that is, as an issue of forced sex.

MacKinnon, Privacy v. Equality: Beyond Roe v. Wade, in Feminism Unmodified 93, 95–96 (1987). For a description, based on interviews with women in abortion clinics, of the variety of reasons women have uncontracepted sex even when they do not want to become pregnant, see Kristin Luker, Taking Chances: Abortion and the Decision Not to Contracept (1991 ed.; orig. pub. 1975). Those reasons include the contradictory images in our culture of female sexuality so that women, although expected to be accessible and responsive to men, are regarded as somehow vulgar if they prepare for sex in advance. Id. at 46–47. Has this context been taken into account in the law of abortion in the U.S.?

10. In another article, MacKinnon asks whether women would still need abortions if sex equality were achieved, so that all sex was genuinely voluntary, and safe and effective contraception were available. At that point, MacKinnon professes, an approach based on privacy might make sense and the father's point of view should perhaps be taken into account as well.

Catharine A. MacKinnon, Reflections on Sex Equality Under Law, 100 Yale L.J. 1281, 1326–27 (1991). What do you think? If there truly were completely safe and effective methods of contraception and women were able to be sexual or not without regard for economic security or social approval, would that change your views about the right to abortion? Why or why not? What if childbearing no longer necessarily meant childrearing, because women and men shared childrearing responsibilities or men performed them exclusively?

11. Andrea Dworkin maintained that birth control and abortion are another way of ensuring male access to women's sexuality. See Andrea Dworkin, Right–Wing Women 93–100 (1978). MacKinnon agrees that "under conditions of gender inequality, sexual liberation in this sense does not free women; it frees male sexual aggression." MacKinnon, above note 9, at 99. If male support for birth control and abortion is based on men's desire for heterosexual intercourse without any consequences, does it follow that women would be better off without birth control and abortion?

12. Robin West argues for a right to reproductive freedom and abortion based upon an ethic of care:

> * * * [R]eproductive freedom, and the abortion rights that at least in the short term must be a part of that freedom, particularly given the continuing climate of hostility toward children and their caretakers that exists in this culture, is a necessary prerequisite for nurturant relationships between the pregnant woman and the fetus, as well as between the mother and child, which an ethic of care seeks to encourage. Without that freedom, the "relationship" is one of nonconsensual servitude, not nurturant, interdependent care. Reproductive freedom is as necessary to nurturance, in other words, as it is to an abstract consistency between the choice of men and women in this culture.
>
> If this is right, then two consequences follow for our constitutional jurisprudence. First, the case for reproductive freedom ought to be cast as precisely that—the case for reproductive *freedom*. As numerous feminists have now pointed out, it should not be cast as an argument for abortion "rights" grounded in an abstract concern for sexual "privacy"—an argument which almost blithely, and indeed almost cruelly, ignores the degree to which sexual privacy has meant, for women, only that their sexual violation is shielded from public scrutiny and legal compensation by a wall of secrecy and privilege. But nor should it be grounded in an equally abstract concern for formal gender equality—which *also* blithely ignores the degree to which women's reproductive nurturant practices, including the practice of nurturing fetal life—is constitutive of the ethic of care.
>
> * * * [R]eproductive freedom might better be viewed, consistently with the nurturant practices at the heart of the ethic of care, as a necessary *positive* liberty to secure women's and children's well-being, and the nurturant practices and values that secure them. If we want nurturant relationships between parents and children to be a part of our social world, and hence a part of the positive liberty each individual is entitled to possess in order to participate in that social world, then we must allow women the freedom to choose to terminate or carry a pregnancy to term. The justification for this freedom, in other words,

> does not stem from a right to violate or abandon fetal life consistently with men's apparent inclination to do so. It must stem, rather, from a right to create materially secure, consensual, and safe nurturant relationships.

West, Caring for Justice 73–74 (1997) (emphasis in original). See also Priscilla J. Smith, Responsibility for Life: How Abortion Serves Women's Interests in Motherhood, 17 J.L. & Pol'y 97, 127 (2008–09) (arguing that "women have abortions because they feel responsible for any life they bring into the world, and because they care about how any child they bear—if they are to bear one—will be mothered"). How is this argument different from arguments based on privacy, self-defense, or equality?

13. West's position includes the argument that children will be best cared for by mothers who can control when their children are born. In fact, the availability of abortion appears to affect not the decision whether to have children so much as the timing of their births. A 1994–1995 national survey of 9,985 abortion patients showed that women who have had a child are more likely to have an abortion than those who have never had a child and that 66% of women who have had an abortion intend to have more children. Stanley K. Henshaw & Kathryn Kost, Abortion Patients in 1994–1995: Characteristics and Contraceptive Use, 28 Family Planning Perspectives 140, 142–44 (1996). Catholics are as likely as other women in the general population to have an abortion. Id.

Other studies suggest that the legalization of abortion has "led to an improvement in the average living conditions of children, probably by reducing the numbers of youngsters who would have lived in single-parent families, lived in poverty, received welfare, and died as infants." Marianne Bitler & Madeline Zavodny, Did Abortion Legalization Reduce the Number of Unwanted Children? Evidence from Adoptions, 34 Perspectives on Sexual & Reproductive Health 25 (2002). See also, e.g., Jonathan Gruber, Phillip Levine & Douglas Staiger, Abortion Legalization and Child Living Circumstances: Who Is The "Marginal Child"?, 114 Q. J. Econ. 263 (1999) (showing that the average living circumstances for cohorts of children born immediately after legalization of abortion improved substantially over the preceding cohorts). Moreover, a 50–state U.S. study shows that the states with the most restrictive abortion laws are also the least likely to provide support for services to children. Jean Reith Schroedel, Is the Fetus a Person?: A Comparison of Policies Across the Fifty States 153–56 (2000). What do you think explains this seeming anomaly?

14. Is making abortion a top priority item on the feminist agenda a form of heterosexism? For one view of the connections between abortion and gay and lesbian rights, see Sylvia A. Law, Homosexuality and the Social Meaning of Gender, 1988 Wisc. L. Rev. 187, 225 ("But individual interest in access to contraception and abortion is not simply a matter of avoiding unwanted procreation. People have a strong affirmative interest in sexual expression and relationships.").

b. Arguments Based on Self–Defense

JUDITH JARVIS THOMSON, A DEFENSE OF ABORTION

1 Phil. & Pub. Aff. 48–49, 52–53, 59–62, 65–66 (1971).

I propose, then, that we grant that the fetus is a person from the moment of conception. How does the argument go from here? Something like this, I take it. Every person has a right to life. So the fetus has a right to life. No doubt the mother has a right to decide what shall happen in and to her body; everyone would grant that. But surely a person's right to life is stronger and more stringent than the mother's right to decide what happens in and to her body, and so outweighs it. So the fetus may not be killed; an abortion may not be performed.

It sounds plausible. But now let me ask you to imagine this. You wake up in the morning and find yourself back to back in bed with an unconscious violinist. A famous unconscious violinist. He has been found to have a fatal kidney ailment, and the Society of Music Lovers has canvassed all the available medical records and found that you alone have the right blood type to help. They have therefore kidnapped you, and last night the violinist's circulatory system was plugged into yours, so that your kidneys can be used to extract poisons from his blood as well as your own. The director of the hospital now tells you, "Look, we're sorry the Society of Music Lovers did this to you—we would never have permitted it if we had known. But still, they did it, and the violinist now is plugged into you. To unplug you would be to kill him. But never mind, it's only for nine months. By then he will have recovered from his ailment, and can safely be unplugged from you." Is it morally incumbent on you to accede to this situation? No doubt it would be very nice of you if you did, a great kindness. But do you *have* to accede to it? What if it were not nine months, but nine years? Or longer still? What if the director of the hospital says, "Tough luck, I agree, but you've now got to stay in bed, with the violinist plugged into you, for the rest of your life. Because remember this. All persons have a right to life, and violinists are persons. Granted you have a right to decide what happens in and to your body, but a person's right to life outweighs your right to decide what happens in and to your body. So you cannot ever be unplugged from him." I imagine you would regard this as outrageous, which suggests that something really is wrong with that plausible-sounding argument I mentioned a moment ago.

In this case, of course, you were kidnapped; you didn't volunteer for the operation that plugged the violinist into your kidneys. Can those who oppose abortion on the ground I mentioned make an exception for a pregnancy due to rape? Certainly. They can say that persons have a right to life only if they didn't come into existence because of rape; or they can say that all persons have a right to life, but that some have less of a right to life than others, in particular, that those who came into existence because of rape have less. But these statements have a rather unpleasant sound. Surely the question of whether you have a right to life at all, or how much of it you have, shouldn't turn on the question of whether or not you are the product of a rape. And in fact the people who oppose abortion on the ground I mentioned do not make this distinction, and hence do not make an exception in case of rape.

* * *

The main focus of attention in writings on abortion has been on what a third party may or may not do in answer to a request from a woman for an abortion. This is in a way understandable. Things being as they are, there isn't much a woman can safely do to abort herself. So the question asked is what a third party may do, and what the mother may do, if it is mentioned at all, is deduced, almost as an afterthought, from what it is concluded that third parties may do. But it seems to me that to treat the matter in this way is to refuse to grant to the mother that very status of person which is so firmly insisted on for the fetus. For we cannot simply read off what a person may do from what a third party may do. Suppose you find yourself trapped in a tiny house with a growing child. I mean a very tiny house, and a rapidly growing child—you are already up against the wall of the house and in a few minutes you'll be crushed to death. The child on the other hand won't be crushed to death; if nothing is done to stop him from growing he'll be hurt, but in the end he'll simply burst open the house and walk out a free man. Now I could well understand it if a bystander were to say, "There's nothing we can do for you. We cannot choose between your life and his, we cannot be the ones to decide who is to live, we cannot intervene." But it cannot be concluded that you too can do nothing, that you cannot attack it to save your life. However innocent the child may be, you do not have to wait passively while it crushes you to death. Perhaps a pregnant woman is vaguely felt to have the status of house, to which we don't allow the right of self-defense. But if the woman houses the child, it should be remembered that she is a person who houses it.

* * *

In sum, a woman surely can defend her life against the threat to it posed by the unborn child, even if doing so involves its death. * * *

* * *

There is room for yet another argument here, however. We surely must all grant that there may be cases in which it would be morally indecent to detach a person from your body at the cost of his life. Suppose you learn that what the violinist needs is not nine years of your life, but only one hour: all you need do to save his life is to spend one hour in that bed with him. Suppose also that letting him use your kidneys for that one hour would not affect your health in the slightest. Admittedly you were kidnapped. Admittedly you did not give anyone permission to plug him into you. Nevertheless it seems to me plain you *ought* to allow him to use your kidneys for that hour—it would be indecent to refuse.

Again, suppose pregnancy lasted only an hour, and constituted no threat to life or health. And suppose that a woman becomes pregnant as a result of rape. Admittedly she did not voluntarily do anything to bring about the existence of a child. Admittedly she did nothing at all which would give the unborn person a right to the use of her body. All the same it might well be said, as in the newly emended violinist story, that she *ought* to allow it to remain for that hour—that it would be indecent in her to refuse.

* * *

So my own view is that even though you ought to let the violinist use your kidneys for the one hour he needs, we should not conclude that he has a right to do so—we should say that if you refuse, you are, like the boy who owns all the chocolates and will give none away, self-centered and callous, indecent in fact, but not unjust. And similarly, that even supposing a case in which a woman pregnant due to rape ought to allow the unborn person to use her body for the hour he needs, we should not conclude that he has a right to do so; we should conclude that she is self-centered, callous, indecent, but not unjust, if she refuses. The complaints are no less grave; they are just different. However, there is no need to insist on this point. If anyone does wish to deduce "he has a right" from "you ought," then all the same he must surely grant that there are cases in which it is not morally required of you that you allow that violinist to use your kidneys, and in which he does not have a right to use them, and in which you do not do him an injustice if you refuse. And so also for mother and unborn child. Except in such cases as the unborn person has a right to demand it—and we were leaving open the possibility that there may be such cases—nobody is morally *required* to make large sacrifices, of health, of all other interests and concerns, of all other duties and commitments, for nine years, or even for nine months, in order to keep another person alive.

* * *

My argument will be found unsatisfactory on two counts by many of those who want to regard abortion as morally permissible. First, while I do argue that abortion is not impermissible, I do not argue that it is always permissible. There may well be cases in which carrying the child to term requires only Minimally Decent Samaritanism of the mother, and this is a standard we must not fall below. I am inclined to think it a merit of my account precisely that it does *not* give a general yes or a general no. It allows for and supports our sense that, for example, a sick and desperately frightened fourteen-year-old schoolgirl, pregnant due to rape, may *of course* choose abortion, and that any law which rules this out is an insane law. And it also allows for and supports our sense that in other cases resort to abortion is even positively indecent. It would be indecent in the woman to request an abortion, and indecent in a doctor to perform it, if she is in her seventh month, and wants the abortion just to avoid the nuisance of postponing a trip abroad. The very fact that the arguments I have been drawing attention to treat all cases of abortion, or even all cases of abortion in which the mother's life is not at stake, as morally on a par ought to have made them suspect at the outset.

NOTES ON ABORTION AND SELF-DEFENSE

1. What do you think of Thomson's argument about the morality of abortion and, in particular, the circumstances when it is not morally acceptable? (Note that the "famous violinist" article was written before Roe v. Wade.) Are there limits, based upon your own moral standards, that you would place on the times and/or reasons a woman should exercise this right? What are they? To what extent do you think that those limits should be embodied in the law? If those limits—and your underlying moral standards—are based upon religious beliefs, does this pose any problems under the First Amendment?

2. Ellen Willis makes a more straightforward argument for abortion based on self-defense:

> * * * Most people would agree * * * that killing in defense of one's life or safety is not murder. And most would accept a concept of self-defense that includes the right to fight a defensive war or revolution in behalf of one's independence or freedom from oppression. * * * The point is that it's impossible to judge whether an act is murder simply by looking at the act, without considering its context. Which is to say that it makes no sense to discuss whether abortion is murder without considering why women have abortions and what it means to force women to bear children they don't want.
>
> We live in a society that defines childrearing as the mother's job; a society in which most women are denied access to work that pays enough to support a family, childcare facilities they can afford, or any relief from the constant, daily burdens of motherhood; a society that forces mothers into dependence on marriage or welfare and often into permanent poverty * * *. Under these conditions the unwillingly pregnant woman faces a terrifying loss of control over her fate. * * * However gratifying pregnancy may be to a woman who desires it, for the unwilling it is literally an invasion * * *. Clearly, abortion is by normal standards an act of self-defense.

Willis, Abortion: Is A Woman A Person?, in Powers of Desire: The Politics of Sexuality 471, 473 (Ann Snitow, Christine Stansell & Sharon Thompson, eds. 1983). What are the elements of the law of self-defense? Do they "fit" the abortion situation? Sylvia Law asks whether the analogy can realistically be extended beyond "the limited circumstances in which the mother reasonably believes that she will suffer death or great bodily harm. Further, even if it is legally justifiable to kill an innocent person who threatens our life or well-being, the morality of such killing seems dubious." Sylvia A. Law, Rethinking Sex and the Constitution, 132 U. Pa. L. Rev. 955, 1022 (1984). Law thus questions the usefulness of self-defense as a basis upon which to defend the right to abortion, while supporting it on other grounds. See also Caitlin E. Borgmann, The Meaning of "Life": Belief and Reason in the Abortion Debate,

18 Colum. J. Gender & Law 551, 563–68 (2009) (arguing, among other things, that the self-defense argument is really about self-preservation and that the most compelling analogy is that of conjoined twins, where only one will live if they are surgically separated). For other situations in which women have sought to use the law of self-defense and sometimes encountered difficulty, see the discussion of women who kill their abusers in Chapter 4.

3. A recent book, What Roe v. Wade Should Have Said (Jack M. Balkin, ed. 2005), includes mock briefs written by persons prominent in the legal debate over abortion, all written under the condition that the author only employ arguments and precedents that were actually available in 1973, when *Roe* was decided. In her brief, Robin West argues, among other things, that restrictions on abortion impose upon pregnant women a duty of "Good Samaritanship" which the law does not impose on other persons. Id. at 129–35. What do you think of this argument? (Note that similar arguments played a key role in the *AC* case, excerpted below, in opposition to the state's compelling a pregnant mother to undergo a caesarean section operation.)

4. Eileen L. McDonagh claims that introducing the notion of consent to pregnancy, and distinguishing it from consent to intercourse, may provide a route out of the irreconcilable arguments in the abortion debate. McDonagh, Breaking the Abortion Deadlock: From Choice To Consent (1996). She argues for a theory of the right to abortion based not upon choice and privacy but instead upon consent to pregnancy, analogizing the intrusion of the fetus to other bodily intrusions, such as rape, which justify a right to self-defense. Thus McDonagh accepts the anti-abortion movement's argument that the fetus is a form of human life but argues that its implanting itself is the direct cause of pregnancy: "if it makes a woman pregnant without her consent, it severely violates her bodily integrity and liberty." Id. at 6. The fetus, in short, is analogized to an assailant, and the right to abortion becomes simply a variant of the right under liberal theory to defend oneself against nonconsensual invasion. The woman may choose to be altruistic and nurture the fetus for nine months, or she may defend herself against the massive bodily changes, risks, and intrusions of pregnancy by using deadly force against it. This changes the terms of the debate away from an emphasis upon negative freedom from the state (privacy doctrine) to "a woman's right to the assistance of the state to stop the fetus as a private party from intruding on her bodily integrity and liberty without consent," thus mandating public funding of abortion as well. Id. How do you react to this argument? Does it offer hope, as McDonagh claims, of breaking the impasse between the absolutist positions in the abortion debate? See Robin West, Liberalism and Abortion, 87 Geo. L.J. 2117 (1999) (reviewing McDonagh's arguments and describing the limitations both of analogical thinking and of liberal constitutionalism in relation to abortion).

5. What is the rationale underlying the exception for abortions in the cases of rape or incest? Does non-consent capture the whole story? Reva Siegel suggests that popular support for rape and incest exceptions rests on normative judgments that ordinarily pregnancy is the "sexual fault" of the woman. Siegel, Reasoning from the Body: A Historical Perspective on Abortion Regulation and Questions of Equal Protection, 44 Stan. L. Rev. 261, 361 (1992).

For those who consider abortion to be murder, isn't it inconsistent to permit it under any circumstances? See Borgmann, note 2 above, at 568–78 (arguing that no position that brackets, and thus fails to take a stand on, fetal personhood, can be consistently held).

6. If anti-abortion advocates are correct that life begins at conception and that doctors commit murder when they abort, then it would seem to follow under criminal law that women obtaining abortions aid and abet murder. Even if the doctor performs the procedure, the woman has actively sought out and participated in the act. Under traditional criminal law principles, one who aids and abets murder (for example, someone who hires another to kill) is as guilty of murder as one who pulls the trigger. If this is right, then every woman in America who has had an abortion is, in theory, a murderer. In many states, there is no statute of limitations on murder prosecutions. Do you think that anti-abortion advocates are willing to put large numbers of women who have had abortions in jail for long periods of time? If they are not, then what does this say about the premise of the argument that it is "life" that is being taken? Is the problem that the very idea of "life" as a coherent entity with a single meaning is problematic?

7. Reva Siegel describes abortion-restrictive regulation as the use of public power to force women to bear children. Siegel, note 5 above, at 277; see also Jed Rubenfeld, The Right of Privacy, 102 Harv. L. Rev. 737, 788–91 (1989) (interpreting anti-abortion laws as enforcing child-bearing and thus radically redirecting women's lives). Can you think how one might develop legal arguments based on the idea that prohibiting abortion is compelling childbirth? Andrew Koppelman has suggested that the Thirteenth Amendment, which prohibits slavery, might be used for this purpose. Koppelman, Forced Labor: A Thirteenth Amendment Defense of Abortion, 84 Nw. U.L. Rev. 480 (1990); see also Nancy J. Hirschmann, Abortion, Self–Defense, and Involuntary Servitude, 13 Tex. J. Women & Law 41 (2003). What do you think of this suggestion?

c. Arguments Based on Equal Protection

AMICUS BRIEF OF 274 ORGANIZATIONS IN SUPPORT OF *ROE v. WADE*, IN *TURNOCK V. RAGSDALE*

Nos. 88–790 and 88–805 (1989).

[This amicus brief was written by law professors Kathleen M. Sullivan and Susan R. Estrich in a case challenging regulations restricting abortion; the case was ultimately settled before argument in the Supreme Court.]

* * * Because abortion restrictions both discriminate uniquely against women, and do so in a way that intrudes on women's basic interests in bodily integrity, procreation, and health, such laws should trigger strict scrutiny.

A. SEX CLASSIFICATIONS THAT INTERFERE WITH BODILY INTEGRITY AND PROCREATION ARE IMPERMISSIBLE IN THE ABSENCE OF COMPELLING JUSTIFICATION.

This Court has held that measures classifying on the basis of gender are unconstitutional unless the party supporting the measure can "carry the burden of showing an 'exceedingly persuasive justification' for the classification." Mississippi University for Women v. Hogan, 458 U.S. 718, 724 (1982). A "searching analysis" is required because gender-based measures often reflect the "mechanical application," of " 'old notions' and 'archaic and overbroad' generalizations," and operate to "put women not on a pedestal, but in a cage." Thus, this Court has repeatedly struck down legislation that restricted the exercise by both men and women of liberty in social roles, recognizing that "[n]o longer is the female destined solely for the home and the rearing of family, and only the male for the marketplace and the world of ideas."

Exacting as it is, this scrutiny escalates to the highest level where, as here, legislation that discriminates on the basis of gender also intrudes on basic interests in bodily integrity, procreation, health, family, and sometimes life itself. The "fundamental rights" branch of equal protection jurisprudence makes clear that, where legislation classifies with respect to such basic interests, any deference that would otherwise be given the legislature attenuates. Rather, such legislation may be upheld only if it survives the strictest and most searching kind of review. Thus, in Skinner v. Oklahoma, 316 U.S. 535, this Court applied strict scrutiny under the Equal Protection Clause to a compulsory sterilization law that discriminated among categories of thieves—a kind of line-drawing that otherwise would not have been suspect. * * * If cases such as Skinner * * * treat impact on the fundamental rights to procreate and to marry as escalating the standard of review from minimal to strict, then surely the impingement of abortion laws on procreation, health, marriage, and family interests should escalate judicial scrutiny the lesser distance from heightened to strict review. Thus, the gender-based discrimination worked by restrictive abortion laws should be reviewed strictly.

B. RESTRICTIVE ABORTION LAWS CLASSIFY ON THE BASIS OF SEX.

The direct impact of abortion restrictions falls, exclusively, on a class of people that consists only of women. Only women get pregnant; only women have abortions; only women will be forced to endure unwanted pregnancies and adverse health consequences if abortions are restricted; only women are injured by dangerous, illegal abortions where legal ones are unavailable; and only women will bear children if abortions are unavailable.

The fact that the laws do not mention "women" is irrelevant. A law restricting "all abortions" is the precise equivalent of a law restricting "all abortions sought by women." A classification based on pregnancy is, by biological definition, a classification based on gender.

* * *

Moreover, abortion restrictions, like the most classic gender-based restrictions on women seeking to participate in the worlds of work and ideas, have historically rested on archaic stereotypes of women as persons whose "paramount destiny and mission ... [is] to fulfill the noble and benign office of wife and mother." Bradwell v. Illinois, 16 Wall. 130, 142 (1873) (Bradley, J., concurring). Legislation prohibiting abortion, largely a product of the years between 1860 and 1880, reflected precisely the same ideas about the natural and proper role of women as did the legislation of the same period—long-since discredited—that prohibited women from serving on juries or participating in the professions, including the practice of law.

Perhaps not surprisingly, modern studies have found that support for laws banning abortion continues to be an outgrowth of the same sort of stereotypical notions that women's only appropriate roles are those of mother and housewife; in many cases, such laws have emerged as a direct reaction to the increasing number of women who work outside the home. See generally K. Luker, Abortion and the Politics of Motherhood 192–215 (1984). It is, of course, precisely such stereotypes, as they are reflected in legislation, that have over and over again been the focus of this Court's modern equal protection cases.

C. THE POLITICAL PROCESS IS INADEQUATE TO PROTECT ACCESS TO ABORTION FOR ALL WOMEN.

* * * This Court has long interpreted the Equal Protection Clause to require even-handedness in legislation, lest the powerful few too casually trade away for others key liberties that they are careful to reserve for themselves. For example, the Court once struck down under the Equal Protection Clause a law permitting castration of recidivist chicken thieves but sparing white-collar embezzlers the knife. Skinner v. Oklahoma, 316 U.S. 535. The implication of Skinner was that, put to an all-or-nothing choice, legislators would rather sterilize no one than jeopardize people like themselves. Thus equality serves as a backstop to liberty.

Every restrictive abortion law has been passed by a legislature in which men constitute a numerical majority. And every restrictive abortion law, by definition, contains an unwritten clause exempting all men from its strictures. To rely on state legislatures to protect women against "abortion regulation reminiscent of the dark ages," Webster, 109 S.Ct. at 3058, ignores the fact that the overwhelming majority of "those who serve in such bodies," like the Oklahoma legislators who supported sterilization for workingmen's crimes, are not directly affected at all by the penalties they are imposing. It is precisely in such cases that strict scrutiny is required, to protect against the very real danger that those in power will too casually impose burdens on others, in this case on women, that they would not have imposed upon themselves.

That is particularly so where, as here, the women most likely to be affected are those whom the political process protects least well. A world without Roe will not be a world without abortion, but a world in which abortion is accessible according to one's constitutional caste. While affluent women will travel to jurisdictions where safe and legal abortion is available, paying whatever is required, restrictive abortion laws—and, with them, the life-threatening prospect of the back-alley abortion—will disproportionately descend upon "those without ... adequate resources" to avoid them. Griswold, 381 U.S. at 503 (White, J., concurring). Those for whom the burdens of an unwanted pregnancy may be the most crushing—the young, the poor, women whose color already renders them victims of discrimination—will be the ones least able to secure a safe abortion.

In the years prior to Roe, "[p]oor and minority women were virtually precluded from obtaining safe, legal procedures, the overwhelming majority of which were obtained by white women in the private hospital services on psychiatric indications."[28] Women denied access to safe and legal abortions often had dangerous and illegal ones. Mishandled criminal abortions were, one detailed study found, the principal cause of maternal deaths in the 1960's, and mortality rates for African–American women were as much as nine times higher than for white women. In 1972, women of color accounted for sixty-four percent of the deaths associated with illegal abortions in this country.

To trust the political process to protect these women is to ignore completely the lessons of history. Time and again, this Court has recognized its special duties to protect minorities whose rights can too easily be trampled by legislative majorities. For in such cases, there are no political checks: legislators can, without difficulty, "escape the political retribution that might be visited upon them if larger numbers were affected." Railway Express Agency v. New York, 336 U.S. 106, 112–13 (1949) (Jackson, J., concurring). Or, if people like them were affected.

NOTES ON EQUAL PROTECTION

1. As we have seen above, the Court in Roe v. Wade rested the right to abortion upon a fundamental right to privacy. Some of its defenders, notably the American Civil Liberties Union Reproductive Rights Project, insisted upon defending it on privacy grounds alone. Many feminists think that this has been a mistake, both because the foundation of privacy has turned out to be somewhat shaky and because it reinforces the public/private distinction which has not served women well. See, e.g., Catharine A. MacKinnon, Privacy v. Equality, in Feminism Unmodified: Discourses on Life and Law 93–102 (1987). The brief above is an attempt to defend the right to abortion while resting it upon grounds of equality instead. What are the advantages and disadvantages of basing legal arguments for abortion on equal protection rather than upon privacy or liberty? Are they likely to succeed, given the current state of equal protection law as applied to women? See Chapter 2. What are the differences between abortion and sterilization in this respect? Does it help or hurt the argument for abortion to link the two issues?

28. Polgar & Fried, The Bad Old Days: Clandestine Abortions Among the Poor in New York City Before Liberalization of the Abortion law, 8 Fam. Plan. Persp. 125 (1976). * * *

2. In a 1985 law review article, Ruth Bader Ginsburg indicated that she believed that Roe v. Wade would not have occasioned such violent opposition if it had been couched in terms of a sex equality rationale rather than as an issue of patient-physician autonomy and that this approach might have changed the treatment of public funding cases as well. Ginsburg, Some Thoughts on Autonomy and Equality in Relation to *Roe v. Wade*, 63 N.C.L. Rev. 375, 382, 386 (1985). Another way of articulating the equality-based argument is as one based on women's right to equal citizenship. In her mock brief in What Roe v. Wade Should Have Said (Jack M. Balkin, ed. 2005), Reva Siegel maintained that the legal grounds upon which to establish that the right to abortion was necessary to women's equal citizenship were available at the time *Roe* was argued. Id. at 71–82.

Other feminist legal scholars have been urging the adoption of a sex equality approach to reproductive rights for some time. See, e.g., Sylvia A. Law, Rethinking Sex and the Constitution, 132 U. Pa. L. Rev. 955, 962 (1984); Catharine A. MacKinnon, Reflections on Sex Equality Under Law, 100 Yale L.J. 1281, 1309–24 (1991). Analyses related to equal protection began to enter the language of Supreme Court opinions in the 1992 joint opinion in *Casey* (see excerpt above); and lower courts have also been adopting versions of the equality-based argument. See Reva B. Siegel, Sex Equality Arguments for Reproductive Rights: Their Critical Basis and Evolving Constitutional Expression, 56 Emory L.J. 815, 830–32 (2007). Has the addition of Justice Ginsburg on the Court since then had any impact on this development? See Gonzales v. Carhart, 550 U.S. 124, 172 (2007) (Ginsburg, J., dissenting) ("legal challenges to undue restrictions on abortion procedures ... center on a woman's autonomy to determine her life's course, and thus to enjoy equal citizenship stature," citing to the Sylvia Law article, above, and to the Reva Siegel article referenced in note 3 below).

3. Perhaps it is necessary to re-envision equal protection law before it will work for women in this context. Reva Siegel has suggested, for example, that abortion-restrictive regulation should be seen as caste legislation, a mode of regulating women's conduct to compel them to perform the work that has traditionally defined their subordinate social role and status, both within the home and in the workplace. Siegel, Reasoning from the Body: A Historical Perspective on Abortion Regulation and Questions of Equal Protection, 44 Stan. L. Rev. 261, 351 (1992). How is the rape exception an example of a legislative determination based on one of these assumptions?

4. Priscilla Smith argues that the equality women are seeking through control over their reproductive rights has been too narrowly defined as equality within the workplace, which appears selfish. Instead, she urges, equality-based arguments should include the aspects in which abortion allows women to raise their children in equality at home, "to mother them in conditions of equality." Priscilla J. Smith, Responsibility for Life: How Abortion Serves Women's Interests in Motherhood, 17 J.L. & Pol'y 97, 137–38, 154–59 (2008–09). How would you construct such an argument? How might such arguments further the repronormativity critiqued by Katherine Franke in chapter 3?

5. The need to build reproductive rights upon equal protection appears particularly urgent in the wake of the Supreme Court's decision in Gonzalez v. Carhart. One commentator argues that the Court's decision in *Gonzalez* may mark the limits of the capacity to protect women's rights with an abortion jurisprudence based upon fundamental rights and privacy. See, e.g., Mary Kathryn Nagle, Abortion Post–*Glucksberg* and Post–*Gonzales*: Applying An Analysis That Demands Equality for Women under the Law, 16 Duke J. Gender L. & Pol'y 293, 296–302 (2009). Nagle believes that the Partial Birth Abortion Act could have been found unconstitutional as sex discrimination under the standard set out by the Supreme Court in United States v. Virginia (excerpt in Chapter 2, above). Id. at 302–13. How would you make such an argument? Do you think that argument would have changed Justice Kennedy's mind?

6. In this chapter, we have examined at least four different approaches to abortion, based on (1) a constitutional right to privacy and liberty (Roe v. Wade and its progeny), (2) the real world, "felt" experiences of women, (3) self-defense, and (4) equal protection. How do these different approaches compare with, or rely upon, the differing feminist theories presented in Chapter 3? For example, is the Voices Brief an example of relational feminism? Where do MacKinnon's views about abortion fit into these categories? Is Judith Jarvis Thomson a formal equality theorist? What about Estrich and Sullivan, in the excerpt above? What would be the approach of a pragmatic feminist? A socialist feminist?

4. FEMINISM AND OPPOSITION TO ABORTION

ELIZABETH FOX–GENOVESE, FEMINISM WITHOUT ILLUSIONS: A CRITIQUE OF INDIVIDUALISM

83–85 (1991).

It is not easy to reconcile the feminist metaphors of motherhood and community with the feminist defense of abortion on the grounds of absolute individual right. Surely, the special sense of human connection and nurture that so many feminists attribute to women derives primarily from women's special roles as the bearers and rearers of children. Jennifer Nedelsky has thus recently proposed that feminists reconceptualize the ideal of autonomy to ground it in child rearing[87].Sara Ruddick has suggested that all women differ from men in their propensity to "maternal thinking.[88]" Either abortion entails the killing of babies or it does not. If it does, then there are no legitimate grounds for allowing it, not even rape or incest. If it does not, then there are only the narrowest of pragmatic grounds for preventing it. The problem remains: Are we dealing with two lives or one? No precedent in individualist theory helps us to understand the issue, for the men upon whom individualism was predicated do not bear children.

87. Nedelsky, "Reconceiving Autonomy[, 1 Yale J. L. & Feminism 7 (1989)]."

88. Ruddick, "Maternal Thinking[: Towards a Politics of Peace (1989)]."

It is not easy to reconcile the defense of women's rights to abortion on the grounds of privacy with sustained attempts on the part of the women's movement to break down other aspects of what was traditionally viewed as the privacy of the family. Most of us applaud the state's growing willingness to help to protect women and children against sexual or physical abuse by husbands and fathers. But only very recently would all interference between a man and a wife have been viewed as an invasion of privacy. In effect, the defense of a woman's right to abortion as a matter of privacy represents a decisive reinforcement of the extreme individualistic view of society as composed of atomized individuals. More frighteningly, by implicitly identifying reproduction as a woman's individual right, it dismisses men's claims and dissolves their responsibilities to the next generation.

Abortion challenges feminists to come to terms with the contradictions in their own thought, notably the contradiction between the commitment to community and nurture and the commitment to individual right. Without doubt, the easiest way would be to reach some determination about our collective definition of life. Most Americans would probably accept a definition of life linked to the notion of viability and accept abortion on demand up to the twentieth week of pregnancy. Without some such agreement on the definition of life, the right to abortion opens the specter of any individual's right to kill those who depend upon her and drain her resources—elderly parents, terminally ill or handicapped children. Without some such agreement, the right to abortion—the woman's rights to sexual self-determination—can logically lead to the right to murder with impunity. How are we to link women as the embodiments of "maternal thinking" with such a position?

* * *

Abortion confronts us with a collective social, economic, political, and moral problem that we can only solve collectively and in frank acknowledgment that no solution will escape intellectual inconsistencies and some unresolved moral tensions. Abortion forces us to recognize provision for children as a collective responsibility. Increasingly, the responsibility for children penalizes women by curtailing their social and economic opportunities. By forcing women to bear and rear children they do not want and for whom they cannot adequately provide, society is pitting women's lives against children's and consigning women to social and economic marginality. But the difficulty and sacrifice do not constitute a moral, or even a political, justification for abortion. They constitute a justification for enhanced medical and educational programs for all children and hence for the acceptance of collective principles.

AMICUS BRIEF OF FEMINISTS FOR LIFE, IN *BRAY v. ALEXANDRIA WOMEN'S HEALTH CLINIC*

No. 90–985 (1991).

One reason for the continuing controversy concerning abortion on demand is that a majority of American women do not agree with respondents' underlying assumption that equal protection under the Fourteenth Amendment requires unlimited abortion on demand. A recent poll conducted by the Gallup Organization revealed that there is no "gender gap" on abortion: indeed, women are as likely, and in some cases, more likely than men to oppose abortion. For example, only 17 percent of women and 20 percent of men believe that an abortion is acceptable, even during the first trimester, if the pregnancy was unplanned and would interrupt a woman's career. A mere 7 percent of women and 11 percent of men believe a first trimester abortion is acceptable as a means of birth control. Only 26 percent of women and 30 percent of men believe first trimester abortion is acceptable if continuing the pregnancy would require a teenager to drop out of school, and 20 percent of women and 30 percent of men approve of abortion where the birth of a child would create a financial burden. And 53 percent of women and 47 percent of men believe the unborn child's "right to be born" outweighs, at the moment of conception, the woman's "right to choose" whether she wants to have a child.

* * *

The broader dispute over abortion is manifested by a division in feminist theory over whether "women can [ ] ever achieve the fulfillment of feminist goals in a society permissive toward abortion." Callahan, Abortion & the Sexual Agenda, Commonweal 232, 232 (April 25, 1986). Respondent N.O.W. holds that abortion is essential to their notion of the feminist agenda. Many others, including, in fact, a majority of American women, hold that a more encompassing and truly feminist vision of justice demands protection for the unborn child. Id. at 234. A contrast is sometimes drawn in feminist theory between "cultural" feminists, who emphasize the importance of women in the creation and nurturing of human life, and "radical" feminists, who identify this very role as the source of oppression of women.[26] These contrary views of feminism offer different conclusions on whether abortion is necessary for the social and political emancipation of women, and whether opposition to abortion is, per se, discrimination against women. Bayles, Feminism and Abortion, The Atlantic Monthly 83, 85 (April 1990).

KRISTIN LUKER, ABORTION AND THE POLITICS OF MOTHERHOOD

193, 199–200, 206–07, 209–10 (1984).

* * * [T]he abortion debate has become a debate about women's contrasting obligations to themselves and others. New technologies and

26. See West, Jurisprudence and Gender, 55 U.Chi.L.Rev. 1, 13 (1989); MacKinnon, Feminism, Marxism, Method, and the State: Toward Feminist Jurisprudence, 8 Signs: Journal of Women in Culture and Society 635, 636, n. 4 (1983).

the changing nature of work have opened up possibilities for women outside of the home undreamed of in the nineteenth century; together, these changes give women—for the first time in history—the option of deciding exactly how and when their family roles will fit into the larger context of their lives. In essence, therefore, this round of the abortion debate is so passionate and hard-fought *because it is a referendum on the place and meaning of motherhood.*

* * *

For example, pro-life women have *always* valued family roles very highly and have arranged their lives accordingly. They did not acquire high-level educational and occupational skills, for example, because they married, and they married because their values suggested that this would be the most satisfying life open to them. Similarly, pro-choice women postponed (or avoided) marriage and family roles because they chose to acquire the skills they needed to be successful in the larger world, having concluded that the role of wife and mother was too limited for them. Thus, activists on both sides of the issue are women who have a given set of values about what are the most satisfying and appropriate roles for women, and they have made *life commitments that now limit their ability to change their minds.* Women who have many children and little education, for example, are seriously handicapped in attempting to become doctors or lawyers; women who have reached their late forties with few children or none are limited in their ability to build (or rebuild) a family. For most of these activists, therefore, their position on abortion is the "tip of the iceberg," a shorthand way of supporting and proclaiming not only a complex set of values but a given set of social resources as well.

* * *

It is stating the obvious to point out that the more limited the educational credentials a woman has, the more limited the job opportunities are for her, and the more limited the job opportunities, the more attractive motherhood is as a full-time occupation. In motherhood, one can control the content and pace of one's own work, and the job is *intrinsically meaningful.* Compared with a job clerking in a supermarket (a realistic alternative for women with limited educational credentials) where the work is poorly compensated and often demeaning, motherhood can have compensations that far transcend the monetary ones. As one woman described mothering: "You have this little, rough uncut diamond, and you're the artist shaping and cutting that diamond, and bringing out the lights . . . that's a great challenge."

All the circumstances of her existence will therefore encourage a pro-life woman to highlight the kinds of values and experiences that support childbearing and childrearing and to discount the attraction (such as it is) of paid employment. Her circumstances encourage her to resent the pro-choice view that women's most meaningful and prestigious activities are in the "man's world."

Abortion also has a symbolic dimension that separates the needs and interests of homemakers and workers in the paid labor force. Insofar as abortion allows a woman to get a job, to get training for a job, or to advance in a job, it does more than provide social support for working women over homemakers; it also seems to support the value of economic considerations over moral ones. Many pro-life people interviewed said that although their commitment to traditional family roles meant very real material deprivations to themselves and their families, the moral benefits of such a choice more than made up for it.

* * *

Pro-life people and pro-life women in particular have very real reasons to fear such a state of affairs. Not only do they see an achievement-based world as harsh, superficial, and ultimately ruthless; they are relatively less well-equipped to operate in that world. A considerable amount of social science research has suggested, at least in the realm of medical treatment, that there is an increasing tendency to judge people by their official (achieved) worth. Pro-life people have relatively fewer official achievements in part because they have been doing what they see as a moral task, namely, raising children and making a home; and they see themselves as becoming handicapped in a world that discounts not only their social contributions but their personal lives as well.

* * *

But pro-life women, like all women, are facing a devaluation of these resources. As American society increasingly becomes a service economy, men can buy the services that a wife traditionally offers. Cooking, cleaning, decorating, and the like can easily be purchased on the open market in a cash transaction. And as sex becomes more open, more casual, and more "amative," it removes one more resource that could previously be obtained only through marriage.

Pro-life women, as we have seen, have both the value orientations and social characteristics that make marriage very important. Their alternatives in the public world of work are, on the whole, less attractive. Furthermore, women who stay home full-time and keep house are becoming a financial luxury. Only very wealthy families *or families whose values allow them to place the nontangible benefits of a full-time wife over the tangible benefits of a working wife* can afford to keep one of its earners off the labor market. To pro-life people, the nontangible benefit of having children—and therefore the value of procreative sex—is very important. Thus, a social ethic that promotes more freely available sex undercuts pro-life women two ways: it limits their abilities to get into a marriage in the first place, and it undermines the social value placed on their presence once within a marriage.

For pro-choice women, the situation is reversed. Because they have access to "male" resources such as education and income, they have far less reason to believe that the basic reason for sexuality is to produce children. They plan to have small families anyway, and they and their husbands come from and have married into a social class in which small families are the norm. For a number of overlapping reasons, therefore, pro-choice women believe that the value of sex is not primarily procreative: pro-choice women value the ability of sex to promote human intimacy more (or at least more frequently) than they value the ability of sex to produce babies. But they hold this view because they can afford to. When they bargain for marriage, they use the same resources that they use in the labor market: upper-class status, an education very similar to a man's, side-by-side participation in the man's world, and, not least, a salary that substantially increases a family's standard of living.

It is true, therefore, that pro-life people are "anti-sex." They value sex, of course, but they value it for its traditional benefits (babies) rather than for the benefits that pro-choice people associate with it (intimacy). Pro-life people really do want to see "less" sexuality—or at least less open and socially unregulated sexuality—because they think it is morally wrong, they think it distorts the meaning of sex, and they feel that it *threatens the basis on which their own marital bargains are built.*

NOTES ON FEMINIST OPPOSITION TO ABORTION

1. Some feminists might say that an anti-abortion feminist is an oxymoron. What do you think? Is it possible to be a feminist and oppose the right to abortion? Why or why not?

2. Does changing the terms of the abortion argument to emphasize abortion as a right flowing from the Equal Protection Clause rather than from the right of privacy address any of the issues raised by Elizabeth Fox–Genovese in the excerpt above? To what extent? What about grounding abortion rights in an ethic of care, as suggested by Robin West?

3. Based upon your reading in this course, do you think it is fair to say that radical feminists see motherhood as a source of oppression, while relational feminists see it as a source of strength? Does it depend at all upon the social and political conditions surrounding childbirth and childrearing? In what ways? Priscilla J. Smith argues that pro-choice women, out of fears of being seen as essentialist, have ceded the discourse of motherhood to anti-abortion advocates and that they should reclaim this ground by emphasizing the relationship between the right to reproductive choice and responsible, caring motherhood. Smith, Responsibility for Life: How Abortion Serves Women's Interests in Motherhood, 17 J.L. & Pol'y 97, 145–59 (2008–09). Would framing the discussion in these terms help to bridge the gap between women who support and women who oppose abortion? What, if any, are the dangers of doing so?

4. Elizabeth Fox–Genovese suggests in the excerpt above that a pro-choice stance is inconsistent with the tenets of relational feminism. Linda C.

McClain points out, however, that relational feminists Carol Gilligan and Robin West strongly support the right to abortion, while themes raised by radical feminists like MacKinnon and Dworkin—abortion as supportive of irresponsible men's sexual access to women and as necessitated by a society that does not accommodate the needs of pregnant women and mothers—are similar to those raised by the Feminists for Life in the excerpt here. McClain, Equality, Oppression, and Abortion: Women Who Oppose Abortion Rights in the Name of Feminism, in Feminist Nightmares: Women At Odds: Feminism and the Problem of Sisterhood 165 (Susan Ostrov Weisser & Jennifer Fleischner, eds. 1994). With which do you agree? Is the Feminists for Life position more in tune with the theoretical foundations of relational feminism or of radical feminism? Is there any common ground based upon these similarities?

5. Is the right to abortion, as Fox–Genovese argues, a slippery slope leading to euthanasia for elderly and handicapped persons? Why or why not? If not, how can you be sure? Does this trouble you? Is this the same point made by the *Gonzalez* majority opinion with its references to the *Glucksberg* case, in the excerpt above? If not, how is it different?

6. One difference between the anti-abortion movement in the 19th century and now is that the modern anti-abortion movement consists primarily of women. See Luker, above, at 194. How do you explain the fact that so many women oppose abortion? Yet the leaders of the anti-abortion movement have been predominantly male. See James Risen & Judy L. Thomas, Wrath of Angels: The American Abortion War 120, 219, 296 (1998). Why? Marilyn Frye suggests that abortion is particularly threatening to men, and thus to male-identified women (whom she calls "patriarchal loyalists"), because it is an example of a woman's willingness to separate from a being that is dependent on her:

> The woman who is free to see the fetus as a parasite might be free to see the man as a parasite. * * * The woman who is capable (legally, psychologically, physically) of decisively, self-interestedly, independently rejecting the one parasite is capable of rejecting, with the same decisiveness and independence, the like burden of the other parasite. In the eyes of the other parasite, the image of the wholly self-determined abortion, involving not even a ritual submission to male veto power, is the mirror image of death.

Frye, The Politics of Reality: Essays in Feminist Theory 100–01 (1983). Is there any truth to this argument? On what do you base your conclusions about its cogency?

7. Kristin Luker's research shows that activists on both sides of the abortion question are in effect representing their own self-interest: pro-choice activists are drawn primarily from upper-income, educated women who are employed, many of them as professionals, while anti-abortion activists tend to be lower-income women with less formal education, who are homemakers. If so, is there any common ground upon which the two groups can meet? Do the facts about the differing class and cultural backgrounds of the two groups suggest any ways in which the debate might be changed in order to make it more fruitful and less divisive?

For a variety of perspectives on the nature of the abortion debate in this country, see, e.g., Faye D. Ginsburg, Contested Lives: The Abortion Debate in an American Community (1989) (viewing the debate as over the meaning of women's lives and the role of nurturance and arguing that the opposing sides have a common interest in helping women with unplanned pregnancies); Laurence H. Tribe, Abortion: The Clash of Absolutes (1990) (arguing that the debate's current focus on "absolutes"—women's right to liberty versus the fetus' right to life—is oversimplified and counterproductive and suggesting that both sides should work toward a world of only wanted pregnancies); Ruth Colker, Abortion & Dialogue: Pro–Choice, Pro–Life, and American Law (1992) (calling for a reshaping of the conversation toward a focus on both sides' interest in love and life and the creation of social conditions which allow women both a meaningful choice and life); Alexander Sanger, Beyond Choice: Reproductive Freedom in the 21st Century (2004) (arguing for supporting reproductive freedom on sociobiological grounds, as necessary to successful reproduction and the survival of children).

D. "FETAL PROTECTION"

DAWN E. JOHNSEN, THE CREATION OF FETAL RIGHTS: CONFLICTS WITH WOMEN'S CONSTITUTIONAL RIGHTS TO LIBERTY, PRIVACY, AND EQUAL PROTECTION

95 Yale L.J. 599, 604–09, 613, 615–17, 620, 624–25 (1986).

* * *

* * * Conceptualizing the fetus as an entity with legal rights independent of the pregnant woman has made possible the future creation of fetal rights that could be used against the pregnant woman. In some instances, this potential has already been realized.

* * *

In one such case, a Michigan court held that a child could sue his mother for taking tetracycline during her pregnancy, allegedly resulting in the discoloration of the child's teeth.[18] The court stated that the appropriate standard for liability was that of the "reasonable" pregnant woman. Another court has suggested that a woman may be sued by her child for not preventing its birth if she had prior knowledge of the probability of its being born "defective."[20] In some states, a woman can be deprived of custody of her child even before its birth if the state feels that her actions during pregnancy endanger the fetus. In Michigan, a state whose laws do not expressly extend to "prenatal abuse," a court held that evidence of a woman's prenatal "abuse" or "neglect" could be considered during proceedings instituted by the state to deprive her of custody of her newborn

18. Grodin v. Grodin, 102 Mich.App. 396, 301 N.W.2d 869 (1980).

20. * * * Curlender v. Bio–Science Laboratories, 106 Cal.App.3d 811, 829, 165 Cal.Rptr. 477, 488 (1980) (dictum).

child.[22] The court further held that this evidence could be obtained by reviewing the woman's medical records without her consent, records whose confidentiality was protected by both federal and state statutes. * * * Perhaps most alarmingly, states have taken direct injunctive action against pregnant women. Courts have seized custody of fetuses (i.e., of pregnant women) in order to enjoin women from taking drugs that are potentially harmful to fetuses. * * *

* * * [A]bsent an increased awareness of the costs to women's autonomy, these rights will almost certainly continue to expand. Given the fetus's complete physical dependence on and interrelatedness with the body of the woman, virtually every act of the pregnant woman has some effect on the fetus. A woman could be held civilly or criminally liable for fetal injuries caused by accidents resulting from maternal negligence, such as automobile or household accidents. She could also be held liable for any behavior during her pregnancy having potentially adverse effects on her fetus, including failing to eat properly, using prescription, nonprescription and illegal drugs, smoking, drinking alcohol, exposing herself to infectious disease or to workplace hazards, engaging in immoderate exercise or sexual intercourse, residing at high altitudes for prolonged periods, or using a general anesthetic or drugs to induce rapid labor during delivery. * * *

In addition to advocating expansion of criminal penalties and tort recovery, commentators have advocated a wide range of new forms of state regulation of pregnant women's behavior. One such suggestion is that public benefits be withheld from pregnant women who refuse to submit to physical examinations or to abstain from drugs or alcohol. "High risk" parents could be required to undergo genetic or post-conception screening. Pregnant women could be prohibited from drinking alcohol and required to submit to breathalyzer tests to ensure compliance. One commentator has even proposed allowing punitive damages against women who intentionally harm their fetuses.

Perhaps the most foreboding aspect of allowing increased state involvement in pregnant women's lives in the name of the fetus is that the state may impose direct injunctive regulation of women's actions. When expanded to cover fetuses, child custody provisions may be used as a basis for seizing custody of the fetus [in utero] to control the woman's behavior. * * * Nevertheless, advocates of fetal rights have proposed that the state increasingly take custody of fetuses and, in some cases, civilly commit pregnant women to "protect" their fetuses.

This threat appears particularly immediate in the area of coerced medical treatment of pregnant women. * * * This phenomenon, troubling in its own right, is susceptible to even more dangerous expansion given new procedures in fetal therapy and fetal surgery. When fully developed, these procedures, which had promised to enhance women's reproductive

22. In re Baby X, 97 Mich.App. 111, 293 N.W.2d 736 (1980) (within twenty-four hours of birth, child began exhibiting signs of drug withdrawal).

freedom, may be used to restrict it. Some in the medical profession advocate compulsory medical treatment, including forced surgery, where it is determined by medical professionals to be in the interest of the fetus. * * *

* * *

Allowing the state to control women's actions in the name of fetal rights, however, reflects a view of the fetus as an entity separate from the pregnant woman, with interests that are hostile to her interests. In fact, by granting rights to the fetus assertable against the pregnant woman, and thus depriving the woman of decisionmaking autonomy, the state affirmatively acts to create an adversarial relationship between the woman and the fetus. By separating the interests of the fetus from those of the pregnant woman, and then examining, often post hoc, the effect on the fetus of isolated decisions made by the woman on a daily basis during pregnancy, the state is likely to exaggerate the potential risks to the fetus and undervalue the costs of the loss of autonomy suffered by the woman.

Where the woman has chosen not to exercise her right to abort her fetus, she is likely to care deeply about the well-being of the child she will bear. It is therefore more rational to assume that women will consider potentially harmful effects to their children resulting from their actions during pregnancy than to subject all women to state regulation of their actions during pregnancy. Furthermore, because the decisions a woman makes throughout her pregnancy depend on her individual values and preferences, complicated sets of life circumstances, and uncertain probabilities of daily risk, the woman herself is best situated to make these complex evaluations.

* * *

There have been few attempts at state intrusion of the magnitude and sweeping nature involved in state regulation of pregnant women's actions. Courts have held unconstitutional even isolated instances of the type of intrusions to which pregnant women would be continually subjected. For example, the Supreme Court has held that the state may not compel criminal suspects to undergo certain medical procedures,[69] and a federal circuit court has recognized the right of even involuntarily committed mental patients to refuse medical treatment.[70] The fact that these prohibited attempts at intrusions have involved those over whom the state traditionally exerts a great deal of authority—criminal defendants and

69. For example, in Rochin v. California, the Court held that the forcible pumping of a criminal suspect's stomach violated the individual's Fourteenth Amendment due process rights, and was "conduct that shocks the conscience." 342 U.S. 165, 172 (1952). * * *

In Winston v. Lee, the court held that to remove surgically a bullet from a suspect's body against his will for use as evidence against him would violate his constitutional rights. 105 S.Ct. 1611 (1985) * * *

70. * * * Rennie v. Klein, 653 F.2d 836 (3d Cir.1981), vacated on other grounds, 458 U.S. 1119 (1982), on remand, 720 F.2d 266 (3d Cir.1983) (reaffirming constitutional right to refuse drugs). * * *

mental patients—suggests the radical nature of the fetal rights trend and its incompatibility with our heritage of civil liberties. * * *

Existing liberty and privacy doctrine recognizes the threat to pregnant women's autonomy posed by fetal rights laws. Yet existing doctrine does not describe the full extent of the injury involved, for it does not identify the sex-specific nature of that injury. Only women can suffer the great intrusions of such laws, for only women have the ability to bear children. Fetal rights laws would not only infringe on constitutionally protected liberty and privacy rights of individual women, they would also serve to disadvantage women as women by further stigmatizing and penalizing them on the basis of the very characteristic that historically has been used to perpetuate a system of sex inequality.

* * *

Granting rights to fetuses in a manner that conflicts with women's autonomy reinforces the tradition of disadvantaging women on the basis of their reproductive capability. By subjecting women's decisions and actions during pregnancy to judicial review, the state simultaneously questions women's abilities and seizes women's rights to make decisions essential to their very personhood. The rationale behind using fetal rights laws to control the actions of women during pregnancy is strikingly similar to that used in the past to exclude women from the paid labor force and to confine them to the "private" sphere. Fetal rights could be used to restrict pregnant women's autonomy in both their personal and professional lives, in decisions ranging from nutrition to employment, in ways far surpassing any regulation of the actions of competent adult men. The state would thus define women in terms of their childbearing capacity, valuing the reproductive difference between women and men in such a way as to render it impossible for women to participate as full members of society. In light of the great threat to women's right to equality posed by legal recognition of the fetus, the state should bear the burden of ensuring that any law granting fetal rights does not disadvantage women or in any way infringe on the autonomy of pregnant women.

DOROTHY E. ROBERTS, PUNISHING DRUG ADDICTS WHO HAVE BABIES: WOMEN OF COLOR, EQUALITY, AND THE RIGHT OF PRIVACY

104 Harv. L. Rev. 1419, 1420–21, 1428–30, 1432–36, 1440–41, 1445–49, 1481 (1991).

A growing number of women across the country have been charged with criminal offenses after giving birth to babies who test positive for drugs. The majority of these women * * * are poor and Black. Most are addicted to crack cocaine. * * *

Crack cocaine appeared in America in the early 1980s, and its abuse has grown to epidemic proportions. Crack is especially popular among inner-city women. Indeed, evidence shows that, in several urban areas in the United States, more women than men now smoke crack. Most crack-addicted women are of childbearing age, and many are pregnant. This phenomenon has contributed to an explosion in the number of newborns affected by maternal drug use. Some experts estimate that as many as 375,000 drug-exposed infants are born every year. * * *

Babies born to drug-addicted mothers may suffer a variety of medical, developmental, and behavioral problems, depending on the nature of their mother's substance abuse. Immediate effects of cocaine exposure can include premature birth, low birth weight, and withdrawal symptoms. Cocaine-exposed children have also exhibited neurobehavioral problems such as mood dysfunction, organizational deficits, poor attention, and impaired human interaction, although it has not been determined whether these conditions are permanent. Congenital disorders and deformities have also been associated with cocaine use during pregnancy. According to NAPARE [National Association for Perinatal Addiction Research and Education], babies exposed to cocaine have a tenfold greater risk of suffering sudden infant death syndrome (SIDS).

* * *

The response of state prosecutors, legislators, and judges to the problem of drug-exposed babies has been punitive. They have punished women who use drugs during pregnancy by depriving these mothers of custody of their children, by jailing them during their pregnancy, and by prosecuting them after their babies are born.

* * *

Poor Black women bear the brunt of prosecutors' punitive approach. These women are the primary targets of prosecutors, not because they are more likely to be guilty of fetal abuse, but because they are Black and poor. Poor women, who are disproportionately Black, are in closer contact with government agencies, and their drug use is therefore more likely to be detected. Black women are also more likely to be reported to government authorities, in part because of the racist attitudes of health care professionals. Finally, their failure to meet society's image of the ideal mother makes their prosecution more acceptable.

To charge drug-addicted mothers with crimes, the state must be able to identify those who use drugs during pregnancy. Because poor women are generally under greater government supervision—through their associations with public hospitals, welfare agencies, and probation officers—their drug use is more likely to be detected and reported. * * * The government's main source of information about prenatal drug use is hospitals' reporting of positive infant toxicologies to child welfare authorities. Hospitals serving poor minority communities implement this testing almost exclusively. Private physicians who serve more affluent women perform less of this screening both because they have a financial stake both in retaining their patients' business and securing referrals from them and because they are socially more like their patients.

* * *

Health care professionals are much more likely to report Black women's drug use to government authorities than they are similar drug use by their wealthy white patients. A study recently reported in The New England Journal of Medicine demonstrated this racial bias in the reporting of maternal drug use.[71] Researchers studied the results of toxicologic tests of pregnant women who received prenatal care in public health clinics and in private obstetrical offices in Pinellas County, Florida. Little difference existed in the prevalence of substance abuse by pregnant women along either racial or economic lines, nor was there any significant difference between public clinics and private offices. Despite similar rates of substance abuse, however, Black women were *ten times* more likely than whites to be reported to public health authorities for substance abuse during pregnancy. * * *

It is also significant that, out of the universe of maternal conduct that can injure a fetus, prosecutors have focused on crack use. The selection of crack addiction for punishment can be justified neither by the number of addicts nor the extent of the harm to the fetus. Excessive alcohol consumption during pregnancy, for example, can cause severe fetal injury, and marijuana use may also adversely affect the unborn. The incidence of both these types of substance abuse is high as well. * * * Therefore, selecting crack abuse as the primary fetal harm to be punished has a discriminatory impact that cannot be medically justified.

* * *

The systematic, institutionalized denial of reproductive freedom has uniquely marked Black women's history in America. An important part of this denial has been the devaluation of Black women as mothers. A popular mythology that degrades Black women and portrays them as less deserving of motherhood reinforces this subordination. * * *

[Here Professor Roberts discusses the brutal denial of Black women's autonomy and reproductive control under slavery.]

The disproportionate number of Black mothers who lose custody of their children through the child welfare system is a contemporary manifestation of the devaluation of Black motherhood. This disparate impact of state intervention results in part from Black families' higher rate of reliance on government welfare. Because welfare families are subject to supervision by social workers, instances of perceived neglect are more likely to be reported to governmental authorities than neglect on the part of more affluent parents. Black children are also removed from their homes in part because of the child welfare system's cultural bias and application of the nuclear family pattern to Black families. Black childrearing patterns that diverge from the norm of the nuclear family have been misinterpreted by government bureaucrats as child neglect. For example, child welfare workers have often failed to respect the longstand-

71. Chasnoff, Landress & Barrett [The Prevalence of Illicit–Drug or Alcohol Use During Pregnancy and Discrepancies in Mandatory Reporting in Pinellas County, Florida, 322 NEW ENG.J.MED. 1202,] 1205 (table 3) [1990].

ing cultural tradition in the Black community of shared parenting responsibility among blood-related and non-blood kin. The state has thus been more willing to intrude upon the autonomy of poor Black families, and in particular of Black mothers, while protecting the integrity of white, middle-class homes.

This devaluation of Black motherhood has been reinforced by stereotypes that blame Black mothers for the problems of the Black family. * * *

Informed by the historical and present devaluation of Black motherhood, we can better understand prosecutors' reasons for punishing drug-addicted mothers. * * *

It is important to recognize at the outset that the prosecutions are based in part on a woman's pregnancy and not on her illegal drug use alone. Prosecutors charge these defendants not with drug use, but with child abuse or drug distribution—crimes that relate to their pregnancy. * * *

When a drug-addicted woman becomes pregnant, she has only one realistic avenue to escape criminal charges: abortion. Thus, she is penalized for choosing to have the baby rather than having an abortion. * * * Thus, it is the *choice of carrying a pregnancy to term* that is being penalized.

* * *

The history of overwhelming state neglect of Black children casts further doubt on its professed concern for the welfare of the fetus. When a society has always closed its eyes to the inadequacy of prenatal care available to poor Black women, its current expression of interest in the health of unborn Black children must be viewed with suspicion. The most telling evidence of the state's disregard of Black children is the high rate of infant death in the Black community. In 1987, the mortality rate for Black infants in the United States was 17.9 deaths per thousand births—more than twice that for white infants (8.6). * * *

The main reason for these high mortality rates is inadequate prenatal care. Most poor Black women face financial and other barriers to receiving proper care during pregnancy. In 1986, only half of all pregnant Black women in America received adequate prenatal care. * * *

The cruelty of this punitive response is heightened by the lack of available drug treatment services for pregnant drug addicts. Protecting the welfare of drug addicts' children requires, among other things, adequate facilities for the mother's drug treatment. Yet a drug addict's pregnancy serves as an obstacle to obtaining this treatment. Treatment centers either refuse to treat pregnant women or are effectively closed to them because the centers are ill-equipped to meet the needs of pregnant addicts. Most hospitals and programs that treat addiction exclude pregnant women because their babies are more likely to be born with health problems requiring expensive care. * * *

Finally, and perhaps most importantly, ample evidence reveals that prosecuting addicted mothers may not achieve the government's asserted goal of healthier pregnancies; indeed, such prosecutions will probably lead to the opposite result. Pregnant addicts who seek help from public hospitals and clinics are the ones most often reported to government authorities. The threat of prosecution based on this reporting forces women to remain anonymous and thus has the perverse effect of deterring pregnant drug addicts from seeking treatment. For this reason, the government's decision to punish drug-addicted mothers is irreconcilable with the goal of helping them.

* * *

A policy that attempts to protect fetuses by denying the humanity of their mothers will inevitably fail. We must question such a policy's true concern for the dignity of the fetus, just as we question the motives of the slave owner who protected the unborn slave child while whipping his pregnant mother. Although the master attempted to separate the mother and fetus for his commercial ends [because the child would become his property], their fates were inextricably intertwined. The tragedy of crack babies is initially a tragedy of crack-addicted mothers. Both are part of a larger tragedy of a community that is suffering a host of indignities, including, significantly, the denial of equal respect for its women's reproductive decisions.

NOTES ON "FETAL PROTECTION"

1. Many of the things predicted in Dawn Johnsen's 1986 article happened. Pregnant women who tested positive for cocaine were arrested, charged with criminal child abuse or "fetal abuse," and imprisoned. By the year 2000, at least 200 women had faced criminal prosecution for using drugs during pregnancy, either for murder or criminal child abuse. See Lynn M. Paltrow, David S. Cohen & Corinne A. Carey, Year 2000 Overview: Governmental Responses to Pregnant Women Who Use Alcohol or Other Drugs 8 (2000). Criminal convictions have been overturned on appeal in most states. See, e.g., Johnson v. Florida, 602 So.2d 1288 (Fla.1992) (overturning conviction for "delivery" of drugs to unborn child under drug trafficking statute). In South Carolina, however, Regina McKnight was sentenced to a 20–year term for murder after she gave birth to a stillborn baby and the autopsy revealed cocaine derivatives. State v. McKnight, 576 S.E.2d 168 (S.C. 2003), cert. denied, 540 U.S. 819 (2003). She was ultimately released after almost 8 years upon a successful post-conviction petition based on ineffective assistance of counsel; the underlying issue was failure to exclude other causes for the death. McKnight v. State, 661 S.E.2d 354 (S.C. 2008). There are, of course, multiple causes for fetal death, including maternal poverty, poor nutrition, lack of prenatal care, domestic violence, and a variety of environmental causes. See, e.g., Linda C. Fentiman, In the Name of Fetal Protection: Why American Prosecutors Pursue Pregnant Drug Users (and Other Countries Don't), 18 Colum. J. Gender & Law 647, 653–54 (2009).

South Carolina is apparently the only state in which criminal convictions against pregnant mothers for drug use have been upheld on appeal. In Whitner v. State, 492 S.E.2d 777 (S.C. 1997), cert. denied, 523 U.S. 1145 (1998), the South Carolina Supreme Court upheld an 8–year sentence for criminal child neglect based on ingestion of cocaine during pregnancy based on a positive drug test of the baby at birth, despite the fact that the baby was in good health. Both McKnight and Whitner were poor Black women; McKnight was homeless. In the late 1980's, South Carolina also initiated a program of cooperation between hospitals and law enforcement agencies, under which pregnant women's urine was tested and the results, if positive for cocaine, were turned over to police. Obstetrical patients who had been arrested brought suit on a number of grounds. The Supreme Court ultimately held that this practice was unconstitutional as a non-consensual and warrantless search. Ferguson v. City of Charleston, 532 U.S. 67 (2001); see also Andrew E. Taslitz, A Feminist Fourth Amendment?: Consent, Care, Privacy, and Social Meaning in Ferguson v. City of Charleston, 9 Duke J. Gender L. & Pol'y 1 (2002).

Prosecutions of drug-addicted mothers continue in South Carolina; three more in 2005–07 resulted in sentences of up to 10 years there and a 15–year sentence in Oklahoma, with many defendants now pleading guilty. See Fentiman, above, at 650 & n.14. What is striking, however, is that such charges continue to be brought in other states, despite the appellate court rulings that have overturned previous convictions. Why should prosecutors bring cases in the face of negative precedent? Linda C. Fentiman, comparing the practice in the United States with that in Canada and France, concludes that the primary reason is that the U.S. elects prosecutors locally and does not subject them to any sort of centralized control. Thus in states where religious conservatives are powerful, these prosecutions thrive; indeed, they may be a necessity for reelection. See Fentiman, above, at 661; see also Linda C. Fentiman, Pursuing the Perfect Mother: Why America's Criminalization of Maternal Substance Abuse Is Not the Answer—A Comparative Legal Analysis, 15 Mich. J. Gender & Law 389 (2009). If pregnant mothers plead guilty, or do not have adequate resources to appeal, what is the result likely to be?

2. On what legal theories can punitive treatment of drug-addicted mothers be challenged? Can you construct an argument based on equal protection? See Julie B. Ehrlich, Breaking the Law By Giving Birth: The War on Drugs, The War on Reproductive Rights, and The War on Women, 32 N.Y.U. Rev. L. & Soc. Change 381, 406–19 (2008); Michelle Oberman, Sex, Drugs, Pregnancy, and the Law: Rethinking the Problems of Pregnant Women Who Use Drugs, 43 Hastings L.J. 505, 526–45 (1992). What arguments might you raise based on the right of privacy? See Note, Maternal Rights and Fetal Wrongs: The Case against the Criminalization of "Fetal Abuse," 101 Harv. L. Rev. 994 (1988). Do you see any due process problems? See Doretta Massardo McGinnis, Prosecution of Mothers of Drug–Exposed Babies: Constitutional and Criminal Theory, 139 U. Pa. L. Rev. 505, 508–16 (1990). Does it violate the cruel and unusual punishment clause of the Eighth Amendment? See Dawn Marie Korver, The Constitutionality of Punishing Pregnant Substance Abusers under Drug Trafficking Laws: The Criminalization of a Bodily Function, 32 B.C.L.Rev. 629, 656–60 (1991). See also Krista Stone–Manista, Protecting

Pregnant Women: A Guide to Successfully Challenging Criminal Child Abuse Prosecutions of Pregnant Drug Addicts, 99 J. Crim. L. & Criminology 823 (2009) (describing successful challenges based on statutory interpretation and lack of fair notice). What argument or arguments might you construct based on Justice Ginsburg's dissent in *Gonzalez*?

3. The most common legal action against drug-addicted mothers is one for child abuse, resulting in removal of the child from the mother's custody soon after birth (and possibly any other children she may have as well). In some states removal of the child is automatic, while others require more evidence of potential harm to the child. Ellen Marrus, Crack Babies and the Constitution: Ruminations about Addicted Pregnant Women after Ferguson v. City of Charleston, 47 Vill. L. Rev. 299, 328–38 (2002). Since these statutes have been in place, the numbers of children in foster care have skyrocketed. Once in the foster care system, only about 25% of children are ever returned to their mothers, who must negotiate a series of onerous requirements in an often unrealistic time frame in order to prevent termination of their parental rights. Id. at 334–36; Janet Ashley Murphy & Robert A. Pugsley, Successful Pregnancy Prevention Program for Addicts Remains under Siege, 5 J. L. Soc'y 155, 180 (2003). Many believe that the trauma of removal and placement in the overburdened foster care system outweighs the potential harm of remaining with a substance-abusing mother, who may in fact be an adequate mother. See Susan C. Boyd, Mothers and Illicit Drugs: Transcending the Myths 14–17 (1999) (describing studies demonstrating that women who use drugs can be adequate parents).

Given the criminal convictions and child abuse actions described above, it is not surprising that drug-addicted mothers are deterred from obtaining the prenatal care that might help them and their babies. Indeed, after the *Whitner* case, above note 1, in which an addicted mother was imprisoned, the number of pregnant women applying for substance abuse treatment in South Carolina declined by as much as 80%. David C. Brody & Heidee McMillin, Combating Fetal Substance Abuse and Governmental Foolhardiness through Collaborative Linkages, Therapeutic Jurisprudence and Common Sense: Helping Women Help Themselves, 12 Hastings Women's L.J. 243, 250 (2001). Infant mortality also increased in the state. Paltrow, Cohen & Carey, above note 1, at 9.

4. For an interesting study of the process by which drug use in pregnancy was discovered by the media as a social problem and then institutionalized both in the legislatures and prosecutors' offices, see Laura E. Gomez, Misconceiving Mothers: Legislators, Prosecutors, and the Politics of Prenatal Drug Exposure (1997). Gomez describes the 1987 Pamela Rae Stewart prosecution, in which a California woman was charged with taking drugs while pregnant, as having ignited a movement among feminists and their allies to defeat the generally very punitive reaction to this social problem. Id. at 42–62. The problem was initially portrayed as particular to poor women of color and connected to other social problems associated by many with this group, as well as to the fetal rights philosophy of the anti-abortion movement. Id. at 117–20. When feminist and reproductive rights groups portrayed it instead as a public health problem deserving of medical rather than criminal treatment, they

were successful, because they were able to define the problem as affecting the reproductive freedom of all women:

> [W]omen's problems are not universally medicalized, and problems linked to white, middle-class women are substantially more likely to be so categorized than those associated with poor or racial-minority women. Part of the strategy to medicalize rather than criminalize prenatal drug exposure, then, depended on recasting it as a more generic women's problem rather than as one limited to a subset of women presumably more apt to be viewed as having criminal propensities.

Id. at 122. Could this strategy be adapted to abortion? Is this a good idea?

5. As it turns out, the "cocaine baby epidemic" did not exist. The statistics about an increase in usage were unreliable, and further medical study has shown little evidence of the negative effects of cocaine use during pregnancy. See Ana Teresa Ortiz & Laura Briggs, The Culture of Poverty, Crack Babies, and Welfare Cheats: The Making of the "Healthy White Baby Crisis," 76 Social Text 39, 44–46 (2003). In most cases, damage is insignificant compared to that caused by drinking alcohol or smoking during pregnancy. Murphy & Pugsley, above note 3, at 156–62. Why do you think people were so willing to believe in the cocaine baby epidemic? Current prosecutions are more often aimed at users of methamphetamines, despite the lack of data showing a nexus between their use by pregnant mothers and damage to the fetus. Fentiman, note 1 above, 15 Mich. J. Gender & Law, at 396–97.

6. Wisconsin and South Dakota statutes also provide that women may be taken into custody if they are pregnant and abusing alcohol. Wis. Stat. § 48.193; S.D. Codified Laws § 34–20A–63. Are there reasons to distinguish between the legal treatment of drugs and alcohol? Between drugs and tobacco? What are they?

7. Professor John A. Robertson has argued that once a woman conceives and then makes the decision not to have an abortion, she loses the liberty to act in ways that would harm the fetus:

> The mother has, if she conceives and chooses not to abort, a legal and moral duty to bring the child into the world as healthy as is reasonably possible. She has a duty to avoid actions or omissions that will damage the fetus and child, just as she has a duty to protect the child's welfare once it is born until she transfers this duty to another.

Robertson, Procreative Liberty and the Control of Conception, Pregnancy, and Childbirth, 69 Va. L. Rev. 405, 438 (1983). What do you think of this argument? If a mother intentionally causes brain damage to her infant after birth, there is no question that she may be prosecuted for child abuse. What, if any, duties do you believe a pregnant woman has to the fetus she is carrying? Fetal surgery is now available to repair many potentially fatal conditions in utero. See Monica J. Casper, The Making of the Unborn Patient: A Social Anatomy of Fetal Surgery (1998) (describing the history, practice, conflicts, and ethical issues involved in fetal surgery). Could women be compelled to consent to prenatal surgery to save the life of a fetus? What constitutional issues are involved? See Rebekah R. Arch, The Maternal–Fetal

Rights Dilemma: Honoring A Woman's Choice of Medical Care during Pregnancy, 12 J. Contemp. Health L. & Pol'y 637 (1996).

8. Does the state have any obligations to the fetus of a drug-addicted mother? If so, is there any inconsistency with DeShaney v. Winnebago County Dep't of Social Services, 489 U.S. 189 (1989) (holding that the state has no obligation to intervene to protect a child from parental abuse, even abuse of which it is aware)? If the state has no obligation under *DeShaney* even *after* the child is born, why are we willing to impose so much on the mother before the child is born?

9. The problem of drug use by women is clearly a serious one. To address it, one must ask why women use drugs in the first place. Drug-addicted women tend to suffer from low self-esteem and severe depression. See Amin N. Daghestani, Psychosocial Characteristics of Pregnant Women Addicts in Treatment, in Drugs, Alcohol, Pregnancy and Parenting 7, 8, 11 (Ira J. Chasnoff, ed. 1988). Moreover, researchers estimate that 50% to 90% of all women drug abusers are victims of childhood sexual abuse. Dr. Ann Boyer, When Pregnant Women Use Drugs: What Are the Real Problems and What Can Society Do to Solve Them?, 5 J.L. Soc'y 137, 138 (2003). To recover from their addiction requires facing the painful memories of this abuse, as well as the reality of racism, sexism, and poverty. While addictive substances are readily accessible to mask this pain, drug rehabilitation is not as available. Moreover, addicts run a high risk of pregnancy. Low self-esteem, coupled with the fact that her partner may be abusive, renders the addicted woman less able to control the circumstances of intercourse, and many contraceptive methods are not well suited to the needs of addicted women. Oberman, above note 2, at 512–13. Are any of these facts legally relevant to defending an addicted mother against criminal charges? How might you raise them in her defense? What conclusions would you draw about the social policies appropriate to address the problem of addiction among young women?

Research shows that women and men in fact require different approaches to treatment, in part because the reasons that drove them to drugs tend to be different (e.g., women's history of physical or sexual violence and low self-esteem) and thus the therapy required is different. A review of 38 studies of treatment outcomes shows that women's outcomes are good in programs with child care, prenatal care, women-only programs, supplemental services and workshops addressing women-focused topics, mental health programming, and comprehensive programming (for example, to enable women who have been abused to live independently). Yet very few programs offer these services. Olivia Silber Ashley, Mary Ellen Marsden & Thomas M. Brady, Effectiveness of Substance Abuse Treatment Programming for Women: A Review, 29 Am. J. Drug & Alcohol Abuse 19, 23, 42 (2003).

10. As Dawn Johnsen describes in the excerpt above, the punitive approach is based on an adversarial model of the mother-child relationship, in which the mother and fetus are viewed as two distinct entities with separate and conflicting interests and rights. Catharine MacKinnon has suggested that the law has never adequately conceptualized either the woman's relationship to her fetus or the fetus itself, because they have been understood from a male perspective, "from the observing outsider." MacKinnon, Reflections on Sex

Equality Under Law, 100 Yale L.J. 1281, 1309 (1991). What do you think is an appropriate conceptualization of the entity represented by the pregnant woman? Are there any analogies or metaphors one could borrow from other fields of law? For a collection of feminist essays analyzing the construction of the fetus as a subject, see Fetal Subjects, Feminist Positions (Lynn M. Morgan & Meredith W. Michaels, eds. 1999).

11. It has been known for quite some time that drug use by the father also poses risks; for example, cocaine may attach itself to the sperm of men who use the drug and enter an egg at the moment of conception, thus damaging the fetus. Ricardo Yazigi, et al., Demonstrations of Specific Binding of Cocaine to Human Spermatozoa, 266 J. Am. Med. Ass'n 1956 (1991); see also Ehrlich, note 2 above, at 389–90. Why do you think people in general and the law in particular have assumed that the woman is the one to be held responsible for damage to the fetus rather than the man? Is it their breadwinner/childcarer roles? The male's distance from gestation? An image of women's bodies as more vulnerable than men's? See Sally Sheldon, *Re*Conceiving Masculinity: Imagining Men's Reproductive Bodies in Law, 26 J. L. & Soc'y 129, 138–45 (1999); Cynthia R. Daniels, Exposing Men: The Science and Politics of Male Reproduction 109–56 (2006). Daniels also points to the fact that research on the connection between fathers and fetal injury was not readily funded or published. Id. at 110.

What about people who smoke tobacco around pregnant women, now that it is clear that passive smoking can have negative effects on the fetus: should they be held liable for potential damage? Why or why not? What about a father who smokes around a pregnant woman? Around a child with asthma? Should the state prosecute him? Do these questions suggest an equal protection argument that could be made in cases of criminal prosecution of addicted mothers?

12. A pregnant woman seeking treatment for her addiction may have difficulty finding it. Some substance abuse treatment programs refuse to accept pregnant women because pregnancy poses additional challenges and may lead to liability; other programs simply do not have the ability to provide prenatal care. See Brody & McMillen, above note 3, at 262–63. Women with children are also not likely to enter a treatment program that does not accept children or, if it is an out-patient program, does not have child care. Yet only about 10% of programs offer child care. Ashley, Marsden & Brady, above note 9, at 23. Women on Medicaid may find it particularly difficult to find treatment during pregnancy; in 2000, 87% of the drug treatment programs in New York City did not provide treatment to Medicaid mothers addicted to crack. By 2010, 19 states had created or funded programs targeted at pregnant women, and nine give pregnant women priority access to publicly funded programs. Guttmacher Institute, State Policies in Brief: Substance Abuse During Pregnancy, June 1, 2010 (including a table detailing policies on substance abuse and treatment during pregnancy on a state-by-state basis). The need still outruns the supply. Class actions have been filed in two states about these issues. See Ehrlich, note 2 above at 383. How might you construct an argument based on equal protection against refusal to accept a pregnant addict into a program that is heavily reliant upon federal research funds?

13. Which of the feminist theories discussed in Chapter 3 is most helpful in analyzing the issues involved in society's treatment of drug-addicted mothers? Which is most helpful in making arguments to a court imposing sanctions upon an addicted mother? Which is, or are, most helpful in making arguments to the legislature?

14. Many women seeking prenatal care are battered women. Julie A. Gazmararian, et al., Prevalence of Violence Against Pregnant Women, 275 J. Am. Med. Ass'n 1915 (1996) (reviewing studies of violence during pregnancy which used differing methodologies and reporting rates of violence during pregnancy ranging from .9% to 20.1%, thus affecting 156,000 to 332,000 women per year). Should fathers who beat pregnant women be jailed for the duration of the pregnancy? By analogy to drug-addicted mothers, should fathers guilty of abusing the mother automatically have their custody rights terminated? See Deborah Tuerkheimer, Conceptualizing Violence Against Pregnant Women, 81 Ind. L. J. 667, 709–11 (2006) (suggesting criminalizing the harm of pregnancy battering).

E. FORCED CAESAREANS

JESSIE MAE JEFFERSON v. GRIFFIN SPALDING COUNTY HOSPITAL

Supreme Court of Georgia, 1981.
247 Ga. 86, 274 S.E.2d 457.

On Thursday, January 22, 1981, the Griffin Spalding County Hospital Authority petitioned the Superior Court of Butts County * * * for an order authorizing it to perform a caesarean section and any necessary blood transfusions upon the defendant, an out-patient resident of Butts County, in the event she presented herself to the hospital for delivery of her unborn child, which was due on or about Monday, January 26. * * *

On Friday, January 23, the Georgia Department of Human Resources, acting through the Butts County Department of Family and Children Services, petitioned the Juvenile Court of Butts County for temporary custody of the unborn child, alleging that the child was a deprived child without proper parental care necessary for his or her physical health, and praying for an order requiring the mother to submit to a caesarean section. After appointing counsel for the parents and for the child, the court conducted a joint hearing in both the superior court and juvenile court cases and entered the following order on the afternoon of January 23:

* * *

"Based on the evidence presented, the Court finds that Jessie Mae Jefferson is due to begin labor at any moment. There is a 99 to 100 percent certainty that the unborn child will die if she attempts to have the child by vaginal delivery. There is a 99 to 100 percent chance that the child will live if the baby is delivered by Caesarean section prior to the beginning of labor. There is a 50 percent chance that Mrs. Jefferson herself will die if vaginal delivery is attempted. There is an almost 100 percent chance that Mrs. Jefferson will survive if a delivery by Caesarean section is done prior to the beginning of labor. The Court finds that as a matter of fact the child is a human being fully capable of sustaining life independent of the mother.

"Mrs. Jefferson and her husband have refused and continue to refuse to give consent to a Caesarean section. This refusal is based entirely on the religious beliefs of Mr. and Mrs. Jefferson. * * *

"Based on these findings, the Court concludes and finds as a matter of law that this child is a viable human being and entitled to the protection of the Juvenile Court Code of Georgia. The Court concludes that this child is without the proper parental care and subsistence necessary for his or her physical life and health.

"Temporary custody of the unborn child is hereby granted to the State of Georgia Department of Human Resources and the Butts County Department of Family and Children Services. The Department shall have full authority to make all decisions, including giving consent to the surgical delivery appertaining to the birth of this child. The temporary custody of the Department shall terminate when the child has been successfully brought from its mother's body into the world or until the child dies, whichever shall happen."

IN RE A.C.

District of Columbia Court of Appeals, 1987.
533 A.2d 611.

A.C. was diagnosed with leukemia when she was thirteen years old. As part of her treatment, she underwent a number of major surgical procedures, therapy, and chemotherapy. When she was twenty-seven years old, after her cancer had been in remission for three years, A.C. married. At the time she became pregnant, she had not undergone chemotherapy for more than a year. In her fifteenth week of pregnancy, she was referred to the hospital's high-risk pregnancy clinic.

When A.C. was approximately twenty-five weeks pregnant, she went to her regularly scheduled prenatal visit complaining of shortness of breath and some pain in her back. Her physicians subsequently discovered that she had a tumor mass in her lung which was most likely a metastatic oxygenic carcinoma. She was admitted to the hospital on June 11 and her prognosis was terminal.

On June 15, during A.C.'s twenty-sixth week of pregnancy, A.C., her physicians, her mother, and her husband discussed the possibility of providing A.C. with radiation therapy or chemotherapy to relieve her pain and to continue her pregnancy. Her physicians believed that her unborn child's chances of viability would be greatly increased if it were delivered when it had reached twenty-eight weeks gestational age. By June 16, the date on which the hospital sought the declaratory order in the Superior

Court, A.C. had been heavily sedated so that she could continue to breathe. Her condition was declining, and the attending medical staff concluded that passive treatment was appropriate because the mother would not survive and the child's chances of survival were grim. The hospital administration then decided to test this decision in the Superior Court.

The trial court appointed counsel for A.C. and the fetus, respectively. The District of Columbia was permitted to intervene for the fetus as parens patriae. A hearing was held at the hospital and was transcribed.

There was some dispute about whether A.C. would have chosen to have a Caesarean section on June 16. Before she was sedated, A.C. indicated that she would choose to relinquish her life so that the fetus could survive should such a choice present itself at the fetus' gestational age of twenty-eight weeks. Her physicians never discussed with her what her choice would be if such a choice had to be made before the fetus reached the twenty-eight-week point. The fetus was suffering oxygen starvation and resultant rapid heart rate. There was at that point less than 20 percent chance that it would be afflicted with cerebral palsy, neurological defects, deafness and blindness. There was not a clear medical consensus on the course of A.C.'s treatment. Those physicians who objected to the proposed surgery did so because A.C. refused her consent to the procedure, not because the surgery was medically objectionable. One physician testified that he believed that A.C. would not have wanted to deliver a baby that might have to undergo the pain of having handicaps that are associated with premature delivery. Another physician believed that A.C. would not have refused permission for the Caesarean section to be performed. During the course of her pregnancy, however, A.C. was aware that a number of medications she was taking might harm the fetus. Nevertheless, she expressed a desire to her physicians to be kept as comfortable as possible throughout her pregnancy and to maintain the quality of her life.

The trial court determined that the fetus was viable and that the District of Columbia had an interest in protecting the potential life of the fetus. See Roe v. Wade, 410 U.S. 113 (1973). * * *

Shortly after the trial judge made his decision, A.C. was informed of it. She stated, during a period of lucidity, that she would agree to the surgery although she might not survive it. When another physician went to A.C. to verify her decision, she apparently changed her mind, mouthing the words, "I don't want it done." There was no explanation for either decision.

After our Clerk was advised of the desire to appeal, a telephonic hearing was had before a hastily assembled division of the court. The trial judge's findings were read to us, and we heard from counsel and an attending physician. The latter answered questions respecting the relative chances of survival of both A.C. and the fetus with and without the surgery. He also informed us of the rapid decline of A.C. and the need to proceed promptly with the surgery, if it was decided to do so. There was no time to have the transcript read or to do effective research. The atypical nature of the appellate hearing included our hearing directly from one of the physicians.

The court based its decision to deny a stay on the medical judgment that A.C. would not survive for a significant time after the surgery and that the fetus had a better, though slim, chance if taken before A.C.'s imminent death. If A.C. died before delivery, the fetus would die as well. Though A.C. might have lived twenty-four to forty-eight hours, the surgery might have hastened her death. The ordinary question of likelihood of ultimate success on the merits was deemed subsumed in the immediate necessity to balance the delicate interests of fetus survival with the mother's condition and options on her behalf.

[The operation was performed; both mother and child died soon after.]

* * *

It is appropriate here to state that this case is not about abortion. * * * [A]s a matter of law, the right of a woman to an abortion is different and distinct from her obligations to the fetus once she has decided not to timely terminate her pregnancy. With a viable fetus, a balancing of interests must replace the single interest of the mother, and as in this case, time can be a critical factor.

We next view this case within the context of its closest legal analogues: the right of an adult to refuse medical treatment and the right of a parent to refuse medical treatment on behalf of offspring.

* * *

The fundamental right to bodily integrity encompasses an adult's right to refuse medical treatment, even if the refusal will result in death. * * *

The state's interest in preserving life usually will not override an adult's right to refuse medical treatment. In most cases where a court orders an adult to receive medical treatment against his consent, it will be to protect innocent third parties who would be harmed by the adult's decision.

* * *

* * * Courts have used this reasoning to hold that parents may not withhold life-saving treatment from their children because of the parents' religious beliefs. The state may intervene even when a parent's refusal of medical treatment for his or her child does not place the child in danger of imminent death.

* * *

There is a significant difference, however, between a court authorizing medical treatment for a child already born and a child who is yet unborn, although the state has compelling interests in protecting the life and health of both children and viable unborn children. Where birth has occurred, the medical treatment does not infringe on the mother's right to bodily integrity. With an unborn child, the state's interest in preserving the health of the child may run squarely against the mother's interest in her bodily integrity.

It can be argued that the state may not infringe upon the mother's right to bodily integrity to protect the life or health of her unborn child unless to do so will not significantly affect the health of the mother and unless the child has a significant chance of being born alive. Performing Caesarean sections will, in most instances, have an effect on the condition of the mother. That effect may be temporary in otherwise normal patients. The surgery presents a number of common complications, including infection, hemorrhage, gastric aspiration of the stomach contents, and postoperative embolism. It also produces considerable discomfort. In some cases, the surgery will result in the mother's death.

Even though we recognize these considerations, we think they should not have been dispositive here. The Caesarean section would not significantly affect A.C.'s condition because she had, at best, two days left of sedated life; the complications arising from the surgery would not significantly alter that prognosis. The child, on the other hand, had a chance of surviving delivery, despite the possibility that it would be born handicapped. Accordingly, we concluded that the trial judge did not err in subordinating A.C.'s right against bodily intrusion to the interests of the unborn child and the state, and hence we denied the motion for stay.

IN RE A.C.

District of Columbia Court of Appeals, 1990 (en banc).
573 A.2d 1235.

We are confronted here with two profoundly difficult and complex issues. First, we must determine who has the right to decide the course of medical treatment for a patient who, although near death, is pregnant with a viable fetus. Second, we must establish how that decision should be made if the patient cannot make it for herself—more specifically, how a court should proceed when faced with a pregnant patient, in extremis, who is apparently incapable of making an informed decision regarding medical care for herself and her fetus. * * *

There was no evidence before the court showing that A.C. consented to, or even contemplated, a caesarean section before her twenty-eighth week of pregnancy. There was, in fact, considerable dispute as to whether she would have consented to an immediate caesarean delivery at the time the hearing was held. * * *

[The court found the case not to be moot, even though A.C. and her baby were dead, because the hospital treated high-risk pregnancy and was likely to face a similar situation again.]

[O]ur analysis of this case begins with the tenet common to all medical treatment cases: that any person has the right to make an informed choice, if competent to do so, to accept or forego medical treatment. * * *

In the same vein, courts do not compel one person to permit a significant intrusion upon his or her bodily integrity for the benefit of another person's health. McFall v. Shimp, 10 Pa. D. & C. 3d 90 (Allegheny County Ct. 1978). In McFall the court refused to order Shimp to donate bone marrow which was necessary to save the life of his cousin, McFall. * * * Even though Shimp's refusal would mean death for McFall, the court would not order Shimp to allow his body to be invaded. It has been suggested that fetal cases are different because a woman who "has chosen to lend her body to bring [a] child into the world" has an enhanced duty to assure the welfare of the fetus, sufficient even to require her to undergo caesarean surgery. Surely, however, a fetus cannot have rights in this respect superior to those of a person who has already been born.[8]

* * *

What we distill from the cases * * * is that every person has the right, under the common law and the Constitution, to accept or refuse medical treatment. This right of bodily integrity belongs equally to persons who are competent and persons who are not. Further, it matters not what the quality of a patient's life may be; the right of bodily integrity is not extinguished simply because someone is ill, or even at death's door. To protect that right against intrusion by others—family members, doctors, hospitals, or anyone else, however well-intentioned—we hold that a court must determine the patient's wishes by any means available, and must abide by those wishes unless there are truly extraordinary or compelling reasons to override them. When the patient is incompetent, or when the court is unable to determine competency, the substituted judgment procedure must be followed.

> [Under the doctrine of substituted judgment, the court attempts to determine what choice the individual would make, if competent, based upon her previously expressed opinions; typically, family members testify about the patient's opinions, predispositions and values.]

* * * The trial court never made any finding about A.C.'s competency to decide. Undoubtedly, during most of the proceedings below, A.C. was incompetent to make a treatment decision; that is, she was unable to give an informed consent based on her assessment of the risks and benefits of the contemplated surgery. The court knew from the evidence that A.C. was sedated and unconscious, and thus it could reasonably have found her

---

8. There are also practical consequences to consider. What if A.C. had refused to comply with a court order that she submit to a caesarean? Under the circumstances, she obviously could not have been held in civil contempt and imprisoned or required to pay a daily fine until compliance. Enforcement could be accomplished only through physical force or its equivalent. A.C. would have to be fastened with restraints to the operating table, or perhaps involuntarily rendered unconscious by forcibly injecting her with an anesthetic, and then subjected to unwanted major surgery. Such actions would surely give one pause in a civilized society, especially when A.C. had done no wrong.

incompetent to render an informed consent; however, it made no such finding. On the other hand, there was no clear evidence that A.C. was competent to render an informed consent after the trial court's initial order was communicated to her.

We think it is incumbent on any trial judge in a case like this, unless it is impossible to do so, to ascertain whether a patient is competent to make her own medical decisions. Whenever possible, the judge should personally attempt to speak with the patient and ascertain her wishes directly, rather than relying exclusively on hearsay evidence, even from doctors. It is improper to presume that a patient is incompetent. We have no reason to believe that, if competent, A.C. would or would not have refused consent to a caesarean. We hold, however, that without a competent refusal from A.C. to go forward with the surgery, and without a finding through substituted judgment that A.C. would not have consented to the surgery, it was error for the trial court to proceed to a balancing analysis, weighing the rights of A.C. against the interests of the state.

* * * An even more serious consequence of court-ordered intervention is that it drives women at high risk of complications during pregnancy and childbirth out of the health care system to avoid coerced treatment. Second, and even more compellingly, any judicial proceeding in a case such as this will ordinarily take place—like the one before us here—under time constraints so pressing that it is difficult or impossible for the mother to communicate adequately with counsel, or for counsel to organize an effective factual and legal presentation in defense of her liberty and privacy interests and bodily integrity. * * *

In this case A.C.'s court-appointed attorney was unable even to meet with his client before the hearing. By the time the case was heard, A.C.'s condition did not allow her to be present, nor was it reasonably possible for the judge to hear from her directly. The factual record, moreover, was significantly flawed because A.C.'s medical records were not before the court and because Dr. Jeffrey Moscow, the physician who had been treating A.C. for many years, was not even contacted and hence did not testify. Finally, the time for legal preparation was so minimal that neither the court nor counsel mentioned the doctrine of substituted judgment, which—with benefit of briefs, oral arguments, and above all, time—we now deem critical to the outcome of this case. * * *

NOTES ON FORCED CAESAREANS

1. The medical condition preventing Jessie Mae Jefferson from natural delivery was placenta previa, that is, the placenta had moved down near the cervix. After the court order, Ms. Jefferson did not return to the hospital, but the placenta shifted and a healthy baby was delivered naturally. Kenneth Jost, Mother versus Child, A.B.A. J. 84, 86 (Apr. 1989). What if the placenta had not moved? Is there any scenario in which you think compelled caesarean section is appropriate? Do you think that legal intervention is appropriate, for example, when a full-term baby is in the birth canal, the cord is wrapped

around her neck, and the parents are opposed to any surgical intervention? If there are some circumstances when compelled caesareans might be appropriate, what procedures would take into account the interests of all parties involved?

2. Does it make any difference if the parents' opposition is based, as it often is, upon religious grounds? See April L. Cherry, The Free Exercise Rights of Pregnant Women Who Refuse Medical Treatment, 69 Tenn. L. Rev. 563 (2002) (describing how both courts and scholars have paid insufficient attention in analyzing these cases to the compelling interest analysis required by the free exercise clause of the First Amendment).

3. One of the interesting aspects of the treatment of the Angela Carder (A.C.) case is the stark difference between the interests taken into account by the different levels of court. At the trial level, the testimony was primarily from doctors, and the court turned to Roe v. Wade's trimester analysis for precedent. By contrast, the en banc appeals court, with more time for briefing and consideration of the issues, considered the woman's rights and turned to an entirely different case law, that of informed consent, reenvisaging the pregnant woman as an autonomous decision-maker. What, if anything, does this say about (1) the treatment women can typically expect from trial level courts, and (2) the importance of litigating precedents concerning issues like this? What other reasons might there be for the difference between the different courts' judgments in this case?

4. Angela Carder's family also filed civil claims against the hospital for deprivation of human rights, discrimination, wrongful death, malpractice, and other claims arising out of the treatment of Ms. Carder; the suit was settled with a monetary award and the development of new policies by the hospital to affirm the autonomy of pregnant patients, announcing its intention to make similar decisions in the future within the doctor-patient relationship and not by involving the courts. ACLU, Reproductive Rights Update, Dec. 7, 1990, at 1–2. Can you think of other legal theories than those set out above and in the opinion upon which to defend women's autonomy in relation to decisions about pregnancy and childbirth? See, e.g., Michelle Oberman, Mothers and Doctors' Orders: Unmasking the Doctor's Fiduciary Role in Maternal–Fetal Conflicts, 94 Nw. U. L. Rev. 451 (2000) (arguing that the typical conflict arises not between mother and fetus but between mother and doctor, in breach of the doctor's fiduciary duty to his patient, and suggesting lawsuits for breach of fiduciary duty as a potential remedy). See also Lidia Hoffman & Monica K. Miller, Inconsistent State Court Rulings Concerning Pregnancy–Related Behaviors, 22 J.L. & Health 279, 281–87 (2009) (describing approaches based on the right to self-determination and bodily integrity, privacy, free exercise of religion, and pregnant women's right to protect their health and lives).

5. Courts in other jurisdictions continued to force caesarean sections and other types of medical treatment upon unconsenting pregnant women. In one case, a woman was seized at home and compelled to return to the hospital for a caesarean section she had refused; the court upheld this decision because the medical testimony had assessed the risk of death from a vaginal delivery after a previous caesarean section as unacceptably high. See, e.g, Pemberton

v. Tallahassee Memorial Regional Medical Center, 66 F. Supp. 2d 1247 (N.D. Fla. 1999). In another case, a woman who refused a transfusion on religious grounds was compelled to submit to one because of the risk to her fetus even though it was not yet viable. In re Jamaica Hospital, 491 N.Y.S.2d 898 (Sup. Ct. 1985). But see In re Baby Boy Doe, 632 N.E.2d 326 (Ill. App. 1994) (refusing to compel a blood transfusion or caesarean for the sake of a viable fetus). In 2004, moreover, Melissa Rowland, a Utah woman, was charged with capital murder because she refused a caesarean section and one of her twins was born dead; after three months in jail, she pled guilty to felony child endangerment. See Linda C. Fentiman, Pursuing the Perfect Mother: Why America's Criminalization of Maternal Substance Abuse Is Not the Answer—A Comparative Legal Analysis, 15 Mich. J. Gender & Law 389, 404–05 (2009).

How may recent developments in the law of abortion by the Supreme Court affect these cases? Should abortion law, relevant to the circumstances when the state may prohibit a woman from aborting a fetus, control in these cases? Why or why not?

6. Most of the cases in which court orders have been sought to compel caesareans involved women who were African American, Asian, or Hispanic, some of whom were immigrant and/or belonged to religious minorities; and most of the women were being treated in a teaching hospital clinic or were receiving public aid. Why are non-white and poor women at a significantly greater risk of this type of compelled medical treatment? See Lisa C. Ikemoto, Furthering the Inquiry: Race, Class, and Culture in the Forced Medical Treatment of Pregnant Women, 59 Tenn. L. Rev. 487, 510–16 (1992) (pointing to the authoritarian nature of medical institutions, the imposition of notions of "good" and "bad" mothers, and the failure to attend to the voice of the woman or to the cultural context of birth). See also Joanne E. Brosh & Monica K. Miller, Regulating Pregnancy Behaviors: How the Constitutional Rights of Minority Women Are Disproportionately Compromised, 16 Am. U.J. Gender Soc. Pol'y & Law 437, 447–51 (2008) (arguing that minority women have lower levels of trust in the medical system and also do not believe that they have the ability to perform behaviors necessary to avoid negative health outcomes).

7. To what extent have the problems presented by forced caesareans been caused by the interaction of new technology and the standard of care in medical malpractice cases? Just because a certain technology is available, does a doctor have to use it? See, e.g., Nancy K. Rhoden, The Judge in the Delivery Room: The Emergence of Court–Ordered Caesareans, 74 Calif. L. Rev. 1951, 2010–23 (1986). Women who are older or who have previously given birth by caesarean section are frequently pressured into having c-sections that they do not desire. Do fears of malpractice liability drive the decisions of doctors and hospitals even where it may involve violating the rights of their patients to make informed decisions about their own medical care? See Lisa L. Chalidze, Misinformed Consent: Non–Medical Bases for American Birth Recommendations as a Human Rights Issue, 54 N.Y.L. Sch. L. Rev. 59 (2009–10); Sylvia A. Law, Childbirth: An Opportunity for Choice That Should Be Supported, 32 N.Y.U. Rev. L. & Soc. Change 345 (2008).

8. This chapter has discussed a large number of attempts to control women in relation to the conception, gestation, and birth of children—restrictions on abortion, compelled contraception, sterilization abuse, a wide variety of "fetal protection" measures, punitive measures taken against drug-addicted mothers, and forced caesareans. Lisa C. Ikemoto has argued that the ideology of motherhood, combined with a tendency to defer to those with "scientific" knowledge, is being transformed by these measures into a "Code of Perfect Pregnancy," institutionalized as legal duties. Ikemoto, The Code of Perfect Pregnancy: At the Intersection of the Ideology of Motherhood, The Practice of Defaulting to Science, and The Interventionist Mindset of Law, 53 Ohio State L.J. 1205 (1992). The resulting model of the good mother, moreover, looks very like the image of a white, middle-class mother and measures "outgroup women" against this standard. Id. at 1305. To the extent that you agree with this description, what may explain this phenomenon?

9. Given recent developments, would you say that women have more, or less, reproductive freedom than they had three decades ago? Which women? See Beth A. Burkstrand–Reid, The Invisible Woman: Availability and Culpability in Reproductive Health Jurisprudence, 81 U. Colo. L. Rev. 97 (2010). Note, for example, that in one case, a mother lost custody of her infant because she refused to consent to a C-section, despite the fact that the child was born vaginally without incident. New Jersey Div. of Youth & Fam. Servs. v. V.M., 974 A.2d 448 (N.J. App. Div. 2009).

F. "SURROGATE" MOTHERHOOD

IN THE MATTER OF BABY M

Supreme Court of New Jersey, 1988.
109 N.J. 396, 537 A.2d 1227.

In February 1985, William Stern and Mary Beth Whitehead entered into a surrogacy contract. It recited that Stern's wife, Elizabeth, was infertile, that they wanted a child, and that Mrs. Whitehead was willing to provide that child as the mother with Mr. Stern as the father.

The contract provided that through artificial insemination using Mr. Stern's sperm, Mrs. Whitehead would become pregnant, carry the child to term, bear it, deliver it to the Sterns, and thereafter do whatever was necessary to terminate her maternal rights so that Mrs. Stern could thereafter adopt the child. * * * Although Mrs. Stern was not a party to the surrogacy agreement, the contract gave her sole custody of the child in the event of Mr. Stern's death. * * *

Mr. Stern, on his part, agreed to attempt the artificial insemination and to pay Mrs. Whitehead $10,000 after the child's birth, on its delivery to him. * * *

* * * William and Elizabeth Stern were married in July 1974, having met at the University of Michigan, where both were Ph.D. candidates. Due to financial considerations and Mrs. Stern's pursuit of a medical degree and residency, they decided to defer starting a family until 1981. Before

then, however, Mrs. Stern learned that she might have multiple sclerosis and that the disease in some cases renders pregnancy a serious health risk. Her anxiety appears to have exceeded the actual risk, which current medical authorities assess as minimal. Nonetheless that anxiety was evidently quite real, Mrs. Stern fearing that pregnancy might precipitate blindness, paraplegia, or other forms of debilitation. Based on the perceived risk, the Sterns decided to forego having their own children. The decision had special significance for Mr. Stern. Most of his family had been destroyed in the Holocaust. As the family's only survivor, he very much wanted to continue his bloodline.

* * *

* * * Mrs. Whitehead's response apparently resulted from her sympathy with family members and others who could have no children (she stated that she wanted to give another couple the "gift of life"); she also wanted the $10,000 to help her family.

* * *

Mrs. Whitehead realized, almost from the moment of birth, that she could not part with this child. She had felt a bond with it even during pregnancy. Some indication of the attachment was conveyed to the Sterns at the hospital when they told Mrs. Whitehead what they were going to name the baby. She apparently broke into tears and indicated that she did not know if she could give up the child. She talked about how the baby looked like her other daughter, and made it clear that she was experiencing great difficulty with the decision.

Nonetheless, Mrs. Whitehead was, for the moment, true to her word. Despite powerful inclinations to the contrary, she turned her child over to the Sterns on March 30 [1986] at the Whiteheads' home.

* * *

Later in the evening of March 30, Mrs. Whitehead became deeply disturbed, disconsolate, stricken with unbearable sadness. She had to have her child. She could not eat, sleep, or concentrate on anything other than her need for her baby. The next day she went to the Sterns' home and told them how much she was suffering.

The depth of Mrs. Whitehead's despair surprised and frightened the Sterns. She told them that she could not live without her baby, that she must have her, even if only for one week, that thereafter she would surrender her child. The Sterns, concerned that Mrs. Whitehead might indeed commit suicide, not wanting under any circumstances to risk that, and in any event believing that Mrs. Whitehead would keep her word, turned the child over to her. * * *

[When the child was not returned, Mr. Stern filed suit to enforce the surrogacy contract, and the Whiteheads fled to Florida with Baby M; the Sterns traced the baby to her grandparents' home in Florida, filed supplementary proceedings, and forcibly removed the child, who was returned to New Jersey and turned over to the Sterns.]

* * * Soon after the conclusion of the [two-month] trial, the trial court * * * held that the surrogacy contract was valid; ordered that Mrs. Whitehead's parental rights be terminated and that sole custody of the child be granted to Mr. Stern; and, after hearing brief testimony from Mrs. Stern, immediately entered an order allowing the adoption of Melissa by Mrs. Stern, all in accordance with the surrogacy contract. * * *

II. INVALIDITY AND UNENFORCEABILITY OF SURROGACY CONTRACT

* * *

The surrogacy contract conflicts with: (1) laws prohibiting the use of money in connection with adoptions; (2) laws requiring proof of parental unfitness or abandonment before termination of parental rights is ordered or an adoption is granted; and (3) laws that make surrender of custody and consent to adoption revocable in private placement adoptions.

* * *

[First,] Mr. Stern knew he was paying for the adoption of a child; Mrs. Whitehead knew she was accepting money so that a child might be adopted; the Infertility Center knew that it was being paid for assisting in the adoption of a child. * * * It strains credulity to claim that these arrangements, touted by those in the surrogacy business as an attractive alternative to the usual route leading to an adoption, really amount to something other than a private placement adoption for money.

* * *

[Second,] where there has been no written surrender to an approved agency * * *, termination of parental rights will not be granted in this state absent a very strong showing of abandonment or neglect. That showing is required in every context in which termination of parental rights is sought, * * * even where the petitioning adoptive parent is, as here, a stepparent. * * *

[Third,] [t]he provision in the surrogacy contract whereby the mother irrevocably agrees to surrender custody of her child and to terminate her parental rights * * * is one more indication of the essential nature of this transaction: the creation of a contractual system of termination and adoption designed to circumvent our statutes.

* * *

The surrogacy contract's invalidity * * * is further underlined when its goals and means are measured against New Jersey's public policy. The contract's basic premise, that the natural parents can decide in advance of birth which one is to have custody of the child, bears no relationship to the settled law that the child's best interests shall determine custody. * * *

The surrogacy contract guarantees permanent separation of the child from one of its natural parents. Our policy, however, has long been that to the extent possible, children should remain with and be brought up by both of their natural parents. * * *

The surrogacy contract violates the policy of this State that the rights of natural parents are equal concerning their child, the father's right no greater than the mother's. * * * The whole purpose and effect of the surrogacy contract was to give the father the exclusive right to the child by destroying the rights of the mother.

* * *

Under the contract, the natural mother is irrevocably committed before she knows the strength of her bond with her child. She never makes a totally voluntary, informed decision, for quite clearly any decision prior to the baby's birth is, in the most important sense, uninformed, and any decision after that, compelled by a pre-existing contractual commitment, the threat of a lawsuit, and the inducement of a $10,000 payment, is less than totally voluntary. Her interests are of little concern to those who controlled this transaction.

* * *

Worst of all, however, is the contract's total disregard of the best interests of the child. There is not the slightest suggestion that any inquiry will be made at any time to determine the fitness of the Sterns as custodial parents, of Mrs. Stern as an adoptive parent, their superiority to Mrs. Whitehead, or the effect on the child of not living with her natural mother.

This is the sale of a child, or, at the very least, the sale of a mother's right to her child, the only mitigating factor being that one of the purchasers is the father. Almost every evil that prompted the prohibition on the payment of money in connection with adoptions exists here.

* * *

Intimated, but disputed, is the assertion that surrogacy will be used for the benefit of the rich at the expense of the poor. In response it is noted that the Sterns are not rich and the Whiteheads not poor. Nevertheless, it is clear to us that it is unlikely that surrogate mothers will be as proportionately numerous among those women in the top twenty percent income bracket as among those in the bottom twenty percent. Put differently, we doubt that infertile couples in the low-income bracket will find upper income surrogates.

In any event, even in this case one should not pretend that disparate wealth does not play a part simply because the contrast is not the dramatic "rich versus poor." At the time of trial, the Whiteheads' net assets were probably negative—Mrs. Whitehead's own sister was foreclosing on a second mortgage. Their income derived from Mr. Whitehead's labors. Mrs. Whitehead is a homemaker, having previously held part-time jobs. The Sterns are both professionals, she a medical doctor, he a biochemist. Their combined income when both were working was about $89,500 a year and their assets sufficient to pay for the surrogacy contract arrangements.

The point is made that Mrs. Whitehead agreed to the surrogacy arrangement, supposedly fully understanding the consequences. Putting aside the issue of how compelling her need for money may have been, and how significant her understanding of the consequences, we suggest that her consent is irrelevant. There are, in a civilized society, some things that money cannot buy. * * *

[The surrogacy contract was thus found to be unenforceable as against public policy.]

* * *

V. CUSTODY

* * * With the surrogacy contract disposed of [having been found unenforceable], the legal framework becomes a dispute between two couples over the custody of a child produced by the artificial insemination of one couple's wife by the other's husband. Under the Parentage Act the claims of the natural father and the natural mother are entitled to equal weight * * *. The applicable rule given these circumstances is clear: the child's best interests determine custody.

* * *

Our custody conclusion is based on strongly persuasive testimony contrasting both the family life of the Whiteheads and the Sterns and the personalities and characters of the individuals. The stability of the Whitehead family life was doubtful at the time of trial. Their finances were in serious trouble (foreclosure by Mrs. Whitehead's sister on a second mortgage was in process). Mr. Whitehead's employment, though relatively steady, was always at risk because of his alcoholism, a condition that he seems not to have been able to confront effectively. Mrs. Whitehead had not worked for quite some time, her last two employments having been part-time. One of the Whiteheads' positive attributes was their ability to bring up two children, and apparently well, even in so vulnerable a household. Yet substantial question was raised even about that aspect of their home life. The expert testimony contained criticism of Mrs. Whitehead's handling of her son's educational difficulties. Certain of the experts noted that Mrs. Whitehead perceived herself as omnipotent and omniscient concerning her children. She knew what they were thinking, what they wanted, and she spoke for them. As to Melissa, Mrs. Whitehead expressed the view that she alone knew what that child's cries and sounds meant. Her inconsistent stories about various things engendered grave doubts about her ability to explain honestly and sensitively to Baby M—and at the right time—the nature of her origin. Although faith in professional counseling is not a sine qua non of parenting, several experts believed that Mrs. Whitehead's contempt for professional help, especially professional psychological help, coincided with her feelings of omnipotence in a way that could be devastating to a child who most likely will need such help. In short, while love and affection there would be, Baby M's life with the Whiteheads promised to be too closely controlled by Mrs. Whitehead. The prospects for wholesome, independent psychological growth and development would be at serious risk.

The Sterns have no other children, but all indications are that their household and their personalities promise a much more likely foundation for Melissa to grow and thrive. There is a track record of sorts—during the one-and-a-half years of custody Baby M has done very well, and the relationship between both Mr. and Mrs. Stern and the baby has become very strong. The household is stable, and likely to remain so. Their finances are more than adequate, their circle of friends supportive, and their marriage happy. Most important, they are loving, giving, nurturing, and open-minded people. They have demonstrated the wish and ability to nurture and protect Melissa, yet at the same time to encourage her independence. Their lack of experience is more than made up for by a willingness to learn and to listen, a willingness that is enhanced by their professional training, especially Mrs. Stern's experience as a pediatrician. They are honest; they can recognize error, deal with it, and learn from it. They will try to determine rationally the best way to cope with problems in their relationship with Melissa. When the time comes to tell her about her origins, they will probably have found a means of doing so that accords with the best interests of Baby M. All in all, Melissa's future appears solid, happy, and promising with them.

[The court awarded custody to the Sterns but held that Mrs. Whitehead was entitled to visitation at some point, to be determined by the trial court.[b]]

NOTES ON BABY M

1. What are the similarities and differences between a surrogacy arrangement and an adoption? See Margaret Jane Radin, Market–Inalienability, 100 Harv. L. Rev. 1849, 1928–29 (1987). Isn't adoption frequently motivated by economic reasons as well?

2. The trial court in *Baby M* had decided the case as one of contract law. After finding that the agreement was not unconscionable or voidable for fraud, it held that Mary Beth Whitehead had breached the contract. Finding that to do so was in the child's best interest, the court ordered specific performance, terminating Mrs. Whitehead's parental rights. In the Matter of Baby M., 525 A.2d 1128 (N.J. Super. 1987). Thus, in both the *Baby M* case and the *A.C.* case, excerpted above, the trial court appears to have ignored basic principles of law: in *Baby M,* principles governing custody, adoption, and

b. The court ordered that Whitehead should have visitation two days a week, every other weekend, and two weeks each summer. See Susan Squire, Whatever Happened to Baby M?, Redbook, Jan. 1994, at 60, 64.

termination of parental rights, and in *A.C.*, the doctrine of informed consent. Why do you think this was so? Is it because the rights of a woman were at stake? Or those of a child? (The time constraints that applied in *A.C.* cannot explain *Baby M,* for the two-month trial attracted a great deal of attention and legal discussion. Mary Beth Whitehead's interests were vigorously pressed at every stage, and many feminists became involved as amici curiae in the New Jersey Supreme Court.)

3. How did considerations of class affect the court's conclusion in *Baby M?* Do you agree with the assumption that low-income infertile women are unlikely to find upper-income surrogates? If so, what conclusions can be drawn from this fact? Was the income differential between the two parties here used differently by the court when it determined the validity of the contract, on the one hand, and when it decided the custody question, on the other? Is the court's treatment of the disparity consistent with usual principles of contract law (which typically do not take the economic positions of the contracting parties into account) and of family law (where custody determinations are not supposed to rest on wealth)? How or how not? Did class considerations determine the outcome in *Baby M?*

4. How was the court's decision to award custody to the Sterns affected, or not affected, by each of the following factors: class bias, cultural bias, bias in favor of a particular parenting style, bias in favor of professionals, especially doctors and psychiatrists, and bias created by the length of the appellate period?

5. Did Mary Beth Whitehead win this case or lose it? What, if any, problems stem from the Parentage Act's provision that the rights of the natural mother and the natural father are to be given equal weight? Should that principle apply differently in the surrogacy situation? How might it be inapt in other situations as well?

6. How should the fact that Mr. Stern's family perished in the Holocaust count in a court's decision of this case? Do you think it influenced the decision here? What about Mrs. Stern's unwillingness to be pregnant, which appears to have been based upon unfounded fears?

7. For a more detailed description of the individuals involved in the *Baby M.* case and of their motivations, see Carol Sanger, Developing Markets in Baby–Making: In the Matter of Baby M., 30 Harv. J.L. & Gender 67 (2007). Sanger believes that the case resulted in so much anguish and litigation because of negligence on the part of the surrogacy broker—specifically, failure to reveal or pay attention to the psychologist's report after interviewing Mary Beth Whitehead that she might have difficulty giving up the child and failure to disclose to Mary Beth that Mrs. Stern was not infertile—and suggests that some of these problems may have receded with the arrival of women as brokers. See id. at 88–95. What types of screening do you think is appropriate of (1) potential surrogate mothers, and (2) families wanting to hire a surrogate?

8. Whatever screening is currently carried on in the United States is by fertility clinics, who refuse about four percent of applicants each year, three percent due to medical concerns and one percent due to psychosocial concerns. Richard F. Storrow, The Bioethics of Prospective Parenthood: In Pursuit of

the Proper Standard for Gatekeeping in Infertility Clinics, 28 Cardozo L. Rev. 2283, 2286 (2007). Because these clinics are largely unregulated in the United States, the standards for approval vary substantially. Storrow argues that any standard based on child welfare should be defined solely in terms of potential harm to the child, measured by parental fitness law, and should not extend to any sort of best interests analysis, which is inappropriate to the preconception context because it depends on judgments about maximizing the interests of a particular child in a particular setting. A best interests standard is also prone to arbitrary and discriminatory decisions, such as to exclude single persons or gays and lesbians. For these reasons, after more than a decade of regulation under the Human Fertilisation and Embryology Act of 1990, which incorporated a more general child welfare analysis, the United Kingdom conducted a study of clinical screening practices and determined in 2005 that nothing beyond fitness screening should be allowed. Id. at 2316–17. Which of these approaches seems most appropriate?

9. The precise problem that occurred in *Baby M.* is much less likely to occur now that 95% of surrogacy arrangements are gestational—that is, a fertilized embryo is implanted in the surrogate mother, who bears no genetic relationship to the child she bears. Sanger, above note 7, at 79. The next case shows how this has changed the nature of the litigation that continues to arise.

TEXT NOTE: FEMINISM AND SURROGACY

Like Mary Beth Whitehead, the first legal surrogate mother, Elizabeth Kane, regretted her decision, went into a major depression touched off by giving up the child, and believed that her decision had a severely negative impact on her other children.[21] Surrogacy, she wrote, "is nothing more than the transference of pain from one woman to another. One woman is in anguish because she cannot become a mother, and another woman may suffer for the rest of her life because she cannot know the child she bore for someone else."[22] Others point out that this situation is no different from adoption and allege that fewer surrogate mothers regret their decision than mothers who give up children for adoption.[23] Lori Andrews argues that prohibiting women from entering into prenatal surrogacy contracts is similar to 19th-century views of women as incompetent to enter into contracts and reflects stereotypes of women as emotional and driven by hormonally caused irrationality.[24] By contrast, sperm donors are regularly held to the pre-conception sale of their parental rights.[25]

Those seeking to obtain genetic children through surrogacy arrangements are almost entirely white married couples in their late thirties or early forties,

---

21. See Elizabeth Kane, Birth Mother: The Story of America's First Legal Surrogate Mother 274–83 (1988).

22. Id. at 275.

23. Lori B. Andrews, Surrogate Motherhood: The Challenge for Feminists, in Surrogate Motherhood 167, 171 (Larry Gostin, ed. 1990) (alleging, without supporting citations, that only 1% of surrogate mothers regret their decision).

24. Id. at 172–73.

25. Id. at 170.

generally well-off and well-educated.[26] Some feminists have expressed concerns that poor women and women of color will be exploited as "breeders."[27] By contrast, Carmel Shalev argues that "A free market [in surrogacy] would allow a new source of productive activity for women who presently have limited income-earning opportunities, with two positive distributive effects: a shift of wealth from the childless consumers to the presumably less advantaged reproducers, and a reallocation of economic returns away from the exploiting intermediaries to the birth mothers."[28]

Since 2002 India has developed a major industry in providing surrogate mothers to persons from countries where ART is subject to restrictions or where it is much more expensive. The cost of surrogacy in the United States can be as high as "$80,000, with about $15,000 going to the surrogate mother and another $30,000 to the surrogacy agency," whereas the cost in India is $10,000 to $30,000, with about $7,500 (nonetheless a substantial sum in India) going to the surrogate.[29] The expectant surrogates are often housed and cared for by the fertility clinic in India, so as to ensure their proper nutrition and prenatal care. To prevent potential problems, the same woman is not allowed to serve as an egg donor and gestational surrogate.[30]

There are a wide variety of approaches states may choose in deciding how to treat surrogacy—for example, making surrogacy contracts enforceable, making them voidable but requiring the payment of damages for breach, making all such contracts void, or even criminalizing surrogacy arrangements. To address concerns about exploitation, especially of gestational mothers (where a woman essentially serves as the "incubator" for the fertilized egg of another couple), and about the negative impact of surrogacy upon adoption, Martha Field has suggested the following approach: Surrogacy contracts should be permitted but non-enforceable. The birth mother could change her mind during pregnancy or shortly after, but the genetic father would be liable for child support, thus creating a disincentive for surrogacy arrangements.[31] Moreover, rather than beginning a child's life with a custody struggle, a bright-line rule would dictate that custody of newborns be given to the birth mother. In this way, surrogacy would remain an option for some, yet society would not encourage an arrangement that has no net social benefit, especially in light of the need for adoptive parents.[32]

More typically, commentators suggest that a variety of surrogacy arrangements be allowed but that the "baby market" be heavily regulated so as to protect egg donors, surrogates, children born though the use of ART, and

---

26. R. Alta Charo, Legislative Approaches to Surrogate Motherhood, in Surrogate Motherhood 88, 88–89 (Larry Gostin, ed. 1990).

27. See, e.g., Gena Corea, The Mother Machine 213–49, 272–82 (1988).

28. Carmel Shalev, Birth Power: The Case for Surrogacy 158 (1989).

29. Jennifer Rimm, Comment, Booming Baby Business: Regulating Commercial Surrogacy in India, 30 U. Pa. J. Int'l L. 1429, 1444 (2009); Amelia Gentleman, India Nurtures Business of Surrogate Motherhood, N.Y. Times, Mar. 10, 2008, at A9.

30. Usha Rengachary Smerdon, Crossing Bodies, Crossing Borders: International Surrogacy Between the United States and India, 39 Cumb. L. Rev. 15, 50 (2008–09).

31. Martha A. Field, Surrogacy Contracts: Gestational and Traditional: The Argument for Nonenforcement, 31 Washburn L.J. 1, 5–13 (1991).

32. See also Martha A. Field, Surrogate Motherhood (1990).

intended parents who belong to groups that may be subject to discrimination. For example, Sonia M. Suter argues that egg donors should be protected by enhanced requirements for informed consent modeled on the type of consent required from human subjects of research and that include disclosure not only of all the possible medical risks (which are substantial for egg donors as well as surrogates) but also of psychological risks.[33] Because the fertility industry is so profit-driven, these requirements will need to be backed up by uniform legislation, such as that passed by New York State to fully inform egg donors, and model consent forms.[34] Better yet, Suter argues, might be a system such as that in England, where a centralized regulatory body, the Human Fertilisation and Embryology Authority, sets requirements and regulations, thus shifting the focus from profit to something more like a public-health model.[35] To protect children, Suter suggests prohibiting anonymity of donors, so that the children of ART may, upon request, obtain genetic information that could be necessary to their future health and also seek out their genetic parents, as adopted children often do, to satisfy their inherent need for self-identity.[36] Discriminatory barriers to access on the part of potential parents, she opines, would need to be prohibited by civil rights laws' adding the provision of fertility services to what is covered by laws prohibiting discrimination based on race or other minority status and marital status and sexual orientation.[37] This has in fact occurred in the state of California, where a fertility clinic that denied services to a lesbian woman was found to have violated the state civil rights law, which in California includes discrimination based on sexual orientation.[38] Most other states would not reach a similar conclusion, however.

Another scholar, Kimberly D. Krawiec, argues that the baby market should be less rather than more regulated. Existing bans on baby selling that require payments to surrogates to be styled as reimbursements and payment for expenses, legal uncertainty about the enforceability of surrogacy contracts, and caps on payments for donor eggs (despite a lively market in designer eggs, Ivy League eggs, and the like), she argues, simply limit the ability of suppliers (typically called "donors" to emphasize the altruistic nature of their services) to share in the profits generated by their labor, which are largely reserved for the middlemen.[39]

NOTES ON FEMINISM AND SURROGACY

1. Mary Beth Whitehead obviously suffered an intense depression touched off by the loss of giving up her birth child, yet Lori Andrews alleges that few surrogate mothers regret their decisions, many fewer than experi-

33. Suter, Giving in to Baby Markets: Regulation Without Prohibition, 16 Mich. J. Gender & L. 217, 237–51 (2009).

34. Id. at 248–49.

35. Id. at 252, 257–58.

36. Id. at 260–77.

37. Id. at 283–91.

38. North Coast Women's Care Medical Group v. Superior Ct., 189 P.3d 959 (Cal. 2008).

39. Krawiec, Altruism and Intermediation in the Market for Babies, 66 Wash. & Lee L. Rev. 203 (2009).

ence major grief over giving up children for adoption. Does it matter how few, if the loss is extreme for some women? Might this perhaps support having nonenforceable contracts, as Martha Field suggests, since most women would go through with the arrangement anyway? On the other hand, should some women's difficulty handling the loss result in prohibiting the arrangement for all women? How do you distinguish this situation from abortion, which, as Justice Kennedy points out in *Gonzalez,* some women may also experience as a loss and occasion for mourning? Is this a problem that could be dealt with simply by psychological screening of potential surrogate mothers?

2. Should sperm donorship and surrogate motherhood be treated similarly, as Lori Andrews argues, or differently, as the *Baby M* court concluded, based upon the different amounts of time invested by the sperm donor and surrogate mother? Do you find the court's analysis of this distinction an adequate one? Does it make a difference if your view of the parent-child relationship is based on biology, genetics, or property notions? What if your theory of property is based upon a labor theory of value (basing the value of a commodity upon the labor mixed with it)? See, e.g., John Locke, Second Treatise on Civil Government, ch. 5, § 27 (1690). How does it change things if you subscribe instead to an exchange theory of value, whereby the value of a commodity is determined by the law of supply and demand? What about property rights conceived as relational? See Margaret Jane Radin, Property and Personhood, 34 Stan. L. Rev. 957 (1982). How, if at all, does the application of these theories change if the surrogacy is gestational rather than genetic?

3. Surrogacy has been analogized, variously, to babyselling (because money is exchanged in the transaction), slavery (because of the surrogate mother's position as a "breeder" for another couple), and prostitution (because of the payment for use of the surrogate's body). Should one be able to sell any of these things—a baby, one's body, a body part? How does surrogacy compare to, and contrast with, prostitution?

4. What is likely to happen if we prohibit surrogacy? Might it continue to exist nonetheless? Would it be harder or easier to protect the most vulnerable potential surrogates if surrogacy is not prohibited and thus can be regulated? What regulations would you suggest? How much should the woman be paid and when? What other regulations are necessary to prevent exploitation? Should the children born of surrogacy be permitted to trace their birth mothers, and vice versa? How about the children of sperm donors? What if they need genetic information relevant to their own health?

5. What do you think of Martha Field's argument that surrogacy contracts should be permitted but nonenforceable? Does this compromise adequately balance the interests of all the parties involved? Do you think it appropriate to expand the interests considered beyond the immediate parties, to consider the interests, for example, of children who might otherwise not be adopted? What is your opinion of Sonia Suter's suggestions for regulation of the baby market industry? Does the requirement for informed-consent disclosure to egg donors and surrogates resemble recent abortion statutes criticized in the previous section? Would a system of centralized regulation such as that in England be possible here? Experience has shown that patients seeking

services merely go to the states with the most liberal standards. Is more regulation the answer, or less, as Kimberly Krawiec argues?

6. How would the course of the *Baby M* case have been changed if the principles Martha Field suggests had been in effect? Would there have been any case at all? How would the actions of the parties have been influenced, do you think? What if the regulations proposed by Sonia Suter had been the law in New Jersey?

7. How would proponents of the various feminist theories presented in Chapter 3 approach the surrogacy issue?

8. Is it fair to make a father who is party to a surrogacy arrangement that falls through pay child support? Why or why not? What rules should govern a surrogacy contract if the child born pursuant to it is born with a disability? See Angela R. Holder, Surrogate Motherhood and the Best Interests of Children, in Surrogate Motherhood 79–80 (Larry Gostin, ed. 1990).

JOHNSON v. CALVERT

Supreme Court of California, In Bank, 1993.
5 Cal.4th 84, 851 P.2d 776, 19 Cal.Rptr.2d 494.

* * *

Mark and Crispina Calvert are a married couple who desired to have a child. Crispina was forced to undergo a hysterectomy in 1984. Her ovaries remained capable of producing eggs, however, and the couple eventually considered surrogacy. In 1989 Anna Johnson heard about Crispina's plight from a coworker and offered to serve as a surrogate for the Calverts.

On January 15, 1990, Mark, Crispina, and Anna signed a contract providing that an embryo created by the sperm of Mark and the egg of Crispina would be implanted in Anna and the child born would be taken into Mark and Crispina's home "as their child." Anna agreed she would relinquish "all parental rights" to the child in favor of Mark and Crispina. In return, Mark and Crispina would pay Anna $10,000 in a series of installments, the last to be paid six weeks after the child's birth. Mark and Crispina were also to pay for a $200,000 life insurance policy on Anna's life.

The zygote was implanted on January 19, 1990. Less than a month later, an ultrasound test confirmed Anna was pregnant.

Unfortunately, relations deteriorated between the two sides. Mark learned that Anna had not disclosed she had suffered several stillbirths and miscarriages. Anna felt Mark and Crispina did not do enough to obtain the required insurance policy. She also felt abandoned during an onset of premature labor in June.

In July 1990, Anna sent Mark and Crispina a letter demanding the balance of the payments due her or else she would refuse to give up the child. The following month, Mark and Crispina responded with a lawsuit, seeking a declaration they were the legal parents of the unborn child. Anna filed her own action to be declared the mother of the child, and the two cases were eventually consolidated. The parties agreed to an independent guardian ad litem for the purposes of the suit.

The child was born on September 19, 1990 * * *. The parties agreed to a court order providing that the child would remain with Mark and Crispina on a temporary basis with visits by Anna.

> [The court first discussed determination of parentage under the standards of the Uniform Parentage Act, concluding that both Anna and Crispina had adduced evidence of a mother-child relationship under the Act but that California law recognizes only one natural mother.]

* * *

Because two women each have presented acceptable proof of maternity, we do not believe this case can be decided without enquiring into the parties' intentions as manifested in the surrogacy agreement. Mark and Crispina are a couple who desired to have a child of their own genetic stock but are physically unable to do so without the help of reproductive technology. They affirmatively intended the birth of the child, and took the steps necessary to effect in vitro fertilization. But for their acted-on intention, the child would not exist. Anna agreed to facilitate the procreation of Mark's and Crispina's child. The parties' aim was to bring Mark's and Crispina's child into the world, not for Mark and Crispina to donate a zygote to Anna. Crispina from the outset intended to be the child's mother. Although the gestative function Anna performed was necessary to bring about the child's birth, it is safe to say that Anna would not have been given the opportunity to gestate or deliver the child had she, prior to implantation of the zygote, manifested her own intent to be the child's mother. No reason appears why Anna's later change of heart should vitiate the determination that Crispina is the child's natural mother.

We conclude that although the Act recognizes both genetic consanguinity and giving birth as means of establishing a mother and child relationship, when the two means do not coincide in one woman, she who intended to procreate the child—that is, she who intended to bring about the birth of a child that she intended to raise as her own—is the natural mother under California law.

Our conclusion finds support in the writings of several legal commentators [citing, among others, Marjorie Maguire Shultz, *Reproductive Technology and Intent–Based Parenthood: An Opportunity for Gender Neutrality* (1990) Wis.L.Rev. 297.]

* * *

The argument that a woman cannot knowingly and intelligently agree to gestate and deliver a baby for intending parents carries overtones of the reasoning that for centuries prevented women from attaining equal economic rights and professional status under the law. To resurrect this view is both to foreclose a personal and economic choice on the part of the surrogate mother, and to deny intending parents what may be their only means of procreating a child of their own genetic stock. Certainly in the present case it cannot seriously be argued that Anna, a licensed vocational nurse who had done well in school and who had previously borne a child, lacked the intellectual wherewithal or life experience necessary to make an informed decision to enter into the surrogacy contract.

* * *

KENNARD, JUSTICE, dissenting.

* * * In my view, the woman who provided the fertilized ovum and the woman who gave birth to the child both have substantial claims to legal motherhood. Pregnancy entails a unique commitment, both psychological and emotional, to an unborn child. No less substantial, however, is the contribution of the woman from whose egg the child developed and without whose desire the child would not exist.

* * *

The proposition that a woman who gives birth to a child after carrying it for nine months is a "substantial factor" in the child's birth cannot reasonably be debated. Nor can it reasonably be questioned that "but for" the gestational mother, there would not be a child. Thus, the majority's reliance on principles of causation is misplaced. Neither the "but for" nor the "substantial factor" test of causation provides any basis for preferring the genetic mother's intent as the determinative factor in gestational surrogacy cases: Both the genetic and the gestational mothers are indispensable to the birth of a child in a gestational surrogacy arrangement.

* * *

The majority's approach entirely devalues the substantial claims of motherhood by a gestational mother such as Anna. True, a woman who enters into a surrogacy arrangement intending to raise the child has by her intent manifested an assumption of parental responsibility in addition to her biological contribution of providing the genetic material. But the gestational mother's biological contribution of carrying a child for nine months and giving birth is likewise an assumption of parental responsibility. A pregnant woman's commitment to the unborn child she carries is not just physical; it is psychological and emotional as well. * * * A pregnant woman intending to bring a child into the world is more than a mere container or breeding animal; she is a conscious agent of creation no less than the genetic mother, and her humanity is implicated on a deep level. Her role should not be devalued.

NOTES ON JOHNSON V. CALVERT

1. Why can't a child have two mothers? What exactly is the state's compelling interest here? In the developing jurisprudence related to lesbian parents, described in more detail in Chapter 7, a child *may* now have two legal

mothers; the question is whether he or she may have multiple parents beyond two—for example, where the donor of sperm to the lesbian couple is known and intends to play a role in the child's life. Assisted reproduction may result in a baby having as many as five parents—two legal, or intentional, parents, two biological parents (an egg donor and a sperm donor), and a gestational mother. The child may want some kind of relationship at some point with all of them. Melanie B. Jacobs argues that the law should make space for multiple parenthood, although all of the parents will not have the same rights; for example, the biological parent may have a right to contact but not to custody. There are many variations on this theme, and some of them have already been recognized by a court either here or in Canada. See Jacobs, Why Just Two? Disaggregating Traditional Parental Rights and Responsibilities To Recognize Multiple Parents, 9 J. L. & Fam. Stud. 309 (2007). See also Susan F. Appleton, Parents by the Numbers, 37 Hofstra L. Rev. 11 (2008). Do you think this is a good idea? Can you see any potential problems?

2. In contrast to Johnson v. Calvert, where the baby arguably had two mothers, in another California case the trial court found that a child born from a surrogacy arrangement had *no* lawful parents. This case, involving a divorcing couple who had caused an embryo, genetically unrelated to either of them, to be implanted in a surrogate mother who carried and gave birth to the child, arose because the husband in the couple argued that he was not liable for child support. Justice Sills, author of the opinion in Johnson v. Calvert, overturned the trial court's finding on appeal based on *Johnson*'s intent test, well-established law that a husband who consents to the artificial insemination of his wife has a duty to support the resulting child, and the state's compelling interest in establishing parentage for all children. In re Marriage of Buzzanca, 72 Cal.Rptr.2d 280 (Cal. App. 1998). In *Buzzanca*, the woman who actually gave birth to the child was not genetically related to it and did not make any claim to parenthood or custody herself. What if either or both of these circumstances were different? Would it affect the court's decision? Would it affect your own evaluation of a just resolution of the case? How and why? What is the state's interest here? Is it the same as or different from that in Johnson v. Calvert?

3. The text of the letter sent by Anna Johnson to the Calverts during her pregnancy, included in a footnote to the appellate court opinion, explains more about the dispute that arose between the two parties to the surrogacy contract:

> I am writing you this letter to inquire if an early payment can be made of what is left to be paid of me. [Anna was to be paid a total of $10,000, but in installments spread out over the pregnancy.] I would not ask if it weren't important and I feel that this is important because it deals with the well-being of the baby. The lady that owns the house in which I reside is selling it, so I must be out by the 10th of August. Since I am to be hospitalized for three weeks due to the pyleonephritis [sic] & premature contractions I need to find another place to live prior to this! Due to the complications of this pregnancy, I am unable to return to work until the delivery of this baby so my income is limited. I do not get enough from disability to make a two month rent deposit plus, the security deposit & have the telephone reconnected. I don't think you'd want your child

> jeopardized by living out on the street. I have looked out for this child's well being thus far, is it asking too much to look after ours?
>
> I'm imploring nicely and trying not to be an ogre about this. But you must admit, you have not been very supportive mentally the entire pregnancy & you've showed a lack of interest unless it came to an ultrasound. I am asking you for help in paying off the final five thousand. There's only two months left & once this baby is born, my hands are free of this deal. But see, this situation can go two ways. One, you can pay me the entire sum early so I won't have to live in the streets, or two you can forget about helping me but, calling it a breach of contract & not get the baby.! I don't want it to get this nasty, not coming this far, but you'd want some help too, if you had no where to go & have to worry about not only yourself but your own child & the child of someone else. Help me find another place & get settled in before your baby's born.

Anna J. v. Mark C., 286 Cal.Rptr. 369, 373 n. 11 (App.1991). Does this letter change your assessment of the rights and obligations of the parties to this case? Could these issues be addressed in the context of surrogacy law? How?

Pamela D. Bridgewater argues that the rational economic actor in this case was Ms. Johnson, yet her economic motivations were held against her, whereas the Calverts are presumed to be rational actors in a market, entitled to enforcement of their contract. Bridgewater, Reconstructing Rationality: Towards A Critical Economic Theory of Reproduction, 56 Emory L.J.1215, 1231–33 (2007). She suggests that gestational surrogates should have the power to rescind the contract, thus altering the balance of power among the parties. What do you think of this suggestion? How is this similar to, or different from, Martha Field's suggestion, described in the text note above, that surrogacy contracts be unenforceable?

4. Does it make any difference to your analysis of the decision in Johnson v. Calvert to know that the couple desiring the baby via the surrogacy arrangement consisted of a white man and a Filipina woman, and that the woman giving birth to the baby was African American? See Dorothy Roberts, Killing the Black Body: Race, Reproduction, and the Meaning of Liberty 280 (1997).

5. The majority opinion above says that "[t]he argument that a woman cannot knowingly and intelligently agree to gestate and deliver a baby for intending parents carries overtones of the reasoning that for centuries prevented women from attaining equal economic rights and professional status under the law." Is this the same argument made by Justice Ginsburg in her dissent in *Gonzalez* about "ancient notions about women's place . . . that have long since been discarded"? Can you consistently argue that gestational mothers should be protected from the consequences of their contracts and that women do not need to be protected from the consequences of their decisions to have an abortion? See also Marjorie Maguire Shultz, Reproductive Technology and Intent–Based Parenthood: An Opportunity for Gender Neutrality, 1990 Wis. L. Rev. 297, 354 ("the argument is not really about pressured choice. Rather, it is either about surrogacy per se, or about women as a group lacking the capacity for free decision-making").

6. Marjorie Shultz, whose article the court cites in *Calvert,* proposed the notion of parenthood by intent as early as 1990, soon after the *Baby M* case (1988). Shultz, above note 5. In it she described how the new reproductive technology, by separating biological reproduction and parenthood, had the potential to support "more flexible, pluralist and non-conventional family arrangements." Id. at 300–01. In case of conflict between genetic and/or gestational parents, Shultz proposed that "intentions that are voluntarily chosen, deliberate, express and bargained-for ought presumptively to determine legal parenthood." Id. at 323. Indeed, she argued, the very intentional character of such parenthood, freely chosen and undertaken at some cost, could be an important indication of capacity for good parenting. Id. at 343. What do you think of this argument? How is it similar to arguments you have encountered in the previous sections about the importance of the right to abortion to good motherhood? Moreover, Shultz argued, use of intention as the default rule might also "offset the biological disadvantages men experience in accessing child-nurturing opportunities" because intention, unlike gestation, for example, was gender-neutral. Id. at 303. Does ART allow, and encourage, parents to escape gender roles? Should this be a goal in setting legal rules to govern it?

7. Justice Kennard, the dissenting judge, argued that the Uniform Status of Children of Assisted Conception Act provided appropriate safeguards in a situation like that in Johnson v. Calvert. The Act provided that "a woman who gives birth to a child is the child's mother" unless a court had approved a surrogacy agreement before conception. In the absence of such court approval, any surrogacy agreement would be void. U.L.A., Uniform Status of Children of Assisted Conception Act §§ 2, 5(b)(1999). If, however, the arrangement for gestational surrogacy has court approval, "the intended parents are the parents of the child." Id., § 8(a)(1). The model legislation also provided for the court to appoint a guardian ad litem for the intended child and legal counsel for the surrogate mother. Before approving a surrogacy arrangement, the trial court was required to conduct a hearing and enter detailed findings, including, among other things, that medical evidence showed the intended mother's inability to bear a child or that for her to do so posed an unreasonable risk to the unborn child or to the physical or mental health of the intended mother and that all parties had received professional mental health counseling pertaining to the effect of the surrogacy arrangement. Id., § 6(b). These provisions, according to Justice Kennard, serve to minimize the potential for overreaching and to ensure that all parties to a surrogacy arrangement understand their respective roles and obligations. Johnson v. Calvert, 19 Cal.Rptr.2d at 512 (Kennard, J., dissenting). "Moreover, by requiring judicial approval, the model act would significantly discourage the rapid expansion of commercial surrogacy brokerage and the resulting commodification of the products of pregnancy." Id. at 516. Do you think this model legislation will take care of all these problems? Is it necessary? Should a couple be required to obtain court approval that surrogacy is a matter of medical necessity? Why or why not? Is it desirable to discourage the expansion of commercial surrogacy? Why or why not?

Almost half the states have passed some legislation concerning surrogacy, some of it quite restrictive. Some states expressly prohibit preconception contracts. See, e.g., Ind. Code Ann. § 31–20–1–1 (2005); Mich. Comp. Laws 722.855 (2005); N.Y. Dom. Rel. Law 121, 122, 124 (2005). Other states allow surrogacy arrangements but prohibit any commercial or paid arrangements; that is, the surrogate cannot be paid more than pregnancy-related expenses. See, e.g., Va. Code Ann. 20–159, 20–160 (2005); Wash. Rev. Code §§ 26.26.725, 26.26.230, 26.26.240 (2005); N.H. RSA 168–B:16(I), (IV) (2004); Fla. Stat. §§ 742.15–16 (2007). A few states, such as Virginia, have adopted some form of the Uniform Status of Children of Assisted Conception Act (which is now, in a slightly revised version from that cited in Johnson v. Calvert, part of the Uniform Parentage Act). Va. Code Ann. §§ 20–156—20–165 (West 2010). What is the law in your state regarding surrogacy? Whose interests does the law protect? Whose does it hurt?

G. REPRODUCTIVE TECHNOLOGY: BOON OR BANE FOR WOMEN?

DAVIS v. DAVIS

Supreme Court of Tennessee, 1992.
842 S.W.2d 588, *cert. denied,* 507 U.S. 911, 113 S.Ct. 1259, 122 L.Ed.2d 657 (1993).

This appeal presents a question of first impression, involving the disposition of the cryogenically-preserved product of in vitro fertilization (IVF), commonly referred to in the popular press and the legal journals as "frozen embryos." The case began as a divorce action, filed by the appellee, Junior Lewis Davis, against his then wife, appellant Mary Sue Davis. The parties were able to agree upon all terms of dissolution, except one: who was to have "custody" of the seven "frozen embryos" stored in a Knoxville fertility clinic that had attempted to assist the Davises in achieving a much-wanted pregnancy during a happier period in their relationship.

I. INTRODUCTION

Mary Sue Davis originally asked for control of the "frozen embryos" with the intent to have them transferred to her own uterus, in a post-divorce effort to become pregnant. Junior Davis objected, saying that he preferred to leave the embryos in their frozen state until he decided whether or not he wanted to become a parent outside the bounds of marriage.

* * *

We note, in this latter regard, that their positions have already shifted: both have remarried and Mary Sue Davis (now Mary Sue Stowe) has moved out of state. She no longer wishes to utilize the "frozen embryos" herself, but wants authority to donate them to a childless couple. Junior Davis is adamantly opposed to such donation and would prefer to see the "frozen embryos" discarded. * * *

* * * IVF involves the aspiration of ova from the follicles of a woman's ovaries, fertilization of these ova in a petri dish using the sperm

provided by a man, and the transfer of the product of this procedure into the uterus of the woman from whom the ova were taken. Implantation may then occur, resulting in a pregnancy and, it is hoped, the birth of a child.

Beginning in 1985, the Davises went through six attempts at IVF, at a total cost of $35,000, but the hoped-for pregnancy never occurred. Despite her fear of needles, at each IVF attempt Mary Sue underwent the month of subcutaneous injections necessary to shut down her pituitary gland and the eight days of intermuscular injections necessary to stimulate her ovaries to produce ova. She was anesthetized five times for the aspiration procedure to be performed. Forty-eight to 72 hours after each aspiration, she returned for transfer back to her uterus, only to receive a negative pregnancy test result each time.

The Davises then opted to postpone another round of IVF until after the clinic with which they were working was prepared to offer them cryogenic preservation, scheduled for November 1988. Using this process, if more ova are aspirated and fertilized than needed, the conceptive product may be cryogenically preserved (frozen in nitrogen and stored at sub-zero temperatures) for later transfer if the transfer performed immediately does not result in a pregnancy. * * * [O]n their last attempt, on December 8, 1988, the gynecologist who performed the procedure was able to retrieve nine ova for fertilization. The resulting one-celled entities, referred to before division as zygotes, were then allowed to develop in petri dishes in the laboratory until they reached the four-to eight-cell stage.

* * *

After fertilization was completed, a transfer was performed as usual on December 10, 1988; the rest of the four- to eight-cell entities were cryogenically preserved. Unfortunately, a pregnancy did not result from the December 1988 transfer, and before another transfer could be attempted, Junior Davis filed for divorce—in February 1989. * * *

* * *

V. THE ENFORCEABILITY OF CONTRACT

* * *

We believe, as a starting point, that an agreement regarding disposition of any untransferred preembryos in the event of contingencies (such as the death of one or more of the parties, divorce, financial reversals, or abandonment of the program) should be presumed valid and should be enforced as between the progenitors. This conclusion is in keeping with the proposition that the progenitors, having provided the gametic material giving rise to the preembryos, retain decision-making authority as to their disposition.

* * *

It might be argued in this case that the parties had an implied contract to reproduce using in vitro fertilization * * *. The problem with such an analysis is that there is no indication in the record that disposition in the event of contingencies other than Mary Sue Davis's pregnancy was ever considered by the parties, or that Junior Davis intended to pursue reproduction outside the confines of a continuing marital relationship with Mary Sue. We therefore decline to decide this case on the basis of implied contract or the reliance doctrine.[21]

* * *

VI. THE RIGHT OF PROCREATIONAL AUTONOMY

* * * We conclude that the answer to this dilemma turns on the parties' exercise of their constitutional right to privacy.

* * *

* * * [T]he right of procreational autonomy is composed of two rights of equal significance—the right to procreate and the right to avoid procreation. Undoubtedly, both are subject to protections and limitations.

The equivalence of and inherent tension between these two interests are nowhere more evident than in the context of in vitro fertilization. None of the concerns about a woman's bodily integrity that have previously precluded men from controlling abortion decisions is applicable here. We are not unmindful of the fact that the trauma (including both emotional stress and physical discomfort) to which women are subjected in the IVF process is more severe than is the impact of the procedure on men. In this sense, it is fair to say that women contribute more to the IVF process than men. Their experience, however, must be viewed in light of the joys of parenthood that is desired or the relative anguish of a lifetime of unwanted parenthood. As they stand on the brink of potential parenthood, Mary Sue Davis and Junior Lewis Davis must be seen as entirely equivalent gamete-providers.

* * *

* * * In this case, the Court must deal with the question of genetic [separated from gestational] parenthood. We conclude, moreover, that an interest in avoiding genetic parenthood can be significant enough to trigger the protections afforded to all other aspects of parenthood. The technological fact that someone unknown to these parties could gestate these preembryos does not alter the fact that these parties, the gamete-providers, would become parents in that event, at least in the genetic sense. The profound impact this would have on them supports their right to sole decisional authority as to whether the process of attempting to

21. We also point out that if the roles were reversed in this case, it is highly unlikely that Junior Davis could force transfer of the preembryos to Mary Sue over her objection. Because she has an absolute right to seek termination of any resulting pregnancy, at least within the first trimester, ordering her to undergo a uterine transfer would be a futility. Ordering donation over objection would raise the other constitutional problems discussed in Section VI.

gestate these preembryos should continue. This brings us directly to the question of how to resolve the dispute that arises when one party wishes to continue the IVF process and the other does not.

VII. BALANCING THE PARTIES' INTERESTS

* * * One way of resolving these disputes is to consider the positions of the parties, the significance of their interests, and the relative burdens that will be imposed by differing resolutions. * * *

Beginning with the burden imposed on Junior Davis, we note that the consequences are obvious. Any disposition which results in the gestation of the preembryos would impose unwanted parenthood on him, with all of its possible financial and psychological consequences. The impact that this unwanted parenthood would have on Junior Davis can only be understood by considering his particular circumstances, as revealed in the record.

Junior Davis testified that he was the fifth youngest of six children. When he was five years old, his parents divorced, his mother had a nervous break-down, and he and three of his brothers went to live at a home for boys run by the Lutheran Church. Another brother was taken in by an aunt, and his sister stayed with their mother. From that day forward, he had monthly visits with his mother but saw his father only three more times before he died in 1976. Junior Davis testified that, as a boy, he had severe problems caused by separation from his parents. He said that it was especially hard to leave his mother after each monthly visit. He clearly feels that he has suffered because of his lack of opportunity to establish a relationship with his parents and particularly because of the absence of his father.

In light of his boyhood experiences, Junior Davis is vehemently opposed to fathering a child that would not live with both parents. Regardless of whether he or Mary Sue had custody, he feels that the child's bond with the non-custodial parent would not be satisfactory. He testified very clearly that his concern was for the psychological obstacles a child in such a situation would face, as well as the burdens it would impose on him. Likewise, he is opposed to donation because the recipient couple might divorce, leaving the child (which he definitely would consider his own) in a single-parent setting.

Balanced against Junior Davis's interest in avoiding parenthood is Mary Sue Davis's interest in donating the preembryos to another couple for implantation. Refusal to permit donation of the preembryos would impose on her the burden of knowing that the lengthy IVF procedures she underwent were futile, and that the preembryos to which she contributed genetic material would never become children. While this is not an insubstantial emotional burden, we can only conclude that Mary Sue Davis's interest in donation is not as significant as the interest Junior Davis has in avoiding parenthood. If she were allowed to donate these preembryos, he would face a lifetime of either wondering about his parental status or knowing about his parental status but having no control over it. He testified quite clearly that if these preembryos were brought to term he would fight for custody of his child or children. Donation, if a child came of it, would rob him twice—his procreational autonomy would be defeated and his relationship with his offspring would be prohibited.

The case would be closer if Mary Sue Davis were seeking to use the preembryos herself, but only if she could not achieve parenthood by any other reasonable means. We recognize the trauma that Mary Sue has already experienced and the additional discomfort to which she would be subjected if she opts to attempt IVF again. Still, she would have a reasonable opportunity, through IVF, to try once again to achieve parenthood in all its aspects—genetic, gestational, bearing, and rearing.

Further, we note that if Mary Sue Davis were unable to undergo another round of IVF, or opted not to try, she could still achieve the child-rearing aspects of parenthood through adoption. The fact that she and Junior Davis pursued adoption indicates that, at least at one time, she was willing to forego genetic parenthood and would have been satisfied by the child-rearing aspects of parenthood alone.

NOTES ON DAVIS V. DAVIS

1. Is Davis v. Davis rightly decided? Why or why not? Is balancing the relative benefits and burdens the appropriate test? If Mrs. Davis intended to have the embryo implanted in her own body, should it have come out differently? If so, why? In a similar Israeli case, the mother wanted to implant the frozen embryos in a gestational surrogate (her own womb having been removed), as the divorcing couple had planned, and raise the child herself. See Daphne Barak–Erez & Ron Shapira, The Delusion of Symmetric Rights, 19 Oxford J. Legal Stud. 297, 300 (1999) (discussing the *Nachmani* case). The Israeli Supreme Court ultimately decided in favor of the mother, primarily on the basis that the right to become a parent is more important than the right to avoid parenthood. Id. at 303. Should an infertile woman's right to attempt to reproduce trump a potential father's right not to do so? Should we defer in general to would-be parents or to those who desire to avoid procreation? What, if any, concerns would you have with this type of balancing approach? Is it better than a contract approach?

2. U.S. courts appear to be uncomfortable with an approach like that taken by the Israeli court in *Nachmani*, and U.S. cases have given priority to the right not to be a genetic parent. See, e.g., In re Marriage of Litowitz, 48 P.3d 261 (Wash. 2002) (allowing destruction of frozen embryos in case where mother argued to have them implanted in a gestational surrogate and father wanted them adopted); In re Marriage of Dahl and Angle, 194 P.3d 834 (Or. 2008) (enforcing agreement to destroy frozen embryos against wishes of husband); Vitakis v. Valchine, 987 So.2d 171 (Fla. Dist. Ct. App. 2008) (enforcing agreement to turn over frozen embryos to husband to dispose of). In the case excerpted above, the court highlighted Mr. Davis's potential distress if there were a biological child of his in existence. One author argues that the courts are overly deferential to the right not to procreate, in the light

of facts about the apparent detachment of sperm donors and large numbers of non-custodial fathers from their biological children. Ellen Waldman, The Parent Trap: Uncovering the Myth of "Coerced Parenthood" in Frozen Embryo Disputes, 53 Am. U.L. Rev. 1021 (2004). Waldman argues that these hypothetical difficulties are much outweighed by the problems of infertility for a woman as she ages and the cost and difficulty of both assisted reproduction and adoption. She also advocates legislation providing that divorcing spouses who object to the implantation of embryos should not be liable for child support. Id. at 1059–61. Should the same approach apply to reluctant unwed fathers who argue unsuccessfully for an abortion? How are the two situations similar or different? See also Glenn Cohen, The Constitution and the Rights Not To Procreate, 60 Stan. L. Rev. 1135 (2008) (arguing that there is no constitutional right not to be a genetic parent if genetic parenthood is detached from legal and gestational parenthood).

3. Do you agree with the *Davis* court that if the parties had entered into a contract at the time of the freezing of the embryos, their intentions expressed in it should govern the situation upon divorce? If so, should IVF (in vitro fertilization) clinics be regulated so as to require entry into such a contract as a condition of treatment? Is it possible to argue consistently that such a contract should be enforced, but that surrogacy contracts should not be? If the contract provided that the embryo would be implanted, even if the couple divorced, could it ever be enforceable? Could the embryo be implanted against the woman's will? See Glenn Cohen, The Right Not To Be A Genetic Parent?, 81 S. Cal. L. Rev. 1115, 1161–84 (2008) (arguing that even if there is a right not to be a genetic parent, it is subject to waiver in advance, but recommending provision of more information to those who sign such agreements, so that consent to such a contract is informed). If the couple fails to execute an agreement, Glenn Cohen argues that the default rule should be non-use of the frozen embryos, subject to a possible exception for cases in which it is impossible for the woman to have a child by other means. Id. at 1187–96. What do you think should be the default terms?

4. United States courts have typically upheld couples' contracts about disposition of frozen embryos, so long as they do not compel implantation of the embryos. For example, the New York Court of Appeals enforced an agreement in a divorce case that provided that the couple's frozen embryos be donated to the IVF clinic for research (Kass v. Kass, 696 N.E.2d 174, 181–82 (N.Y. 1998)), but the Supreme Judicial Court of Massachusetts held that a prior agreement regarding disposition of frozen preembryos was unenforceable if it compelled one of the parties to become a parent against his or her will. A.Z. v. B.Z., 725 N.E.2d 1051, 1057–58 (Mass. 2000). The New Jersey Supreme Court has held that these agreements should be enforced, but subject to the right of either party to change his or her mind up to the moment of implantation. J.B. v. M.B., 783 A.2d 707, 719 (N.J. 2001). See also Tex. Fam. Code Ann. § 160.706 (2003) (consent of former spouse to assisted reproduction may be withdrawn by that individual at any time before placement of eggs, sperm, or embryos).

5. A number of states have enacted statutes intended to prevent a *Davis*-type conflict from arising; their approaches have varied. Florida, for example, requires couples undertaking IVF to execute a written agreement for

disposition of the embryos in the event of divorce, death of either party, or other unforeseen circumstances. Fla. Stat. Ann. § 742.17 (West 2005). New Hampshire, by contrast, simply sets a 14–day limit for the maintenance of ex utero prezygotes. N.H. Rev. Stat. Ann. § 168–B:15 (2010). Which of these approaches do you think is preferable?

TEXT NOTE: REPRODUCTIVE TECHNOLOGY

Assisted reproductive technology ("ART") has become a large and profitable business in the United States, but it is virtually unregulated. By 1998, artificial insemination contributed to 60,000 births, with a large increase in its use attributed to single women and lesbian couples.[40] In 2005, ART accounted for almost three percent of all births.[41] Its increase is due in part to the entry of women into the workplace and the accompanying delay of childbearing, with its attendant risk of infertility.[42]

Unless it is performed without the use of ovulation-stimulating drugs, IVF produces multiple embryos; given the cost and discomfort of the procedures of egg-extraction and embryo-implantation, most couples choose to implant more than one embryo and/or to freeze and preserve numbers of them for future use if the first attempt at pregnancy fails. There is a 10.6 to 37.3% success rate of IVF leading to the birth of a child, decreasing with the age of the mother.[43] The question of what to do with the extra embryos has become highly politicized in light of the debate over abortion and the status of life after conception.[44] The father in one of the cases referred to in the notes above, for example, was Roman Catholic and believed that the embryos constituted a form of life that was sacred; for that reason, he argued that the frozen embryos should either be used by his ex-wife or donated to an infertile couple. While the court found that the wife's right not to procreate trumped the husband's desire to use or donate the embryos, it held that the embryos would not be destroyed if he was willing to pay the fees for continuous storage.[45]

Embryonic stem cell research has long been seen as a possible source of cures for a variety of serious diseases because stem cells are undifferentiated and can develop into almost any cell in the human body, thus containing the potential capacity to repair a number of parts of the body.[46] Because stem cell research involves the destruction of an embryo, many (though not all) anti-abortion activists have opposed any governmental funding of it since at least

---

40. See Judith F. Daar, Accessing Reproductive Technologies: Invisible Barriers, Indelible Harms, 23 Berkeley J. Gender L. & Just. 18, 27–28 (2008).

41. Id.

42. See Sonia M. Suter, The "Repugnance" Lens of *Gonzales v. Carhart* and Other Theories of Reproductive Rights: Evaluating Advanced Reproductive Technologies, 76 Geo. Wash. L. Rev. 1514, 1561 (2008) (citing Judith Daar, Reproductive Technologies and the Law 13, 16 (2006)).

43. See Amy B. Monahan, Value–Based Mandated Health Benefits, 80 U. Colo. L. Rev. 127, 160–61 (2009).

44. See Janet L. Dolgin, Surrounding Embryos: Biology, Ideology, and Politics, 16 Health Matrix 27 (2006).

45. J.B. v. M.B., 783 A.2d 707, 719 (N.J. 2001).

46. See Janet L. Dolgin, Embryonic Discourse: Abortion, Stem Cells, and Cloning, 31 Fla. St. U. L. Rev. 101, 111 (2003).

the Reagan Administration.[47] President George W. Bush, despite his anti-abortion stance, reached a compromise on this issue, ordering in 2001 that research on stem cell lines that were already in existence would be funded, while prohibiting the funding of any research based on newly-created embryos.[48] At the same time, the Bush Administration sponsored a $1 million initiative to promote embryo "adoption"—that is, donation of unused frozen embryos to a recipient who wants to use them to have a child.[49] In March 2009, President Barack Obama issued an executive order aimed at lifting the Bush Administration's restrictions on stem cell research, but as of August 2010 federal government money was still flowing to agencies for embryo adoption.[50]

Given its high cost, most types of ART are effectively available to address infertility only for wealthy individuals or for those who have insurance that covers it. The cost of a cycle of IVF can range between $10,000 and $20,000, and the total cost per delivery may range from $44,000 to $211,000, much beyond the range of economic possibility for most people.[51] Usage rates are therefore low, especially compared to countries with national health insurance.[52] Currently, only 15 states—Arkansas, California, Connecticut, Hawaii, Illinois, Louisiana, Maryland, Massachusetts, Montana, New Jersey, New York, Ohio, Rhode Island, Texas, and West Virginia—have laws that require insurance coverage for treatment of infertility; they differ as to the extent of coverage required, and many cover only married couples using their own genetic material.[53]

The EEOC found in April 1999 that an employer had violated federal disability laws and the Civil Rights Act when it denied medical insurance coverage for a woman's infertility treatments and the care necessitated by her

---

47. Id. at 135–41.

48. Id. at 141–47.

49. Paula J. Manning, Baby Needs a New Set of Rules: Using Adoption Doctrine to Regulate Embryo Donation, 5 Geo. J. Gender & Law 677, 678 (2004).

50. Sheryl Gay Stolberg, Obama Lifts Bush's Strict Limits on Stem Cell Research, N.Y. Times, Mar. 10, 2009; for information on current funding see http://www.usaspending.gov/search?query=% 22embryo+adoption% 22&Search=Search.

51. Daar, above note 40, at 36; Martha M. Ertman, What's Wrong With A Parenthood Market? A New and Improved Theory of Commodification, 82 N.C.L. Rev. 1, 13 (2003).

52. See Daar, above note 40, at 36–37.

53. Ark. Code Ann. §§ 23–85–137, 23–86–118 (1987) (requiring that patient's eggs be fertilized with her spouse's sperm); Cal. Health & Safety Code, § 1374.55 (West 1989) (not covering IVF); 2006 Conn. Pub. Act 05–196 (including lifetime maximum of two IVF cycles with no more than two embryos implanted per cycle); Haw. Rev. Stat. §§ 431.10A–116.5, 432.1–604 (2003) (covering only one IVF cycle and must be with spouse's sperm); 215 Ill. Comp. Stat. 5/356m (1997) (including lifetime maximum of six egg retrievals); La. Rev. Stat. Ann. § 22:1036 (2008); Md. Code Ann., Ins. § 15–810 (2000); Md. Code Ann., Health-Gen. § 19–701 (2000) (covering cost of three IVFs per live birth with lifetime maximum of $100,000 and eggs must be fertilized with spouse's sperm); Mass. Gen. Laws Ann. Ch. 175, § 47H; Ch. 176A, § 8K; Ch. 176B, § 4J; Ch. 176G, § 4, 211 CMR 37.00 (1987) (comprehensive); Mont. Code Ann. §§ 33–22–1521, 33–31–102(2)(v) (1987); N.J. Stat. Ann. § 17B:27–46.1x (2001) (covering four completed egg retrievals per lifetime and only for person less than 46 years old and not covering cryopreservation); N.Y. Ins. Law, §§ 3216(13), 3221 (2002) (limiting to persons 21 to 44 and excluding IVF); Ohio Rev. Code Ann. § 1751.01(A)(7)(1991) (allowing but not requiring to cover IVF); R.I. Gen. Laws §§ 27–18–30, 27–19–23, 27–20–20, 27–41–33 (1989) (covering only women between 25 and 40); Tex. Ins. Code Ann. §§ 1366.003–1366.006 (2003) (only requiring to offer IVF); W.Va. Code § 33–25A–2 (1995).

resulting miscarriage.[54] It based its ruling on a Supreme Court case, Bragdon v. Abbott (524 U.S. 624 (1998)), finding that reproduction was "a major life activity" in the context of the Americans with Disabilities Act.[55] The federal courts have split on whether infertility is covered by the Pregnancy Discrimination Act.[56]

Elizabeth Bartholet has argued, based on her own unsuccessful experience with IVF, that this form of technology reinforces and exploits women's socialization that fertility, pregnancy, childbirth, and mothering are critical to their identities.[57] Bartholet herself went through eight unsuccessful IVF cycles, accompanied by a considerable amount of physical and emotional pain, over a ten-year period.[58] She argues for substantial regulation of IVF and against coverage of the procedure by insurance. She also maintains that the legal system as a whole is massively biased in favor of biological parenthood and against adoption, which is accompanied by extremely onerous regulations, and advocates that this situation should be reversed.[59]

Dorothy Roberts suggests that the enormous resources directed into reproductive technology by insurance coverage would be better spent on research about infertility and improvement of the conditions that lead to it. Women of color and poor women have substantial infertility problems yet are unlikely to have access to the high-tech treatments now available; the majority population fails to see this as an issue, based on the perception that poor women are already "too fertile."[60] Yet fertility and genetic parenthood may be even more heavily charged issues within many minority communities and cultures. Motherhood may be central to a woman's status and to a man's sense of masculinity, which is defined at least in part by the ability to father children. Moreover, whereas infertile white couples have a relatively easy time finding donors, African Americans and other people of color may find that their options are extremely limited because of a lack of Black and racial minority donors of eggs or sperm.[61]

---

54. Randy Kennedy, U.S. Agency Says Employer Should Pay for a Woman's Infertility Treatments, N.Y. Times, Apr. 29, 1999, at B5.

55. See also Note, Reproduction Constitutes a "Major Life Activity" Under the ADA: Implications of the Supreme Court's Decision in *Bragdon v. Abbott*, 32 Creighton L. Rev. 1357 (1999) (arguing against inclusion of reproduction under the ADA).

56. See Krauel v. Iowa Methodist Medical Center, 95 F.3d 674 (8th Cir. 1996) (holding that infertility is not covered under PDA and thus insurance company is not discriminating if it does not offer coverage); Saks v. Franklin Covey Co., 316 F.3d 337 (2d Cir. 2003) (distinguishing infertility from pregnancy and thus finding denial of insurance benefits for infertility on a gender neutral basis not to be sex discrimination). But see Pacourek v. Inland Steel Co., 858 F.Supp. 1393 (N.D. Ill. 1994) (holding that infertility is covered by the PDA in a case involving an adverse employment action). See also Elizabeth A. Pendo, The Politics of Infertility: Recognizing Coverage Exclusions as Discrimination, 11 Conn. Ins. L.J. 293 (2004); James B. Roche, After Bragdon v. Abbott: Why Legislation Is Still Needed to Mandate Infertility Insurance, 11 B.U. Pub. Int. L.J. 215 (2002).

57. Bartholet, Family Bonds: Adoption and the Politics of Parenting 29–30, 187–98 (1993); see also Sarah Franklin, Embodied Progress: A Cultural Account of Assisted Conception 101–97 (1997) (describing women's experience of IVF); Silvia Tubert, How IVF Exploits the Wish to Be a Mother: A Psychoanalyst's Account, 14 Genders 33 (1992).

58. Bartholet, above note 57, at 28, 192–98.

59. Id. at 62–85, 201–17.

60. Dorothy Roberts, Killing the Black Body: Race, Reproduction, and the Meaning of Liberty 290–92 (1997).

61. Dov Fox, Note, Racial Classification in Assisted Reproduction, 118 Yale L.J. 1844, 1852–53 (2009) (describing scarcity of Black donors in pool of sperm donors in the leading California

Many fear that the new reproductive technology may lead to a number of other harms to women. The long-term risks to the genetic mother from ovarian hyperstimulation are unknown, and the chance of a dangerous ectopic pregnancy is doubled.[62] ART also makes it possible to select the sex of a child, either by deciding to implant only embryos that pre-implantation testing shows are of that sex or by subsequent abortion. Although we know that in some countries, like India and China, female fetuses are regularly aborted, it is unclear that sex selection would be similarly sex-discriminatory in the United States. Nonetheless, two states have already prohibited sex-selective abortions.[63]

Gays and lesbians who wish to become parents without adopting have an obvious need for assisted reproduction of various sorts—lesbians for artificial insemination, sometimes for egg or embryo donation, and for IVF if they wish to divide genetic and gestational motherhood between them, and gay males for surrogacy arrangements. Access can be a problem for these groups as private fertility clinics may deny service to single people or to any persons they regard as unfit to parent. It has been estimated that 80% of clinics provide services to single and lesbian women, while only 20% serve males.[64]

Scholars have also begun to focus on the potential harms to children of assisted reproduction. Because of the ovulation-stimulating hormones used on their mothers and the implantation of multiple embryos, there is a very high rate of multiple births, which can result in serious health problems.[65] Multiple births increase from 3% to 33% with IVF, and perinatal death rates are four times higher for twins than for single births, six times higher for triplets and higher multiple births.[66] Moreover, IVF infants are more likely to be preterm and low birth weight (24% versus 4.8% in natural conception) and have higher rates of mortality and congenital disabilities.[67] Another problem arises from the anonymity of egg, sperm, and embryo donors: the resulting children do not have information about their genetic past that may be important to their health or that of their future children. For this reason, one author suggests that embryo donation should be treated legally like an open adoption.[68]

---

sperm bank). See also Nanette R. Elster, ART for the Masses? Racial and Ethnic Inequality in Assisted Reproductive Technologies, 9 DePaul J. Health Care L. 719, 730 (2005) (describing comparative donor scarcity found in one 2003 study); Charis Thompson, Skin Tone and the Persistence of Biological Race in Egg Donation for Assisted Reproduction, in Shades of Difference: Why Skin Color Matters 131–47 (Evelyn Nakano Glenn, ed. 2009) (discussing ethnoracial matching with egg donors).

62. Jaime King, Predicting Probability: Regulating the Future of Preimplantation Genetic Screening, 8 Yale J. Health Pol'y L. & Ethics 283, 306–12 (2008).

63. 720 Ill. Comp. Stat. 510/6–6(8)(2003); 18 Pa. Cons. Stat. Ann. § 3204(c)(2000).

64. John A. Robertson, Gay and Lesbian Access to Assisted Reproductive Technology, 55 Case W. Res. L. Rev. 323 (2004). See also Richard F. Storrow, Medical Conscience and the Policing of Parenthood, 16 Wm. & Mary J. Women & Law 369 (2010) (discussing medical ethics of refusing treatment because of sexual orientation or marital status).

65. Jennifer L. Rosato, The Children of ART (Assisted Reproductive Technology): Should the Law Protect Them From Harms?, 2004 Utah L. Rev. 57, 77–79; see also John A. Robertson, Procreative Liberty and Harm to Offspring in Assisted Reproduction, 30 Am. J. L. & Med. 7 (2004).

66. See Marsha Garrison, Regulating Reproduction, 76 Geo. Wash. L. Rev. 1623, 1644 (2008).

67. King, above note 62, at 304–5.

68. Manning, above note 49.

The problems with ART described above have led to calls for its regulation in the United States, especially after the extensive publicity given to one unemployed single mother in California, Nadya Suleiman, who had octuplets after already having six previous children, all born with the assistance of IVF.[69] IVF is already heavily regulated in Europe. Germany and Italy prohibit freezing embryos; a maximum of three may be created at one time and all must be implanted.[70] The United Kingdom, by contrast, has a national agency that must approve, on a case by case basis, every use of IVF, storage of embryos, and research involving them.[71] Louisiana law provides that a pre-zygote is to be considered a juridical person and must be implanted, but ART largely takes place in the United States with little regulation.[72] The only regulations by the federal government are requirements that fertility centers report their success rates to the Centers for Disease Control on an annual basis and that donated gametes be tested for HIV, sexually-transmitted diseases, and a variety of other disorders before they are used.[73]

Scholars debate whether and to what extent regulation of ART would be constitutional. John Robertson argues that there is a constitutional right to procreate that includes using ART, subject only to limits necessary to prevent tangible harm to others.[74] Marsha Garrison, by contrast, argues that a constitutional right to procreate could not possibly extend to means that circumvent the limitations inherent in sexual conception, such as a right to methods that allow childbirth postmenopause or after death of the father and to choose a child's specific traits in advance; she recommends regulation of ART by a quasi-public entity along the lines that are currently employed in the United States for organ donation and implantation.[75] Jaime King makes an extensive and detailed proposal for a regulatory regime in the United States, suggesting that an independent agency similar to the SEC be created that would license all ART clinics, monitor their use of the new technologies, collect evidence concerning their risks, and write regulations concerning their appropriate uses based on this data, prohibiting uses only when their harms clearly outweigh their benefits.[76] Naomi Cahn, author of an exhaustively researched and informative 2009 book written from the perspective of a feminist legal scholar, recommends the following more specific substantive requirements, among other things: (1) limiting payment of gamete donors to their costs; (2) counseling and extensive informed-consent procedures for both

---

69. See, e.g., Stephanie Saul, Birth of Octuplets Puts Focus on Fertility Clinics, N.Y. Times, Feb. 12, 2009, at A1. See also June Carbone & Naomi Cahn, Embryo Fundamentalism, 18 Wm. & Mary Bill of Rts J. 1015, 1037–43 (2010).

70. See Radhika Rao, Equal Liberty: Assisted Reproductive Technology and Reproductive Equality, 76 Geo. Wash. L. Rev. 1457, 1458–59 (2008).

71. For a description of the UK's HFEA, see King, above note 62, at 350–51.

72. La. Rev. Stat. Ann. § 9:123 (2005).

73. See King, above note 62, at 333; Naomi R. Cahn, Test Tube Families: Why the Fertility Market Needs Legal Regulation 55–59 (2009).

74. John A. Robertson, Children of Choice: Freedom and the New Reproductive Technologies (1994).

75. Garrison, above note 66, at 1627, 1648–51.

76. King, above note 62, at 331–57. Cf. Kimberley M. Mutcherson, Making Mommies: Law, Pre–Implantation Genetic Diagnosis, and the Complications of Pre–Motherhood, 18 Colum. J. Gender & Law 313, 386–90 (2008) (opposing regulation).

sperm and egg donors; (3) imposition of limits upon the number of times both sperm and egg donors may donate; and (4) disclosure of donor identities to a federal registry that would allow children of ART access to information about their genetic parentage upon their majority.[77]

The developing technology of pre-implantation embryonic diagnosis and genetic screening (PGS) has added to the legal and ethical issues presented by ART. It is now possible to test the embryos produced in the IVF process for chromosomal abnormalities that can lead to death or serious disorders in children; and fertility centers regularly select the healthiest embryos to implant.[78] Pre-implantation screening can also identify a variety of genetic disorders, such as Tay–Sachs disease and cystic fibrosis, for which there is no cure and which lead to premature death; testing can also identify the genes predisposing an individual to develop other diseases later in life, such as Huntington's disease and Alzheimer's.[79] Disability rights activists express concerns about the impact of PGS on persons with non-fatal disabilities, as well as about the spreading of inaccurate notions about the quality of life of disabled persons.[80] There are concerns, as well, that fertility services will refuse to assist persons with disabilities who wish to become parents.[81]

Widespread use of PGS may be self-limiting, given the cost, discomfort, and risks of the procedures involved (e.g., harm to the embryo from embryo biopsy) and current limitations on the accuracy of the testing.[82] It is presently unregulated in the United States, but PGS is totally banned in Germany, Austria, Italy, and Switzerland (presumably for its eugenic implications in the first three) and other European countries limit its use to testing for genetic or chromosomal disorders that would lead to a serious impairment of the fetus, decided on a case by case basis.[83] Some feminist scholars worry that the availability of prenatal testing will put pressure on pregnant women to undergo tests even if they do not want to and create expectations of a "Good Mother" who protects the welfare of her future child in this way.[84]

Radical feminists were early critics of the new reproductive technologies, pointing to the dangers, for example, of "reproductive brothels" for eugenic breeding and the potential for international traffic in reproduction based upon exploitation of third-world women.[85] There is evidence that this may be happening, such as the surrogacy industry in India, described above. Repro-

---

77. Naomi Cahn, Test Tube Families: Why the Fertility Market Needs Legal Regulation 194–99, 236 (2009).

78. See King, above note 62, at 292–95.

79. Id. at 295–96.

80. See id. at 317–18; Mutcherson, above note 76, at 324.

81. Kimberly M. Mutcherson, Disabling Dreams of Parenthood: The Fertility Industry, Anti-discrimination, and Parents with Disabilities, 27 Law & Ineq. 311 (2009).

82. King, above note 62, at 310–12.

83. Id. at 346.

84. See Mutcherson, above note 76, at 339–40.

85. See, e.g., Gena Corea, The Reproductive Brothel, in Man–Made Women: How New Reproductive Technologies Affect Women 38, 43–44 (Corea et al., eds. 1985) (the term "reproductive brothel" is Andrea Dworkin's). See also Corea, The Mother Machine 213–15, 245 (1985).

duction has indeed gone global, with patients seeking out jurisdictions where the price and regulations favor their needs.[86]

Socialist feminists, on the other hand, have criticized the radical feminists' stance on this issue as based upon an image of women as passive victims, of patriarchy as simply a male plot, and of technology as having a force of its own, separate from the social conditions of its control.[87] The solution, from this perspective, is to alter the conditions under which the technology is used and to employ it in the interests of women.[88] More recently, the debate has revolved around concerns about the commodification of human life, which is usually considered to be per se bad. Martha Ertman, however, argues that a free private market has liberatory potential for women, as it allows them to construct non-conventional families and even to do without the inclusion of a male, after purchasing the sperm—unlike situations like prostitution, where men are always the purchasers of women's body parts.[89] This is particularly important, Ertman argues, for groups such as lesbians who desire to construct new forms of family.[90]

NOTES ON FEMINISM AND REPRODUCTIVE TECHNOLOGY

1. Why do you think the public reaction to Nadya Suleiman's octuplets was so negative? Is it because she was single? Because she was on public assistance? Because she had too many children? Because she was the sort of person who should not have that many children (in contrast with Jon and Kate Gosselin, on the television program "Jon and Kate Plus Eight")?

2. Given the burdens on IVF created by policies like those in Germany and Italy, which greatly diminish the possibility of a pregnancy resulting from it, how would you regulate the creation and storage of prezygotes? Which European policy, if any, do you favor and why?

3. Should infertility be recognized either as a disability or as sex discrimination and thus covered by prohibitions against discrimination on those bases? What legal challenges can be made to legislation that requires insurance companies to pay for IVF but not for abortions? What principles should guide whether infertility should or should not be covered by insurance? See, e.g., Amy B. Monahan, Value–Based Mandated Health Benefits, 80 U. Colo. L. Rev. 127 (2009) (applying cost-benefit, efficiency analysis to the issue).

---

86. See Lisa C. Ikemoto, Reproductive Tourism: Equality Concerns in the Global Market for Fertility Services, 27 Law & Ineq. 277, 295–300 (2009). In Europe, the sperm donor nation is Denmark, because anonymity is allowed; and Spain is the preeminent destination for IVF, because laws governing it there are not as strict as in other European nations. Id.

87. See, e.g., Rosalind Pollack Petchesky, Fetal Images: The Power of Visual Culture in the Politics of Reproduction, 13 Feminist Studies 263, 278–80 (1987).

88. For an early description of this debate among feminists from the admittedly biased perspective of a radical feminist, see Janice G. Raymond, Reproductive Technologies, Radical Feminism, and Socialist Liberalism, 2 Reproductive & Genetic Engineering 133 (1989).

89. Ertman, above note 51. Marjorie Maguire Schultz also pointed to this potential of reproductive technology for women as early as 1990. See Schultz, Reproductive Technology and Intent-based Parenthood: An Opportunity for Gender Neutrality, 1990 Wis. L. Rev. 297.

90. See also Kimberly D. Krawiec, Altruism and Intermediation in the Market for Babies, 66 Wash. & Lee L. Rev. 203 (2009) (arguing for deregulation of ART so that donors will be able to share in the profits generated by their labor, now largely reserved for the middlemen).

4. What do you think of Bartholet's suggestions, described in the text note above, that IVF be subjected to strict regulation and that adoption regulations be eased? What regulations would you suggest?

5. Should parents have a right to choose the sex of their child? Should they have a right to select for disabilities? If so, for which ones? For Alzheimer's disease? What, if any, legal checks should be placed on this virtually unregulated and very profitable industry to prevent parents who can afford it from genetic manipulation of their offspring, thus exacerbating current inequalities? See Michael J. Malinowski, Choosing the Genetic Make-up of Children: Our Eugenics Past–Present, and Future?, 36 Conn. L. Rev. 125 (2003); Mary Crossley, Dimensions of Equality in Regulating Assisted Reproductive Technologies, 9 J. Gender Race & Just. 273 (2005). If the mother has a right to abort the fetus for any reason during early pregnancy, how can one prohibit her from deciding, on any basis whatsoever, what embryos to implant?

6. Can you construct a legal argument that gay and lesbian individuals have a right to reproduce that may not be denied based on sexual orientation? See John A. Robertson, Gay and Lesbian Access to Assisted Reproductive Technology, 55 Case W. Res. 323 (2004).

7. Apart from banning the procedure or limiting the number of embryos to be implanted, is there any way to prevent the potential harms to children of ART? Given the mounting evidence of harm to the fetus from the mother's taking ovulation stimulating drugs and implanting multiple embryos, why has public attention focused instead on the risks of taking cocaine, which turns out to be comparatively minor in comparison with the risks of ART? In South Carolina, where drug-addicted mothers can be convicted of murder, over 70% of births in 2002 to women over 35 were multiple births resulting from the use of ART. Michele Goodwin, Prosecuting The Womb, 76 Geo. Wash. L. Rev. 1657, 1660 (2008). See also Dorothy E. Roberts, Privatization and Punishment in the New Age of Reprogenetics, 54 Emory L.J. 1343, 1348 (2005).

8. Should we prohibit anonymity of sperm donors? Of egg donors? Substantial problems of gamete supply would result, as they have in European countries that do not allow anonymity. See Vanessa L. Pi, Note, Regulating Sperm Donation: Why Requiring Exposed Donation Is Not The Answer, 16 Duke J. Gender L. & Pol'y 379, 394–95 (2009). Identification of a donor may prove important to future health decisions of the child, but most clinics do extensive interviews and testing, and this information could be maintained without disclosing the identity of the donor. It may also be important, especially when a sperm donor has "fathered" many children over a period of time, for children conceived in this fashion to obtain information so as to avoid incest when choosing their own partners. They could, of course, undergo DNA testing for this purpose, but only if their parents have told their children how they were conceived. Id. at 398–99. For two points of view on whether anonymity should be permitted, compare Michelle Dennison, Revealing Your Sources: The Case for Non-anonymous Gamete Donation, 21 J.L. & Health 1 (2008) (arguing for the prohibition of anonymous donation), with Pi, above (arguing for anonymity while giving donor-conceived children access to information about donor identity by court order upon a showing of good cause).

9. The text note above describes the differing perspectives of radical and socialist feminists concerning reproductive technology. How would other feminists come down on this question? Are the problems envisaged by many feminists in connection with the new reproductive technologies ones that can be solved only by pushing the genie back into the bottle? Are some of them produced by the law's inability to handle the problems of the new technology? Will they be adequately addressed after our legal categories adapt to the new technology? Or would other changes be necessary as well? What are they?

10. The new reproductive technologies have led to mix-ups and concomitant legal and ethical problems. One white woman, for example, brought suit against a fertility clinic for having inseminated her with a Black man's sperm, instead of her husband's. See Dorothy Roberts, Killing the Black Body: Race, Reproduction, and the Meaning of Liberty 251 (1997). In another case, a fertility doctor mistakenly implanted fertilized eggs from two different women—one white and one Black—into one of the two during an in vitro procedure. Five months after the babies' birth, the couples agreed to hand the Black baby over to the Black couple, although they subsequently went to court over visitation; the New York appellate court decision held that the genetic parents had exclusive custody and thus the gestational mother had no standing to claim visitation rights, despite the fact that she had raised the Black child since birth and the court's holding separated twins from one another almost half a year after their birth. Perry–Rogers v. Fasano, 715 N.Y.S.2d 19 (2000). Leslie Bender argues that this decision was profoundly marred by genetic essentialism (by giving no rights at all to the white mother who had nurtured the baby through pregnancy, birth, and early infancy), sex bias (because privileging genetic ties is biased in favor of men), and racism. Would DNA testing ever have been done if the baby were not black? Why was the court so certain that the child's best interests lay with its genetic, race-matched family? Bender, Genes, Parents, and Assisted Reproductive Technologies: ARTs, Mistakes, Sex, Race, & Law, 12 Colum. J. Gender & Law 1 (2003). What sorts of remedies do you think should be available in cases of mistake?

11. The possibilities and potential drawbacks of repro-tech have been the subject of a good deal of interdisciplinary literature and analysis from a number of perspectives. Here is a sampling of some of this literature:

- Cyborg Babies: From Techno–Sex to Techno–Tots (Robbie Davis–Floyd & Joseph Dumit, eds. 1998) (including cultural anthropologists' arguments that the "cyborgification" of modern life has fundamentally changed reproduction and child-rearing, requiring our society to face new ethical and moral problems)
- Valerie Hartouni, Cultural Conceptions: On Reproductive Technologies and the Remaking of Life (1997) (describing ways in which cultural "shaping" affects contemporary debates over reproductive practices and processes)
- Swasti Bhattacharyya, Magical Progeny, Modern Technology: A Hindu Bioethics of Assisted Reproductive Technology (2006) (reproductive technology from a Hindu perspective)

- Morgan Clarke, Islam and New Kinship: Reproductive Technology and the Shariah in Lebanon (2009) (discussing whether reproductive technology creates new forms of Islamic kinship)
- Deborah Spar, The Baby Business: How Money, Science, and Politics Drive the Commerce of Conception (2006) (discussing how socioeconomic factors drive the market for reproductive technology)
- Charis Thompson, Making Parents: The Ontological Choreography of Reproductive Technologies (2005) (examining impact of reprotech on gender roles of parenting)

For a good collection of essays discussing many of the issues involved, see Baby Markets: Money and the New Politics of Creating Families (Michele Bratcher Goodwin, ed. 2010).

CHAPTER 6

LAW, WOMEN, AND INTIMATE RELATIONSHIPS

■ ■ ■

A. INTRODUCTION

How would intimate relationships be structured in a just society? Would marriage exist at all? What would family mean? What would intimacy mean? Western political philosophy has tended either to ignore these questions or to presume that the patriarchal family is the basis of any society. In contrast, feminists have long criticized the patriarchal family and attempted to imagine new frameworks for personal life. For example, Susan Moller Okin argued: "In a just society, the structure and practices of families must give women the same opportunities as men to develop their capacities, to participate in political power and influence social choices, and to be economically secure."[1]

Prior to the 1970's, family law in the United States dictated a deeply gendered family. As Martha Fineman has summarized, "[T]he sexes had distinct and well-defined gender roles: husbands were economic providers, disciplinarians, and the heads of families, while wives were nurturers, caretakers, and subservient to their husbands."[2] In the 1970's, in large part due to grassroots feminist activism, legislators and courts began to eliminate laws that mandated official gender roles within the family, as discussed in Chapter 2. Family law now does not restrict family functions to one gender or another, with the exception of different-sex marriage requirements in force in many states. This means that once a family is recognized by the state, the law no longer assigns legal functions to family members according to restrictive notions of gender roles. Both men and women are permitted, and often required, to perform all of the functions the law traditionally reserved for (male) husbands and (female) wives or (female) mothers and (male) fathers.

Feminist family law scholars have praised this revolution toward gender-neutral family law, but they have questioned whether gender neutrality necessarily leads to gender equality. Feminists have questioned

1. Okin, Justice, Gender, and the Family 22 (1989).

2. Fineman, Progress and Progression in Family Law, 2004 U. Chi. Legal F. 1, 2.

what a gender-neutral family law means for marriage and divorce, as well as what it means for intimate relationships outside of marriage:

> At least for several years after the advent of gender-neutral divorce and alimony laws, most middle-class wives continued to forego full-time wage work in order to engage in childcare and other care work, leaving them with limited bargaining power upon divorce. Jill Hasday, among others, has analyzed how these women were harmed by state legislatures' assumptions that divorce law no longer needed to take women's particular status into account upon divorce but simply needed to treat both spouses equally. Hasday uses this example to urge family law scholars to continue to work toward the goal of gender equality instead of assuming that equality has already been achieved through gender-neutral laws.
>
> Other concerns about the effects of gender-neutral laws go beyond debates about formal and substantive equality. These concerns are grounded in a consideration of the power of the existing boundaries of the legal family. Scholars engaged in this type of critique examine how the law's placement of certain relationships and activities outside of the legal family could itself perpetuate gender inequality. * * *
>
> Other scholars have extended this argument about the boundaries of the legal family to other groups of people, including unmarried opposite-sex cohabitants, unmarried cohabitants whose living arrangements do not involve sex, and single and other unmarried parents. Although formal gender distinctions are not the cause of these groups' placement outside family law's privileged family forms, women and their children in these "outsider" family forms tend to suffer disproportionately more than similarly situated men. * * * [T]he existing boundaries of the legal family fail to encompass the diverse ways that families function, and therefore states support some families more than others.[3]

This chapter begins with a discussion of the ways law and society have long encouraged women to marry men and how this emphasis on marriage potentially harms various groups of women and men to this day. We then explore the distribution of power and well-being within different-sex marriage, including the division of household labor, the movement toward same-sex marriage, and the economic impact of divorce. We discuss a variety of suggestions for change in the law's regulation of relationship dissolution, from substantial "tinkering" with post-divorce remedies based on contract, partnership, or commercial law, to major legal changes, including taxation of housework and the total abolition of all legal privileges accorded to marriage. We conclude by considering the regulation of intimate relationships outside of marriage, including cohabitation, friendship, and other relationships outside of the marital couple form.

3. Laura A. Rosenbury, Friends with Benefits?, 106 Mich. L. Rev. 189, 196–98 (2007).

B. MARRIAGE, POWER, AND WELL-BEING

Prior to the 1970's, middle-class white women experienced extreme pressure to marry men, given their economic and political subordination and the widely held view that "[m]arital status defined women's worth."[4] This worth was largely determined by women's sexual and domestic care of men within the home. In return, women received financial support and social acceptance. Or, as Adrienne Rich emphasized, women "have married because it was necessary, in order to survive economically, in order to have children who would not suffer economic deprivation or social ostracism, in order to remain respectable, in order to do what was expected of women because coming out of 'abnormal' childhoods they wanted to feel 'normal,' and because heterosexual romance has been represented as the great female adventure, duty, and fulfillment."[5] Black and working class women, in contrast, were often denied access to marriage because lawmakers assumed that they either could not provide the requisite level of care or their male counterparts did not deserve that care.[6]

Given women's increased access to education and employment, women are now thought to choose marriage more freely. Large cohorts of women have the means to delay marriage or other long-term domestic commitment until they find the partner of their choice. But many gendered and heteronormative aspects of marriage remain. This section examines the law's role in encouraging marriage even to this day; what women tend to find once they enter different-sex marriage; and the effects of legal recognition or rejection of same-sex marriage.

1. CHOOSING MARRIAGE

NANCY POLIKOFF, BEYOND (STRAIGHT AND GAY) MARRIAGE: VALUING ALL FAMILIES UNDER THE LAW

3, 5, 8–9, 123, 126, 132–33, 141 (2008).

I propose family law reform that would recognize all families' worth. Marriage as a family form is not more important or valuable than other forms of family, so the law should not give it more value. Couples should have the choice to marry based on the spiritual, cultural, or religious meaning of marriage in their lives; they should never *have to* marry to reap specific and unique legal benefits. I support the right to marry for same-sex couples as a matter of civil rights law. But I oppose discrimination against couples who do not marry, and I advocate solutions to the needs all families have for economic well-being, legal recognition, emotional peace of mind, and community respect.

* * *

4. Rachel F. Moran, How Second–Wave Feminism Forgot the Single Woman, 33 Hofstra L. Rev. 223, 229–30 (2004).

5. Rich, Compulsory Heterosexuality and Lesbian Existence, 5 Signs 631, 654 (1980).

6. Moran, above note 4, at 225–28.

It is possible to envision family law and policy without marriage being the rigid dividing line between who is in and who is out. Keeping the state out of marriage entirely, making marriage only a religious, cultural, and spiritual matter, would be one way to accomplish this. But the law would still have to determine how to allocate rights and responsibilities in families and when relationships among people would create entitlements or obligations. This necessity, coupled with the disruption of expectations that ending the state's involvement in marriage would produce, suggests another approach.

I call this approach valuing all families. The most important element in implementing this approach is identifying the purpose of a law that now grants marriage unique legal consequences. By understanding a law's purpose, we can identify the relationships that would further that purpose without creating a special status for married couples.

* * *

Laws that distinguish between married couples and everyone else need to be reexamined. They stem from the days when a husband was the head of his household with a dependent wife at home, when a child born to an unmarried woman was a social outcast, and when virtually every marriage was for life regardless of the relationship's quality. It was a very different time.

When the Supreme Court declared the laws differentiating between men/husbands and women/wives unconstitutional, the laws became gender-neutral. This created a new problem. It left distinctions between married couples and everyone else without assessing the justness of that approach. It's time to make that assessment. Today more people live alone, more people live with unmarried partners, and more parents have minor children who live neither with them nor with their current spouse. The laws that affect families need to be evaluated in light of contemporary realities. A valuing-all-families approach does this by demanding a good fit between a law's purpose and the relationships subject to its reach.

* * *

Marriage brings with it a staggering number of legal consequences. A 2004 U.S. Government Accountability Office report identified 1,138 provisions of federal law that treat a relationship between two people who are married differently from any other relationship. The same is true at the state level. * * *

Advocates for same-sex marriage invoke these facts as evidence of the justness of same-sex couples' demand to be permitted to marry. They present the stories of couples whose family life mirrors that of married couples. They document the undesirable—sometimes tragic—consequences of excluding these couples from a legal status uniquely available to different-sex couples who marry. In the stories they tell, the *harm* is exclusion from marriage, and so the *remedy* is allowing same-sex couples to marry.

But the injustice same-sex couples suffer is not unique. When law makes marriage the dividing line, it harms all unmarried people, including those with children. The harm is the dividing line. The remedy is drawing a different line more closely tailored to achieving the law's purpose.

* * *

Laws that make marriage—only marriage and always marriage—different from all other relationships must be reevaluated. Many laws apply only to marriage because of marriage's historically gendered nature; these stray far from their original purpose. Until recently "husband" and "wife" remained distinctly gendered states, backed by distinctly gendered laws. In the 1970s the Supreme Court struck down gender-based distinctions. This left two options: extend a law equally to husbands and wives or eliminate it. Courts and legislatures did both. When they extended the laws, husbands and wives were then treated the same—a legal framework that would have shocked societies and legislatures and judges of previous centuries—but unlike everyone else.

These laws no longer serve their original purpose, which was tied to legally mandated sex roles in marriage. Laws enacted before no-fault divorce, the end of illegitimacy, and the elimination of rigid norms of gender and sexual expression must be reevaluated. When children are involved, the law already ties rights and responsibilities to *parenthood*, not to *marriage*; when a law's purpose is to protect children, marriage is never an appropriate dividing line. * * *

* * *

The valuing-all-families legal system keeps marriage and extends it to same-sex couples, although with a new official name—civil partnership. Over the past four decades, family laws have shed words laden with outmoded and undesirable meanings. The change in nomenclature symbolizes a break with the past.

* * *

"Marriage" has a long history of exclusion; slaves, interracial couples, and same-sex couples have been denied it. "Marriage" has a long, sex-stereotyped past that is both unconstitutional and inconsistent with modern values. For many people, "marriage" is moored to religious doctrine that belongs in churches, synagogues, and mosques. The terminology of civil partnership distances this legal status from its past and from the components of marriage that religions define. The legal terms "husband" and "wife" should also change, making way for the gender-neutral terms "spouse" and "partner."

A valuing-all-families approach will alter marriage's legal consequences, something the law has done repeatedly over the centuries. In this instance, with the relationships included in a law dependent on that law's purpose, a law might encompass some marriages and not others. If a law is designed to recognize or facilitate childrearing, for example, a marriage without children would be excluded and any household raising children would be included. While divorcing couples now have one set of rules for the economic consequences of separation and unmarried couples who split have another, laws might instead differentiate not based on marriage but based on whether the couple has raised a child or on some other criteria.

California's domestic partnership law, for example, which confers a status equal to that accorded spouses, allows dissolution of a domestic partnership by filing of a notice with the secretary of state, without having to go to court, if the couple meets certain criteria. These include that they have been registered for less than five years, have no children, own no real property, have relatively little money or other assets, and have a signed property settlement agreement.[a] The scheme reflects the sound principle that not all marriages should trigger the same legal consequences.

Finally, with marriage neither necessary nor sufficient to access particular laws, marriage would be a real *choice*. While the movement for marriage equality has insisted it is fighting for same-sex couples to have the choice to marry, marriage is not a choice if it is the *only* way to achieve economic well-being and peace of mind.

NOTES ON CHOOSING MARRIAGE

1. According to the 2000 Census, 52.9% of men and 49.5% of women in the United States were legally married with a present, different-sex spouse. However, these percentages vary by racial group. The largest percentage is the 56.8% of white men who are married with a present spouse, compared with 53.3% of Asian men, 44.0% of Native Hawaiian/Pacific Islander, 42.7% of Hispanic/Latino men (of any race), 41.0% of mixed-race men, 40.6% of another race alone, 40.1% of American Indian/Alaskan native, and 34.2% (by far the lowest) of Black men. The numbers are similar for women of different racial groups. Interestingly, however, the largest group of married women is Asians, with 55.8% of Asian women married with a present spouse, compared with 53.2% of white women, 46.2% of Hispanic/Latino women (of any race), 45.1% of Native Hawaiian/Pacific Islander, 45.0% of another race alone, 41.2% of mixed-race women, 40.0% of American Indian/Alaskan native, and only 27.5% of Black women. U.S. Census Bureau, Marital Status: 2000 3 tbl.1 (Oct. 2003).

A 2002 study conducted by the Centers for Disease Control and Prevention (CDC) did not consider Asian women, but largely confirmed the statistics above. The percentage of Black women increased, however, to 35.4% when the survey asked if women between 15 and 44 were presently in a marital or different-sex cohabiting union, and to 39.3% when the survey asked if those women had "ever married." CDC, Marriage and Cohabitation in the United States: A Statistical Portrait Based on Cycle 6 (2002) of the National Survey of Family Growth 19–25 (Feb. 2010). Why do you think Asian and white women and men are more likely to marry than women and men of other races? Why do you think Black women are so unlikely to marry? How might

---

a. California's divorce law is similar in this respect, allowing a summary divorce proceeding to couples without children or property who have been married five years or less. Cal. Fam. Code § 2400 (2009).

legal, economic, cultural, and religious factors be at work? What about different incarceration rates across race?

What role does race play in marriage and intimate relationships more generally? How might interracial relationships still be stigmatized? Studies reveal that the number of interracial marriages has increased in recent years. Jeffrey S. Passel, Wendy Wang & Paul Taylor, Pew Research Center, Marrying Out: One-in-Seven New U.S. Marriages is Interracial or Interethnic ii (2010). Do you think that acceptance and prevalence of interracial relationships varies according to the race of each partner? Are men and women of certain races more likely to enter into interracial relationships, and more likely to choose partners of certain other races? Karyn Langhorne Folan provides accounts of various notions that keep "black women from exploring relationships outside of their race, forty-three years after the Lovings' marriage was recognized as a legal union." Folan, Don't Bring Home a White Boy: And Other Notions That Keep Black Women from Dating Out 12 (2010). These notions include perceptions of attractiveness, concerns about children, familial acceptance, and societal perceptions of Black women as gold-diggers or sellouts. Might there be similar concerns for Black men dating women who are not Black? Or for women and men of other races?

2. The 2002 CDC study, above note 1, also found significant differences in marriage rates across class. The majority of women (55.1%) and men (51.5%) in the United States age 15–44 were presently in a different-sex union, defined as marriage or cohabitation. When surveying women between the age of 22 and 44, however, those percentages increased to 72.9% of women at 300% of the poverty level and above, and 70.3% of women between 150% and 299% of the poverty level. In contrast, only 53.9% of women in that age cohort living below 149% of the poverty level and 52.3% of women in the cohort living below 99% of the poverty level were presently in an different-sex union. The differences among men of various classes were less significant: for men in the 22 to 44 age cohort, 64.5% at 300% of the poverty level and above were in a different-sex union, compared to 66.7% between 150% and 299% of the poverty level, 64.5% below 149% of the poverty level and 61.4% below 99% of the poverty level. CDC, Marriage and Cohabitation in the United States: A Statistical Portrait Based on Cycle 6 (2002) of the National Survey of Family Growth 17–18 (Feb. 2010).

In 2008, the median income for all households in the United States was $50,303. That number rose to $62,621 for family households (two or more family members living together related by blood, adoption or marriage), and $73,010 for married-couple households (a subset of family households). In contrast, the median income for family households with a female householder and no husband present was $33,073, while the median for male householders with no wife present was $49,186. The numbers were even more dramatic for nonfamily households, who had a median income of $30,078. For households that did not fall under the family definition, male householders earned a median income of $36,006, while female householders earned only $25,014. U.S. Census Bureau, Income, Poverty, and Health Insurance Coverage in the United States: 2008 6 tbl.1 (Sept. 2009).

What do you think explains these differences across class and gender? What are the possible relationships between marriage and wealth? Might the statistics simply reveal that women living with or married to men tend to be wealthier than other women? Or do they imply that working-class women see their wealth decrease upon marriage? Either way, how might the potential links between marriage and wealth influence women's choices to enter marriage? How might women's increased earning power change the distribution of power within marriage?

3. In response to studies that report a correlation between marriage and happiness, Ruthann Robson argues:

> * * * [I]t is important to remember that the state itself creates the conditions that allow the married to be wealthier and healthier, and therefore perhaps happier, through a legal regime that benefits and promotes marriage. * * *
>
> The most obvious of the forces that maintain marriage are those that provide financial benefits to marital partners. The prevalent modern legal view of marriage in our capitalist state is that marriage is an economic partnership. The partnership is not necessarily an equal one, however, because implicit in this partnership idea remains the notion of economic dependency within the relationship and the existence of wider inequalities in capitalist society. * * *
>
> * * *
>
> Overall, U.S. economic policies foster and subsidize the economics of marriage. If we accept the notion that people will conform their behavior to maximize their economic gain, then the present legal regime operates as one of the forces that "organize" and "manage" people's "choice" whether or not to marry.

Ruthann Robson, Compulsory Matrimony, in Feminist and Queer Legal Theory: Intimate Encounters, Uncomfortable Conversations 313, 314, 316 (Martha Albertson Fineman, Jack E. Jackson & Adam P. Romero, eds. 2009). Given the statistics in note 2 above, are the pressures to marry largely financial? Would Polikoff agree? How do economic considerations intersect with other incentives to marry?

4. Given that women no longer necessarily need to be economically dependent on men, why do you think so many women continue to view marriage to a man as a desirable goal? See Hillary Frey, Why Ms. Independent Still Wants to Get Hitched; The Rules of Attraction, Nation, July 5, 2004, at 42. Is love the primary reason? What about social acceptance or other factors? Lori Gottlieb provides this advice to unmarried women over the age of 30:

> Settle! That's right. Don't worry about passion or intense connection. Don't nix a guy based on his annoying habit of yelling "Bravo!" in movie theaters. Overlook his halitosis or abysmal sense of aesthetics. Because if you want to have the infrastructure in place to have a family, settling is the way to go. Based on my observations, in fact, settling will probably make you happier in the long run, since many of those who marry with great expectations become more disillusioned with each passing year.

Gottlieb, Marry Him!, Atlantic Monthly, Mar. 2008, at 76. What do you think of Gottlieb's advice? What does it reveal about various factors that may influence women's choices to marry? See Claudia Card, Against Marriage and Motherhood, 11 Hypatia 1, 7 (1996) (describing marriage under current conditions as "not a totally free choice"). What implicit assumptions is Gottlieb making about men's relationship to marriage? Why do you think so many men continue to view marriage to a woman as a desirable goal? Or is marriage less of a goal for men? Instead of striving for marriage, are heterosexual men more likely to agree to marriage in order to maintain a relationship or receive care?

5. Many people think of marriage as a private institution existing outside of the law. How does Polikoff challenge that assumption? In her view, what are the main ways the law encourages individuals to choose marriage over other forms of relationship? What are some other ways the law induces individuals to marry? How might these inducements operate differently for women rather than men? How might they operate differently across race and class?

Why is Polikoff concerned about legal inducements to marry? What is their harm? Might there be any benefits from a feminist perspective?

6. What are some of the ways unmarried women are ignored by law and society? How might being "single" be viewed as a status to be pitied or a prelude to marriage? Bella DePaulo argues that "[p]eople who do not have a serious coupled relationship (my definition, for now, of single people) are stereotyped, discriminated against, and treated dismissively." DePaulo, Singled Out: How Singles are Stereotyped, Stigmatized, and Ignored, and Still Live Happily Ever After 2 (2006). The two most recently appointed Supreme Court Justices, Sonia Sotomayor and Elena Kagan, have been unmarried, which sparked questions of whether they were lesbians. See Maureen Dowd, All the Single Ladies, N.Y. Times, May 18, 2010, at A27. Why do people assume an unmarried woman is lesbian? Do perceptions change if a woman has been partnered with a man in the past? Do unmarried men face similar problems?

7. Polikoff does not seek to end state recognition of marriage, but instead calls on states to confer benefits on multiple forms of relationships between adults in order to promote more freedom to choose or not choose marriage. In contrast, many queer theorists argue that the state should not recognize marriage or otherwise confer benefits on some relationships to the exclusion of others. For example, Michael Warner writes:

> As long as people marry, the state will continue to regulate the sexual lives of those who do not marry. It will continue to refuse to recognize our intimate relations—including cohabiting partnerships—as having the same rights or validity as a married couple. It will criminalize our consensual sex. It will stipulate at what age and in what kind of space we can have sex. It will send the police to harass sex workers and cruisers. It will restrict our access to sexually explicit materials. All this and more the state will justify because these sexual relations take place outside of marriage. In the modern era, marriage has become the central legitimating institution by which the state regulates and permeates people's most

> intimate lives; it is the zone of privacy outside of which sex is unprotected. In this context, to speak of marriage as merely one choice among others is at best naïve.

Warner, The Trouble With Normal: Sex, Politics, and the Ethics of Queer Life 96 (2000). What are the advantages and disadvantages of Warner's approach compared to Polikoff's valuing-all-families approach? Who might be left out or harmed under either approach? Can you think of additional ways to address Polikoff's and Warner's concerns?

8. Polikoff also discusses the legal agenda of the so-called marriage movement, which "wants to make divorces harder to obtain," opposes same-sex marriage, and "supports distinguishing the legal consequences of marriage from those associated with any other relationship":

> In other words, it favors "special rights" for married couples unavailable to other families or relationships. It justifies this special status in order to create a "marriage culture" that will result in more children being born to married parents, thereby, it claims, reducing a host of social problems.
>
> * * *
>
> Given their emphasis on how good marriage is for children, secular marriage-movement proponents have had to articulate why it should be unavailable to gay and lesbian couples who raise children. Their response has been insistence on the specialized roles of husbands and wives. * * *
>
> In literature and court briefs, marriage-movement proponents argue that, unlike mothers, good fathers are "made, not born," and heterosexual marriage is what makes them. Whitehead and Popenoe call marriage the "glue" that binds fathers to children. Proponents also claim that only marriage tames men's innately promiscuous and antisocial nature. As Glenn Stanton of Focus on the Family put it, "marriage is . . . the way societies socialize men and protect women from predatory males."

Polikoff, above, at 80–81. What might this marriage movement reveal about the link between gender-neutral family laws and gender equality? Even if the law removed all gender distinctions, would biology and culture still support differentiated gender roles within the family?

9. How does different-sex marriage shape or construct our understandings of gender? Historically, the state recognized marriage, and only marriage, as a means of privatizing women's and children's dependency in an era when women had few political and economic rights. Individual men, as opposed to the state, assumed responsibility for this dependency through marriage and generally received the full range of citizenship rights in return. See Nancy F. Cott, Public Vows: A History of Marriage and the Nation 7 (2000). Wives had to rely on their husband's financial and political support, and they provided the domestic support that made their husband's participation in the market and political realm possible. Given these roots, the state's recognition of marriage may be more about gender than love, intimacy or companionship. See Herma Hill Kay, "Making Marriage and Divorce Safe for Women" Revisited, 32 Hofstra L. Rev. 71, 89–91 (2003) (arguing that the law of marriage is a "codification of society's attitudes about women"). Do you think

marriage can ever transcend this gendered history? If it can, how would conceptions of gender change?

10. Do you agree with Polikoff that the state should treat spouses and other partners with children differently than spouses and other partners without children? What are the advantages of the current one-size-fits-all approach to marriage? What are some of the potential harms? How might the current approach affect individuals' choices to marry and their choices within marriage? Do you think Gottlieb would change her advice in note 4 above if the state supported childrearing outside of marriage on the same terms as childrearing within marriage? How might the current approach devalue marriages that do not involve children? Polikoff emphasizes:

> Adults build relationships for purposes other than childrearing. Whether married or unmarried, sexual or platonic, connected through biology, adoption, extended family, or choice, adults create relationships that contribute to their health, happiness, well-being, identity, and security. A society that cares about the welfare of its people will make laws that value and support those relationships. Laws must also justly address the consequences of these relationships when they end through death or dissolution.

Polikoff, above, at 141. Would her valuing-all-families approach reduce the pressure to have children that many women experience? Would that be a good or bad result?

2. DYNAMICS WITHIN MARRIAGE

CAROLE PATEMAN, THE SEXUAL CONTRACT

116–117, 118, 128, 167 (1988).

The old, domestic contracts between a master and his (civil) slave and a master and his servant were labour contracts. Slaves and servants labour at the behest of their masters. The marriage contract, too, is a kind of labour contract. To become a wife entails becoming a housewife; that is, a wife is someone who works for her husband in the marital home. But what kind of labourer is a (house)wife? How does the conjugal labour contract resemble or differ from other domestic labour contracts, or from the present-day employment contract? What form of subordination is involved in being a (house)wife? What is the significance of the fact that only women become (house)wives? * * *

* * *

* * * Contract is the specifically modern means of creating relationships of subordination, but, because civil subordination originates in contract, it is presented as freedom. * * *

Private domestic relations also originate in a contract—but the meaning of the marriage contract, a contract between a man and a woman, is very different from the meaning of contracts between men in the public sphere. The marriage contract reflects the patriarchal ordering of nature embodied in the original contract. A sexual division of labour is constituted through the marriage contract. * * *

* * *

A (house)wife now performs the tasks once distributed between servants of different rank or undertaken by the maid of all work. Her 'core' jobs are cleaning, shopping, cooking, washing-up, laundering and ironing. She also looks after her children, frequently cares for aged parents or other relatives, and is sometimes incorporated to a greater or lesser degree as an unpaid assistant in her husband's work. * * * The problem is not that wives perform valuable tasks for which they are not paid (which has led some feminists to argue for state payment or wages for housework). Rather, what being a woman (wife) *means* is to provide certain services for and at the command of a man (husband). In short, the marriage contract and a wife's subordination as a (kind of) labourer, cannot be understood in the absence of the sexual contract and the patriarchal construction of 'men' and 'women' and the 'private' and 'public' spheres.

* * *

* * * Unlike other contracts, the marriage contract cannot be entered into by any two (or more) sane adults, but is restricted to two parties, one of whom must be a man and the other a woman (and who must not be related in certain prescribed ways). Not only does a 'husband' obtain a certain power over his wife whether or not he wishes to have it, but the marriage contract is sexually ascriptive. A man is always a 'husband' and a woman is always a 'wife'. * * * Freedom of contract (proper contract) demands that no account is taken of substantive attributes—such as sex. If marriage is to be truly contractual, sexual difference must become irrelevant to the marriage contract; 'husband' and 'wife' must no longer be sexually determined. Indeed, from the standpoint of contract, 'men' and 'women' would disappear.

SUSAN MOLLER OKIN, JUSTICE, GENDER, AND THE FAMILY

135–136, 138–139, 141 (1989).

* * * [M]arriage and the family, as currently practiced in our society, are unjust institutions. They constitute the pivot of a societal system of gender that renders women vulnerable to dependency, exploitation, and abuse. When we look seriously at the distribution between husbands and wives of such critical social goods as work (paid and unpaid), power, prestige, self-esteem, opportunities for self-development, and both physical and economic security, we find socially constructed inequalities between them, right down the list.

* * *

* * * Few people would disagree with the statement that marriage involves, in some respects, especially emotionally, mutual vulnerability

and dependence. It is, clearly, also a relationship in which some aspects of unequal vulnerability are not determined along sex lines. For example, spouses may vary in the extent of their love for and emotional dependence on each other; it is certainly not the case that wives always love their husbands more than they are loved by them, or vice versa. Nevertheless [in] crucial respects gender-structured marriage involves women in a cycle of socially caused and distinctly asymmetric vulnerability. The division of labor within marriage (except in rare cases) makes wives far more likely than husbands to be exploited both within the marital relationship and in the world of work outside the home. To a great extent and in numerous ways, contemporary women in our society are made vulnerable by marriage itself. They are first set up for vulnerability during their developing years by their personal (and socially reinforced) expectations that they will be the primary caretakers of children, and that in fulfilling this role they will need to try to attract and to keep the economic support of a man, to whose work life they will be expected to give priority. They are rendered vulnerable by the actual division of labor within almost all current marriages. They are disadvantaged at work by the fact that the world of wage work, including the professions, is still largely structured around the assumption that "workers" have wives at home. They are rendered far more vulnerable if they become the primary caretakers of children, and their vulnerability peaks if their marriages dissolve and they become single parents.

* * *

* * * Part of the peculiarity of contemporary marriage comes from its very lack of definition. The fact that society seems no longer to have any consensual view of the norms and expectations of marriage is particularly apparent from the gulf that exists between the continued perception of most men and women that it is still the primary responsibility of husbands to "provide for" their wives by participating in wage work and of wives to perform a range of unpaid "services" for their husbands, and the fact that most women, including mothers of small children, are both in the labor force and performing the vast majority of household duties. In addition, the persistent perception of the male as provider is irreconcilable with both the prevalence of separation and divorce and the fact that, more and more, women and children are not being provided for after divorce. Between the expectations and the frequent outcome lies an abyss that not only is unjust in itself but radically affects the ways in which people behave within marriage. * * *

* * *

The traditional idea of sex-differentiated marital responsibility, with its provider-husband and domestic-wife roles, continues to be a strong influence on what men and women think and how they behave. * * * Given the emphasis our society places on economic success, belief in the male provider role strongly reinforces the domination of men within marriage. Although * * * many wives actually work longer hours (counting paid and unpaid work) than their husbands, the fact that a husband's work is predominantly paid gives him not only status and prestige, both within and outside the marriage, but also a greater sense of entitlement. As a consequence, wives experiencing divorce, especially if they have been housewives and mothers throughout marriage, are likely to devalue their own contributions to the marriage and to discount their right to share its assets. * * * In ongoing marriages too, it is not uncommon for husbands to use the fact that they are the primary breadwinners to enforce their views or wishes.

ROBIN WEST, MARRIAGE, SEXUALITY, AND GENDER

181–88 (2007).

* * * Study after study after study has shown, with almost mind-numbing-regularity, that working married women continue to do considerably more domestic work than their husbands—they do considerably more childcare and vastly more housework. They work a "second shift," while their husbands do not: they come home from their paid job, as do their husbands, and put in another four, six, or eight hours of work at home, while their husbands do not. They have less leisure time, as a result, and they also earn less money in their paid work, as well: as mothers, these women take more time out of the paid labor force to accommodate their domestic and child-care duties. * * * Mothers work less at work, and so they earn less. That alone, of course, doesn't seem odd, or particularly unfair. They also, however, work considerably more at home, and earn nothing for it. Overall, wives work more hours than husbands, and earn considerably less.

So—is this injustice a problem? Plenty of people think not. The whole arrangement is fully voluntary. * * * She didn't have to enter this marriage, and she can always leave. At every point that brought her to this stage in her life, [she] has had options. She wanted to get married, and she wanted to marry this man, and she obviously prefers to stay with him than to leave. So again, is this injustice a problem?

The short answer is that of course it is. Whether or not both consent to it—whether or not both view the arrangement as preferable to alternatives—it is transparently and flagrantly unfair for one of two adults living intimately and with a sense of shared mutual responsibility for the well-being of the other, to do the bulk of undesirable work from which they both benefit. Any child knows this, including the children raised in these second-shift households, who nevertheless, over time, and for the most easily understood reasons, come to view both the distribution of labor, and the unfairness of it, as natural. The second shift represents a continual, day-to-day, gnawing, exhausting, self-denigrating injustice. Every load of laundry, every dirty dish, every changed diaper, every unmade bed, every overgrown flower bed, addressed by one partner with no help from the other, and with no anticipation of help, and with no eventual balancing of the books, is an injustice. * * * It has adverse effects on the woman herself; on our societal understanding of the value of caregiving labor, and on the children who absorb it * * *.

First, consider the psychic effect of the second shift on the woman herself. * * * When you're treated unjustly day by day by day, the net effect will be not only rising and perfectly rational doubts about your own self-worth—you must not be deserving of basic justice—but also, an increasing willingness to be treated as subordinate. A lack of self-regard and a lack of due regard from others we hold in high esteem unsurprisingly results in a willingness to submit, a willingness to dispossess the self, to enlist the self in the service of others.

Second, consider the effect of the second shift on the larger society, and particularly on its valuation of caregiving and domestic labor. Wives work the second shift for nothing. * * * Nannies, babysitters, day-care workers, elder-care providers, and house cleaners earn the lowest wages going—except, of course, the wage rate for the housewife herself, which is zero. If a man can get a woman to do work for free by marrying her, it is not likely that he will choose to pay someone a substantial amount to do it for pay, when push comes to shove and he's forced to. * * * It is very hard to see how this cycle can be brought to heel, by private action, or market transactions, alone.

Third, consider the effect of the second shift on the children raised in the families that foster it. Children born into a family in which a mother but not a father works an uncompensated second shift are the direct beneficiaries—along with the father—of structural domestic injustice. * * *

* * * Women who can work good jobs for fair compensation, bring home half or more of a family's income, and have no serious impediment to separation or divorce should they so choose, nevertheless remain in marriages where they do a disproportionate amount of domestic labor. The alternatives for these women are obviously either worse or perceived to be worse: ending the marriage, loneliness, a losing struggle with one's mate that will diminish the quality of the marriage, or a filthy house and neglected children.

Hardy though it may be, however, the second shift is neither inevitable nor impervious to change. * * * In our own marriages, the wives do more domestic labor than our husbands, but at the same time, our husbands do more—even far more—domestic labor than did their own fathers. That these two lived realities are being experienced jointly, I think, is significant, both for our politics and for the quality of our lives. It suggests a straightforward explanation for what is otherwise puzzling, and that is that women in "second-shift" households often report themselves relatively satisfied with their marriages. Perhaps that is not so odd. Our own marriages, in spite of their manifest injustice, are more just than the home environment in which we were ourselves raised. * * *

That doubled experience might explain some degree of complacency, then. It also, though, suggests a moral imperative. We know, from the very fact of the distance between our own upbringing and the distribution of labor in our current marriages, that that distribution is both unjust and can be rectified. The second shift, like marriage generally, is a constructed institution. It can be changed. Thus, the imperative. Injustice that truly can't be changed perhaps should be tolerated * * * but injustice that can be changed, should be. The injustice within marriage is demonstrably of the latter sort. I reach this conclusion: contemporary civil marriage is very good for most participants, and it sure works for me. But marriage must also be made just—both the institution and my own. The injustice of this institution, even conceding its manifest social utility, should be addressed and rectified.

A nascent movement for egalitarian marriage—what is sometimes called the "just marriage" movement—seeks to do so, and to explore and remedy related injustices intertwined with marriage as well. Political philosopher Mary Shanley, and law Professor Linda McClain, now argue that the challenge facing us regarding contemporary marriage, both as an institution and as a legal structure, is to figure a way to retain it, but to remake it justly. * * * Our public institutions and work relations, we assume, should be regulated by norms that must themselves be just, and when they are not, they are properly criticized by reference to that virtue. In private intimate life, by contrast, it is widely believed that relations should be regulated not by reference to the virtue of justice, but rather, by reference to the domestic virtues of altruism, devotion, sacrifice, and love. This division of not only labor, but also of virtues, has been terrible for the public sphere: the public worlds of politics, commerce, and industry could use a healthy dollop of compassion, care, community responsibility, and altruism. But this same division of critical labor and virtue has also been a bad deal for women and family members in the private sphere: an unjust household is not particularly humane. So long as the ideal of "just marriage" continues to strike many as odd, or paradoxical, marriage will be unjust, and so long as marriage is unjust, its participants will have lesser lives because of it.

So, what would just marriage entail? Minimally, it would mean an end to the undue privatization and underenforcement of criminal laws against domestic violence and marital rape. Ending violence within marriage would correct a double injustice: the injustice of the violence, and violation, itself, but second, the injustice of the state's neglect of it—it is the latter, rather than the former, that reflects women's debased status as secondary citizens. But second, just marriage would require an end to the undue privatization, the unjust distribution, and the undercompensation, of the caregiving and domestic labor that wives specifically, and women more generally, perform. It would require an end to the second shift. * * *

How to achieve that? Reform proposals proliferate. Paychecks in single-wage households could be required, by law, to be issued to both spouses as payees, rather than one, where a spouse is at home with children, and not in the wage market. Fathers could be either encouraged or required to take advantage of paternity and family leaves, upon the birth or adoption of a baby. Employers could be required to provide flexibility to workers who are parents, as well as to workers who are children of aging parents, as well as workers who are partners of sick or disabled loved ones, and who need hours in a week, or weeks in a year, or years over the course of a working career, to provide for the essential needs of dependents. Women who stay at home through substantial parts of their adulthood to care for small children or aging parents could be better protected through the Social Security system, by earning entitlements to their own Social Security through their own caregiving labor, rather than earning those entitlements only parasitically through their husbands. Most important, we could societally pick up part of the tab, through tax dollars, of some of the costs of caregiving, and we could do this either through compensating mothers or fathers who do this work for infants, in the form of paid family leaves, or by heavily subsidizing universal prekindergarten childcare. * * *

Just marriage cannot possibly come to be solely through changing the internal work distribution within family. Rather, as Law Professor Joan Williams has amply demonstrated, the workforce must undergo fundamental change as well. The modern workforce is designed to serve the interests of ideal breadwinning male employees: the nine-to-five workday; the heightened demands on workers in their twenties and thirties when women, but not men, are experiencing their years of greatest reproductive capacity; the now expanding expectation (because of technology that brings work home) that a worker will willingly devote undivided attention to an employer's needs and demands through the day, week, and year; the apparent inability—or simple refusal—of the work world and the public sector to jointly create a daily and yearly school schedule that accommodates working parents. These patterns of work life presuppose an ideal, male, breadwinning employee, freed from the demands of his dependents by virtue of having a nonworking wife at home. Such an ideal couple, consisting of a breadwinning husband and nonworking wife, of course, is no longer the norm, and was never particularly functional even when it was. What we now have, then, is a work life and home life structured by law, by social expectation, by custom, and by the economic- and market-driven demands of employers, to meet the needs of a dysfunctional and discarded norm. * * *

* * *

* * * If the political, democratic will is there to render civil marriage more just, law can be put to the task. Marriage in the year 2000 is no more a child of nature, divine providence, intelligent design, than was the unregulated labor contract between capitalist and worker in 1900. We—meaning, "we humans"—created the common law of contract that made the worker's labor agreement look so misleadingly natural, benign, and mutually rewarding. Then, we remade our law to make it ever so slightly more rewarding, or at least less dangerous and dehumanizing, for workers. Likewise, here. We—"we humans"—created the laws of marriage,

property, divorce, contract, and inheritance that have made the traditional marriage contract appear the same. We radically changed the labor contract, and we did it through law, democratically imposed, upon the will of capitalists and employees both. We can surely do the same thing here. Liberal scholars of the family, of marriage, and justice—Susan Okin and Molly Shanley in philosophy, Linda McClain and Joan Williams, in law—are showing us how.

NOTES ON DYNAMICS WITHIN MARRIAGE

1. What different dynamics within marriage are identified by Pateman, Okin, and West? How do their concepts of power and well-being within marriage differ? How are they similar? What would a just conception of marriage look like for Pateman, Okin, and West? Is egalitarian marriage the only feminist marriage? How would the feminist theorists discussed in Chapter 3 answer that question? What does equality mean in the marriage context? What are other paths toward achieving feminist marriage?

2. Nancy Fraser criticizes Pateman for focusing on the master/subject relationship within the marital dyad, and instead finds Okin's analysis of the institutional context of marriage persuasive. Fraser, Beyond the Master/Subject Model: Reflections on Carole Pateman's Sexual Contract, 37 Soc. Text 173, 175 (1993). Which approach do you find more persuasive? Which seems more accurate? Are the two approaches reconcilable? Is it easier to address the problems posed by Pateman or by Okin? What solutions could you find to address each? How does West extend Okin's discussion of the institutional context of marriage?

3. Various social science studies have attempted to measure spouses' well-being within marriage. Studies in the 1980's and 1990's found that many wives were dissatisfied with their disproportionate share of domestic housekeeping responsibilities, yet few of them attempted to negotiate with their husbands for a more equitable division of such tasks. See Roberta S. Sigel, Ambition & Accommodation: How Women View Gender Relations 96–98, 167–68 (1996). Somewhat surprisingly, studies also found that employed mothers reported more sadness and dissatisfaction with their marriages when their husbands took on a larger share of housekeeping responsibilities, although the same mothers reported more happiness and satisfaction with their marriages when they had an equal say in decisionmaking and their husbands shared in the responsibilities of child care and childrearing. Janice M. Steil, Marital Equality: Its Relationship to the Well–Being of Husbands and Wives 32–35, 39–42 (1997). Some commentators viewed such findings as "consistent with the hypothesis that gender differences in emotional well-being and mental health are associated with gender differences in power and status," although they do not "tell the whole story." Id. at 42. Other commentators, interpreting similar data, have concluded that married women are happier if they eschew gender equality and instead embrace traditional expectations of marriage. W. Bradford Wilcox & Steven L. Nock, What's Love Got To Do With It? Equality, Equity, Commitment & Women's Marital Quality, 84 Soc. Forces 1321, 1339–40 (2006).

If you received a grant to study the issue of power and well-being within different-sex marriage among spouses of different races, what questions would you want to ask? Would you ask different questions of the wives than of the husbands? How would race alter the questions you asked to wives and husbands? What about class or religion? How would the following factors be likely to influence power and well-being within marriage: emotional dependence; commitment to the marriage; expectations of the marriage; options at divorce; economic dependence (especially in light of divorce options); age; membership in a socially dominant group (such as men, whites, upper class, Harvard graduates, J.D.'s, etc.); children who need care; appearance; or the need to be socially accepted as a "couple." Which partner would each factor likely empower in most marriages?

4. Is there an accurate way to measure power in marriage? What factors would you consider to determine who has more power in marriage? Should we measure power in marriage by comparing differences in money from wage work; or by comparing hours spent on household chores and care work (the more hours, the less power); or by comparing hours of leisure (the more leisure, the more power)? How would such approaches implicitly value wage work and leisure over care work?

Although women's hours working outside the home have risen dramatically over the last 40 years, there has been no dramatic change in men's domestic labor. See Liana C. Sayer, Gender, Time and Inequality: Trends in Women's and Men's Paid Work, Unpaid Work and Free Time, 84 Soc. Forces 285, 286 (2005); Michael Selmi, Family Leave and the Gender Wage Gap, 78 N.C. L. Rev. 707, 709 (2000). Instead, in marriages where both spouses are engaged in wage work, the total amount of housekeeping decreases (although wives still perform more than their husbands) and wives generally perform twice as much child care work as their husbands. Suzanne M. Bianchi, John P. Robinson & Melissa A. Milkie, Changing Rhythms of American Family Life 91 (2006). What does this suggest about the relative distribution of power in marriage?

5. In 2008, the median income for full-time year-round male workers was $46,367, compared with $35,745 for female workers. The female-to-male earnings ratio in 2008 was 0.771. U.S. Census Bureau, Income, Poverty, and Health Insurance Coverage in the United States: 2008 36 tbl. A–2 (Sept. 2009). Note that these figures do not include part-time workers, and that women are more likely to be part-time workers than men. In addition to receiving less money by working fewer hours, part-time workers also generally do not receive health and other employment benefits.

There is some evidence that men's higher wages, more than the distribution of housework or other care work, support men's unequal power within different-sex marriage. Cathleen Zick, W. Bryant & Sivithee Srisukhumbowornchai, Does Housework Matter Anymore? The Shifting Impact of Housework on Economic Inequality, 6 Rev. Econ. of the Household 1 (2008). If this is true, should feminists spend less time worrying about care work and more time focused on increasing women's wages? Or are women married to men stuck in a double bind? For example, another study found that wives began to do a greater share of housework once they earned more than their husbands.

Theodore N. Greenstein, Economic Dependence, Gender, and the Division of Labor in the Home: A Replication and Extension, 62 J. Marriage & Fam. 322, 333 (2000). Why might higher wages actually increase a woman's domestic responsibilities? The authors of the study attributed the phenomenon to the greater importance of conforming to gendered roles with regard to unpaid work if the couple does not conform to those roles with regard to paid work. See id. at 333; see also Michael Bittman, Paula England, Nancy Folbre, Liana Sayer & George Matheson, When Does Gender Trump Money? Bargaining and Time in Household Work, 109 Am. J. Soc. 186, 192 (2003) (also finding that couples in which women earn more money than men seem to compensate with a more traditional division of household work); Allen M. Parkman, Bargaining Over Housework: The Frustrating Situation of Secondary Wage Earners, 63 Am. J. Econ. & Soc. 765 (2004) (finding that both spouses respond to changes in relative earnings when making decisions about the amount of housework to perform but the response of husbands, who tend be the higher earners, is smaller than that of wives).

6. Does West assume that marriage is inevitable? Note that she describes "[t]he expectation that women will and should perform extra labors for free," when in fact she is talking about wives, as opposed to women in general. Later, West refers to "the caregiving and domestic labor that wives specifically, and women more generally, perform." Which women is West referring to, if not wives? Mothers? Daughters? Cohabitants? Sisters? Lesbians? Friends? Girlfriends? Domestic workers or nannies? How might West be read to privilege wives over these other women? How do assumptions about the inevitability of marriage affect West's analysis of power within marriage?

7. West states that "[s]o long as the ideal of 'just marriage' continues to strike many as odd, or paradoxical, marriage will be unjust, and so long as marriage is unjust, its participants will have lesser lives because of it." Do you agree with this statement? What does this statement say about the role of marriage in people's lives? Notice that she refers to "participants," implying that both parties will suffer. Do you think that one participant will suffer more than the other? Who and why? How do men suffer from unjust marriages?

Do you share West's optimism about the possibility of just marriage? How would Mary Joe Frug likely respond to such optimism? As you may recall from Chapter 3, Frug stated that "[t]he question ... is not whether sex differences exist—they do—or how to transcend—we can't." Frug, A Postmodern Feminist Legal Manifesto (An Unfinished Draft), 105 Harv. L. Rev. 1045, 1052 (1992). Is West suggesting that we can transcend traditional sex roles? If so, how might that relate to the value West places on women's connectedness, as discussed in Chapter 3?

8. In what other ways can we look at power dynamics within marriage? Elizabeth Emens approaches the issue under the framework of name-changing at marriage. She observes that:

> Under current conventions, women's choices in this area are sharply limited. This is true in the obvious sense that social costs accompany unconventional choices, thereby creating the collective action problem surrounding any attempt to change social meaning. Women's choices are

> also limited in the sense that what men do with their names constrains the overall marital naming options: since men almost never change their names, and since children typically take their father's name even when their mother makes an unconventional naming choice for herself, women lack a naming option that creates continuity among their parents, their spouses, and their children.

Emens, Changing Name–Changing: Framing Rules and the Future of Marital Names, 74 U. Chi. L. Rev. 761, 764 (2007). Emens further notes that for women, changing their name to "Mrs. His Name" is the norm (the "social default"), despite the current legal default of "keeping" her name. "Although no longer required to do so, the majority of women take their husbands' names at marriage. This suggests that something other than law is largely driving behavior, at least for women. So what role is law playing, and what role should it play?" Id. at 763. How would you answer these questions? In other areas of the law, legal default rules encourage behavior to conform to the default. Why does that not happen in this context? Why do women so often change their name upon marriage, despite the onerous steps required? (Emens identifies 33 different types of entities that a woman must inform of her marital name change.) How do Emens' observations relate to power within marriage? How are the dynamics of name-changing different from the second shift and other allocations of time to paid, unpaid and leisure activities within marriage? How might name-changing nonetheless affect how spouses allocate their time to paid, unpaid, and leisure activities within marriage?

Emens argues that states should institute laws or procedures designed to encourage spouses to discuss and negotiate their marital-name options instead of relying on social conventions. Do you think this would alter name-changing practices? What costs would such a negotiation involve? Do you think people would be willing to incur those costs in the name of equality? Might laws and procedures designed to encourage spouses to discuss other aspects of their marriage alter power dynamics within marriage? How would you extend Emens' proposal to issues involving the allocation of wage work, care work, and leisure?

9. How do relationships with children affect power in marriage? How might custody standards at divorce affect power during marriage? (For more on custody standards, see Chapter 7.) How might concern about the economic well-being of children after divorce affect power during marriage? How might concern about one's own economic status after divorce affect power in marriage? See, e.g., Penelope Eileen Bryan, The Coercion of Women in Divorce Settlement Negotiations, 74 Denv. U. L. Rev. 931, 931–35 (1997) (describing how a variety of unfair background conditions, including custody standards, concern for children, and unequal economic power affect divorce negotiations and settlements). See also Bryan, Women's Freedom to Contract at Divorce: A Mask for Contextual Coercion, 47 Buff. L. Rev. 1153 (1999).

10. Researchers have long reported that married individuals, women as well as men, enjoy a marriage bonus: they are healthier, happier, and better off financially than those who are single or cohabiting. See Alois Stutzer & Bruno S. Frey, Does Marriage Make People Happy or Do Happy People Get Married?, 35 J. Soc.-Econ. 326, 342 (2006) (finding that marriage continues to

be highly correlated with happiness for both men and women and that "[i]t is unlikely that * * * selection effects can explain the entire difference in well-being between singles and married people"); Linda J. Waite & Maggie Gallagher, The Case for Marriage (2000). However, "new research is increasingly presenting a more nuanced view of the so-called marriage advantage." Tara Parker–Pope, Is Marriage Good for Your Health?, N.Y. Times, Apr. 12, 2010, Magazine §, at 46. As Parker–Pope reports:

> Several new studies, for instance, show that the marriage advantage doesn't extend to those in troubled relationships, which can leave a person far less healthy than if he or she had never married at all. One recent study suggests that a stressful marriage can be as bad for the heart as a regular smoking habit. And despite years of research suggesting that single people have poorer health than those who marry, a major study released last year concluded that single people who have never married have better health than those who married and then divorced. Both married women and married men tend to be healthier than single individuals, although marriage leads to a greater physical health advantage for men than women.
>
> * * *
>
> Perhaps the most striking finding concerned single people who had never married. For more than 100 years, scientists have speculated that single people, because they generally have fewer resources, lower income and perhaps less logistical and emotional support, have poorer health than the married. But in the Chicago study, people who had divorced or been widowed had worse health problems than men and women who had been single their entire lives. In formerly married individuals, it was as if the marriage advantage had never existed.

Id.; see also Charlotte N. Markey, Patrick M. Markey, Carl Schneider & Susan Brownlee, Marital Status and Health Benefits: Different Relations for Men and Women, 53 Sex Roles 443, 444 (2005) (examining possible explanations for the significant disparity in health benefits that marriage has for men as compared to women). What might such studies reveal about why individuals "choose" marriage? What might these studies reveal about power dynamics within marriage?

3. SAME–SEX MARRIAGE

TEXT NOTE: CAMPAIGNS FOR SAME-SEX MARRIAGE PRIOR TO 2000

The issue of same-sex marriage is currently at the forefront of American politics. Despite the visibility of the debate, gay and lesbian activists only recently placed the fight to gain access to legal marriage at the top of their legislative, judicial, and public relations agendas. Many earlier activists instead questioned the desirability of legal marriage, finding it to be a "problem because it channeled everyone into only one approved relationship, it regulated the lives of men and women along gender lines, and it policed the boundary between acceptable and unacceptable sexual expression."[7]

Despite this internal debate, increasing amounts of litigation brought by lesbian and gay couples beginning in the 1990's brought the issue of same-sex marriage out of the gay and lesbian community and into the spotlight of national politics. These cases drew on a few earlier cases brought in the 1970's, which made one or both of two arguments, one statutory and the other constitutional. Courts facing the statutory challenge—that plaintiffs were entitled to a marriage license under the relevant state marriage statutes—relied on an ordinary understanding of marriage as an institution reserved for different-sex couples to dismiss the plaintiffs' claims, even when the relevant statute contained no language suggesting a requirement that couples be of different sex to marry.[8]

Early courts facing the constitutional argument—that different-sex marriage requirements discriminated on the basis of sex much like the Supreme Court found that same-race marriage requirements discriminated on the basis of race in Loving v. Virginia, 388 U.S. 1 (1967)—were forced to engage in more analysis. In *Loving*, the Supreme Court held that Virginia's criminal law against marriages between members of the "white race" and of "other races" discriminated on the basis of race, impermissibly denying individuals seeking to enter marriages involving a white and non-white spouse the fundamental right to marry. The state of Virginia had argued that because anti-miscegenation "statutes punish equally both the white and the Negro participants in an interracial marriage, these statutes, despite their reliance on racial classifications do not constitute an invidious discrimination based upon race."[9] The Court rejected this argument:

> There can be no question but that Virginia's miscegenation statutes rest solely upon distinctions drawn according to race. The statutes proscribe generally accepted conduct if engaged in by members of different races. * * * At the very least, the Equal Protection Clause demands that racial classifications, especially suspect in criminal statutes, be subjected to the "most rigid scrutiny," and, if they are ever to be upheld, they must be shown to be necessary to the accomplishment of some permissible state objective, independent of the racial discrimination which it was the object of the Fourteenth Amendment to eliminate. * * *
>
> There is patently no legitimate overriding purpose independent of invidious racial discrimination which justifies this classification. The fact that Virginia prohibits only interracial marriages involving white persons demonstrates that the racial classifications must stand on their own justification, as measures designed to maintain White Supremacy.[10]

By analogy, gay and lesbian challengers to different-sex marriage requirements argued that if race-based restrictions discriminate on the basis of race, then sex-based restrictions discriminate on the basis of sex. Early courts also rejected this argument, but only after explaining why facial classifications on

7. Nancy D. Polikoff, Equality and Justice for Lesbian and Gay Families and Relationships, 61 Rutgers L. Rev. 529, 530 (2009).

8. See, e.g., Jones v. Hallahan, 501 S.W.2d 588 (Ky. App. 1973).

9. 388 U.S. at 8.

10. Id. at 11.

the basis of sex were different from such classifications on the basis of race, most obviously because, in those courts' view, different-sex marriage requirements were not designed to maintain male supremacy over women.[11]

In three of the cases brought in the 1990's, however, judges in Hawaii, Alaska, and Vermont ruled in favor of same-sex couples on various constitutional claims. The Supreme Court of Hawaii held that the denial of a marriage license to a same-sex couple was a violation of the Equal Rights Amendment to the Hawaii Constitution.[12] The court reasoned that if a statute banning interracial marriage discriminated on the basis of race, as the United States Supreme Court had held in *Loving*, then a statute banning same-sex marriage discriminated on the basis of sex in violation of the provision against sex discrimination in the Hawaiian Constitution. The Hawaii Supreme Court remanded the case to provide the state with an opportunity to justify the sex-based classification on the ground that it served compelling governmental purposes. At trial, Hawaii failed to bear this burden, and the state's ban on same-sex marriage was therefore held unconstitutional.[13] While this decision was on appeal, however, a referendum amended the state constitution to provide that the legislature could limit marriage to different-sex couples, thus mooting the case. A similar course of successful litigation and constitutional amendment to reverse its results occurred in Alaska in 1998.[14]

In 1999, however, the Supreme Court of Vermont held in Baker v. Vermont that Vermont's marriage law was unconstitutional.[15] The Vermont Constitution contains a Common Benefits Clause, which the *Baker* Court interpreted to hold that same-sex couples could not be excluded from all the benefits associated with marriage under state law. The Court left it up to the legislature to decide how to address this holding of unconstitutionality by extending either full marriage recognition or the benefits of marriage under another name. In April, 2000, the Vermont legislature responded by passing An Act Relating to Civil Unions.[16]

The Act did not, however, provide federal benefits to those united in a civil union. Under the Defense of Marriage Act enacted by Congress in 1996, "marriage" for purposes of federal law "means only a legal union between one man and one woman as husband and wife and the word 'spouse' refers only to a person of the opposite sex who is a husband or wife." Because of this provision, Vermont couples in a civil union were excluded from Social Security coverage, marital status for federal tax purposes, and a host of other federal benefits which DOMA limits explicitly to different-sex marriage.

NOTES ON CAMPAIGNS FOR SAME-SEX MARRIAGE PRIOR TO 2000

1. Why do you think the lesbian and gay community ultimately pursued same-sex marriage? Jane Schacter believes the anti-gay backlash to the

11. See, e.g., Baker v. Nelson, 191 N.W.2d 185, 187 (Minn.1971).

12. Baehr v. Lewin, 852 P.2d 44 (Haw.1993).

13. Baehr v. Miike, 910 P.2d 112 (Haw.1996).

14. Brause v. Bureau of Vital Statistics, 1998 WL 88743 (Alaska Super. 1998).

15. 744 A.2d 864 (Vt.1999).

16. Vt. Stat. Ann. tit. 15 § 1204 (2009).

Hawaii decision played a large role. Once anti-gay forces were mobilized in greater numbers, many gay and lesbian activists who were once wary of the same-sex marriage movement preferred to align themselves with same-sex marriage activists rather than implicitly support the anti-gay movement. Schacter, The Other Same–Sex Marriage Debate, 84 Chi–Kent L. Rev. 379, 394 (2009). Do you find Schacter's explanation convincing? What else might explain the decision to pursue same-sex marriage?

2. Do you think same-sex marriage has the potential to alter the gendered nature of marriage? How? Is same-sex marriage a form of the "drag," imitation and subversion that Judith Butler emphasizes (as discussed in Chapter 3)? Will such an alteration benefit same-sex couples or only women and men who choose different-sex marriage? How might the "choice" of different-sex marriage be altered by same-sex marriage? How might notions of gender be changed by same-sex marriage? If the last remaining gendered aspect of family law is eliminated, will there be a gender panic?

Or is same-sex marriage more likely to channel gay culture and gay sex into the gendered and domesticated institution of marriage? Michael Warner argues that the "definition of marriage, from the presupposition of the state's special role in it to the culture of romantic love—already includes so many layers of history, and so many norms, that gay marriage is not likely to alter it fundamentally, and any changes that it does bring may well be regressive." Warner, The Trouble With Normal: Sex, Politics, and the Ethics of Queer Life 129 (2000). Do you find yourself agreeing with Butler or Warner or neither of them? Why?

3. Should a marriage statute that does not explicitly define marriage as the union of a man and a woman be interpreted as so limited? What if—as is true of some state marriage laws—there are no words anywhere in the marriage statutes even suggesting a man and a woman? How do laws and policies reinforce the notion of marriage as an institution for heterosexuals? Is marriage really limited only to heterosexuals, even in states that prohibit same-sex marriage? What other implicit or explicit restrictions apply to marriage?

4. What was the purpose of marriage in the societies from which we inherited the contemporary American notion of marriage? Mary Becker suggests that the ancient pre-Christian cultures of Israel, Greece, Rome and Germany viewed marriage as necessarily the union of a man and a woman because its purpose was to assure the man that the woman's children were his children, to assure her family that her children would be his legitimate heirs, and to give her the status of wife, rather than the lower status of concubine. Christianity—specifically, medieval canon law—has been even more influential on our notions of marriage than these ancient cultures. The medieval Roman Catholic church regarded all sex as inferior to virginity; the only sex that was not sin was uncontracepted sex in marriage. Because the only licit sex was procreative, marriage was necessarily limited to different-sex couples. Becker, Family Law in the Secular State and Restrictions on Same–Sex Marriage: Two Are Better Than One, 2001 U. Ill. L. Rev. 1, 17–27.

In contrast, Michael Warner writes that marriage:

is a contradictory amalgamation of histories and contexts, including:

- a stone-age economic structure of household formation and the traffic in women;
- a pagan and Christian symbolic order for male domination;
- the central institution that justifies the state's power to restrict sex in all other contexts;
- a distinctively modern contractual relationship of individuals, certified by the state and other third parties but usually understood as a private relationship of equality and intimacy; and
- an ancient ritual vocabulary of recognition and status—one that has a nonstate performativity quite apart from issues of state regulation.

Warner, above note 2, 129–30. How should these histories affect marriage regulation today? Which aspects of the original purposes behind marriage remain, if any?

5. Is a requirement that men marry women and that women marry men a form of overt, facial sex discrimination? Would the Supreme Court regard a statute requiring all girls to go to girls' schools and all boys to boys' schools as something other than sex discrimination? What of a statute that required employers to have separate departments for female and male employees? Or a statute that required women to possess green drivers' licenses and men to possess yellow drivers' licenses? Would these statutes discriminate on the basis of sex, or would they simply apply the same treatment to women and to men? What are the potential harms of categorizing individuals by gender?

6. What do you think of the strength of the analogy between race discrimination in Loving v. Virginia, the miscegenation case described above, and sex discrimination in same-sex marriage cases? In Baker v. Nelson, discussed in the text note above, the court regarded *Loving* as totally irrelevant:

> Virginia's antimiscegenation statute, prohibiting interracial marriages, was invalidated solely on the grounds of its patent racial discrimination. * * *
>
> Loving does indicate that not all state restrictions upon the right to marry are beyond reach of the Fourteenth Amendment. But in commonsense and in a constitutional sense, there is a clear distinction between a marital restriction based merely upon race and one based upon the fundamental difference in sex.

191 N.W.2d at 187. See also Dean v. District of Columbia, 653 A.2d 307 (D.C. 1995) (engaging in a similar analysis). Can you articulate the difference the court refers to here? Do you find this convincing?

Do you think that bans on same-sex marriage are analogous to antimiscegenation statutes? Andrew Koppelman argues that discrimination on the basis of sexual orientation is necessarily discrimination on the basis of sex. In states where same-sex marriage is prohibited, a man can marry a woman, but a woman cannot marry a woman. Therefore, a woman is treated differently on the basis of her sex. She is prohibited from doing the same action as a man, solely because of her sex. Similarly, a woman can marry a man, but a man cannot. Seemingly, under the heightened scrutiny applied to sex discrimination, different-sex marriage requirements would be unconstitutional. Koppelman, Why Discrimination against Lesbians and Gay Men is Sex Discrimination, 69 N.Y.U. L. Rev. 197 (1994). Do you find this equal protection analysis convincing? What might be some of the harms of a sex discrimination analysis? See Edward Stein, Evaluating the Sex Discrimination Argument for Lesbian and Gay Rights, 49 UCLA L. Rev. 471 (2001). Why do you think so many courts rejected the *Loving* analogy?

7. One possible reason that courts have rejected the *Loving* analogy is that the *Loving* Court focused on how the racial classification at issue perpetuated white supremacy. Simply differentiating between the races thus may not have been enough to invalidate the statute. Do different-sex marriage requirements promote the supremacy of one group over another? Which groups? In addition to his formal equality argument, Andrew Koppelman also argued that:

> [O]ne effect of the miscegenation taboo, intended or not, is the maintenance of the boundary between the races on which the system of racism depends. Similarly, compulsory heterosexuality keeps women in relationships in which men exert power over their lives. The symbolic message of the miscegenation taboo associates racial equality with sexual danger and endorses the idea that the boundaries enforced by the taboo are terribly important ones. An analogous message can be seen in the homosexuality taboo. Sex equality is dangerous; it will reduce men to the level of women; thus, maintaining the boundary between the sexes is a terribly important undertaking.

Koppelman, above note 6, at 248–49; see also Susan Frelich Appleton, Missing In Action? Searching for Gender Talk in the Same–Sex Marriage Debate, 16 Stan. L. & Pol'y Rev. 97 (2005). Carrie G. Costello argues:

> The process of defining legitimate bonds and unnatural unions fortified a system of racial caste, and both the caste system and the definitional process long outlived racial bondage. The tactics employed in the control of racial Others remain effective today. These tactics are currently being utilized in the control of other groups, including queer people; the Order destabilizes the Other through the denial of familial rights. Spurred on in the struggle to secure these familial rights, lesbians and gay men, among others, provide the threat of subversion against which the hegemonic Order needs to unite itself. Control of the definition of the family is a powerful tool, and the Order will continue to seek to employ it to constitute itself and control its Others far into the future.

Costello, Legitimate Bonds and Unnatural Unions: Race, Sexual Orientation, and Control of the American Family, 15 Harv. Women's L.J. 79, 171 (1992).

Why is same-sex marriage seen as such a threat to heterosexuality and different-sex marriage? Is heterosexuality so fragile? Is gender so fragile? Is the purpose of limiting marriage to heterosexuals to regulate sexual behavior or to enforce gender norms? Is it both? How do you think Adrienne Rich, discussed in Chapter 3, would respond to the arguments and questions in this note?

8. In Turner v. Safley, 482 U.S. 78 (1987), the Supreme Court recognized, and constitutionally protected, the non-procreative purposes of marriage, holding that the fundamental right to marry extends to prisoners even though inmates have no constitutional right to conjugal visits, noting that: (1) marriage is "an expression of emotional support and public commitment"; (2) marriage has spiritual significance to many people and "the commitment of marriage may be an exercise of religious faith as well as an expression of personal dedication"; and (3) marriage is often "a precondition to government benefits (e.g., Social Security benefits), property rights (e.g., tenancy by the entirety, inheritance rights), and other, less tangible benefits." Id. at 95–96. Can you distinguish same-sex marriage claims from those in *Turner*?

At the time of the *Turner* decision (1987), it is clear that the Supreme Court would have affirmed a ban on same-sex marriage; it had just decided Bowers v. Hardwick, 478 U.S. 186 (1986) (upholding a state law applied to criminalize consensual sodomy in private between two men). *Bowers* left no room for doubt on how the 1986 Court would have ruled in a same-sex marriage case. *Bowers* was overruled, however, in 2003, so states can no longer argue that permitting same-sex marriage would be condoning criminal behavior. Lawrence v. Texas, 539 U.S. 558 (2003) (invalidating laws criminalizing sodomy). Despite its holding, the Supreme Court in *Lawrence* specifically stated that it was not determining the question of same-sex marriage. Id. at 574–75.

How do you think today's Court would rule in a same-sex marriage case, given both *Lawrence* and Romer v. Evans, 517 U.S. 620 (1996) (holding unconstitutional a Colorado constitutional amendment that prohibited the state and all its subdivisions from banning discrimination on the basis of "homosexual, lesbian or bisexual orientation, conduct, practices or relationships")? The *Romer* Court found that there was no explanation for the statute other than "animosity toward the class of persons affected." Id. at 634. It is unclear how far *Romer* might reach in protecting lesbians and gay men from legislative classifications singling them out for disfavored treatment. Does *Romer* suggest that the Court might regard denial of marriage to same-sex couples as unconstitutional? What distinctions might be made between the Colorado amendment and denial of marriage to same-sex couples? Is there an argument that the federal Defense of Marriage Act (DOMA), which denies federal benefits to gay and lesbian couples even if they are married under state law, is unconstitutional under *Romer*? See Andrew Koppelman, Dumb and DOMA: Why the Defense of Marriage Act Is Unconstitutional, 83 Iowa L. Rev. 1 (1997).

9. Which argument do you think would have the greatest chance of success: that denial of same-sex marriage rights (a) discriminates on the basis of sex; (b) discriminates impermissibly against homosexuals; or (c) interferes with the fundamental right to marry? What are the strongest arguments you could make for each? What are the potential weaknesses of each argument?

10. Why do you think the Vermont legislature created civil unions for same-sex couples and limited marriage to different-sex couples? Is a deliberately-created status differential based on sexual orientation constitutional under *Romer*? See Jane S. Schachter, Romer v. Evans and Democracy's

Domain, 50 Vand. L. Rev. 361, 381 (1997) ("The [*Romer*] opinion also raises, but does not answer clearly, the critical question whether intolerance of homosexuality framed in terms of traditional values is the same thing as anti gay animus."). Does the different name necessarily lead to a difference in social status and acceptance? Or, as in the Scandinavian countries, will people refer to civil unions as gay marriage? Are civil unions and other second tier approaches necessary steps on the road to full marriage rights? Or obstacles?

GOODRIDGE v. DEPARTMENT OF PUBLIC HEALTH

Supreme Judicial Court of Massachusetts, 2003.
440 Mass. 309, 798 N.E.2d 941.

MARSHALL, C.J.

* * * The question before us is whether, consistent with the Massachusetts Constitution, the Commonwealth may deny the protections, benefits, and obligations conferred by civil marriage to two individuals of the same sex who wish to marry. We conclude that it may not. The Massachusetts Constitution affirms the dignity and equality of all individuals. It forbids the creation of second class citizens. In reaching our conclusion we have given full deference to the arguments made by the Commonwealth. But it has failed to identify any constitutionally adequate reason for denying civil marriage to same sex couples.

* * *

III

A

* * *

Tangible as well as intangible benefits flow from marriage. The marriage license grants valuable property rights to those who meet the entry requirements, and who agree to what might otherwise be a burdensome degree of government regulation of their activities. * * *

The benefits accessible only by way of a marriage license are enormous, touching nearly every aspect of life and death [including property benefits, evidentiary rights, health care rights, and parental rights].

* * *

Where a married couple has children, their children are also directly or indirectly, but no less auspiciously, the recipients of the special legal and economic protections obtained by civil marriage. Notwithstanding the Commonwealth's strong public policy to abolish legal distinctions between marital and nonmarital children in providing for the support and care of minors, the fact remains that marital children reap a measure of family stability and economic security based on their parents' legally privileged status that is largely inaccessible, or not as readily accessible, to nonmarital children. Some of these benefits are social, such as the enhanced approval that still attends the status of being a marital child. Others are material, such as the greater ease of access to family based State and Federal benefits that attend the presumptions of one's parentage.

* * *

B

* * *

The department argues that no fundamental right or "suspect" class is at issue here, and rational basis is the appropriate standard of review. For the reasons we explain below, we conclude that the marriage ban does not meet the rational basis test for either due process or equal protection. Because the statute does not survive rational basis review, we do not consider the plaintiffs' arguments that this case merits strict judicial scrutiny.

The department posits three legislative rationales for prohibiting same sex couples from marrying: (1) providing a "favorable setting for procreation"; (2) ensuring the optimal setting for child rearing, which the department defines as "a two parent family with one parent of each sex"; and (3) preserving scarce State and private financial resources. We consider each in turn.

* * * Our laws of civil marriage do not privilege procreative heterosexual intercourse between married people above every other form of adult intimacy and every other means of creating a family. General Laws c. 207 contains no requirement that the applicants for a marriage license attest to their ability or intention to conceive children by coitus. Fertility is not a condition of marriage, nor is it grounds for divorce. People who have never consummated their marriage, and never plan to, may be and stay married. * * *

Moreover, the Commonwealth affirmatively facilitates bringing children into a family regardless of whether the intended parent is married or unmarried, whether the child is adopted or born into a family, whether assistive technology was used to conceive the child, and whether the parent or her partner is heterosexual, homosexual, or bisexual. If procreation were a necessary component of civil marriage, our statutes would draw a tighter circle around the permissible bounds of nonmarital child bearing and the creation of families by noncoital means. * * *

* * *

* * * Protecting the welfare of children is a paramount State policy. Restricting marriage to opposite sex couples, however, cannot plausibly further this policy. * * * The "best interests of the child" standard does not turn on a parent's sexual orientation or marital status.

The department has offered no evidence that forbidding marriage to people of the same sex will increase the number of couples choosing to enter into opposite sex marriages in order to have and raise children. There is thus no rational relationship between the marriage statute and the Commonwealth's proffered goal of protecting the "optimal" child rearing unit. Moreover, the department readily concedes that people in same sex couples may be "excellent" parents. * * * But the task of child rearing for same sex couples is made infinitely harder by their status as outliers to the marriage laws. While establishing the parentage of children as soon as possible is crucial to the safety and welfare of children, same sex couples must undergo the sometimes lengthy and intrusive process of second parent adoption to establish their joint parentage. While the enhanced income provided by marital benefits is an important source of security and stability for married couples and their children, those benefits are denied to families headed by same sex couples. While the laws of divorce provide clear and reasonably predictable guidelines for child support, child custody, and property division on dissolution of a marriage, same sex couples who dissolve their relationships find themselves and their children in the highly unpredictable terrain of equity jurisdiction. Given the wide range of public benefits reserved only for married couples, we do not credit the department's contention that the absence of access to civil marriage amounts to little more than an inconvenience to same sex couples and their children. Excluding same sex couples from civil marriage will not make children of opposite sex marriages more secure, but it does prevent children of same sex couples from enjoying the immeasurable advantages that flow from the assurance of "a stable family structure in which children will be reared, educated, and socialized."

* * *

In this case, we are confronted with an entire, sizeable class of parents raising children who have absolutely no access to civil marriage and its protections because they are forbidden from procuring a marriage license. It cannot be rational under our laws, and indeed it is not permitted, to penalize children by depriving them of State benefits because the State disapproves of their parents' sexual orientation.

* * *

The department suggests additional rationales for prohibiting same sex couples from marrying, which are developed by some amici. It argues that broadening civil marriage to include same sex couples will trivialize or destroy the institution of marriage as it has historically been fashioned. Certainly our decision today marks a significant change in the definition of marriage as it has been inherited from the common law, and understood by many societies for centuries. But it does not disturb the fundamental value of marriage in our society.

Here, the plaintiffs seek only to be married, not to undermine the institution of civil marriage. They do not want marriage abolished. They do not attack the binary nature of marriage, the consanguinity provisions, or any of the other gate keeping provisions of the marriage licensing law. Recognizing the right of an individual to marry a person of the same sex will not diminish the validity or dignity of opposite sex marriage, any more than recognizing the right of an individual to marry a person of a different race devalues the marriage of a person who marries someone of her own race. If anything, extending civil marriage to same sex couples reinforces the importance of marriage to individuals and communities. That same sex couples are willing to embrace marriage's solemn obligations of exclusivity, mutual support, and commitment to one another is a testament to the enduring place of marriage in our laws and in the human spirit.

* * *

IV

* * *

We construe civil marriage to mean the voluntary union of two persons as spouses, to the exclusion of all others. This reformulation redresses the plaintiffs' constitutional injury and furthers the aim of marriage to promote stable, exclusive relationships. It advances the two legitimate State interests the department has identified: providing a stable setting for child rearing and conserving State resources. It leaves intact the Legislature's broad discretion to regulate marriage.

In their complaint the plaintiffs request only a declaration that their exclusion and the exclusion of other qualified same sex couples from access to civil marriage violates Massachusetts law. We declare that barring an individual from the protections, benefits, and obligations of civil marriage solely because that person would marry a person of the same sex violates the Massachusetts Constitution. We vacate the summary judgment for the department. We remand this case to the Superior Court for entry of judgment consistent with this opinion. Entry of judgment shall be stayed for 180 days to permit the Legislature to take such action as it may deem appropriate in light of this opinion.

So ordered.

GREANEY, J. (concurring).

I agree with the result reached by the court, the remedy ordered, and much of the reasoning in the court's opinion. In my view, however, the case is more directly resolved using traditional equal protection analysis.

* * *

Because our marriage statutes intend, and state, the ordinary understanding that marriage under our law consists only of a union between a man and a woman, they create a statutory classification based on the sex of the two people who wish to marry. That the classification is sex based is self evident. The marriage statutes prohibit some applicants, such as the plaintiffs, from obtaining a marriage license, and that prohibition is based solely on the applicants' gender. As a factual matter, an individual's choice of marital partner is constrained because of his or her own sex. Stated in particular terms, Hillary Goodridge cannot marry Julie Goodridge because she (Hillary) is a woman. Likewise, Gary Chalmers cannot marry Richard Linnell because he (Gary) is a man. Only their gender prevents Hillary and Gary from marrying their chosen partners under the present law.

* * *

The equal protection infirmity at work here is strikingly similar to (although, perhaps, more subtle than) the invidious discrimination perpetuated by Virginia's antimiscegenation laws and unveiled in the decision of Loving v. Virginia. In its landmark decision striking down Virginia's ban on marriages between Caucasians and members of any other race on both equal protection and substantive due process grounds, the United States Supreme Court soundly rejected the proposition that the equal application of the ban (i.e., that it applied equally to whites and blacks) made unnecessary the strict scrutiny analysis traditionally required of statutes drawing classifications according to race, and concluded that "restricting the freedom to marry solely because of racial classifications violates the central meaning of the Equal Protection Clause." That our marriage laws, unlike antimiscegenation laws, were not enacted purposely to discriminate in no way neutralizes their present discriminatory character.

With these two propositions established (the infringement on a fundamental right and a sex based classification), the enforcement of the marriage statutes as they are currently understood is forbidden by our Constitution unless the State can present a compelling purpose furthered by the statutes that can be accomplished in no other reasonable manner. This the State has not done. The justifications put forth by the State to sustain the statute's exclusion of the plaintiffs are insufficient for the reasons explained by the court * * *.

> [Three justices dissented, on the grounds, inter alia, that this was a question for the legislature. They also found no violation of either equal protection or due process (fundamental right) and that the state's interest was sufficient to pass the very deferential rational relationship test.]

HERNANDEZ v. ROBLES

Court of Appeals of New York, 2006.
7 N.Y.3d 338, 821 N.Y.S.2d 770, 855 N.E.2d 1.

We hold that the New York Constitution does not compel recognition of marriages between members of the same sex. Whether such marriages should be recognized is a question to be addressed by the Legislature.

* * *

New York's statutory law clearly limits marriage to opposite-sex couples. The more serious question is whether that limitation is consistent with the New York Constitution.

* * *

III

It is undisputed that the benefits of marriage are many. * * *

The critical question is whether a rational legislature could decide that these benefits should be given to members of opposite-sex couples, but not same-sex couples. * * * [T]here are at least two grounds that rationally support the limitation on marriage that the Legislature has enacted. * * *

First, the Legislature could rationally decide that, for the welfare of children, it is more important to promote stability, and to avoid instability, in opposite-sex than in same-sex relationships. * * * The Legislature could also find that such relationships are all too often casual or temporary. It could find that an important function of marriage is to create more stability and permanence in the relationships that cause children to be born. It thus could choose to offer an inducement—in the form of marriage and its attendant benefits—to opposite-sex couples who make a solemn, long-term commitment to each other.

The Legislature could find that this rationale for marriage does not apply with comparable force to same-sex couples. These couples can become parents by adoption, or by artificial insemination or other technological marvels, but they do not become parents as a result of accident or impulse. The Legislature could find that unstable relationships between people of the opposite sex present a greater danger that children will be born into or grow up in unstable homes than is the case with same-sex couples, and thus that promoting stability in opposite-sex relationships will help children more. * * *

There is a second reason: The Legislature could rationally believe that it is better, other things being equal, for children to grow up with both a mother and a father. Intuition and experience suggest that a child benefits from having before his or her eyes, every day, living models of what both a man and a woman are like. * * *

* * *

Plaintiffs seem to assume that they have demonstrated the irrationality of the view that opposite-sex marriages offer advantages to children by showing there is no scientific evidence to support it. * * * In the absence of conclusive scientific evidence, the Legislature could rationally proceed on the commonsense premise that children will do best with a mother and father in the home. And a legislature proceeding on that premise could rationally decide to offer a special inducement, the legal recognition of marriage, to encourage the formation of opposite-sex households.

In sum, there are rational grounds on which the Legislature could choose to restrict marriage to couples of opposite sex. Plaintiffs have not persuaded us that this long-accepted restriction is a wholly irrational one, based solely on ignorance and prejudice against homosexuals. * * *

* * *

IV

Our conclusion that there is a rational basis for limiting marriage to opposite-sex couples leads us to hold that that limitation is valid under the New York Due Process and Equal Protection clauses, and that any expansion of the traditional definition of marriage should come from the Legislature.

* * *

We find no inconsistency that is significant in this case between our due process and equal protection decisions and the Supreme Court's. * * *

A. Due Process

In deciding the validity of legislation under the Due Process Clause, courts first inquire whether the legislation restricts the exercise of a fundamental right, one that is "deeply rooted in this Nation's history and tradition." In this case, whether the right in question is "fundamental" depends on how it is defined. The right to marry is unquestionably a fundamental right. The right to marry someone of the same sex, however, is not "deeply rooted"; it has not even been asserted until relatively recent times. The issue then becomes whether the right to marry must be defined to include a right to same-sex marriage.

* * *

* * * Plaintiffs here do not, as the petitioners in *Lawrence [v. Texas]* did, seek protection against state intrusion on intimate, private activity. They seek from the courts access to a state-conferred benefit that the Legislature has rationally limited to opposite-sex couples. We conclude that, by defining marriage as it has, the New York Legislature has not restricted the exercise of a fundamental right.

Where no fundamental right is at issue, legislation is valid under the Due Process Clause if it is rationally related to legitimate government interests. * * *

B. Equal Protection

Plaintiffs claim that the distinction made by the Domestic Relations Law between opposite-sex and same-sex couples deprives them of the equal protection of the laws. This claim raises, first, the issue of what level of scrutiny should be applied to the legislative classification. The plaintiffs argue for strict scrutiny, on the ground that the legislation affects their fundamental right to marry—a contention we rejected above. Alternatively, plaintiffs argue for so-called intermediate or heightened scrutiny on two grounds. They say that the legislation discriminates on the basis of sex, a kind of discrimination that has been held to trigger heightened scrutiny. They also say that discrimination on the basis of sexual preference should trigger heightened scrutiny * * *.

By limiting marriage to opposite-sex couples, New York is not engaging in sex discrimination. The limitation does not put men and women in different classes, and give one class a benefit not given to the other. Women and men are treated alike—they are permitted to marry people of the opposite sex, but not people of their own sex. * * * Plaintiffs do not argue here that the legislation they challenge is designed to subordinate either men to women or women to men as a class.

However, the legislation does confer advantages on the basis of sexual preference. Those who prefer relationships with people of the opposite sex and those who prefer relationships with people of the same sex are not treated alike, since only opposite-sex relationships may gain the status and benefits associated with marriage. This case thus presents the question of what level of scrutiny is to be applied to legislation that classifies people on this basis. * * *

We resolve this question in this case on the basis of the Supreme Court's observation that no more than rational basis scrutiny is generally appropriate "where individuals in the group affected by a law have distinguishing characteristics relevant to interests the State has the authority to implement". Perhaps that principle would lead us to apply heightened scrutiny to sexual preference discrimination in some cases, but not where we review legislation governing marriage and family relationships. A person's preference for the sort of sexual activity that cannot lead to the birth of children is relevant to the State's interest in fostering relationships that will serve children best. In this area, therefore, we conclude that rational basis scrutiny is appropriate.

* * *

V

We hold, in sum, that the Domestic Relations Law's limitation of marriage to opposite-sex couples is not unconstitutional. * * *

The dissenters assert confidently that "future generations" will agree with their view of this case. We do not predict what people will think generations from now, but we believe the present generation should have a chance to decide the issue through its elected representatives. We therefore express our hope that the participants in the controversy over same-sex marriage will address their arguments to the Legislature; that the Legislature will listen and decide as wisely as it can; and that those unhappy with the result—as many undoubtedly will be—will respect it as people in a democratic state should respect choices democratically made.

KERRIGAN v. COMMISSIONER OF PUBLIC HEALTH

Supreme Court of Connecticut, 2008.
289 Conn. 135, 957 A.2d 407.

On appeal, the plaintiffs challenge the trial court's determination that Connecticut's civil union law does not discriminate against gay persons because same sex couples who have entered into a civil union are entitled to the same legal rights under state law as married couples. The plaintiffs also renew the various state constitutional claims that they raised in the trial court. We conclude, first, that the trial court improperly determined that the distinction between civil unions and marriage is constitutionally insignificant merely because a same sex couple who enters into a civil union enjoys the same legal rights as an opposite sex couple who enters into a marriage. We also conclude that our statutory scheme governing marriage impermissibly discriminates against gay persons on the basis of their sexual orientation.

I

* * * The trial court predicated its determination on the fact that a couple who enters into a civil union has the same legal rights under state law as a couple who enters into a marriage. The court reasoned that the difference in labels afforded marriage and civil unions is not, in itself, sufficient to trigger an analysis of the constitutionality of that statutory scheme as applied to same sex couples.

The plaintiffs * * * contend that [marriage] is an institution of unique and enduring importance in our society, one that carries with it a special status. * * * We agree with the plaintiffs that, despite the legislature's recent establishment of civil unions, the restriction of marriage to opposite sex couples implicates the constitutional rights of gay persons who wish to marry a person of the same sex.

A cognizable constitutional claim arises whenever the government singles out a group for differential treatment. The legislature has subjected gay persons to precisely that kind of differential treatment by creating a separate legal classification for same sex couples who, like opposite sex couples, wish to have their relationship recognized under the law. Put differently, the civil union law entitles same sex couples to all of the same rights as married couples except one, that is, the freedom to marry, a right that "has long been recognized as one of the vital personal rights essential to the orderly pursuit of happiness by free men [and women]" and "fundamental to our very existence and survival." Loving v. Virginia, 388 U.S. 1, 12 (1967). * * *

Especially in light of the long and undisputed history of invidious discrimination that gay persons have suffered, we cannot discount the plaintiffs' assertion that the legislature, in establishing a statutory scheme consigning same sex couples to civil unions, has relegated them to an inferior status, in essence, declaring them to be unworthy of the institution of marriage. In other words, "[b]y excluding same-sex couples from civil marriage, the [s]tate declares that it is legitimate to differentiate between their commitments and the commitments of heterosexual couples. Ultimately, the message is that what same-sex couples have is not as important or as significant as 'real' marriage, that such lesser relationships cannot have the name of marriage." Lewis v. Harris, 188 N.J. 415, 467 (2006) (Poritz, C.J., concurring and dissenting). * * *

Accordingly, we reject the trial court's conclusion that marriage and civil unions are "separate" but "equal" legal entities. * * *

We do not doubt that the civil union law was designed to benefit same sex couples by providing them with legal rights that they previously did not have. If, however, the intended effect of a law is to treat politically unpopular or historically disfavored minorities differently from persons in the majority or favored class, that law cannot evade constitutional review under the separate but equal doctrine. In such circumstances, the very existence of the classification gives credence to the perception that separate treatment is warranted for the same illegitimate reasons that gave rise to the past discrimination in the first place. Despite the truly laudable effort of the legislature in equalizing the legal rights afforded same sex and opposite sex couples, there is no doubt that civil unions enjoy a lesser status in our society than marriage. We therefore conclude that the plaintiffs have alleged a constitutionally cognizable injury, that is, the denial of the right to marry a same sex partner.

VARNUM v. BRIEN

Supreme Court of Iowa, 2009.
763 N.W.2d 862.

In turning to the courts, the twelve plaintiffs filed this lawsuit in the Polk County District Court. They claimed the statutory same-sex marriage ban violates certain liberty and equality rights under the Iowa Constitution. The individual rights claimed by plaintiffs to be adversely affected [by the action of the legislative branch in enacting the same-sex marriage ban and the action of the government officials of the executive branch in enforcing the ban] included the fundamental right to marry, as well as rights to privacy and familial association. Additionally, plaintiffs claimed the legislative and the executive actions unconstitutionally discriminated against them on several bases, including sexual orientation.

* * *

This class of people asks a simple and direct question: How can a state premised on the constitutional principle of equal protection justify exclusion of a class of Iowans from civil marriage?

* * *

* * * [W]e have said our marriage laws "are rooted in the necessity of providing an institutional basis for defining the fundamental relational rights and responsibilities of persons in organized society." These laws also serve to recognize the status of the parties' committed relationship.

Therefore, with respect to the subject and purposes of Iowa's marriage laws, we find that the plaintiffs are similarly situated compared to heterosexual persons. Plaintiffs are in committed and loving relationships, many raising families, just like heterosexual couples. Moreover, official recognition of their status provides an institutional basis for defining their fundamental relational rights and responsibilities, just as it does for heterosexual couples. Society benefits, for example, from providing same-sex couples a stable framework within which to raise their children and the power to make health care and end-of-life decisions for loved ones, just as it does when that framework is provided for opposite-sex couples.

* * *

Plaintiffs believe Iowa Code section 595.2 classifies on the bases of gender and sexual orientation. The County argues the same-sex marriage ban does not discriminate on either basis. The district court held section 595.2 classifies according to gender. As we will explain, we believe the ban on civil marriages between two people of the same sex classifies on the basis of sexual orientation.

* * *

* * * Under such a law, gay or lesbian individuals cannot simultaneously fulfill their deeply felt need for a committed personal relationship, as influenced by their sexual orientation, and gain the civil status and attendant benefits granted by the statute. Instead, a gay or lesbian person can only gain the same rights under the statute as a heterosexual person by negating the very trait that defines gay and lesbian people as a class—their sexual orientation. The benefit denied by the marriage statute—the status of civil marriage for same-sex couples—is so "closely correlated with being homosexual" as to make it apparent the law is targeted at gay and lesbian people as a class. The Court's decision in Romer v. Evans, 517 U.S. 620 (1996), supports this conclusion. Romer can be read to imply that sexual orientation is a trait that defines an individual and is not merely a means to associate a group with a type of behavior.

By purposefully placing civil marriage outside the realistic reach of gay and lesbian individuals, the ban on same-sex civil marriages differentiates implicitly on the basis of sexual orientation. Thus, we proceed to analyze the constitutionality of the statute based on sexual orientation discrimination.

* * * To determine if this particular classification violates constitutional principles of equal protection, we must next ask what level of scrutiny applies to classifications of this type. * * *

Although neither we nor the United States Supreme Court has decided which level of scrutiny applies to legislative classifications based on sexual orientation, numerous Supreme Court equal protection cases provide a general framework to guide our analysis under the Iowa Constitution. * * *

* * *

Instead of adopting a rigid formula to determine whether certain legislative classifications warrant more demanding constitutional analysis, the Supreme Court has looked to four factors. The Supreme Court has considered: (1) the history of invidious discrimination against the class burdened by the legislation; (2) whether the characteristics that distinguish the class indicate a typical class member's ability to contribute to society; (3) whether the distinguishing characteristic is "immutable" or beyond the class members' control; and (4) the political power of the subject class.

* * *

* * * [W]e analyze each of the four factors and assess how each bears on the question of whether the Iowa Constitution requires a more searching scrutiny be applied to the specific classification at issue. We note the first two factors—history of intentional discrimination and relationship of classifying characteristic to a person's ability to contribute—have always been present when heightened scrutiny has been applied. They have been critical to the analysis and could be considered as prerequisites to concluding a group is a suspect or quasi-suspect class. However, we consider the last two factors—immutability of the characteristic and political powerlessness of the group—to supplement the analysis as a means to discern whether a need for heightened scrutiny exists.

Guided by the established framework, we next consider each of the four traditional factors and assess how each bears on the question of whether the constitution demands a more searching scrutiny be applied to the sexual-orientation-based classification in Iowa's marriage statute.

1. *History of discrimination against gay and lesbian people.* * * * [G]ay and lesbian people as a group have long been the victim of purposeful and invidious discrimination because of their sexual orientation. * * *

The Iowa General Assembly has recognized the need to address sexual-orientation-based discrimination by including sexual orientation as a characteristic protected in the Iowa Civil Rights Act, by defining hate crimes to include certain offenses committed because of the victim's sexual orientation, and by prohibiting "harassing or bullying" behavior in schools based on sexual orientation. * * *

In sum, this history of discrimination suggests any legislative burdens placed on lesbian and gay people as a class "are more likely than others to reflect deep-seated prejudice rather than legislative rationality in pursuit of some legitimate objective." This observation favors an elevated scrutiny to uncover any such prejudice.

2. *Sexual orientation and the ability to contribute to society.* * * *

* * * [T]he Iowa legislature has recently declared as the public policy of this state that sexual orientation is not relevant to a person's ability to contribute to a number of societal institutions other than civil marriage. [Here the court cites to various Iowa statutes forbidding discrimination on the basis of sexual orientation in employment, public accommodations, housing, education, and credit practices.] * * * [These statutes] demonstrate sexual orientation is broadly recognized in Iowa to be irrelevant to a person's ability to contribute to society. Those statutes and regulations reflect at least some measure of legislative and executive awareness that

discrimination based on sexual orientation is often predicated on prejudice and stereotype and further express a desire to remove sexual orientation as an obstacle to the ability of gay and lesbian people to achieve their full potential. Therefore, we must scrutinize more closely those classifications that suggest a law may be based on prejudice and stereotype. * * *

3. *Immutability of sexual orientation.*

* * *

* * * The constitutional relevance of the immutability factor is not reserved to those instances in which the trait defining the burdened class is absolutely impossible to change. * * *

* * * [B]ecause sexual orientation is central to personal identity and " 'may be altered [if at all] only at the expense of significant damage to the individual's sense of self,' " classifications based on sexual orientation "are no less entitled to consideration as a suspect or quasi-suspect class than any other group that has been deemed to exhibit an immutable characteristic." * * *

4. *Political powerlessness of lesbian and gay people.*

* * *

Notwithstanding the lack of a mathematical equation to guide the analysis of this factor, a number of helpful general principles related to the political power of suspect classes can be culled from the Supreme Court's cases. First, these cases show absolute political powerlessness is not necessary to subject legislative burdens on a certain class to heightened scrutiny. For example, females enjoyed at least some measure of political power when the Supreme Court first heightened its scrutiny of gender classifications.

Second, Supreme Court jurisprudence establishes that a group's current political powerlessness is not a prerequisite to enhanced judicial protection. * * * Race continues to be a suspect classification, even though racial minorities enjoy growing political power. Likewise, gender classifications receive various forms of heightened scrutiny, even though women continue to gain political power.

* * * Rather, the touchstone of the analysis should be "whether the group lacks sufficient political strength to bring a prompt end to the prejudice and discrimination through traditional political means."

* * *

* * * Gays and lesbians certainly possess no more political power than women enjoyed four decades ago when the Supreme Court began subjecting gender-based legislation to closer scrutiny. Additionally, gay and lesbian people are, as a class, currently no more powerful than women or members of some racial minorities. These facts demonstrate, at the least, the political-power factor does not weigh against heightened judicial scrutiny of sexual-orientation-based legislation.

* * * The factors established to guide our determination of the level of scrutiny to utilize in our examination of the equal protection claim in this case all point to an elevated level of scrutiny. Accordingly, we hold that legislative classifications based on sexual orientation must be examined under a heightened level of scrutiny under the Iowa Constitution.

* * * Because we conclude Iowa's same-sex marriage statute cannot withstand intermediate scrutiny, we need not decide whether classifications based on sexual orientation are subject to a higher level of scrutiny. Thus, we turn to a discussion of the intermediate scrutiny standard.

* * *

Thus, the question we must answer is whether excluding gay and lesbian people from civil marriage is substantially related to any important governmental objective.

Governmental objectives. The County has proffered a number of objectives supporting the marriage statute. These objectives include support for the "traditional" institution of marriage, the optimal procreation and rearing of children, and financial considerations.

* * *

First, the County argues the same-sex marriage ban promotes the "integrity of traditional marriage" by "maintaining the historical and traditional marriage norm ([as] one between a man and a woman)." This argument is straightforward and has superficial appeal. A specific tradition sought to be maintained cannot be an important governmental objective for equal protection purposes, however, when the tradition is nothing more than the historical classification currently expressed in the statute being challenged. * * *

* * *

Another governmental objective proffered by the County is the promotion of "child rearing by a father and a mother in a marital relationship which social scientists say with confidence is the optimal milieu for child rearing." This objective implicates the broader governmental interest to promote the best interests of children. The "best interests of children" is, undeniably, an important governmental objective. Yet, we first examine the underlying premise proffered by the County that the optimal environment for children is to be raised within a marriage of both a mother and a father.

Plaintiffs presented an abundance of evidence and research, confirmed by our independent research, supporting the proposition that the interests of children are served equally by same-sex parents and opposite-sex parents. On the other hand, we acknowledge the existence of reasoned opinions that dual-gender parenting is the optimal environment for children. These opinions, while thoughtful and sincere, were largely unsupported by reliable scientific studies.

Even assuming there may be a rational basis at this time to believe the legislative classification advances a legitimate government interest, this assumed fact would not be sufficient to survive the equal protection analysis applicable in this case. In order to ensure this classification based on sexual orientation is not borne of prejudice and stereotype, intermediate scrutiny demands a closer relationship between the legislative classification and the purpose of the classification than mere rationality. * * *

* * *

We begin with the County's argument that the goal of the same-sex marriage ban is to ensure children will be raised only in the optimal milieu. In pursuit of this objective, the statutory exclusion of gay and lesbian people is both under-inclusive and over-inclusive. The civil marriage statute is under-inclusive because it does not exclude from marriage other groups of parents—such as child abusers, sexual predators, parents neglecting to provide child support, and violent felons—that are undeniably less than optimal parents. Such under-inclusion tends to demonstrate that the sexual-orientation-based classification is grounded in prejudice or "overbroad generalizations about the different talents, capacities, or preferences" of gay and lesbian people, rather than having a substantial relationship to some important objective. If the marriage statute was truly focused on optimal parenting, many classifications of people would be excluded, not merely gay and lesbian people.

* * *

The ban on same-sex marriage is substantially over-inclusive because not all same-sex couples choose to raise children. Yet, the marriage statute denies civil marriage to all gay and lesbian people in order to discourage the limited number of same-sex couples who desire to raise children. * * *

* * * Same-sex couples currently raise children in Iowa, even while being excluded from civil marriage, and such couples will undoubtedly continue to do so. * * *

If the statute was truly about the best interest of children, some benefit to children derived from the ban on same-sex civil marriages would be observable. Yet, the germane analysis does not show how the best interests of children of gay and lesbian parents, who are denied an environment supported by the benefits of marriage under the statute, are served by the ban. Likewise, the exclusion of gays and lesbians from marriage does not benefit the interests of those children of heterosexual parents, who are able to enjoy the environment supported by marriage with or without the inclusion of same-sex couples.

* * *

The County also proposes that government endorsement of traditional civil marriage will result in more procreation. * * * While heterosexual marriage does lead to procreation, the argument by the County fails to address the real issue in our required analysis of the objective: whether exclusion of gay and lesbian individuals from the institution of civil marriage will result in more procreation? * * *

* * *

Conceptually, the promotion of procreation as an objective of marriage is compatible with the inclusion of gays and lesbians within the definition of marriage. Gay and lesbian persons are capable of procreation. * * * [T]he link between exclusion of gay and lesbian people from marriage and increased procreation is far too tenuous to withstand heightened scrutiny. Specifically, the statute is significantly under-inclusive with respect to the objective of increasing procreation because it does not include a variety of groups that do not procreate for reasons such as age, physical disability, or choice.

* * *

A fourth suggested rationale supporting the marriage statute is "promoting stability in opposite sex relationships." * * * The County offers no reasons that it does, and we can find none. * * *

The conservation of state resources is another objective arguably furthered by excluding gay and lesbian persons from civil marriage. The argument is based on a simple premise: couples who are married enjoy numerous governmental benefits, so the state's fiscal burden associated with civil marriage is reduced if less people are allowed to marry. * * * Thus, the ban on same-sex marriages may conserve some state resources. Excluding any group from civil marriage—African-Americans, illegitimates, aliens, even red-haired individuals—would conserve state resources in an equally "rational" way. Yet, such classifications so obviously offend our society's collective sense of equality that courts have not hesitated to provide added protections against such inequalities.

* * *

* * * While the objectives asserted may be important (and many undoubtedly are important), none are furthered in a substantial way by the exclusion of same-sex couples from civil marriage. Our equal protection clause requires more than has been offered to justify the continued existence of the same-sex marriage ban under the statute.

* * *

While unexpressed, religious sentiment most likely motivates many, if not most, opponents of same-sex civil marriage and perhaps even shapes the views of those people who may accept gay and lesbian unions but find the notion of same-sex marriage unsettling. * * *

* * *

* * * Our constitution does not permit any branch of government to resolve these types of religious debates and entrusts to courts the task of ensuring government *avoids* them. The statute at issue in this case does not prescribe a definition of marriage for religious institutions. Instead,

the statute declares, "Marriage is a civil contract" and then regulates that civil contract. Thus, in pursuing our task in this case, we proceed as civil judges, far removed from the theological debate of religious clerics, and focus only on the concept of civil marriage and the state licensing system that identifies a limited class of persons entitled to secular rights and benefits associated with civil marriage.

We, of course, have a constitutional mandate to protect the free exercise of religion in Iowa, which includes the freedom of a religious organization to define marriages it solemnizes as unions between a man and a woman. This mission to protect religious freedom is consistent with our task to prevent government from endorsing any religious view. State government can have no religious views, either directly or indirectly, expressed through its legislation. This proposition is the essence of the separation of church and state.

* * *

* * * These principles require that the state recognize both opposite-sex and same-sex civil marriage. Religious doctrine and views contrary to this principle of law are unaffected, and people can continue to associate with the religion that best reflects their views. A religious denomination can still define marriage as a union between a man and a woman, and a marriage ceremony performed by a minister, priest, rabbi, or other person ordained or designated as a leader of the person's religious faith does not lose its meaning as a sacrament or other religious institution. The sanctity of all religious marriages celebrated in the future will have the same meaning as those celebrated in the past. The only difference is civil marriage will now take on a new meaning that reflects a more complete understanding of equal protection of the law. This result is what our constitution requires.

* * *

Iowa Code section 595.2 is unconstitutional because the County has been unable to identify a constitutionally adequate justification for excluding plaintiffs from the institution of civil marriage. A new distinction based on sexual orientation would be equally suspect and difficult to square with the fundamental principles of equal protection embodied in our constitution. * * * Consequently, the language in Iowa Code section 595.2 limiting civil marriage to a man and a woman must be stricken from the statute, and the remaining statutory language must be interpreted and applied in a manner allowing gay and lesbian people full access to the institution of civil marriage.

NOTES ON SAME-SEX MARRIAGE LITIGATION SINCE 2000

1. How do *Goodridge*, *Hernandez*, *Kerrigan*, and *Varnum* change your assessment of the campaign for same-sex marriage through litigation? Do you think it's likely that more states will recognize same-sex marriage? Or will anti-same-sex-marriage sentiments become more entrenched? How, if at all,

did the cases change your prediction about how the Supreme Court would rule in a same-sex marriage case?

In 2009, Vermont became the first state to extend legal marriage to same-sex couples legislatively. By 2011, civil unions will be phased out, and Vermont will end its distinction between civil unions and marriage. New Hampshire soon followed with same-sex marriage legislation of its own. As of the summer of 2010, five states—Connecticut, Iowa, Massachusetts, New Hampshire and Vermont—as well as the District of Columbia recognize same-sex marriage. Ten other states currently extend marriage-like benefits to same-sex couples who register for domestic partnerships, civil unions, or beneficiary agreements. Those states are California, Colorado, Hawaii, Maine, Maryland, Nevada, New Jersey, Oregon, Washington, and Wisconsin. Maine, Maryland, and Nevada permit both same-sex and different-sex couples to register for domestic partnerships on the same terms; Colorado permits two persons of the same sex or opposite sex to register as designated beneficiaries; and the other states limit registration to same-sex couples or, in a few instances (California, New Jersey, and Washington), to same-sex couples and older different-sex couples. In addition to recognizing same-sex marriage, the District of Columbia permits two people to register for domestic partnerships without regard to gender or the nature of the relationship. New York and Maryland extend marriage recognition to same-sex couples legally wed in other jurisdictions.

2. After its decision in *Goodridge,* the Supreme Judicial Court gave the state of Massachusetts 180 days to bring its law into conformity with its decision, above. State senators introduced a bill to establish civil unions instead of marriages, and the Senate submitted the bill to the Supreme Judicial Court for an advisory opinion. In response, the Court held 4 to 3 (with the dissenting justices in *Goodridge* now inclined to uphold civil unions) that civil unions would still relegate same-sex couples to a second-class status and violate the Massachusetts Constitution. Despite agitation for a state constitutional amendment barring same-sex marriage, same-sex couples began to marry on May 17, 2004.

Same-sex married couples in Massachusetts may also begin to receive federal marriage benefits. In July, 2010, a federal district court in Massachusetts declared unconstitutional Section 3 of the federal Defense of Marriage Act (DOMA), which defines the terms "marriage" and "spouse" for purposes of federal law to include only the union of one man and one woman. Gill v. Office of Personnel Management, 699 F.Supp.2d 374 (D. Mass. 2010). The court found that the federal statute violated equal protection because "there exists no fairly conceivable set of facts that could ground a rational relationship" to a legitimate government interest. Id. at 387. After disposing of various purported government interests that supported DOMA at the time of its passage, the court stated:

> What remains, therefore, is the possibility that Congress sought to deny recognition to same-sex marriages in order to make heterosexual marriage appear more valuable or desirable. But to the extent that this was the goal, Congress has achieved it "only by punishing same-sex couples who exercise their rights under state law." And this the Constitution does

> not permit. "For if the constitutional conception of 'equal protection of the laws' means anything, it must at the very least mean" that the Constitution will not abide such "a bare congressional desire to harm a politically unpopular group."

Id. at 389. It is unclear whether the decision will be upheld upon appeal. If it is, what will be the implications for federal recognition of same-sex marriage? Will the Supreme Court be more likely to require states to recognize same-sex marriage?

3. The backlash to same-sex marriage has been substantial. As of 2010, at least 37 states have passed their own "defense of marriage" acts, two more states have strong legislative language that defines marriage as a union between a man and woman, and 30 states have passed state constitutional amendments banning same-sex marriage. Only five states have neither a statute nor a constitutional provision prohibiting same-sex marriage. Defense of Marriage Act (DOMA): Legal Resources and Information, available at http://www.domawatch.org. Two proposed amendments to the U.S. Constitution have been introduced, one of which would prohibit any state or federal law from extending "the legal incidents" of marriage, as well as marriage itself, to same-sex couples. The issue played a role in the 2008 presidential election. Both Obama and McCain stated that they opposed same-sex marriage. However, both also opposed an amendment to the U.S. Constitution prohibiting same-sex marriage. Their primary point of disagreement on the issue concerned the federal Defense of Marriage Act, with Obama opposing it and McCain in support.

On the other hand, there has been an increase in the number of private and public employers extending limited benefits to same-sex partners. By early 2010, 59% of Fortune 500 companies offered benefits to domestic partners. Also as of early 2010, 23 states, the District of Columbia, and more than 150 local governments provided benefits to domestic partners of public employees, compared to 10 state governments and 130 local governments in 2004. The Domestic Partnership Benefits and Obligations Act, available at http://www.hrc.org/issues/marriage/5662.htm. Additionally, the Domestic Partnership Benefits and Obligations Act is currently being considered by Congress and, if passed, would provide benefits to domestic partners of federal employees. Id.

4. In *In re Marriage Cases*, 183 P.3d 384 (Cal.2008), the California Supreme Court considered the question of whether the relegation of same-sex relationships to domestic partnership status, rather than marriage, violated the state's constitution. California's existing domestic partnership laws granted same-sex couples nearly all of the same rights as marriage. The court, analogizing to its past invalidation of anti-miscegenation laws, found that history alone was insufficient to exclude same-sex couples from the institution of marriage. The court concluded that marriage is a fundamental liberty right which cannot be denied to same-sex couples. The court further held that to reserve the title of "marriage" for different-sex couples, while denying it to same-sex couples, "poses at least a serious risk of denying the family relationship of same-sex couples such equal dignity and respect," and that such a distinction violated the state constitution's equal protection clause on the

basis of sexual orientation (but not on the basis of sex or gender). Id. at 400. The court addressed the "accidental procreation" argument embraced by the *Hernandez* court, but held that argument insufficient to limit the fundamental liberty right of marriage.

Almost six months later, California voters approved Proposition 8, which amended the California Constitution to read "[only] marriage between a man and a woman is valid or recognized in California." The following day, three lawsuits were filed in the Supreme Court of California, which were consolidated in Strauss v. Horton, 207 P.3d 48 (Cal.2009). The Court concluded that the amendment was permissible, but not retroactive, and therefore the marriages that had taken place between the decision in *In Re Marriage Cases* and the passage of Proposition 8 (estimated by the court at 18,000) remained valid. Id. at 64, 122.

In 2010, the United States District Court for the Northern District of California found Proposition 8 unconstitutional on both due process and equal protection grounds. Findings of Fact and Conclusions of Law, Perry v. Schwarzenegger, No. 09–cv–02292–VRW (N.D. Cal. Aug. 4, 2010). The court found that Proposition 8 violated due process because it infringed on the fundamental right to marry. In refuting arguments posed by the defendants, the court reasoned that "the movement of marriage away from a gendered institution and toward an institution free from state-minded gender roles reflects an evolution in the understanding of gender rather than a change in marriage." Id. at 113. The court also found that Proposition 8 violated equal protection, discriminating impermissibly on the basis of sex and sexual orientation, because its classifications could not survive rational basis review. As of September 2010, the case is pending appeal in the Ninth Circuit, although it is uncertain whether appellants have standing to appeal. Neither the attorney general nor the governor of California participated in defending Proposition 8, instead permitting private intervenors to litigate on their behalf. After reaching its decision on the merits, the district court questioned whether these intervenors have standing to appeal or if California officials must bring the appeal. Order at 5–6, Perry v. Schwarzenegger, No. 09–cv–02292–VRW (N.D. Cal. Aug. 12, 2010). Although the district court refused to stay its decision, the Ninth Circuit issued a stay pending appeal, so same-sex marriage has not recommenced in California. In light of the cases discussed thus far, on what grounds do you think the Ninth Circuit might affirm or reverse the district court's ruling? How might the *Perry* court's gender analysis affect future cases regarding same-sex marriage?

Notwithstanding the *Perry*'s court's statements, how might evolving understandings of gender change marriage?

5. How do the decisions in *Goodridge*, *Kerrigan*, and *Varnum* differ from one another? Do you find one court's analysis more compelling than the others? How does the analysis in each of those decisions differ from the analysis in *Hernandez*? Which decision do you most support? What are the strongest legal and policy arguments for prohibiting same-sex marriage? What are the strongest legal and policy arguments for recognizing same-sex marriage?

The same month that *Hernandez* was decided, the Supreme Court of Washington similarly upheld its 1998 Defense of Marriage Act. Even in the face of a state Equal Rights Amendment that subjected classifications based on sex to strict scrutiny, the court held that the legislature's limitation of marriage to different-sex couples did not violate the ERA, equal protection, or the privileges and immunities clause or implicate a fundamental right. The Washington court found that "the legislature was entitled to believe that limiting marriage to opposite sex couples furthers procreation, essential to survival of the human race, and furthers the well being of children by encouraging families where children are reared in homes headed by the children's biological parents." Andersen v. King County, 138 P.3d 963 (Wash. 2006). What do you think of the five courts' differing views of the connection between marriage and procreation? How do their attitudes differ as to the appropriate weight to be given to the evidence submitted on this subject?

6. The *Hernandez* court emphasized that gays and lesbians "do not become parents as a result of accident or impulse" and therefore "[t]he Legislature could find that unstable relationships between people of the opposite sex present a greater danger that children will be born into or grow up in unstable homes than is the case with same-sex couples, and thus that promoting stability in opposite-sex relationships will help children more." Do you find this "accidental procreation" rationale persuasive? Kerry Abrams and Peter Brooks draw on anthropological theory, literature, history, and constitutional law to refute the claim that marriage was designed to address accidental procreation. Instead, marriage served other purposes, including "the exchange of women through marriage [which] served not only the function of creating alliances for purposes of survival but also for maintaining control over private property" by separating legitimate heirs from children conceived outside of marriage. As such, marriage was "more specifically a way for men to determine how to transmit wealth *independent* of accidental procreation." Abrams & Brooks, Marriage as a Message: Same–Sex Couples and the Rhetoric of Accidental Procreation, 21 Yale J.L. & Human. 1, 9 (2009). Abrams and Brooks also note that even when the Supreme Court began to link procreation to marriage, in the early twentieth century, it was not until Justice Cordy's dissent in *Goodridge* that the accidental procreation rationale for marriage was proposed:

> Admittedly, heterosexual intercourse, procreation, and child care are not necessarily conjoined (particularly in the modern age of widespread effective contraception and supportive social welfare programs), but an orderly society requires some mechanism for coping with the fact that sexual intercourse commonly results in pregnancy and childbirth. The institution of marriage is that mechanism.

Goodridge v. Department of Public Health, 798 N.E.2d 941, 995 (Mass. 2003) (Cordy, J., dissenting).

What visions of gender and sexual orientation underlie the accidental procreation rationale for marriage? Does the accidental procreation argument necessarily lead to the conclusion that same-sex couples are more responsible procreators? Or that heterosexuals are less responsible, and need legal marriage to induce them to care for the byproducts of their sexual pleasure?

Consider Abrams' and Brooks' observation that "[a]t the heart of the argument is a paradox: gay couples are seen as hyper-responsible, and yet what they are doing is disturbingly unnatural." Abrams & Brooks, above, at 26. Do you agree? The authors also note the way that accidental procreation arguments promote patriarchal roles for fathers: "[f]or the accidental procreationists, marriage is just as much about enforcing a patriarchal role for fathers as it is about preventing their abandonment of mothers; *responsible* procreation is all about masculine control of the family." Id. at 27. Does the accidental procreation rationale for marriage imply that heterosexual men view sex as a source of pleasure whereas women view sex as a source of family, and therefore the state needs to intervene to encourage men to take responsibility and privatize dependency? Do you think this is true? If so, is it a valid basis for excluding same-sex couples from marriage? Would it also exclude infertile or celibate heterosexuals from marriage? How could you use the accidental procreation argument as an attorney for the state? How would you refute it as an attorney for same-sex couple plaintiffs seeking the right to marry?

7. Do the recent same-sex marriage cases shed any more light on the substantive connection between sex discrimination and the ban on same-sex marriage? What connections do you see between the social inequality of women and men and bans on same-sex marriage? Are there connections other than the historical origins of marriage as a patriarchal institution? Whose interests are served by keeping same-sex unions socially unacceptable?

8. Should bans on same-sex marriage primarily be challenged as a form of discrimination on the basis of sexual orientation? Is this the strongest argument in favor of same-sex marriage? Are there more effective strategies to use in the campaign for same-sex marriage? As a litigator advocating to abolish a ban on same-sex marriage, would you choose to advance an equal protection argument, a due process argument, or both? See Jean C. Love, The Synergistic Evolution of Liberty and Equality in the Marriage Cases Brought by Same-Sex Couples in State Courts, 13 J. Gender, Race & Just. 275 (2010).

Should gay men and lesbians be regarded as a suspect class for purposes of constitutional analysis? The Supreme Court has often discussed immutability as an important factor in finding that classifications based on sex and race are subject to heightened scrutiny. Is immutability a necessary factor for heightened scrutiny? See Janet E. Halley, Sexual Orientation and the Politics of Biology: A Critique of the Argument From Immutability, 46 Stan. L. Rev. 503, 507–16 (1994) (arguing that the Supreme Court has never stated it is a necessary finding and noting its absence in religion and alienage cases). Why is immutability—or a genetic basis for homosexuality—so important in the national debate? Should it be? See Andersen v. King County, 138 P.3d, above note 5, at 974 (gay and lesbian plaintiffs seeking to marry fail to make the showing of immutability necessary to qualify as a suspect class).

If some women experience more fluid sexuality than men do, as discussed in Chapter 3, how might standards relying on immutability hurt women more than men?

9. What do you see as the appropriate role of the state in regulating marriage? What are some legitimate reasons that a secular state may be involved in marriage in a diverse society in the 21st century? Given your view

of the state's legitimate role in regulating marriage, do you think that as a matter of sound family law policy marriage itself should be extended to same-sex couples? Or should some alternative form of union recognition be extended instead of marriage? Should neither be extended in order to protect and preserve the institution of marriage? Should other forms of relationships between adults be accorded state recognition?

Should state recognition of marriage be abolished? Robin West argues that civil unions should become the norm, available in every state and open to any two persons as a way to recognize relationships of intimacy and care that are not necessarily sexual. Civil unions would be granted the same privileges, rights, and benefits that are currently granted to marriage, with the only legal difference being the openness of entry requirements. Symbolically, civil unions would preserve the state's legitimate interest in promoting the care of dependents without permitting state intrusion into individuals' sexual behavior. West imagines a gradual change leading to a clear delineation between faith-based marriage and state-based civil unions. West, Marriage, Sexuality, and Gender 205–211 (2007). For proposals similar to West's, see Katherine K. Baker, The Stories of Marriage, 12 J.L. & Fam. Stud. 1, 2, 43–48 (2010) (offering "a definition of marriage which suggests that marriage can be beneficial to the state, beneficial to the couple, and integrated into the rich social history of marriage without necessarily being gendered"); Cass R. Sunstein & Richard H. Thaler, Nudge: Improving Decisions about Health, Wealth and Happiness 217 (2008) (proposing that state recognition of marriage be replaced with state recognition of civil unions for all couples, same-sex and different-sex). Would these proposals solve the current controversies in the same-sex marriage debate? Would they create more controversy? Do they go far enough? Would they transform gender hierarchy within relationships? How do such proposals relate to the proposals made by Nancy Polikoff in the excerpt at the beginning of this chapter?

10. Does the campaign for same-sex marriage limit the range of possibilities for relationship recognition? Discussion about the goal of legal marriage within the gay and lesbian community exploded in the 1989 debate between Thomas Stoddard and Paula Ettelbrick in Out/Look Magazine. Gay Marriage: A Must or Bust? Out/Look, Fall 1989, at 9–17. Stoddard argued that until marriage was available to lesbian and gay couples, all lesbians and gay men would continue to face inequality and second class status. In his view, expanding the definition of marriage to include same-sex couples could also make the institution of marriage less gendered and oppressive. Stoddard, Why Gay People Should Seek the Right to Marry, Out/Look, Fall 1989, at 9. Ettelbrick, on the other hand, argued that same-sex marriage was a path toward assimilating gays and lesbians to dominant heterosexual norms. Ettelbrick urged gays and lesbians to instead embrace functional approaches to relationship recognition and more general programs like universal health insurance. Ettelbrick, Since When Is Marriage A Path to Liberation?, Out/Look, Fall 1989, at 14.

What do you think of the same-sex marriage campaign? Do you think it would have been better to focus on a more universal progressive agenda? How can feminists and gay rights activists promote relationship equality outside of marriage? Do any of the proposals presented in this section offer a satisfying solution? If marriage were available to same-sex couples, would non-married same-sex couples receive even less recognition because they did not take advantage of the available legal mechanisms? What about non-married different-sex couples? What about individuals living outside the couple form? Might the recognition of same-sex marriage leave even less room for a functional approach?

TEXT NOTE: CHOICE OF LAW QUESTIONS AND RESPONSES ABROAD

In July 2005, the Canadian federal government passed a statute recognizing same-sex marriage. The recognition of same-sex marriages in Massachusetts, Canada, the subsequent four states, and the District of Columbia have raised substantial questions about whether those marriages will be recognized elsewhere. What happens if a couple from another state goes to one of the states where marriage is recognized for a combined wedding and honeymoon? Will they be married in their home state when they return? Initially, activists on both sides of the issue seemed to believe that couples would be married in their home states when they returned, arguing that Article IV of the United States Constitution, requiring each state to give "Full Faith and Credit * * * to the public Acts, Records, and judicial proceedings of every other State," would require other states to recognize same-sex marriages validly performed elsewhere. Opponents of same-sex marriage argued that legislation "protecting" marriage was therefore desperately needed. They proposed DOMA's (Defense of Marriage Acts) in each state expressly providing that the state would not recognize same-sex marriages when their residents traveled to another state to marry. As previously discussed, the vast majority of states have enacted such provisions. Congress also passed a national DOMA, which provides that no state need recognize a same-sex marriage from another state and defines marriage for purposes of federal regulations and benefits as limited to different-sex couples.

Although advocates and opponents of same-sex marriage tended to agree that, unless states passed DOMA legislation, they would be bound to recognize the same-sex marriages of their residents who went to another state to get married, the law was uniformly to the contrary. The general (common law, not constitutional law) choice of law rule is that a marriage valid where performed is valid everywhere. But there is a public policy exception: if a state considers its restrictions on marriage a serious enough concern (for example, incest prohibitions), it need not give full faith and credit to a marriage performed in another state that violates the local state's marriage statute. A marriage is more vulnerable to challenge under this public policy exception if it involves residents who went to another state for their wedding ceremony in order to evade restrictions in their home state than in cases where legally married residents of one state move to another. This public policy exception has not been seen as unconstitutional under the Full Faith and Credit Clause; the clause "has never been much of a constraint on states' power to fashion choice of law rules."[17] (Note also that a marriage license—unlike a divorce, to which full faith and credit does apply—is not a judicial judgment.)

---

17. Andrew Koppelman, Same Sex, Different States: When Same-Sex Marriages Cross State Lines 118 (2006).

Other questions are raised when a same-sex couple resident in one of the six jurisdictions recognizing same-sex marriage marries there and later moves to another state—a situation involving migration rather than evasion of their home state law. Despite state DOMA's, it is difficult to imagine that all aspects of a legal same-sex marriage will be wholly ignored when the couple moves. Imagine, for example, a married lesbian couple with three children who move from Massachusetts to Illinois. One partner has been a full time homemaker. Under the law of Massachusetts, both have become legal parents of the children, though the children are biologically related only to the stay-at home-parent. All the assets are titled in the breadwinning partner's name. It seems unlikely that every judge in Illinois would actually be willing to hold that the breadwinning partner has no link to the children, no right to argue for custody or visitation, and no obligation to support them, or to hold that the stay-at-home partner has no claim to the assets titled in the breadwinning partner's name or to spousal support (if appropriate) when they split up. These results would, however, be mandated by current Illinois law, given the Illinois DOMA, 750 ILCS 5/213.1 (1996), and Hewitt v. Hewitt (described in excerpt on law of cohabitation, below).

Andrew Koppelman suggests that courts will be inclined to decide these cases, as southern states did during the period of miscegenation laws, based on the particular incident of marriage at issue and weighing the interests involved. He suggests that any incident that the couple could otherwise establish by contract (such as inheritance or the right to make medical decisions) should be recognized, because it was clearly not against the public policy of the forum. On the other hand, incidents arising out of operation of law, such as joint taxation, might not be recognized.[18] Rights of third parties such as children, however, even if arising out of state law, should not be subject to invalidation. What of the rights of a third party (let us assume a person of the different sex for purposes of argument) whom a party to a legal same-sex marriage wants to marry, if the spouse has moved and is ineligible to divorce in the new state? Moreover, considerable hardship could arise for legally married same-sex couples who are simply on a vacation trip to another state should they become involved in an accident that results in injury or death to one partner, thus implicating the hospital visitation and health care decision making statutes, and potentially the wrongful death and negligent infliction of emotional distress law of the state they are visiting. In short, this area of the law is still in a state of development, and there is likely to be much litigation in the future.

Abroad

According legal recognition of some sort to same-sex couples appears to be a general trend. The Netherlands made a form of domestic partnership available to same-sex couples and then became the first country to offer full marriage rights, including the word "marriage," to same-sex couples in 2001. Belgium, Sweden, Norway, Iceland, Portugal, Spain, South Africa, and Argentina all allowed same-sex couples to marry by the summer of 2010. In the United Kingdom, same-sex couples can enter into civil partnerships with the benefits and responsibilities of marriage. Other European countries offer

18. Id. at 107–10.

domestic partnerships with more limited rights. For example, the German Life Partnerships Act, effective in 2001, confers many rights upon same-sex couples, including inheritance tax exemptions, next of kin rights, eligibility for some social security benefits, tenancy rights, and immigration concessions for a foreign partner. In 1999, France adopted a law allowing any couple who share a home to enter into a "civil solidarity pact" (known as PACS, an acronym in French), offering many rights (tax, social security, and the right to succeed to tenancies, for example) and requiring mutual support.

4. DISSOLUTION OF MARITAL RELATIONSHIPS

TEXT NOTE: THE ECONOMIC CONSEQUENCES OF DIVORCE AND DEATH

Supporters of same-sex marriage often cite the legal default rules attaching to marital dissolution as one of the primary benefits of legal marriage. Although such default rules are reserved exclusively for couples who are legally married (or in some states, in a legally recognized domestic partnership), feminists have long debated whether such rules adequately protect women when a marriage ends by divorce or death, particularly those women who have devoted significant amounts of time to care work within the home.

Upon marital dissolution, property accumulated during a marriage is subject to two sets of default rules governing property distribution. In the nine states known as community property states,[19] all property accumulated by either spouse from wages during the marriage is considered to be the joint or community property of the spouses. Each spouse therefore owns an equal, undivided share in all acquisitions from earnings during marriage, regardless of which spouse holds the title of those acquisitions. Similarly, title does not control the distribution of community property upon divorce or death. Rather, divorce courts in these states generally apply a rule or presumption of equal division of the community property upon divorce,[20] and probate rules provide that the surviving spouse retains at least her half of the community property.[21]

In contrast, in the remaining 41 states, property accumulated by either spouse during marriage remains the separate property of that spouse unless the spouses agree to hold the property jointly. Upon divorce in these separate property states, default rules traditionally permitted spouses to keep the property titled in their individual names; if a divorcing spouse needed more property for living expenses than was titled in her name, courts would order

19. These states are Arizona, California, Idaho, Louisiana, Nevada, New Mexico, Texas, Washington, and Wisconsin. See Laura A. Rosenbury, Two Ways to End a Marriage: Divorce or Death, 2005 Utah L. Rev. 1227, 1234 & n.19 (providing citations).

20. Although equal division of community property is now the norm in all of the community property states, it became the governing principle only after California introduced it in 1969. Herma Hill Kay, An Appraisal of California's No-Fault Divorce Law, 75 Cal. L. Rev. 291, 299–304 (1987). Prior to that time, courts took fault into account when dividing the community property, leading to many unequal divisions, often in women's favor. Id.

21. If the deceased spouse executed a valid will before death, community property states respect his power to give the other half of the community property to anyone he desires. If the deceased spouse died without a valid will, intestacy laws give the surviving spouse a significant portion (sometimes all) of the deceased spouse's community property in addition to her half of the community property.

alimony payments for a specified period of time or on an ongoing basis. The separate property states' current approach to property division upon divorce is dramatically different from this traditional approach. Over the past 40 years, all of the separate property states have adopted equitable distribution approaches that require courts to look beyond title when dividing property upon divorce. Courts are now instructed to make an equitable distribution of virtually all of the property acquired by the spouses during marriage, which is referred to as marital property, and alimony is disfavored.[22] Therefore, although title continues to govern the ownership of property during the marriage, ownership is redefined at divorce. When a marriage ends by death, however, different rules apply. Ownership of assets is not redefined; instead, the deceased spouse has the ability to devise through will the property titled in his name at death to anyone he chooses, subject only to the surviving spouse's right to make a claim against the deceased spouse's estate. These "elective share" rights generally give the surviving spouse much less than one half of the assets accumulated by wages during the marriage, making such rights more analogous to alimony than current equitable distributions of property.[23]

Feminists have generally praised the partnership theory of marriage that underlies modern notions of both community property and equitable distribution of assets upon divorce. In fact, the current default rules are in part the result of feminist calls to reform divorce law upon the advent of no-fault divorce, which initially adversely affected many wives because they no longer could use fault as a bargaining tool if they were dissatisfied with title-based distributions of property.[24] Pursuant to the partnership theory, marriage is no longer a hierarchical relationship, but rather is an enterprise freely chosen by two equal individuals who may nonetheless contribute to marriage in different ways. As such, nontangible contributions to the marriage, particularly the care work traditionally performed by wives, are now valued equally with tangible contributions in order to promote cooperation and sharing within the marriage and limit incentives for financial opportunism and oppression.[25]

22. In 12 of the separate property states, equitable distribution means, in most cases, that all marital property is divided equally upon divorce, much like what would happen in a community property state. In the remaining 29 separate property states, courts are given discretion to distribute the marital property equitably, meaning equal divisions of marital property are less likely to occur. However, even in these states, ownership is redefined at divorce because spouses cannot automatically exercise control over the assets titled in their name, as they could during marriage, but rather must wait for the court to make an equitable distribution of the marital property or approve a settlement purporting to make an equitable distribution. See Rosenbury, above note 19, at 1236–37 (providing citations).

23. In one state, Georgia, the elective share right is one of support only: surviving spouses are entitled to an allowance from the deceased spouse's estate designed to cover the surviving spouse's living expenses during the first year after the spouse's death. In most of the other separate property states, surviving spouses are entitled to one-third of the deceased spouse's separate property, although a few separate property states have attempted to revise their elective share laws to more closely mirror default rules governing equitable distribution at divorce. See Rosenbury, above note 19, at 1245–60.

24. See, e.g., Lenore J. Weitzman, The Divorce Revolution: The Unexpected Social and Economic Consequences for Women and Children in America 16–41, 323–56 (1985); Jill Elaine Hasday, The Canon of Family Law, 57 Stan. L. Rev. 825, 869–70 & n.171 (2004).

25. See Rosenbury, above note 19.

Given the potential of the partnership theory of marriage to transform hierarchical relations within marriage and to better protect women who engage in care work upon divorce or the death of their spouse, many feminists focus on how both separate property and community property states might more faithfully implement the theory at dissolution than is now the case. These feminists argue, for example, that assets owned by spouses before marriage should be considered community property or marital property subject to equitable distribution, that alimony should reflect partnership theory principles when marital assets are not sufficient to value women's intangible contributions to the marriage, or that inheritance law should come to mirror divorce law's embrace of the partnership theory.[26] Other feminists, most notably Martha Fineman, argue that the partnership theory does not go far enough because its presumption of equal division fails to acknowledge that many women actually "over-participate" in marriage.[27]

Laura Rosenbury questions which women benefit from the partnership theory. Employing an anti-essentialist analysis, and drawing upon critiques of alimony[28] and tax and Social Security law,[29] Rosenbury argues:

> [T]he underlying premise of the partnership theory is that intangible contributions to a marriage, such as child care, housework and other care work, should be valued on par with tangible financial contributions, thus leading to an equal or equitable division of tangible assets. This premise most advances the material well-being of those wives who forego market work in order to do care work. Indeed, these women would own no property but for the partnership theory of marriage. But, as feminists have acknowledged in other contexts, historically only certain women—namely white middle- to upper-middle-class women—could afford to forego market work, and, increasingly, many of those women have found that they must work to make ends meet. Thus, today, the partnership theory of marriage most benefits only those women who can afford to stay at home and choose to do so.
>
> In addition, the amount of the material benefit received by these women is directly tied to the amount of money earned by their husbands. Under the partnership theory, the value of care work is not independently set. Rather, wives who forego market work receive half of every dollar earned by their husbands. Therefore, the more money earned by the husband, the more the wife benefits from the partnership theory of marriage. The partnership theory of marriage thus most benefits not only

26. See, e.g., Shari Motro, Labor, Luck, and Love: Reconsidering the Sanctity of Separate Property, 102 Nw. U. L. Rev. 1623 (2008); Cynthia Lee Starnes, One More Time: Alimony, Intuition and the Remarriage–Termination Rule, 81 Ind. L.J. 971 (2006); Alicia Brokars Kelly, Rehabilitating Partnership Marriage as a Theory of Wealth Distribution at Divorce: In Recognition of a Shared Life, 19 Wis. Women's L.J. 141 (2004); Susan N. Gary, Marital Partnership Theory and the Elective Share: Federal Estate Tax Law Provides a Solution, 49 U. Miami L. Rev. 567 (1995).

27. Martha Albertson Fineman, The Illusion of Equality: The Rhetoric and Reality of Divorce Reform 2–6, 29, 47 (1991); Fineman, Equality: Still Illusive After All These Years, in Gender Equality: Dimensions of Women's Equal Citizenship 251, 253–66 (Linda C. McClain & Joanna L. Grossman, eds. 2009).

28. See Twila L. Perry, Alimony: Race, Privilege, and Dependency in the Search for Theory, 82 Geo. L.J. 2481, 2486–95 (1994).

29. See Martha T. McCluskey, Caring for Workers, 55 Me. L. Rev. 314, 326–29 (2002).

those women who can afford to stay at home, but the subset of those women who are married to wealthy men.

Of course wives who do not forego market work can also benefit from the partnership theory of marriage, but their care work is valued less than the care work of the wives who forego market work. Every dollar earned by a wife in the market translates into a dollar by which her care work is undervalued, at least when compared to the wife who foregoes market work. Thus, women who both work outside of the home and do the bulk of the care work within the home may not benefit from the partnership theory of marriage and may even be harmed by it. For example, the intangible contributions of a wife who earns as much as her husband yet also does most of the housework and child-care coordination—a situation that is increasingly common—will be completely unvalued pursuant to the partnership theory of marriage. Similarly, in the rare situations where a husband earns as much as his wife and also does the bulk of the care work, the husband's care work will be completely unvalued. And a wife who earns more than her husband yet also does most of the housework and child-care coordination will be hurt by the partnership theory because she must share her wages with her husband even though he did not make significant intangible contributions to the marriage.

Therefore, it is beyond dispute that the women who benefit most from the partnership theory of marriage are those who forego market work and are married to wealthy men. In addition to being privileged by wealth, these women also tend to be white, primarily because most women of color do not forego market work and those who do tend not to be married to wealthy men. Moreover, although lesbians are not permitted to marry their same-sex partners in most states, if same-sex marriages were more widely recognized, it is doubtful that married lesbians would benefit from the partnership theory in the same way that straight women married to wealthy men do because women tend to earn less than men, particularly at the highest levels of the professions, and lesbians tend not to adopt the traditional division of care work and market work that maximizes the material benefits of the partnership theory. The partnership theory of marriage thus seems to be a vestige from the time when feminist reforms primarily benefited privileged women.[30]

Despite that critique, feminists have not developed alternatives to the partnership theory of marriage. Instead, most feminist considerations of the economic consequences of divorce or death explore how the law can better value women's nontangible contributions to marriage. In addition, as discussed below, Fineman argues that the state should stop assigning benefits to marital couples altogether and other feminists have argued that private ordering should replace state default rules. It is unclear how the increased legal recognition of same-sex marriage will affect these trends.

---

30. Rosenbury, above note 19, at 1283–85.

NOTES ON THE ECONOMIC CONSEQUENCES OF DIVORCE AND DEATH

1. In 2003, 3.5% of married white women over age 65 and 12.4% of married Black women over age 65 fell below the poverty line as compared to 16.9% of white women over age 65 and 40.3% of Black women over age 65 who were in households with no spouse present. U.S. Census Bureau, 65+ in the United States 105–106 fig. 4–13 (2005). Part of the problem for elderly women is that women are generally less likely than men to be firmly attached to the labor market throughout their adult lives and, even when working, are less likely to hold jobs in sectors with good pensions; they are also likely to earn less during life, and pension benefits tend to be tied to lifetime earnings. Gov't Accountability Office, Retirement Security: Women Face Challenges in Ensuring Financial Security in Retirement 4–6 (Oct. 2007); Angela O'Rand & John C. Henretta, Midlife Work History and Retirement Income, in Women's Retirement: Policy Implications of Recent Research 25 (Maximiliane Szinovacz, ed. 1982). These factors cannot, however, explain the economic similarities between widows and divorcees, since husbands might be expected to ensure the well-being of widows, since their marriages lasted until death.

Why aren't widows better protected by (1) their husbands, (2) inheritance laws, or (3) welfare safety nets? How might these meager protections reflect a norm of wifely sacrifice? See Rosenbury, excerpt above, cited in footnote 19, at 1278–82. Should feminists continue to expect that women need to be taken care of at dissolution, or should we instead focus on opportunities that allow women to be self-sufficient? Which women would benefit from each approach?

2. In most divorces, the husband walks away with significantly better Social Security protection than the wife, though it would be easy enough to divide Social Security entitlements equally as they are earned during marriage. In marriages conforming to the male wage-earner/female caretaker model, only the husband walks away from a marriage lasting less than ten years (the average marriage lasts only seven years) with a Social Security claim for the contributions made to the fund during the marriage. Even if the marriage lasts ten years, the wife walks away with 50% of his claim; his increases to 150% if he remarries, whereas hers is likely to end if she remarries. At retirement, a woman must choose between filing a claim based on her own earnings record and on her status as ex-wife. What does this choice mean for her autonomy both during marriage and post-divorce? Does this correspond to the partnership theory of marriage discussed above?

Because of this provision, women often receive no increase in their Social Security benefit from combining years in the wage labor market with years of caretaking, though many women combine years of caretaking (with perhaps part-time wage work) with years of full-time wage work. If a couple stays married until death (usually of the husband), the widow's draw after his death will be only two-thirds of their joint draw, though for one person to live on the same level as a couple, that person needs 80% of the couple's income. See Mary E. Becker, Obscuring the Struggle: Sex Discrimination, Social Security, and Stone, Seidman, Sunstein, & Tushnet's *Constitutional Law*, 89 Colum. L. Rev. 264, 286–87 (1989). Given women's lower pay and weaker attachment to the wage-labor market because of their caretaking responsibilities, combined with the structure of Social Security, it is not surprising that in 1999 16.9% of women over 85 years of age as compared to 9.6% of men over age 85 lived in poverty. U.S. Census 2000 Special Report, We the People: Aging in the United States 9 (2004). See also Nadia Karamcheva & Alicia H. Munnell, Ctr. for Retirement Research at Boston Coll., Why are Widows So Poor? Brief No. 7–9, (July 2007); Martha T. McCluskey, Caring for Workers, 55 Me. L. Rev. 314, 328–30 (2002); Karen C. Burke & Grayson M.P. McCouch, The Impact of Social Security Reform on Women's Economic Security, 16 N.Y.L. Sch. J. Hum. Rts. 375, 375–87 (1999). Current reform proposals suggest replacing survivor benefits with an earnings sharing model, in which Social Security benefits would depend on assumed shared income between spouses. Studies and models released by the Social Security Administration show, however, that for widowed women in particular, the earnings sharing model would result in a decrease in benefits for 93% of widows. Howard M. Iams, Gayle L. Reznik & Christopher R. Tamborini, Earnings Sharing in Social Security: Projected Impacts of Alternative Proposals Using the MINT Model, 69 Soc. Security Rev. 1 (2009). What underlying values and assumptions are reflected in the structure of our Social Security system? Do they correspond to reality? What conceptions of marriage are reflected by the Social Security system?

3. Many ex-wives' wealth decreases considerably after divorce. There are several key components to this post-divorce poverty including the facts that (1) almost no ex-wives get alimony, and those few who do receive only short-term "rehabilitative" alimony; (2) ex-wives get at most half the couple's accumulated property at divorce, which tends to be little in most families; (3) ex-husbands usually walk away with the largest family asset, his future income stream; and (4) fathers may extract economic concessions by threatening custody challenges. A fifth component is that child support awards are low and poorly enforced. See Chapter 7, Section G, below. A sixth problem, as described in note 2 above, is that in most families, the husband walks away with better Social Security protection than the wife. Additional problems are presented by disparities between male and female wages in the labor market and the limitations imposed on mothers' labor market participation by their child care responsibilities as (in most instances) single custodial parents. The absence of affordable child care exacerbates this problem. See Chapter 7, Section E2, below. What changes would you propose to address any or all of these problems? How many of them can be brought about through litigation? How many through legislation? Who would benefit from your proposals? Who might be harmed?

4. Do you agree with Rosenbury's critique of the partnership theory of marriage? Can you imagine ways that the law could better value both wage work and care work within marriage? How might the current system encourage both men and women to conform to conventional gender roles? What alternative systems might value men's care work? How might such systems change the distribution of labor within marriage?

5. Many feminists have proposed that private contractual ordering, rather than state default rules attaching to marital status, govern family relationships. See, e.g., Marjorie M. Shultz, Contractual Ordering of Marriage: A New Model for State Policy, 70 Cal. L. Rev. 207, 253 (1982) (arguing that contract offers an approach to individual fulfillment and gender neutrality through negotiation between equal parties); Margaret Brinig & June Carbone,

The Reliance Interest in Marriage and Divorce, 62 Tul. L. Rev. 855 (1988) (evaluating remedies available upon divorce under reliance theory of contract damages); Jana B. Singer, The Privatization of Family Law, 1992 Wis. L. Rev. 1443 (tracing and critiquing the increasing privatization of family law in a variety of areas, including court approval of both premarital contracts and contracts between cohabitants); Katharine B. Silbaugh, Marriage Contracts and the Family Economy, 93 Nw. U. L. Rev. 65 (1998) (arguing that monetary contracts should not be enforced if nonmonetary contracts are not); Howard Fink & June Carbone, Between Private Ordering and Public Fiat: A New Paradigm for Family Law Decision–Making, 5 J. Law & Fam. Studies 1 (2003) (arguing for an administrative process encouraging ex ante contract formation by married couples which would then be binding on both the parties and courts deciding future disputes). However, as discussed in the excerpt from Carol Pateman above, the marriage contract has long been resistant to actual contractual principles. Many feminists also see substantial problems with contractual ordering, stemming both from power differentials between the parties and from couples' refusal to recognize the statistical risks of divorce at the time of entry into marriage. Jana Singer suggests that privatization could bring further problems, including the potential to divert attention from attempts to reform family law doctrine and "to imagine alternative forms of public ordering," including advocacy of sharing principles in both marriage and divorce. Singer, above, at 1556–60. Privatization also reinforces the notion of the public/private split, which has harmed women in many ways by isolating women within families and supporting the position that the public has little interest in what goes on within the hearth. Id. at 1560–64.

If the protections of current family law were unavailable, would women bargain for adequate safeguards and avoid entry into relationships of dependency if they could not obtain them? Why or why not? See Robin West, Sex, Law, and Consent, in The Ethic of Consent: Theory and Practice 221, 236 (Franklin G. Miller & Alan Wertheimer eds., 2010) (analyzing the ways that women often consent to things they do not want). Would some women have more ability to bargain for adequate safeguards than others? If so, which ones? In contrast to losing safeguards, might women be freed from some of the burdens of marriage under a private ordering approach? Which ones?

6. Another model that has been suggested for the private-law ordering of family relationships is to analogize them to business partnerships. Thus, for example, Cynthia Starnes advocates treating the dissolution of marriage like the dissolution of a partnership prior to expiration of its "term." Under this model, the dissociated spouse would receive the right to a buyout of her interest in any income-generating marital enterprise that continues after dissociation as a result of the human capital of her spouse, capital enhanced during the marriage by education or labor force participation. Starnes also proposes a mathematical model for calculating enhanced earnings and a sliding scale basing the buyout price on the length of the marriage. See Starnes, Divorce and the Displaced Homemaker: A Discourse on Playing with Dolls, Partnership Buyouts and Dissociation Under No–Fault, 60 U. Chi. L. Rev. 67, 131–37 (1993). See also Cynthia Lee Starnes, Mothers, Myths and the Laws of Divorce: One More Feminist Case for Partnership, 13 Wm. & Mary J. Women & L. 203 (2006) (arguing that partnership principles will help reduce

the effects of the myth that "mothering just happens, mothering is free, and mothering is for babies"). How is this approach similar to and different from the partnership theory of marriage? Do you think this remedy is appropriate? Does a spouse have an "ownership" interest in the education, training, and skills of the other spouse? Does it make a difference if the couple does or does not have children? Which women will benefit from Starnes's proposal and which women will be left out or harmed?

7. Other feminists have turned to commercial law in the search for remedies for caretaker-spouses. For example, Martha M. Ertman suggests the use of security agreements to protect the primary homemaker's interest in her "loan" to the primary wage-earning spouse. These "Premarital Security Agreements" would grant the creditor homemaker a security interest in post-divorce income as well as in marital property, on the ground that this income includes the extension of credit from the primary homemaker by her specialization in domestic labor—a debt that will go unpaid if the marriage does not last. Ertman, Commercializing Marriage: A Proposal For Valuing Women's Work Through Premarital Security Agreements, 77 Tex. L. Rev. 17 (1998). See also Ertman, Marriage as a Trade: Bridging the Private/Private Distinction, 36 Harv. C.R.-C.L. L. Rev. 79 (2001) (arguing in favor of using business models rather than naturalized models to describe marriage arrangements because the former provide enhanced equity and flexibility). Although Ertman's formula and collection mechanism are perhaps the most elaborately described, a variety of proposals for post-divorce income sharing have gained the support of feminist scholars. See, e.g., Alicia Brokars Kelly, Rehabilitating Partnership Marriage as a Theory of Wealth Distribution at Divorce: In Recognition of a Shared Life, 19 Wis. Women's L.J. 141 (2004) (suggesting that the contributions and sacrifices of spouses in marriage create intangible burdens and benefits which must be divided during divorce); June Carbone, Income Sharing: Redefining the Family in Terms of Community, 31 Hous. L. Rev. 359 (1994) (supporting the idea that the post-divorce family is an ongoing community entitled to a share in the income and support of the absent parent); Jane Rutherford, Duty in Divorce: Shared Income As a Path to Equality, 58 Fordham L. Rev. 539 (1990) (arguing that a permanent equal sharing of income after a divorce can encourage a more equitable division of labor and power during the marriage); Jana Singer, Divorce Reform and Gender Justice, 67 N.C. L. Rev. 1103 (1989) (viewing marriage as an investment partnership, requiring intangible career assets to be equitably divided at divorce along with property, most simply through a set period of income sharing). What do you think the impact of a commercial arrangement like Ertman's would be upon intimate relationships? Do you find it a promising avenue to protect the interests of the more vulnerable spouse? Would such proposals address Rosenbury's critiques of the partnership theory or only reinforce them?

C. INTIMACY OUTSIDE OF MARRIAGE

As discussed above, laws recognizing marriage to the exclusion of other relationships necessarily also regulate intimacy outside of marriage. Such regulation takes the form of neglect at best and stigmatization at worst. This section considers intimacy outside of legal marriage in light of the principles of gender equality and women's well-being developed throughout this book. We begin by considering a proposal to decenter the current sexual family, then move to an examination of cohabitation outside of marriage, before ending with ways to re-imagine intimacy through friendship and other relationships outside the couple form.

1. DE-CENTERING THE SEXUAL FAMILY

MARTHA ALBERTSON FINEMAN, THE NEUTERED MOTHER, THE SEXUAL FAMILY AND OTHER TWENTIETH CENTURY TRAGEDIES

228–35 (1995).

* * * Concurrently (and complementarily), the legal roles of Husband–Father, Wife–Mother, and Child–Adult are formulated in the context of the relationship that resides in the contrived institution of the official family, which is entitled to privacy and protection from intervention, regulation, and the state. Dependency is naturally assigned to this private family by the state. Within the family, this dependency is further directed by continued gendered role division.

Because we are concerned with this institution from a functional perspective, as a complement to the state designated to care for dependencies, we must consider the natural family a failure. In its historic form it is not adequate to handle both the demands for equality and the contemporary manifestations of inevitable and derivative dependency.[b] It is essential that we begin to reconceptualize the relationship between law and the family in regard to these dependencies. In doing so, we should keep a few basic principles in mind. First, we must abandon the pretense that we can achieve gender equality through family-law reform. The egalitarian family myth remains largely unassisted by other ideological and structural changes in the larger society and is belied by the statistics reflecting the ways women and men live.

We also should recognize that family policy is a form of state regulation. We must therefore, be explicit about the norms and values motivating public and legal decisions about what should be protected or encouraged through social and economic subsidies. Furthermore, family policy must be secular, not based on a religious model. It should reference the functional aspirations we have for families in our society and be supportive of those aspirations. I, therefore, propose two recommendations for legal reform: the abolition of the legal supports for the sexual family and the construction of protections for the nurturing unit of caretaker and dependant exemplified by the Mother/Child dyad. These proposals are intended to direct policy discussions toward support for caretaking.

---

b. By "inevitable and derivative dependencies" Fineman means the dependency of the human infant and child, the elderly, and the sick or handicapped, on the one hand, and the dependency of the person who is the caretaker of other dependents, on the other hand.

A. ENDING MARRIAGE AS A LEGAL CATEGORY

Consistent with the first goal, we should abolish marriage as a legal category and with it any privilege based on sexual affiliation. I want to emphasize I am addressing only the legal significance of marriage. There would be no special legal rules governing the relationships between husband and wife or defining the consequences of the status of marriage as now exist in family law. In fact, these categories would no longer have any legal meaning at all. Instead, the interactions of female and male sexual affiliates would be governed by the same rules that regulate other interactions in our society—specifically those of contract and property, as well as tort and criminal law. The illusive equality between adults in sexual and all other areas would thus be asserted and assumed, a result that to many will be symbolically appealing. Women and men would operate outside of the confines of marriage, transacting and interacting without the fetters of legalities they did not voluntarily choose. Of course, people would be free to engage in "ceremonious" marriage; such an event would, however, have no legal (enforceable in court) consequences. If they didn't execute a separate contract, there would be no imposed terms as now operate in the context of marriage. Any legal consequences would have to be the result of a separate negotiation. Mere agreement to form a live-in sexual relationship would not suffice.

This proposal is actually not very farfetched. We already encourage antenuptual [sic] agreements that are contractual deviations from state-imposed marriage consequences. No-fault divorce makes marriage a "tenuous" relationship. Opportunities for individual bargaining about economic and other aspects of sexual relations typically now occur at the termination of the relationship. Separation agreements (contracts) are the norm, not judicial decrees. My proposal would merely mandate that such bargaining occur prior to the termination of the relationship, ideally before the couple becomes too "serious." This is what occurs in some nonmarital cohabitation cases. Many states have begun to recognize such contractual commitments (promises) about sharing assets or providing compensation for "services" in marriage-like arrangements. Even if promises are not explicit, equity sometimes intervenes to protect "expectations" or to reimburse and compensate contributions to the accumulation of property.

One benefit of abolishing marriage as a legal category (upon which a whole system of public and private subsidies and protections is based) is that the state interest in bolstering the institution would dissolve. Adult, voluntary sexual interactions would be of no concern to the state since there would no longer be a state-preferred model of family intimacy to protect and support. Therefore, all such sexual relationships would be permitted—nothing prohibited, nothing privileged. Of course, children would continue to be protected by incest and other laws, and rape would continue to be subject to criminal sanctions. Voluntary sexual relationships between adults would be unregulated, however.

* * *

This proposal to abolish marriage as a legal category, which I realize may be viewed as quite radical, is necessary given the ideological position of the sexual family and its role in maintaining inequality. This very position, however, forces the conclusion that the institution is incapable of reform. As long as it exists, it will continue to occupy a privileged status and be posited as the ideal, defining other intimate entities as deviant. Instead of seeking to eliminate this stigma by analogizing more and more relationships to marriage, why not just abolish the category as a legal status and, in that way, render all sexual relationships equal with each other and all relationships equal with the sexual?

B. MOTHER/CHILD DYAD

The second objective—securing protections for the nurturing units—reflects concern for the "weaker" members of society, the dependents who need protection. If marriage has no legal significance and the traditional family is not state subsidized and supported, these dependencies will be more visible. Hopefully, they will also become the object of generalized societal concern. One solution to inevitable dependencies unanchored by the private family would be the direct assumption of responsibility by the state through public institutions. I am uncomfortable with such unmediated state power, and would therefore want to maintain the concept of family privacy, merely drawing the line around a non-traditional configuration of family. * * * In my newly redefined legal category of family, I would place inevitable dependents along with their caregivers. The caregiving family would be a protected space, entitled to special, preferred treatment by the state.

The new family line, drawn around dependency, would mark the boundaries of the concept of family privacy. The unit would also have legitimate claims on the resources of society. Specifically, I envision a redistribution or reallocation of social and economic subsidies now given to the natural family that allow it to function "independently" within society. Family and welfare law would be reconceived so as to support caretaking as the family intimacy norm.

This re-envisioning reflects current empirical and social reality as to evolving family form. Instead of being a society where our ideals and our ideology (the private, natural family) are out of sync with the real lives of many of our citizens, we would become a society that recognized and accepted the inevitability of dependency. We would face, value, and therefore subsidize, caretaking and caretakers.

* * *

C. MOTHER AND METAPHOR

As a concluding matter, I want to explicitly address my device of the Mother/Child metaphor. Abandoning myself to ideological utopianism, I have concluded that what is necessary in order to confront the hegemony of the sexual-natural family is an equally powerful cultural symbol. The most vivid and shared image of connection is the Mother/Child dyad. This is the prototypical nurturing unit, a fitting substitute for the Husband/Wife dyad that forms the basic unit of the sexual family. I propose Mother/Child as the substitute core of the basic family paradigm. Our laws and policies would be compelled to focus on the needs of this unit. Mother/Child would provide the structural and ideological basis for the transfer of current societal subsidies (both material and ideological) away from the sexual family to nurturing units.

The need for a positive societal vision is the reason the Mother/Child metaphor is appropriate. In excavating the image, I want to pull in the powerful resonances it has across a variety of discourses. Sara Ruddick combines positive images of Mother in arguing for "peace politics" based on maternal practices: "Preservative love, singularity in connection, the promise of birth and the resilience of hope, the irreplaceable treasure of vulnerable bodily being—these cliches of maternal work are enacted in public, by women." Mother is an embodied concept with biological, anthropological, theological, and social implications that give it strength in the public sphere. It is also a concept that embodies the dependency that is inevitable in the form of the Child. The Child is part of the Mother—the embodiment of the idea of derivative dependency now hidden in the private family. Mother is a metaphor with power to make the private visible.

I have deliberately (even defiantly) chosen not to make my alternative vision gender neutral by substituting terms such as "caretaker" and "dependent" for "Mother" and "Child," although that is the interrelationship in all its forms that I seek to address. Historically, and in terms of its cultural cachet, mothering is a gendered concept and, partly for that reason, is qualitatively different from terms currently (incorrectly) substituted for it such as "caretaker."

I realize that affirmatively introducing Mother into a feminist debate will be considered by many to be too dangerous, but I believe it is essential that we reclaim the term. Motherhood has unrealized power—the power to challenge the hold of sexuality on our thinking about intimacy; the power to redefine our concept of the family, which may be why men have tried for so long to control its meaning. The Mother/Child metaphor represents a specific practice of social and emotional responsibility. The strength of the image is in its redistributive potential, grounded on empirical evidence ("reality") about the need for and the assumption of caretaking.

* * *

Two additional theoretical caveats are necessary. First, I believe that men can and should be Mothers. In fact, if men are interested in acquiring legal rights of access to children (or other dependents), I argue they must be Mothers in the stereotypical nurturing sense of that term—that is, engaged in caretaking. Second, the Child in my dyad stands for all forms of inevitable dependency—the dependency of the ill, the elderly, the disabled, as well as actual children. The child is an embodied concept, exemplifying the need for physical caretaking.

NOTES ON DE-CENTERING THE SEXUAL FAMILY

1. Fineman suggests restructuring our treatment of the family around the mother/child dyad rather than the sexual couple, positing that such a radical move would either force individuals into private contractual ordering of their relationships or force society to subsidize the caretaking of dependents of all sorts, or both. What do you think of this suggestion? Do you think we need new and powerful symbols like the mother/child metaphor in order to change the ways in which we order our intimate relationships by law? Should we re-focus our attention upon relationships of dependency?

Who benefits under Fineman's proposal and who is left out? Does Fineman necessarily support the repronormativity that Katherine Franke critiques, as discussed in Chapter 3? Which women might be harmed by Fineman's proposal? What power dynamics might Fineman overlook? How might children be harmed if parents' positions in vertical parent-child relationships are strengthened by the state?

2. How might Fineman's proposal transform marriage? Fineman emphasizes that marriage, standing alone, no longer necessarily involves dependency, or at least the type of dependency that should be facilitated by the state. Do you agree? What dependencies might still arise within marriage, or other relationships with adults, even in the absence of children?

3. How does Fineman's proposal relate to the current construction of gender? Might it reinforce the assignment of carework to women? For discussions of this possibility, see Mary Anne Case, Commentary, How High the Apple Pie? A Few Troubling Questions About Where, Why, and How the Burden of Care for Children Should be Shifted, 76 Chi.-Kent L. Rev. 1753, 1753–62 (2001). Could Fineman's proposal instead challenge the assignment of carework to women? Note that Fineman emphasizes that "men can and should be Mothers." For a discussion of how Fineman's proposal could better help the law recognize and support "transgressive caregiving," see Laura Kessler, Transgressive Caregiving, 33 Fla. St. U. L. Rev. 1 (2005). How might women of different races and classes be affected by Fineman's proposal?

4. Remedies discussed in the notes in the previous section—contract, partnership, and commercial law—essentially return the regulation of intimate relationships to the private sphere. Fineman's preferred solution, however, is to make many of the responsibilities involved in dependency relationships into public obligations, ones the society would subsidize. This approach to family support is consonant with that taken by most European countries. See, e.g., Barbara A. Bergman, Saving Our Children From Poverty: What the United States Can Learn From France (1996) (contrasting French government child care programs, direct payments to raise children's living standards, and provision of free medical services to children with the lack of such programs in the U.S.). Do you think a similar approach could work in the United States? Why or why not?

5. Other feminists envisage the problems attendant upon dependency as a subcase of our legal system's treatment of unpaid domestic labor not as work, but simply a gift of love. See, e.g., Katherine Silbaugh, Turning Labor into Love: Housework and the Law, 91 Nw. U. L. Rev. 1 (1996). Unlike the fields of sociology and of economics, which have in recent years turned their attention to the wealth produced by housework (economists estimate the value of housework to be between 24% and 60% of the Gross Domestic Product, id. at 17), the law continues to ignore the value of domestic labor across the board—not only in property distribution and maintenance at divorce, but also as consideration for premarital contracts, in bankruptcy and estates, in the structure of Social Security payments, in actions for loss of consortium, in taxation, in labor law, and in the bases for welfare reform, which assume that a poor woman's caring for her children does not constitute productive labor. Id. at 8–21, 27–79. One way to address this problem is suggested by Nancy Staudt, who proposes that houseworkers' labor be recognized by imputing it as income to the couple and subjecting it to taxation. Staudt, Taxing Housework, 84 Geo. L.J. 1571 (1996). This would result in ensuring women independent social welfare benefits, such as Social Security accounts, based on the economic value of their own labor rather than their spouses'. Id. at 1574, 1598–99.

Staudt's proposal is different from much of the previous literature on the gendered basis of the Tax Code, which focused instead on how the tax structure creates disincentives for women to enter the labor force and thus encourages them to be economically dependent upon men. See, e.g, Grace Blumberg, Sexism in the Code: A Comparative Study of Income Taxation of Working Wives and Mothers, 21 Buff. L. Rev. 49 (1972); Edward J. McCaffery, Slouching Toward Equality: Gender Discrimination, Market Efficiency, and Social Change, 103 Yale L.J. 595 (1993); McCaffery, Taxation and the Family: A Fresh Look at Behavioral Gender Biases in the Code, 40 UCLA L. Rev. 983 (1993). Commentators like Blumberg and McCaffery advocate tax reform that encourages women to enter the workforce, while Staudt argues that women's workforce participation does not in fact respond in a major way to tax incentives. Women, especially poor women and women of color, work because they have to. Perhaps paradoxically, these women also value the work involved in household labor differently than women who do not engage in wage work because they have little time to devote to their families. See Staudt, above, at 1586–92; Kessler, above note 3, at 12–27. In your opinion, who has the better of this debate? Should the tax structure encourage women's entry into the paid labor force or assign value to household labor as an independent economic enterprise, even at the price of requiring the payment of taxes on it? What would Fineman likely say? See also Patricia C. Bradford, Taxing Women: Thoughts on a Gendered Economy, 6 S. Cal. Rev. L. & Women's Stud. 397 (1997) (using game theory to analyze the likely effects on decision-making within marriage due to specific changes in the tax code); Michael A. Johnson, A Gap in the Analysis: Income Tax and Gender–Based Wage Differentials, 85 Geo. L.J. 2287 (1997) (arguing that the Code reinforces the gendered distribution of labor by requiring joint filing in the progressive income tax system and separate tax calculations in the regressive FICA system, not treating the value of imputed labor as taxable income, and disallowing deductions for household expenditures).

6. In recent years, Fineman has shifted her focus from women's dependencies to all individuals' vulnerability. Fineman, Equality: Still Illusive After All These Years, in Gender Equality: Dimensions of Women's Equal Citizenship 251, 253–66 (Linda C. McClain & Joanna L. Grossman, eds. 2009); Fineman, The Vulnerable Subject: Anchoring Equality in the Human Condition, 20 Yale J.L. & Feminism 1 (2008). What do you think of this move away from gender to shared humanity? Might it paradoxically alter constructions of gender and promote gender equality and egalitarian relationships? How might the focus on shared vulnerability better address individuals' dependencies both within relationships and outside of them? Who might be harmed?

2. THE LEGAL TREATMENT OF COHABITATION

CYNTHIA GRANT BOWMAN, LEGAL TREATMENT OF COHABITATION IN THE UNITED STATES

26 Law & Pol'y 119, 125–31, 134–37 (2004).

A. No Rights for Cohabitants

Before the development of contractual and status-based remedies for cohabitants, the traditional position was that cohabitants simply had no rights vis-à-vis one another or third parties. Three states—Illinois, Georgia and Louisiana—continue to adhere to this position. *Hewitt v. Hewitt* [394 N.E.2d 1204] (1979), the case frequently used to illustrate the Illinois position, is a stark one. Victoria and Robert Hewitt began cohabiting as students at Grinnell College. Subsequently they moved to Illinois, where he established a lucrative medical practice and she served as homemaker and mother to their children, while assisting him in building his practice. After fifteen years, they separated. Apparently believing that they were married (perhaps by common law), Victoria Hewitt sued for divorce. The court not only dismissed the divorce action but also, when she amended to add causes of action in contract and for equitable remedies, held that Mrs. Hewitt was entitled to no remedy at all, neither property distribution nor alimony. To give her any rights, the court reasoned, would be to denigrate the institution of marriage and in effect bring back common law marriage, which Illinois had abolished in 1905. In short, Mrs. Hewitt, after a fifteen-year period of reliance upon and contribution to the relationship, was left without anything.

Although *Hewitt* was decided in 1979, it appears still to be alive and well in Illinois. It was followed and, indeed, extended in *Ayala v. Fox* [564 N.E.2d 920] (1990). Illinois courts have also consistently refused to give any legal protection to cohabitants in other contexts, turning down, for example, claims for loss of consortium by cohabitants and holding that cohabitation may constitute appropriate grounds to remove children from the custody of cohabiting parents, all based on *Hewitt*.

The *Hewitt* court's reasoning that extension of recognition to cohabitants would somehow harm the institution of marriage is open to dispute. In *Hewitt,* protections for the female cohabitant were denied even though the relationship was virtually identical to the most traditional of marriages, as Mrs. Hewitt stayed home to raise their children and assist her partner in his career. To deny property and support rights to cohabitants in a case like that in fact creates an incentive to *avoid* marriage—Mr. Hewitt was able to extract the benefit of his partner's contributions and get away with all the couple's accumulated wealth.

In states like Illinois, it is risky for a cohabitant to make any investment in a nonmarital relationship. As the leading cases show, the cohabitants most likely to make such investments—either because they simply trust the men they love or because they do not have the bargaining power to insist either upon marriage or even joint title for property—are women. The law's refusal to protect their investments leaves these women extremely vulnerable at the termination of a cohabiting relationship. The men in these relationships clearly benefit from such a legal rule.

B. Cohabitants' Rights Based on Contract

With the exception of Illinois, Georgia and Louisiana, almost every state will now recognize express contracts between cohabitants, especially if they are written. This state of affairs required the breakthrough of the *Marvin v. Marvin* "palimony" case in 1976. Prior to that time, cohabitants' contracts were considered unenforceable because they rested upon "meretricious" consideration, that is, the exchange of sex. The *Marvin* court, however, held that cohabitants could enter into contracts with one another just as other individuals could and, indeed, that the courts would enforce both written and oral express contracts; in dicta the court also indicated that recovery might be based upon contracts implied from the conduct of the parties and a variety of equitable grounds as well (*Marvin I* 1976 [134 Cal. Rptr. 815] at 122–23).

Michelle Triola alleged that the well-known actor Lee Marvin had entered into a contract to support her for the rest of her life, in return for her service as his homemaker, entertainer and companion, and that she had given up her own career to do so. When they separated after six years, Marvin argued that such a contract was unenforceable under California law. In *Marvin I*, the court ruled against him on these grounds, thus establishing the cause of action, and remanded, but in *Marvin II* found that no such contract existed. Thus the *Marvin* case, which was attended by a great deal of publicity, in fact resulted in no recovery at all for the plaintiff; it simply established the principle that cohabitants' rights in California could be based upon express or implied contracts and that the consideration for them could include homemaking services.

While many states have adopted the *Marvin* approach, other states reacted with alarm to the long and messy *Marvin* litigation, especially because it required the court to examine and weigh highly intimate details of the couple's relationship. The Illinois court in *Hewitt* declined to adopt similar contract-based rights; other states moved to accept *Marvin* but to limit its application. * * *

* * *

* * * [G]ay or lesbian cohabitants have sued for remedies upon dissolution of their relationships; courts have been very reluctant to grant support rather than property distribution in such cases. * * * This may reflect the fact that courts find it difficult to envisage a male in the role of a homemaker or a more general distaste for same-sex cohabitant cases; but it does not derive from *Marvin,* in which compensation for homemaking services was approved in gender-neutral terms. * * *

A much more profound problem with the use of contract principles to redress inequities that may arise on termination of a cohabiting relationship is that cohabiting couples—like married couples—typically do not make contracts; they simply proceed trusting that their relationship will endure and that each party will treat the other fairly. * * * Most cohabitants simply proceed under vague agreements to pool resources and make no provision for remedies upon termination.

* * *

In sum, a contractual approach to cohabitants' rights returns to them the rights and remedies they would have had as individuals to enter into contracts of various sorts with one another, in a sense commodifying their relationships. The more the arrangement looks to the court like a business deal, the more likely it is to be recognized and compensated. By contrast, women's traditional contributions to relationships continue to be underrecognized and uncompensated. Although postrelationship support is theoretically available under a contract doctrine, it needs to have been a quite explicit expectation of the parties. * * *

* * *

C. Cohabitants' Rights Based on Status

* * *

1. Meretricious Relationships in Washington

The Washington Supreme Court rejected a contract approach to the thorny legal issues presented upon dissolution of cohabitant relationships. Its approach instead confers rights generally upon couples in what it calls a "meretricious relationship," defined as "a stable, marital-like relationship where both parties cohabit with knowledge that a lawful marriage between them does not exist" (*Connell v. Francisco* [898 P.2d 831] 1995 at 834; see also *In re Marriage of Lindsey* [678 P.2d 328] 1984 at 331). Upon dissolution or death, property of individuals in such relationships which would have been community property if they were married is to be divided between them in a just and equitable distribution. Thus all income and property acquired by either party during the relationship is presumed to be owned by both—a type of community property by analogy. This legal rule, which protects vulnerable parties at the end of a relationship if they have property to divide, has been extended to same-sex couples (*Vasquez v. Hawthorne* [33 P.3d 735] 2001).

* * * Unlike a contract-based system, the Washington approach, rather than assuming (and encouraging) individual autonomy, presumes that a couple in such a relationship is in fact a joint economic unit, thus encouraging the type of sharing behavior typical of marriage. If a couple in a long-term unmarried relationship do not wish to pool their income and undertake economic responsibility for one another, they need to contract *out* of such obligations in the state of Washington, unlike in California and other states following *Marvin*, where such obligations are undertaken by contracting *in*. Because registration is not required, Washington residents who are not well-versed in the law may have an unpleasant surprise upon ending their relationships.

Evaluating the status-based approach taken in Washington from the touchstone of protection for vulnerable parties, it clearly improves upon contract schemes in this respect, imposing upon cohabitants who have become interdependent an obligation to share their property upon termination of the relationship without the necessity of proving a contract. Washington's approach is limited in several ways, however. First, it only applies to property distribution; so if the couple have not accumulated property, it is worthless. Second, it pertains only to rights against one another, thus excluding, for example, both standing for tort claims and the plethora of government benefits tied to marital status. Third, it is activated only upon termination of the relationship by dissolution or death; the pseudo-community property does not attach during the relationship.

* * *

* * * Although now applicable in only a relatively small part of the United States, this is the general approach recommended by the American Law Institute (ALI) for adoption in all states. Under the ALI *Principles of the Law of Family Dissolution*, the same rules that apply upon divorce of married persons are to be applied to either same-sex or heterosexual cohabitants if they qualify as "domestic partners" within the statute; those rules presume equal division of property acquired during the relationship and also provide for compensatory payments—alimony or spousal maintenance—to dependent parties in long-term unions (ALI 2002: §§ 6.04–6.05, 4.09–4.10, 5.04). Individuals are presumed to qualify either if they have cohabited continuously for a state-defined period and act jointly with respect to household management or if they have a common child; if not, they are entitled to establish a domestic partnership by proof of a number of factors having to do with financial interdependence, intimacy and reputation as a couple. Although ALI formulations have been influential upon state law in the past, thus far no state has moved to adopt its most recent recommendations in this respect.

* * *

3. Domestic Partnership Laws * * *

The demand for equal benefits has also resulted in a plethora of domestic partnership schemes throughout the United States, often passed by municipal or county ordinances; many apply to heterosexuals as well as same-sex cohabitants. Many such programs provide merely a system of registration and dissolution, with no attendant benefits except for municipal or county employees, who may receive family leave, family medical insurance and the like. * * * Nonetheless, domestic partnership ordinances have proliferated, driven in large part by a desire to obtain employee benefits. Eligibility to enter into such a status may be relatively stringent, requiring nonrelationship, indefinite commitment, common residence and an agreement to joint responsibility for basic living expenses.

More recently, a number of statewide domestic partnership laws have originated as a direct response to the litigation campaign for gay marriage. * * *

* * *

In response to demand for equal benefits, the California legislature passed its first domestic partnership law in 2001, under which both same-sex cohabitants and heterosexual cohabitants over the age of sixty-two may register (Domestic Partner Registration Act, Cal Family Code § 297). * * * Under the new partnership act, domestic partners received the right to sue for [wrongful death], as well as to make health care decisions for one another, to receive sick leave and unemployment benefits for reasons related to a partner, to adopt a partner's child as though a stepparent, and to administer a partner's estate.

* * *

In September 2003 California passed a second partnership act, the Domestic Partner Rights and Responsibilities Act, which is to go into effect in January 2005. In the meantime, currently registered domestic partners are being given notice that as of that date the rights and obligations they have toward one another will be radically changed if they do not opt out. The new act will give the most extensive rights to cohabitants outside of Vermont and Massachusetts; indeed, it will affect many more people, both because such a large proportion of cohabitants live in California and because it includes opposite-sex couples over the age of sixty-two.

The provisions of the new California act are simple:

> Registered domestic partners shall have the same rights, protection, and benefits, and shall be subject to the same responsibilities, obligations, and duties under law, whether they derive from statutes, administrative regulations, court rules, government policies, common law, or any other provisions or sources of law, as are granted to and imposed upon spouses [or former spouses, widows and widowers].

In short, a regime equivalent to marriage will become available to same-sex and certain opposite-sex couples in California for all purposes of state law * * *.

NOTES ON THE CURRENT LEGAL TREATMENT OF COHABITATION

1. Do you agree with the result in *Hewitt,* the Illinois case described in the excerpt above? Would you find a contractual basis for recovery in this situation? Why should a long-term homemaker wife be entitled to a division of the marital property, rehabilitative maintenance and/or other remedies, but not Victoria Hewitt?

2. What would Martha Fineman, whose work is excerpted above, think of the result reached by the *Hewitt* court? Would she believe that Victoria Hewitt should be treated as though the couple had been married? Would she prefer a return to recognition of common law marriage, an approach the *Hewitt* court raises? What would Fineman's remedy for the *Hewitt* situation be? How do you predict Fineman's remedy would change if the Hewitts did not have children?

3. The Hewitts lived together at Grinnell College in Iowa and would have been eligible for a common law marriage if they had remained in Iowa long enough to establish the element of "holding out" as a married couple. Common law marriage is still recognized in 11 U.S. jurisdictions. Cynthia Grant Bowman has suggested that the non-recognition or abolition of common law marriage has had harmful effects on women, and especially upon poor women and women of color. Bowman, A Feminist Proposal to Bring Back Common Law Marriage, 75 Or. L. Rev. 709 (1996). The common law marriage doctrine protected women in Mrs. Hewitt's position—that is, women who had invested heavily in a relationship recognized by the community as a marriage—by granting them not only remedies upon divorce but also inheritance rights, Social Security, and workers' compensation benefits, among other benefits. Id. at 754–70. Is it a good idea to try to resuscitate common law marriage, or should we devise other remedies for cohabitants? Are modern-day cohabitants likely to fulfill the legal elements of common law marriage? As a normative matter, do you believe we should treat cohabitants as though they were married? If we did so, would it improve the power of women (even in marriage)?

4. Does the prohibition on common law marriage necessarily mean that the consequences of terminating a relationship include the absence of any property rights whatsoever? If so, are persons who live together on notice of this fact and thus assumed to know that they should make contractual provisions for their property? Can they do so under *Hewitt?* Do you think this is a realistic assumption in most instances? Apparently many cohabitants persist in a mistaken belief that they are in fact married under common law and entitled to all the benefits of marriage after a certain period of cohabitation. See, e.g., ALI, Principles of the Law of Family Dissolution: Analysis and Recommendations 907–943 (2002). See also Anne Barlow, Simon Duncan & Grace James, Cohabitation, Marriage and the Law: Social Change and Legal Reform in the 21st Century 27–47 (2005) (reporting, based on a large-scale

survey of cohabitants in the U.K., where common law marriage was abolished in 1753, that over half the respondents thought they were entitled to the rights of marriage after a period ranging from six months to six years).

5. Do you agree with the result in Marvin v. Marvin? What if Michelle and Lee had had children and Michelle had spent her time caring for them as well as serving as Lee's companion and hostess?

6. What if Victoria Hewitt or Michelle Marvin had made economic rather than domestic contributions to their relationships, but the property ended up titled in the names of Mr. Hewitt and Mr. Marvin? Would you allow recovery in that situation? Would your analysis turn on contract notions? All courts give recovery when the non-title-holding partner has contributed cash. But recovery is uncertain or denied in many jurisdictions when the contributions are domestic, i.e., women's traditional work in the home. What might explain the traditional presumption that "services performed in the context of a 'family or marriage relationship' were presumed gratuitous"? Watts v. Watts, 405 N.W.2d 303, 312 n.19 (Wis.1987). Should an opposite presumption apply in the absence of marriage?

7. What is the likely result of the court's decision in *Hewitt*? Do you think economically dominant partners avoid marriage in order to avoid the economic consequences of divorce? If so, is the *Hewitt* result likely to increase or decrease cohabitation outside of marriage? In other words, does cohabitation substitute for marriage among those seeking to maintain their economic positions? If, by contrast, cohabitants are treated as though they were married for purposes of property distribution and spousal support, will this increase cohabitation relative to marriage, as the *Hewitt* court assumes, or decrease it? What roles do emotions and social norms, as opposed to economics, play in cohabitation and marriage decisions? How might that interplay differ across gender, sexual orientation, race and class?

8. What are the problems with contract (whether explicit or implicit) as *the* solution for non-married cohabitants? Consider the problems, discussed in the previous section, of using pre-marital contracts to address the economic problems of divorcing women. Are there fewer or more problems with expecting contract law to resolve how the courts should decide disputes upon separation of people who do not marry? Do you agree with the *Hewitt* court that denying Victoria Hewitt a recovery will encourage marriage? Doesn't this result give breadwinners, like Robert Hewitt, an incentive *not* to marry? How does the state incentivize men and women to marry? How do those strategies have different effects across gender, sexual orientation, race, and class?

9. What do you think of the law on meretricious relationships in the state of Washington and the ALI's proposal concerning cohabitants' property relationships, as they are described in the excerpt above? Should cohabitants have to contract *in* to obligations to one another or contract *out*? Is there a third option? What are the potential harms of measuring all couples against the married couples recognized by the state?

Several states permit couples, same-sex and different-sex, to opt into domestic partnerships, as discussed above in the same-sex marriage section. See also Cynthia Grant Bowman, Unmarried Couples, Law, and Public Policy 59–69 (2010). Do you think couples should be required to register as partners in order to obtain any state benefits? What are the advantages and disadvantages of such a registry system as compared to an opt-out system? Who is unlikely to register? Who benefits under each approach? Who is harmed? What policies is the state attempting to further under each approach? What would be your ideal strategy for supporting couples living outside of marriage?

TEXT NOTE: COHABITATION IN THE U.S. AND ABROAD

Cohabitation grew at a rapid pace in the United States over a relatively brief period of time. In 1960, there were fewer than 500,000 cohabiting couple households, but by 2008, there were 6.8 million; in other words, 13.6 million individuals.[31] The groups who tend to cohabit are diverse but include disproportionately large numbers of younger people, lower-income people, Black women and men, Puerto Ricans, divorced people, and, increasingly, the elderly.[32]

Cohabitation has been the subject of a great deal of study by sociologists and demographers over the last two decades. Their research about different-sex couples who live together shows that cohabiting unions do not last as long as marriages, with the average duration about 1.5 years in the United States, and the unions are not accompanied by levels of satisfaction as high as those shared by married couples. There is also a higher level of domestic violence among cohabitants than among married couples.[33] Even though their relationships are less enduring and unprotected by the law, some studies have found that the majority of cohabitants pool their income, and virtually all do if they have a child.[34] About 40% of cohabiting couples have children in the household, about equally split between the biological children of the couple and children for whom one of the cohabitants is in the position of a stepparent.[35]

Some scholars argue that the law should discourage cohabiting relationships by giving no benefits at all to cohabiting couples.[36] Others argue that these groups include some of the most vulnerable individuals in our society and that they need protection at the end of their relationships as well as benefits from the government and third parties, such as unemployment

---

31. Pamela J. Smock & Wendy D. Manning, Living Together Unmarried in the United States: Demographic Perspectives and Implications for Family Policy, 26 Law & Pol'y 87, 88 (2004); U.S. Census Bureau, Current Population Survey, 2008 Annual Social and Economic Supplement tbl.UC1 (2009).

32. Cynthia Grant Bowman, Unmarried Couples, Law, and Public Policy 102–20 (2010).

33. Id. at 131–38, 146–58.

34. See Kristen R. Heimdal & Sharon K. Houseknecht, Cohabiting and Married Couples' Income Organization: Approaches in Sweden and the United States, 65 J. Marriage & Fam. 525, 533 (2003); Carolyn Vogler, Cohabiting Couples: Rethinking Money in the Household at the Beginning of the Twenty First Century, 53 Soc. Rev. 1, 12–13 (2005).

35. See Larry L. Bumpass, James A. Sweet & Andrew Cherlin, The Role of Cohabitation in Declining Rates of Marriage, 53 J. Marriage & Fam. 913, 919 (1991); Rose M. Kreider & Jason Fields, U.S. Dep't of Commerce, Living Arrangements of Children: 2001 5 tbl. 2 (2005).

36. See, e.g., William C. Duncan, The Social Good of Marriage and Legal Responses to Non-Marital Cohabitation, 82 Or. L. Rev. 1001, 1031 (2003); Maggie Gallagher, Rites, Rights, and Social Institutions: Why and How Should the Law Support Marriage?, 18 Notre Dame J.L. Ethics & Pub. Pol'y 225, 238–240 (2004).

compensation and the availability of tort actions for negligent infliction of emotional distress and loss of consortium.[37]

Cohabitants are given more protections in other developed industrial democracies than in the United States. In England, for example, cohabitants receive advantageous treatment under laws concerning tenancies, pensions, and workers compensation, as well as coverage under the Fatal Accidents Act and certain rights upon inheritance.[38] In the Netherlands, both same-sex and different-sex couples may now choose between marriage and registration as domestic partners, which is virtually identical to marriage in legal status. And recall that since 1999, French couples of the same or different sex have been able to enter into a "civil solidarity pact," under which they undertake financial responsibility for one another, own any purchases or debts jointly, and are eligible for one another's employment benefits, among other things; the pact can be dissolved unilaterally with three months' notice.[39] In Canada, cohabitants are entitled to post-relationship support (but not to property distribution) in almost every province if they have lived in a marriage-like relationship for a defined period of time, and to all the rights of married couples under federal law if they have lived together for at least one year.[40] In all of these countries, unlike in the United States, cohabitants are also covered by universal health insurance and many other government benefits as individuals.

NOTES ON COHABITATION IN THE U.S. AND ABROAD

1. How, if at all, do the statistics about the people most likely to cohabit in the United States affect your opinion about what legal remedies should be afforded to cohabitants? Should the state attempt to encourage these individuals to marry by denying state support, or should the state support these individuals in their current situations? Are different approaches warranted if children are involved? How would Martha Fineman likely approach these questions?

2. In choosing to provide, or not to provide, legal remedies for cohabitants, should the law treat different-sex and same-sex couples the same or differently? What grounds might there be to distinguish between the two groups? Do you find those grounds valid? Why or why not?

3. What do you think underlies the attitude of many courts, and of many people more generally, toward the legal status of cohabitants? Notions of morality? Economic calculations of some sort? Protection of the public fisc? Age and personal experience of life? Traditional views of the family? Devaluation of relationships that are assumed to end before death? What else? What

---

37. See, e.g., Bowman, above note 32, at 221–42; Grace Ganz Blumberg, Cohabitation Without Marriage: A Different Perspective, 28 UCLA L. Rev. 1125 (1981).

38. See Rebecca Probert, Cohabitation in Twentieth Century England and Wales: Law and Policy, 26 Law & Pol'y 13, 15, 17, 22–23 (2004); Anne Barlow, Regulation of Cohabitation, Changing Family Policies and Social Attitudes: A Discussion of Britain Within Europe, 26 Law & Pol'y 57, 71 (2004).

39. See Barlow, above note 38, at 63–66.

40. Modernization of Benefits and Obligations Act, S.C. 2000, chap. 12 (Can.).

considerations do you think should appropriately form the basis for deciding upon the appropriate legal treatment of cohabitants?

4. A growing phenomenon in many countries is that of couples who live apart together, often called LAT's. These people think of themselves as couples although they do not live together for a variety of reasons, such as having children or aged parents to look after, dissatisfaction with a previous cohabiting relationship, not wanting to risk their relationship by too much togetherness, wanting to maintain their independence and friendships with other people, or working or studying in different cities. See Sasha Roseneil, On Not Living With a Partner: Unpicking Coupledom and Cohabitation, 11 Soc. Res. Online, no. 3, Sept. 2006 (dividing LAT's into "living apart regretfully," "living apart gladly," and "living apart undecidedly"). See also Simon Duncan & Miranda Phillips, People Who Live Apart Together (LATs)—How Different Are They?, 58 Soc. Rev. 1 (2010); John Haskey & Jane Lewis, Living-apart-together in Britain: Context and Meaning, 2 Int'l J. Law in Context 37 (2006). How should the law treat these couples? Does marriage, domestic partnership, or cohabitation provide a potential model? What kinds of information would you like to have about them before making a recommendation for legal treatment? What factors should make a relationship worthy of state recognition and support? Should living together be a requirement for state recognition? See Laura A. Rosenbury, Friends with Benefits?, 106 Mich. L. Rev. 189, 201 (2007) (suggesting no). What about married couples who do not live together?

5. Sweden is the country with the longest experience with cohabitation and also the highest rate of cohabitation; about half of all Swedish couples are unmarried. See Gören Lind, Common Law Marriage: A Legal Institution for Cohabitation 788–89 (2008). Yet Swedish law gives very little protection to cohabitants per se, instead opting to detach as many legal and/or financial consequences as possible from an individual's choice to marry or not; this is known as the principle of neutrality. Individuals are presumed to be self-sufficient, so, for example, support is unavailable from a former cohabitant or from a former spouse, and Swedes are taxed as individuals rather than as family units. At the same time, individuals are protected by a thoroughgoing system of state welfare benefits, including health insurance, child care, pensions, and the like. The primary legal protection given to cohabitants is a shared interest in the couple's joint home, regardless of legal ownership. Cohabitants are defined simply as persons who live together as a couple on a permanent basis and share a household; they are not required to register, on the theory that those who most need protection would be least likely to register. See Cynthia Grant Bowman, Unmarried Couples, Law, and Public Policy 214–19 (2010). What do you think of this model of legal treatment of cohabitants? Would it work in the United States? Why or why not?

6. Cynthia Grant Bowman has proposed that cohabitants be treated as though they were married after two years or the birth of a child. Bowman, above note 5, at 224–28. Couples would be allowed to opt out of this status by mutual agreement, however. What are your reactions to this proposal? What objections to it do you anticipate? What are the advantages and disadvantages of such legal reform in the United States? What conceptions of relationships underlie this proposal?

3. FRIENDSHIP

LAURA A. ROSENBURY, FRIENDS WITH BENEFITS?

106 Mich. L. Rev. 189, 202–08, 212, 230–33 (2007).

II. The Place of Friendship

Given family law's focus on domestic caregiving within the home, it is not surprising that friendship has been largely ignored by family law scholars. Friendship is generally viewed as utterly distinct from domesticity and hence from family. Friends are assumed to share a home only at times of family limbo, for instance in the years between leaving a childhood home and establishing a home with a sexual partner or one's own children. In addition, dependency is often seen as anathema to friendship. Instead, friendship is often assumed to embody norms of equality and autonomy.

* * * There is no reason why the state must maintain a strict divide between family and friends, a divide that places friends, acquaintances, and strangers alike in the nonfamily category, thereby obscuring the ways that friends are more like family than strangers. * * *

* * *

A. The Law's Role in Defining Friendship

Although the law has traditionally placed friendship outside of its domain, the law matters to friendship. In the views of many, the benefits of friendship derive from its "out-law" status. * * *

Why is lack of regulation perceived to be good for friendship? On the most basic level, the state does not specify the terms of friendship, leaving it up to individuals to define the interaction. This creates multidimensional freedom. On one level, the state imposes no obligations on friends; therefore, any obligations arise from the parties themselves. On another level, the state does not privilege one definition of friendship over another. Many types of friendships can develop and coexist, and individual friendships can be fluid and shifting. * * *

Although the freedom to define friendship in diverse ways is attractive and powerful, it is incorrect to view it as flowing from lack of state regulation. Instead, as discussed below, the placement of friendship outside of the legal family is a decision of the state. Some individuals may choose to embrace friendship in an attempt to escape the power of the state, but such escape can be only partial because the state has created the very divide sought to be exploited. Friendships are thus not intrinsically free relationships; rather, their freedom derives in part from the state, and that freedom is limited by various state decisions.

1. The Limits of Friendship's "Out-Law" Status

The law currently intervenes in friendships in multiple ways. * * * The most obvious context is in the denial of various benefits that the law reserves for family. Even if friends are performing many, or all, of the functions traditionally ascribed to spouses, parents, or children, friends are not eligible, for example, to take leave to care for each other pursuant to the Family and Medical Leave Act ("FMLA"), to require hospitals to allow them to visit each other or to make decisions about each other's medical care, to bring a viable suit for negligent infliction of emotional distress when they witness the other being harmed, or to inherit each other's estates under state intestacy rules. * * * Of course, not all friends would want state recognition, but those who would are denied benefits that the states bestow on other types of intimate adult relationships.

* * *

* * * [T]he law also intervenes in friendships by setting outer boundaries: marriage and, increasingly, marriage-like relationships. If friends obtain a marriage license or, in some states, if a friendship (generally opposite-sex) takes on the qualities of a marriage-like relationship through sexual cohabitation, then it is no longer a friendship in the law's eyes. Rather, a friend in such a friendship can appeal to the state and often receive benefits reserved for parties in marriage and marriage-like relationships.

2. Consequences of the Law's Role

Given the law's role in creating the distinction between friendship and marriage, friendship has been experienced differently by straight and gay communities. Because gay men and lesbians have traditionally been denied same-sex marriage, the line between friendship and romance or between friendship and family is not as stark in many gay and lesbian communities as it is in straight culture. In addition, friendship is less likely to be implicitly devalued by comparisons to marriage. * * *

In contrast, straight culture has, at least until recently, perpetuated a strict divide between individuals who are viewed as dating and those who are "just friends." This distinction implies that the dating relationship may lead to the privileged state of marriage, whereas the friendship will not. Recently, the distinction has been blurred somewhat with the popularity of the term "friends with benefits." In contrast to "just friends," this term implies that the relationship embodies at least one of the attributes of marriage, namely sex. In many ways, this term devalues friendship even more than the term "just friends" because it implies that friendship has no benefits unless sex is involved. At the same time, the term also safely maintains the privileging of marriage and dating relationships that might lead to marriage. * * * After all, "friends with benefits" are still "just" friends, implying that sex alone does not place a relationship on the path to marriage.

These differences in the experiences of friendship in turn reinforce the fact that friendship is not inherently free. Instead, freedom is conferred, and limited, by the decision of the state to recognize some relationships and not others. The state's distinction between friendship and legal marriage affects friendship as well as marriage, by defining marriage in opposition to other adult intimate relationships, including friendship. * * *

* * *

C. The Role of Marriage and Domesticity

* * *

This silence does more than potentially stigmatize friendship. Rather, the silence can also perpetuate gender inequality, because the preferred form of attachment and connection is marriage and, increasingly, relationships that embrace many aspects of traditional marriage by providing care within the home. Elevating such relationships over friendships contributes to gender inequality by encouraging individuals to engage in domestic coupling rooted in a history of patriarchy and then stigmatizing those who live outside of that coupling.

* * *

In order to recognize that people can and do rely on multiple people to perform different functions in their lives, and that these people and functions can shift over time, family law would have to go well beyond proposals permitting individuals to name one designated friend or even a spouse plus a best friend. For example, one relatively aggressive approach would gather all of the benefits, default rules, and obligations attaching to marriage and permit individuals to assign some or all of those forms of legal support to the individuals of their choice. For example, an individual could choose for default property division rules to apply to the person with whom they are living, joint health insurance benefits to be shared with a noncohabitating friend or lover, hospital visitation rights to be given to yet another person, and protections under the FMLA to be available to care for a sibling.

Such an approach would be difficult to implement, given the complexity of the current regulatory regime of marriage. The benefits, default rules, and obligations attaching to marriage are a patchwork of federal, state, and local law. However, despite the fragmented nature of marriage recognition and regulation, all levels of government are united in their silence with respect to friendship. Permitting individuals to assign certain benefits, obligations, or default rules to friends would therefore be an innovation throughout the entirety of the complex regulatory regime of marriage, minimizing conflicts among the levels of government. Moreover, the complexity of the regime could permit experimentation at the various levels of government and with respect to the specific benefit, obligation, or default rule in question. For example, a state could initially provide individuals with the flexibility to designate friends as eligible for certain benefits, obligations, or default rules but not other benefits, obligations, or default rules.

Individuals can currently achieve some of this flexibility through private contracting (for example through living-together agreements, prenuptial agreements, or health care proxies), but not all of the consequences of marriage can currently be assigned by contract (including, most importantly, health insurance benefits, social security benefits, and rights under the FMLA). Therefore, such a proposal would change the current substance of the law to a great extent but not radically. The more radical aspect of this type of proposal would be its rejection of private contracting to readjust the current consequences of marriage determined by the state. Instead, some or all of the benefits, obligations, and default rules currently reserved for spouses would be available alike to spouses, friends, or the other individuals designated. Such a proposal would therefore allow all individuals, not just married couples, to decide how they would like the state to support their personal relationships, if at all. Unlike the current state of the law, marriage or a marriage-like relationship would not be a prerequisite for taking on the packages of benefits, obligations, and default rules provided by federal, state and local governments. Instead, individuals could choose to apply those packages to other types of personal relationships without engaging in private contracting. In addition, individuals would not be required to take or leave entire packages but rather could divide the packages among multiple individuals, also without engaging in private contracting.

Such an approach could go a long way toward supporting the diverse forms of care performed by multiple individuals in many people's lives and encouraging other people to consider new ways to live their lives. State support would no longer hinge on the performance of types of domestic caregiving rooted in a history of state-supported patriarchy. The care and support provided and received outside of that framework would no longer be ignored or negated. The boundaries of family law would be expanded, making them much less likely to constrain individual preferences and practices. Unlike other proposals, however, friendship would not be pushed to take on the defining aspects of family in order to be let into family law's domain. Rather, individuals could choose how they would like the state to support and recognize both their friendships and family relationships.

* * *

* * * When guided by the principles of nonexclusivity and fluidity, new constructions of family law can begin to blur the line between friends and family, providing individuals with more freedom to structure their personal lives in diverse ways. In the process, existing notions of both family and friendship could be transformed. This transformation has particularly strong implications for gender equality.

NOTES ON FRIENDSHIP

1. How might explicit legal recognition of friendship promote gender equality? Is it because more women will choose egalitarian friendships over

patriarchal marriage? If so, is this proposal simply an application of Adrienne Rich's work on compulsory heterosexuality and the lesbian continuum, described in Chapter 3? Or do you agree that legal recognition could transform both friendship and marriage? What would these transformations look like? Which women would likely benefit the most from such transformations? Which women might be harmed?

2. Rosenbury also argues that legal recognition could promote gender equality by changing the nature of friendships between women, between men, and between women and men: "Women might receive more care in female friendships, men might receive more care in male friendships, and men and women might come to experience opposite-sex friendships free from many of the constraints of heteronormativity." Rosenbury, above, at 233. How does this focus on care compare to Fineman's focus? Is there a difference between dependent and non-dependent care? Does Rosenbury assume that non-dependent care is always egalitarian? Or that dependencies that arise outside of the home are of a different quality than those within the home? What are your experiences of the power dynamics within friendship? How do gender, sexual orientation, race and class influence those dynamics?

Rosenbury further argues that recognition of friendship, and the transformation of friendships between women, between men, and between women and men might relieve some of the pressure placed on marriage to serve all of the spouse's emotional and physical needs, leading to longer, happier marriages. Do you think these outcomes are likely? What are other potential outcomes?

3. What are some of the dangers of legal recognition of friendship? Might friendship come to be regulated by the state in much the same way marriage is regulated? Katherine M. Franke, Longing for *Loving*, 76 Fordham L. Rev. 2685, 2703 (2008) (arguing that calls for the law to regulate friendship are "radically wrongheaded"). Does legal recognition always lead to legal regulation? Would Fineman's proposal to end all legal recognition of relationships between adults be preferable to Rosenbury's approach?

4. How might Rosenbury be read as privileging non-sexual friendships over sexual relationships, including friendships that involve sex? Is Rosenbury's focus on friendship necessarily anti-sex? Why has straight culture maintained such a line between friendship and sex? Is Rosenbury challenging that line or reinforcing it? How are friendships that involve sex distinguishable from friendships that do not (yet?) involve sex? Does it matter if those friendships are same-sex or different-sex? How do the dynamics of friendship and sex differ based on the sexual orientation and gender of one or more of the friends? For one popular account rooted in psychology, see The Ladder Theory, available at http://www.laddertheory.com/ ("cover[ing] such topics as why women sometimes just want to be friends but men always want sex").

In a subsequent article, Rosenbury and co-author Jennifer E. Rothman argue that the state should more fully protect both sex outside of intimacy and intimacy not involving sex. Rosenbury & Rothman, Sex In and Out of Intimacy 59 Emory L.J. 809 (2010). In other words, just as the state should recognize relationships not defined by sex, it should also protect sex not defined by relationship. Although some may see the latter as harmful to women, Rosenbury and Rothman argue that it could alter constructions of gender: "Women could experience less pressure to take on the traditional role of taming male desire through domesticity and intimacy, and men could escape the assumption that they always want sex." Id. at 853. Do you think this is likely? Should feminists overlook potential harm to individual women in order to challenge the gender system more broadly? Can that system really be challenged through friendship or sex?

5. How might friendship help us reimagine relationships outside of the couple form? Elizabeth Emens challenges the norm of monogamous coupledom by drawing upon the work of Adrienne Rich in order "to question the idea of monogamy as a choice, indeed as the only viable choice for many, and to engage in the work of thinking critically about its margins." Emens, Monogamy's Law: Compulsory Monogamy & Polyamorous Existence, 29 N.Y.U. Rev. L. & Soc. Change 277, 286 (2004). Emens proposes that:

> [T]he practice of polyamory as "ethical nonmonogamy" bears serious consideration at a moment when the terms and conditions of intimate relationships are such a focus of discussion. Polyamory is a lifestyle embraced by a minority of individuals who exhibit a wide variety of relationship models and who articulate an ethical vision that I understand to encompass five main principles: self-knowledge, radical honesty, consent, self-possession, and privileging love and sex over other emotions and activities such as jealousy. Contrary to the common view of multiparty relationships as either oppressive or sexual free-for-alls, at least some set of individuals—polyamorists, or "polys" for short—seems to be practicing nonmonogamy as part of an ethical practice that shares some of its aspirations with more mainstream models of intimate relationships.

Id. at 283. How do the five principles of ethical nonmonogamy relate to feminists' explorations of just marriage? How might polyamory be a feminist issue? Can polyamory transform power dynamics within marriage? In what ways have norms of monogamy perpetuated compulsory heterosexuality and influenced women's choice to marry? How might monogamy be a feminist issue? In what ways have women achieved comfort, safety, and maternal creativity through monogamous marriage, as Mary Joe Frug discussed in Chapter 3? Which women and men do you think benefit from norms of monogamy? Which women and men might be harmed? Is polyamory a potential solution to that harm?

What are some other ways that women might flourish outside of the couple form? Must women engage with multiple partners or any partners at all? Must women engage in sexual relationships? See Sally Cline, Women, Passion, and Celibacy 253 (1993) (arguing that "purposeful" and "passionate" celibacy is "about a rejection of the sexual and material roles which women are still required to play. Celibacy stands firm as a revolt against a set of male definitions about women's sexuality in a society that is genitally focused and geared to coupledom.").

6. Emens argues that opposition to nonmonogamy stems from a failure of monogamy:

> Many people engage in nonmonogamous behavior; many more have nonmonogamous fantasy lives. Indeed, one might go so far as to say that it is the rare person whose sexual thoughts only ever involve his or her

> partner in monogamy. * * * Rather than prompting outsiders to identify with polyamorists, the potential of nearly everyone to imagine him or herself engaging in nonmonogamous behavior leads outsiders to steel themselves against polyamory and to eschew the idea of legitimizing such relationships through law. This I call the paradox of prevalence.

Emens, above note 5, at 283–84. How does denial of nonmonogamy sustain marriage and other forms of monogamous relationships? Why do such relationships take monogamy as their norm even when many individuals cannot live up to monogamy, and thus practice a secret or nonethical form of nonmonogamy? Who is hurt by nonethical nonmonogamy? How might that harm be greater than the perceived harm of polyamory? Emens further argues:

> [P]olyamory may prompt an egalitarian objection that the traditional form of polygamy involves one man dominating multiple wives. From a feminist perspective, traditional polygyny looks like the archetype of the oppressive patriarchal family writ large. But economists and legal scholars, as well as practitioners of polygyny such as Elizabeth Joseph, have made the opposite claim: polygyny may actually benefit women. * * * [S]ome polyamorists specifically embrace the practice of nonmonogamy as part of a feminist commitment to self-possession. In this light, feminist objections cannot entirely ground the opposition to multiparty marriage, unless one is also inclined to oppose marriage altogether on the ground that its traditional form oppresses women. And even this sort of feminist opposition to marriage would not necessarily explain a negative response to the idea of nonmarital relationships of more than two.

Id. at 333–34. What are the potential benefits of polyamory for women? Why have feminists spent so much time analyzing the power dynamics of marriage instead of the potential promise of polyamory? What would a feminist agenda look like that gave women more freedom to choose between monogamous marriage or monogamous marriage-like relationships and ethical nonmonogamy?

7. How do norms of monogamy participate in the construction of gender? How is marriage a form of regulation of desire based on assumptions of dangerous male sexuality? Adrienne Davis argues that cultural and radical feminists might support legal recognition of polygamous marriage because "increasing the ratio of women to men in a household might be a more effective solution than pressuring husbands to 'change' and conform to women's expectations" regarding housework. Davis, Regulating Polygamy: Intimacy, Default Rules, and Bargaining for Equality, 110 Colum. L. Rev., forthcoming (2010). In addition, some conservative women argue that polygamy "permits men's basic (base?) instincts while using the marital structure to domesticate and discipline them. Following this logic, men may serve their biological impulses for multiplicity, but may not be deceitful or disrespectful." Id. Do you agree that recognized polygamy could alter power dynamics within marriage? How do you predict the feminist theorists in Chapter 3 would respond to Davis's analysis? How do you predict Emens would respond? Would such an approach to polygamy reinforce or challenge constructions of gender?

8. How does legal recognition of some relationships to the exclusion of others influence individuals' choices to enter both recognized and nonrecognized relationships? Can legal recognition be more inclusive or will it always necessarily leave some relationships out? How can both recognition and nonrecognition be harmful? How can they both promote freedom? If you were devising a feminist relationship recognition system, what laws and policies would you propose?

CHAPTER 7

WOMEN AND CHILDREN

■ ■ ■

A. INTRODUCTION

Most children are reared by women, and this fact has a profound effect upon those children as adults and, through them, upon gender relations in society. Indeed, Susan Moller Okin argues that our society will not be just until children are raised by just families:

> In a just society, * * * families must be just because of the vast influence that they have on the moral development of children. The family is the primary institution of formative moral development. And the structure and practices of the family must parallel those of the larger society if the sense of justice is to be fostered and maintained. * * * A society that is committed to equal respect for all of its members, and to justice in social distributions of benefits and responsibilities, can neither neglect the family nor accept family structures and practices that violate these norms, as do current gender-based structures and practices. It is essential that children who are to develop into adults with a strong sense of justice and commitment to just institutions spend their earliest and most formative years in an environment in which they are loved and nurtured, *and* in which principles of justice are abided by and respected. What is a child of either sex to learn about fairness in the average household with two full-time working parents, where the mother does, at the very least, twice as much family work as the father? What is a child to learn about the value of nurturing and domestic work in a home with a traditional division of labor in which the father either subtly or not so subtly uses the fact that he is the wage earner to "pull rank" on or to abuse his wife? What is a child to learn about responsibility for others in a family in which, after many years of arranging her life around the needs of her husband and children, a woman is faced with having to provide for herself and her children but is totally ill-equipped for the task by the life she agreed to lead, has led, and expected to go on leading?[1]

1. Susan Moller Okin, Justice, Gender, and the Family 22–3 (1989).

In addition to shaping society, women's childrearing role affects the daily lives of many women in numerous ways from pregnancy, to the need for parental leave and other support at the birth or adoption of children, to the demands of providing ongoing care for children, to the rigors of the "second shift" of housework and childcare at the end of the working day for women employed outside of the home. Feminists question whether it is desirable that women primarily perform the nurture of children in society, or that motherhood results in the kinds of consequences it has traditionally carried in our culture. For a genuine emancipation of women, including their effective integration into the world of work, it may prove necessary to contemplate alternatives to the traditional concept of family as a unit within which women almost exclusively tend to the emotional and physical needs of its members. In other words, it may be necessary to separate childbearing from childrearing.

Numerous issues of law and policy arise in connection with caregiving and women's relationship to children and child care. We deal with those issues in this chapter under three broad rubrics: (1) childrearing, (2) parental leave and child care, and (3) custody and support of children whose parents are not married. In all of these debates over law and policy, one theme reappears: the legal, economic, and social devaluation of the work of raising children—either because the care of children has traditionally been "women's work" or because child care is undervalued in its own right and has therefore become women's work. By contrast, many women themselves value their relationships to their children with an intensity the economic system does not share. In most instances, women are children's primary caregivers within different-sex marriages[2] and their primary physical custodians after divorce.[3] Additionally, single parents are over five times more likely to be women than men.[4]

For all of these reasons, legal issues concerning women and children have been of special interest to feminist legal scholars. The panoply of issues raised by feminists concerning women in their role as mothers is the subject of this chapter.

B. GENDERED CHILDREARING

TEXT NOTE: CLASSICAL FEMINIST THEORIES OF MOTHERING

Adrienne Rich's book, Of Woman Born: Motherhood As Experience and Institution, published in 1976, has influenced generations of feminists. Rich

2. Within marital households in 2007, there were 5.6 million stay-at-home mothers compared with 165,000 stay-at-home fathers. Census Bureau, Current Population Reports, America's Families and Living Arrangements: 2007 12 (Sept. 2009).

3. In 2007, mothers retained primary physical custody of children after divorce 82.6% of the time. Census Bureau, Current Population Reports, Custodial Mothers and Fathers and Their Child Support: 2007 2 (Nov. 2009).

4. In 2007, there were nearly 10 million households comprised of a mother living only with children under age 18 but less than 2 million households of a father living only with his children. Census Bureau, Current Population Reports, Sept. 2009, America's Families and Living Arrangements: 2007 7 (Sept. 2009).

argues that the fact that all persons, male or female, are born of a woman has a major influence on their lives. Virtually everyone has experienced mothering by a woman, either their birth mother or some other woman. By "mothering," Rich denotes the continuing presence of a woman from pregnancy, childbirth, and nursing, through the physical and emotional care and education necessary during the extended period of human childhood. Fathers, by contrast, are an "elusive" presence; a man may even "father" a child, for example, by rape and then disappear. As a result, "[f]or most of us a woman provided the continuity and stability—but also the rejections and refusals—of our early lives, and it is with a woman's hands, eyes, body, voice, that we associate our primal sensations, our earliest social experience."[5] This two-sided association of love and authority, Rich believes, may lead men to deny their dependence on women, but it has also formed women's lives and status. Rich suggests that we:

> distinguish between two meanings of motherhood, one superimposed on the other: the *potential relationship* of any woman to her powers of reproduction and to children; and the *institution*, which aims at ensuring that potential—and all women—shall remain under male control. This institution has been a keystone of the most diverse social and political systems. It has withheld over one-half the human species from the decisions affecting their lives; it exonerates men from fatherhood in any authentic sense; it creates the dangerous schism between "private" and "public" life; it calcifies human choices and potentialities. In the most fundamental and bewildering of contradictions, it has alienated women from our bodies by incarcerating us in them. At certain points in history, and in certain cultures, the idea of woman-as-mother has worked to endow all women with respect, even with awe, and to give women some say in the life of a people or a clan. But for most of what we know as the "mainstream" of recorded history, motherhood as institution has ghettoized and degraded female potentialities.[6]

In her groundbreaking 1978 book, The Reproduction of Mothering, Nancy Chodorow drew upon classical psychoanalytic theory to explain how a gendered division of parental labor is reproduced generation after generation. Although both male and female children originally identify with the mother, boys shift to identify with their father at Freud's Oedipal stage of development. They define themselves in opposition to the mother, devaluing—indeed, feeling contempt for—women in general and for the feminine within themselves. Because men have had the power to define culture, those perceptions become general norms and are seen as natural. On the level of the individual boy, "[m]asculine identification processes stress differentiation from others, the denial of affective relation, and categorical universalistic components of the masculine role. Feminine identification processes are relational, whereas masculine identification processes tend to deny relationship."[7]

---

5. Adrienne Rich, Of Woman Born: Motherhood as Experience and Institution 12 (2d ed. 1986).

6. Id. at 13.

7. Nancy Chodorow, The Reproduction of Mothering: Psychoanalysis and the Sociology of Gender 176 (2d ed. 1999).

Therefore, while boys' development requires differentiation, girls define themselves by a continuing identification with the mother. As a result:

> Women's mothering * * * produces psychological self-definition and capacities appropriate to mothering in women, and curtails and inhibits these capacities and this self-definition in men. The early experience of being cared for by a woman produces a fundamental structure of expectations in women and men concerning mothers' lack of separate interests from their infants and total concern for their infants' welfare. Daughters grow up identifying with these mothers, about whom they have such expectations. This set of expectations is generalized to the assumption that women naturally take care of children of all ages and the belief that women's "maternal" qualities can and should be extended to the nonmothering work that they do. All these results of women's mothering have ensured that women will mother infants and will take continuing responsibility for children.[8]

In short, mothering is "reproduced" as girls, but not boys, grow up with "the particular psychological capacities and stance which go into primary parenting."[9]

LAURA T. KESSLER, TRANSGRESSIVE CAREGIVING

33 Fla. St. U. L. Rev. 1, 3–4, 12–13, 27, 44–45, 49, 83–84, 86 (2005).

* * * [C]are work can constitute an affirmative political practice of resistance to a host of discriminatory institutions and ideologies, including the family, workplace, and state, as well as patriarchy, racism, and homophobia. I label such political work "transgressive caregiving" and locate it most centrally—although not exclusively—in the care work of ethnic and racial minorities, gays and lesbians, and heterosexual men.

Transgressive caregiving occurs all around us, despite widespread attempts by state and federal lawmakers to domesticate it. Unmarried parents now make up one-third of households with children less than eighteen years old, and unmarried parenthood is the predominant family form in the African–American community. Somewhere between one million and nine million children have at least one gay or lesbian parent in the United States. In 2003, 4.6 million couples cohabited outside of marriage, and children were present in about forty percent of those households. Finally, although I hesitate to paint too rosy a picture of recent improvements in the gendered division of household labor within marriage, men have increased their share of housework over the past few decades. These contexts illustrate that the conventional wisdom that caregiving is experienced primarily as a condition of patriarchal oppression, or even as a benign activity benefiting children and society, tells only part of the story.

* * *

---

8. Id. at 208.

9. Id. at 206.

The state has heavily regulated black women's sexuality, reproduction, family caregiving work, and wage work from slavery to the present. Black women resisted and sought refuge from this structural discrimination in part through family and community relationships. Caregiving work within black families and communities is thus imbued with significant political meaning that derives from blacks' historical materials tracing black women's activism, as well as by contemporary social science research.

* * *

Gay men and lesbians also have long suffered state-sponsored discrimination with regard to their reproduction, sexuality, and family life. As in the race context, the state has effected this discrimination through the denial of substantial rights and benefits of citizenship. Gay men and lesbians have challenged this discrimination in part through their intimate relationships, not solely outside of them as traditional liberal theory would suggest. Given the possibility of a radical alternative to the hetero-patriarchal family presented by same-sex intimacy, the potential for political emancipation (as well as oppression) through family and intimate life is well understood by gay men and lesbians and by the larger society. This understanding of the political significance of intimacy within the gay community is supported by historical materials and contemporary social science research.

* * *

* * * In the twentieth century, [the] quest for manhood was defined primarily through the family wage system. Under this economic and gender system, earning was the sole responsibility of husbands and unpaid domestic labor was the only proper long-term occupation of women. * * * Today, as an empirical matter, the family wage system is almost completely eroded. In an environment of rapid economic globalization the real wages of men have stagnated—or in the case of the least skilled men, substantially declined. Given the breakdown of the family wage system, married women's paid work is necessary to provide just the basics for their families.

Despite this breakdown, the family wage ideal remains as a powerful norm that structures the workplace and the division of household labor within married families.

* * *

* * * [W]hen men engage in care work—even men in traditional marriages with relatively traditional gender patterns—they resist the male breadwinner ideal, the current structure of work, and the continued construction of men as inauthentic caregivers within family and social welfare law. Thus, again, we see that family caregiving may be subversive of patriarchy when manifested in the form of transgressive care practices.

* * *

The impulse at this historic moment of recognition for transgressive caregivers, such as people of the same sex who wish to marry, is to use the language of equality. There are arguments for this approach. As a colleague suggested at the beginning of this project, wouldn't it be much simpler and more straightforward simply to argue that transgressive caregivers are, upon closer examination, really just like traditional caregivers? Or, as many legal feminists have argued, if the goal is increased support for care, could we simply emphasize family values and the importance of children to society? Or describe the problem as one of sex discrimination, for which there already exists a comprehensive system of regulation? Although these strategies may have more appeal to lawmakers than the "transgressive caregiving as politics" conception, they are also more likely to reify the very hierarchies they seek to undermine. Explicitly adding the political dimensions of transgressive caregiving to the current rights discourse over same-sex marriage may counteract some of its assimilatory effects by maintaining the difference of gay people while also avoiding sociobiological conceptions of "difference."

Beyond same-sex marriage, family law would be greatly enriched and the quality of people's lives improved if the law recognized and protected transgressive care practices as a form of valuable political expression. For example, although many states now permit a child to have two legal parents of the same sex—a significant step forward for transgressive caregiving practices—American family law generally takes the position that a child can have no more than two legal parents. Where consensual and in the best interests of the child, why not allow more than two adults to serve as the legal parents of a child, with designated primary and secondary parents, which as a practical matter reflects the arrangement of many families within minority communities already? Along the same lines, in the case of family dissolution, why not augment a child's right to receive child support from only one noncustodial parent—typically a male, biological parent? If we look to the parenting practices in African–American and gay communities, a whole range of individuals are likely to have economic and affective ties to a child worth preserving. Recognizing such care practices, which can be highly functional and are constitutive of such communities, would represent long-deserved recognition of the value of that care.

* * *

Much of the legal feminist and law reform discourse on care has been characterized by a split between those women who benefit from market-based solutions to the problem of devalued family labor and those who do not. For example, many middle-class women support punitive welfare reforms because they have experienced wage work as a positive source of liberation from the burdens of domestic labor, and because they can pass on their domestic labor to less privileged women. * * * Yet, many of these same women may be transgressive caregivers. Perhaps they are unmarried cohabitants or lesbian caregivers. Perhaps they are married to men who do significant care work, thereby enabling them to see the importance of recognizing transgressive care work. Similarly, although African Americans as a class generally are more conservative on certain issues implicating "family values," transgressive care practices are quite prevalent in African–American communities. The explicit linkage of gay and minority care practices may thus serve to forge important coalitions across race lines that will strengthen both the gay liberation and welfare rights movements. Finally, although the legal feminist discourse on care has largely conceptualized the interests of men and women as adverse, to the extent that men are transgressive caregivers in certain contexts, they too potentially can be part of law reform efforts aimed at valuing care.

KATHERINE M. FRANKE, THEORIZING YES: AN ESSAY ON FEMINISM, LAW, AND DESIRE

101 Colum. L. Rev. 181, 183–186 (2001).

I. The Repronormativity of Motherhood

Motherhood and its implications figure centrally in virtually all feminist agendas. However, for much of first and second wave legal feminism, issues of gender collapse quite quickly into the normative significance of our roles as mothers. Grounding feminist legal theory in object relations theory and demanding that women's participation in the wage labor market be compatible with our responsibilities as mothers are only two salient examples of how the legal feminist frame tends to collapse women's identity into motherhood. The centrality, presumption, and inevitability of our responsibility for children remain a starting point for many, if not most, legal feminists.

Consider two propositions: The overwhelming majority of women are heterosexual. The overwhelming majority of women are mothers. The degree to which social preferences and prohibitions—otherwise known as compulsory heterosexuality—contribute to the "fact" stated by the first proposition has become relatively accepted within feminist, and certainly queer, theory circles. Feminists have become, to varying degrees, sensitive to the technologies of power that steer, suggest, coerce, and demand that women be heterosexual and that abjection lies in the refusal of such a demand.

Yet the same cannot be said of the second proposition laid out above: Most women are mothers. Why is it that we are willing to acknowledge that heteronormative cultural preferences play a significant role in sexual orientation and selection of sexual partners, while at the same time refusing to treat repronormative forces as warranting similar theoretical attention? If you believe the statistics, women are more likely not to have borne a child in their lifetimes than to be lesbian. Is there any principled reason why legal feminists might not want to devote some attention to exposing the complex ways in which reproduction is incentivized and subsidized in ways that may bear upon the life choices women face? To ask such a question is to risk being labeled unfeminist. To suggest that we reconceptualize procreation as a cultural preference rather than a biological imperative, and then explore ways in which to lessen or at least modify the demand to conform to that preference, is to initiate a conversation within feminism that has been explicitly and curtly rejected by some legal feminists. However, it is a conversation that necessarily demands feminist discussants, for only by positing the possibility of female identity divorced from mothering can we make mothering ethically and politically intelligible. Surely mothering grounds the lives of many women, but that ground, once taken for granted, risks obscuring the figure of woman, whose identity extends beyond her role as mother.

Notwithstanding the prevalence of both childlessness and lesbianism, somehow reproduction continues to be regarded as more inevitable and natural than heterosexuality. That is to say, repronormativity remains in the closet even while heteronormativity has stepped more into the light of the theoretical and political day. Reproduction has been so taken for granted that only women who are not parents are regarded as having made a choice—a choice that is constructed as nontraditional, nonconventional, and for some, non-natural. In a telling switch, the issue of choice flips for lesbians, who are constructed as choosing motherhood, given that lesbians continue to have an identity understood as non-reproductive in nature. Similarly, the official story of reproduction as a natural drive is deeply racialized, as women of color have struggled against social forces that have at times coercively appropriated, and at other times coercively discouraged their reproduction in numerous ways. So too, in recent debates over welfare reform, poor mothers have been vilified for having borne children strategically. While a claim not borne out by any reliable studies, it has justified the punishment of women who reproduce for the wrong reasons.

Thus, reproduction raises numerous sticky normative questions, yet underexplored within feminism, with respect to choice, coercion, and policies that incentivize and disincentivize reproductive uses of women's sexual bodies-not only for women who occupy law's margins, such as lesbians and women of color, but also for women whose reproduction we regard as unproblematic.

NOTES ON GENDERED CHILDREARING

1. What does Adrienne Rich mean when she describes mothering as an institution? What are the rules of this institution insofar as you have been able to infer them from your own life experiences? Who legislates those rules? Are the rules a product of your race and class as well as your gender? How? How can men be mothers? How do these rules affect your life as a student and/or lawyer? Is it possible to escape the "institution" of motherhood in our culture, that is, can one "mother" without being controlled by its rules?

2. Rich points to the very different meanings ascribed to the verbs "to mother" and "to father." Given this difference, what do we mean when we use the term "to parent" (as in "parental leave")? Some feminists object to

the use of the term "parenting" or "caregiving," opting instead to speak of "mothering," whether performed by a woman or a man, to underscore the different meanings of these terms, as well as the reality that most nurturing is still performed by women and to emphasize the central importance of the functions described by "mothering." See, e.g., Martha Albertson Fineman, The Neutered Mother, The Sexual Family and Other Twentieth Century Tragedies 233–35 (1995). "Parenting," on the other hand, points to a future where both men and women share the nurturing of children, thereby challenging the current gendered nature of childrearing. Which terminology do you prefer and why?

3. Does Chodorow's theory adequately explain why women are the primary caregivers and nurturers of children? What other explanations can you think of for this near universal phenomenon? Do the different approaches to feminist theory discussed in Chapter 3 suggest any different explanations?

Might Chodorow's psychological theories provide an explanatory underpinning for Gilligan's "different voice" theory? For relational feminism? Why or why not?

4. Does Chodorow's theory of gender differentiation account for male domination in society in general? How can we explain change between historical periods and differences among cultures? See Iris Marion Young, Is Male Gender Identity the Cause of Male Domination?, in Throwing Like a Girl and Other Essays in Feminist Philosophy and Social Theory 36–61 (1990). What other explanations can you offer for the persistence of these almost universal institutions?

5. How does Chodorow's theory relate to the theories of Kessler and Franke? Is Chodorow considering normative childrearing, while Kessler is considering transgressive childrearing? How does Chodorow's analysis apply to lesbian parents? Black parents? Men who are already engaging in childrearing? Is Chodorow supporting the repronormativity that Franke critiques? How might a feminist support each of the approaches?

6. Dorothy E. Roberts argues that Black women's experience of motherhood and the family contrasts with the feminist image of the home as oppressive for women. Roberts, Motherhood and Crime, 79 Iowa L. Rev. 95 (1993). First, the separate spheres ideology has never described Black women's lives, as Black mothers have always worked outside the home as well. Thus "Black women have viewed work outside the home as an aspect of racial subordination and the family as a site of solace and resistance against white oppression." Id. at 131. Indeed, the mothering of Black children, devalued by the majority community, may be seen as a "radical vocation." In addition, Black women have a more communal notion of childrearing, as female relatives and friends help to raise each others' children. "Black women historically have practiced mothering in a way that overcomes some of the burdens of motherhood and holds the potential for the collective transformative action of mothers." Id. at 132.

What are the implications of Roberts' description of motherhood as a liberatory—even a political—experience? Do these implications pertain only to women of color? In what ways might the interests and attitudes of white and Black, professional, middle-class, and working-class mothers, as well as mothers receiving public assistance, differ with respect to the role of motherhood in a woman's life? Can you think of ways in which their interests are congruent? What lessons might our society draw from the more collective/communal childrearing practices of the Black community described by Roberts? How do you think Kessler would answer that question?

7. One Black writer, bell hooks, has criticized white middle-class feminists for having alienated poor and non-white women by attacking motherhood in the early years of the current women's movement and then for romanticizing motherhood in a new version of the 19th-century cult of domesticity. hooks, Revolutionary Parenting, in Feminist theory from margin to center 133–36 (1984). This romanticization is dangerous, in hooks's opinion, both because it "reinforce[s] central tenets of male supremacist ideology" and because it undermines women's involvement in other types of work at a time when many teenagers are bearing children rather than developing a connection to the world of work. Why do you think contemporary feminists may have "flip-flopped" in their views of mothering? Is what hooks describes as a new cult of domesticity the same as the 19th century variety (which exalted the role of the woman—at least the middle-class white woman—within the home, at the price of disqualifying her from playing any role in the public world), given that the new domesticity takes place in a context in which most women have entered the paid labor force?

How do you think hooks would respond to Franke's call for an interrogation of repronormativity? Franke emphasizes that only certain women—white, non-immigrant, financially secure women—are encouraged to reproduce. How might Franke and hooks work together to interrogate the emphasis on mothering in feminist legal theory? What might the work of Zillah Eisenstein, discussed in Chapter 3, add to their project?

8. Chodorow seems to suggest that men are the solution and that women cannot be adequate caregivers for a nonsexist future generation. Her solution is to bring men more fully into the "mothering" process and thus create a system of dual or more egalitarian parenting. How does this relate to Kessler's project? How well do you think this will work, given the characteristics of adult males and females described by Chodorow? Do we have any reason to believe that men, as a group, can be good "mothers," given that many men aren't very interested in caregiving? How might this change? Would changes in the nature and organization of work be necessary? What about changes in the attitude of the two genders toward work? Do you think Chodorow and Kessler are overly optimistic?

9. Adrienne Rich states that "large numbers of men could, in fact, undertake child care on a large scale without radically altering the balance of male power in a male-identified society." Rich, Compulsory Heterosexuality and Lesbian Existence, 5 Signs 631, 638 (1980). Who is right on this point, Chodorow or Rich? Would having men mother make that much difference in a world in which whatever men do is valued more than what women do? In other words, is women's mothering the cause of social inequality, or is inequality simply replicated by women's mothering under conditions of inequality between mothers and fathers?

10. Several authors have suggested that mothering can offer a fruitful model for political and legal relationships. Sara Ruddick, for example, argues that the injection into public life of a mother's interests in preserving life, fostering growth, and loving attentively could transform society. Sara Ruddick, Maternal Thinking (1989). Is this simply a new version of the suffragists' argument that giving the vote to women would lead to a new morality in public life? How is it different? Virginia Held points to the revolutionary potential of replacing the contractual paradigm underlying much of Western social and political thought (e.g., the foundation of the state through an original social contract hypothesized by philosophers such as Hobbes, Locke, and Rousseau, whereby rational individuals decided to trade the unlimited freedom of the state of nature for the security of the civil state) with a paradigm of the mother-child relationship as the primary social relationship—one which involves dependence, vulnerability, caring, and responsibility, rather than autonomy, self-interest, privacy, and the exercise of power. Virginia Held, Mothering versus Contract, in Beyond Self–Interest 287–304 (Jane J. Mansbridge ed., 1990). What might the social contract look like if it had been designed by women? Or by individuals who do not yet know what gender role they will be assigned to play in society? What social contract would the various theorists in Chapter 3 design? What different strategies might these theorists suggest for women now?

11. Franke encourages feminist legal theorists to question the "taken-for-grantedness" of motherhood, to "reconceptualize procreation as a cultural preference rather than a biological imperative." Indeed, the number of women who are not mothers or mothers-to-be has increased steadily in the past few decades. Roughly 20% of women between the ages of 40 and 44 have no children, twice the level of thirty years ago. Katie Zezima, More Women Than Ever Are Childless, Census Finds, N.Y. Times, Aug. 18, 2008, at A12. Despite this dramatic increase, however, women who are childless by choice are often treated with scorn or suspicion. For example, members of the media commented extensively on the fact that Supreme Court Justices Sonia Sotomayor and Elena Kagan are both childless women. Some critics fear that female judges without children will not be able to relate to the 80% of American women who have (or plan to have) children; others are concerned that women who are not mothers lack certain qualities associated with childrearing, such as compassion or tolerance. Lisa Belkin, Judging Women, N.Y. Times Magazine §, May 17, 2010.

How can feminists recognize the role of childrearing in many women's lives without reinforcing repronormativity? Do feminist legal theorists contribute to the construction of women as mothers? Recall Robin West's discussion of marriage in Chapter 6. Does she consider women without children? Does she assume that all marriages will produce children? How might suspicion of, or silence about, childless women perpetuate the idea that to be a woman is to be a mother, and hence childless women are not really women? How might this book contribute to repronormativity by containing an entire chapter on women and children?

C. LESBIAN AND GAY PARENTING

DAVID L. CHAMBERS & NANCY D. POLIKOFF, FAMILY LAW AND GAY AND LESBIAN FAMILY ISSUES IN THE TWENTIETH CENTURY

33 Fam. L.Q. 523, 532–42 (1999).

Many gay men and lesbians have children. They have them in the course of marriages and other relationships with a person of the opposite sex. They have them, by artificial insemination or adoption, when single or during relationships with a same-sex partner. There is very little statutory law explicitly addressing the gay parent. Lesbians and gay men who are parents or who want to become parents come into contact with the law in the same way that most heterosexuals do: when they divorce or become involved in a custody struggle with another person who claims the rights of a parent and when they apply for adoption or seek to become foster parents. Over the last thirty years, as more and more women and men have revealed themselves as lesbian or gay, these encounters with the legal system have become more frequent.

A parent's homosexuality was explicitly acknowledged in a handful of reported cases going back to 1952, but custody cases involving a homosexual parent first began appearing with some frequency in the early and mid–1970s, as the women's liberation movement and changing attitudes towards divorce made it easier for all women to leave marriages and as the gay liberation movement enabled substantial numbers of gay men and lesbians to embrace an identity they had earlier been taught to despise.

When the cases first arose in the 1970s, courts applying the prevailing "best interests of the child" standard ruled both for and against lesbian and gay parents [but usually against]. * * *

During the late 1970s, the first mental health research on the well-being of children raised by lesbian mothers was published. Using expert witnesses, advocates were in a better position to dispel recurring myths about lesbians as mothers—that lesbians were mentally ill or emotionally unstable; that a lesbian mother was likely to sexually molest her child or engage in sexual behavior in front of her child; that children raised by lesbian mothers would probably become gay or lesbian, would be confused about their gender identity, would be socially stigmatized, or would suffer other psychological harm.

By the late 1970s, numerous factors coincided to encourage a new form of lesbian and gay parenthood not tied to heterosexual marriage. The gay rights movement enabled many young adults to embrace, rather than reject, their sexual orientation. Many gay men and lesbians who, in an earlier period, would have married a person of the opposite sex out of convention, fear, or denial, no longer did so. While it may have initially appeared that parenthood would never be an option for such men and women, other cultural and medical phenomena soon resulted in a new frame of mind. Specifically, births of out-of-wedlock children no longer carried the stigma they did in earlier decades, and medical technology opened the possibilities for conception without sexual intercourse. Although there are accounts of decisions by lesbian couples to raise children together as far back as 1965, it was at some point in the late 1970s that lesbians in significant numbers, first in the San Francisco area and then around the country, began contemplating planned motherhood, primarily using alternative insemination as the means of conception, but also adopting as individual parents. Into the early 1980s, even as the conservative Christian right emerged and its influence grew, the openness, pride, and numbers of lesbian and gay families also grew.

Meanwhile, the number of reported cases of custody and visitation disputes between a heterosexual parent and a gay or lesbian parent also increased. About twenty states had reported appellate decisions in the first half of the 1980s. Decisions during this period were as mixed as those of the 1970s. In 1980, for example, the Massachusetts Supreme Court ruled that a lesbian mother could not lose her children simply because she had a lifestyle "at odds with the average."[35] The Alaska Supreme Court ruled in 1985 that a mother's lesbian relationship should be considered only if it negatively affected the child and that it was "impermissible to rely on any real or imagined social stigma attaching to mother's status as a lesbian."[36] * * *

Most courts, however, continued to rule against gay parents. Cases from appellate courts in North Dakota, South Dakota, and Virginia overturned trial court judges who had awarded custody to lesbian, gay, or bisexual parents. * * *

In May 1985, neighbors of a gay foster parent couple in Boston went to the Boston Globe to express their disapproval. The ensuing publicity sparked widespread national debate about gay men and lesbians raising children. The Massachusetts Department of Social Services removed the children from the home, and changed its policy, issuing regulations that made it almost impossible for lesbians and gay men to become foster parents. In the wake of that controversy, New Hampshire in 1986 enacted a law prohibiting adoption, foster parenting, or ownership of a child care facility by lesbians or gay men. Although the child care facility provisions were struck down as unconstitutional, the bans on adoption and foster parenting were upheld. New Hampshire became the second state with an adoption ban and the first with a legislatively mandated ban on gay foster parenting.

In the latter half of the 1980s, state courts continued to decide substantial numbers of custody disputes between a lesbian or gay parent and a heterosexual parent and continued the prior pattern of widely divergent attitudes toward parenting by lesbians and gay men. During this

35. Bezio v. Patenaude, 410 N.E.2d 1207 (Mass. 1980).

36. S.N.E. v. R.L.B., 699 P.2d 875 (Alaska 1985).

same period of time, advocates for gay and lesbian parents developed new approaches to protect gay and lesbian families in which, from birth, a child had two parents of the same gender. Lawyers advocated for "second-parent adoption," a term describing the equivalent of a stepparent adoption, in which a biological parent's partner adopts her child. The term "joint adoption" was used to designate adoption of a child by both members of a couple, a practice unheard of earlier unless the couple was married. The first second-parent adoption was granted in Alaska in 1985; within months others were granted in Oregon, Washington, and California.

The mid–1980s also saw the first disputes between separating lesbian mothers who had raised a child together, between a surviving nonbiological mother and family members of a deceased biological mother, and between a lesbian mother and a semen donor, often a gay man, when disagreements arose about the donor's relationship with the child. These cases would become more prominent in the late 1980s and into the 1990s. In a particularly poignant 1989 case, a trial court judge in Broward County, Florida, awarded custody of ten year old Kristen Pearlman to Janine Ratcliffe, her nonbiological mother, reversing a decision made four years earlier, upon the death of Kristen's biological mother, Joanie, that had granted custody to Joanie's parents. In chambers, the child pleaded with the judge to permit her to live with Janine. The judge found that Kristen continued to view Janine as her primary parent figure, that it would be detrimental to Kristen to continue her separation from Janine, and that there was no evidence Janine's sexual orientation would have any detrimental effect on Kristen.

Although there have been a handful of other cases arising upon the death of a child's only legal parent, disputes about parenthood in planned lesbian and gay families have arisen primarily in two other contexts. The first is a claim by a legally unrecognized parent to continue a relationship with a child when she and the child's biological or adoptive parent separate. The second is a claim by a biological father, usually a semen donor, who demands legal parental status in disregard of an agreement with the lesbian couple that he would not assert parental rights based on biology. These cases have presented courts with two options—recognize planned lesbian and gay families and modify family law principles to protect the interests of parents and children in such families, or maintain a rigid definition of parenthood that often fails to recognize the reality of children's actual relationships with parenting figures. Courts, sometimes claiming that legislative language gave them no choice, have usually taken the latter option. * * * While appellate courts in Wisconsin, New Mexico, and Massachusetts have allowed the non-biological parent to request visitation,[49] these states are in the minority, and even they have not authorized a claim for sole or joint custody by the legally unrecognized parent, even if she was the child's primary caretaker.

---

49. *In re* H.S.H.–K., 533 N.W.2d 419 (Wis. 1995); A.C. v. C.B., 829 P.2d 660 (N.M. 1992); E.N.O. v. L.M.M., 711 N.E.2d 886 (Mass. 1999).

The 1990s, like the preceding two decades, were filled with incongruity for lesbian and gay parents. The number of planned lesbian and gay families skyrocketed, bringing broad visibility in the media, in schools, in churches and synagogues, and in the courts. With this visibility came an increased number of heterosexual allies, people in positions of power able to influence mainstream organizations, as well as ordinary people whose children became friends with children of gay and lesbian parents, thereby learning about gay and lesbian families in ways that break down myths, stereotypes, and fear. In 1995, the American Psychological Association issued Lesbian and Gay Parenting: A Resource for Psychologists, a review of forty-three empirical studies and numerous other articles that concluded that "[n]ot a single study has found children of gay and lesbian parents to be disadvantaged in any significant respect relative to children of heterosexual parents."[50] In 1996 and 1999, the American Bar Association passed resolutions opposing use of sexual orientation as a basis for denying custody and adoption, respectively. In some parts of the country, joint and second-parent adoptions for lesbian and gay couples became routine, and lesbians and gay men were welcomed as adoptive and foster parents for the growing number of children needing good homes.

With increased visibility came increased political volatility. Legislatures had more opportunities to debate lesbian and gay parenting. Related issues concerning children and homosexuality, such as the content of school curricula, the sexual orientation of teachers and school board members, and whether gay men can serve as Boy Scout leaders, increasingly became subjects of public controversy. The debates over same-sex marriage often included heated discussion of childrearing by lesbians and gay men. Courts today considering the fate of lesbian and gay parents issue their rulings in this volatile context.

The greatest legal accomplishment for lesbian and gay parents in the 1990s was the availability in some parts of the country of joint and second-parent adoption. After many unreported trial court decisions in the last half of the 1980s, the first reported second-parent adoption by a lesbian couple occurred in 1991 in the District of Columbia.[51] Other reported decisions came shortly thereafter, and in early 1992 the first New York decision granting a second-parent adoption to a lesbian couple was reported in the New York Times and applauded on its editorial page.[52] Appeals courts in New York, New Jersey, Vermont, Massachusetts, Illinois, and the District of Columbia have approved such adoptions and instructed trial judges to grant them under the same best-interests-of-the-child standard used in all adoptions.[53] Appellate courts in only four states,

---

50. American Psychological Association, Lesbian and Gay Parenting: A Resource for Psychologists 8 (1995).

51. *In re* Adoption of Minor (T. and M.), 17 Fam. L. Rep. (BNA) 1523 (D.C. Super. 1991).

52. *In re* Adoption of Evan, 583 N.Y.S.2d 997 (N.Y. Sup. Ct. 1992); Ronald Sullivan, Judge Lets Gay Partner Adopt Child, N.Y. Times, Jan. 31, 1992, at B1; James D. Marks, A Victory for the New American Family, N.Y. Times, Feb. 1, 1992, at 21.

53. *In re* Dana, 660 N.E.2d 397 (N.Y. 1995); *In re* Adoption of Two Children by H.N.R., 666 A.2d 535 (N.J. Super. Ct. App. Div. 1995); *In re* Adoptions of B.L.V.B. and E.L.V.B., 628 A.2d

Wisconsin, Colorado, Ohio, and Connecticut, have rejected such adoptions, in decisions narrowly construing their adoption statutes.[54] Trial courts in more than a dozen other states have granted such adoptions, and in some counties, such as those in the San Francisco Bay area, there have been hundreds, perhaps thousands, over the last fifteen years. In a 1997 settlement of a class action law suit, New Jersey became the first state in the country with a written agency policy requiring that gay, lesbian, and unmarried heterosexual couples be evaluated for joint adoption of children using the same criteria used for married couples.

From the mid–1990s on, the increasing, high profile coverage of lesbian and gay families provoked an escalation of efforts to prevent lesbians and gay men from adopting children and serving as foster parents. Legislation proposing statewide bans on adoption and/or foster parenting was introduced between 1995 and 1997 in Oklahoma, Missouri, South Carolina, Tennessee, and Washington. None passed. In 1998, however, on the heels of the nationwide publicity accorded the settlement of the New Jersey litigation, prohibitions were proposed in Arkansas, Indiana, Texas, and Utah. Restrictions passed in Utah and Arkansas in 1999.

Despite these setbacks, there were also positive legislative developments. In 1999 New Hampshire repealed its ban on lesbian and gay adoption and foster parenting. Upon signing the bill into law, Governor Jeanne Shaheen commented that foster and adoptive families would now be selected based on fitness, "without making prejudicial assumptions." Later in 1999, the Republican-controlled House of Representatives defeated an amendment that would have prohibited joint adoption by unmarried gay and heterosexual couples in the District of Columbia, even though the same language had passed in 1998.

Although childrearing by openly gay men and women has become increasingly common, and although young gay men and lesbians have an increasing number of positive images and role models that allow them to affirm their sexual orientation, large numbers of adults still do not come out as gay or lesbian until after they have married and had children within heterosexual marriages. Their life stories look strikingly like those of their counterparts in the 1970s, and, as in earlier decades, their fate will be determined more than anything else by the state in which they live and the judge who hears their case.

The most visible custody dispute in the 1990s was the battle between Sharon Bottoms and her mother, Kay Bottoms, who challenged Sharon's right to continue raising her two year old son, Tyler, even though Sharon's former husband believed that Sharon should retain custody of the boy. Sharon lost at trial, but won in the Virginia Court of Appeals, in a

---

1271 (Vt. 1993); *In re* Adoption of Tammy, 619 N.E.2d 315 (Mass. 1993); *In re* Petition of K.M. and D.M., 653 N.E.2d 888 (Ill. App. Ct. 1995); *In re* M.M.D. & B.H.M., 662 A.2d 837 (D.C. 1995).

54. *In re* Angel Lace M., 516 N.W.2d 678 (Wis. 1994); *In re* Adoption of T.K.J., 931 P.2d 488 (Colo. 1996); *In re* Adoption of Doe, 1998 WL 904252 (Ohio Ct. App. 1998); *In re* Adoption of Baby Z., 724 A.2d 1035 (Conn. 1999).

decision that credited the years of research on the well being of children living with lesbian mothers.[59] The victory was short-lived, however, as the Virginia Supreme Court in 1995 reinstated the trial court's ruling, which included a prohibition on Sharon's visitation with Tyler in the presence of her partner.[60]

The continuing vulnerability of lesbian and gay parents in some parts of the country was reinforced by a series of state supreme court decisions in 1998 and 1999 from Indiana, Missouri, North Carolina, Alabama, and Mississippi.[61] Each affirmed either a change in custody or a severe restriction on visitation rights based upon the parent's homosexuality. * * *

To be sure, there were positive court decisions during the 1990s. A 1998 opinion from the highest court in Maryland overturned a trial judge's order that a gay father's partner be prohibited from being present during the father's visitation with his children,[63] in the process citing similar 1990s decisions from Illinois, Pennsylvania, and Washington.[64] Nonetheless, a review of reported disputes between gay and straight parents in the 1990s demonstrates that neither the increased visibility of lesbian and gay families, nor the mental health research on the well-being of children raised by lesbian and gay parents, nor the successes in the areas of adoption and foster-parenting have decreased the risks to a lesbian mother or gay father battling a heterosexual former spouse over custody or visitation. It is as true at the turn of the millennium as it was in the 1970s that the result of such a dispute depends largely on where the case goes to court.

NOTES ON LESBIAN AND GAY PARENTING

1. How does the analysis of Chambers and Polikoff illustrate the ways that childrearing is not only gendered but also constructed around norms of compulsory heterosexuality? Is it possible to escape those norms? Studies generally report that the children of lesbian and gay men do not differ in statistically significant ways from the children of heterosexuals on measures of sexual orientation, gender identity, self-esteem, psychological health, and social adjustment. Rachel H. Farr, Stephen L. Forssell & Charlotte J. Patterson, Parenting and Child Development in Adoptive Families: Does Parental Sexual Orientation Matter?, 14 Applied Dev. Sci. 164 (2010); Charlotte J. Patterson & Jennifer L. Wainright, Adolescents with Same–Sex Parents: Findings from the National Longitudinal Study of Adolescent Health, in Lesbian and Gay Adoption: A New American Reality (D. Brodzinsky, A.

---

59. Bottoms v. Bottoms, 444 S.E.2d 276 (Va. Ct. App. 1994).

60. Bottoms v. Bottoms, 457 S.E.2d 102 (Va. 1995).

61. Marlow v. Marlow, 702 N.E.2d 733 (Ind. Ct. App. 1998); J.A.D. v. F.J.D., 978 S.W.2d 336 (Mo. 1998) (en banc); Pulliam v. Smith, 501 S.E.2d 898 (N.C. 1998); *In re* J.B.F and J.M.F., 730 So. 2d 1190 (Ala. 1998); Weigand v. Houghton, 730 So. 2d 581 (Miss. 1999).

63. Boswell v. Boswell, 721 A.2d 662 (Md. 1998).

64. *In re* Marriage of Pleasant, 628 N.E.2d 633 (Ill. App. Ct. 1993); Blew v. Verta, 617 A.2d 31 (Pa. Super. Ct. 1992); *In re* Marriage of Wicklund, 932 P.2d 652 (Wash. Ct. App. 1996).

Pertman & D. Kunz eds., 2007); In re Adoption of Doe, 2008 WL 5006172 (Fla. Cir. Ct. Nov. 25, 2008) (relying on such studies to invalidate Florida's categorical ban on adoption by individuals who identify as homosexual). Researchers have also found no deficits in children of lesbian mothers in other areas of "personal development, including separation-individuation, locus of control, self-concept, intelligence, or moral judgment," and many studies show that "children of lesbian mothers have normal, healthy relationships with other children as well as with adults." See Mary Becker, Family Law in the Secular State and Restrictions on Same-Sex Marriage, 2001 U. Ill. L. Rev. 1, 50–52. In light of these studies, why do you think parenting is still organized around norms of compulsory heterosexuality?

2. Commentators differ as to whether it is a mistake to highlight differences between children raised by gay and lesbian parents and those raised by heterosexual parents. The Committee on Psychosocial Aspects of Child and Family Health of the American Academy of Pediatrics issued a report saying that there were no meaningful differences and that parents' sexual orientation simply does not predict children's development. See Ellen C. Perrin, et al., Technical Report: Coparent or Second-Parent Adoption by Same-Sex Parents, 109 Pediatrics 341, 343 (2002). A controversial essay published in 2001, on the other hand, highlights differences that emerge from a review of the studies, for example, that children of gay and lesbian parents conform less to gender norms and that daughters of lesbians are more interested in "male" occupations and "dress, play and behave in ways that do not conform to sex-typed cultural norms." Judith Stacey & Timothy J. Biblarz, (How) Does the Sexual Orientation of Parents Matter?, 66 Am. Soc. Rev. 159, 168 (2001). Elsewhere, Stacey has said that "boys raised by gay parents tend to be less aggressive, more nurturing and more sexually restrained than those raised in heterosexual families. Girls raised by gay parents tend to be more sexually adventurous and self-confident * * *." Barri Bronston, Children of Same–Sex Parents Fare Well in Research, New Orleans Times-Picayune, Nov. 14, 2004, Living §, at 6. At least one study also suggests that children raised by lesbian mothers may be somewhat more likely to become lesbian or gay for a number of reasons, including being raised in an environment more accepting of same-sex relationships. See Becker, above note 1, at 52–53. Should we be concerned about these differences or celebrate them? See Carlos A. Ball, Lesbian and Gay Families: Gender Nonconformity and the Implications of Difference, 31 Cap. U. L. Rev. 691 (2003). If children raised by lesbian mothers do as well as other children in measures of well-being and development, should it matter whether these children are more likely (or feel free) to identify as lesbian or gay themselves?

3. Polikoff has recently written about the options currently available to gay and lesbian parents who are not biologically related to their children:

> At the moment, the lesbian partner of a woman who bears a child can become a parent without adopting the child under two different statutory schemes. The first derives from a formalized relationship between the two women that provides the couple with all the state-based legal consequences of marriage, including the marital presumption. The

second occurs when a court determines that its existing statutes confer parentage on a biological mother's partner.

* * *

Ten states and the District of Columbia allow (or are set to allow) same-sex couples to enter a formal legal status that grants the couple all or virtually all the state-based legal consequences of marriage. * * * In all instances, a female spouse or domestic/civil union partner of a woman who bears a child receives the same presumption of parentage that a husband receives.

* * *

A presumption based on a couple's formal status is not the only method of extending parentage to the partner of a woman who gives birth. All states establish legal parentage by statute. Courts have been asked to apply existing law to parentage questions, and, in a few instances, they have found that a nonbiological mother is a parent.

Nancy D. Polikoff, A Mother Should Not Have to Adopt Her Own Child: Parentage Laws for Children of Lesbian Couples in the Twenty–First Century, 5 Stan. J. C.R. & C.L. 201 (2009). For many commentators, adoption and the so-called marital presumption are not entirely satisfactory methods of determining when parents should be legally recognized. The California Supreme Court has recognized the rights and obligations of non-biological, non-marital, non-adoptive social or functional parents, even though existing state "statutes that did not explicitly contemplate two mothers for a child." Id. at 224 (referencing Elisa B. v. Superior Court, 117 P.3d 660 (Cal. 2005)). In 2009, with gay and lesbian parents in mind, the Delaware state legislature amended its Uniform Parentage Act to explicitly recognize de facto parents. Id. at 224.

4. On August 22, 2005, the California Supreme Court handed down a series of cases holding that lesbian partners who plan a family and raise a child together should both be regarded as legal parents in the event of separation, with the same rights and responsibilities as heterosexual parents, including, inter alia, custody, visitation, and support. In K.M. v. E.G., 117 P.3d 673 (Cal. 2005), a woman donated eggs to her partner, who was the gestational mother; the two lived together and were domestic partners under California law. The court held that "a woman who supplies ova to be used to impregnate her lesbian partner, with the understanding that the resulting child will be raised in their joint home, cannot waive her responsibility to support the child." Id. at 682. In the second case, the biological mother and her partner had entered into a stipulated judgment that the non-biological mother was the second parent and would have joint custody; the couple subsequently separated. Applying the doctrine of equitable estoppel, the court held that the biological mother could not challenge the validity of the prior judgment determining that both women would be legal parents. Kristine H. v. Lisa R., 117 P.3d 690 (Cal. 2005). The third case of the trilogy involved a lesbian partner who agreed to raise twins conceived by artificial insemination of her partner and then sought to be relieved of the obligation to support the twins (one of whom had Downs syndrome) when the couple separated two years later. The court held that she was the presumed mother within the

meaning of the Uniform Parentage Act and was obligated to pay child support, because she had supported her partner's artificial insemination, received the twins into her home, and held them out as her own. Elisa B. v. Superior Ct., 117 P.3d 660 (Cal. 2005). To the extent that these decisions were inconsistent with other California decisions, the court disapproved those prior decisions. Id. at 672.

The series of decisions was widely heralded as a major victory for the LGBT community. Anna Marie Smith, Reproductive Technology, Family Law, and the Postwelfare State: The California Same–Sex Parents' Rights "Victories" of 2005, 34 Signs 826, 829, 832 (2009). However, many commentators question whether the cases would have come out the same way had the birth mother not applied for government assistance. Anna Marie Smith has argued that *Elisa B.*, in addition to being a case about recognizing social or functional parents, was a poverty law case that expanded the state of California's power to enforce rules that require a parent applying for government assistance to identify the absent second parent and "assist[ ] in the collection of support payments from him or her." Id. at 832. Do you think same-sex parents should be subject to the same child support regimes as different-sex parents, even when the same-sex parent has no biological connection to the child? How might such a rule alter both the gender and sexual orientation of dominant notions of parenting? For more on child support and poverty prevention, see Sections E and G, below.

5. In 2010, the Court of Appeals of New York declined to follow any of the approaches adopted by the California courts, but nonetheless recognized the parental rights of a non-biological lesbian mother pursuant to the presumption of legitimacy. Janice R. and Debra H., residents of New York, had entered into a civil union in the state of Vermont after Janice R. had become pregnant through artificial insemination but before the child was born. The women separated when the child was two-years-old, with no second-parent adoption in place (in fact Janice R. had refused to permit an adoption), and Debra H. petitioned the court for joint physical and legal custody. The Court held that, by virtue of their civil union, Debra H. was a parent of the child under Vermont law and that, under the doctrine of comity, the state of New York would similarly recognize Debra H. as a parent. Debra H. v. Janice R., 930 N.E.2d 184 (N.Y. 2010). What are the advantages and disadvantages of the New York approach compared with the California approach? How do both approaches compare with that taken in jurisdictions that recognize only those non-biological parents who have undertaken second-parent adoptions, as discussed by Chambers and Polikoff? Which approach do you think is preferable? In your opinion, which approach best accommodates the interests of the partners and children involved?

6. When a lesbian couple gives birth as a result of artificial insemination, there are three parents: two mothers (one biologically related to the child) and a sperm donor. Who do you think should have a stronger claim, a sperm donor who has not given up all his parental rights in writing or the non-birth mother who has mothered the child? Why have courts been more willing to recognize the claims of the sperm donor than those of the non-birth mother when she and the birth mother separate after years of co-mothering?

Although the California Supreme Court in 2005 reiterated the widely accepted rule that a child cannot have more than two legally recognized parents, in 2007 the Pennsylvania Superior Court held that three people—two lesbian mothers and a sperm donor—could all be considered parents for the purposes of physical custody and child support. Jacob v. Shultz-Jacob, 923 A.2d 473 (Pa. Super. 2007). The majority was unconvinced that child support guidelines could not be reworked to include three parents in order to accommodate the best interests of the children. Id. at 482. How does this change your answers to the questions immediately above? How might this change the gender and sexual orientation of parenting?

7. The law is changing so rapidly that it is impossible to give an accurate snapshot of the state of the law on lesbian and gay parenting issues, although Polikoff's 2009 article, as summarized above in note 3, chronicles many of the developments up until that time. Gay and Lesbian Defenders (GLAD), a Boston gay rights organization, created a working group of lawyers "to develop standards to guide attorney and client conduct in queer dissolution situations." William B. Rubenstein, Divided We Propagate: An Introduction to Protecting Families: Standards for Child Custody in Same-Sex Relationships, 10 UCLA Women's L.J. 143, 147–48 (1999) (describing development of the standards). For the standards, see id. at 151. If a lesbian couple came to you to draft a waiver of all parental rights to be signed by a sperm donor, what provisions would you suggest to try to protect the non-biological mother's link to the child in a jurisdiction in which second-parent adoption is not possible? What might be done to minimize her risk? How would your advice change if you were instead advising a gay male couple?

D. PARENTAL LEAVE: GOOD OR BAD FOR WOMEN?

The issues involved in provision of maternity and parental leave have provoked substantial debate among feminists. We have already encountered this debate in Chapter 3, in connection with the disagreement among feminist lawyers over whether to support legislation requiring employers to provide their employees with leave for childbirth when other temporary disabilities are not covered by an employer's benefit package. As we have seen above, formal equality theorists answered "no," on the grounds that such laws, if not applied to women and men alike, reinforce stereotypes about women and deter employers from hiring them. Other feminists answered "yes," arguing that inadequate leave policies constitute sex discrimination in employment and also substantially burden women's procreative rights. Maternity and parental leave policy, however, goes beyond provision for the period of disability caused by pregnancy as a physical condition. As the excerpts below show, what is at stake is not only the place of women within the workplace during their years of childbirth and childrearing but also the priorities our society places upon the relationship between children and those who care for them in the earliest months of life.

1. THE FAMILY AND MEDICAL LEAVE ACT

FAMILY AND MEDICAL LEAVE ACT OF 1993

Pub. L. 103–03, 107 Stat. 6; 103d Cong., 1st Sess., Feb. 5, 1993.
29 U.S.C. § 2601 et seq.

[The Family and Medical Leave Act (FMLA) was first introduced into Congress in 1985. Although the bill was passed by both houses of Congress, it was vetoed by President George H.W. Bush in 1991 and in 1992, but was signed into law in the early weeks of the Clinton Administration in 1993.]

SEC. 2. FINDINGS AND PURPOSES.

(a) FINDINGS.—Congress finds that—

(1) the number of single-parent households and two-parent households in which the single parent or both parents work is increasing significantly;

(2) it is important for the development of children and the family unit that fathers and mothers be able to participate in early childrearing and the care of family members who have serious health conditions;

(3) the lack of employment policies to accommodate working parents can force individuals to choose between job security and parenting;

(4) there is inadequate job security for employees who have serious health conditions that prevent them from working for temporary periods;

(5) due to the nature of the roles of men and women in our society, the primary responsibility for family caretaking often falls on women, and such responsibility affects the working lives of women more than it affects the working lives of men; and

(6) employment standards that apply to one gender only have serious potential for encouraging employers to discriminate against employees and applicants for employment who are of that gender.

(b) PURPOSES.—It is the purpose of this Act—

(1) to balance the demands of the workplace with the needs of families, to promote the stability and economic security of families, and to promote national interests in preserving family integrity;

(2) to entitle employees to take reasonable leave for medical reasons, for the birth or adoption of a child, and for the care of a child, spouse, or parent who has a serious health condition;

(3) to accomplish the purposes described in paragraphs (1) and (2) in a manner that accommodates the legitimate interests of employers;

(4) to accomplish the purposes described in paragraphs (1) and (2) in a manner that, consistent with the Equal Protection Clause of the Fourteenth Amendment, minimizes the potential for employment discrim-

ination on the basis of sex by ensuring generally that leave is available for eligible medical reasons (including maternity-related disability) and for compelling family reasons, on a gender-neutral basis; and

(5) to promote the goal of equal employment opportunity for women and men, pursuant to such clause.

* * *

SEC. 102. LEAVE REQUIREMENT.

(a)(1) ENTITLEMENT TO LEAVE.—* * * [A]n eligible employee shall be entitled to a total of 12 workweeks of leave during any 12–month period for one or more of the following:

(A) Because of the birth of a son or daughter of the employee and in order to care for such son or daughter.

(B) Because of the placement of a son or daughter with the employee for adoption or foster care.

(C) In order to care for the spouse, or a son, daughter, or parent, of the employee, if such spouse, son, daughter, or parent has a serious health condition.

(D) Because of a serious health condition that makes the employee unable to perform the functions of the position of such employee.

* * *

(c) UNPAID LEAVE PERMITTED.—* * * [L]eave granted under subsection (a) may consist of unpaid leave.

* * *

SEC. 104. EMPLOYMENT AND BENEFITS PROTECTION.

(a) RESTORATION TO POSITION.—

(1) * * * [A]ny eligible employee who takes leave under section 102 for the intended purpose of the leave shall be entitled, on return from such leave—

(A) to be restored by the employer to the position of employment held by the employee when the leave commenced; or

(B) to be restored to an equivalent position with equivalent employment benefits, pay, and other terms and conditions of employment.

(2) LOSS OF BENEFITS.—The taking of leave under section 102 shall not result in the loss of any employment benefit accrued prior to the date on which the leave commenced.

* * *

(c) MAINTENANCE OF HEALTH BENEFITS.—

(1) * * * [D]uring any period that an eligible employee takes leave under section 102, the employer shall maintain coverage under any

"group health plan" * * * for the duration of such leave at the level and under the conditions coverage would have been provided if the employee had continued in employment continuously for the duration of such leave.

* * *

[The Act provides that an employee may bring suit for noncompliance directly under the statute, or the Secretary of Labor may sue on her behalf; it also provides for civil damages equal to lost wages and benefits, plus interests and costs, in addition to injunctive remedies such as reinstatement.]

NOTES ON THE FAMILY AND MEDICAL LEAVE ACT

1. Review the "Findings" and "Purposes" sections of the Family Leave Act, above. Which feminist theorists studied in Chapter 3 would be most likely to write those sections? Do you see the influence of several strands of feminist theory? Which ones, and where? If you were to rewrite the legislative findings and purposes of the legislation based on what you know, both from this course and other sources, what, if anything, would you add or change?

2. The FMLA has a number of shortcomings from the perspective of expansive coverage, among them that the leave is unpaid and that private employers are required to comply with its provisions only if (1) they employ fifty or more workers within a 75 mile radius, and (2) the employee has been employed for at least 12 months. 29 U.S.C. § 2611(2)(B)(ii), (4)(A) (2009). In 2005, about 76.1 million employees—roughly 54% of all U.S. employees—were eligible for unpaid leave under the FMLA. Family and Medical Leave Act Regulations: A Report on the Department of Labor's Request for Information, 72 Fed. Reg. 35549, 35551, 35622 (June 28, 2007) (to be codified at 29 C.F.R. pt. 825). However, lower-income workers were much less likely to be covered than other workers. Thirty-nine percent of workers earning less than $20,000 were covered, compared with roughly 65% of workers earning between $20,000 and $49,999, and 74% of workers earning $100,000 or more. Dep't of Labor, Balancing the Needs of Families and Employers: Family and Medical Leave Surveys: 2000 Update App. A–2 (2001).

Even if available, how realistic is parental leave if it is unpaid? Which groups of women benefit most from such a provision? Only those whose income is secondary to another wage earner's income? The majority of eligible employees who need leave cannot afford to take it, either because it is unpaid or because of the restrictions on coverage. See, e.g., Note, Family and Medical Leave Act Reform: Is Paid Leave the Answer?, 51 Clev. St. L. Rev. 65, 70 (2004). By 2007, over 29% of American families with children under 18 were considered single-parent households. Of those single parents, over 85% of them were single mothers. Roughly 58% of Black families were considered single-parent in 2007. US Census Bureau, America's Families and Living Arrangements: 2007 10 (2009). One study found that "77 percent of employees who needed leave but decided not [to] take it made that decision for financial reasons, and 88 percent of this group said they would have taken leave had some wage replacement been available." Sarah Fass, National Center for Children in Poverty, Paid Leave in the States 5 (2009). How does the FMLA help poor women, if at all? How might the FMLA hurt poor women? Should feminists support unpaid leave programs if they benefit only some women? Why not hold out for the ultimate goal of paid leave?

3. About 35 million people took leave under the Act between 1993 and 2000, 58% of them women, 49% of those for their own illness and 29% for maternity. See Lindsay R.B. Dickerson, "Your Wife Should Handle It": The Implicit Messages of the Family and Medical Leave Act, 25 B.C. Third World L.J. 429, 438 n.75 (2005), and sources cited therein. Although employers predicted that the Act would be too costly in terms of replacement workers and administrative costs and strenuously opposed its passage, subsequent surveys show that most have found compliance with the Act relatively easy, and most report no noticeable impact on productivity, profit, and growth. Gillian Lester, A Defense of Paid Family Leave, 28 Harv. J.L. & Gender 1, 51 (2005); Balancing the Needs, above note 2, at 6–5 tbl.6.3. This is true even though the FMLA also requires the employer to maintain health insurance for employees on leave, a considerable benefit. See FMLA, § 104(c), above. Cost predictions may not have been accurate due to the savings produced by avoiding costly turnover of employees. Indeed, studies show that continuity of female participation in the workforce correlates with employer supportiveness about the length of childbearing leave provided and the ability to avoid mandatory overtime and inconvenient shifts (unpredictable or in the late afternoon) upon returning to work. Jennifer L. Glass & Lisa Riley, Family Responsive Policies and Employee Retention Following Childbirth, 76 Soc. Forces 1401 (1998).

Despite the workplace continuity that flows from supportive parental leave policies, the Act has mostly been invoked to provide leave to care for an employee's own illness. Such illnesses accounted for 52.4% of all FMLA leaves in 2000, while only 18.5% were to care for a new child. Michael Selmi, Is Something Better than Nothing? Critical Reflections on Ten Years of the FMLA, 15 Wash. U. J.L. & Pol'y 65, 74 (2004). A 2000 Department of Labor report showed that only 5.7% of all covered female employees took leave to care for a new child, but they were more than twice as likely to take such a leave than male employees: 68.2% of female employees with young children took leave, compared to 34.1% of male employees with young children. See Joanna L. Grossman, Job Security Without Equality: The Family and Medical Leave Act of 1993, 15 Wash. U. J.L. & Pol'y 17, 54 (2004). How might this gender difference indicate that the unpaid nature of the leave adversely impacts even middle-class women? See id. at 38 ("[T]o the extent available parental leave is unpaid, there exists a clear incentive for a couple to prefer maternal leave over paternal leave, given the likelihood that a husband out-earns his wife.").

4. Before passage of the FMLA, one commentator predicted that "[t]he cost of providing some employees with parental leave will be borne by low-skill female employees who lose their jobs or fail to obtain employment because of the increased wage bill faced by the employer." Maria O'Brien Hylton, "Parental" Leaves and Poor Women: Paying the Price for Time Off, 52 U. Pitt. L. Rev. 475, 493 (1991). Thus, Hylton argued, the price of the FMLA would be paid by the most vulnerable members of the workforce, especially by Black and Hispanic women. Id. at 501. Do you agree? Are

employers likely to substitute male for female employees to avoid any potential costs (though the leave is unpaid)? Has this happened when employers have initiated voluntary leave programs? Consider that the wage gap between male and female workers makes men more costly employees even in relatively low-skilled positions. See Chapter 9, below. Will men take these low-paying "women's" jobs?

How many low-skilled women will actually be able to take unpaid leave for a longer period under such a statute than they could take in the absence of any such law? If most unskilled women can't afford to stay away longer than absolutely necessary to their health, won't employers realize this and hire them anyway? (Note, for example, that the statute allows men to take leave; yet there is no argument that its passage will deter employers from hiring men.) Won't *some* poor women in fact be helped by the Act, since their employers won't be able to fire them for taking off whatever time is absolutely necessary? As discussed in Chapter 3, this was the situation of Lillian Garland, the plaintiff in the *Cal Fed* case. Garland, a Black woman, was a receptionist; she first lost her job, due to the lack of maternity leave, then her housing, because she had no job; due to her lack of housing, she lost custody of the daughter whose birth had incapacitated her in the first place. See Mary E. Becker, Prince Charming: Abstract Equality, 1987 Sup. Ct. Rev. 201, 202–03.

5. What might be some other potentially gendered implications of the FMLA? Joanna Grossman argues:

> Other provisions of the FMLA reinforce traditional leave-taking patterns as well. For example, employers are permitted to deny leave to 'key employees,' defined as the most highly paid ten percent of the workforce, if they can show that granting leave would cause the employer a substantial hardship. Because of the gender-imbalanced power structures of the workplace, this primarily exempts men (and deprives them of leave), and, for the women it does affect, the exemption reinforces the notion that mother is inconsistent with employment success.

Grossman, above note 3, at 38–39. Lindsay Dickerson argues that the Act, although formally gender-neutral, actually reinforces the "Mommy myth": by being unpaid, it assumes that the caretaker's income is secondary and that the leave-taker (probably female) will always be available to look after very young children. See Dickerson, above note 3. Do you think this is a problem? Can you think of other ways that the FMLA may reinforce traditional patterns of caregiving?

6. Some scholars argue that the FMLA is largely symbolic and has made little difference to women's lives. Studies show that although the Act has had a significant impact on employers' leave policies (primarily by making them gender-neutral), it has not had a major impact on leave-taking behavior, largely because women take time off for childbirth and newborn care with or without protected leave whereas men do not. Grossman, above note 3, at 51; see also Charles L. Baum, Has Family Leave Legislation Increased Leave Taking?, 15 Wash. U. J.L. & Pol'y 93, 112 (2004) (finding little to no effect of FMLA on the incidence of leave-taking). Indeed, some argue that passage of the FMLA may have stalled more positive activity by the states and private

employers, who were active in this field and might have passed more generous leave policies if they were not lulled into inactivity by passage of the FMLA. Selmi, above note 3, at 82–83. About 40% of women had maternity leave prior to passage of the FMLA, either due to state law, union contract, or voluntary employer action. Jane Waldfogel, The Family Gap for Young Women in the United States and Britain: Can Maternity Leave Make a Difference?, 16 J. Lab. Econ. 505, 508 (1998). Do you think it is better to have passed the FMLA, even if its effects have been minimal and its coverage inadequate, than to be without any family leave policy at all on the federal level? Why or why not?

7. Despite the FMLA's gender-neutrality, do you think many men in this country will take leave at the time of childbirth? See Deborah J. Anthony, The Hidden Harms of the Family and Medical Leave Act: Gender-Neutral Versus Gender-Equal, 16 Am. U. J. Gender Soc. Pol'y & L. 459, 479–80 (2008) (summarizing Department of Labor statistics on FMLA usage demonstrating that men use FMLA leave less often than women and when men do use it, they do so not to care for others but to address their own health needs); Rosemarie Feuerbach Twomey & Gwen E. Jones, The Family and Medical Leave Act of 1993: A Longitudinal Study of Male and Female Perceptions, 3 Emp. Rts. & Emp. Pol'y J. 229 (1999) (describing study showing continuing belief that caregiving leave is for female employees). The fact that the leave is unpaid is a substantial deterrent, along with the fact that it is limited to 12 weeks, a period typically associated with recovery from childbirth and adjustment to breastfeeding. Nancy E. Dowd, Family Values and Valuing Family: A Blueprint for Family Leave, 30 Harv. J. on Legis. 335, 347–50 (1993). Some commentators point out that this leads to a vicious cycle with respect to care of children, as parenting skills are very much learned "on the job." When the mother stays home with the newborn, she both gains competence and becomes known as the one who knows how to perform the relevant tasks, ultimately leading both parents and the children to look to her for these functions. Angie K. Young, Assessing the Family and Medical Leave Act in Terms of Gender Equality, Work/Family Balance, and the Needs of Children, 5 Mich. J. Gender & L. 113, 124–25 (1998). In Sweden, by contrast, parental leave can extend up to eighteen months (540 days), and the state provides a wage replacement for up to 480 days of the leave, but those days must be shared by the parents or else some of the wage replacement is forfeited. Julie Suk, Are Gender Stereotypes Bad for Women? Rethinking AntiDiscrimination Law and Work-Family Conflict, 110 Colum. L. Rev. 1, 24–40 (2010). Should we perhaps consider giving twelve weeks paid leave for each parent, nontransferable, so that to take advantage of twenty-four weeks of paid leave, the father as well as the mother would have to take twelve weeks off? Do you think that men would take leave under these conditions?

Michael Selmi believes that men will not take leave unless they are virtually forced to and suggests a government contract set-aside program which would require employers to establish generous leave policies and get at least 50% of their male employees to take at least six weeks of leave in order to qualify for federal contracts of a certain size. Selmi, Family Leave and the Gender Wage Gap, 78 N.C. L. Rev. 707, 775–76 (2000). He argues that:

> [I]ncreasing workplace equality will require persuading men to behave more like women, rather than trying to induce women to behave more like men. Achieving this objective would create a new workplace norm where all employees would be expected to have and spend time with their children, and employers would adapt to that reality.

Id. at 708. In other words, if women's current experiences, rather than men's, were taken as the norm, and men were required to share the experience of balancing work and family, employers would quickly see that paid family leave should be part of the regular package of employee benefits. Do you agree? Is this the only way to change what appear to be deeply-ingrained patterns of caregiving and worklife?

8. Other commentators surmise that men will begin to take more leave only if federal legislation permits employees to take leave for both caregiving and noncaregiving activities, thereby reducing "the stigma associated with the special needs of caregivers." Rachel Arnow–Richman, Incenting Flexibility: The Relationship Between Public Law and Voluntary Action in Enhancing Work/Life Balance, 42 Conn. L. Rev. 1081, 1109 (2010). These commentators therefore support the passage of the Working Families Flexibility Act, H.R. 1274, 111th Cong. § 3(a) (2009), which would create and protect an employee's right to apply for a change in schedule, if the change relates to "(1) the number of hours the employee is required to work; (2) the times when the employee is required to work; or (3) where the employee is required to work," although the bill imposes no obligation on the employer to agree to the change. Id. Vicki Schultz questions why most feminists are not supporting that bill but instead are "continuing to advocate for programs that offer flexibility to individual employees rather than for policies that would promote more predictable, more reasonable working hours for employees across the board." Schultz, Feminism and Workplace Flexibility, 42 Conn. L. Rev. 1203, 1211–12 (2010). What are the advantages and disadvantages of such an approach? Why do you think feminists have been slow to support the Working Families Flexibility Act? How might feminist attempts to achieve flexibility for women and mothers specifically, instead of for all workers, reinforce stereotypes of mothers and fathers? How would you compare such attempts to woman-specific protective labor legislation in the early 1900s?

9. In 2003, the Supreme Court decided a case upholding the FMLA as a constitutional exercise of legislative power in the face of an 11th Amendment challenge, holding that state employees may recover money damages in federal court if the state did not comply with the FMLA because Congress had clearly abrogated the states' immunity by passing the Act. Nevada Dep't of Human Res. v. Hibbs, 538 U.S. 721 (2003). The decision, written by then Chief Justice Rehnquist, was notable for emphasizing that the FMLA was designed to protect the right to be free of gender discrimination in employment by promoting the sharing of parental responsibilities:

> Stereotypes about women's domestic roles are reinforced by parallel stereotypes presuming a lack of domestic responsibilities for men. Because employers continued to regard the family as the woman's domain, they often denied men similar accommodations or discouraged them from taking leave. These mutually reinforcing stereotypes created a self-fulfill-

> ing cycle of discrimination that forced women to continue to assume the role of primary family caregiver, and fostered employers' stereotypical views about women's commitment to work and their value as employees. Those perceptions, in turn, Congress reasoned, lead to subtle discrimination that may be difficult to detect on a case-by-case basis.
>
> * * *
>
> * * * [T]he FMLA attacks the formerly state-sanctioned stereotype that only women are responsible for family caregiving, thereby reducing employers' incentives to engage in discrimination by basing hiring and promotion decisions on stereotypes.

Id. at 736–37. In light of Justice Rehnquist's earlier views in sex discrimination cases, as discussed in Chapter 2, are you surprised to see him articulate these arguments? Some surmise that his consciousness may have been raised by his wife's terminal illness and the needs of his single-parent lawyer daughter, who needed him to leave work several times to pick up his grandchildren when her own arrangements failed. See Joan C. Williams, *Hibbs* as a Federalism Case; *Hibbs* as a Maternal Wall Case, 73 U. Cin. L. Rev. 365, 374–75 (2004). Based on what you know about the structure of the FMLA, above, do you think this rhetoric reflects reality? Why or why not? Has use of the Act, described in note 3 above, achieved the goals Justice Rehnquist described in *Hibbs*?

10. A good deal of litigation over the FMLA has centered on the definition of a "serious health condition." The case law is mixed, but a case holding that the flu could be a serious health condition for purposes of taking family leave alarmed many employers. Miller v. AT&T, 250 F.3d 820 (4th Cir. 2001). Feminist commentators argue that the courts' permissive interpretation of a serious health condition could transform the FMLA into "a broader family accommodation statute." Katharine B. Silbaugh, Is the Work–Family Conflict Pathological or Normal Under the FMLA? The Potential of the FMLA to Cover Ordinary Work–Family Conflicts, 15 Wash. U. J.L. & Pol'y 193, 204–06 (2004). Do you think it is possible that the FMLA could evolve into such a statute? Why or why not? Would this be preferable to the Working Families Flexibility Act?

11. Prior to passage of the FMLA, Nadine Taub pointed out that a leave program tied to traditional family relationships would prove inadequate in a society where the pool of formally related, and thus statutorily qualified, caregivers has been heavily reduced by divorce, step-parenting, cohabitation, extended family, and other networking arrangements for child care. See Taub, From Parental Leaves to Nurturing Leaves, 13 N.Y.U. Rev. L. & Soc. Change 381, 391–94 (1984–85). Taub argued, in addition, that "[t]o structure a benefit program around membership in the family is to reward and attempt to channel people into an institution that has proved oppressive to many, generally women." Id. at 393. How can these problems be addressed? The only attempt made to address these issues on the federal level is through administrative regulations defining a child under the FMLA as a "biological, adopted, or foster child, a stepchild, a legal ward, or a child of a person standing in loco parentis...." 29 C.F.R. § 825.113(a),(c) (1993). Does the Act reflect the diversity of family structures in our society, including both the frequency of

cohabitation and family-like relationships in Black communities, as described by Laura Kessler in the previous section? The District of Columbia Family and Medical Leave Act, adopted as a result of the efforts of a broad coalition including both the lesbian and gay communities and the Black community contains a very broad definition of family, including anyone with whom a worker shares a residence and has a "committed relationship." D.C. Code § 32–501(4)(c) (2001). How, if at all, would you change the definition of who is to qualify for leave under the FMLA?

12. Care of the elderly is a task that also falls disproportionately upon women in our society. Women provide about 70% of all elder care, and the burden is expected to rise with the aging of the population. Peggie R. Smith, Elder Care, Gender, and Work: The Work–Family Issue of the 21st Century, 25 Berkeley J. Emp. & Lab. L. 351, 355–64 (2004). See also Nat'l Alliance for Caregiving & AARP, Caregiving in the U.S. 8, 23 (2004) (reporting that female caregivers provide more hours of care and more intensive care than male caregivers). Data from the 1988 National Survey of Families and Households showed that 14.4% of women respondents who both work and fulfill traditional caregiving roles also report caring for someone with a serious illness or disability. See Carol L. Jenkins, Women, Work, and Caregiving: How Do These Roles Affect Women's Well-being?, 9 J. Women & Aging 27, 34–40 (1997). This unpaid care by women allows elderly persons to remain in the community rather than be institutionalized and/or dependent upon society at large for financial support. Id. at 40. The impact of such care on employment is substantial: 16% of elder caregivers quit their jobs; 38% take time off; 30% rearrange work schedules; and 21% work fewer hours. Smith, above, at 370–71. One author suggests that policymakers should consider the social benefits of this unpaid caregiving for the elderly and provide aid in the form of adult day care, meals-on-wheels, and respite care. Jenkins, above, at 41–42.

FMLA provides a limited response to this problem, constrained by the facts that it is unpaid and only applies to employers with fifty or more employees, among other things. The nuclear family-based definition of family also is a problem, in part because many elderly persons are cared for by their daughters-in-law (this is particularly common among some ethnic groups, such as Koreans) and they are not eligible for leave under the Act. Smith, above, at 393–97. Why do you think the lion's share of caring for the elderly falls upon women in our society? What additional public or legal responses to this problem can you imagine? Why don't we hear more about the need to get men to care for the elderly?

2. PAID LEAVE

GILLIAN LESTER, A DEFENSE OF PAID FAMILY LEAVE

28 Harv. J.L. & Gender 1, 31–33, 36, 38, 50, 54, 61, 64–66, 72–76, 78, 82–83 (2005).

The problem of combining work and family life is perhaps the central challenge for the contemporary American family. In this Article, I evaluate and defend government provision of paid family leave, a benefit that would allow workers to take compensated time off from work for purposes of family caregiving.

A legal intervention in the arena of work-family accommodation can only build on some prior normative understanding of the family, and embedded within that, contested value choices about women's identities and entitlements in workplace, family, and society.

* * *

The effects of caregiving obligations on women are intimately tied to their labor market participation and to the qualitative features of their employment in terms of pay and career advancement. * * * The text of the FMLA explicitly acknowledges that unequal family care burdens affect the working lives of women, and that promoting the goal of equal employment opportunity for women and men is consistent with the Equal Protection Clause of the Fourteenth Amendment. Recently, the Supreme Court spoke very powerfully to the importance of the preventative remedial measures embodied in the FMLA for achieving gender equality in the distribution of family caregiving obligations and paid employment opportunities.[136] If the social norm that women bear the bulk of family caregiving obligations plays a causal role in producing inequality between men and women in paid labor markets, then addressing this causal link is a concern for *all of society,* not just for working women. Work-family policies that erode gender inequality in paid employment will in turn enhance solidarity in a society that values such equality.

At the same time, participation in paid employment may have significant psychological benefits for women. Increasing women's opportunities to engage in market work may enhance their ability to live a life free from dependency, and thus create the conditions for reaching their fullest human potential.

Although both of these reasons might justify labor market interventions designed to erode the existing differentiation in men's and women's market and family roles, they may implicate different mechanisms for *financing* these interventions. An argument for financing a social program in a way that redistributes wealth is best supported with evidence that the program will confer a benefit on society as a whole rather than just on those who receive the specific program benefits. When the societal benefits of a program are highly targeted, it is normatively easier to justify state intervention if the method for financing the program involves cost-internalization by program beneficiaries. * * * I have offered a basis for defending labor market intervention to increase equality between men and women in the domestic and market spheres on both grounds. Such intervention would confer benefits on women themselves, in the form of their greater autonomy, and society as a whole, in the form of upholding the fundamental societal value of equality in the paid labor economy.

136. Nev. Dep't of Human Res. v. Hibbs, 538 U.S. 721, 736 (2003). * * *

IV. THE EFFECT OF PAID FAMILY LEAVE ON WOMEN'S WORKFORCE PARTICIPATION

* * *

* * * [E]conomic theory predicts that government mandates requiring paid leave for maternity purposes will affect different mothers differently: some will be unaffected, some will take longer leaves, some will take leaves instead of quitting, and some will enter the workforce who would not have done so otherwise. How aggregate labor supply (and demand) will change are empirical questions. Certainly, paid leave may confer benefits on workers and society aside from its effects on women's workforce participation. For example, it may have the beneficial effects of improving parent-infant bonding, and improve the health outcomes of sick children and disabled elders. However, from the normative perspective of encouraging women's involvement in market work, a leave program that results in some women taking more and longer leaves, thus decreasing their workforce experience, will have a net positive effect only so long as it: (1) does not actually lead them to quit or take extremely long leaves, and (2) has the offsetting effect of encouraging other women to join the workforce or refrain from quitting.

* * *

* * * [E]mpirical studies suggest that paid leave policies increase the likelihood that women will take leave. At the same time, modestly generous leave policies appear to hasten women's return to work and increase the likelihood that they will return to their former employer. Such returns are associated with higher pay, greater use of skill, and more hours of work. Looking at labor market supply generally, paid leave policies appear to increase women's overall labor market participation.

* * *

VI. FINANCING PAID LEAVE

The cost of a paid family leave policy and who will pay for it are both issues central to my proposal. I argue in this Part that at least some of the costs of paid leave should be spread beyond leave-takers, in part to avoid undermining the normative goal of work-attachment that informs this analysis, and in part in keeping with the ethical argument made earlier that society has a broad interest in this form of social provision.

* * *

Two common ways to finance social welfare benefits to redistribute wealth are payroll taxes and general revenue financing. Relying on payroll taxes allows for the redistribution of costs between workers, and using general revenues can produce an even broader spreading of costs. The next two sections discuss each of these mechanisms in light of the social objectives of paid family leave.

1. Payroll Taxes

In the United States, social insurance programs have historically been financed using payroll taxes rather than general revenues. All the major social insurance programs—Social Security, Medicare, federal long-term disability insurance, state temporary disability insurance, and unemployment insurance—are financed in whole or in large part through payroll taxes. Moreover, the trend is toward increasing reliance on the payroll tax.

A payroll tax may be imposed on employers, employees, or both. The focal point of public debates about payroll taxes often centers on whom, as between employers and employees, should bear the tax, the assumption being that it will have implications for wealth distribution. Such debates, however, overlook the important issue of tax incidence. The economic burden of a payroll tax may differ from the legal burden. Both theory and empirical evidence suggest that whatever the statutory burden may be, a payroll tax does not significantly redistribute wealth from employers to employees.

* * *

2. General Revenues

General tax revenues, either state or federal, are a common source of funding for social insurance programs outside of the United States. For example, many European Union countries have paid family leave programs financed at least partly by general revenues.

Financing through general funds distributes the economic costs of a benefit most broadly. Included in general revenues are all income taxes (not just wage income), corporate taxes, excise and sales taxes, estate and gift taxes, and payroll taxes. In essence, all taxpayers contribute to general revenues in proportion to their tax burdens. Therefore, this method of financing draws revenues from a broader swath of the population than a payroll tax, which targets employers and workers alone.

* * *

3. Empirical Evidence of Cost–Shifting Effects of Paid Leave Policies on Women's Wages

* * *

Ruhm's twenty-four-year survey of paid parental leave mandates in Europe * * * examined wage effects.[137] Recall that in the period analyzed, entitlements tripled in generosity. The overall average wage replacement rate by the end of the period analyzed was about 80%. Paid, job-protected leaves of relatively short duration (ten weeks) had little consequence for women's wages (not just mothers), although leaves of longer duration (twenty to forty weeks) were associated with a 2%–3% wage reduction. Ruhm's study suggests that paid leave policies, at least those that permit

137. *See* [Christopher J.] Ruhm, *Economic Consequences of Parental Leave* [*Mandates: Lessons from Europe,* 113 Q.J. ECON. 285 (1998)].

shorter-duration leaves (somewhere between ten and twenty weeks), can increase women's workforce participation without significantly reducing their wages. The absence of a wage effect suggests that either the costs to employers of short leaves are trivial, or that for shorter duration leaves, the positive wage effects of increased workforce attachment—and the employee's attachment to a particular employer—may offset any costs shifted to female workers.

* * *

* * * [P]aid leave policies may result in wage costs to workers most likely to take leave—women in their childbearing years. This is not necessarily bad for women. If women want paid leave benefits, but the market does not provide them, they may be more willing to work, even at a reduced wage, in a regime that mandates these benefits. In that case, the beneficiaries of the program would essentially internalize its costs. Still, there is a strong normative claim that the costs of paid leave benefits should be more widely spread. * * *

VII. IMPLEMENTING PAID FAMILY LEAVE

* * *

A number of models have been proposed for implementing a paid family leave program. These include expanding existing state UI [unemployment insurance] programs, expanding existing state TDI [temporary disability insurance] programs and creating new ones, creating separate family leave insurance programs, providing incentives for employers to expand sick leave policies, and reimbursing employers who voluntarily create paid leave programs.

* * * Building on to an existing administrative infrastructure is likely to be more efficient than starting a program from the ground up. * * *

* * *

In terms of both conceptual fit and practical design features * * * the TDI model seems more adaptable than the UI model to the aims of a paid family leave program. In general, TDI programs tend to have a higher taxable wage base than UI programs (meaning there is greater progressivity of the tax and benefit schedule), and would require less dramatic modifications of the basic features of the program than if UI were adapted to accommodate family leaves (e.g., there is no experience rating and no "able and available" requirement in TDI programs). The "pay or play" concept in several of the TDI schemes is particularly attractive in its capacity to give employers the opportunity to experiment with private plans, possibly offering greater incentives for some employers to set an example by offering programs that exceed the minimum. Only five states currently have TDI programs, but several administer them through the state UI infrastructure. Thus it would be possible to create a paid family leave insurance program that tapped state UI administrative infrastructure without being subject to the constraints of the UI program itself.

As an example, consider the new California Family Temporary Disability Insurance ("FTDI"), which adds family illness and nonmaternity parental benefits to the existing State Disability Insurance ("SDI") benefits of personal illness and maternity leave. The SDI program, although conceptually distinct from UI, is operated through the state's UI administrative apparatus. The new benefits are financed with a fairly low tax on employees' wages. In 2004 and 2005, it will be .08% of their wages up to the taxable wage limit of $68,829 in 2004 and $79,418 in 2005; it is subject to further increase in later years, up to a maximum of 1.5%. This is an average of about $70 per employee per year. The program covers about 70% of California's workforce, with eligibility requiring wage earnings of at least $300 in a twelve-month base period prior to application for benefits. It provides wage replacement at approximately 55% for up to six weeks, with weekly benefits in 2004 ranging from a minimum of $50 to a maximum of $728. Personal illness and maternity leave benefits in California's preexisting state disability insurance program provide up to fifty-two weeks' wage replacement (on the same terms as above).

B. *Financing*

* * *

If financed through a payroll tax, there is a question of whether the nominal tax should fall on employers, workers, or both. I mentioned that although in theory a nominal tax on employers will be passed fully to workers, in practice, employers may find it difficult to pass the tax fully to workers. This leads to fuller cost-sharing, at least in the short run, than if the tax is imposed entirely on workers. At the same time, imposing the nominal tax at least partly on workers may have stronger political appeal and facilitate buy-in by the public and pro-business legislators. As I have argued, cost internalization by the class of individuals covered by the benefit may be acceptable, and perhaps appropriate, as long as the degree of cost-shifting to leave-takers is not so great as to undermine the work incentive effects that I argue are so central to the value of paid leave. An across-the-board payroll tax, by tolling workers while at the same time spreading costs beyond the subclass of workers most likely to take leaves, may strike a reasonable balance in this regard. There should also be a relatively high ceiling on the taxable wage base, closer to what we see for Social Security than for UI, to avoid regressivity.

I have also argued that at least some degree of general revenue financing is ethically justified. States may be open to funding paid leave at least partly through general funds: in the wake of BAABUC [the Clinton Administration's regulations allowing states to fund leave out of unemployment insurance, repealed by President Bush], several states considered bills for paid family leave that would be financed in part through direct general fund allocations or state tax credits. Thus general revenue financing may be more politically plausible than some commentators have suggested. One appealing suggestion is to use a general fund allocation to reimburse employers based on how many workers actually take leaves, and in doing so, reduce the likelihood of employers shifting "disruption costs" to leave-takers in the form of targeted wage or employment reductions.

A program of paid family leave insurance, then, could be funded by a payroll tax on employers, workers, or both. The resulting trust fund could also be augmented with general tax revenues, although it seems unrealistic and perhaps imprudent to advocate for a system funded entirely through general funds.

C. Wage Replacement

* * *

There are a number of ways to structure benefits aimed at progressivity while also satisfying competing concerns. I recommend benefits paid as a percentage of pre-leave earnings with a floor and ceiling imposed, rather than flat rate payments based on average wages, as some have proposed. Because they are less likely to under-or overcompensate workers whose wages deviate from the average, wage-proportional benefits are better suited than flat benefits to sustaining workers' standard of living and avoiding the necessity of major structural changes to the family economy during leave. For this to hold true, the percentage of wage replacement should be fairly generous, perhaps 70% of pre-leave earnings. Less than full wage replacement is also [a] classic check against moral hazard; a slight but not excessive drop in earnings allows workers to avoid major shocks to their standard of living while also minimizing frivolous leave-taking and maintaining work incentives. One risk of providing only partial wage replacement is that lower-earning workers will receive benefits that are too low to enable them to take leave, and that the benefit may therefore be skewed toward middle-and upper-income workers. A floor and ceiling on benefits ensures provision that is both sufficient at the low end and simultaneously limited at the high end where workers are most likely to have an adequate personal safety net or private employer benefits. In addition, exempting lower-income workers from the payroll tax would help avoid the potential for regressivity in the program.

D. Eligibility

* * *

* * * Paid family leave insurance should include workers whose work hours are substantial and whose attachment to the workforce is stable, even if they fail to meet the work-hours test for any single employer. Including workers who piece together full or substantial work hours with multiple employers seems unlikely to create significant incentives for workers to become "trapped" in such arrangements because these workers likely prefer more stable employment and will continue to seek such opportunities. Furthermore, paid leave may facilitate the move toward more stable workforce attachment in these workers if it helps them avoid downward mobility and family restructuring in the event of work inter-

ruption. Therefore, eligibility requirements for paid leave should permit the aggregation of hours worked across employers.

* * *

F. Duration of Benefits

* * * [B]enefits of excessive duration may undermine the goal of increasing women's workforce attachment. Examples from the European literature of excessively generous benefits may be found in the three-year paid programs offered in France and Germany. While some speculation is required, three to four months' wage replacement per year for all covered work interruptions seems more sensible. The California program, which offers six weeks' compensation, may reflect a more realistic picture of what is politically possible.

VIII. CONCLUSION

* * *

* * * [B]oth theory and existing empirical work suggest that the effectiveness of paid leave policies in increasing women's workforce attachment may require limiting the duration of leaves and financing benefits in a way that avoids shifting excessive costs of the program to women. The argument for spreading the costs of leave policies is driven in part by the practical observation that the very incentive to enter into or remain attached to the workforce may be thwarted if the full cost of caregiving accommodations is borne by women workers. However, the argument for cost spreading also has an ethical element: increasing women's workforce participation will advance the broader social project of reducing gender inequality in paid employment.

NOTES ON PAID LEAVE

1. Lester states that her main goal is to increase the attachment of women to the labor force, both in order to avoid dependency on male breadwinners and for a variety of additional psychological benefits. See Lester, above, at 25–32. Do you think this should be a major objective of family leave policy? Why or why not? What other goals do you think should be central to such a policy? See, e.g., Christopher J. Ruhm, Parental Leave and Child Health, 19 J. Health Econ. 931 (2000) (finding strong correlation between generous paid leave in European countries and reduction in post-neonatal deaths, that is, in infants and young children). How, if at all, would Lester's analysis be different if other goals were central to it?

2. Lester's article contains much more detail about the different empirical studies summarized in the excerpt above, as well as about the economics of the various proposed arrangements. The two models discussed for financing such a leave in the U.S. are temporary disability insurance (TDI) and unemployment insurance (UI). TDI is funded by a payroll tax imposed on a relatively high wage base (up to $35,495, compared to $9,000 for UI on the

average). Lester, above, at 70. Both TDI and UI replace about half an employee's weekly wages. Id. at 68. The average duration of disability leaves is about eight weeks, and that under UI is 13.8 weeks, though the maximum duration can be 26 weeks. Id. at 71. UI addresses an involuntary situation in which the person is actively seeking work. Id. at 69. Which of these models seems more appropriate for funding family leave?

Sweden finances its comprehensive system through a combination of payroll tax and general government revenue. Arielle Horman Grill, The Myth of Unpaid Family Leave: Can the United States Implement a Paid Leave Policy Based on the Swedish Model?, 17 Comp. Lab. L.J. 373, 380 (1996). The Canadian system relies upon unemployment insurance to provide payment for family leave. Donna Lenhoff & Claudia Withers, Implementation of the Family and Medical Leave Act: Toward the Family–Friendly Workplace, 3 J. Gender & L. 39, 54 (1994). Which of these systems seems to you to be the fairest? The most economically feasible? The most politically feasible in the U.S.?

3. Most employees taking leave under the FMLA cobble together some kind of wage replacement through use of accrued vacation pay, disability pay, or sick pay. About 42% of private employers provide at least partly paid leave during the period of physical disability for maternity; women in high-wage employment are especially likely to get generous treatment. See Lester, above, at 9, 75. These methods place the costs of leave upon either the individual employee or the employee and the employer. Some commentators urge direct governmental financing, both because the benefits accrue to society as a whole and in order not to promote sex segregation in the workplace or overburden businesses that have a limited ability to pass on costs. Angie K. Young, Assessing the Family and Medical Leave Act in Terms of Gender Equality, Work/Family Balance, and the Needs of Children, 5 Mich. J. Gender & L. 113, 156 (1998). What problems would you foresee in pressing for payment out of general revenue in the United States?

4. President Clinton proposed that states be permitted to fund paid family leave through their unemployment insurance programs, a proposal that was withdrawn by the Bush Administration. Peter A. Susser, The Employer Perspective on Paid Leave & the FMLA, 15 Wash. U. J.L. & Pol'y 169, 179–86 (2004). In 2007, then Senator Edward Kennedy sponsored the Unemployment Insurance Modernization Act, S. 1871, 110th Cong. (2007), which lapsed and never reached a vote. It has been proposed again in the House as H.R. 290, 111th Cong. (2009). The bill seeks to incentivize states to expand their unemployment benefits to part-time workers and to workers who need to take time off from work because of domestic violence. On the executive level, President Obama's budget includes funding for states to start paid family leave programs. See Jennifer Ludden, Obama Budget Pushes Paid Leave Programs, NPR (May 10, 2010), http://www.npr.org/templates/story/story.php?storyId=126557919.

As of 2009, five states (California, Hawaii, New Jersey, New York, and Rhode Island) had programs funding childbirth leave through TDI. See Sarah

Fass, National Center for Children in Poverty, Paid Leave in the States: 6 (2009). Should the federal government do more to encourage states to experiment with paid leave programs, or would it be better to pursue a federal paid leave law? Or should feminists pursue litigation? Which path is likely to gain more support from employers and workers? See Patricia A. Shiu & Stephanie M. Wildman, Pregnancy Discrimination and Social Change: Evolving Consciousness About a Worker's Right to Job-Protected Paid Leave, 21 Yale J.L. & Feminism 119, 158–59 (2009) (suggesting that while litigation is useful for raising consciousness, true support for California's paid pregnancy leave came from the will of the people through the legislature).

5. California was the first state to pass a state-supported paid family leave law, in contrast to childbirth leave. Since then, New Jersey and Washington have followed suit. All three states offer between five and six weeks of leave upon the birth or adoption of a child or to care for a sick family member. California's maximum weekly benefit is by far the most generous (nearly four times that of Washington's, and twice that of New Jersey's). See Fass, above note 4, at 8 fig.2.

California passed its legislation, the California Family Temporary Disability Insurance Law, in 2002, providing six weeks of leave paid at 55% of an employee's average salary. The act, unlike the FMLA, covers all employees, not just those working for employers of fifty employees or more, and defines the family member entitled to the leave as a child, spouse, parent, or domestic partner. See Cal. Unemp. Ins. Code § 3301 (2004); Jennifer Thompson, Family and Medical Leave for the 21st Century?: A First Glance at California's Paid Family Leave Legislation, 12 U. Miami Bus. L. Rev. 77, 92–94 (2004).

In 2008, New Jersey adopted a paid leave system similar to California's, N.J. Stat. Ann. § 34:11B–1 et seq. (West 2010), which provides six weeks of benefits to covered individuals to "bond" with newborn or newly adopted children, or to care for sick family members. The New Jersey Department of Labor reports that the program, known as Family Leave Insurance, has proven to be successful so far, in that the state has collected nearly double the amount in payroll deductions that it has paid out in benefits. The majority of those taking leave in New Jersey are women ages 25 to 44 working in the private sector. The average length of leave has been only 4.5 weeks, less than the projected 5.5 weeks and also less than the maximum amount of paid leave permitted, six weeks. See Editorial, Family Business, Phila. Inquirer, July 10, 2010. Additionally, in the one-year period between July 2009 and June 2010, 80% of the eligible claims were "bonding" claims for birth or adoption of children. N.J. Dep't of Labor & Workplace Dev., Family Leave Insurance Program Statistics, http://lwd.dol.state.nj.us/labor/fli/content/monthly_report_fli.html.

The state of Washington has also passed legislation providing for paid leave upon the birth or adoption of a child, but the law has yet to go into effect, in large part because Washington, unlike California and New Jersey, did not have a pre-existing temporary disability insurance program. Fass, above note 4, at 9. Do you think any of these states provide good models for other states to follow? What type of benefits, if any, would you be entitled to in your state and/or from your employer if you wanted to take leave after bringing a child into your family?

6. Many studies consider the so-called "family gap"—that is, the difference between male and female pay that is caused by family status and, in particular, motherhood. In the U.S., this gap is 20%; that is, mothers earn about 70% of men's pay while nonmothers earn 90%. Jane Waldfogel, The Family Gap for Young Women in the United States and Britain: Can Maternity Leave Make a Difference?, 16 J. Lab. Econ. 505, 532 (1998). Waldfogel's study found that women with leave coverage received a wage premium that offset the negative wage effect of having children because they were more likely to return to their previous employer. Id. at 529–30, 534. See also Jean Kimmel & Catalina Amuedo–Dorantes, The Effects of Family Leave on Wages, Employment, and the Family Wage Gap: Distributional Implications, 15 Wash. U. J.L. & Pol'y 115, 139 (2004) (finding that the job protective effect of the FMLA overcomes the potential wage-depressing effect). Christopher J. Ruhm's 24-year survey of paid parental leave mandates in Europe found that leaves of relatively short duration (10 to 20 weeks) can increase women's workforce participation without significantly reducing their wages. Ruhm, The Economic Consequences of Parental Leave Mandates: Lessons from Europe, 113 Q.J. Econ. 285, 311–15 (1998). (Of course, leaves in Europe are subsidized from general revenues so that the cost does not fall directly upon the employer.) A recent study published by the Swedish Institute for Labour Market Evaluation looks at the effect of enforced paternal parental leave on maternal wages, namely that "[e]ach additional month that the father stays on parental leave increases mothers' earnings by 6.7 percent." Elly–Ann Johannson, The Effect of Own and Spousal Parental Leave on Earnings 28 (Inst. for Labour Mkt. Evaluation, Working Paper No. 2010:4), http://www.ifau.se/upload/pdf/se/2010/wp10–4–The-effect-of-own-and-spousal-parental-leave-on-earnings.pdf. Is family leave essential to effectuate the goals of the Equal Pay Act?

7. Even if paid family leave was instituted in all states, it is unlikely that women and men would take leave in equal numbers. Should feminists be concerned about that possibility? The Center for Economic and Policy Analysis postulates that "[i]f parental leave does not replace a substantial portion of fathers' earnings, families will bear a greater financial burden when fathers take leave than when mothers take leave." Rebecca Ray, Janet G. Gornick & John Schmitt, Ctr. for Econ. & Policy Research, Parental Leave Policies in 21 Countries: Assessing Generosity and Gender Equality 13 (2008). Should feminists urge states to incentivize fathers to take parental leave through increasing benefit amounts? Without such an incentive, do you think men would be willing to take paid leave? With an increased benefit, do you think employers would be more or less receptive to fathers taking leave upon the birth or adoption of a child?

3. SOME INTERNATIONAL COMPARISONS

JULIE SUK, ARE GENDER STEREOTYPES BAD FOR WOMEN? RETHINKING ANTIDISCRIMINATION LAW AND WORK-FAMILY CONFLICT

110 Colum. L. Rev. 1, 24–40 (2010).

III. The Social Welfare State's Support for Parenthood

* * * In European countries, comprehensive social welfare policies promote the well-being of children raised by their mothers and fathers. These policies include maternity and parental leave that are separately categorized and treated much more generously than all other forms of leave, including sick leave. * * *

The European approach demonstrates that it is possible to be generous with maternity and parental leave without being equally generous with medical leave. This understanding of European family and sick leave policies exposes the dysfunction of the United States's single regime that links together family and medical leave.

A. The European Directive

A 1992 EU directive imposed minimum standards on the member states regarding the legal protection of the "safety and health at work of pregnant workers and workers who have recently given birth or are breastfeeding." This directive required at least fourteen weeks of maternity leave "in accordance with national legislation and/or practice." The article on maternity leave also stipulates that the fourteen weeks of leave "must include compulsory maternity leave of at least two weeks allocated before and/or after confinement in accordance with national legislation and/or practice."

The directive also requires member states to adopt measures to ensure that pregnant workers can receive paid time off of work for prenatal care. Furthermore, to protect pregnant workers from discrimination, the directive requires member states to adopt laws protecting employees from dismissal from the beginning of their pregnancy until the end of their maternity leave, except in "exceptional cases not connected with their condition."

* * *

B. Family Policy in France

In comparative studies, social scientists often identify France as a country with extensive, generous policies that help women combine paid work and family responsibilities. The policies that support working mothers in France originated in the state's early twentieth-century attempts to protect mothers and children. These early attempts were largely justified by a desire to stimulate birth rates and protect infant health. Since the

1970s, gender equality has also been raised as a reason for improving work-family reconciliation policies, but policymakers have been ambivalent about this goal. Therefore, the protection of mothers and children continues to be emphasized even in current proposals to lengthen maternity leave. * * *

1. Maternity Leave.—The Labor Code entitles female employees to various absences from work due to pregnancy and maternity. These entitlements are more extensive than those available to employees who are otherwise temporarily disabled by physical illness. First, every female employee is entitled to a congé de maternité, or "maternity leave," totaling sixteen weeks, of which six may be taken before the due date. During the maternity leave, the employment contract is suspended, but the leave period is still taken into account for purposes of seniority. * * * At the end of the leave, the employee is entitled to "her previous job or a similar job with, at the very least, equivalent pay." * * *

A portion of the maternity leave is mandatory for both the employee and the employer. While American women are applauded for working until they go into labor, French women are normally not permitted to do so. An employee may, with the permission of the medical professional monitoring her pregnancy, shorten the leave prior to birth to three weeks, in which case the period of leave to which she is entitled following the birth is augmented. In a similar paternalistic vein, the Code prohibits employers from employing pregnant women and postnatal women too close to the time of giving birth. By making eight weeks of maternity leave mandatory, the Labor Code sets aside two months during which female employees cannot choose to work, thereby making it impossible for employers to encourage women to take shorter leave or to reward those who forego leave altogether.

The Labor Code does not require the employer to pay the employee during maternity leave. Rather, female employees are guaranteed wage replacement through a regime known as Assurance Maternité, or "Maternity Insurance." * * * In addition to wage replacement, Maternity Insurance covers, first and foremost, all the medical and pharmaceutical expenses related to pregnancy, childbirth, and postpartum, including laboratory tests and hospitalization. Maternity Insurance also includes a daily cash benefit to replace wages for six weeks before the due date and ten weeks after, provided that the woman has stopped paid work during this period, with augmentations for multiple births or the birth of a third child. This provision also reiterates the rule that the pregnant employee must stop working for at least eight weeks around the time of the birth.

* * *

3. Paternity Leave.—Unlike U.S. law, French law treats paternity leave differently from maternity leave. The father of a newborn, upon giving his employer one month's notice, has the right to a congé de paternité, or "paternity leave," of eleven consecutive days of leave (eigh-

teen in the case of multiple births), during which time the employment contract is suspended. * * * In addition, the Labor Code guarantees that a father can return to his previous job or a similar job, with pay that is at least equal. As with maternity leave, the provisions for pay during paternity leave are found in the Social Security Code. Provided that he stops working, the father is entitled to a daily stipend equivalent to that received by mothers on maternity leave. However, fathers are entitled to leave that is comparable in length to those enjoyed by mothers only if the mother dies. If the mother dies during her maternity leave, fathers become entitled to ten weeks of leave and a suspension of their employment contract. But, unlike maternity leave, paternity leave is never compulsory.

4. Support for Parenthood and Childrearing.—In addition to maternity and paternity leave, for up to a year, French employees, regardless of gender, are entitled to take a congé parental d'éducation, or "parental leave for education," during which either the employment contract is suspended, or, if they choose, their working hours are reduced to no less than sixteen hours a week. Persons on such leave are entitled to monthly, flat-rate childrearing benefits. The parental leave can be prolonged twice, up until the third birthday of the child. Employees who are on parental leave are not permitted to engage in any professional activities, but they are permitted to engage in training and education. Half of the period of the parental leave is counted towards the employee's seniority, and the employee is entitled to his or her previous job, or a similar job with at least equivalent pay, upon return.

* * *

In addition to employment laws guaranteeing various forms of leave related to caring for children, the French state provides cash benefits to support parenthood. Some of these benefits are only available to persons whose income is below a certain ceiling, but several benefits, which I shall outline here, are available to all parents, so long as they have worked for statutorily required amounts of time. A person who interrupts his or her professional activities to look after a child under the age of three is entitled to a monthly stipend for libre choix d'activité, or "free choice of activity," for up to six months. The person must have worked for at least two years to be eligible. A separate category of benefit, with higher stipend awards, is available for a person who interrupts professional activities for a year to take care of at least three children. For dual-earner households, a benefit for libre choix du mode de garde, or "free choice of form of care," is available. This benefit covers the social security taxes that the parent owes when hiring a home-based caregiver for a child under the age of six years.

The government also provides early schooling to assist with childcare. Nursery schools for children between the ages of two and six, known as écoles maternelles, are part of the national education system. These schools both provide childcare and educational services. About twenty-five percent of all two year olds, and almost all children between the ages of three and six, are enrolled. The écoles maternelles are administered, free of charge to parents, by municipal governments.

* * *

For children under two years of age, regional and municipal governments provide a variety of childcare options that are generously subsidized. For example, the crèches collectives are daycare centers that care for babies from ten weeks of age. There are also crèches familiales, or "family daycares," in which an assistante maternelle, a state-licensed childcare provider, cares for children in her home. Unlike the écoles maternelles, the crèches collectives are not free. Parents are charged according to a formula that calculates the fee based on the parents' income.

The various forms of parental leave in France, in addition to cash support for childrearing, state-subsidized childcare, and early childhood education, support the conclusion that French law and public policy affirmatively support parenthood and childrearing within the nuclear family. Taken together, these policies make it easier for women to work and raise children.

5. The Separate Medical Leave Regime.—Unlike American law, French law treats pregnancy and maternity differently from illness and medical incapacity. Although the funds for maternity insurance come from sickness insurance funds, a separate set of rules applies only to sick leave. Although the law recognizes important commonalities between maternity and temporary disability, it nonetheless administers them through separate legal rules. * * *

French legal thinkers * * * justify the separation of the sick leave regime from the maternity leave regime on two grounds. First, maternity protections are special because they necessarily implicate the well-being of the future child. Second, a sick leave system needs rules that curb the dangers of fraud, which are far less relevant to maternity protections. The upshot of these differences between maternity and sickness benefits is that generosity is more appropriate to the former.

* * *

Sick leave is distinct from maternity leave. French case law makes clear that the annual vacation days accrued by a female employee are to be taken separately from maternity leave; an employer cannot deny a woman her thirty days of paid vacation on the grounds that she has already taken them while on maternity leave. But taking days off for one's own illness can decrease the number of vacation days to which an employee is entitled annually.

* * * An employer cannot fire a person simply on the basis of their state of health, but can ultimately fire an employee whose absences due to illness disrupt the functioning of the enterprise. By contrast, an employer

cannot fire a pregnant employee, short of serious fault on the employee's part.

In this regime, the employee's incentive to abuse sick leave is limited, as compared with the American regime. For one thing, if he "calls in sick," his day off is somewhat dampened by a trip to the doctor's office to get a medical certificate. By contrast, * * * under the FMLA, American employers can require medical certificates from employees, but once a doctor certifies an "intermittent" condition, employees have the right to take leave whenever they themselves deem it necessary, without additional certification for each absence, until they exhaust the twelve weeks per year allotted by statute. Until the twelve weeks are exhausted, adverse actions against the employee constitute an interference with the exercise of his FMLA rights. By contrast, in France, taking such significant sick leave could lead to an employee's termination for cause, provided that such behavior was sufficiently disruptive to the enterprise.

C. Family Policy in Sweden

Swedish family policy is similar to French family policy in some respects. It, too, offers maternity leave immediately before and after the birth of a newborn as a special category of protection for female employees. Like the French state, the Swedish state provides a variety of subsidies to support parents, as well as a system of public daycare and early childhood education. Unlike France, however, Sweden has pursued the explicit purpose of bringing about a more equitable division of labor within families and homes, by using both gender specific and gender neutral initiatives. Like the French policies, Swedish maternity leave originated in early twentieth-century initiatives designed to protect women and children and to stabilize decreasing birth rates. However, reforms in the 1960s and 1970s reframed the purpose of paid parental leave as gender equality in the family. As a result, Swedish parental leave law provides long periods of paid gender neutral parental leave, with added incentives for men to take parental leave.

1. Parental Leave.—The Swedish parental leave scheme attracts much attention and discussion, as it is thought to be among the most generous in the world. The Parental Leave Act provides for maternity leave for female employees in connection with childbirth or breastfeeding, but paid parental leave is available to both mothers and fathers. The maternity leave consists of job-protected leave for fourteen weeks, seven of which may be used prior to the due date. There is no specific requirement that the maternity leave be paid, but normally women are paid because they simultaneously take maternity leave and paid parental leave, the latter of which is available to both sexes.

The Parental Leave Act enables Swedish parents to take "full leave for the care of a child until the child reaches eighteen months, irrespective of whether the parent receives parental benefit." The parental benefit is paid by the state, pursuant to the National Insurance Act, for up to 480 days that a parent forgoes gainful employment to look after a child. The

480 days of pay are allocated per child, to be shared by the parents. Thus, in a two-parent household, each parent is entitled to 240 days of the benefit. One parent may transfer all but sixty days of his or her allocation to the other parent. In other words, if only the mother takes leave, the family's total allocation of parental benefits in connection with care for one child is reduced to 420 days, and the father's sixty days of leave are lost to the family. Furthermore, as of July 2008, there is a "gender equality bonus" in the form of a tax rebate, with greater rebates for parents who share the leave as evenly as possible. The Parental Leave Act also makes it possible for parents to reduce their working hours during the period that they receive the parental benefit, with a proportionate reduction of the benefit.

* * *

3. Support for Parenthood and Childrearing.—Every child who lives in Sweden is entitled to a child allowance beginning the month after birth. The allowance is not taxed, and it is paid monthly until the child reaches the age of sixteen. The Swedish government also provides a childcare allowance for parents who care for sick or disabled children in their homes. In addition, as of July 2008, a new program provides for a childraising allowance to assist parents in their transition from parental leave to work. The childraising allowance, which is administered by municipal governments, is available to parents of children between the ages of one and three and can be combined with paid work.

Like France, the Swedish state provides extensive support for daycare and early childhood education. A 1999 study indicated that seventy-five percent of all Swedish children between the ages of one and five participate in public daycare. Every child over the age of one year is legally entitled to public childcare and preschool. As in France, these preschools are seen as having an educational, as well as a childcare, function. According to the Ministry of Education, "[t]he task of the pre-school is to make the most of this thirst for knowledge and lay the foundations for a lifelong learning process." The Education Act also imposes standards with regard to the quality of care: Over half of all preschool employees have university degrees in preschool education.

4. The Separate Medical Leave Regime.—Like France, Sweden has a sick leave regime that is separate from its family leave regime. Unlike France, Sweden has been struggling over the last few years with its paid sick leave policy, due to widespread concerns about its overuse and abuse. In Sweden, the law effectively allows workers to take paid sick leave for up to seven days whenever they deem it necessary, since employers can only require medical certification for absences lasting longer than a week. The first day of sick leave is unpaid, but the next fourteen days are paid by the employer at a rate of eighty percent of the employee's wages. When an employee takes sick leave, the employer must inform the Swedish Social Insurance Agency. The employer's obligation to pay ends after two weeks.

At that point, the worker is entitled to the government's sickness benefit, equal to eighty percent of the employee's usual wages.

* * *

* * * [B]ecause sick leave and family leave are completely separate legal entitlements with separate administrative regimes, controversies about sick leave excess do not cast doubt on the legitimacy of Sweden's generous and ever-expanding family-friendly policies. In the last decade, despite ongoing controversies about the government's excessive spending on sick leave benefits, and a growing consensus that sick-leave taking needs to be reduced in Sweden, changes to the parental leave system have made parental leave more generous. For example, a 2002 reform increased the "daddy month" from one month to two months, and also increased the total number of days for which parental benefits can be paid to the parents of a child, from 450 to 480 days. Reforms in 2006 also expanded family leave. First, the monthly cap on the parental leave benefit was increased to motivate more fathers to use extra days for parental leave. Similarly, one new law prohibits employers from refusing to employ someone on the grounds that he or she wishes to take parental leave in the near future. Another protects employees in termination proceedings by preventing employers from commencing a term of notice for termination for just cause until an employee has returned to work after parental leave.

The situation in Sweden shows how the expansion of family-friendly policies need not be accompanied by an expansion of sick leave benefits. It also demonstrates that problems with the overuse and possible abuse of sick leave need not detract from legislative initiatives to protect and promote parental leave. It is possible for the government to aim to halve sick leave while simultaneously increasing paid parental leave taking. This lesson is an important one for members of Congress and advocates of women and families in the United States, who seem incapable of imagining the expansion of parental leave without including the costly appendage of medical leave on equal terms.

NOTES ON SOME INTERNATIONAL PERSPECTIVES ON PARENTAL LEAVE

1. The passage of Australia's first paid parental leave plan in 2010 made the United States the only industrialized nation without nationally legislated paid leave for parents. Tina Liptai, Parental Leave Scheme Passed, The Standard (June 19, 2010) http://www.standard.net.au/news/local/news/general/parental-leave-scheme-passed/1862989.aspx. According to statistics issued by the United Nations in June, 2010, the United States is one of only four countries in the world that do not guarantee at least some form of paid parental leave; the other three countries are Lesotho, Papua New Guinea, and Swaziland. United Nations Statistics Division, Statistics and Indicators On Women and Men: Maternity Leave Benefits tbl.5g (2010). Why do you think the United States' parental leave policies differ so dramatically from those of other developed nations?

An Equal Opportunities Unit attorney for the European Community Commission has commented that the U.S. "seems to assume that pregnancy is a sort of private hobby, which must be borne at your own expense." Sabra Craig, The Family and Medical Leave Act of 1993: A Survey of the Act's History, Purposes, Provisions, and Social Ramifications, 44 Drake L. Rev. 51, 79 (1995) (quoting Orlagh O'Farrell). Do you think the leave policies of the United States reflect a societal view that childbearing and rearing are private family matters? Does such a belief coexist easily with the political rhetoric about "family values"? Do the French or Swedish models suggest that other countries may view childbearing and childrearing as the responsibility of society at large? In Sweden, for example, the population is willing to pay very high taxes to fund the system described by Suk above. As a result, children in Sweden are cared for by their parents during infancy, whereas fewer than 10% of U.S. families now consist of one wage-earning parent and a homemaker. Arielle Horman Grill, The Myth of Unpaid Family Leave: Can the United States Implement a Paid Leave Policy Based on the Swedish Model?, 17 Comp. Lab. L.J. 373, 385–88 (1996). In short, although Sweden regards childrearing as a responsibility of the society at large, the family is the social unit charged with carrying out the tasks involved. At the same time, Sweden has the world's highest labor market participation rate for females: 91% of women between 25 and 49 are employed. Id. at 381. Infant health in Sweden is among the best in the world. Jennifer Thompson, Family and Medical Leave For the 21st Century?: A First Glance at California's Paid Family Leave Legislation, 12 U. Miami Bus. L. Rev. 77, 100 (2004).

2. Does it make a difference what policy goals (gender equality, pronatalism, children's welfare, employment of women, etc.) underlie a parental leave policy? Suk contends that, in drafting their leave policies, French lawmakers were motivated by a desire to protect women and children while Sweden's concern was gender equality in homes. Family leave policy in the United States has also been characterized as a women's rights issue. See, e.g., Nancy Dowd, Envisioning Work and Family: A Critical Perspective on International Models, 26 Harv. J. on Legis. 311, 316–19, 328–31 (1989). Paolo Wright-Carozza suggests that the American focus on gender discrimination has had a detrimental effect upon the development of parental policy in the U.S., by emphasizing formal equality abstracted from parental responsibilities and family relationships. Wright-Carozza, Organic Goods: Legal Understandings of Work, Parenthood, and Gender Equality in Comparative Perspective, 81 Calif. L. Rev. 531, 574 (1993).

While the paradigm of pregnancy as an individual employment disability reigned in the U.S., Italian postwar legislation providing for childbearing and childrearing benefits was premised upon a more complex combination of goals, including not only equal employment but also a restructuring of family roles, so as to effectuate societal concerns about the welfare of children and families. U.S. law, by contrast, "rested on a thin notion of equality that separates individuals from the full context of their lives and on a neglect for the interrelationship of human goods implicit in these areas of life [market, work, and family care] and law." Id. at 532. As a result of the broader focus in Italy, additional legislation was passed to establish nurseries on the premises of all major employers. Id. at 543. Wright–Carozza concludes that "[i]n Italy, the struggle for women's equality has been a struggle to share and socialize the responsibilities and obligations that society historically has imposed on women alone and that helped keep women out of the workforce,'' thus reflecting a vision of equality that sees persons—male and female—as integral wholes, participating in multiple but interconnected aspects of life. Id. at 579, 581.

How do the differences in the French and Swedish leave policies described by Suk reflect their different motivations? Is the Italian approach described in the previous paragraph better or worse? Given the quite different historical and social background in the United States, can you think of strategies to encourage such a paradigm shift here? Is the FMLA, an excerpt from which is included above, structured in a way likely to achieve the stated goals Congress set forth in its preamble?

3. Fathers' participation rates in Sweden have improved in recent years, though they are still less likely to take leave than mothers and do so for shorter periods. Participation by Swedish fathers increased from 3% in 1974, to 23% in 1979, to 44% of fathers taking an average of 45 days parental leave by 1992. Grill, above note 1, at 377–78. Under the current Swedish leave-taking scheme, in a two-parent household both parents must take at least some leave (60 days) in order to utilize the entire amount of time allowed, a provision that reflects the desire of lawmakers to encourage gender equality in the home. Presumably, this requirement has led to the dramatic recent increase in the rate of paternal leave-taking in Sweden: as of 2010, nearly 85% of Swedish fathers take parental leave. Katrin Beinhold, In Sweden, Men Can Have It All, N.Y. Times, June 15, 2010, at A6. Many speculate that after elections to be held later this year, the amount of time each parent would be required to take in order to use the full 480 days could be doubled. Id. Under the new legislation, in order to use 480 days of leave in a two-parent household, each parent would be required to take 120 days, with the remaining 240 days to be split between them as they saw fit. As the Swedish law is now, if only one parent in a two-parent household takes parental leave, the maximum number of days available is 420. Under the new legislation, that number would drop to 360. Do you think this new legislation will achieve even more gender equality? Or will fathers stop taking the full amount of leave available because too much time is required? Could the total amount of paid leave taken actually decrease as a result of the new legislation?

4. Suk is critical of the combination of parental leave and sick leave in the FMLA. As discussed earlier in this chapter, prior to the passage of the FMLA, commentators paid much attention to the parental leave provisions of the Act, but in practice employees have primarily used the Act to take leave for personal illnesses. See Michael Selmi, Is Something Better than Nothing? Critical Reflections on Ten Years of the FMLA, 15 Wash. U. J.L. & Pol'y 65, 74 (2004). One of the reasons French and Swedish lawmakers separated parental leave from sick leave is because the latter is more susceptible to abuse. Should Congress have made separate provisions for parental leave and personal illness? Does it make a difference that leave under the FMLA is unpaid, unlike parental leave in France or Sweden?

5. As Suk points out, France's leave policy requires women to take eight weeks of maternity leave, without the option to work during this period. What are the advantages and disadvantages of compulsory maternity leave? Does this make it more likely that women will be discriminated against in hiring? Should paternity leave be compulsory as well?

6. Now that you've read about some of the possibilities, what do you think an ideal policy for parental leave in the United States would provide? Answering the following questions may provide a good starting point:

* Should it be paid or unpaid?

* What employers should be covered?

* What employees should be covered?

* How should it be funded and administered?

* Should it be linked to a percentage of the employee's wages? Is this fair to lower paid women?

* How else might the level of pay be determined?

* Should costs be borne by the employer, by the social security system, by unemployment insurance, or by general tax revenues?

* How long a period of time should be provided and at what level of income?

* Should it cover both men and women? Should women and men be forced to take leave?

* Should it also cover sick leave?

How does your proposed policy differ from the policies of your classmates? What goals is your policy designed to further?

E. CHILD CARE

Leave at the time a child joins a family is only the first step in policies designed to address the needs of families with young children. After the initial period of recuperation by a formerly pregnant mother and incorporation of the child into the life of the family, infants have many needs that must be fulfilled by adults over a long period of time. How these needs are met has profound implications for both the structure of power and well-being within the family and for women's subsequent ability to participate effectively in the workforce and in civic and political life. The current options for child care in the United States are relatively limited. In single-parent or dual-earner homes—now the vast majority of all families with children—the option to care for the child oneself during the work day, even in infancy, is generally not available. Lacking an infrastructure of public institutions to care for preschool-aged children, parents are forced to choose among care by relatives or friends, a "nanny," day care provided in the home of another woman, and institutional day care facilities, all with very little public subsidy or support.

In this section, we address a number of issues: (1) the division of labor for child care within the family; (2) child care by third parties, including the American ambivalence about day care in general and the gender, race, and class issues implicated in the widespread employment of women of color to look after other women's children; and (3) the limited social supports that exist for child care in this country. We also discuss the implications of welfare "reform" legislation for mothers of small children and compare the arrangements in the United States with those available in other industrialized nations.

1. WHO TAKES CARE OF CHILDREN WITHIN THE FAMILY?

ARLIE HOCHSCHILD, THE SECOND SHIFT

33–39, 43–44 (1989).

[Together with Anne Machung, Arlie Hochschild carried out extensive interviews of fifty two-job couples, most of them consisting of multiple interviews over the period from 1980 to 1988, and observed many of the couples in their homes, all in order to study the division of domestic labor and child care responsibilities when husbands and wives both work. Based upon her observations and interviews, Hochschild concluded that women in a two-job couple work roughly fifteen hours longer each week than men, or an extra month of 24-hour days over the course of a year.]

Nancy Holt arrives home from work, her son, Joey, in one hand and a bag of groceries in the other. As she puts down the groceries and opens the front door, she sees a spill of mail on the hall floor, Joey's half-eaten piece of cinnamon toast on the hall table, and the phone machine's winking red light: a still-life reminder of the morning's frantic rush to distribute the family to the world outside. Nancy, for seven years a social worker, is a short, lithe blond woman of thirty who talks and moves rapidly. She scoops the mail onto the hall table and heads for the kitchen, unbuttoning her coat as she goes. Joey sticks close behind her, intently explaining to her how dump trucks dump things. Joey is a fat-cheeked, lively four-year-old who chuckles easily at things that please him.

Having parked their red station wagon, Evan, her husband, comes in and hangs up his coat. He has picked her up at work and they've arrived home together. Apparently unready to face the kitchen commotion but not quite entitled to relax with the newspaper in the living room, he slowly studies the mail. Also thirty, Evan, a warehouse furniture salesman, has thinning pale blond hair, a stocky build, and a tendency to lean on one foot. In his manner there is something both affable and hesitant.

From the beginning, Nancy describes herself as an "ardent feminist," an egalitarian (she wants a similar balance of spheres and equal power). Nancy began her marriage hoping that she and Evan would base their identities in both their parenthood and their careers, but clearly tilted toward parenthood. Evan felt it was fine for Nancy to have a career, if she could handle the family too.

As I observe in their home on this evening, I notice a small ripple on the surface of family waters. From the commotion of the kitchen, Nancy calls, "Eva-an, will you *please* set the table?" The word *please* is thick with irritation. Scurrying between refrigerator, sink, and oven, with Joey at her feet, Nancy wants Evan to help; she has asked him, but reluctantly. She seems to resent having to ask. (Later she tells me, "I *hate* to ask; why should I ask? It's begging.") Evan looks up from the mail and flashes an irritated glance toward the kitchen, stung, perhaps, to be asked in a way so barren of appreciation and respect. He begins setting out knives and forks, asks if she will need spoons, then answers the doorbell. A neighbor's child. No, Joey can't play right now. The moment of irritation has passed.

Later as I interview Nancy and Evan separately, they describe their family life as unusually happy—except for Joey's "problem." Joey has great difficulty getting to sleep. They start trying to put him to bed at 8:00. Evan tries but Joey rebuffs him; Nancy has better luck. By 8:30 they have him *on* the bed but not *in* it; he crawls and bounds playfully. After 9:00 he still calls out for water or toys, and sneaks out of bed to switch on the light. This continues past 9:30, then 10:00 and 10:30. At about 11:00 Joey complains that his bed is "scary," that he can only go to sleep in his parents' bedroom. Worn down, Nancy accepts this proposition. And it is part of their current arrangement that putting Joey to bed is "Nancy's job." Nancy and Evan can't get into bed until midnight or later, when Evan is tired and Nancy exhausted. She used to enjoy their love-making, Nancy tells me, but now sex seems like "more work." The Holts consider their fatigue and impoverished sex life as results of Joey's Problem.

The official history of Joey's Problem—the interpretation Nancy and Evan give me—begins with Joey's fierce attachment to Nancy, and Nancy's strong attachment to him. On an afternoon walk through Golden Gate Park, Nancy devotes herself to Joey's every move. Now Joey sees a squirrel; Nancy tells me she must remember to bring nuts next time. Now Joey is going up the slide; she notices that his pants are too short—she must take them down tonight. The two enjoy each other. (Off the official record, neighbors and Joey's baby-sitter say that Nancy is a wonderful mother, but privately they add how much she is "also like a single mother.")

For his part, Evan sees little of Joey. He has his evening routine, working with his tools in the basement, and Joey always seems happy to be with Nancy. In fact, Joey shows little interest in Evan, and Evan hesitates to see that as a problem. "Little kids need their moms more than they need their dads," he explains philosophically; "All boys go through an oedipal phase."

Perfectly normal things happen. After a long day, mother, father, and son sit down to dinner. Evan and Nancy get the first chance all day to talk to each other, but both turn anxiously to Joey, expecting his mood to deteriorate. Nancy asks him if he wants celery with peanut butter on it. Joey says yes. "Are you sure that's how you want it?" "Yes." Then the fidgeting begins. "I don't like the strings on my celery." "Celery is made up of strings." "The celery is too big." Nancy grimly slices the celery. A certain tension mounts. Every time one parent begins a conversation with the other, Joey interrupts. "I don't have anything to drink." Nancy gets him juice. And finally, "Feed me." By the end of the meal, no one has obstructed Joey's victory. He has his mother's reluctant attention and his father is reaching for a beer. But talking about it later, they say, "This is normal when you have kids."

Sometimes when Evan knocks on the baby-sitter's door to pick up Joey, the boy looks past his father, searching for a face behind him: "Where's Mommy?" Sometimes he outright refuses to go home with his father. Eventually Joey even swats at his father, once quite hard, on the face for "no reason at all." This makes it hard to keep imagining Joey's relation to Evan as "perfectly normal." Evan and Nancy begin to talk seriously about a "swatting problem."

Evan decides to seek ways to compensate for his emotional distance from Joey. He brings Joey a surprise every week or so—a Tonka truck, a Tootsie roll. He turns weekends into father-and-son times. One Saturday, Evan proposes the zoo, and hesitantly, Joey agrees. Father and son have their coats on and are nearing the front door. Suddenly Nancy decides she wants to join them, and as she walks down the steps with Joey in her arms, she explains to Evan, "I want to help things out."

Evan gets few signs of love from Joey and feels helpless to do much about it. "I just don't feel good about me and Joey," he tells me one evening, "that's all I can say." Evan loves Joey. He feels proud of him, this bright, good-looking, happy child. But Evan also seems to feel that being a father is vaguely hurtful and hard to talk about.

The official history of Joey's problem was that Joey felt the "normal" oedipal attachment of a male child to his mother. Joey was having the emotional problems of growing up that any parent can expect. But Evan and Nancy add the point that Joey's problems are exacerbated by Evan's difficulties being an active father, which stem, they feel, from the way Evan's own father, an emotionally remote self-made businessman, had treated him. Evan tells me, "when Joey gets older, we're going to play baseball together and go fishing."

As I recorded this official version of Joey's Problem through interviews and observation, I began to feel doubts about it. For one thing, clues to another interpretation appeared in the simple pattern of footsteps on a typical evening. There was the steady pacing of Nancy, preparing dinner in the kitchen, moving in zigzags from counter to refrigerator to counter to stove. There were the lighter, faster steps of Joey, running in large figure eights through the house, dashing from his tonka truck to his motorcycle man, reclaiming his sense of belonging in this house, among his things. After dinner, Nancy and Evan mingled footsteps in the kitchen, as they cleaned up. Then Nancy's steps began again; click, click, click, down to the basement for laundry, then thuck, thuck, thuck up the carpeted stairs to the first floor. Then to the bathroom where she runs Joey's bath, then into Joey's room, then back to the bath with Joey. Evan moved less—from the living room chair to Nancy in the kitchen, then back to the living room. He moved to the dining room to eat dinner and to the kitchen to help clean up. After dinner he went down to his hobby shop in the basement to sort out his tools; later he came up for a beer, then went back down. The footsteps suggest what is going on: Nancy was at work on her second shift.

Behind the Footsteps

* * * Between 8:05 a.m. and 6:05 p.m., both Nancy and Evan are away from home, working a "first shift" at full-time jobs. The rest of the time they deal with the varied tasks of the second shift: shopping, cooking, paying bills; taking care of the car, the garden, and yard; keeping harmony with Evan's mother who drops over quite a bit, "concerned" about Joey, with neighbors, their voluble baby-sitter, and each other. And Nancy's talk reflects a series of second-shift thoughts: "We're out of barbecue sauce.... Joey needs a Halloween costume.... The car needs a wash...." and so on. She reflects a certain "second-shift sensibility," a continual attunement to the task of striking and restriking the right emotional balance between child, spouse, home, and outside job.

When I first met the Holts, Nancy was absorbing far more of the second shift than Evan. She said she was doing 80 percent of the housework and 90 percent of the childcare. Evan said she did 60 percent of the housework, 70 percent of the childcare. Joey said, "I vacuum the rug, and fold the dinner napkins," finally concluding, "Mom and I do it all." A neighbor agreed with Joey. Clearly, between Nancy and Evan, there was a "leisure gap": Evan had more than Nancy. I asked both of them, in separate interviews, to explain to me how they had dealt with housework and childcare since their marriage began.

One evening in the fifth year of their marriage, Nancy told me, when Joey was two months old and almost four years before I met the Holts, she first seriously raised the issue with Evan. "I told him: 'Look, Evan, it's not working. I do the housework, I take the major care of Joey, *and* I work a full-time job. I get pissed. This is *your* house too. Joey is *your* child too. It's not all *my* job to care for them.' When I cooled down I put to him, 'Look, how about this: I'll cook Mondays, Wednesdays, and Fridays. You cook Tuesdays, Thursdays, and Saturdays. And we'll share or go out Sundays.' "

According to Nancy, Evan said he didn't like "rigid schedules." He said he didn't necessarily agree with her standards of housekeeping, and didn't like that standard "imposed" on him, especially if she was "sluffing off" tasks on him, which from time to time he felt she was. But he went along with the idea in principle. Nancy said the first week of the new plan went as follows. On Monday, she cooked. For Tuesday, Evan planned a meal that required shopping for a few ingredients, but on his way home he forgot to shop for them. He came home, saw nothing he could use in the refrigerator or in the cupboard, and suggested to Nancy that they go out for Chinese food. On Wednesday, Nancy cooked. On Thursday morning, Nancy reminded Evan, "Tonight it's your turn." That night Evan fixed hamburgers and french fries and Nancy was quick to praise him. On Friday, Nancy cooked. On Saturday, Evan forgot again.

As this pattern continued, Nancy's reminders became sharper. The sharper they became, the more actively Evan forgot—perhaps anticipating even sharper reprimands if he resisted more directly. This cycle of passive refusal followed by disappointment and anger gradually tightened, and before long the struggle had spread to the task of doing the laundry. Nancy said it was only fair that Evan share the laundry. He agreed in principle, but anxious that Evan would not share, Nancy wanted a clear, explicit agreement. "You ought to wash and fold every other load," she had told him. Evan experienced this "plan" as a yoke around his neck. On many weekdays, at this point, a huge pile of laundry sat like a disheveled guest on the living-room couch.

In her frustration, Nancy began to make subtle emotional jabs at Evan. "I don't know *what's* for dinner," she would say with a sigh. Or "I can't cook now, I've got to deal with this pile of laundry." She tensed at the slightest criticism about household disorder; if Evan wouldn't do the housework, he had absolutely *no* right to criticize how she did it. She would burst out angrily at Evan. She recalled telling him: "After work *my* feet are just as tired as *your* feet. I'm just as wound up as you are. I come home. I cook dinner. I wash and I clean. Here we are, planning a second child, and I can't cope with the one we have."

* * *

Upstairs-Downstairs: A Family Myth as "Solution"

* * * Not long after this crisis in the Holts' marriage, there was a dramatic lessening of tension over the issue of the second shift. It was as if the issue was closed. Evan had won. Nancy would do the second shift. Evan expressed vague guilt but beyond that he had nothing to say. Nancy had wearied of continually raising the topic, wearied of the lack of resolution. Now in the exhaustion of defeat, she wanted the struggle to be over too. Evan was "so good" in *other* ways, why debilitate their marriage by continual quarreling. Besides, she told me, "women always adjust more, don't they?"

One day, when I asked Nancy to tell me who did which tasks from a long list of household chores, she interrupted me with a broad wave of her hand and said, "I do the upstairs, Evan does the downstairs." What does that mean? I asked. Matter-of-factly, she explained that the upstairs included the living room, the dining room, the kitchen, two bedrooms, and two baths. The downstairs meant the garage, a place for storage and hobbies—Evan's hobbies. She explained this as a "sharing" arrangement, without humor or irony—just as Evan did later. Both said they had agreed it was the best solution to their dispute. Evan would take care of the car, the garage, and Max, the family dog. As Nancy explained, "the dog is all Evan's problem. I don't have to deal with the dog." Nancy took care of the rest.

For purposes of accommodating the second shift, then, the Holts' garage was elevated to the full moral and practical equivalent of the rest of the house. For Nancy and Evan, "upstairs and downstairs," "inside and outside," was vaguely described like "half and half," a fair division of labor based on a natural division of their house.

The Holts presented their upstairs-downstairs agreement as a perfectly equitable solution to a problem they "once had." This belief is what we might call a "family myth," even a modest delusional system. Why did they believe it? I think they believed it because they needed to believe it, because it solved a terrible problem. It allowed Nancy to continue thinking of herself as the sort of woman whose husband didn't abuse her—a self-conception that mattered a great deal to her. And it avoided the hard truth that, in his stolid, passive way, Evan had refused to share. It avoided the truth, too, that in their showdown, Nancy was more afraid of divorce than Evan was. This outer cover to their family life, this family myth, was jointly devised. It was an attempt to agree that there was no conflict over the second shift, no tension between their versions of manhood and womanhood, and that the powerful crisis that had arisen was temporary and minor.

M. RIVKA POLATNICK, WHY MEN DON'T REAR CHILDREN: A POWER ANALYSIS

In Mothering: Essays in Feminist Theory
23, 24–25, 26, 27–28, 31, 33, 37 (Joyce Trebilcot ed., 1983).

* * * [M]en (as a group) don't rear children because they don't *want* to rear children. (This implies, of course, that they are in a position to enforce their preferences.) It is to men's advantage that women are assigned childrearing responsibility, and it is in men's interest to keep things that way.

* * *

* * * Full-time childrearing responsibility limits one's capacity to engage in most other activities. However, the most important thing, in power terms that childrearers can't do is to be the family breadwinner. This is the job that men prefer as their primary family responsibility. It offers important power advantages over the home-based childrearing job.

* * *

* * * First, and of signal importance, breadwinners earn money. "Money is a source of power that supports male dominance in the family.... money belongs to him who earns it, not to her who spends it, since he who earns it may withhold it."[5]

5. Reuben Hill and Howard Becker, eds., *Family, Marriage, and Parenthood* (1955), p. 790.

Second, occupational achievement is probably the major source of social status in American society.

> In a certain sense the fundamental basis of the family's status is the occupational status of the husband and father. [The wife/mother] is excluded from the struggle for power and prestige in the occupational sphere [while the man's breadwinner role] carries with it ... the primary prestige of achievement, responsibility, and authority.[6]

Even if one's occupation ranks very low in prestige and power, other tangible and intangible benefits accrue to wage earners, such as organizational experience, social contacts, "knowledge of the world," and feelings of independence and competence. Moreover, the resources that breadwinners garner in the outside world do not remain on the front porch; breadwinning power translates significantly into power within the family. This is in direct contradiction to the notion of "separate spheres": The man reigning supreme in extrafamilial affairs, the woman running the home-front show. * * *

The correlation between earning power and family power has been substantiated concretely in a number of studies of family decision-making. These studies show that the more a man earns, the more family power he wields; and the greater the discrepancy between the status of the husband's and wife's work, the greater the husband's power. When the wife works too, there is a shift toward a more egalitarian balance of power and more sharing of household burdens.

* * *

* * * Men have good reason, then, to try to monopolize the job of principal family breadwinner (much as they may appreciate a second income). Husbands' objections to wives working "stem from feelings that their dominance is undermined when they are not the sole or primary breadwinners."[11] There is also

> the feeling of being threatened by women in industry, who are seen as limiting opportunities for men, diminishing the prestige of jobs formerly held only by men, and casting a cold eye on masculine pretentions to vocational superiority.[12]

These feelings are quite justified; as Benson so neatly understates it, "the male fear of competition from women is not based solely on myth."[13]

Where outright forbidding of the wife to work is no longer effective, the continued allocation of childrearing responsibility to women accomplishes the same end: assuring male domination of the occupational world.

---

6. Talcott Parsons, "Age and Sex in the Social Structure" in *The Family: Its Structure and Functions*, edited by Rose Laub Coser (1964), pp. 258, 261–62.

11. Phyllis Hallenbeck, "An Analysis of Power Dynamics in Marriage," *Journal of Marriage and the Family* 28 (May 1966): 201.

12. Helen Mayer Hacker, "The New Burdens of Masculinity," *Marriage and Family Living* 19 (August 1957): 232.

13. Leonard Benson, *Fatherhood: A Sociological Perspective* 293 (1968).

Should all other barriers to economic power for women suddenly vanish, childrearing responsibility would still handicap them hopelessly in economic competition with men.

Of course, children are not just a handy excuse to keep women out of the job market. Most people—male and female—want to have them, and somebody has to rear them. Men naturally prefer that women do it, so that having children need not interfere with their own occupational pursuits.

* * *

* * * By propagating the belief that women are the ones who really desire children, men can then invoke a "principle of least interest": that is, because women are "most interested" in children, they must make most of the accommodations and sacrifices required to rear them. Benson says that "fatherhood . . . is less important to men than motherhood is to women, in spite of the fact that maternity causes severe limitations on women's activities." My own version would be that fatherhood is less important to men than motherhood is to women *because* childrearing causes severe limitations on the childrearer's activities.

* * *

Women too imbibe the ideology of motherhood, but men seem to be its strongest supporters. By insuring that the weight of childrearing responsibility falls on women's shoulders, they win for themselves the right of "paternal neglect." As Benson observes, "The man can throw himself into his work and still fulfill male obligations at home, mainly because the latter are minimal. [Men have] the luxury of more familial disengagement than women."

Of course, men as family breadwinners must shoulder the *financial* burden involved in raising children: they may have to work harder, longer hours, and at jobs they dislike. But even factory workers enjoy set hours, scheduled breaks, vacation days, sick leave, and other union benefits. To the extent that men *can* select work suited to their interests, abilities, and ambitions, they are in a better position than women arbitrarily assigned to childrearing. And to the extent that breadwinning gains one the resources discussed earlier (money, status, family power, etc.), financial responsibility is clearly preferable, in power terms, to "mothering" responsibility.

* * *

Performing well at the job of childrearer may be a source of feminine credentials, but it is not a source of social power or status. Of all the possible adult roles for females, "the pattern of domesticity must be ranked lowest in terms of prestige," although "it offers perhaps the highest level of a certain kind of security."[29] When a woman bears and raises children, therefore, she is fulfilling social expectations and avoiding negative sanctions, but she "is not esteemed, in the culture or in the small

29. Parsons, "Age and Sex in the Social Structure," p. 261.

society of her family, in proportion to her exercise of her 'glory,' childbearing."[30]

The rewards for rearing children are not as tangible as a raise or a promotion, and ready censure awaits any evidence of failure: "if the child goes wrong, mother is usually blamed."[31] Thus the male preference for the breadwinner role may reflect (among other things) an awareness that "it's easier to make money than it is to be a good father.... The family is a risky proposition in terms of rewards and self-enhancement."[32]

* * *

* * * Childrearing, I have argued, is not a source of money, status, power in the society, or power in the family. The childrearing job is disadvantageous in terms of these major assets, but there are also drawbacks inherent in the nature of the work itself. The rearing of children "involves long years of exacting labor and self-sacrifice," but

> the drudgery, the monotonous labor, and other disagreeable features of childrearing are minimized by "the social guardians." On the other hand, the joys and compensations of motherhood are magnified and presented to consciousness on every hand. Thus the tendency is to create an illusion whereby motherhood will appear to consist of compensations only, and thus come to be desired by those for whom the illusion is intended.[33]

The responsibilities of a childrearer/homemaker are not confined to a 40–hour work-week. Margaret Benston estimates that for a married woman with small children (excluding the very rich), "the irreducible minimum of work ... is probably 70 or 80 hours a week."[40] In addition to the actual hours of work, there is the constant strain of being "on call." Thus, another consideration in why the husband's power is greatest when the children are young "may be the well-described chronic fatigue which affects young mothers with preschoolers."[42]

* * *

* * * The allocation of childrearing responsibility to women, I have argued, is no sacred fiat of nature, but a social policy which supports male domination in the society and in the family.

Whatever the "intrinsic desirability" of rearing children, the conditions of the job as it's now constituted—no salary, low status, long hours, domestic isolation—mark it as a job for women only. Men, as the superor-

---

30. Judith Long Laws, "A Feminist Review of Marital Adjustment Literature," *Journal of Marriage and the Family* 33 (August 1971): 493.

31. Benson, *Fatherhood,* p. 12.

32. Myron Brenton, *The American Male* (1966), p. 133.

33. Leta S. Hollingworth, "Social Devices for Impelling Women to Bear and Rear Children," *The American Journal of Sociology* 22 (July 1916): 20–21, 27.

40. Margaret Benston, "The Political Economy of Women's Liberation" in Garskof, Roles Women Play, p. 199.

42. Hallenbeck, "An Analysis of Power Dynamics in Marriage," p. 201.

dinate group, don't want childrearing responsibility, so they assign it to women. Women's functioning as childrearers reinforces, in turn, their subordinate position. Thus we come back again to the causal model of my Introduction—

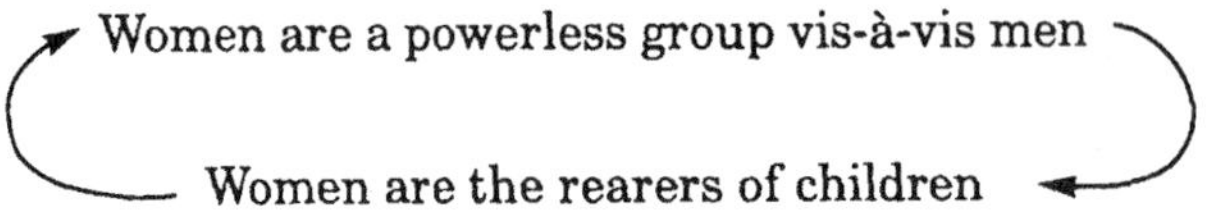

Women are a powerless group vis-à-vis men

Women are the rearers of children

—a vicious circle that keeps male power intact.

NOTES ON CHILD CARE

1. In a more recent study, Arlie Hochschild described how the hours left over for the second shift in our society have been decreasing, as the average worker, by various estimates, has added a month of work to his or her work year. Hochschild, The Time Bind: When Work Becomes Home and Home Becomes Work (1997) (citing Juliet Schor, The Overworked American: The Unexpected Decline of Leisure (1991)). Official data highlight this problem, concluding that families on average have experienced a decrease of twenty-two hours a week (14%) in parental time available to spend with their children; this creates a "time crunch" that falls virtually entirely on women. Council of Economic Advisers, Families and the Labor Market, 1969–1999: Analyzing the "Time Crunch" 3–6, 11–13 (1999). A startling result of Hochschild's study is that many workers, especially women, report that they feel more "at home" at work—more relaxed, emotionally supported, and appreciated—than they do at home. Hochschild, The Time Bind, at 200–01. Why might women feel this way more than men? Is it likely true for all women? See Lucy Williams, Poor Women's Work Experiences, in Labour Law, Work, and Family 195, 198 (Joanne Conaghan & Kerry Rittich eds., 2005) (emphasizing that the current discourse on the second shift and time crunch assumes that the labor force has only recently been feminized by the entry of middle- and upper-class women). Why might some women feel more supported at work than at home and others not? Should feminists be concerned about this reversal of home and work for some women? Why or why not?

2. What options did Nancy Holt, who "chooses" to lose the battle over the second shift, have? Why didn't she exercise them? Is she doing more than her own share in part because she wants to? A national survey of 1100 mothers in the late 1980s reported that only about one in four thought that fathers should play a 50–50 role in raising children (although most wanted fathers to do more child care than they currently did), and two out of three mothers seemed threatened by the idea of equal participation, leading the authors to conclude that "*mothers themselves may be subtly putting a damper on men's involvement with their children* because they are so possessive of their role as primary nurturer." Louis Genevie & Eva Margolies, The Motherhood Report: How Women Feel About Being Mothers 358 (1987) (emphasis in original). What do you think explains these results? Do you think they would be different now? See Lisa Belkin, When Mom and Dad Share it All, N.Y.

Times, June 15, 2008, Magazine §, at 74 (describing different-sex couples who "work equal hours, spend equal time with their children, take equal responsibility for their home. Neither would be the keeper of the mental-to-do lists; neither of their careers would take precedence."). What do you think you would have done if you were in Nancy Holt's place? How is your answer influenced by your gender, race, sexual orientation, and class?

3. Why do you think women rather than men are typically the primary caregivers of children? Do you find the explanations offered by Chodorow (discussed in the text note in Section B above) or by Polatnick more persuasive? What would the various feminists discussed in Chapter 3 likely think causes this allocation of responsibility?

4. If women "mother" because of influences upon them in early childhood, how can this system be changed? Hochschild reported that sex-role socialization had not changed much in the younger generation with respect to who is to be breadwinner and who is to be primarily responsible for caregiving and other domestic labor. Hochschild, The Second Shift, at 266 (discussing 1986 study of Berkeley seniors which found that "54 percent of the women and 13 percent of the men expected to be the one who would miss an important meeting at work for a sick child"). A more recent study of "care orientation" in students in grades 6, 8, 10, and 12 found a larger percentage of the females had a value orientation characterized by, among other things, a higher priority given to children. Kimberly Badger, Rebecca Simpson Craft & Larry Jensen, Age and Gender Differences in Value Orientation among American Adolescents, 33 Adolescence 591–96 (1998). See also Miriam Lewin & Lilli M. Tragos, Has the Feminist Movement Influenced Adolescent Sex Role Attitudes? A Reassessment After A Quarter Century, 16 Sex Roles 125 (1987) (finding no significant change in sex role stereotyping by high school students between 1956 and 1982). What do you think explains the persistence of these attitudes? How can feminism address them?

What sort of a father is Joey (Nancy and Evan's son in the excerpt from The Second Shift) likely to be? How can he change?

5. Hochschild concluded, based on her observations of Nancy and Evan Holt's "family myth" and those constructed by other couples whose marriages she observed, that highly educated, professional, higher-income couples tend to engage more in the rhetoric of equality, without any more actual equality, than couples at the other end of the socioeconomic scale. (One of the couples Hochschild observed to be *most* equitably sharing the tasks of the "second shift" also voiced very traditional and non-egalitarian rhetoric about the roles of husbands and wives in marriage.) Hochschild, The Second Shift, at 59–74. Similarly, although Black men tend to hold very traditional views about gender roles, they are also the most likely to help out with children and housework. See M. Belinda Tucker, Marital Values and Expectations in Context: Results from a 21–City Survey, in The Ties That Bind: Perspectives on Marriage and Cohabitation 184 (Linda J. Waite ed., 2000). Why do you think middle- and upper-middle-class couples feel the need to obscure reality with a myth?

6. How can one break the vicious cycle Polatnick describes, in which women have less power than men and are therefore assigned the task of

childrearing, which in turns keeps them from gaining more power in the workplace, and thus in the home? Can one woman do it as an individual or does society as a whole have to change in order for any one to do so? What kinds of changes would be necessary?

7. Although it is a violation of Title VII not to provide disability benefits for maternity leave if other disabilities are covered by an employer, no court has ever found that the statute is violated by structuring a job so as to effectively preclude its performance by someone with child care responsibilities. Thus, for example, a law firm that requires new associates to bill 2500 hours per year does not violate Title VII. Can you make an argument that such practices do constitute sex discrimination? How would you go about proving your allegations? What evidence would you bring into court? Is it admissible?

For a discussion of the possibility of an employment discrimination case seeking to require an employer to provide child care assistance, see Lucinda M. Finley, Legal Aspects of Child Care: The Policy Debate Over The Appropriate Amount of Public Responsibility, in Parental Leave and Child Care: Setting a Research and Policy Agenda 149–52 (Janet Shibley Hyde & Marilyn J. Essex eds., 1991). See also Joan Williams, Unbending Gender: Why Family and Work Conflict and What To Do About It 104–08 (2000) (suggesting a number of antidiscrimination claims to file, such as Title VII disparate-impact claims and Equal Pay Act claims, to require employers to provide family-friendly policies and to protect workers who work part-time, refuse overtime or travel, and otherwise seek to accommodate work with familial responsibilities); Joan C. Williams & Elizabeth S. Westfall, Deconstructing the Maternal Wall: Strategies for Vindicating the Civil Rights of "Carers" in the Workplace, 13 Duke J. Gender L. & Pol'y 31, 31 (2006) (discussing "maternal wall" cases from the perspective of plaintiffs' employment lawyers).

2. CHILD CARE BY THIRD PARTIES

RUTH SIDEL, WOMEN & CHILDREN LAST: THE PLIGHT OF POOR WOMEN IN AFFLUENT AMERICA

115–18, 128–30, 179, 184–87 (1986).

* * * Day care is one of those murky issues on which many Americans do not really know where they stand. Are we for it or against it? Is it good for children or harmful to them? Will it facilitate their social and intellectual development or undermine their emotional well-being? Is it perhaps somewhat "un-American" for a mother to leave her child during the first few years of life? * * * Why do we seem so very ambivalent about this important topic?

* * * [T]he rhetoric of the Reagan administration and its allies has undermined public perception of the need for day care by nostalgically recalling and mythologizing another era—perhaps the 1950s, more likely the 1920s—and longingly trying to recapture it.

In this image of small-town America, we are led to believe that father went to work every morning and returned home every evening to hugs and shouts of joy, that mother had hot cocoa and homemade cookies ready for well-behaved children returning from school, and that in case of an emergency grandmother was down the block, only too glad to help out when needed. Children set up lemonade stands on tree-lined streets, large families gathered for Thanksgiving dinner, and friends of long standing were available to provide mutual aid and support in times of hardship—perhaps a scene out of a Jimmy Stewart movie, with everything working out just fine in the end. There is little evidence that this Norman Rockwell image of America ever existed except, possibly, for a limited number of middle- and upper-middle-class families; it surely is not the reality of today. But this image, this rhetoric, has been used by an administration that has tried, and succeeded to a remarkable extent, in removing supports from families under the guise that they will be encouraged to return to an idyllic Never-Never Land.

Other voices, from other viewpoints, also attack day care. Recent allegations of sexual abuse of children by workers in day-care centers in California and New York have shocked parents, professionals, and the public. These incidents highlight a critical problem that has existed in American society for many years: The flagrant disregard for the well-being of children resulting in the absence of a responsible, coherent child-care policy.

* * *

Marion Blum, educational director of the Wellesley College Child Study Center, has recently written a powerful critique of day care. She points out that in our extraordinarily materialistic society, children are viewed as things, as commodities around which others can make a profit. She rightly condemns such equipment as cage-like cribs, harnesses and leashes that treat children as though they were animals rather than humans in order to minimize the number of caretakers and to maximize profits. She points out that because of the high turnover of preschool teachers, and the fact that teachers work shifts that may not coincide with the children's hours at the center, children must relate to a variety of adults during their day-care experience. She points out that eight hours or more is a long time for a three- or four-year-old to be away from home and to be required, for the most part, to behave according to preset schedules. She and others have pointed out the difficulties for overworked caregivers trying to maintain proper sanitation, particularly in younger age groups in which the children may not be toilet trained. She points out the higher rates of colds, flu, diarrhea, and even hepatitis A in children who attend day-care centers.

Finally, Blum notes that day care has involved a "transfer of roles from one group of exploited women—mothers—to another group of exploited women—day-care staff." Day-care workers are among the lowest paid adult wage earners in our society, with little or no opportunity for advancement, little or no prestige, and very little in the way of benefits. According to the Children's Defense Fund, "Two out of three center-based caregivers earn below poverty level wages and 87 percent of family day-care workers earn below the minimum wage." The status of preschool teachers clearly indicates the lack of value we place on women and children in our society.

Why is day care so inadequate in the United States? Why is it so exploitive of children, of day-care workers, of the parents themselves who often have no other choice? Is it because day care is seen as "nonproductive" in a society so geared to materialism and productivity? Is it because it serves the needs of two groups—women and children—who are particularly powerless? Is it because in a system not committed to full employment, decision-makers really do not want women in the labor force possibly taking jobs away from men? Is it because many, particularly people in positions of power, want to maintain the patriarchal family, and day care is seen as a force undermining that power relationship? * * *

Perhaps the most significant development over the past few years has been the emergence of employer-supported child care. * * * Child-care support by employers takes many forms. It includes providing or participating in the provision of direct services. * * * Some companies join together to form a consortium to run a center; others sponsor family day-care arrangements.

A second form of employer participation in their employees' child-care concerns is the provision of information and referral services, either offered on the work premises or through an existing community agency. Yet another form of involvement is employer-financed subsidy. The establishment of a Dependent Care Assistance Plan was made possible by the Economic Recovery Tax Act of 1981, making child care a nontaxable benefit for employees. The fourth mechanism whereby employers help their employees with child care is through more flexible working hours—flextime, job sharing, part-time work, or home work, also called "flexiplace."

* * *

There is no doubt that employer involvement in child care is a positive development; it has, for example, undoubtedly legitimized day care in the eyes of many who may have felt doubt or even antipathy. But there are problems with relying on employers to be major providers of child care. One major difficulty is that the current wave of employer-sponsored activity is generally voluntary. Most firms or unions or institutions that move into the area of day care do it because they need to recruit and retain skilled employees, because they feel their employees will, in the long run, have more stable work histories if some of their family problems are solved, or because they feel it is good public relations. As Friedman points out, industries that cater to the family market, such as Gerber Foods and Stride Rite children's shoes, feel a greater commitment to family issues. But what of other working people in the country? Most of the companies that offer child-care options are nonunionized. Child-care benefits are, therefore, often not a right won through negotiation and guaranteed through a contract but rather a result of enlightened self-interest on the part of industry. But what happens when the industry's self-interest changes—if its profit margin shrinks and executives feel such services can be eliminated?

Which segment of the population is most likely to benefit from industry involvement in child care? Will this be yet another way of separating services for the poor from services for working people, many of whom are middle class? Corporate child-care programs are usually found in high-technology companies, insurance companies, banks and hospitals. Are we moving simultaneously toward improved child care for the fortunate few and reduced, often inferior care for the poor, the unemployed, and those workers unfortunate enough to work for companies that are either unenlightened or not making sufficient profit to consider breaking new ground in the area of child care? In addition, many of the companies now offering child-care services offer them as part of a "cafeteria" plan, whereby the worker must choose one benefit over another. Should a parent have to choose dental coverage over child care or vice versa?

Child care is still a two-class system in the United States. Those with adequate income can generally purchase first-rate care for their preschool children; those without adequate income are left at the mercy of the political and economic forces that determine social policy. While the poor, the near poor, and the working class sometimes have access to good care, more often than not they are faced with long waiting lists, inadequate teacher-child ratios, and a rapid turnover of caregivers.

* * *

Lessons From Sweden

* * *

During the 1970s the single most important family policy issue [in Sweden] was child care. Since the Swedish government, and indeed most institutions within Swedish society, had made a serious commitment both to equality between men and women and to enhancing the well-being of the family unit, the expansion of child-care facilities was considered an urgent priority.

Child-care programs are a municipal responsibility in Sweden. Facilities are generally located in residential areas, near where the children live. Unlike the pattern in countries such as China, preschool facilities at the workplace are rare in Sweden.

There are several different kinds of facilities for young children. Day nurseries, generally open from 6:30 A.M. to 6:30 P.M., take children from six months to seven years. Because of the availability of parental leave until the child is one year old and because of waiting lists for available places, relatively few children as young as six months attend.

Part-time groups generally care for older preschoolers, children ages four to six. In 1975 a law was passed requiring all municipalities to provide a preschool place for all six-year-olds. These programs usually run three hours a day, five days a week, and are comparable to kindergarten in the United States.

Yet another alternative is the family day nursery. In this instance, the municipality hires a woman to care for up to four children in her home. These facilities are supervised by the municipality.

Recreation centers, also known as "leisure time centers," are available after school and during school vacations to care for school-age children, ages seven to twelve, whose parents are working or studying full time.

* * *

Although Swedish policymakers have recognized over the past ten to fifteen years the urgent need for additional preschool facilities, particularly with increasing numbers of young women entering the labor force, their commitment to day care of extraordinarily high quality has often meant an inability to move ahead in numbers of places as rapidly as many would have liked. Swedish day nurseries are surely among the best day-care facilities in the world. From the modern, relatively spacious and somewhat avant-garde centers in Stockholm, stocked with the most up-to-date equipment, to day nurseries such as the one in the suburbs of the small city of Västerås, located in a lovely old wooden house surrounded by trees and grass, which prides itself on the close relationships among children, parents, and staff, preschool facilities in Sweden are indeed enviable. They are, almost unfailingly, warm and welcoming, and decorated colorfully, ingeniously, sometimes with Scandinavian fabrics and always with stunning posters and the children's artwork. Close attention is paid not only to the children's physical environment but to their individual development, to their health and well-being, and to their social development.

The children are sometimes grouped by age, more often today into sibling groups ages two-and-one-half to seven. The notion is that, by mixing different ages, children can have the experience of playing different roles in the group, of helping one another and of being helped, of caring for others and being cared for. The caregivers include preschool teachers, who have been trained in a two-year course following upper secondary school, and children's nurses, who are trained through a two-year program within upper secondary school or through a special one-year program. The most common ratio is one adult for every four or five children, with the infant programs having even fewer children per adult. Creative play is stressed, with children working both in small groups and singly if they prefer. The development of the individual and the child's ability to be part of the larger group are both felt to be essential learning experiences.

Special facilities are available for immigrant children ages five and six who speak a language other than Swedish in the home. These children have priority in obtaining places in preschool facilities and are offered training in their "home language." For at least four hours a week children may, on a voluntary basis, be taught by a teacher who speaks their native tongue; participate in unilingual part-time groups from the age of four; and join unilingual sibling groups at day nurseries or in a variety of other settings in which their original language is used.

* * * Parents' fees vary from municipality to municipality and are dependent upon income, but the average fee paid by parents was approximately 4,000 kronor ($460) in 1981. Part-time preschools are free for six-year-olds and for younger children needing special care. There is no fixed fee for after-school care; the amount is often linked to the day nursery fee but is set at perhaps 40 to 50 percent of that amount.

In addition to benefits that stem from Sweden's family policy, Swedish citizens are entitled to a comprehensive variety of other benefits under their social insurance system. These include health insurance, sickness benefits, old-age pension, disability pension, work-injury insurance, unemployment insurance, and a variety of special measures to help to care for the elderly. In addition, "social assistance" is available for those individuals who are still in need after receiving other benefits.* * *

NOTES ON THE PROVISION OF CHILD CARE

1. We've encountered two instances of the power of myths in these readings: the Holt family's myth of equality described by Arlie Hochschild in Section E1 and the national myth of the Golden Age of the nuclear family described by Ruth Sidel in the excerpt above. What is the function of these myths? Why are they so powerful? Is there a relationship between the national myth and the individual one? How, if at all, are they related?

2. Parents obtain child care during work hours from a variety of options available in this society—from relatives, from women they pay (in the child's or the other woman's home), in family day care homes, and in institutionalized day care facilities. U.S. Dep't of Commerce, U.S. Census Bureau, Who's Minding the Kids? Child Care Arrangements: Summer 2006 (2008); see also Melissa Murray, The Networked Family: Reframing the Legal Understanding of Caregiving and Caregivers, 94 Va. L. Rev. 385, 386 (2008) ("Although family law understands caregiving to be the work of the nuclear family—and parents, in particular—families routinely enlist the assistance of outside caregivers, who claim no parental role, to help discharge their caregiving responsibilities."). In dual earner families, the parents may work different shifts and then relieve one another on child care shifts. Kathleen Snyder & Sarah Adelman, The Use of Relative Care While Parents Work: Findings from the 1999 National Survey of America's Families 25 (Urban Institute Discussion Paper 2004), http://www.urban.org/UploadedPDF/311131_DP04-09.pdf.

The most common arrangement for non-parental care is care by relatives, often by grandmothers, which is either free or very low-cost and relatively flexible in hours. This is particularly common among low-income and single-parent families. Id.; see also Jeffrey Capizzano & Gina Adams, Children in Low-Income Families Are Less Likely to Be in Center-Based Child Care

(Urban Institute Snapshots of America's Families III, No. 16) (updating previous Urban Institute study with 2002 data), http://www.urban.org/UploadedPDF/310923_snapshots3_no16.pdf. Because the caregivers are often persons with little education or training in child care, the quality of relative care may vary; this becomes a problem for children three to four years old, when studies show that center-based care is valuable for both educational and social development. Snyder & Adelman, above, at 6. At any rate, relative care is fast declining with the increase in female labor force participation. Jennifer L. Glass & Lisa Riley, Family Responsive Policies and Employee Retention Following Childbirth, 76 Soc. Forces 1401, 1406 (1998). It is nonetheless still the primary source of child care for both Black and Hispanic children, in part because it is consistent with cultural patterns, in part because they cannot afford center-based care, and in part because center hours do not suit persons who work irregular shifts. See Natalia Sarkisian & Naomi Gerstel, Kin Support Among Blacks and Whites: Race and Family Organization, 69 Am. Soc. Rev. 812, 812 (2004); Deborah J. Johnson et al., Studying the Effects of Early Child Care Experiences on the Development of Children of Color in the United States: Toward a More Inclusive Research Agenda, 74 Child Dev. 1227, 1231, 1234, 1236 (2003).

Family day care is another option. Family day care runs the gamut from one woman offering to look after another woman's child along with her own for some compensation while the other woman works, to structured in-home environments that are licensed to look after a small group of preschoolers and are subject to regulation. It is difficult to estimate how many of these arrangements are used by working women because a portion of this labor takes place in the underground economy. See Nat'l Research Council, Who Cares for America's Children?: Child Care Policy for the 1990s 151 (Cheryl D. Hayes, John L. Palmer & Martha J. Zaslow eds., 1990). The Census Bureau estimated that family day care accounted for about 5.2% of child care arrangements for children under the age of five in 2006; another 4.9% of children were cared for by nonrelatives who may have been paid. U.S. Dep't of Commerce, U.S. Census Bureau, Who's Minding the Kids? Child Care Arrangements: Summer 2006 (2008). The quality of care available in family day care homes varies substantially, leading many to suggest more stringent health and quality regulation and monitoring of this in-home "industry," a move resisted by many care providers. Anywhere from 50 to 90% of family day care is thought to be unregulated. See Margaret K. Nelson, The Regulation Controversy in Family Day Care: The Perspective of Providers, in Parental Leave and Child Care: Setting a Research and Policy Agenda 354–55 (Janet Shibley Hyde & Marilyn J. Essex eds., 1991). What are the race and class implications of increased regulation of this type of caregiving? See Johnson et al., above (arguing for more sensitivity to cultural and class contexts affecting early child care for families of color); see also Peggie R. Smith, Laboring for Child Care: A Consideration of New Approaches to Represent Low-Income Service Workers, 8 U. Pa. J. Lab. & Emp. L. 583, 585 (2006) ("Far too frequently, enhanced funding for child care has privileged child care consumers while ignoring the child care workforce.").

3. During World War II, when it was perceived to be necessary to the national economy and defense, child care was provided in some workplaces

and subsidized by the government. For example, centers established under the Lanham Act included two at the Kaiser Shipbuilding plant in Portland, Oregon, which were open 24 hours a day and provided numerous services, including care for children with minor illnesses, shopping and low cost carry-out dinners. Sidel, Women & Children Last, excerpt above, 119–20.

Today, only about 9% of employers of fifty or more employees provide child care at or near the workplace. Ellen Galinsky, James T. Bond, Kally Sakai with Stacy S. Kim & Nicole Giuntoli, Families and Work Institute, 2008 National Study of Employers 21 (2008). Those employers that do provide child care tend to employ higher-skilled women, particularly in jobs that are personnel-intensive and require scarce skills. For example, on-site child care has come to be seen as a cheap and efficient way of retaining nurses. Sonya Michel, The Politics of Child Care in America's Public/Private Welfare State, in Families in the U.S.: Kinship and Domestic Politics 841–42 (Karen V. Hansen & Anita Ilta Garey eds., 1998).

What are the advantages of on-site child care provided by the employer? For the employer? For the parent? For the child? What are the disadvantages for each group?

4. Most European countries have for a long time devoted substantial attention and public resources to the provision of services to support persons who are raising children, by way of direct grants or family allowances, direct provision of services such as publicly funded and publicly run nurseries, or some combination of the two. Julie Suk, Are Gender Stereotypes Bad for Women? Rethinking AntiDiscrimination Law and Work–Family Conflict, 110 Colum. L. Rev. 1, 24–40 (2010). Despite an economic downturn and the replacement of the Social Democratic government by a more conservative administration, Sweden has remained committed to providing high-quality publicly subsidized day care for all children. Id. Despite the commitment to sex equality at home and at work, however, gender segregation in the workplace does persist to some extent in Sweden, and women remain more likely to care for children than men. Would the Swedish system of child care work in the United States? Why or why not?

France, an industrialized country without the extensive social democratic political background of Sweden, also has a comprehensive program of publicly funded child care. After sixteen weeks of paid maternity leave, infant care is available in crèches collectives (infant day care centers whose directors have training equivalent to that of a registered nurse or midwife, with additional training in administration of infant care) and crèches familiares (clusters of fifteen in-home care providers who look after three children each and are trained, supervised, and monitored by directors comparable to those acting as supervisors in the collective centers); the centers, which are available only to working parents, are subsidized and charge according to ability to pay. Suk, above, at 32. Free full-time nursery schools are provided for children between the ages of two and six and form an integral part of the public educational system. Id.

Perhaps because European industrialized countries provide these and comparable child care benefits to parents in all income classes, use of these benefits is not stigmatized and does not reinforce class differences. Nancy E.

Dowd, Family Values and Valuing Family: A Blueprint for Family Leave, 30 Harv. J. on Legis. 335, 362 (1993). Could the same thing happen in the United States?

5. Some studies have shown powerful long-term effects of quality child care programs, including greater likelihood of college attendance, lower rates of juvenile criminal activity and less likelihood of arrest by age 27, almost a doubling of monthly earnings, and vastly decreased likelihood of receiving public assistance. Deborah Lowe Vandell & Barbara Wolfe, U. of Wisc. Inst. for Res. on Poverty, Child Care Quality: Does It Matter and Does It Need to Be Improved? v (2000). Given these substantial societal benefits, why is it so hard to make arguments for government funding of child care in the United States? Might there be additional values to a mother's employment in that her children may be less likely to form traditional attitudes about the proper role of women?

Apart from the American anti-tax, anti-government political culture and ideology of individualism, Barbara R. Bergmann suggests that unwillingness to pay for child care in this country relates to the history of racism. For one thing, "Americans are accustomed to think[ing] that the primary beneficiaries of child care, income supplementation, and medical care programs are parents, and in particular, mothers, rather than children." Bergmann, Saving Our Children From Poverty: What The United States Can Learn from France 19 (1996). Moreover, Bergmann states, "The anger against poor children's parents is in part connected to the problem of race relations in the United States. * * * But the widespread antagonism against black people undoubtedly contributes to the opposition to giving poor families—widely but falsely perceived to be black—any more help." Id. at 10. Do you agree with this explanation?

6. Does it make a difference *why* the government adopts a particular child care policy—that is, whether it is seen as a question of sex equality, as in Sweden; of employment necessity, as in wartime Britain and the United States; or of child welfare? How are the resulting programs likely to differ? Does it make a difference if the child care policy and programs stand alone or form part of a broader family support policy including, as in Sweden and France, comprehensive national health insurance, social insurance against unemployment, provisions for care for the elderly, etc.? Although France has a substantial commitment to early childhood care and education, French women nonetheless lag those in the U.S. in terms of both labor force participation and gender equality in the home. See Michael Selmi & Naomi Cahn, Caretaking and the Contradictions of Contemporary Policy, 55 Me. L. Rev. 290, 302–03 (2003). What, in your opinion, is missing?

7. A report on the structure and attitudes of American families was released by the National Opinion Research Center (NORC) in late 1999. Tom W. Smith, Nat'l Opinion Res. Ctr., Social Change Report 42: The Emerging 21st Century American Family (1999). NORC reported that American attitudes toward government assistance for child care and other types of government social welfare programs have changed with the changing structure of the American family from the previously typical single-earner couple to a predominance of dual-earner couples and single-parent families. Single-earner

couples are the most traditional in their attitudes toward gender roles, women working, and social welfare policies to assist working parents; dual-earner parents are more liberal (NORC calls them more "modern") on all these fronts; and single parents are the most supportive in their orientation to all of these issues. Id. at 16–18. NORC predicts that support for gender equality and government assistance will increase with the continuing structural changes in the family, especially as more children are raised by working mothers. Id. at 19–20. How would you assess this prediction? Do you think that structural changes will inexorably lead to a change in American views on all these subjects?

8. There has by now been a substantial amount of research concerning the effects of maternal employment and nonparental care upon children. Contrary to popular assumptions, the overwhelming results of longitudinal studies show that children whose mothers work suffer no detrimental effects from maternal employment. See, e.g., Adele Eskeles Gottfried & Allen W. Gottfried, eds., Maternal Employment and Children's Development, Longitudinal Research (1988). Controlling for other differences, including socioeconomic status, children whose mothers are employed and children whose mothers are not employed are equivalent in infant developmental status, security of attachment in infancy, toddlerhood and kindergarten years, cognitive, language and intellectual development in the preschool through school-age years, problem solving in toddlerhood, social reasoning during preschool and social maturity during the school years, emotional expressiveness during kindergarten, behavioral adjustment from ages four through seven, academic performance in the early school years, school motivation, and sex role development in adolescence. Id. at 270. Indeed, there appear to be benefits from maternal employment beyond purely economic ones, including higher educational aspirations and attitudes, paternal involvement, and variety of children's experience. Id. at 273. This research was used by the California Supreme Court as a basis for holding that a mother's employment status could not be used to discriminate against her in deciding about child custody. Burchard v. Garay, 724 P.2d 486, 493 (Cal. 1986) (Rose Bird, J., concurring).

A large-scale longitudinal study by the National Institute of Child Health and Human Development (a division of the National Institutes of Health) [NICHD] has now yielded a host of reports on the effects of child care upon the emotional and educational development of children, their peer relations, and the variable effects of different types of child care arrangements. Child care appears to be largely unrelated to infant-mother attachment, for which maternal sensitivity is the strongest predictor. NICHD Early Child Care Research Network, Child-Care and Family Predictors of Preschool Attachment and Stability From Infancy, 37 Developmental Psychol. 847, 848–49 (2001). Moreover, quality child care, especially center-based care, is consistently linked to the development of cognitive and linguistic skills and academic skills important to subsequent success in school. NICHD, The Relation of Child Care to Cognitive and Language Development, 71 Child Dev. 960, 975 (2000); NICHD, Early Child Care and Children's Development Prior to School Entry: Results from the NICHD Study of Early Child Care, 39 Am. Ed. Res. J. 133, 157 (2002). It is also conducive to positive and skilled interaction with peers. NICHD, Child Care and Children's Peer Interaction at 25 and 36

Months: The NICHD Study of Early Child Care, 72 Child Dev. 1478, 1496 (2001). The benefits of high-quality, center-based care is particularly important for children in lower-income groups, although they are less likely than higher-income families to place their children in center-based care. See Vandell & Wolfe, note 5 above, at iii; NICHD 2002, above, at 158. Given all these advantages, why is there not more government investment in quality child care for preschool children? Should universal compulsory education begin at age three?

9. Note that the advantages described above correlate with child care that is of high quality, which itself correlates with certain structural characteristics, such as the adult-child ratio, training and education of caregivers, low turnover of caregivers, and the provision of a safe and stimulating environment. Unfortunately, much of the child care effectively available to most American children is not of high quality, for a variety of reasons—primarily because parents can't afford it and because caregivers are unskilled and undercompensated. See, e.g., Vandell & Wolfe, above note 5, at vi-viii, 74–78; Peggie R. Smith, Caring for Paid Caregivers: Linking Child Care with Improved Working Conditions, 73 U. Cin. L. Rev. 399, 404–07 (2004). The average child care worker made about $17,610 a year in 2005, resulting in turnover of 50% or more employees per year at many centers. Children's Defense Fund, Child Care Basics, April 2005 (citing Department of Labor statistics); Vandell & Wolfe, above, at viii, 80 fig.5. Vandell and Wolfe argue that the only solution to this market failure is government subsidy, regulation, and/or direct provision of care. Id. at viii-xi, 82–86. How would you address this market failure, where parents need care yet cannot afford it and child care work is so devalued? See Smith, above, at 422–30 (arguing for unionization of center-based child care workers).

10. If California were to pass a law requiring employers to provide day care for female employees' children, how would the formal equality theorists who opposed the maternity leave statute in the *Cal Fed* case (see Chapter 3) respond? Would such a law be constitutional? Would it violate Title VII? What if it were written in a gender-neutral fashion, even though the state contemplated that only women employees were likely to take advantage of it? *Should* California pass such a law?

11. The cost of child care in the U.S. is substantial but varies according to the region of the country, the type of care facility, and the age of the child receiving care for. In 2009, for example, the average cost of full-time care for an infant in a center ranged from $4550 in Mississippi to $18,750 in Massachusetts. National Ass'n of Child Care Resource & Referral Agencies, Parents and the High Cost of Child Care (2010 Update): Executive Summary 1 (2010). Family day care, as discussed above in note 2, is generally less expensive than care within a designated child care center. Id. The annual cost of infant care, cited above, would drop significantly in a family child care home to between $3550 and $11,900. Id. Care for preschool children is generally lower than for infants; in 2009, full-time, center-based care for a four-year old ranged from $4050 to $13,150. Id; see also Children's Defense Fund, State of America's Children 2010 F–6 (June 2010) (setting forth similar statistics for 2008). Despite these variations, child care costs are undoubtedly high. To put these costs in perspective, consider that the average center-based child care fees for

an infant exceeded the annual cost of "tuition and related fees at a four-year public university in 40 states." Parents and the High Cost of Child Care, above, at 2.

The race and immigration status of a caregiver may also influence the cost of child care. See Taunya Lovell Banks, Toward a Global Critical Feminist Vision: Domestic Work and the Nanny Tax Debate, 3 J. Gender, Race & Just. 1, 31 nn.139–40 (1999) (reporting that the going rate for an inexperienced woman from the Caribbean working as a live-in "nanny" in New York City in the 1990s was $150 per week plus room and board, that Haitians were cheaper, due to both language difficulties and Americans' fear of AIDS, but that Hispanics started at $200 per week because they were white). Moderate-income families are the least able to get high-quality care, because they don't make enough to afford it but make too much to be eligible for subsidies. Jane Waldfogel, Child Care, Women's Employment, and Child Outcomes, 15 J. Population Econ. 527, 537 (2002).

How would you address the race and class issues raised by the types of child care available in the United States? What would be the provisions of an ideal child care policy in this country, and how would it address these problems? How would such a policy be financed? How would you describe the child care policy we have now? What sort of child care program would you want available for the children in your life? For a comprehensive description of the history of child care in the United States and discussion of the studies about its effect, see Alison Clarke-Stewart & Virginia D. Allhusen, What We Know About Childcare (2005).

MARY ROMERO, MAID IN THE U.S.A.

98–103, 32–34, 37, 39–41 (1992).

Domestic service reveals the contradiction in a feminism that pushed for women's involvement outside the home, yet failed to make men take responsibility for household labor. Employed middle- and upper-middle class women escaped the double day syndrome by hiring poor women of color to perform housework and child care, and this was characterized as progress. Some feminists defined domestic service as progressive because traditional women's work moved into the labor market and became paid work. However, this definition neglects the inescapable fact that when women hire other women at low wages to do housework, both employees and employers remain women. As employers, women continued to accept responsibility for housework even if they supervised domestics who performed the actual labor. If we accept domestic service as central to women's oppression, the contradiction, as Linda Martin and Kerry Segrave have pointed out, is that "every time the housewife or working woman buys freedom for herself with a domestic, that very same freedom is denied to the domestic, for the maid must go home and do her own housework."[4]

---

4. Linda Martin and Kerry Segrave, *The Servant Problem: Domestic Workers in North America*, pp. 32–33.

Although the system of gender domination places the burden of housework on women, middle class women have financial resources to escape the drudgery of housework by paying someone else to do her work. * * * In other words, hire a woman of color and pay her as little as possible to fulfill your housework duties and responsibilities. The most exploitative form of domestic service is maintained through systems of gender, class and racial domination. Thus, middle-class American women aim to "liberate" themselves by exploiting women of color—particularly immigrants—in the underground economy, for long hours at relatively low wages, with no benefits.

* * * In *Las Mujeres*, Ida Gutierrez recounted the ways in which women employers determined her working conditions:

> Some of the ladies pay Social Security, but some of them don't. It all depends. If you're lucky, you find a woman that is real nice to you. If you get to meet one of those ladies, you got it made—they pay for your gas, or they give you money. But not all people are the same. I've worked for rich ladies who thought they'd go broke if they gave me a Coca–Cola. And they make you work real hard for your money, too—clean the walls, get down on your knees and scrub the floor.[9]

The present chapter draws upon my research with Chicana domestic workers as well as studies of African American, West Indian, Japanese American, and Central American immigrant women. Interviews with domestic workers describe interactions between white middle-class women employers and working class women of color that take place outside the public eye. The accounts describe working conditions and work relations and provide insight into the function of gender in shaping interclass and interracial social relationships. Investigating daily rituals and practices involving employer and employee provides a microperspective on the process whereby systems of gender, class, and race domination are reproduced in domestic service.

WHY DO WOMEN HIRE OTHER WOMEN

Why do white middle class employers hire working-class women of color as domestics? * * *

Let us overlook, for now, the illusion common among white middle-class women that hiring a woman of color to clean their toilets is a form of social benefit, reducing the unemployment rate. It is clear that African American, West Indian, Chicana, and Japanese American domestics describe working arrangements that challenge the thesis that personal service and status are vanishing needs no longer fulfilled in the occupation. They report a broad range of tasks including personal service and emotional labor, suggesting that servitude and traditional demeanor are still expected by some employers. * * *

---

9. Nan Elsasser, Kyle MacKenzie and Yvonne Tixier y Vigil, *Las Mujeres: Conversations from a Hispanic Community*, p. 70–1.

Physical Labor

* * *

In their efforts to escape the diffuse duties of their housewife roles, employers do not acknowledge work boundaries. Even when the worker's tasks were agreed upon in a verbal contract, employees frequently reported that employers requested additional duties. For instance, household workers commonly complained that employers did not differentiate between housework and child care. In her interviews with women hired to do child care in New York City, Kathy Dobie found that "many of the women are hired as nannies and then asked if they wouldn't mind straightening up a bit. They are asked if they wouldn't clean, then shop, then do the laundry, then, etc." One child care worker told Dobie:

> I give her coffee, I take care of Stephen. I do the laundry. I go out and do the shopping. I buy her birth control tablets. I couldn't believe that ... Even the light bulbs in the ceiling, I change. Even her panties, I pick them up when she drops them on the floor.[13]

Soraya Moore Coley reported similar findings in her study on African American private household workers. Mrs. Green described how her job description changed:

> When she hired me, she told me I was to only take care of the children. Then, the woman starts leaving the house and asking me if I would do this or that. Before you know it, I'm taking care of the baby and doing the work. I enjoy the children and I guess I stayed because they become so attached to me—but the woman probably knew when she hired me, she wanted me to do other work.[14]

* * *

Not all housewives structured the work to relieve themselves of the burden of housework. Workers encountered employers who disregarded their years of experience and treated them as unskilled labor that required detailed instruction and supervision. * * * In her interview with Studs Terkel, Maggie Holmes described the demeaning and unnecessary nature of supervision:

> I don't like nobody checkin' behind me. When you go to work, they want to show you how to clean. I been doin' it all my life. They come and get the rag and show you how to do it. [laughs.] I stand there, look at 'em. Lotta times I ask her, "you finished?" I say, "if there's anything you gotta go and do, I'd wish you'd go." I don't need nobody to show me how to clean.[20]

* * *

---

13. Kathy Dobie, "Black Women, White Kids, A Tale of Two Worlds," p. 23.

14. Soraya Moore Coley, " 'And Still I Rise': An Exploratory Study of Contemporary Black Private Household Workers," p. 213.

20. Studs Terkel, *Working: People Talk About What They Do All Day and How They Feel About What They Do*, p. 118.

CHICANA PRIVATE HOUSEHOLD WORKERS AS WORKING MOTHERS

* * *

For Chicana private household workers, having a job meant doing paid housework during the day and returning to do unpaid housework in their own homes. At home or on the job, there was no respite from housework.

* * *

These women understood all too well the plight of working women. Homemaking activities ranged from the usual housecleaning, cooking, laundry, and shopping to endless errands, nursing, and child care. Although tasks and the amount of work differed among families, mothers with younger children were faced with additional tasks related to child care, including extra laundry, cooking, and housecleaning. Child care duties were frequently socialized to other family members by women who lived near their families of orientation; babysitting nephews, nieces, and grandchildren was not unusual.

* * *

In many cases the women arranged the job so that they were always at home when their families were there. Husbands' and children's schedules were rarely inconvenienced or altered. Consequently, husbands were not faced with the need to change the division of household labor. Like so many other mothers and wives, Chicanas were expected to cook, wash, iron, vacuum, dust, and care for children. For the most part, they did not escape the sexual division of labor that dominates household work today. About half of the women described a rigid sexual division of labor in household duties. * * *

All of the women approved of their husbands helping with housework, child care, cooking and other household chores; yet this did not mean that they voiced dissatisfaction with the division of labor between wife and husband. To some degree, the issue of equity was related to the husbands' perceived position as breadwinners. The women tended to discount the importance of their economic contributions to the family, characterizing their wages as "pin money." They described their wages as providing "extras" not afforded by their husbands' incomes. Objectively, however, the items included food, clothes, tuition, and bills. Clearly, the "extras" purchased by these wage-earning mothers are necessities rather than extras. They may not indeed be necessary for survival, but these items, which husbands' paychecks cannot cover, would be considered necessary by most middle-class families.

* * *

My inquiries about husbands helping with housework were usually interpreted as having to do with child care. Descriptions of the ways in which husbands "helped out" were almost uniformly the same: when wives were not home, husbands were responsible for the children. They watched the children and sometimes fed them if the wife had prepared food before she left. However, "watching the kids" did not necessarily involve the broad range of tasks such as bathing or cleaning up after the children. Husbands were more likely to supervise older children and make sure that their chores were done. In fact, most of the married women with school age children mentioned that their husbands helped with the housework by telling the children to do their chores. Mrs. Segura's response was typical:

> No he don't [do housework]. He'll tell the kids "that doesn't go there," "pick it up and take to the hamper" or "put it in your room."

* * *

In sum, the division of household labor left all these women with the double day. Like many other working mothers, Chicanas did not have enough help with housework, child care, laundry, and cooking. Mrs. Chacon voiced a wish to be able to afford to hire someone to help her with the spring-cleaning in her own home.

> I would appreciate someone—to be able to afford someone to come in and help me instead of taking one or two weeks to do the job. Instead you'd be able to pay someone to come in and have it done the way you want it done too.

Unlike higher-paid workers, they were unable to gain relief from the double day by replacing their labor with the labor of another. As workers in a poorly-paid occupation, Chicana household workers had limited resources and certainly could not afford the same solutions as middle-class women. Rarely could they afford to take the family to restaurants, order take-out, or fill the refrigerator with expensive frozen or precooked food. Nor could they afford to pay for child care. The cost of day care can be a burden for middle class women; it is especially onerous for low-paid workers. The lack of bilingual and bicultural services was also a problem in purchasing child-care services.

* * *

For the majority of women whose extended families lived in the city, female relatives were an important resource. Relatives—particularly grandmothers and sisters—were frequently called upon to care for the children during the day. Five of the women mentioned exchanging child-care services with relatives and neighbors. Relatives were especially helpful in preparing for the holidays. However, only women residing fairly close to their relatives were able to obtain regular assistance. More frequently, relatives were a source of aid only during a crisis. Sisters and mothers provided help during sickness, childbirth and emergencies. And, of course, relatives dropping in from out of town often created additional housework rather than provided additional help.

The Chicanas that I interviewed represented their choice of employment as a conscious strategy. When I asked, "Why did you start doing housework?" their response was not, "I couldn't find any other job." Rather, they began by comparing housework with previously held unskilled jobs. Jobs as line workers, nurse's aides, waitresses, or dishwashers had fixed schedules. Taking days off from fast-food restaurants, car washes or turkey farms jeopardized their employment. Explanations about the way in which domestic service was compatible with taking care of their families followed.

They emphasized that domestic service allowed them to arrange their own hours, and they could easily add or drop employers to lengthen or shorten the workweek. As private household workers, they were able to arrange hours and the workweek to care for sick children, to attend PTA meetings, or to take children to the dentist. The flexible schedule also permitted women to participate in school functions or be active in church and community activities. Having control over their own schedules permitted the women to get their children off to school in the morning and be back home when school was over. Domestic service did not demand rigid commitments of time, nor did the occupation force women to make the job their first priority. Mrs. Garcia explained:

> You can change the dates if you can't go a certain day and if you have an appointment, you can go later, and work later, just as long as you get the work done.... I try to be there at the same time, but if I don't get there for some reason or another, I don't have to think I'm going to lose my job or something.

Two-thirds of the interviewees said that they selected domestic service over other low-paying jobs because the occupation offered the flexibility to fulfill family obligations. As Mrs. Lopez related:

> That's one thing with doing daywork—the children are sick or something, you just stayed home because that was my responsibility to get them to the doctor.

Mothers with preschool children preferred domestic service over other low-paying jobs that they had held in the past. Unable to afford a sitter or day-care, domestic service offered an alternative. Mrs. Rodriquez, a thirty-three-year-old mother of two, took her preschool children to work with her:

> I could take my kids with me. There were never any restrictions to taking the children. Most of the people I've worked for like kids, so I just take the kids with me. It's silly to have to work and pay a sitter. It won't work.

Mrs. Cordova also mentioned this aspect of domestic service as grounds for selecting the occupation:

> So that's what I enjoyed about housework is that I could take the kids along and not worry about not having a reliable baby-sitter. So that's mainly the reason I did it [domestic service], because I knew the kids

were going to be all right and they were with me and they were fed and taken care of.

Flexibility was not an inherent characteristic of domestic service. Neither was taking children to the job. Provisions for both had to be negotiated in informal contracts and labor arrangements with employers. * * *

NOTES ON WOMEN OF COLOR AS CHILD CARE WORKERS

1. In the excerpt above, Romero implies that the employment of women of color by middle-class women to care for their children and do their housework is exploitative per se; she argues that this reveals a contradiction in feminism whereby some women obtain freedom from traditional roles as housekeepers and caregivers only by requiring *other* women to assume these roles for them. Do you agree or disagree with her position? Why? What is the exact nature of the contradiction? Is it that domestic workers are forced to do their own housework and childcare, as Linda Martin describes in the text accompanying footnote 4 of the excerpt, or that they are asked to perform the traditional roles from which their female employers are fleeing?

2. How might the interests of women of color employed as household workers and women who employ them be congruent? Can you reconcile these shared interests, if any, with the contradiction Romero describes?

3. Taunya Lovell Banks suggests that only socialist feminism, with its emphasis upon multiple systems of oppression, the need for significant structural changes, and collective action, provides an adequate framework for analyzing the intersecting issues involved in working women's employment of other women to care for their children. Banks, Toward a Global Critical Feminist Vision: Domestic Work and the Nanny Tax Debate, 3 J. Gender, Race & Just. 1, 38–40 (1999). Do you agree? How would other feminist legal theorists studied in Chapter 3 address the problems raised by the employment of women of color as child care workers?

4. As Romero points out, upper-income and professional women in the U.S. deal with their dual roles in the home and in the economy by shifting the burden of child care onto another group of women, many of them undocumented workers employed at or below the minimum wage and with no benefits. The nomination in late 1992 by President Clinton of corporate lawyer Zoe Baird to be Attorney General focused national attention on the fact that many of these child care arrangements take place in the underground economy, without payment of taxes or Social Security for the child care worker. Indeed, Clinton's first two nominees for Attorney General both withdrew over irregularities concerning the employment of women to care for children in their homes; he ultimately appointed a woman without children, Janet Reno, as the first female Attorney General. See Mona Harrington, Care and Equality: Inventing a New Family Politics 11–24 (1999). According to Mona Harrington, the Clinton Administration was surprised by the resulting uproar because its policymakers had focused upon the gender issue and failed to notice the class issues involved; the Administration was thus unprepared for the outrage of many Americans about Baird's domestic arrangements. The

central problem, Harrington says, is that "we have not devised any equality-respecting system to replace the full-time caretaking labor force of women at home." Id. at 17. What do you think of this analysis? Whose equality counts the most? That of women in the workplace required to compete with men who have no caretaking duties, or that of the women looking after those women's children? How can these problems, which Harrington calls "care-equality problems," be addressed? Taunya Banks points out that feminists also missed an opportunity at the time of the so-called "Nannygate" controversy to force a more general public debate about the gendered nature of mothering and other domestic work. Banks, note 3 above, at 5.

5. In the first part of the 20th century, there was in fact a movement to improve the conditions of domestic workers by encouraging employers to use voluntary, standardized labor contracts and by lobbying for passage of labor legislation applicable to domestic service. See Peggie R. Smith, Regulating Paid Household Work: Class, Gender, Race, and Agendas of Reform, 48 Am. U. L. Rev. 851, 882–917 (1999). A National Committee on Household Employment, chaired by Eleanor Roosevelt, drafted labor standards to govern the employment relationship. Id. at 884–85. When the New Deal labor legislation was passed, however, domestic service was excluded from the Fair Labor Standards Act (FLSA), the National Labor Relations Act (NLRA), and the Social Security Act (SSA). Id. at 888–89. Smith attributes these failures to a number of factors, including the economic devaluation of housework in general as "non-productive" work; reluctance to think of the home as a unit of production or of household employers, who were women, as requiring regulation; and unwillingness to accept interference with family privacy. Id. at 898–912. Moreover, as white women left domestic service and were increasingly replaced by women of color, political support for protection of domestic workers decreased. Id. at 915–16.

The NLRA still explicitly excludes domestic service, 29 U.S.C. § 152(3), but the FLSA was amended in 1974 to provide minimum wage and overtime benefits to domestic workers, with some exceptions ("casual" babysitters, companions for the sick and elderly, and live-in domestic workers are all exempt from overtime requirements, and the former two are also exempt from minimum wage requirements). 29 U.S.C. § 213(a)(15), (b)(21). In addition, other key pieces of legislation that work to protect employees' rights, such as Title VII of the Civil Rights Act, the Americans with Disabilities Act, the Age Discrimination in Employment Act, and the Occupational Safety and Health Act, implicitly exclude domestic workers by requiring that an "employer" employ generally at least fifteen to twenty people, thereby excluding the average working mother who hires domestic workers from the definition. See 42 U.S.C. § 2000e(b); 42 U.S.C. § 12111(5)(A); 29 U.S.C. § 630(b); 29 C.F.R. § 1975.6 (2010). Given the current legislative environment, do you think this labor legislation would pass if brought before Congress today? What about legislation that provides more protection to domestic workers?

6. How can conditions be improved for the women who care for other women's children? Domestic workers are now covered by Social Security, thanks to the 1950 amendments to the act, but compliance with domestic employment laws is very low. Although Congress simplified the payment of employment taxes after the Zoe Baird fiasco described in note 4 above, by

eliminating quarterly reporting requirements, increasing the threshold amount, and exempting wages paid to certain family members, the number of household employers filing employment tax returns fell from 500,000 in 1994 to 300,000 in 1995. Debra Cohen-Whelan, Protecting the Hand That Rocks the Cradle: Ensuring the Delivery of Work Related Benefits to Child Care Workers, 32 Ind. L. Rev. 1187, 1192–93 (1999). It has been estimated that fewer than 25% of household employers comply with the requirements of the SSA on behalf of their domestic employees. Smith, above note 5, at 921. One commentator suggests a carrot-and-stick approach to enforcing the law—selecting income tax returns of dual-income couples with high salaries and exemptions for dependents for special scrutiny, and increasing the incentive to comply by providing a deduction for child care as a business expense, thus defraying much of the cost of paying employment taxes. Cohen-Whelan, above, at 1205–07, 1213–15. In this way, domestic workers would be able to claim Social Security benefits when they retire or are disabled, as well as unemployment compensation. These measures may not address the treatment of undocumented immigrant workers, however, who typically work for lower wages and do not want their employment relationships revealed. This is not surprising, as Taunya Banks notes, given that the Congressional debates following the "Nannygate" controversy focused primarily on the problems of affluent working women. Even when the interests of the women employed as child care workers were considered, the focus was only upon the needs of native-born minority workers and not of foreign-born resident child care providers. Banks, note 3 above, at 14–15. How can a political coalition be constructed around these issues?

7. On June 1, 2010, the New York State Senate passed the Domestic Workers Bill of Rights, which provides basic labor protections to domestic workers, such as overtime pay, paid sick days, and the right to organize. If the bill passes the State Assembly, New York will become the first state to afford labor protections to domestic workers. Assem. 1470, Reg. Sess. (N.Y. 2009); Russ Buettner, For Nannies, Hope for Workplace Protection, N.Y. Times, June 3, 2010, at A1. In other states, such as California and Colorado, movements to pass similar bills of rights for domestic workers have sprung up and are gaining momentum. See National Domestic Worker Alliance, CA Domestic Workers' Bill of Rights, http://www.nationaldomesticworkeralliance.org/campaigns/ca-domestic-workers-bill-of-rights; El Centro Humanitario, Campaigns, http://www.centrohumanitario.org/campaigns.php; see also National Domestic Worker Alliance, Regulatory Reforms at the U.S. Dep't of Labor, http://www.nationaldomesticworkeralliance.org/campaigns/us-dept-of-labor-reforms. There are also moves to amend U.S. Department of Labor regulations to require employers to keep records of hours worked by live-in workers and to provide wholesome meals for their employees if they want to claim meal and lodging credits. Advocates also hope to create a specialized Domestic Worker's Bureau in the Department of Labor. See National Domestic Worker Alliance, above. What other reforms or new legislation should be introduced to maximize the rights of domestic workers? How should feminists participate in this movement?

8. Perhaps the worst case scenario for a domestic worker is exemplified in United States v. Sabhnani, 599 F.3d 215 (2d Cir. 2010). From 2001 to 2007,

defendants Mahender and Varsha Sabhnani "employed" first one and then two Indonesian women to cook, clean, and perform other such chores in their household. The women were forced to sleep on the floor, dress in rags, and work long hours with little sleep or food. They were punished for any mistakes by being burned with scalding water, beaten by household objects, mutilated by knives and even Varsha Sabhnani's own hands, and, perhaps most perversely, forced to eat large quantities of hot chili peppers until physically ill. Varsha Sabhnani also threatened one of the women, forcing her to write embarrassing but false letters to her family in Indonesia, which Sabhnani kept along with both women's expired passports. The Sabhnanis were charged and convicted of multiple counts of forced labor, harboring aliens, peonage, and document servitude, among others. On appeal, the convictions were affirmed.

Another less violent but still disturbing case is Hernandez v. Attisha, No. 09–CV–2257–IEG, 2010 WL 816160 (S.D. Cal. 2010). The victim, Rosa Hernandez, crossed the border between Mexico and the United States without a visa in order to work for the defendants, Samad and Yvonne Attisha, who promised they would "fix [Hernandez's] papers." After arriving illegally in the country, Hernandez was forced to perform household duties for the Attishas without monetary compensation—her "employers" claimed it was to reimburse their secretary for the costs of Hernandez's transportation into the country. She was required to work extremely long hours for less than the state and federal minimum wage and was essentially under the Attishas' complete control as they held her passport and made it clear she was not free to go. As of late 2010, the Attishas stand charged with involuntary servitude and human trafficking.

How do these cases change your perception of the lives and rights of domestic workers? Are your views still rooted in the same theory of women's oppression and the contradiction of feminism that Romero discusses? Through what other lenses might we view these women's situations?

3. THE STATE AND CHILD CARE

In contrast to other major industrialized countries, the United States has no comprehensive policy on child care. In its absence, the outlines of a policy of sorts can nonetheless be discerned indirectly, for example, in the structure of the Family and Medical Leave Act, above; in the indirect subsidization of child care expenses through the tax code; and in the implications of recent welfare legislation for the care of children born to poor women. In this section we focus on the policy implications for child care of provisions in the Internal Revenue Code and of welfare reforms requiring mothers to work.

TEXT NOTE: CHILD CARE AND THE INTERNAL REVENUE CODE

The cost of caring for young children is an expense incurred by parents who are employed in the wage labor market. However, it has never been classified as a business expense under the Internal Revenue Code. In a 1939 case, a working couple claimed a deduction for the expenses of employing others to look after their young child. The Tax Court rejected classification of these costs as a business expense, explaining that:

> * * * We are not prepared to say that the care of children, like similar aspects of family and household life, is other than a personal concern. The wife's services as custodian of the home and protector of its children are ordinarily rendered without monetary compensation. There results no taxable income from the performance of this service and the correlative expenditure is personal and not susceptible of deduction. Here the wife has chosen to employ others to discharge her domestic function * * *. But that does not deprive the same work performed by others of its personal character nor furnish a reason why its cost should be treated as an offset in the guise of a deductible item.
>
> * * * It may for practical purposes be said to constitute a distinction between those activities which, as a matter of common acceptance and universal experience, are "ordinary" or usual as the direct accompaniment of business pursuits, on the one hand; and those which, though they may in some indirect and tenuous degree relate to the circumstances of a profitable occupation, are nevertheless personal in their nature, of a character applicable to human beings generally, and which exist on that plane regardless of the occupation, though not necessarily of the station in life, of the individuals concerned.
>
> In the latter category, we think, fall payments made to servants or others occupied in looking to the personal wants of their employers. And we include in this group nursemaids retained to care for infant children.[10]

Another argument against granting a tax deduction for child care is that the greatest benefit would flow to those individuals who earn the most, whose income is therefore likely to be taxed at a higher rate, and for whom a deduction from income is thus likely to provide a greater benefit. Such a deduction would have the same regressive effect, it is argued, as if the federal government were to provide cash payments for child care that increased as income increased. However valid this point may be, it has not prevailed with respect to those expenses which tax law has decided to treat as business expenses, including automobiles, home offices, and business meals.

Although child care is still not deductible as a business expense, the Taxpayer Relief Act of 1997 introduced a per-child credit against taxes owed for those with dependent children under the age of 17. In addition, the Internal Revenue Code now includes a limited provision for a tax credit for child care expenses.[11] A credit against taxes theoretically eliminates the disparity between higher- and lower-bracket taxpayers since everyone gets the same benefit, while a deduction would provide more benefit to higher-bracket taxpayers. However, the credit is of no value if the taxpayer makes so little as to not have a positive tax liability against which to offset the credit. Moreover, the credit is capped, regardless of how much is actually spent, and decreases as income increases, thus making the credit worth less or nothing to middle-

10. Smith v. Commissioner, 40 B.T.A. 1038, 1039–40 (1939), aff'd, 113 F.2d 114 (2d Cir. 1940).

11. See 26 U.S.C. § 21 (2010).

and upper-income taxpayers who spend large sums on child care. In addition, the credit may not be taken if the caregiver could be claimed as a dependent on the taxpayer's return, thus generally excluding payments to any relative living in the household. Hence the credit may not be available for child care by a relative, although such care, typically by a female relative, is a very common support system for poor women.

Families who do not qualify for tax credits may nonetheless take advantage of what are called "flexible spending plans" to receive a tax break on dependent care—if they work for the right employer. The current Internal Revenue Code allows an employee to pay in pretax dollars for up to $5000 in child care, if his or her employer maintains a plan providing for the setting aside and reimbursement of such expenses, a provision which gives higher-bracket taxpayers a larger benefit by shielding their marginal income. The amount is taken out of the employee's pretax income, placed in an account by the employer, and not reported as taxable income for that year; the employee then receives the amounts set aside only when she presents evidence of payments actually made for dependent care during that calendar year. By 2008, about 46% of companies with fifty or more employees offered this type of plan (37% of companies with fifty to ninety-nine employees and 76% of companies with 1000 or more employees), thus allowing their employees to pay for child care with untaxed income.[12] The tax code also allows an employer to provide child care directly in an equivalent amount, without taxing the benefit to the employee.[13]

In addition to denying a business expense deduction for child care, the Internal Revenue Code supports a traditional division of labor within the family by creating other disincentives for wives to work, for example, by (1) taxing the income of the secondary earner (usually the wife, who is typically paid less, is more likely to work part time, and may enter and leave the paid workforce at various points in her life cycle) at the marginal rate of the primary earner; (2) imposing regressive Social Security tax rates (the same percentage of income is paid by all wage earners, until they reach the annual maximum amount) and providing survivors' benefits for spouses who never participate in paid labor; and (3) failing to impute income for unpaid labor by caregivers.[14]

NOTES ON CHILD CARE AND THE INTERNAL REVENUE CODE

1. According to the Tax Court in *Smith*, child care should not be deductible as a business expense in part because it is not one of "those activities which, as a matter of common acceptance and universal experience, are 'ordinary' or usual as the direct accompaniment of business pursuits," but rather is an activity which though it "may in some indirect and tenuous degree relate to the circumstances of a profitable occupation, [is] nevertheless personal * * *, applicable to human beings generally, * * * regardless of the

12. Families and Work Institute, 2008 National Study of Employers 21 tbl.9 (surveying a representative sample of 1,100 companies with 50 or more employees).

13. 26 U.S.C. § 129 (2010).

14. See Nancy C. Staudt, Taxing Housework, 84 Geo. L.J. 1571, 1590–92, 1607–10 (1996); Edward J. McCaffery, Taxing Women 91–93, 120–22, 137–60 (1997).

occupation, though not necessarily of the station in life, of the individuals concerned." Deconstruct this argument. What are the interests underlying the distinction being made? With what is the court really concerned? Is this argument gender-based? Is the description by the *Smith* court dated, or does it still describe the attitude toward child care in our society?

2. The Canadian Supreme Court considered the issue of child care as a business expense more recently, in light of its constitutional prohibition of sex discrimination, but reached essentially the same decision as the *Smith* court. Symes v. Canada, 110 D.L.R. 4th 470 (1993). Ironically, although the case discussed the issue in light of the right to equality on the basis of sex as explicitly guaranteed by the Canadian Charter of Rights and Freedoms, these arguments failed on the ground that men with primary child care responsibilities were equally disadvantaged by the limitations on the deductibility of child care costs. Id. at 559. What do you think of this argument? How would the various theorists discussed in Chapter 3 analyze this issue?

Not all foreign courts agree with *Smith* and *Symes*. Recently, an Israeli court allowed attorney Vered Pery to deduct childcare expenses from her income taxes. The court ruled that the expenses Pery incurred for care of her children while she was at work were business-related because she would not have been able to work without them. The court reasoned that were it not for Pery's need to work outside the home, she would have been with her children, thus the tax deduction was appropriate. See Ido Baum, Court: Child-care Expenses are Tax Deductible, Haaretz (July 4, 2008), http://www.haaretz.com/print-edition/business/court-child-care-expenses-are-tax-deductible–1.243496. What do you think of this approach? How might it both help and hurt women?

3. Mary Louise Fellows asserts that the author of the opinion in *Smith* "relies on accepted roles based on class, gender, and, in a less obvious way, race to create the appearance of applying tax rules objectively." Fellows, Rocking the Tax Code: A Case Study of Employment-Related Child-Care Expenditures, 10 Yale J.L. & Feminism 307, 311, 374–79 (1998). Among other things, the opinion fails to address that a dual-earner family forgoes the tax benefit of the imputed income available to families where one spouse stayed at home and performed child care for the family unit. The mother's payment of another individual to perform these services instead is treated as a personal choice. Which is the choice involved: to have children or to enter the workforce? Or to care for one's children or outsource that task? Does the mother go to work to earn the money to consume child care or purchase child care in order to go to work? In what sense should these be treated as personal choices?

Judge Richard A. Posner suggests that the imputed tax benefit keeps women in the home and out of the workforce. Posner, Conservative Feminism, 1989 U. Chi. Legal F. 191 (1989). He argues that:

> Because the housewife's "earnings" in the home are not taxed, however, women will stay home even when they would be worth more in the market. For example, suppose the value of a housewife's work is $40,000 a year; her earnings in the market (net of all expenses associated with market work—commuting costs, etc.) would be $50,000; and she

would be in the 28 percent income tax bracket if she did enter the market. Then her after-tax income would be lower in the market than at home, and she will stay home even though she is worth more in the market.

Although this distortion could be eliminated, or at least reduced by taxing housewives' imputed earnings, the measurement problems would be formidable, to say the least. * * * A tax on housewives' imputed income * * * would * * * eliminate tax incentives from the decision whether to work within or outside the home. * * * [T]he economic or libertarian perspective * * * shows that things are not always as they seem; legislation superficially inimical to women's interests may actually serve those interests—and vice versa as we shall see. Feminists who are not libertarians may not like the vocabulary, methods, and assumptions of economics, but if they refuse to consider the economic consequences of policies affecting women they may end up hurting rather than helping women.

Id. at 193–94. Do you agree with Posner that taxing housewives' imputed income would remove some incentives for women to work within the home, allowing them to make freer market-based choices? Socialist feminists such as Eisenstein, excerpt in Chapter 3 above, argue that women's oppression is part and parcel with the oppression of their social classes, and that in order to combat such oppression, domestic work needs to be recognized alongside work in the formal economy. Do you think Posner's means of recognizing domestic work is what Eisenstein had in mind? If not, what are alternative means for acknowledging domestic work?

4. Should feminists support an income tax deduction for child care, if it benefits some groups of women more than others? Why or why not? How does this relate to your views of whether feminists should support a tax on housework, as discussed in Chapter 6?

5. Allowing flexible spending plans for dependent care provides a subsidy for some mothers—those who are employed by large institutional employers who set up such an account—and shuts out those employed part-time or by smaller employers who do not have such accounts, with a detrimental effect on many lower-income mothers who need child care in order to find employment. Such plans may sufficiently placate higher-income mothers so that they do not place pressure on Congress to treat child care as a business expense for which a deduction should be allowed. Should feminists oppose flexible spending plans for these reasons? Why or why not? How might you alter such programs in the interests of fairness and equality?

6. There are some indications that the reasoning in *Smith* may not hold up to more modern sensibilities. In Brown v. Comm'r, 73 T.C. 156 (1979), the tax court found the expense of sending the taxpayer's child to boarding school was deductible because it enabled the taxpayer to work. In a slightly different context, the tax court in Zoltan v. Comm'r, 79 T.C. 490 (1982), found the expense of sending a taxpayer's child to day camp qualified as an "employment-related expense" for purposes of the child care credit. More recently, the 10th Circuit in NLRB v. Velocity Exp., Inc., 434 F.3d 1198, 1203 (10th Cir. 2006), though not deciding an issue of child support, stated that "[e]xpenses

incurred permitting an employee to work (transportation and child care) seem just as essential as an employee's vehicle operating expenses." The dissent in this case also recognized that child care was "essential to allowing an employee to work," although it pointed out that neither child care nor vehicle operating expenses are currently deductible from an individual's income tax. Id. at 1206.

7. As discussed in the text note above, the Internal Revenue Code now includes a limited tax credit for a percentage of the money that qualifying parents spend on child care. 26 U.S.C. § 21 (2010). The credit depends on income; it begins at 35% and is reduced by one percentage point for every $2000 over $15,000 the taxpayer earns, with 20% as the minimum for qualifying taxpayers. Id. Several bills have been introduced in recent years to increase the amount of the credit for certain parents, but none have passed. The American Recovery and Reinvestment Act of 2009 increased the availability of the child tax credit (a credit against tax liability for taxpayers with qualifying children), but did not change the current child care tax credit. I.R.S., ARRA and the Additional Child Tax Credit (2009), http://www.irs.gov/newsroom/article/0,,id=205670,00.html. The Act did, however, provide nearly $2 billion for the Child Care and Development Fund, which supports child care services for lower-income families. U.S. Dep't Health & Hum. Services, Child Care and Development Fund, http://www.hhs.gov/recovery/programs/acf/childcare.html. It is unclear whether these provisions, and other tax cuts introduced by George W. Bush, will be extended past 2010.

Attempting to make good on his campaign promises, President Obama has proposed an increase of the minimum child care credit rate from 20% to 35% for any family making under $85,000 a year. Council on Women and Girls, Obama Administration Initiatives to Help Americans Meet Work and Family Responsibilities 2 (July 28, 2010), http://www.whitehouse.gov/sites/default/files/rss_viewer/Work-Family-fact-sheet.pdf. Members of Congress have introduced a similar proposal in the Support Working Parents Act of 2010, H.R. 5260, 111th Cong. (2010), which would increase the credit rate to 35% for qualifying parents in order to "repeal the phasedown of the credit percentage for dependent care tax credit." Id. More generous reforms have also been proposed, such as the Family Tax Relief Act, which would increase the percentage of child care expenses that could be claimed by low- and middle-income families to 50%. S. 997, 111th Cong. (2009). Given that even with these proposed increases, the child care credit makes up only a minute portion of the average family's child care expenses, do you think these reforms are worthwhile expenditures in an economic downturn? How else could Congress alleviate the burden of child care for America's middle- and lower-income families?

8. In one case, the Tax Court held that welfare payments paid to a mother for care of her disabled adult child were taxable as income to the mother, although welfare payments are generally nontaxable. Bannon v. Comm'r, 99 T.C. 59 (1992). Why must a related caregiver who uses those payments to care for the welfare recipient pay tax on them, when the welfare recipient herself is not required to do so? Why is this "income," if money given to a mother who is a homemaker by the child's father is not imputed as income to her? (Note: Child support after divorce is not taxable to the mother,

although maintenance or alimony must be included in her taxable income. See Lamb v. Dep't of Rev., TC–MD 080910C, 2008 WL 5147140 (Or. T.C. 2008) (providing a discussion of why child support payments do not qualify for the child care credit).) What are the assumptions underlying these distinctions? See, e.g., Grace Blumberg, Sexism in the Code: A Comparative Study of Income Taxation of Working Wives and Mothers, 21 Buff. L. Rev. 49 (1971).

9. The Earned Income Tax Credit (EITC) is a means by which the IRC implicitly supports parents, by providing tax credits to low-income individuals who file taxes. See 26 U.S.C. § 32 (2010). After welfare reform, EITC became the largest welfare expenditure, twice the amount expended on Temporary Assistance to Needy Families (TANF) and greater than the amount expended on the Food Stamp Program and Supplemental Security Income. Michael A. O'Connor, The Earned Income Tax Credit: Eligible Families at Risk of Losing Benefits, 33 Clearinghouse Rev. 433, 433 (1999). However, anywhere from 14–58% of those eligible for the credit do not receive it. Id. at 433–34. Barriers include the complex tax preparation process, language barriers for immigrants, and not wanting to be liable for taxes if self-employed. Id. at 435–36. Given the barriers to claiming the EITC, do you think it is an effective means of providing government support to poor parents with children?

10. When the Internal Revenue Code creates a disincentive for wives to work, whom does this advantage? Whom does it disadvantage? Should government be creating such incentives? Why or why not? How can they be eliminated? Compare Efrem Fischer, Note, Child Care: The Forgotten Tax Deduction, 3 Cardozo Women's L.J. 113 (1996) (advocating an increase in tax benefits to compensate for the "marriage penalty" as opposed to abolishing the joint return) and Tonya Gauff, Note & Comment, Eliminating the Secondary Earner Bias: Lessons from Malaysia, the United Kingdom, and Ireland, 4 Nw. J.L. & Soc. Pol'y 424 (2009) (identifying the separate filing option as not economically feasible because it results in higher taxes than if the couple filed jointly) with Laura Davis, Note, A Feminist Justification for the Adoption of an Individual Filing System, 62 S. Cal. L. Rev. 197 (1988) (advocating for the replacement of the joint filing system with a mandatory separate filing system to eliminate the marriage penalty) and Jessica Kornberg, Comment, Jumping on the Mommy Track: A Tax for Working Mothers, 17 UCLA Women's L.J. 187 (2008) (proposing an end to the joint filing system and a reinstatement of the separate filing system to alleviate the work disincentive which stems from the marriage penalty). Would removing the "marriage penalty" remove the disincentive for wives to work or to marry? See also Henry E. Smith, Intermediate Filing in Household Taxation, 72 S. Cal. L. Rev. 145 (1998) (proposing that taxpayers be allowed to file splitting income between spouses, so long as they commit to that division for state law purposes on divorce).

In Congress, bills have been introduced in both houses to eliminate or at least reduce the impact of the marriage penalty. The Marriage Tax Penalty Permanent Elimination Act of 2009, H.R. 85, 111th Cong. (1st Sess. 2009), was introduced in the House and the Permanent Marriage Penalty Relief Act of 2009, S. 74, 111th Cong. (1st Sess. 2009), was introduced in the Senate. Both bills, if passed, would repeal the sunset on the marriage penalty relief.

11. In addition to the various tax breaks described above, the federal government has also contributed to the development of corporate child care by tax write-offs and loans to corporations which provide child care directly to their employees. The 2011 United States budget allocates an estimated $28 billion this year and an estimated $22 billion next year between the relative values of tax incentives for employer run child care programs and tax credits for individual taxpayers. (Over $23 billion of the $28 billion in 2010 and over $18 billion of the $22 billion in 2011 is solely from the Child Tax Credit.) Office of Mgmt & Budget, Exec. Office of the President, Analytical Perspectives, Budget of the United States Government, Fiscal Year 2011 211 (2010). Do you think this policy is an adequate response to the need for child care in the United States? What are the shortcomings of such a policy? What are its race and class implications?

12. A 1954 amendment to the Internal Revenue Code provided a "limited deduction for certain child care expenses" for a brief period of time. Nammack v. Commissioner, 56 T.C. 1379, 1381 (1971). That deduction was expanded in 1964 to allow a woman, widower, or husband whose wife was incapacitated or institutionalized to claim up to a $600 deduction for one dependent and up to a $900 deduction for two or more dependents. Id. at 1381–82. However, the Tax Reform Act of 1976 repealed the deduction and enacted the child care credit that is still in place today. Do you think feminists could reinstate a similar deduction? Why or why not? What strategies would you pursue? How would such strategies relate to the feminist theories discussed in Chapter 3?

Text Note: Welfare Reform

Relatively recent changes in the U.S. welfare system have had a dramatic impact upon the relationship of women to their children. These "reforms" also mark a dramatic break from traditional views about the value of women caring for their own children at home. The previous welfare system, Aid to Families with Dependent Children (AFDC), had its origins in New Deal social security legislation. The program was designed primarily with white women in mind—widows or women who had been abandoned—and it assumed that these women would not work.[15] Thus AFDC provided a type of income support for the children of these mothers, although it was never as generous as the level of support given to former wage-earners under Social Security and was in fact inadequate to support a woman and her family.

AFDC was a federal program that reimbursed states for part of the benefits provided under a state welfare scheme, so long as the state scheme complied with federal requirements. It was a so-called entitlement program, that is, there was a federally guaranteed entitlement to assistance for persons covered by its terms, and states were guaranteed a matching share of whatever amount was necessary to provide benefits to all who qualified for the program.[16]

---

15. Dorothy Roberts, Killing the Black Body: Race, Reproduction and the Meaning of Liberty 205–06 (1997).

16. Jane C. Murphy, Legal Images of Motherhood: Conflicting Definitions from Welfare "Reform," Family, and Criminal Law, 83 Cornell L. Rev. 688, 737 (1998).

Initially, virtually all AFDC recipients were white; indeed, Blacks were largely excluded from the program's benefits until the 1960's.[17] After such exclusions were eliminated, work requirements gradually began to be added to the program. In the 1970s, women with school-age children were required to register to work, and the Family Support Act of 1988 required women whose children were three or older to work or enter training to work.[18]

A stereotype of the Black welfare mother was exploited by the New Right in the 1980s to attack the system of welfare as a whole, and presidential candidate Bill Clinton also vowed to "end welfare as we know it."[19] The Personal Responsibility and Work Opportunity Reconciliation Act (PRWORA) of 1996 was the result.[20] PRWORA abolished the federal entitlement system, replacing it with a block-grant program under which states were given a fixed sum, regardless of the level of need, and the states were given authority to decide eligibility requirements as well as the overall structure of the state program. However, PRWORA required two major changes in all state programs receiving funding. First, absolute time limits were imposed upon the receipt of benefits: a five-year cumulative lifetime maximum for any family, and a two-year deadline for all current recipients to find other means of support. Second, all recipients were required to work, regardless of the age of their children. Many states also added so-called "Family Caps," providing that no additional amounts would be included in a family's benefits upon the birth of a child to a mother who was already receiving benefits.[21]

In sum, the welfare reforms of the 1990s contradicted both the original assumptions of the AFDC program and the family values rhetoric of the New Right—that a young child was best cared for by his or her mother. At the same time, the new program made woefully inadequate provision for child care. Although PRWORA included funding to states for child care purposes (42 U.S.C. § 601), the Congressional Budget Office estimated that it fell $13.1 billion short of meeting the needs of mothers faced with the new work requirements during the period from 1997 to 2002.[22] The Department of Health and Human Services reported that only about 15% of low-and moderate-income children eligible for this federal assistance were receiving any aid in 1998, in part due to variations in state definitions of eligibility.[23] As a result, according to one study, "[a]bout a million additional toddlers and preschoolers are in child care because of changes in the welfare laws, but many are in low-quality care and are lagging in language and social development."[24]

---

17. See Linda Gordon, Pitied But Not Entitled: Single Mothers and the History of Welfare 1890–1935 15, 276 (1994).

18. Murphy, above note 16, at 734.

19. Id. at 735.

20. 42 U.S.C. §§ 601–607.

21. Roberts, above note 15, at 210–25.

22. Murphy, above note 16, at 740 n.281.

23. Child Care Bureau, Access to Child Care for Low-Income Working Families (1999) available at http://www.researchconnections.org/childcare/resources/180?q=access+to+child+care.

24. Tamar Lewin, Study Finds Welfare Changes Lead a Million Into Child Care, N.Y. Times, Feb. 4, 2000, at A16 (describing a Berkeley/Yale study of 1000 single mothers moving from welfare to work).

DOROTHY E. ROBERTS, THE VALUE OF BLACK MOTHERS' WORK

26 Conn. L. Rev. 871–78 (1994).

I. WHY MUST WELFARE MOTHERS WORK?

The common ground of contemporary welfare reform discourse is the belief that single mothers' dependence on government support is irresponsible and should be remedied by requiring these mothers to get jobs. "Workfare" is a refrain of the general theme that blames the poor, because of their dependence mentality, deviant family structure, and other cultural depravities, for their poverty. Martha Minow reveals workfare's injustice by asking the unspoken question, "why should single mothers responsible for young children be expected to work outside the home?"[2] Why does society focus on welfare mothers' dependence on public assistance rather than on their children's dependence on them for care?

Minow correctly points out that the focus on welfare mothers' dependence rather than their valuable care reflects a radical departure from the original welfare policy towards mothers. During the late nineteenth century, women successfully lobbied for public relief for widowed mothers. In her recent book, Protecting Soldiers and Mothers: The Political Origins of Social Policy in the United States, Theda Skocpol demonstrates how women's organizations and their allies exploited the ideology of motherhood to attain mothers' pensions and other "maternalist" legislation. The logic that propelled maternalist welfare policy was precisely the opposite of that backing workfare: widowed mothers needed government aid so that they would not have to relinquish their maternal duties in the home in order to join the work force. This maternalist rhetoric was powerful enough to mobilize disenfranchised women, defeat conservative opponents, and convince American legislatures to embark on social welfare programs far ahead of those of most European countries.

The current workfare proposals, then, reflect an unprecedented depreciation of welfare mothers' contribution to society. The rhetoric of motherhood has lost all of the persuasive force it wielded during the Progressive Era. The modern welfare state has increasingly degraded the work all mothers perform. It has abandoned the moral mother ideology and diminished the control of mothers over child care. As increasing numbers of women join the work force, society decreasingly rewards mothers' socially productive labor in the home. An individual's entitlement to welfare benefits now depends on his or her relationship to the market. Former workers are entitled to compensation by social insurance programs for their prior participation in the wage labor force. As unpaid caregivers with no connection to a male breadwinner, single mothers are considered undeserving clients of the welfare system.

---

2. Martha Minow, The Welfare of Single Mothers and Their Children, 26 Conn. L. Rev. 817 (1994). * * *

This universal devaluation of mothers' work, however, does not explain entirely the revolution in welfare reform. When welfare reformers devise remedies for maternal irresponsibility, they have Black single mothers in mind. Although marital status does not determine economic well-being, there is a strong association between Black single motherhood and family poverty. The image of the lazy Black welfare queen who breeds children to fatten her allowance shapes public attitudes about welfare policy. Part of the reason that maternalist rhetoric can no longer justify public financial support is that the public views this support as benefitting primarily Black mothers. Society particularly devalues Black mothers' work in the home because it sees these mothers as inherently unfit and their children as inherently useless.

II. THE VALUE OF BLACK MOTHERING

Maternalist rhetoric has no appeal in the case of Black welfare mothers because society sees no value in supporting their domestic service. The public views these mothers as less fit, less caring, and less hurt by separation from their children. First, workfare advocates fail to see the benefit in poor Black mothers' care for their young children. To the contrary, contemporary poverty rhetoric blames Black single mothers for perpetuating poverty by transmitting a deviant lifestyle to their children. Far from helping children, payments to Black single mothers merely encourage this transgenerational pathology. Dominant images have long depicted Black mothers as unfit. * * * Modern social pundits from Daniel Patrick Moynihan to Charles Murray have held Black single mothers responsible for the disintegration of the Black family and the Black community's consequent despair.[15]

Second, workfare advocates fail to see the injury in requiring Black mothers to leave their young children. Welfare reform discourse gives little attention to the relationship between poor Black mothers and their children. The forced separation of Black mothers from their children began during slavery, when Black family members faced being auctioned off to different masters. Slave mothers knew the regular pain of seeing their loved ones "rented out, loaned out, bought up, brought back, stored up, mortgaged, won, stolen or seized."[18] The disproportionate state disruption of Black families through the child welfare system reflects a continuing depreciation of the bond between Black mothers and their children.

Finally, workfare advocates are not hindered by any disharmony in the idea of a Black working mother. The conception of motherhood confined to the home and opposed to wage labor never applied to Black women. Slave women's hard labor in the field defied the Victorian norm of female domesticity. Even after Emancipation, political and economic conditions forced many Black mothers to earn a living outside the home.

---

15. See Charles Murray, Losing Ground: American Social Policy, 1950–1980, at 154–66 (1984) (claiming that welfare induces Black women to refrain from marriage and to have babies)* * *.

18. Toni Morrison, Beloved 23 (1987).

Americans expected Black mothers to look like Aunt Jemima, working in somebody else's kitchen: "(*o*)utfitted in an unflattering dress, apron, and scarf (a 'headrag'), she is always ready for work and never ready for bed."[22] American culture reveres no Black madonna; it upholds no popular image of a Black mother nurturing her child. Given this history, it is not surprising that policymakers do not think twice about requiring welfare mothers to leave their young children in order to go to work.

III. THE VALUE OF BLACK CHILDREN

The state often uses the pretext of helping children to justify regulating their mothers. What is striking about recent welfare proposals is that they do not even claim the traditional justification of promoting children's welfare. Indeed, they mandate or encourage practices traditionally regarded as harmful to children, such as mothers working outside the home and abortion. Welfare reformers cannot demonstrate that it is better for poor children to make their mothers work. Minow convincingly describes the extra dangers these children face. Their mothers' employment may actually reduce the amount of money available for their needs and jeopardize their health care; it may deprive them of their only protection against a myriad of environmental hazards. Thus, it is not mothers' wage labor itself that is harmful to children; rather, workfare's harm lies in its failure to provide meaningful support for working mothers, such as day care, jobs, housing, health care, education and a guaranteed income.

Underlying the consensus that welfare mothers should work is often the conviction that their children are socially worthless, lacking any potential to contribute to society. Welfare reform rhetoric assumes that these children will grow up to be poor and, consequently, burdens to society. The proposals dismiss any possible reason to nurture, inspire, or love these children. Minow asks at the end of her essay, "why not consider paying mothers of especially young children to care for their children?" In addition to the historic resistance to compensating mothers' work, society's response is, "because these children are not worth it."

The reason for society's bleak assessment is not only the belief that Black mothers are likely to corrupt their children, but that Black children are predisposed to corruption. * * * The powerful Western image of childhood innocence does not seem to benefit Black children. Black children are born guilty. They are potential menaces—criminals, crackheads, and welfare mothers waiting to happen. * * *

This devaluation of Black children, like the devaluation of Black mothering, is older than recent poverty discourse. It stems from a racial caste system based on white superiority and racial purity that has endured for three centuries. In this supposedly natural hierarchy, Black mothers inevitably pass down to their children a whole set of inferior traits. Racist ideology dictates that Black bodies, intellect, and character are all inher-

22. Regina Austin, Black Women, Sisterhood, and the Difference/Deviance Divide, 26 New Eng. L. Rev. 877, 883 (1992).

ently vulgar. This history enhances Stephanie Coontz's account of the family's political role.[34] American society's embrace of the private family as its model for social accountability is particularly devastating for Black children. According to Coontz, society's empathy extends only to people "whom we can imagine as potential lovers or family members."[35] America's legacy of racial separation makes it especially difficult—if not impossible—for most white Americans to imagine Black children as part of their family.

NOTES ON WELFARE REFORM AND CHILD CARE

1. Is the public opposition to mothers on welfare because they are single, because they do not work, or because they are assumed to be Black? (In fact, only 39.5% of AFDC recipients in 1990 were Black; non-Hispanic whites were 38.1%. Lucy A. Williams, The Ideology of Division: Behavior Modification Welfare Reform Proposals, 102 Yale L.J. 719, 744 (1992).) Linda C. McClain also notes the gendered assumptions underlying the critique of welfare, with its emphasis upon the "irresponsibility" of mothers who procreate without either a husband or adequate economic resources, rather than upon men's failure to take responsibility for contraception, to be involved and nurturing parents, and to pay child support. McClain, "Irresponsible" Reproduction, 47 Hastings L.J. 339, 422–25 (1996).

2. The welfare reform legislation was premised upon the belief that it is possible to modify the behavior of welfare recipients by the terms of a statute. Rebekah Smith challenges this reasoning by examining the false assumptions under an idea like a family cap, which limits the number of children for whom aid may be given. Smith, Family Caps in Welfare Reform: Their Coercive Effects and Damaging Consequences, 29 Harv. J.L. & Gender 151 (2006). The legislation assumes, among other things, that: welfare mothers have many children; they have viable family planning options; they get pregnant in order to receive additional benefits; and that welfare promotes intergenerational dependence. In reality, as of 1990, 72.5% of AFDC families had only one or two children; only about 10% had more than three. Id. at 159. Moreover, childbearing decisions appear not to correlate with economics in general; and birthrates among welfare recipients are not higher where benefits are high. Williams, above note 1, at 739–40. Indeed, the increase in benefits for a new child is hardly significant enough to affect behavior: "As one welfare director stated: 'anyone who thinks that a woman goes through nine months of pregnancy . . . for $45 more a month . . . has got to be a man.' " Smith, above, at 158. In addition, as noted in Chapter 5, poor women often have little control over the conditions under which they become pregnant and are unable to obtain government funding for abortions. Finally, with regard to intergenerational dependence, only a quarter of welfare recipients receive benefits on a long-term basis; most are on welfare for less than two years. That time typically marks a period of transition for the family, such as a divorce or

34. See Stephanie Coontz, The Way We Never Were: American Families and the Nostalgia Trap (1992).

35. Id. at 115.

losing a job. Id. at 161. Why do you think so many false assumptions persist in the face of evidence to the contrary?

3. The welfare reform legislation also assumed that welfare recipients do not work because they do not want to; the new law was expected to modify behavior in this respect as well. In fact, poor women who are mothers do work, or try to, although there are simply not enough jobs in the economy for unskilled workers without experience. Most welfare recipients have a strong work ethic, and those who do not work are often faced with significant obstacles, such as mental or physical impairment. Smith, above note 2, at 162. Jody Raphael suggests that one reason women may not be able to keep jobs, or join training programs, is domestic violence; the abuser may deliberately sabotage any attempt by the woman to establish economic independence of him. Raphael, Domestic Violence and Welfare Receipt: Toward A New Feminist Theory of Welfare Dependency, 19 Harv. Women's L.J. 201, 203–07 (1996). See also Joan Meier, Domestic Violence, Character, and Social Change in the Welfare Reform Debate, 19 Law & Pol'y 205, 209–12 (1997) (summarizing empirical research showing that over 50% of women on welfare are presently or have recently been victims of domestic violence and describing the causal connection between the abuse and women's inability to participate in welfare-to-work programs or become economically self-sufficient). What policies are necessary to address this problem?

4. Is the fact that women in general are moving into the workforce a good reason to require women who are on welfare to be employed as well? Why or why not? Do you believe that mothers in general should work outside the home, or only those who wish to do so? Should it depend upon whether they are able to find work that yields a benefit greater than their caretaking in the home would yield? How would you measure this?

5. Is there any way to reconcile the New Right rhetoric of family values, namely its opposition to working mothers and day care, with its support for requiring mothers on assistance to work? To what extent do patriarchal notions play a role in this rhetoric? Should the wife be at home because she has a husband or because she has a child? Is racism the only explanation for this seeming anomaly among conservatives?

6. Is the conservative critique of welfare consistent with opposition to abortion? What alternatives are assumed to be available to a young woman without economic resources who becomes pregnant, is abandoned by the father of her children, or leaves him to escape domestic violence? See McClain, above note 1, at 396–408 (describing the intersection of arguments about abortion and "irresponsible" reproduction).

7. As Roberts points out in the excerpt above, the welfare reforms "mandate or encourage practices traditionally regarded as harmful to children, such as mothers working outside the home and abortion * * *. Their mothers' employment may actually reduce the amount of money available for their [poor children's] needs and jeopardize their health care; it may deprive them of their only protection against a myriad of environmental hazards." Do the values embedded in the welfare reform legislation reflect a more general abandonment of the notion that it is important for mothers to care for their children and a denigration of the value of mothers' work? Or only for Black

mothers and their children? If the latter, would that abandonment pertain to all Black mothers or merely those on or close to being on welfare?

Several times over the course of the excerpt, Roberts implies that motherhood is incompatible with work outside the home, that a mother cannot care for her children and maintain a 9–to–5 job, and that by requiring her to have such a job, welfare reform is forcing her to abandon her role as a mother. Is this always true, or is Roberts emphasizing that it is particularly true for poor women? How might Roberts be read to suggest that mothers who work are not truly caring for their children, whereas men in the same position would be praised as responsible breadwinners? If the things a mother needs to care for her children have a market price, isn't she fulfilling her role as a caregiver when she enters the market as a worker to obtain them? Or is Roberts arguing that women on assistance cannot afford to obtain that care?

8. When PRWORA was reauthorized in 2003, it was accompanied by a variety of "marriage-promotion" initiatives proposed by the Bush Administration and an "illegitimacy bonus," a financial incentive of up to $25 million granted to states that have the largest decrease in births to unwed mothers. Phoebe G. Silag, To Have, To Hold, To Receive Public Assistance: TANF and Marriage–Promotion Policies, 7 J. Gender Race & Just. 413, 416–27 (2003). Congress authorized almost $2 billion to be spent over 5–6 years on marriage promotion and "responsible fatherhood" activities. Judith E. Koons, Motherhood, Marriage, and Morality: The Pro–Marriage Moral Discourse of American Welfare Policy, 19 Wis. Women's L.J. 1, 17–19 (2004). What is the relationship between marriage and the perceived problems toward which PRWORA/TANF is directed? What are those problems perceived to be? How do they relate to marriage or its absence? Will marriage solve them? Why or why not?

Since PRWORA first passed, legal scholars have debated both the social and constitutional problems with the marriage promotion aspect of welfare reform. Just as the work requirement and family cap provisions of the act were based on assumptions about women and families on welfare that are not necessarily true, the promotion of marriage in modern welfare programs seems to be based on the stigmatization of single motherhood and the belief that marriage can magically reduce or even eliminate poverty. See Parvin Huda, Singled Out: A Critique of the Representation of Single Motherhood in Welfare Discourse, 7 Wm. & Mary J. Women & L. 341 (2001) (discussing stigma through various feminist lenses); Angela Onwuachi–Willig, The Return of the Ring: Welfare Reform's Marriage Cure as the Revival of Post–Bellum Control, 93 Cal. L. Rev. 1647, 1679 (2005). Most recently, Aly Parker points out a plethora of problems with marriage promotion. Aside from the constitutional problems—namely the coercion factor and religious undertones—these problems include the threat of abusive marriage, the likelihood of barriers to marriage for poor women, the mixed messages sent to women about being both caretaker and breadwinner, and the reality that children of single parents are not doomed to be criminals. Parker, Can't Buy Me Love: Funding Marriage Promotion Versus Listening to Real Needs in Breaking the Cycle of Poverty, 18 S. Cal. Rev. L. & Soc. Just. 493, 505 (2009). What other problems may arise from government promotion of marriage as a "cure" for poverty? Can these problems be solved only by abolishing marriage promotion programs, or could there be a feminist marriage program? What would such a program look like?

9. The recession that began in 2008 may, ironically, eliminate some of these concerns by ending welfare itself. In California, Governor Arnold Schwarzenegger has proposed eliminating the entire welfare-to-work program and corresponding state subsidies for child care. See Jack Dolan, Budget Analyst Advises Lawmakers to Reject Schwarzenegger's Plan to Cut Welfare, L.A. Times, May 19, 2010. What might this trend in state spending reveal about public and political perceptions of welfare? Is it because welfare is publicly perceived—despite evidence to the contrary—as largely benefiting Blacks that politicians are willing to reduce spending or scrap their programs all together? What other programs should states cut before gutting welfare?

10. President Obama has been criticized for allegedly destroying welfare reform with his recent stimulus bill, which included a TANF Emergency Fund designed to reimburse states that increase spending on assistance, short-term non-recurrent benefits, or subsidized employment between 2009 and 2010. See U.S. Dept. of Health and Human Services: Administration for Children and Families, Temporary Assistance for Needy Families Program Instruction, Apr. 3, 2009, http://www.acf.hhs.gov/programs/ofa/policy/pa-ofa/2009/pa200901.htm. Critics argue that the increased spending essentially eliminates the marriage promotion policies of the Bush administration and erases the benefits of the Clinton-era welfare reform by encouraging states to increase welfare caseloads. Given that the work requirement is still in place, however, is it truly the case that welfare reform is dead? What would make it dead in Roberts's view? In your view?

F. CUSTODY

TEXT NOTE: THE DEVELOPMENT OF CUSTODY PREFERENCES

Well into the 19th century, fathers of children born into a marriage automatically retained custody of children at divorce or separation because the law viewed these children as their father's property and under his control at all times. By the end of the 19th century, this paternal preference was replaced in most jurisdictions by a presumption that children "of tender years" (somewhere between the ages of five and twelve depending on the child and the judge) were best off in the custody of their mothers. When a judge regarded a child as no longer of tender years, custody was awarded pursuant to the best interest of the child standard, which directed the judge to place the child in the household which, in the judge's view, would be best for the child. During the late 1960s and 1970s, the tender years doctrine came under attack because it treated women and men differently, in violation of the emerging norm of formal equality. As a result, between 1970 and 1990, the maternal preference was replaced in almost all jurisdictions by some version of the "best interest of the child" standard.

Several other approaches have been used in recent years. Many jurisdictions have moved toward joint custody, which can mean either joint *legal* custody only—joint decisionmaking on matters such as education and health care with a primary custodial parent and visitation for the noncustodial parent—or joint legal custody combined with joint *physical* custody, meaning that the child resides half the time with each parent. Although parents initially developed the concept of joint custody in privately negotiated settlement agreements that were merely tolerated by the courts, in many jurisdictions it began to be pressed upon divorcing parents by mediators and judges even when the parents did not desire it, on the theory that continued close contact with both parents is always in the best interest of the child. Another approach, the "primary-caretaker" standard, was adopted in West Virginia and Minnesota, though it has now been abandoned in both jurisdictions. Minnesota returned to the best-interest standard, and West Virginia adopted the standard of the American Law Institute's Principles of Family Dissolution. The ALI standard is akin to the primary-caretaker standard in that it provides that, whenever possible, the court is to apportion custody so as to approximate the proportion of time each parent spent caring for the child during marriage. The apparent assumption is that most children—not just those children with a *primary* caretaker—are likely to be best off after divorce in the care of the parents who cared for them prior to the divorce. Each of these approaches is discussed in the article which follows. Katharine Bartlett, the author, was the Reporter for the ALI's Principles of Family Dissolution.

KATHARINE T. BARTLETT, CHILD CUSTODY IN THE 21ST CENTURY: HOW THE AMERICAN LAW INSTITUTE PROPOSES TO ACHIEVE PREDICTABILITY AND STILL PROTECT THE INDIVIDUAL CHILD'S BEST INTERESTS

35 Willamette L. Rev. 467, 468–81 (1999).

I. The Open–Ended Best–Interests-of-the-Child Test

Let us consider the case of Jane and David. Like most couples today, both work outside the home, and both are actively involved in the caretaking of their two children, Sara, 8, and Jamelle, 10. David works longer hours and earns more money than Jane. Jane, who works thirty hours per week outside the home, assumes primary responsibility for the children. She makes the after-school arrangements, goes to the parent-teacher conferences, sees to the children's doctor's appointments, and performs a majority of the bedtime and morning routines, weekend care, and meal preparation.

Jane and David have different parenting styles. David believes in firm rules, high expectations, and regular chores. He will not negotiate bedtimes, dinner menus, homework routines, or the children's choice of movies. Jane is a freer spirit who is more spontaneous and creative with the children. She does not interrupt her quality time with the children with an artificial bedtime or rigid schedule for homework and chores. The children have more fun when they are with Jane, but they are better behaved when with David. There are other differences as well. David goes to church; Jane does not. David reads voraciously and has tried to pass on his love of literature, fine art, and classical music to the children; Jane enjoys board games, cards, television, and rock and roll.

A year ago, Jane had an affair, for which David has not forgiven her. Their relationship has deteriorated, they have decided to divorce, and now they each want custody of the children. Who should win? What rule should govern the case?

For a long time, the rule thought to best serve the child's interests at divorce was the best-interests-of-the-child test. This test simply adopts the goal as the standard itself, leaving it to the judge to determine what custodial arrangement, on a case-by-case basis considering all of the relevant facts, produces the best result for the child. The advantages of the test are obvious: (1) it relies on individualized determinations for Sara and Jamelle specifically, not generalizations about what is good for all children or the average child; (2) it focuses decisionmaking on the child, rather than on the interests of the state of Oregon or on Jane's or David's own desires; and (3) it creates the greatest amount of flexibility in decisionmaking.

As many others have pointed out, this broad, individualized standard also has a number of flaws. Most especially, the standard allows so much judicial discretion that Jane and David may find it hard to predict what the court will do. Either party may win and, thus, each has reason to secure his or her respective advantage, most likely at the expense of cooperation with the other. For example, David may ask for primary custody, even if he does not want it, to create some negotiating room. He may attempt to build his reputation as the more responsible parent by alienating Jane from the court-appointed psychiatrist, the children's teachers, or the parents of the children's friends. Jane, for her part, may begin to exclude David from decisionmaking, or suggest to the children in subtle, or not-so-subtle, ways, that their father is a real drag. None of these strategies is likely to benefit the children.

To convince the court that he or she is the better parent, David and Jane will each hire experts. These experts can be expensive. What will they do to earn their fees? Jane is likely to want experts who will give testimony in open court about how flexible, caring, and nurturing she is, and what a cold, uncaring, rigid and distant figure their father is. David's experts, in turn, will attempt to highlight Jane's irresponsibility, her sexual immorality, and her lack of discipline of the children, while emphasizing David's rock-steady parenting skills. This dirty linen will be aired in custody reports or in open court, furthering the alienation between the parents.

After hearing from the experts, the teachers, the friends, Jane and David themselves, and perhaps even the children, how will the court decide? Under the best-interests test, any sense the court makes of the evidence will be determined by what it determines is best for children. The judge cannot separate that determination from the judge's beliefs about what matters to the child's welfare. If the judge thinks organized religion is beneficial for children, he or she will favor David on that account. If the judge thinks that what matters most is how much time a parent has spent caring for the child, Jane will have the edge, unless the judge believes that a good mother would have stayed home and spent her time caring for children rather than trying to advance her career. If the judge thinks that spontaneity and creativity are better for children than firm routines, Jane wins. On the other hand, if Jane's extramarital affair makes her a bad parent in the judge's eyes, she is more likely to lose.

No matter who gets custody, the matter is not necessarily over, for the facts may change. For example, assume Jane wins primary custody, but then her boyfriend moves in with her and the children. While the judge may have been willing to overlook Jane's marital infidelity episode before the divorce, he may feel differently about her engaging on an ongoing basis in behavior he deems immoral. David may think it is worth a try to find out. If so, the whole case will be relitigated—as it may be also if Jane decides to relocate to Idaho or takes a job that requires her to rely more heavily on day care.

II. Alternatives to the Best Interests Test

Any standard example like the one outlined demonstrates a number of difficulties with the best-interests test: uncertainty and unpredictability, stimulation of strategic behavior, encouragement of litigation, and the requirement of costly experts in a setting that emphasizes finger-pointing over cooperation. In light of these and related difficulties, policy-makers and scholars have been attempting for years to refine the best interests test, in order to achieve, with a greater degree of predictability, decisions that are best for children. It is important to see that these refinements are alternatives to the best-interests test, not alternatives to the child's best interests. They represent efforts to determine the child's interests without producing the "anti-child consequences." After examining the alternatives, this Part explains why the ALI approach is the most promising one.

A. "Laundry List" Approach

The first—and by far the most common—way legislators have attempted to make the best-interests test more specific and predictable is to detail a "laundry list" of factors that courts must consider in applying the best-interests test. Oregon's statute, for example, lists the following factors: (1) the emotional ties between the child and other family members; (2) the parties' interest in and attitude toward the child; (3) the desirability of continuing an existing relationship; (4) the abuse of one parent by the other; and (5) the willingness and ability of each parent to facilitate and encourage a close and continuing relationship between the other parent and the child. Other statutes mention the child's physical, emotional, mental, religious, and social needs and the capability and desire of each parent to meet these needs, the child's preferences, and the stability of each home environment.

The laundry-list approach to determining the child's best interests appears to add specificity and concreteness. Two difficulties, however, make this approach less likely to produce a predictable result than the best-interests test itself. First, the lists focus on factors such as parenting abilities and the quality of relationships, which are as intangible and difficult to measure as the child's best interests. Second, the approach fails to prioritize the factors under consideration. A court may decide that Jane has a stronger emotional bond with her children, but that David is more mature and has better parenting abilities. Who, then, should win? When the factors do not all point in a single direction—that is, when guidelines are needed most—they leave the decisionmaker to decide which factors matter most, with no useful guidance from the rule itself.

B. Primary Caretaker Presumption

A different approach for operationalizing the best-interests test, an approach popular among scholars and commentators, is a primary caretaking presumption. A primary caretaker presumption requires a court to identify the parent who has spent the greatest amount of time caring for the child and then award custody to that parent, unless the other parent establishes that the primary caretaking parent is unfit. The approach is defended on the grounds that the parent who has been taking primary care of the child has the better parenting skills and the stronger emotional connection with the child. If the presumption is applied to the facts set forth above, Jane would win custody because she spent more time during the marriage caring for the children than did David.

The primary caretaker approach has been criticized as favoring women because women are most often the primary caretakers of children. This claim of bias is an interesting topic in itself: Should the fact that women have assumed (or been assigned) the primary responsibility for raising children in this society mean that when they get custody, the system is biased in favor of them? * * *

Ironically, the experiences of the only two states that have worked with a primary caretaking presumption—West Virginia, from 1981 through 1999,[8] and Minnesota for four years between 1985 and 1989—appear to show that gender bias against mothers, especially those who do not conform to gender role stereotypes, is at least as serious a problem as bias against fathers. The problem comes from the fact that in identifying who has been the primary caretaking parent, many courts tend to reward fathers for doing more than judges expect them to do, while tending to penalize mothers who work or who are otherwise less available to their

---

8. See Garska v. McCoy, 278 S.E.2d 357 (W. Va. 1981). [The court identified a number of factors to be considered under the primary-caretaker standard:

> In establishing which natural or adoptive parent is the primary caretaker, the trial court shall determine which parent has taken primary responsibility for, *inter alia,* the performance of the following caring and nurturing duties of a parent: (1) preparing and planning of meals; (2) bathing, grooming and dressing; (3) purchasing, cleaning, and care of clothes; (4) medical care, including nursing and trips to physicians; (5) arranging for social interaction among peers after school, i.e., transporting to friends' houses or, for example, to girl or boy scout meetings; (6) arranging alternative care, i.e., babysitting, day-care, etc.; (7) putting child to bed at night, attending to child in the middle of the night, waking child in the morning; (8) disciplining, i.e., teaching general manners and toilet training; (9) educating, i.e., religious, cultural, social, etc.; and (10) teaching elementary skills, i.e., reading, writing and arithmetic.

Id. at 363.]

children than the traditional stay-at-home mother.[11] A number of trial courts have characterized a woman who intends to put her child in day care as an uncaring mother, while treating a father who intends to do so as simply a responsible provider.[12] Courts are also said to be harder on mothers who have had an extramarital affair than they are on fathers who have done so, or to find mothers more emotionally unstable even when that instability might be due to severe domestic abuse.

If gender bias in the application of the presumption could be eliminated, the primary caretaker approach would produce more determinate results than the best-interests test. The primary caretaker approach, however, * * * presupposes that every family has a primary caretaker or, if not, that it should have one. I am talking about two different types of norms here: an empirical one—how a child has been cared for, before the divorce—and a normative one—how the child should be cared for, after the divorce. A primary caretaker rule perpetuates a particular norm—that one parent specializes (and should) in childrearing while the other parent specializes (and should) in supporting the family economically. That is a reasonable description of many families. But it is not the only reasonable reality or ideal, and it is not a reality or ideal that should be sponsored by a society that prides itself on—indeed, gives constitutional recognition to—the importance of family diversity and cultural pluralism.

* * *

C. Joint Custody Approach

Another alternative to the best-interests test, and the favored solution of many legislators, is joint custody. Joint custody, its advocates argue, serves the child's best interests by treating both parents as important to the child, with their own strengths and unique contributions to the child's well-being.

Reformers have sought to make joint custody a more likely option in custody cases by enacting measures that require judges to consider, or to prefer, joint physical custody. The strength of the presumption varies. Some states, such as Oregon, recognize a presumption in favor of joint custody only when parents agree to it. Other states have rules that affect

---

11. See, e.g., Patricia Ann S. v. James Daniel S., 435 S.E.2d 6 (W. Va. 1993) (upholding the trial court finding that neither the father, who was a full-time architect, nor the mother, who was a stay-at-home parent, was the children's primary caretaker, because father typically made the children's breakfast, cooked some weekend meals, attended some school functions, and engaged in weekend activities with the children). This same bias also affects how the trial courts apply the best-interest test. See, e.g., *In re* Marriage of Holcomb, 888 P.2d 1046 (Or. Ct. App.1995) (overturning trial court decision to place a child with the father based in part on the conclusion that the mother's plans to attend graduate school out of state, as well as her continued breastfeeding of the 19–month–old child, demonstrated that she placed her concerns for herself above those of her child); Prost v. Greene, 652 A.2d 621 (D.C. 1995) (accepting trial court findings that the father assumed the greater portion of parental obligations for the children, based on evidence that focused more on what the mother did not do than on what the father did).

12. See, e.g., Tresnak v. Tresnak, 297 N.W.2d 109 (Iowa 1980) (reversing custody award to the father that had been based, in part, on an assumption that the mother's pursuit of a legal education would be detrimental to the children, while no such assumption was made about the father, who was engaged in full-time employment outside the home).

only the burden of proof, making joint custody the default rule but allowing an order other than joint custody if one parent establishes that joint custody is not in the child's best interests. A few states impose a stronger presumption. In Florida, for example, shared parenting responsibility is required unless shown to be detrimental to the child.

Leaving aside the special practical difficulties of working out equally shared physical responsibility in many family circumstances, a joint custody rule is inadequate for the same reason a primary caretaker rule is inadequate: it presumes that one particular form of custody is best in all cases. A joint custody rule represents a judgment by the state that both parents should have equal caretaking roles with respect to their children. While this norm, again, might make sense to many of us in our individual lives, it is not the choice many families have exercised and should not be imposed as a general standard.

D. Why the Alternatives to the Best–Interests Tests Have Not Replaced It

Although both a primary caretaker presumption and a joint custody approach have their adherents, neither approach has caught on as the way to implement the goal of the child's best interests. * * *

The mismatch between the ideals of each of these presumptions and the family realities within which they must be implemented has caused substantial difficulties for courts. Few states have enacted a primary caretaker presumption. Those that have—West Virginia and Minnesota—have had a disproportionate number of appellate cases in which trial court decisions have been reviewed and often overturned. The joint custody movement has produced new laws in at least thirteen states but has not made child custody decisions substantially more predictable and certain. As noted above, those legislatures enamored of the notion of joint custody as an ideal have enacted legislation that is largely symbolic, applying only when the parties have agreed to joint custody, or as a burden of proof rule. The few states that have a stronger presumption in favor of joint custody typically follow rules that counteract its effects. * * * Because joint custody does not suit the individual needs and circumstances of many families, interest in joint custody seems to be subsiding. Montana recently repealed its joint custody preference.

E. The ALI Alternative

The ALI has proposed a set of default rules or "Principles" in the custody area that go some way toward avoiding the difficulties described above. These Principles provide that, unless parents agree otherwise, a parent should be allocated custodial responsibility in rough proportion to the share of responsibility the parent assumed before the divorce or the circumstances giving rise to the custody action. Exceptions to this rule exist, but these exceptions for the most part are either clear and easily applicable, or require that the necessary findings be established under a heightened standard of proof. * * * The Principles also require reasonable limits in access to a child to protect the child or child's parent where the other parent, regardless of the past level of caretaking, is found to have engaged in child abuse, domestic abuse, or drug or alcohol abuse. In fact, when domestic abuse is established, the abusing parent cannot be allocated custodial access without findings that the child and the other parent can be protected.

* * *

The ALI approach to allocating custodial responsibility prioritizes a factor that courts increasingly emphasize in applying the best-interest test: past parenting involvement. The approach, however, makes this reliance more explicit and predictable. In effect, it amounts to a primary caretaker presumption when one parent has been exercising a substantial majority of the past caretaking, and it amounts to a joint custody presumption when past caretaking has been shared equally in the past. It responds to all variations and combinations of past caretaking patterns between those two poles, declining to impose some average, idealized family form on all families and instead favoring solutions that roughly approximate the caretaking shares each parent assumed before the divorce or before the custody issue arose.

The benefits of the ALI alternative are substantial. First, it focuses a factfinder on historical facts rather than on subjective questions about what is good for children, comparative judgments about the quality of emotional bonds and parental abilities, or future speculation about the different outcomes that might result from different custodial arrangements. Questions about who did what in the past can be contentious, but courts and court procedures are set up to resolve what happened in the past; they are not accustomed to predicting the future.

Because questions about past parenting patterns are factual and do not require normative judgments or speculative predictions, they should be answerable in most cases without resort to experts. At the same time, past caretaking patterns likely are a fairly reliable proxy of the intangible qualities such as parental abilities and emotional bonds that are so difficult for courts to ascertain. If the parent has been more involved with the child in the past, it may reasonably be supposed that parent is more experienced and emotionally connected to the child. Past caretaking patterns also are likely to mirror the strength of each parent's preference to spend time with the child, which means less distortion in the bargaining process.

Relying on past caretaking patterns also reduces the potential for bias in custody decisions, which may be based on gender, race, religion, and other prejudicial factors. Under the best interests test, it is difficult to eliminate the bias stemming from an unconscious belief that a mother's primary occupation should be raising her children, while a father should be engaged in the full-time economic support of the family. If custody must be apportioned based on each parent's past share of caretaking efforts, however, this bias has far less room to operate. A parent who obtains a greater share of custodial time because of a more extensive prior role as the caretaking parent does so not because of the court's gender bias but because of the parents' own past choices about the best way to care for the child.

NOTES ON CHILD CUSTODY

1. Does the best-interest-of-the-child standard provide sufficient guidelines for judges? What does Bartlett think? What do you think? Who are the people serving as family court judges in your jurisdiction? Do they have any special training in family law issues? Did they ask to be placed in family court, or do they view their current role as a necessary stepping stone to becoming a judge in other courts? How do you predict the judges in your jurisdiction would come out in Bartlett's hypothetical involving Jane and David under a best-interest standard? Compare your answer with your classmates. Is there consensus on what "best interests" would mean in this hypothetical? What guidance does the standard provide when there are two fit parents with different values, parenting styles, lifestyles, interests, religious commitments, etc.?

2. According to the readings earlier in this chapter, do mothers or fathers typically perform most of the functions outlined in the West Virginia primary caretaker standard quoted in footnote 8 in the excerpt above? As Bartlett reports, some commentators claim this standard is biased against men "because women are most often the primary caretakers of children." Bartlett asks: "Should the fact that women have assumed (or been assigned) the primary responsibility for raising children in this society mean that when they get custody, the system is biased in favor of them?" What do you think? Under a standard without this alleged bias, would men be as likely to win custody as women? What would make a standard bias-free in your view?

3. As Bartlett indicates, during the more than 18 years in which West Virginia used the primary caretaker standard, the standard as applied often favored fathers. Bartlett cites one of these cases, Patricia Ann S. v. James Daniel S., 435 S.E.2d 6 (W.Va. 1993). In this case, the court awarded custody to a father who worked 12–hour days as an architect with frequent out-of-town business trips rather than to the mother who quit working as a kindergarten teacher to work as a full-time mother when she had children. Incredibly, both the trial court and the West Virginia Supreme Court found that there had been no primary caretaker because both parents had been equally involved in caretaking. The appropriate standard was therefore the best-interest standard, and the trial court, affirmed by the West Virginia Supreme Court, held that the father won under the standard. What explains cases in which judges find that the parents shared parenting equally when one gave up her career to care for the children full-time at home? What does Bartlett see as the problem? How might we all tend to expect more of mothers than fathers and to be quite impressed when fathers do more than the average father does? How can we protect children and mothers from such bias in custody decisions?

4. As Bartlett points out, the bias apparent in *Patricia Ann S.*—the tendency to be over-impressed when a father does *any* caretaking—"also affects how the trial courts apply the best-interests test." As examples, she cites an Oregon trial court opinion, later overruled, awarding custody to the father because, among other things, the mother planned to go to graduate school in another state (evidence, according to the trial judge, that she placed her own needs above those of her child) and a District of Columbia trial court award, also later overruled, of custody to a father based on its conclusion that he had done most of the parenting though the evidence focused on what the mother did *not* do rather than what the father *did*. Bartlett, excerpt above, at 474. Many other cases could be cited to illustrate this common phenomenon. Do you think that the ALI approach will eliminate this problem? How might the determination of the relative proportions of caretaking performed by each parent during the marriage be tainted by precisely the same bias?

5. Fathers who come out as gay do not enjoy a similar bias. Cliff J. Rosky illustrates the ways that gay fathers are stereotyped as agents of HIV and as child molesters in custody and visitation proceedings. Rosky, Like Father, Like Son: Homosexuality, Parenthood, and the Gender of Homophobia, 20 Yale J.L. & Feminism 257, 279–94 (2009). Because lesbian mothers are much less likely to be stereotyped in these ways—although mothers who come out as lesbian are at times accused of abusing their daughters, they are almost never portrayed as child molesters or HIV agents—Rosky argues that these stereotypes involve both gender and sexual orientation. How should a judge take sexual orientation into account when making custody determinations? See Michael S. Wald, Adults' Sexual Orientation and State Determinations Regarding Placement of Children, 40 Fam. L.Q. 381 (2006) (arguing that sexual orientation should play no role unless an older child thinks it is relevant). What are the various ways that sexual orientation is likely to intersect with gender in these cases? Given that custody law often stereotypes gay fathers while praising heterosexual fathers who do more caregiving than is expected, what role does custody law play in the construction of both sexual orientation and gender?

Rosky also illustrates the ways the gender of the child, as well as the gender of the parent, affect custody determinations of gay and lesbian parents. Although both gay and lesbian parents are stereotyped as homosexual "recruiters," courts are most concerned that gay men will encourage their sons to be gay, somewhat less concerned that lesbians will encourage both their sons and daughters to be gay, and relatively unconcerned that gay men will encourage their daughters to be gay. Rosky, above, at 298. Rosky argues that this phenomenon reveals that litigants, experts, and judges have adopted a male supremacy principle, according to which they value boys' adoption of heterosexual masculinity more than girls' adoption of femininity. Id. at 311. Do you agree? How else might the custody system encourage or reward masculinity over femininity?

6. Polikoff and Chambers, excerpted above in Section C, describe the shift in some jurisdictions from a per se rule that lesbian mothers and gay fathers are unfit parents in custody disputes with heterosexual ex-spouses to a rule that sexual orientation is irrelevant to custody and visitation issues except to the extent that the heterosexual parent shows a link between sexual

orientation and harm to the child (the nexus test). This sounds like a decided shift in favor of lesbian mothers and gay fathers. But Susan J. Becker reports that hostile judges find harm based solely on sexual orientation; before these judges, there is no difference between the per se rule and the nexus test. See Becker, Court-Created Boundaries Between a Visible Lesbian Mother and Her Children, 12 Wis. Women's L.J. 331 (1997); Susan J. Becker, Child Sexual Abuse Allegations Against a Lesbian or Gay Parent in a Custody or Visitation Dispute: Battling the Overt and Insidious Bias of Experts and Judges, 74 Denv. U. L. Rev. 75 (1996). Here is an example from a 2002 Alabama Supreme Court opinion:

> The Court of Civil Appeals erred in reversing the judgment of the trial court and holding that there was *no* evidence indicating that the mother's homosexual relationship would have a detrimental effect on the children. From its earliest history, the law of Alabama has consistently condemned homosexuality. The common law adopted in this State and upon which our laws are premised likewise declares homosexuality to be a detestable and abominable sin. Homosexual conduct by its very nature is immoral, and its consequences are inherently destructive to the natural order of society. Any person who engages in such conduct is presumptively unfit to have custody of minor children under the established laws of this State.

Ex parte H.H., 830 So.2d 21, 37–38 (Ala. 2002) (Moore, C.J., concurring) (emphasis in original). What rules would best protect relationships between children and their gay and lesbian parents with respect to (1) the relevance of sexual orientation and (2) the underlying custody standard (best interest, primary caretaker, ALI proposal, etc.)?

7. Heterosexual fathers, including unwed fathers, are increasingly successful in obtaining custody of newborns under the best-interest standard. See Mary Becker, The Rights of Unwed Parents: Feminist Approaches, 63 Soc. Serv. Rev. 496 (1989). What is the ALI standard for newborn babies? Does the ALI regard pregnancy as caretaking? Should pregnancy be regarded as caretaking? Should the ability or desire of the mother to breastfeed be relevant? See Kristen D. Hofheimer, Breastfeeding as a Factor in Child Custody and Visitation Decisions, 5 Va. J. Soc. Pol'y & L. 433 (1998) (illustrating that judges are prone to give lip service to the importance of breastfeeding but to award custody without regard to this factor). What do you think should be the proper standard of custody for a newborn?

How might your proposed standard for newborns change if you considered the issue from the perspective of the newborn rather than the perspective of her biological parents? See James G. Dwyer, A Constitutional Birthright: The State, Parentage, and the Rights of Newborn Persons, 56 UCLA L. Rev. 755 (2009) (arguing that the state should assign custody for all newborn children in order to exclude unfit birth parents from legal parentage, because children have a constitutional right not to be forced into relationships that are likely to be harmful to them and biological parents have no constitutional right to force their association on children). Do all newborns have an interest in breastfeeding? Or an interest in maintaining a connection with the woman who carried them in utero? How might other interests of the newborn trump those interests? What are the gender implications of considering the standard from the perspective of the newborn rather than the perspective of her biological parents?

8. As we have seen in Chapter 6, there are many financial hazards and long-term economic risks attached to foregoing wage work in favor of care work in an era when marriage is frequently not forever. As we have seen in this chapter and will see again in Chapter 9, being the primary caretaker of children also causes serious problems for mothers who work. Ann Laquer Estin and Martha Albertson Fineman have both criticized the general silence in our society about the financial hazards of economic dependence and caregiving. Estin, Maintenance, Alimony, and the Rehabilitation of Family Care, 71 N.C. L. Rev. 721, 779 (1993); Fineman, The Vulnerable Subject: Anchoring Equality in the Human Condition, 20 Yale J.L. & Feminism 1 (2008). Given that fathers have also become much more likely to gain custody when they seek it, even when the mother has been a full-time homemaker like Patricia Ann S., discussed in note 3 above, caregivers also lack protection for their relationships to their children. How would proponents of the various feminist theories described in Chapter 3 respond to this problem? Would all of them see it as equally problematic? How would the various feminist theorists discussed in Chapter 3 address the question of selecting the appropriate custody standard? What factors would they consider? Which approaches would be most concerned with the desires of majority of women? Which would be most concerned with the economic position of women during and after marriage? Which would be concerned about the role of custody standards in constructing gender?

9. The award to the father in *Patricia Ann S.* ignored not only clear evidence that the stay-at-home mother had been the primary caretaker, but also evidence that the father had physically and emotionally abused the mother, alienated the children from her, used excessive force on the children, and generally exerted a high level of control over mother and children. For example, the dissenting judge reports:

> It is clear from Mr. S.'s testimony that he ran this family with an iron hand, a significant trait in abusive relationships being the total power and control of one party. The evidence reflects that for some period of time Mrs. S. was not allowed to have a cent, not even grocery money. She was permitted to write a grocery list, and if her husband was ever-so-gracious, he would include her requests. Once she attempted to take $20 from his wallet and wound up in the emergency room after he wrestled her over it. Mr. S. testified that he actually found the whole episode rather humorous, likening his wife clinging desperately to the $20 bill by hiding it in her mouth as resembling a lizard with lettuce sticking out of its mouth.

435 S.E.2d at 19 (Workman, C.J., dissenting). Abusive fathers often seek custody to maintain control over their wives as well as their children; family court judges, who tend not to be well-trained in domestic violence, often award custody to abusive fathers, either ignoring classic indicators of abuse or, as in *Patricia Ann S.*, ignoring explicit evidence of abuse. What explains this treatment of domestic violence?

10. Most states now require courts to consider domestic violence as part of their best-interest determinations in custody cases. The Oregon best interest statute described by Bartlett, for example, mentions "abuse of one parent by the other" as one factor a court *can* consider. These statutes do not mandate that abuse be taken into account or given any particular weight in determining the child's best interest. In light of overwhelming evidence of serious harm to children who live in households in which one adult abuses another, a growing number of states have gone beyond the best interest approach, creating a rebuttable presumption against awarding custody to an abusive parent. See Linda D. Elrod & Milfred D. Dale, Paradigm Shifts and Pendulum Swings in Child Custody: The Interests of Children in the Balance, 42 Fam. L.Q. 381, 395 (2008) (indicating 24 such states); see also Mary Becker, Double Binds Facing Mothers in Abusive Families: Social Support Systems, Custody Outcomes, and Liability for Acts of Others, 2 U. Chi. Roundtable 13, 19–20 (1995) (stating that children who live in households with domestic violence are more likely than other children to abuse others or be abused themselves as adults, may have trouble forming healthy adult intimate relationships, or may avoid intimate relationships). In fact, Oregon now has such a rebuttable presumption; domestic violence is just one factor among many in a best-interest analysis only if the presumption is not invoked. Or. Rev. Stat. § 107.137 (West 2009); see also Am. Bar Ass'n, Custody Decisions in Cases with Domestic Violence Allegations, http://www.abanet.org/legalservices/probono/childcustody/domestic_violence_chart1.pdf (providing a state-by-state analysis).

What do you think is the ideal approach? Is a best-interest analysis enough? Or should evidence of abuse be rebuttable evidence that the abusive parent should not receive custody? Irrebuttable? If rebuttable, what evidence would be sufficient to rebut the presumption? Under the Louisiana statute, for example, the presumption that an abusive parent should not have sole or joint custody arises when "the court finds that one incident of family violence has resulted in serious bodily injury or the court finds more than one incident of family violence." La. Rev. Stat. § 9:364 (West 2009). It is rebuttable only upon a showing that the abuser has completed a treatment program, is not abusing alcohol or illegal drugs, and the child's best interest requires custody with the abuser "because of the other parent's absence, mental illness, or substance abuse, or such other circumstances which affect the best interest of the child or children." Under what circumstances do you think an abusive parent should receive custody?

11. Mothers who have been in abusive relationships may look like less than ideal parents for a number of reasons. See, e.g., Naomi R. Cahn, Civil Images of Battered Women: The Impact of Domestic Violence on Child Custody Decisions, 44 Vand. L. Rev. 1041, 1072 (1991); Martha R. Mahoney, Legal Images of Battered Women: Redefining the Issue of Separation, 90 Mich. L. Rev. 1, 49 (1991). Many abused women are angry and some are fragile after their experience; their partners may appear stable, calm, controlled, and often quite charming. The children, especially once they are over the age of five or six, may identify with and prefer to live with the abuser. The abused mother, whom they have seen demeaned and derided all their lives, may be unable to control them. See, e.g., *Patricia Ann S.*, above note 3 (court

finding that the mother was angry and unable to control the older two children—both boys—who now shared their father's attitude toward her, whereas the father was calm and totally in control).

How should feminists respond to these difficulties? The Louisiana statute, discussed in note 10 above, includes the following provision: "The fact that the abused parent suffers from the effects of the abuse shall not be grounds for denying that parent custody." La. Rev. Stat. § 9:364 (West 2009). Is that enough to curb judicial discretion? Should we never take the effects of abuse into account? What if the mother's experience of domestic violence makes her a less fit parent?

12. What reasons might a parent have for seeking custody other than to participate in the childrearing of his or her children? Bartlett suggests that her hypothetical "David may ask for primary custody, even if he does not want it, to create some negotiating room." Negotiating room over what? See Herma Hill Kay, No-Fault Divorce and Child Custody: Chilling Out the Gender Wars, 36 Fam. L.Q. 27, 34 (2002) ("Of the five divorce issues, only two remain open in most states today: spousal support and child custody."). If a parent doesn't want custody, why would he or she use the threat of seeking custody in divorce negotiations? Is this a problem? What if we considered the issue from the perspective of the child?

13. Many best-interest statutes have friendlier-parent provisions like the Oregon statute described by Bartlett, which states that one factor a court can consider is "the willingness and ability of each parent to facilitate and encourage a close and continuing relationship between the other parent and the child." What is the effect of such statutes on women fighting for custody against abusive or controlling partners? See Margaret K. Dore, The "Friendly Parent" Concept: A Flawed Factor for Child Custody, 6 Loy. J. Pub. Int. L. 41, 42 (2004); Joan Zorza, Recognizing and Protecting the Privacy and Confidentiality Needs of Battered Women, 29 Fam. L.Q. 273, 285 (1995). Oregon attempted to address such effects by amending its friendlier-parent provision as follows: "However, the court may not consider such willingness and ability if one parent shows that the other parent has sexually assaulted or engaged in a pattern of behavior of abuse against the parent or a child and that a continuing relationship with the other parent will endanger the health or safety of either parent or the child." Or. Rev. Stat. § 107.137 (West 2009). What do you think of that solution? Does it strike the appropriate balance between the interests of abused women and the interests of children?

TEXT NOTE: MOTHERS AND CUSTODY

In 1968, just prior to the abandonment of the maternal preference standard in California, mothers received sole physical custody about 90% of the time at divorce.[25] Despite dramatic changes in custody doctrine in recent decades with the demise of the maternal preference standard and the rise of joint custody, mothers still receive sole physical custody at very high rates,

25. Lenore J. Weitzman & Ruth B. Dixon, Child Custody Awards: Legal Standards and Empirical Patterns for Child Custody, Support and Visitation After Divorce, 12 U.C. Davis L. Rev. 473, 484, 489 (1979) (1968 data shows mothers receiving custody 88.4% of the time in San Francisco and 87.7% of the time in Los Angeles).

whether as a result of settlement or of litigation. (Most custody arrangements are the result of the parents' agreement rather than a judge's application of a custody standard in a litigated case.) Yet in some jurisdictions, mothers are less likely to receive sole physical custody today than in the past; there is clearly a great deal of variation from jurisdiction to jurisdiction.[26] In many, probably most, jurisdictions, there have been dramatic increases in awards of joint *legal* custody even when mothers continue to receive sole physical custody at traditional rates.[27]

An early California study looked at outcomes in litigated cases from 1972 and 1976 (before and after the elimination of the maternal preference). Between these dates, there was no change in the percentage of fathers requesting custody, but there was a dramatic increase in their likelihood of obtaining custody over the period of the study: from 37% in 1972 to 63% in 1977. Yet because so few fathers sought custody, there was no significant change in the proportion of cases overall in which mothers received custody between 1972 and 1977 (88–90%).[28] Two years after abolition of the maternal preference standard, 98% of attorneys surveyed from Los Angeles said that judges still used a maternal preference in deciding who would have custody of pre-school aged children; about 33% said that judges also used the preference in deciding custody for older children.[29]

One empirical study of litigated cases in San Diego identified only two factors that were strongly predictive of judges' decisions: the recommendation of a counselor ordered by the court to investigate the family (75% of the time the judge ordered the custodial arrangement recommended by the counselor) and the child's preference. The mother was more likely to get custody when the counselor's report described her as having "good" physical appearance, social skills, and social adjustment. If a father lived with a woman, whether a girlfriend, wife, or mother, he had a 50% chance of obtaining custody.[30]

These studies suggest that more has changed in terms of doctrine and the language of opinions than in terms of outcomes in settled cases or in the actual grounds on which judges make decisions. With respect to *legal* custody, changes have been dramatic in some jurisdictions: the number of cases in which parents share legal responsibility for decisionmaking has skyrocketed, and the number of cases in which only the mother has legal responsibility has correspondingly plummeted. With respect to *physical* custody, the change has been in the same direction—toward more paternal custody—but is more modest, though in some counties and regions women are at significant risk of

---

26. See Robert H. Mnookin, Eleanor E. Maccoby, Catherine R. Albiston & Charlene E. Depner, Private Ordering Revisited: What Custodial Arrangements Are Parents Negotiating?, in Divorce Reform at the Crossroads 37, 54, 74 (Stephen D. Sugarman & Herma Hill Kay, eds. 1990) (in the California counties fathers received sole physical custody 10% of the time, and physical custody was joint 25% of the time).

27. See Stephen J. Bahr, Jerry D. Howe, Meggin Morrill Mann & Matthew S. Bahr, Trends in Child Custody Awards: Has the Removal of Maternal Preference Made a Difference?, 28 Fam. L.Q. 247, 256–57, 259 (1994).

28. Weitzman & Dixon, above note 48, at 475–77, 502–04.

29. Id. at 506–08.

30. Carla C. Kunin, Ebbe B. Ebbesen & Vladimir J. Konečni, An Archival Study of Decision-Making in Child Custody Disputes, 48 J. Clinical Psychol. 564, 567, 569, 572 (1992).

losing custody of the children they have mothered when a father fights for custody.

Mary Becker notes that (1) judges often have a great deal of difficulty appreciating how much caretaking is done by mothers rather than fathers, (2) most fathers will not actually be primary caretakers after getting custody (their new wives or mothers are likely to care for the child), and (3) stepmothers are not as likely as birth mothers to be committed to the child.[31] Becker therefore recommends the adoption of a maternal *deference* standard, under which judges would defer to a fit mother's judgment of what custodial arrangement is best for her children.[32] In the vast majority of cases, it is the mother who has demonstrated most concern for this child and the greatest commitment to the child's well-being, she argues. The mother's recommendation as to the best custodial arrangement should therefore be adopted by the court unless she is an unfit parent.

Other feminists have been concerned that Becker's approach and others like it reinforce the social assignment of caregiving to women upon childbirth or adoption.[33] In fact, some scholars are concerned that *existing* custody laws may overly privilege women's connection with their children, leading to the disengagement of fathers upon divorce.[34] Although stronger emotional bonds may exist between mothers and their children, those bonds are, at least in part, likely the consequence of social construction and constrained choices. The law can either conform to the construction of motherhood and fatherhood, and femininity and masculinity, or try to reconstruct it.

By contrast, Penelope Bryan identifies women's needs at divorce, particularly with respect to child custody and post-divorce support, as an important but unfinished piece of feminist business. Given the "pain, loss, and humiliation" of many women at divorce, she urges feminists to listen to divorced women and then put aside their differences with respect to the ideal custody standard and join in supporting a primary caretaker standard. She believes that such a standard would "honor the caretaking that mothers provide" and protect women from the loss they fear most.[35]

NOTES ON MOTHERS AND CUSTODY OUTCOMES

1. Is it a mistake to mention the strength of women's emotional bonds with their children because doing so reinforces stereotypes? Is it true, in your opinion, that women have stronger emotional bonds with their children and are more likely to plan and organize to ensure children's needs are met

---

31. Becker, Maternal Feelings: Myth, Taboo, and Child Custody, 1 S. Cal. Rev. L. & Women's Stud. 133, 181–82, 201, 208 (1992).

32. Id. at 203–22.

33. Nancy Levit, Feminism for Men: Ideology and the Construction of Maleness, 43 UCLA L. Rev. 1037, 1077–78 (1996) (arguing that Becker's article "silences the male voice" and "disparages the emotional bonds between fathers and children"); Deborah Rhode, Justice and Gender 155 (1989) (critiquing earlier maternal preference laws).

34. Solangel Maldonado, Beyond Economic Fatherhood: Encouraging Divorced Fathers to Parent, 153 U. Pa. L. Rev. 921, 964–75 (2005).

35. Penelope E. Bryan, Re-asking the Woman Question at Divorce, 75 Chi.–Kent L. Rev. 713, 742, 751–52 (2000).

(including, for example, health care)? Even if true, is it dangerous to mention these emotional realities? Or is it dangerous to embrace such "realities" without questioning how they are constructed? How would various feminist approaches described in Chapter 3 deal with this double bind? How would they evaluate Becker's maternal deference proposal?

2. What are the potential dangers of custody laws that relegate fathers to minor roles in their children's lives? Instead of arguing for maternal deference, should feminists attempt to create a norm of "nurturing fatherhood," as Solangel Maldonado urges in her article cited in footnote 34 above? What would such a norm look like? How might children benefit? How might they be harmed? Would it be possible to implement a nurturing fatherhood norm without hurting women?

3. Is it sex discrimination under the Constitution for a judge to consider (1) whether a father seeking custody is living with a woman or (2) the evidence that children in general seem to be better off with their mother than with a stepmother? If yes, is it because such classifications cannot survive intermediate scrutiny? Or is it because these factors should be irrelevant? If the primary concern is the best interests of children, should judges ignore the results of the stepmother studies?

4. Were you surprised that the elimination of the maternal preference standard did not affect custody outcomes as much as one might have expected? What explains these results?

5. What explains the fact that judges still rely on an unspoken maternal preference, especially for young children? Do the studies described above suggest that the parents' sex *is* still relevant to custody decisions? Is it realistic to think that judges actually decide custody cases as though the issue were which of two sexless parents should have custody rather than whether a mother or a father should have custody? Could you, for example, determine custody of a newborn or a toddler without reference to parental sex? Would it be better to have a more honest rule? What would a more honest rule look like? Would it be constitutional? What role would such "honesty" play in the construction of gender?

6. Most mothers receive custody of their children at divorce because most fathers agree to it. But if a father chooses to fight for custody against a mother who has been a primary caretaker, he is likely to have a number of advantages in litigation. Custody litigation is extremely expensive, and he is likely to have more money for lawyers and expert witnesses because he was likely to have been the primary breadwinner and not the primary caretaker, even if she also worked. If he is remarried and she is not (and men remarry at higher rates than women), his household may look better for the child because it is a traditional two-parent family. There are many decisions changing custody from a single mother to a remarried father. See, e.g., Carla C. Kunin, Ebbe B. Ebbesen & Vladimir J. Konecni, An Archival Study of Decision-Making in Child Custody Disputes, 48 J. Clinical Psychol. 564, 569 (1992) (reporting on study finding that if father was living with another woman, his wife, girlfriend, or mother, his chances of obtaining custody in litigated cases rose to 50%). Biases against mothers, particularly those who do not conform to judges' images of good mothers, are also likely to hurt mothers. If the

husband is abusive, he may be able to use the divorce process, as many abusive men do, to continue his abuse and ultimately obtain custody. For stay-at-home mothers as well as working mothers who have sacrificed fast-track careers to care for their children, but especially for mothers in abusive relationships, these are frightening possibilities, and loss of custody can be devastating. Given the importance of children to women and the potential inequities in the current custody system, why isn't the appropriate standard for child custody at divorce a priority item on the political agenda?

7. What custody standard would you urge your state to adopt? Would you choose an existing standard or propose a new one? How would your standard better protect women and their relationships with children at divorce, if at all? What do your classmates think of your standard?

G. CHILD SUPPORT

LENORE WEITZMAN, THE ECONOMICS OF DIVORCE: SOCIAL AND ECONOMIC CONSEQUENCES OF PROPERTY, ALIMONY, AND CHILD SUPPORT AWARDS

28 UCLA L. Rev. 1181, 1233, 1235–40, 1241, 1249, 1250–52 (1981).

[The statistics upon which Lenore Weitzman relied in this classic article were derived from a massive study using data from court records and interviews Weitzman conducted with judges, matrimonial lawyers and divorced individuals in California between 1968 and 1978.]

IV. Child Support

A. The Amount of Child Support

* * *

Another way of looking at the typical child support award is as a percentage of husband's income. In Ted Byrd's case, $250 out of a net monthly income of $1,000 is 25% of Ted's net income for child support. That was about the average percentage in Los Angeles in 1977, but was slightly below the average in San Francisco where child support averaged about a third of the husband's net income.

* * *

B. The Adequacy of Child Support Awards

I would suggest three standards for evaluating the adequacy of child support awards. One is to compare them with the actual costs of raising children. A second is to assess their reasonableness in terms of the husband's financial resources. Each of these standards is embodied in California law, which specifies that support be set in accordance with the parties' needs and ability to pay. A third way to evaluate them is to compare the husband's financial contribution to child support with the financial contribution of his former wife.

1. The Cost of Raising Children

Economist Thomas Espenshade has calculated that it would cost $85,163 to raise a child to age eighteen in a moderate income family in 1980. In a low income family in the United States it would cost $58,238. His calculations include only the direct maintenance costs: out-of-pocket expenditures on the child's birth, food, clothing, housing, transportation, medical care, education, and other expenses. A final component is the cost of a four-year college education at a tax-supported institution. * * *

If we use Espenshade's conservative estimates, and eliminate the cost of college (since college costs may not be included in child support), we find that it averages $4,200 a year to raise one child at a moderate income level. Because of economies of scale, a second child increases the costs roughly half as much as the first child so that the total childrearing cost for two minor children would be over $6,000 a year. Similarly, if we calculate the cost for a low income standard of living, we find the cost close to $3,000 a year for one child and over $4,500 for two children.

* * * If we assume that our hypothetical Pat Byrd would raise her children at the moderate standard, we find that her court-ordered child support award would give her $2,700 less than what she needs. Even at the poverty standard, her court-ordered child support would leave her $1,200 short.

The inadequacy of court-ordered child support is underscored by another relevant comparison. Pat Byrd's total support award of $450 per month for child and spousal support is lower than she would get from the Aid to Families with Dependent Children (AFDC) program. The AFDC level of support for a household with two children is $463 per month plus $73 in food stamps, or a total of $536 per month. The Federal Government has determined this sum to be necessary for families at the lowest economic levels; hence we see that Pat Byrd, our average divorced woman, obviously will not be able to rear her children, even at the poverty level, on the court-ordered support.

One problem with Espenshade's calculations is that they omit a major child care expense that Pat Byrd will have to bear. Since Espenshade's calculations are based on two-parent families, he assumes that one parent, typically the mother, is available full time to care for the child. But if the mother in a single-parent family has to work, she typically has to pay someone else to take care of her children. These child care costs have to be added to Espenshade's estimates in order to determine adequate child support for such single-parent families.

* * *

If we assume that Pat Byrd will work full time, then her child care costs would be about $200 a month for her daughter and $138 a month for her son. That adds up to over $333 a month—more than her entire child support award. Of course, if she is lucky enough to get the children into a public day care center with a sliding fee scale, her costs will be much less, but that typically entails a long waiting list and places her under pressure to go to work immediately.

2. The Husband's Ability to Pay

A second way to evaluate the adequacy of child support awards is in terms of the husband's financial resources. In a classic study of child support enforcement, Professor David Chambers established a procedure for evaluating the reasonableness of the court awards in terms of the husband's resources.[36] Chambers first looked at the father's postdivorce standard of living *without* any deductions. Following his procedures with our California data, we find, as Chambers did, that most fathers would be relatively well off. In Michigan, over 90% of the divorced fathers would be living at a level above the higher standard budget if they did not pay any support. In California, close to two-thirds of the fathers would be living at this level if no support were paid. When a father moves out, "separating himself from his family and hoarding all income to himself, the father improves his standard of living dramatically."

Next, Chambers asked what would happen to the father's standard of living if he paid the full amount of child support ordered. At the same time he asked how ex-wives and dependent children would fare on the amount of support ordered by the court. Obviously, if the family income stays constant, both units cannot maintain their former standard when living apart. In Michigan, Chambers found that "under the levels of child support that are ordered by the court ... it is only the women and children whose standards of living decline even when the father is making payments." Chambers concluded that 80% of the fathers could maintain a comfortable standard of living (at or above the intermediate standard budget) after paying court-ordered support.

In California, we found that close to three-quarters of the fathers had the "ability to pay" the amount the court ordered without a substantial reduction in their standard of living. * * * 61% of the California fathers would be able to comply fully with the court order and still live above the high standard budget. An additional 12% would be living above the lower standard budget. Thus 73% of the men could live at a level above the lower standard budget. In contrast only 7% of the women would be living at this level. Almost all the women and children—fully 93%—would be living below the poverty level.

* * *

V. Social and Economic Consequences for the Family

A. Postdivorce Incomes of Husbands and Wives

The awards made in * * * two hypothetical cases illustrate how support awards structure large disparities in the postdivorce incomes of men and women. * * * [I]f Victor Thompson is ordered to pay $2,000 a

36. D. Chambers, Making Fathers Pay (1979).

month spousal support, he retains $4,000 a month or twice as much income for himself. And if Ted Byrd is ordered to pay $450 a month for spousal and child support, he retains $550 for himself or 55% of the family's income. That leaves 45%—less than half—to be shared by the three other members of his family. Judges are reluctant to consider taking more than half of a man's net income for support, but when there are children in the family, the consequences can be grossly inequitable: a wife and two children are expected to live on less than the husband has for himself.

Thus one result of the support awards discussed above is that husbands are much better off after divorce than are their former wives and children. * * *

B. The Impoverishment of Women and Children

* * *

These data * * * show a radical change in the two families' [those of the former husband and wife] standard of living just one year after legal divorce. Men experienced a 42% improvement in their postdivorce standard of living, while women experienced a 73% loss.[a]

* * * [D]ivorce is a financial catastrophe for most women: in just one year they experience a dramatic decline in income and a calamitous drop in their standard of living. It is difficult to imagine how they survive the severe economic deprivation: every single expenditure that one takes for granted—clothing, food, housing, heat—must be cut to one-half or one-third of what one is accustomed to. No wonder that more divorced women report that they are in a constant financial crisis after divorce and that they are perpetually worried about not being able to pay their bills. This financial crisis cannot help but affect their socio-emotional lives, and it is not surprising that divorced women report more stress and less satisfaction with their lives than any other group of Americans.

ADRIENNE JENNINGS LOCKIE, MULTIPLE FAMILIES, MULTIPLE GOALS, MULTIPLE FAILURES: THE NEED FOR "LIMITED EQUALIZATION" AS A THEORY OF CHILD SUPPORT

32 Harv. J.L. & Gender 109, 112–13, 121–22, 133–36 (2009).

The structure of the American family has changed since the first federal child support laws were passed in 1974. Many children are expect-

a. Richard R. Peterson reanalyzed Weitzman's data and demonstrated that these percentages were inaccurate. Peterson, A Re-Evaluation of the Economic Consequences of Divorce, 61 Am. Soc. Rev. 528 (1996). Weitzman acknowledged that there were errors, but insisted that there was still a wide disparity between men and women—about a 30% decline for women in the first year and a 10% increase for men, resulting in a 40% disparity. Weitzman, The Economic Consequences of Divorce Are Still Unequal: Comment on Peterson, 61 Am. Soc. Rev. 537 (1996). Others disagree about the exact percentages, but all do agree that women's standard of living does drop substantially in the aftermath of divorce, while men's rises. See, e.g., Suzanne M. Bianchi, Lekha Subaiya & Joan R. Kahn, The Gender Gap in the Economic Well-Being of Nonresident Fathers and Custodial Mothers, 36 Demography 195 (1999).

ed to live apart from "at least one biological parent, usually the father, before they reach the age of 18."[11] Numerous children are born to parents who are not married, and the number of single-parent families has steadily increased. In the child support system, there are significant numbers of custodial parents who have never been married. Having children with multiple partners is also increasingly common, particularly in unmarried families. * * * Stepparenting is also increasingly common, with one study suggesting that one-third of Americans are members of a stepfamily. Same-sex partners are also increasingly raising children together: according to the 2000 Census, over ninety-five percent of U.S. counties have at least one same-sex couple with children under the age of eighteen. These statistics demonstrate the decreasing prevalence of the two-parent heterosexual model and the rise in single-parent households, blended families, adoptive families, families headed by gays and lesbians, and extended families.

* * *

For all parents in the child support system, hidden assumptions about family are embedded in the gender-neutral child support laws: child support policy contains assumptions about motherhood and fatherhood, which often differ based on race. One attitude implicit in current child support policy is that single motherhood is a problem that needs to be "fixed" by marriage. Fathers are frequently portrayed as deadbeats whose only value as a parent is economic. Child support enforcement policies punish women by "simultaneously offer[ing] women access to resources while reinscribing traditional gender roles."[71] * * *

Child support laws implicitly assume a particular vision of the family: mothers are the custodial parents and fathers are the child support obligors. Although child support laws have become gender-neutral over time, * * * the reality of child support is highly gendered: most recipients of child support are mothers while most obligors are fathers. According to a recent demographic survey sponsored by the Office of Child Support Enforcement ("OCSE"), close to ninety-five percent of custodial parents in the child support system are mothers.[77] Moreover, the current failures of child support may not receive the attention they deserve because the responsibility for child care is typically seen as the duty of mothers.

* * *

---

11. Anne C. Case, I-Fen Lin & Sara McLanahan, Explaining Trends in Child Support: Economic, Demographic, and Policy Effects, 40 Demography 171, 171 (2003).

71. Jyl J. Josephson, Gender, Families, and State: Child Support Policy in the United States, 128 (1997); see also Martha Albertson Fineman, Child Support is Not the Answer: The Nature of Dependencies and Welfare Reform, in Child Support: The Next Frontier 209, 210–11 (J. Thomas Oldham & Marygold S. Melli eds., 2000) (indicating that government preferences like tax breaks serve as a form of welfare assistance for everyone, but that only traditional nuclear families receive "unstigmatized assistance").

77. Elaine Sorenson & Tess Tannehill, Dep't of Health and Human Servs., Demographic Survey Results from Nine State IV–D Programs (2007) (on file with Harvard Law School Library).

Current support laws do not serve the goal of improving children's economic well-being and have further damaged the economic well-being of poor and complex families. * * *

First, the child support system fails to achieve this goal because it only applies to a small subset of families: the goal is designed to protect the financial situation of children in one cohabitating family that is dissolving. The premise is that children should not be economically harmed by the dissolution of a family and that children should not bear the brunt of the extra costs associated with establishing two homes. While this goal may, at most, serve children whose parents were living together at some point, it ignores the interests of children raised in other settings. Additionally, this goal frequently fails even under the standard paradigm because "child support policies do not actually contemplate 'equalization' of the standards of living in the residential and nonresidential households."[153] * * *

Although child support laws attempt to protect children from the economic costs associated with family dissolution, this goal is challenging in multiple families, even if one believes it is a legitimate goal. * * * If income is divided equally, two (or more) households may end up in poverty. Absent substantial resources, economic well-being is difficult to achieve where there are numerous households requiring financial support.

Moreover, the child support system has not met the goal of enhancing children's economic well-being for many of the low-income complex families in the child support system. Economic well-being is narrowly defined to address only the child's immediate financial needs and does not account for poverty prevention. "Economic well-being" exists in the context of protecting the economic situation of one family at dissolution, while "poverty prevention" is a larger and more expansive goal. * * * Although inadequate child support certainly contributes to poverty of complex families, even full enforcement of all existing support orders would have a minimal effect on reduction of poverty or welfare dependency. Moreover, child support laws usually ignore the actual financial needs of poor women; these laws also tend to prefer the interests of the nonresident parent. * * *

Enhanced enforcement measures are also insufficient to address the problem of children living in poverty. Problems with compliance are particularly difficult in low-income families, partially because low-income fathers may have disproportionately higher child support awards than higher-income fathers. In multiple families without resources, compliance with support orders is even less likely. Child support awards based on parental income cannot support children's economic well-being if the parents have no income or are unable to comply with multiple child support orders. * * * Instead of a definition of "economic well-being" that

---

153. Am. Law Inst., Principles of the Law of Family Dissolution: Analysis and Recommendations § 3.04 cmt. i (2000).

is unattainable given family demographics, child support policy should be refocused on poverty prevention.

* * *

Although child support laws are likely to remain gender-neutral, gender neutrality may obscure the reality that women typically receive child support and that "the child support regime is . . . based on gendered ideas of family life."[303] While being mindful of not reinforcing stereotypes, federal and state governments should examine how child support laws and policies affect obligors and obligees differently. The current gender-neutral regime often masks the important ways that mothers are treated differently than nonresident fathers. For example, in some states, obligors may receive a deduction for subsequent children, but obligees do not receive a deduction for their subsequent children. In effect, this different treatment allows obligors to receive an offset for having new children while the non-obligor receives no comparable benefit. Because fathers comprise the majority of obligors, they receive preferential treatment. Even as child support laws are based on outdated assumptions about the roles of women, the gendered reality of who receives child support suggests that gender cannot be ignored.

NOTES ON CHILD SUPPORT

1. A number of commentators disagreed with Weitzman's conclusions in whole or in part. Weitzman attributed the economic situation of women after divorce to the passage of reformed divorce laws and, in particular, to no-fault divorce, because they treated men and women as economic equals when in reality men and women still have different earning capacities and women still assume a disproportionate share of childcare. Others pointed out that the economic situation of women and children was bad both before and after the change. See, e.g., Marygold S. Melli, Constructing A Social Problem: The Post-Divorce Plight Of Women And Children, ABF Res. J., Fall 1986, at 759, 770. Martha Fineman criticized the notion that *any* legal reforms grounded in the concept of marriage as an equal partnership could provide a remedy for the post-divorce situation of women. Fineman, Illusive Equality: On Weitzman's *Divorce Revolution*, ABF Res. J., Fall 1986, at 781, 783. This was so, in Fineman's view, because such reforms are based upon a liberal feminist ideal of gender equality and independence, while the real life situation of women and children is one of need and dependence. Id. at 786. Fineman continues to hold this view, even though she concedes that inequalities post-divorce have lessened to some degree. Fineman, Equality: Still Illusive After All These Years, in Gender Equality: Dimensions of Women's Equal Citizenship 251, 254–57 (Linda C. McClain & Joanna L. Grossman eds., 2009). What types of child support arrangements do you think would be supported by the various

303. Josephson, supra note 71, at 143–44. As Susan Moller Okin has noted in discussing gender neutrality historically, "gender-neutral terms frequently obscure the fact that so much of the real experience of 'persons,' so long as they live in gender-structured societies, does in fact depend on what sex they are." Susan Moller Okin, Justice, Gender, and the Family 11 (1989).

feminist approaches described in Chapter 3? What arrangements do you think would achieve equality for mothers and their children?

2. What might be some other goals of a child support system? See Ira Mark Ellman & Tara O'Toole Ellman, The Theory of Child Support, 45 Harv. J. on Legis. 107 (2008) (articulating four principles of any effective child support system: ensuring that parents rather than the state provide for children; protecting the child's well-being; enforcing the social consensus that both parents have a support obligation; and limiting the size of the gap between the child's living standard and that of the support obligor). Which of those goals would be consistent with a feminist child support system and which would not? What goals does Lockie promote? How are these goals both similar to Weitzman's and different? Are Weitzman and Lockie focused on the same groups of women? How might a child support system help some women at the expense of others?

3. Why is the child support system still designed around a heterosexual, two parent model? What would alternative systems look like if they instead took single-parent households, blended families, adoptive families, families headed by gays and lesbians, cohabitants, or extended families as their norm? See, e.g., Sara R. David, Turning Parental Rights into Parental Obligations–Holding Same-Sex, Non-Biological Parents Responsible for Child Support, 39 New Eng. L. Rev. 921 (2005). Would such alternatives better address child poverty? Would they be less likely to reinforce traditional gender roles? How might they make women's care more visible, as Lockie desires?

4. Jane Rutherford suggests a per capita division of income upon divorce, dividing the total post-divorce family income equally among the family members. For example, in a family consisting of a mother, father and three children with the mother earning $20,000 and the father earning $30,000, the following division would result if the mother had custody: the mother and children would receive a total of $40,000 ($10,000 each, necessitating a $20,000 transfer from the father) and the father would receive $10,000. Rutherford, Duty in Divorce: Shared Income as a Path to Equality, 58 Fordham L. Rev. 539, 566–67 (1990). Is this a fair division? Why or why not? Would it address Weitzman's concerns? Lockie's?

5. Data compiled by the Bureau of the Census show that in 2007 only about 46% of custodial parents (83% of whom were women) who were awarded child support in fact received the full payment awarded; this percentage had increased from 36.9% in 1993. More than 24% of those supposed to receive payments in 2007 received no payment at all (relatively unchanged since 1993), while 29.5% received only partial payment. Census Bureau, Current Population Reports, Custodial Mothers and Fathers and Their Child Support: 2007 8 (Nov. 2009). These statistics show only the extent of nonpayment of child support where an award of child support has in fact been made, either by court order or by voluntary agreement. About 53% of the 13.7 million custodial parents in April 2007 had never received any award in the first place, for a variety of reasons, most commonly that they did not feel the need for a legal agreement or that the child's other parent could not afford to pay. Id. at 6–8. Not surprisingly, the Census Bureau reported that 30.7% of

custodial parents who did not receive child support due were living below the 2007 poverty level. Id. at 8 fig.4.

In the last decades, Congress has enacted legislation to strengthen the enforcement of child support awards, requiring state enforcement agencies, among other things, to attempt to track down absent fathers, to require mandatory withholding of support from paychecks, and to establish guidelines to determine child support obligations. See 42 U.S.C. §§ 651–659. By contrast, in Sweden, if a noncustodial parent does not or cannot pay a child support award, the government steps in and pays a "maintenance advance" to the child, which the parent must repay; if the amount of child support awarded is clearly inadequate, the government will also pay a supplementary allowance which the noncustodial parent is not required to repay. See Sidel, Women & Children Last: The Plight of Poor Women in Affluent America 180–81 (1986). How does the Swedish arrangement differ from that in this country? What are the conceptual underpinnings of the two programs? Who do you think should be primarily responsible for the support of young children? On what grounds?

6. Federal law requires that the states review their child support guidelines every four years in light of data about the cost of raising children, such as the Espenshade study described in the Weitzmann excerpt, above. See Ira Mark Ellman, Fudging Failure: The Economic Analysis Used to Construct Child Support Guidelines, 2004 U. Chi. Legal F. 167, 169–70. A common source for this evaluation is the statistics issued by the Department of Agriculture. In 2009, the Department of Agriculture estimated that the average cost of raising a child to age 18 (housing, food, transport, clothing, health care, child care, and education, etc.) was $160,410 for dual-parent families earning less than $56,670, $222,360 for couples earning from $56,670 to $98,120, and $369,360 for those whose income was more than $98,120. The cost varies with the age of the child, with teenagers the most expensive. Dep't of Agric., Expenditures on Children by Families, 2009 26 tbl.1 (2010). (The Department of Agriculture also has a program that allows you to calculate the cost of having a child: http://www.cnpp.usda.gov/calculator.htm.) What does this tell us about the costs of raising children when the mother and father are not in the same household? And what does that tell us about the appropriate amount of child support? See Ellman, above, for a detailed critique of the "continuity of marginal expenditure" assumption upon which child support calculations are based—the premise that child support should be based on what parents spend on their children in intact families.

7. Why do you think so many fathers fail to pay child support? Harry D. Krause believes that the main reason is that defaulting fathers simply don't have the money to pay. Krause, Child Support Reassessed: Limits of Private Responsibility and the Public Interest, in Divorce Reform at the Crossroads 175 (Stephen D. Sugarman & Herma Hill Kay, eds. 1990). However, Weitzman's data from California and other data gathered by David Chambers in Michigan during the 1970s indicated that inability to pay was certainly not the only cause. Weitzman found little relationship between income and noncompliance with child support orders. Weitzman, above, at 1256. Chambers' study showed that strong enforcement procedures, including automatic monitoring of payment or nonpayment of child support by court personnel, a self-starting system of collection, and a high incarceration rate, correlate with

high rates of compliance. David L. Chambers, Making Fathers Pay: The Enforcement of Child Support 90–93 (1979). More recent studies show that compliance is highly associated with ability to pay, with noncompliance becoming a problem when fathers owe more than 35% of their income each month. Daniel Meyer & Judi Bartfeld, Compliance with Child Support Orders in Divorce Cases, 58 J. Marriage & Fam. 201, 210 (1996). Imprisonment continues to be one of the most effective remedies for nonpayment of child support, however, as are cancellation of a non-paying parent's driver's license and putting a "Denver boot" on his or her car (which immobilizes it until unlocked by the authorities). See, e.g., Drew A. Swank, Das Boot! A National Survey of Booting Programs' Impact on Child Support Compliance, 4 J.L. & Fam. Stud. 265 (2002). What do these studies show, if anything, about the reasons for nonpayment? About appropriate remedies? Why do you think courts are reluctant to jail fathers for nonpayment of child support? Do you think they should do so?

8. One reason frequently cited for the federal government's intense focus on collection of child support is that this will enable the movement of women and children off welfare. See, e.g., Inst. for Women's Policy Research, How Much Can Child Support Provide? Welfare, Family Income and Child Support 1 (Mar. 1999) (quoting President Clinton). Careful analysis of the factors associated with the receipt of child support challenges this hypothesis, for a number of reasons. First, women who in the past received AFDC were in fact the women least likely to be awarded child support or to collect it if awarded. Id. at 1–3. Moreover, the amount of support these women could potentially collect is quite limited; child support constituted only about 11.8% of family income for this group (in contrast with 21.3% for non-AFDC but low-income families), hardly enough to move the family out of poverty. Id. at 5–6. The authors of the study conclude: "This points to the limitation of using child support as a safety net or replacement of government transfers for single-mother families on welfare, because those single-mothers who are disadvantaged in the labor market are also disadvantaged in obtaining child support." Id. at 6. What are the policy implications of this study? How might child support be one part of a larger poverty prevention plan, as Lockie urges, instead of a replacement for such a plan?

9. Krause suggests that our society's emphasis on collecting child support from absent fathers is essentially misplaced in an era when the only familial relationship may be founded upon (1) consanguinity based on permissible recreational sex or (2) the essentially terminated post-divorce relationship between the typical father and his child. Krause, above note 7, at 181. Providing indirect support for this theory, the Census Bureau reports that noncustodial parents who had visitation or joint custody were more likely to make child support payments: 78.3% with those provisions made some support payments versus 67.2% without them. Census Bureau, Current Population Reports, Custodial Mothers and Fathers and Their Child Support: 2007 9 (Nov. 2009). Krause concludes that responsibility for child support should be undertaken by the public now that there is no real social link between many fathers and their children, much like caring for the elderly has been taken over by the government, through Social Security and Medicare. What do you think of this argument? Is it likely that the government, state or federal, will

undertake the responsibility for adequate child support in the United States? Do you think Lockie would support this proposal?

A number of different proposals resting upon some notion of collective responsibility for the support of children have been made. Among the most influential was one made by Irwin Garfinkel for a child support assurance (CSA) program. Garfinkel, Assuring Child Support: An Extension of Social Security (1992). Under this plan, the caretaker of a child would receive either the amount paid by the noncustodial parent pursuant to a child support award or an assured benefit amount set by the government (Garfinkel proposed $2000–2500 for one child per year), whichever is higher; if child support lower than the assured benefit is paid, the government would make up the difference between the two. Id. at 47. Unlike child support allowances given to all families in a country like France, regardless of need or marital status, CSA would be available only to single parents and only to the extent the amount was not covered by the noncustodial parent. Stephan Sugarman makes a less broad-reaching proposal, suggesting that children of absent parents be covered by benefits under the Social Security system that are currently reserved for the children of parents whose absence is the result of death. Sugarman, Financial Support of Children and the End of Welfare As We Know It, 81 Va. L. Rev. 2523, 2561 (1995). This plan, of course, would only cover children whose fathers are themselves insured under the Social Security system, leaving out, for example, many teen mothers. Id. at 2562. Which of these alternatives do you prefer? Which, if any, seems politically feasible? Can you think of other ways in which our society might undertake to protect and support these children?

10. Other scholars are concerned about federal efforts to collect child support from low-income fathers, fearing that such efforts may drive away men who in fact are making important contributions to children's lives, through emotional involvement and a variety of in-kind contributions, such as groceries, gifts, and help with child care. Some of these men may not even be biological fathers but they nevertheless have stepped into an important role in children's lives. Fear of the mandated paternity testing that is part of child support enforcement efforts may cause these men to distance themselves from children in their lives, despite the bonds they have developed. Solangel Maldonado, Deadbeat or Deadbroke: Redefining Child Support for Poor Fathers, 39 U.C. Davis L. Rev. 991, 1005–1007 (2006). If very little child support may be collectable in any event, the goals of child support enforcement and parental involvement may be diametrically opposed. What, if any, solutions do you see to this problem? Are there any solutions that address both the problems of non-paying middle-class fathers and the problems of low-income or unemployed fathers? In cases of conflict, whose interests should prevail? How would Lockie address these concerns? How would Weitzman?

11. Studies show that within three years of divorce 50% of fathers see their children not at all or infrequently, with only 25% of children seeing their fathers at least weekly. See Solangel Maldonado, Beyond Economic Fatherhood: Encouraging Divorced Fathers to Parent, 153 U. Pa. L. Rev. 921, 924, 946–48 (2005), and studies cited therein. Citing various educational, social and emotional advantages to children with continued paternal involvement, some scholars have proposed legal changes to address this problem. Id. at

949–61 (describing studies concerning benefits of paternal engagement). Maldonado proposes, among other things, making visitation legally enforceable through contempt and other measures. Id. at 991–98. What do you think of this proposal?

Another author recommends that states follow California's example and adjust child support awards based on the amount of time the non-custodial parent spends with the child. A father who has extensive visitation would receive a deduction from child support for the periods the child is with him; fathers who aren't active in their children's lives could perhaps be required to pay a surcharge. Geoffrey P. Miller, Parental Bonding and the Design of Child Support Obligations, in The Law and Economics of Child Support Payments 219–28 (William S. Comanor ed., 2004). Do you think that fathers' child support should be reduced for the time they spend visiting their children? What, if any, problems do you see with this approach? What is the likely impact on mothers? What are its race and class implications? How might such laws affect the construction of gender?

12. Even if the full amount of child support is collected, the amounts may be meager in relation to the costs of raising a child. Different states calculate the support due in different ways. See, e.g., Ellman, above note 2, at 111–13. One system bases the amount presumed due upon a percentage of the noncustodial parent's income, for example, 20% for one child, 28% for two, 32% for three, and up to 50% for six or more children. 750 Ill. Comp. Stat. 5/505(a)(1) (2005). Thus, if a parent obliged to pay support earns $40,000 per year and takes home $32,000 as statutorily defined net income, he would owe approximately $533 per month for one child, $747 for two, $853 for three children, and so on. The custodial parent's income would not be taken into account in calculating the amount due, but she would presumably work, given the meager resources otherwise available to the diminished family unit, and thus contribute to the children's support both monetarily and by her caretaking. Even under the rather low national averages reported by the Children's Defense Fund in 2005 described above (in Section D2), the custodial parent will be required to pay between $333 and $833 per month for child care while she works, not leaving an adequate amount for other costs, such as housing, food, clothes, and medical care. In other states, the income of both parents is taken into account, and the calculation would assume contributions by both toward support of the child. Which of these systems of calculating child support obligations seems fairer? Why? Is either approach feminist? What would be your ideal feminist child support system?

CHAPTER 8

WOMEN AND EDUCATION

■ ■ ■

A. INTRODUCTION

Historically, women have suffered discrimination at every level of education. It was not until the latter part of the 19th century that almost all public elementary schools admitted both boys and girls. In 1837 (200 years after the first American college was founded), Oberlin College admitted women, becoming the first coeducational institution of higher learning. That same year the first all-female baccalaureate program began at Mt. Holyoke.[1] Education for female slaves did not come until after Emancipation; it was a crime to teach slaves to read.[2] As Florence Howe describes, in the 19th century education was deemed dangerous to girls' health and to the health of future generations:

> * * * Scientific belief held not only that the brains of women were smaller than those of men, but also that brain size was directly related to intelligence, and that hence women were less capable than men of academic learning. More important, however, was the medical assumption that only one bodily organ functioned optimally at any one time. Thus, if women used their brains during adolescence, their uterine development would be disturbed and their child-bearing abilities impaired, perhaps so severely as to cause the production of malformed or dead infants. Indeed, higher education might in and of itself sterilize women. * * * [F]or the female scholar, intense study directly inhibited her ability to bear children, or to bear healthy normal ones, capable of surviving past infancy.[3]

It was not until 1972 with the passage of the Education Amendments to the Civil Rights Act ("Title IX") that discrimination in public education was formally prohibited. Title IX mandated that women shall not "be excluded from participation in, be denied the benefits of, or be subjected to

1. Deborah L. Rhode, Association and Assimilation, 81 Nw. U.L. Rev. 106, 128–136 (1986).

2. Angela Y. Davis, Women, Race & Class 106 (1981) ("with the exception of Maryland and Kentucky, every Southern state absolutely prohibited the education of slaves").

3. Florence Howe, Myths of Coeducation 210 (1984).

discrimination under any education program or activity receiving Federal financial assistance."[4]

Despite this history of discrimination women's educational advancement over the last 30 years has been dramatic. Girls and women currently outperform boys and men on many academic indices. At the elementary and high school levels, girls consistently outperform boys in reading and writing. While boys have traditionally outperformed girls in math and science these gaps are smaller and more variable than those that exist in reading and writing.[5] Moreover, high school girls currently take as demanding math and science classes as do boys,[6] and girls participate more frequently than boys in every type of school-related activity other than athletics.[7]

Women are also currently participating in and graduating from college at higher rates than men. As of 2006, 57 percent of all undergraduates were female.[8] Among those who enrolled in college for the first time in 1995–96 seeking a bachelor's degree, 66 percent of women as compared to 59 percent of men had earned a bachelor's degree by the spring of 2001.[9] In 2001 women earned more than half of the bachelor's degrees awarded.[10] The increase in women's postsecondary educational partic-

---

4. 20 U.S.C.A. § 1681 et seq. (1988). The statute continues, *inter alia,* to exclude from coverage (1) religious schools; (2) U.S. military schools; (3) public undergraduate schools that have been single sex since inception; and (4) limited other special programs. See also regulations implementing Title IX, 45 C.F.R. Pt. 86 (1992). Three other federal statutes deal with sex discrimination in education: the Women's Educational Equity Act of 1974, 20 U.S.C.A. § 3041 (2000) (providing for federal financial and technical support to local efforts to remove barriers for females in all areas of education); Title IV of the Civil Rights Act of 1964, 42 U.S.C.A. § 2000c (1994) (providing for support to schools to comply with the mandate of nondiscrimination by providing funds for regional Desegregation Assistance Centers and grants to state education departments for providing more equitable education to students); and the 1976 amendments to the Vocational Education Act of 1963, 20 U.S.C.A. § 1371 (2000) (requiring states to act affirmatively to eliminate sex bias, stereotyping, and discrimination in vocational education).

5. National Center for Education Statistics, Trends in Educational Equity of Girls & Women: 2004 4–8 (2004).

6. Id. While overall females' high school academic programs in math and science are as demanding as males', there are some differences in the classes the two sexes tend to take. "Female high school graduates in 2000 were more likely than their male peers to have taken algebra II, biology, AP/honors biology, and chemistry. Males, by contrast, were more likely than females to have taken physics." Id. at 7. Boys continue, to make up a higher proportion of students taking AP exams in science and calculus and score higher on these examinations than girls. Id. at 6.

7. Id. at 48. In 2001, 6 percent of male students as compared to 13 percent of female students participated in school newspaper/yearbook activities; 19 percent of male students as compared to 31 percent of female students were involved in music/performing arts; 12 percent of male students as compared to 19 percent of female students were involved in academic clubs; 8 percent of male students as opposed to 13 percent of female students were involved in student council/government; and 26 percent of male students as opposed to 44 percent of female students were involved in other types of school-related activities. The only extracurricular activity in which male students participated at higher rates than female students was athletics: 45 percent of boys participated as compared to 32 percent of girls. Id.

8. The National Science Foundation, table B–1, Undergraduate enrollment at all institutions, by race/ethnicity, citizenship, sex and enrollment status: 2000–2007, available at http://www.nsf.gov/statistics/wmpd/pdf/tabb–1.pdf.

9. Supra note 5, at 76.

10. Women earned 57 percent of the bachelor degrees awarded in 2001. Id. at 78. This proportion reflects the fact that the female-male graduation disparity is even more significant

ipation has meant that among the general population ages 25–29 in 2006, a slightly higher percentage of women than men (31.6 percent as compared to 25.3 percent) had attained a bachelor's degree or higher degree.[11]

Women have likewise made tremendous progress at the graduate and professional school level. In 2006, women made up 58 percent of all graduate students.[12] In terms of professional degrees, in 2006 women earned 46 percent of law degrees, 21 percent of engineering degrees, 51 percent of medical degrees and 41 percent of MBA's awarded.[13] The tide has so turned that the stream of books and articles from the 1980's and 1990's arguing that schools were shortchanging girls has been replaced, in large part, by a literature arguing that boys, not girls, are suffering from educational neglect.[14]

Despite these considerable advances, however, girls continue to lag behind boys on high-stakes tests such as the SAT and Advanced Placement Exams as well as on entrance exams to medical and law schools. In fact, boys outperform girls on all areas of Advanced Placement Exams except art history and foreign languages.[15] The gap between girls and boys on standardized math and science tests, while narrowing, persists.[16]

Moreover, women's academic achievements continue to have a traditionally sex-based hue. Women and men continue to major in stereotypically gendered fields, with women overrepresented in fields that often lead to lower paying occupations such as education and health professions and underrepresented in areas that often lead to higher paying occupations such as computer science and engineering.[17]

Significant questions remain about whether female (and male) students perform better, and in less gender-stereotypical manners, in single-sex rather than co-educational schools. Concerns also remain about sexual harassment and intimidation of girls in schools. A 2005 report on sexual harassment on college campuses found that 62 percent of students had

---

among blacks and Hispanics than among whites. In 2001, 66 percent of black college graduates were female and 60 percent of Hispanic college graduates were female. Id. at 80.

11. US Census Bureau, Educational Attainment in the United States: 2006, Table 1a: percentage of high school and college graduates of the population 15 years and over, by age, sex, race and Hispanic origin: 2006.

12. Id. at 82.

13. American Council on Education, Gender Equality in Higher Education: 2006, available at http://www.acenet.edu/bookstore/pdf/Gender_Equity_6_23.pdf.

14. Compare Mary Bray Pipher, Reviving Ophelia: Saving the Selves of Adolescent Girls (1994); Myra Sadker & David Sadker, Failing at Fairness: How America's Schools Cheat Girls (1994), and American Association of University Women, How Schools Shortchange Girls: A Study of Major Findings on Girls and Education (1992), with David S. Cohen, No Boy Left Behind? Single-sex Education and the Essentialist Myth of Masculinity, 84 Ind L.J. 135(2009); Christina Hoff Sommers, The War Against Boys (2000); Ben Gose, Liberal–Arts Colleges Ask: Where Have the Men Gone? The Chron. of Higher Educ., June 6, 1997, at A35–36; William Pollack, Real Boys: Rescuing Our Sons from the Myths of Boyhood (1998); Dan Kindlon & Michael Thompson, Raising Cain: Protecting the Emotional Life of Boys (1999).

15. Supra note 5, at 6.

16. Rosemary C. Salomone, Feminist Voices in the Debate over Single–Sex Schooling: Finding Common Ground, 11 Mich. J. Gender & L. 63, 76 (2004).

17. Supra note 5, at 78.

been sexually harassed and 66 percent said they knew someone personally who had had been harassed. 62 percent of female students were likely to encounter sexual harassment and females students were more likely to experience sexual harassment that involved physical contact than men, 35 percent versus 29 percent.[18] Finally, despite large advances in women's athletic participation since the passage of Title IX,[19] women continue to participate at lower rates in varsity college athletics than do men and receive a lower proportion of college athletic scholarships.[20]

The definition of "equality" in education seems more elusive the more we learn. Some educators are turning to separatism as a solution for both women and minorities. Although the results are by no means uniform, several studies have measured the value of single-sex colleges in terms of both external achievements and internal satisfaction and have found them superior to coeducation. This forces us to ponder the following complicated question: is the concept "separate but equal," rejected for race in 1954,[21] nonetheless viable when considering gender?

This chapter will address a wide variety of issues involved in equality of education for women, beginning with single-sex education and proceeding to affirmative action. After discussing equality in athletic programs, the chapter concludes with an examination of two areas that are very important for the acceptance of women into educational institutions on an equal footing with men: the regulation of hate speech and sexual harassment on campus.

---

18. See American Association of University Women Education Foundation, Hostile Hallways: Bullying, Teasing, and Sexual Harassment in School (2001). American Association of University Women Educational Foundation, Drawing the Line: Sexual Harassment on Campus (2005), available at http://www.aauw.org/learn/research/upload/DTLFinal.pdf.

19. U.S. Dept. of Educ., Title IX: 25 Years of Progress (1997). In 1971, fewer than 300,000 high school girls participated in interscholastic sports; in 1997, over 2.4 million did. Women's basketball illustrates this dramatic development: from 1972 to 1994, girls playing high school basketball increased 300 percent. Girls and women are also participating in greater numbers in sports traditionally viewed as male only—lacrosse, wrestling, soccer, rugby, and ice hockey. Id. at 15.

20. See Women's Sports Foundation, Women's sports and Physical Activity Facts and Statistics 2007, available at http://www.womenssportsfoundation.org/binary-data/WSF_ARTICLE/pdf_file/191.pdf. See also Warren A. Whisenant, How Women Have Fared as Interscholastic Athletic Administrators Since the Passage of Title IX, 49 Sex Roles: A Journal of Research 179, 180 (2003) (noting that women made up 41.9 percent of the student athlete population in colleges in 2001); American Association of University Women, Equity in School Athletics 2 (2003) (reporting while women make up more than half the undergraduate student body, they make up only 42 percent of student athletes and that, as of 2000, women's teams received less than 40 percent of recruiting dollars and less than 43 percent of athletic operating dollars). See also Glenn George, Title IX and the Scholarship Dilemma, 9 Marq. Sports L. J. 273 (1999) (explaining the difficulties under current NCAA rules of providing equivalent financial assistance for male and female athletes).

21. Brown v. Board of Education, 347 U.S. 483, 74 S.Ct. 686, 98 L.Ed. 873 (1954).

B. SINGLE–SEX EDUCATIONAL INSTITUTIONS

MISSISSIPPI UNIVERSITY FOR WOMEN v. HOGAN

United States Supreme Court, 1982.
458 U.S. 718, 102 S.Ct. 3331, 73 L.Ed.2d 1090.

JUSTICE O'CONNOR delivered the opinion of the Court.

This case presents the narrow issue of whether a state statute that excludes males from enrolling in a state-supported professional nursing school violates the Equal Protection Clause of the Fourteenth Amendment.

The facts are not in dispute. In 1884, the Mississippi Legislature created the Mississippi Industrial Institute and College for the Education of White Girls of the State of Mississippi, now the oldest state-supported all-female college in the United States. The school, known today as Mississippi University for Women (MUW), has from its inception limited its enrollment to women.

* * *

The School of Nursing [established in 1971] has its own faculty and administrative officers and establishes its own criteria for admission.

Respondent, Joe Hogan, is a registered nurse but does not hold a baccalaureate degree in nursing. * * * In 1979, Hogan applied for admission to the MUW School of Nursing's baccalaureate program. Although he was otherwise qualified, he was denied admission to the School of Nursing solely because of his sex. School officials informed him that he could audit the courses in which he was interested, but could not enroll for credit.

Hogan filed an action * * *, claiming the single-sex admissions policy of MUW's School of Nursing violated the Equal Protection Clause of the Fourteenth Amendment. * * * Because the challenged policy expressly discriminates among applicants on the basis of gender, it is subject to scrutiny under the Equal Protection Clause of the Fourteenth Amendment. That this statutory policy discriminates against males rather than against females does not exempt it from scrutiny or reduce the standard of review. Our decisions also establish that the party seeking to uphold a statute that classifies individuals on the basis of their gender must carry the burden of showing an "exceedingly persuasive justification" for the classification. The burden is met only by showing at least that the classification serves "important governmental objectives and that the discriminatory means employed" are "substantially related to the achievement of those objectives."

* * *

The State's primary justification for maintaining the single-sex admissions policy of MUW's School of Nursing is that it compensates for discrimination against women and, therefore, constitutes educational affirmative action. As applied to the School of Nursing, we find the State's argument unpersuasive.

In limited circumstances, a gender-based classification favoring one sex can be justified if it intentionally and directly assists members of the sex that is disproportionately burdened.

* * *

* * * Mississippi has made no showing that women lacked opportunities to obtain training in the field of nursing or to attain positions of leadership in that field when the MUW School of Nursing opened its door or that women currently are deprived of such opportunities. In fact, in 1970, the year before the School of Nursing's first class enrolled, women earned 94 percent of the nursing baccalaureate degrees conferred in Mississippi and 98.6 percent of the degrees earned nationwide. * * * As one would expect, the labor force reflects the same predominance of women in nursing. When MUW's School of Nursing began operation, nearly 98 percent of all employed registered nurses were female.

Rather than compensate for discriminatory barriers faced by women, MUW's policy of excluding males from admission to the School of Nursing tends to perpetuate the stereotyped view of nursing as an exclusively woman's job.[15] By assuring that Mississippi allots more openings in its state-supported nursing schools to women than it does to men, MUW's admissions policy lends credibility to the old view that women, not men, should become nurses, and makes the assumption that nursing is a field for women a self-fulfilling prophecy. * * *

The policy is invalid also because it fails the second part of the equal protection test, for the State has made no showing that the gender-based classification is substantially and directly related to its proposed compensatory objective. To the contrary, MUW's policy of permitting men to attend classes as auditors fatally undermines its claim that women, at least those in the School of Nursing, are adversely affected by the presence of men.

* * *

The uncontroverted record reveals that admitting men to nursing classes does not affect teaching style, that the presence of men in the classroom would not affect the performance of the female nursing students, and that men in coeducational nursing schools do not dominate the classroom. In sum, the record in this case is flatly inconsistent with the claim that excluding men from the School of Nursing is necessary to reach any of MUW's educational goals.

* * *

Accordingly, we hold that MUW's policy of denying males the right to enroll for credit in its School of Nursing violates the Equal Protection Clause of the Fourth Amendment.

---

15. Officials of the American Nurses Association have suggested that excluding men from the field has depressed nurses' wages. To the extent the exclusion of men has that effect, MUW's admissions policy actually penalizes the very class the State purports to benefit.

JUSTICE POWELL, with whom JUSTICE REHNQUIST joins, dissenting.

The Court's opinion bows deeply to conformity. Left without honor—indeed, held unconstitutional—is an element of diversity that has characterized much of American education and enriched much of American life. The Court in effect holds today that no State now may provide even a single institution of higher learning open only to women students.

* * *

By applying heightened equal protection analysis to this case, the Court frustrates the liberating spirit of the Equal Protection Clause. It prohibits the States from providing women with an opportunity to choose the type of university they prefer. And yet it is these women whom the Court regards as the *victims* of an illegal, stereotyped perception of the role of women in our society. The Court reasons this way in a case in which no woman has complained, and the only complainant is a man who advances no claims on behalf of anyone else. His claim, it should be recalled, is not that he is being denied a substantive educational opportunity, or even the right to attend an all-male or a coeducational college. It is *only* that the colleges open to him are located at inconvenient distances.

NOTES ON HOGAN

1. The majority opinion in *Hogan* states that when a man alleges that he has been discriminated against because of his sex in violation of Equal Protection, courts are to apply the "intermediate scrutiny" standard of review applicable in similar suits brought by women, rather than the rational basis standard generally applicable to claims under the Equal Protection Clause. Which do you think is the appropriate standard when discrimination against men is alleged? Do you agree with the majority or dissent? Does it matter which standard is applied? How does this case fit with the early liberal feminist strategy of the Women's Rights Project discussed in Chapter Two?

2. In his dissent in *Hogan,* Justice Powell states that "[t]he Court in effect holds today that no State now may provide even a single institution of higher learning open only to women students." Is this a correct reading of the majority opinion?

3. Justice O'Connor warns in *Hogan* against "benign" legislation that is based on paternalistic stereotypes. Is it possible to characterize sex-specific rules, like MUW's, as benign *or* harmful? Don't such rules help some women at some times in some ways and hurt some women at some times in other ways? How did MUW's policy (a) help and (b) hurt women? How would you decide whether the costs outweigh the benefits? How should courts approach such difficult issues? Can the courts be trusted to make these determinations?

Consider Justice Powell's view that MUW's women-only policy is benign because it conforms to an honored tradition which gives women the benefit of diversity in their choice of school, i.e., it expands women's choices. David Hoffman points to three problems with this characterization:

> First, it is clearly a mistake to assume that women, or men, have unlimited freedom of choice as to the school they attend. Many students are forced, as Joe Hogan was, to attend school where their families or jobs are located. Moreover, the notion that a woman's decision to attend a sex-segregated school is truly voluntary is deeply undercut by the reality, recognized even by Justice Powell, that one of the factors that make single-sex schools attractive for women is the sexist treatment they receive at coeducational schools.
>
> Second, separate schools for women have historically been significantly inferior to comparable male facilities. This second-class status may affect not only the self-esteem of students who attend women's schools, but their careers and salaries as well.
>
> Third, the Justices' invocation of ancient tradition on behalf of single-sex schools probably does more to undermine the legitimacy of the schools than to bolster it. Women's schools were originally founded in the United States because of the exclusion of women from the established colleges and universities, and bore an unmistakable stigma on that account. Their curricula, moreover, were defined by traditional, stereotyped notions of "women's place." To the extent that women's schools have transcended these limitations, they have generally done so in spite of their heritage rather than because of it.
>
> * * *
>
> "Choice" is relatively unmeaningful for women when the range of options is largely determined by men.

Hoffman, Challenge to Single–Sex Schools Under Equal Protection: *Mississippi University for Women v. Hogan*, 6 Harv. Women's L.J. 163, 172 (1983). What criteria do you think Hoffman would utilize to determine if a single-sex school benefited women or not? What criteria does Justice Powell use? How persuasive do you find the argument made by the American Nurses Association, referred to in note 15, that excluding men from nursing disadvantages women by depressing wages in the field? See U.S. Department of Labor, Women in the Labor Force: A Databook (2009) (reporting that as of 2008, women still made up 91.7 percent of registered nurses).

4. How would the feminist theorists examined in Chapter 3 approach the problems raised in *Hogan*?

5. Are women's colleges discriminatory by their very nature? Should our society approve of separatism when it is chosen by the less powerful group as a means of empowerment, rather than imposed upon it by the dominant group, and is a means toward empowerment? See Lisa Denise Gladke, The Fate of Women's Colleges: An Anti–Subordination Analysis, 18 B.C. Third World L.J. 195 (1998); Deborah L. Rhode, Association and Assimilation, 81 Nw. L. Rev. 106 (1986); Janella Miller, The Future of Private Women's Colleges, 7 Harv. Women's L.J. 153, 179–80 (1984); Jillian Kinzie, Auden D. Thomas, Megan M. Palmer, Paul D. Umbach, George D. Kuh, Women Students at Coeducational and Women's Colleges: How do their Experiences Compare?, Journal of College Student Development, vol. 48, no.2, 145–165 (2007).

6. A San Francisco coeducational academic high school adopted a policy that the student body should be divided 50/50 between boys and girls. In order to achieve this balance, it was necessary to set an admission standard of a 3.50 grade point average on a scale of 4 for girls and only 3.25 for boys. Is this constitutional? What does this policy do to a definition of equality? Is this simply "affirmative action" in reverse? See Berkelman v. San Francisco Unified Sch. Dist., 501 F.2d 1264 (9th Cir.1974).

7. Should it matter whether the government operates a sex-specific school? What arguments can you make for allowing only private single-sex institutions?

TEXT NOTE: COMPARISONS BETWEEN SINGLE-SEX FEMALE AND COEDUCATIONAL HIGHER EDUCATION

In the late 1970's Elizabeth Tidball published an influential study showing that from 1910 to 1960 "graduates of women's colleges were twice as likely as women graduates of coeducational institutions to be cited for career achievements in *Who's Who of American Women*."[22] She later found similar results, i.e., greater numbers of women's college graduates among men and women entering medical school and obtaining natural science doctorates. These findings seemed especially true for graduates of the Seven Sisters colleges of Barnard, Bryn Mawr, Radcliffe, Mount Holyoke, Smith, Vassar, and Wellesley. This higher career achievement was explained by Tidball to be the result of greater numbers of women faculty who could act as role models at women's colleges. These and similar assertions of success and achievement by graduates of women's colleges, contributed to the resurgence of women's colleges in the 1980's following the closing of many women's colleges in the mid-sixties and seventies.[23]

Two other researchers, Joy K. Rice and Annette Hemmings, have updated Tidball's studies. According to their study:

> Women's colleges flourished before the turn of the century, offering women who wanted to obtain a higher education the choice of a single-sex environment. Many of these early colleges justified their mission to educate women with the social rationale that educated women would become teachers, reformers, and culture bearers, as well as "better" mothers and wives. Although in the first half of this [the twentieth] century elite women's colleges were largely accessible only to the wealthy, they often provided a rigorous curriculum for women that was comparable to that received by men at coeducational institutions. By the late 1960s, however, federal cutbacks and economic constraints on higher education prompted many small colleges to close and universities and colleges to reduce their budgets. Educational equity and the integration of minorities and women was publicly debated, and women's colleges increasingly were seen by professionals in educational policy studies as an

---

22. Joy K. Rice & Annette Hemmings, Women's Colleges and Women Achievers: An Update, in Reconstructing the Academy: Women's Education and Women's Studies 220 (Elizabeth Minnich et al, eds. 1988).

23. Id. at 220–23.

> elitist anachronism. In 1960 there were about three hundred colleges for women; by 1970 only half of those colleges remained single-sex institutions. The majority of these were church-related schools, primarily Roman Catholic. As financial pressures grew and coeducation attracted many women to previously all-male schools, many women's colleges began admitting men. The six-month period between June and December 1968, when an astounding sixty-four women's colleges either became coeducational institutions or closed their doors, was a watermark in higher education. Today [1988], 116 women's colleges educate about 125,000 students, roughly 1 percent of all college students and 2 percent of all women college students.[24]

The researchers found data consistent with Tidball's results and noted that other studies essentially replicated Tidball's major findings using *Who's Who in America* instead of *Who's Who of American Women*.[25] However, these studies also suggested a possible role for factors other than single-sex environment—i.e., college admissions selectivity and prior student academic achievement. Nonetheless, when Tidball reanalyzed her own data, she found that: (1) highly selective women's colleges had twice as many graduates who were high achievers as did highly selective coeducational colleges; and (2) all other women's colleges were twice as likely to have high-achieving women alumnae as were all other coeducational colleges. Still, a key variable, the student's socioeconomic status, was not taken into account.

Opponents of single-sex education argue that these studies are flawed because: (1) they failed to control for such factors as pre-college backgrounds, institutional recruitment efforts, and institutional selectivity; and (2) because women were not admitted to many men's colleges until the 1970's, women's colleges had the best and brightest women from which to draw their student bodies.[26] Furthermore, because studies consistently conclude that boys benefit from the presence of girls and that the "severest forms of sexism [are] found in boys' schools,"[27] opponents believe that coeducational settings are the best way to fight discrimination.

Studies are inconsistent in their findings of when single-sex schools lead to improved academic performance for girls.[28] However, it is incontrovertible that single-sex education offers greater opportunities for girls to be in leadership positions. Furthermore, one effect of single-sex women's education, positive self-esteem, has remained constant in both older and more current studies: "At both secondary and postsecondary schools, female students self-report that single-sex educational environments are academically advantageous * * *. Two fairly well-accepted advantages of single-sex education are

---

24. Id. at 221–22. By 1998, there were approximately 80 women's colleges remaining. Irene Harwarth et al., U.S. Dep't of Ed., Women's Colleges in the United States: History, Issues and Challenges (1997).

25. Id. at 222–23. See also Harwarth et al., above note 25, at 83 (finding that women who attend women's colleges are more likely to have studied math, science or economics, more than two times as likely to receive doctoral degrees, and more likely to attend medical and law school than their coed counterparts).

26. Nancy Levit, Separating Equals: Educational Research and the Long–Term Consequences of Sex Segregation, 67 Geo. Wash. L. Rev. 451, 475–76 (1999).

27. Id. at 499.

28. Id. at 485–92.

the effect of an all-girl environment on self-esteem and students' satisfaction with their academic * * * life."[29] In fact, in one poll 91 percent of women who attended an all-girls' school believed single-sex education helped them.[30]

NOTES ON COLLEGE STUDIES

1. What do you think are the reasons why graduates of the Seven Sisters women's colleges are such high achievers? Have you experienced single-sex education? How do you evaluate its benefits? What, if any, are its disadvantages?

2. Do you think that reliance on inclusion in *Who's Who,* as used by Tidball and others, is a satisfactory indicator of achievement? What other measures would you use? Rice and Hemmings note that women's colleges have increased their ethnic and socioeconomic diversity by attracting and providing support for ethnic and racial minorities and disadvantaged women. Do you agree with their conclusion that this might decrease the influence of socioeconomic status as a determinant of career achievement for women's college graduates?

3. Rather than being isolated from half the population, is it important for women to learn to relate to men during the educational process? Do you think that attending women's schools inhibits females from developing survival skills necessary for a "man's" world? What arguments can you make in support of coeducation for women? Does the strength of those arguments vary with the maturity of the students? With their level of self-esteem? Do the arguments supporting single-sex women's education also support single-sex men's education? Are there reasons why males should be educated alongside females? Can you develop an optimal model for education for both sexes? What role should the law play in these issues?

UNITED STATES v. VIRGINIA

United States Supreme Court, 1996.
518 U.S. 515, 116 S.Ct. 2264, 135 L.Ed.2d 735.

[This case, known as *VMI*, is excerpted in Chapter Two, above.]

NOTES ON SINGLE-SEX EDUCATION

1. Is *VMI* consistent with *Hogan*? Does *Hogan* support sex-specific schools when such schools add diversity to a state's educational offerings?

29. Id. at 481, 496. Research by Cornelius Riordan suggests that the positive effects of single-sex schools are the greatest for black and Hispanic females from low socioeconomic levels. See Cornelius Riordan, The Future of Single–Sex Schools, in Separated by Sex: A Critical Look at Single Sex Education for Girls 53 (Am. Ass'n Univ. Women Educ. Found., ed., 1998); Cornelius Riordan, Single–Gender Schools: Outcomes for African and Hispanic Americans, 10 Res. Soc. Educ. & Socialization 177, 192–202 (1994); Cornelius Riordan, Girls and Boys in School: Together or Separate? 61 (1990); US Department of Education, Single–Sex versus Coeducational Schooling: a Systematic Review (2005), (available at http://www2.ed.gov/rschstat/eval/other/single-sex/single-sex.pdf, last visited May 10, 2010).

30. Josette Shiner & Bonnie Erbe, Are All–Girl Schools Good for Education?, Wash. Times, Apr. 17, 1999, § A12 (citing a 1990 Yankelovich poll). See also Lea Hubbard & Amanda Datnow, Do Single–Sex Schools Improve the Education of Low–Income and Minority Students? An Investigation of California's Public Single–Gender Academies, Anthropology and Education Quarterly, vol. 36 115–131 (2005).

What of *Hogan*'s rejection of traditional sexual stereotypes? Does the Court in *VMI* accept such stereotypes? In *Hogan,* the Supreme Court went out of its way to emphasize that men in the classrooms did not affect teaching style or the performance of female students; does it address that concern in *VMI*? Is the difference in how the sexes learn relevant to these cases?

2. How would the *VMI* issue, i.e., whether women must be admitted to a male-only state-supported college, be analyzed under the various feminist theories explored in Chapter 3? How would proponents of each of these approaches respond to the point that VMI will be changed, if not destroyed, if women are admitted?

3. Does *VMI*, as Scalia indicates, sound the death knell for public, single-sex education? What about footnote 7, in which the Court stated it did "not question the Commonwealth's prerogative *evenhandedly* to support diverse educational opportunities" (emphasis added)? What criteria will such a school have to meet to pass muster after *VMI*? What about private single-sex schools? Will they be affected by *VMI*?

4. *VMI* was decided on constitutional grounds. Does Title IX impose identical requirements, i.e., are "equal protection" and non-discrimination on the basis of sex in education identical concepts? Are there differing standards?

5. In recent years, public, single-sex education has experienced something of a revival. In 2004 there were twenty-five single-sex public primary and secondary schools. Sixty-three other schools offered single-sex classrooms within co-ed schools. The majority of these schools serve primarily students of color. See Verna L. Williams, Reform or Retrenchment? Single–Sex Education and the Construction of Race and Gender, 2004 Wis. L. Rev. 15, 20 n. 31 (2004).

(a) Consider, for example, New York City's Young Women's Leadership High School, opened in 1996. The school now has over 300 middle and high school students. As soon as the school opened, the New York Civil Liberties Union, the National Organization for Women, and the New York Civil Rights Coalition filed a Title IX complaint. No legal challenge has yet succeeded in closing the school or forcing it to admit boys. See Rosemary C. Salomone, Same, Different, Equal: Rethinking Single–Sex Schooling 10–25 (2003). The school graduated its first class, 32 girls, in 2001. Every student, with the exception of one who chose to join the Air Force, was accepted by and enrolled at a four year college. See Lawrence G. Sager, Cool Federalism and the Life Cycle of Moral Progress, 46 Wm & Mary L. Rev. 1385, 1397 n. 41 (2005). What arguments would you make in defense of the school? How much of the school's success do you think is attributable to its single-sex nature and how much to other characteristics like a clear mission, small size, above-average student spending? Does the school violate Title IX? Does the school violate the constitutional guarantee of equal protection or guarantee it? See Michael Heise, Are Single–Sex Schools Inherently Unequal? 102 Mich. L. Rev. 1219 (2004); Denise C. Morgan, Anti–Subordination Analysis after *United States v.*

Virginia: Evaluating the Constitutionality of K–12 Single–Sex Public Schools, [1999] U. Chi. Leg. F. 381.

(b) California's former governor, Pete Wilson, set aside $5 million dollars in 1996 to fund experimental, single-sex public school academies on sites of existing middle and high schools. This program required that districts receiving funds must spend equal amounts on boys' and girls' programs, and that the money must be spent for equivalent items or purposes. See Tamar Lewin, In California, Wider Test of Same–Sex Schools, N.Y. Times, Oct. 9, 1997, at A1. Is this constitutional? Is it a violation of Title IX?

(c) In 1991, the Detroit School Board Task Force recommended establishing all-male, African American high school academies, citing the following statistics: (1) in 1989, the unemployment rate for African American males living in Detroit was 18.3 percent, compared with 7.1 percent for all males in Michigan; (2) the homicide rate for black males between ages 15 and 24 in the county in which Detroit is located was 14 times the national rate for all males, twice the rate for African American males in Michigan, and 47 times the rate for white males in Michigan; (3) 54 percent of Detroit boys eventually drop out of school, and over 66 percent are suspended; (4) boys fall farther behind the national average academically in almost every successive year of elementary and secondary school; (5) boys in the first grade perform at or above grade level on academic achievement tests, but by the twelfth grade they are over two grades behind in reading and over three grades behind in mathematics; and (6) the Detroit male dropout rate is approximately 10 percent higher than the female dropout rate. Note, Inner–City Single–Sex Schools: Educational Reform or Invidious Discrimination?, 105 Harv. L. Rev. 1741, 1742–43 (1992). Moreover, the Detroit public school student population is 90 percent black. Id. at 1743, n. 10. However, girls, too, suffer from remarkably high dropout rates and low academic performance in the Detroit school system. Nearly 50 percent of female students drop out, and, on average, twelfth-grade girls score only at a ninth-grade level on standardized math tests and at a tenth-grade level on standardized reading tests. Id. at 1745, n. 32. High levels of violence, teen-age pregnancy and other social problems are correlated with low academic performance. Id. at 1756.

Do you think these statistics justify the Detroit School Board's establishment of three male academies? Does the Constitution forbid dealing with one *part* of a problem before solving the whole? Especially when the alternative may be to take *no* action? What if the Detroit School Board had a plan in place to open a similar number of Female Academies on a specific date, rather than simply saying that it would do so "soon"? Would that change your opinion? See Garrett v. Board of Education, Detroit, 775 F.Supp. 1004 (E.D.Mich.1991) (granting a preliminary injunction preventing the opening of all-male educational facilities on the ground that the important purpose of the all-male academies is insufficient to override the rights of females to equal opportunities).

What does the Detroit School Board mean when it states that African American boys are "at-risk" students? Does it mean "at risk" of committing a crime, at risk of dropping out, or at risk of not being educated? In what ways are the Detroit African American girls also "at risk"? What can you infer from the School Board's decision to address the male students' problems first?

The boys' "Rites of Passage" curriculum in the Detroit schools included topics such as "men master their emotions," "men need a vision and a plan for living," and "men acquire skills and knowledge to overcome life's obstacles." What would be included in a "Rites of Passage" curriculum for adolescent girls?

Many parents desperately wanted their children to go to the Male Academies. Within four months of the announcement that the Academies would be established, nearly 1200 children had applied for 560 slots. Accord in Detroit Would Let Girls Attend All–Boys Schools, N.Y. Times, Aug. 26, 1991, at A16. Following the ruling in *Garrett,* the Detroit School Board approved a compromise plan and admitted 38 girls to the experimental schools with the Afrocentric curriculum for the 1991–92 school year. Ron Russell, Single–Sex Schools Get New Approach in Detroit, Detroit News, Nov. 18, 1991. Does that settlement satisfy Equal Protection concerns?

6. Are there dangers in an all-male institution that are absent in an all-female institution? Are there benefits to an all-female institution that are absent from an all-male institution? What arguments can you make for permitting female-only institutions while disallowing male-only institutions? What arguments would the various feminist theorists discussed in Chapter 3 make?

7. Would separate but equal grade schools be permissible under the feminist theories explored in Chapter 3? What are the benefits and harms likely to be associated with such schools?

8. Michael Kimmel, one of the founders of the masculinities movement, addressed why boys are at risk in a speech he gave in January of 2000:

> Are boys in trouble in school? At first glance, the statistics would suggest that they are. Boys commit suicide four times more often than girls, get into fights twice as often, get lower grades on standardized tests of reading and writing, and have lower class rank and fewer honors than girls. Given these gender differences, it's not surprising that we're having a national debate. After all, boys seem to be both doing badly and doing worse than girls.
>
> * * *
>
> Introducing masculinities into the discussion alleviates several of the problems with the "what about the boys?" debate. It enables us to explore the ways in which class and race complicate the picture of boys' achievement and behaviors. It also reveals that boys and girls are on the same side in this struggle, not pitted against each other. Making masculinity visible also enables us to understand what I regard as the *real* boy crisis in America. We call it "teen violence," "youth violence." Just who do we think is doing it—girls? Imagine if the killers in schools in Littleton and Jonesboro were all black girls from poor families. The entire focus would be on race, class, and gender. Yet the obvious fact that at these schools the killers were all middle-class white boys seems to have escaped

> everyone's notice. From an early age, boys learn that violence is not only an acceptable form of conflict resolution, but one that is admired.
>
> If we really want to rescue boys, protect boys, promote boyhood, then our task must be to find ways to reveal and challenge this ideology of masculinity, to disrupt the facile "boys will be boys" model, and to erode boys' sense of entitlement. Because the reality is that this ideology of masculinity is the problem for *both* girls *and* boys. * * *

Kimmel, "What About the Boys?" What the Current Debates Tell Us, and Don't Tell Us, About Boys in School, Wellesley Centers for Women, 21 Research Rpt. 6 (2000). Can public education "reveal and challenge this ideology of masculinity?" How?

9. What criteria should be used to determine if public single-sex schools are "equal?" Identical curriculum? Identical pedagogical styles? The same budget? The same achievement levels? The same number of students, the same class sizes, the same number of teachers and administrators? See, e.g., Bray v. Lee, 337 F.Supp. 934 (D.Mass.1972) (to obtain admission to Boston Latin Schools, girls had to score at least 133 out of 200 on an admissions test but the boys only had to score 120 or better because Boys Latin had twice as much capacity as Girls Latin; court held that the use of separate and different standards to evaluate the examination results to determine the admission of boys and girls constituted a violation of the Equal Protection Clause). Does *VMI* provide guidance about what "comparability" in Equal Protection cases means? Are "comparability" and "equality" interchangeable?

10. Several commentators question the assimilation of women into male society through coeducation, claiming that it fails to challenge the existing structure of society in any meaningful way. See, e.g., Nancy E. Shurtz, Lighting the Lantern: Visions of a Virtual All–Women's Law School, 16 Hastings Women's L.J. 63 (2004); Jennifer Gerarda Brown, "To Give Them Countenance": The Case for a Women's Law School, 22 Harv. Women's L.J. 1 (1999); Deborah L. Rhode, Association and Assimilation, 81 Nw. U. L. Rev. 106 (1986); Janella Miller, The Future of Private Women's Colleges, 7 Harv. Women's L.J. 153 (1984). Adrienne Rich acknowledges that women who try to change the university will be accused of "reverse chauvinism":

> Women in the university therefore need to address themselves—against the opprobrium and obstruction they do and will encounter—to changing the center of gravity of the institution as far as possible; to work toward a woman-centered university because only if that center of gravity can be shifted will women really be free to learn, to teach, to share strength, to explore, to criticize, and to convert knowledge to power.

Rich, Toward a Woman–Centered University, in On Lies, Secrets, and Silence: Selected Prose 1966–1978 125, 128 (1979). There is no doubt that education is a powerful tool of socialization. What is the best strategy to address this issue? Does a college that admits women only offer the answer? Even if it uses a "male" curriculum? What solution would you propose?

TEXT NOTE: CLASSROOM EXPERIENCES, LANGUAGE, LEARNING STYLES, AND SELF-ESTEEM

Many researchers have puzzled over the drop in girls' self-esteem as they go through school, even though they get better grades than boys. At least one teacher trainer, Cathy Nelson, attributes this effect to the negative messages delivered to girls by school curricula, messages that women's lives count for less than men's. The historian Linda Kerber states: "Lowered self-esteem is a perfectly reasonable conclusion if one has been subtly instructed that what people like oneself have done in the world has not been important and is not worth studying."[31]

In a year-long study designed to determine if specific day-to-day teacher practices of equity are linked to student achievement in a seventh grade classroom, researchers discovered that:

> While boys and girls reported fair treatment, both in surveys and in focus groups and interviews, they also described their experiences at school in terms of differential treatment, which *they* considered fair because boys and girls are different and "that's just the way it is." For these adolescents an understanding of differences being "natural" also led to expectations that boys did not have to pay attention during lessons but could later rely on teachers and girls in the class (since girls are "smarter") to provide extra help. Both boys and girls thought that the greater amount of time teachers spend working with boys individually or in small groups was fair because boys need more attention. Girls said that boys are "louder," "more disruptive," "more outgoing" while girls are "more shy than boys" and "normally quiet."
>
> Boys said that girls are "smarter," naturally faster at their schoolwork, better listeners, and are easily embarrassed and therefore do not like too much attention while boys "want more attention," are "more outgoing," and "don't study as much." When we asked boys if it was difficult for them to attend classes when they thought they weren't as smart as their female classmates, one boy told us, "In elementary and middle school, [girls are] like way smarter than boys, but then like when it comes to like high school and college I think boys start to get even smarter because like most of the famous scientists are like the boys * * * but you don't really see that much famous, smart girl scientists."[32]

The researchers concluded that culture both constructs and reinforces these inequities under the guise of progress. Additionally, they found that:

> Consistent with national data, the girls in this study had lower self-esteem than boys, despite the fact that they got consistently higher grades in every subject area. Boys, on the other hand, felt little motivation to do well and take responsibility for their own learning, especially in subjects deemed more feminine such as language arts.[33]

---

31. The AAUW Report: How Schools Shortchange Girls 67 (1992).

32. Michelle V. Porche & Renee Spencer, "We've Come a Long Way . . . Maybe?" Wellesley Center for Women, 21 Research Rpt. 22–23 (2000).

33. Id.

This study thus presents a complicated picture: boys and girls perceive teachers to be fair and equitable when boys and girls are treated differently.[34] Apparently, by the seventh grade, gender stereotypes are firmly embedded.

These classroom inequities occur in an environment in which learning styles may vary in gendered ways. Some research suggests, for example, that girls and boys have different learning styles and benefit from different educational environments. For girls and women, successful learning may be more likely to take place in an atmosphere that enables students empathetically to enter into the subject they are studying, an approach called "connected knowing."[35] On the other hand, it is suggested that boys thrive in an adversarial, individualistic classroom. Even though there are no studies indicating that boys would not learn better through "connected knowing," few teachers employ it. Competition, not collaboration, is the mode of learning.

Language and communication issues further complicate the classroom experience for females. Research indicates that men tend to (1) do more talking; (2) interrupt more; and (3) choose the topics of discussion in conversations with women.[36] In all-women conversations, the speakers regard the conversation as cooperative, not competitive; in all-men conversations, speakers view the conversation as individualistic. What is the result? According to Sally McConnell–Ginet:

> How does inequality in discourse affect what can be meant and by whom? First, men are more likely than women to have a chance to express their perspective on situations, not only because they have more frequent access to the floor but also because they are more actively attended to. This distinction is especially important, since comprehension goes well beyond simple recognition of the linguistic structures used. In other words, where the sexes have somewhat different perspectives on a situation, the man's view is more likely to be familiar to the woman than hers is to him. This observation leads directly to the second point: men are much more likely than women to be unaware that their own view is not universally shared.[37]

Many researchers have pointed to hypercorrect grammar, super polite forms, and questioning as distinctive characteristics of women's speech. Specifically, women were found to: (a) ask more questions; (b) make statements in a

---

34. Id.

35. See Mary Field Belenky et al., Women's Ways of Knowing: The Development of Self, Voice and Mind 102 (1986). See also American Association of University Women, Girls In The Middle (1996) (stating that girls fare better in cooperative learning environments); American Association of University Women, Growing Smart: What's Working for Girls in Schools (1994) (linking cooperative learning in single-sex girls' classes to increases math and science scores); Malkah T. Notman & Carol C. Nadelson, A Review of Gender Differences in Brain and Behavior, in Women and Men: New Perspectives on Gender Differences 24 (Malkah T. Notman & Carol C. Nadelson eds., 1990) ("[W]omen favor a 'communicative mode' in gaining knowledge about the world and in dealing with others.").

36. Sally McConnell–Ginet, The Sexual (Re)Production of Meaning: A Discourse–Based Theory in Language, Gender, and Professional Writing: Theoretical Approaches and Guidelines for Nonsexist Usage 35, 43 (Francine Wattman Frank & Paul A. Treichler, eds. 1989). See also Elizabeth Mertz et al., What Difference Does Difference Make? The Challenge for Legal Education, 48 J. Legal Educ. 1, 14–15 (1998) (reviewing several studies finding that men talk more in class than women and that women are more vulnerable to interruption).

37. Id.

questioning tone; (c) use more tag questions ("don't you think?"); (d) lead off with questions to ensure a listener's attention; and (e) use more "hedges" or qualifiers and intensifiers ("really").[38]

Coeducation appears to require women to alter the communication patterns they utilize in all-women conversations in order to participate fully in the classroom. Linguists note this dilemma:

> The collaborative patterns which are central to talk among women—drawing out other speakers, supportive listening and head nods, mutual sharing of emotions and personal knowledge, respect for one another's conversational space—are weak or "powerless" only when contrasted with their opposites. For example, open, sharing behaviors become weak only when another person in an interaction refuses to reciprocate them. Being sensitive to another's need—inviting them to take turns at talk, drawing out the topics they raise—is heard as ineffectual only when this sensitivity is not reciprocated. Revealing emotions is a disadvantage only when others are being reserved and refusing to share or to show emotion. The "powerlessness" of the speech patterns women more often use exists only relative to the power of so-called masculine patterns. When only women are told to change their behavior, and essentially to adopt "male forms," the characteristics of male speech are ignored, and the assumption of power as domination is reproduced.[39]

Thus, the classroom experience remains a difficult one for girls and women to negotiate successfully.

NOTES ON THE CLASSROOM EXPERIENCE

1. How should teachers respond to the findings about differential treatment of girls and boys in the classroom? What *does* equity mean in the classroom? "Identical" treatment? How can we ensure that gender differences don't make a difference in fair treatment in the classroom?

2. The linguists discuss women's collaborative communication patterns in positive terms; are these really survival skills of the oppressed? If so, should we be valorizing them? Do you agree that there is a hierarchy in communication patterns, with male forms considered superior? Are women taken more seriously if they use a more male speech style? However, if a woman speaks more directly and assertively, will she be dismissed as "unfeminine"? Do women, in effect, need to be bilingual—using their first language (female) when speaking on a personal level or with other women and their foreign language (male) when they need to be "taken seriously"? How do you assess the likelihood of reforming coeducational communication patterns?

3. What are the implications of the findings about communication patterns? Do women express their thoughts more tentatively? Do women have to work harder to get someone's attention? Have women internalized men's assumptions that what they have to say is not very interesting or intellectual-

---

38. See generally Mary Crawford, Talking Difference: On Gender & Language 23–26 (1995); Robin Lakoff, Language and Woman's Place 53–6 (1975).

39. Barrie Thorne et al., Language, Gender and Society: Opening a Second Decade of Research in Language, Gender and Society 7, 19 (Thorne, Kramarae & Henley, eds. 1983).

ly rigorous? In your experience, do these patterns impact women's performance in law school? What is their likely impact in litigation? What is the implication of this data for coeducation?

4. The *VMI* case, excerpted in Chapter 2, above, acknowledged gendered ways of learning, holding that the "adversative" system of teaching utilized at VMI would have to be changed if women were enrolled since it negatively affected women's learning. If men and women learn differently, which system of teaching should be used? The one that favors men or women? For a more complete discussion of feminist pedagogy, see Charlotte Bunch & Sandra Pollack, eds., Learning Our Way: Essays in Feminist Education (1983); Margo Culley & Catherine Portuges, eds., Gender Subjects: The Dynamics of Feminist Education (1985); Susan L. Gabriel & Isaiah Smithson, eds., Gender in the Classroom: Power and Pedagogy (1990); Frances A. Maher & Mary Kay Thompson Tetreault, The Feminist Classroom: Dynamics of Gender, Race, and Privilege (2001); Elizabeth Minnich, Jean O'Barr & Rachel Rosenfeld, eds., Reconstructing the Academy: Women's Education and Women's Studies (1988); Judith Resnick, A Continuous Body: Ongoing Conversations About Women and Legal Education, 53 L. Legal Educ. 564 (2003).

5. Do you think it is possible to transform the power dynamics of the coeducational classroom from masculinist ("domination or control") to feminist ("power as energy, effective interaction or empowerment")—a solution offered by Barrie Thorne et al., Language, Gender and Society: Opening a Second Decade of Research in Language, Gender and Society 7, 19 (Thorne, Kramarae and Henley, eds. 1983). How could this be accomplished?

C. STANDARDIZED TESTING

SHARIF v. NEW YORK STATE EDUCATION DEPARTMENT

United States District Court, Southern District of New York, 1989.
709 F.Supp. 345.

This case raises the important question of whether New York State denies female students an equal opportunity to receive prestigious state merit scholarships by its sole reliance upon the Scholastic Aptitude Test ("SAT") to determine eligibility. To the Court's knowledge, this is the first case where female students are seeking to use the federal civil rights statute prohibiting sex discrimination in federally-funded educational programs to challenge a state's reliance on standardized tests. This case also presents a legal issue of first impression: whether discrimination under Title IX can be established by proof of disparate impact without proof of intent to discriminate.

* * *

[The court reviewed the evolution of the New York State Scholarship Awards and how they are determined. After utilizing special Regents examinations for decades, in 1977, as a cost-cutting measure, the program was instructed to use a nationally established competitive examination to decide awards. The State Education Department ("SED") chose the Scholastic Aptitude Test ("SAT"), the test taken by the greatest number of students. In response to allegations that the SED's practice of relying solely on the SAT discriminated against females who consistently score below males, the legislature directed that the awards be based in part upon the student's grade point average as a measure of high school achievement. Under this procedure, using a combination of grades and SAT scores, women received substantially more scholarships than in the prior years in which the SAT had been the sole criterion. Although use of the GPA reduced the disparity between the number of men and women receiving awards, the SED recommended that the practice be discontinued, as soon as a new exam was developed, because: (1) use of GPA put an increased burden on school staff; (2) use of GPA did not provide an equitable way to compare students from different schools; and (3) use of GPA would encourage students to avoid more challenging courses in order to obtain better grades for scholarship purposes. The legislature failed to provide funds to develop a new exam or to renew its directive to use GPA's in the scholarship determination.]

The Educational Testing Service ("ETS") developed the SAT in order to predict academic performance in college. The ability of the SAT to serve this purpose has been statistically "validated." It is undisputed, however, that the SAT predicts the success of students differently for males and females. In other words, while the SAT will predict college success as well for males within the universe of males as for females within the universe of females, when predictions are within the combined universe of males and females, the SAT *underpredicts* academic performance of females in their freshman year of college, and *overpredicts* such academic performance for males. The SAT has never been validated as a measure of past high school performance.

* * *

Both the Empire and Regents Scholarships are intended to reward past academic achievement of high school students, and to encourage those students who have demonstrated such achievement to pursue their educations in New York State. It is undisputed, however, that the SAT was developed and validated to serve a different purpose—*predicting* performance *in college*. * * *

Males have outscored females on the verbal portion of the SAT since 1972, with an average score differential of at least 10 points since 1981. Males have also consistently outscored females on the mathematics portion, with an average differential of at least 40 points since 1967. In 1988, for example, girls scored 56 points lower than boys on the test. The probability that these score differentials happened by chance is approximately about one in a billion and the probability that the result could consistently be so different is essentially zero.

Statisticians have attempted to explain the score differentials between males and females by removing the effect of "neutral" variables, such as ethnicity, socioeducational status (parental education), high school classes, and proposed college major. However, under the most conservative studies presented in evidence, even after removing the effect of these factors, at least a 30 point combined differential remains unexplained.

* * *

Plaintiffs do not claim that defendants have intentionally discriminated against them based on their sex. Rather, they claim that defendants' practice of sole reliance upon SAT scores to award prestigious state scholarships disparately impacts female students. * * *

Plaintiffs * * * have established that the probability, absent discriminatory causes, that women would consistently score 60 points less on the SAT than men is nearly zero. Defendants concede that at least half of this differential cannot be explained away by "neutral" variables. Based upon the totality of evidence, then, this Court finds that plaintiffs have demonstrated that the State's practice of sole reliance upon the SAT disparately impacts young women.

* * *

The SED cannot justify its discriminatory practice because any alternative would be more difficult to administer. All states giving merit scholarship awards, with the exception of New York and Massachusetts, use GPAs, without concern for either administrative difficulties, grade inflation or the comparability of grades. Any administrative difficulties that the SED experienced in 1988, when it used a combination system, were attributable to the SED's own failure to implement and clarify specific guidelines for the collections of grades, and to provide any enforcement mechanisms to guard against cheating. * * *

Defendants' practice of relying solely upon SAT scores in awarding Regents and Empire Scholarships deprives young women of the opportunity to compete equally for these prestigious scholarships in violation of both Title IX and the Constitution's equal protection clause. Defendants are hereby ordered to discontinue such discriminatory practices and, instead, to award Regents and Empire Scholarships in a manner that more accurately measures students' high school achievement. For the present year, the best available alternative is a combination of grades and SATs. The SAT component is justified, not as a measure of achievement, but to weight the GPA component. The Court, however, does not limit the SED's discretion to develop other alternatives in the future, including a statewide achievement test.

NOTES ON STANDARDIZED TESTING

1. Are there feasible alternatives to using standardized national tests for admission to college and graduate school, scholarship selection, and placement

in advanced courses? Peter Sacks reports that a "student's high school record alone is the best predictor of performance in the first year of college." Sacks, Standardized Minds: The High Price of America's Testing Culture and What We Can Do to Change It 7 (2000). What about personal interviews? Essays about how an applicant has overcome adversity in their life? Evaluate the costs and benefits of each alternative.

2. Some scholars argue that standardized tests currently are androcentric in format and content and should be replaced by "gynocentric" tests, dominated by or emphasizing feminine interests or point of view. See Phyllis Teitelbaum, Feminist Theory and Standardized Testing, in Gender/Body/Knowledge: Feminist Reconstructions of Being and Knowing, 324, 325–33 (Alison M. Jaggar & Susan R. Bordo, eds. 1989). Do you think standardized tests are androcentric? What might a gynocentric standardized test look like? Will it harm men if we substitute a test based on "gynocentric" knowledge? If so, which should be used—the one that favors men or the one that favors women? How would a proponent of the various feminist theories discussed in Chapter 3 respond to this question? Is there another alternative?

3. In 1995 the SAT was revised, due in part to the criticism of the test's gender-related prediction differences, i.e., the overprediction of college grades of males and underprediction for females. Despite the 1995 revisions of the SAT, colleges continued to express dissatisfaction and some stopped requiring the test for admission. In order to stem the tide of colleges who no longer required SAT scores as part of their admissions requirements, the College Board in 2005 again revamped the SAT. The new test, administered for the first time in March 2005, included a new writing section as well as more advanced math questions. The goal of the changes was to have the SAT reflect what is actually learned in high school classrooms, reinforcing the shift in the SAT's mission from being an aptitude test to being an achievement test. See Tamar Lewin, College Board to Revise SAT After Criticism by University, N.Y. Times, Mar. 23, 2002, at A10. Do you think modifying the SAT to look more like a traditional subject matter achievement test, rather than an aptitude test, will benefit women and minorities or harm them? What types of bias might such changes minimize and what types might such changes exacerbate? Do you think the new test will be more or less susceptible to coaching than the old test?

4. Would a possible solution to the dilemma in *Sharif* be a quota on scholarships—50 percent each to men and women? How would a proponent of the various feminist theories discussed in Chapter 3 respond to this question? Would such a quota violate any law? What is more persuasive to you, the plaintiffs' argument against relying solely on SAT scores because they discriminate against girls or the defendants' argument against using GPA's because they are not uniform, put an extra burden on school staff, and encourage students to take "easy" courses? Why?

5. Standardized tests are also used by the National College Athletic Association (NCAA) to deny eligibility to college athletes. In 1995, the NCAA required that to qualify for play, student-athletes must have a 2.0 GPA in 13 approved academic core courses and a combined SAT score of 1010 or an ACT score of 86; if they do not, they are precluded from competition and may be

denied athletic scholarships. A similar, moderately less restrictive rule, Proposition 48, was in effect from 1986 until 1995. According to data provided by the NCAA, had Prop. 48 been applicable in 1984 and 1985, it would have denied full eligibility to 47 percent of African American student-athletes who went on to graduate, but just 8 percent of white athletes who graduated. Research by the NCAA itself demonstrates that African American student-athletes are disqualified at a rate 9 to 10 times the rate for white students. Moreover, using an SAT cut-off score disproportionately harms low-income students. According to the Department of Education, Prop. 48's test score cut-off denied full eligibility to more than one-third of lower-income students, despite their classroom success. The comparable percentage was only one-tenth for higher-income students. FairTest, What's Wrong with the NCAA's Test Score Requirements?, available at http://www.fairtest.org/facts/prop48.htm. Sports ethicist Russ Gough noted:

> There is a strong correlation between family income and standardized test scores. The NCAA's own studies have completely ignored this well-documented and well-known correlation. The upshot here is that, under the present rule structure, the NCAA might as well throw out its standardized test score requirements and simply allow a freshman to play or not play on the basis of his family's income.

Gough, A Sporting Chance, Wash. Post, Nov. 29, 1994, at A23.

In response to such criticism, as well as several lawsuits alleging that the test-based eligibility requirements discriminated based on race, the NCAA in 2003 modified its test eligibility requirements so as to make test scores play a weaker role. The new requirements increased the number of required core courses to 16 for Division I schools but allowed students to be eligible to play with significantly lower SAT/ACT scores if their GPA's were relatively higher. The new requirements established a sliding scale of combined GPA's and test scores which permitted low test scores if compensated for by higher high school grades. See Jeffrey M. Waller, A Necessary Evil: Proposition 16 and Its Impact on Academics and Athletics in the NCAA, 1 DePaul J. Sports L. & Contemp. Probs. 189 (2003); 2009–2010 NCAA Guide for the College–Bound Student–Athlete, available at http://www.ncaapublications.com/productdownloads/CB10.pdf; Pryor v. NCAA, 288 F.3d 548 (3d Cir. 2002) (reversing the district court's dismissal of plaintiffs' claim that the NCAA's eligibility requirements intentionally discriminated based on race); Cureton v. NCAA, 198 F.3d 107 (3d Cir. 1999) (dismissing plaintiffs' claim that the NCAA's minimum SAT requirements had a disparate impact based on race in violation of Title VI). Do you think the changes will diminish racial disparities in athletic eligibility? Do you think they are a better measure of student-athletes' ability to perform successfully in college? What should the rules be?

6. The focus on testing seems only to be increasing. In 2001 Congress passed the No Child Left Behind Act which tied federal funds to the ability of state school districts to meet rigid, and explicitly race-conscious, testing requirements. 20 U.S.C.A § 6301 (West 2000 & Supp. 2003). As Daniel J. Losen explains: "the law requires that all major racial and ethnic groups achieve 100 percent proficiency in reading and math [by the 2013–2014 school

year] while meeting specified benchmarks of 'adequate yearly progress' along the way. Failure by any racial or ethnic group to meet the benchmarks (over two or more consecutive years) mandates increasingly harsh interventions. These actions can include firing staff, taking over school boards, or closing schools completely." Losen, Challenging Racial Disparities: The Promise and Pitfalls of the No Child Left Behind Act's Race–Conscious Accountability, 47 How. L. J. 243, 258–59 (2004). In the years since its passage the Act has come under increasing fire for its high-stakes emphasis on testing. Parents and teachers have criticized the time spent "teaching to the test" as taking away from the teaching of higher order or more complex skills. Others challenge the arbitrariness in the Act, which allows states to set their own accountability standards such that what is considered proficient in one state is failing in other. Finally, some educators criticize the Act for imposing unrealistic achievement expectations without recognizing the important differences among certain groups of children, particularly those in special education programs and those who are not native English speakers. See Mark Goldberg, Losing Students To High–Stakes Testing, 70 Educ. Dig. 10 n.7 (2005); Editorial, Selfishness Rules as Rich Parents, Schools Reject Reform, USA Today, April 23, 2001, at A11; Sam Dillon, Obama Proposes Sweeping Change in Education Law, New York Times, Mar. 14, 2010, at A1.

WILLIAM C. KIDDER, PORTIA DENIED: UNMASKING GENDER BIAS ON THE LSAT AND ITS RELATIONSHIP TO RACIAL DIVERSITY IN LEGAL EDUCATION

12 Yale J.L. & Feminism 1, 6–14, 18, 22, 24–25, 29–35 (2000)

Although women confront myriad barriers before they commit to law school, after they start their legal education and once they enter the profession, this article focuses on the persistent barrier that the Law School Admission Test (LSAT) poses for women—and women of color in particular—who apply to law school. The LSAT is most frequently treated by law school admission decision-makers as the single most significant element of an applicant's file. Consistent with other standardized tests in higher education, women trail men on the LSAT by an average of approximately one-tenth of a standard deviation.

Table 1: 1992–96 Average Scores on the LSAT for Male and Female Applicants to ABA Law Schools

Applicants		1991–92	1992–93	1993–94	1994–95	1995–96
Male	Avg. Number	152.6 55,460	152.9 51,458	153.2 49,682	152.4 45,945	152.6 41,081
Female	Avg. Number	151.0 41.140	151.3 39,899	151.5 39,531	150.6 37,933	150.7 35,173
Gender Gap	Avg. Male–Avg. Female	1.6 pts.	1.6 pts.	1.7 pts.	1.8 pts.	1.9 pts.

II. The Current State of LSAT–Related Bias in Law School Admissions

A. *The Paucity of Reliable Studies on Gender Bias*

In general, far too little attention has been given to the admission consequences of women's lower LSAT scores. Despite a growing body of academic literature analyzing women's experiences in legal education, no contemporary independent studies assess the impact of the LSAT on women's admission chances. A recent study by Linda Wightman of the Law School Admission Council (LSAC) concluded that the LSAT does not cause gender bias in ABA law school admissions. Yet, there are reasons to believe this conclusion is misleading.

B. *The LSAT's Impact on Admissions Opportunities for Racial and Ethnic Minorities*

An appropriate investigation of the claim that the LSAT disproportionately lowers opportunities for women would measure women's admission chances based on a UGPA [undergraduate grade-point average] model, then study whether including the LSAT increases or restricts opportunities. On this point, much can be learned from Wightman's other major study using the same 1991 database, where she calculated admission chances for racial and ethnic groups. Table 2 summarizes Wightman's findings, after making the two models comparable by adjusting the number of total admits in each model to be the same as the number of actual admits in 1991. Including the LSAT in law school admissions disadvantages every racial/ethnic minority group in Wightman's study.

Bearing in mind that both models are "race blind," it is highly significant that Table 2 indicates that more than twice as many African Americans would be admitted to law school under a UGPA model compared to an LSAT/UGPA model. Puerto Rican applicants are also particularly hard-hit by the LSAT. A similar, if less dramatic, pattern occurs for other groups of color. Even Asian Americans, celebrated by some as the so-called "model minority," would see a not-insignificant 13 percent increase in admits under a UGPA model compared to an LSAT/UGPA model. Overall, the admission chances of people of color would increase by 41 percent under a UGPA admission model compared to an LSAT/UGPA model. This difference of 1,638 students is particularly important when the representation of people of color is already small under "race-blind" admissions.

TABLE 2: Projected 1991 Admission Figures by Racial Group UGPA Model Compared to LSAT/UGPA Model

Racial Group	UGPA Only	LSAT/UGPA	Difference (UGPA–LSAT/UGPA)
African American	1,769	822	+947
Mexican American	398	300	+98
Hispanic	1,062	810	+252

American Indian	199	177	+22
Asian American	1,954	1,727	+227
Puerto Rican	210	118	+92
People of Color Total	5,592	3,954	+1638
White	45,048	46,684	-1636
Overall Total	50,640	50,638	same

III. Results of an Analysis of LSAT–Related Gender Bias in Law School Admissions

A. *Are Men and Women with the Same UGPAs Equally Likely To Be Accepted?*

LSAC annually provides summary information broken down by LSAT and UGPA bands for all applicants to ABA law schools. This permits a fairly straightforward analysis of the disparate impact of the LSAT on women's and people of color's admission opportunities. If the principle of ceteris paribus—hold everything else constant—is applied, do men and women, or Whites and minorities, have equal admission chances when they apply with equivalent UGPAs? Table 3 reveals the sizeable and systematic preference the LSAT affords male candidates in law school admissions, as evidenced by the fact that men are admitted at a higher rate than women with the same grades. Over the last five years—the 1993–94 to 1997–98 admission cycles—women were disadvantaged relative to men by the LSAT in each of the sixteen UGPA bands. The gender gap in admission rates was remarkably consistent from year to year even though overall applications dropped by one fifth between 1993–94 and 1997–98, and even though the proportion of female applicants climbed modestly during this period.

* * *

Table 3: Male & Female Acceptance Rates to Law School (All Applicants to ABA–Accredited Schools) 1993–94 to 1997–98 Admission Cycles

GPA RANGE	MEN (#Applicants)	WOMEN (#Applicants)
3.75+	89.9% (15,130)	88.8% (16,171)
3.50–3.74	85.0% (26,538)	82.5% (28,066)
3.25–3.49	79.4% (34,046)	76.4% (33,802)
3.00–3.24	73.1% (38,118)	67.1% (33,373)
2.75–2.99	63.9% (33,901)	55.8% (26,683)
2.50–2.74	55.0% (26,995)	44.7% (18,670)
2.25–2.49	44.7% (17,875)	33.7% (10,713)
2.00–2.24	35.5% (8,850)	23.1% (4,729)
TOTALS	68.9% (201,453)	66.0% (172,207)

The disparities between male and female admission rates increase as UGPAs decrease, so the women who are least likely to be admitted to law school are also the ones whose admission rates lag furthest behind men with the same UGPA. Women often need UGPAs a quarter-point higher than men merely to equalize their admission chances. Just as important, women with 2.0 or higher UGPAs do not have overall admission rates that are equal to men. This means that in terms of admission consequences, even the appreciably better performance of women in college is insufficient to counterbalance the negative impact produced by modest LSAT score differences.

B. Race and Gender: A Double Burden for Women of Color Applying to Law School?

* * * What may be more surprising to some is that even when diversity is a factor in admission decisions, the negative impact of the LSAT is so severe that among applicants with approximately the same UGPAs, Whites consistently have the greatest chance of being accepted into ABA law schools.

* * * The gap in overall admission rates between Asian Americans and Whites, for example, is about the same magnitude as the gap between men and women in admission rates. However, all other minority subgroups—Native American, Hispanic, Mexican American and African American—face a substantially greater barrier to opportunity. For example, Black law school applicants with 2.5–2.74 UGPAs are slightly less likely to be offered admission than are Whites with more modest 2.0–2.24 UGPAs. The far greater difference in overall admission rates of people of color reflects the combined consequences of lower UGPAs and even lower LSAT scores.

* * *

IV. Consequences Versus Significance of Gender Bias

* * *

C. Consequences of a Two–Point Gap in Admission Decisions

Unfortunately, neither the lack of statistical significance of the LSAT gender gap between individual applicants, nor LSAC's Cautionary Policies, guarantee that small score differences will not be given excessive weight in law school admission decisions. Examples abound of schools overrelying on minute LSAT score differences to such a degree that two points can literally make or break one's chances to become a lawyer. For instance, at one Midwest law school, the difference between admits at the 75th percentile of the class and those at the 25th percentile—spanning 261 admission offers—was only two points. An admissions policy report prepared by Boalt Hall students found that a mere one point increase on the LSAT raised admission chances from 13 to 31 percent. At many highly competitive law schools the difference between the 75th and 25th percentile of admits is only three or four points.

* * *

V. Sources of Test Bias Against Women and Minorities

The persistence of the LSAT gender and racial/ethnic gaps—bearing in mind the issue of statistical significance between two test-takers—requires investigating the possible causes of such test performance differences. This is especially true for those looking for ways to reduce the score gaps (and thus LSAT-related gender and racial/ethnic bias) and those seeking policy justifications for adjusting admission criteria to counteract LSAT gender and racial/ethnic bias. Test bias occurs when two populations differ in ways picked up by the predictor (LSAT) but which are not intended to be part of the construct (aptitude for the study of law) which the criterion variable (first-year law school grades) is intended to tap into. Possible forms of LSAT test bias linked to gender and race/ethnicity include stereotype threat, speededness, differential guessing, subject matter selection and item bias.

* * *

A. *Stereotype Threat*

One plausible explanation of gender and racial/ethnic bias on the LSAT is what educational psychologists call stereotype threat. Studies in this field show that the mere self-awareness of a possibility that one's test performance could confirm a negative suspicion about the intellectual ability of one's group is itself sufficient to adversely effect performance on standardized tests. When the same test (derived from GRE questions) was either announced as being diagnostic of intellectual ability or portrayed as simply a non-diagnostic problem-solving task, African Americans (in this case the group facing stereotype threat) performed significantly lower in the diagnostic cohort when in the non-diagnostic cohort their performance was equal to Whites. In addition to those of African Americans, similar results have been found for standardized test performance of Latinos, women and students from low socioeconomic backgrounds.

* * *

B. *Speededness and Differential Guessing*

Two potential sources of gender-specific LSAT test bias discussed by Wightman are differences in speededness and differences in omitting rather than guessing on items. Wightman found there to be a "consistently higher rate of omitting items by women than men" on the LSAT. Similar results occur on the GRE general test. Furthermore, for Black, Puerto Rican and Hispanic test takers the LSAT has been found to produce "particularly dramatic" speededness differences compared to White students. An earlier LSAC study found that when time pressures were eased on the LSAT, African Americans demonstrated greater score gains than did Whites, suggesting a differential impact. It may also be the case that speededness is as much a symptom of other forms of test bias as it is a cause in its own right. Steele and Aronson, for example, found that invoking stereotype threat impaired the rate at which African Americans completed GRE questions. Recent research also suggests that the LSAT is more speeded for female test takers than for male test takers.

C. Gendered Effects of Subject Matter Selection

Content coverage on the LSAT, like other standardized tests, can be altered to either increase or diminish the performance differences between groups. One important but little discussed example involves changes over time in the gender gap on the SAT. Prior to the 1970s, women tended to score slightly higher than men on the SAT verbal section. Since that time, women have fallen behind men about one-tenth of a standard deviation, which is the same magnitude of difference as on the LSAT. Why did this occur? Both testing critics and Educational Testing Service (ETS) researchers who were there at the time of the changes credit alterations in the subject matter of the SAT verbal section with causing men to obtain higher verbal scores, though this has been disputed by Nancy Cole, the current president of ETS. Supporting the interpretation that the introduction of more science passages lowered women's scores are findings that scientific-oriented reading comprehension passages are differentially more difficult for women than comparable men. The latest review of the literature cites six recent studies to this effect, without any contrary findings.

* * * In fact, a close look at Wightman and Muller's study of 40,000 LSAT test takers reveals that the reading comprehension section alone accounted for 79 percent of the overall gender gap. This is significant because it is presumably in the area of reading comprehension that the selection of content is most directly related to performance.

LSAT subject matter selection patterns should be subjected to greater scrutiny because the performance differences favoring men on reading comprehension are at variance with evidence about verbal abilities more generally. Hyde and Linn's 1988 meta-analysis of 165 studies (and 441,000 subjects) of gender differences on verbal ability tests found essentially uniform results in favor of women by one-tenth of a standard deviation. This raises the question of whether much of the gender gap could be eliminated simply by, for example, replacing the usual science passage with a literature passage.

Recent events support the conclusion that the LSAT could easily be altered to lessen or eliminate the gender gaps. For example, minor changes on the PSAT in 1999 resulted in dramatically more gender equity in the allocation of National Merit Scholarships. As a result of complaints to OCR, the College Board agreed to add a multiple choice "writing" section. Subsequently, women garnered 45 percent of the National Merit Scholarships instead of the usual 40 percent. Bob Schaeffer, who spearheaded Fairtest's complaint to OCR, noted that since the gender gap on the PSAT was so quickly narrowed, "Why, for example, have similar changes not been made on the SAT, the GRE and related exams which show comparable bias?"

* * *

D. Biased Questions

Another source of possible gender and racial/ethnic bias on the LSAT is the presence of biased questions. Since other authors have vivisected the race/gender/class implications of myriad LSAT questions, narrative analysis of item bias will be limited. An addendum is included with some examples of LSAT questions that are potentially biased against women and minorities. Despite claims by LSAC officials that biased and offensive questions were eliminated by the expansion of sensitivity review panels in the early 1980's possibly offensive and/or distracting LSAT questions persist long after the sensitivity review policies were adopted. An interesting example of bias is an LSAT question addressing women's and minorities' opportunities in higher education. The passage, question and answer choices are as follows:

The universities should not yield to the illiberal directives of the Office of Civil Rights [sic] that mandate affirmative action in hiring faculties. The effect of the directives to hire minorities and women under threat of losing crucial financial support is to compel universities to hire unqualified minorities and women and to discriminate against qualified nonminorities and men. This is just as much a manifestation of racism, even if originally unintended, as the racism the original presidential directive was designed to correct. The consequences of imposing any criterion other than that of qualified talent on our educational establishments are sure to be disastrous in the quest for new knowledge and truth, as well as subversive of our democratic values.

Which of the following, if true, would considerably weaken the argument above?

I. The directive requires universities to hire minorities and women when no other applicant is better qualified.

II. The directive requires universities to hire minorities and women only up to the point that these groups are represented on faculties in proportion to their representation in the population at large.

III. Most university employees are strongly in favor of the directive.

(A) I only

(B) II only

(C) III only

(D) I and II only

(E) II and III only

The answer credited as being correct is choice A (option I only). A major problem with this question deals with option II. Unfortunately, if a reader assumes that women and minorities possess equal "qualified talent" she may reasonably conclude that affirmative action hiring practices which are capped by the proportion of women and minorities in the population at large weakens the argument that affirmative action forces "universities to hire unqualified minorities and women." A reader who assumes that hiring in proportion to population statistics ushers in hordes of unqualified women and minorities is rewarded for having "legal aptitude." Secondly, readers must first work through the distraction and disorientation of this passage, which is more likely to adversely affect outsider students precisely because they are outsiders.

E. Critique of Item Bias Detection Methods: The Indifference of DIF

For decades now, each question that appears on the LSAT goes through a rigorous, multi-staged statistical and sensitivity review process. Yet, the continued presence of insensitive and distracting questions despite the sincere and comprehensive efforts of LSAC researchers suggests that current bias detection methods are flawed. Typically, LSAC researchers assume that, if an individual question creates racial or gender disparities similar to disparities in overall test scores, then that item must not be biased. In other words, bias is treated as a discrete, accidental deviation from the overall absence of bias on the test.

The psychometric procedure for measuring item bias is called "differential item functioning" (DIF), which is an attempt to match people of approximately equal knowledge and skill to see whether different groups perform in substantially different ways on a test question. After conducting DIF analysis on the LSAT, Wightman and Muller concluded: "There is no evidence that any one item type particularly disadvantages minority test takers nor are there individual items that exhibit statistical evidence of bias toward any subgroup."

The assumptions underlying the use of DIF as a remedy for item bias, and thus Wightman and Muller's conclusion, are questionable. Because LSAC DIF analysis does not provide for a standard of unbiasedness that is external to the LSAT, the claim that DIF establishes the absence of item bias against women and minorities has been criticized as seriously misleading, even tautological. If gender or racially biased questions have spillover consequences affecting performance on subsequent questions, or if stereotype threat creates a constant bias permeating the entire test (or both), the LSAC's bias detection methods would reveal no bias precisely when bias was most severe and systematic. Even Cole, the current ETS president, admits that there "is no statistic that can prove whether or not a test question is biased" and that DIF cannot "guarantee that there is no gender bias in the questions."

NOTES ON GENDER BIAS AND THE LSAT

1. Were you surprised at how important the LSAT was to law school admissions and how significantly it alters the admissions prospects of women and men with the same undergraduate grade point average? Do you think law schools should rely wholly on undergraduate grades in making admissions decisions? What are the advantages and disadvantages of such an approach?

2. Kidder identifies three possible explanations for the gender disparity in LSAT scores, 1. stereotype threat, 2. speededness and differential guessing,

and 3. gendered effects of subject matter selection. Based on your own experience, which factor do you think has the most significant gendered impact? Why? What changes to the test do you think would help minimize the sex disparity? What would be the potential disadvantages of changing the test in those ways?

3. As the article notes, the Educational Testing Service (ETS) in 1997 added a "writing" section to the three-hour, multiple-choice Preliminary SAT/National Merit Scholarship Qualifying Test (PSAT/NMSQT), the scores of which are an important factor in awarding about $28 million in annual National Merit Scholarships. Even though females earn higher grades than their male counterparts in both high school and college when matched for identical courses, they won fewer than 40 percent of the prestigious National Merit Scholarships before this change. As of 1999, women, who represent 56 percent of students taking the PSAT/NMSQT, were awarded 45 percent of the scholarships. FairTest made this statement:

> The narrowing of the National Merit gender gap raises several important questions. Why, for example, have similar changes not been made on the SAT, the GRE and related exams which show comparable bias? Even more fundamentally, why are instruments on which results can be so quickly "adjusted" ever used as the sole or primary factor to determine college admissions or award scholarships?

FairTest: National Center for Fair & Open Testing, State-by-State Study Shows Hundreds More Females Will Win Scholarships, Apr. 21, 1999, available at http://www.fairtest.org/pr/psat4.21.htm. See also Kristen Poe, Note: Blinded by Results: Is Looking to GPA in Addition to Standardized Test Scores Truly a Less Discriminatory Solution to Merit Scholarship Selection?, 19 Women's Rts. L. Rptr. 181 (1998). How would you answer the question posed above by FairTest? Do you think a writing portion would make the LSAT more fair? Do you think it might improve the LSAT's predictive accuracy for law school and career success?

4. Title IX regulations forbid recipients of federal funds from administering or operating any test for admission "which has a disproportionately adverse effect on persons on the basis of sex unless the use of such test or criterion is shown to predict validly success in the education program or activity in question and alternative tests or criteria which do not have such a disproportionately adverse effect are shown to be unavailable." 45 C.F.R. § 86.21(b)(2) (1992). The Office for Civil Rights of the Department of Education issued a draft Resource Guide in May of 1999 (revised in December of 1999) that summarized current law and professional guidelines concerning standardized test score misuse. In order to use such tests properly, "if an exam has a significant disparate impact on minorities and women, then it is the obligation of the institution requiring it to show that the use of test scores is an 'educational necessity,' that the exam is technically sound (valid and reliable), and that there is no practical alternative mechanism of equivalent or better quality that achieves the same educational goal with less disparate impact." FairTest Examiner: Federal Standards for Standardized Tests, available at http://fairtest.org/examarts/summer99/FederalStandards.htm. Do you

think colleges can justify continued use of the SAT and LSAT under this standard?

D. AFFIRMATIVE ACTION

TEXT NOTE: AFFIRMATIVE ACTION

One approach to remedying past discrimination, both sex and race-based, is through affirmative action. While race-based affirmative action programs have been the focal point of political debate and legal challenge in recent years, sex-based programs have become similarly vulnerable.

Racial and gender preferences and emphases in recruitment, retention, scholarships, admission, hiring, and awarding of contracts are known as different things in different contexts, e.g., affirmative action in higher education, affirmative action in employment, and so-called minority set-asides in government contracts. Many of these programs have resulted in greater representation of women and minorities in jobs, schools, and businesses in which they were previously excluded, tokenized, or minimally represented. However, in the late 1980's several attacks were launched against affirmative action, arguing that these programs discriminated against whites and men ("reverse discrimination") or that the programs actually harmed those they were intended to benefit (primarily through stigmatization). The strength of the anti-affirmative action movement became clear in 1996 when the people of California, by referendum, adopted the California Civil Rights Initiative (Proposition 209) as an amendment to their constitution. Proposition 209 sweeps wide and far, providing that:

> the state shall not discriminate against, or grant preferential treatment to, any individual or group on the basis of race, sex, color, ethnicity, or national origin in the operation of public employment, public education, or public contracting.

Fearing the impact of this prohibition on affirmative action upon minority admissions to higher education, a lawsuit was brought to enjoin its implementation. The Ninth Circuit Court of Appeals, however, held that Proposition 209 passed muster under the Fourteenth Amendment.[40] The impact of the law was felt immediately. For example, a year after its passage there was only one African American student at Boalt Hall, Berkeley's law school.[41] Following the anti-affirmative action success in California, several bills were introduced into Congress to "nationalize" Proposition 209, and numerous states are considering or have enacted similar legislation.

Another prong of the anti-affirmative action attack has been individual so-called reverse discrimination suits against numerous state colleges and universities, arguing that racial and/or gender preferences treat non-minorities unfairly, resulting in denial of their admission. In 1978 in Regents of

---

40. Coalition for Economic Equity v. Wilson, 110 F.3d 1431 (9th Cir.), cert. denied, 522 U.S. 963 (1997).

41. In the fall of 1996, 20 African Americans matriculated at Boalt Hall; in fall of 1997, only one did. In the fall of 1996, there were 19 African Americans who entered UCLA Law School; in the fall of 1997 only two did. In Texas, the year after the *Hopwood* decision, see note 45 below, African American enrollment at the University of Texas dropped from 29 to four, Hispanic enrollment dropped from 46 to 31. R.A. Lenhardt, Understanding the Mark: Race, Stigma, and Equality in Context, 79 N.Y.U. L. Rev. 803, 905 n. 489 (2004).

California v. Bakke, the Supreme Court held that race was a valid consideration in the admissions process for graduate school.[42] Throughout the 1990's, however, circuit courts issued conflicting rulings on the continued constitutionality of such plans.[43]

In 2003 the Supreme Court reaffirmed the constitutionality of properly tailored affirmative action plans in higher education, in two reverse discrimination lawsuits challenging affirmative action policies at the University of Michigan Law School and the University of Michigan College of Literature, Science and the Arts. *Gratz v. Bollinger* involved a challenge to the College's use of racial preferences in undergraduate admissions by two white students who were both denied admission. The Supreme Court held that the college's affirmative action plan—which involved adding points to application files of students who were members of racial or ethnic minority groups—was not narrowly tailored to meet the college's interest in diversity and hence violated the Equal Protection Clause of the 14th Amendment. 539 U.S. 244 (2003). *Grutter v. Bollinger* involved a challenge to Michigan Law School's use of race as a factor in admissions by a white female student who was denied admission. In *Grutter*, the Supreme Court upheld the law school's affirmative action plan—which considered an applicant's race as one factor among many in making admissions decisions but did not allocate specific points to applications because of race or ethnicity—on the grounds that diversity is a compelling state interest in the context of higher education and that the affirmative action plan in this case was narrowly tailored to further that interest. 539 U.S. 306 (2003). The Supreme Court's holding in *Grutter* made clear that educational affirmative action plans would be constitutional as long as properly structured.

Underlying the question of affirmative action is the fundamental issue of "merit." Generally, admission or employment is determined by "neutral" evaluative methods, e.g., standardized tests, and by subjective assessments, e.g., interviews. There is an assumption that this system of evaluation is fair and functional, that all applicants have an equal opportunity to compete, and that the resulting meritocracy identifies the people most qualified for the position. Departures from these traditional and conventional methods to determine who is most qualified are said to be unfair to those who are ranked as most qualified under this system. The dominance of "objective" criteria is a relatively recent phenomenon, dating from the 1950's.[44]

Affirmative action challenges both the norms inherent in this system of meritocracy as well as the implicit understanding that all people have an

42. Regents of Univ. of Cal. v. Bakke, 438 U.S. 265 (1978).

43. See, e.g., Hopwood v. Texas, 78 F.3d 932 (5th Cir.), cert. denied, 518 U.S. 1033 (1996) (holding that the University of Texas School of Law may not use race as a factor in deciding which applicants to admit either 1. in order to achieve a diverse student body, 2. to combat the perceived effects of a hostile environment at the law school, 3. to alleviate the law school's poor reputation in the minority community, or 4. to eliminate any present effects of past discrimination by actors other than the law school); Wooden v. Board of Regents of the Univ. of Ga., 32 F. Supp.2d 1370 (S.D. Ga.1999) (holding unconstitutional a dual track admission system in which the objective academic criteria to be admitted was lower for the black applicants). But see Smith v. University of Washington Law School, 233 F.3d 1188 (9th Cir.2000) (upholding an admissions policy considering race as a factor).

44. James Crouse & Dale Trusheim, The Case Against the SAT 31–37 (1988).

equal opportunity to achieve under these norms. The following excerpt argues that the "affirmative action" debate provides an opportunity to re-examine our commitment to racial and gender fairness and questions the legitimacy of the predictive measurements that have traditionally been a focal point of the affirmative action debate.

SUSAN STURM AND LANI GUINIER, THE FUTURE OF AFFIRMATIVE ACTION: RECLAIMING THE INNOVATIVE IDEAL

84 Calif. L. Rev. 953–58, 1010 (1996)

We are witnessing a broad-based assault on affirmative action—in the courts, the legislatures, and the media. Opponents have defined affirmative action as a program of racial preferences that threatens fundamental American values of fairness, equality, and democratic opportunity. Opponents successfully depict racial preferences as extraordinary, special, and deviant—a departure from prevailing modes of selection. They also proceeded on the assumption that, except for racial or gender preferences, the process of selection for employment or educational opportunity is fair, meritocratic, and functional. Thus, they have positioned affirmative action as unnecessary, unfair, and even un-American.

* * *

It is time, we argue, for those of us committed to racial and gender equity to advance a more fundamental critique of existing selection and admission conventions. It is time to discuss how conventional assessment and predictive criteria do not function fairly, democratically, or even meritocratically for many Americans who are not members of racial or gender minorities. To reclaim the moral high ground, we must broaden and expand the terms of engagement. By revealing faulty assumptions about the concept of affirmative action and the system of selection in which it operates, we can move from an incrementalist strategy of inclusion for a few to a transformative vision of reform for the many.

To reopen the conversation on race, gender, and democratic opportunity, it is necessary to change the paradigm. Certainly, we must challenge out loud the basic assumption that affirmative action is a departure from an otherwise sound meritocracy. At the same time, we must challenge existing add-on practices of affirmative action as too conservative a remedy. The experience of women and people of color offers insights beyond showing how and why those particular people have been excluded. We need to show that the current one-size-fits-all ranking system of predicting "merit" is no longer justified or productive for anyone.

The present system of selection is unfair for people who are neither women nor people of color. It denies opportunity for advancement to many poor and working-class Americans of all colors and genders who could otherwise obtain educational competence. It is underinclusive of those who can actually do the job. It is deeply problematic as a predictor of actual job performance. Across-the-board, it does violence to fundamental principles of equity and "functional merit" in its distribution of opportunities for admission to higher education, entry-level hiring, and job promotion.

Typical among the existing criteria and selection methods are paper-and-pencil tests, such as the Scholastic Assessment Test (SAT), the Law School Admissions Test (LSAT), and civil service exams. These tests, which are used to predict future performance based on existing capacity or ability, do not correlate with future performance for most applicants, at least not as a method of ranking those "most qualified." These tests and informal criteria making up our "meritocracy" tell us more about past opportunity than about future accomplishments on the job or in the classroom.

In challenging the way these tests are used, we are not proposing a critique of merit per se. Nor are we advancing an entirely original argument. Simply stated, we seek to highlight the way that certain paper-and-pencil tests have been used as "wealth preferences" or poll taxes to determine who gets to participate as full citizens in our democracy. As Michael Lind argues in a slightly different context, these tests are used, in conjunction with subjective assessments and informal networks, to develop a class-linked opportunity structure that credentializes "a social oligarchy."[19]

* * *

Patterns of exclusion experienced primarily by women and people of color are, nevertheless, still important. They serve as signals. Patterns of race-and gender-based exclusion signal the possibility that bias or unfair advantage has operated in the ostensibly neutral selection process. They also signal the inadequacy of traditional methods of selection for everyone, and the need to rethink the process used to allocate opportunities to participate in work and school. In other words, patterns of exclusion provide a window on the methods for "inclusion." They are an important source of continuous critique of monolithic and monochromatic ranking and selection processes.

[The authors then provide an extensive analysis of what they call the "testocracy," in which applicants are scored, ranked, and their future performance predicted based on static, closed-book, timed paper-and-pencil assessments of past ability. First, they argue that the tests are extremely limited and do not measure qualities necessary to succeed, such as motivation, creativity, perseverance and teamwork skills. Second, they note that studies have consistently shown that the tests are only weakly correlated to what they are intended to measure. Finally, they discuss the racial, gender and class discriminatory impact of these tests.]

* * *

19. Michael Lind, Prescriptions for a New National Democracy, 110 POL. SCI. Q. 563, 582 (1995–96).

We are proposing a shift in the model of selection from prediction to performance. This model builds on the insight that the opportunity to participate creates the capacity to perform, and that actual performance offers the best evidence of capacity to perform. There simply is no substitute for experience, both in equipping people to perform and in producing informed judgments about the functional capacity of candidates. This approach shifts the emphasis away from the design of an instrument that is separate from the performance of the job, but that can be correlated with success in that job. Instead, the emphasis is on thinking creatively about how evaluation can proceed through the observation of applicants engaged in the work of those positions. The model also emphasizes the importance of creating opportunities to succeed and of structuring fair, inclusive, and participatory mechanisms to define and assess successful performance. This approach thus embeds performance and inclusion in the design of the selection process.

NOTES ON AFFIRMATIVE ACTION

1. In a highly publicized book published in 1998, William G. Bowen (former President of Princeton University) and Derek Bok (former President of Harvard University) strongly supported affirmative action after analyzing the College and Beyond Database, containing the academic, employment, and personal histories of more than 45,000 students of all races who entered certain academically selective universities in the falls of 1951, 1976, and 1989. Bowen & Bok, The Shape of the River: Long–Term Consequences of Considering Race in College and University Admissions (1998). They found that utilizing race as a criterion for admission resulted in increased educational opportunities for all students as well as increasing the number of graduates involved in volunteer activities, especially in leadership positions. Emphasizing the civic responsibilities of educational institutions, the authors argue that "[w]hat admissions officers must decide is which set of applicants, *considered individually and collectively*, will take fullest advantage of what the college has to offer, contribute most to the educational process in college, and be most successful in using what they have learned for the benefit of the larger society." Id. at 277. In agreeing that admissions must be "fair," Bowen and Bok define "fairness" as follows: "each individual is to be judged according to a consistent set of criteria that reflect the objectives of the college or university. Fairness should not be misinterpreted to mean that a particular criterion has to apply—that, for example, grades and test scores must always be considered more important than other qualities and characteristics so that no student with a B average can be accepted as long as some students with As are being turned down." Id. at 277–78. Is their position consistent with Sturm and Guinier? In what ways? Although both support affirmative action, is one argument more persuasive to you than the other? Why?

2. Sturm and Guinier contend that standardized tests are not very good at predicting future performance in the classroom or on the job. Richard H. Sander disagrees and argues that test scores are good predictors of future grades and professional success. Sander, A Systemic Analysis of Affirmative Action in American Law Schools, 57 Stan. L. Rev. 367 (2004). Sander's article

has generated considerable debate. See, e.g., David B. Wilkins, A Systematic Response to Systematic Disadvantage: A Response to Sander, 57 Stan. L. Rev. 1915 (2005) (challenging Sander's contention that blacks are hurt more than they are helped by affirmative action by emphasizing the significant prestige-related benefits gained by those who attend the most elite law schools); Ian Ayres & Richard Brooks, Does Affirmative Action Reduce the Number of Black Lawyers?, 57 Stan. L. Rev. 1807 (2005) (challenging Sander's contention that black beneficiaries of affirmative action learn less than they would have had they attended less selective law schools without affirmative action); Michele Landis Dauber, The Big Muddy, 57 Stan. L. Rev. 1899 (2005) (arguing that Sander has no evidence to support his finding that black students do not benefit from affirmative action and acceptance into better law schools due to methodological errors in his modeling); David L. Chambers et. al., The Real Impact of Eliminating Affirmative Action in American Law Schools: An Empirical Critique of Richard Sander's Study, 57 Stan. L. Rev. 1855 (2005) (finding that without affirmative action, both the enrollment of black law students, particularly at the 50 or 80 most selective schools, and the production of black lawyers would significantly decline). To what degree does your view of affirmative action programs that admit women and minority applicants with lower standardized test scores than white men depend on the predictive accuracy of these tests in terms of long term career success? What measures of career success would you use? What factors other than future career success affect your view of affirmative action?

3. Are there "affirmative action" plans in place for whites or males? What about legacies, in which children of alumni are granted admission? For example, for several decades 20 percent of Harvard students have been admitted as legacies even though they may not be as well qualified as regular applicants under the traditional academic criteria. Laura M. Padilla, Intersectionality and Positionality: Situating Women of Color in the Affirmative Action Dialogue, 66 Fordham L. Rev. 843, 867 (1997). What about athletic scholarships and admissions? An analysis of data of 90,000 students from 30 selective colleges and universities in the 1950s, 1970s, and 1990s found that athletes receive significantly more admissions advantage than do racial minorities. James L. Shulman et al., The Game of Life: College Sports and Educational Values 40–41 (2001); See also William G. Bowen et. al., Reclaiming the Game: College Sports & Educational Values (2003). Why aren't these preferences recognized as a type of affirmative action?

4. After concluding that affirmative action preferences exacerbate intergroup tensions and perpetuate certain subtle forms of intergroup bias, Linda Hamilton Krieger nonetheless argues that they are essential in addressing societal discrimination:

> [T]endencies towards intergroup discrimination are much more subtle, stable, and pernicious than these assumptions ["that discrimination is conscious, intentional, and reasonably easy to identify" and "that absent state-sanctioned or overt discrimination by private actors* * *, intergroup relations in the United States will improve or at least remain relatively tranquil"] or their reflection in anti-affirmative action rhetoric admit. Social cognition teaches that much intergroup discrimination is both unintentional and unconscious. It occurs spontaneously as an un-

wanted artifact of normal cognitive functions associated with the processing of information about other people and can be corrected, if at all, only through further deliberate mental effort. Social identity theory and related research in experimental social psychology indicates that the tendencies to assist or excuse those with whom we feel closely identified and to subordinate the socially distant are far less tractable than we might wish.

These more subtle, incremental forms of discrimination are difficult to recognize, and neither our cultural understanding nor our jurisprudential models of discrimination illuminate or provide ways to reckon with them. Without affirmative action, it remains to be seen how powerfully they will operate to exclude minorities and women from large segments of the academy, public contracting, or labor markets.

Krieger, Civil Rights Perestroika: Intergroup Relations After Affirmative Action, 86 Calif. L. Rev. 1251, 1332–33 (1998). Are you persuaded by this additional justification for affirmative action? Are there distinctions to be made between gender and racial intergroup discrimination which would justify variations in affirmative action? Recall the discussions in Chapter Two about comparing race and gender discrimination, appropriate standards, and remedies.

TEXT NOTE: AFFIRMATIVE ACTION IN THE CLASSROOM

On a substantive level, during the early 1970s women in higher education began to create and offer courses with an interdisciplinary emphasis that focused on women and were critical of the subordination of women and minorities. The Women's Studies Movement was a direct attack on the narrowness and exclusivity of the traditional male-dominated curriculum. Additionally, this new concentration was premised on effecting social change, sometimes even including an activist component. In a sense, women's studies is a type of classroom affirmative action.[45]

Florence Howe describes the basic curriculum in a mature women's studies program:

1. an understanding of patriarchy in historical perspective, philosophically and sociologically, its relationship to the religions of the world, and to ideas of knowledge and power—hence, an understanding of what it means to be born "permanently" into a subordinate or dominant status; a knowledge of feminist theory

2. an understanding of the complex, confusing, and still chaotic area of biological psychological sex differences; the importance of null findings

3. an understanding of socialization and sex roles, as well as of sex-role stereotyping; the relationships among gender, race, and class—all from a cross-cultural perspective

45. See generally Florence Howe, Myths of Coeducation: Selected Essays 1964–1983 (1984). Howe notes the novelty of this challenge to the "men's curriculum," and explains it as follows: "It is difficult to criticize adversely an institution you want access to. It is difficult also to criticize an institution you have access to but want equality in." Id. at 218.

4. an understanding of women in history, not only in the United States, but throughout the world, recognizing that such study includes legal as well as medical history—the history of birth control, for example, which is essential to the study of women, even to the study of fiction about women

5. an understanding of women as represented in the arts they have produced, some of which have been buried or ignored as arts—quilt-making, for example, or the pottery of North American Indian women; and as represented in the significant literature by women of all races and nationalities that never was included in the literary curriculum; as well as an awareness that the images of women portrayed by the male-created arts have helped to control the dominant conceptions of women—hence, the importance of studying images of women on TV, in film and the theatre, and in advertising

6. an understanding of the ways in which post-Freudian psychology has attempted to control women's destiny; an awareness that other male-centered psychological constructs like those of Erikson and Kohlberg are potentially damaging to women; an understanding of new women-centered theories of female development

7. an understanding of female sexuality, including perspectives on both heterosexuality and lesbianism; special issues involved in birth control and reproduction

8. an understanding of the history and function of education as support and codifier of sex segregation and of limited opportunities for women; some perspectives on education as an agent for change in the past and present

9. an understanding of the history and function of the family in the United States and cross-culturally; of the current variety of family structures, and of the conflict between beliefs and research findings with reference especially to issues surrounding children

10. an understanding of women in the workforce through history, in the present, and cross culturally; the economy in relation to women; the relationship between money and power in personal interactions, in the family, and in society

11. an understanding of the relationship between laws affecting women and social change; the history of women and social movements.[46]

What further distinguishes this approach from the male curriculum is that class, race, and sexual orientation issues are addressed as well.

Of course, even after the need for women's studies is established, there are serious issues about implementation strategy. Should the interdisciplinary courses and materials remain segregated under "Women's Studies," or should there be a curriculum mainstreaming them in an integrationist approach? There are some very serious concerns with each approach. For instance, only the converted may take segregated courses unless they are mandatory. There are problems, as well, with the integrationist approach: "What happens to a body of feminist knowledge that is distributed by non-feminists because they

46. Howe at 275–76.

have to incorporate it into their course? And what happens to the student who gets her or his feminist education from such a teacher?"[47] These concerns are equally applicable to teaching feminist theory in law schools.

Similar to gender preference programs, women's studies has been criticized as devaluing or harming men. These innovations have frequently met with resistance, which are explained by Carolyn Heilbrun, referring to Christine Froula's work, in terms of power politics:

> Why are men so afraid? "I think the answer to this question," Christine Froula, a young feminist critic writes, "has to do with the fact that woman's voice threatens to discredit that masculinist culture upon which [men have] modeled their identity." Many works of the canon have constructed their "speech on the bedrock of woman's silence." "Men very commonly express the fear that feminist criticism will invert that hierarchy in which they have invested so much—will, in other words, silence *them* as patriarchal discourse has silenced women. * * * But a woman speaking does not reverse the conditions of her own silencing. She does not demand that men be silent: she only asks that men cease speaking in such a way as to silence her."
>
> All the jokes in literature about women-dominated marriages, all the horrible wives in Dickens, Trollope, and others speak to the male fear of hierarchical reversal. If men are not boss, women will be. But this is what men fear, not what women want. Women ask men only to "grant women's voices an equal position with male discourse, rescuing it from the now inevitable reactive position of either assimilation or opposition."[48]

This male fear has resulted in vitriolic attacks on attempts to reform the male curriculum, traditionally known as the "canon," in which the works of particular authors, almost exclusively white and male, establish the standards of excellence.

Another aspect of affirmative action in the classroom is what has become known as the Political Correctness (PC) Wars, a reaction to the demands of women and minorities that the canon be opened to non-white, non-male authors, issues and concerns; that racist and sexist speech which inhibits learning and poisons the learning environment not be tolerated; and that what constitutes excellence not be determined by an elite few. During the 1990's many conservative academics and politicians decried "political correctness," which, according to them, was an ideological movement stifling free discussion, destroying academic standards, and threatening the First Amendment.[49] Katherine T. Bartlett gave a spirited response to these critics:

> In any social organization, the views of the dominant tend to be taken for granted as objective and neutral. Challenges to these views—like those we

47. Gloria Bowles & Renate Duelli Klein, Introduction: Theories of Women's Studies and the Autonomy/Integration Debate, in Theories of Women's Studies 1, 9 (Bowles & Klein, eds. 1983).

48. Heilbrun, The Politics of Mind: Women, Tradition, and the University, in Gender in the Classroom: Power and Pedagogy 28, 30–31 (Susan L. Gabriel & Isaiah Smithson, eds. 1990).

49. See, e.g., William J. Bennett, The De-Valuing of America: The Fight for Our Culture and Our Children (1995); Jeffrey Winters, ed., PC Wars: Politics and Theory in the Academy (1994); Dinesh D'Souza, Illiberal Education: Political Correctness and the College Experience (1992).

are now hearing in the universities—appear to seek special favors for the "less qualified," or some compromising of academic standards.

* * *

Some PC critics dismiss as interest-group politics requests that authors such as Toni Morrison or Mary Wollestonecraft be included in the curriculum; others malign courses in feminist theory or black studies as a "Balkanization" of the curriculum.

In contrast, assignments of writings by Nathaniel Hawthorne or T.S. Eliot draw no notice and require no defense; neither does the "basic" political philosophy course that begins with Aristotle and ends with John Rawls. The difference is *not* that the standard "Western civilization" courses are apolitical. In fact, it is precisely the alignment of these courses with particular points of view—the dominant ones in our society—that makes them appear neutral. This is not to argue that such courses should be abolished, but nobody should pretend that only feminist and minority-studies courses have political content.[50]

In fact, according to Bartlett, it is the PC critics who are utilizing personal denunciation and caricature instead of honest discussion in an attempt to divert the debate. They are "using a double standard to judge those who do not respect their authority. These critics invoke important principles of academic freedom to shield themselves from criticism of classroom remarks that some students find racist or sexist."[51]

E. ATHLETIC PROGRAMS

In no area has unequal treatment been more open, and defended, than sports. The early legal challenges to sex inequality in school athletics were based primarily on state and federal constitutional protections. These cases most frequently concerned the legality of rules that classified persons as eligible to participate in sports on the basis of their sex. In general, courts had little difficulty concluding that public school regulations prohibiting girls from participating in particular sports denied girls Equal Protection.[52] Nonetheless, many states have lawful policies prohibiting females from participating with males in contact sports.[53] In addition, when a school provides teams in particular sports for both sexes,

50. Bartlett, Some Factual Correctness About Political Correctness, Wall St.J., June 6, 1991, § A, at 19.

51. Id.

52. See Hoover v. Meiklejohn, 430 F.Supp. 164 (D.Colo.1977) (soccer); Brenden v. Independent Sch. Dist., 477 F.2d 1292 (8th Cir.1973) (tennis, cross country skiing, and cross country running); Carnes v. Tennessee Secondary Sch. Athletic Ass'n, 415 F.Supp. 569 (E.D.Tenn.1976) (baseball); Reed v. Nebraska Sch. Activities Ass'n, 341 F.Supp. 258 (D.Neb.1972) (golf); Lantz v. Ambach, 620 F.Supp. 663 (S.D.N.Y.1985) (football); Clinton v. Nagy, 411 F.Supp. 1396 (N.D.Ohio 1974) (football); but see Lafler v. Athletic Bd. of Control, 536 F.Supp. 104 (W.D.Mich.1982) (finding that even though no women's division existed, female plaintiff was constitutionally denied the right to box in the flyweight division of the Golden Gloves boxing competition).

53. Title IX regulations also seem to permit this, defining contact sports broadly to include "boxing, wrestling, rugby, ice hockey, football, basketball and other sports the purpose or major activity of which involves bodily contact." 34 C.F.R. § 106.41(b) (1995).

most courts have approved the sex-segregated teams.[54] On the other hand, decisions have been inconsistent when rules prohibiting boys from participating on girls' teams are at issue. All of these reported cases involve situations in which there is no separate boys' team. Courts upholding such regulations usually rely on arguments that the exclusionary rules were substantially related to the important governmental interest in redressing overall equality of athletic opportunity and to redress past discrimination against women.[55]

More recently, plaintiffs have asserted broader claims of discrimination in athletic programs, especially in the areas of funding and scholarships. For example, in 1987 female students at Washington State University were successful in their suit, based on Washington's Equal Rights Amendment (ERA), seeking more equal funding. The trial court ordered WSU to increase incrementally the funds and scholarships allocated to the intercollegiate athletic program until it matched the percentage of women undergraduates at the university; however, the football program was to be excluded from the calculations. On appeal, the Washington Supreme Court held that the trial court had abused its discretion, stating that the state ERA "contains no exception for football."[56]

With the enactment of Title IX in 1972, it was widely predicted that equality in athletics finally was within reach.[57] Indeed, the increase in girls' and women's participation in competitive athletics has been dramatic since the passage of the Act. Nonetheless, participation rates for girls at the high school level continues to lag behind that of boys and both

54. See O'Connor v. Board of Educ. of Sch. Dist. No. 23, 645 F.2d 578 (7th Cir.1981), cert. denied, 454 U.S. 1084 (1981); but see Yellow Springs Exempted Village Sch. Dist. Bd. of Educ. v. Ohio High Sch. Athletic Ass'n, 443 F.Supp. 753 (S.D.Ohio 1978). See also Glenn M. Wong and Richard J. Ensor, Sex Discrimination in Athletics: A Review of Two Decades of Accomplishments and Defeats, 21 Gonzaga L. Rev. 345 (1985–86). Regulations under Title IX also permit separate teams for males and females "where selection for such teams is based upon competitive skill." 34 C.F.R. § 106.41(b) (1995).

55. See Clark v. Arizona Interscholastic Ass'n, 695 F.2d 1126 (9th Cir.1982), cert. denied, 464 U.S. 818 (1983) (excluding boys from girls' volleyball teams is a permissible means to insure equal opportunity for girls and to redress past discrimination); but see Gomes v. Rhode Island Interscholastic League, 469 F.Supp. 659 (D.R.I.), vacated as moot, 604 F.2d 733 (1st Cir.1979) (holding that Fourteenth Amendment and Title IX require school to allow plaintiff to compete on girls volleyball team); Attorney General v. Massachusetts Interscholastic Athletic Ass'n, 393 N.E.2d 284 (Mass. 1979) (holding that exclusion of boys from girls team violates state Equal Rights Amendment).

56. Blair v. Washington State Univ., 740 P.2d 1379, 1383 (Wash. 1987).

57. Women have made extraordinary improvements in performance. For example, in "swimming and long-distance running, women have come to within ten percent of the best male times. Joan Benoit won the women's marathon in the 1984 Olympics in 2 hours, 24 minutes, 52 seconds, a time that would have captured the gold medal in the men's marathon in 1948, and would have won a silver medal in the men's marathon in 1952. On the other hand, gold medal-winner Don Schollander's world record-setting time in the 400–meter freestyle in the 1964 Olympics would have placed him fifth in the women's event in the 1980 Moscow Games." Karen L. Tokarz, Separate But Unequal Educational Sports Programs: The Need for a New Theory of Equality, 1 Berkeley Women's L.J. 201, 221 (1985). In 1926, the first woman to swim the English Channel, nineteen-year-old Gertrude Ederle, shattered the previous record by almost two hours. Pia Sarkar, She Was the Wave of the Future, The Record, Jan. 25, 2000, News § , at 1. The current world record of 7 hours and 40 minutes was set by female Penny Lee Dean in 1978. http://home.istar.ca.

participation and funding for women's college level sports falls short of that for men's sports.

In 1971, for example, 294,015 girls as compared to 3,666,917 boys participated in high school athletics while in 2003, 2.9 million girls as compared to 4 million boys participated.[58] College statistics are similar. In 1997 the NCAA released a sequel report to its 1992 "Gender Equity Study." In reviewing the progress made at Division I schools, the NCAA found that although 53 percent of the undergraduates were women, they constituted only 37 percent of student-athletes, with women's teams receiving only 23 percent of expenditures. Coaches of men's teams received 60 percent of the compensation for Division I schools; there were no female coaches in the major men's teams of football, basketball and baseball.[59] By 2006, women made up 55.3 percent of the Division I athletes but received only 22 percent of expenditures.[60]

Under Title IX, there are three main sources of gender equity: the law itself, implementing regulations, and the Title IX Athletics Investigator's Manual used by the Department of Education's Office for Civil Rights (OCR), the federal agency with responsibility for interpreting and enforcing Title IX. The OCR has identified three compliance areas: (1) athletic financial assistance; (2) equivalence in other athletic benefits and opportunities; and (3) effective accommodation of athletic interests and abilities. The second area—equivalence—has ten components: effective accommodation of interest and ability; provision and maintenance of equipment and supplies; scheduling of games and practice times; travel and per diem allowances; opportunity to receive coaching and academic tutoring; assignment and compensation of coaches and tutors; provisions of locker rooms, practice and competitive facilities; provision of medical and training facilities and services; provision of housing and dining facilities and services; and publicity. The Final Policy Interpretation adds two other factors: recruitment and provision of support services.

In 1979, the OCR issued a Policy Interpretation intended to provide colleges with further guidance on how to effectively accommodate the athletic interests and abilities of female and male students to the extent necessary to provide equal opportunity to both sexes and comply with the Act. The Policy Interpretation provided that compliance would be assessed in one of the following ways:

1. Whether intercollegiate level participation opportunities for male and female students are provided in numbers substantially proportionate to their respective enrollments; or

---

58. Nat'l Fed'n of State High School Ass'ns, 2003–04 High School Athletics Participation Survey, available at http://www.nfhs.org/ scriptcontent/VA_Custon/SurveyResources/2003_04_Participation_Summary.pdf.

59. Diane Heckman, ScoreBoard: A Concise Chronological Twenty–Five Year History of Title IX Involving Interscholastic and Intercollegiate Athletics, 7 Seton Hall J. Sport L. 391, 416–18 (1997).

60. NCAA 2005–2006 Gender–Equity Report, available at www.ncaa.org/wps/wcm/connect/.../GenderEquityRept–Final.pdf ....

2. Where the members of one sex have been and are underrepresented among intercollegiate athletes, whether the institution can show a history and continuing practice of program expansion which is demonstrably responsive to the developing interest and abilities of the members of that sex; or

3. Where the members of one sex are underrepresented among intercollegiate athletes, and the institution cannot show a continuing practice of program expansion such as that cited above, whether it can be demonstrated that the interests and abilities of the members of that sex have been fully and effectively accommodated by the present program.[61]

In practice, compliance with respect to participation has most often come down to the first test. The proportionality requirement, for two reasons. First, in light of the thirty years since Title IX's passage it is difficult for any college to boast a history and continuing practice of program expansion for women if the school still does not provide proportionally equal opportunities for both sexes. Second, when female students bring a Title IX lawsuit arguing that they are entitled to have a particular athletic team funded, it is difficult for a college to defend its lack of proportional opportunities by arguing that it has fully accommodated women's interest and abilities.[62]

The proportionality requirement has come under attack in recent years by male athletes who blame Title IX for cuts made to men's teams and by scholars who argue that proportionality unfairly favors women in the distribution of varsity athletic resources.[63] In response to such criticism, in June 2002, the Secretary of the Department of Education created a Commission on Opportunity in Athletics charged with the mission of reevaluating Title IX's application to college athletics.[64] On February 26, 2003, the Commission issued its report, "Open to All": Title IX at Thirty, which offered twenty-three recommendations to the Secretary of Education regarding how the current enforcement of Title IX should be modified.[65] On July 11, 2003, the Department of Education issued a public letter effectively maintaining the three prong test for Title IX compliance, but emphasizing that proportionality was not the only acceptable means of

61. See U.S. Dept. of Ed., Office for Civil Rights, Title XI 1979 Policy Interpretation, available at http:// www.ed.gov/about/offices/list/ocr/docs/t9interp.html (1979).

62. Kimberly A. Yuracko, One for You and One for Me: Is Title IX's Sex-Based Proportionality Requirement for College Varsity Athletic Positions Defensible?, 97 Nw. U. L. Rev. 731, 741 (2003).

63. See National Wrestling Coaches Ass'n v. Department of Educ., 263 F.Supp.2d 82 (D.D.C. 2003); William E. Thro & Brian A. Snow, The Conflict Between the Equal Protection Clause and Cohen v. Brown University, 123 Educ. L. Rep. 1013, 1025 (1998); Earl C. Dudley & George Rutherglen, Ironies, Inconsistencies, and Intercollegiate Athletics: Title IX, Title VII, and Statistical Evidence of Discrimination, 1 Va. J. Sports & L. 177, 213–14 (1999).

64. Valerie Strauss & Mike Allen, Panel Named to Study Title IX: Law's Fairness to be Examined, Wash. Post, June 28, 2002, at A27.

65. See the Commission's report, available at http://www.ed.gov/about/bdscomm/list/athletics/ title9report. doc.

compliance.[66] In March, 2005, however, the Department of Education quietly issued another clarification which undermined the proportionality requirement and made showing compliance with the third prong of the Policy Interpretation significantly easier than it had previously been. The clarification put the burden on students and government investigators to show that a college was not fully and effectively satisfying female students' athletic interest and abilities, and it allowed colleges to defend such allegations simply by pointing to the results of an online survey to show that female students had no unmet athletic interests. According to the clarification, if the rate of female student response to the survey was low, that would be evidence of female students' lack of interest in athletics.[67] In 2010, the Obama administration reversed this policy and said universities could no longer rely solely on student surveys to prove they were meeting the requirements of Title IX.[68]

The OCR has never withdrawn federal funds from any educational institution as a result of noncompliance in athletics. Private parties, however, have become much more active in filing lawsuits in federal court under Title IX.

NOTES ON GENDER EQUITY IN ATHLETICS

1. Why do you think girls' and women's participation rates in competitive athletics continues to lag behind that of boys and men? Do you think it is a result of historical and lingering discrimination? Would you imagine females' and males' rates of athletic participation to be the same in the absence of discrimination?

2. What do you view as the appropriate purpose of Title IX with respect to athletics? Is the purpose of the Act to end discriminatory treatment of girls and women in athletics and/or to affirmatively encourage girls and women toward athletics? In other words, is Title IX aimed at changing girls' and women's preferences regarding sports or simply breaking down barriers to entry for those who already know they want to participate?

3. Does nondiscrimination in the context of competitive athletics require that females and males compete against each other on the same teams? Does it require that females and males be given athletic opportunities in proportion to their numbers in the study body? Does it require that females and males be given athletic opportunities in proportion to their relative interest in athletic participation? What does nondiscrimination in this context look like? What are the advantages and disadvantages of each approach?

---

66. See "Dear Colleague" Letter from Gerald Reynolds, Assistant Secretary for Civil Rights, available at http://www2.ed.gov/about/offices/list/ocr/letters/colleague- 20100629.html.

67. See Additional Clarification of Intercollegiate Athletics Policy: Three-Part Test-Part Three, available at http://www.themat.com/section.php?section_id=3&page=showarticle&Art icle ID=12052; Editorial, A New Attack on Women's Sports, N. Y. Times, April 12, 2005, at A20.

68. Katie Thomas, Rule Change Takes Aim at Loophole in Title IX, New York Times, April 20, 2010 at B11.

4. Should Title IX protect girls who want to play on boys' athletic teams because there is no girls' team available? Does your opinion change depending upon whether the sport at issue involves physical contact or not? Should Title IX protect girls who want to play on boys' teams in order to get a higher level of competition? Do your answers change when analyzing claims by boys who want to play on girls' teams?

TEXT NOTE: TITLE IX SPORTS LITIGATION

Many cases have been litigated by private parties showing unequal treatment in intercollegiate sports. In a 1987 class action, female students participating in (or deterred from participating in) the intercollegiate athletic program at Temple University asserted violations of both state and federal equal protection clauses as well as Title IX.[69] In considering the defendant's motion for summary judgment, the court stated that its task was "to define the 'equality' that is required, and then to determine whether defendants offer equivalent athletic programs to men and women student athletes."[70]

First, the court noted that during the relevant time periods, in terms of opportunities to compete, although Temple's student body was fifty percent female, only one-third of its athletes were. Second, Temple spent $2,100 more on male athletes that it did on female athletes. Third, 84 percent of recruiting funds, or $236 more per capita, was spent on male athletes. Fourth, men's teams paid coaches more, had more coaches assigned to them, and received superior coaching (although, as the defendant noted, the proportion of women's coaches to total coaches was higher than the proportion of women athletes to total athletes). Fifth, Temple spent over twice as much on team travel for men's teams (e.g., even when teams, such as men's and women's basketball, were traveling to the same destination, the men's team flew and the women's team took a bus). Sixth, male athletes were provided superior support in the areas of uniforms; equipment; locker rooms; supplies; facilities and scheduling for both practice and competition; housing and dining facilities, including for pre-season and holidays; preference in provision of athletic trainers and training services; academic tutoring support; and publicity. In defense of these economic disparities, Temple argued that (a) women's teams still had a higher win rate and (b) that if the "revenue" teams of football, men's basketball and women's basketball were excluded, expenditures on nonrevenue men's teams were equivalent to that spent on women's nonrevenue teams. The court rejected the proposition that comparable "win" rates meant equal treatment as well as the "revenue" team argument (or so-called "football defense") since the Temple football team lost more money than the entire expenditure on the women's sports program. Finally, the court refused to impose an intent requirement in order to find a violation of Title IX and, based upon the above facts, denied the motion for summary judgment.

After eight years of litigation, and about two months after the trial in *Haffer* began, the district court approved a settlement negotiated by the parties. In the landmark consent decree, Temple agreed to alter its athletic

---

69. Haffer v. Temple University, 678 F.Supp. 517 (E.D.Pa.1987).

70. Id.

program over five years beginning with the 1988–89 academic year, and plaintiffs agreed to withdraw their demand for $1.8 million dollars in damages. Temple agreed, among other things, to: (a) keep the percentage of athletic scholarships granted to women equal to the percentage of female participants in the school's athletic programs and (b) keep the percentage of athletic expenditures for women within ten percentage points of the percentage of women participating (excluding coaches' salaries and benefits, home game expenses and post-season competition), e.g., if one third of the school's athletes are women, then the women's athletic program must receive at least 23 percent of the total athletic budget. Temple was required to file annual reports with the court and was subject to contempt if it fails to meet the terms of the decree. The University also had to pay over $700,000 in fees and costs.[71]

The *Haffer* case has been followed by many other Title IX suits brought by private parties. One of the most publicized cases was a class action filed against Brown University after it demoted the women's gymnastics and volleyball teams from university-funded varsity status to donor-funded varsity status, a downgrade which cost the teams not only university funding but also most of the other forms of support and privileges accompanying university-funded varsity sports at Brown. Two men's teams, water polo and golf, were similarly downgraded.[72] During a trial on the merits, the district court found that:

> [I]n 1993–94, there were 897 students participating in intercollegiate varsity athletics, of which 61.87 percent were men and 38.13 percent (342) were women. During the same period, Brown's undergraduate enrollment comprised 5,722 students, of which 48.86 percent (2,796) were men and 51.15 percent (2,926) were women. * * * [I]n 1993–94, Brown's intercollegiate athletics program consisted of 32 teams, 16 men's teams and 16 women's teams. Of the university-funded teams, 12 were men's teams and 13 were women's teams; of the donor-funded teams, three were women's teams and four were men's teams. At the time of trial, Brown offered 479 university-funded varsity positions for men, as compared to 312 for women; and 76 donor-funded varsity positions for men, as compared to 30 for women. In 1993–94, then, Brown's varsity program—including both university-and donor-funded sports—afforded over 200 more positions for men than for women. Accordingly, * * * Brown maintained a 13.01 percent disparity between female participation in intercollegiate athletics and female student enrollment, and "although the number of varsity sports offered to men and women are equal, the selection of sports offered to each gender generates far more individual positions for male athletes than for female athletes."[73]

The trial court then held that Brown did not meet the OCR Policy Interpretation concerning effective accommodation because it did not provide opportunities for male and female students in numbers substantially proportionate to

71. Steve Springer, After 16 Years, Title IX's Goals Remain Unfulfilled, L.A. Times, Oct. 30, 1988, Sports §, at 12.

72. Cohen v. Brown Univ., 101 F.3d 155 (1st Cir. 1996), cert. denied, 520 U.S. 1186 (1997).

73. 101 F.3d at 163 (recounting district court findings from Cohen III, 879 F.Supp. 185 (D.R.I. 1995)).

their respective enrollments nor did it maintain an ongoing program of expansion for the underrepresented sex, women. Continuing, the court held that simply eliminating or demoting several men's teams did not constitute program expansion for women. Finally, the court found that Brown had not fully and effectively accommodated female student athletes' interests and abilities.

On appeal, the First Circuit recognized that sex discrimination under Title IX imposes differing standards for athletics, admissions and employment. It rejected Brown's argument that the gender disparity was caused not by discrimination but by a lack of interest on the part of female students unrelated to lack of opportunities. The court explained:

> [T]o allow a numbers-based lack-of-interest defense to become the instrument of further discrimination against the underrepresented gender would pervert the remedial purpose of Title IX. We conclude that, even if it can be empirically demonstrated that, at a particular time, women have less interest in sports than do men, such evidence, standing alone, cannot justify providing fewer athletics opportunities for women than for men. Furthermore, such evidence is completely irrelevant where, as here, viable and successful women's varsity teams have been demoted or eliminated.[74]

Furthermore, the court noted that since Title IX there has been a tremendous growth in women's participation in sports, a fact that rebuts Brown's argument that women are less interested in sports for reasons other than lack of opportunity.[75] In another case the court held that male athletes do not have a cause of action when, in response to a significant deficit in the athletic budget, the college decided to eliminate the men's, but not the women's, swimming team.[76]

When seven female University of Texas–Austin athletes filed a class action against the school claiming intentional discrimination under Title IX, the UT student body was 47 percent women, although their sports participation was a mere 23 percent. The men's annual athletic budget for nine sports was $16 to $20 million, while the women's budget for eight sports was $4.3 million. Men received $1.78 million in athletic scholarship dollars, while women received $449,000. The attorney representing the plaintiffs, Diana Henson, said the lawsuit did not seek monetary damages but rather to force UT to add softball, soccer, rowing and gymnastics to the women's athletic competitions. In 1993 the UT settled the lawsuit, agreeing to devote 44 percent of its varsity athletic roster spots to women and to give women more than 42 percent of its athletic scholarship money. In order to accomplish this goal, UT added three women's varsity teams and slightly reduced the roster sizes of its men's varsity teams without eliminating any of them.[77]

---

74. Id. at 179.

75. Cohen v. Brown Univ., 101 F.3d 155, 179–80 (1st Cir. 1996).

76. Kelley v. Board of Trustees, Univ. of Illinois, 35 F.3d 265, 270 (7th Cir. 1994) (holding that this was not a Title IX violation "because even after the cuts, 'men's participation in athletics would continue to be more than substantially proportionate to their presence in the university's student body.' ").

77. Carol Herwig, Female Athletics Sue Texas for Gender Bias, USA Today, July 2, 1992, Sports §, at 2; Citing Title IX, 7 Women File Suit Against Texas, Wash. Post, July 3, 1992, Sports §, at 2.

In 2005, the Supreme Court considered the question of whether a coach who faces retaliation for complaining about unequal treatment of female and male athletes has a cause of action under Title IX. The lawsuit was filed by Roderick Jackson, a former girls' high school basketball coach who believed his team was being denied equal funding and equal access to sports facilities as compared with the boys' teams at his school. Jackson complained to his supervisors about the discrimination, after which he began receiving negative performance evaluations and was then removed from his position. Jackson sued under Title IX for retaliation based on his complaints of sex discrimination. The Supreme Court held that Title IX's private right of action does encompass claims of retaliation for complaints about sex discrimination. The Court explained that this holding was necessary in order to give the Act's sex equality goal real effect. According to the Court:

> Congress enacted Title IX not only to prevent the use of federal dollars to support discriminatory practices, but also "to provide individual citizens effective protection against those practices." We agree with the United States that this objective "would be difficult, if not impossible, to achieve if persons who complain about sex discrimination did not have effective protection against retaliation." If recipients were permitted to retaliate freely, individuals who witness discrimination would be loathe to report it, and all manner of Title IX violations might go unremedied as a result.[78]

NOTES ON TITLE IX LITIGATION

1. Brown offered an argument that a remedy with numerical requirements was a "quota" and hence unconstitutional according to Adarand Constr., Inc. v. Pena, 515 U.S. 200, 115 S.Ct. 2097, 132 L.Ed.2d 158 (1995). Do you think that the successes of the anti-affirmative action movement, discussed in the previous section, will affect remedies imposed *after* findings of liability? Are numerically-based remedies a type of quota in the context of separate sports teams for women and men?

2. One of the defenses asserted by Temple was that "revenue" teams, most particularly football, should be excluded from any comparisons. Many commentators believe that college football is the biggest obstacle to Title IX compliance. According to Deidre G. Duncan:

> Many coaches and athletes fear that "Title IX will be the end of major college football." College football has been referred to as the "golden goose" of college athletics. Football's attendance levels and television ratings far surpass those of any other sport. Likewise, there is no sport, men's or women's, that equals the number of players and scholarships given to football programs by university athletic departments. All of these numbers pose great problems for a university attempting to achieve Title IX compliance.

* * *

78. Jackson v. Birmingham Bd. of Ed., 544 U.S. 167, 181 (2005) (quoting Cannon v. University of Chicago, 441 U.S. 677, 704 (1979); Brief for United States as Amicus Curiae 13).

> In Division I college football, eighty-eight scholarships are permitted per university and participation often exceeds one hundred athletes. This problem virtually precludes universities from having a ratio of male to female athletes proportionate to the general student body. With such large teams, football often costs far more money than the entire women's athletic budget. Athletic departments worry that if schools were forced to offer an equitable number of men's and women's scholarships, some schools would be able to operate only three men's sports: football, basketball, and baseball.
>
> The problem seems deceptively simple to solve—exempt college football from the proportionality requirement. However, football cannot legally be exempted. When Congress passed Title IX, the late Senator John Tower of Texas proposed an amendment that would have excluded revenue-producing sports from the Title IX equity requirement. The bill was summarily rejected. Proponents of gender equity interpret this rejection as imposing a requirement that Title IX analysis must include college football.
>
> * * *
>
> Aside from the proportionality problem, football also raises the issue of how to give credit to revenue-generating sports. Because football often contributes revenue and provides financial support for other men's and women's athletics, football supporters claim it should be exempted from Title IX analysis. They point to the fact that money raised from college football, along with the revenue earned from the NCAA Division I men's basketball tournament, assists in supporting several other nonrevenue generating sports, men's and women's. An NCAA study released in August of 1994 revealed that men's sports programs, with football at the top of the list, generated an average of sixty-nine percent of Division I–A athletic department revenue. Women's programs average only four percent of total revenues, with the remaining [revenue] coming from nongender specific sources.

Duncan, Gender Equity in Women's Athletics, 64 U. Cin. L. Rev. 1027, 1046–49 (1996). There is significant disagreement as to how often college football teams are in fact revenue generating. See, e.g., Richard Haglund, Staring Down the Elephant: College Football and Title IX Compliance, 34 J.L. & Educ. 439, 439–452 (2005); Ross A. Jurewitz, Playing at Even Strength: Reforming Title IX Enforcement in Intercollegiate Athletics, 8 Am. U.J. Gender Soc. Pol'y & L. 283 (2000); Brian L. Porto, Completing the Revolution: Title IX as Catalyst for an Alternative Model of College Sports, 8 Seton Hall J. Sport L. 385 (1998). Should football be exempt from Title IX proportionality compliance requirements? Why or why not? How strong is the revenue generation argument? What is the role of the media in deciding which sports generate the most revenue? Does the revenue generation argument come dangerously close, as a practical matter, to elevating college sports from amateur to professional status? Is this desirable? Is it reality?

3. In 1992 after investigating allegations of sex discrimination the OCR found Brooklyn College in violation of Title IX. The findings included the fact that women made up 30 percent of Brooklyn College's athletes, while they

were 56 percent of the student body. The equipment budget for men's teams was nearly seven times that for women's teams; and men's teams played more games, e.g., the men's baseball schedule included 46 games while the women's softball team played 12. Men's teams had more experienced coaches, more experienced trainers, higher food stipends, more publicity and 87 percent of the money spent on recruiting. Malcolm Moran, Brooklyn College at Crossroads, N.Y. Times, June 23, 1992, § B, at 15. Several months after receiving the OCR decision, the College decided to terminate its entire athletic department. Roscoe Nance, Colleges, USA Today, July 2, 1992, Sports §, at 13. Women and men would be treated equally with respect to athletic options after Brooklyn College's decision. Does the decision, nonetheless, seem discriminatory to you? If so why? Is there any legal remedy for this? What arguments could you make? See Deborah L. Brake, When Equality Leaves Everyone Worse Off: The Problem of Leveling Down in Equality Law, 46 Wm & Mary L. Rev. 513 (2004).

4. How should non-discrimination be defined in athletic scholarships and funding? Title IX regulations require only substantial proportionality in scholarships based on the percentage of females with respect to the total group of athletic participants. 34 C.F.R. § 106.37(a) (1995). Is one effect of these regulations to provide an incentive to schools not to promote participation by women? Is this regulation consistent with Title IX?

MICHAEL A. MESSNER, POWER AT PLAY: SPORTS AND THE PROBLEM OF MASCULINITY

24, 33, 34, 35–37, 62, 68–69, 91, 159–60, 166–68, 170–72 (1992)

[The author conducted semi-structured interviews, ranging from one and one-half to six hours, with 30 male former athletes, aged 21 to 48, in order to "discover how masculine gender identities develop and change as boys and men interact with the socially constructed world of organized sport."]

Zane Grey once said, "All boys love baseball. If they don't, they're not real boys." This is, of course, an ideological statement: Some boys do not love baseball, or any other sports, for that matter. There are millions of males who at an early age are rejected by, become alienated from, or lose interest in organized sport. Yet, studies in the 1970s and the 1980s consistently showed that sport remains the single most important element of the peer-status system of U.S. adolescent males. The fact is, boys are, to a greater or lesser extent, judged according to their ability, or lack of ability, in competitive sport.

* * *

Young boys may initially find that playing competitively gives them the opportunity to experience emotionally "safe" connections with others. But once enmeshed in sport as an institution, they are confronted by two interrelated realities—hierarchy and homophobia—that undermine the possibility of boys' transcending their fears of intimacy and developing truly close relationships with others.

* * *

* * * The extent of homophobia in the sports world is staggering. Boys learn early that to be gay, to be suspected of being gay, or even to be unable to prove one's heterosexual status is not acceptable. Though athletes are cultural symbols of masculine heterosexual virility, however, it is not true that there are no gay men and boys in sports. There is growing evidence that many (mostly closeted) gay males are competing in organized sport at all levels.

* * *

Indeed, boys learn early that if it is difficult to define masculinity in terms of what it *is*, it is at least clear what it is *not*. A boy is not considered masculine if he is feminine. In sport, to be told by coaches, fathers, or peers that one throws "like a girl" or plays like a "sissy" or a "woman" is among the most devastating insults a boy can receive, and such words can have a powerful impact upon his actions, relationships, and self-image. Sociologist Gary Alan Fine spent three years studying Little League baseball teams and noted clear and persistent patterns of homophobic banter and sexual talk about females among eleven-and twelve-year-old boys. * * *

Fine's observations demonstrate how homophobia and the sexual objectification of females together act as a glue that solidifies the male peer group as separate from females, while at the same time establishing and clarifying hierarchical relations within the male peer group. In short, homophobia polices the boundaries of narrow cultural definitions of masculinity and keeps boys—especially those in all-male environments such as organized sport—from getting too close. Through sport, a young boy learns that it is risky—psychologically as well as physically—to become too emotionally open with his peers: he might be labeled a "sissy," a "fag," or even be beaten up or ostracized from the group. He also finds that he had better not become too close to girls; he must, of course, establish his masculine status by making (and laughing at) heterosexist jokes, but he "must never let girls replace boys as the focus of [his] attention."

* * *

Indeed, my research suggests that a young man's imperative to prove himself, to perform, achieve, and win, dovetails with the hierarchic world of athletic careers in such a way that he tends to develop a certain kind of relationship to his own body. It's not simply that an athlete's body becomes "the focus of the self," but that the athlete is often encouraged to see his body as an instrument. An "instrumental male" is an alienated creature: he is usually very goal-oriented (in his work and in his personal relations), and he frequently views other people as objects to be manipulated and defeated in his quest to achieve his goals. The ultimate extension of instrumental rationality is the alienation from one's own body—the tendency to treat one's body as a tool, a machine to be utilized (and "used up") in the pursuit of particular ends. Tender feelings (toward oneself and toward others) come to be seen as an impediment, something that needs to be repressed or "worked on." Physical or emotional pain are experienced as a nuisance to be ignored or done away with (often through the use of alcohol or other drugs). A common result of this focus on the body as an instrument is violence expressed toward others, and ultimately toward oneself.

* * *

Mary Duquin and Brenda Bredemeier [sociologists], in two separate studies aimed at testing Gilligan's theory of gender difference [excerpted and discussed in Chapter 3, above], found that male and female athletes indeed engaged in different kinds of moral reasoning around issues such as rule-breaking and aggression. Female athletes tended to fear that aggression—even "within the rules"—threatened their connection with others, and thus the basis of their identities. By contrast, male athletes tended to feel affirmed by, and comfortable with, rule-bound athletic aggression.

These social-psychological analyses of athletic aggression reveal the affinity between developing masculine identities and the structure of values of the institution of sport. Within the athletic context, young males can develop a certain kind of closeness with each other while not having to deal with the kinds of (intimate) attachments that they tend to fear. Here individuals' roles and separate positions within hierarchies are determined by competition within a clearly defined system of rules that governs the interaction of participants. Although many athletes will "stretch" the rules as much as they can to gain an advantage over their opponents, most have a respect, even a reverence, for the importance of rules as a code of conduct that places safe boundaries around their aggression and their relationships with others. Without the rules, there would be chaos—both physical and psychological; there would be a frightening need to negotiate and renegotiate relationships constantly. This is what feels truly dangerous to men.

* * *

For most of the men whom I interviewed, this sort of aggression "within the rules" was considered legitimate—even desirable. In fact, sociologist Peter Lyman has observed that aggression is usually not defined by men as "violent" so long as it is rule-governed, rather than anger-induced.

* * *

An interesting consensus has emerged among those who have studied gender and friendship in the United States: Women have deep, intimate, meaningful, and lasting friendships, while men have a number of shallow, superficial, and unsatisfying "acquaintances." Several commentators have concluded that men's relationships are shallow because men have been taught to be highly homophobic, emotionally inexpressive, and competitive "success objects."

* * *

Organized sport, as we know it, emerged largely as a masculinist response to a crisis in the gender order of the late nineteenth and early twentieth centuries. The world of sport gave men a retreat from what they feared was a "feminized" modern culture, and it gave white upper-class men (initially), and working-class and minority men (eventually), a means of "naturalizing" dominant forms of masculinity. Throughout most of the twentieth century, this masculine institution of sport existed alongside a vibrant but much less visible tradition of women's sport. In the early 1970s, there emerged what Stephanie Twin has called a "second wave of athletic feminism." The explosion of girls' and women's athletics in the next two decades served notice that female athletes could no longer be ignored to the extent that they once were.

How have men responded to women's recent movement into sport? There is some evidence that increasing female athleticism has caused many boys and men to adjust—and sometimes radically alter—their preconceptions of what women are capable of. Personally confronting the reality of female athleticism has caused some boys and men to question what sociologist Nancy Theberge has called "the myth of female frailty." On the other hand, there is also considerable evidence that women's sport has been institutionally contained, and thus its potential challenge to sport's construction of hegemonic masculinity has been largely defused.

* * *

Increased athletic participation for girls and for women does partially undermine sexist attitudes and assumptions among some men. Yet as long as we are simply attempting to incorporate women within an institution that is, in its dominant structure and values, a masculine construction, "equal opportunity" for females will ultimately serve to affirm and naturalize masculine superiority. The reason is this: Today's sports media—and, indeed, liberal feminists who are intent on gaining equal opportunities for female athletes—often ignore the fact that male and female bodies do tend to differ in potential physical strength, endurance, agility, and grace. Despite considerable overlap, the average adult male is about five inches taller than the average female. Can women really hope to compete with men at the highest levels of basketball or volleyball? Males average 40 percent muscle and 15 percent body fat, while females average 23 percent muscle and 25 percent body fat. Can women possibly compete at the highest levels with men in football, track and field, hockey, or baseball? On the other hand, women have some physical differences from men that can be translated into athletic superiority. For instance, * * * women's different skeletal structures and greater flexibility make for superior performances on a balance beam. In addition, women's higher body fat ratio gives them greater buoyancy in water and greater insulation against heat loss, which has translated into women's times in distance swimming, especially in cold water, being considerably faster than men's.

In other words, as long as we are intent on measuring the highest levels of physical performance, males are likely to excel in some activities, females in others. Yet given our present values and institutional arrangements, these average physiological differences between the sexes nearly always end up being translated into female physical "inferiority." The reason for this is simple: The most highly valued sports in the U.S. (especially the "money sports" like football) are at present organized according to the most extreme possibilities of the male body. "Equal opportunity" for women within these masculine-defined sports puts women at a decided disadvantage.

Significantly, though coverage of women's sport lags far behind coverage of men's sport, the sport media increasingly appear to be employing liberal conceptions of equal opportunity in their presentations of the athletic performances of women. With women competing in male-defined sports, the media can employ statistics as "objective measures of performance." Spectators can see for themselves that, for instance, though the women competitors in the Olympics are impressive athletes, the medal winners' performances would rarely be good enough to qualify them for the finals in the men's events. Equal opportunity within this system thus provides support for the ideology of meritocracy, while subtly supplying incontrovertible evidence of the "natural superiority" of males over females. Clearly, if equal opportunity for women is not to serve simply as the basis for a reconstituted ideology of male superiority, the institution of sport itself must be transformed from a masculine construction to a human construction.

* * *

What does televised sport mean to male viewers? The mythology and symbolism of today's most popular spectator sports are probably meaningful to viewers on a number of levels: patriotism, militarism, violence, and meritocracy are all dominant themes. But it is reasonable to speculate that gender is a salient organizing theme in the construction of meanings, especially with respect to the more aggressive and violent aspects of sport. For example, when I was interviewing a thirty-two-year-old white professional-class male, and I asked him how he felt about the fact that recently a woman had been promoted to a position of authority in his workplace, he replied, "A woman can do the same job as I can do—maybe even be my boss. But I'll be *damned* if she can go out on the 'football' field and take a hit from Ronnie Lott [legendary retired San Francisco 49'er safety football player who was known for being a 'hard hitter' and who had part of his little finger amputated in order to play in a scheduled game]."

At the most obvious level, we can read this man's statement as an indication that he is identifying with Ronnie Lott as a man, and the basis of the identification is the violent male body. Football, based as it is on the fullest potential of the male body (muscular bulk, explosive power) is clearly a world apart from women, who are relegated to the roles of sex objects on the sidelines, rooting their men on. In contrast to the bare and vulnerable bodies of the cheerleaders, the armored male bodies of the football players are elevated to mythical status and thus give testimony to the undeniable "fact" that here is at least one place where men are clearly superior to women. Yet it is also significant that this man was quite aware that he (and perhaps 99 percent of the rest of the male population of the United States) was probably equally incapable of taking a "hit" from the likes of Ronnie Lott and living to tell of it. I would speculate that by recognizing the simultaneous construction of identification and difference among men, we may begin to understand the major role that televised sport plays in the current gender order.

* * *

Since the institution of sport is both constructed by, and in turn helps to construct, the overall gender order, it makes no sense to speak of transforming sport in the abstract. Any fundamental changes in the values and structure of organized sport necessarily must take place within a larger movement to transform other social institutions (economy, politics, family, education, etc.). But this does not mean that attempts to change sport have no worth. I have argued here that sport is a key component of our current gender order. Further, though sport's major impact appears to support the status quo of hegemonic masculinity, there are also internal contradictions in men's experiences with athletic careers. These problems have been given potential new meaning by women's recent challenge to sport as a masculine institution.

* * *

It is possible for sport to be reorganized in such a way that its positive potentialities—which all of the men I interviewed experienced to a degree, but which, for many of them, were eclipsed by anxiety and pain—can rise to the surface. But if, as I have suggested, the current affinity between boys' and men's developing masculine identities and the institution of sport continues, then simply attempting to reorganize sport will be an exercise in futility. There are two fundamental requisites for the humanization of sport: First, boys and girls should be brought up and nurtured in an equal manner, and this work must be shared equally by men and women. Second, all of our social institutions—schools, workplaces, families, the state—must be reorganized in ways that maximize equality for all people. Girls and boys, women and men who are raised in such an egalitarian world might finally be able to enjoy sport for all that it really has to offer.

NOTES ON SPORTS, GENDER, AND MASCULINITIES

1. Do you agree with Messner that the institution of sport is premised upon hierarchy and homophobia? If so, can you provide examples? Is the same true for "girls'" sports? Can you think of other ways in which sports

perpetuate male domination? After reading the Messner excerpt, do you perceive a relationship between sports and violence against women? A 1998 study found that college football and basketball players were more abusive to women than other college students: "[f]rom 1991–93, male student athletes comprised 3.3 percent of the male population at 10 major universities but accounted for 19 percent of the men reported to campus officials for sexual assault ... Of those, 76 percent were football or basketball players." Paul Ruffins, The Fumble of a Lifetime, 17 Black Issues in Higher Education 34 (2000). Another study documented findings "that male college students who engaged in formal athletics were more likely than other men to feel hostile towards women and engage in sexual aggression." Id. Do you think such aggression is a function of sport per se, or of how society has constructed male athletics and masculinity more generally?

2. Do you agree with Messner that organized sport was a "masculinist response to a crisis in the gender order of the late nineteenth and early twentieth centuries?" Does it continue to assert male superiority and dominance? In what ways? What role does the media play in perpetuating views about proper gender roles through the use of sports? Figure skating is one of the most often televised women's sports; why?

3. When she was a student at Harvard Law School, Lyn Lemaire, former member of the U.S. Women's Cycling Team, noted that the prevailing model of athletics today is "combative." According to her analysis, the fundamental reason for engaging in sports under this combative model was best expressed by Vince Lombardi, long time coach of the National Football League champion Green Bay Packers: "Winning isn't everything; it's the only thing." Lemaire points out that "this narrow view posits victory and dominance as the goals of athletic competition and thereby creates a dichotomy between the winners and the losers in sports competition." Lemaire, Women and Athletics: Toward a Physicality Perspective, 5 Harv. Women's L.J. 121, 123 (1982). She urged a new model for sports:

> In contrast to the "traditional model" of sports, which emphasizes competition for the sake of winning, the "physicality model" focuses on the value of athletic participation per se, regardless of winning or losing. The author [Lemaire] thus advocates a shift from a goal-oriented to a process-oriented view of the benefits of athletic activity. The argument does not suggest that women are incapable of competing successfully with men, that competition in itself is undesirable, or that physicality is mere recreation devoid of rigorous training. Rather, the point is advanced that competition and exertion engaged in for the joy of athletic participation could increase the number and elevate the status of women athletes.

Id. at 122. Is this a substantive equality argument? Is Lemaire's proposal similar to what is occurring in other areas of education, i.e., not just obtaining access for women to play by men's rules but serious evaluation of the game itself? How is her proposal similar to or dissimilar from Messner's sports analysis?

F. SEXUAL HARASSMENT

GEBSER v. LAGO VISTA INDEPENDENT SCHOOL DISTRICT

Supreme Court of the United States, 1998.
524 U.S. 274, 118 S.Ct. 1989, 141 L.Ed.2d 277.

JUSTICE O'CONNOR delivered the opinion of the Court.

[The facts alleged in this case were that petitioner, eighth-grade student Alida Star Gebser, in 1991 joined a high school book discussion group led by a teacher at Lago Vista's high school, Frank Waldrop. At meetings of the book club Waldrop often made sexually suggestive comments. Later that fall, when Gebser entered high school, she was assigned to classes taught by Waldrop. His sexual comments continued; he began to direct them specifically to Gebser, including at times when they were alone in the classroom. The next spring he initiated sexual conduct with her, and the two of them had sexual intercourse several times over the next year, although never on school property. Gebser did not report the relationship to school officials because she was uncertain how to react and wanted to keep Waldrop as a teacher. When other parents complained of Waldrop's comments in class, the principal met with the teacher and advised him to be careful about his class comments. The principal did not report the complaint to the superintendent, who was the Title IX coordinator. A few months later police discovered Waldrop having sex with Gebser and arrested him. He was fired and his teaching license was revoked. During this time Lago Vista School District did not have an official sexual harassment policy or grievance procedure.]

The question in this case is when a school district may be held liable in damages in an implied right of action under Title IX of the Education Amendments of 1972 for the sexual harassment of a student by one of the district's teachers. We conclude that damages may not be recovered in those circumstances unless an official of the school district who at a minimum has authority to institute corrective measures on the district's behalf has actual notice of, and is deliberately indifferent to, the teacher's misconduct.

* * *

Gebser and her mother filed suit against Lago Vista and Waldrop in state court in November 1993, raising claims against the school district under Title IX and state negligence law, and claims against Waldrop primarily under state law. They sought compensatory and punitive damages from both defendants. After the case was removed, the United States District Court for the Western District of Texas granted summary judgment in favor of Lago Vista on all claims, and remanded the allegations against Waldrop to state court. [The Fifth Circuit affirmed.]

* * *

[The Court began its analysis by noting that although Title IX's express statutory means of enforcement is administrative, it recognized an implied private cause of action in 1979 and specifically established in Franklin v. Gwinnett County Public Schools, 503 U.S. 60, 112 S. Ct. 1028, 117 L.Ed.2d 208 (1992), that monetary damages are available in sexual harassment claims under Title IX. However, *Franklin* did not articulate the standard for liability, which is the issue in this case. Petitioners, joined by the United States as amicus curiae, argued that Title VII employment discrimination standards used in cases involving a supervisor's sexual harassment of an employee in the workplace should be adopted; they relied on language in *Franklin* which analogized teachers sexually abusing students to supervisors sexually harassing a subordinate in the workplace. Because Meritor Sav. Bank v. Vinson [excerpted in Chapter 10] directed courts to apply common law agency principles in determining employer liability under Title VII, they argued agency principles should also apply under Title IX. Specifically, they advanced two possible standards under which Lago Vista would be liable for Waldrop's conduct: (1) vicarious or imputed liability and (2) constructive notice, i.e., where the district knew or "should have known" about the harassment but failed to uncover and eliminate it. Both of these theories are broader than that adopted by the Fifth Circuit's rule requiring actual notice.]

Congress enacted Title IX in 1972 with two principal objectives in mind: "to avoid the use of federal resources to support discriminatory practices" and "to provide individual citizens effective protection against those practices." The statute was modeled after Title VI of the Civil Rights Act of 1964, which is parallel to Title IX except that it prohibits race discrimination, not sex discrimination, and applies in all programs receiving federal funds, not only in education programs. The two statutes operate in the same manner, conditioning an offer of federal funding on a promise by the recipient not to discriminate, in what amounts essentially to a contract between the Government and the recipient of funds.

That contractual framework distinguishes Title IX from Title VII, which is framed in terms not of a condition but of an outright prohibition. Title VII applies to all employers without regard to federal funding and aims broadly to "eradicat[e] discrimination throughout the economy." Title VII, moreover, seeks to "make persons whole for injuries suffered through past discrimination." Thus, whereas Title VII aims centrally to compensate victims of discrimination, Title IX focuses more on "protecting" individuals from discriminatory practices carried out by recipients of federal funds. * * *

Title IX's contractual nature has implications for our construction of the scope of available remedies. When Congress attaches conditions to the award of federal funds under its spending power, as it has in Title IX and Title VI, we examine closely the propriety of private actions holding the recipient liable in monetary damages for noncompliance with the condition. Our central concern in that regard is with ensuring "that the receiving entity of federal funds [has] notice that it will be liable for a monetary award." * * * If a school district's liability for a teacher's sexual harassment rests on principles of constructive notice or respondeat superior, it will likewise be the case that the recipient of funds was unaware of the discrimination. It is sensible to assume that Congress did not envision a recipient's liability in damages in that situation.

Most significantly, Title IX contains important clues that Congress did not intend to allow recovery in damages where liability rests solely on principles of vicarious liability or constructive notice. Title IX's express means of enforcement—by administrative agencies—operates on an assumption of actual notice to officials of the funding recipient. * * *

Presumably, a central purpose of requiring notice of the violation "to the appropriate person" and an opportunity for voluntary compliance before administrative enforcement proceedings can commence is to avoid diverting education funding from beneficial uses where a recipient was unaware of discrimination in its programs and is willing to institute prompt corrective measures. The scope of private damages relief proposed by petitioners is at odds with that basic objective. When a teacher's sexual harassment is imputed to a school district or when a school district is deemed to have "constructively" known of the teacher's harassment, by assumption the district had no actual knowledge of the teacher's conduct. Nor, of course, did the district have an opportunity to take action to end the harassment or to limit further harassment.

It would be unsound, we think, for a statute's express system of enforcement to require notice to the recipient and an opportunity to come into voluntary compliance while a judicially implied system of enforcement permits substantial liability without regard to the recipient's knowledge or its corrective actions upon receiving notice. Moreover, an award of damages in a particular case might well exceed a recipient's level of federal funding. (Lago Vista's federal funding for 1992–1993 was roughly $120,000). Where a statute's express enforcement scheme hinges its most severe sanction on notice and unsuccessful efforts to obtain compliance, we cannot attribute to Congress the intention to have implied an enforcement scheme that allows imposition of greater liability without comparable conditions.

Because the express remedial scheme under Title IX is predicated upon notice to an "appropriate person" and an opportunity to rectify any violation, we conclude, in the absence of further direction from Congress, that the implied damages remedy should be fashioned along the same lines. An "appropriate person" under § 1682 is, at a minimum, an official of the recipient entity with authority to take corrective action to end the discrimination. Consequently, in cases like this one that do not involve official policy of the recipient entity, we hold that a damages remedy will not lie under Title IX unless an official who at a minimum has authority to address the alleged discrimination and to institute corrective measures on the recipient's behalf has actual knowledge of discrimination in the recipient's programs and fails adequately to respond.

We think, moreover, that the response must amount to deliberate indifference to discrimination. The administrative enforcement scheme presupposes that an official who is advised of a Title IX violation refuses to take action to bring the recipient into compliance. The premise, in other words, is an official decision by the recipient not to remedy the violation. That framework finds a rough parallel in the standard of deliberate indifference. Under a lower standard, there would be a risk that the recipient would be liable in damages not for its own official decision but instead for its employees' independent actions. * * *

Applying the framework to this case is fairly straightforward, as petitioners do not contend they can prevail under an actual notice standard. * * *

Petitioners focus primarily on Lago Vista's asserted failure to promulgate and publicize an effective policy and grievance procedure for sexual harassment claims. They point to Department of Education regulations requiring each funding recipient to "adopt and publish grievance procedures providing for prompt and equitable resolution" of discrimination complaints, and to notify students and others "that it does not discriminate on the basis of sex in the educational programs or activities which it operates." Lago Vista's alleged failure to comply with the regulations, however, does not establish the requisite actual notice and deliberate indifference. And in any event, the failure to promulgate a grievance procedure does not itself constitute "discrimination" under Title IX. Of course, the Department of Education could enforce the requirement administratively: Agencies generally have authority to promulgate and enforce requirements that effectuate the statute's non-discrimination mandate, even if those requirements do not purport to represent a definition of discrimination under the statute. We have never held, however, that the implied private right of action under Title IX allows recovery in damages for violation of those sorts of administrative requirements.

The number of reported cases involving sexual harassment of students in schools confirms that harassment unfortunately is an all too common aspect of the educational experience. No one questions that a student suffers extraordinary harm when subjected to sexual harassment and abuse by a teacher, and that the teacher's conduct is reprehensible and undermines the basic purposes of the educational system. The issue in this case, however, is whether the independent misconduct of a teacher is attributable to the school district that employs him under a specific federal statute designed primarily to prevent recipients of federal financial assistance from using the funds in a discriminatory manner. Our decision does not affect any right of recovery that an individual may have against a school district as a matter of state law or against the teacher in his individual capacity under state law or under 42 U.S.C. § 1983. Until Congress speaks directly on the subject, however, we will not hold a school district liable in damages under Title IX for a teacher's sexual harassment of a student absent actual notice and deliberate indifference. We therefore affirm the judgment of the Court of Appeals.

DAVIS v. MONROE COUNTY BOARD OF EDUCATION

Supreme Court of the United States, 1999.
526 U.S. 629, 119 S.Ct. 1661, 143 L.Ed.2d 839.

JUSTICE O'CONNOR delivered the opinion of the Court.

Petitioner brought suit against the Monroe County Board of Education and other defendants, alleging that her fifth-grade daughter had been the victim of sexual harassment by another student in her class. Among petitioner's claims was a claim for monetary and injunctive relief under Title IX of the Education Amendments of 1972. The District Court dismissed petitioner's Title IX claim on the ground that "student-on-student," or peer, harassment provides no ground for a private cause of action under the statute. The Court of Appeals for the Eleventh Circuit, sitting en banc, affirmed. We consider here whether a private damages action may lie against the school board in cases of student-on-student harassment. We conclude that it may, but only where the funding recipient acts with deliberate indifference to known acts of harassment in its programs or activities. Moreover, we conclude that such an action will lie only for harassment that is so severe, pervasive, and objectively offensive that it effectively bars the victim's access to an educational opportunity or benefit.

* * *

Petitioner's minor daughter, LaShonda, was allegedly the victim of a prolonged pattern of sexual harassment by one of her fifth-grade classmates at Hubbard Elementary School, a public school in Monroe County, Georgia. According to petitioner's complaint, the harassment began in December 1992, when the classmate, G.F., attempted to touch LaShonda's breasts and genital area and made vulgar statements such as " 'I want to get in bed with you' " and " 'I want to feel your boobs.' " Similar conduct allegedly occurred on or about January 4 and January 20, 1993. LaShonda reported each of these incidents to her mother and to her classroom teacher, Diane Fort. Petitioner, in turn, also contacted Fort, who allegedly assured petitioner that the school principal, Bill Querry, had been informed of the incidents. Petitioner contends that, notwithstanding these reports, no disciplinary action was taken against G.F.

G.F.'s conduct allegedly continued for many months. In early February, G.F. purportedly placed a door stop in his pants and proceeded to act in a sexually suggestive manner toward LaShonda during physical education class. LaShonda reported G.F.'s behavior to her physical education teacher, Whit Maples. Approximately one week later, G.F. again allegedly engaged in harassing behavior, this time while under the supervision of another classroom teacher, Joyce Pippin. Again, LaShonda allegedly reported the incident to the teacher, and again petitioner contacted the teacher to follow up.

Petitioner alleges that G.F. once more directed sexually harassing conduct toward LaShonda in physical education class in early March, and that LaShonda reported the incident to both Maples and Pippen. In mid-April 1993, G.F. allegedly rubbed his body against LaShonda in the school hallway in what LaShonda considered a sexually suggestive manner, and LaShonda again reported the matter to Fort.

The string of incidents finally ended in mid-May, when G.F. was charged with, and pleaded guilty to, sexual battery for his misconduct. The complaint alleges that LaShonda had suffered during the months of harassment, however; specifically, her previously high grades allegedly dropped as she became unable to concentrate on her studies, and, in April 1993, her father discovered that she had written a suicide note. The complaint further alleges that, at one point, LaShonda told petitioner that she " 'didn't know how much longer she could keep [G.F.] off her.' "

Nor was LaShonda G.F.'s only victim; it is alleged that other girls in the class fell prey to G.F.'s conduct. At one point, in fact, a group composed of LaShonda and other female students tried to speak with Principal Querry about G.F.'s behavior. According to the complaint, however, a teacher denied the students' request with the statement, " 'If [Querry] wants you, he'll call you.' "

Petitioner alleges that no disciplinary action was taken in response to G.F.'s behavior toward LaShonda. In addition to her conversations with Fort and Pippen, petitioner alleges that she spoke with Principal Querry in mid-May 1993. When petitioner inquired as to what action the school intended to take against G.F., Querry simply stated, " 'I guess I'll have to threaten him a little bit harder.' " Yet, petitioner alleges, at no point during the many months of his reported misconduct was G.F. disciplined for harassment. Indeed, Querry allegedly asked petitioner why LaShonda " 'was the only one complaining.' "

Nor, according to the complaint, was any effort made to separate G.F. and LaShonda. On the contrary, notwithstanding LaShonda's frequent complaints, only after more than three months of reported harassment was she even permitted to change her classroom seat so that she was no longer seated next to G.F. Moreover, petitioner alleges that, at the time of the events in question, the Monroe County Board of Education had not instructed its personnel on how to respond to peer sexual harassment and had not established a policy on the issue.

* * *

There is no dispute here that the Board is a recipient of federal education funding for Title IX purposes. Nor do respondents support an argument that student-on-student harassment cannot rise to the level of "discrimination" for purposes of Title IX. Rather, at issue here is the question whether a recipient of federal education funding may be liable for damages under Title IX under any circumstances for discrimination in the form of student-on-student sexual harassment.

* * *

[The Court noted that in *Gebser* it articulated a Title IX standard in which money damages will be available only where federally-funded recipients had notice of liability. The School Board argued that Title IX provides no such notice that a recipient could be liable not for its misconduct but that of a third party over whom it exercises little control. Although the Court agreed that a recipient may be liable only for its own misconduct, it disagreed that the plaintiff in this case was holding the School Board responsible for G.F.'s actions. Rather, the petitioner was seeking "to hold the Board liable for its own decision to remain idle in the face of known student-on-student harassment in its schools."]

We consider here whether the misconduct identified in *Gebser*—deliberate indifference to known acts of harassment—amounts to an intentional violation of Title IX, capable of supporting a private damages action, when the harasser is a student rather than a teacher. We conclude that, in certain limited circumstances, it does. * * * [T]he regulatory scheme surrounding Title IX has long provided funding recipients with notice that they may be liable for their failure to respond to the discriminatory acts of certain non-agents. The Department of Education requires recipients to monitor third parties for discrimination in specified circumstances and to refrain from particular forms of interaction with outside entities that are known to discriminate.

The common law, too, has put schools on notice that they may be held responsible under state law for their failure to protect students from the tortious acts of third parties. In fact, state courts routinely uphold claims alleging that schools have been negligent in failing to protect their students from the torts of their peers.

* * * If a funding recipient does not engage in harassment directly, it may not be liable for damages unless its deliberate indifference "subject[s]" its students to harassment. That is, the deliberate indifference must, at a minimum, "cause [students] to undergo" harassment or "make them liable or vulnerable" to it. Moreover, because the harassment must occur "under" "the operations of" a funding recipient, the harassment must take place in a context subject to the school district's control.

These factors combine to limit a recipient's damages liability to circumstances wherein the recipient exercises substantial control over both the harasser and the context in which the known harassment occurs. Only then can the recipient be said to "expose" its students to harassment or "cause" them to undergo it "under" the recipient's programs. * * *

Where, as here, the misconduct occurs during school hours and on school grounds—the bulk of G.F.'s misconduct, in fact, took place in the classroom—the misconduct is taking place "under" an "operation" of the funding recipient. In these circumstances, the recipient retains substantial control over the context in which the harassment occurs. More importantly, however, in this setting the Board exercises significant control over the harasser. We have observed, for example, "that the nature of [the State's] power [over public schoolchildren] is custodial and tutelary, permitting a degree of supervision and control that could not be exercised over free adults." * * *

We stress that our conclusion here—that recipients may be liable for their deliberate indifference to known acts of peer sexual harassment—does not mean that recipients can avoid liability only by purging their schools of actionable peer harassment or that administrators must engage in particular disciplinary action. We thus disagree with respondents' contention that, if Title IX provides a cause of action for student-on-student harassment, "nothing short of expulsion of every student accused of misconduct involving sexual overtones would protect school systems from liability or damages." * * *

* * * We believe, however, that the standard set out here is sufficiently flexible to account both for the level of disciplinary authority available to the school and for the potential liability arising from certain forms of disciplinary action. A university might not, for example, be expected to exercise the same degree of control over its students that a grade school would enjoy, and it would be entirely reasonable for a school to refrain from a form of disciplinary action that would expose it to constitutional or statutory claims.

* * *

* * * We thus conclude that funding recipients are properly held liable in damages only where they are deliberately indifferent to sexual harassment, of which they have actual knowledge, that is so severe, pervasive, and objectively offensive that it can be said to deprive the victims of access to the educational opportunities or benefits provided by the school.

* * *

Whether gender-oriented conduct rises to the level of actionable "harassment" thus "depends on a constellation of surrounding circumstances, expectations, and relationships," including, but not limited to, the ages of the harasser and the victim and the number of individuals involved. Courts, moreover, must bear in mind that schools are unlike the adult workplace and that children may regularly interact in a manner that would be unacceptable among adults. Indeed, at least early on, students are still learning how to interact appropriately with their peers. It is thus understandable that, in the school setting, students often engage in insults, banter, teasing, shoving, pushing, and gender-specific conduct that is upsetting to the students subjected to it. Damages are not available for simple acts of teasing and name-calling among school children, however, even where these comments target differences in gender. Rather, in the context of student-on-student harassment, damages are available only where the behavior is so severe, pervasive, and objectively offensive that it denies its victims the equal access to education that Title IX is designed to protect.

* * *

Moreover, the provision that the discrimination occur "under any education program or activity" suggests that the behavior be serious enough to have the systemic effect of denying the victim equal access to an educational program or activity. Although, in theory, a single instance of sufficiently severe one-on-one peer harassment could be said to have such an effect, we think it unlikely that Congress would have thought such behavior sufficient to rise to this level in light of the inevitability of student misconduct and the amount of litigation that would be invited by entertaining claims of official indifference to a single instance of one-on-one peer harassment. By limiting private damages actions to cases having a systemic effect on educational programs or activities, we reconcile the general principle that Title IX prohibits official indifference to known peer sexual harassment with the practical realities of responding to student behavior, realities that Congress could not have meant to be ignored. * * *

Applying this standard to the facts at issue here, we conclude that the Eleventh Circuit erred in dismissing petitioner's complaint. Petitioner alleges that her daughter was the victim of repeated acts of sexual harassment by G.F. over a 5–month period, and there are allegations in support of the conclusion that G.F.'s misconduct was severe, pervasive, and objectively offensive. The harassment was not only verbal; it included numerous acts of objectively offensive touching, and, indeed, G.F. ultimately pleaded guilty to criminal sexual misconduct. Moreover, the complaint alleges that there were multiple victims who were sufficiently disturbed by G.F.'s misconduct to seek an audience with the school principal. Further, petitioner contends that the harassment had a concrete, negative effect on her daughter's ability to receive an education. The complaint also suggests that petitioner may be able to show both actual knowledge and deliberate indifference on the part of the Board, which made no effort whatsoever either to investigate or to put an end to the harassment.

* * * Accordingly, the judgment of the United States Court of Appeals for the Eleventh Circuit is reversed, and the case is remanded for further proceedings consistent with this opinion.

NOTES ON SEXUAL HARASSMENT IN SCHOOLS

1. The cases discussed above show the Supreme Court developing the jurisprudence of private litigation under Title IX, a progression from establishing sexual harassment as discrimination under Title IX (*Franklin*, 1992), to adding the requirement of actual notice to an official with authority to

institute corrective measures and who responds with deliberate indifference in order to impose liability (*Gebser*, 1998), to establishing liability for peer harassment if there is actual notice to an official with authority who is deliberately indifferent and the harassment alleged is "so severe, pervasive, and objectively offensive that it can be said to deprive the victims of access to the educational opportunities or benefits provided by the school" (*Davis*, 1999). Do you think that the Court was correct to imply a private cause of action under Title IX in the first place? What would have been the effect if the Court had not recognized such a right? See Cannon v. University of Chicago, 441 U.S. 677 (1979). When a court implies a cause of action not explicitly provided for by statute, what kinds of problems occur? What does a plaintiff have to allege now to survive a motion to dismiss in cases involving (a) teacher and (b) peer sexual harassment in schools?

2. In *Davis*, even though the Court affirmed a cause of action for peer sexual harassment, it appeared to impose three highly restrictive elements: (a) the defendant must have actual notice and act with deliberate indifference; (b) liability will be limited to circumstances in which the school exercises substantial control over both the harasser and the context in which the known harassment occurs; and (c) the harassment has to be so severe, pervasive, and objectively offensive that it deprives the victim of access to the educational opportunities or benefits provided by the school. What kinds of problems do you anticipate with these restrictions?

Interestingly, the Court seemed to recognize potential problems with the third aspect, noting that "schools are unlike the adult workplace and that children may regularly interact in a manner that would be unacceptable among adults," and that "[d]amages are not available for simple acts of teasing and name-calling among school children * * * even where these comments target differences in gender." Is this standard too high to protect targets, usually girls? At a time when personalities and social interaction are being developed, should there be greater rather than lesser sensitivity to harassment?

When a North Carolina school disciplined a six-year-old boy for kissing a female classmate on the cheek, there was public criticism that the innocence of childhood was being punished. See, e.g., Dan Rollins, A Kiss Is Just a Kiss ... Or Is It?, Charleston Gazette, Dec. 4, 1996, Metro § at 5. What action should the school take in such a situation? What legal action, if any, was the school required to take? What more would you want to know before making a recommendation?

3. What does the *Davis* requirement of the educational institution's substantial control over both the harasser and context mean for colleges and universities? Is there a different standard for liability and damages? What about student interns who, as part of a college course, report for a learning experience at a placement outside of the university in order to obtain practical experience? Will a university be responsible for sexual harassment that occurs in that context? See Cynthia Grant Bowman & MaryBeth Lipp, Legal Limbo of the Student Intern: The Responsibility of Colleges and Universities to Protect Student Interns Against Sexual Harassment, 23 Harv. Women's L.J. 95 (2000).

4. In contrast to claims that sexual harassment is not really a problem, surveys of college students in the United States have revealed that between 30 percent and 70 percent of women undergraduates think they have been victims of some form of sexual harassment. See, e.g., Judith Berman Brandenburg, Confronting Sexual Harassment: What Schools and Colleges Can Do 15–16 (1997). For example, in relatively early studies, 30 percent of the female seniors at Berkeley in 1980 reported harassment by at least one male instructor, and over 43 percent of graduate and undergraduate female students at Iowa State University in 1983 believed they received undue attention from a professor. Elisabeth A. Keller, Consensual Amorous Relationships Between Faculty and Students: The Constitutional Right to Privacy, 15 J.C. & U.L. 21 (1988). In study released in 2006 by the American Association of University Women, 62 percent of college students said they had experienced sexual harassment, which the survey defined as "unwanted and unwelcome sexual behavior that interferes with your life." American Association of University Women, Drawing the Line: Sexual Harassment on Campus (2006). Moreover, the 2006 AAUW study found that only 7 percent of students reported sexual harassment to a faculty member or other college employee. Does a lack of reported complaints justify inaction in this area? Why or why not? What is the problem with a sexual harassment policy that is complaint-driven? What do you think of the AAUW's definition of harassment? Is it too narrow or too broad?

5. Other studies have addressed sexual harassment in primary and secondary schools. A 2000 study conducted by the American Association of University Women of students in grades eight through eleven found that 80 percent of the students surveyed said they had experienced some form of sexual harassment. AAUW Educational Foundation, Hostile Hallways: Bullying, Teasing, and Sexual Harassment in School 2–3 (2001). The study found that while three-quarters of students had experienced nonphysical types of harassment, more than half the students surveyed had experienced some form of physical harassment during their school lives with 33 percent of students experiencing such physical harassment often or occasionally. Sixty percent of students experienced some form of sexual harassment often or occasionally, with 25 percent of students experiencing it often. Id. at 3. In addition, a 2007 study found that 17.1 percent of girls in secondary school had experienced sexual harassment and 13.4 percent of boys had. International Network on School Bullying, Bullying Among Pupils at Primary and Secondary Schools (2007). Do these studies suggest that sexual harassment policies are necessary for kindergarten through twelfth grade? If so, should those policies have a greater emphasis on education about what sexual harassment is? Would you make other adjustments for young children?

6. Will the holding in *Davis* apply to college date rape? A woman is more likely to be the victim of a sexual assault while at college than at any other time in her life. Nonetheless, college age women are less likely to report their rapes than victims in other age groups; only one in ten campus rape victims reports her attack to the college administration. See Terry Nicole Steinberg, Rape on College Campuses: Reform Through Title IX, 18 J.C. & U.L. 39 (1991); see also Michelle J. Anderson, The Legacy of the Prompt Complaint Requirement, Corroboration Requirement, and Cautionary Instructions on

Campus Sexual Assault, 84 B. U. L. Rev. 945, 978 (2004) (reporting that "[a] 1997 Bureau of Justice Statistics random sample survey of 4,446 college-aged women found that, although about one in ten had been raped and another one in ten had experienced an attempted rape, fewer than five percent of those victims reported their rapes or attempted rapes to police or other campus authorities"). Can you make an argument under *Davis* that campus rape is sexual harassment violative of Title IX? What would you have to prove after *Davis*? Is campus rape sex discrimination? If a college investigates and punishes other campus crimes, but not rape, is it violating any provision of Title IX? Would it be necessary to amend Title IX to cover campus rape?

7. As early as the 1980 report by the National Advisory Council on Women's Educational Programs, researchers discovered that victims of sexual harassment in schools try to manage incidents on their own. Frank J. Till, National Advisory Council on Women's Educational Programs, Sexual Harassment: A Report on the Sexual Harassment of Students (1980). Many victims suffer in isolation; when they go "public," they express surprise to discover that they were not alone. Id. The report concluded:

> Why do victims keep silent or try to cope without invoking the authority of the school administration or the courts? Our responses and the work of almost all researchers indicate that there are several primary causes: fear that they—as victims—are somehow responsible for the incident, fear that they will not be believed, shame at being involved in any form of sexual incident, fear that by protesting they will call attention to their sex rather than to their work, a belief that no action will be taken, and fear of reprisals by the initiator and his colleagues.

Id. Do you think this "silencing" continues to this day? Why do you think victims of sexual harassment feel this way? Are they right in their assumptions? Are there similar responses by women to rape and sexual harassment in the workplace? See discussions in Chapters 4 and 9, respectively. Do you think the Court in *Gebser* and *Davis* was aware of this data when it imposed an actual notice standard before liability could be found? If so, what do you think motivated the requirement?

JANE GALLOP, FEMINIST ACCUSED OF SEXUAL HARASSMENT

31–35, 38–39 (1997).

Just last week, I was gossiping with a friend of mine about the department she teaches in. My friend, who is a feminist, confessed that she supported a junior colleague "even though he is a sexual harasser." Being pretty sensitive about the issue, I confronted her: "Is he really a sexual harasser, or does he just date students?"

She only meant that he dated students. Thanks to an administrative stint, my friend is very familiar with academic policy. Her casual use of the term "sexual harasser" was not aberrant but, in fact, represents a new sense of sexual harassment operative in the academy today.

Nowadays, most campus sexual-harassment policies include a section on "consensual relations" between teachers and students. These range from outright prohibitions of teacher-student relationships to warnings that a consensual relationship will not protect the teacher from the student's claims of harassment. Although the range suggests some uncertainty about the status of consensual relations, *their very inclusion within harassment policies* indicates that consensual relations are themselves considered a type of sexual harassment.

Sexual harassment has always been defined as *unwanted* sexual attention. But with this expansion into the realm of consensual relations, the concept can now encompass sexual attention that is reciprocated and very much welcome. This reconfigures the notion of harassment, suggesting that what is undesirable finally is not unwelcome attention but sexuality per se. Rather than some sexuality being harassing because of its unwanted nature, the inference is that sexuality is in and of itself harassment.

I have reason to be sensitive to this slippage in meaning. When I was accused of sexual harassment by two students, my relation to one of the complainants was deemed to be in violation of the university's policy on "consensual relations."

The two students charged me with classic quid pro quo sexual harassment. They both claimed that I had tried to get them to have sex with me and that when they rejected me, I had retaliated by withdrawing professional support (in one case with negative evaluations of work, in the other with a refusal to write letters of recommendation). The university's affirmative-action office conducted a lengthy investigation which resulted in a pretty accurate picture of my relations with these students. I had not tried to sleep with them, and all my professional decisions regarding them seemed clearly based in recognizable and consistent professional standards. No evidence of either "sexual advances" or "retaliations" was to be found.

What the investigation did find was that I indulged in so-called sexual behavior that was generally matched by similar behavior directed toward me on the part of the students. Not only did they participate in sexual banter with me, but they were just as likely to initiate it as I was. With one of the students, this banter was itself so minimal that the case was dismissed. But because my relationship with the other complainant was much more elaborate, it was determined that this mutual relationship of flirtatious banter and frank sexual discussion violated the consensual-relations policy.

The woman who conducted the investigation thought that because I had a consensual "sexual relation" with a student, I should be considered guilty of sexual harassment. My lawyer argued that if this were a consensual relation, I was at most guilty of violating a university policy, not of breaking the federal law prohibiting harassment. While campus harassment policies increasingly encompass consensual relations, the laws that make harassment illegal not only do not concern themselves with such mutual relations, but would seem specifically to exclude them.

This confrontation between my lawyer and the university investigator (both specialists in the area of discrimination) demonstrates the gap opening up between a general understanding of harassment as unwanted sexual attention and this new sense of harassment operating in the academy today—which includes all teacher-student sexual relations, regardless of the student's desires.

After the investigation had been conducted, but before the findings were released, the university hired a lawyer from off-campus to head the affirmative-action office. It was she who wrote the final determination of my case. This lawyer found no probable cause to believe that I had sexually harassed anyone. But her determination does go on to find me guilty of violating university policy because I engaged with one of my students in a "consensual amorous relation."

The document explains the choice of "amorous" (a word that appears in the policy) as denoting a relation that was "sexual" but did not involve sex acts. Much less serious than quid pro quo harassment (trading professional support for sexual favors), less serious than hostile-environment harassment (discrimination by emphasis on sexuality), less serious even than consensual *sexual* relations, the precise finding of "consensual amorous relations" is, in fact, the slightest infraction comprised within the policy.

It was as if I had been accused of "first-degree harassment," and the charge had been reduced to something like "fourth-degree harassment." The distinction between sexual harassment and consensual relations becomes not a difference in kind but merely a difference in degree. The university found no evidence of compromised professional judgments, or of discrimination, unwanted sexual attention, or any sort of harassment; it found I wasn't even having sex with students. But the investigation revealed that I did not in fact respect the boundary between the sexual and the intellectual, between the professional and the personal. It was as if the university, seeing what kind of relations I did have with students, felt I must be *in some way* guilty and was able, through this wrinkle in the policy, to find me *slightly guilty of sexual harassment.*

* * *

As a feminist, I am well aware of the ways women are compelled to sexual relations with men by forces that have nothing to do with our desire. And I see that students might be in a similar position with relation to teachers. But, as a feminist, I do not think the solution is to deny women or students the right to consent. Denying women the right to consent reinforces our status as objects rather than desiring subjects. That is why I believe the question of whether sexual advances are wanted is absolutely crucial.

Prohibition of consensual teacher-student relations is based on the assumption that when a student says yes she really means no. I cannot help but think that this proceeds from the same logic according to which when a woman says no she really means yes. The first assumption is protectionist; the second is the very logic of harassment. What harassment and protectionism have in common is precisely a refusal to credit women's desires. Common to both is the assumption that women do not know what we want, that someone else, in a position of greater knowledge and power, knows better.

ROBIN L. WEST, THE DIFFERENCE IN WOMEN'S HEDONIC LIVES: A PHENOMENOLOGICAL CRITIQUE OF FEMINIST LEGAL THEORY

3 Wis. Women's L. J. 108–111 (1987).

Sexual harassment of women students by male professors;12684;12684 is now recognized as a discriminatory injury and an actionable harm. And, although it constitutes a triumph of radical—not liberal—feminism, the prohibition of coercive, academic sexual harassment is nevertheless fully consistent with liberal and liberal feminist premises. The sex-for-a-grade that follows sexual harassment by a teacher of a student is characterized by liberals and liberal feminists as "coercive" because it is for a grade. Thus, whatever other reason might exist for prohibiting sex-for-grade transactions (and there are others), prohibition of these sexual transfers is fully consistent with liberal premises: the sex is a compensable assault because it is non-consensual.

This liberal feminist reconstruction of what was originally a more radical insight, I believe, rather significantly misses the mark. The greater damage done on college campuses, to women, by men, and through sex, is precisely what the liberal conception of academic sexual harassment definitionally excludes. Women who are faced with the choice of sleeping with the teacher to get the A they academically earned, or settling instead for a C, have undoubtedly been injured. But with all due respect for the harm done to those students, there is a deeper tragedy, a more profound loss, and a greater harm done daily in campus bedrooms, and these relatively astute women who "know what they should have gotten" are decidedly not the victims. The greater misery, I believe, is a product of the fully consensual and highly regarded romantic attachments of female graduate students and assistant professors, or undergraduates and research assistants. It is a mistake to infer, as the liberal feminist is inclined to do, from the wrongness of coercive, for-grade campus sex that consensual sex between male teachers and female students is therefore good. We cannot and should not so infer.

Smart male students view themselves as all sorts of things, including young intellectuals. A good male student will often attach himself to a brilliant professor, and will aspire to be like him. A smart female student who defines herself as "giving" might attach herself in this way to a brilliant professor and aspire to be like him. But it's not very likely. Unlike the male student, she is far more likely to be attracted to the brilliant professor, and aspire not to be like him, but to give herself to him. In her own way the "giving" female student will seek the recognition and praise which all students crave, by offering her sexuality. She may be intellectually gifted and she may perceive herself as such. But to the extent that the female student who is a "giving self" tries to define herself as an intellectual, she does so at the cost of internal war. For the definition of "self" as a sexually giving self rather than an academically demanding self is always there, always in competition, always available. For the female student, the intellectual self must fight the giving self, both in external and internal reality. The women who lose this battle have lost far more than the women who lost the A to which they were entitled, and so has the world.

All good students, male and female, love their professor's displays of intellectual brilliance; this is part of the joy of being a student. For the giving woman, however, that love is dangerous and ambiguous. Like male students, she craves recognition by her teachers. Her intellectual self craves recognition for intellectual work done. Her "giving self" though, craves the recognition that can only come through the teacher's acceptance of her gift of self. Consequently, male professors have a power which I suspect they often do not know they have, and when they do, they don't understand it. The male professor, as authority, is in a position to validate one or the other of the woman's conflicting self-definitions. If he reinforces the intellectual self, the woman's self-definition as intellectual is encouraged. If he reinforces the giving self, by accepting the woman's offered sexuality, the woman's internal war is over. The woman receives an authoritative pronouncement to the effect that her contribution to art, history, music or whatever will be in a form that she has always suspected and even hoped for—that it will be, at root, sexual. Her contribution will not be in the delivery of ideas—which after all will most likely not be the work of genius—but will be instead through her giving of herself to one whose intellectual contribution, unlike her own, may be. She is a jewel whose intellectual talents will be used to make all the more perfect her rare gift. The female student who loves intellect, and who is aware of herself as a sexual being, will not only consent to these romantic entanglements. She will crave them—fiercely, continuously, and with heart, mind and soul.

The pleasure to be had in such a relationship bears a disconcerting similarity to that of a cocaine high. Furthermore, both are damaging and addictive, although only cocaine is recognized as such. The woman feels pleasure in making a contribution to the culture she respects—even deeply respects—through a fusion of intellectuality and sexuality. It can feel like a mystical blend: a transcendental, transformative experience. Self-objectification can feel beautiful. It feels palpably meaningful to enrich the life of someone who is admirable and immersed in a discipline you value by merely being, and by giving what you are. The gift of self can feel more significant, universal, transcendental, and religious than the paltry competition for status in the seminar rooms in which one's (ex)-peers are engaged.

The pain of these relationships—as well as the damage they do—far exceeds their Cassandra-like high. The woman's self-respect will hit a new low with which she is probably unfamiliar and for which she is totally unprepared, for at least three reasons. First, for a life of such servitude to feel of value, the man being served must be perceived as truly superior. The more skeptical the woman becomes of the man's genius, the more she must downgrade her own potential in order to maintain what is really central to these relationships—the distance between them. Whatever intellectual insecurities she brought with her are multiplied. This is a very bad way to feel about oneself. Second, the life of servitude to genius is likely to be a lazy, privileged, and pampered life. The woman will lose whatever employable skills she once had. She becomes unable to support herself. A given, empty self will not have the self-possession it takes to work. This sort of self-imposed, consensual unemployability is debilitating and infantilizing. This is also a bad way to feel about oneself. And finally, the woman who is using the relationship as a means of entrance into a discipline is being manipulative, and knows it. This too is not a good way to feel about oneself. The cumulative effect is a smothering blanket of self-contempt. You lose your respect for your intelligence, your competency in the world, and your moral character, and all for good reason: you have lost yourself.

This is not a subtle point, nor an invisible loss. "Falling-in-love" with high school teachers, college professors, or research assistants really does destroy the productivity, the careers, the earning potential, and eventually the self respect of many gifted women. Smart women drop out of high school, college and graduate school (and pretty women are at highest risk) to date, to marry, to help, and to serve those they perceive as intellectual giants. Eventually they learn boredom, the weariness of inactivity, and the self-contempt of nonproductivity. But in spite of its incredible familiarity, most academic men and many academic women do not see this as a harm at all, and if they do see it as a harm, they do not see it as worth discussing. This ignorance must be ideological. My guess is that we cannot see the harm of these consensual relationships to precisely the degree to which we have adopted the blinders of liberalism. It is a harm caused not by coercive, occasional acts, but by the way we have defined the self that consents to the non-coercive relationships in which we engage. It is a harm that a liberal legal regime which resolutely regards the giving of consent as the infallible proxy of an increase in self-regarded and self-assessed value cannot possibly address.

School Sexual Harassment Policies

[The following are portions of various sexual harassment policies that have been enacted at different universities at different times.]

UNIVERSITY OF CHICAGO

Sexual advances, requests for sexual favors, or sexually-directed remarks constitute harassment when:

1. submission to or rejection of such conduct is made, explicitly or implicitly, a basis for an academic or employment decision, or a term or condition of either; or

2. such conduct directed against an individual persists despite its rejection.

3. such conduct has the purpose or effect of unreasonably interfering with an individual's academic or professional performance by creating what a reasonable person would view as an intimidating or hostile environment.

A person's subjective belief that behavior is offensive, intimidating or hostile does not make that behavior sexual harassment. The behavior must be objectively unreasonable. Moreover, expression occurring in an academic, educational or research context is broadly protected by academic freedom. Such expression will not constitute sexual harassment unless (in addition to satisfying the above definition) it is targeted at a specific person or persons, is abusive and serves no bona fide academic purpose.

ANTIOCH COLLEGE FACULTY-STUDENT CONSENSUAL SEXUAL RELATIONS POLICY

The faculty-student relationship, however warm or caring, inherently involves disproportionate power and influence on one side and is thus liable to abuse. A sexual relationship between a faculty member and a student can not only exploit this imbalance but also distort and inhibit the learning environment. For these reasons, it is the agreement of the Antioch College faculty that sexual relationships between Antioch College faculty members and Antioch College students are unacceptable and constitute professional misconduct.

DEPAUL UNIVERSITY EXAMPLES OF SEXUAL/GENDER HARASSMENT

1. Sexual harassment includes, but is not limited to, any unwelcome sexual advances, direct or indirect requests for sexual favors and other verbal or physical conduct of a sexual nature when: submission to or rejection of such conduct is made or is threatened to be made, either explicitly or implicitly, a term or condition of instruction, employment or participation in other University activity; submission to or rejection of such conduct by an individual is used or is threatened to be used as a basis for evaluation in making academic or employment decisions affecting that individual; or such conduct has the intent, purpose or can reasonably be expected to have the effect of interfering with an individual's academic or professional performance or advancement, or creating an intimidating, hostile or offensive educational living or working environment.

2. The University's Sexual Harassment Policy and Procedures also apply to gender harassment. Gender harassment includes verbal or physical harassment which is based on the person's gender but which is not sexual in nature.

3. It may be a violation of this policy for any administrative, faculty or staff member of the University to offer or request sexual favors, make

sexual advances or engage in sexual conduct, consensual or otherwise, while the other individual involved is enrolled in the faculty member's class or is working under the supervision of, or subject to evaluation by, the administrative person, faculty or staff member. In such circumstances, consent may not be considered a defense against a charge of sexual harassment in any proceeding conducted under the University's Sexual Harassment Policy. The determination of what constitutes sexual harassment depends upon the specific facts and the context in which the conduct occurs.

NOTES ON SEXUAL HARASSMENT IN HIGHER EDUCATION

1. Which of the sexual harassment policies excerpted above is best, and why? In particular, answer the following questions:

(a) *Conduct prohibited.* What behaviors do the policies cover? Do they all cover both quid pro quo (i.e., sex in exchange for favors) and hostile or offensive environment situations? Do you think most people know what conduct "has the purpose or effect of unreasonably interfering with an individual's academic or professional performance by creating what a reasonable person would view as an intimidating or hostile environment?" This language in the University of Chicago policy tracks that of the Equal Employment Opportunity Commission's Guidelines on Sexual Harassment in Employment. 29 C.F.R. § 1604.11 (1992). Is it preferable to be very specific about the conduct prohibited? Why or why not? What are "sexually-directed remarks" as referred to by the Chicago policy? Is it necessary to give some examples to educate people governed by such policies? Must the remarks be repeated in order to violate the Chicago policy?

(b) *Harassment by peers.* Do all the policies cover harassment by peers? After *Davis*, shouldn't a policy address students harassing other students? The explicit, or implicit, reason for sexual harassment policies is to protect the victim from the abuse of the harasser's power or authority over her. Is it a necessary element that the harasser be in a position of power over the victim? Do male students have power over female students? What is the nature of such power?

(c) *Consensual relationships.* The Antioch College policy prohibits sexual relationships between faculty and students, even those presumably "consensual." Should consensual sexual relationships between teachers and students be prohibited? If so, under what circumstances? For what reasons? Should such relationships be barred only if the student is under the direct supervision of the faculty member? What about future reliance on the faculty member for references and the like? Is there always a disparity of power between teacher and student? If so, can there be true "consent"? What if the sexual relationship preceded the teacher-student relationship? Even if the teacher is not in an immediate position of authority over the student, is there a possibility that a student's judgment may be compromised by her feelings of trust and respect? What is the impact on other students if a peer has a sexual relationship with a teacher? Do faculty members have a right of privacy to have a sexual relationship with whomever they wish, including students? See

Paul M. Secunda, Getting to the Nexus of the Matter: A Sliding Scale Approach to Faculty–Student Consensual Relationship Policies in Higher Education, 55 Syracuse L. Rev. 55 (2004) (arguing that professors are entitled to private consensual relationships with students as long as the effects of those relationships do not spill over into the academic arena in ways that are harmful to the university); Margaret H. Mack, Regulating Sexual Relationships Between Faculty and Students, 6 Mich. J. Gender & L. 79 (1999) (arguing that sexual relationships should be prohibited as long as faculty have supervisory or evaluative control over a student); Gary E. Elliott, Consensual Relationships and the Constitution: A Case of Liberty Denied, 6 Mich. J. Gender & L. 47 (1999) (arguing that professors should be as free from regulation in their sexual relations with students as they are in their speech rights); Elisabeth A. Keller, Consensual Amorous Relationships Between Faculty and Students: The Constitutional Right to Privacy, 15 J.C. & U.L. 21 (1988) (contending that the constitutional right to privacy applies to consensual amorous relationships between faculty and students at public colleges and universities).

2. Jane Gallop and Robin West view consensual teacher-student relationships in starkly different terms. Gallop sees such relationships as intellectually stimulating while West sees them as intellectually stifling for the students involved. Gallop then adopts a libertarian approach to such relationships while West adopts a paternalistic approach to them. With whom do you agree? Is it possible to have truly free and voluntary sexual relationships between unequals? How would consensual teacher-student relationships be analyzed under the various feminist theories explored in Chapter 3? What kind of sexual harassment policies would Gallop and West each favor?

3. What is the most appropriate legal description of the teacher-student relationship? Is it one of fiduciary and beneficiary? What legal obligation does that characterization imply? Or is the relationship more like professional and client? Are sexual relationships appropriate under either characterization? Why or why not? See Caroline Forell, What's Wrong With Faculty–Student Sex? The Law School Context, 47 J. Legal Educ. 47 (1997); Ronna Greff Schneider, Sexual Harassment and Higher Education, 65 Tex. L. Rev. 525, 552–53 (1987).

4. Does your school have a sexual harassment policy? Is it adequate in your view? If your school fails to issue a policy or grievance mechanisms to address sexual harassment complaints, can you assert a viable claim under Title IX after *Gebser*? Pursuant to its authority under Title IX, the Department of Education has issued a regulation requiring schools receiving federal funds to "adopt and publish grievance procedures providing for prompt and equitable resolution of student and employee complaints alleging any action which would be prohibited by this part [proscribing sex discrimination]." 45 C.F.R. § 86.8(b) (1992).

5. Draft what you think would be an ideal sexual harassment policy for your institution. Be sure to consider the role of education and the need for an enforcement mechanism in constructing the policy, as well as the problem of retaliation. Under guidelines proposed by Women Organized Against Sexual Harassment, a student group at Berkeley, an adequate sexual harassment

policy must: "(1) acknowledge sexual harassment as sex discrimination, not as isolated misconduct; (2) refer to a full range of harassment from subtle innuendos to assault; (3) refer to ways in which the context of open and mutual academic exchange is polluted by sexual harassment; and (4) refer to sexual harassment as the imposition of sexual advances by a person in a position of authority." Phyllis L. Crocker, An Analysis of University Definitions of Sexual Harassment, in Reconstructing the Academy: Women's Education and Women's Studies 24, 35 (Elizabeth Minnich, Jean O'Barr & Rachel Rosenfeld, eds. 1988). Do you agree with these guidelines? Are they too expansive or limited?

6. Do sexual harassment policies infringe on academic freedom of speech by limiting the exploration of ideas in the classroom? If so, how should we determine which concern should be superior? Should the answer be determined by which group is hurt more if its right is denied? Who is to decide?

G. HATE SPEECH REGULATION

Some universities responded to the incidents of hostility towards students of color and women students at the end of the last century by adopting "hate speech" codes. Following a series of racial incidents at the University of Wisconsin, that school prohibited students from making remarks that demeaned others and created a hostile or intimidating educational environment. Within two years the regulation had been invoked 35 times. In October of 1991, however, a federal judge declared the rule unconstitutionally overbroad and unduly vague.[79] Two years earlier another federal district court struck down a campus hate speech code in Doe v. University of Michigan on the same grounds.[80] In 1993, Central Michigan University's speech code was declared unconstitutional, and Stanford University's rule was thrown out in 1995.[81] Because First Amendment free speech concerns are only applicable when state action is present, these decisions are limited to public institutions; private colleges and universities are normally free to issue and enforce hate speech regulations without running afoul of the First Amendment.[82]

After the court challenges, many public colleges and universities drafted new hate speech policies which address the constitutional issues.

79. UWM Post, Inc. v. Board of Regents of Univ. of Wisconsin, 774 F.Supp. 1163, 1164, 1167, 1181 (E.D.Wis.1991).

80. 721 F.Supp. 852 (E.D.Mich. 1989) (holding that code was unconstitutionally overbroad both on its face and as applied and unduly vague).

81. Dambrot v. Central Mich. Univ., 839 F.Supp. 477, 481 (E.D.Mich. 1993) (overturning a campus rule that prohibited any "verbal * * * behavior that subjects an individual to an intimidating, hostile or offensive educational * * * environment by demeaning or slurring individuals * * * because of their racial or ethnic affiliation"); Corry v. Leland Stanford Jr. Univ., No. 740309 (Cal. Sup.Ct. filed Feb. 27, 1995) (holding that even though policy was restricted to "fighting words," it was an impermissible content-based regulation because it proscribed only fighting words "based on sex, race, color and the like"), available at http://www.ithaca.edu/faculty/cduncan/265/corryvstanford.htm (last updated Sept. 2, 2010).

82. Stanford's speech code was invalidated as a violation of a California statute applying the First Amendment to private universities. See Burton Caine, The Trouble with "Fighting Words": Chaplinsky v. New Hampshire is a Threat to First Amendment Values and Should be Overruled, 88 Marq. L. Rev. 441, 528 (2004).

These revised speech codes are carefully tailored to satisfy the fighting words doctrine, enunciated by the Supreme Court in Chaplinsky v. New Hampshire, 315 U.S. 568, 62 S.Ct. 766, 86 L.Ed. 1031 (1942), as modified by Cohen v. California, which requires the fighting words to be "directed to the person of the hearer," 403 U.S. 15, 20, 91 S.Ct. 1780, 1785, 29 L.Ed.2d 284, 291 (1971).[83]

These attempts to regulate racist speech on school campuses are not unique; the international community has long recognized the real harms caused by racist speech propaganda and has chosen to outlaw it. The members of the United Nations have adopted an International Convention on the Elimination of All Forms of Racial Discrimination, which requires states to criminalize racial hate messages. Additionally, the United Kingdom, Canada, Australia and New Zealand all have laws restricting racist speech, leaving the United States alone among major common law jurisdictions in its complete tolerance of such speech.[84]

This section first looks at the Supreme Court's decision concerning hate crimes, and then at two authors who address what they view as the real harms that result from hate speech on college campuses.

R.A.V. v. CITY OF ST. PAUL

Supreme Court of the United States, 1992.
505 U.S. 377, 112 S.Ct. 2538, 120 L.Ed.2d 305.

JUSTICE SCALIA delivered the opinion of the Court.

In the predawn hours of June 21, 1990, petitioner and several other teenagers allegedly assembled a crudely-made cross by taping together broken chair legs. They then allegedly burned the cross inside the fenced yard of a black family that lived across the street from the house where petitioner was staying. * * * [St. Paul charged the juvenile petitioner under the St. Paul Bias–Motivated Crime Ordinance, which provides:]

> "Whoever places on public or private property a symbol, object, appellation, characterization or graffiti, including, but not limited to, a burning cross or Nazi swastika, which one knows or has reasonable grounds to know arouses anger, alarm or resentment in others on the basis of race, color, creed, religion or gender commits disorderly conduct and shall be guilty of a misdemeanor."

* * *

> [The Supreme Court of Minnesota interpreted this statute as proscribing only "fighting words," a category of words the Supreme

---

83. See Jon. B. Gould, The Precedent that Wasn't: College Hate Speech Codes and the Two Faces of Legal Compliance, 35 Law and Soc'y Rev. 345 (2001).

84. Mari J. Matsuda, Public Response to Racist Speech: Considering the Victim's Story, 87 Mich. L. Rev. 2320, 2341 (1989). The Convention was unanimously adopted by the General Assembly on December 21, 1965, and entered into force on January 4, 1969. The U.S. was an early signatory but, although President Carter submitted the convention to the Senate for ratification in 1978, the Senate has not yet done so. Id. at 2345, 2346–48. See also Richard Delgado, Campus Antiracism Rules: Constitutional Narratives in Collision, 85 Nw. U. L. Rev. 343, 364–71 (1991).

Court had in the past held could be proscribed because "by their very utterance [they] inflict injury or tend to incite an immediate breach of the peace." Chaplinsky v. New Hampshire, 315 U.S. 568, 572 (1942). The Supreme Court was, of course, bound by the narrowing interpretation of the Minnesota Supreme Court.]

The First Amendment generally prevents government from proscribing speech, or even expressive conduct, because of disapproval of the ideas expressed. Content-based regulations are presumptively invalid. From 1791 to the present, however, our society, like other free but civilized societies, has permitted restrictions upon the content of speech in a few limited areas, which are "of such slight social value as a step to truth that any benefit that may be derived from them is clearly outweighed by the social interest in order and morality." We have recognized that "the freedom of speech" referred to by the First Amendment does not include a freedom to disregard these traditional limitations. Our decisions since the 1960's have narrowed the scope of the traditional categorical exceptions for defamation, and for obscenity, but a limited categorical approach has remained an important part of our First Amendment jurisprudence.

* * *

Our cases surely do not establish the proposition that the First Amendment imposes no obstacle whatsoever to regulation of particular instances of * * * proscribable expression [such as "fighting words"], so that the government "may regulate [them] freely." That would mean that a city council could enact an ordinance prohibiting only those legally obscene works that contain criticism of the city government or, indeed, that do not include endorsement of the city government. Such a simplistic, all-or-nothing-at-all approach to First Amendment protection is at odds with common sense and with our jurisprudence as well. * * *

Even the prohibition against content discrimination that we assert the First Amendment requires is not absolute. It applies differently in the context of proscribable speech [such as "fighting words"] than in the area of fully protected speech. The rationale of the general prohibition, after all, is that content discrimination "rais[es] the specter that the Government may effectively drive certain ideas or viewpoints from the marketplace." But content discrimination among various instances of a class of proscribable speech often does not pose this threat.

When the basis for the content discrimination consists entirely of the very reason the entire class of speech at issue is proscribable, no significant danger of idea or viewpoint discrimination exists. Such a reason, having been adjudged neutral enough to support exclusion of the entire class of speech from First Amendment protection, is also neutral enough to form the basis of distinction within the class. To illustrate: A State might choose to prohibit only that obscenity which is the most patently offensive *in its prurience—i.e.,* that which involves the most lascivious displays of sexual activity. But it may not prohibit, for example, only that obscenity which includes offensive *political messages.* And the Federal

Government can criminalize only those threats of violence that are directed against the President, * * *—since the reasons why threats of violence are outside the First Amendment (protecting individuals from the fear of violence, from the disruption that fear engenders, and from the possibility that the threatened violence will occur) have special force when applied to the person of the President. But the Federal Government may not criminalize only those threats against the President that mention his policy on aid to inner cities. * * *

Another valid basis for according differential treatment to even a content-defined subclass of proscribable speech is that the subclass happens to be associated with particular "secondary effects" of the speech, so that the regulation is "*justified* without reference to the content of the ... speech." A State could, for example, permit all obscene live performances except those involving minors. * * *

Applying these principles to the St. Paul ordinance, we conclude that, even as narrowly construed by the Minnesota Supreme Court, the ordinance is facially unconstitutional. Although the phrase in the ordinance, "arouses anger, alarm or resentment in others," has been limited by the Minnesota Supreme Court's construction to reach only those symbols or displays that amount to "fighting words," the remaining, unmodified terms make clear that the ordinance applies only to "fighting words" that insult, or provoke violence, "on the basis of race, color, creed, religion or gender." Displays containing abusive invective, no matter how vicious or severe, are permissible unless they are addressed to one of the specified disfavored topics. Those who wish to use "fighting words" in connection with other ideas—to express hostility, for example, on the basis of political affiliation, union membership, or homosexuality—are not covered. The First Amendment does not permit St. Paul to impose special prohibitions on those speakers who express views on disfavored subjects.

In its practical operation, moreover, the ordinance goes even beyond mere content discrimination, to actual viewpoint discrimination. Displays containing some words—odious racial epithets, for example—would be prohibited to proponents of all views. But "fighting words" that do not themselves invoke race, color, creed, religion, or gender—aspersions upon a person's mother, for example—would seemingly be usable *ad libitum* in the placards of those arguing *in favor* of racial, color, etc. tolerance and equality, but could not be used by that speaker's opponents. One could hold up a sign saying, for example, that all "anti-Catholic bigots" are misbegotten; but not that all "papists" are, for that would insult and provoke violence "on the basis of religion." St. Paul has no such authority to license one side of a debate to fight freestyle, while requiring the other to follow Marquis of Queensbury Rules.

* * *

Despite the fact that the Minnesota Supreme Court and St. Paul acknowledge that the ordinance is directed at expression of group hatred, Justice Stevens [in a concurring opinion] suggests that this "fundamentally misreads'' the ordinance. It is directed, he claims, not to speech of a particular content, but to particular ''injur[ies]'' that are ''qualitatively different'' from other injuries. This is word-play. What makes the anger, fear, sense of dishonor, etc., produced by violation of this ordinance distinct from the anger, fear, sense of dishonor, etc., produced by other fighting words is nothing other than the fact that it is caused by a distinctive idea, conveyed by a distinctive message. The First Amendment cannot be evaded that easily. It is obvious that the symbols which will arouse ''anger, alarm or resentment in others on the basis of race, color, creed, religion or gender'' are those symbols that communicate a message of hostility based on one of these characteristics. * * *

Finally, St. Paul and its *amici* defend the conclusion of the Minnesota Supreme Court that, even if the ordinance regulates expression based on hostility towards its protected ideological content, this discrimination is nonetheless justified because it is narrowly tailored to serve compelling state interests. Specifically, they assert that the ordinance helps to ensure the basic human rights of members of groups that have historically been subjected to discrimination, including the right of such group members to live in peace where they wish. We do not doubt that these interests are compelling, and that the ordinance can be said to promote them. But the ''danger of censorship'' presented by a facially content-based statute, requires that that weapon be employed only where it is ''*necessary* to serve the asserted [compelling] interest.'' The existence of adequate content-neutral alternatives thus ''undercut[s] significantly'' any defense of such a statute, casting considerable doubt on the government's protestations that ''the asserted justification is in fact an accurate description of the purpose and effect of the law.'' The dispositive question in this case, therefore, is whether content discrimination is reasonably necessary to achieve St. Paul's compelling interests; it plainly is not. An ordinance not limited to the favored topics, for example, would have precisely the same beneficial effect. In fact the only interest distinctively served by the content limitation is that of displaying the city council's special hostility towards the particular biases thus singled out. That is precisely what the First Amendment forbids. The politicians of St. Paul are entitled to express that hostility—but not through the means of imposing unique limitations upon speakers who (however benightedly) disagree.

NOTES ON R.A.V.

1. Can you find support for upholding the Minnesota statute in the language in *Chaplinsky* that fighting words can be proscribed because ''by their very utterance [they] inflict injury or tend to incite an immediate breach of the peace''? 315 U.S. at 572, 62 S.Ct. at 769. Why didn't the Court use this language to uphold the Minnesota law?

2. Justice Scalia seems confident that the state is unlikely to be discriminating on the basis of viewpoint when ''the basis for the content discrimination consists entirely of the very reason the entire class of speech at issue is

proscribable." He illustrates this point by noting that a state can "prohibit only that obscenity which is most patently offensive in its prurience." Do you think that such regulation is likely to be neutral with respect to viewpoint? Think, for example, of the effect of such an approach, when applied by jurors, on gay or lesbian erotica relative to straight erotica.

3. Can you describe the distinction Justice Scalia sees between threats of violence against the President, which can be singled out from other threats of violence and punished more severely, and threats of violence against a member of a specific racial group on the basis of race, which cannot? Would it matter that a threat of violence was targeted against women rather than against a racial group? What are the implications of this reasoning for (a) the MacKinnon–Dworkin ordinance, discussed above in Chapter 4, or (b) the hostile environment prong of a sexual harassment cause of action, discussed in Chapter 9? Does Scalia consider the Title VII limits on sex discrimination in employment to be different from the statute at issue in *R.A.V.*? How is the harassing-environment prong of sexual harassment different from the St. Paul ordinance?

4. Justice Scalia seems to see the *R.A.V.* outcome as necessary to protect unpopular speakers from the tyranny of the majority: "majority preferences must be expressed in some fashion other than silencing speech on the basis of content." Is it possible that Scalia's decision is in fact counter-majoritarian in a more basic sense, i.e., it tends to support the power of white men, a minority group? How might a decision like *R.A.V.* support the status quo, tending to perpetuate the subordinate status of women and racial minorities?

5. Under the Supreme Court's approach, are the costs and benefits of the Free Speech provision of the First Amendment borne by different groups? Are the groups harmed most by racist and sexist speech as likely to have their own speech effectively protected by the First Amendment? Are they likely to have less power in the private arena, e.g., control of media, or in the public arena? See Richard Delgado & Jean Stefancic, Understanding Words that Wound (2004); Chris Demaske, Modern Power and the First Amendment: Reassessing Hate Speech, 9 Comm. L. & Pol'y 273 (2004); Helen Ginger Berrigan, "Speaking Out" About Hate Speech, 48 Loy. L. Rev. 1 (2002); Frederick Schauer, The Political Incidence of the Free Speech Principle, 64 U. Colo. L. Rev. 935 (1993). Consider the reasons for, and effects of, movies in which 80 percent to 85 percent of the characters are male and "[t]he few female roles are dominated by three major images: 'child temptress' (as in the film 'Crush'), 'commodity' ('Honeymoon in Vegas') and 'psycho-killer' ('Hand That Rocks The Cradle')." See Merilee S. Novinson, Stop Feeding the Exploitation–Film Monster, Chi.Trib., May 9, 1993, § 6, at 11.

6. Why is the constitutional commitment to racial and sexual equality irrelevant in cases involving speech? Given that the Fourteenth Amendment (containing the equality commitment) was enacted after the First Amendment, could you argue that the latter should be read in light of the former? How might such a reading affect the analysis in a case like *R.A.V.*? See, e.g., Akhil Reed Amar, Comment: The Case of the Missing Amendments: R.A.V. v. City of St. Paul, 106 Harv. L. Rev. 124 (1992); Akhil Reed Amar, The Bill of Rights and the Fourteenth Amendment, 101 Yale L.J. 1193 (1992). Would you

agree with such an approach? See also Morrison Torrey, Thoughts About Why the First Amendment Operates to Stifle the Freedom and Equality of a Subordinated Majority, 21 Women's Rts. Rptr. 25 (1999) (arguing that both the Fourteenth and Nineteenth Amendments should outweigh the First Amendment since the later amendments represent participation by a more inclusive group in the democratic process).

7. Justice Scalia seems to believe that government is unlikely to suppress speech it considers undesirable by restrictions on conduct rather than speech. Is this equally true for all groups? Would it be true for lesbians and gay men? Are some government rules—such as the military ban on lesbians and gay soldiers—designed to silence them? In recent debates, much of the support for the ban is from those who wish not to exclude valuable soldiers from service, but to keep them quiet. Why does the ban look like a restriction on conduct rather than speech (or expressive conduct, which is protected as speech)?

8. MacKinnon argues that there are speech issues on both sides of the pornography debate, and that the speech of pornographers silences women (see pornography section in Chapter 4). Could a similar point be made about cross burnings? Isn't part of the message of burning a cross in the yard of an African American family that they should move away without complaint, that they most definitely should *not* continue challenging the status quo by either speech or action? Why doesn't Justice Scalia see the burning cross as an attempt to stop political action and to silence political speech of African Americans who would change the status quo? If you do see speech issues on both sides of the case, how would you resolve them? Why does the Court analyze the case as though speech issues arise only on one side?

CHARLES R. LAWRENCE III, IF HE HOLLERS LET HIM GO: REGULATING RACIST SPEECH ON CAMPUS

1990 Duke L.J. 431, 452–55.

The fighting words doctrine anticipates that the verbal "slap in the face" of insulting words will provoke a violent response with a resulting breach of the peace. When racial insults are hurled at minorities, the response may be silence or flight rather than a fight, but the preemptive effect on further speech is just as complete as with fighting words. Women and minorities often report that they find themselves speechless in the face of discriminatory verbal attacks. This inability to respond is not the result of oversensitivity among these groups, as some individuals who oppose protective regulation have argued. Rather, it is the product of several factors, all of which reveal the non-speech character of the initial preemptive verbal assault. The first factor is that the visceral emotional response to personal attack precludes speech. Attack produces an instinctive, defensive psychological reaction. Fear, rage, shock, and flight all interfere with any reasoned response. Words like "nigger," "kike," and "faggot" produce physical symptoms that temporarily disable the victim, and the perpetrators often use these words with the intention of producing this effect. Many victims do not find words of response until well after the assault when the cowardly assaulter has departed.

A second factor that distinguishes racial insults from protected speech is the preemptive nature of such insults—the words by which to respond to such verbal attacks may never be forthcoming because speech is usually an inadequate response. When one is personally attacked with words that denote one's subhuman status and untouchability, there is little (if anything) that can be said to redress either the emotional or reputational injury. This is particularly true when the message and meaning of the epithet resonates with beliefs widely held in society. This preservation of widespread beliefs is what makes the face-to-face racial attack more likely to preempt speech than are other fighting words. The racist name-caller is accompanied by a cultural chorus of equally demeaning speech and symbols.

The subordinated victim of fighting words also is silenced by her relatively powerless position in society. Because of the significance of power and position, the categorization of racial epithets as "fighting words" provides an inadequate paradigm; instead one must speak of their "functional equivalent." The fighting words doctrine presupposes an encounter between two persons of relatively equal power who have been acculturated to respond to face-to-face insults with violence. The fighting words doctrine is a paradigm based on a white male point of view.[85] In most situations, minorities correctly perceive that a violent response to fighting words will result in a risk to their own life and limb. Since minorities are likely to lose the fight, they are forced to remain silent and submissive. This response is most obvious when women submit to sexually assaultive speech or when the racist name-caller is in a more powerful position—the boss on the job or the mob. Certainly, we do not expect the black women crossing the Wisconsin campus to turn on their tormentors and pummel them. Less obvious, but just as significant, is the effect of pervasive racial and sexual violence and coercion on individual members of subordinated groups who must learn the survival techniques of suppressing and disguising rage and anger at an early age.

NOTES ON HATE SPEECH AND HATE SPEECH CODES

1. Is the following hate speech code constitutional?

Speech or other expression constitutes harassment by personal vilification if it:

(a) is intended to insult or stigmatize an individual or a small number of individuals on the basis of their sex, race, color, handicap, religion, sexual orientation, or national and ethnic origin; and

(b) is addressed directly to the individual or individuals whom it insults or stigmatizes; and

---

85. The fighting words doctrine captures the "macho" quality of male discourse. It is accepted, justifiable, and even praiseworthy when "real men" respond to personal insult with violence.

* * * The fighting words doctrine's responsiveness to this "male" stance in the world and its blindness to the cultural experience of women is another example of how "neutral" principles of law often reflect the values of those who are dominant. * * *

> (c) makes use of insulting or "fighting" words or non-verbal symbols.
>
> In the context of discriminatory harassment by personal vilification, insulting or "fighting" words or non-verbal symbols are those "which by their very utterance inflict injury or tend to incite to an immediate breach of the peace," and which are commonly understood to convey direct and visceral hatred or contempt for human beings on the basis of their sex, race, color, handicap, religion, sexual orientation, or national and ethnic origin.

If you believe this policy to be unconstitutional, can you amend it to make it constitutional? How? Does the policy cover what teachers might say in the classroom, or does it only regulate peer behavior? Should that make a difference? Is it restricted to face-to-face insults? What about academic freedom?

2. How can the harms of hate speech be established? Is the harm of hate speech more persuasive when it is put into context, i.e., when we are told the stories of specific incidents and how the victims felt? Richard Delgado writes about incidents at eight selected campuses in his article, Campus Antiracism Rules: Constitutional Narratives in Collision, 85 Nw. U. L. Rev. 343, 349–58 (1991). Would litigants be more effective if they did this type of "storytelling?" See also Cynthia Grant Bowman, Street Harassment and the Informal Ghettoization of Women, 106 Harv. L. Rev. 517 (1993).

3. What exactly are the harms of hate speech in the campus setting? It has been suggested that hate speech disrupts an equal learning environment:

> when, for example, black students hear that they "don't belong in classrooms, they belong hanging from trees," when an Asian student is told, "Die, Chink. Hostile Americans want your yellow hide," or when women students are described as "fat housewives." Such demeaning expression injures self-image, undermines self-confidence, and alienates the victimized student from her school. Hate speech hinders learning and participation in and out of class. It may also frustrate efforts to attract minority faculty and students.

First Amendment—Racist and Sexist Expression on Campus—Court Strikes Down University Limits on Hate Speech.—*Doe v. University of Michigan,* 721 F.Supp. 852 (E.D.Mich.1989), 103 Harv. L. Rev. 1397, 1399–1400 (1990). Can you identify any other harms? Have you ever been targeted for "hate speech"? If so, how did you feel?

4. Delgado also argues that how you frame the issue determines the outcome: Is it a First Amendment problem of free speech or a Fourteenth Amendment problem of equality? Delgado, above note 2, at 345–46. He summarizes the conflict as follows:

> One often hears that the problem of campus antiracism rules is that of balancing free speech and equality. But more is at stake. Each side wants not merely to have the balance struck in its favor; each wants to impose its own understanding of what is at stake. Minority protectors see the injury of one who has been subject to a racial assault as not a mere isolated event, but as part of an interrelated series of acts, by which persons of color are subordinated, and which will follow the victim wherever she goes. First Amendment defenders see the wrong of silencing

> the racist as much more than a momentary inconvenience: protection of his right to speak is part of the never-ending vigilance necessary to preserve freedom of expression in a society that is too prone to balance it away.

Id. at 347–48. Is there any way to reconcile the First and Fourteenth Amendments in this context? Is there the same conflict in regulating pornography? Is pornography a form of "hate speech"?

5. Do you think hate speech codes are a good idea? Haven't universities always regulated speech? Aren't the following regulations of speech essentially less explicit classroom speech codes: grades, syllabi, reading and writing assignments, and unspoken understandings about what is relevant to discussions? What, if any, are the differences? Why do hate speech codes look like censorship to many, resulting in successful First Amendment challenges, though there never have been First Amendment "censorship" challenges to the assignment of "the male curriculum" or the exclusion of women's perspectives or issues from academic courses? See Mary E. Becker, Conservative Free Speech and the Uneasy Case for Judicial Review, 64 U. Colo. L. Rev. 975 (1993).

Is the problem that speech codes make universities' expectations of students explicit? Intelligent discussions are possible only if there is a shared understanding of what is relevant and worthwhile. Incoherent diatribes, for example, are understood as out of place in the classroom because they are inconsistent with worthwhile intellectual discussions in an atmosphere conducive to learning. Why aren't speech codes, even in public institutions, just explicit statements of such understanding and judgments, at least when applicable to classroom discussions? A student who repeatedly engages in incoherent diatribes might receive a low grade for classroom participation or a reprimand from the teacher, but would certainly be "disciplined" in some manner, although that word probably would not be used. Is this censorship?

6. Would the proponents of the various feminist theories explored in Chapter 3 support hate speech regulation? On what grounds would each support or oppose it?

7. Where do civil libertarians stand on this issue? Charles R. Lawrence III, expresses his view of this dilemma:

> But I am deeply concerned about the role that many civil libertarians have played, or the roles we have failed to play, in the continuing, real-life struggle through which we define the community in which we live. I fear that by framing the debate as we have—as one in which the liberty of free speech is in conflict with the elimination of racism—we have advanced the cause of racial oppression and have placed the bigot on the moral high ground, fanning the rising flames of racism. Above all, I am troubled that we have not listened to the real victims, that we have shown so little empathy or understanding for their injury, and that we have abandoned those individuals whose race, gender, or sexual orientation provokes others to regard them as second class citizens. These individuals' civil liberties are most directly at stake in the debate.

Lawrence, above at 436. See Nadine Strossen, Regulating Racist Speech on Campus: A Modest Proposal?, 1990 Duke L.J. 484 (describing the ACLU position on hate speech).

In testimony before the Senate Judiciary Committee hearings on S.622, the Hate Crimes Prevention Act of 1999, the ACLU stated it could not support the proposed bill making violent conduct directed at a person because of race, color, national origin, religion, gender, sexual orientation, or disability a federal civil rights violation *unless* the bill was amended by adding the following evidentiary provision:

> In any prosecution under this section, (i) evidence proving the defendant's mere abstract beliefs or (ii) evidence of the defendant's mere membership in an organization, shall not be admissible to establish any element of an offense under this section.

Available at http://www.aclu.org/free-speech/letter-reps-hyde-and-conyers-hate-crimes-prevention-act-1999.

8. In an article comparing the status of university sexual harassment and hate speech codes, Jon Gould concludes that, even though the speech codes were virtually identical to Title VII's sexual harassment laws, courts strike down speech codes while enforcing sexual harassment policies. Gould, The Triumph of Hate Speech Regulation: Why Gender Wins But Race Loses in America, 6 Mich. J. Gender & L. 153 (1999). He also expresses surprise that the universities whose hate speech codes were found unconstitutional did not exert strong defenses and failed to appeal the adverse rulings:

> Perhaps, even supporters had only intended the codes as a symbolic statement—in this case, as a vehicle to highlight their concern over a receding national interest in civil rights. In either case, it is abundantly clear that the codes did not have the same level of committed support that Title VII did.
>
> What's more, the universities were in the difficult position of playing defense against an organized opposition. Contrary to the experience of sexual harassment litigants, the universities were not joined by any legal advocacy groups, nor did the EEOC enter the litigation on their behalf. Rather, the universities found themselves pitted against an unbending wall of attorneys affiliated with the American Civil Liberties Union and the Individual Rights Foundation.

Id. at 195–96. The court decisions were met with little protest on college campuses. Id. at 196. The author suggests that the political climate might explain the situation, citing a 1990 Gallup poll finding that almost two-thirds of Americans believe that racial equality has been achieved and that white Americans consider the civil rights crusade complete and express little willingness to address the problems faced by black Americans; 2/3 of whites oppose new civil rights laws and 77 percent of whites think blacks overestimate the amount of discrimination. Id. at 216–17. However, the opposite is true for women: a significant number of Americans believe women do not have equal job opportunities as men and only 29 percent think there has been too much attention paid to the civil rights of women. Id. at 217. Do you think public opinion is influencing these decisions? How do you explain the lack of support for hate speech codes and the substantial support for sexual harassment policies? Do you agree that the two types of speech regulation are essentially the same?

CHAPTER 9

WOMEN AND WAGE LABOR

■ ■ ■

A. INTRODUCTION

From the settling of the first colonies until the industrial revolution, most Americans, women as well as men, worked in family businesses and on farms. Women and men often specialized in different chores, but women were major producers of necessities consumed by families: cloth, clothing, candles, soap, fresh vegetables and fruits from the kitchen garden, eggs and chickens, canned food, as well as meals. There were important variations in labor and conditions across race and class. Privileged, upper class women supervised slaves and servants involved in these activities. But relatively few Americans of any race, sex, or class worked for wages. As late as 1780, "64 percent of the non-native population lived in families engaged in self-employment, 20 percent were slaves, and only 16 percent were wage workers or indentured servants."[1]

In a little over 100 years, the situation changed dramatically: "[B]y 1890, there were twice as many people working for wages or salaries as there were self-employed; by 1970, there were nine times as many."[2] This astonishing transition was accompanied by the movement of much production from the home to the factory. As producer activity left the home in the 19th century, the cult of domesticity developed as the ideal for "real" women (white middle or upper class women who were not immigrants); a woman's place was in the home nurturing her children and creating a haven to which the weary breadwinner could return at night.[3] Although relatively few white women born in this country worked for wages once they were married, many women of color, immigrant, lower class, and single women worked for wages in order to survive. For example, as late as 1920, only 6.5% of married European American women worked for wages, though 32.5% of married African American women did so and 18.5% of married Asian American women. In each of these categories, employment rates were much higher for unmarried women: 45% for

1. Teresa L. Amott & Julie A. Matthaei, Race, Gender, and Work: A Multicultural Economic History of Women in the United States 295 (1991).

2. Id.

3. See Barbara Welter, The Cult of True Womanhood: 1820–1860, 18 Am.Q. 151 (1966).

European American women; 58.8% for African American women; and 38.7% for Asian American women.[4]

The single most important change in the labor force in the 20th century was the increase in female wage workers, the fastest growing segment of the wage workforce. Today, most women with children work in the wage labor market either full or part time, and African and European American women are about equally likely to work for wages. Most women continue also to be primarily responsible for the domestic sphere. Information about women's labor force participation rates are detailed in the tables that follow.

Table 1: Women's Labor Force Participation Rates Civilians Age 16 and Over[5]

1942—2008

Year	Percentage of Women in Labor Force[6]	Women as Percentage of Labor Force	Year	Percentage of Women in Labor Force	Women as Percentage of Labor Force
1948	32.7%	28.6%	1980	51.5%	42.5%
1952	34.7%	31.0%	1984	53.6%	43.8%
1956	36.9%	32.2%	1988	56.6%	45.0%
1960	37.7%	33.4%	1992	57.8%	45.4%
1964	38.7%	34.8%	1996	59.3%	46.2%
1968	41.6%	37.1%	2000	59.9%	46.5%
1972	43.9%	43.9%	2003	59.5%	46.6%
1976	47.3%	40.5%	2008	59.5%	46.4%

Table 2: Civilian Labor Force Participation Rates for Persons Age 16 and Over by Sex, Race, and Hispanic Origin,[7] Selected Years, (in percentages).[8]

	Women					Men				
	All races	White	Black	Asian	Hispanic	All races	White	Black	Asian	Hispanic
1980	51.5%	51.2%	53.1%	—	47.4%	77.4%	78.2%	70.3%	—	81.4%
1990	57.5%	57.4%	58.3%	—	53.1%	76.4%	77.1%	71.0%	—	81.4%

4. Amott & Matthaei, above note 1, at 300, Table 9–2.

5. Information from Cynthia B. Costello, Shari Miles & Anne J. Stone, The American Woman 1999–2000: A Century of Change—What's Next table 4–1 at 264 (1998). Information for years 2000 through 2008 from United States Department of Labor, Civilian Labor Force Participants by age, sex, race and ethnicity (2009), available at http://www.bls.gov/emp/ep_table_% 1F303.htm.

6. Percentage of civilian women aged 16 and older who were in the labor force.

7. Persons of Hispanic origin may be of any race.

8. Information from U.S. Department of Labor, Bureau of Labor Statistics, "Women in the Labor Force: A Databook (2008 edition)." Report 1011 (2008), Table 3 "Employment status by race, age, sex, Hispanic or Latino ethnicity", available at http://www.bls.gov/cps/wlf-databook 2008.htm.

	All races	White	Black	Asian	Hispanic	All races	White	Black	Asian	Hispanic
2000	59.9%	59.5%	63.1%	59.2%	57.5%	74.8%	75.5%	69.2%	76.1%	81.5%
2003	59.5%	59.2%	61.9%	58.3%	55.9%	73.5%	74.2%	67.3%	75.6%	80.1%
2004	59.2%	58.9%	61.5%	57.6	56.1%	73.3%	73.3%	66.7%	75.0%	80.4%
2007	59.4%	59.0%	61.1%	58.6%	56.5%	72.9%	74.0%	66.8%	75.1%	80.5%

Table 3: Labor Force Participation Rates for Mothers with Infants[9]

1976	31%	1992	54%
1980	38%	1998	49%
1984	47%	2002	55%
1988	51%	2009	56.6%

Among mothers with infants in 2009, 56.6% were employed. For women with school-aged children (6–17), labor-force participation rates were higher, at 77.3%. Women with higher levels of education and wages are more likely to return to work (and to work longer hours) after the birth of a child than other women.[10]

Although women's labor force participation is substantial, women and men continue to engage in paid work in different ways and at different levels. Women are likely to spend fewer hours per week than men at paid labor while spending more hours per week than men on unpaid domestic work.[11]

Antidiscrimination law has both responded to and facilitated women's entrance into the work force. The focus of this chapter is Title VII, 42 U.S.C.A. § 2000e et seq., the primary federal law prohibiting sex discrimi-

9. United States Census Bureau, Fertility of American Women, Current Population Reports June 2002 at 7, Fig. 2 (October 2003) (mothers 15–44 years of age who have had a child within the last year and were working or looking for work); United States Department of Labor, Bureau of Labor Statistics, Employment Characteristics of Families–2009, available at www.bls.gov/news.release/pdf/famee.

10. Sharon R. Cohany and Emy Sok, "Trends of labor force participation of married mothers of infants" *Monthly Labor Review* (2007) 9–16 http://www.bls.gov/opub/mlr/2007/02/art2abs.htm last visited June 10, 2010 and United States Department of Labor, Bureau of Labor Statistics, Employment Characteristics of Families–2009, available at www.bls.gov/news.release/pdf/famee.

11. See Scott Coltrane, Research on Household Labor: Modeling and Measuring the Social Embeddedness of Routine Family Work, 62 J. Marriage & the Fam. 1208 (2000) (noting that women perform two to three times the amount of caretaking work as men); Joan Williams, Toward a Reconstructive Feminism: Reconstructing the Relationship of Market Work and Family Work, 19 N. Ill. U. L. Rev. 89 (1998) (explaining that women perform 80% of childcare and two-thirds of housework); Michael Selmi, Family Leave and the Gender Wage Gap, 78 N.C. L. Rev. 707, 709 (2000) (noting that women participate less in the paid labor market than do men because women overwhelmingly continue to be primarily responsible for child care and child rearing. Moreover, "strikingly few men take any significant paternity leave or assume equal responsibility for child rearing. As a result, women have less of an attachment to the labor force than men (though the differences are narrowing), miss more work than men, take more time off when they have children, and generally work fewer hours. All of these factors contribute to a cumulative workplace disadvantage that exacts a heavy price in terms of salary, promotions, and responsibility."); Vicki Schultz & Allison Hoffman, Precarious Work and Working Time: The Case for a Reduced Workweek in the United States, in Precarious Work, Women and the New Economy: The Challenge to Legal Norms (Judy Fudge & Rosemary Owens eds., 2006).

nation in employment. Two types of discrimination claims can be brought under Title VII: disparate treatment and disparate impact. Disparate treatment is proscribed by § 703(a):

> a) It shall be an unlawful employment practice for an employer—
>
> (1) to fail or to refuse to hire or to discharge any individual, or otherwise to discriminate against any individual with respect to his compensation, terms, conditions, or privileges of employment, because of such individual's race, color, religion, sex, or national origin; or
>
> (2) to limit, segregate, or classify his employees or applicants for employment in any way which would deprive or tend to deprive any individual of employment opportunities or otherwise adversely affect his status as an employee, because of such individual's race, color, religion, sex, or national origin.

42 U.S.C.A. § 2000e–2. Discrimination based on sex is permissible only when sex is "a bona fide occupational qualification ["BFOQ"] reasonably necessary to the normal operation of that particular business or enterprise." 42 U.S.C.A. § 2000e–2(e).

Disparate impact is proscribed by § 703(k)(1)(A):

> An unlawful employment practice based on disparate impact is established under this title only if—
>
> > (i) a complaining party demonstrates that a respondent uses a particular employment practice that causes a disparate impact on the basis of race, color, religion, sex, or national origin and the respondent fails to demonstrate that the challenged practice is job related for the position in question and consistent with business necessity * * *

42 U.S.C.A. § 2000e–2(k)(a)(A).

Title VII provides both for individual suits by "aggrieved individuals" and for suits by the Equal Employment Opportunity Commission ("EEOC"), a federal administrative agency charged with enforcement of Title VII. Aggressive enforcement by the EEOC against targeted industries has had significant effects in desegregating traditionally male jobs. For example, during the 1970's significant desegregation occurred when the banking and insurance industries were targeted for enforcement actions.[12] Unfortunately, as explored in the next section, Title VII has had only limited effect in helping women combine wage work and caretaking.

B. MOTHERS IN THE WORKPLACE

TEXT NOTE: THE EARLY CASES

The first sex-discrimination case to come before the Supreme Court, Phillips v. Martin Marietta Corp., 400 U.S. 542 (1971), was as important as

12. Barbara F. Reskin & Patricia A. Roos, Job Queues, Gender Queues: Explaining Women's Inroads into Male Occupations 54–55 (1990).

any subsequent case. The Fifth Circuit, known at that time for its firm commitment to racial equality, had held that an employer did not violate Title VII's ban on sex discrimination by refusing to hire women with preschool children. 411 F.2d 1 (5th Cir.1969). The employer argued that this policy was not "per se discrimination on the basis of sex," presumably because some women (those without preschool children) were hired. The Fifth Circuit accepted this argument:

> A per se violation of the Act can only be discrimination based solely on one of the categories, i.e., in the case of sex, women vis-a-vis men. When another criterion of employment is added to one of the classifications listed in the Act, there is no longer apparent discrimination based solely on * * * sex * * *. It becomes the function of the courts to study the conditioning of employment on one of the elements outlined in the statute coupled with the additional requirement and to determine if any individual or group is being denied work due to his * * * sex * * *.
>
> As to the case *sub judice,* as [sic] assembly trainee, among other disqualifications, cannot be a woman with pre-school age children. The evidence presented in the trial court is quite convincing that no discrimination against women as a whole or the appellant individually was practiced by Martin Marietta. The discrimination was based on a two-pronged qualification, i.e., a woman with pre-school age children. Ida Phillips was not refused employment because she was a woman nor because she had pre-school age children. It is the coalescence of these two elements that denied her the position she desired. In view of the above, we are convinced that the judgment of the District Court [for the defendant] was proper * * *.

Id. at 4. The court saw congressional intent as crucial, but concluded that "[t]he common experience of Congressmen is surely not so far removed from that of mankind in general as to warrant our attributing to them such an irrational purpose" as to require that employers treat mothers and fathers of young children "exactly alike." Id.

Had the Supreme Court affirmed this decision, Title VII's ban on sex discrimination would have been nearly meaningless. But in a brief unanimous opinion the Court held that Martin Marietta had violated Title VII by adopting "one hiring policy for women and another for men." 400 U.S. at 544.

Since this initial Supreme Court decision, the courts have charted a wavering course, sometimes seeing sex discrimination and sometimes missing it. In 1976 the Supreme Court held that Title VII's prohibition on sex discrimination did not include distinctions based on pregnancy. General Electric Co. v. Gilbert, 429 U.S. 125 (1976). The Court's decision prompted considerable outrage. Congress responded with the Pregnancy Discrimination Act of 1978 ("PDA"), which amended Title VII to provide that sex discrimination includes discrimination

> because of or on the basis of pregnancy, childbirth, or related medical conditions; and women affected by pregnancy, childbirth, or related medical conditions shall be treated the same for all employment-related purposes, including receipt of benefits under fringe benefit programs, as

other persons not so affected but similar in their ability to work or inability to work * * *.

42 U.S.C.A. § 2000e(k). However in AT & T v. Hulteen, ___ U.S. ___, 129 S.Ct. 1962 (2009), the Supreme Court held that a company did not violate the PDA or Title VII by denying retirement benefits to women who took temporary disability leave while pregnant when the leave was taken before the PDA came into effect.

The Supreme Court addressed an important question regarding the PDA's effect on protectionist employment policies in International Union, UAW v. Johnson Controls, Inc., 499 U.S. 187 (1991). The question raised was whether an employer could exclude women who could not prove sterility from the factory floor where workers were exposed to lead. To prove sterility, a woman had to produce a document from her doctor certifying that she could not conceive because she was post-menopausal or for some other reason. Men received no similar protection even though there was evidence of risk to the offspring of male workers. Precise levels of risk for children of women and men were unknown, but the plaintiffs included a 50–year old divorcee (most unlikely to have a child in the future) and a young married man whose wife was trying to become pregnant. Clearly the risk of harm to future life was greater as a result of the exposure of this man than of this woman.

The Court held that Johnson Controls' policy overtly, facially, violated Title VII:

> Johnson Controls' policy classifies on the basis of gender and childbearing capacity, rather than fertility alone. Respondent does not seek to protect the unconceived children of all its employees. Despite evidence in the record about the debilitating effect of lead exposure on the male reproductive system, Johnson Controls is concerned only with the harms that may befall the unborn offspring of its female employees. * * * This Court faced a conceptually similar situation in Phillips v. Martin Marietta Corp., and found sex discrimination because the policy established "one hiring policy for women and another for men—each having pre-school-age children." Johnson Controls' policy is facially discriminatory because it requires only a female employee to produce proof that she is not capable of reproducing.
>
> Our conclusion is bolstered by the Pregnancy Discrimination Act of 1978 (PDA), in which Congress explicitly provided that, for purposes of Title VII, discrimination "on the basis of sex" includes discrimination "because of or on the basis of pregnancy, childbirth, or related medical conditions." * * * In its use of the words "capable of bearing children" in the 1982 policy statement as the criterion for exclusion, Johnson Controls explicitly classifies on the basis of potential for pregnancy. Under the PDA, such a classification must be regarded, for Title VII purposes, in the same light as explicit sex discrimination. Respondent has chosen to treat all its female employees as potentially pregnant; that choice evinces discrimination on the basis of sex.
>
> * * * [T]he absence of a malevolent motive does not convert a facially discriminatory policy into a neutral policy with a discriminatory effect.

> Whether an employment practice involves disparate treatment through explicit facial discrimination does not depend on why the employer discriminates but rather on the explicit terms of the discrimination. * * * The beneficence of an employer's purpose does not undermine the conclusion that an explicit gender-based policy is sex discrimination under § 703(a) and may thus be defended only as a BFOQ.

Id. at 198–200.

Johnson Controls tried to use Title VII's BFOQ defense, which allows an employer to discriminate on the basis of sex when sex "is a bona fide occupational qualification reasonably necessary to the normal operation of that business or enterprise." The Court rejected this argument. Although there had been cases in which a BFOQ was recognized on the basis of safety concerns, the Court explained that safety concerns justify sex discrimination only when the issue is safety of those in contact with the employee during the course of her job, such as customers. Thus, a BFOQ defense is available only when "sex or pregnancy actually interferes with the employee's ability to perform the job." Id. at 204.

In claiming a BFOQ defense, Johnson Controls had argued that women employees were more costly than male employees because of the risk to offspring during pregnancy. The court rejected the relevance of cost:

> The tort-liability argument reduces to two equally unpersuasive propositions. First, Johnson Controls attempts to solve the problem of reproductive health hazards by resorting to an exclusionary policy. Title VII plainly forbids illegal sex discrimination as a method of diverting attention from an employer's obligation to police the workplace. Second, the specter of an award of damages reflects a fear that hiring fertile women will cost more. The extra cost of employing members of one sex, however, does not provide an affirmative Title VII defense for a discriminatory refusal to hire members of that gender. Indeed, in passing the PDA, Congress considered at length the considerable cost of providing equal treatment of pregnancy and related conditions, but made the "decision to forbid special treatment of pregnancy despite the social costs associated therewith." * * *
>
> We, of course, are not presented with, nor do we decide, a case in which costs would be so prohibitive as to threaten the survival of the employer's business. We merely reiterate our prior holdings that the incremental cost of hiring women cannot justify discriminating against them.

Id. at 208, 210–211. Thus, as a general matter, increased costs cannot justify the blanket exclusion of women from a class of jobs.

NOTES ON THE EARLY TITLE VII CASES

1. Why would a company allow young married men whose wives were trying to conceive to work in a lead exposure area but exclude 50–year–old divorced women?

2. How would you decide a case in which there is firm scientific evidence that risk associated with maternal exposure is significantly higher than the

risk associated with paternal exposure? (There was no such evidence in *Johnson Controls.*) What would the outcome be under the various feminist approaches described in Chapter 3?

3. Would firing the pregnant worker from a hazardous job necessarily be in the best interest of the child? What if the fired pregnant woman would lose her insurance and no longer be able to afford adequate medical care? What if she would be unable to make mortgage payments or pay her rent?

In Hunt–Golliday v. Metropolitan Water Reclamation District of Greater Chicago, 104 F.3d 1004 (7th Cir.1997), a pregnant woman was fired after experiencing cramps (and "threatening to miscarry," according to hospital personnel who treated her) while doing heavy lifting. Hunt–Golliday had just returned from a period of disability caused by a back injury. The near miscarriage occurred on her first day back on the job; she left and went to the hospital for treatment, and then called in sick the next day. The Seventh Circuit affirmed the grant of summary judgment for the employer on her pregnancy discrimination claim, noting that she had "presented no evidence showing, for instance, that a nonpregnant employee returning from extended leave who left her job and called in sick after one day back would not have been suspended." Id. at 18. Do you think that there should have been a trial to see if her pregnancy was a factor in the decision to fire her? Under *Johnson Controls*, can an employer fire a pregnant worker with a perfect attendance record after she has cramps and almost miscarries after doing heavy lifting?

4. Suzanne Harvender learned she was pregnant in February of 1996 with a due date in late September. She was a staff technician with the Norton Company and worked with chemicals. When she informed her employer of her pregnancy, the employer asked her to obtain a letter from her doctor stating that "she should be protected from chemical exposure." She thought that Norton "requested the note so that they could place her on a light duty program as they had done before when she had gone through an earlier pregnancy." Harvender v. Norton Co., 1997 WL 793085, 4 Wage & Hour Cas.2d (BNA) 560 (N.D.N.Y.1997). Harvender gave Norton the requested letter from her doctor, and Norton responded by placing her on FMLA leave (which totals only 12 unpaid weeks of leave in a calendar year), explaining that they could not place her on light duty because of restructuring and downsizing. Norton also indicated that if she did not return to work after her 12–week unpaid FMLA leave (May 15), her employment would be terminated. Suzanne Harvender miscarried and returned to work in April. She also brought suit alleging that Norton had (1) knowingly and intentionally violated the FMLA; (2) intentionally inflicted emotional distress; and (3) breached its contract of employment. The district court granted the employer's motion for summary judgment on all three claims, holding that employers as well as employees can invoke the FMLA because "nowhere in the act does it provide that FMLA leave must be granted only when the employee wishes it to be granted." Would Suzanne Harvender have fared better had she filed suit for pregnancy discrimination under Title VII, citing *Johnson Controls*?

As the decisions below show, courts require that women alleging sex discrimination present evidence showing that they were treated differently than similarly situated men. Plaintiffs who cannot find a similarly situated man who was treated differently are likely to lose their Title VII claim. What would be the chances that Havender could find a similarly situated male (regardless of how he was treated)?

5. Consider Armstrong v. Flowers Hospital, 812 F.Supp. 1183 (M.D.Ala. 1993). Pamela Armstrong was a nurse working for a hospital that provided home services to patients. During her pregnancy, she was assigned to a patient with cryptococal meningitis, an infectious and serious illness common among AIDS patients. AIDS patients tend to suffer from a number of opportunistic infections likely to be more dangerous to a child in utero than to a healthy adult. Armstrong told her supervisor that because she was in the first trimester of pregnancy she should not treat this patient. Her supervisor replied that it was not hospital policy to reassign nurses on the basis of unusual risks. Armstrong was given two days in which to decide whether to treat the patient or lose her job. She refused to treat the patient and was fired. As a result, she lost her health insurance prior to childbirth. She sued claiming both disparate treatment and disparate impact discrimination on the basis of pregnancy. The district court held that there had been no disparate treatment since pregnant workers were treated precisely like nonpregnant workers, a straightforward application of formal equality.

Should employers be required to offer employees particularly vulnerable to fetal hazards—typically pregnant workers and male workers whose wives are trying to conceive—safe employment during the period of vulnerability at no loss of pay? The Americans with Disability Act ("ADA") requires that employers accommodate disabilities; however, the EEOC, in an interpretive guidance, has said that pregnancy is not a disability under the meaning of the ADA. 29 C.F.R. pt. 1630 app. Should Title VII be amended to require accommodation of the needs of workers hoping to be parents in the near future? On a theoretical level, is there any link between employers' failure to afford such accommodation and inequality between women and men? For discussions of the need to require such accommodation, see Mary Becker, Reproductive Hazards After *Johnson Controls*, 31 Hous. L. Rev. 43 (1994); Ruth Colker, Pregnancy, Parenting, and Capitalism, 58 Ohio State L. J. 61, 75–76 (1997).

TROUPE v. MAY DEPARTMENT STORES CO.

United States Court of Appeals, Seventh Circuit, 1994.
20 F.3d 734.

POSNER, CHIEF JUDGE.

In 1978, Congress amended Title VII of the Civil Rights Act of 1964 to prohibit discrimination on account of pregnancy: "women affected by pregnancy, childbirth, or related medical conditions shall be treated the same for all employment-related purposes, including receipt of benefits under fringe benefit programs, as other persons not so affected but similar in their ability or inability to work." * * *

The plaintiff, Kimberly Hern Troupe, was employed by the Lord & Taylor department store in Chicago as a saleswoman in the women's accessories department. She had begun working there in 1987, initially working part time but from July 1990 full time. Until the end of 1990 her work was entirely satisfactory. In December of that year, in the first trimester of a pregnancy, she began experiencing morning sickness of unusual severity. The following month she requested and was granted a return to part-time status, working from noon to 5:00 p.m. Partly it seems because she slept later under the new schedule, so that noon was "morning" for her, she continued to experience severe morning sickness at work, causing what her lawyer describes with understatement as "slight" or "occasional" tardiness. In the month that ended with a warning from her immediate supervisor, Jennifer Rauch, on February 18, she reported late to work, or left early, on nine out of the 21 working days. The day after the warning she was late again and this time received a written warning. After she was tardy three days in a row late in March, the company on March 29 placed her on probation for 60 days. During the probationary period Troupe was late eleven more days; and she was fired on June 7, shortly after the end of the probationary period. She testified at her deposition that on the way to the meeting with the defendant's human resources manager at which she was fired, Rauch told her that "I [Troupe] was going to be terminated because she [Rauch] didn't think I was coming back to work after I had my baby." Troupe was due to begin her maternity leave the next day. We do not know whether it was to be a paid maternity leave but at argument Lord & Taylor's counsel said that employees of Lord & Taylor are entitled to maternity leave with half pay. We must assume that after Troupe was fired she received no medical benefits from Lord & Taylor in connection with her pregnancy and the birth of her child, for she testified without contradiction that she received no monetary benefits of any kind, other than unemployment benefits, after June 7, 1991. We do not know whether Lord & Taylor was less tolerant of Troupe's tardiness than it would have been had the cause not been a medical condition related to pregnancy. There is no evidence on this question, vital as it is.

* * *

Different kinds and combinations of evidence can create a triable issue of intentional discrimination ("disparate treatment," in the jargon of discrimination law), the only kind of discrimination alleged in this case. One kind is evidence that can be interpreted as an acknowledgment of discriminatory intent by the defendant or its agents * * *. Such evidence is indeed direct evidence as distinct from circumstantial; and since intent to discriminate is a mental state and mind reading not an accepted tool of judicial inquiry, it may be the only truly direct evidence of intent that will ever be available. But circumstantial evidence is admissible too, to provide a basis for drawing an inference of intentional discrimination.

* * *

[In order to survive] summary judgment a plaintiff must produce * * * evidence from which a rational trier of fact could reasonably infer that the defendant had fired the plaintiff because the latter was a member of a protected class, in this case the class of pregnant women.

We must examine the record in the light of these principles. The great, the undeniable fact is the plaintiff's tardiness. Her lawyer argues with great vigor that she should not be blamed—that she was genuinely ill, had a doctor's excuse, etc. That would be pertinent if Troupe were arguing that the Pregnancy Discrimination Act requires an employer to treat an employee afflicted by morning sickness better than the employer would treat an employee who was equally tardy for some other health reason; this is rightly not argued. If an employee who (like Troupe) does not have an employment contract cannot work because of illness, nothing in Title VII requires the employer to keep the employee on the payroll.

Against the inference that Troupe was fired because she was chronically late to arrive at work and chronically early to leave, she has only two facts to offer. The first is the timing of her discharge: she was fired the day before her maternity leave was to begin. Her morning sickness could not interfere with her work when she was not working because she was on maternity leave, and it could not interfere with her work when she returned to work after her maternity leave because her morning sickness would end at the latest with the birth of her child. Thus her employer fired her one day before the problem that the employer says caused her to be fired was certain to end. If the discharge of an unsatisfactory worker were a purely remedial measure rather than also, or instead, a deterrent one, the inference that Troupe wasn't really fired because of her tardiness would therefore be a powerful one. But that is a big "if." We must remember that after two warnings Troupe had been placed on probation for sixty days and that she had violated the implicit terms of probation by being as tardy during the probationary period as she had been before. If the company did not fire her, its warnings and threats would seem empty. Employees would be encouraged to flout work rules knowing that the only sanction would be a toothless warning or a meaningless period of probation.

Yet this is only an interpretation; and it might appear to be an issue for trial whether it is superior to Troupe's interpretation. But what is Troupe's interpretation? Not (as we understand it) that Lord & Taylor wanted to get back at her for becoming pregnant or having morning sickness. The only significance she asks us to attach to the timing of her discharge is as reinforcement for the inference that she asks us to draw from Rauch's statement about the reason for her termination: that she was terminated because her employer did not expect her to return to work after her maternity leave was up. We must decide whether a termination so motivated is discrimination within the meaning of the pregnancy amendment to Title VII.

Standing alone, it is not. (It could be a breach of contract, but that is not alleged.) Suppose that Lord & Taylor had an employee named Jones, a black employee scheduled to take a three-month paid sick leave for a kidney transplant; and whether thinking that he would not return to work when his leave was up or not wanting to incur the expense of paying him while he was on sick leave, the company fired him. In doing so it might be breaking its employment contract with Jones, if it had one, or violating a state statute requiring the payment of earned wages. But the company could not be found guilty of racial discrimination unless (in the absence of any of the other types of evidence of discrimination that we have discussed) there was evidence that it failed to exhibit comparable rapacity toward similarly situated employees of the white race. We must imagine a hypothetical Mr. Troupe, who is as tardy as Ms. Troupe was, also because of health problems, and who is about to take a protracted sick leave growing out of those problems at an expense to Lord & Taylor equal to that of Ms. Troupe's maternity leave. If Lord & Taylor would have fired our hypothetical Mr. Troupe, this implies that it fired Ms. Troupe not because she was pregnant but because she cost the company more than she was worth to it.

The Pregnancy Discrimination Act does not, despite the urgings of feminist scholars, e.g., Herma Hill Kay, "Equality and Difference: The Case of Pregnancy," 1 Berkeley Women's L.J. 1, 30–31 (1985), require employers to offer maternity leave or take other steps to make it easier for pregnant women to work—to make it as easy, say, as it is for their spouses to continue working during pregnancy. Employers can treat pregnant women as badly as they treat similarly affected but nonpregnant employees, even to the point of "conditioning the availability of an employment benefit on an employee's decision to return to work after the end of the medical disability that pregnancy causes." Maganuco v. Leyden Community High School Dist. 212, 939 F.2d 440, 445 (7th Cir.1991). *Maganuco* and other cases hold that disparate impact is a permissible theory of liability under the Pregnancy Discrimination Act, as it is under other provisions of Title VII. But, properly understood, disparate impact as a theory of liability is a means of dealing with the residues of past discrimination, rather than a warrant for favoritism.

The plaintiff has made no effort to show that if all the pertinent facts were as they are except for the fact of her pregnancy, she would not have been fired. So in the end she has no evidence from which a rational trier of fact could infer that she was a victim of pregnancy discrimination. The Supreme Court noted recently that the age discrimination "law requires the employer to ignore an employee's age ...; it does not specify *further* characteristics that an employer must also ignore," such as pension expense. Hazen Paper Co. v. Biggins, 507 U.S. 604, 612, 113 S.Ct. 1701, 1707, 123 L.Ed.2d 338 (1993) (emphasis in original). The Pregnancy Discrimination Act requires the employer to ignore an employee's pregnancy, but * * * not her absence from work, unless the employer overlooks the comparable absences of nonpregnant employees * * * in which event it would not be ignoring pregnancy after all. Of course there may be no comparable absences, but we do not understand Troupe to be arguing that the reason she did not present evidence that nonpregnant employees were treated more favorably than she is that * * * there is no comparison group of Lord & Taylor employees. What to do in such a case is an issue for a case in which the issue is raised. (We do not even know how long Troupe's maternity leave was supposed to be.) We doubt that finding a comparison group would be that difficult. Troupe would be halfway home if she could find one nonpregnant employee of Lord & Taylor who had not been fired when about to begin a leave similar in length to hers. She either did not look, or did not find. Given the absence of other evidence, her failure to present any comparison evidence doomed her case.

NOTES ON TROUPE

1. How would you characterize the tone of this opinion? Do you think it is condescending and hostile to Kimberly Troupe? What assumptions does Posner make about "morning" sickness? See Ann C. McGinley & Jeffrey W. Stempel, Condescending Contradictions: Richard Posner's Pragmatism and Pregnancy Discrimination, 46 Fla. L. Rev. 193 (1994).

2. In *Troupe*, Posner uses a hypothetical (the African American male employee in need of a kidney transplant) to dismiss any inference that Lord & Taylor discriminated against Troupe on the basis of her pregnancy even though her boss had said that she was being fired because she was not expected to return to work after her baby was born. According to Posner, his hypothetical kidney patient "implies that [Lord & Taylor] fired Ms. Troupe not because she was pregnant but because she cost the company more than she was worth to it." But is Posner's hypothetical kidney patient actually on point? Do you think that Lord & Taylor would have been as likely to infer that the kidney patient would not return from short-term disability leave as it was to infer that Troupe would not return from maternity leave? Wouldn't a closer analogy be a man who had a recent record of tardiness related to medical problems, who was about to go on a medical leave which would entirely cure those problems, and who expected to become a new father during his leave? Do you think that Lord & Taylor would have been as likely to fire the about-to-be father? In the non-hypothetical real world, is there any truly analogous comparison group Troupe could use?

3. The *Troupe* case reached the Seventh Circuit on appeal from a district court decision granting summary judgment for the employer. Thus, affirmance was appropriate only if no reasonable fact finder could conclude that Troupe was dismissed because she was pregnant or a woman. Further, once a plaintiff shows that either sex or pregnancy played a part in an employment decision, the burden shifts to the employer to prove "by a preponderance of the evidence that it would have made the same decision even if it had not taken the plaintiff's gender into account." Price Waterhouse v. Hopkins, 490 U.S. 228, 258 (1989). In *Price Waterhouse*, the plaintiff's evidence that gender had played a part consisted of evidence of sexual stereotyping. Hopkins was told that she did not make partner because she was too macho and aggressive and that her chances would improve if she would "walk more femininely, talk more femininely, dress more femininely, wear make-up, have her hair styled, and wear jewelry." Id., 490 U.S. at 278. On the basis of this and similar evidence, the Court held that Hopkins demonstrated

that sex was a factor, and the burden was now on her employer to demonstrate that it would have reached the same decision had it not considered her sex.

Did Troupe present evidence of sex stereotyping analogous to that presented in *Price Waterhouse*? Do you think that a reasonable fact finder might conclude that Kimberly Troupe had at least presented evidence that sex (which includes pregnancy) played a role in Lord & Taylor's decision? Is it credible (given her supervisor's explanation) that her pregnancy played no role in the decision to fire her? Isn't it likely that Lord & Taylor's assessment of the odds of Troupe returning from leave were affected by the fact that it was pregnancy leave and that she would be a new mother at the end of it? Can one seriously argue that an employer would be as likely to conclude that a male worker, about to become a father while on an extended medical leave, would not return to his job? How does Posner handle the social expectations and stereotypes about pregnant women and new mothers? For a discussion of stereotyping missed by the courts in *Troupe* and similar cases, see Judith G. Greenberg, The Pregnancy Discrimination Act: Legitimating Discrimination Against Pregnant Women in the Workforce, 50 Me. L. Rev. 225 (1998).

4. How does Posner justify the result in *Troupe*? Why does he conclude that his interpretation is the only possible one and that there is no issue for trial? Why didn't Troupe have enough evidence to survive summary judgment with her combination of the timing of her firing (when her morning sickness could no longer be a problem) and her supervisor's statement that she was being terminated because she was not expected to return to work after her leave? Does Posner pick her case apart by looking at one element at time and dismissing each because it, standing alone, would not be sufficient, though of course the plaintiff has not relied only on any one fact?

5. Look carefully at Posner's decision, beginning with the sentences just before his assertion that the "great, the undeniable fact is the plaintiff's tardiness." In the preceding paragraphs, Posner has explained that various combinations of evidence can create a triable issue of fact so that summary judgment is inappropriate. His first analytical sentence, applying Title VII law to the facts before him, is: "the great, the undeniable fact is the plaintiff's tardiness." How is this great fact relevant (on the employer's motion for summary judgment) given Troupe's testimony that her supervisor told her she was being fired because she was not expected to return to work from her maternity leave?

6. Was Kimberly Troupe discriminated against because she was about to become a new mother and hadn't even been tough enough to work her scheduled hours during her pregnancy? For other cases in which women seem to have lost their jobs for being new mothers, see Piantanida v. Wyman Center, Inc. 116 F.3d 340 (8th Cir.1997) (affirming dismissal on summary judgment of plaintiff's claim that she had been discriminated against because she was a "new mom" on the ground that discrimination against new parents is gender-neutral); Bass v. Chemical Banking Corp., 1996 WL 374151 (S.D.N.Y.1996) (dismissing on summary judgment plaintiff's claim that she had been discriminated against because she was the mother of young children with respect to a promotion opportunity—which went to a woman without

children—because the plaintiff failed to show that men with young children were treated more favorably than she). Are the cases in which about-to-be new mothers lose consistent with Phillips v. Martin Marietta, 400 U.S. 542, 91 S.Ct. 496, 27 L.Ed.2d 613 (1971) (described in the introduction to this section on mothers in the workplace)? For a discussion of recent new mother cases, see Martha Chamallas, Mothers and Disparate Treatment, 44 Will. L. Rev. 337 (1999).

7. The FMLA had yet to be enacted at the time Kimberly Troupe was fired. Would it have helped her?

8. How would a formal equality feminist analyze *Troupe*? Would she find discrimination in violation of Title VII? What about a dominance feminist? A relational feminist?

9. Would it surprise you to learn that Posner is not a supporter of the PDA?

> The requirement that the employer not differentiate among its employees on the basis of pregnancy is analytically the same as a requirement that the employer pay the same retirement benefits to male and female employees despite women's superior longevity, or a requirement that the employer grant maternity leave (in other words, agree to reinstate female employees who take time off to have or take care of their babies). In all three cases, the law compels the employer to ignore a real difference in the average cost of male and female employees. The result is inefficient, but a more interesting point is that it may not benefit women as a whole.

Richard A. Posner, An Economic Analysis of Sex Discrimination Laws, 56 U. Chi. L. Rev. 1311, 1332 (1989). Posner's point is that employers may be reluctant to hire women of child-bearing age if they must ignore real costs associated with employing them. Do you agree that the PDA has likely done more harm than good? In deciding *Troupe*, was Posner influenced by his antipathy to the statute he was interpreting? See McGinley & Stempel, above note 1, at 245–251 (noting that Posner also regards bans on sex discrimination as unlikely to help women).

TEXT NOTE: PREGNANCY AND DISPARATE IMPACT

In *Troupe*, Posner cites his earlier decision in Maganuco v. Leyden Community High School Dist. 212, 939 F.2d 440, 445 (7th Cir.1991), for the position that "[e]mployers can treat pregnant women as badly as they treat similarly affected but nonpregnant employees, even to the point of conditioning the availability of an employment benefit on an employee's decision to return to work after the end of the medical disability that pregnancy causes." Rebecca Maganuco claimed that her employer had discriminated on the basis of pregnancy both in terms of disparate treatment (the type of discrimination analyzed in *Troupe*) and in terms of disparate impact. As noted earlier, disparate impact occurs when an employer adopts a rule or standard that has a negative impact on a protected group; once the plaintiff shows that a policy has such an impact, the employer must drop the policy unless it demonstrates that it is sufficiently "job related" or a "business necessity." Disparate impact was first recognized and is most likely to be applied in the context of an occupational qualification or selection procedure. In that context, the question is whether a requirement or procedure disproportionately leaves out of the candidate pool qualified candidates who are (depending on the claim) African American, female, etc. In order to establish a disparate impact case, the plaintiff must show, for example, that 50% of graduates of law schools are women but that only 20% of those hired by the defendant law firm are women. Note that there are two figures for comparison here: the percentage of women in the applicant pool and the percentage of those hired who are women.

Although plaintiffs have tried to bring disparate impact claims based on pregnancy-discrimination challenges to employer rules of various kinds, these claims tend to fail. One problem is that in pregnancy cases, unlike disparate impact claims in other settings, there is no obvious way to determine impact. In *Maganuco*, for example, the plaintiff was a high school teacher who challenged a provision in the union contract prohibiting the use of accrued sick days for a (paid) disability leave followed by an (unpaid) maternity leave. Thus, a pregnant teacher had to choose between using her accrued sick days (accumulated at the rate of 17 days a year) and taking a maternity leave (of up to one and a half semesters without pay). If these leaves could be combined, many pregnant women would be able to take a leave for a full school year to care for a newborn. But under the policy, women had to choose between one and a half semesters of unpaid leave and paid leave for the period of their accrued sick days. In a sense, such a policy had a disparate impact on women, since only women qualified for maternity leave and only maternity leave could not follow a period of disability during which the employee used accrued sick days. Women were obviously worse off under the school district's policies than they would have been under a policy that allowed women to combine maternity leave with disability leave using accrued sick days. But there are other possible comparisons. Women were better off under the school district's policy than they would have been if the employer provided no maternity leave, just leave during the period of actual disability associated with childbirth.

There are no two obvious numbers to compare in this situation. Indeed, Rebecca Maganuco argued that the "leave policy leads women who choose to have children to accumulate a greater number of sick days than men or than women who choose to forego childbirth," 939 F.2d at 444. However, the Seventh Circuit noted that Maganuco failed to present evidence demonstrating this alleged disparate impact. The case therefore lacked the "gross statistical disparities" necessary for a disparate impact case.

Maganuco also argued that the school district's leave policies had a discriminatory impact "by forcing women to choose between using their accumulated sick days for pregnancy-related disability and taking maternity leave subsequent to childbirth." Id. But the court rejected this argument on the ground that the PDA only requires that pregnant women be given the same benefits available to others. Moreover, noted Posner, the impact Maganuco was challenging depended not just on the district's policies and the biological fact of pregnancy, but on the teacher's "choice to forego returning to work immediately in favor of spending time with her newborn child." Id.

(Posner noted that the school district's policy extending a one and a half semester leave to new mothers and not to new fathers probably did violate Title VII. See id. at 445 n.1.)

Although the *Maganuco* court held that a disparate impact pregnancy discrimination claim was possible, it did not see a valid one in the case before it. This seems to be the general fate of such claims.

NOTES ON PREGNANCY AND DISPARATE IMPACT

1. What role does the fact that a woman "chooses" to spend some time with her new baby play in Posner's analysis? Do you think the use of this term is fair? Is this choice the equivalent of a vacation in Tahiti or is it itself a productive and labor-intensive enterprise which can be expected to contribute to the general good? If you were writing the opinion, what would you say about the relevance of the mother's "choice" to the question of whether her needs and those of her baby should receive some accommodation from an employer?

2. Although Posner talks about the function served by disparate impact claims and states "that disparate impact is a permissible theory of liability under the Pregnancy Discrimination Act," he did not apply it in *Troupe*. Why not? What does he see as the problem with applying disparate impact in that case?

3. Would you regard as favoritism policies designed to make it as easy for women to combine pregnancy and parenting with wage work as it is for men to combine childbirth and and parenting with wage work? Would Posner?

4. Although there is no obvious comparison to use to determine impact in pregnancy cases, courts could interpret Title VII's ban on policies having a disparate impact on pregnant women as requiring employers to make reasonable accommodations to the needs of pregnant workers. After all, when pregnant workers need accommodation (including jobs less hazardous to the fetus), it is because a rule or policy makes it more difficult for them than for other workers to continue to work. This approach has been taken by Canadian courts interpreting very similar statutes. Why haven't American courts taken such an approach? Ruth Colker suggests that the explanation is the prevalence of "judges who are imbued in the philosophy of law and economics" in American courts. Colker, Pregnancy, Parenting, and Capitalism, 58 Ohio State L. J. 61, 82 (1997). What do you think explains this difference? Would you favor the Canadian approach?

IN RE: CARNEGIE CENTER ASSOCIATES

United States Court of Appeals, Third Circuit, 1997.
129 F.3d 290.

GREENBERG, CIRCUIT JUDGE.

[Deborah Rhett, an unmarried African American woman working as a secretary, was fired during her maternity leave. The employer needed to eliminate a secretarial position, and picked Rhett's, not on the basis of seniority or merit, but because she was out of the office.

When Rhett informed her supervisors and coworkers of her pregnancy, the company controller and financial officer asked if she planned on marrying, and one said that getting married was "the right thing to do." Carnegie had an informal policy under which it tried to hold jobs open for workers on maternity leave when possible, and had done so for two others in the past. The district court affirmed the order of the Bankruptcy Court which had dismissed Rhett's claim of discrimination on the basis of race and sex.]

* * *

Rhett argues that Carnegie terminated her employment solely because of her absence and her absence was due solely to her pregnancy and related medical conditions. Consequently, in her view Carnegie terminated her employment because of her pregnancy. The Supreme Court has held that under the Age Discrimination in Employment Act an employer must ignore an employee's age in certain employment decisions, but not any other characteristics such as pension expense. Hazen Paper Co. v. Biggins, 507 U.S. 604, 612, 113 S.Ct. 1701, 1707, 123 L. Ed. 2d 338 (1993). The Court of Appeals for the Seventh Circuit has held, by analogy to *Hazen*, that the PDA "requires the employer to ignore an employee's pregnancy, but ... not her absence from work, unless the employer overlooks the comparable absences of non-pregnant employees...." *Troupe, 20 F.3d at 738.* This holding is entirely consistent with the plain language of the PDA * * *. This view eliminates Rhett's theory of transitivity, that if A (termination) is caused by B (absence) which is caused by C (pregnancy), then C causes A. Other courts similarly have held that "the PDA does not force employers to pretend that absent employees are present whenever their absences are caused by pregnancy."

* * *

This case is unusual in that Carnegie terminated an employee who had performed satisfactorily solely because of an economically justified reduction in force while she was away on maternity leave.

Nevertheless, the law covering this case is clear from the view of the Court of Appeals of the Seventh Circuit which it set forth in *Troupe*, that an employer legitimately can consider an employee's absence on maternity leave in making an adverse employment decision; [this view] is consistent with and, indeed, is compelled by the plain language of the PDA. Thus, *Troupe* properly requires the plaintiff employee seeking to recover under the PDA to show that the employer treated her differently than non-pregnant employees on disability leave. * * * Thus, we cannot find, as Rhett urges, that the mere consideration of an employee's absence on maternity leave is a per se violation of the PDA. In short, the PDA does not require an employer to reinstate an employee merely because she has been absent on maternity leave. Rather, the PDA is a shield against discrimination, not a sword in the hands of a pregnant employee.

Rhett has not made a showing that Carnegie treated her differently than it would have treated a non-pregnant employee absent on disability leave. Of course, it was difficult for her to make such a showing because Carnegie never has had an employee on disability leave for a protracted period for a reason other than pregnancy. Thus, we must affirm the district court's denial of her PDA claim for the reasons indicated.

* * *

In reaching our result, we have not overlooked Rhett's argument that this case is somehow different than a case based on a claim of discrimination predicated either on race or gender, because she bases her claim on both race and gender. This argument adds nothing to her case because regardless of the basis for her claim of discrimination, she cannot establish that the legitimate reason that Carnegie proffered for terminating her was pretextual. Furthermore, we have not ignored Rhett's argument that Carnegie's termination of her position had a discriminatory impact on her based on her race. Rather, we reject this contention as entirely insubstantial for an employee is not insulated from having her position lawfully terminated merely because she happens to be a minority.

* * *

Conclusion

We hold, in agreement with the Court of Appeals for the Seventh Circuit [and] the plain language of the PDA, * * * that an employee alleging a PDA violation must show that her employer treated her differently than it would have treated an employee on leave for a temporary disability other than pregnancy. It is not a violation of the PDA for an employer to consider an employee's absence on maternity leave in making an adverse employment decision if it also would have considered the absence of an employee on a different type of disability leave in the same way. Inasmuch as Carnegie asserted that Rhett's absence from work, rather than her pregnancy, was the reason for her termination, and Rhett has failed to show that this assertion was pretextual, her claim fails.

In view of our conclusions, we will affirm the judgment of the district court * * *.

MCKEE, CIRCUIT JUDGE, dissenting.

I agree that Deborah Rhett's claim of racial discrimination was properly dismissed. However, I respectfully dissent because I believe that the district court erred in affirming the bankruptcy court's dismissal of Rhett's claim of sex discrimination. * * *

Relying upon Hazen Paper Company v. Biggins, 507 U.S. 604, 113 S.Ct. 1701, 123 L. Ed. 2d 338 (1993), the majority states that "the Supreme Court has held that under the Age Discrimination in Employment Act an employer must ignore an employee's age in certain employment decisions, but not any other characteristics such as pension expense." However, I believe that *Hazen Paper* [supports the plaintiff in this case.] * * *

> [In *Hazen Paper*, the plaintiff was fired a few weeks before his pension rights would have vested based on his years of service. The Supreme Court held that firing an employee to prevent his pension rights from vesting under a plan providing for vesting based on years of service did not necessarily violate the ADEA (though it would violate ERISA). The Court explained that such a termination would violate the ADEA only if the employer fired the employee because of his age, which was analytically distinct from his years of service. The Court did remand for consideration of whether the jury had sufficient evidence to find a violation of the ADEA.]

Pregnancy and absence are not, however, analytically distinct, and an employer cannot punish for the absence occasioned by pregnancy under Title VII. As noted above, that statute states that it is an unlawful employment practice to "discharge any individual ... or otherwise discriminate ... because ... of sex," and, after the PDA, that includes discrimination "on the basis of pregnancy ... or related medical conditions." That protection is meaningless unless it is intended to extend to the "temporary" absence from employment that is unavoidable in most pregnancies. Thus, the absence endemic to pregnancy, unlike factors that may sometimes be a proxy for age, has to be protected under the facts of this case. In *Hazen Paper,* it was the employee's years of service, not his age, that occasioned the vesting of his pension. The Court was very careful to note that

> We do not consider the special case where an employee is about to vest ... as a result of his age, rather than years of service, and the employer fires the employee in order to prevent vesting. That case is not presented here. Our holding is simply that an employer does not violate the ADEA just by interfering with an older employee's pension benefits that would have vested by virtue of years of service.

507 U.S. at 613. I believe that Rhett's situation under the PDA is much closer to the situation of an employee whose pension is vesting because of age than to the plight of the plaintiff in *Hazen Paper*. Accordingly, the holding in *Hazen Paper* does not assist the majority nearly as much as first appears.[4]

"In using the broad phrase 'women affected by pregnancy, childbirth and related medical conditions,' the [PDA] makes clear that its protection

---

4. I do not mean to suggest by this that the PDA requires an employer to necessarily take affirmative steps to make it easier for a pregnant employee to work. See *Troupe,* 20 F.3d at 738 ("The Pregnancy Discrimination Act does not ... require employers to ... take ... steps to make it easier for pregnant women to work."). The PDA does not provide for accommodation as does the ADA.

Nor do I suggest that an employee who is pregnant can not be fired for reasons that are not occasioned by pregnancy. For example, if Carnegie decided, in good faith, to eliminate everyone with a certain salary grade based upon its business judgment, Rhett could be terminated if she was at that salary grade whether she was on pregnancy leave or not because the termination would not be based upon a factor endemic to her pregnancy.

extends to the whole range of matters concerning the childbearing process." H.R. Rep. 95–948. The holding in *Troupe*, and the majority's holding here, remove a substantial portion of the protection Congress intended. *Troupe*'s position was terminated because of conditions related to pregnancy (tardiness occasioned by her morning sickness). I do not understand, therefore, why she was not terminated "because of ... her pregnancy," in violation of Title VII.

* * *

Carnegie clearly did not put Rhett's departure on maternity leave to one side when deciding to terminate her. Rhett's absence from work was so inextricably intertwined with pregnancy, her protected trait, as to make the two inseparable. In its "theory of transitivity," the majority separates the events in this case into discrete entities that suggest the causal relationship between Rhett's pregnancy and her termination. The majority too easily rejects [Rhett's] position. See Maj. Op. ("This view eliminates Rhett's theory of transitivity, that if A (termination) is caused by B (absence) which is caused by C (pregnancy), then C causes A.").

TERMINATION BECAUSE OF PREGNANCY

An employer can not insulate itself from the reach of Title VII by an action that appears neutral, yet has the functional effect of disparately treating an individual based upon a protected trait. See *Griggs*, 401 U.S. at 430. Carnegie's action is the functional equivalent of terminating Rhett because she was pregnant.

* * *

CONCLUSION

For the reasons stated above, I would reverse the decision of the district court and remand this matter to the bankruptcy court for a determination of whether Rhett would have been terminated had her pregnancy-related absence been put aside.

NOTES ON CARNEGIE

1. Do you think that Rhett's race and pregnancy were in all likelihood factors in Carnegie's choice of whom to fire? How might her race have been relevant; what stereotypes about African American women might have been in play? Why does even the dissent agree that her race claim was properly dismissed? What would Rhett have to show to prove that race and pregnancy (particularly for a black woman outside of marriage) likely influenced Carnegie's decision to fire her rather than the least competent secretary? Why does it seem to be so difficult to frame that combined claim in a way recognizable by Title VII?

2. Take a close look at paragraphs two and three of the dissent in *Carnegie*. Is firing a worker because she is about to go on pregnancy leave (and therefore costs more to the employer than she is worth, as Posner

describes the situation in *Troupe*) or because she is on leave and someone has to be cut from the payroll (as in *Carnegie*), more like firing an older worker whose pension rights are about to vest because of years in service (analytically distinct from age) or one whose rights are about to vest with age (obviously not analytically distinct from age)? What point does Judge McKee make in these paragraphs?

3. With whom do you agree, the *Carnegie* majority or dissent, on the causation point? Was Rhett fired because of her pregnancy when she was fired because of her absence which occurred because of her pregnancy?

4. In this case the court concedes that the plaintiff could not possibly compare the employer's treatment of her with the employer's treatment of other workers; the company had never had anyone on extended disability who was not pregnant. Does the PDA protect women only at employers large enough to have a history of extended disability leaves for workers in varying circumstances? Or is finding a comparison group for pregnant workers likely to be impossible in many cases even at large employers?

5. Protection of pregnant workers is important for a number of reasons. The woman and her baby may need the medical insurance routinely given during leaves and may be uninsured without leave. Both may need the income that would come with her return to work after the baby's birth. Losing one's job at any time can be traumatic, and losing one while pregnant and facing unusual costs as well as the inability to work for some period of time is likely to be particularly traumatic. Trauma can have all sorts of negative effects on pregnancy and its outcome. A significant part of the persistent wage gap between women and men is attributable to the fact that many women take time off from wage work when and after their children are born. Being able to combine childcare (including pregnancy) and wage work is essential for women's economic equality. See Samuel Issacharoff & Elyse Rosenblum, Women and the Workplace: Accommodating the Demands of Pregnancy, 94 Colum. L. Rev. 2154 (1994). Can you think of more effective ways to protect women during pregnancy than the PDA? See Gillian Lester, A Defense of Paid Family Leave, 28 Harv. J. L. & Gender 1 (2005) (arguing on behalf of paid family leave as a way to increase women's workforce participation).

BROWN v. RENTOKIL

European Court of Justice, 1998.
Case C–394/96, 1998 ECR I–4185.

[In each case before it, the Court of Justice of the European Union is advised by one of nine Advocates General. The Advocate General delivers an opinion in open court recommending an outcome and rationale. As in this case, the Court routinely adopts the Advocate General's recommendations. The decision below begins with the recommendation of the Advocate General and ends with the judgment of the European Court of Justice.]

Opinion of Mr. Advocate General Ruiz–Jarabo Colomer delivered on 5 February 1998.

* * * Mrs. Brown, the appellant in the main proceedings, was employed as a driver for Rentokil Limited * * * (hereinafter "Rentokil"), the

respondent in those proceedings. Her job was mainly to transport and change Sanitact units in shops and other centres. She became pregnant and informed Rentokil in August 1990.

Her pregnancy later became complicated through a number of interrelated causes, of which details are not given in the documents before the Court. As from 16 August 1990 she submitted a succession of four-week medical certificates mentioning various diagnoses such as "symptoms of pregnancy," "bleeding in pregnancy" or "pregnant backache." From that time, until her dismissal, the appellant remained unable to work.

The respondent included a clause in the contract of employment under which any employee, man or women, who was incapable of work for more than 26 weeks without interruption would be dismissed. On 9 November 1990 Mrs. Brown had a meeting with two executives of the company, who informed her that half of the 26–week period had passed and reminded her that her employment contract would be terminated on 8 February 1991 if she was not back at work by that time, following an independent medical examination confirming that she was able to work. Those details were confirmed to her by letter of the same date.

The appellant did not go back to work after receiving that letter. The parties agree that there was never any question of her being able to return to work prior to the [expiration] of the 26–week period. [She gave birth on 22 March 1991.]

* * *

[The courts of Great Britain held that Rentokil did not discriminate on the basis of sex when it fired Mrs. Brown.]

The Community Legislation

The Community provisions of which an interpretation is needed for judgment to be given in this dispute are all contained in [the Equal Treatment Directive], namely Article 2(1) and (3) and Article 5(1) and (2), which provide as follows:

[The Equal Treatment Directive]

Article 2

(1) For the purposes of the following provisions, the principle of equal treatment shall mean that there shall be no discrimination whatsoever on grounds of sex either directly or indirectly by reference in particular to marital or family status.

* * *

(3) This Directive shall be without prejudice to provisions concerning the protection of women, particularly as regards pregnancy and maternity.

Article 5

(1) Application of the principle of equal treatment with regard to working conditions, including the conditions governing dismissal, means that men and women shall be guaranteed the same conditions without discrimination on grounds of sex.

(2) To this end, Member States shall take the measures necessary to ensure that:

(a) any laws, regulations and administrative provisions contrary to the principle of equal treatment shall be abolished

(b) any provisions contrary to the principle of equal treatment which are included in collective agreements, individual contracts of employment, internal rules of undertakings or in rules governing the independent occupations and professions shall be, or may be declared, null and void or may be amended.

* * *

On 19 October 1992 the Council adopted [the Maternity Leave and Pregnancy Discrimination Directive] in order to protect the health and safety of pregnant workers who have given birth or are breastfeeding * * *, which requires the Member States to adopt, before 19 October 1994, among others provisions needed to ensure that female workers enjoy a continuous period of maternity leave of at least 14 weeks, allocated before and/or after confinement, including two weeks compulsory leave. It also prohibits dismissal of a pregnant worker, in the following terms:

[The Pregnancy Directive]

Article 10

(1) Member States shall take the necessary measures to prohibit the dismissal of workers [who are pregnant, have recently given birth or are breastfeeding] during the period from the beginning of their pregnancy to the end of the maternity leave ... save in exceptional circumstances not connected with their condition which are permitted under national legislation and/or practice and, where applicable, provided that the competent authority has given its consent....

However, since Mrs. Brown was dismissed at the beginning of 1991, there is no need to interpret [the Pregnancy Directive in this case].

* * *

The National Legislation

* * *

[At the time of Mrs. Brown's dismissal, a woman was entitled to return to her job after pregnancy provided that she had been working for her employer for at least two years at the start of her 11th week of pregnancy, but Mrs. Brown had not been working for her employer long enough for this provision to apply to her. In addition, pregnant women, including Mrs. Brown, are entitled to up to 18 weeks paid leave at birth under British law.]

* * *

[Observations and Recommendation to the European Court of Justice]

* * * [This Court's earlier decisions in this area] illustrate well the thesis of Lucinda M. Finley, which can be summarized in the following statement:

> The fact that women bear children and men do not has been the major impediment to women becoming fully integrated into the public world of the workplace.[14]

* * *

What is involved here, ultimately, is the duty incumbent upon us all of progressively removing all traces of the discrimination which women have suffered over the centuries, a duty to which the institutions of the European Union are so deeply committed.

* * *

Starting from the premise that equality, as defined by the Constitutional Court of one of the Member States, "is not a reality or an abstract mathematical concept but rather unequal treatment of that which is unequal or equal treatment of that which is similar or alike" * * * and having regard to the settled case-law of the Court of Justice to the effect that "discrimination can arise only through the application of different rules to comparable situations or the application of the same rule to different situations," * * * I shall now consider whether the dismissal of a pregnant woman on grounds of incapacity for work arising from her condition occurs under the same conditions as dismissal of a man for incapacity for work of the same duration, arising from an illness.

* * *

I wonder whether it is still necessary, at this stage, to repeat the self-evident fact that pregnancy is a situation which affects only women, since only they can become pregnant. Pregnancy, besides being a biological situation pertaining exclusively to women, is a period limited in time, during which there may occur not only the well-known phenomenon of morning sickness but also complications such as risks of miscarriage or premature contractions associated with stress, which may compel the woman to rest absolutely for periods which may extend from two or three months to the whole of the period of pregnancy.

This Court emphatically stated, [in an earlier decision], that "the dismissal of a female worker on account of repeated periods of sick leave which are not attributed to pregnancy or confinement does not constitute

---

14. Lucinda M. Finley, "Transcending Equality Theory: A Way out of the Maternity and the Workplace Debate," Columbia Law Review, Vol. 86:1118, p. 1119.

direct discrimination on grounds of sex, inasmuch as such periods of sick leave would lead to the dismissal of a male worker in the same circumstances."

Can it be said, however, that the dismissal of a pregnant woman on account of repeated periods of sick leave attributable to pregnancy occurs under the same conditions as the dismissal of a man who has been on sick leave for the same period? In my opinion the answer is no.

Without wishing to meddle in matters which are the province of doctors, I should make it clear that, although * * * pregnancy is not in any way comparable with a pathological condition, no one is unaware of the existence of "high-risk pregnancies" which occur—the following being examples, not an exhaustive list—when there is a history of premature or still-births, when the placenta is lower than normal, when the woman has undergone in vitro fertilization treatment, and in cases where the woman suffers from a heart condition or diabetes. The main characteristic of such pregnancies is not that they cause the woman to be "ill" but that, normally, they require her to remain under strict medical supervision and, in some of the cases mentioned above, to rest absolutely for several months or, sometimes, throughout her pregnancy.

I cannot share the view that, in situations of that kind, where the woman is not suffering from any illness but is simply pregnant, it can be said that, in the event of dismissal for repeated absences, she is dismissed under the same conditions as a man who has been absent through illness for the same period of time. The same reasoning will apply where the incapacity for work derives from the fact that pregnancy has aggravated an existing illness or brought about conditions which may be classified as real illness.

Whilst the situation of a pregnant worker whose pregnancy prevents her from working and that of a male worker who is ill coincide in so far as neither of them can, for a period, carry out the tasks involved in her or his employment, important differences distinguish them: only women may find themselves at some time during their working life in a situation where they are prevented from working because of incapacity arising from a pregnancy and, in most cases, a woman's incapacity for work arising from pregnancy will end on a date known in advance with more or less accuracy, when she gives birth.

These factors appear to have been taken into account by the domestic law applicable in most Member States at the time of the material events in this case, which was fairly similar—only the legislation in the United Kingdom and Ireland differed radically.

Thus, [for example,] in Germany there was specific protection for women from the start of pregnancy until after confinement, whereby in that period dismissal was subject to administrative authorisation. In Denmark, the Ministry of Employment considered it discriminatory to take account, for the purposes of dismissal, of absences due to incapacity for work attributable to pregnancy, before a woman gave birth. In France, the employer could not dismiss a woman during pregnancy, during maternity leave or during the four weeks thereafter. * * *

I consider that the dismissal of a woman whilst she is pregnant, on account of unfitness for work caused by her pregnancy, by taking into consideration a situation in which only women can find themselves, constitutes direct discrimination contrary to Article 5(1) of [the Equal Treatment Directive].

* * *

[Judgment of the European Court of Justice]

* * *

According to settled case-law of the Court of Justice, the dismissal of a female worker on account of pregnancy, or essentially on account of pregnancy, can affect only women and therefore constitutes direct discrimination on grounds of sex.

* * *

It was precisely in view of the harmful effects which the risk of dismissal may have on the physical and mental state of women who are pregnant, women who have recently given birth or women who are breastfeeding, including the particularly serious risk that pregnant women may be prompted voluntarily to terminate their pregnancy, that the Community legislature, pursuant to Article 10 of [the Pregnancy Directive] on the introduction of measures to encourage improvements in the safety and health at work of pregnant workers and workers who have recently given birth or are breastfeeding * * * provided for special protection to be given to women, by prohibiting dismissal during the period from the beginning of their pregnancy to the end of their maternity leave. Article 10 of [the Pregnancy Directive] provides that there is to be no exception to, or derogation from, the prohibition of dismissal of pregnant women during that period, save in exceptional cases not connected with their condition.

* * *

* * * [D]ismissal of a woman during pregnancy cannot be based on her inability, as a result of her condition, to perform the duties which she is contractually bound to carry out. If such an interpretation were adopted, the protection afforded by Community law to a woman during pregnancy would be available only to pregnant women who were able to comply with the conditions of their employment contracts, with the result that the provisions of [the Equal Treatment Directive] would be rendered ineffective.

* * *

It is also clear from all the foregoing considerations that * * * where a woman is absent owing to illness resulting from pregnancy or childbirth, and that illness arose during pregnancy and persisted during and after maternity leave, her absence not only during maternity leave but also during the period extending from the start of her pregnancy to the start of her maternity leave cannot be taken into account for computation of the period justifying her dismissal under national law. As to her absence after maternity leave, this may be taken into account under the same conditions as a man's absence, of the same duration, through incapacity for work.

* * *

It is well settled that discrimination involves the application of different rules to comparable situations or the application of the same rule to different situations. * * *

Where it is relied on to dismiss a pregnant worker because of absences due to incapacity for work resulting from her pregnancy, * * * a contractual term, applying both to men and to women, is applied in the same way to different situations since * * * the situation of a pregnant worker who is unfit for work as a result of disorders associated with her pregnancy cannot be considered to be the same as that of a male worker who is ill and absent through incapacity for work for the same length of time.

Consequently, application of that contractual term in circumstances such as the present constitutes direct discrimination on grounds of sex.

* * *

[Ruling]

On those grounds, THE COURT * * * hereby rules: Articles 2(1) and 5(1) of [the Equal Treatment Directive], on the implementation of the principle of equal treatment for men and women as regards access to employment, vocational training and promotion, and working conditions, preclude dismissal of a female worker at any time during her pregnancy for absences due to incapacity for work caused by illness resulting from that pregnancy.

The fact that a female worker has been dismissed during her pregnancy on the basis of a contractual term providing that the employer may dismiss employees of either sex after a stipulated number of weeks of continuous absence does not affect the answer given.

NOTES ON THE EUROPEAN LAW OF SEX AND PREGNANCY DISCRIMINATION

1. Compare the tone of the decision of the European Court of Justice and that of the Seventh Circuit in *Troupe* and *Maganuco* and the Third Circuit in *Carnegie* in terms of their attitudes toward the pregnant worker. How and where does the European Court express its concern for the well-being of the woman and the child? Are similar concerns ever expressed by the American courts? What do you think explains this difference? See Ruth Colker, Pregnancy, Parenting, and Capitalism, 58 Ohio State L. J. 61, 72–73 (1997) (discussing dominance of economic analysis in PDA discussions com-

bined with a failure to consider the needs of the newborn, and noting in particular Posner's "uncaring and callous consideration of the needs of the newborn" in *Maganuco*). Should the needs of the newborn be considered in creating rights for pregnant workers?

2. In reaching its decision, the European Court of Justice considers "the harmful effects which the risk of dismissal may have on the physical and mental state of women who are pregnant, women who have recently given birth or women who are breastfeeding, including the particularly serious risk that pregnant women may be prompted voluntarily to terminate their pregnancy." Are these concerns paternalistic or troubling in any other way?

3. Compare the references to American feminists in *Troupe* (Herma Hill Kay) and *Brown* (Lucinda Finley), particularly the attitude with which they are cited. Compare the United States and Europe in terms of their commitment to social safety nets and rugged individualism. Why might European culture be more open to feminist arguments on these issues?

4. Compare the American decisions throughout this text (and those you have read elsewhere) with the European Court of Justice in terms of strength of commitment to equality in the real world. In *Brown*, the Advocate General states: "What is involved here, ultimately, is the duty incumbent upon us all of progressively removing all traces of the discrimination which women have suffered over the centuries, a duty to which the institutions of the European Union are so deeply committed." The European Court of Justice has itself "expanded the equal pay principle [of the Treaty governing the European Union] into a general equality right between women and men which exists at the core of EU law." Elizabeth F. Defeis, The Treaty of Amsterdam: The Next Step Towards Gender Equality, 23 B.C. Int'l & Comp. L. Rev. 1, 6 (1999). Can you imagine any justice on our Supreme Court describing sex equality as "existing at the core of our constitutional framework"?

5. Compare the benefits and protections available to a pregnant worker in Great Britain before *Brown* and after *Brown* with those available to a pregnant worker in the United States today.

6. In his opinion, Advocate General Colomer states that equality "is not a reality or an abstract mathematical concept but rather unequal treatment of that which is unequal or equal treatment of that which is alike." What does he mean by stating that equality is not a reality and not a "mathematical concept"? Is it fair or accurate to state that American courts regard equality as both a reality and a mathematical concept?

7. The *Brown* opinion stresses that equality requires that comparable situations be treated comparably and that different situations be treated differently. (This notion of equality can be traced back to Aristotle.) American courts adopt essentially the same account of nondiscrimination but with very different outcomes. How do the American courts perceive pregnancy in terms of its comparability or distinctness from other nonpregnancy-related illnesses? How do the European courts perceive pregnancy?

8. Under the European approach, the fact that only women experience pregnancy and childbirth is the basis for regarding discrimination on the basis of pregnancy, childbirth, or any factor related to them (such as being unable

to work for a time because of morning sickness or childbirth) as direct sex discrimination. Sex equality demands such a rule because otherwise women workers who become parents would face handicaps not faced by male workers who become parents. In the United States, the fact that only women experience pregnancy and childbirth dooms claims of discrimination unless a woman can find a similarly situated male, an often impossible task. Does the European approach level the playing field for female and male workers or is it a form of favoritism protecting women when men are not protected? What would Posner think?

9. What do you think would happen were legislation proposed in Congress defining pregnancy discrimination as including any negative employment decision based on pregnancy, childbirth, or maternity leave or on any factor related to pregnancy and childbirth (including inability to work)? What arguments would be used to oppose such legislation? Who would support it?

10. Joan Williams proposes the use of Title VII to challenge employer norms structured for ideal workers without any significant caretaking or domestic responsibilities. For example, she suggests that a Title VII disparate impact case be used to challenge the low numbers of women in higher-level jobs because of such norms. The plaintiff would argue that the standards for promotion have a disparate impact on women workers and would begin by showing "that, say, 50 percent of entry-level positions but only 20 percent of jobs in the top four corporate levels and a mere 5 percent of top management positions are held by women." Williams, Unbending Gender: Why Family and Work Conflict and What To Do About It 106 (2000). The second issue would be "whether the relative paucity of women in higher-level jobs is caused by the actions of the employer or by women's choice to quit." Id. She suggests that, even if many women regard their failure to stay on the high-powered career track as a matter of their own personal choice, judges need not:

> [The courts'] mandate is to consider whether the constraints women face constitute discrimination. If they do, the fact that many women may have internalized those constraints does not provide employers with an excuse for continuing the discrimination.

Id. Finally, the plaintiff would explain how specific policies, such as not considering part-time employees for partnership, contribute to the disappearance of women at higher level jobs. The burden would then shift to the defendant to show that the challenged practice is a business necessity. Williams concedes that the availability of the business necessity defense in her hypothetical case is arguable either way, but notes that even if the plaintiff loses on this issue, she "can win if she can prove the existence of a less discriminatory alternative, an alternative way of structuring the promotion track that has a less harsh effect on women." Id. at 107.

Given what you have seen of judicial interpretations of Title VII so far in this chapter, what do you think of Williams' proposal? Can you imagine judges concluding that even though women state that they choose not to compete on the partnership track, the employer's failure to consider part-time workers for partner constitutes sex discrimination? See Kathryn Abrams, Cross–Dressing in the Master's Clothes, 109 Yale L. J. 745, 756–57 (2000) (expressing some doubts).

On May 23, 2007, the Equal Employment Opportunity Commission issued guidance on caregiver discrimination. See http://www.eeoc.gov/policy/docs/caregiving.pdf. The guidance explained that "[a]lthough the federal EEO laws do not prohibit discrimination against caregivers per se, there are circumstances in which discrimination against caregivers might constitute unlawful disparate treatment." Examples of such discrimination, according to the EEOC, include treating women and men with young children differently or basing business decisions on stereotyped assumptions that mothers are not as committed to their jobs. The most commonly used basis for protecting family caregivers in the workplace is Title VII and the PDA. However, the Family and Medical Leave Act, Americans with Disabilities Act, Employee Retirement Income Security Act and state anti-discrimination statutes have all been used as well. See Joan C. Williams, The Evolution of "FRED": Family Responsibilities Discrimination and Developments in the Law of Stereotyping and Implicit Bias, 59 Hastings L. J. 1311 (2008).

In what kinds of cases is the EEOC guidance likely to be most helpful? What are the limits of Family Responsibilities Discrimination protection?

Can you think of ways to promote change that might be more effective than those discussed above? What about legislative changes giving American women paid maternity leave and the right not to be fired during pregnancy or maternity leave for any pregnancy-related reason, rights parallel to those now enjoyed by European women? Can you think of ways to increase the numbers of women in higher positions? Consumers, clients, shareholders, and government can all exert pressure (in different ways) on employers to adopt affirmative action policies to increase the number of women in higher-level jobs. Return to this after reading the following text note comparing attitudes toward affirmative action in the United States and the European Union.

TEXT NOTE: AFFIRMATIVE ACTION IN THE UNITED STATES AND THE EUROPEAN UNION

As Elizabeth F. Defeis describes, European law has been far more supportive of affirmative action for women than American law.[13] The only United States Supreme Court decision directly addressing affirmative action in employment for women, Johnson v. Transportation Agency, Santa Clara County, California, 480 U.S. 616 (1987), upheld the legality of the plan before the Court, but that plan was very limited in scope. The Santa Clara plan allowed the county agency to take sex into account as one factor in selecting between qualified applicants for traditionally male jobs "in which women have been significantly underrepresented." Id., 480 U.S. at 620–621. The case involved a challenge from a qualified man when, in mid–1980, a qualified woman became the first woman ever to hold a Skilled Craft Worker Position (prior to her promotion, all 238 of the Skilled Craft Workers were men). In upholding the plan, the Court pointed to the "manifest imbalance" of women in these positions and stressed that the plan did not "unnecessarily trammel the interests" of male employees (during the period from 1978–1982, there

13. Elizabeth F. Defeis, The Treaty of Amsterdam: The Next Step Towards Gender Equality, 23 B.C. Int'l & Comp. L. Rev. 1, 21–33 (1999).

were 111 new Skilled Craft positions and 105 went to men), that sex was only one factor taken into account in selecting among qualified applicants, and that the plan was not permanent but a temporary means to reach a balanced workforce, allowing sex to be considered as a factor when considering promotion to positions held disproportionately by men.

Since *Johnson*, the Supreme Court has been increasingly hostile to affirmative action in the context of race, making clear that such policies would be subject to strict scrutiny despite their intention to aid traditionally disadvantaged groups.[14]

European law is moving in the opposite direction on affirmative action for women. Article 141 of the Treaty of Rome, the original treaty of the European Union, contained a single provision mandating sex equality: a provision mandating equal pay for equal work regardless of sex.[15] This provision is the basis for the Equal Treatment Directive quoted and interpreted in *Brown* to ban the firing of a worker during pregnancy or maternity leave for any reason connected to pregnancy or maternity leave, including inability to do the job because of temporary disability. The European Court of Justice has interpreted this directive as consistent with a German law giving a preference for civil-service promotions to women—if as qualified as male candidates "unless reasons specific to an individual male candidate tilt the balance in his favor"—for positions in which women are underrepresented. Case C–409/95, Marschall v. Land Nordrhein–Westfalen, [1997] All ER (EC) 865 (1997). The European Court of Justice noted that "such a rule may counteract the prejudicial effects on female candidates" of continuing stereotypes, including the expectation "that women will interrupt their careers more frequently, that owing to household and family duties they will be less flexible in their working hours, or that they will be absent from work more frequently because of pregnancy, childbirth, and breastfeeding." Id. at ¶¶ 28, 29, 31.

The Amsterdam Treaty of 1997 amended the original Treaty of Rome by, among other things, strengthening the commitment to achieving actual equality between women and men. In the words of Elizabeth Defeis:

> The Amsterdam Treaty goes beyond existing EU legislation regarding gender equality in employment and imposes a general obligation on the Union in all of its activities to eliminate inequalities and to promote equality. In addition to clarifying, developing and expanding the EC Treaty provisions on equality, the Amsterdam Treaty adopts the comparable worth concept first set out in [EU legislation] and requires "equal pay for work of equal value."
>
> The Amsterdam Treaty also adds two new provisions to the Article 141 equality principle. The first provision requires the Council [of Europe]

14. See Adarand Constructors, Inc. v. Pena, 515 U.S. 200, (1995) (holding unconstitutional Small Business Administration regulations creating a financial incentive for contractors to hire minority subcontractors); City of Richmond v. J.A. Croson Co., 488 U.S. 469 (1989) (holding unconstitutional a city's affirmative action plan to set aside a portion of city contracts for minority contractors). But see Grutter v. Bollinger, 539 U.S. 306 (2003) (finding constitutional a race-based affirmative action plan in law school admissions).

15. Id. at 2.

* * * to adopt measures to ensure equal opportunity and equal treatment of men and women in employment. The second provision allows Member States to adopt and maintain positive action provisions. It states:

> With a view to ensuring full equality in practice between men and women in working life, the principle of equal treatment shall not prevent any Member State from maintaining or adopting measures providing for specific advantages in order to make it easier for the underrepresented sex to pursue a vocational activity or to prevent or compensate for disadvantages in professional careers.

Although the term "underrepresented sex" replaces the term "women" as the focus of positive action, a declaration by Member States stipulates that such action should in the first instance aim at improving the situation of women in working life. * * *

Finally, the Amsterdam Treaty expands the scope of the equality principle and allows the Council to take action against discrimination based on sex, race or ethnic origin, religion or belief, disability, age, or sexual orientation within the limits of its powers. * * *

NOTES ON AFFIRMATIVE ACTION IN THE UNITED STATES AND THE EUROPEAN UNION

1. In Marschall v. Land Nordrhein–Westfalen, the European Court of Justice referred to continuing prejudice against and stereotyping of women in justifying a law requiring affirmative action for women against a challenge that it violated the Equal Treatment Directive. In contrast, American courts justify affirmative action as a remedy for past, rather than ongoing discrimination. In Johnson v. Transportation Agency, the American sex-based affirmative action case discussed in the text note above, the woman who was promoted under the challenged plan and became the only woman ever to hold a Skilled Craft Worker position in the Santa Clara County Transportation Agency had herself faced discrimination and stereotyping on the job as well as in the selection process. For example, one member of an interviewing team that rated the candidates was a man who had referred to Joyce as a "rebel-rousing, skirt-wearing person." *Johnson*, 480 U.S. at 624 n. 5. Yet the justification the Court offered for allowing affirmative action in that case was the substantial gender imbalance in the workplace resulting from past discrimination. The Court never once mentioned continuing discrimination as a good reason for affirmative action. And the Court's stress, in *Johnson* and other cases, on the temporary nature of the plan suggests an assumption that discrimination is over, so that once a balanced work force is achieved, there is no continuing need for affirmative action.

As *Troupe* illustrates, American judicial decisions, again unlike European decisions, ignore that employment has been and continues to be structured to accommodate workers without significant caretaking abilities, i.e., people who are not likely to be mothers. These structural barriers to equality for women do not constitute legal discrimination in the United States, as *Troupe* again illustrates. Why has the Supreme Court been unwilling to date to recognize that both traditional forms of discrimination and structural barriers are substantial and continuing obstacles to women's equality? Do American courts believe that equality is a reality and inequality *cannot*, therefore, be continuing on any systemic basis? Why do European courts see inequality as continuing? Is the difference one only of perspective rather than reality? Which of the theoretical views of equality discussed in Chapter 3 do the American courts seem to adopt and which do the European courts seem to adopt?

2. Have you been surprised by what you have learned about European law in this chapter? Is it consistent with the self-image of the United States as a leader in women's rights? What explains our conviction that we are at the forefront of sex equality around the world and our parochialism, i.e., our inattention—in the news or elsewhere in popular culture—to more expansive approaches to sex equality?

3. What are the downsides of affirmative action for women? How can individual women be hurt by such policies? What are the advantages of affirmative action for women? Do you support or oppose affirmative action for women? Would you support actual quotas or absolute preferences in any circumstances?

C. SEXUAL HARASSMENT

With the passage of the Equal Pay Act in 1963, women were entitled to equal pay for equal work. The next year, after the passage of the Civil Rights Act of 1964, employers were prohibited from making employment decisions based on sex. Yet, despite these legislative enactments ensuring equal treatment for women, many workplaces remained hostile to women. Women talking about problems in their workplaces identified a variety of practices, including demands for sex in exchange for promotions and constant sexual comments, which created a hostile work environment. Creative practitioners, working with women workers and activists, crafted a theory of "sexual harassment" as a type of sex discrimination prohibited by Title VII. Beginning in the 1970's, women brought sexual harassment test cases under Title VII's prohibition of sex discrimination. These early cases were rejected by trial courts for a variety of reasons, including that (1) the activity at issue was a matter of "nothing more than a personal proclivity, peculiarity or mannerism" and not company policy;[16] (2) the company did not derive a benefit from the conduct; and (3) recognition of sexual or amorous activity at the workplace as a violation of Title VII would open the floodgates to vast litigation.[17] Employers also argued that if sexual harassment was sex discrimination because the harasser harassed only people of the opposite sex (and not members of the same sex), then a bisexual supervisor could harass with impunity both men and women since he would not be discriminating between one sex and another.

16. Corne v. Bausch and Lomb, Inc., 390 F.Supp. 161, 163 (D. Ariz. 1975), vacated without op., 562 F.2d 55 (9th Cir. 1977).

17. See generally Catharine A. MacKinnon, Sexual Harassment of Working Women (1979); Fred Strebeigh, Equal: Women Reshape American Law (2009).

Because this seemed odd, sexual harassment must be something other than sex discrimination.

Despite a number of early dismissals, plaintiffs persisted in bringing claims of sexual harassment and a court finally recognized sexual harassment as a form of sex discrimination in 1976.[18] Two types of sexual harassment claims emerged: (1) quid pro quo, in which submission to sexual advances is a condition of an individual's hiring, firing, promotion, or receipt of an employment benefit, and (2) hostile environment, in which sexual conduct and/or speech unreasonably interferes with an individual's work performance or creates an intimidating, hostile or offensive working environment.[19]

In 1998, however, in a pair of cases, the Supreme Court moved away from this division and began to focus instead on whether the harassment involved a tangible employment action.[20] The question of whether there was a tangible employment action as part of the alleged harassment became critical to whether an employer would be held liable for the harassing conduct of its supervisors. Excerpts from some of the key cases in this area of the law follow.

MERITOR SAVINGS BANK v. VINSON

Supreme Court of the United States, 1986.
477 U.S. 57, 106 S.Ct. 2399, 91 L.Ed.2d 49.

JUSTICE REHNQUIST delivered the opinion of the Court.

* * *

In 1974, respondent Mechelle Vinson met Sidney Taylor, a vice president of what is now petitioner Meritor Savings Bank (bank) and manager of one of its branch offices. When respondent asked whether she might obtain employment at the bank, Taylor gave her an application, which she completed and returned the next day; later that same day Taylor called her to say that she had been hired. With Taylor as her supervisor, respondent started as a teller-trainee, and thereafter was promoted to teller, head teller, and assistant branch manager. She worked at the same branch for four years, and it is undisputed that her advancement there was based on merit alone. In September 1978, respondent notified Taylor that she was taking sick leave for an indefinite period. On November 1, 1978, the bank discharged her for excessive use of that leave.

Respondent brought this action against Taylor and the bank, claiming that during her four years at the bank she had "constantly been subjected to sexual harassment" by Taylor in violation of Title VII. She sought

18. Williams v. Saxbe, 413 F.Supp. 654 (D.D.C.1976).

19. See, e.g., Miller v. Bank of America, 600 F.2d 211 (9th Cir.1979) (quid pro quo); Meritor Savings Bank v. Vinson, 477 U.S. 57 (1986) (harassing environment).

20. See Burlington Indus. v. Ellerth, 524 U.S. 742 (1998); Faragher v. City of Boca Raton, 524 U.S. 775 (1998).

injunctive relief, compensatory and punitive damages against Taylor and the bank, and attorney's fees.

At the 11–day bench trial, the parties presented conflicting testimony about Taylor's behavior during respondent's employment. Respondent testified that during her probationary period as a teller-trainee, Taylor treated her in a fatherly way and made no sexual advances. Shortly thereafter, however, he invited her out to dinner and, during the course of the meal, suggested that they go to a motel to have sexual relations. At first she refused, but out of what she described as fear of losing her job she eventually agreed. According to respondent, Taylor thereafter made repeated demands upon her for sexual favors, usually at the branch, both during and after business hours; she estimated that over the next several years she had intercourse with him some 40 or 50 times. In addition, respondent testified that Taylor fondled her in front of other employees, followed her into the women's restroom when she went there alone, exposed himself to her, and even forcibly raped her on several occasions. These activities ceased after 1977, respondent stated, when she started going with a steady boyfriend.

* * *

Taylor denied respondent's allegations of sexual activity, testifying that he never fondled her, never made suggestive remarks to her, never engaged in sexual intercourse with her, and never asked her to do so. He contended instead that respondent made her accusations in response to a business-related dispute. The bank also denied respondent's allegations and asserted that any sexual harassment by Taylor was unknown to the bank and engaged in without its consent or approval.

* * *

Respondent argues, and the Court of Appeals held, that unwelcome sexual advances that create an offensive or hostile working environment violate Title VII. Without question, when a supervisor sexually harasses a subordinate because of the subordinate's sex, that supervisor "discriminate[s]" on the basis of sex. Petitioner apparently does not challenge this proposition. It contends instead that in prohibiting discrimination with respect to "compensation, terms, conditions, or privileges" of employment, Congress was concerned with what petitioner describes as "tangible loss" of "an economic character," not "purely psychological aspects of the workplace environment." * * *

We reject petitioner's view. First, the language of Title VII is not limited to "economic" or "tangible" discrimination. The phrase "terms, conditions, or privileges of employment" evinces a congressional intent " 'to strike at the entire spectrum of disparate treatment of men and women' " in employment. Petitioner has pointed to nothing in the Act to suggest that Congress contemplated the limitation urged here.

Second, in 1980 the EEOC issued Guidelines specifying that "sexual harassment," as there defined, is a form of sex discrimination prohibited by Title VII. * * *

Of course, * * * not all workplace conduct that may be described as "harassment" affects a "term, condition, or privilege" of employment within the meaning of Title VII. For sexual harassment to be actionable, it must be sufficiently severe or pervasive "to alter the conditions of [the victim's] employment and create an abusive working environment." Respondent's allegations in this case—which include not only pervasive harassment but also criminal conduct of the most serious nature—are plainly sufficient to state a claim for "hostile environment" sexual harassment.

* * *

[T]he District Court's conclusion that no actionable harassment occurred might have rested on its earlier "finding" that "[i]f [respondent] and Taylor did engage in an intimate or sexual relationship . . ., that relationship was a voluntary one." But the fact that sex-related conduct was "voluntary," in the sense that the complainant was not forced to participate against her will, is not a defense to a sexual harassment suit brought under Title VII. The gravamen of any sexual harassment claim is that the alleged sexual advances were "unwelcome." While the question whether particular conduct was indeed unwelcome presents difficult problems of proof and turns largely on credibility determinations committed to the trier of fact, the District Court in this case erroneously focused on the "voluntariness" of respondent's participation in the claimed sexual episodes. The correct inquiry is whether respondent by her conduct indicated that the alleged sexual advances were unwelcome, not whether her actual participation in sexual intercourse was voluntary.

* * * [T]he Court of Appeals stated that testimony about respondent's "dress and personal fantasies," which the District Court apparently admitted into evidence, "had no place in this litigation." The apparent ground for this conclusion was that respondent's voluntariness vel non in submitting to Taylor's advances was immaterial to her sexual harassment claim. While "voluntariness" in the sense of consent is not a defense to such a claim, it does not follow that a complainant's sexually provocative speech or dress is irrelevant as a matter of law in determining whether he or she found particular sexual advances unwelcome. To the contrary, such evidence is obviously relevant.

* * *

Finding that "the bank was without notice" of Taylor's alleged conduct, and that notice to Taylor was not the equivalent of notice to the bank, the court concluded that the bank therefore could not be held liable for Taylor's alleged actions. The Court of Appeals took the opposite view, holding that an employer is strictly liable for a hostile environment created by a supervisor's sexual advances, even though the employer neither knew nor reasonably could have known of the alleged misconduct. The court held that a supervisor, whether or not he possesses the authority to hire, fire, or promote, is necessarily an "agent" of his employer for all Title VII purposes, since "even the appearance" of such authority may enable him to impose himself on his subordinates.

* * *

This debate over the appropriate standard for employer liability has a rather abstract quality about it given the state of the record in this case. We do not know at this stage whether Taylor made any sexual advances toward respondent at all, let alone whether those advances were unwelcome, whether they were sufficiently pervasive to constitute a condition of employment, or whether they were "so pervasive and so long continuing . . . that the employer must have become conscious of [them]."

We therefore decline the parties' invitation to issue a definitive rule on employer liability, but we do agree with the EEOC that Congress wanted courts to look to agency principles for guidance in this area. While such common-law principles may not be transferable in all their particulars to Title VII, Congress' decision to define "employer" to include any "agent" of an employer surely evinces an intent to place some limits on the acts of employees for which employers under Title VII are to be held responsible. For this reason, we hold that the Court of Appeals erred in concluding that employers are always automatically liable for sexual harassment by their supervisors. For the same reason, absence of notice to an employer does not necessarily insulate that employer from liability.

Finally, we reject petitioner's view that the mere existence of a grievance procedure and a policy against discrimination, coupled with respondent's failure to invoke that procedure, must insulate petitioner from liability. While those facts are plainly relevant, the situation before us demonstrates why they are not necessarily dispositive. Petitioner's general nondiscrimination policy did not address sexual harassment in particular, and thus did not alert employees to their employer's interest in correcting that form of discrimination. Moreover, the bank's grievance procedure apparently required an employee to complain first to her supervisor, in this case Taylor. Since Taylor was the alleged perpetrator, it is not altogether surprising that respondent failed to invoke the procedure and report her grievance to him. Petitioner's contention that respondent's failure should insulate it from liability might be substantially stronger if its procedures were better calculated to encourage victims of harassment to come forward.

NOTES ON MERITOR

1. Do you think Congress intended to address sexual harassment when it passed Title VII in 1964? Why or why not? Under principles of statutory construction, should Title VII be interpreted to cover this kind of sex discrimination?

2. Did the Supreme Court perceive the *Meritor* case to be a quid pro quo or hostile environment case? Do you agree with its perception of the case? What are the practical effects of how the issue is cast? Are there differing proof problems? Is quid pro quo harassment easier to recognize? Do you think that quid pro quo harassment is less controversial, i.e., that most people agree that it is wrong? It is estimated that quid pro quo constitutes only a small portion (about 5%) of sexual harassment. See Morrison Torrey, We Get the Message—Pornography in the Workplace, 22 S.W.U. L. Rev. 53, n.17 (1992).

3. Do you think the Court adequately defined hostile environment sexual harassment? Based on the *Meritor* opinion, would you feel comfortable advising a client about what constitutes a hostile environment? Compare Mendoza v. Borden, Inc., 195 F.3d 1238 (11th Cir. 1999) (finding no actionable sexual harassment as a result of plaintiff's being followed, constantly stared at, looked up and down and sniffed at, and rubbed up against by her supervisor and granting summary judgment for defendant), with Rorie v. United Parcel Serv., Inc., 151 F.3d 757 (8th Cir. 1998) (holding that plaintiff's allegations that manager patted her on the back, brushed up against her, and told her that she smelled good were sufficient to survive a motion for summary judgment). Do you think men and women might perceive what occurs in the workplace differently?

4. Differences in gendered perspectives and experiences of harassment have been documented in numerous studies. See Torrey, above note 2, at 60–66. Every study that has found gender differences has concluded that women are more likely than men to perceive behaviors as harassing. See Jeremy A. Blumenthal, The Reasonable Woman Standard: A Meta-Analytic Review of Gender Differences in Perceptions of Sexual Harassment, 22 L. & Hum. Behav. 33, 46 (1998); Richard L. Wiener, Linda Hurt, Brenda Russell, Kelley Mannen & Charles Gasper, Perceptions of Sexual Harassment: The Effects of Gender, Legal Standard, and Ambivalent Sexism, 21 L. & Hum. Behav. 71 (1997); Jennifer L. Hurt, et al., Situational and Individual Influences on Judgments of Hostile Environment Sexual Harassment, 29 J. Applied Soc. Psychol. 1395 (1999).

For example, Barbara Gutek, in her 1985 book, Sex and the Workplace: The Impact of Sexual Behavior and Harassment on Women, Men and Organizations, discussed the findings of her study based on a large random sample survey of 1,257 working men and women in Los Angeles County. She discovered that men and women had significantly different reactions to and attitudes about overtures from the opposite sex, e.g., 67% of men said they would be flattered by a woman at work making a proposition to them while only 17% of women responded they would be flattered while the remaining 63% of the women said they would be insulted. Gutek concluded that sexual harassment is generally not a problem for men even though they report receiving social and sexual overtures from women. The majority of the male subjects indicated that young, attractive, unmarried, co-workers or subordinate women made most of the advances to them, and they neither felt coerced to submit to keep their jobs or felt that their work or opportunity for advancement was affected. Women, on the other hand, reported a completely different experience. The average male harasser was older (almost half were forty or over), married, and less attractive. In response to the harassment, over 20% of the women in the study quit a job, transferred, were fired, or quit applying for a job. Torrey, above note 2, at 61–62. See also Barbara A. Gutek & Maureen O'Connor, The Empirical Basis of the Reasonable Woman Standard, 51 J. Soc. Issues 151, 154 (1998) (noting that studies indicate that women are "more liberal, broad, and inclusive in their definitions of harassment" than are men). What do you make of these differences? How can you explain them? Do they help to explain why men and women may have such different views of sexual harassment? Are men more likely to see "sex" at work as sex, while women perceive it to be an abuse of power over them? What problems do these differences cause in litigating sexual harassment cases? In what ways would you address these problems?

5. Do you agree with the Court's distinction between "voluntary" and "welcome"? What difference, if any, does it make? How can a court determine if sexual activity was "unwelcome"? Is consent the same thing as welcomeness? Note that, in general, an employee may not sign a form waiving her right to be free from unlawful discrimination on the basis of race or sex; if she could, as a practical matter, employers might require all employees to execute such a waiver on day one of the job. See generally, Charles A. Sullivan, Michael J. Zimmer & Richard F. Richards, Employment Discrimination, III 336 (2d ed. 1988). What are the risks for women of recognizing welcomeness as a defense? How can a woman demonstrate unwelcomeness? By changing the subject? Leaving the room? Or does she have to expressly tell the harasser that his behavior is unwelcome? Must she "resist"? What are the risks (for men and employers) of not recognizing such a defense? Which alternative is better and more fair? Which alternative is likely to yield the lowest number of errors?

6. Susan Estrich believes that the requirement of "unwelcomeness" imports some of the worst doctrines of rape law into Title VII cases: "Unwelcomeness has emerged as the doctrinal stepchild of the rape standards of consent and resistance, and shares virtually all of their problems." Estrich, Sex at Work, 43 Stan. L. Rev. 813, 827 (1991). Estrich argues that the consent standard shifts the focus from the behavior of the defendant to that of the plaintiff. Id. Do you agree that this is its effect? Is there any way that a welcomeness standard could empower women? Or does the notion of "unwelcomeness" necessarily incorporate female stereotypes? For instance, does posing nude for magazines mean that the plaintiff "welcomes" questions from her employer about her willingness to pose nude for him in the plant? Why or why not? What assumptions underlie the positions on each side? See Burns v. McGregor Electronic Industries, 955 F.2d 559 (8th Cir.1992) (reversing the lower court's conclusion that an employee's objections to alleged sexual harassment in the workplace were not credible in light of her having posed nude for motorcycle magazines).

7. Why does the Supreme Court in *Meritor* consider how a plaintiff dresses relevant? What assumptions must the Court be making? What effect does admission of such evidence have on women plaintiffs? In a 1989 prosecution for rape in Florida, the jury acquitted the defendant explaining that the woman who had worn a lace miniskirt with no underwear "asked for it the way she was dressed." AP, Jury: Woman in Rape Case "asked for it," Chi.

Trib., Oct. 6, 1989, News §, at 11. What are the risks of allowing or disallowing such evidence?

8. The *Meritor* Court says that "sexually provocative speech" is "obviously relevant." Why should the content of a plaintiff's conversations be relevant? How should a woman communicate and be an effective employee when sexual language is prevalent in the workplace? If she is non-responsive, will there be a negative impact on her employment? On the other hand, if she responds in similar language, is she indicating that the environment is "welcome"? See Ukarish v. Magnesium Elektron, 31 F.E.P. 1315 (D.N.J.1983) (dismissing claim because plaintiff appeared to accept the sexual banter at the workplace and even to join in it).

9. How should the rules of discovery and evidence be applied in sexual harassment cases? For instance, should evidence of prior or contemporaneous sexual conduct outside the workplace be admissible? See B.K.B. v. Maui Police Dept., 276 F.3d 1091, 1105 (9th Cir. 2002) (holding in sexual harassment case that evidence regarding plaintiff's alleged sexual fantasies concerning co-workers and sexual behavior while off-duty were barred by federal rules of evidence); Priest v. Rotary, 98 F.R.D. 755 (N.D.Cal.1983) (ruling that defendant in sexual harassment case could not inquire as to the names of plaintiff's sexual partners during the previous ten years since any evidence obtained would be inadmissible under Federal Rule of Evidence 404, which excludes evidence of character or past acts offered to show that a person acted in conformity). Is the issue similar to the problems addressed by rape shield statutes in the criminal context? (See discussion of rape shield statutes, above Chapter 4D(3), note 3.) In 1995, Congress revised F.R.E. 412 to extend "rape shield" protection to civil actions that claim sexual misconduct, including sexual harassment. The rule deems inadmissible, subject to exceptions, evidence offered to prove (1) that any alleged victim engaged in other sexual behavior or (2) any alleged victim's sexual predisposition. However, when Jane Harris Aiken analyzed how the courts were utilizing Rule 412, she found that while "[c]ourts are more willing to be suspicious of broad inquiries into a plaintiff's sexual history even at discovery," "they are finding new relevance for such evidence when evaluating damage claims." Aiken, Sexual Character Evidence in Civil Actions: Refining the Propensity Rule, 1997 Wis. L.Rev. 1221, 1224. In other words, even after Rule 412, when a plaintiff asserts a claim for mental or emotional damages, her sexual history and predisposition are likely to be discoverable and admissible.

10. Under the Civil Rights Act of 1991, Pub.L. 102–166 (Nov. 21, 1991), 105 Stat. 1071, plaintiffs under Title VII can demand (1) punitive damages if the employer acted with malice or reckless indifference to the plaintiff's federal rights; (2) compensatory damages for future pecuniary losses, emotional pain, suffering, inconvenience, mental anguish, loss of enjoyment of life, and other nonpecuniary losses, subject to varying caps from $50,000 to $300,000 depending upon the number of workers employed by the defendant; and (3) a trial by jury. How does this amendment to Title VII change what is at stake in sexual harassment cases? Might there be an even greater emphasis on the mental status of the plaintiff?

11. African American women have played a dominant role as plaintiffs in litigating sexual harassment claims. See Susan Brownmiller & Dolores Alexander, From Carmita Wood to Anita Hill, Ms., Jan./Feb. 1992, at 70. Why do you think this is so? Is it possible to separate sexual harassment from racism? Is this a continuing legacy of slavery? See Sumi Cho, Converging Stereotypes in Racialized Sexual Harassment: Where the Model Minority Meets Suzie Wong, 1 J. Gender, Race & Just. 177, 182 (1997) (arguing that Asian Pacific American women "are at particular risk of being racially and sexually harassed because of the combustible and recombinant reaction of race with gender that produces sexualized racial stereotypes and racialized gender stereotypes").

12. In one of the most important events to publicize sexual harassment, Professor Anita Hill testified in October of 1991 before the Senate Judiciary Committee considering the nomination of Clarence Thomas to be a Supreme Court justice. Hill, who as a young lawyer had worked under the supervision of Thomas at the Equal Employment Opportunity Commission, spoke of numerous unwanted sexual overtures made to her by Thomas. Much of the hearing was televised, with Thomas claiming he was being victimized by a "media lynching." In the first six months following Hill's testimony, the EEOC logged a record number of harassment complaints, 50% more than the previous six months. Jane Mayer & Jill Abramson, Strange Justice: The Selling of Clarence Thomas 352 (1994). Nonetheless, research has found that less than 10% of women in an organization who say they have been harassed reported it to a supervisor. Gail Schmoller Philbin, The Unspoken Accusation: Decades into the Women's Movement, Victims of Sexual Harassment are Still Suffering in Silence, Orlando Sentinel, Mar. 24, 2004, at G1. See also Laura Beth Nielson & Robert Nelson, Rights Realized? An Empirical Analysis of Employment Discrimination Litigation as a Claiming System, 2005 Wis. L. Rev. 663 (2005) (discussing underreporting of discrimination claims generally). How do you explain this? See Edward A. Marshall, Excluding Participation in Internal Complaint Mechanisms From Absolute Retaliation Protection: Why Everyone, Including Employers, Loses, 5 Employee Rts. & Emp. Pol'y J. 549, 587 (2001) (reporting on a study finding that 70 percent of women who did not report their sexual harassment claimed that fear of retaliation was a moderate or strong reason for their failure to do so). Should women feel a moral obligation to enforce Title VII by filing sexual harassment suits? What concerns militate against pursuing a lawsuit? What would you advise a client? What would you do yourself?

HARRIS v. FORKLIFT SYSTEMS, INC.

Supreme Court of the United States, 1993.
510 U.S. 17, 114 S.Ct. 367, 126 L.Ed.2d 295.

JUSTICE O'CONNOR delivered the opinion of the Court [which was unanimous, with concurring opinions by JUSTICES SCALIA and GINSBURG].

In this case we consider the definition of a discriminatorily "abusive work environment" (also known as a "hostile work environment") under Title VII of the Civil Rights Act of 1964.

* * *

Teresa Harris worked as a manager at Forklift Systems, Inc., an equipment rental company, from April 1985 until October 1987. Charles Hardy was Forklift's president.

The Magistrate found that, throughout Harris' time at Forklift, Hardy often insulted her because of her gender and often made her the target of unwanted sexual innuendos. Hardy told Harris on several occasions, in the presence of other employees, "You're a woman, what do you know" and "We need a man as the rental manager"; at least once, he told her she was "a dumb ass woman." Again in front of others, he suggested that the two of them "go to the Holiday Inn to negotiate [Harris'] raise." Hardy occasionally asked Harris and other female employees to get coins from his front pants pocket. He threw objects on the ground in front of Harris and other women, and asked them to pick the objects up. He made sexual innuendos about Harris' and other women's clothing.

In mid-August 1987, Harris complained to Hardy about his conduct. Hardy said he was surprised that Harris was offended, claimed he was only joking, and apologized. He also promised he would stop, and based on this assurance Harris stayed on the job. But in early September, Hardy began anew: While Harris was arranging a deal with one of Forklift's customers, he asked her, again in front of other employees, "What did you do, promise the guy . . . some [sex] Saturday night?" On October 1, Harris collected her paycheck and quit.

Harris then sued Forklift, claiming that Hardy's conduct had created an abusive work environment for her because of her gender. The United States District Court for the Middle District of Tennessee, adopting the report and recommendation of the Magistrate, found this to be "a close case," but held that Hardy's conduct did not create an abusive environment. The court found that some of Hardy's comments "offended [Harris], and would offend the reasonable woman," but that they were not

> "so severe as to be expected to seriously affect [Harris'] psychological well-being. A reasonable woman manager under like circumstances would have been offended by Hardy, but his conduct would not have risen to the level of interfering with that person's work performance.
>
> "Neither do I believe that [Harris] was subjectively so offended that she suffered injury. . . . Although Hardy may at times have genuinely offended [Harris], I do not believe that he created a working environment so poisoned as to be intimidating or abusive to [Harris]."

* * *

When the workplace is permeated with "discriminatory intimidation, ridicule, and insult," that is "sufficiently severe or pervasive to alter the conditions of the victim's employment and create an abusive working environment," Title VII is violated.

This standard, which we reaffirm today, takes a middle path between making actionable any conduct that is merely offensive and requiring the conduct to cause a tangible psychological injury. As we pointed out in *Meritor*, "mere utterance of an ... epithet which engenders offensive feelings in a employee," does not sufficiently affect the conditions of employment to implicate Title VII. Conduct that is not severe or pervasive enough to create an objectively hostile or abusive work environment—an environment that a reasonable person would find hostile or abusive—is beyond Title VII's purview. Likewise, if the victim does not subjectively perceive the environment to be abusive, the conduct has not actually altered the conditions of the victim's employment, and there is no Title VII violation.

But Title VII comes into play before the harassing conduct leads to a nervous breakdown. A discriminatorily abusive work environment, even one that does not seriously affect employees' psychological well-being, can and often will detract from employees' job performance, discourage employees from remaining on the job, or keep them from advancing in their careers. Moreover, even without regard to these tangible effects, the very fact that the discriminatory conduct was so severe or pervasive that it created a work environment abusive to employees because of their race, gender, religion, or national origin offends Title VII's broad rule of workplace equality. The appalling conduct alleged in *Meritor*, and the reference in that case to environments " 'so heavily polluted with discrimination as to destroy completely the emotional and psychological stability of minority group workers,' " merely present some especially egregious examples of harassment. They do not mark the boundary of what is actionable.

We therefore believe the District Court erred in relying on whether the conduct "seriously affect[ed] plaintiff's psychological well-being" or led her to "suffe[r] injury." Such an inquiry may needlessly focus the factfinder's attention on concrete psychological harm, an element Title VII does not require. Certainly Title VII bars conduct that would seriously affect a reasonable person's psychological well-being, but the statute is not limited to such conduct. So long as the environment would reasonably be perceived, and is perceived, as hostile or abusive, there is no need for it also to be psychologically injurious.

This is not, and by its nature cannot be, a mathematically precise test. We need not answer today all the potential questions it raises, nor specifically address the Equal Employment Opportunity Commission's new regulations on this subject, see 58 Fed.Reg. 51266 (1993) (proposed 29 CFR §§ 1609.1, 1609.2); see also 29 CFR § 1604.11 (1993). But we can say that whether an environment is "hostile" or "abusive" can be determined only by looking at all the circumstances. These may include the frequency of the discriminatory conduct; its severity; whether it is physically threatening or humiliating, or a mere offensive utterance; and whether it unreasonably interferes with an employee's work performance. The effect on the employee's psychological well-being is, of course, relevant to determining whether the plaintiff actually found the environment abusive.

But while psychological harm, like any other relevant factor, may be taken into account, no single factor is required. * * *

We therefore reverse the judgment of the Court of Appeals, and remand the case for further proceedings consistent with this opinion.

NOTES ON HARRIS

1. The Court in *Harris* tries to provide greater guidance by indicating that "hostile" or "abusive" can only be determined by looking at all the circumstances, including "frequency of the discriminatory conduct; its severity; whether it is physically threatening or humiliating, or a mere offensive utterance; and whether it unreasonably interferes with an employee's work performance." Do you agree that these factors are important? Are there others that you think are relevant? What are they?

2. Two of the many ironies about sexual harassment are that it both undermines a woman's self-esteem, making it less likely that she will complain about the harassment, and increases stress, which may in fact negatively affect her performance, giving her employer "legitimate" business reasons for terminating her if she does speak out. See James E. Gruber & Lars Bjorn, Women's Responses to Sexual Harassment: An Analysis of Sociocultural, Organizational, and Personal Resource Models, 67 Soc. Sci. Q. 814, 817 (1986); Sandy Lim & Lilia M. Cortina, Interpersonal Mistreatment in the Workplace: The Interface and Impact of General Incivility and Sexual Harassment, 90 J. Applied Psychol. 483 (2005); Joy A. Livingston, Responses to Sexual Harassment on the Job: Legal, Organizational, and Individual Actions, 38 J. Soc. Issues 5, 16 (1982). How are judges likely to respond to evidence of these reactions to harassment? As counsel for plaintiff, how might you try to handle these problems?

3. How might coping responses of victims of sexual harassment further complicate the situation? Women typically try to manage incidents on their own by ignoring the behavior, avoiding the harasser, asking the harasser to stop, or trivializing the incidents by making a joke of the harassment in the hope it will put an end to the behavior. Morrison Torrey, We Get the Message—Pornography in the Workplace, 22 Sw. U. L. Rev. 53, 69–70 (1992). How are these responses likely to affect subsequent litigation?

4. Why do most victims remain silent, or blame themselves for an incident of sexual harassment, rather than complain to management? How would you respond if your supervisor commented on your breasts? What if you were a waitress, and a customer grabbed you and kissed you; what would you do? What if you went out with a group from your office, and a supervisor from another department told you that if you slept with him he would "take care of you?" Would you report the incident to your supervisor, who is a friend of the harasser?

5. Both parties put on expert witnesses about whether pornography in the workplace was sexual harassment in Robinson v. Jacksonville Shipyards, 760 F.Supp. 1486 (M.D.Fla.1991). The pornography that Lois Robinson and other women had to deal with on a daily basis included totally or partially nude women involved in sexually submissive behavior, including "a drawing

depicting a frontal view of a nude female body with the words 'U.S.D.A. Choice' written on it ... a dart board with a drawing of a woman's breast, with her nipple as the bull's eye ... a picture of a woman's pubic area with a meat spatula pressed on it ... multiple centerfold-style pictures ... a picture of a nude woman with long blonde hair wearing high heels and holding a whip [Robinson had long blonde hair and worked with a welding tool called a whip]." Id. at 1495–98. The court found that one of plaintiff's experts, Dr. Susan Fiske, an expert on sexual stereotyping, presented testimony supporting "a sound, credible theoretical framework from which to conclude that the presence of pictures of nude and partially nude women, sexual comments, sexual joking, and other behaviors * * * creates and contributes to a sexually hostile work environment." Id. at 1505. Should expert testimony be necessary to obtain such a conclusion? Is it likely to be necessary?

6. How free is speech at work? Are employees free to speak their minds? Who regulates speech at work? In the *Jacksonville Shipyards* case, discussed above, note 5, the employer banned all political speech at work, including campaign posters, buttons, etc. Why wasn't that ban a violation of the First Amendment? Would the ban on political speech, posters, etc., have violated the First Amendment if the employer had been a government entity? Why would an employer adopt a policy banning political speech but tolerating (or even encouraging) wide-spread displays of pornography, including the type of pornography at Jacksonville Shipyards? See Mary Becker, How Free Is Speech at Work?, 29 U.C. Davis L. Rev. 815 (1996).

On appeal in *Jacksonville Shipyards*, one of the employer's arguments was that pornography alone, if not directed against any particular woman, cannot constitute sexual harassment because it is speech protected by the First Amendment. (Following the employer's bankruptcy, the case settled before an appellate decision was issued.) Except for early cases challenging restrictions on sex-based employment ads, e.g., Pittsburgh Press Co. v. Pittsburgh Comm. on Human Relations, 413 U.S. 376 (1973) (finding sex-specific employment advertisements discriminatory), the First Amendment has been relatively dormant in the employment discrimination context. However, in the 1990's a few scholars began to argue that the First Amendment protected workplace speech from Title VII liability. See generally Eugene Volokh, What Speech Does "Hostile Work Environment" Harassment Law Restrict?, 85 Geo. L. J. 627 (1997); Eugene Volokh, Freedom of Speech and Workplace Harassment, 39 U.C.L.A. L. Rev. 1791 (1992); Kingsley R. Browne, Title VII as Censorship: Hostile–Environment Harassment and the First Amendment, 52 Ohio St. L.J. 481 (1991). To date, however, courts have *not* applied the First Amendment so as to insulate sexual harassment employment discrimination from Title VII remedies. The Supreme Court in *Harris* failed to mention First Amendment concerns even though several amici curiae addressed the issue. See generally Richard H. Fallon, Jr., Sexual Harassment, Content Neutrality, and the First Amendment Dog That Didn't Bark, 1994 Sup. Ct. Rev. 1.

According to Cynthia L. Estlund, perspectives on this issue range from essentially First Amendment absolutism, see, e.g., Browne, above, to a position that "harassment law [is] both necessary to workplace equality and entirely consistent with free speech principles and doctrine," see, e.g., Becker, above. Estlund, Freedom of Expression in the Workplace and the Problem of Discriminatory Harassment, 75 Tex. L. Rev. 687, 693 (1997). Estlund proposes an alternative: "a conception of the workplace as a 'satellite domain' of public discourse—a domain that lies outside the core of public discourse but contributes to that discourse in unique and important ways." Id. at 693–94. Specifically, she proposes:

> a compromise in the form of certain constraints on the *manner* of expression in the workplace forum. Admittedly these constraints would not be constitutional in the public forum. In particular, the proposal would leave unprotected, first, speech that is directed at a listener whom the speaker knows to be offended on the basis of race, sex, or religion, and, second, speech the manner of which is manifestly offensive on the basis of race, sex, or religion—independent of the viewpoint expressed—and that is uttered at a time and place that could not reasonably be avoided by listeners who are thus offended.

Id. at 695.

Should Title VII restrictions on workplace speech be insulated from First Amendment limitations? What would be the advantages and disadvantages of recognizing speech claims in such settings? Do you think the Estlund proposal is a good compromise? How does her approach vary from regarding Title VII regulations as insulated from the First Amendment?

7. Sexual harassment often is prevalent when women attempt to work in traditionally male-dominated occupations. See Elvia R. Arriola, "What's the Big Deal?" Women in the New York City Construction Industry and Sexual Harassment Law, 1970–1985, 22 Colum. Hum. Rts. L. Rev. 21 (1990). Why might men harass women in such situations? Why might such harassment be especially frightening in industries like construction—and hence effective in forcing women out of the job? See, e.g. Vicki Schultz, Reconceptualizing Sexual Harassment, 107 Yale L.J. 1683, 1694–95 (1998) (describing the effect of men's harassment of women workers at a Stroh's Brewery bottling plant in St. Paul, Minnesota).

8. Describe the harm of quid pro quo sexual harassment as a violation of (a) formal equality, (b) MacKinnon's dominance feminism, (c) relational equality, and (d) critical race feminism, all of which are presented in Chapter 3. What does each see as the core harm?

9. Sexual harassment is not just a problem in the United States. According to the International Labor Organization, "[o]ne in 12 women in the industrialized world is forced out of her job after being sexually harassed at work." Job Sex Harassment Hits Industrial World, ILO Washington Focus, Winter 1993, at 1. Research involving 23 industrialized countries showed pervasive sexual harassment against women. However, at that time only seven of the countries had statutes specifically mentioning the term sexual harassment (Australia, Canada, France, New Zealand, Spain, Sweden and some states in the United States); in six countries the term has been defined by judicial opinions (Australia, Canada, Ireland, Switzerland, United Kingdom, and the United States); in many other countries laws concerning unfair dismissal, tort or criminal law have implied prohibitions against sexual harassment. Id. However, in only four years there were dramatic changes: 36

countries adopted sexual harassment legislation by 1997. See ILO, World of Work, No. 19 (Mar. 1997). In May 2002, the European Union Parliament passed legislation defining sexual harassment as a form of discrimination and requiring member states to take steps to promote equality and enforce anti-discrimination laws. Mary Ellen Tsekos, The New European Union Directive on Sexual Harassment and its Implications for Greece, 10 Human Rights 31, 31 (2003).

ONCALE v. SUNDOWNER OFFSHORE SERVICES, INC.

Supreme Court of the United States, 1998.
523 U.S. 75, 118 S.Ct. 998, 140 L.Ed.2d 201.

JUSTICE SCALIA delivered the opinion for a unanimous Court.

This case presents the question whether workplace harassment can violate Title VII's prohibition against "discriminat[ion] . . . because of . . . sex," when the harasser and the harassed employee are of the same sex.

* * *

The precise details are irrelevant to the legal point we must decide, and in the interest of both brevity and dignity we shall describe them only generally. In late October 1991, Oncale was working for respondent Sundowner Offshore Services on a Chevron U.S.A., Inc., oil platform in the Gulf of Mexico. He was employed as a roustabout on an eight-man crew which included respondents John Lyons, Danny Pippen, and Brandon Johnson. Lyons, the crane operator, and Pippen, the driller, had supervisory authority. On several occasions, Oncale was forcibly subjected to sex-related, humiliating actions against him by Lyons, Pippen and Johnson in the presence of the rest of the crew. Pippen and Lyons also physically assaulted Oncale in a sexual manner, and Lyons threatened him with rape. [According to the appellate opinion, the rig was an all-male environment, and the harassment included "Pippen and Johnson restraining Oncale while Lyons placed his penis on Oncale's neck, on one occasion, and on Oncale's arm, on another occasion;" and "the use of force by Lyons to push a bar of soap into Oncale's anus while Pippen restrained Oncale as he was showering on Sundowner premises." 83 F.3d 118, 118–19 (5th Cir.1996).]

Oncale's complaints to supervisory personnel produced no remedial action; in fact, the company's Safety Compliance Clerk, Valent Hohen, told Oncale that Lyons and Pippen "picked [on] him all the time too," and called him a name suggesting homosexuality. Oncale eventually quit—asking that his pink slip reflect that he "voluntarily left due to sexual harassment and verbal abuse." When asked at his deposition why he left Sundowner, Oncale stated "I felt that if I didn't leave my job, that I would be raped or forced to have sex."

* * * [T]he district court held that "Mr. Oncale, a male, has no cause of action under Title VII for harassment by male co-workers."

* * *

Title VII's prohibition of discrimination "because of ... sex" protects men as well as women, and in the related context of racial discrimination in the workplace we have rejected any conclusive presumption that an employer will not discriminate against members of his own race. "Because of the many facets of human motivation, it would be unwise to presume as a matter of law that human beings of one definable group will not discriminate against other members of that group." * * * If our precedents leave any doubt on the question, we hold today that nothing in Title VII necessarily bars a claim of discrimination "because of ... sex" merely because the plaintiff and the defendant (or the person charged with acting on behalf of the defendant) are of the same sex.

Courts have had little trouble with that principle in cases [in which] * * * an employee claims to have been passed over for a job or promotion. But when the issue arises in the context of a "hostile environment" sexual harassment claim, the state and federal courts have taken a bewildering variety of stances. Some, like the Fifth Circuit in this case, have held that same-sex sexual harassment claims are never cognizable under Title VII. Other decisions say that such claims are actionable only if the plaintiff can prove that the harasser is homosexual (and thus presumably motivated by sexual desire). Still others suggest that workplace harassment that is sexual in content is always actionable, regardless of the harasser's sex, sexual orientation, or motivations.

We see no justification in the statutory language or our precedents for a categorical rule excluding same-sex harassment claims from the coverage of Title VII. As some courts have observed, male-on-male sexual harassment in the workplace was assuredly not the principal evil Congress was concerned with when it enacted Title VII. But statutory prohibitions often go beyond the principal evil to cover reasonably comparable evils, and it is ultimately the provisions of our laws rather than the principal concerns of our legislators by which we are governed. Title VII prohibits "discriminat[ion] ... because of ... sex" in the "terms" or "conditions" of employment. Our holding that this includes sexual harassment must extend to sexual harassment of any kind that meets the statutory requirements.

* * *

Courts and juries have found the inference of discrimination easy to draw in most male-female sexual harassment situations, because the challenged conduct typically involves explicit or implicit proposals of sexual activity; it is reasonable to assume those proposals would not have been made to someone of the same sex. The same chain of inference would be available to a plaintiff alleging same-sex harassment, if there were credible evidence that the harasser was homosexual. But harassing conduct need not be motivated by sexual desire to support an inference of discrimination on the basis of sex. A trier of fact might reasonably find such discrimination, for example, if a female victim is harassed in such sex-specific and derogatory terms by another woman as to make it clear that the harasser is motivated by general hostility to the presence of women in the workplace. A same-sex harassment plaintiff may also, of course, offer direct comparative evidence about how the alleged harasser treated members of both sexes in a mixed-sex workplace. Whatever evidentiary route the plaintiff chooses to follow, he or she must always prove that the conduct at issue was not merely tinged with offensive sexual connotations, but actually constituted "discrimina[tion] ... because of ... sex."

* * * The prohibition of harassment on the basis of sex requires neither asexuality nor androgyny in the workplace; it forbids only behavior so objectively offensive as to alter the "conditions" of the victim's employment. "Conduct that is not severe or pervasive enough to create an objectively hostile or abusive work environment—an environment that a reasonable person would find hostile or abusive—is beyond Title VII's purview." We have always regarded that requirement as crucial, and as sufficient to ensure that courts and juries do not mistake ordinary socializing in the workplace—such as male-on-male horseplay or intersexual flirtation—for discriminatory "conditions of employment."

We have emphasized, moreover, that the objective severity of harassment should be judged from the perspective of a reasonable person in the plaintiff's position, considering "all the circumstances." In same-sex (as in all) harassment cases, that inquiry requires careful consideration of the social context in which particular behavior occurs and is experienced by its target. A professional football player's working environment is not severely or pervasively abusive, for example, if the coach smacks him on the buttocks as he heads onto the field—even if the same behavior would reasonably be experienced as abusive by the coach's secretary (male or female) back at the office. The real social impact of workplace behavior often depends on a constellation of surrounding circumstances, expectations, and relationships which are not fully captured by a simple recitation of the words used or the physical acts performed. Common sense, and an appropriate sensitivity to social context, will enable courts and juries to distinguish between simple teasing or roughhousing among members of the same sex, and conduct which a reasonable person in the plaintiff's position would find severely hostile or abusive.

NOTES ON ONCALE

1. The Court notes that some courts had held that only homosexual same-sex harassment was cognizable, because it was "motivated by sexual desire." In either *Meritor* or *Harris* did the Court describe or require a motive for harassment? What do you think motivates a harasser? A variety of reasons have been suggested for male-female harassment: many men, as a result of socialization, can only relate to women as sex objects, not professional colleagues; others perceive women as unwanted competition and hope to force their exit; still others do not understand that their conduct is unwelcome. See generally Morrison Torrey, We Get the Message—Pornography in the Work-

place, 22 Sw. U. L. Rev. 53 (1992); Maria L. Ontiveros, Three Perspectives on Workplace Harassment of Women of Color, 23 Golden Gate U.L. Rev. 817 (1993). What do you think motivated the harassers in *Oncale*?

2. What are the three ways the Supreme Court in *Oncale* says that a plaintiff can show that same-sex sexual harassment is "because of" sex? How successful would Oncale be on remand under each approach?

3. According to one study, men often harass other men to enforce "the traditional heterosexual male gender role." Craig R. Waldo, et al., Are Men Sexually Harassed? If So, by Whom?, 22 Law & Hum. Behav. 59, 61 (1998). According to the authors,

> [t]his form of behavior includes ridiculing men for acting too "feminine" and pressuring them to engage in stereotypical forms of "masculine" behavior. Such behavior can be interpreted as arising from the societal devaluation of femininity and the complementary valorization of male heterosexuality and masculinity. Thus, for men, gender harassment includes not only negative and derogatory remarks about men, and the lewd and obscene comments that also offend women, but also enforcement of the traditional male gender role.

Id. The study also discovered that such harassment between men occurs more often than previously assumed. Id. at 72. See also Hilary S. Axam & Deborah Zalesne, Simulated Sodomy and Other Forms of Heterosexual "Horseplay:" Same Sex Sexual Harassment, Workplace Gender Hierarchies, and the Myth of the Gender Monolith Before and After *Oncale*, 11 Yale J. L. & Feminism 155 (1999). Does this provide an explanation for the occurrences in *Oncale*? Joseph "Jody" Oncale, married with two children, is only 5′4″ tall. Neither he, nor the men who harassed him, are homosexual; Oncale asserted that he is "not a standard-bearer for gay rights," although he was not a "gay-basher." See Mary Judice, LA Offshore Worker Settles Sex Suit, Times–Picayune, Oct. 24, 1998, at C1; Joanna Weiss, Same–Sex Harassing Illegal Too, Court Says, Times–Picayune, Mar. 5, 1998, at A1.

4. Catharine MacKinnon filed an amicus brief on behalf of the National Organization on Male Sexual Victimization, Inc.; Men Stopping Rape, Inc.; et al. in support of Joseph Oncale. 1997 WL 471814. In that brief she argued that "sexual abuse of men by men is a serious social problem of gender inequality" since "sex-discriminatory norms long endemic to such settings [all-male work environments]—under which men may sexually victimize others—must also be addressed to make sex equality real." Id. at 12–13. More specifically, she stated:

> The denial that interactions among men can have a sexual component, and that sexual abuse of men is gendered, are twin features of the social ideology of male dominance with which amici are familiar as experts. In this ideology, men are seen as sexually invulnerable. This image protects men from much male sexual violence and naturalizes the sexual abuse of women, making it seem that women, biologically, are sexual victims. Denying that men can be sexually abused as men thus supports the gender hierarchy of men over women in society. The illusion is preserved that men are sexually inviolable, hence naturally superior, as the sexual abuse of men by men is kept invisible.

Id. at 11. In addressing sexual orientation issues, she asked:

> By definition, sexual harassment is unwanted, so victim sexual orientation is as irrelevant on same-sex facial challenges on sex-basis as it is on opposite-sex ones. The sexual orientation of the victim cannot convert aggression that is sex-based into aggression that is not, or vice-versa.
>
> Will Title VII access now turn on the sexual feelings and imagined or real sexual identities of perpetrators? Will it have one sexual harassment rule for gay sexual harassers and another for straight ones? One for those whose sexual feelings have coalesced, another for those whose sexual feelings are diverse, diffuse, denied, deniable, unknown, or simply unprovable? Oncale sued for forced sex. Why should the gender of those with whom Lyons and Pippen are sexual, when others want to be sexual with them, determine Oncale's rights against them for violating (what is conventionally considered) his manhood?

Id. at 25. Do you agree with MacKinnon that the interactions in *Oncale* had a sexual component (though all the men were heterosexual) and that their interactions were "gendered"? What does MacKinnon mean by "gendered"? What does the Supreme Court mean by "gender discrimination"? Is her approach one that you could have predicted under dominance theory?

5. Scalia gives the following as an example of how a plaintiff might show that same-sex harassment occurred because of sex (though it was not sexually motivated): "a female victim is harassed in such sex-specific and derogatory terms by another woman as to make it clear that the harasser is motivated by general hostility to the presence of women in the workplace." Is this example likely to be of any use to Joseph Oncale, working with other men in an all-male job site? What is the issue on remand in *Oncale*? What could Joseph Oncale introduce as evidence that he was harassed "because of sex" in an all-male environment where most men were not treated the way he was?

Even in an environment with women as well as men, how could Oncale prove discrimination on the basis of sex? Would similar harassment of women (by the men who harassed Oncale) support or undermine Oncale's claim? Would evidence that women were not harassed support his claim that he was harassed because of sex if *most* men as well as *all women* were *not* harassed? Or would evidence that all or some women were harassed support his claim that he was harassed because of sex if no other men were harassed? (The case was settled on the eve of the trial in October of 1998.) See Richard F. Storrow, Same–Sex Sexual Harassment Claims After *Oncale*: Defining the Boundaries of Actionable Conduct, 47 Am. Univ. L.R. 677 (1998).

6. If Oncale shows that he was harassed because he was regarded as an effeminate man, would he prove a violation of Title VII using the sex stereotyping theory announced by the court in Price Waterhouse v. Hopkins, 490 U.S. 228 (1989) (excerpt below this chapter)? (In *Price Waterhouse* the Supreme Court held that it was actionable sex discrimination for an employer to penalize a woman for being aggressive and competitive when it did not penalize men with the same characteristics.) Or would recovery be denied under the cases holding that discrimination on the basis of sex under Title VII does not reach discrimination on the basis of sexual orientation? Lower courts have consistently held that Congress did not intend to reach discrimination on

the basis of sexual orientation when it enacted Title VII's ban on discrimination on the basis of sex. See, e.g., DeSantis v. Pacific Tel. & Tel., 608 F.2d 327, 329–331 (9th Cir.1979); Samuel Estreicher & Michael C. Harper, Cases and Materials on Employment Discrimination and Employment Law 209 (2000). Nonetheless, courts are increasingly interpreting Title VII as providing protection for men harassed because they were perceived as effeminate. See Nichols v. Azteca Restaurant Enterprises, Inc., 256 F.3d 864 (9th Cir. 2001); Doe v. City of Belleville, 119 F.3d 563 (7th Cir.1997); Rene v. MGM Grand Hotel, Inc., 305 F.3d 1061 (9th Cir. 2002).

Despite the fact that the Supreme Court in *Oncale* did not refer to the holding in *Price Waterhouse*, courts since *Oncale* have consistently used the *Price Waterhouse* sex-stereotyping rationale as a fourth method to show sexual harassment is because of sex.

7. Does *Oncale* support the proposition—an argument actually made by employers in early sexual harassment cases and described above in this section—that Title VII cannot reach sexual harassment by the hypothetical non-discriminatory bisexual supervisor who does not discriminate on the basis of sex in selecting targets? Does this suggest that sexual harassment is not a form of sex discrimination? Or does it suggest that the Court in *Oncale* missed some key point about sexual harassment? If the latter, what are they?

8. Under *Oncale* and the interpretation of Title VII as not reaching sexual orientation discrimination is it likely that a gay man harassed by straight men (or a lesbian harassed by straight women) will have a cause of action under Title VII? What difficulties would such a plaintiff have in proving discrimination on the basis of sex? How can the victim of same-sex harassment show sex discrimination other than by showing that someone of the opposite sex would not have been harassed sexually by the harasser(s)? And won't the sexual orientation of the harasser be key to that determination, under traditional ways of thinking, so that gay male harassers of straight men will be violating Title VII whereas straight harassers of gay men will not be violating Title VII? See Steven L. Willborn, Taking Discrimination Seriously: *Oncale* and the Fate of Exceptionalism in Sexual Harassment Law, 7 Wm. & Mary Bill Rts. J. 677 (1999) (noting that nowhere else in discrimination law is such an exacting search of the "true" reason required); see also Dabney D. Ware & Bradley R. Johnson, Oncale v. Sundowner Offshore Services, Inc.: Perverted Behavior Leads to a Perverse Ruling, 51 Fla. L. Rev. 489 (1999) (noting that presumption of sexual desire is available to plaintiff if he can show the harasser was a homosexual). Do you agree with Mary Coombs that "gay workers may well find that *Oncale* has made them more, rather than less, vulnerable in the workplace." Coombs, Title VII and Homosexual Harassment After *Oncale*: Was it a Victory?, 6 Duke J. Gender L. & Pol'y 113, 114 (1999).

9. How would a formal equality feminist describe the harm of sexual harassment? Under what circumstances would a formal equality feminist consider sexual harassment a form of sex discrimination? For example, would heterosexual-male sexual harassment be a form of sexual harassment? What of the bisexual supervisor who harasses both men and women? The heterosexual male who sexually harasses a gay man? A gay man who sexually harasses

a straight man? How would a dominance anti-subordination feminist answer these questions? A relational feminist? How, if at all, is sexual orientation relevant under the various approaches?

10. Did Oncale have alternatives to a Title VII suit? What about criminal charges (rape or assault and battery) or a tort action (assault, battery, invasion of privacy, intentional infliction of emotional distress)? Is this true for other victims of harassment? Why not rely on a torts action? Mark McLaughlin Hager, for example, has argued that victims of hostile environment sexual harassment by non-supervisory co-workers should seek redress through tort suits (primarily outrage and intentional infliction of emotional distress) against the perpetrators rather than a Title VII suit against the employer. Hager, Harassment as a Tort: Why Title VII Hostile Environment Liability Should Be Curtailed, 30 Conn. L. Rev. 375 (1998). He believes that the offense is one to personal dignity and autonomy and is not a type of gender discrimination. Is a tort action a better alternative? Why or why not? Could a tort suit be brought against an employer for negligence, i.e., the supervisor did nothing when informed of the conduct? See also Catharine A. MacKinnon, Sexual Harassment of Working Women 88, 164–74 (1979) (arguing against the personalization and privatization of sexual harassment law through tort actions).

11. Should an employer simply prohibit *all* sexual activity or conversation in the workplace? Is that a feasible, or desirable, response? Recent studies indicate that 70 to 80 percent of people date or wed people they meet at work. See Rocky Mountain News, Looking for Love? Survey Shows It's in Workplace, Bus. §, at 2G (Feb. 14, 1999); Florida Times–Union, First Business, at 12 (Sept. 21, 1998). A 1994 poll by the American Management Association found that about half of workplace romances lead to marriage or a long-term relationship. U.S. Chamber of Commerce, 86 Nation's Business No. 7 (July 1, 1998). In fact many employers believe that workplace romance can benefit companies since "people involved in office romance were more interested in their work, more motivated, more energized, more creative, and extra productive because they didn't want to get criticized by their peers that the romance was causing a fall off in productivity." Id. What do you think of this argument? How can employers allow romance but discourage harassment? Can you draft rules reflecting this difference? Can romance gone sour become harassment?

KATHRYN ABRAMS, THE NEW JURISPRUDENCE OF SEXUAL HARASSMENT

83 Cornell L. Rev. 1169, 1205–1213 (1998).

* * *

Even before the workplace emerged as a site of struggle over gender equality, sexual harassment functioned to preserve male supremacy and reinforced masculine norms. Many "pink collar" jobs and jobs traditionally held by women were defined in order to replicate or draw on the roles women performed in the home or in sexual encounters or relationships. Furthermore, the gendered role of women workers also permitted male employees to enjoy many of the male privileges which men enjoyed outside the workplace. Some attributes of female employment roles perpetuated advantages that were not sexual in nature. A secretary, for example, made her boss's coffee, organized his worklife, and assumed responsibility for social amenities, such as the purchase of gifts. Other female employment roles perpetuated male prerogatives that were characteristically sexual. From office worker to stewardess, women were expected to dress and conduct themselves so as to be aesthetically pleasing or stimulating to male sexual desires. The men who supervised or worked with such women often considered it appropriate to comment on this physical presentation or to act on the desire it was intended to arouse, without any particular reference to the desires of the woman involved. It is in this sense that Catharine MacKinnon wrote in 1979 that sexual harassment was built into the job descriptions of many women in traditionally female jobs. Sexual harassment, along with sex segregation and the specific job requirements of women's work, was a part of the work environment that conditioned the expectations of workers and reinforced the gender hierarchy—of men over women and of masculine power and sexual subjectivity over female service and sexual objectification—that permeated the rest of society.

As more women have begun to claim equal status in society and have sought access to a wider range of jobs, male control over the workplace is no longer so hegemonic that sexualization and sexual availability are built uncontroversially into women's job descriptions. Women now realize that work roles need not replicate the roles prescribed in broader society at large. They have begun to see demands for sexual availability or titillation as extraneous, though they have not always recognized such demands as illegitimate or illegal. In the face of women's demands for equality in the workplace and their tentative exploration of new roles that secured some degree of independence from the roles of wife, mother, or sex object, harassment has begun to both follow different patterns and take on different meanings.

In some cases, sexual harassment has emerged as a means of preserving male control over the workplace, particularly where the entry of women into a particular workforce appears to call that control into question. A prime example is sexual harassment directed at women who have entered predominantly male fields. Some types of harassment within this category are particularly flagrant, including physical or sexual aggression or persistent, targeted verbal abuse so severe as to serve unequivocal notice that women are not welcome. Women targeted in this way are often compelled to leave the workplace or transfer to a job with different coworkers or another supervisor. Even when they stay, it is clear that they remain at the sufferance of their male coworkers; they have no hope of getting sufficient purchase on the workplace to make it in any sense their own.

Other forms of harassment aimed at preserving male control are slightly subtler. Supervisors or coworkers may sexualize women employees by either propositioning them directly or treating them in a manner that highlights their sexuality, as opposed to other, work related characteristics. Supervisors may demand that women workers conform to dominant feminine stereotypes that operate outside the workplace by making repeated comments or suggestions regarding the employees' physical appearance, or through instructions to behave in a feminine manner. In some cases, it may be applied categorically to signal that women are not taken seriously: that they are considered sex objects or "pets" instead of competent workers. These latter forms of harassment may not be sufficient to compel all women to leave any particular workplace. Yet they make clear—to women and the men who work with them—that mere presence is not equal to influence or control. These forms of harassment suggest that whatever professional goals women pursue, they will continue to be viewed and judged by reference to more traditional female roles and whatever careers they enter, they still will occupy subordinate roles.

A distinctive feature of these control oriented forms of sexual harassment is that they operate against women as a group. While the harassment may be directed at a particular target who suffers individual employment detriment, most harassment within this category treats individual women as representatives of their sex based group. The message communicated is not simply about a particular woman but about the suitability of all women for employment in a particular job or work environment.

Other forms of harassment are concerned not with resisting women directly but with asserting the primacy of male prerogatives or norms in the workplace. Sexism involves a hierarchy between men and women, but it is rarely concerned simply with the relations between the biological sexes. Most forms of sexism also involve a valuation of masculine norms—those practices or characteristics associated with men—and a devaluation of feminine norms—those practices or characteristics associated with women. Similarly, most forms of sexism involve a confinement of men and women to paradigmatically masculine and feminine roles. This confinement prevents women from partaking of the privilege that may flow from manifesting more socially valued characteristics. It also prevents men from compromising the hierarchy among values by embracing devalued norms. Discouraging or disciplining instances of nonconformity creates the illusion, as Franke notes, that "femininity is . . . the authentic expression of female agency and masculinity is . . . the authentic expression of male agency."[211] The apparently inevitable association of males with valued (or superordinate) norms and of females with devalued (or subordinate) norms also rationalizes as "natural" the subordination of women to men.

Some forms of harassment seek to enforce this gender hierarchy or gender confinement in the workplace, as they might in other spheres of life. One coworker may devalue a woman who performs a traditionally

211. [Katherine M.] Franke, * * * [What's Wrong with Sexual Harassment?, 49 Stan. L. Rev. 691,] 762 [(1997)].

feminine task (such as secretarial work or food service) by sexualization or derogation. Another may harass a nonfeminine woman or nonmasculine man. These actions may have little to do with workplace relations between the sexes and much to do with social struggles over normative hierarchy and gender conformity.

Yet, there are other forms of sexual harassment which relate to a particular expression of gender hierarchy that occurs in the workplace. The social power of men and the social valuation of masculine norms are expressed, as they are in other social and institutional settings, through the creation of work environments that reflect these norms. Not only do masculine qualities define the effective or successful worker, but also masculine tastes and prerogatives shape the environment in which people do their jobs. Some of this male interaction, such as roughhousing, sexualized talk or pornographic images in the workplace, may not seem "masculine" so much as "the way things are done." Other examples of the entrenchment of masculine norms, such as the toleration of unilateral or even predatory sexual expression, may be recognized as such but are given little thought. All of these norms, however, may be called into question when women, to whom such norms are frequently less natural or less congenial, enter the workplace. When this occurs, male workers may assert these norms more vigorously in order to re-entrench them in the workplace. Some portion of this entrenching behavior may be sexual harassment.

Workers may engage (or engage more intensely) in talk that sexualizes or derogates women. They may circulate or post sexually explicit or pornographic visual images. They may engage in practices such as bagging [unexpectedly grabbing a male's genitals] that express a vaguely sexualized form of masculine camaraderie. Such practices not only make "masculine" male workers more comfortable, but they also mark the workplace as an arena in which masculinity is appropriate or even constitutive. Workers may also express the traditionally male prerogative for initiating sex in a range of contexts and without particular reference to the desires of the target. A number of forces may motivate such practices, including actual sexual desire, the impulse to affirm a previously unchallenged prerogative of masculinity, or both. What is distinctive about this last category of behavior, for purposes of sexual harassment analysis, is not the particular motivation (i.e., sexual desire or nonsexual desire) but that the perpetrator feels sufficiently authorized to express himself in this way that he fails to consider the possibility of either contextual inappropriateness or injury to the target. Finally, workers may engage in vigorous disciplinary action against colleagues whose action or self-presentation threatens to undermine the primacy of masculine norms. Men or women who object to these norms or practices may be targeted, as may men who manifest nonmasculine traits.

Some of this behavior appears to be almost reflexive: it is conditioned by a structural arrangement that suggests the centrality or naturalness within the workplace of certain masculine norms, and that may suggest, at some subconscious level, the need to reassert them if workers perceive these norms to be in danger. However, some of this behavior may also be more self-aware and explicitly responsive, aimed as retaliating against women intruders or signaling that the demographic composition of the workplace may have changed but the organizing norms have not. Nevertheless, such behavior as a whole seeks to restore a balance, an orientation around masculine normative lines, that workers perceive disturbed. These norm entrenching forms of sexual harassment may be directed at women as a group—insofar as sexualization or derogation of women is an accepted mode of expressing masculinity or masculine camaraderie. They also may be directed at individual men or women whose actions or modes of self-presentation seem to pose a threat to the unquestioned (or embattled) predominance of masculine norms.

NOTES ON SEXUAL HARASSMENT JURISPRUDENCE

1. Kathryn Abrams views sexual harassment as being not primarily about sex but about using sex for instrumental ends—namely to preserve male dominance in the workplace. What does Abrams mean by "control oriented" forms of sexual harassment? How does sexual harassment, according to Abrams, reinforce gender norms and reinstantiate the hierarchy of masculine over feminine roles?

2. Why in Abrams's view is sexual harassment of a particular woman a form of discrimination against women as a group? Do you agree? Would Abrams treat as actionable sex discrimination sexual harassment against a woman in a workplace in which no other women are similarly harmed? Would you adopt a similar or different approach? How does Abrams view the harms of less targeted "norm entrenching" forms of sexual harassment that reinforce the masculine ethos of a workplace?

3. An alternative theory of sexual harassment is offered by Anita Bernstein:

> How, then, to understand sexual harassment? * * * Hostile environment sexual harassment, I argue, is a type of incivility or—in the locution that I prefer—disrespect. For purposes of doctrine, accordingly, hostile environment complaints should refer to respect; the plaintiff should be required to prove that the defendant—a man, or a woman, or a business entity—did not conform to the standard of a respectful person. This respectful person standard would rightly supplant references to reason and reasonableness; respect is integral to the understanding and remedying of sexual harassment, whereas reason is not.
>
> In giving content to the ideal of equality behind Title VII as well as the ideal of individual autonomy behind dignitary—tort law, this respectful person standard would fit within the two most important legal bases for redressing sexual harassment in the workplace. Focus on respect addresses the concerns of both those who identify with the imperfect humanity of the accused harasser and those who seek foremost to purge sexual coercion from the workplace. Respect also reconciles competing perspectives on fault, simultaneously recognizing the tort—like wrong of sexual

> harassment and the Title VII emphasis on workplace discrimination. It gives shape to a problem whose outlines have been blurred and contested. Despite its apparent novelty, the respectful person standard is intelligible, easy to execute, and not especially vulnerable to abuse or confusion. In short, it is likely to help reduce the incidence of hostile environment sexual harassment and to provide a remedy for injured plaintiffs.

Bernstein, Treating Sexual Harassment with Respect, 111 Harv. L. Rev. 445, 450–51 (1997). Do you share Bernstein's optimism that the courts will easily be able to comprehend and apply her "respectful person" standard? Do you think there is a universal understanding of what "respect" is? How would you advise an employer client to convey to her employees what would be required under Bernstein's theory of sexual harassment? Would Bernstein's approach eliminate the "because of sex" element from Title VII and replace it with a requirement that all employees be treated with respect? Is there any way to reconcile her approach with the language of Title VII? How precisely is the respect standard different from the current standard? Which one is better for plaintiffs? For defendants? Why?

4. Katherine Franke offers a view of the problems with how sexual harassment jurisprudence is currently articulated and offers yet another alternative:

> Although the Supreme Court has not provided such a theory [of sexual harassment], feminist theorists and lower courts have attempted to do so. Over time, three principal justifications have emerged for considering workplace sexual harassment a violation of Title VII's proscriptions against discrimination "on the basis of sex": (1) it is conduct that would not have been undertaken but for the plaintiff's sex; (2) it is conduct that violates Title VII precisely because it is sexual in nature; and (3) it is conduct that sexually subordinates women to men.
>
> Each of these approaches to the wrong of sexual harassment has formed the foundation for successful litigation challenging sexually hostile working environments under Title VII. Yet to varying degrees, all three of these paradigms fail to provide an adequate account of why sexual harassment is a form of sex discrimination. * * * When pressed, they provide indeterminate and unprincipled outcomes to both central and marginal cases of sexual harassment. What is more, these theories misdirect attention from the real problem: sexual harassment is a sexually discriminatory wrong because of the gender norms it reflects and perpetuates.
>
> According to the theory I develop * * *, the sexual harassment of a woman by a man is an instance of sexism precisely because the act embodies fundamental gender stereotypes: men as sexual conquerors and women as sexually conquered, men as masculine sexual subjects and women as feminine sexual objects. If a "technology" is a manner of accomplishing a task, or the specialized aspect of a particular field, then sexual harassment is both the manner of accomplishing sexist goals, and the specialized instantiation of a sexist ideology. Sexual harassment is a technology of sexism. It is a disciplinary practice that inscribes, enforces, and polices the identities of both harasser and victim according to a

> system of gender norms that envisions women as feminine, (hetero)sexual objects, and men as masculine, (hetero)sexual subjects. This dynamic is both performative and reflexive in nature. Performative in the sense that the conduct produces a particular identity in the participants, and reflexive in that both the harasser and the victim are affected by the conduct. The account I suggest provides a better theoretical context from which to draw the inference that, in cases like *Meritor*, the sexual harassment of women by men, "without question," is discrimination "because of sex." At the same time, this framework has the advantage of furnishing a principled way to approach the increasing number of new sexual harassment cases at the margin involving same-sex sexual harassment. Neither the existing Supreme Court account of sexual harassment, nor the three dominant theories of the wrong of sexual harassment can provide an adequate or principled answer to these two questions: (1) why should we draw the inference, in cases like *Meritor*, that sexual harassment is sex discrimination?; and (2) does the sexual harassment of a man by another man constitute sex discrimination?
>
> * * *
>
> On my account, sexual harassment—between any two people of whatever sex—is a form of sex discrimination when it reflects or perpetuates gender stereotypes in the workplace. I suggest a reconceptualization of sexual harassment as gender harassment. Understood in this way, sexual harassment is a kind of sex discrimination not because the conduct would not have been undertaken if the victim had been a different sex, not because it is sexual, and not because men do it to women, but precisely because it is a technology of sexism. That is, it perpetuates, enforces, and polices a set of gender norms that seek to feminize women and masculinize men. * * * As a tool of sexism, sexual harassment can do its dirty work in either a different-sex or a same-sex context. Thus, the sexism in sexual harassment lies not in the fact that it is sexual, but in what it does as a disciplinary, constitutive, and punitive regulatory practice.

Katherine M. Franke, What's Wrong with Sexual Harassment?, 49 Stan. L. Rev. 691, 695–96 (1997). How precisely does Franke's analysis differ from Abrams' or from MacKinnon's in her brief in *Oncale*? Which of these approaches to sexual harassment do you think is the best? Why? Which is the easiest to apply? Which best covers and explains every permutation of sexual harassment? Can you articulate an even better theory, or might different theories be needed to describe different types of sexual harassment?

TEXT NOTE: EMPLOYER LIABILITY

After sexual harassment was recognized as an actionable form of sex discrimination under Title VII, the question remained as to when and under what conditions employers would be held liable for such harassment. In traditional cases of sex discrimination, in which an employee was refused a job or fired because of sex, employers were always held liable for the actions of their agents under the doctrine of respondeat superior. In sexual harassment cases, however, courts were more ambivalent about the appropriateness of holding employers liable for sexually harassing conduct of supervisors and co-workers, particularly in instances in which the harassment was not accompanied by some tangible employment action such as a termination or demotion.

As a general matter in the years after *Meritor*, courts imposed liability upon employers for quid pro quo harassment by supervisors, whether or not the employer actually knew of the conduct or the supervisor acted outside the scope of his employment.[21] However, in hostile environment cases—whether the hostile environment was created by supervisors or co-workers—lower federal courts often applied a negligence standard, holding employers liable only if they knew or should have known of the hostile environment.[22]

In 1998, the Supreme Court issued two opinions on the same day addressing the issue of employer liability for hostile environment sexual harassment committed by supervisors. The cases were Faragher v. City of Boca Raton, 524 U.S. 775 (1998), and Burlington Industries, Inc. v. Ellerth, 524 U.S. 742 (1998). In *Faragher*, the plaintiff was a college student who worked during the summers as a lifeguard for Boca Raton. She asserted that her supervisors repeatedly subjected her and other female lifeguards to uninvited and offensive touching as well as lewd and demeaning remarks addressed to them personally and about women generally. Even though the City had a sexual harassment policy, it failed to disseminate it to her supervisors, and they were unaware of it. While the plaintiff talked about the offensive behavior with a supervisor, she considered these discussions to be personal and not a formal complaint; and the supervisor did not report the conversations to any City official. Later, however, another female lifeguard wrote to the City's Personnel Director to complain about the harassing supervisors' behavior. As a result, the City investigated and punished them.

The trial court found sexual harassment and held the City liable because: (1) the harassment was pervasive enough that the City had "constructive knowledge" of it; (2) under traditional agency principles, the supervisors were acting as agents; and (3) another supervisor had knowledge of the harassment and did not take any action. On appeal, the Eleventh Circuit agreed with the finding of discrimination, but reversed the imposition of liability on the employer, finding that the supervisors were acting outside the scope of their employment when they were harassing; that they were not aided in their actions by the agency relationship; and that the City did not have constructive knowledge of the unlawful activity.

The Supreme Court refused to impose automatic liability on employers for supervisors who harass. Instead, the Court held that an employer could raise the following affirmative defenses to shield itself from liability:

> (a) that the employer exercised reasonable care to prevent and correct promptly any sexually harassing behavior, and (b) that the plaintiff employee unreasonably failed to take advantage of any preventive or corrective opportunities provided by the employer or to avoid harm

---

21. See, e.g., Katz v. Dole, 709 F.2d 251, 256 n. 6 (4th Cir.1983); 29 C.F.R. § 1604.11(c); EEOC Policy Guidance on Current Issues of Sexual Harassment D(1) (Mar. 19, 1990).

22. See, e.g., EEOC v. Hacienda Hotel, 881 F.2d 1504 (9th Cir.1989) (harassment by supervisors); Hall v. Gus Constr. Co., 842 F.2d 1010, 1016 (8th Cir.1988) (harassment by co-workers).

> otherwise. While proof that an employer had promulgated an antiharassment policy with complaint procedures is not necessary in every instance as a matter of law, the need for a stated policy suitable to the employment circumstances may appropriately be addressed in any case when litigating the first element of the defense. And while proof that an employee failed to fulfill the corresponding obligation of reasonable care to avoid harm is not limited to showing an unreasonable failure to use any complaint procedure provided by the employer, a demonstration of such failure will normally suffice to satisfy the employer's burden under the second element of the defense. No affirmative defense is available, however, when the supervisor's harassment culminates in a tangible employment action, such as discharge, demotion, or undesirable reassignment.

Id. at 807. The Court thus established two distinct tests for employer liability for harassment by supervisors of subordinates. First, in instances in which the harassment resulted in a tangible employment action, the employer would be strictly liable for the harassment. Second, in instances involving no tangible employment action, the employer would be liable unless it could satisfy the two prong affirmative defense (exercise of care by employer and failure of plaintiff to minimize the harm). *Faragher* involved no "tangible job action," and the Court imposed liability on the City because it failed to meet the requirements of the affirmative defense since its sexual harassment policy was not distributed to the many city departments and the policy was an inadequate precaution against hostile environment discrimination.

The plaintiff in the second case, *Ellerth,* alleged constant sexual harassment by one of her supervisors who threatened to make her work life harder but did not take any specific adverse actions against her. The plaintiff did not complain to anyone in authority at Burlington Industries. In its analysis, the Supreme Court noted that the former division of sexual harassment claims into those in which the employee faces actual or threatened adverse consequences if she does not comply with sexual demands (quid pro quo) and those premised upon "bothersome attentions or sexual remarks that are sufficiently severe or pervasive" (hostile work environment) was not useful in determining employer liability. Instead, the Court reiterated the principle in *Faragher* that employers would be liable in cases in which sexual harassment by supervisors resulted in tangible employment actions against the employee, but that employers have a possible affirmative defense to sexual harassment by supervisors when no tangible employment action is taken. The case was remanded to permit the trial court to determine whether to allow the plaintiff to amend her pleading or supplement her discovery based on the rulings in *Ellerth* and *Faragher*; the employer would then have an opportunity to assert and prove an affirmative defense. In dissent, Justices Thomas and Scalia were willing to impose liability upon the employer only if it was negligent in permitting the supervisor's conduct to occur.

In *Ellerth*, the Court offered additional guidance on what it meant by tangible employment action and explained why employers were vicariously liable for supervisor harassment whenever the supervisor took a tangible job action against the harassed employee. (The affirmative defense described in

Faragher is not available when there has been an adverse and tangible job action.) The Court explained:

> Tangible employment actions are the means by which the supervisor brings the official power of the enterprise to bear on subordinates. A tangible employment decision requires an official act of the enterprise, a company act. The decision in most cases is documented in official company records, and may be subject to review by higher level supervisors. The supervisor often must obtain the imprimatur of the enterprise and use its internal processes.
>
> For these reasons, a tangible employment action taken by the supervisor becomes for Title VII purposes the act of the employer.

524 U.S. at 762.

> In the context of this case, a tangible employment action would have taken the form of a denial of a raise or a promotion. * * * A tangible employment action constitutes a significant change in employment status, such as hiring, firing, failing to promote, reassignment with significantly different responsibilities, or a decision causing a significant change in benefits. Compare Crady v. Liberty Nat. Bank & Trust Co. of Ind., 993 F.2d 132, 136 (7th Cir.1993) ("a materially adverse change might be indicated by a termination of employment, a demotion evidenced by a decrease in wage or salary, a less distinguished title, a material loss of benefits, significantly diminished material responsibilities, or other indices that might be unique to a particular situation"), with Flaherty v. Gas Research Institute, 31 F.3d 451, 456 (7th Cir.1994) (a "bruised ego" is not enough); Kocsis v. Multi–Care Management, Inc., 97 F.3d 876, 887 (6th Cir.1996) (demotion without change in pay, benefits, duties, or prestige insufficient) and Harlston v. McDonnell Douglas Corp., 37 F.3d 379, 382 (8th Cir.1994) (reassignment to more inconvenient job insufficient).

Id. at 761.

NOTES ON EMPLOYER LIABILITY

1. The Court in *Ellerth* holds that the employer is automatically liable for a supervisor's harassment only when it culminates in a tangible employment action. This is a significant change from pre-*Ellerth* law. As described above, both the lower federal courts and the EEOC had imposed automatic liability on employers for quid pro quo harassment by a supervisor. And quid pro quo harassment was understood, by at least some courts, as including implicit as well as explicit threats by supervisors. See, for example, the EEOC definition of sexual harassment at the beginning of this section. After *Ellerth*, what is the current standard of employer liability for harassment by a supervisor involving threats that are implicit or never acted upon? Is the current affirmative defense adequate to protect employees? Is it necessary to protect employers from unjustified liability? What standard would you impose for supervisor threats (implicit or explicit) that do not result in "tangible job action"?

2. Subsequent to *Ellerth* and *Faragher*, at least one court has "concluded that extra work assignments, 'inappropriate' work assignments, and denial of the opportunity to attend a professional conference did not rise to the level of 'tangible employment action.'" Reinhold v. Virginia, 151 F.3d 172, 174–75 (4th Cir.1998). Is this consistent with *Ellerth*'s explanation of tangible job action? Is the Reinhold decision cause for concern? Do you find the court's notion of tangible job action too narrow? Recall that automatic liability is imposed on the employer for supervisor harassment only when there has been an adverse employment action because it is the adverse action that makes the supervisor's act the company's act. But does this necessitate a conclusion that reassignment to a more inconvenient job is *not* a tangible job action? Can you suggest any explanation for the narrowness of the Court's standard for tangible job action?

3. When there has been supervisor harassment but no tangible employment action is taken, the employer can raise an affirmative defense (to be proven by a preponderance of the evidence): "(a) that the employer exercised reasonable care to prevent and correct promptly any sexually harassing behavior, and (b) that the plaintiff employee unreasonably failed to take advantage of any preventive or corrective opportunities provided by the employer or to avoid harm otherwise." *Faragher*, 524 U.S. at 807. How would you advise an employer who wishes to avoid liability? Should the employer hold special training sessions for all supervisors? Write, circulate and enforce a sexual harassment policy? What can an employer do to encourage victims to use the procedures of such a policy? If you experienced sexual harassment from a partner at a law firm, would you make use of the complaint procedure of a sexual harassment policy? Why or why not? Can an employer anticipate and address these concerns? How?

4. Left unaddressed by the Supreme Court is the standard for establishing employer liability for hostile environment harassment created by co-workers. What do you think the standard should be? Perhaps the Supreme Court has not been concerned about this issue because, as noted above, the lower courts have consistently held that employers are liable for hostile environments created by co-workers, customers, vendors, etc. only when the employer knew or should have known about the harassment and did not respond appropriately. Do you agree that this is the appropriate standard? Under what conditions would you consider an employer negligent in this respect?

5. In the late 1990's another development occurred in the area of sexual harassment: high-profile class action suits. Three highly visible suits filed against Smith Barney, Merrill Lynch and Mitsubishi Motors affirmed the effectiveness of such suits. The actions against the two brokerage houses were groundbreaking in another way—the two employers agreed not to enforce the security industry's arbitration contract forfeiting employee rights to a court forum, leading the National Association of Securities Dealers (NASD) to allow job discrimination suits to bypass the mandatory arbitration requirement. The multi-million dollar settlements in the brokerage cases also made use of creative mediation, arbitration and judicial options for individual plaintiffs in the class. See Martens v. Smith Barney, Inc., 194 F.R.D. 113 (S.D.N.Y.2000); Cremin v. Merrill Lynch Pierce Fenner & Smith, Inc., 957 F.Supp. 1460

(N.D.Ill.1997); EEOC v. Mitsubishi Motor Manufacturing of America, 990 F.Supp. 1059 (C.D.Ill.1998). Publicity played a major role in all three of these lawsuits, applying enormous pressure on the defendants to settle. The National Organization for Women (NOW), a key player in public demonstrations in the cases, is now implementing a "direct action" campaign, asking the country's top 500 employers to sign a NOW pledge that "ensures a women-friendly workplace," including a workplace free of discrimination. While several major companies have signed the pledge, nearly 97% have not. See Carol Kleiman, Making an Enemy of Workplace Discrimination, Chi. Tribune, Aug. 17, 1999, Business §, at 1. Litigation, coupled with media campaigns, can be more effective than litigation alone. What kinds of strategies should we be implementing in the 21st Century?

6. How would you assess the current state of sexual harassment law? Would you recommend a Congressional response to the Supreme Court opinions establishing employer liability or do you think they have struck the right balance between protecting employee rights and employer interests? Do they give employers the appropriate incentives to stop harassment in their organizations? If not, what kind of legislation would you propose?

7. Perhaps the most notorious sexual harassment case to date arose when Paula Jones claimed that then-Governor Bill Clinton, among other things, exposed his erect penis to her and asked her to "kiss it" after she went to his hotel room to meet him during a convention she was staffing as an Arkansas employee. Contrary to Ms. Jones' allegations of adverse employment actions taken after she refused, the judge found that the plaintiff received every cost-of-living and merit increase subsequent to the event, as well as receiving a job upgrade. After discovery was complete, and upon remand from the Supreme Court after it rejected a finding of temporary immunity for the President for a civil action arising before he assumed that office until after he leaves that office, Clinton v. Jones, 520 U.S. 681 (1997), the judge granted summary judgment to the defendant on the ground that plaintiff did not establish a sexual harassment claim. Jones v. Clinton, 990 F.Supp. 657 (E.D.Ark.1998). Why were Jones's allegations insufficient to establish sexual harassment? See Susan S. Blaha, Feminism in the Wake of Jones v. Clinton: Theory, Politics, and the Law, 1 DePaul Women's L.J. 1 (1998). It was President Clinton's testimony during discovery in that case that led to Independent Counsel Kenneth Starr's accusations that the President obstructed justice and committed perjury, ultimately resulting in the House of Representatives bringing impeachment charges against the President. After the failure of impeachment proceedings in the Senate, President Clinton settled the *Jones* suit to foreclose subsequent appeals. Unfortunately, the *Jones* case, including the information contained in the deposition of White House intern Monica Lewinsky, arguably created an atmosphere in which sexual harassment became more of a joke (or cliché) than a serious societal problem. See Christina E. Wells, Essay: Hypocrites and Barking Harlots: The Clinton–Lewinsky Affair and the Attack on Women, 5 Wm. & Mary J. Women & L. 151 (1998). Do you agree that sexual harassment has become a joke? How is it portrayed? It seems to be more and more the subject for television sit-coms and late night comedian monologues. What consequences does this have for working women?

8. Vicki Schultz has argued that human resources personnel in companies have used sexual harassment law as an excuse to sterilize the workplace of sexualized conduct even though such conduct is often not illegal and may actually be both enjoyable and energizing for employees. See Schultz, The Sanitized Workplace, 112 Yale L. J. 2061 (2003). Do you agree that sexual harassment law has been taken too far and is being used by employers (if not by courts) to sterilize and unnecessarily inhibit women's and men's relations in the workplace? Alternatively, do you think that most companies are not interpreting their sexual harassment policies broadly enough? Compare Schultz with Kimberly A. Yuracko, Private Nurses and Playboy Bunnies, Explaining Permissible Sex Discrimination, 92 Cal. L. Rev. 147 (2004) (warning of the dangers to women of being explicitly sexualized in mainstream jobs).

D. SEXUALITY, STEREOTYPING, FEMININITY, AND PROFESSIONAL APPEARANCE

PRICE WATERHOUSE v. HOPKINS

Supreme Court of the United States, 1989.
490 U.S. 228, 109 S.Ct. 1775, 104 L.Ed.2d 268.

JUSTICE BRENNAN announced the judgment of the Court and delivered an opinion, in which JUSTICE MARSHALL, JUSTICE BLACKMUN, and JUSTICE STEVENS join.

* * *

Ann Hopkins had worked at Price Waterhouse's Office of Government Services in Washington, D.C., for five years when the partners in that office proposed her as a candidate for partnership. Of the 662 partners at the firm at that time, 7 were women. Of the 88 persons proposed for partnership that year, only 1—Hopkins—was a woman. Forty-seven of these candidates were admitted to the partnership, 21 were rejected, and 20—including Hopkins—were "held" for reconsideration the following year. * * *

In a jointly prepared statement supporting her candidacy, the partners in Hopkins' office showcased her successful 2–year effort to secure a $25 million contract with the Department of State, labeling it "an outstanding performance" and one that Hopkins carried out "virtually at the partner level." Despite Price Waterhouse's attempt at trial to minimize her contribution to this project, Judge Gesell specifically found that Hopkins had "played a key role in Price Waterhouse's successful effort to win a multi-million dollar contract with the Department of State." Indeed, he went on, "[n]one of the other partnership candidates at Price Waterhouse that year had a comparable record in terms of successfully securing major contracts for the partnership."

The partners in Hopkins' office praised her character as well as her accomplishments, describing her in their joint statement as "an outstanding professional" who had a "deft touch," a "strong character, independence and integrity.'' Clients appear to have agreed with these assessments. At trial, one official from the State Department described her as ''extremely competent, intelligent,'' ''strong and forthright, very productive, energetic and creative.'' Another high-ranking official praised Hopkins' decisiveness, broadmindedness, and ''intellectual clarity''; she was, in his words, ''a stimulating conversationalist.'' Evaluations such as these led Judge Gesell to conclude that Hopkins ''had no difficulty dealing with clients and her clients appear to have been very pleased with her work'' and that she ''was generally viewed as a highly competent project leader who worked long hours, pushed vigorously to meet deadlines and demanded much from the multidisciplinary staffs with which she worked.''

On too many occasions, however, Hopkins' aggressiveness apparently spilled over into abrasiveness. Staff members seem to have borne the brunt of Hopkins' brusqueness. Long before her bid for partnership, partners evaluating her work had counseled her to improve her relations with staff members. Although later evaluations indicate an improvement, Hopkins' perceived shortcomings in this important area eventually doomed her bid for partnership. Virtually all of the partners' negative remarks about Hopkins—even those of partners supporting her—had to do with her ''interpersonal skills.'' Both ''[s]upporters and opponents of her candidacy,'' stressed Judge Gesell, ''indicated that she was sometimes overly aggressive, unduly harsh, difficult to work with and impatient with staff.''

There were clear signs, though, that some of the partners reacted negatively to Hopkins' personality because she was a woman. One partner described her as ''macho''; another suggested that she ''overcompensated for being a woman''; a third advised her to take ''a course at charm school.'' Several partners criticized her use of profanity; in response, one partner suggested that those partners objected to her swearing only ''because it's a lady using foul language.'' Another supporter explained that Hopkins ''ha[d] matured from a tough-talking somewhat masculine hard-nosed mgr [manager] to an authoritative, formidable, but much more appealing lady ptr [partner] candidate.'' But it was the man who, as Judge Gesell found, bore responsibility for explaining to Hopkins the reasons for the Policy Board's decision to place her candidacy on hold who delivered the coup de grace: in order to improve her chances for partnership, Thomas Beyer advised, Hopkins should ''walk more femininely, talk more femininely, dress more femininely, wear make-up, have her hair styled, and wear jewelry.''

Dr. Susan Fiske, a social psychologist and Associate Professor of Psychology at Carnegie–Mellon University, testified at trial that the partnership selection process at Price Waterhouse was likely influenced by sex stereotyping. Her testimony focused not only on the overtly sex-based comments of partners but also on gender-neutral remarks, made by partners who knew Hopkins only slightly, that were intensely critical of her. One partner, for example, baldly stated that Hopkins was ''universally disliked'' by staff, and another described her as ''consistently annoying and irritating"; yet these were people who had had very little contact with Hopkins. According to Fiske, Hopkins' uniqueness (as the only woman in the pool of candidates) and the subjectivity of the evaluations made it likely that sharply critical remarks such as these were the product of sex stereotyping—although Fiske admitted that she could not say with certainty whether any particular comment was the result of stereotyping. * * *

In previous years, other female candidates for partnership also had been evaluated in sex-based terms. As a general matter, Judge Gesell concluded, "[c]andidates were viewed favorably if partners believed they maintained their femin[in]ity while becoming effective professional managers"; in this environment, "[t]o be identified as a 'women's lib[b]er' was regarded as [a] negative comment." * * *

* * *

In passing Title VII, Congress made the simple but momentous announcement that sex, race, religion, and national origin are not relevant to the selection, evaluation, or compensation of employees. Yet, the statute does not purport to limit the other qualities and characteristics that employers may take into account in making employment decisions. * * * Title VII eliminates certain bases for distinguishing among employees while otherwise preserving employers' freedom of choice. This balance between employee rights and employer prerogatives turns out to be decisive in the case before us.

Congress' intent to forbid employers to take gender into account in making employment decisions appears on the face of the statute. In now-familiar language, the statute forbids an employer to "fail or refuse to hire or to discharge any individual, or otherwise to discriminate with respect to his compensation, terms, conditions, or privileges of employment," or to "limit, segregate, or classify his employees or applicants for employment in any way which would deprive or tend to deprive any individual of employment opportunities or otherwise adversely affect his status as an employee, because of such individual's . . . sex." We take these words to mean that gender must be irrelevant to employment decisions. * * *

* * *

We need not leave our common sense at the doorstep when we interpret a statute. It is difficult for us to imagine that, in the simple words "because of," Congress meant to obligate a plaintiff to identify the precise causal role played by legitimate and illegitimate motivations in the employment decision she challenges. We conclude, instead, that Congress meant to obligate her to prove that the employer relied upon sex-based considerations in coming to its decision.

* * *

To say that an employer may not take gender into account is not, however, the end of the matter, for that describes only one aspect of Title

VII. The other important aspect of the statute is its preservation of an employer's remaining freedom of choice. We conclude that the preservation of this freedom means that an employer shall not be liable if it can prove that, even if it had not taken gender into account, it would have come to the same decision regarding a particular person. The statute's maintenance of employer prerogatives is evident from the statute itself and from its history, both in Congress and in this Court.

* * *

[W]e hold that the plaintiff retains the burden of persuasion on the issue whether gender played a part in the employment decision * * *. [T]he employer's burden is most appropriately deemed an affirmative defense: the plaintiff must persuade the fact finder on one point, and then the employer, if it wishes to prevail, must persuade it on another.

* * *

In saying that gender played a motivating part in an employment decision, we mean that, if we asked the employer at the moment of the decision what its reasons were and if we received a truthful response, one of those reasons would be that the applicant or employee was a woman. In the specific context of sex stereotyping, an employer who acts on the basis of a belief that a woman cannot be aggressive, or that she must not be, has acted on the basis of gender.

Although the parties do not overtly dispute this last proposition, the placement by Price Waterhouse of "sex stereotyping" in quotation marks throughout its brief seems to us an insinuation either that such stereotyping was not present in this case or that it lacks legal relevance. We reject both possibilities. As to the existence of sex stereotyping in this case, we are not inclined to quarrel with the District Court's conclusion that a number of the partners' comments showed sex stereotyping at work. As for the legal relevance of sex stereotyping, we are beyond the day when an employer could evaluate employees by assuming or insisting that they matched the stereotype associated with their group, for " '[i]n forbidding employers to discriminate against individuals because of their sex, Congress intended to strike at the entire spectrum of disparate treatment of men and women resulting from sex stereotypes.' " An employer who objects to aggressiveness in women but whose positions require this trait places women in an intolerable and impermissible Catch–22: out of a job if they behave aggressively and out of a job if they do not. Title VII lifts women out of this bind.

* * *

It takes no special training to discern sex stereotyping in a description of an aggressive female employee as requiring "a course at charm school." Nor, turning to Thomas Beyer's memorable advice to Hopkins, does it require expertise in psychology to know that, if an employee's flawed "interpersonal skills" can be corrected by a soft-hued suit or a new shade of lipstick, perhaps it is the employee's sex and not her interpersonal skills that has drawn the criticism.

* * *

We hold that when a plaintiff in a Title VII case proves that her gender played a motivating part in an employment decision, the defendant may avoid a finding of liability only by proving by a preponderance of the evidence that it would have made the same decision even if it had not taken the plaintiff's gender into account. Because the courts below erred by deciding that the defendant must make this proof by clear and convincing evidence, we reverse the Court of Appeals' judgment against Price Waterhouse on liability and remand the case to that court for further proceedings.

NOTES ON PRICE WATERHOUSE

1. On remand, Price Waterhouse declined an opportunity, offered by the district court, to submit additional evidence. The district court then concluded that Price Waterhouse had not met its burden of showing that Hopkins would not have been admitted to partnership even absent sexist stereotyping. It therefore ordered Price Waterhouse to admit Hopkins to partnership, not to retaliate against her in the future, to pay her back compensation of $371,175 and lawyers' fees and costs of $422,460.32. In addition, Price Waterhouse was ordered to award her the appropriate number of partnership shares in return for Hopkins' contribution of the appropriate amount of capital to the partnership. Hopkins v. Price Waterhouse, 737 F.Supp. 1202 (D.D.C.1990), affirmed, 920 F.2d 967 (D.C.Cir.1990).

2. Many of Hopkins' subordinates were women. Price Waterhouse argued on remand that this meant that the subordinates' objections to her treatment of them were nonsexist. Do you agree that women cannot be sexist? What would be the key question in determining whether the subordinates' negative reactions were discriminatory?

3. What does it mean "to walk more femininely, talk more femininely," etc.? What is the content and meaning of "femininity" in the context in which Hopkins was given this advice? Do you think that feminine women are more likely to wear make-up, jewelry, and have their hair styled? Is there any link on psychological levels (independent of physical appearance) between being the kind of person others would consider "feminine" and being the kind of person likely to appear feminine in terms of physical appearance (by wearing make-up, etc.)? What is that link? Is there a racial element to determinations about femininity?

4. Both Mary Anne Case and Katherine Franke discuss the relationship between sex and gender in articles critical of the courts' interpretations of Title VII. As discussed in Chapter 2, courts often use "gender discrimination" as a synonym for "sex discrimination." But these terms are understood as discrete phenomena in other disciplines. "Gender" refers to socially constructed norms appropriate for members of one sex: the two sexes are defined as female and male by physical characteristics, whereas the two genders are sets

of social norms we call "femininity" (which we expect to see displayed by people whose physical sex is female) and "masculinity" (which we expect to see displayed by people whose physical sex is male).

Mary Anne Case explains the relationship between sex and gender in law:

> [A]s things now stand, the concept of gender has been imperfectly disaggregated in the law from sex on the one hand and sexual orientation on the other. * * * When individuals diverge from the gender expectations for their sex—when a woman displays masculine characteristics or a man feminine ones—discrimination against her is now treated as sex discrimination while his behavior is generally viewed as a marker for homosexual orientation and may not receive protection from discrimination. * * *
>
> This differential treatment * * * marks the continuing devaluation, in life and in law, of qualities deemed feminine.* * *
>
> We are in danger of substituting for prohibited sex discrimination a still acceptable gender discrimination, that is to say, discrimination against the stereotypically feminine, especially when manifested by men, but also when manifested by women. Ann Hopkins, I fear, may have been protected only because of the doubleness of her bind: It was nearly impossible for her to be both as masculine as the job required and as feminine as gender stereotypes require. But the Supreme Court seems to have had no trouble with the masculine half of Hopkins's double bind; there is little indication, for example, that the Court would have found it to be sex discrimination if a prospective accounting partner had instead been told to remove her makeup and jewelry and to go to assertiveness training class instead of charm school.

Case, Disaggregating Gender from Sex and Sexual Orientation: The Effeminate Man in the Law and Feminist Jurisprudence, 105 Yale L. J. 1, 2–3 (1995).

Katherine Franke argues for a reconceptualization in the law of the relationship between sex and gender:

> Antidiscrimination law is founded upon the idea that sex, conceived as biological difference, is prior to, less normative than, and more real than gender. Yet in every way that matters, sex bears an epiphenomenal relationship to gender; that is, under close examination, almost every claim with regard to sexual identity or sex discrimination can be shown to be grounded in normative gender rules and roles. Herein lies the mistake. In the name of avoiding "the grossest discrimination," that is, "treating things that are different as though they were exactly alike," sexual equality jurisprudence has uncritically accepted the validity of biological sexual differences. By accepting these biological differences, equality jurisprudence reifies as foundational fact that which is really an effect of normative gender ideology. This jurisprudential error not only produces obvious absurdities at the margin of gendered identity, but it also explains why sex discrimination laws have been relatively ineffective in dismantling profound sex segregation in the wage-labor market, in shattering "glass ceilings" that obstruct women's entrance into the upper

echelons of corporate management, and in increasing women's wages, which remain a fraction of those paid men. The targets of antidiscrimination law, therefore, should not be limited to the "gross, stereotyped distinctions between the sexes" but should also include the social processes that construct and make coherent the categories male and female. In many cases, biology operates as the excuse or cover for social practices that hierarchize individual members of the social category "man" over individual members of the social category "woman." In the end, biology or anatomy serve as metaphors for a kind of inferiority that characterizes society's view of women.

* * * Given the epiphenomenal relationship between identity and equality, the Fourteenth Amendment and Title VII should apply with equal force to acts of classification as well as to disparate treatment of classes. Rather than accepting sexual differences as the starting point of equality discourse, sex discrimination jurisprudence should consider the role that the ideology of sexual differences plays in perpetuating and ensuring sexual hierarchy.

A reconceptualization of the two most fundamental elements of sexual equality jurisprudence is necessary to correct this foundational error. First, sexual identity—that is, what it means to be a woman and what it means to be a man—must be understood not in deterministic, biological terms, but according to a set of behavioral, performative norms that at once enable and constrain a degree of human agency and create the background conditions for a person to assert, I am a woman. To say that someone is a woman demands a complex description of the history and experience of persons so labeled. This conception of sexual identity ultimately provides the basis for a fundamental right to determine gendered identity independent of biological sex.

Second, what it means to be discriminated against because of one's sex must be reconceived beyond biological sex as well. To the extent that the wrong of sex discrimination is limited to conduct or treatment which would not have occurred but for the plaintiff's biological sex, antidiscrimination law strives for too little. Notwithstanding an occasional gesture to the contrary, courts have not interpreted the wrong of sex discrimination to reach rules and policies that reinforce masculinity as the authentic and natural exercise of male agency and femininity as the authentic and natural exercise of female agency.

Franke, The Central Mistake of Sex Discrimination Law: The Disaggregation of Sex from Gender, 144 U. Penn. L. Rev. 1, 2–3 (1995). Are Case and Franke making similar or opposite points? Why is Case's article about the need to disaggregate sex and gender whereas Franke's is about the need to see the interconnection?

Do you agree with Franke that biological differences are "really only an effect of normative gender ideology"? What does she mean? Is she arguing that having a child is the same physical event for women and men? What would Franke say if presented with evidence that high levels of testosterone make people more upbeat and confident (with definite advantages in employment)? See Andrew Sullivan, Why Men Are Different, N.Y. Times Magazine, Apr. 2, 2000, at 46 (describing such evidence). Do you agree with Franke's definition of sexual identity as what it means to be a woman or man in social performative terms? Is that what sexual identity means to you? Franke suggests that "[t]he targets of antidiscrimination law * * * should include the social processes that construct and make coherent the categories male and female." Can you give examples of how this suggestion would work: what kinds of cases could be brought? Would you advocate this approach? How would the various feminist approaches described in Chapter 3 view this proposal? How would judges react?

5. Are there problems analogous to the courts' failure to see masculine norms as sex discrimination with respect to race and cultural background? What are they?

6. There is considerable evidence that elite women who seem to be rising to the top of professions or corporations hit a glass ceiling well before reaching the top. As one researcher reports:

> Surveys indicate consistently that although 30–40% of all entry level management positions are held by women, their proportions decline to 20% at middle ranks, and plummet to only 2–5% of the top positions (i.e., within three levels of management of the CEO's office). Stated differently, the higher one goes, the greater one's opportunities if one is male; the more opportunity shrinks if one is female.

Mark Maier, Gender Equity, Organizational Transformation and Challenges, 16 J. Bus. Ethics 943, 943 (June 1997). An article published in October, 2000, reports that "[a]lthough women in the United States comprise approximately 40% of all managers, in the largest corporations women hold less than 0.5% of the highest paid management jobs." Judith G. Oakley, Gender–Based Barriers to Senior Management Positions: Understanding the Scarcity of Female CEOs, 27 J. Bus. Ethics 321, 321 (Oct. 2000). In 2010, only fifteen of the CEOs of Fortune 500 companies were women and only one of these women was African American. "fortune 500 Women CEOs" CnnMoney.com, available at http://money.cnn.com/galleries/2010/fortune/1004/gallery.fortune500_women_ceos.fortune/index.html. Anita Bruzzese, On the Job: women in the workplace, USA Today (June 18, 2009), available at http://www.usatoday.com/money/workplace/2009-06-18-on-the-job_N.htm?loc=interstitialskip,.

The glass ceiling is a metaphor for the many barriers women of all colors and men of color face as they attempt to rise through the management ranks. One problem discussed by both Maier and Oakley is that managers are supposed to exercise traits regarded as masculine, though there is no evidence that in fact these traits are effective in managing. Could Title VII be used to challenge the masculine norms of corporate culture? Or the fact that workplaces are structured for workers without significant caretaking responsibilities? Why or why not?

7. Might women and minorities tend to have skills that might make them more effective at managing than the politically-adept white men who tend to be promoted to higher levels? What is your reaction to Sally Helgesen's conclusion—after examining the leadership styles of four successful women leaders—that women as leaders have "particular aptitudes for long-term negotiating, analytic listening, and creating an ambiance in which people

work with zest and spirit"? Helgesen, The Female Advantage: Women's Ways of Leadership 249 (1990). If these qualities are so effective, why are they not valued more in promotion?

8. Some scholars have interpreted *Price Waterhouse* as requiring courts to find actionable sex discrimination anytime a person of one sex is penalized for engaging in behavior that would not be penalized if the person was of the other sex. Just as Hopkins could not be terminated for being masculine where such behavior was deemed acceptable for men, neither can a man be terminated for being effeminate when such behavior is deemed acceptable in women. According to Mary Anne Case, the logic of *Price Waterhouse* requires that it is an actionable form of sex discrimination to punish a man for wearing a pink frilly dress to work if female workers are permitted to do so. See Case, note 4 above, at 68–69; compare Kimberly A. Yuracko, Trait Discrimination as Sex Discrimination: An Argument Against Neutrality, 83 Tex. L. Rev. 167 (2004). Courts have not adopted the *Price Waterhouse* logic as completely as Case would wish. Courts increasingly use the *Price Waterhouse* logic to protect effeminate men from harassment but do not use it to strike down sex-specific grooming requirements. Compare Nichols v. Azteca Restaurant Enterprises Inc., 256 F.3d 864 (9th Cir. 2001) (holding that discrimination of man based on effeminacy is discrimination based on sex); Centola v. Potter, 183 F.Supp.2d 403 (D. Mass. 2002) (same): with Tavora v. New York Mercantile Exchange, 101 F.3d 907 (2d Cir. 1996) (upholding sex-specific short hair requirement for men against sex discrimination challenge); Pecenka v. Fareway Stores, Inc., 672 N.W.2d 800 (Iowa 2003) (upholding sex-specific no earring rule against sex discrimination challenge). Is there any justification consistent with Title VII's purpose for drawing the line in this place?

9. In 2004 a panel of the Ninth Circuit ruled that it was not a violation of Title VII for Harrah's Casino to impose sex-specific grooming requirements on female and male employees. The plaintiff, a bartender, challenged the employer's requirement that she wear makeup and nail polish to work and have her hair styled since men did not face the same requirements. Men were required to be clean and well shaven. See Jespersen v. Harrah's Operating Company, Inc., 392 F.3d 1076 (9th Cir. 2004). An en banc panel of the Ninth Circuit affirmed the panel's decision. Jespersen v. Harrah's Operating Company, Inc., 444 F.3d 1104 (9th Cir. 2006). Can you reconcile the Ninth Circuit's holding with *Price Waterhouse*? See also Devon Carbado, Mitu Gulati & Gowri Ramachandran, The Jespersen Story: Makeup and Women at Work, in Employment Discrimination Stories 105 (Joel Wm. Friedman ed., 2006); David Cruz, Making Up Women: Casinos, Cosmetics, and Title VII, 5 Nev. L. J. 240 (2004).

10. Also in 2004 the Sixth Circuit in the case of Smith v. City of Salem, OH, 378 F.3d 566 (6th Cir. 2004), held in what was the first decision of its kind, that a pre-operative male-to-female transsexual could state a claim for sex discrimination as a result of adverse treatment he suffered when he began coming to work with a more feminine appearance. The court explained: "After *Price Waterhouse*, an employer who discriminates against women because, for instance, they do not wear dresses or makeup, is engaging in sex discrimination because the discrimination would not occur but for the victim's sex. It follows that employers who discriminate against men because they *do* wear

dresses and makeup, or otherwise act femininely, are also engaging in sex discrimination, because the discrimination would not occur but for the victim's sex." Id. at 574. A year later in Barnes v. City of Cincinnati, 401 F.3d 729 (6th Cir. 2005) the Sixth Circuit affirmed a jury verdict of sex discrimination in favor of a male-to-female transsexual penalized for his feminine appearance at work. District courts in other circuits have begun to follow suit. See Schroer v. Billington, 424 F.Supp.2d 203 (D. D. C. 2006) (holding that a male-to-female transsexual could state an actionable sex discrimination claim when employer rescinded job offer after learning that plaintiff would be presenting a female appearance at work); Mitchell v. Axcan Scandipharm, Inc., 2006 WL 456173 (W.D. Pa. Feb. 17, 2006) (holding that a pre-operative male-to-female transsexual who alleged harassment and termination based on failure to conform to gender stereotypes could state a claim for sex discrimination).

11. How important or trivial do you think sex specific grooming cases are to Title VII's sex equality mandate? See Marc Linder, Smart Women, Stupid Shoes, and Cynical Employers: The Unlawfulness and Adverse Health Consequences of Sexually Discriminatory Workplace Footwear Requirements for Female Employees, 22 J. Corp. L. 295, 308 (1997). If you are a woman, compare how you feel in a skirt and in pants (assuming that both are part of comparable professional outfits). What are the differences? Would you feel more competent or confident or feminine in one or the other? What are some of the disadvantages of skirts of various lengths on the job? Of feeling feminine on the job?

12. Many of the grooming code cases have been brought by men who want to wear earrings or long hair. For a case in which a male optometrist lost his job for wearing one small earring to work, see Kleinsorge v. Eyeland Corp., 81 Fair Empl. Prac. Cas. (BNA) 1601 (E.D.Pa. 2000) (dismissing claim though female employees were allowed to wear earrings). Why would an employer care whether an employee wore one small (presumably tasteful) earring? What is the cultural meaning of a man wearing one earring? Of a woman wearing one earring? Of a man wearing two earrings? Of a woman wearing two earrings?

For cases in which men lost jobs because of long hair, see, e.g., Tavora v. New York Mercantile Exchange, 101 F.3d 907 (2d Cir.1996) (upholding dismissal though women employees allowed to wear long hair); Harper v. Blockbuster Entertainment Corp., 139 F.3d 1385 (11th Cir.1998) (same); Austin v. Wal–Mart Stores, Inc., 20 F.Supp.2d 1254 (S.D.Ind.1998) (same). Why would an employer allow women to wear long hair and forbid men to wear long hair? What is the cultural meaning of a woman with long hair? Of a man with long hair?

13. In writing about the dress code cases, Katharine T. Bartlett makes this point:

> The real problem with the assumptions courts make about the trivial impact of dress and appearance requirements on employees and their importance to employers is not that they are never right; nor is it a problem of inconsistency. The problem is that they rely on unexamined, culture-bound stereotypes. Such judgments reflect more about the high

> degree of societal consensus regarding dress and appearance expectations than the value that individuals or businesses attach to dress and appearance. That a woman should wear knee-length skirts and high heels and a man should not can be understood as trivial to the employee but important to the employer only from within a culture in which women commonly wear knee-length skirts and high heels and men do not. In such a culture, a requirement that men wear knee-length skirts and high heels could not be so easily dismissed [as trivial].

Bartlett, Only Girls Wear Barrettes: Dress and Appearance Standards, Community Norms, and Workplace Equality, 92 Mich. L. Rev. 2541, 2558–59 (1994). Do you agree with Bartlett? Which way does Bartlett's point cut?

14. Does sex equality demand that men be permitted to wear everything that women are permitted to wear and vice versa? See e.g., Case, note 4 above; Cruz, note 9 above. Are there any potential dangers to not permitting employers ever to implement sex specific grooming standards? If employers are required to have one unisex standard, what is it likely to look like? See Yuracko, note 8 above.

TEXT NOTE: HOW DISCRIMINATION OPERATES

The standard for sex discrimination in disparate treatment cases under Title VII is the same as in cases under the Equal Protection Clause of the Fourteenth Amendment, described above in Chapter 2. For both kinds of cases, discriminatory "intent" or "purpose" is often said to be a requirement: the defendant must "intend" to discriminate. An explicitly sex-based classification—such as one rule for men and another for women—satisfies this standard. In the absence of such overt discrimination, however, evidence of an intent to discriminate on the basis of sex helps to establish that in fact this person was treated differently because she was a woman rather than, for example, because she was incompetent.

In *Price Waterhouse,* the Court explains what it means by intent, i.e., that gender was a motivating factor:

> In saying that gender played a motivating part in an employment decision, we mean that, if we asked the employer at the moment of the decision what its reasons were and if we received a truthful response, one of those reasons would be that the applicant or employee was a woman. In the specific context of sex stereotyping, an employer who acts on the basis of a belief that a woman cannot be aggressive, or that she must not be, has acted on the basis of gender.

Conflict theory, the prominent sociological explanation of discrimination, is consistent with this notion of discrimination as intentional:

> According to a conflict-theory perspective, the beneficiaries of systems of inequality protect their privileges by using the resources they control to exclude members of subordinate groups. Thus, these theories explain discrimination in terms of the strategic, self-interested actions by members of privileged groups who intentionally exclude and exploit subor-

dinate-group members to protect or advance their own interests.[23] Conflict theory, however, leaves much discrimination unexplained.

By contrast, social cognition theory, from social psychology, explores discrimination in terms of cognitive processing rather than intentional acts. Sociologist Barbara Reskin describes social cognition theory:

> In brief, social cognition theory holds that people automatically categorize others into ingroups and outgroups. The visibility and cultural importance of sex and race and their role as core bases of stratification make them almost automatic bases of categorization. Having categorized others, people tend to automatically "feel, think and behave toward [particular members of the category] the same way they ... feel, think, and behave toward members of that social category more generally." Importantly, categorization is accompanied by stereotyping, attribution bias, and evaluation bias. These, in turn, introduce sex, race, and ethnic biases into our perceptions, interpretations, recollections, and evaluations of others. These biases are cognitive rather than motivational; in other words, they occur independently of decision makers' group interests or their conscious desire to favor or harm others.[24]

Laboratory experiments reveal that when people are categorized into groups on any basis, bias results. Employment discrimination lawyer and scholar Linda Krieger describes these processes:

> [Experimental] subjects are grouped according to what they are told is some minimal similarity, and are then asked to evaluate members of their own and the other group or to allocate rewards between the two groups. In some studies, subjects were told that they had been grouped according to whether they tended to underestimate or overestimate the sizes of dots. In other studies, subjects were told that their group assignment had been based on preferences for different paintings or photographs, and in yet others, subjects were informed that group assignment was random.
>
> The experiments showed that, as soon as people are divided into groups—even on a trivial or random basis—strong biases in their perception of differences, evaluation, and reward allocation result. As soon as the concept of "groupness" is introduced, subjects perceive members of their group as more similar to them, and members of other groups as more different from them, than when those same persons are viewed as noncategorized individuals. Indeed, when offered a choice, * * * subjects prefer to view information indicating their similarity with ingroup members and their distinctiveness from outgroup members.
>
> While ingroup members perceive similarities between themselves and others in their group, they perceive outgroup members as being even more homogeneous. In other words, subjects tend to perceive outgroup

23. Barbara F. Reskin, The Proximate Causes of Employment Discrimination, 29 Contemporary Sociol. 319, 320–21 (2001).

24. Id. (quoting Susan T. Fiske, Monica Lin & Steven Neuberg, The Continuum Model: Ten Years Later in Dual Process Theories in Social Psychology (Shelly Chaiken & Yaacov Trope, eds. 1999)).

members as an undifferentiated mass, while ingroup members are more highly differentiated.[25]

Grouping people, things, events, into categories is a normal and necessary cognitive process; without it the world would be a vast wilderness of discrete phenomena. We would see no forests. But, as noted above, categorization results in stereotyping, evaluation bias, and attribution bias. Barbara Reskin explains how these occur:

> Stereotyping
>
> Stereotypes are unconscious habits of thought that link personal attributes to group membership. Stereotyping is an inevitable concomitant of categorization: As soon as an observer notices that a "target" belongs to a stereotyped group (especially an outgroup), characteristics that are stereotypically linked to the group are activated in the observer's mind, even among people who consciously reject the stereotypes. To appreciate the importance of stereotyping for discriminatory outcomes, it is helpful to distinguish descriptive and prescriptive stereotypes.
>
> Descriptive stereotypes, which characterize how group members are, influence how we perceive others and interpret their behavior. Descriptive stereotyping can precipitate discrimination because it predisposes observers toward interpretations that conform to stereotypes and blinds them to disconfirming possibilities, especially when the behavior that observers must make sense of is subject to multiple interpretations (e.g., she worked late because women are helpful, rather than she worked late because she wants a promotion). Thus, descriptive stereotypes distort observers' impressions of the behavior of members of stereotyped groups.
>
> Prescriptive stereotypes are generalizations about how members of a group are supposed to be, based usually on descriptive stereotypes of how they are. These normative stereotypes serve as standards against which observers evaluate others' behavior. Both descriptive and prescriptive stereotypes influence what we remember about others and the inferences we draw about their behavior. Thus, stereotypes serve as "implicit theories, biasing in predictable ways the perception, interpretation, encoding, retention, and recall of information about other people."
>
> * * * Research on people's efforts to suppress stereotypes is relevant. In one study, subjects instructed to avoid sexist statements in a sentence-completion task could comply when they had enough time, but when they had to act quickly the statements they constructed were more sexist than those of subjects who had not been told to avoid making sexist statements. And according to a comparison of subjects who were and were not instructed to suppress stereotypes, the former could refrain from expressing stereotypes, but in a "rebound effect," they expressed stronger stereotypes in subsequent judgments than did subjects who had not tried to suppress their stereotypes in the first place.

---

25. Linda Hamilton Krieger, The Content of Our Categories: A Cognitive Bias Approach to Discrimination and Equal Employment Opportunity, 47 Stan. L. Rev. 1161, 1191–92 (1995). See also Linda Hamilton Krieger, Civil Rights Perestroika, 86 Cal. L. Rev. 1251 (1998).

Evaluation Bias and Attribution Bias

Stereotype-based expectations and ingroup favoritism act as distorting lenses through which observers assess others' performance and account for their successes and failures. Descriptive stereotypes affect observers' expectations and hence the explanations they construct. When the actions of others conform to our expectations, we tend to attribute their behavior to stable, internal propensities (e.g., ability), while we attribute actions that are inconsistent with our stereotype-based expectations to situational (i.e., external) or transient factors (e.g., task difficulty, luck, or effort). In this way, stereotype-based expectations give rise to biased attributions. For example, given the stereotype that men are good at customarily male tasks, competent performance doesn't require an explanation; men's failures do, however, and observers tend to attribute these unexpected outcomes to situational factors such as bad luck or lack of effort, none of which predict future failure. In contrast, women are stereotypically not expected to do well at customarily male endeavors, so explaining their failure is easy: They lack the requisite ability (an internal trait) and hence are likely to fail in the future. In contrast, their successes are unexpected, so they must have resulted from situational factors that do not predict future success.

Ingroup preference and outgroup derogation lead to similar attribution processes. Because observers expect ingroup members to succeed and outgroup members to fail, they attribute ingroup success and outgroup failure to internal factors [such as ability or lack of ability], and ingroup failure and outgroup success to situational factors [such as luck]. Observers also tend to characterize behavior that is consistent with their expectations in abstract terms and unexpected behavior in concrete terms. For example, give the same act—arriving late for a meeting—an observer would recall that an ingroup member was delayed, but that an outgroup member is a tardy person. Once behavior has been interpreted and encoded into memory, it is the interpretation, not the initial behavior, to which people have ready access. Thus, observers would predict that the outgroup member, but not the ingroup member, would be tardy in the future.

Power and Cognitive Biases

* * * [P]ower affects the degree to which people act on the propensity to stereotype. People can't afford to stereotype others on whom they depend because they need to assess them accurately, but they can afford to stereotype subordinate groups and are more likely to do so than subordinate group members are to stereotype members of dominant groups. In addition, under conditions of perceived threat, the more stake observers have in the status quo, and hence the more to lose, the more likely they are to stereotype outgroups. The sense of entitlement that accompanies dominant-group status is likely to give dominant group members particular confidence in their stereotypes. This propensity is reinforced by the fact that powerful observers actively seek information that confirms their stereotypes and disregard disconfirming information. However, priming the powerful with egalitarian values leads them to pay closer attention to

information that contradicts outgroup stereotypes. Finally, members of high-status ingroups show more bias in favor of ingroup members than do members of low-status groups.[26]

Disproportionately, white men are at the top of most workplaces, and they are likely to perceive women and minorities as members of outgroups. One should therefore expect that performance evaluations will serve to advantage subordinate males over subordinate females. One should also expect "the devaluation of jobs that are predominantly female and predominantly minority" and the overvaluation of jobs held predominantly by white men.[27] When members of outgroups are present in low numbers in jobs held predominantly by white men, stereotyping is likely to be particularly powerful.[28]

These psychological facts are not taken into account by the legal standard for discrimination. Courts assume that discrimination is motivational, and also that decisionmakers know what factors influence or determine a decision. Recall that in *Price Waterhouse*, the Supreme Court explains that by "saying that gender played a motivating part in an employment decision, we mean that, if we asked the employer at the moment of the decision what its reasons were and if we received a truthful response, one of those reasons would be that the applicant or employee was a woman." In reality, decisionmakers do not have access to such insight, explains Linda Krieger:

> [P]eople are actually quite poor at identifying the effects of various stimuli on their evaluations, judgments, choices, and predictions. In a series of experiments, [researchers] systematically manipulated some component of a complex stimulus situation such that the impact of a particular stimulus component on subjects' choices and actions could be assessed. They found that subjects were virtually never accurate in identifying the causal efficacy of the manipulated stimulus. Where the stimulus had a significant effect on their responses, subjects typically reported that it was noninfluential; in cases where a particular stimulus component had no significant causal effect, subjects reported it as having determined their response.[29]

Martha Chamallas identifies cultural domination as another important component of discrimination in the workplace. Consider a law school that admits minorities and women as students and even hires some as members of the faculty, but the law school's values and perspectives do not change to incorporate the values and perspectives of the newcomers.[30] For example, the school is reluctant to offer courses on feminism and critical race theory. When such courses are offered, they are regarded as "fluff," and those teaching

26. Reskin, above note 23, at 322–23 (third paragraph of extract in text quotes Krieger, above note 27, at 1188).

27. Id. at 322.

28. Martha Chamallas, Structuralist and Cultural Domination Theories Meet Title VII: Some Contemporary Influences, 92 Mich. L. Rev. 2370, 2379–83 (1994).

29. Krieger, above note 25, at 1214–15.

30. Chamallas, above note 28, at 2388–2389. See also David A. Thomas & Robin J. Ely, Making Differences Matter: A New Paradigm for Managing Diversity, Harv. Bus. Rev., Sept.–Oct. 1996, at 79 (describing three stages of workplace diversity; only in the third do the values and perspectives of the newcomers become part of the institution itself).

them are seen as teaching odd "boutique" courses of interest to a few rather than anything either analytically rigorous or important for a quality legal education. A similar kind of cultural domination and marginalization may affect the valuation of jobs, career paths, and management styles in the workplace.

NOTES ON HOW DISCRIMINATION OPERATES

1. Barbara F. Reskin and Debra Branch McBrier suggest that certain personnel policies, such as formal evaluation and recruitment procedures with express standards (even if still subjective, such as "works well with others"), increase the numbers of women promoted to management. Reskin & McBrier, Why Not Ascription? Organizations' Employment of Male and Female Managers, 65 Am. Sociol. Rev. 210 (2000). Thus, good employment practices—designed to counteract cognitive biases—can decrease the amount of discrimination within an organization. Is there any way this insight could be incorporated into anti-discrimination law?

2. Describe the culture at places you have gone to school or worked. If cultural domination was present, can you describe how it operated and who benefited?

3. Do you agree with Linda Hamilton Krieger that "[i]t is probably no accident that legal policymakers interpreting Title VII have constructed all disparate treatment discrimination as manifesting a conscious, discriminatory purpose." Krieger, The Content of Our Categories: A Cognitive Bias Approach to Discrimination and Equal Employment Opportunity, 47 Stan. L. Rev. 1161, 1247 (1995). She suggests that courts prefer this understanding of discrimination because it "holds the problem of intergroup bias at a safe distance, something those 'other people,' that is, 'bad people' do." Id. Do you agree? Do you think that the justices are unaware of the evidence about how discrimination operates on a cognitive level? Can you think of other explanations for the courts' holding fast to a motivational theory of discrimination despite mounting evidence over the last few decades that "discrimination is not one thing, but many"? Id. at 1248.

4. This conception of discrimination as necessarily conscious and intentional may have contributed to the Supreme Court's decision in Ledbetter v. Goodyear Tire & Rubber Co., 550 U.S. 618 (2007). The plaintiff in the case, Lily Ledbetter, was a longtime employee of Goodyear. Near the end of her career, she received an anonymous tip that she was earning less than her male colleagues. Over the course of her career, she had received smaller annual pay increases than her male counterparts. She sued for sex discrimination. A jury ruled in her favor and awarded her over $200,000 in back salary. The Supreme Court overturned the jury's decision holding that Ledbetter's claim was time-barred. Specifically, the court held that the statute of limitations for filing a claim for unequal pay begins to run at the time of the intentionally discriminatory decision and not each time that a paycheck affected by the decision is issued, even if the employee does not discover the discriminatory pay decision until several years after the fact.

In January 2009, President Obama signed into law the Lilly Ledbetter Fair Pay Act which effectively overturned the Supreme Court's decision. The Act clarifies that the 180 day statute of limitations is extended every time an employer violates the law by issuing a paycheck that discriminates. Therefore, if an employee alleges that she received a salary 20 years ago that was less than that of male co-workers because of sex discrimination, each new paycheck since that occurrence would be a new unlawful practice that resets the statute of limitation. What are the different conceptions of discrimination motivating the Supreme Court's decision and the Act? Which conception fits most squarely with the goals of Title VII?

5. Ann C. McGinley discusses the implications of insights from the masculinities literature for Title VII:

> In her groundbreaking work on male behavior in the workplace, Professor Patricia Martin observes that men "mobilize masculinities" in their evaluation of women (and men) at work.[157] Professor Martin identifies a number of ways that men, perhaps unconsciously, establish and maintain their dominance over equally qualified women in the workplace by conflating masculinity with social relations at work and with work performance. Professor Martin identifies three gender-based evaluation frames (or lenses) through which males evaluate female workers: (1) potential; (2) legitimacy; and (3) performance. For example, in evaluating potential, male managers typically see women and men workers as different. These frames, according to Professor Martin, are used generally without the manager's awareness. Male managers tend to judge men's talents and abilities as "more consonant with more valued jobs and opportunities." With respect to legitimacy, men "framed women as lacking legitimacy to hold powerful positions." This was apparent, for example, when a group of men on a search committee for a university president, missed the formal job presentation of the only woman candidate, while attending the presentations of all of the male candidates. This action was a public enactment of masculinity, according to Martin, "declaring for all to see their assumption that men are better (more important) than women." Finally, men observe women's performance through a "gender lens," frequently devaluing women's performance relative to men's. Even when men evaluate women positively, they still actively favor men by promoting them over women.[164]

McGinley, !Viva La Evolucion!, 9 Cornell J. L. & Pub. Pol'y 415, 440–441 (2000). See also Ann C. McGinley, Masculinities at Work, 83 Or. L. Rev. 359 (2004). In your experience at law school or at law firms, have you seen men judge men's "talents and abilities" as "more consonant with" being a good lawyer or law professor? Have you seen women as lawyers or law professors face legitimacy challenges not faced by their male peers? Have you seen women's performance as law students devalued by men relative to their valuation of men who are law students? Have you seen similar phenomena along racial lines? If you did observe any of these phenomena, would you

157. See Patricia Y. Martin, Gendering and Evaluating Dynamics: Men, Masculinities, and Managements, in Men As Managers, Managers As Men 186, 190 (David L. Collinson & Jeff Hearn eds., 1996).

164. See id. [at 202.]

describe them as conscious? Should they be seen as violating Title VII even if not conscious?

6. How would you craft a statute to try to reach unconscious discrimination? See McGinley, above note 5, at 481–84 (suggesting legislation that would define intent to include unconscious discrimination; "expand the stereotypes doctrine established in *Price Waterhouse*"; and create a strong inference of discrimination from "discriminatory racial or sexual remarks" even when not direct evidence of discrimination). Can you make other suggestions?

E. THE INTERSECTION OF RACE AND SEX

ROGERS v. AMERICAN AIRLINES, INC.

United States District Court, Southern District of New York, 1981.
527 F.Supp. 229.

Plaintiff is a black woman who seeks $10,000 damages, injunctive, and declaratory relief against enforcement of a grooming policy of the defendant American Airlines that prohibits employees in certain employment categories from wearing an all-braided hairstyle. Plaintiff has been an American Airlines employee for approximately eleven years, and has been an airport operations agent for over one year. Her duties involve extensive passenger contact, including greeting passengers, issuing boarding passes, and checking luggage. She alleges that the policy * * * discriminates against her as a woman, and more specifically as a black woman. * * *

[Defendant's motion to dismiss is] meritorious with respect to the statutory claims insofar as they challenge the policy on its face. The statutory bases alleged, Title VII and section 1981, are indistinguishable in the circumstances of this case, and will be considered together. The policy is addressed to both men and women, black and white. Plaintiff's assertion that the policy has practical effect only with respect to women is not supported by any factual allegations. Many men have hair longer than many women. Some men have hair long enough to wear in braids if they choose to do so. Even if the grooming policy imposed different standards for men and women, however, it would not violate Title VII. It follows, therefore, that an evenhanded policy that prohibits to both sexes a style more often adopted by members of one sex does not constitute prohibited sex discrimination. This is because this type of regulation has at most a negligible effect on employment opportunity. It does not regulate on the basis of any immutable characteristic of the employees involved. It concerns a matter of relatively low importance in terms of the constitutional interests protected by the Fourteenth Amendment and Title VII, rather than involving fundamental rights such as the right to have children or to marry. The complaint does not state a claim for sex discrimination.

The considerations with respect to plaintiff's race discrimination claim would clearly be the same, except for plaintiff's assertion that the "corn row" style has a special significance for black women. She contends that it has been, historically, a fashion and style adopted by Black American women, reflective of the cultural, historical essence of the Black women in American society. The style was "popularized" so to speak, within the larger society, when Cicely Tyson adopted the same for an appearance on nationally viewed Academy Awards presentation several years ago * * *. It was and is analogous to the public statement by the late Malcolm X regarding the Afro hair style * * *. At the bottom line, the completely braided hair style, sometimes referred to as corn rows, has been and continues to be part of the cultural and historical essence of Black American women.

There can be little doubt that, if American adopted a policy which foreclosed Black women/all women from wearing hair styled as an "Afro/bush," that policy would have very pointedly racial dynamics and consequences reflecting a vestige of slavery unwilling to die (that is, a master mandate that one wear hair divorced from one's historical and cultural perspective and otherwise consistent with the "white master" dominated society and preference thereof).

Plaintiff is entitled to a presumption that her arguments, largely repeated in her affidavit, are true. But the grooming policy applies equally to members of all races, and plaintiff does not allege that an all-braided hair style is worn exclusively or even predominantly by black people. Moreover, it is proper to note that defendants have alleged without contravention that plaintiff first appeared at work in the all-braided hairstyle on or about September 25, 1980, soon after the style had been popularized by a white actress in the film "10." Plaintiff may be correct that an employer's policy prohibiting the "Afro/bush" style might offend Title VII and section 1981. But if so, this chiefly would be because banning a natural hairstyle would implicate the policies underlying the prohibition of discrimination on the basis of immutable characteristics. In any event, an all-braided hairstyle is a different matter. It is not the product of natural hair growth but of artifice. An all-braided hair style is an "easily changed characteristic," and, even if socioculturally associated with a particular race or nationality, is not an impermissible basis for distinctions in the application of employment practices by an employer.

* * *

Moreover, the airline did not require plaintiff to restyle her hair. It suggested that she could wear her hair as she liked while off duty, and permitted her to pull her hair into a bun and wrap a hairpiece around the bun during working hours. * * * Plaintiff has done this, but alleges that the hairpiece has caused her severe headaches. A larger hairpiece would seem in order. But even if any hairpiece would cause such discomfort, the policy does not offend a substantial interest.

Plaintiff has failed to allege sufficient facts to require defendants to demonstrate that the policy has a bona fide business purpose. In this regard, however, plaintiff does not dispute defendant's assertion that the policy was adopted in order to help American project a conservative and business-like image, a consideration recognized as a bona fide business purpose. Rather she objects to its impact with respect to the "corn row" style, an impact not protected against by Title VII or section 1981.

PAULETTE M. CALDWELL, A HAIR PIECE: PERSPECTIVES ON THE INTERSECTION OF RACE AND GENDER

In Critical Race Feminism: A Reader 297, 297–305 (Adrien Katherine Wing, ed. 1997) (originally published in [1991] Duke L. J. 365).

I want to know my hair again, to own it, to delight in it again, to recall my earliest mirrored reflection when there was no beginning and I first knew that the person who laughed at me and cried with me and stuck out her tongue at me was me. I want to know my hair again, the way I knew it before I knew that my hair is me, before I lost the right to me, before I knew that the burden of beauty—or lack of it—for an entire race of people could be tied up with my hair and me.

I want to know my hair again, the way I knew it before I knew Sambo and Dick, Buckwheat and Jane, Prissy and Miz Scarlett. Before I knew that my hair could be wrong—the wrong color, the wrong texture, the wrong amount of curl or straight. Before hot combs and thick grease and smelly-burning lye, all guaranteed to transform me, to silken the coarse, resistant wool that represents me. I want to know once more the time before I denatured, denuded, denigrated, and denied my hair and me, before I knew enough to worry about edges and ditches and burrows and knots, when I was still a friend of water—the rain's dancing drops of water, a swimming hole's splashing water, a hot, muggy day's misty invisible water, my own salty, sweaty, perspiring water.

When will I cherish my hair again, the way my grandmother cherished it, when fascinated by its beauty, with hands carrying centuries-old secrets of adornment and craftswomanship, she plaited it, twisted it, cornrowed it, finger-curled it, olive-oiled it, on the growing moon cut and shaped it, and wove it like fine strands of gold inlaid with semiprecious stones, coral and ivory, telling with my hair a lost-found story of the people she carried inside her?

Mostly, I want to love my hair the way I loved hers, when as granddaughter among grandsons I stood on a chair in her room—her kitchen-bed-living-dining room—and she let me know her hair, when I combed and patted it from the crown of her head to the place where her neck folded into her shoulders, caressing steel gray strands that framed her forehead before falling into the soft, white cottony temples at the border of her cheekbones.

* * *

ON BEING THE SUBJECT OF A LAW SCHOOL HYPOTHETICAL

The case of *Rogers v. American Airlines* upheld the right of employers to prohibit the wearing of braided hairstyles in the workplace. The plaintiff, a black woman, argued that American Airlines' policy discriminated against her specifically as a black woman. In effect, she based her claim on the interactive effects of racial and gender discrimination. The court chose, however, to base its decision principally on distinctions between biological and cultural conceptions of race. More important, it treated the plaintiff's claims of race and gender discrimination in the alternative and independent of each other, thus denying any interactive relationship between the two.

Although *Rogers* is the only reported decision that upholds the categorical exclusion of braided hairstyles, the prohibition of such styles in the workforce is both widespread and long-standing. I discovered *Rogers* while reading a newspaper article describing the actual or threatened firing of several black women in metropolitan Washington, D.C., solely for wearing braided hairstyles. The article referred to *Rogers* but actually focused on the case of Cheryl Tatum, who was fired from her job as a restaurant cashier in a Hyatt Hotel under a company policy that prohibited "extreme and unusual hairstyles."

The newspaper description of the Hyatt's grooming policy conjured up an image of ludicrous and outlandishly coifed Cheryl Tatum, one clearly bent on exceeding the bounds of workplace taste and discipline. But the picture that accompanied the article revealed a young, attractive black woman whose hair fell neatly to her shoulders in an all-American, common, everyday pageboy style, distinguished only by the presence of tiny braids in lieu of single strands of hair.

Whether motivated by politics, ethnic pride, health, or vanity, I was outraged by the idea that an employer could regulate or force me to explain something as personal and private as the way I groom my hair.

My anger eventually subsided, and I thought little more about *Rogers* until a student in my course in Employment Discrimination Law asked me after class to explain the decision. I promised to take up the case when we arrived at that point in the semester when the issues raised by *Rogers* fit most naturally in the development of antidiscrimination law.

Several weeks passed, and the student asked about *Rogers* again and again (always privately, after class), yet I always put off answering her until some point later in the semester. After all, hair is such a little thing. Finally, in a class discussion on a completely unrelated topic, the persistent one's comments wandered into the forbidden area of braided-hair cases. As soon as the student realized she had publicly introduced the subject of braided hair, she stopped in midsentence and covered her mouth in embarrassment, as if she had spoken out of turn. I was finally forced to confront what the student had obviously sensed in her embarrassment.

I had avoided private and public discussions about braided hair not because the student had asked her question at the wrong point in the semester. Nor had I avoided the subject because cases involving employer-mandated hair and grooming standards do not illustrate as well as other cases the presence of deeply ingrained myths, negative images, and stereotypes that operate to define the social and economic position of blacks and women. I had carefully evaded the subject of a black woman's hair because I appeared at each class meeting wearing a neatly braided pageboy, and I resented being the unwitting object of one in thousands of law school hypotheticals.

WHY WOULD ANYONE WANT TO WEAR THEIR HAIR THAT WAY?

In discussing braided hairstyles, I was not prepared to adopt an abstract, dispassionate, objective stance on an issue that so obviously affected me personally; nor was I prepared to suffer publicly, through intense and passionate advocacy, the pain and outrage that I experience each time a black woman is dismissed, belittled, and ignored simply because she challenges our objectification. Should I be put to the task of choosing a logical, credible, "legitimate," legally sympathetic justification out of the many reasons that may have motivated me and other black women to braid our own hair? Perhaps we do so out of concern for the health of our hair, which many of us risk losing permanently after years of chemical straighteners; or perhaps because we fear that the entry of chemical toxins into our bloodstreams through our scalps will damage our unborn or breast-feeding children. Some of us choose the positive expression of ethnic pride not only for ourselves but also for our children, many of whom learn, despite all our teachings to the contrary, to reject association with black people and black culture in search of a keener nose or bluer eye. Many of us wear braids in the exercise of private, personal prerogatives taken for granted by women who are not black.

The persistent student's embarrassed questioning and my obfuscation spoke of a woman-centered silence: she, a white woman, had asked me, a black woman, to justify my hair. She compelled me to account for the presence of legal justifications for my simultaneously "perverse visibility and convenient invisibility." She forced me and the rest of the class to acknowledge the souls of women who live by the circumscriptions of competing beliefs about white and black womanhood and in the interstices of racism and sexism.

Our silence broken, the class moved beyond hierarchy to a place of honest collaboration. Turning to *Rogers*, we explored the question of our ability to comprehend through the medium of experience the way a black woman's hair is related to the perpetuation of social, political, and economic domination of subordinated racial and gender groups; we asked why issues of experience, culture, and identity are not the subject of explicit legal reasoning.

TO CHOOSE MYSELF: INTERLOCKING FIGURATIONS IN THE CONSTRUCTION OF RACE AND GENDER

* * *

My initial outrage notwithstanding, *Rogers* is an unremarkable decision. Courts generally protect employer-mandated hair and dress codes, and they often accord the greatest deference to codes that classify individuals on the basis of socially conditioned rather than biological differences.

But *Rogers* is regrettably unremarkable in an important respect. It rests on suppositions that are deeply embedded in American culture. *Rogers* proceeds from the premise that, although racism and sexism share much in common, they are nonetheless fundamentally unrelated phenomena—a proposition proved false by history and contemporary reality. Racism and sexism are interlocking, mutually reinforcing components of a system of dominance rooted in patriarchy. No significant and lasting progress in combating either can be made until this interdependence is acknowledged, and until the perspectives gained from considering their interaction are reflected in legal theory and public policy.

Among employment discrimination cases that involve black female plaintiffs, at least three categories emerge.

In one category, courts have considered whether black women may represent themselves or other race or gender discriminatees. Some cases deny black women the right to claim discrimination as a subgroup distinct from black men and white women.[4] Others deny black women the right to represent a class that includes white women in a suit based on sex discrimination, on the ground that race distinguishes them.[5] Still other cases prohibit black women from representing a class in a race discrimination suit that includes black men, on the ground of gender differences.[6] These cases demonstrate the failure of courts to account for race-sex intersection, and are premised on the assumption that discrimination is based on either race or gender, but never both.

A second category of cases concerns the interaction of race and gender in determining the limits of an employer's ability to condition work on reproductive and marital choices associated with black women.[7] Several courts have upheld the firing of black women for becoming pregnant while unmarried if their work involves association with children—especially black teenage girls. These decisions rest on entrenched fears of and distorted images about black female sexuality, stigmatize single black mothers (and by extension their children), and reinforce "culture of poverty" notions that blame poverty on poor people themselves. They also reinforce the notion that the problems of black families are attributable to the deviant and dominant roles of black women and the idea that racial progress depends on black female subordination.

---

4. *See, e.g.,* Degraffenreid v. General Motors Assembly Div., 413 F.Supp. 142, 145 (E.D.Mo. 1976) (Title VII did not create a new subcategory of "black women" with standing independent of black males).

5. *See, e.g.,* Moore v. Hughes Helicopters, Inc., 708 F.2d 475, 480 (9th Cir.1983).

6. *See, e.g.,* Payne v. Travenol, 673 F.2d 798, 810–812 (5th Cir.1982) (interests of black female plaintiffs substantially conflict with interests of black males, since females sought to prove that males were promoted at females' expense notwithstanding the court's finding of extensive racial discrimination).

7. *See* Chambers v. Girls Club of Omaha, 834 F.2d 697 (8th Cir.1987).

A third category concerns black women's physical images. These cases involve a variety of mechanisms to exclude black women from jobs that involve contact with the public—a tendency particularly evident in traditionally female jobs in which employers place a premium on female attractiveness—including a subtle, and often not so subtle, emphasis on female sexuality. The latter two categories sometimes involve, in addition to the intersection of race and gender, questions that concern the interaction of race, gender, and culture.

The failure to consider the implications of race-sex interaction is only partially explained, if at all, by the historical or contemporary development of separate political movements against racism and sexism. Rather, this failure arises from the inability of political activists, policy makers, and legal theorists to grapple with the existence and political functions of the complex myths, negative images, and stereotypes regarding black womanhood. These stereotypes, and the culture of prejudice that sustains them, exist to define the social position of black women as subordinate on the basis of gender to all men, regardless of color, and on the basis of race to all other women. These negative images also are indispensable to the maintenance of an interlocking system of oppression based on race and gender that operates to the detriment of all women and all blacks. Stereotypical notions about white women and black men are developed not only when they are compared to white men, but also when they are set apart from black women.

THE *ROGERS* OPINION

The court gave three principal reasons for dismissing the plaintiff's claim. First, in considering the sex discrimination aspects of the claim, the court disagreed with the plaintiff's argument that, in effect, the application of the company's grooming policy to exclude the category of braided hairstyles from the workplace reached only women. Rather, the court stressed that American's policy was evenhanded and applied to men and women alike. Second, the court emphasized that American's grooming policy did not regulate or classify employees on the basis of an immutable gender characteristic. Finally, American's policy did not bear on the exercise of a fundamental right. The plaintiff's racial discrimination claim was analyzed separately but dismissed on the same grounds: neutral application of American's antibraid policy to all races and absence of any impact of the policy on an immutable racial characteristic or of any effect on the exercise of a fundamental right.

The court's treatment of culture and cultural associations in the racial context bears close examination. It carefully distinguished between the phenotypic and cultural aspects of race. First, it rejected the plaintiff's analogy between all-braided and Afro, or "natural" hairstyles. Stopping short of concluding that Afro hairstyles might be protected under all circumstances, the court held that "an all-braided hairstyle is a different matter. It is not the product of natural hair growth but of artifice." Second, in response to the plaintiff's argument that, like Afro hairstyles, braids reflected her choice for ethnic and cultural identification, the court again distinguished between the immutable aspects of race and characteristics that are "socioculturally associated with a particular race or nationality." However, given the variability of so-called immutable racial characteristics such as skin color and hair texture, it is difficult to understand racism as other than a complex of historical, sociocultural associations with race.

In support of its view that the plaintiff had failed to establish a factual basis for her claim that American's policy had a disparate impact on black women, thus destroying any basis for the purported neutral application of the policy, the court pointed to American's assertion that the plaintiff had adopted the prohibited hairstyle only shortly after it had been "popularized" by Bo Derek, a white actress, in the film 10. Notwithstanding the factual inaccuracy of American's claim, and notwithstanding the implication that there is no relationship between braided hair and the culture of black women, the court assumed that black and white women are equally motivated (i.e., by the movies) to adopt braided hairstyles.

Wherever they exist in the world, black women braid their hair. They have done so in the United States for more than four centuries. African in origin, the practice of braiding is as American—black American—as sweet potato pie. A braided hairstyle was first worn in a nationally televised media event in the United States—and in that sense "popularized"—by a black actress, Cicely Tyson, nearly a decade before the movie 10. More important, Cicely Tyson's choice to popularize (i.e., to "go public" with) braids, like her choice of acting roles, was a political act made on her own behalf and on behalf of all black women.

The very use of the term "popularized" to describe Bo Derek's wearing of braids—in the sense of rendering suitable to the majority—specifically subordinates and makes invisible all the black women who for centuries have worn braids in places where they and their hair were not overt threats to the American aesthetic. The great majority of such women worked exclusively in jobs where their racial subordination was clear. They were never permitted in any affirmative sense of the word any choice so closely related to personal dignity as the choice—or a range of choices—regarding the grooming of their hair. By virtue of their subordination—their clearly defined place in society—their choices were simply ignored.

The court's reference to Bo Derek presents us with two conflicting images, both of which subordinate black women and black culture. On the one hand, braids are separated from black culture and, by implication, are said to arise from whites. Not only do blacks contribute nothing to the nation's or the world's culture, they copy the fads of whites. On the other hand, whites make fads of black culture, which, by virtue of their popularization, become—like all "pop"—disposable, vulgar, and without lasting value. Braided hairstyles are thus trivialized and protests over them made ludicrous.

To narrow the concept of race further—and, therefore, racism and the scope of legal protection against it—the *Rogers* court likened the plaintiff's claim to ethnic identity in the wearing of braids to identity claims based on the use of languages other than English. The court sought refuge in *Garcia v. Gloor,* a decision that upheld the general right of employers to prohibit the speaking of any language other than English in the workplace without requiring employers to articulate a business justification for the prohibition.[15] By excising the cultural component of racial or ethnic identity, the court reinforces the view of a homogeneous, unicultural society, and pits blacks and other groups against each other in a battle over minimal deviations from cultural norms. Black women cannot wear their hair in braids because Hispanics cannot speak Spanish at work. The court cedes to private employers the power of family patriarchs to enforce a numbing sameness, based exclusively on the employers' whim, without the obligation to provide a connection to work performance or business need, and thus deprives employees of the right to be judged on ability rather than on image or sound.

HEALING THE SHAME

Eliminating the behavioral consequences of certain stereotypes is a core function of antidiscrimination law. This function can never be adequately performed as long as courts and legal theorists create narrow, inflexible definitions of harm and categories of protection that fail to reflect the actual experience of discrimination. Considering the interactive relationship between racism and sexism from the experiential standpoint and knowledge base of black women can lead to the development of legal theories grounded in reality, and to the consideration by all women of the extent to which racism limits their choices as women and by black and other men of color of the extent to which sexism defines their experiences as men of subordinated races.

* * *

NOTES ON A HAIR PIECE

1. Why do you think the employer in *Rogers* prohibited cornrows? Do you think that cornrows are unprofessional or inconsistent with a "conservative and business-like image"? Do employers regard "white" hair as more professional than "black" hair? What sorts of problems does any difference in our perceptions of professional hair create for African Americans in general and, in particular, for African American women?

2. Does the prohibition of cornrows in this case seem relevant or irrelevant to the plaintiff's job performance? Does job relevance affect your view of the legitimacy of the requirement?

3. If you think the prohibition on cornrows is irrelevant to job performance, do you think that employers should only be able to impose job relevant

---

15. Garcia v. Gloor, 618 F.2d 264, 267–69 (5th Cir.1980).

employment criteria? Should an employer not be permitted to refuse to hire employees with blue hair who are qualified for the job? Is a prohibition on cornrows, even if job irrelevant, different? If so how?

4. If you think the prohibition on cornrows is job relevant because cornrows lead to diminished customer satisfaction, would you also permit employers to only hire people over six feet tall as customer service representative if they discovered that tall employees left customers feeling more satisfied and secure about the service they received?

5. The court distinguishes between a prohibition on Afros and a prohibition on cornrows by focusing on the mutability of each. Are cornrows really more mutable than an Afro? Why do you think the court is more uncomfortable allowing employers to prohibit Afros than cornrows? Does the distinction seem meaningful to you?

6. How would you respond to an employer who refuses to employ individuals who speak Black English. Is the case easier or harder for you than the no-cornrows case? Why?

7. How do you think Paulette Caldwell would have written *Rogers* if she had been the judge? What reasoning would she have used?

8. Does social cognition theory explain why the judge in *Rogers* thinks of a white actress when he thinks of cornrows?

9. Is *Rogers* the inevitable result of formal equality? How would various feminist approaches discussed in Chapter 3 analyze the question? Would it matter to your analysis that cornrows were worn once by a white actress in a movie? Would the result in *Rogers* have changed if Bo Derek had never worn cornrows in "10"? Why did the judge consider this factor relevant? What is the scope of what the judge sees as discrimination on the basis of race or on the basis of race and sex? What is the scope of what Caldwell sees as discrimination?

10. What does Caldwell mean when she states that the negative images of black women "are indispensable to the maintenance of an interlocking system of oppression based on race and gender that operates to the detriment of all women and all blacks"? Later, she says that black women will not "be the exclusive or primary beneficiaries" of a society that treats black women better. What is her point here? Can you give examples that illustrate these points?

11. Caldwell also states that "considering the interactive relationship between racism and sexism from the experiential standpoint and knowledge base of black women can lead to the development of legal theories grounded in reality." Why is this needed? Can you give an example?

JUDGE v. MARSH

United States District Court, District of Columbia, 1986.
649 F.Supp. 770.

[Plaintiff, an African American woman, seeks redress for, among other things, two promotions she did not receive as a civilian employee of the Army. The excerpt below deals with her failure to be promoted to the position of Equal Employment Opportunity Officer in 1981.]

The protected group upon which plaintiff's claims are based is that of black women. Disparate treatment of subclasses of women, based on an immutable characteristic or the exercise of a fundamental right, has been held unlawful under Title VII. Extrapolating from such "sex-plus" cases, the Fifth Circuit has determined that black women are a distinct subgroup, protected by Title VII. This outcome is logical: while accepted "sex-plus" discrimination is based on ostensibly neutral factors, both factors allegedly involved in the present case are separately accorded Title VII protection. Race discrimination directed solely at women is not less invidious because of its specificity. Thus, the Court concludes that employment actions directed against black women as a group may violate Title VII.

The difficulty with this position is that it turns employment discrimination into a many-headed Hydra, impossible to contain within Title VII's prohibition. * * * [P]rotected subgroups would exist for every possible combination of race, color, sex, national origin and religion. It is questionable whether any employer could make an employment decision under such a regime without incurring a volley of discrimination charges. For this reason, * * * [protected subgroups are] appropriately limited to employment decisions based on one protected, immutable trait or fundamental right, which are directed against individuals sharing a second protected, immutable characteristic. The benefits of Title VII thus will not be splintered beyond use and recognition; nor will they be constricted and unable to reach discrimination based on the existing unlawful criteria. Further, recognition of a new subgroup does not alter the employer's burden in a disparate treatment case. The employer still need establish merely a legitimate, non-pretextual basis for the employment decision. Plaintiff herein retains the burden, difficult though it may be, of establishing by a preponderance of the evidence that her employer's challenged decisions were based on this narrowly defined subgroup.

* * *

Failure to select Ms. Judge as EEO Officer was also not based on her status as a black woman. The testimony at trial did not reveal any unlawful discrimination at either level of the two-tiered decision-making process. General Cadoria indicated that the applicants' records were evaluated as a whole. General Rogers testified that, in ranking the top three applicants, he reviewed each applicant's record as a whole, and gave weight to the fact that both Anita Gomez Troughten and Luther Santiful were EEO Officers at the time, while Ms. Judge was an assistant EEO Officer. Further, Ms. Judge's SKAP [employee evaluation instrument] rating sheet had five Cs and no As, while neither Santiful nor Troughten had any ratings lower than B. General Kroesen accepted the Review Panel's recommendations. The respect General Kroesen accorded the selection process is further evidenced by his decision to reconvene the Review Panel once Anita Troughten declined the EEO Officer position.

Without doubt, the decisions of the evaluation panel members in ranking the applicants, and General Kroesen in twice relying upon the panel reflect subjective choices. Although the Court is sensitive to the possibility that subjective criteria in a hiring or promotion process may produce discrimination, it recognizes that such criteria "are not to be condemned as unlawful per se, for in all fairness to applicants and employers alike, decisions about hiring and promotion in supervising and managerial jobs cannot realistically be made using objective standards alone." The employer's judgment in selecting and applying subjective criteria may be poor, and it may be erroneous, but the only relevant inquiry for the Court is whether the given reasons mask unlawful discrimination. The steps in the evaluation and selection process of EEO Officer reflected only the subjectivity inherent in employment decisions. The preponderance of the evidence does not reveal that plaintiff's status as a black woman was a factor in her ranking or her non-selection. Thus, the Court finds that plaintiff has not met the ultimate burden of showing by a preponderance that her 1977 SKAP rating or her non-selection were based on her race and sex.

TEXT NOTE: INTERSECTIONALITY CLAIMS UNDER TITLE VII

As Paulette Caldwell points out in her essay on hair, women of color do not face a simple combination of sex discrimination plus race discrimination. The discrimination they face is the result of a complex interaction of racism and sexism, an interaction fueled by "myths, negative images, and stereotypes regarding black womanhood." Caldwell, above, at 302.

Caldwell identifies three problems for black women bringing intersectional claims: their perceived inability to represent all African Americans or all women; bias against unwed black mothers; and bias against black women's physical appearance. Another serious problem is that courts rarely hold for plaintiffs on claims of discrimination based on both sex and race. For example, in Judge v. Marsh, the plaintiff claimed that she had been discriminated against as an African American woman. Although the court admitted that "employment actions directed against black women as a group may violate Title VII," the court regarded this position as turning "employment discrimination into a many-headed hydra." And it held that the plaintiff had failed in the end to prove discrimination on the basis of both sex and race. The court explained that once the employer articulated a legitimate non-discriminatory reason for its failure to promote the plaintiff, the burden shifted to the plaintiff to show that she was discriminated against "based on this narrowly defined subgroup." And, in the end, she lost because she had "not met the ultimate burden of showing that" the decisions not to promote her "were based on her race and sex."

In Re: Carnegie Center Associates, 129 F.3d 290 (3d Cir. 1997) (excerpt above § B), is another example. There, an unwed African American mother lost her job when the employer had to eliminate one secretarial position while she was on maternity leave. Two employees in high positions had expressed discomfort with her marital status. The plaintiff alleged discrimination on the basis of sex and race, and apparently tried to show the connection between what happened to her and stereotypes of unwed black mothers, but the court said that her intersectional claim added nothing.

As these cases illustrate, although women of color routinely face complicated forms of discrimination that cannot easily be disentangled into race discrimination and sex discrimination, it is very difficult to win such a claim. Almost always, the combined claim comes to nothing once the plaintiff has presented the available proof and the court has applied the burden of proof rules of Title VII. To win, the plaintiff bringing an intersectionality claim would have to show that she was treated differently than white women and that she was also treated differently from men of color. This is not an easy task if the discrimination has been subtle rather than overt, and discrimination is seldom overt nowadays.

NOTES ON INTERSECTIONALITY CLAIMS UNDER TITLE VII

1. As noted by Caldwell in the excerpt above, although many classes of racial minorities or women have been certified with only one person (someone who necessarily has only one sex and only one race) as a class representative, some courts have refused to certify African American women as class representatives for classes of either all African Americans or all women. See, e.g., Payne v. Travenol Lab., 673 F.2d 798 (5th Cir.1982) (African American women cannot represent a class including African American men); Moore v. Hughes Helicopters, Inc., 708 F.2d 475, 480 (9th Cir.1983) (African American women cannot represent a class including white women). Why might the status of African American women as representatives seem more suspect than representation of all women by white women or of all African Americans by an African American man? See Kimberle Crenshaw, Demarginalizing the Intersection of Race and Sex: A Black Feminist Critique of Antidiscrimination Doctrine, Feminist Theory and Antiracist Politics, 1989 U. Chi. Legal F. 139. Why might African American women in fact be *better* able to represent a class of all women or all African Americans than a white woman or an African American man? Does the discussion earlier in this chapter of social cognition theory help explain the willingness of courts to certify white women or minority men, but not minority women, as representatives of classes including members of other races or of the other sex?

2. Often plaintiffs do not have the types of "smoking gun" evidence present in *Price Waterhouse*. What are the difficulties faced by a plaintiff like Judge? Do you think she might have been discriminated against, despite the court's ruling? Why might she have trouble winning on a discrimination claim even if the denial of the promotion was discriminatory?

3. What is the Judge court getting at when it talks about the "many-headed Hydra"? Where does the court draw the line? Do you agree? Note that courts routinely allow white men to sue for reverse discrimination under Title VII without any such discussion. See, e.g., Johnson v. Transportation Agency, 480 U.S. 616 (1987); United Steelworkers v. Weber, 443 U.S. 193 (1979). Why

aren't such suits regarded as equally problematic because they are brought by a distinct "sex-plus" subgroup?

4. Does the fact that one belongs to multiple "subgroups" strengthen or weaken the need for a Title VII remedy? Why, in practice, is it almost impossible to win an intersectionality claim?

5. Should discrimination against a black woman because of her race and sex be regarded as just another form of "sex-plus," equivalent to discriminating against any other subset of women, such as women with pre-school children? Is there a difference between these two "subgroups"? Is such analysis equivalent to eliminating race from the plaintiff's claim? See Peggie R. Smith, Separate Identities: Black Women, Work, and Title VII, 14 Harv. Women's L.J. 21, 40–45 (1991).

6. Should the presence of African Americans and women in the workforce be interpreted as evidence that an employer does not discriminate against black women? For a discussion of cases suggesting yes, see Smith, above note 5, at 35–37.

7. As Virginia W. Wei has pointed out, like African American women, Asian American women have had "difficulties with their Title VII claims based on combined factors of race and sex." Asian Women and Employment Discrimination: Using Intersectionality Theory To Address Title VII Claims Based on Combined Factors of Race, Gender and National Origin, 37 B.C.L. Rev. 771, 780 (1996). She notes that Asian women experience the convoluted interaction of at least three forms of discrimination: race, sex, and national origin. How would national origin complicate discrimination for Asian women? What other women are likely to face this triple intersection? Would you expect such claims to be easier or harder to establish under Title VII than claims of African American women that they have been discriminated against on the basis of race and sex?

8. It is often assumed that minority women, as a "double minority," have an advantage in obtaining good jobs because they "count twice" for affirmative action purposes. Do you think that this is true? See Deborah J. Merritt & Barbara F. Reskin, The Double Minority: Empirical Evidence of a Double Standard in Law School Hiring of Minority Women, 65 S. Cal. L. Rev. 2299, 2301 (1992) (study reveals that "minority women who joined law school faculties during this period [between Fall 1986 and Spring 1991] began teaching at significantly lower ranks than the minority men, obtained positions at significantly less prestigious schools, and were significantly more likely to teach low-status courses like legal writing or trusts and estates"). Why are perceptions and reality so different?

9. Can an employer, say a law school, take into account the advantages of a diverse faculty—in terms of sex and race—to the effectiveness of its educational mission in hiring decisions? See David A. Thomas & Robin J. Ely, Making Differences Matter: A New Paradigm for Managing Diversity, Harv. Bus. Rev., Sept.–Oct. 1996, at 79 (suggesting that organizations can profit from a diverse workforce); Steven A. Ramirez, The New Cultural Diversity and Title VII, 6 Mich. J. Race & L. 127 (2000) (arguing that diversity hiring aimed at improving corporate profitability should be legal under Title VII). How do you think the Supreme Court's decision in Grutter v. Bollinger, 539

U.S. 306, 123 S.Ct. 2325, 156 L.Ed.2d 304 (2003), described in Chapter 8 above, affects the legality of diversity-based hiring in higher education?

10. Camille Hebert has noted that sexual harassment claims and racial harassment claims can both be traced to the same Supreme Court decisions, and that racial harassment analogies have helped some "courts to understand and to demonstrate the unlawful and discriminatory nature of sexually harassing behavior." Hebert, Analogizing Race and Sex in Workplace Harassment Claims, 58 Ohio St. L. J. 819, 820 (1997). But she warns that, in recent years, courts have imported restrictive rules from sexual harassment law to racial harassment law, making it "increasingly difficult for employees to successfully establish the existence of a racially hostile or abusive work environment." Id. According to Hebert:

> one of the dangers that needs to be guarded against when analogizing race and sex is the suggestion that racism and sexism, or racial harassment and sexual harassment, are identical, rather than merely comparable in certain respects. If drawing analogies between race and sex is seen as an attempt to belittle, or even has the unintended result of belittling, the importance of race and the evil of racism, then the use of analogies between race and sex could pose more dangers than are justified by the potential benefits of such comparison.

Id. at 880. Do you agree with Hebert? How are racial harassment and sexual harassment different? How are they similar? What arguments can you make against extending the limitations emerging in the law of sexual harassment to the law of racial harassment?

FOSTER v. DALTON

United States Court of Appeals, Fifth Circuit, 1995.
71 F.3d 52.

Plaintiff-appellant Sharon C. Foster, an African-American woman, sued the Secretary of the Navy on the ground that the Newport Naval Hospital (the Hospital) denied her a job due to her race. Following a bench trial, the district court rendered judgment for the Secretary. Although the record makes it painfully clear that this episode is light years away from the Navy's finest hour, we have no principled choice but to affirm.

I. BACKGROUND

The subsidiary facts are largely undisputed. The United States Navy maintains a substantial presence in Newport, Rhode Island. In the summer of 1989, the appellant found civilian employment at the Naval War College. Seeking to advance through the ranks, she assiduously applied for other, more attractive jobs in the Newport naval establishment. Since most facilities located at the base adhered to a policy of filling vacancies by selecting internal candidates (i.e., candidates already employed within the particular facility) where possible, the appellant had no luck until the Hospital hired her as its professional affairs coordinator. She reported for duty in July of 1990.

Shortly after the appellant came on board, the Hospital's director of administration, Commander William Travis, sought to fill a newly created opening for a management analyst. Because he believed that available funding would be jeopardized if the position remained open at the start of the next fiscal year (October 1, 1990), Commander Travis eschewed the hiring procedure ordinarily used to recruit civilian staff and undertook a non-competitive search. This process consisted mainly of culling the names of aspirants for advancement from existing files and assembling a list of potential candidates. Staff personnel compiled a roster of five such candidates (including the appellant). As among the five nominees, the appellant was twice distinguished: she was the only non-Caucasian and the only person already employed at the Hospital. Thus, had Commander Travis adhered to the usual policy of preferring in-house aspirants, the appellant who was plainly qualified for the postwould have been selected.

When George Warch, the Hospital's civilian program specialist, presented Commander Travis with the list, Travis inquired why James Berry's name was omitted from it. Warch informed Travis that Berry—Warch's "fishing buddy" and Travis's acquaintance—could not be offered employment at the grade specified for the position. Travis promptly directed Warch to rewrite the job description, specify a lower grade (at which Berry would be eligible), and generate a new list. Leaving little to chance, Travis also decreed that candidates for the position should have certain computer expertise—expertise that Berry possessed—and intimated that he would invoke the Veterans Readjustment Act (VRA).[2]

The modified job description yielded a fresh list with only one name on it: James Berry. Although Warch mused that the revisions made it appear that the powers-that-be had connived to preselect Berry for the vacancy, Travis brushed these concerns aside and named Berry to the management analyst position.

In the wake of Berry's hiring, the appellant filed an administrative complaint with the Navy, alleging that the Hospital had discriminated against her on the basis of her race and gender. Receiving no satisfaction, she brought suit in Rhode Island's federal district court, charging discrimination in contravention of Title VII of the Civil Rights Act of 1964. Following a bench trial that focused on allegations of race discrimination, the district court ruled in the Secretary's favor. The court thought that the appellant proved a prima facie case * * * and also thought that she was better qualified for the position than Berry * * *. But the court determined that the Secretary had successfully rebutted the prima facie case by proffering a nondiscriminatory, if unsavory, reason for the personnel action: preselection of a friend of the appointing officer. * * * Overriding Travis's and Warch's pious assurances that cronyism played no role in Berry's recruitment, the court concluded that this was a near-classic

2. Under the VRA, veterans receive preference in certain governmental employment. * * * Not coincidentally, Berry had served in the United States Navy.

case of an old boy network in operation, but not a situation in which the employment decision was motivated by racial animus. This appeal ensued.

* * *

This case is troubling in that we, if writing on a pristine page, might well have reached a different conclusion as to the impetus behind the refusal to hire. But that is not the test. * * * While the record, read objectively, shows that the district court could have drawn an inference of discriminatory intent, it does not show that such an inference is compelled. That raises the stakes appreciably. It is common ground that, "when there are two permissible views of the evidence, the factfinder's choice between them cannot be clearly erroneous." *Johnson v. Watts Regulator Co.,* 63 F.3d 1129, 1138 (1st Cir.1995) (citing *Anderson v. City of Bessemer City,* 470 U.S. 564, 574, 105 S.Ct. 1504, 1511–12, 84 L.Ed.2d 518 (1985)). So it is here.

First: We start at a high level of generality. The appellant does not seriously dispute the district court's account of the facts, but vigorously attacks the inferences that the court saw fit to draw from them. * * * While the record, read objectively, shows that the district court could have drawn an inference of discriminatory intent, it does not show that such an inference is compelled.

Second: Turning to specifics, the appellant says that preselection (which, according to the court below, dictated the adverse employment decision) occurred only after the decisionmaker learned that the management analyst post would go to an African–American woman, virtually by default, if he failed to adopt an alternative means of candidate selection. This is a plausible rendition of the facts, but not the only permissible one. Though Berry's name first surfaced after Commander Travis received an initial list, Travis could well have expected all along to see Berry in that lineup and, when his hopes were dashed, attempted to regain lost ground by altering the rules. * * *

Third: The appellant insists that Commander Travis's abandonment of the Hospital's wonted policy of preferring in-house candidates itself gives rise to an irresistible inference of racial animus. The appellant weaves a complicated tapestry with the threads of this argument, hinting that the policy often operated in the past to exclude minority candidates from elevation, thus making the Hospital's disregard of it in a case where that policy would redound to the advantage of a minority candidate all the more cruel. In her view, this abrupt departure from past practice can only be explained on the basis of racial bias. We do not agree.

The district court treated this departure as suspicious, but concluded that Commander Travis tweaked the ordinary praxis to benefit a friend rather than to thwart a person of color. Two obvious propositions spring to mind. One is that cronyism is deplorable, especially when it is allowed to infect public sector employment decisions. The other obvious proposition is that Title VII does not have a limitless remedial reach. An employer can hire one person instead of another for any reason, fair or unfair, without transgressing Title VII, as long as the hiring decision is not spurred by race, gender, or some other protected characteristic. * * * As we explain *infra,* Title VII does not outlaw cronyism—and, in this case, cronyism provides a sufficient alternative explanation for the challenged deviation from the standard hiring protocol. Thus, the district court's assessment of the proffered evidence was not clearly erroneous.

Fourth: At trial, Commander Travis stalwartly maintained that he hired Berry because he was the best qualified aspirant. Judge Pettine understandably discounted this testimony. * * * slip op. at 14–15. Although the appellant concedes that a court is not legally bound to find for a Title VII plaintiff simply because it rejects the employer's proffered reason for an employment decision, she maintains that, here, the court's disbelief of the explanation, coupled with the deviation from the standard policy of in-house preferment, compels an inference that the decision was race-driven. To shore up this contention, the appellant points to the naval officials' repeated denials of favoritism. Noting that the district court declined to credit these denials because they were self-serving, * * *, the appellant asseverates that, since preselection was the only alternative rationale that could sidetrack a finding of racial discrimination, the district court erred; the denials of preselection were, in fact, against self-interest, and the employer should be held to them.

This argument is too clever by half. We do not believe it is implausible that veteran bureaucrats—and, in our view, "bureaucrat" and "naval officer" are not mutually exclusive terms—would deny preselection to avoid the stigma of having failed to follow neutral hiring procedures. Indeed, Travis's and Warch's on-the-stand denials are replete with clues from which the district judge reasonably could have deduced that the two men collogued to tilt the process in Berry's favor. In all events, actions speak louder than words. In a bench trial "what an actor says is not conclusive on a state-of-mind issue. Notwithstanding a person's disclaimers, a contrary state of mind may be inferred from what he does and from a factual mosaic tending to show that he really meant to accomplish that which he professes not to have intended." *Anthony v. Sundlun,* 952 F.2d 603, 606 (1st Cir.1991).

In one sense, the district court's finding that an old boy network was in operation though the old boys denied it amounts to a credibility call. By and large, such calls are for the district court, not for the court of appeals. * * * There is no reason to apply a different rule in this case.

Fifth: The appellant argues passionately that even if Commander Travis fished Berry from the applicant pool simply because he was spawned by the old boy network, such a hiring decision itself contravenes the mandate of Title VII. Though this construct, which rests on the premise that cronyism is the primary means by which employers perpetuate workplace apartheid, possesses a certain superficial appeal, it cannot withstand close perscrutation.

Indeed, the construct lacks any vestige of precedential support. The very cases on which the appellant relies explicitly reject it. * * * Thus, her argument amounts to nothing more than a plea that we impose the construct by judicial fiat. But that is not our province. Given the state of the law, appellant's construct should be debated before the Congress, not argued before the courts.

Relatedly, the appellant suggests that Title VII must be read to bar cronyism because that tawdry practice assures continued white domination in the workplace. But this suggestion challenges as discriminatory a facially race-neutral (if offensive) policy, and necessarily depends for support on an examination of multiple hiring decisions. It is, therefore, better tailored to cases alleging disparate impact as opposed to disparate treatment. * * *

Where, as here, a disappointed applicant has made no systematic effort to prove *pervasive* cronyism or to show that cronyism, when practiced in a particular workplace, regularly yields a racially discriminatory result, a disparate impact claim goes by the boards. So here: at trial, appellant's counsel, responding to the district court's insightful questioning, characterized the suit as one involving disparate treatment, not disparate impact. That characterization binds the appellant in the present venue as well.

This brings us full circle. While the facts of this disparate treatment case can support an inference of discriminatory intent, they can equally support a finding of undiluted favoritism, unmixed with racial animus. On such a record, it is the trial court's prerogative—indeed, its duty—to select the inference that it deems appropriate. Because we cannot accept the appellant's invitation to create a presumption that the use of an old boy network in hiring constitutes per se racial discrimination, we are powerless to subvert the district court's election between conflicting inferences.

III. CONCLUSION

We need go no further. Title VII "does not presume to obliterate all manner of inequity, or to stanch, once and for all, what a Scottish poet two centuries ago termed '[m]an's inhumanity to man.' " *Keyes,* 853 F.2d at 1026 (quoting Robert Burns, *Man Was Made to Mourn* (1786)). Like the court below, we find the conduct of the naval hierarchy in this case to be deserving of opprobrium, but two wrongs seldom make a right. Discerning no clear error in the district court's finding that favoritism, not racism, tainted Commander Travis's decisionmaking, we reject Foster's appeal.

NOTES ON FOSTER

1. The court disbelieved the employer's stated reason for its hiring decision. It did not believe the decision was made based on merit. Why then does the plaintiff lose?

2. Assuming the court was right in finding that the decision was based on nepotism, not race, should this be conduct that Title VII prohibits? If so, on what grounds? How would you frame the prohibition?

3. Should Title VII require that all applicants must be treated only on the basis of merit? Alternatively and more narrowly, should Title VII ensure that members of minority groups are always treated on the basis of on job relevant merit? Why or why not?

4. Compare *Foster* with the Supreme Court's holding in Personnel Administrator of Massachusetts v. Feeney, excerpted and discussed in Chapter 2 above. Do you find the conduct at issue in *Foster* more or less troubling from an antidiscrimination perspective than the veterans' preference statute at issue in *Feeney*? Would you have treated the conduct at issue in either case as actionable discrimination? If not, how would you define the contours of Title VII's prohibition on race and sex discrimination?

F. SUMMARY JUDGMENT AND TITLE VII

TEXT NOTE ON SUMMARY JUDGMENT AND TITLE VII

Paul Mollica reports on a study of the change in summary judgment standards in federal courts over the last thirty years and on the importance of this change to Title VII cases.[31] When a judge grants a defendant's (or more rarely a plaintiff's) motion for summary judgment, the case is decided on the basis of documents (including affidavits) filed with the court together with the parties' pleadings.[32] There is no trial.

Over the last thirty years, trials of any kind have become increasingly rare in federal courts in civil suits as increasing numbers of cases are dismissed on motions for summary judgment. This trend was already visible at the district court level by the mid 1980's, but was strengthened by three cases decided by the Supreme Court in 1985. Although none of these cases involved a civil rights or employment discrimination issue,[33] they have been interpreted by the lower federal courts as changing the standard for summary judgment in all kinds of cases, including those arising under Title VII.[34]

Mollica's study examines ten volumes of the Federal Reporter from 1973 and ten volumes from 1997–98 and finds a dramatic difference in the standard for summary judgment between these dates. In 1973, most appeals were from trials. In the cases in which the trial court had granted summary judgment, the reversal rate on appeal was 45.5%. In 1973, federal appellate courts showed:

> extreme vigilance against treading on contested fact issues or mixed questions of law and fact—even arguable ones—reversing them for evidentiary hearings. Only a modest proffer by the non-movant was enough to demonstrate the necessity of a trial. This was especially true in cases applying indeterminate legal standards, such as reasonableness. * * *

31. Paul Mollica, Federal Summary Judgment at High Tide, 84 Marq. L. Rev. 141 (2000).

32. Fed. R. Civ. Pro. 56.

33. See Matsushita Electric Industrial Co., Ltd. v. Zenith Radio Corp., 475 U.S. 574 (1986) (antitrust suit); Anderson v. Liberty Lobby, Inc., 477 U.S. 242 (1986) (libel action); Celotex Corp. v. Catrett, 477 U.S. 317 (1986) (wrongful death action).

34. Mollica, above note 31, at 141–170.

> With only one exception [a defamation case], state-of-mind issues (such as intent and malice) did not terminate in summary judgment in the sample cases.[35]

In the 1997–98 sample, by contrast, most appeals were from grants of summary judgment, not trials:

> It has become common to evaluate such legal standards as intent and reasonableness on summary judgment—to evaluate, on occasion, even issues of credibility—and to default non-movants under Rule 56. [Rule 56 is the procedural rule on summary judgment.] * * *
>
> The reach of summary judgment * * * is especially pernicious in the field of employment discrimination law, where the ultimate issue in most cases is whether the employer (or, more pointedly, its agent) intended to discriminate on the basis of a protected classification * * *.
>
> In a fair number of the employment cases, the summary judgment went to the heart of the employer's alleged discriminatory intent. A few cases found that plaintiffs failed to prove even a prima facie case of discrimination. A larger number of decisions affirmed summary judgment by holding that the plaintiff could not establish discriminatory intent, either directly or indirectly.[36]

The pressure on lower federal courts to use summary judgment to eliminate Title VII cases from their dockets has increased greatly in the 1990's as the number of employment discrimination cases has gone through the roof. In the year ending December 31, 1990, 8,290 employment discrimination cases were filed. Less than a decade later, in the year ending March 31, 1997, the number filed was 23,547.[37] These numbers are high enough to overwhelm the federal courts and create great pressure on district courts to dispose of employment discrimination claims on motions for summary judgment.

As increasing numbers of Title VII cases are decided on summary judgment, it is likely to become ever harder for plaintiffs to prevail. *Troupe*, for example, held that, as a matter of law, a plaintiff cannot prevail on a pregnancy-discrimination claim when an employer alleges that she was fired for absenteeism even if she can show that her supervisor said she was being fired because she was not expected to return from maternity leave. Over time, as more and more such cases are decided by summary judgment in order to control dockets and avoid trials, it will become more and more difficult for plaintiffs to prevail. In light of the numbers of employment discrimination cases filed every year in federal court, judicial determination to use summary judgment to eliminate most of these suits is understandable. But the result is the diminution of Title VII as an effective remedy for employment discrimination.

---

35. Id. at 147–150.

36. Id. at 166–169.

37. Rebecca Hanner White, De Minimis Discrimination, 47 Emory L. J. 1121, 1124 n.14 (1998). Paul Mollica reports that in 1973, 8.5% of pending federal civil cases resulted in a trial, for a total of 8,297 civil trials. In 1999, 2.3% of pending federal civil cases resulted in a trial, for a total of 6,228 civil trials in a year. Mollica, above note 32, at 141.

NOTES ON SUMMARY JUDGMENT AND TITLE VII

1. In 1989, the Supreme Court decided several Title VII cases limiting the ability of plaintiffs to seek remedies for employment discrimination in federal courts. The decisions were widely criticized and, for the most part, overturned by the Civil Rights Act of 1991. Ann C. McGinley has argued that the phenomenon of increasing summary judgment dispositions "is less obvious but equally destructive of Title VII, silently curtail[ing] workers' civil rights claims." There is, however, no outcry over this change nor any movement to amend the statute. McGinley, Credulous Courts and the Tortured Trilogy: The Improper Use of Summary Judgment in Title VII and ADEA Cases, 34 B.C.L. Rev. 203, 205–206 (1993).

2. The viability of sexual harassment complaints is also threatened by the federal court's increasing use of summary judgment. Isabel Medina has argued that this trend "frustrates enforcement of gender antidiscrimination norms by preventing juries, the most diverse, and most experienced in the workplace actors in the legal system, from participating in the development of [sexual harassment] norms and assisting American society to reach consensus on gender issues." Medina, A Matter of Fact: Hostile Environments and Summary Judgments, 8 S. Cal. Rev. Law & Women's Studies 311, 311 (1999). See also Ann Juliano & Stewart J. Schwab, The Sweep of Sexual Harassment Cases, 86 Cornell L. Rev. 548 (2001). Given the cases you have read in this chapter, why might it be important that Title VII suits be decided in trials before juries rather than in summary judgment proceedings before judges?

3. Rebecca Hanner White suggests that, in an increasingly determined effort to clear their dockets of the avalanche of employment discrimination cases, federal courts are increasingly holding that employers are liable for discrimination only when it is more than de minimis, i.e., only when it results in a tangible and adverse employment action. Rebecca Hanner White, De Minimis Discrimination, 47 Emory L. J. 1121 (1998). Although the Supreme Court has required tangible employment action in cases in which employers are held vicariously liable for harassment by a supervisor, White suggests that lower courts may be starting to require tangible (and negative) employment action generally for discrimination to be actionable. Can you suggest other solutions to the avalanche of cases? And to the standard for proving discrimination, given what we now know about human decisionmaking from cognitive theory?

G. COMPARABLE WORTH

TEXT NOTE: COMPARABLE WORTH

Although there is a great deal of variation in what jobs are considered women's and men's across various cultures and economic systems, men and women tend to do different things, and the construction of difference seems of great importance in all cultures and economic systems. Gayle Rubin suggests that "[t]he division of labor by sex can * * * be seen as a 'taboo': a taboo against the sameness of men and women, a taboo dividing the sexes into two mutually exclusive categories, a taboo which exacerbates the biological differences between the sexes and thereby *creates* gender."[38] And in all industrial or capitalist societies (where wages make values easy to compare), what men do is valued more than what women do.

Despite women's increasing participation in the wage labor market and the enactment of Title VII and the Equal Pay Act,[39] most women still work in women's jobs for women's wages.[40] In the Bible, women are valued at about 60% of the value of men.[41] This gender wage gap has been surprisingly persistent over the centuries, as suggested by the table below, which reports that in 1951, women workers (working full-time year-round) earned 63.9 cents for every dollar earned by male workers (working full-time year-round). As the table also illustrates, women workers in the United States have made significant gains since then, particularly in the 1980's.

Table 4: 2006 Median Annual Earnings by Race and Sex[42]

Race/Sex	Earnings	Wage ratio
White men	$47, 814	100%
Black men	$34,480	72.1%
White women	$35,151	73.5%
Black women	$30,398	63.6%
Hispanic men	$27, 490	57.5%
Hispanic women	$24,738	51.7%
All men	$42,210	
All women	$32,649	
Overall wage gap		77.4%

Table 5: 1951–2008 Wage Gap between Women and Men[43]

Year	Percent	Year	Percent	Year	Percent	Year	Percent
1951	63.9%	1965	59.9%	1978	59.4%	1991	69.6%
1952	63.9%	1966	57.6%	1979	59.7%	1992	70.8%

38. Rubin, The Traffic in Women: Some Notes on the "Political Economy" of Sex, in Toward an Anthropology of Women 157, 178 (Rayna R. Reiter, ed. 1975).

39. 29 U.S.C.A. § 206(d). The Act prohibits employers from paying less to women than men for "equal work on jobs the performance of which requires equal skill, effort, and responsibility, and which are performed under similar working conditions * * *." Id. at § 206(d)(1).

40. U.S. Dept. of Labor, Women's Bureau, 20 Leading Occupations of Employed Women Full-time Wage and Salary Workers, 2004 Annual Averages, available at http://www.infoplease.com/ipa/Ao922455. html. As Diane Balser notes, "[a]long with the massive entry of women into the wage-work force, a parallel and equally revolutionary phenomenon has been the development of a *sex-segregated wage-work force*, with men, in general, occupying the higher status and better paid positions and the majority of women holding the lower status and lower paid positions." Balser, Sisterhood & Solidarity: Feminism and Labor in Modern Times 19 (1987).

41. Leviticus 27: 3:4.

42. The Learning Network, available at http://www.infoplease.com/us/census/median-earnings-by-race–2006.html.

43. The Learning Network, available at http://www.infoplease.com/ipa/A0193820.html.

Year	Percent	Year	Percent	Year	Percent	Year	Percent
1953	63.9%	1967	57.8%	1980	60.2%	1993	71.5%
1954	63.9%	1968	58.2%	1981	59.2%	1994	72.0%
1955	63.9%	1969	58.9%	1982	61.7%	1995	71.4%
1956	63.3%	1970	59.4%	1983	63.6%	1996	73.8%
1957	63.8%	1971	59.5%	1984	63.7%	1997	74.2%
1958	63.0%	1972	57.9%	1985	64.6%	1998	73.2%
1959	61.3%	1973	56.6%	1986	64.3%	1999	72.2%
1960	60.7%	1974	58.8%	1987	65.2%	2000	73.3%
1961	59.2%	1975	58.8%	1988	66.0%	2001	76.3%
1962	59.3%	1976	60.2%	1989	68.7%	2002	76.6%
1963	58.9%	1977	58.9%	1990	71.6%	2003	75.5%
1964	59.1%	2004	76.6%	2005	77.0%	2006	76.9%
				2007	77.8%	2008	77.1%

The wage gap diminished by about 13% between 1970 and 1996 for two reasons: women's wages rose *and* men's fell. Between these dates, women's real wages rose by 17.1% *and* men's real wages fell by 3%. For the least educated women (those with a high school education or less), real wages fell between 1980 and 1998.[44]

Job Segregation

The continuation of the wage gap is associated with persistent segregation by sex and race, with jobs held by women and minorities tending to pay less than other jobs. It is true that there have been significant declines in the level of job segregation in recent decades. But, as with the wage gap, job segregation is amazingly persistent. A few examples will illustrate this point. Between 1983 and 2008, women employed as lawyers rose from 15.8% to 34.4%; women employed as physicians rose from 15.8% to 30.5%; and women employed as clergy rose from 5.6% to 14.8%. But even in 2008, women were 97.6% of preschool and kindergarten teachers, 81.2% of grade school teachers (almost the same percentage as in 1983), 91.7% of registered nurses (down from 95.8% in 1983), and 96.3% of dental assistants. And in 2008, men were 95.2% of firefighters (down from 99% in 1983), and 97.4% of airplane pilots and flight engineers.[45]

Thus far, we have only described national data which combine information across workplaces. But even when national data report that a job is *not* segregated by race or sex, at many (sometimes most) workplaces, the job will be held only by members of one group. For example, both women and men work as textile, apparel and finishing machine operators. But they tend to

44. Costello et al., above note 5, at 303; Jane Waldfogel & Susan Mayer, Differences Between Men and Women in the Low-wage Labor Market, 20 Focus 11, 16 (1998–1999) (published by University of Wisconsin–Madison Institute for Research on Poverty, available at http://www.irp.wisc.edu/publications/focus/pdfs/foc201.pdf#page=11.

45. Costello et al., above note 5, at 287. See also U.S. Census Bureau, Statistical Abstract of the United States: 2004–2005, table 597, available at http://www.census.gov/prod/2004pubs/04statab/labor.pdf.

work at different firms. About 64% of women in this occupation would have to work at a different job for this occupation to be integrated on a workplace-by-workplace basis. And when women and men work at the same occupation at different firms, the workers at the firms employing men tend to pay higher wages.[46]

There are few studies reporting on levels of actual segregation on a workplace basis. A 1989 survey of North Carolina workers asked about the race and sex of coworkers and reported that for 70% of all jobs, the jobs were held entirely by men or by women at the respondent's workplace. Of the 30% of jobs held by both men and women at particular work sites, most (16%) were held almost entirely by men or women. In only 15% of jobs did people actually work in workplaces in which women and men both held the position in proportion to their numbers in the workforce.[47]

Racial segregation was reported at somewhat lower levels. A majority (56%) of workers held jobs which were held only by blacks or only by whites at their workplaces. Some 30% worked at jobs that were almost entirely segregated. In only 14% of jobs were workers of both races present in numbers approximately proportional to their numbers in the work force.[48]

The Case for Comparable Worth

Segregation by race and sex would be less troubling were jobs held by men and women of various races equivalent in terms of pay, status, and opportunities for advancement. Unfortunately, that is not the reality. Many attempts have been made to explain the wage gap in terms of differences in education, training, labor force attachment, and so forth. These studies consistently report that white men earn more than women and minorities with the same education.[49]

Many studies have tried to explain the wage gap between women and men in terms of differences in education and work patterns. Men tend to have greater labor force attachment, and women are more likely to take time off to care for young children full time and temporarily, including when children are sick. Also, women are likely to work fewer hours for wages, though women who work for wages work more hours in toto (homemaking and wage employment combined) than working men. Researchers have concluded, however, that such differences explain only about one fourth to one half of the wage gap for the hours women do work for wages.[50] The remaining disparity would seem to be the result of differential opportunities afforded men and

46. Id. at 22.

47. Barbara A. Bergman, In Defense of Affirmative Action 42–43(1996) (describing study by Donald Tomaskovic-Devey, Gender and Racial Inequality at Work: The Sources and Consequences of Job Segregation (1993)).

48. Id. at 43–44.

49. Id. See also Income Gaps Found Among the College–Educated, N.Y. Times, Mar. 28, 2005, at A12 (describing Census Bureau data showing that college-educated white men earn "far more than any similarly educated man or woman").

50. See, e.g., Greg J. Duncan, et al., Years of Poverty, Years of Plenty: The Changing Economic Fortunes of American Workers and Families 161 (1984); Heidi Hartmann, Women are Paid Less—They and Their Families Deserve Pay Parity, Civ. Rts. J., Fall 1999, at 31; Joni Hersch & Leslie S. Stratton, Housework & Wages, 37 J. Human Resources 217 (2002).

women by employers and unconscious undervaluation of work done by women.[51]

To the extent differences between women and men do explain the pay gap, the explanation may still reflect discrimination and the disparate choices facing women and men. Observed differences would not necessarily *justify* the wage gap. For example, if many workplaces are structured to reflect men's life styles but not women's, though women's could readily be accommodated, then the fact that women caretake more than men or take off more time at childbirth, will "explain" the wage gap though employers could accommodate this difference and thereby diminish the gap.[52] Indeed, a comprehensive study of the relationship between sex segregation and the wage gap from the mid–990's reports that the gap would almost disappear were women to work in the same occupations at the same establishments as men,[53] suggesting that it is occupational segregation that causes the gap rather than differences between the sexes.

"Comparable worth" is a term of art describing a remedy for the fact that workers in jobs held predominantly by women of any color and other members of minority groups tend to pay less than jobs held by whites and by men. Although a comparable worth standard could be formulated in many ways, it is typically described as requiring equal pay for "comparable" jobs, that is, jobs requiring equivalent knowledge and skills, mental demands, accountability, and working conditions. For example, a 1974 study for the state of Washington analyzed each job and awarded a maximum of 280 points for the knowledge and skills required for the job, a maximum of 140 points for the job's mental demands, a maximum of 160 points for accountability, and a maximum of 20 for working conditions. These points were then added together to yield a composite point value representing the value of the job to the employer. Values of various jobs were then compared to wages of various jobs, making it possible to identify jobs for which the pay was low relative to the rate at which the employer paid jobs of comparable value.

Large employers often set internal wages for many jobs according to assessments of the worth of various jobs, assessments obtained in a formal job evaluation study such as that performed by the state of Washington. The pay for some jobs, especially entry-level jobs, may be pegged to market wages. But the pay for most jobs is set by an internal formal analysis of the worth of various jobs.

---

51. Cross-cultural studies support this explanation. In almost all cultures, women and men do different work, though what women do in one culture men often do in another (and vice versa). Yet whatever it is that men do in a culture is what is most valued. See, e.g., Sherry B. Ortner, Is Female to Male as Nature Is to Culture?, in Woman, Culture, and Society 67 (Michelle Z. Rosaldo & Louise Lamphere, eds. 1974); Gayle Rubin, The Traffic in Women: Notes on the "Political Economy" of Sex, in Toward an Anthropology of Women 157, 178 (Rayna R. Reiter, eds. 1975).

52. See Joan C. Williams & Nancy Segal, Beyond the Maternal Wall: Relief for Family Caregivers Who Are Discriminated Against on the Job, 26 Harv. Women's L. J. 77, 78 (2003) (arguing that eliminating a workplace ideal of a worker with a man's body and men's "traditional immunity from caregiving" "is not 'accommodation,' it is the minimum requirement for gender equality").

53. Trond Peterson & Laurie A. Morgan, Separate and Unequal: Occupation–Establishment Sex Segregation and the Gender Wage Gap, 101 Am. J. Sociol. 329 (1995).

A comparable worth standard cannot be expected to eliminate entirely that portion of the wage gap attributable to the undervaluation of women's work. All valuations are likely to be tainted by the fact that those with privilege have written the rules to value most the qualities and skills they see themselves as displaying.[54] For example, sociologist Arlie Hochschild has explored the relationship between gender and waged emotional work. In her study of stewards and stewardesses, she found that women (stewardesses) were more likely to be the recipients of hostile feelings from passengers and more likely to perform supportive emotional labor than stewards. Women's extra emotional work was not, however, compensated, though it is work.[55] Given current cultural values, however, emotional work performed by women will often be invisible or seen as something other than valuable work. Indeed, jobs involving caring work, such as child care, teaching, therapy, and nursing, "offer low pay relative to their requirements for education and skill."[56]

Although comparable worth cannot eliminate all gender-linked pay disparities, there is evidence that a comparable worth standard does result in a diminished gap between the wages paid to workers in men's jobs and the wages paid to those in women's jobs. Minnesota adopted a comparable worth standard for state employees some time ago, and 90% of the wage increases went to people (mostly women) in the following occupations: "secretaries, other clerical employees, teacher aides, other school aides, cooks, other food service employees, non-nursing medical employees, nurses (RN, LPN), social services employees, library employees, city clerks and clerk-treasurers, and liquor store employees."[57]

Comparable Worth Around the World

In the United States, the first federal legislation banning discrimination against women in employment was the Equal Pay Act of 1963, but it only prohibits wage discrimination between women and men "for equal work on jobs the performance of which requires equal skill, effort, and responsibility, and which are performed under similar working conditions."[58] It applies only when women and men hold the same job in the same establishment, and thus does not reach the wage gap associated with women and men holding different jobs.

---

54. See Barbara F. Reskin, Bringing the Men Back In: Sex Differentiation and the Devaluation of Women's Work, 2 Gender & Soc'y 58 (1988). Reskin argues that "[d]ominant groups remain privileged because they write the rules," and the rules they write "enable them *to continue to write the rules.*" Id. at 60 (emphasis in original). Reskin maintains that "the basic cause of the income gap is not sex segregation but men's desire to preserve their advantaged position and their ability to do so by establishing rules to distribute valued resources in their favor." Id. at 61.

55. Hochschild, The Managed Heart: The Commercialization of Human Feeling (1983). For an article discussing the failure of traditional job evaluation systems to value emotional labor and suggesting how emotional labor might be valued in a job evaluation system, see Ronnie J. Steinberg, Emotional Labor in the Service Economy: Emotional Labor, its Measurement and Repercussions, 561 Annals Am. Acad. Polit. & Soc. Sci. 143, 143 (1999).

56. Paula England & Nancy Folbre, Emotional Labor in the Service Economy: The Contours of Emotional Labor: The Cost of Caring, 561 Annals Am. Acad. Polit. & Soc. Sci. 39, 39 (1999).

57. Sara M. Evans & Barbara J. Nelson, Wage Justice: Comparable Worth and the Paradox of Technocratic Reform 159 (1989).

58. 29 U.S.C. § 206(d)(1) (with exceptions for differential payments "made pursuant to (i) a seniority system; (ii) a merit system; (iii) a system which measures earnings by quantity or quality of production; or (iv) a differential based on any other factor other than sex").

Nor does Title VII reach this problem. An early and leading case is the decision of the Ninth Circuit in AFCSME v. State of Washington, 770 F.2d 1401 (9th Cir. 1985). In 1974, Washington commissioned a study, described above, to consider whether there was a wage disparity between state employees working in women's jobs (jobs held predominantly by women) and those working in men's jobs. The study reported a disparity of about 20% in pay between jobs held mostly by women and those held mostly by men. After conducting similar studies in 1976 and 1980, Washington enacted legislation requiring that state employees doing jobs of comparable worth receive equal pay, with comparable worth being determined according to the four factors mentioned above: knowledge and skills, mental demands, accountability, and working conditions. This comparable worth scheme—i.e., a plan to pay equal pay to workers holding (different) jobs of comparable worth—was to be implemented over a ten-year period. AFSCME, a union of state workers, sued alleging sex discrimination in Washington's failure to pay women and men equal salaries for jobs of comparable worth during the ten-year phase-in period. The district court ruled for AFSCME finding that there was discrimination on the basis of sex in violation of Title VII on the basis of both disparate treatment and disparate impact.

The Ninth Circuit reversed, holding that there had been no discrimination on the basis of sex under Title VII. In rejecting the disparate treatment claim, the court stated:

> AFSCME contends discriminatory motive may be inferred from the Willis study, which finds the State's practice of setting salaries in reliance on market rates creates a sex-based wage disparity for jobs deemed of comparable worth. AFSCME argues from the study that the market reflects a historical pattern of lower wages to employees in positions staffed predominantly by women; and it contends the State of Washington perpetuates that disparity, in violation of Title VII, by using market rates in the compensation system. The inference of discriminatory motive which AFSCME seeks to draw from the State's participation in the market system fails, as the State did not create the market disparity and has not been shown to have been motivated by impermissible sex-based considerations in setting salaries.
>
> The requirement of intent is linked at least in part to culpability. That concept would be undermined if we were to hold that payment of wages according to prevailing rates in the public and private sectors is an act that, in itself, supports the inference of a purpose to discriminate. Neither law nor logic deems the free market system a suspect enterprise. Economic reality is that the value of a particular job to an employer is but one factor influencing the rate of compensation for that job. Other considerations may include the availability of workers willing to do the job and the effectiveness of collective bargaining in a particular industry. * * * [E]mployers may be constrained by market forces to set salaries under prevailing wage rates for different job classifications. We find nothing in the language of Title VII or its legislative history to indicate Congress intended to abrogate fundamental economic principles such as the laws of supply and demand or to prevent employers from competing in the labor market.

> While the Washington legislature may have the discretion to enact a comparable worth plan if it chooses to do so, Title VII does not obligate it to eliminate an economic inequality that it did not create. * * *

770 F.2d at 1406–07. In rejecting the disparate impact claim, the court stated:

> AFSCME's disparate impact argument is based on the contention that the State of Washington's practice of taking prevailing market rates into account in setting wages has an adverse impact on women, who, historically, have received lower wages than men in the labor market. * * * [T]he decision to base compensation on the competitive market, rather than on a theory of comparable worth, involves the assessment of a number of complex factors not easily ascertainable, an assessment too multifaceted to be appropriate for disparate impact analysis. In the case before us, the compensation system in question resulted from surveys, agency hearings, administrative recommendations, budget proposals, executive actions, and legislative enactments. A compensation system that is responsive to supply and demand and other market forces is not the type of specific, clearly delineated employment policy contemplated by [the Supreme Court's disparate impact cases]. * * *

Id. at 1405–06.

Although federal anti-discrimination law does not require equal pay for jobs of equal value, comparable worth has been adopted by some states as the pay standard for state employees, i.e., state employees must be paid according to a comparable worth assessment.[59]

In addition, many other industrialized countries have some sort of comparable worth standard, including Ontario, Canada, Europe, and Australia, and apply their standards to *all* employers (not just state employees). The Ontario plan has been described by its drafter:

> [T]he *Pay Equity Act* has application in both the public and private sectors (to firms with ten employees or more), and it follows a proactive rather than a complaint-driven model which requires each employer to create plans to achieve pay equity for employees in predominantly female job classes. This means that employers must carry out job comparisons of all predominantly female job classes with predominantly male job classes on the basis of the skill, effort, responsibility and working conditions inherent in the job. Where jobs are determined to be of equal or comparable value, the female job class must be paid at least at the same rate as the lowest paid male job class of equal value. The *Act* allows for varied approaches to job comparison by employers, as long as the system used is gender-neutral.
>
> Separate plans must be posted for employees in each bargaining unit in the establishment, and for non-bargaining employees. Each plan must identify the group covered by the plan, define the establishment, and identify all job classes which formed the basis of the comparisons. The plan must also describe the gender-neutral comparison system used and

59. See Martha Chamallas, Deepening the Legal Understanding of Bias: On Devaluation and Biased Prototypes, 74 S. Cal. L. Rev. 747, 768 n. 87 (2001) (noting that by 1987 twenty states had made comparable worth adjustments for state employees).

the results of the comparisons. Finally, it must identify all the female job classes for which pay equity adjustments are required and state the date on which the first pay adjustments will be made.[60]

The European Union also has a standard requiring equal pay "for work to which equal value is attributed."[61] This standard is enforced by the European Court of Justice in suits between employees and private employers.[62] The European Court of Justice has held, for example, that an employer cannot give lower hourly wages or lower (per hour worked) benefits to part-time workers than full-time workers if (as is often the case) there are significantly more women working part time than full time.[63] (Such differentials would be legal in the United States unless a woman employee could make the difficult showing that the policy was intentionally adopted to discriminate against women.)

Once a plaintiff in the EU shows that women are paid less than men for jobs of equal value, the burden shifts to the employer to show that the differential is justified.[64] The employer can prevail only on a showing that differentials "correspond to a real need on the part of the undertaking, are appropriate with a view to achieving the objectives pursued, and are necessary to that end."[65] More is needed than a subjective belief on the employer's part that the differentials are necessary, and the employer's objective justification must be proportionate to the pay differentials.[66] An economic defense is therefore possible, though the ECJ "has made little attempt to explain where it sees the balance lying as between commercial profitability of an organization and the elimination of discrimination."[67]

Table 7: International Comparisons (2003)[68]

Country	Wage gap
Austria	83%

60. Elaine M. Todres, Women's Work in Ontario: Pay Equity and the Wage Gap, 22 Ottawa L. Rev. 555, 561–62 (1990). For additional information about the Ontario experience, see Judy Fudge, Limiting Equity: The Definition of "Employer" under the Ontario Pay Equity Act, 4 Can. J. Women & L. 556 (1990–1991); Patricia C. McDermott, Pay Equity in Ontario: A Critical Legal Analysis, 28 Osgoode Hall L.J. 381 (1990). For a description of comparable worth in the various Canadian provinces as well as at the federal level, see M. Neil Brown & Michael D. Meuti, Individualism and the Market Determination of Women's Wages in the United States, Canada, and Hong Kong, 21 Loy.L.A. Int'l & Comp.L.J. 355, 372–87 (1999).

61. Council Directive 75/117 (Equal Pay Directive) art. 1, 1975 O.J. (L45), 19 (interpreting article 119 of the Treaty of Rome).

62. Case 61/81, Commission v. U.K., [1982] 3 C.M.L.R. 284.

63. See Evelyn Ellis, EC Sex Equality Law 112–19 (1998) (discussing cases).

64. Id. at 119–122 (discussing cases).

65. Case 170/84, Bilka–Kaufhaus GmbH v. Weber Von Hartz, [1986] ECR 1607, 1628.

66. Case C–127/92, Enderby v. Frenchay Health Authority, [1993] ECR I–5535, 5576; see also Ellis, above note 62, at 125–126 (discussing cases and standard).

67. Ellis, above note 62, at 126.

68. The data from the EU is from The Social Situation in the European Union: 2006 (showing women's wages as a percentage of men's wages), available at http://ec.europa.eu/employment_social/social_situation/socsit_en.htm#2005–2006 last visited 6/15/2010. The U.S. data for 2003 is from U.S. Women's Bureau and the National Commission on Pay Equity, available a http://www.infoplease.com/ipa/A0882775.html.

Country	Wage gap
Belgium	88%
Denmark	82%
Finland	80%
France	88%
Germany	77%
Greece	89%
Ireland	86%
Italy	94%
The Netherlands	82%
Portugal	91%
Spain	82%
Sweden	84%
United Kingdom	88%
United States	75.6%
Cyprus	75.0%

In most, though not all, of the countries in the EU, the wage gap between women and men is lower than in the United States, as the table above illustrates. All countries in the chart, other than the United States and parts of Canada, have a comparable-worth standard applicable to some private employers.

NOTES ON COMPARABLE WORTH

1. What are the arguments for and against a comparable worth standard applicable to all employers? In particular, what are the difficulties with this sort of standard? Would it be judicially manageable? Do you think it requires comparison of apples and oranges? Can you think of other (existing) legal standards presenting similar difficulties?

2. One limit on the effectiveness of a comparable worth standard in eliminating the wage gap between women and men is that it only allows challenges to wage disparities within a single employer. To the extent manufacturing jobs pay more than service jobs "of equal value," comparable worth will not provide a remedy. Can you think of a way to structure a remedy that would reach across industries?

3. Do you agree with the reasoning in AFSCME v. State of Washington (rejecting comparable-worth arguments in Title VII cases)? Do you agree with the court's assertion that "[n]either law nor logic deems the free market system a suspect enterprise"? If you regard the free market system with some suspicion, given the evidence of persistent wage gaps by race and sex, together with job segregation by race and sex, how would you analyze the questions presented in *AFSCME*? Would you have found disparate treatment? Disparate impact?

4. Comparable worth accepts market driven wages with some minor adjustments. What problems and inequities does comparable worth thereby ignore? How would women of various classes and races fare under comparable worth? One commentator has observed: "it would be better, for the women's movement and for society, for feminist lawyers developing their legal theory to have as their goal a redefinition of human worth that challenges the market-based definition more directly than a pay equity [or comparable worth] theory does, and to seek a remedy that calls for some plausible modification in the organization of a workplace aimed at realizing a more nurturant and socially confirming conception of the nature of socially valuable labor." Peter Gabel, Dukakis's Defeat and the Transformative Possibilities of Legal Culture, Tikkun, Mar.–Apr. 1989, at 13, 113. In what ways is comparable worth conservative? What might a more radical claim look like? See Johanna Brenner, Feminist Political Discourses: Radical Versus Liberal Approaches to the Feminization of Poverty and Comparable Worth, 1 Gender & Soc'y 447 (1987), Paula England, Comparable Worth: Theories and Evidence, Aldine de Gruyter Publishing (1992), Elaine Sorenson, The Crowding Hypothesis and Comparable Worth, The Journal of Human Resources 55–89 (1990).

5. How would the various feminist approaches presented in Chapter 3 analyze and explain the wage gap? What remedy or remedies would each consider appropriate? Which explanation is, in your view, most accurate? Which remedies are most likely to be effective?

6. Why do you think the United States, unlike other countries such as Australia, Canada, and the EU, has not adopted comparable worth? Should it?

CHAPTER 10

WOMEN AND THE LEGAL PROFESSION

■ ■ ■

A. INTRODUCTION

Women have entered the legal profession in large numbers only since the 1970's. In 1971, just 3% of all lawyers were women; this figure had risen to 8% by 1980 and to 27% by 2000,[1] due in large part to the passage of Title VII of the Civil Rights Act of 1964.[2] After meeting the challenge of outright exclusion, women also faced other forms of bias in law schools, courts, and law firms. The impact of women upon the legal profession and whether they will make it into positions of power in proportion to their numbers remain to be seen.

In 1869, Belle Mansfield became the first woman admitted to the bar in the United States, when she applied for and received a license to practice law in Iowa.[3] Women in other states did not fare as well. Although Ada H. Kepley was the first woman to graduate from a law school in the United States when she received her degree from Union College of Law (now Northwestern) in 1870, she was denied admission to the Illinois bar until 1881.[4] Courts that considered the petitions of women seeking the right to practice law found that woman's "nature" was unsuited for a profession that "has essentially and habitually to do with all that is selfish and malicious, knavish and criminal, coarse and brutal, repulsive and obscene, in human life."[5]

---

1. Clara N. Carson, The Lawyer Statistical Report: The U.S. Legal Profession in 2000 3 (2004). Women were 34% of all lawyers in 2008. U.S. Dep't of Labor, Current Population Survey, Table 11: Employed persons by detailed occupation and sex, 2008 annual averages, available at http://www.bls.gov/cps/wlf-table11-2009.pdf.

2. See Karen Berger Morello, The Invisible Bar: The Woman Lawyer in America: 1638 to the Present 210–15 (1986); Cynthia Fuchs Epstein, Women in Law 184–86 (1981).

3. Morello, above note 2, at 11–14.

4. Epstein, above note 2, at 50; Morello, above note 2, at 49–50 (Morello asserts that Kepley graduated from the University of Chicago Law School, but Northwestern's claim of historical and legal connection seems clearer than that of the University of Chicago, which was not founded until 1891 (the law school in 1902). Moreover, Northwestern has long laid claim to Kepley, while Chicago has not.)

5. In re Goodell, 39 Wis. 232, 245–46 (1875). See also Bradwell v. Illinois, 83 U.S. (16 Wall.) 130, 130 (1872).

Even after the passage of acts guaranteeing the right of women to practice the occupations of their choice, women who chose to become lawyers faced other barriers. Law schools were slow to admit women. Harvard, one of the last holdouts, did not admit women students until 1950, and a few other schools continued to exclude women until the 1960's and 1970's.[6] Until the 1970's, moreover, admissions quotas severely limited the numbers of women at most law schools. Even after being admitted, women experienced hostility to their presence on the part of professors and male students alike.[7] Nonetheless, with the assistance of federal anti-discrimination laws, the number of women studying law has increased sharply during the last few decades. While never more than 4% until 1967, women were 20% of law students by 1974–75 and 40% by 1985–86, and their number has hovered between 40% and 50% ever since.[8]

Fierce discrimination continued to face women who sought positions with large law firms. Wall Street was particularly hostile territory, and until the 1970's firms readily admitted that they did not hire women.[9] Sandra Day O'Connor, who in 1981 became the first woman justice on the Supreme Court, was unable to obtain employment as a lawyer in 1952, although she had graduated from Stanford Law School with honors and served as an editor on the Stanford Law Review.[10]

In the early 1970's, a group of women law students at NYU Law School, together with others at Columbia Law School, represented by the Columbia legal clinic's Employment Law Project, sued ten major Wall Street firms for discrimination in interviewing and hiring women. Three of the firms settled after the cases against them were investigated by the New York City Human Rights Commission, and the two cases that went on to be litigated in federal district court ultimately resulted in settlements as well, on terms ensuring that women would be interviewed and hired on the same basis as men. The number of women hired by large law firms climbed during the 1970's. Those women lucky enough to be hired, however, did not advance within large law firms as men did. The prestigious firm of Sullivan & Cromwell, for example, hired its first woman associate in 1930 but did not make any woman partner until 1982.[11] Although women have been entering the profession in substantial num-

6. Epstein, above note 2, at 50. Notre Dame did not admit women until 1969 and Washington and Lee until 1972. Id.

7. Id. at 63–67; Morello, above note 2, at 103–05.

8. Richard K. Neumann Jr., Women in Legal Education: What the Statistics Show, 50 J. Leg. Educ. 313, 314 (2000). Women made up approximately 47% of all first-year law students enrolled in 2008–2009. Percentage extrapolated from American Bar Association statistics available at http://www.abanet.org/legaled/statistics/charts/stats% 20–% 201.pdf.

9. Epstein, above note 2, at 83–95; Morello, above note 2, at 194–217.

10. Epstein, above note 2, at 84 n.; Morello, above note 2, at 194.

11. Morello, above note 2, at 197; Epstein, above note 2, at 214–15. See also Cynthia Grant Bowman, The Entry of Women into Wall Street Law Firms: The Story of *Blank v. Sullivan & Cromwell*, in Women and the Law Stories (Elizabeth M. Schneider & Stephanie M. Wildman eds., 2011).

bers since the 1970's, their representation among partnerships is still disproportionately low.[12]

In the 1980's and early 1990's, task forces were set up in many states to study the question of gender bias in the law. The reports issued by these groups concluded that outright exclusion of women had been replaced by subtler forms of discrimination against them by both judges and male lawyers—by sexist remarks and practices, by derogatory treatment and forms of address, and by numerous other messages that conveyed that women were still not completely welcome in the profession.[13]

The entry of women into the legal profession in increasing numbers brought demands for change. In a society in which women are still the primary caretakers of both the very young and the very old, female lawyers have confronted a profession structured around the norm of a male attorney with little or no responsibility for caretaking. This confrontation led to demands for maternity leave, part-time work, and flexible tracks to partnership, which in turn occasioned fears about a "glass ceiling," a "Mommy track," and the relegation of women to second-class status within the profession.[14]

Women lawyers change jobs sooner and more frequently than men, typically moving in a direction that would be considered downwardly mobile and are consistently paid less than men.[15] Whether women will simply leave law firms or will stay and restructure the legal workplace to meet their needs remains an open question. Yet, although women's attrition rates from private law firms are disproportionately high, women lawyers responding to longitudinal studies report that they are at least as happy with their career choice over time as men are, and perhaps more so—apparently because they have made job changes that accommodate their personal lives in terms of hours and stress, if at the cost of lower pay.[16]

---

12. In 2009, women were 19.21% of partners and 45.66% of associates. National Association for Law Placement statistics available at http://www.nalp.org/oct09lawfirmdiversity (Table 1).

13. See Ann J. Gellis, Great Expectations: Women in the Legal Profession, A Commentary on State Studies, 66 Ind. L.J. 941 (1991); Jeannette F. Swent, Gender Bias at the Heart of Justice: An Empirical Study of State Task Forces, 6 S. Cal. Rev. L. & Women's Stud. 1 (1996).

14. The "glass ceiling" refers to an invisible barrier that prevents women from scaling the upper rungs on the ladder of success while allowing them to see what they are missing; the phrase "Mommy track" is used to describe the career path of women who choose to work fewer hours because of child care obligations and may therefore be shunted into less prestigious work with fewer opportunities for advancement. See, e.g., Felice Schwartz, Management Women and the New Facts of Life, 67 Harv.Bus.Rev., Jan.–Feb. 1989, at 65, 68; Women in Law, 74 A.B.A. J., June 1, 1988, at 49; Judith S. Kaye, "Mommy Track" in Practice, Nat'l L.J., May 22, 1989, at 13; Jennifer A. Kingson, Women in the Law Say Path Is Limited by "Mommy Track," N.Y. Times, Aug. 8, 1988, at A1.

15. See, e.g., Nancy J. Reichman & Joyce S. Sterling, Recasting the Brass Ring: Deconstructing and Reconstructing Workplace Opportunities for Women Lawyers, 29 Cap. U.L. Rev. 923, 930, 938 (2001–2003) (concerning job movement); Nancy J. Reichman & Joyce S. Sterling, Sticky Floors, Broken Steps, and Concrete Ceilings in Legal Careers, 14 Tex. J. Women & L. 27, 30–37 (2004) (concerning the pay gap).

16. See Kenneth G. Dau–Schmidt, Marc S. Galanter, Kaushik Mukhopadhaya & Kathleen Hull, Men and Women of the Bar: The Impact of Gender on Legal Career, 16 Michigan J. Gender & Law 49, 117–26 (2009) (study summarizing the literature on job satisfaction as well as

Some claim that women will substantially change the legal profession, not only by restructuring the workplace but also by contributing a "different voice" to lawyering—a more collaborative, cooperative, and contextual approach, with a preference for non-adversarial modes of dispute resolution, such as mediation.[17] Critics, on the other hand, point out that women, like minorities, may suffer in informal settings if the parties are unequal in power or only one of the two is socialized to think in terms of the other party's interest rather than her own.[18] Others wonder how it is possible to fight the necessary battles over the many legal issues that affect women's lives without learning to fight "like men."[19]

Whatever their impact upon the structure and practice of law, it seems clear that unless women enter the profession and use its tools, they will be excluded from an important source of power in our society. As Cynthia Fuchs Epstein has pointed out, law provides access to important positions in business, government, and politics in the United States: "Members of the legal elite preside over power and property relationships. They play a leading role in the legislative and regulative bodies that write the law; they direct the executive agencies responsible for enforcing the law; they rule the courts that elaborate and apply the law; they guide the corporate and financial institutions that constitute the most important property interests."[20] In short, the role of women within the legal profession may prove central to their capacity to structure the rules and institutions that affect women's lives in every sphere.

B. WOMEN AND LEGAL EDUCATION

LANI GUINIER, MICHELLE FINE, AND JANE BALIN, WITH ANN BARTOW AND DEBORAH LEE STACHEL, BECOMING GENTLEMEN: WOMEN'S EXPERIENCES AT ONE IVY LEAGUE LAW SCHOOL

143 U. Pa. L. Rev. 1, 2–5, 47–55, 61–62, 65, 80, 82, 99 (1994).

In this Article we describe preliminary research[a] by and about women law students at the University of Pennsylvania Law School—a typical, if

reporting that women law graduates of the University of Michigan in the late 1970's were more satisfied than men with both their careers and the balance of work and family in their lives fifteen years after graduation); John Monahan & Jeffrey Swanson, Lawyers at Mid–Career: A 20–Year Longitudinal Study of Job and Life Satisfaction, 6 J. Empirical Legal Stud. 451 (2009) (same finding based on 20–year study of 1990 graduating class from the University of Virginia School of Law); John P. Heinz, Kathleen E. Hull & Ava A. Harter, Lawyers and Their Discontents: Findings from a Survey of the Chicago Bar, 74 Ind. L.J. 735, 746 (1999) (finding no statistically significant gender difference in overall job satisfaction). But see NALP Foundation & Am. Bar Foundation, After the J.D. II: Second Results from a National Study of Legal Careers 70 (2009) (women's job satisfaction within large law firms was significantly lower than that of men).

17. See, e.g., Carrie Menkel–Meadow, Portia in a Different Voice: Speculations on a Women's Lawyering Process, 1 Berkeley Women's L.J. 39 (1985).

18. See, e.g., Lisa Lerman, Mediation of Wife Abuse Cases: The Adverse Impact of Informal Dispute Resolution on Women, 7 Harv. Women's L.J. 57 (1984); Richard Delgado et al., Fairness and Formality: Minimizing the Risk of Prejudice in Alternative Dispute Resolution, 1985 Wis. L. Rev. 1359. See also excerpt from Trina Grillo, below.

19. See, e.g., Sarah E. Burns, Notes from the Field: A Reply to Professor Colker, 13 Harv. Women's L.J. 189 (1990).

20. Epstein, above note 2, at 13.

elite, law school stratified deeply along gender lines. Our database draws from students enrolled at the Law School between 1987 and 1992, and includes academic performance data from 981 students, self-reported survey data from 366 students, written narratives from 104 students, and group-level interview data of approximately eighty female and male students. From these data we conclude that the law school experience of women in the aggregate differs markedly from that of their male peers.

First, we find strong academic differences between graduating men and women. Despite identical entry-level credentials, this performance differential between men and women is created in the first year of law school and maintained over the next three years. By the end of their first year in law school, men are three times more likely than women to be in the top 10% of their law school class.

Second, we find strong attitudinal differences between women and men in year one, and yet a striking homogenization by year three. The first-year women we studied are far more critical than their first-year male peers of the social status quo, of legal education, and of themselves as students. Third-year female students, however, are less critical than their third-year male colleagues, and far less critical than their first-year female counterparts. A disproportionate number of the women we studied enter law school with commitments to public interest law, ready to fight for social justice. But their third-year female counterparts leave law school with corporate ambitions and some indications of mental health distress.

Third, many women are alienated by the way the Socratic method is used in large classroom instruction, which is the dominant pedagogy for almost all first-year instruction. Women self-report much lower rates of class participation than do men for all three years of law school. Our data suggest that many women do not "engage" pedagogically with a methodology that makes them feel strange, alienated, and "delegitimated." These women describe a dynamic in which they feel that their voices were "stolen" from them during the first year. Some complain that they can no longer recognize their former selves, which have become submerged inside what one author has called an alienated "social male."

* * *

Finally, we document substantial material consequences for those women who exit the Law School after sustaining what they describe as a crisis of identity. These women graduate with less competitive academic credentials, are not represented equally within the Law School's academic and social hierarchies, and are apparently less competitive in securing prestigious and/or desirable jobs after graduation.

* * *

a. Guinier, Fine, and Balin subsequently published their research in the book Becoming Gentlemen: Women, Law School, and Institutional Change (1997).

The hierarchy within the large first-year Socratic class also includes a hierarchy of perspectives. Those who most identify with the institution, its faculty, its texts, and its individualistic perspectives experience little dissonance in the first year. On the other hand are students who import an ambivalent identification with the institution, who resist competitive, adversarial relationships, who do not see themselves in the faculty, who vacillate on the emotionally detached, "objective" perspectives inscribed as "law," and who identify with the lives of persons who suffer from existing political arrangements. These students experience much dissonance.

A disproportionate number of women of all racial and ethnic groups also experience alienation in that they enter law school with a zeal for public interest work, but end having opted for corporate or other private sector employment. Our data suggest that there is an academic cost, and perhaps a mental health cost, to discarding passions, politics, emotions, and community-based identities that were once central to the student's identity. * * *

With remarkable consistency, students indicate that law school taught them to be "less emotional," "more objective," and to "put away ... passions." For some, this ability to suppress feelings [is] considered an enormous accomplishment; for others, it is considered a defeat. Second only to the skills of "objectivity," students report that over time they have learned to stop caring about others and have become more conservative. Some men indicate they have grown more aggressive and abrasive over their three years in law school; some women see themselves as more "humble" and "nitpicking." One woman concluded her interview by saying, "Here [at the Law School], it's okay to be intolerant."

The competitive, hierarchical format of the Law School's dominant pedagogy is also used by peers to put down some women. Many women who complained that their voices are pushed back and down, suffocated early on by hostile first-year classrooms, described how those women who spoke out felt humiliated by male, and some female, contemporaries who silenced those who publicly dared to "act like gentlemen." Ideas about women's sexuality, for example, became a basis for ridiculing individual women, especially those who spoke out in class. These putdowns may occur in informal networks that exist outside the classroom, but they are normalized by and may reproduce behavior that is performed within the classroom.

* * *

Many men attempt to "explain away" the gender and institutional aspects of the data. These men, who include students and faculty, often resort to alternative explanations, all of which identify a source unrelated to the Law School for the differences we found. For example, they proffered age, undergraduate major, and even participation in varsity sports in college as possible explanations for the differential between women's and men's performances as measured by grades in law school.

We found no statistically significant difference between women and men in these categories. * * * We explored these intuitions and found that, when controlled for incoming demographics, gender alone predicted third-year law school class rank.

* * *

A. Alienation and Academic Performance Within the Formal Structure of the Institution

"Becoming gentlemen" appears to exact an academic cost for many women. Women's enfeebled participation within the formal structure of legal education occurs simultaneously with their less successful performance on the anonymously-graded examinations from which law school grades are derived. In other words, low levels of class participation in the formal, structured pedagogy correlate with weak performance on the formal, structured evaluation system.

There is also a psychological dimension to women's relatively weak academic performance. Along with a formal link between classroom participation and examination success, we suspect that there exists a psychological link between self-confidence, alienation, and academic performance. Students who are alienated by the formal classroom methodology, hierarchy, and size are arguably not psychologically prepared to succeed on the formal examinations. Those who doubt themselves or doubt whether they belong in the Law School do not perform as well.

Many students, especially many women, have simply not been socialized to thrive in the type of ritualized combat that comprises much of the legal educational method. * * *

* * *

It is important to recognize that peer relations reinforce women's silence via "hazing" imposed on women by white males. Students describe hazing as taking the form of "laughing at what I said" or "lesbian-baiting." Apparently, merely being called a "feminist" is sometimes considered sufficiently insulting to silence women who try to challenge prevailing interpretations of legal texts.

* * *

B. The Alienation and Exclusion of Women from Informal Learning Networks

[In this section the authors describe women's discomfort in various informal networks within the law school community and, in particular, their lack of interaction with and mentoring by male faculty.]

C. Women Who Do Not Become Gentlemen Are Less Valued Members of the Law School Community

* * *

According to the difference hypothesis, women's difference makes them less equipped for law school. The way things are done in law school (the Socratic method, issue-spotting exams, large classrooms, unpatroled and informal networks) devalues and distorts those characteristics traditionally associated with women such as empathy, relational logic, and nonaggressive behavior. In this understanding, law school unintentionally uses a male-oriented baseline to measure male/female differences.

* * *

Most of this paper is about a group of women at the Law School who cannot or do not want to "become gentlemen." It is important to recognize, however, that even within this group of females, "women" is not a monolithic category. We have sought to identify the fact that some women who are alienated nevertheless do well academically; these women successfully function in the hierarchy and norms of the Law School. Accordingly, we identify two distinct "groups" of women. The first group of women fails academically as well as personally. The second group of women succeeds academically. These are women who do "become gentlemen." Within this category of successful women, there is also a subset who do well but feel alienated. This subset of women resents the sacrifices of self that law school requires them to make. These women perceive that law school is a "game." These women learn the rules in order to play the game, but they are acutely aware of the price they are paying. These women are those who have been described in some of our secondary literature as "bicultural" or "bilingual." They can act both as "women" and as "gentlemen" and they are acutely aware of the difference.

* * *

We believe that our research raises the second-generation diversity issue. If the first generation of women was challenged to demonstrate the need for access into existing, previously all-male institutions, the current (second) generation is challenged to demonstrate that mere access, especially in comparatively low status positions, is inadequate. As now designed, law school fails to equalize the experience and outcomes for all law students across gender. Whether because of difference or domination, legal education at an Ivy League institution exacts a disproportionate toll on almost half the law student population.

Formerly all-male educational institutions cannot incorporate and take advantage of difference without changing from within. Yet, the institution we studied has admitted more women students without adequately transforming itself. The major changes we observed occurred within the women who attend the school, not within or by the institution.

Second-generation diversity, however, requires some institutional transformation as a precondition for genuine inclusion. We argue that the purpose of legal education should be reconsidered critically. The problem is not simply "difference" or gendered domination—both of which play a role in the stories we have told. Nor is the problem simply that women are outsiders who opt for a powerful, stony silence. The problem lies in the system of evaluation in law schools, which functions to rank students on a hierarchy that prospective employers then use to choose who they will actually train to be a lawyer. In addition to ensuring selectivity, the law school's pedagogy socializes students to a certain adversarial practice of law. In these complementary ways, law schools perpetuate a vision of legal practice that has contributed to a crisis in the public trust of lawyers.

NOTES ON WOMEN AND LEGAL EDUCATION

1. A pioneering study of women's experience in legal education was written by two women in the Yale Law School class of 1987, based on documenting the experiences of 20 women students in that class. The resulting article showed substantial amounts of alienation on the part of women students from the law school community, from their classroom experiences, and from the content of legal education in general, including low rates of classroom participation and distress at law school pedagogy. Catherine Weiss & Louise Melling, The Legal Education of Twenty Women, 40 Stan. L. Rev. 1299 (1988). The Weiss and Melling study was repeated in the class of 1997 at Yale, with similar results. Paula Gaber, "Just Trying To Be Human in This Place": The Legal Education of Twenty Women, 10 Yale J. L. & Feminism 165 (1998). Another, still later study reported lower class participation by women, less contact with and mentoring by faculty, and underrepresentation on the Yale Law Journal. Sari Bashi & Maryana Iskander, Why Legal Education Is Failing Women, 18 Yale J. L. & Feminism 389 (2006). Yale is not unique in this respect. A study carried out in the spring of 2003 at Harvard Law School also showed lower class participation, less self-confidence, lower first-year course grades, less representation on the law review (36%), and less probability of graduating with honors for the 45% of students who were women than for their male counterparts. Adam Neufeld, Costs of an Outdated Pedagogy? Study on Gender at Harvard Law School, 13 Am. U. J. Gender Soc. Pol'y & Law 511 (2005). If you are a law student, how has your experience been similar to or different from that of the women students described in these studies or in the Guinier excerpt above? How many of these problems do you believe are related to whether you are male or female? How is the pedagogy at your law school different from that described in the Guinier excerpt, if at all? What ideas do you have for changes in legal education that might address the problems identified in these studies?

2. Law school studies have consistently reported significant differences in class participation by gender, with women speaking far less frequently in class than men. See, e.g., Claire G. Schwab, A Shifting Gender Divide: The Impact of Gender on Education at Columbia Law School in the New Millennium, 36 Colum. J.L. & Soc. Probs. 299, 316, 320–24 (2003); Lisa A. Wilson & David H. Taylor, Surveying Gender Bias At One Midwestern Law School, 9 Am. U.J. Gender Soc. Pol'y & L. 251, 265–66 (2001); Joan M. Krauskopf, Touching the Elephant: Perceptions of Gender Issues in Nine Law Schools, 44 J. Legal Educ. 311, 325–26 (1994); Suzanne Homer & Lois Schwartz, Admitted But Not Accepted: Outsiders Take an Inside Look at Law School, 5 Berkeley Women's L.J. 1, 10, 12, 29, 37–38 (1990); Taunya Lovell Banks,

Gender Bias in the Classroom, 38 J. Legal Educ. 137, 141–43 (1988). Testing these reports, Elizabeth Mertz carried out a quantitative analysis of patterns in first-year contracts classes at eight law schools (recorded and coded by observers and verified by tapes); in six out of the eight classes studied, men had between 10% and 54% more turns to speak in class than women and took between 12% and 38% more time speaking. See Elizabeth Mertz, Wamucii Njogu & Susan Gooding, What Difference Does Difference Make? The Challenge for Legal Education, 48 J. Legal Educ. 1, 45–46 (1998). What do you believe causes the different rates of participation of men and women in law school classrooms? Have you experienced it?

Some posit that women's silence reflects the fact that "they feel excluded and alienated from the law school classroom * * * [and] subtle aspects of traditional legal education deny or even denigrate certain aspects of women's personal beliefs and values * * *." Janet Taber et al., Gender, Legal Education, and the Legal Profession: An Empirical Study of Stanford Law Students and Graduates, 40 Stan. L. Rev. 1209, 1256 (1988). Others suggest that "[f]or many students the choice of silence is not a passive act; it is an expression of anger." Stephanie M. Wildman, The Question of Silence: Techniques to Ensure Full Class Participation, 38 J. Legal Educ. 147, 149 (1988). Whether passive withdrawal or act of rebellion, the problem is especially common among students of color whose life experiences and interpretations are not recognized by traditional legal discourse. See, e.g., Margaret E. Montoya, *Mascaras, Trenzas, y Grenas:* Un/masking The Self While Un/braiding Latina Stories and Legal Discourse, 17 Harv. Women's L.J. 185 (1994).

What strategies might professors and students adopt to ensure full class participation? See, e.g., Wildman, above, at 152–55. At a summit conference on women in legal education held at Mills College in November 1997, women law professors debated whether establishing an all-women's law school would be a way to confront the problems of alienation, silence, and underachievement reported among women law students. See Jennifer Gerarda Brown, "To Give Them Countenance": The Case for a Women's Law School, 22 Harv. Women's L.J. 1 (1999). What do you think of this idea? Would it be constitutional?

3. Linda Wightman's extensive empirical study of almost 29,000 students entering 163 law schools in the fall of 1991 showed that both women and men suffer drops in self-esteem, or academic self-concept, during law school; the drop is about the same for both, although women start law school with lower self-esteem. Linda F. Wightman, Women in Legal Education: A Comparison of the Law School Performance and Law School Experiences of Women and Men 54–59, 73 (1996). Why does this drop occur, in your opinion? What would be different at a law school that increased students' self-esteem rather than lowering it?

According to Wightman, African American women suffer a disproportionate drop in their self-esteem during the first year of law school. Id. at 58. Why do you think the negative impact of law school upon academic self-confidence has a stronger effect on African American women than on other groups? How does this happen? What might be some remedies for this problem? Law school appears to be an especially difficult experience for Latinas as well. See

Montoya, above note 2 Maureen Ebben & Norma Guerra Gaier, Telling Stories, Telling Self: Using Narrative to Uncover Latinas' Voices and Agency in the Legal Profession, 19 Chicano–Latino L. Rev. 243 (1998). A recent survey of Latina attorneys reported that they felt isolated and alienated both socially and academically in law school and that this contributed to feelings of self-doubt. Hispanic National Bar Ass'n, Few and Far Between: The Reality of Latina Lawyers 8 (2009). See also Nancy Dowd, Race, Gender, and Ethnicity in Legal Education, 15 J. L. & Pub. Pol'y 11 (2003) (describing University of Florida survey substantiating the differential response of women and minorities to law school and emphasizing the intersection of race and gender in this respect).

Gay and lesbian students also report that law school can be an alienating experience. Janice L. Austin, Patricia A. Cain, Anton Mack, J. Kelly Strader & James Vaseleck, Results from a Survey: Gay, Lesbian, and Bisexual Students' Attitudes About Law School, 48 J. Legal Educ. 157, 166–67 (1998) (describing, among other things, defacement of posters and problematic in-class discussions of gay and lesbian issues). See also Scott Ihrig, Sexual Orientation in Law School: Experiences of Gay, Lesbian, and Bisexual Law Students, 14 Law & Ineq. 555 (1996); Kim Brooks & Debra Parkes, Queering Legal Education: A Project of Theoretical Discovery, 27 Harv. Women's L.J. 89 (2004) (discussing problems faced by lesbian professors as well). How can law school be made a more comfortable place for "outsider" groups? How would it be changed if it were? Different groups may have different reasons for their discomfort in law school. One author argues that only reforms of legal education informed by the insights of post-structuralist feminist theory are adequate to the task of inclusion, lest changes designed to include one group result in excluding another. Banu Ramachandran, Re–Reading Difference: Feminist Critiques of the Law School Classroom and the Problem with Speaking from Experience, 98 Colum. L. Rev. 1757 (1998).

4. Law school studies also discuss significant psychological distress experienced by women law students. See Morrison Torrey, Jennifer Ries & Elaine Spiliopoulos, What Every First–Year Female Law Student Should Know, 7 Colum. J. Gender & L. 267, 288–91 (1998) (summarizing the findings of various studies on stress and self-esteem in women law students). Psychological distress is apparently widespread among law students, as compared to other types of graduate students and the population at large, and women law students are an especially high-risk group. See Matthew M. Dammeyer & Narina Nunez, Anxiety and Depression Among Law Students: Current Knowledge and Future Directions, 23 Law & Hum. Behav. 55 (1999) (finding law students report higher rates of psychiatric distress than either medical students and the general population); Stephen B. Shanfield & G. Andrew H. Benjamin, Psychiatric Distress in Law Students, 35 J. Legal Educ. 65, 68–72 (1985) (women law students exhibit higher level of psychiatric symptoms than men law students, a finding not duplicated with medical students); Nancy J. Soonpaa, Stress in Law Students: A Comparative Study of First–Year, Second–Year, and Third–Year Students, 36 Conn. L. Rev. 353, 377–79 (2004) (reporting that female third-year students had the highest mean stress score). To what would you attribute this phenomenon? What do you think can be done to address this problem? Would smaller classes and more frequent

feedback help? Would some of these changes make law school a better place for male students as well?

5. What do you think of Guinier et al.'s findings about the differential success of women and men in law school? Would a study of your school yield similar results? Linda Wightman's study of almost 29,000 students entering 163 law schools in fall 1991 revealed, consistent with Guinier's findings, that women underperform in law school, both in comparison with male students and with their own undergraduate grade point averages. Linda F. Wightman, Women in Legal Education: A Comparison of the Law School Performance and Law School Experiences of Women and Men 5, 26–27 (1996). A study of 13 years of entering classes at the University of Texas School of Law also confirmed Guinier's findings. Allison L. Bowers, Women at the University of Texas School of Law: A Call for Action, 9 Tex. J. Women & L. 117 (2000) (finding that men outperformed women in both first-year grades and law review). See also William C. Kidder, Portia Denied: Unmasking Gender Bias on the LSAT and Its Relationship to Racial Diversity in Legal Education, 12 Yale J.L. & Feminism 1 (2000) (excerpt in Chapter 8, above) (reporting and discussing disparity in LSAT scores by gender and race). If women enter law school with higher grade point averages than men but underperform on both the LSAT and in law school GPA, is the problem with women or with our system of legal education? How might these problems be addressed? Is affirmative action a solution, or should the entire system be redesigned?

A number of formal and informal replication studies carried out at several other law schools contradicted Guinier's finding that women law students underachieve academically. One study, at Brooklyn Law School, where many of the pedagogical innovations recommended by Guinier (small sections in the first year, varied teaching techniques, non-exam-based feedback, and the like) had already been instituted, demonstrated that women students there both enter and graduate with academic credentials equivalent to men (though they still participate significantly less in class and experience more symptoms of distress). Marsha Garrison, Brian Tomko & Ivan Yip, Succeeding in Law School: A Comparison of Women's Experiences at Brooklyn Law School and the University of Pennsylvania, 3 Mich. J. Gender & Law 515 (1996). See also Shanie Latham, Iowa Study Defies Trend, Nat'l Jurist, Oct./Nov. 1995, at 28 (reporting that women law students at Iowa perform as well as men). What do you think can explain the differences in results among schools?

6. Linda Hirshman devised a ranking called the "Femscore" of 158 accredited law schools based on two measures of how well women succeed at each school—the percentage of female tenured or tenure-track faculty and the percentage of women who make the school's law review. Hirshman, A Woman's Guide to Law School 125–54 (1999). Do you think that the percentage of women who make law review is an accurate reflection of women succeeding in law school? What about graduation rate, grade point average, or simple happiness with one's chosen field? What makes law school a successful endeavor for women? Hirshman found that women "underperform" in relation to their presence within the student body as a whole in 90 of the schools she examined, including such elite institutions as Yale, Harvard, and Stanford. When choosing a law school, should women look to the statistical pattern

of female students' success? How does the woman-friendliness of a school compare to its job placement or location as a persuasive reason to attend that institution?

One study of the 15 top-ranked law schools reported that women law students were underrepresented on law reviews and that fewer student notes authored by females were published in those schools' law reviews than notes authored by men. The author of this study examined likely explanations for this disparity, including the proportions of women and men in those law schools, and concluded that it was because women were less likely to go through the process of applying for law review membership and also less likely to submit notes for consideration, to revise them if conditionally accepted, or to run for editorial positions; she attributed this to their alienation by their experience of the first year of law school. Because these positions and publication of a student note are so important to subsequent career success and especially to obtaining clerkships and positions as law faculty, she argues that women law students should be encouraged to hold their noses and jump into this competition. Nancy Leong, A Noteworthy Absence, 59 J. Legal Educ. 279 (2009).

7. Traditionally, law school teachers have used what is loosely termed the Socratic method of teaching. The theory is that law students learn better if they have to infer generalities from questions posed to them in discussions about specific cases. Yet Guinier et al., in the study excerpted above, point to use of the Socratic method as one source of women's distress in law school, and other observers agree. See, e.g., Torrey et al., above note 4; Deborah L. Rhode, Missing Questions: Feminist Perspectives on Legal Education, 45 Stan. L. Rev. 1547, 1554–57 (1993). Why do you think law professors rely on the Socratic method? Various cynical answers have been offered—for example, that it maintains the mystification of the legal process, is an exercise of power in hierarchical relationships, and furthers the patriarchal power of the teacher while simultaneously devaluing students and undermining their confidence and self-esteem. Jennifer Jaff, Frame–Shifting: An Empowering Methodology for Teaching and Learning Legal Reasoning, 36 J. Legal Educ. 249, 260–61 (1986). See also Elizabeth Mertz, Teaching Lawyers the Language of Law: Legal and Anthropological Translations, 34 J. Marshall L. Rev. 91 (2000) (discussing how use of Socratic method erases context and narrative, while rendering moral and cultural perspectives irrelevant). See also Mertz, The Language of Law School: Learning to "Think Like a Lawyer" (2007).

Others argue that the Socratic method, used well, is the most effective pedagogy to teach women proficiency in the language of doctrinal legal analysis, so that they become "bilingual" in the type of discourse that models intellectual exchanges that take place when approaching legal problems and in the practice of law. Jennifer L. Rosato, The Socratic Method and Women Law Students: Humanize, Don't Feminize, 7 S. Cal. Rev. L. & Women's Stud. 37 (1997). What is your experience of the Socratic method? In what ways is it effective? Can it be used in a nonabusive fashion? If you were teaching, would you use the Socratic method? Why or why not? What pedagogical method would you use? More lecture? Discussion? Small group work? Simulation? Other methods?

8. Sandra Janoff, a psychologist, carried out a study of modes of moral reasoning among law students at the beginning and end of their first year at Temple Law School. Janoff, The Influence of Legal Education on Moral Reasoning, 76 Minn. L. Rev. 193 (1991). She found, consonant with Carol Gilligan's findings described in Chapter 3 above, that entering women law students reasoned predominantly from a care-oriented perspective, concerned with connection, prevention of harm, maintaining relationships, and responding to need, while male students were more likely to use rights-oriented moral reasoning. By the end of the first year, however, rights orientation was significantly more pronounced, and there was no significant difference in the care orientations of women and men. Are you surprised by Janoff's results? Does law school institutionalize a "male" method of moral reasoning? What changes would be necessary to eliminate this effect of law school education? Is it desirable to do so?

Might there be some advantages to approaching law school with an ethic of care? For example, many law professors complain that students spend too much time on exams regurgitating abstract black letter law rather than applying the law to the particular facts before them. This might be addressed by encouraging the inclusion of more references to context and particular facts in class discussion. Would requiring clinical courses or other pro bono work also help? What other differences would you foresee based upon a care-based approach to legal education? Susan P. Sturm suggests that the "gladiator" paradigm of the legal profession upon which legal education is premised be replaced by a professional paradigm of lawyers as problem-solvers—a more team-oriented and contextual approach that would present fewer barriers to full participation by women. Sturm, From Gladiators to Problem–Solvers: Connecting Conversations About Women, The Academy, and The Legal Profession, 4 Duke J. Gender L. & Pol'y 119 (1997). What do you think of this idea? How could it be carried out?

9. In The Alchemy of Race and Rights: Diary of a Law Professor 8–9 (1991), Patricia J. Williams identified three features of legal thought: dichotomization, abstract universality, and objective norms. Are these concepts idealized in legal analysis? Do they account for women's discomfort with legal education? Are those the methods necessary to "think like a lawyer"? Does the law thereby avoid the truth of life's complexities? How? Is the law's attempt to universalize and objectify authority a device to avoid responsibility? What is the antidote?

These characteristics of legal education, and especially the assumption of objectivity, or perspectivelessness, present particular problems for law students of color—either they begin all legal analysis from a perspective that denies their identity or they are seen as biased by their special interest and their views disregarded, even when they are put on the spot and asked to add their particular approach to a classroom discussion. Kimberlé Williams Crenshaw, Foreword: Toward a Race–Conscious Pedagogy in Legal Education, 4. S. Cal. Rev. L. & Women's Stud. 33 (1994).

10. How often does a law teacher ask the class how the students feel rather than how they think about a case's outcome? Should emotion have a greater role in the law? What about the role of empathy? Professor Lynne N.

Henderson has argued that the law would be more just if it were more empathetic. Do you think she is right? See Henderson, Legality and Empathy, 85 Mich. L. Rev. 1574 (1987). See also Robin West, Caring for Justice (1997). Contra Toni M. Massaro, Empathy, Legal Storytelling, and The Rule of Law: New Words, Old Wounds?, 87 Mich. L. Rev. 2099 (1989) (questioning the value of empathy in decision-making because, among other things, of judges' limited capacity for empathy and the dangers of discretionary adjudication). Can you think of an experience you have had that allowed you to empathize more with others? Has it enlarged your perspective? Made you a fairer person? A better lawyer? Would it make you a better judge?

When Justice David Souter resigned from the Supreme Court, President Obama described empathy as "an essential ingredient for arriving at just decisions and outcomes" and a quality he would seek in a judge. Peter Slevin, Obama Makes Empathy a Requirement for Court, Wash. Post, May 13, 2009, at A3. As Souter's replacement, he selected Sonia Sotomayor, who had stated in a 2001 speech that she "would hope that a wise Latina woman with the richness of her experiences would more often than not reach a better conclusion than a white male who hasn't lived that life." Charlie Savage, A Judge's View of Judging Is on the Record, N.Y. Times, May 15, 2009, at A21. These remarks occasioned sharp criticism from conservatives, who interpreted empathy as betokening bias in favor of certain groups. To rescue her nomination, Sotomayor distanced herself from her previous remark and from the gender/race stereotypes the criticism invoked.

What do you think of this controversy? Can you distinguish empathy from bias? How?

TEXT NOTE: WOMEN LAW FACULTY

Women students traditionally had few role models among the professoriat. Women were absent for a long time from any positions of power within law schools.[21] By 1986, more than 40% of law students were women, but women made up only about 20% of full-time faculty in American law schools.[22] By 2008–2009 37.3% of faculty members listed in the Association of American Law Schools Directory were women, but this figure masked substantial inequality. Many of these women are in fact legal writing and clinical instructors, largely untenured fields that became feminized in the 1980s and 1990s.[23] Women made up 61% of clinical and skills instructors by the fall of 1995 and 70% of legal writing teachers; they were 50.4% of clinical instructors and 56% of legal writing instructors by 2007–08.[24] (Men seem to be moving

21. See, e.g., Herma Hill Kay, The Future of Women Law Professors, 77 Iowa L. Rev. 5, 5–14 (1991).

22. Marina Angel, Women in Legal Education: What It's Like to Be Part of a Perpetual First Wave or the Case of the Disappearing Women, 61 Temp. L. Rev. 799, 803 (1988).

23. Id. See also Richard Chused, The Hiring and Retention of Minority and Female Faculty in American Law Schools, 137 U. Pa. L. Rev. 537, 548 (1988). The 2008–09 statistics are available at http://www.aals.org/statistics/2009dlt/gender.html.

24. See Richard K. Neumann Jr., Women in Legal Education: What the Statistics Show, 50 J. Leg. Educ. 313, 329 (2000). The 2007–08 statistics are taken from the AALS Statistical Report on Law Faculty 2007–2008 29, 32, available at http://www.aals.org/resources_statistical.php.

into these previously unattractive fields.) Moreover, in this segmented profession, men are more likely than women to succeed in moving from non-tenured to tenured positions. Choices resulting from women's commitments to their families do not explain the disparity because women take tenured over non-tenured jobs when available, and non-tenured positions like legal writing and clinical skills courses are in fact more labor-intensive and inflexible in their time demands than tenured slots.[25]

Over the period of women's entry into law teaching, law schools have restructured themselves so that non-tenured personnel now carry out a large proportion of instruction; they include not just legal writing teachers and clinical instructors but also lecturers and instructors without job security, who receive less pay than those in tenured or tenure-track positions.[26] The ranks of these new positions are filled with women. Women were 51.8% of all new hires in 2007–08, but held a lopsided 59.5% of non-tenure-track positions.[27] Despite their improved numbers in entry-level tenure-track positions (between 47% and 52% of all new assistant professors since 1991–92), in 2007–08 women were still only 29.3% of the full tenured professors in the U.S.[28] This was a big improvement over 13% in 1991, but, as one journalist remarked, "with that rate of growth—roughly 1 percent a year—it will take another 25 years for women to reach the 50–percent mark."[29] Moreover, although women formed 29.3% of the pool of professors, they were only 19.8% of law school deans.[30]

Given that entry-level candidates for law teaching positions have typically been out of law school only a few years, these statistics represent a clear gender imbalance on law faculties, especially over a period when many have assumed that law schools were exercising affirmative action to hire both women and minorities. In fact, an extensive analysis of law faculty hired between 1986 and 1991 showed little to no evidence of affirmative action.[31] Indeed, male candidates for faculty positions were significantly more likely than women to enter teaching at a higher professorial rank, controlling for other factors.[32] According to one 1993

25. Debra Branch McBrier, Gender and Career Dynamics within a Segmented Professional Labor Market: The Case of Law Academia, 81 Social Forces 1201 (2003).

26. See, e.g., Marina Angel, The Glass Ceiling for Women in Legal Education: Contract Positions and the Death of Tenure, 50 J. Leg. Educ. 1 (2000); Jan M. Levine & Kathryn M. Stanchi, Women, Writing & Wages: Breaking the Last Taboo, 7 Wm. & Mary J. Women & Law 551 (2001).

27. The 2007–08 statistics are taken from the AALS Statistical Report on Law Faculty 2007–2008 24, 34, available at http://www.aals.org/resources_statistical.php. See also Marjorie E. Kornhauser, Rooms of Their Own: An Empirical Study of Occupational Segregation by Gender Among Law Professors, 73 U.M.K.C. L. Rev. 293 (2004).

28. Richard K. Neumann, Jr., Women in Legal Education: A Statistical Update, 73 U.M.K.C. L. Rev. 419, 427 (2004); AALS Statistical Report on Law Faculty 2007–2008 18, available at http://www.aals.org/resources_statistical.php.

29. Christine Garton, A Tough Market for Women, Legal Times, Sept. 6, 2004, at 32.

30. AALS Statistical Report on Law Faculty 2007–2008 18, available at http://www.aals.org/resources_statistical.php. See also Laura M. Padilla, A Gendered Update On Women Deans: Who, Where, Why, and Why Not?, 15 Am. U. J. Gender Soc. Pol'y & Law 443 (2007).

31. Deborah Jones Merritt & Barbara F. Reskin, Sex, Race, and Credentials: The Truth About Affirmative Action in Law Faculty Hiring, 97 Colum. L. Rev. 199, 280–82 (1997).

32. Id. at 205, 252.

study, family ties and geographic constraints did not explain the failure of recently hired women to attain positions at prestigious law schools.[33] African American women have been doing better in the hiring process recently than African American men and other minorities.[34]

Moreover, women appear to be tenured at a lower rate than men.[35] One early study indicated that things seemed to be improving, except at the elite law schools, where the numbers of women faculty remained very low.[36] However, Richard Neumann's extensive analysis of the statistics for men and women hired onto the tenure track in 1990–91 showed, through 1997–98, that the "tenuring gap" between men and women had in fact grown from 6% to 11% since 1979–1989: that is, while 65% of women and 71% of men were awarded tenure in the 1979–89 period, only 61% of women starting in 1990–91 obtained tenure in contrast to 72% of men.[37] Some opine that the courses law schools assign women to teach may have something to do with this. Men are substantially more likely to teach constitutional law courses (77.6% taught by male faculty in 2007–08), and women to teach family law courses (61.6% taught by women in the same year), with their assignment to teach these courses having little to do with their credentials, particular expertise, or prior work experience. Women are also more likely than men to teach critical legal studies, critical race theory, feminist legal theory, juvenile law, race and the law, and women and the law. The authors of one study suggest that law schools reserve high-status courses that enhance a professor's career prospects for men.[38]

What can explain these disparities? Professors Angel and Chused believe that women are underrepresented on law faculties at least in part because initial appointments rely heavily upon old boy networks, because the factors considered in the tenure decision are extremely subjective in nature, and because they are underrepresented in the feeder pipelines, such as Supreme Court clerkships.[39] Neumann points also to the facts that

---

33. Deborah J. Merritt, Barbara F. Reskin & Michelle Fondell, Family, Place, and Career: The Gender Paradox in Law School Hiring, 1993 Wis. L. Rev. 395.

34. African American women were 10.3% of all female faculty in 2007–08, while African American men made up only 5.2% of male faculty members; African American women also did substantially better than other non-white groups in general. AALS Statistical Report on Law Faculty 2007–2008 11, available at http://www.aals.org/resources_statistical.php. But see Deborah J. Merritt & Barbara F. Reskin, The Double Minority: Empirical Evidence of a Double Standard in Law School Hiring of Minority Women, 65 S. Cal. L. Rev. 2299 (1992) (concluding at that time that minority women were particularly disadvantaged in the hiring process, even in relation to minority men).

35. Angel, above note 22, at 805.

36. Robert Borthwick & Jordan Schau, Gatekeepers of the Profession: An Empirical Profile of the Nation's Law Professors, 25 Mich. J.L. Reform 191, 199–212 (1991).

37. Neumann, above note 24, at 357.

38. See Merritt & Reskin, above note 31, at 258–73. The 2007–08 statistics are taken from the AALS Statistical Report on Law Faculty 2007–2008 29–33, available at http://www.aals.org/resources_statistical.php.

39. Chused, above note 23, at 552; Angel, above note 22, at 829; David H. Kaye & Joseph L. Gastwirth, Where Have All The Women Gone? The Gender Gap in Supreme Court Clerkships, 49 Jurimetrics 411 (2008–09) (reporting that there are two men for every woman Supreme Court clerk, an imbalance the authors attribute to the lower numbers of women who come through the traditional hiring pipeline, having served as high officers on law reviews at a limited number of

(1) there are so few women faculty at the producer schools (the law schools from whose graduates most faculty are drawn) that female students there lack role models and mentors, and (2) the ranks of tenured law professors are top-heavy with males who will not retire or die for years.[40] Women law faculty interviewed by the author of a popular press book about women and the law reported that women, especially feminist scholars, were seen by older male professors as rocking the boat and/or threatening to their egos.[41] Catharine MacKinnon, excerpts from whose path-breaking scholarly work pervade these pages, was turned down for tenure at Yale and taught at five different law schools before obtaining tenure at Michigan in 1990.[42] One scholar, basing her conclusions on masculinities studies and social science research about women in the business world, opines that law school teaching remains a job that it is gendered male in its expectations.[43]

Once they have been hired, women law faculty may face still other obstacles, based on their lack of similarity to the traditional image of a law professor. There is a marked difference between student evaluations given to male and female law professors, with the ones given to women faculty being not as positive, praising the women for quite different characteristics (such as approachability instead of mastery of subject matter), including comments about their personal appearance, and holding the women professors to standards that are different from, if not higher than, those applied to men.[44] Articles by women are also underrepresented in the top law reviews, causing one author to suggest blind review of all submissions to student-edited law reviews to prevent bias.[45] Moreover, the initial results of one survey of 1,176 tenured law professors indicate that, even after receiving tenure, smaller percentages of women than men feel that they are respected by their colleagues or are listened to with respect during hiring and promotion decisions.[46] At the same time, the tenured women reported doing a larger share of giving advice and emotional support to students, performing an unfair amount of committee work, and not being as likely to receive salary increases, leaves, or other perqs from their law schools.[47]

---

elite law schools and then having clerked for a federal appellate court judge who is a major feeder of clerks to the Supreme Court).

40. Neumann, above note 24, at 350, 347.

41. Lorraine Dusky, Still Unequal: The Shameful Truth About Women and Justice in America 84–131 (1996).

42. Id. at 97–99.

43. Ann C. McGinley, Reproducing Gender on Law School Faculties, 2009 B.Y.U. L. Rev. 99 (2009).

44. See, e.g., Christine Haight Farley, Confronting Expectations: Women in the Legal Academy, 8 Yale J. L. & Feminism 333 (1996). See also Deborah J. Merritt, Bias, the Brain, and Student Evaluations of Teaching, 82 St. John's L. Rev. 235 (2008).

45. Jonathan Gingerich, A Call for Blind Review: Student Edited Law Reviews and Bias, 59 J. Legal Educ. 269, 276–78 (2009).

46. Am. Bar Found., After Tenure: Post-Tenure Law Professors in the U.S. 7, 26–27 (2010).

47. Id. at 28–30.

Women of color who enter the legal academy face unique obstacles and stresses. One study based on interviews with ten prominent African American women law professors reveals the hostile environment most of them have had to confront, including presumptions of their incompetence by both students and fellow faculty, which often made them feel disempowered and marginalized.[48] Despite this hostile treatment, these women have played a large role in producing the literature of critical race theory that has enriched the pages of this book, accomplishing this in part by setting up informal support networks among themselves.

Hostile treatment of women faculty in law schools, including their underrepresentation and segregation to certain courses, cannot help but affect what is taught in the legal academy. Quite apart from the impact of these disparities on the lives and egos of the women scholars involved, consider the impact this may also have on the pedagogy employed in law schools and the research reflected in law review articles throughout this book.

C. BIAS AGAINST WOMEN AS ATTORNEYS

CYNTHIA GRANT BOWMAN AND ELIZABETH M. SCHNEIDER, FEMINIST LEGAL THEORY, FEMINIST LAWMAKING, AND THE LEGAL PROFESSION

67 Fordham L. Rev. 249, 260–63 (1998).

C. Attempts by Women Lawyers and Academics to Attack the Problem of Gender Bias in the Profession: Task Forces and Commissions

In the 1980s and 1990s, a new form of literature began to emerge—reports from task forces and commissions established by women practitioners under the aegis of state supreme courts or bar associations.[58] The gender bias task force movement provides the most striking example of this development, which compiled and described the experiences of women in the legal system both as lawyers and litigants. The material assembled by the task forces provided data about the problems women lawyers continued to experience in the profession, and some included suggestions for change. In addition, publication of the reports was official recognition that discrimination against women in the legal profession continued to exist and thus legitimized the claims that had been emerging from the academy.

The task forces undertaking these independent investigations typically consisted of a mix of judges, practitioners, and academics; their methods

48. See, e.g., Elwood Watson, Outsiders Within: Black Women in the Legal Academy after *Brown v. Board* 49–64, 81–89 (2008).

58. The first reports were published in the early 1980s by task forces established by the New Jersey and New York supreme courts, at the instigation of women judges and practitioners. See The First Year Report of the New Jersey Supreme Court Task Force on Women in the Courts—June 1984, 9 Women's Rts. L. Rep. 129 (1986); Report of the New York Task Force on Women in the Courts (1986), 15 Fordham Urb. L.J. 1 (1986–1987). By now, a total of 34 states and five federal judicial circuits have issued reports as well. * * *

of research included surveys, public hearings, and round-tables. Among other topics, each task force undertook an investigation of gender bias in the courtroom. The ABA Commission on Women in the Profession extended the investigation to discrimination against women in law firms and other settings, held public hearings, and published reports in 1988 and 1995.[59] * * *

The findings presented in these reports are astonishingly similar, lending persuasion from their sheer cumulative effect. The state court task force reports describe continuing discrimination against women lawyers in the courtroom by male attorneys and judges—for example, inappropriate and derogatory treatment, assumptions that women are less credible than men, and a variety of forms of sexual harassment. In addition, the findings demonstrate how women's and men's perceptions of discrimination differ (in effect, women see it and men don't notice).[61] Although the task force reports were largely essentialist with regard to their conclusions about the experiences of women, some included brief references to the effect, for example, that the experiences of African American women were even worse.[62] Most of the state task forces deliberately chose to set aside questions of race or other discrimination in the legal profession for separate study, leaving the experiences of women of color (or of other marginalized groups) to fall between the cracks.[63]

Bar association studies pointed repeatedly to job segregation, pay differentials, glass ceilings, sexual harassment, and overwhelming work/family conflicts encountered by women lawyers. The 1988 ABA Report described testimony by women in law firms to the effect that they lacked mentors, were excluded from socialization with clients, were not assigned to "plum" cases or only given minor roles on them, and were required to overcome a presumption of incompetence. Moreover, the Glass Ceiling Report published by the New York City Bar Association in 1995 indicated that things might be getting worse rather than better: whereas

59. ABA 1988 Report [Commission on Women in the Profession, American Bar Ass'n, Report to the House of Delegates (1988)]; ABA 1995 Report [Commission on Women in the Profession, American Bar Ass'n, Unfinished Business: Overcoming the Sisyphus Factor (1995)]. * * * [The ABA Commission on Women has continued to publish such reports and best practices manuals, including The Unfinished Agenda: Women and the Legal Profession (2001); Balanced Lives: Changing the Culture of Legal Practice (2001); Walking The Talk: Creating A Law Firm Culture Where Women Succeed (2004).]

61. For descriptions of the reports of the state task forces, see Ann J. Gellis, Great Expectations: Women in the Legal Profession, A Commentary on State Studies, 66 Ind. L.J. 941 (1991); Judith Resnik, Asking about Gender in Courts, 21 Signs: J. of Women in Culture and Soc'y 952 (1996); Jeannette F. Swent, Gender Bias at the Heart of Justice: An Empirical Study of State Task Forces, 6 S. Cal. Rev. L. & Women's Stud. 1 (1996).

62. See, e.g., Illinois Task Force on Gender Bias in the Courts, The 1990 Report of the Illinois Task Force on Gender Bias in the Courts 221 (1990) (reporting instances of patronizing, demeaning, and dismissive conduct by male judges toward African-American female attorneys). California, Michigan, and Florida, as well as the federal task forces for the Ninth and D.C. Circuits, made the experiences of women of color a more direct subject of study. See Resnik, supra note 61, at 974.

63. See id. at 973–77. Indeed, a number of manuals for both gender bias as well as race and ethnic bias task forces counseled separate treatment, for fear of distracting attention paid from one to the other. See id. at 975.

15.25% of female hires became partners between 1973 and 1981, only 5% of post–1981 hires did.[66]

Some have argued that the work of the various task forces and commissions constituted an exercise in feminist theory—essentially, cultural feminism—in that they listened to women's voices and focused upon women's experiences as different from men's. The theoretical grounding of the various studies carried out by the bench and the bar, however, was formal equality; this was perhaps inevitable, given the composition of the groups that authored them, which included powerful "insiders." Thus, discrimination against women was regarded primarily as an aberration perpetrated against individuals, the continuation of outdated stereotypes, and an irrationality rather than a structural problem requiring radical change in the profession. As a result of this theoretical grounding, recommendations for change tended to be incremental, partial, and aimed at a particular manifestation of the problem. As a remedy for in-court discrimination, for example, task forces recommended judicial education and better control by judges of their courtrooms. To remedy problems faced by women in law firms, recommendations included part-time work and flexible schedules.

At the same time, however, practitioners for whom these incremental changes had not worked told their stories in the legal press. Lawyers who had worked part-time or flexible hours, for instance, described how "part-time" was interpreted as forty hours a week and resulted in guilt on their own part and resentment by others, loss of benefits and desirable work assignments, and either delay or complete derailment from the partnership track. In short, if the theory behind the task force recommendations was formal equality, the real-life experience of women lawyers was proving its limits.

NOTES ON GENDER BIAS IN THE LEGAL PROFESSION

1. How should one evaluate the absence of women in positions of power in law firms? Past studies have shown that women are much less likely than men to be in private practice seven to ten years after law school, which has traditionally been the amount of time it takes to become a partner in a large law firm. Mona Harrington reported, concerning women who graduated in the class of 1980 from Harvard Law School and were in practice in New York City in 1982 and 1989, that 54% of these women were in large firms in 1982, but only 33% remained there in 1989. By contrast, 70% of men from that class in New York City were in large firms in 1982 and 78% in 1989. Harrington, Women Lawyers: Rewriting The Rules 37 (1994). This disparity appears to be getting worse. A 1995 study of eight large New York firms—the "Glass Ceiling Report"—reported increasing gender disparity in the route to partnership. Although approximately 21% of male associates and 15% of female associates made partner between 1973 and 1981, after 1981 only 17% of males

---

66. See [Cynthia Fuchs Epstein et al., Report, Glass Ceilings and Open Doors: Women's Advancement in the Legal Profession, 64 Fordham L. Rev. 291 (1995)] at 358–59.

made partner, and the female rate declined to 5%. Cynthia Fuchs Epstein, Robert Saute, Bonnie Oglensky & Martha Gever, Glass Ceilings and Open Doors: Women's Advancement in the Legal Profession, 64 Fordham L. Rev. 291, 358–59 (1995).

Although 40% to 50% of law school graduates in the last decades have been women, as of 2009, women made up 19.21% of law firm partners and 45.66% of associates. Nat'l Ass'n for Law Placement statistics, available at http://www.nalp.org/oct09lawfirmdiversity, Table 1. Indeed, a 2003 study by the EEOC estimated the "odds ratio" for a woman versus a man becoming a partner and concluded that men were five times more likely than women to succeed at this. U.S. Equal Employment Opportunity Comm'n, Diversity in Law Firms 29 (2003). What, in your opinion, has caused this phenomenon?

2. Women of color are almost absent from top positions in the private sector. In 2004, for example, they were fewer than 1% of law firm equity partners and 2.1% of non-equity partners in 64 large Chicago firms, and filled only 1.1% of general counsel positions in Fortune 1000 companies. ABA Comm'n on Racial and Ethnic Diversity in the Legal Profession (by Elizabeth Chambliss), Miles to Go: Progress of Minorities in the Legal Profession (2004). Astonishingly, their attrition rate from large law firms has been reported to approach 100% after eight years. ABA Comm'n on Women in the Profession, The Unfinished Agenda: Women and the Legal Profession 23 (2001) (citing NALP Foundation, Beyond the Bidding Wars: A Survey of Associate Attrition, Departure, Destinations, and Workplace Initiatives 23 (2000)). A more recent survey of 93 New York City law firms reports that little has changed. Only 1.7% of partners, without differentiating between equity and non-equity partners, were women of color. New York City Bar, 2006 Diversity Benchmarking Study: A Report to Signatory Law Firms (2006), in Beyond Diversity 101: Navigating the New Opportunities 230 (2008). Moreover, women of color had the highest attrition rate of all associates—22.2% among junior associates (versus 18.5% for white women and 19% for white men), 45% among mid-level associates (versus 40.7% for white women and 32.4% for white men), and 41.8% among senior associates (versus 31.8% for white women and 31.6% for white men). Id. at 234. What do you think causes this higher attrition rate for women of color?

In a study by the American Bar Association in 2004 and 2005 involving both a scientific survey and focus groups of attorneys in firms of 25 lawyers or more, large percentages of women of color reported being subjected to demeaning comments or other types of harassment (49%), lack of effective mentoring (67%) and exclusion from internal support networks (62%), and limited access to client development and client relationship opportunities (43%), largely because senior partners preferred to work with white male lawyers. ABA Comm'n on Women in the Profession, Visible Invisibility: Women of Color in Law Firms 10, 12, 19, 21 (2006). Forty-four percent of women of color reported being passed over for desirable assignments (versus 39% of white women, 25% of men of color, and 2% of white men), and 31% reported unfair performance ratings (versus 25% of white women, 21% of men of color, and 1% of white men). Id. at 21, 26. The resulting stress made many of them decide to leave; the retention rate for women of color in the law firms studied was 53% and that for white men was 72%. Id. at 30.

Latina lawyers are particularly underrepresented in leadership positions within the profession, even though they can now count one Supreme Court justice, Sonia Sotomayor. A large-scale survey of Latina attorneys in 2008–09 reported that they believe their qualifications are often devalued by employers and clients and that they feel isolated, as tokens, in their workplaces. Hispanic National Bar Ass'n, Few and Far Between: The Reality of Latina Lawyers 9 (2009). Only 1.9% of associates and 0.4% of partners in law firms are Latina, the lowest proportion of any racial or ethnic group. Id. at 10. The attorneys responding to this survey or commenting at focus group discussions identified the sources of discrimination against them as three-fold, based on gender, ethnicity, and race; of the three, they identified the gender barriers as the most salient. Id. at 48–49.

Women of color who are lawyers report serious problems with derogatory treatment in court—regularly being mistaken for secretaries or clerks in the presence of their clients, being addressed in a patronizing fashion, and the like. See, e.g., The 1990 Report of the Illinois Task Force on Gender Bias in the Courts 221; Maureen Ebben & Norma Guerra Gaier, Telling Stories, Telling Self: Using Narrative to Uncover Latinas' Voices and Agency in the Legal Profession, 19 Chicano–Latino L. Rev. 243, 258–62 (1998). How are the problems women of color face similar to, or different from, those faced by white women who are lawyers?

3. There is also a pay gap between male and female attorneys. See "Unfinished Agenda," above note 2, at 14 (reporting that women in legal practice made about $20,000 a year less than men, and that the gap persists when controlling for position and experience). See also NALP Foundation & Am. Bar Foundation, After the JD II: Second Results from a National Survey of Legal Careers 67 (2009) (reporting that women working full time in law firms make on average about 85% of men's salaries); Kenneth G. Dau–Schmidt, Marc S. Galanter, Kaushik Mukhopadhaya & Kathleen E. Hull, Men and Women of the Bar: The Impact of Gender on Legal Careers, 16 Mich. J. Gender & L. 49, 103 (2009) (reporting that average hourly wage of female University of Michigan law alumni was 71.9% that of their male counterparts); Nancy J. Reichman & Joyce S. Sterling, Sticky Floors, Broken Steps, and Concrete Ceilings in Legal Careers, 14 Tex. J. Women & L. 27, 30–37 (2004) (reporting on pay gap in studies of both Colorado and Michigan lawyers). One study, based on a nationally representative sample of lawyers in all work settings, reported a gender pay gap of 5.2%; even after controlling for job setting, hours worked, legal market (lawyers are paid more in large cities), and credentials; about three quarters of this gap was unexplained, leading the authors to surmise that women lawyers' work is consistently devalued and that of men overrated. Ronit Dinovitzer, Nancy Reichman & Joyce Sterling, The Differential Valuation of Women's Work: A New Look at the Gender Gap in Lawyers' Incomes, 88 Social Forces 819, 843–48 (2009). See also Neil H. Buchanan, Why Do Women Lawyers Earn Less than Men? Parenthood and Gender in a Survey of Law School Graduates, GWU Legal Studies Research Paper No. 449 (2008), available at http://ssrn.com/abstract=1280464 (reporting that fathers receive higher salaries than non-fathers and mothers earn less than non-mothers but that there is also a penalty associated purely with gender, independent of parenthood). Even if women lawyers make equity

partner, which is increasingly rare, their average median compensation in 2007 was almost $90,000 less than that of a male equity partner. Judith S. Kaye & Anne C. Reddy, The Progress of Women Lawyers at Big Firms: Steadied or Simply Studied?, 76 Fordham L. Rev. 1941, 1946–67 (2008) (citing a survey sent to the top 200 law firms in the United States).

What might explain this disparity in pay between men and women lawyers? One report suggests that male law firm lawyers, based on their socialization into a "masculine mystique," respond to having multiple children by working longer hours in order to support their families in an extravagant style and do this by spending increasing numbers of hours with corporate clients, while their female counterparts cut down their work with corporate clients as they have more children, although they still work comparably long hours. John Hagan & Fiona Kay, The Masculine Mystique: Living Large from Law School to Later Life, Law School Admission Council Research Report Series, Oct. 2007. Others suggest that law firms need to address the problem of unconscious bias in the highly subjective evaluations used to mark the progress of young lawyers. See, e.g., Joan C. Williams & Consuela A. Pinto, Fair Measure: Toward Effective Attorney Evaluations 15–31 (2d ed. 2008).

4. The American Bar Foundation Statistical Report stated that:

> In 2000 the three employment settings in which female lawyers were over-represented were government (women 36% of government lawyers), legal aid and defender programs (women 44% of program lawyers), and judicial departments (women 43% of lawyers in judicial departments excluding judges). The total number of female lawyers employed in government was one-third higher than expected based on representation of women in the 2000 lawyer population. Over-representation was even greater in legal service programs and among judicial support staff (well over 50% higher than expected) * * * in every age cohort.

Clara N. Carson, The Lawyer Statistical Report: The U.S. Legal Profession in 2000 11 (2004). The second wave of the *After the J.D.* study also found heavy concentrations of women lawyers in public or non-profit employment; in addition, about 11% of women attorneys were now inside corporate counsel (versus 4% in the early 2000s). NALP Foundation & Am. Bar Foundation, After the JD II: Second Results from a National Survey of Legal Careers 62–63 (2009). What might account for the higher percentages of women in government, legal aid, and similar settings than in private practice? Do you think this overrepresentation is a good or bad thing? Why?

5. Another finding in numerous gender bias reports and surveys has been that women attorneys were repeatedly subjected to sexual harassment by judges, opposing counsel, and partners and associates in their own firms. See, e.g., ABA Comm'n on Women in the Profession (by Deborah L. Rhode & Jennifer A. Drobac), Sex–Based Harassment 5 (2002) (describing surveys finding that between 2/5 and 2/3 of women lawyers report experiencing or observing sexual harassment); Marina Angel, Sexual Harassment by Judges, 45 U. Miami L. Rev. 817, 821–23 (1991) (describing numerous studies as well as individual cases in which judges harassed women in the courtroom); Lisa Pfenninger, Sexual Harassment in the Legal Profession: Workplace Education

and Reform, Civil Remedies, and Professional Discipline, 22 Fla. St. U. L. Rev. 171, 179–81 (1994) (describing instances of men harassing women within law firms). Given that sexually harassing behavior is both unethical and can be a violation of federal and state civil rights laws, can you think of effective remedies for women experiencing such conduct?

In 2004, Indiana conducted a follow-up survey to their 1990 gender bias report. While finding that many things had not changed even though the number of women lawyers had doubled, the later study found "a significant increase in the percentage of female respondents who report not having observed or experienced physical sexual harassment." However, 10.6% of women respondents did report physical sexual harassment and 41% reported verbal sexual harassment. Maria Pabón López, The Future of Women in the Legal Profession: Recognizing the Challenges Ahead by Reviewing Current Trends, 19 Hastings Women's L.J. 53, 60, 76 (2008). What do you think could be causing this change?

6. How should women lawyers respond when they are the object of or observe sexist comments, innuendo, or other forms of derogatory treatment in court? Should the response differ if the offending remarks are made by a judge or by opposing counsel? Does it make a difference if the woman's client is present at the time? What if the attorney has to appear before the same judge repeatedly? What factors should women lawyers take into account when responding in such situations? Are any of these factors potentially conflicting, for example, feminist convictions versus the interest of the client? How should one decide in case of conflict? Would you report such an incident to a bar disciplinary committee? Is it unethical according to the rules governing attorneys in your state? What other routes are open to female attorneys who believe they have been the object of sex discrimination? Do the Code of Professional Responsibility and complaints filed with local disciplinary committees offer any potential for relief? See Kandis Koustenis, Sexual Trial Tactics: The Ability of the *Model Code* and *Model Rules* to Discipline Discriminatory Conflicts Between Adversaries, 4 Geo. J. Legal Ethics 153 (1990).

7. What are the effects of male and female speech characteristics in the courtroom? In two experiments college students listened to the testimony of a female or male witness who used either "powerless" speech (e.g., speech patterns associated with women's speech, such as frequent use of intensifiers, hedges, and questioning intonation) or "power" speech (more assertive style associated with men) to deliver the same basic evidence. Both the experiment using tape-recorded testimony and the one using trial transcripts found that listeners evaluated the witness (regardless of actual sex) using the "powerless" style more negatively. See William M. O'Barr, Linguistic Evidence: Language, Power, and Strategy in the Courtroom 61–75 (1982). What are the implications of this research for the success of women in litigation? As litigators? Is the answer to teach women to speak and act more like men in order to challenge the status quo? Or should we be attempting to challenge the hierarchical structure that places "male" speech at the top and "female" speech at the bottom?

8. Samantha, a fourth year associate, has done most of the discovery and trial preparation work on a case for Calvin Client, whose work represents

a substantial portion of the billings at the law firm. Henry, also a fourth year associate, has also worked on the case but has done considerably less on it than Samantha. Two months prior to trial, Sam Senior Partner tells Samantha that Calvin Client wants Henry to do all the in-court work because he feels uncomfortable being represented by a woman attorney in court. What should Samantha do? What should the firm do (1) as a question of law and of ethics, (2) as a question of justice, and (3) as a question of the best representation for the client? In an article discussing the removal of a female associate from a case at the client's request and analyzing it as a question of both legal ethics and Title VII, Ernest L. Lidge III concludes that law firms should be allowed to comply with the client's demand when necessary to maintain the client's trust and confidence in the attorney. Lidge, Law Firm Employment Discrimination in Case Assignments at the Client's Insistence: A Bona Fide Occupational Qualification?, 38 Conn. L. Rev. 159 (2005). What do you think of this conclusion?

LESLIE BENDER, SEX DISCRIMINATION OR GENDER INEQUALITY?

57 Fordham L. Rev. 941, 941–45, 949–52 (1989).

The prestigious male bastions of Wall Street law firms have finally done the honorable thing and opened their conclaves to significant numbers of women. Women who conform to male expectations and predictions of success may now enter and play by their rules. These institutional rules of the game, by which one "wins" success, power, prestige, security and money, were designed for persons like the named partners themselves, people without primary interpersonal caregiving responsibilities. * * * [A]s more women have been granted admission to the world of professional lawyering, the rules have changed. The required billable hours have escalated so that it has become physically impossible to participate in a big firm practice while taking personal responsibility for the care of others, be they children, parents, lovers, siblings, friends or the needy in our communities. Women (and men), unencumbered by such responsibilities, may be able to adjust their lifestyles to meet these unreasonable professional demands, at least temporarily. They are required to make their work the entire focus of their lives. Women (and men) who are primary caregivers and take those responsibilities seriously, whether because of externally-imposed or internalized gender role stereotypes, natural inclination, happenstance, or unfettered choice, often are forced to seek alternative career choices. Such alternatives include part-time employment; flextime and job-sharing; career "sequencing"; more flexible legal practices in small firms or as sole practitioners; teaching; in-house corporate counsel positions; government lawyering; perhaps public interest work; or even to drop out of law entirely.

* * *

Is there an important distinction between including more women lawyers in law firms and affirming gender equality? Between avoiding sex discrimination and eliminating gender inequality? I would argue that there is.

* * *

Women ought not be satisfied with being allowed into male-created big law firm practices and playing by their rules, or with being given less empowered, less prestigious, less remunerative options. We should not commend law firms for offering permanent part-time, temporary part-time, or dead-end tracks to accommodate those of us not willing or able to make our careers our entire lives. We ought not accept the implicit assumptions of the current construction of law practice that depend on dichotomies between devotion to family and to career, and that require unswerving fealty to work over all else. Women should demand no less than an opportunity to redefine the meanings of lawyering, law firm practice, professionalism, and professional success, all of which were created without our input, insights, needs and gender culture taken into account. The elimination of sex discrimination is not enough. We must have gender equality.

* * *

Our business/professional world has been constructed by men to reinforce and reward their gendered male characteristics. Interpersonal caregiving, which was not part of the male gender culture, was excluded and perceived as inappropriate or interruptive of the important functions of professional work. Although women have succeeded in entering the pre-constructed professional world and sharing it with men, we have not succeeded as well in shedding our primary responsibility for caregiving and in sharing the interpersonal caregiver role equally with men. Our entrance into the professional world has also not succeeded in bringing our gender culture into accepted facets of the professional culture. Interpersonal caregiving to our friends, family and community remains separate and distinct from our activities in the office. Women are now permitted to do both (participate in the professional world and continue in our caregiving), so long as we do not integrate them. The parts of our daily activities that reflect our gender culture are specifically excluded from and deemed inappropriate to our professional environment. As a consequence, in our professional communities, and, in particular, in the world of high-powered law firms, gender inequality predominates. Therefore, our goal must be to reconstruct legal institutions based on gender equality—empowering both genders and eliminating the privilege/power of one gender over another.

Feminism has approached the issues of gender inequality and sex discrimination in several ways. The women's liberation, liberal-humanist feminist approach began with the assimilationist premise that women can do anything men can do and can do it at least as well if given a fair opportunity and equal access to positions and offices. The goal of this model of feminism was getting women accepted into the big law firms based on traditional criteria of merit, competing on existing terms, and being treated equally to, that is the same as, men. A later variation on this theme developed the idea that where there are biological differences in women from men, for example, pregnancy and childbirth, women should be treated specially and not disadvantaged by these female physical differences, so that they could continue to compete equally for the brass rings.

Both models accept the implicit male norm of existing legal institutions and attempt to mold women to its expectations and demands. If success as a lawyer requires women to be aggressive, competitive, superrational, emotionally detached; to work at our careers for more than ten or twelve hours a day; to depend upon others to care for our families and our homes; to perpetuate status hierarchies within our working environment; and to create sharp divisions between family and career, then so be it. Even though we add more and more females to the quotient of persons doing the job, women who demonstrate aspects of the gendered women's culture are discouraged, badly evaluated, and seen as unfit. This is the infamous "add women and stir" model of reform. We add members of our sex to a profession, but we do not add "acceptance" of gender differences. Those women who can make themselves act and think most like the gendered male culture succeed. One of the surest ways to do this is to remain unencumbered by caregiving responsibilities. Women's participation and complicity in this structure perpetuate its inequalities for women who seek to maintain their interconnectedness with others and their women's gender culture identities, and for men who resist many of the traditional male gender traits. Despite gender assimilation, we find that these women do not "succeed" at equal paces and in equal numbers with their male counterparts. Women who have tried to deemphasize their female-gendered characteristics to prove their worth in the male world are nonetheless disadvantaged by their physical differences and the politics of gender power relations.

It is not gender equality for women to assume characteristics of the male gender or to attempt to take a male perspective and then do those jobs. Just because we are talented enough to assimilate male characteristics for the business world does not mean that that is what we want or what is best. Getting inside the law firms is a start, but if the only women who succeed and achieve the power to change the institutions are the women who are most like men and least woman-identified, then gender inequality continues unabated. Sex discrimination may be eliminated in the workforce, but gender inequality still cries out for response.

Some other feminists have advocated a modification of existing institutional requirements to accommodate women's traditional caregiving responsibilities. This approach moves beyond sex discrimination to issues of gender difference. While it recognizes women's gendered role expectations and choices, it does not solve the problem of gender inequality. This model argues that the practice of law must incorporate or accommodate the reality of women's actual life experiences—not as viewed from the outside, but as lived and experienced. It offers an option for women (and men) who want an alternative career choice to meet their family or interpersonal responsibilities, but it leaves the rest of the system intact. It does not question institutional assumptions about the gendered characteristics for or definitions of the norms of professional conduct and success.

The addition of a "mommy track," "parenting track," or "family track," which this analysis suggests as a solution, does not end gender inequality. It is an exception to the "normal" work style, a less valued (in terms of money, power, prestige), genderized woman track. This approach fails to consider the power aspects of gender-based norms and privileges, and looks only to accommodating difference. Women (and men) who are caregivers and spend time out of the wage force (or in lower paying jobs while caring for others) are subordinated and undervalued because of it. At best, with extraordinary effort and hard work, they can "rehabilitate" their careers after their aberrational and deviant behavior.

Had women been included in designing our workplaces, opportunities for caregiving and sensitivities to its requirements would have been an integral part of their structure. Since primary and cooperative caregivers now participate in legal practices and professional institutions, it has become eminently clear that the structure is deficient. We must collectively decide that caregiving is something we value as a constitutive aspect of our ideal lawyer/citizen/worker and then re-imagine a professional world that fosters that value. We must restructure the professional world of law firm practice (for that matter, the entire wage work world) from the perspective of people responsible for others in an actual caregiving sense.

NOTES ON SEX DISCRIMINATION AND GENDER INEQUALITY IN THE LEGAL PROFESSION

1. How do you think large law firms would have been structured if women had played a major role in setting them up? If women were to restructure or redesign the lawyering profession, what modifications might they make other than accommodating or integrating caregiving? How should the ideal law firm be structured? How would it handle the demands of clients with fast-paced litigation? Would it need to confine itself to certain types of legal work? What are the economics of such a practice? The fairness?

2. Are the phenomena described above—the initial exclusion of women from the legal profession, informal ways of keeping them out or of making them uncomfortable within the profession, the difficulty of combining a legal career with domestic caretaking duties, and the discomfort many women may feel with the law's distance and adversariness—all appropriately described as gender bias? Sex discrimination? Gender inequality? If so, what precisely do we mean by these terms? What would a proponent of formal equality say? A dominance/inequality theorist? A relational feminist? A pragmatic feminist?

3. The unequal positions of men and women in the legal profession have been the subject of repeated empirical studies. One such study examined whether women's different career experiences (1) would disappear with their

increasing numbers in the profession (the assimilation over time thesis), (2) were the result of choice (related primarily to the unequal domestic division of labor), or (3) amounted to continuing structural discrimination (the "gendered constraint" theory). Kathleen E. Hull & Robert L. Nelson, Assimilation, Choice, or Constraint? Testing Theories of Gender Differences in the Careers of Lawyers, 79 Social Forces 229, 231–33 (2000). This study, of 788 lawyers in Chicago in 1995 (34% of them women), concluded that the third thesis had most explanatory power; the results suggested "that gender differences in careers of lawyers are in significant part the product of the dynamics of gender inequality within legal employment * * *." Id. at 253.

A study of Colorado lawyers argues that women's "choices" are really more a question of being pushed out by unyielding and unfriendly organizations than being pulled toward family responsibilities. Nancy J. Reichman & Joyce S. Sterling, Recasting the Brass Ring: Deconstructing and Reconstructing Workplace Opportunities for Women Lawyers, 29 Cap. U.L. Rev. 923 (2002). This study showed that women lawyers move from one workplace to another earlier and more frequently than men, often in the direction of downward mobility, leaving their first placement long before the question of partnership comes up. The authors opine that women encounter "sticky floors" rather than "glass ceilings," in the form of "gendered work practices and compensation systems that do not allow women to progress." Id. at 930, 938. In particular, Reichman and Sterling condemn socially constructed and gendered notions of both productivity and commitment that lead to the devaluation of women lawyers. The model rewarded by partnership is one that assumes a linear and continuous career (no pregnancy leave or part-time work) and a definition of commitment that amounts to virtually unlimited availability for work, often confusing "face time" with the productivity and genuine commitment that women lawyers offer. Id. at 935–38, 948–55. Is there any way to address this type of gender-biased treatment that occurs in private law firms? How?

4. Given the hierarchical nature of most large law firms, the disproportionate numbers of men at the top of the hierarchy, and the subjective nature of evaluations, how should women attorneys respond to sex discriminatory treatment when it happens to them? What can women subjected to such treatment expect from a Title VII suit? See, e.g., Ezold v. Wolf, Block, Schorr and Solis–Cohen, 751 F.Supp. 1175 (E.D. Pa. 1990); 983 F.2d 509 (3d Cir. 1992); see also Deborah L. Rhode, "What's Sex Got To Do With It?": Diversity in the Legal Profession (2006) (discussing the *Ezold* case from perspective of both plaintiff and defendants); Hishon v. King & Spalding, 467 U.S. 69 (1984) (holding that Title VII applies to law partnership decisions).

Joan C. Williams and Nancy Segal propose that the primary discrimination against women now is based on pregnancy and caregiving and suggest a variety of causes of action, including Title VII disparate treatment, disparate impact, hostile work environment, constructive discharge and retaliation actions, along with cases based on the Equal Pay Act, Family and Medical Leave Act, Americans with Disabilities Act, Section 1983, and a variety of state statutes protecting employees. Williams & Segal, Beyond the Maternal Wall: Relief for Family Caregivers Who Are Discriminated Against on the Job, 26 Harv. Women's L.J. 77, 122–61 (2003). One lawyer sued under Title VII, alleging that she had suffered a variety of negative consequences, including negative job evaluations and termination, based on sex, pregnancy and motherhood; the court held that her complaint stated a claim for sex discrimination under Title VII, noting also the disproportionate number of lawyers who were pregnant or mothers who left during that time. Sigmon v. Parker Chapin Flattau & Klimpl, 901 F.Supp. 667, 676–78 (S.D.N.Y. 1995). Although Title VII does not prohibit discrimination based on caregiving responsibility, it does bar making employment decisions based on stereotypes about women with children that would not be made about men with children, such as that women are likely to neglect their job duties in favor of childcare. See Chadwick v. Wellpoint, Inc., 561 F.3d 38 (1st Cir. 2009). Williams and Segal urge that lawyers arguing discrimination cases should make use of the human resources literature showing the irrationality of practices based on gender stereotypes and the profitability of family-friendly policies. Williams & Segal, above, at 79. What are the advantages and disadvantages of the different possible legal remedies set out above? How do you predict Bender would respond to such strategies?

5. Women's entry into the legal profession coincided with substantial changes in the profession itself, none of them favorable to women's success. The time to partnership has been extended; decreasing percentages of associates are promoted to partner; the billable hours required per year have risen to the point where 60 to 80 hours a week at work may be necessary to fulfill expectations; and new categories of attorneys have been created—permanent associates, contract attorneys, non-equity partners, and "of counsel" positions, all heavily populated by women. See, e.g., Fiona M. Kay & John Hagan, Cultivating Clients in the Competition for Partnership: Gender and the Organizational Restructuring of Law Firms in the 1990s, 33 Law & Soc'y Rev. 517, 548–49 (1999); ABA Comm'n on Women, Unfinished Agenda: Women and the Legal Profession 23–24 (2001). Kay and Hagan opine that the resulting attrition of women lawyers, though wasteful of training and talent, is in fact functional for law firms because it reduces the competition for partnership and allows previously exclusive groups to maintain their dominant position without directly excluding newcomers, which is now illegal. Kay & Hagan, above, at 518–19, 527. How can women succeed in the face of these challenges? Reichman and Sterling argue that genuine equality requires that law firms reframe evaluative procedures, requirements for partnership, and definitions of commitment, as well as provide greater flexibility in working conditions. Reichman & Sterling, note 3 above, at 962. What might Bender think about such a strategy? How will law firms reform if women are not represented in substantial numbers among law firm equity partners?

6. Eli Wald argues that the problems women lawyers face in large law firms have been greatly exacerbated as the competitive meritocracy ideology of the 1960's and 1970's, under which they could succeed, has been replaced by a hypercompetitive professional ideology that clashes with persistent stereotypes of women. This new professional ideology—a 24/7 mentality requiring not only exceptional merit but also a willingness to sacrifice one's personal life—is inherently incompatible with gender stereotypes of women as not sufficiently committed to the firm and its clients because of their commitments to family, and these remaining stereotypes affect retention decisions

despite women's willingness to take advantage of modern technology and work from home. Eli Wald, Glass Ceilings and Dead Ends, Professional Ideologies, Gender Stereotypes, and the Future of Women Lawyers at Large Law Firms, 78 Fordham L. Rev. 101 (2010). Combined with the recent economic downturn and its impact on the legal market, which has resulted in mass firings, hiring freezes, and deferral of job offers to the best of law students, he suggests that "women lawyers are facing not a formidable glass ceiling but a dead end." Id. at 114. Judith Kaye, one of the early women pioneers in large firm practice, agrees, seeing the following as the causes of the lack of progress for women in law firms: (1) the persistence of gender stereotypes of women as less committed; (2) a consequent resistance to flexible work arrangements that would allow them to balance the demands on their time; and (3) the billable hour economic model. Judith S. Kaye & Anne C. Reddy, The Progress of Women Lawyers at Big Firms: Steadied or Simply Studied?, 76 Fordham L. Rev. 1941, 1954–64 (2008). The one hopeful sign to which she points is a recent focus on recruiting from a reentry pool of women lawyers—women who have left the workforce to raise their young children and are now returning. Id. at 1968. What sources of change do you see in these patterns and their impact on the success of women in law? Would Bender be hopeful?

7. Cynthia Fuchs Epstein has said that the application of a "differences approach" to the problems encountered by women lawyers, resulting in forms of special treatment for them, such as maternity leave, part-time work, and a flexible partnership track, is just a new form of the protective attitude displayed by the 19th-century judges who denied women admission to the bar on the grounds that woman's nature and natural role did not fit her for work in the courtroom. Epstein, Faulty Framework: Consequences of the Difference Model for Women in the Law, 35 N.Y.L. Sch. L. Rev. 309, 317–27 (1990). What do you think of this argument? How would Bender respond? How are the forms of "special treatment" sought by women today different from the spheres to which they were consigned by Victorian paternalism? Do you think there is any danger that these accommodations may backfire and result in second-class status for women within the legal profession? Is there any way to prevent this from happening?

8. Women are also underrepresented in the judiciary. As of 2009 women comprised about 26.9% of federal court of appeals judges, 24.7% of federal district court judges, and 32.4% of state supreme court justices. ABA Comm'n on Women in the Profession, A Current Glance at Women in the Law 3 (2009). The political party of the president makes a great difference to the numbers of women appointed to the federal judiciary: 32.8% of Clinton's appointees to the U.S. courts of appeals and 28.5% to the U.S. district courts were women, as compared with about 19% and 20% to each of these courts by both the first and second Presidents Bush. Sourcebook of Criminal Justice Statistics 2003 75–76, available at http://www.albany.edu/sourcebook/pdf/t182.pdf and /t181.pdf. Half of President Obama's nominees to the U.S. courts of appeal as of April 2010 have been women. Alliance for Justice, The State of the Judiciary: The Obama Administration: 2009 6 (2010).

9. What do female judges bring to the judiciary? Suzanna Sherry has opined that women's presence shatters stereotypes; their participation injects

women's perspectives, insight into women's problems, and greater empathy; and their decision-making displays greater attention to context and connection. Sherry, The Gender of Judges, 4 Law & Ineq. 159, 160–65 (1986). Studies attempting to test some of these hypotheses have had mixed results. Some of those studying the voting patterns of women judges have concluded that they lean toward the interests of their gender on "women's issues," especially on sex discrimination claims. See, e.g., Sue Davis, Susan Haire & Donald R. Songer, Voting Behavior and Gender on the U.S. Courts of Appeals, 77 Judicature 129, 131–32 (1993); David W. Allen & Diane E. Wall, Role Orientations and Women State Supreme Court Justices, 77 Judicature 156, 158, 161–62, 164–65 (1993). Other studies disagree with these conclusions. See, e.g., Sarah Westergren, Gender Effects in the Courts of Appeals Revisited: The Data Since 1994, 92 Geo. L.J. 689 (2004) (finding no significant difference between voting patterns of male and female judges on sex discrimination cases and concluding that party of appointing president is the key factor). Yet another study has found that female state supreme court justices are likely to vote to support the female litigant in divorce cases 75.6% of the time, while male justices do so 53.6% of the time. Elaine Martin & Barry Pyle, State High Courts and Divorce: The Impact of Judicial Gender, 36 Univ. Toledo L. Rev. 923, 936 (2005).

A study of 556 federal appellate cases on sexual harassment and sex discrimination claims in 1999–2001 found that plaintiffs were two times as likely to prevail if a female judge was included in the panel, leading the author to surmise that "the presence of female judges may influence male judges before or during oral argument, in conference after argument, in informal conversations about the case, or in writing as judges exchange drafts of their opinions." Jennifer L. Peresie, Female Judges Matter: Gender and Collegial Decisionmaking in the Federal Appellate Courts, 114 Yale L.J. 1759, 1761, 1780 (2005). The author surmised about possible explanations for this influence, including a simple tendency to reach a consensus view, that the other (male) judges were persuaded by the female judge's arguments, that they simply deferred to the women judges on matters they thought were within their expertise, or that the presence of a woman made male judges feel constrained to silence their anti-plaintiff views.

Other studies have examined whether women bring a different decisional style to the bench, regardless of case outcome—a more contextual style with more attention given to care, connection, and community. Authors conflict over whether the jurisprudence of Supreme Court Justice Sandra Day O'Connor displayed such characteristics. Cf. Suzanna Sherry, Civic Virtue and the Feminine Voice in Constitutional Adjudication, 72 Va. L. Rev. 543 (1986), with Sue Davis, The Voice of Sandra Day O'Connor, 77 Judicature 134, 138–39 (1993). See also Sue Davis, Do Women Judges Speak "In A Different Voice?": Carol Gilligan, Feminist Legal Theory, and the Ninth Circuit, 8 Wis. Women's L.J. 143 (1992–1993) (finding, based on comparison of male and female opinions on the Ninth Circuit, no support for theory that women judges bring a different voice to adjudication).

Based on a comparison with Canada, where the Supreme Court has had a majority of women members since 2005, Rosalind Dixon questions whether the substantive insights women bring to the judiciary will continue in the long run, as younger women lawyers have not had the experience of discrimination that their predecessors did. Consequently, she recommends that feminists emphasize the substantive positions rather than the gender of judicial candidates, preferring feminist male judges to conservative females. Dixon, Female Justices, Feminism and the Politics of Judicial Appointment: A Re-Examination, 21 Yale J.L. & Feminism 297 (2010). Even if the decisions of male and female judges are similar, are there arguments for inclusion of women in larger numbers on the bench? What do you think are the best reasons for doing so?

D. LAWYERING IN A DIFFERENT VOICE?

CARRIE MENKEL-MEADOW, PORTIA IN A DIFFERENT VOICE: SPECULATIONS ON A WOMEN'S LAWYERING PROCESS

1 Berkeley Women's L.J. 39, 49–55, 57–59 (1985).

[The Portia of the title is the character in Shakespeare's play The Merchant of Venice who pleads (in Act IV, Scene 1) for mercy to temper justice.]

[Carol] Gilligan's observations about male-female differences in moral reasoning may have a great deal to suggest about how the legal system is structured, how law is practiced and made, and how we reason and use law in making decisions. * * *

Two sets of questions illustrate how we might think about the impact of two voices on our legal system as presently constituted and as it might be transformed. First, how has the exclusion, or at least the devaluation, of women's voices affected the choices made in the values underlying our current legal structures? When we value "objectivity," or a "right" answer, or a single winner, are we valuing male goals of victory, exclusion, clarity, predictability? What would our legal system look like if women had not been excluded from participating in its creation? What values would women express in creating the laws and institutions of a legal system? How would they differ from what we see now? How might the different male and female voices join together to create an integrated legal system? Second, can we glimpse enclaves of another set of values within some existing legal structures? Is the judge "male," the jury "female?" Is the search for facts a feminine search for context and the search for legal principles a masculine search for certainty and abstract rules? * * *

These two sets of questions explore a central issue, which is whether, to the extent that there are value choices to be made in the legal system, those choices will be differently made and with different results when the people who make decisions include a greater representation of women among their numbers. * * * But even if the choices of values are not themselves gendered, it may be that women will favor one set of values over another in sufficient numbers, or with sufficient intensity, to change the balance at times. Although existing structures give a glimpse of what the legal system could look like, we cannot yet know what the consequences of women's participation in the legal system will be—some fear the women's voice will simply be added on and be drowned out by the louder male voice; others fear an androgynous, univoiced world with no interesting differences.

Perhaps by examining these issues in their concrete forms we can see how Portia's different voice might expand our understanding of the lawyering process. * * *

* * * The basic structure of our legal system is premised on the adversarial model, which involves two advocates who present their cases to a disinterested third party who listens to evidence and argument and declares one party a winner. In this simplified description of the Anglo–American model of litigation, we can identify some of the basic concepts and values which underlie this choice of arrangements: advocacy, persuasion, hierarchy, competition, and binary results (win/lose). The conduct of litigation is relatively similar (not coincidentally, I suspect) to a sporting event—there are rules, a referee, an object to the game, and a winner is declared after the play is over. * * * The adversarial model affects the way in which lawyers advise their clients ("get as much as you can"), negotiate disputes ("we can really get them on that") and plan transactions ("let's be sure to draft this to your advantage"). All of these activities in lawyering assume competition over the same limited and equally valued items (usually money) and assume that success is measured by maximizing individual gain. Would Gilligan's Amy create a different model?[b]

By returning to Heinz's dilemma we see some hints about what Amy might do. Instead of concluding that a choice must be made between life and property, in resolving the conflict between parties as Jake does, Amy sees no need to hierarchically order the claims. Instead, she tries to account for all the parties' needs, and searches for a way to find a solution that satisfies the needs of both. In her view, Heinz should be able to obtain the drug for his wife and the pharmacist should still receive payment. So Amy suggests a loan, a credit arrangement, or a discussion of other ways to structure the transaction. In short, she won't play by the adversarial rules. She searches outside the system for a way to solve the problem, trying to keep both parties in mind. Her methods substantiate Gilligan's observations that women will try to change the rules to preserve the relationships.

Furthermore, in addition to looking for more substantive solutions to the problem (i.e., not accepting the binary win/lose conception of the problem), Amy also wants to change the process. Amy sees no reason why she must act as a neutral arbiter of a dispute and make a decision based only on the information she has. She "belie[ves] in communication as the mode of conflict resolution and [is convinced] that the solution to the

---

b. See excerpt from Gilligan, In a Different Voice, in Chapter 3, above.

dilemma will follow from its compelling representation...."[69] If the parties talk directly to each other, they will be more likely to appreciate the importance of each other's needs. Thus, she believes direct communication, rather than third party mediated debate, might solve the problem, recognizing that two apparently conflicting positions can both be simultaneously legitimate, and there need not be a single victor.

The notion that women might have more difficulty with full-commitment-to-one-side model of the adversary system is graphically illustrated by Hilary, one of the women lawyers in Gilligan's study. This lawyer finds herself in one of the classic moral dilemmas of the adversary system: she sees that her opponent has failed to make use of a document that is helpful to his case and harmful to hers. In deciding not to tell him about the document because of what she sees as her "professional vulnerability" in the male adversary system, she concludes that "the adversary system of justice impedes not only the supposed search for truth (the conventional criticism), but also *the expression of concern for the person on the other side.*"[70] * * *

So what kind of legal system would Amy and Hilary create if left to their own devices? They might look for ways to alter the harshness of win/lose results; they might alter the rules of the game (or make it less like a game); and they might alter the very structures and forms themselves. Thus, in a sense Amy and Hilary's approach can already be found in some of the current alternatives to the adversary model such as mediation. Much of the current interest in alternative dispute resolution is an attempt to modify the harshness of the adversarial process and expand the kinds of solutions available, in order to respond better to the varied needs of the parties. Amy's desire to engage the parties in direct communication with each other is reflected in mediation models where the parties talk directly to each other and forge their own solutions. The work of Gilligan and Noddings, demonstrating an ethic of care and a heightened sense of empathy in women, suggests that women lawyers may be particularly interested in mediation as an alternative to litigation as a method of resolving disputes.

Even within the present adversarial model, Amy and Hilary might, in their concern for others, want to provide for a broader conception of interested parties, permitting participation by those who might be affected by the dispute (an ethic of inclusion). In addition, like judges who increasingly are managing more of the details of their cases, Amy and Hilary might seek a more active role in settlement processes and rely less on court-ordered relief. Amy and Hilary might look for other ways to construct their lawsuits and remedies in much the same way as courts of equity mitigated the harshness of the law courts' very limited array of remedies by expanding the conception of what was possible.

69. Id. [Carol Gilligan, In A Different Voice: Psychological Theory and Women's Development (1982)] at 30.

70. Id. at 135–36.

The process and rules of the adversary system itself might look different if there were more female voices in the legal profession. If Amy is less likely than Jake to make assertive, rights-based statements, is she less likely to adapt to the male-created advocacy mode? * * *

Amy and Hilary might create a different form of advocacy, one resembling a "conversation" with the fact finder, relying on the creation of a relationship with the jury for its effectiveness, rather than on persuasive intimidation. * * *

In sum, the growing strength of women's voice in the legal profession may change the adversarial system into a more cooperative, less war-like system of communication between disputants in which solutions are mutually agreed upon rather than dictated by an outsider, won by the victor, and imposed upon the loser. * * *

TRINA GRILLO, THE MEDIATION ALTERNATIVE: PROCESS DANGERS FOR WOMEN

100 Yale L.J. 1545, 1600, 1601, 1603–07 (1991).

[The late Trina Grillo, a law professor, had extensive experience as a mediator in California, where mediation is mandatory in all child custody cases. The italicized stories included in the article from which this is an excerpt are composites drawn from her own observation of many mediation cases.]

Emma has been in a marriage which in its early years seemed to be a good one for both Emma and her husband. She has been the primary caretaker of the children, and she is very committed to them. She has lived much of her life through her husband and her children, and has not worked outside her home. Increasingly, however, she has begun to feel that she and her husband have grown apart, and that he does not see her as a person but rather as a repository of various roles. After much agony, she has decided to end her marriage. Her departure from the marriage is a first step toward seeing her life as having separate dimensions from her husband's and children's, but her right to individuation does not seem clear to her; in fact, there are many times when it seems selfish and wrong. It is hard for her even to find the language to describe what is propelling her to turn her life, and her children's lives, upside down, but propelled she is. The marital separation was an early step toward defining her own physical and psychological boundaries. She now finds herself, however, feeling guilty, frightened, and unsure of how she will survive in the world alone.

Joan has been in a marriage in which she has been physically abused for ten years. She and her husband David have two children, whom David has never abused. She is afraid, however, that if she leaves David, he will begin to abuse the children whenever he is caring for them. Joan has been afraid to leave her marriage because David has threatened to harm her if she does so. When she separated briefly from him previously, he followed her and continually harassed her. Each time David beats Joan he shows great remorse afterwards and promises never to do it again. He is a man of considerable charm, and she has often believed him on these occasions. Nonetheless, Joan has finally decided to leave her husband. She is worried about what will happen, economically and physically, to her children and herself.

* * *

A. The Ethic of Care in Mediation

* * *

Carrie Menkel–Meadow has suggested that the ethic of care can and should be brought into the practice of law—that the world of lawyering would look very different from the perspective of that ethic. Some commentators have identified mediation as a way to incorporate the ethic of care into the legal system and thereby modify the harshness of the adversary process. And, indeed, at first glance, mediation in the context of divorce might be seen as a way of bringing the woman-identified values of intimacy, nurturance, and care into a legal system that is concerned with the most fundamental aspects of women's and men's lives.

If mediation does not successfully introduce an ethic of care, however, but instead merely sells itself on that promise while delivering something coercive in its place, the consequences will be disastrous for a woman who embraces a relational sense of self. If she is easily persuaded to be cooperative, but her partner is not, she can only lose. If it is indeed her disposition to be caring and focused on relationships, and she has been rewarded for that focus and characterized as "unfeminine" when she departs from it, the language of relationship, caring, and cooperation will be appealing to her and make her vulnerable. Moreover, the intimation that she is not being cooperative and caring or that she is thinking of herself instead of thinking selflessly of the children can shatter her self-esteem and make her lose faith in herself. In short, in mediation, such a woman may be encouraged to repeat exactly those behaviors that have proven hazardous to her in the past.

In the story above, Emma is asked to undergo a forced engagement with the very person from whom she is trying to differentiate herself at a difficult stage in her life. She may find it impossible to think of herself as a separate entity during mediation, while her husband may easily be able to act on behalf of his separate self. "When a separate self must be asserted, women have trouble asserting it. Women's separation from the other in adult life, and the tension between that separation and our fundamental state of connection, is felt most acutely when a woman must make choices, and when she must speak the truth."[274]

Emma will be asked to talk about her needs and feelings, and respond to her husband's needs and feelings. Although in the past her valuing

274. [Robin] West, Jurisprudence and Gender, 55 U.Chi.L.Rev. 1, 55 (1988).

relationships above all else may have worked to the detriment of her separate self, Emma will now be urged to work on the future relationship between herself and her ex-husband. Above all, she will be asked to put the well-being of the children before her own, as if she and her children's well-being were entirely separate. Her problem in addressing her future alone, however, may be that she reflexively puts her children before herself, even when she truly needs to take care of herself in order to take care of her children. For Emma, mediation may play on what are already her vulnerable spots, and put her at a disadvantage. She may begin to think of herself as unfeminine, or simply bad, if she puts her own needs forward. Emma may feel the need to couch every proposal she makes in terms of the needs of her children. In sum, if she articulates her needs accurately, she may end up feeling guilty, selfish, confused, and embarrassed; if she does not, she will be moving backwards to the unbounded self that is at the source of her difficulties.

For Joan, the prescription of mediation might be disastrous. She has always been susceptible to her husband's charm, and has believed him when he has said that he would stop abusing her. She has also always been afraid of him. She is likely, in mediation, to be susceptible and afraid once again. She may continue to care for her husband, and to think that she was responsible for his behavior toward her. Joan, and not her husband, will be susceptible to any pressure to compromise, and to compromise in her situation might be very dangerous for both her and her children.

B. Sexual Domination and Judicial Violence

Women who have been through mandatory mediation often describe it as an experience of sexual domination, comparing mandatory mediation to rape. Catharine MacKinnon's work provides a basis for explaining why, for some women, this characterization is appropriate. MacKinnon has analyzed gender as a system of power relations, evidenced primarily with respect to the control of women's sexuality. While MacKinnon recognizes the sense in which women are fundamentally connected to others, she does not celebrate it. Rather, she sees the potential for connection as invasive and intrusive. It is precisely the potential for physical connection that permits invasion into the integrity of women's bodies. It is precisely the potential for emotional connection that permits intrusion into the integrity of women's lives.

Men do not experience this same fear of sexual domination, according to MacKinnon; they do not live in constant fear of having the very integrity of their lives intruded upon. Men may not comprehend their role in this system of sexual domination any more than women may be able to articulate the source of their feeling of disempowerment. Yet both of these dynamics are at work in the mediation setting. It may seem a large leap, from acts of physical violence and invasion to the apparently simple requirement that a woman sit in a room with her spouse working toward the resolution of an issue of mutual concern. But that which may be at stake in a court-ordered custody mediation—access to one's children—may be the main reason one has for living, as well as all one's hope for the future. And because mandatory mediation is a forced engagement, ordinarily without attorneys or even friends or supporters present, it may amount to a form of "psychic breaking and entering" or, put another way, psychic rape.

There is always the potential for violence in the legal system: "A judge articulates her understanding of a text, and as a result, somebody loses his freedom, his property, his children, even his life.... When interpreters have finished their work, they frequently leave behind victims whose lives have been torn apart by these organized, social practices of violence."[281]

The reality of this background of judicial violence cannot be discounted when measuring the potential trauma of the mandatory mediation setting. Although the mediation system is purportedly designed in part to help participants *avoid* contact with the violence that must come from judicial decisions, in significant ways the violence of the contact is more direct. Since the parties are obliged to speak for themselves in a setting to which the culture has not introduced them and in which the rules are not clear (and in fact vary from mediator to mediator), the potential violence of the legal result, combined with the invasiveness of the setting, may indeed end up feeling to the unwilling participant very much like a kind of rape. Moreover, in judging, it is understood that the critical view of the quarrel is that of the judge, the professional third party. Mediation is described as a form of intervention that reflects the *disputants'* view of the quarrel. But having the mediation take place on court premises with a mediator who might or might not inject her prejudices into the process may make it unlikely that the disputants' view will control. Thus, a further sense of violation may arise from having another person's view of the dispute characterized and treated as one's own.

That many reportedly find mediation helpful does not mean everyone does. * * *

When I have suggested to mediators that even being forced to sit across the table and negotiate, unassisted, with a spouse might be traumatic, their reaction has been almost uniformly dismissive. Some mediators have denied that this could possibly be the case. Even mediators who acknowledge the possibility of trauma have said, in effect, "So what?" A few hours of discomfort seems not so much to ask in return for a system that, to their mind, serves the courts and the children much better than the alternative. But a few hours of discomfort may not be all that is at stake; the trauma inflicted upon a vulnerable party during mediation can be as great as that which occurs in other psychologically violent confrontations. As such, it should not be minimized. People frequently take months or years to recover from physical or mental abuse, rape, and other traumatic events. Given the psychological vulnerability of people at the

281. [Robert] Cover, Violence and the Word, 95 Yale L.J. 1601, 1601 (1986).

time of a divorce, it is likely that some people may be similarly debilitated by a mandatory mediation process.

Moreover, because the mandatory mediation system is more problematic for women than for men, forcing unwilling women to take part in a process which involves much personal exposure sends a powerful social message: it is permissible to discount the real experience of women in the service of someone else's idea of what will be good for them, good for their children, or good for the system.

SARAH E. BURNS, NOTES FROM THE FIELD: A REPLY TO PROFESSOR COLKER

13 Harv.Women's L.J. 189, 193–195 (1990).

[At the time she wrote this article, Sarah E. Burns was Legal Director of the NOW Legal Defense and Education Fund and had extensive experience litigating women's rights cases at the trial, appellate, and United States Supreme Court levels. The excerpt is taken from a comment by Ms. Burns on an article by law professor Ruth Colker, entitled "Feminist Litigation: An Oxymoron?," 13 Harv. Women's L.J. 137 (1990), in which Professor Colker argued that feminist attorneys should consciously make use of feminist arguments and methods in their litigation practice.]

II. Feminist Litigation: What Is It?

In describing feminist litigation, Professor Colker mistakes feminine stereotypes—a gentleness that eschews fighting, a valuation of feeling, a concern for others and their relationships—as indicia of the truly "feminist." However, feminist litigation is not measured by its form, but rather is governed by its contribution to the larger feminist enterprise of transforming established social, economic, political, and legal power relations that work to the detriment of women.

Feminist litigation is not, and cannot be, as Professor Colker would have it, a dialogue. Litigation is a conflict between two or more adverse parties who seek to deploy the state's coercive power in favor of one party's interests over the interests of the other. The application or restraint of the force of the state is the direct result of litigation.

In some instances, litigation is necessary to avoid an application of state power in favor of a predetermined interest. In fact, virtually all of the litigation involving issues of sexual equality or reproductive rights has concerned efforts to alter a state-mandated outcome that works to the disadvantage of women. For example, Jane Roe was in court because Texas law coerced her either to undergo an unintended, financially and emotionally disastrous pregnancy or to obtain a legally and medically treacherous, expensive illegal abortion.[11]

11. See Jane Roe v. Henry Wade, 410 U.S. 113 (1973).

Feminist litigation appeals to the state to apply or restrain its power in a manner consistent with the aims of feminism. The common goal of all branches of feminism is to right the wrongs of sex-based oppression and transform society so that women have full and equal share of resources and opportunities. In the abortion context, feminist litigation concerns whether and to what extent the state, or others acting through the state's mechanisms, may coerce women to function as vessels for the fetus.

Feminism is rooted in the basic premise that liberty and equality are moral rights, whatever the similarities and differences between the sexes. Feminism is not necessarily an effort to make the world conform more to "women's ways" of doing things, although the increased inclusion and involvement of women as a result of feminist action may bring about such an end. Indeed, feminism may require us to note that differences among women may be great as may be the similarities between women and men. Thus, while it may inspire us to counteract the denigration of women, and the status and actions associated with women, feminism is neither necessarily a celebration nor a rejection of women's cultures and norms. It is, however, always a rejection of women's subjugation.

Feminists litigate not because we have some fondness for courts or a belief that courts provide a special haven for us, but because circumstances require us to be there or to be silenced. We know gender bias in court is a severe and widespread problem. We know that there are limitations on litigation's power to transform society. Given the exclusion from and subordination of women by the legislatures, we cannot avoid advocacy in the courts on some theory that courts are elitist and that elected branches, being majoritarian, are our proper venue. Indeed, suggestions that feminists should shy away from litigation reflect naiveté concerning how political outcomes are orchestrated by those with money and access to public opinion, who are generally not women. * * *

NOTES ON LAWYERING IN A DIFFERENT VOICE

1. What do you think of Menkel–Meadow's speculations about the ways in which women might change the structure of the law? See also Naomi R. Cahn, Styles of Lawyering, 43 Hastings L.J. 1039 (1992); Jennifer A. Freyer, Women Litigators in Search of a Care–Oriented Judicial System, 4 J. Gender & Law 199 (1995). Can you think of areas in which women might want to maintain adversarial approaches and formal procedures? What are they? Do you think the response of women of color to this question is likely to be different from that of other women? What would be the approach taken by a formal equality theorist, a dominance theorist, and a pragmatic feminist?

2. Rand Jack and Dana Crowley Jack, an attorney and a developmental psychologist, interviewed practicing attorneys about who they were, what they did, and what they thought about practicing law; they were interested, among other things, in whether women attorneys bring a different point of view to the practice of law and how they reconcile personal values with the conflicting demands of legal practice. Jack & Jack, Moral Vision and Professional

Decisions: The Changing Values of Women and Men Lawyers (1989). They described a number of different ways in which care-oriented women lawyers adjust to practicing law: (1) by emulating the "male" rights-oriented model and denying the relational self, subjugating personal concerns to demands of the professional role; (2) by "splitting the self" into a detached lawyer at work and the caring self at home; and (3) attempting to reshape the role of lawyer to conform with their personal morality. See id. at 130–51. One woman lawyer pursuing the third alternative, by designing her own domestic relations practice which reflected both her caring self and her feminist values, reported that the emotional toll was high. The authors concluded that "emotional vulnerability is one reason lawyers erect barriers of detachment and objectivity. The price of involved concern and the anxiety attached to caring may be more than they are able or willing to bear." Id. at 151. What are the advantages and disadvantages of the three paths described? Which path or approach do you think will achieve the most for women in the long run? In the short run? How would a formal equality theorist approach this question? A dominance/inequality theorist like MacKinnon? A pragmatic feminist? A relational feminist?

3. Can you think of ways to address the personal costs and potential burnout of being a caring lawyer without learning to adopt the stance of distance from one's client? Isn't this a problem law shares with other professions that involve caretaking roles, such as social workers and doctors? Can relationships among women practitioners play a role in addressing any of the problems women face in the practice of law?

4. Catharine MacKinnon has said that the role of a successful lawyer in our society is fundamentally a "male" role:

> Being a lawyer is also substantially more consistent with the content of the male role, with what men are taught to be in this society: ambitious, upwardly striving, capable of hostility, aggressive not just assertive, not particularly receptive or set off from the track of an argument by what someone else might be saying or, god forbid, feeling. It also requires one to be unserious. By this I mean what I think Virginia Woolf meant when she spoke of "unreal loyalties." Not being present in what you say in a way that might make you vulnerable, skilled at false and manipulative passion and manufactured intensity. The lawyer role has as its implicit norms the same qualities that are the explicit norms of masculinity as it is socially defined. It is a power role.

MacKinnon, On Exceptionality: Women as Women in Law, in Feminism Unmodified 74 (1987). If this is so, is there any way that women can feel comfortable as lawyers? Or is law, in the words of the Wisconsin Supreme Court which denied Lavinia Goodell's application for admission to the bar, simply too "selfish and malicious, knavish and criminal" a profession for women? In re Goodell, 39 Wis. 232, 245–46 (1875).

5. A number of writers, like Trina Grillo in the excerpt above, express concern about requiring mediation in the context of cases involving domestic violence. Domestic violence victims, in addition to their socialization to place the interests of other parties before their own, may also have been rendered passive by repeated and arbitrary beatings. Quite apart from the sheer

trauma of being forced to negotiate or participate in a mediation with her abuser, all of these factors may place an abused woman at a substantial disadvantage in the context of alternative dispute resolution (ADR). See, e.g., Lisa Lerman, Mediation of Wife Abuse Cases: The Adverse Impact of Informal Dispute Resolution on Women, 7 Harv.Women's L.J. 57 (1984); Robert Geffner & Mildred Pagelow, Mediation and Child Custody Issues in Abusive Relationships, 8 Behav. Sci. & Law 151, 152–53 (1990). Moreover, some studies have shown that battered women are more likely to be abused after mediation. Karla Fischer, Neil Vidmar & Rene Ellis, The Culture of Battering and the Role of Mediation in Domestic Violence Cases, 46 S.M.U. L. Rev. 2117, 2153 (1993) (citing study comparing repeated abuse to that occurring after a trial); Sarah Krieger, The Dangers of Mediation in Domestic Violence Cases, 8 Cardozo Women's L.J. 235, 252 (2002) (citing Dianne Post, Mediation Can Make Bad Worse, Nat'l L.J., June 8, 1002, at 2). But see Rene L. Rimelspach, Mediating Family Disputes in a World with Domestic Violence: How To Devise a Safe and Effective Court–Connected Mediation Program, 17 Ohio St. J. Disp. Resol. 95, 103 (2001) (reporting a lessening of incidents of abuse in a Canadian mediation project). Is there any way to ensure that mediation will take account of these and other power imbalances between the parties? Does it make any difference if it is mandatory or not?

6. California remains one of the only states with mandatory mediation, and the only one that allows no exemptions, although it does provide for separate meetings by the mediator with the parties and allows them to bring their attorneys if they wish. Alana Dunnigan, Restoring Power to the Powerless: The Need to Reform California's Mandatory Mediation for Victims of Domestic Violence, 37 U.S.F.L. Rev. 1031, 1036–37, 1043–44 (2003). Commentators have called for reform of the California mandatory system. Others believe that substantial reforms are necessary to make *any* system of mediation safe for victims of domestic violence. See, e.g., Rimelspach, note 5 above, at 104–10 (recommending pre-screening to eliminate inappropriate cases from mediation, private caucuses or telephone mediation, elaborate security measures and training for mediators, giving parties the ability to terminate mediation at any point, and judicial review of all agreements for fairness). Do you think that these measures, if taken, will address the concerns expressed in the Grillo excerpt above? If not, what do you think should be done? See Jane C. Murphy & Robert Rubinson, Domestic Violence and Mediation: Responding to the Challenges of Crafting Effective Screens, 39 Fam. L.Q. 53 (2005); Lauri Boxer–Macomber, Revising the Impact of California's Mandatory Custody Mediation Program on Victims of Domestic Violence Through a Feminist Positionality Lens, 15 St. Thomas l. Rev. 883 (2003).

7. How is negotiation different from mediation with respect to the potential for gender bias? In negotiation, either the parties or their attorneys bargain directly with one another, while in mediation a trained third party facilitates the discussion, often without attorneys present. Empirical studies of students in simulated negotiation exercises have not shown any statistically significant difference between the negotiating results achieved by men and women. See, e.g., Charles Craver, The Impact of Gender on Clinical Negotiating Achievement, 6 Ohio St. J. Disp. Resol. 1 (1990). See also Lloyd Burton et al., Feminist Theory, Professional Ethics, and Gender–Related Distinctions in

Attorney Negotiating Styles, 1991 J. Disp. Resol. 199 (based on surveys and interviews with practicing attorneys); Sandra R. Farber & Monica Rickenberg, Under–Confident Women and Over–Confident Men: Gender and Sense of Competence in a Simulated Negotiation, 11 Yale J. L. & Feminism 271, 292–93 (1999) (reporting that men and women had comparable outcomes although women felt less confident about their competence). Women may be more cooperative and less competitive in negotiation than are men. Amy E. Walters, Alice F. Stuhlmacher & Lia L. Meyer, Gender and Negotiator Competitiveness: A Meta–Analysis, 76 Org. Behav. & Human Decision Processes 1, 20 (1998). Recent literature has also tended to show that women negotiating on their *own* behalf do not achieve as favorable results as men with respect to salaries and automobile prices, either because they simply don't ask or are the subject of active discrimination. See Linda Babcock & Sara Laschever, Women Don't Ask: Negotiation and the Gender Divide (2003); Ian Ayres & Peter Siegelman, Race and Gender Discrimination in Bargaining for a New Car, 85 Am. Econ. Rev. 304 (1995). What are the implications of these findings for women as lawyers? As litigants?

8. Some commentators have argued that informal procedures such as mediation place persons of color at a disadvantage in general. Richard Delgado, Chris Dunn, Pamela Brown, Helena Lee & David Hubbert, Fairness and Formality: Minimizing the Risk of Prejudice in Alternative Dispute Resolution, 1985 Wis. L. Rev. 1359. Delgado et al. based this conclusion on social scientific studies that show that people who hold prejudiced attitudes are more likely to act on those attitudes in informal than in formal settings and suggest that ADR should be reserved for disputes in which the parties are of comparable status and power. Are there any ways to address these problems short of retreating to formal adversarial settings?

9. There are some indications that women may be systematically disadvantaged by mediation in substantive ways as well as those discussed by Trina Grillo in the excerpt above. For example, higher levels of joint custody result from mediation than from adjudication, apparently because mediators tend to push the concept. Jana B. Singer, The Privatization of Family Law, 1992 Wis. L. Rev. 1443, 1543–44; see also Elizabeth Ellen Gordon, What Role Does Gender Play in Mediation of Domestic Relations Cases?, 86 Judicature 134, 137 (2002–2003). Mediation theory also urges focusing upon the future, rather than upon a couple's past behavior. Singer, above, at 1544–45. How may women be disadvantaged by this fact? Finally, as Jana Singer points out, "mediation is touted most enthusiastically as a substitute for adjudication in precisely those areas—custody and visitation—where the prevailing legal standards are perceived to favor women." Id. at 1545. One Georgia study, however, reports no significant differences in the experience or evaluation of the procedures and outcome of their mediations by male and female participants in court-ordered mediation, where their attorneys were present. Gordon, above, at 137–42. Should we care if the outcomes were fair in the long run, so long as the participants are satisfied (and not traumatized by the experience)?

10. Who has the best of the Colker–Burns debate? In other words, is lawyering according to feminist principles in our current legal system like being a pacifist in a world of warriors? Is it suicidal not to fight with the

weapons other participants typically use in a legal system currently organized around adversarial, win-or-lose principles? Power and litigation involve the controlled use of violence, and the legal system is a monopoly. Hence, if "women's ways of doing" are not the ways things are done, is there any way to achieve change without sacrificing important individual and group battles along the way? On the other hand, can women ever change the way things are done if they simply adopt the methods by which the legal system has always proceeded; can they, in Audre Lorde's phrase, dismantle the master's house using the master's tools? Audre Lorde, The Master's Tools Will Never Dismantle The Master's House, in Sister Outsider: Essays and Speeches 110 (1984).

11. Are there any types of cases feminist lawyers should refuse to take? What are they? Are women attorneys who defend rapists being "used"? How can feminist attorneys who object to the traditional methods of courtroom defense (such as impugning the virtue of a rape victim) register their protest and reform the process? Is it possible to do so while actively representing defendants?

Is it ethical to represent only certain types of clients in divorce cases—or only one gender? See Joan Mahoney, Using Gender as a Basis of Client Selection: A Feminist Perspective, 20 W. New Eng. L. Rev. 79 (1998) (analyzing under different schools of feminist legal theory—equal treatment, radical feminism, and cultural feminism—a Massachusetts case in which a female attorney refused to represent a male divorce client).

CHAPTER 11

WOMEN AND THE STATE

■ ■ ■

A. INTRODUCTION

What do women want from the state? What should women expect from the state? The state has traditionally denied women many of the rights guaranteed to men and has given men power over women. Only in 1919 did women win the right to vote in all elections. At common law, husbands had total control of the property of their wives; married women had no rights to own, control, or use property and could not contract. Prior to recent reforms in some states, the state interpreted a marriage license as license to rape. To this day, social safety nets and a variety of legal rules, from the consent standard in rape to economic rules at divorce, protect men better than women.

On the other hand, women tend to have fewer resources, lower status, and less power than men of their class and race in "private" realms. It is often impossible for women to exert pressure for change within private institutions at more than a snail's pace. Women have, for example, been excluded from leadership in mainstream religious organizations and even today are allowed to be clergy only in the more liberal branches and are rare in the upper echelons even there. In education, business, and the professions, women are disproportionately at the bottom of the hierarchies. The media, arguably the most powerful institution in the United States today, is dominated by men. Sports, an arena of great cultural importance, is dominated by male heroes, coaches, and commentators. Men continue to have more power than women in families. Women have, therefore, often looked to the state for assistance in improving their well-being.

As a majority of voters today, women have the potential to use the state to force legal change and have sometimes been able to do so. Many institutions are more likely to change as a result of government intervention than as a result of women's attempts to change the balance of power by efforts entirely within the "private" sphere. For example, anti-discrimination laws applicable to private employers and educational institutions have increased considerably women's opportunities in employment, education, and school athletics. The Family and Medical Leave Act of 1993, mandating that employers with more than 50 employees give up to 12 weeks of unpaid leave during any 12 month period if a family member needs care, gives family leaves to more women than entirely "private" efforts have done to date. Although women's political power does not reflect women's majority status, it is often greater than women's power to change powerful private institutions, including market mechanisms.

This chapter explores a number of key issues related to the complex relationship of women and government. Three basic strategic questions are presented. First, is there a connection between the persistent inequality of women and the lack of supports for caregivers in the United States? Second, should women focus on increasing their share of government power and favor elimination of judicial limits on majoritarian processes? Third, how can women's share of political power be increased to reflect women's majority status?

We begin with the connection many feminists have come to see between persistent sex inequality and lack of public supports for caretakers. We then look at political equality, the extent to which women are present in governmental decisionmaking bodies in proportion to their presence in the population. We then turn to consider political reforms, beginning with insights from global feminism.

B. CARE AND EQUALITY: THE MISSING SAFETY NETS

We have a number of income support systems, the most important being Unemployment Insurance, Social Security Old–Age and Disability Insurance (Social Security), Temporary Assistance to Needy Families (TANF, which replaced Aid to Families with Dependent Children (AFDC)), and Supplemental Security Income (SSI). Two of these systems were designed for (male) breadwinners: Unemployment Insurance and Social Security. These are the premier American income support systems. Both are understood to be state-run insurance plans, though the extent to which Social Security can accurately be classified as a form of insurance, rather than a transfer of income from the young to the old, is questionable.[1] Nevertheless, beneficiaries of these systems are not perceived as the recipients of charity; they are collecting insurance proceeds. Beneficiaries do not have to prove that they are poor to qualify, and benefits are not based on need. In contrast, TANF is the descendant of Mothers' Aid programs which were designed to aid the "white impoverished widows of men like those eligible for Workmen's Compensation."[2] SSI was designed

1. For discussions of whether Social Security is an insurance or welfare system, see Nancy J. Altman, The Reconciliation of Retirement Security and Tax Policies: A Response to Professor Graetz, 136 U.Pa.L.Rev. 1419, 1424–32 (1988); William H. Simon, Rights and Redistribution in the Welfare System, 38 Stan.L.Rev. 1431, 1458–59 (1986).

2. Barbara J. Nelson, The Origins of the Two–Channel Welfare State: Workmen's Compensation and Mothers' Aid in Women, the State, and Welfare 123, 133 (Linda Gordon, ed. 1990). For additional discussion of these points, see Virginia Sapiro, The Gender Basis of American Social Policy, in Women, the State, and Welfare 36 (Linda Gordon, ed. 1990).

as a safety net for the aged and disabled who do not qualify for Social Security—people who were not successful breadwinners. Not surprisingly, most SSI recipients are women.

There are a number of ways in which the systems designed for successful breadwinners are better than the systems designed for mothers and others.[3] Both TANF and SSI are means-tested and perceived as forms of charity (or redistribution) rather than insurance. Income support levels are generally much lower for SSI and TANF (women's systems) than for Social Security and Unemployment Insurance (men's systems). For example, the maximum monthly TANF benefits for a family of three as of January, 2005, was $215 per month in Alabama, $704 per month in California, and $396 per month in Illinois.[4] In contrast, the average Unemployment Insurance benefit was $723.67 per month in Alabama, $940.33 per month in California, and $1213.33 per month in Illinois irrespective of need. The maximum Unemployment Insurance benefit was $910 per month in Alabama, $1603.33 per month in California, and $1412.67 to $1898 per month (depending on the number of dependents) in Illinois.[5]

Formal equality does apply to social insurance and welfare systems but only requires that similarly situated women and men be treated similarly.[6] Given the differences between most women and most men, it is easy to treat similar women and men identically, yet leave most women with inferior income protection. Formal equality does nothing about the fact that breadwinners have better safety nets than caretakers, including caretakers who also work for wages.

Although most women now work in the wage-labor force for much of their lives, Unemployment Insurance and Social Security continue to work better for men than for women. Unemployment Insurance offers unemployment benefits to eligible workers who lose their jobs through no fault of their own. Only 37% of unemployed men receive Unemployment Insurance, but even fewer—33%—of unemployed women do. There are two major problems. First, women workers who lose their jobs or are forced to quit for reasons associated with caretaking—such as childbirth or inability to find reliable childcare—are not usually eligible for benefits because

3. For early discussions of how safety nets for men are structured as social insurance whereas those for women are structured as welfare, see Nancy Fraser, Women, Welfare and The Politics of Need Interpretation, 2 Hypatia 103, 108–13 (1987); Barbara J. Nelson, Women's Poverty and Women's Citizenship: Some Political Consequences of Economic Marginality, 10 Signs 209, 221–23 (1984); Diana M. Pearce, Toil and Trouble: Women Workers and Unemployment Compensation, in Women and Poverty 141 (Barbara Gelpi, et al. eds. 1986). For a discussion of Unemployment Insurance problems from the perspective of women workers, see, e.g., Pearce, above, at 141.

4. National Center for Children in Poverty 2010, available at http://www.nccp.org/tools/policy/.

5. Staff of the U.S. House of Representatives Ways and Means Committee, Amount and Duration of Weekly Benefits for Total Employment Under the Regular State Programs, Table 4.5, in The Green Book, above note 4, at 4–16—4–17. Recent data is not available on both UI averages and TANF maximums for precisely the same period, so we have used January 2003 amounts for TANF and 2002 averages for UI.

6. See, for example, Califano v. Goldfarb, 430 U.S. 199 (1977).

their job loss is seen as the result of their own choice. Unemployment Insurance does not support leave for childbirth even though the FMLA (the Family and Medical Leave Act described in Chapter 7) gives slightly more than 50% of workers the right to 12 weeks of unpaid caretaking leave every year.[7]

The second major problem is that eligibility for Unemployment Insurance is based on earnings, rather than hours worked, with a relatively high minimum earnings requirement. As a result, many part-time and low-wage workers are not covered. And, disproportionately, women work for low-wages and/or on a part-time basis.[8]

In June of 2000 the Department of Labor issued regulations allowing states to use Unemployment Insurance to cover paid leaves for workers to care for infants and newly adopted children. In 2003, with no state yet implementing the program, the regulations were rescinded.[9] To date only six states afford any form of paid leave at childbirth, and these states do so through Temporary Disability Insurance programs not available in other states.[10] (These programs are described in more detail in Chapter 7.) While forty-three percent of women are able to utilize some form of paid leave during childbirth, just over half of them are able only to access unused vacation and sick days.[11] Most workers who take leave for family care cannot afford to take time off without pay, and nearly 10% of workers who have to take leave to care for family members must use welfare for support.[12]

Leave policies providing pay for childbirth and infant care (it is virtually impossible to find day care for an infant younger than three months) make it much easier to combine mothering and wage work; significantly more mothers return to work when paid leave is available. And 85% of Americans support paid leave to care for a new child or seriously ill family member.[13] With TANF severely limiting the availability of welfare for women between jobs, Unemployment Insurance coverage is more important than ever. California enacted a provision in 2002 providing all workers with six weeks of partially paid leave to care for a new child or seriously ill family member. Payments amount to 55% of wages. Washington State's Family Leave Insurance Law (S 5659), passed in 2007,

7. Vicky Lovell, Women and Unemployment: Better Check Your Insurance Coverage, Institute for Women's Policy Research, Quarterly Newsletter, Winter 2000, at 1, 3; Institute for Women's Policy Research, Fact Sheet: Paid Family and Medical Leave: Essential Support for Working Women and Men (Nov. 2000), available at http://www.iwpr.org/pdf/famlve2.pdf, (hereinafter Paid Family Leave Fact Sheet).

8. Lovell, above note 7, at 1, 3; Unemployment Insurance Fact Sheet, above note 7.

9. Labor Project for Working Families, Quarterly Newsletter, Winter 2004, available at http://www.laborproject.org/newsletter/winter04.html#bu.

10. Institute for Women's Policy Research, Maternity Leave in the United States Fact Sheet, August 2007, available at http://www.iwpr.org/pdf/parentalleaveA131.pdf.

11. National Partnership for Women and Families, Expecting Better: A State by State Analysis of Parental Leave Programs 9 (2005).

12. Id. at 7.

13. Id.

called for the creation of a Leave Insurance Program. This program would provide $250 per week for five weeks to full time workers to care for newborn or newly adopted children.[14]

Like Unemployment Insurance, Social Security is designed for workers without significant caretaking responsibilities, though it is particularly important for women, who are less likely than men to qualify for employer-provided pensions. But Social Security does a much better job of ensuring financial security in old age for men than for women. Benefits are based on earnings over a 35–year career, and the average man works 39 years. But the average woman works only 27 years, and her years without earnings severely depress her draw based on her own employment record when she retires. In addition, benefit levels are tied to wages, and thus are higher for men.[15] (Recall the discussion of the wage gap in Chapter 9.) The combination of lower wages and fewer years in the wage-labor market means that most married women draw benefits based not on their own earnings record, but as their husband's dependent spouse. For these couples, their Social Security benefits at retirement are calculated without any consideration of the wife's years working for wages; wives draw not a penny more than they would have had they never worked outside the home.[16]

Another problem is that in most divorces, the husband walks away with significantly better Social Security protection than the wife, though it would be easy enough to divide Social Security entitlements equally as they are earned during marriage. (This problem is described in more detail in Chapter 6.)

Poverty rates are the strongest evidence that safety nets protect men better than women (and children). Overall, 14.4% of women are poor, whereas 12.0% of men are poor.[17] But elderly women, particularly unmarried elderly women, and women heads of households with children—those most in need of safety nets—are poor at very high rates. Almost twice as many elderly (defined as age 65 and over) women (11.9%) than men (6.7%) are poor. For elderly women living alone, the rate is an astounding 20.4%. Black and Hispanic elderly women living alone have more than a one in three chance of being poor. For elderly black women living alone the poverty rate is 34.7%; for elderly Hispanic women living alone the poverty rate is 43.1%.[18] The overall rate of poverty for elderly women is has not changed much in the last fifteen years.[19]

14. Institute for Women's Policy Research, Maternity Leave in the United States Fact Sheet, August 2007, available at http://www.iwpr.org/pdf/parentalleaveA131.pdf.

15. Susan B. Garland, Making Social Security More Women–Friendly, Business Week, May 22, 2000, at 103.

16. Id.; Mary Becker, Obscuring the Struggle, 89 Colum. L. Rev. 264, 276–86 (1989); Karen C. Burke & Grayson M.P. McCouch, The Impact of Social Security Reform on Women's Economic Security, 16 N.Y.L. Sch. J. Hum. Rts. 375, 375–87 (1999).

17. US Census Bureau, Current Population Survey, 2009 Annual Social and Economic Supplement, 2009, available at http://www.census.gov/prod/2009pubs/p60–236.pdf.

18. U.S. Census Bureau, Current Population Survey, 2009 Annual Social and Economic Supplement, *Age and Sex of All People, Family Members and Unrelated Individuals Iterated by Income-to-Poverty Ratio and Race: 2008*)

Similarly, women living with children and without men are at particular risk, as Table 1 illustrates.

Table 1: Families Below Poverty Level by Selected Characteristics: 2007[20]

ALL FAMILIES	9.8%	HISPANIC FAMILIES<18	19.7 %
Married couple	4.9 %	Married couple	13.4 %
Male head only	28.3 %	Male head only	15.3 %
Female head only	13.6 %	Female head only	38.4 %
ANGLO[21] FAMILIES WITH	7.9 %		
Married couple	4.5 %		
Male head only	11.6 %		
Female head only	24.7%		
BLACK FAMILIES	22.1%		
Married couple	6.8 %		
Male head only	25.7 %		
Female head only	37.3 %		

Women heading households with children under 18, whether African American, Hispanic, or non-Hispanic white, are much more likely to be poor than married women and are also much more likely to be poor than single African American, Hispanic, or non-Hispanic white men heading households with children under 18.

After an unprecedented period of economic prosperity in the 1990's, when the overall poverty rate of 11.8% in 1999 was the lowest it had been in 20 years, the poverty rate rose steeply in 2008 to 13.2% after the country fell into a severe recession.[22] Similarly, while the poverty rate for children under 18 was 16.9% in 1999, the lowest rate of any year since 1979, this rate rose to 19.0% in 2008.[23] As Table 3 indicates, even before the 2008 recession hit, children living with single mothers faced a shockingly high risk of poverty, ranging from 22% *after cash transfers* (and before the effects of the stringent time limits for receipt of TANF benefits pinch[24]) for all such children to a rate of 27.3% for African American children and 28.3% for Hispanic children.

19. Cynthia V. Costello, Shari Miles & Anne J. Stone, The American Woman 1999–2000 104 (1998).

20. U.S. Census Bureau Table 700: Poverty Families Below Poverty Level by Selected Characteristics: 2007, available at http://www.census.gov/compendia/statab/cats/income_% 1F expenditures_poverty_wealth.html. See also http://www.census.gov/ hhes/www/macro/032008/pov/toc.htm>.

21. This entry is for non-Hispanic white families.

22. 2008 rate (13.2%) according to Census data, "first statistically significant annual increase in the poverty rate since 2004." (http://www.census.gov/hhes/www/poverty/poverty08/pov08hi.html).

23. US Census Bureau, Income, Poverty, and Health Insurance Coverage in the United States: 2008, available at http://www.census.gov/prod/2009pubs/p60–236.pdf.

24. Federal law requires that states limit benefits to a family to a total of two years at a time, with a lifetime limit of 5 years of benefits. The effects of these stringent limitations will not be

Persistent poverty in the United States is associated with an increasing gap between the rich and the poor in recent decades, as illustrated in Table 2.

Table 2: Selected Measures of Income Inequality 1967–2008 in 2008 CPI–U–RS adjusted dollars[25]

Measures of Income Inequality	2008	2003	1998	1993	1988	1975	1967
MEAN (AVERAGE) HOUSEHOLD INCOME BY QUINTILE**26**							
Top quintile (top 20%)	171,057	172,035	168,230	148,567	137,741	109,443	100,441
Second quintile	79,760	80,770	79,499	71,308	72,149	61,987	55,813
Third quintile	50,132	51,027	3,751,404	44,885	47,729	42,661	39,891
Fourth quintile	29,517	30,060	30,721	27,374	28,537	26,002	24,984
Fifth quintile	11,656	11,702	12,166	10,798	11,306	10,586	9,017
SHARES OF HOUSEHOLD INCOME BY QUINTILE**27**							
Top quintile (top 20%)	50.1%	49.4%	48.7%	46.6%	45.3%	43.2%	43.8%
Second quintile	23.2%	23.2%	23.3%	24.0%	24.6%	24.8%	24.2%
Third quintile	14.7%	14.9%	15.2%	15.9%	16.3%	17.1%	17.3%
Fourth quintile	8.7%	8.9%	9.1%	9.6%	9.7%	10.5%	10.8%
Fifth quintile	3.4%	3.6%	3.7%	3.9%	4.0%	4.4%	4.0%
Gini coefficient of income inequality**28**	0.466	0.457	0.450	0.428	0.419	0.397	0.399

Table 2 shows that income disparities have increased dramatically in the United States between 1967 and 2008. Although real household income for the top fifth of households rose by 70.31% (an increase of $70,616), income for the lowest 20% of households increased by 29.27% (an increase of $2,639). And household income for the middle quintile increased by 25.7% ($10,241).

When wealth is considered, disparities are even more startling. In 2001 the richest one percent of households owned 33.4% of the financial wealth of the country, and the richest 10% owned 71.5% of the wealth. The share owned by the wealthiest one percent in 2001 was almost identical to that in 1983, when they owned 33.8% of financial wealth, though it is lower than the 38.1% owned by the top one percent in 1998.[29] The temporary decline in this percentile's financial wealth ownership can likely be explained by the fact that these households had a much higher

known for several more years. Jason DeParle & Steven A. Holmes, A War on Poverty Subtly Linked to Race, N.Y. Times, Dec. 26, 2000, at A1, A16.

25. U.S. Census Bureau, Income, Poverty, and Health Insurance Coverage in the United States: 2008 (P1–74–229) 40 (Table A–3) (2009).

26. The next five rows give average household income for selected years for each quintile (one-fifth) of the population. The top quintile is the 20% of households with the highest incomes, and the bottom quintile is the 20% of households with the lowest incomes.

27. These figures report the percentage of total household income going to each quintile. Thus, in 2004, the 20% of families with the highest household income received 50.1% of total household income for all households.

28. A frequently used measure of income inequality which varies between one (absolute inequality: one person receives all income) and zero (perfect equality: everyone receives the same income).

29. Edward N. Wolff, International Perspectives on Household Wealth 113 (2006).

percentage of their financial wealth concentrated in stock ownership over a period when stock prices generally fell, whereas other percentiles had their financial wealth largely concentrated in the much stronger housing market over this period.[30] Almost all financial wealth is owned by whites. In 2001 the median[31] net financial wealth of Hispanic households was $200, and the figure for African American households was $1,100. For white households, the median was $42,100.[32]

Real income from 1984 to 2006 rose substantially for households headed by married couples with working wives, rising by $18,711 (based on median incomes, in 2006 dollars), or $30,284 (based on mean incomes, in 2006 dollars).[33] In contrast, for married couples with non-working wives, real income only rose by $2170 (based on median incomes, in constant 2006 dollars), or $14151 (based on mean incomes, in 2006 dollars) over the same period. For families headed by women, 2006 median income ($28,829) was also not much higher than median income in 1984 (23,664, in 2006 dollars)).[34] Thus, the increase in income to families over the last two decades has largely been the result of married women working more hours in the wage-labor market.

Children in the United States are at very high risk of being poor, particularly, as the data above suggests, if living with a single mother. This is true both before and after all cash and non-cash benefits under existing safety nets as Table 3 reports.

Table 3: Children in Poverty in the United States 2007[35]

	Prior to taxes but including cash benefits	After taxes and non cash benefits
ALL RACES[36]		
All children < 18	18.0%	12.0%
Children < 6	20.8%	14.4%
Living with single mother	30.7	22.0%
BLACK[37]		

30. Id. at 32.

31. Median household wealth refers to the wealth of a household that is half way between the highest in terms of household wealth and the lowest in terms of household wealth.

32. Wolff, above note 27, at 35–36.

33. U.S. Census Bureau, Historical Income Tables—Families, available at http://www.census.gov/hhes/www/income/histinc/f07ar.html.

34. U.S. Census Bureau, Historical Income Tables—Families, available at http://www.census.gov/hhes/www/income/histinc/f07ar.html.

35. U.S. Census Bureau, Alternative Measures of Income and Poverty, Table 2: Percent of Persons in Poverty, by Definition of Income and Selected Characteristics: 2007, available at http://www.census.gov/macro/032008/rdcall/2_001.htm.

36. Id., Table 2: Percent of Persons in Poverty, by Definition of Income and Selected Characteristics: 2007 (All Races), available at http://www.census.gov/macro/032008/rdcall/2_001.htm.

37. Id., Table 2: Percent of Persons in Poverty, by Definition of Income and Selected Characteristics: 2007 (Black Alone), available at http://www.census.gov/macro/032008/rdcall/2_006.htm.

	Prior to taxes but including cash benefits	After taxes and non cash benefits
All children < 18	34.5%	22.9%
Children < 6	40.8%	28.3%
Living with single mother	39.7%	27.3%
HISPANIC[38]		
All children < 18	28.6%	18.7%
Children < 6	31.2%	21.4%
Living with single mother	39.6%	28.3%
NON-HISPANIC WHITE[39]		
All children < 18	10.1%	7.0%
Children < 6	11.8%	8.4%
Living with single mother	21.4%	16.1%

Of families with children, 12.7% of white families were maintained by women alone in 2000 whereas 23.4% of Hispanic families and 44% of African American Families were maintained by women alone.[40] About 9.9% (as of 2008) of American children are not covered by any form of health insurance.[41]

Children in the United States are particularly likely, relative to children in other industrialized nations, to be living in households headed by single mothers. Not surprisingly, given this fact and the weakness of American safety nets for mothers and children, children are more likely to be poor in the United States than in other industrialized nations.

---

38. Id., Table 2: Percent of Persons in Poverty, by Definition of Income and Selected Characteristics: 2004 (Hispanic Origin), available at http://pubdb3.census.gov/macro/032005/rdcall/2_009.htm.

39. Id., Table 2: Percent of Persons in Poverty, by Definition of Income and Selected Characteristics: 2007 (White alone, not Hispanic), available at http://www.census.gov/macro/032008/rdcall/2_004.htm.

40. U.S. Census Bureau, Population Profile 16–3 (2000), available at http: //www.census.gov/population/pop-profile/2000/chap16.pdf.

41. *U.S. Census Bureau, Income, Poverty and Health Insurance Coverage in the United States: 2008, press release September 10, 2009, available at* http://www.census.gov/Press-Release/www/releases/archives/income_wealth/014227.html,. *Healthcare bill:* http://thomas.loc.gov/cgi-bin/query/z?c111:H.R.4872: Bill H.R. 4872

Table 4: Child Poverty Selected Industrial Nations 2007[42]

Country	Children living below national poverty lines
United States	21.7%
Italy	15.7%
United Kingdom	16.2%
Canada	13.6%
Australia	11.6%
Germany	10.9%
Netherlands	9.0%
France	7.3%
Sweden	3.6%
Denmark	2.4%

The disparity between poverty rates for women and men is also larger in the United States than in many other nations. A study comparing poverty rates for women and men in eight industrialized nations reports that the United States has the highest disparity between male and female poverty rates of any nation studied. In the United States 38% more women than men are poor, yielding a poverty ratio of 1.38 (women to men). By contrast, as Table 5 illustrates, women are *less* likely than men to be poor in Sweden (where only 73 women are poor for every 100 men). Of the industrialized nations in this study, with the exception of Australia, all have considerably better poverty ratios for women than the U.S. The Australian ratio is lower than that of the United States, but not nearly as low as the other countries studied. The findings of this study are summarized in Table 5.

Table 5: Poverty Ratios (Women to Men) in Selected Industrialized Countries After Cash Transfers[43]

Country	Poverty ratio (women to men)
Australia	1.30
Canada	1.13
France	1.11
Germany	1.18
Netherlands	1.14
Sweden	0.73
United Kingdom	1.20
United States	1.38

42. UNICEF Innocenti Research Centre, Report No. 7 Child Poverty in perspective: An Overview of Child Well-being in Rich Countries 2007, available at http://www.unicef-irc.org/publications/pdf/rc7_eng.pdf. Percentage of children living in poverty is defined as households with income below 50 percent of the national median income.

43. Karen Christopher, Paula England, Katherin Ross, Tim Smeeding & Sara McLanahan, Women's Poverty Relative to Men's in Affluent Nations: Single Motherhood and the State, Table 2 (2000).

Because people sharing a household are assumed to share income, a poverty ratio other than 1 (one poor woman for every poor man) reflects the extent to which women are not living with men. Women living in households without men are likely to be poor for three reasons. First, as discussed in Chapter 9, women earn less than men in the wage-labor market. Second, women living without a male partner are more likely than men living without a female partner to be living with and supporting children. And third, being a parent depresses women's wages, though not men's. Indeed, motherhood depresses women's earnings even after taking into account time off for child care. Men tend to earn more when they become fathers.

Feminist Arguments for Social Support of Caretaking

Many feminists from various disciplines have argued in recent years that the state should provide better support systems for caretakers and their dependents. Their positions are discussed more fully in Chapter 7. Here we briefly describe two forms of this argument.

Arguments Based on Morality and Equality

A number of feminists have made moral arguments for a social commitment to care for society's dependents and their caretakers and have seen such a commitment as essential to equality between the sexes. In Chapter 3, we described Robin West's argument for a politics centered on care and empathy rather than equality. Philosopher Eva Kittay emphasizes the link between acknowledging dependency and valuing caregiving, on the one hand, and equality for women, on the other:

> The call for sexual equality has been with us for a long time. But until relatively recently, the demands of even the most farsighted women have assumed very traditional and gendered arrangements of dependency work. Radical visions in which dependency work is taken out of the family have left many women cold—largely, I suggest, because they have failed to respect the importance of the dependency relationship. A view of society as consisting of nested dependencies, so constituted as to provide all with the means to achieve functioning that respects the freedom and relatedness of all citizens, is a view that can only emerge now, as women taste the fruits of an equality fashioned by men—and find it wanting. This equality has not left room for love's labors and love's laborers. It is time to shape a new vision by creating new theories and by forging the requisite political will. We need to revise our social and political commitment to ourselves as dependents and as dependency workers. Only through these efforts may we come to see what it means for men and women to share the world in equality.[44]

In her book, Care and Equality: Inventing A New Family Politics, political scientist Mona Harrington argues that care should be "a national political value":

44. Eva Kittay, Love's Labor: Essays on Women, Equality, and Dependency 188 (1999).

> The key idea for a new politics of family care * * * is to add care to the pantheon of national social values. That is, to assure good care to all members of the society should become a primary principle of our common life, along with the assurance of liberty, equality and justice.
>
> We need to elevate care to this level of importance for the basic reason that it is essential to human health and balanced development. It is also crucial to developing human moral potential, to instilling and reinforcing in an individual a sense of positive connection to others. And it is this sense of connection that makes possible the whole range of mutual responsibilities that allow the people of a society to respect and work toward common goals. As political theorist Joan Tronto puts it, thinking about care seriously, recognizing that everyone at different times is both a giver and receiver of care, underscores for people the fact of their personal and social interdependence. And, she says, this insight can enhance a commitment to the responsibilities of democratic citizenship.[45]

West's, Kittay's, and Harrington's arguments can all be seen as building on the work of Amartya Sen and Martha Nussbaum, who identify as the primary goal of government the creation of an environment in which each individual is given the ability to develop her or his capabilities for connections to others, autonomy, and competency.[46]

Arguments Based on Women's Production of a Public Good

Feminist lawyers and economists have also argued that women are disproportionately poor because their productive caretaking labor is under-or uncompensated. Although the costs of raising children and developing their capabilities are disproportionately borne by women, the whole society benefits from a new generation of capable workers, citizens, and taxpayers.[47]

Economists Paula England and Nancy Folbre begin with the proposition that women invest more in children in terms of both time and money than men do. Women have significantly increased their hours working in the market to support their families in recent decades, while men have only slightly increased their caretaking and household labor. Increasing numbers of families are headed by women who receive inadequate or no child support from absent fathers. At the same time, it has become increasingly costly to develop the capabilities of children as education becomes increasingly important for economic success and the costs of college rise. According to England and Folbre, "[t]hat many other traditional obstacles to gender inequality have been overturned means that

45. Mona Harrington, Care and Equality: Inventing a New Family Politics 48–49 (1999) (citing Joan Tronto, Moral Boundaries: A Political Argument for an Ethic of Care (1993) (arguing for recognition of care as a basic element of political morality)).

46. Amartya Sen, Capability and Well Being, in The Quality of Life 30 (Martha C. Nussbaum & Amartya Sen, eds. 1993); Martha C. Nussbaum, Sex and Social Justice 39–47 (1999).

47. In addition to the work discussed in the text making this argument, see Martha Albertson Fineman, Cracking the Foundational Myths: Independence, Autonomy, and Self-Sufficiency, 8 Am.U.J. Gender, Soc. Pol'y, & L. 13 (2000).

parental responsibilities loom large as a current cause of lower earnings and restrictions on career advancement for women."[48] They point out, as Table 4 indicates, that children in the United States are more likely to be poor than in most other industrialized countries and "[p]arents in general and mothers in particular remain highly susceptible to poverty in the United States."[49]

Traditionally, economists have viewed children as a consumption item; adults have children because the benefits they derive from doing so outweigh the costs. England and Folbre characterize this as the "children-as-pets approach."[50] But children raised in an environment allowing them to develop their capabilities benefit society as a whole, not just their caretakers. They actually pay into Social Security the money used to support the elderly population, yet Social Security benefits are calculated without regard to whether recipients have invested in children.[51] We also benefit personally from the caretaking work of others; we have spouses, friends, neighbors, employers, employees, and coworkers who have been raised by others.[52]

In short, children are a "public good," that is, a benefit to the general society like a good defense system or good roads.[53] Yet society as a whole pays less than 38% of the costs of raising children. Instead, the costs are disproportionately borne by individual women who are, for that reason, more likely to be poor. Further, when children are raised by caretakers without the assets needed in today's society to develop their children's capabilities, too little is invested. Better supports would be economically efficient in the long term, though not the short term. And better supports would distribute to all taxpayers the costs of the benefits they enjoy as a result of others raising children. As this suggests, adequate supports for children and their caretakers should be seen as a long-term investment in the future, one that should be publicly supported to avoid free riders (those able to enjoy the benefits of a public good without paying the costs).[54]

Although this argument uses economic analysis to demonstrate that children are a value to society as a whole, and their costs should therefore not be borne disproportionately by a group likely to be poor because of their caretaking of children, proponents do not mean to imply that economic factors should dominate decisions and relationships within the

48. Paula England & Nancy Folbre, The Silent Crisis in U.S. Child Care: Who Should Pay for the Kids?, 563 Annals 194, 197 (1999). See generally Nancy Folbre, Who Pays for the Kids?: Gender and the Structures of Constraint (1994).

49. Id.

50. Id.

51. Id. at 198–201.

52. Nancy Folbre, Children as Public Goods, 84 Am. Econ. Rev. 86, 87–88 (1994).

53. See England & Folbre, above note 46, at 195 ("Economists define a public good as one that is difficult to put a price on because it is nonexcludable (someone can enjoy it without paying for it) and nonrival (one person can enjoy it without diminishing someone else's enjoyment of it.").

54. Id. at 201–04.

family. Rather, they simply mean to point out "the economic consequences of the organization of family life, which has become increasingly costly for women in the United States over time."[55]

England and Folbre point to France as one of the European countries which "impose higher taxes on the entire working-age population to defray the costs of child care."[56] Such policies, they note, can be thought of as a loan from the current generation of workers to the next, to be repaid through taxes on income earned as adults. We turn next to consider the programs supporting children and their caretakers in France.

Supports for Families

In France, many supports are available to all parents and children regardless of income. Free nursery schools are available for children (regardless of whether the mother works) from the time they are toilet trained (about 2½ years) until they enter first grade. Parents who use private centers receive cash benefits and tax breaks. When mothers of younger children work, the government heavily subsidizes placements in day care centers.[57]

France and several other continental European countries combine somewhat shorter periods of paid leave with dual systems of public child care (for the under–3s) and preschool (from 3 until school age). In the French policy package, mothers are entitled to 16 weeks of paid leave at the birth of first and second children (26 weeks at the birth of subsequent children), with 100–percent wage replacement; fathers have a right to 11 days of paid paternity leave. French parents are also entitled to share three years of job-protected parental leave with low flat-rate benefits. Leave benefits are coupled with a dual system of early child care and later public preschool. About 20 percent of children aged 1 and 2 attend a public crèche or other subsidized care; from the ages of 2 1/2 to 3, children are entitled to a place in free public preschools (écoles maternelles), and nearly all children attend. Quality standards are set by national policy and curricula, and teachers in French écoles have the equivalent of graduate training in early education and earn wages that are above the average for all employed women.[58]

All education is free in France, from nursery school through university. And "supervised recreational programs for school-age children for the

55. Id. at 196.

56. Id.

57. Barbara R. Bergmann, Saving Our Children from Poverty: What the United States Can Learn From France 27–41 (1996). Subsidies for care of infants and toddlers vary with income level. In 1991, a family with a monthly income under $681 and one child would pay the equivalent of $4.15 per day for care of an infant or young toddler; such a family would pay the equivalent of $3.38 per day per child for two children in such care. A family with a monthly income of $1,286 would pay $7.68 and $6.45, respectively. A family with a monthly income of $2,496 would pay $15.21 and $12.60. Id., at 40 (Table 3.7).

58. Marcia K. Meyers & Janet C. Gornik, The European Model: What we can learn from how other nations support families that work, American Prospect Magazine, Nov. 2004.

after-school hours, and during summers and school vacations, subsidized by the government, are common."[59]

The French government also provides a supplement that allows a parent to either reduce or stop his/her employment in order to look after a child. In 2009, a supplement of $693.60 (554.88 Euros) per month was given to a parent who ceased to work and a supplement of $527.41(421.93 Euros) per month was given to a parent who worked less than 50%. For the first child, the supplement is paid for six months, and for any additional children, the supplement is paid until the child's third birthday.[60] Handicapped children also receive an additional allowance independent of family income. In 2009, a base allowance for a severely disabled child under 20 years of age was $155.68 (124.54 Euros) a month. Depending upon the incapacity of the child, supplements are also available and range from $116.76 (93.41 Euros) per month to $1286.38(1,029.10 Euros) per month.[61]

For mothers who temporarily leave work after the birth of a child, cash benefits are paid by the local Sickness Insurance Funds, and in 2006 were "equal to the insured person's basic daily wages after deduction of the employee's share of all legal social contributions."[62] In France, all families are covered by national health insurance.[63]

Finally, caretaking is made easier by the fact that the French, like other Europeans, work significantly fewer hours per year than do Americans. Many American workers receive only 10 paid vacation days a year. In Europe, including France, the norm is at least four to six paid weeks of vacation. In 2008, workers in the United States averaged 44 hours per week, compared to the French who worked only 37.55 hours per week.[64] Thus, the French worker works an average of 5.99 fewer hours per week.

Moreover, the gap between men's and women's pay is smaller in France than in the United States: In the United States, full-time year-round wage-earning women earn an average of $0.77 for every dollar earned by similar men, but full-time year-round wage-earning women in France earn about $0.88 for every $1.00 earned by such men.[65]

---

59. Bergmann, above note 57, at 28.

60. Centre of European and International Liaisons for Social Security (CLEISS), The French Social Security System, III. Family Benefits, available at http://www.cleiss.fr/docs/regimes/regime_france/an_3.html.

61. Id.

62. Id.

63. Id.

64. International Labour Organization, Bureau of Statistics' Databases, LABORSTA Internet, Yearly Data of Total and Economically Active Population, Employment, Unemployment, Hours of Work, Wages, Labour Cost, Consumer Price Indices, Occupational Injuries, Strikes and Lockouts: 1969–2008, Table 4A: Hours of work, by economic activity, available at http://laborsta.ilo.org/STP/guest.

65. American data found at http://www.infoplease.com/ipa/A0882775.html. French data found at http://ec.europa.eu/employment_social/social_situation/socsit_en.htm#2005–2006.

Under France's Social Security Code, families with two or more children are entitled to a family allowance. In 2009 families with two children received $155 (124 Euros) per month, families with three children received $352.5 (282 Euros) per month plus $198.75 (159 Euros) per month for each additional child. The single-parent's allowance ensures that a single parent (unmarried, widowed, divorced, or deserted) receives a minimum income. Under the single-parent allowance, a single parent with one dependent child receives $972.5 (778 Euros) per month plus $235 (188 Euros) per month for each additional child.[66]

All of these state-provided subsidies for child raising have two important effects:

1. By working, even at a minimum wage job, parents who work can pull their families out of poverty. Good supports provide no disincentive to work in France, because families remain poor unless parents work, but can rise above the poverty level if parents work.
2. Many of the supports needed by poor families are either available to all families or to all but wealthy families. Because these supports are available to all or most families, they are broadly supported.

BARBARA R. BERGMANN, SAVING OUR CHILDREN FROM POVERTY: WHAT THE UNITED STATES CAN LEARN FROM FRANCE

117–19 (1996).

How are we to design and pay for a system of programs in the United States that would enable more families to live above the poverty line? * * * French programs accomplish this by giving a great deal of help to parents who hold low-paying jobs. In order to do that, the French spend heavily in three areas: providing child care, providing health care, and providing income supplements, including help with rent. * * * [G]overnment help with child care and health insurance, covered by vouchers rather than by cash grants, are the necessary ingredients for protecting American children from deprivation.

Any system of programs will reflect the values of those devising the system. Many Americans put heavy weight on discouraging births outside of marriage and getting single parents to take jobs. The aim of reducing child poverty in the short and medium run goes largely unmentioned in the debate on reforming American welfare. On the other hand, many of those on the right appear willing to adopt policies that would increase child deprivation in the short run, on the ground that treating single parents harshly will teach them and others not to produce more children destined to be poor.

The French clearly put the greatest weight on keeping all children out of deprivation and do not put a great deal of emphasis on reducing

66. Europa European Alliance for Families, Country profiles: France, available at http://ec.europa.eu/employment_social/emplweb/families/index.cfm?id=4&policyId=78&langId=en&countryId=5. Europe to US Dollar conversion based on $1.25= 1 Euro.

improvident births. In fact, most of the components of their child welfare system were constructed with French-born married couples in mind, in the apparently vain hope that they would be induced to have more children. The unmarried are eligible for all of these pronatally motivated benefits, which—if they have an effect on births to unwed couples—might be expected to increase rather than reduce such births. On the other hand, increasing the labor force participation of single mothers, as these benefits do, may have a negative effect on the number of children they have, since women in jobs generally desire fewer children than those who do not. As we have seen, birthrates outside marriage are very similar in France and the United States, suggesting that the more generous benefits to single parents in France have not resulted in a flood of children to unmarried couples. Nonetheless, an American system more like the French one might not discourage births as effectively as would reduced benefits, promoted by U.S. politicians on the right. A system along French lines would provide a single mother who has low labor-market skills with an option she does not have under the present system—she and her children could live above the poverty line, provided she works for pay.

Even though the French system has achieved both low child-poverty rates and relatively high job-holding among single parents, would it work in the United States, with its very different history and culture? The fact is, the basic needs of families in the two countries are not at all different. Whether they live in France or the United States, preschool children must be cared for—by parents, by other family members, or by paid nonrelatives. Good child care is expensive to buy or provide in both countries. American children, like French children, have health-care needs, which are met or not met depending on their access to care. Whatever the incentives parents have to take jobs, there will be parents in both countries with low wages or no wages. Even if child care and medical care are provided, such children live in families that need financial help to purchase sufficient food, clothing, and shelter.

What is different in the two countries is not children's needs, but the sense of public responsibility for the welfare of the nation's children, the feelings of generosity toward those who are poor, the willingness to pay taxes, racial antipathies, the proportion of public funds devoted to armaments, the degree of faith in the government's ability to deliver effective and high-quality programs, and beliefs about the importance and means of limiting "dysfunctional" behavior, such as births to unmarried teenage mothers. These attitudinal differences do not preclude the design of an effective American program to fight child poverty, but they do create roadblocks to the acceptance of such a program.

While the unsatisfactory state of current American programs for health care and income supplementation is well known, the child-care issue has only recently been recognized as an important component in solving the problem of child poverty. Critical to the argument that follows is the idea that health care and good-quality child care are "big-ticket items," and that most of the jobs open to women on welfare will not provide them as fringe benefits or, alternatively, do not pay high enough wages to enable their purchase.

CAN WE AFFORD IT?

Another crucial roadblock in the way of a large-scale government program to reduce child poverty is the idea that, given the current budgetary situation, the United States cannot afford to spend more on social welfare programs, even those that would be of high value. But "cannot afford" has two quite different meanings: it can mean literally financially impossible or imprudent, or it can mean that the desire to purchase the item in question is not strong enough to warrant restructuring one's budget.

A program that would provide child care and health insurance for lower-and middle-income families could be financed by a modest rearrangement of the budget. When the politicians are saying (and the citizens are echoing) that we "cannot afford" to spend more on such programs, they are playing a word game—pretending to use the phrase in its "imprudence" sense, rather than in its "insufficient desire" sense. No politician wants to say that we have better things to do with our resources than mobilizing them to improve child welfare in this country (through higher taxes, or reducing other expenditures, or borrowing). By all measures, the United States is an extremely wealthy country, and one of the least taxed in the developed world. Saying that we "cannot afford" the programs simply rings hollow in light of our country's vast resources.

The example of France, a country very like ours, and with somewhat fewer resources than we have at our disposal, shows that the "can't afford it" rationale for continuing to tolerate widespread child poverty is one that deserves questioning. Certainly, it is possible that the French programs, and the heavy taxes that support them, detract somewhat from economic performance and raise unemployment rates. Nevertheless, the French example should prompt us to ask whether it would be worth sacrificing some aspects of high economic performance in favor of reducing the child poverty rate approaching one in four to a rate of one in eighteen, as the French have done.

A costly and activist program is the only way we will be able to make progress against child poverty. We cannot create, through government policy or moral suasion or religious revival, a society in which single mothers and their children will not need some help. We are unlikely to move anytime soon to a situation where all or almost all children are born to married couples, where almost all marriages last until death, and where all children have parents who earn enough to support them adequately. Such an alternative is closed to us, at least as the expected outcome of any series of actions by the government. If we are to make a serious attempt to design a government program to rescue millions of poor children whose predicament "cannot be countenanced by a wealthy nation, a caring people, or a prudent society," we must choose from the alternatives that are available to us. The passage of such a program must await the time when we have a president who can effectively frame and forward the required agenda, a time when generosity toward the "have-nots" is greater, and when antigovernment rhetoric has been overcome by an even more obvious need for action.

NOTES ON CARE AND EQUALITY

1. In 2010 President Obama passed comprehensive healthcare reform legislation which will guarantee health insurance coverage for children and will automatically increase coverage for adults. How do you think such coverage will affect the lives of women and children in particular? Is it likely to help diminish the economic separation between women and men?

2. Do you agree that caregiving is a moral act? If it is a moral act, should caretaking be its own reward? Many caretakers enjoy their work and love those for whom they care. Shouldn't the compensations associated with enjoying the work you do for those you love be sufficient? What are the strongest arguments for better public supports of caregivers? What are the strongest arguments against?

3. Do you agree with Kittay, Harrington, West, and others that women cannot attain equality without more social support for caretakers? What, if anything, do you see as the links between caretaking and inequality between the sexes?

4. Is valuing caretaking and supporting caregivers generally seen as an important aspect of social justice or gender equality in philosophy, political science, or constitutional law courses, ordinary politics, or the culture at large? If not, why do you think this is so? What do you see as the major obstacle to better public support for caretaking in the United States?

5. Are women full citizens today? Are caretakers full citizens? What does full citizenship mean to you?

6. What, if anything, do you see as the links between caretaking and inequalities based on race and class? Do you see inadequate support for paid and unpaid caretakers and caretaking as linked to race and class inequality as well as sex inequality? How would poor or minority women be affected by better supports for caretakers, particularly those who work as caretakers in their own families and in other women's families?

7. What do you think of England and Folbre's economic argument for support of children and their caretakers? Is it dangerous because it encourages us to view children in economic terms? Or is it necessary because caretaking *is* productive labor, though it is seldom viewed as such?

8. What reforms of Social Security might be appropriate from the perspective of England and Folbre's analysis? Social Security, though seen as an insurance scheme, with each worker earning benefits for himself and his dependents, is actually a pyramid scheme, with younger generations paying benefits to older generations and a considerable amount of redistribution. Should women receive Social Security credits for each year they live with a child under 18? Would such a change be constitutional? Would it raise equal protection problems?

Some reform proposals have suggested that unemployed workers (mostly women) with children under the age of six receive some sort of Social Security credit. Other reform ideas would give partial credits to part-time workers (mostly women) with older children. Current proposals for such credits would not help most women, however, since even with these reforms (the proposed credits are not large) they would be better off drawing Social Security benefits as their husband's dependents rather than on their own Social Security account. Moreover, many women work full time *and* care for children. How could Social Security be adjusted to credit their disproportional contributions to the capabilities of those who will actually be supporting the elderly? Can you think of Social Security reforms that would be effective and constitutional?

9. Nancy C. Staudt has argued that women's unpaid caretaking and domestic work should be subject to income and payroll taxes, thus earning Social Security credits. Staudt, Taxing Housework, 84 Geo. L.J. 1571 (1996). Is this a solution? Could it be structured to give extra credits to mothers who are working full-time for wages *and* investing disproportionally in their children's capabilities? If it were so structured, would it be constitutional? Do you see other problems?

10. In September of 2000, the Center for Policy Alternatives and Lifetime Television published the results of a national poll on women's concerns. The poll showed very high levels of support for (1) policies making it easier to combine caretaking and wage work, such as shorter working hours and flexible time; (2) job-independent health care; (3) equal pay and retirement security; and (4) greater availability of affordable quality child care. According to the published findings, 59% of mothers with children under six reported that it is harder to balance the demands of family and work than it was four years earlier. Women were also concerned about the growing economic gap between the rich and the poor and supported an increase in the minimum wage. Center for Policy Alternatives and Lifetime Television, Women's Voices 2000: The Most Comprehensive Polling and Research Project on Women's Values and Policy Priorities for the Economy 14, 18, 19, 26–29, 32 (2000). Why haven't women, a majority group, been more successful in demanding the kind of changes suggested by these poll results?

11. How would the various feminist theories in Chapter 3 approach the issue of the missing safety nets? Would all of them see the system of current safety nets as problematic? Which theoretical approaches would place the need for better safety nets for women and children high on their agenda? Which would not place better safety nets anywhere on their agenda?

C. POLITICAL EQUALITY IN THE UNITED STATES

Although women are a majority of citizens and voters, women are not, and have never been, present in elective office in numbers that reflect these facts. Since 1975, women's numbers in elective office have been increasing. But the numbers remain low relative to the number of women in the population and relative to the one third that many women in politics regard as the critical mass necessary to make a difference in legislative bodies. When diversity is considered in terms of both race *and* sex, the picture of who is in government is even more unlike the picture of the governed.

Executive Branches

Although Hillary Rodham Clinton ran a close race in 2008, and was long considered the frontrunner, no woman has been President or Vice President of the United States. In 2010, there were five female governors out of 50. Of the other 315 statewide elected officials, including lieutenant governors, state attorneys general, treasurers, and secretaries of state, 72 (22.9%) were women, down from 89 (32.6%) prior to the 2000 election.[67] Of the 72 female statewide elected officials including governor, seven were women of color.[68]

Legislative Branches

It is extremely difficult to get information about the racial composition of state legislatures, but such information is available about Congress. Tables 6 and 7 demonstrate the overwhelming overrepresentation of white men relative to their numbers in the general population and the underrepresentation of women of all colors and other African, Asian, Hispanic, and Native American citizens in Congress. Non–Hispanic white men have more than twice their share of political power in both the House and the Senate. Indeed, non-Hispanic white men are only 36.9% of the general population but nearly 80% of the Senate.

Table 6: Voices in the United States Congress 2010[69]

	% Population (2000)[70]	% House	% Senate
Non–Hispanic white men	36.9%	68.0%	79%
Women of all colors	20.7%	3.5%	17.0%
Black & African American men	12.3%	6.2%	1.0%
Hispanic American men	12.5%	5.1%	1.0%
Asian American men	2.3%	1.4%	2.0%
Native American men	0.9%	0.2%	0%

67. National Foundation for Women Legislators, "Women in Elective Office 2010 Fact Sheet", 2010, available at http://www.womenlegislators.org/women-legislator-facts.php.

68. CAWP, Fact Sheet: Women of Color in Elective Office 2010, available at http://www.cawp.rutgers.edu/fast_facts/levels_of_office/documents/color.pdf.

69. Women's data is from CAWP, Fact Sheet: Women in the U.S. House of Representatives 2010, available at http://www.cawp.rutgers.edu/fast_facts/levels_of_office/documents/house. pdf. Men's data is from Mildred Amer, Membership of the 111th Congress: A Profile (Feb. 4, 2010), available at http://www.fas.org/sgp/crs/misc/R40086.pdf.

70. General population numbers and population data on race are from Census 2000 Demographic Profile Highlights, U.S. Census Bureau American FactFinder Fact Sheet, available at http://factfinder.census.gov. Population numbers represent those people who indicated only one race in the Census 2000 survey.

Table 7: Women in the United States Congress 2010[71]

	% Population (2000)[72]	% House	% Senate
All Women %	16.8%	17.0%	
Non–Hispanic white women	38.3%	12.0%	17.0%
Black & African American women	2.8%	%	0.0%
Hispanic American women	6.1%	1.4%	0.0%
Asian American women	0.7%	0.3%	0.0%
Native American women	0.0%	0.0%	0.0%

Only one woman of color has ever been a member of the Senate, Carol Moseley Braun, who served from 1992–1998.

Overall, women are present in state legislatures in higher proportions than in Congress. Table 8 gives the proportions of women in color in state legislative bodies alongside their percentage in the population. Table 9 gives the overall proportions of women in the five states with the highest percentage of women in the state legislature and the five states with the lowest percentage. Women are present in the five state legislatures with the fewest women in even smaller percentages than they are in Congress.

Table 8: Women in State Legislatures 2010[73]

	% Population (2000)[74]	% State Legislatures
All Women	50.9%	24.4%
Non–Hispanic White women	38.3%	18.4%
Black & African American Women	6.5%	4.7%
Hispanic American Women	6.1%	0.9%
Asian American Women	0.4%	0.3%
Native American Women	0.3%	0.1%

71. CAWP, Fact Sheet: Women in the U.S. House of Representatives 2010, available at http://www.cawp.rutgers.edu/fast_facts/levels_of_office/documents/house.pdf.

72. Census 2000 Demographic Profile Highlights, U.S. Census Bureau American FactFinder Fact Sheet, available at http://factfinder.census.gov/.

73. CAWP Women of Color in Elective Office 2010, available at http://www.cawp.rutgers.edu/fast_facts/levels_of_office/documents/color.pdf.

74. Census 2000 Demographic Profile Highlights, U.S. Census Bureau American FactFinder Fact Sheet, available at http://factfinder.census.gov/.

Table 9: States with the Highest and Lowest Percentages of Women in Their Legislatures 2009[75]

HIGHEST STATES	% women	LOWEST STATES	% women
New Hampshire	37.3%	South Carolina	10.0%
Vermont	37.2%	Oklahoma	11.4%
Colorado	37.0%	Alabama	12.1 %
Minnesota	34.8 %	Mississippi	14.4 %
Nevada	31.7%	Pennsylvania	14.6%

NOTES ON POLITICAL EQUALITY

1. Why might it matter that women of all colors and other members of minority groups are underrepresented in positions as governmental decision-makers? Would only an "essentialist" (i.e., someone who believes that differences between women and men or between various racial groups are innate and universal) see a need for more women of all colors and members of other minority groups in government? In the context of representation in legislatures, Anne Phillips argues that "any system that claims to be democratic should be able to ensure that its representatives mirror the ethnic and sexual composition of the population," though at the same time she maintains that "these representatives should not then be viewed as 'representing' their ethnic group or their sex." She believes that it would be "profoundly *un*democratic if women representatives were considered to be speaking only or even mainly for women, particularly when there are no substantial mechanisms for establishing what their 'constituents' support." Anne Phillips, Engendering Democracy 155–56 (1991). Despite this reservation, Phillips believes it is necessary to adopt "procedures [such as quotas] that will ensure a more balanced result," i.e., procedures that will ensure that those represented mirror the sex of the population. Id. at 151–52. Do you agree with any of these points? Is Phillips necessarily inconsistent in advocating adequate representation of women by women, as judged by the numbers, and *also* insisting that women representatives should not be seen as speaking only or mainly for women? Could (and should) similar points be made about members of racial minorities?

2. Do you think that people who have been primary caretakers of dependents are likely to be underrepresented as elected officials? Why? Why might it matter that primary caretakers are underrepresented in elective office?

3. A number of reasons have been given for women's underrepresentation in elected office. In some states, party bosses and political culture are barriers. Sex role socialization may inhibit women from seeking careers in politics, and women's family responsibilities may limit their participation. Bias against women on the part of voters may be another problem. The fact that most incumbents are men is a major problem. Incumbents have a

75. National Conference of State Legislatures, Women in State Legislatures: 2009 State Legislation, 2009, available at http://www.ncsl.org/default.aspx?tabid=15398.

tremendous advantage in an election, and in recent years women have been as likely to win as men once incumbency and other factors are considered. As will be discussed in greater detail below, the American electoral system is also part of the problem, since women tend to do less well with single-member winner-take-all electoral schemes than schemes using some form of proportional representation. For a discussion of these possible explanations, see Janet Clark, Getting There: Women in Political Office, 515 Annals 63 (May, 1991). Clark ends with the problem of power and prestige:

> Finally, the power and prestige of the political office also seem to be factors in determining the level of representation of women. That is, the more desirable the office and/or the greater the competition for the office, the less likely that women will be well represented. In legislatures that are large relative to the population represented, women have more seats. Also the degree of the professionalism of the legislature determines the relative representation of women. In legislatures where the members sit full-time, receive a relatively large salary, and hold greater prestige, there will be fewer women. The hypothesis that the level of competitiveness and prestige of the legislative body affects the number of women in office seems to be confirmed by the fact that there are more women in local and state offices than in national offices. Also, even at the same level of government, women have been more likely to be elected in places where the office is considered less desirable.

Id. at 75. The higher the position, whether in government, religion, industry, education, etc., the less likely it is that a woman will hold it. What do you think explains the dwindling number of women as one ascends any hierarchy?

4. Do you think—perhaps because of socialization or perhaps because of genetic differences—that women are less likely to run for public office because they are less competitive and have less confidence (or perhaps less arrogance)? Senator Susan Collins of Maine describes a conversation among Democratic and Republican women Senators: "At one dinner we were talking about all the men running for president—a lot of them Senators—and here we were, nine women Senators, and not a single one of us thinks of herself as president." Collins continues:

> That's got to be gender-related. I remember Lynn Martin speaking at a women's Campaign Fund event saying a man who sells Toyotas thinks he's an expert in international trade while a woman thinks she needs a Ph.D. in economics before she can comment. We went down the list of men who were running, and they weren't more experienced or more capable. They have a confidence, or is it an arrogance? I don't know what it is. We got up to about a dozen Senators, both sides of the aisle. We laughed about it, but the essential truth of it struck all of us.

Eleanor Clift & Tom Brazatis, Madam President: Shattering the Last Glass Ceiling 132 (2000). This is a description of the *women in the United States Senate*, nine of the most powerful women in the world. And *they* feel lacking in confidence (arrogance?) relative to their colleagues. Do you think this is part of the problem for women in politics, particularly with respect to higher positions? What are the underlying causes? Might testosterone give men an edge in competition for high positions? In a controversial essay, Andrew

Sullivan argued, based on his own experience with testosterone injections, that testosterone explains some of the persistent inequities between the sexes, especially in high-risk professions, such as "the military, contact sports, hazardous exploration, venture capitalism, politics, gambling." Sullivan, The He Hormone, N.Y. Times Magazine, Apr. 2, 2000, at 47, 69. Whatever its source, what can be done to overcome this aspect of the problem?

5. Do you think that there is continued bias against women running for office, particularly high office? Can you think of media reactions to women candidates that would not have occurred had the candidate been a man? Can you think of voter reactions to women candidates that would not have occurred had the candidate been a man? Is it, for example, as easy for a woman as a man to appear to be an authority on military and international affairs? Do you think these issues played a role in Hillary Rodham Clinton's 2008 Presidential campaign? Describe the kind of woman you think is likely to be the first woman president. What constraints would she face? See Clift & Brazatis, note 4 above (discussing many problems). Are women, for example, more likely to be seen as "too" ambitious than male candidates for high office? Soft on defense? Too liberal on spending for social welfare?

6. A woman politician is expected to have children, but is also expected to be their primary caretaker. Women who have run for office with small children or while pregnant face a double bind: trying to appear capable of devoting the necessary time to the job *and* trying to appear to be good mothers. To date, most women have avoided this dilemma by entering politics about ten years later than men, when their children are no longer young. See Clark, above note 3, at 72; Clift & Brazatis, above note 4, at 143–61, 212–27, 255–59. How can we offset the structural disadvantages caretakers face?

7. In recent elections women who run have had as much chance of winning *open* seats (seats without an incumbent) as men. Part of the problem with women's continuing underrepresentation is that so few women run. Part of the explanation may be that fewer women are asked to run: 90% of men who run have been asked to run by party leaders and activists, whereas only 30% of women who run have been asked. See Clift & Brazatis, above note 4, at 305. Have you ever considered running for the House of Representatives or the United States Senate? What would deter you? Are the things which would deter you in any way linked to being a woman or a man? Compare your responses with those of others in your class.

8. Can you think of advantages men who are simply voters (not candidates for office) might have over women with respect to political power? See Karen Burns, Kay Hehman Schlozman & Sidney Verba, The Public Consequences of Private Inequality: Family Life and Citizen Participation, 91 Am. Poli. Sci. Rev. 373, 373 (1997) (considering political power of husbands and wives in light of domestic inequalities and concluding that husbands have more power than would be expected on the basis of their other characteristics because of their "control over major financial decisions and autonomy in using small amounts of time").

TEXT NOTE: WOMEN MAKE A DIFFERENCE

The Center for American Women and Politics (CAWP) at the Eagleton Institute of Politics at Rutgers has done a series of important empirical studies of women in government, asking whether women make a difference.[76] They have consistently found that, in fact, women do make a difference whether as members of the executive, judicial, or legislative branches. Two of these studies looked at women in legislatures during the late 1980's and the 1990's. The first surveyed and interviewed women and men in state legislatures in 1988. This study found that, independent of party and ideology, women are more likely than men to support and work on issues important to women. For example, 76% of liberal women (but only 67% of liberal men) were working on women's rights bills; 58% of moderate women (but only 35% of moderate men) were working on such bills; 39% of conservative women (but only 26% of conservative men) were working on such bills. Note that *conservative* women tend to be more committed to women's issues than *moderate* men. African American women were especially likely to be working on women's bills: 85% of African American women legislators (but only 57% of white women legislators) were working on such bills. Id. at 40–41. Non-feminist women were only slightly less likely (46%) than feminist men (49%) to be working on women's rights bills. In contrast, 73% of feminist women were working on such bills, as were 34% of non-feminist men.[77]

A second study looks at women in the 103rd Congress (1993–95). This was an unusual term. The numbers of women in Congress rose dramatically in the 1992 elections for a number of reasons. One factor was the unusually high number of open seats. Another was that the 1992 election followed the hearings over Clarence Thomas' nomination to the Supreme Court. At the hearings, Anita Hill testified—before an all-male Senate Judiciary Committee—that Thomas had repeatedly harassed her sexually when he was her boss at the EEOC. A number of Senators on the Committee brutally attacked Hill, enraging and mobilizing many women. In the next election, women were determined to make the Senate less of a boys' club. The number of women in the Senate increased in the 1992 election from 2 (2%) to 6 (6%), a threefold increase. And the number of women in the House increased from 28 (6.4%) to 47 (10.8%). Altogether the number of women in Congress almost doubled in a single election. Not coincidentally, this is the Congress that enacted the Violence Against Women Act (VAWA) which we looked at in Chapter 4.[78]

The CAWP study on women in Congress found that, like women in state legislatures, women in Congress were more likely to support and work on

---

76. In addition to the studies described in the text, see Gender and Policymaking: Studies of Women in Office (Debra L. Dodson, ed., CAWP 1991) (an analysis of a number of studies of women in executive, judicial, and executive positions which concludes that across the board, women make a difference). See also John Gruhl, Cassia Spohn & Susan Welch, Women as Policymakers: The Case of Trial Judges, 25 Am.J.Pol.Sci. 308 (1981); Alison Morris, Women, Crime and Criminal Justice (1987).

77. Debra L. Dodson & Susan J. Carroll, Reshaping the Agenda: Women in State Legislatures 38–47 (CAWP 1991).

78. Debra L. Dodson, Susan J. Carroll, Ruth B. Mandel, Katherine E. Kleeman, Ronnee Schreiber & Debra Liebowitz, Voices, Views, Votes: The Impact of Women in the 103rd Congress 2–3 (CAWP 1993).

causes important to women than were their male colleagues, as illustrated by the following table:

Table 10: Selected Votes of Male and Female House Members in the 103rd Congress[79]

	Republican Men	Republican Women	Democratic Men	Democratic Women
For Crime Bill (including VAWA)]	23%	67%	72%	89%
For Assault Weapons Ban	19%	58%	66%	91%
For FACE Conference Report (access to abortion clinics)	20%	75%	80%	97%
For Brady Bill (gun control)	30%	67%	70%	89%
Against Amendment to Ask Recruits if Gay, Bisexual	32%	67%	87%	100%
For Family and Medical Leave Act	21%	50%	87%	100%
Against Hyde Amendment (no federal funds for abortions for poor women)	6%	50%	58%	86%
Against Version of Don't Ask, Don't Tell	6%	17%	41%	78%

Women's presence was, however, far more important than simply the numbers of votes they were able to cast on issues important to women:

> Women members of Congress can influence the nature of the debate, the policy agenda, or the content of bills, women can also influence the face of legislation by blocking a bill in committee, extricating bills from committee, forcing a vote on a bill, participating in a "whipping" plan to muster votes, holding press conferences to influence public perception of a bill, meeting with leadership to express a collective point of view, or getting added to a bill certain provisions their male colleagues might not have considered. Women in the 103rd Congress took all these steps, thereby exerting important influences in addition to any impact to be discerned through analysis of their voting behavior of bill sponsorship.[80]

Congresswomen in the 103rd Congress felt a special responsibility to represent women. Congressman Nydia Velazquez (D–NY) describes this commitment:

> Before I came here, I worked for a Congressman. And while I worked for him, I saw that women's issues were not part of the national agenda. And that is ... true today. It hasn't changed. So it is our responsibility to participate in every single issue that we have here, and every debate that we have here, but I understand that if we don't force others to focus on women's issues, then it will not be a part of the debate. And that is a responsibility that all of us share, especially women.[81]

And, in the words of Congresswoman Nancy Johnson (R–CT):

---

79. Id. at 9.

80. Id. at 9–10.

81. Id. at 15.

> We need to integrate the perspective of women into the policy-making process, just as we have now successfully integrated the perspective of environmental preservation, the perspective of worker safety.... Now, whenever something comes up, we automatically think, "Gee, how will this affect the environment? How will this affect the working people at the work site?" But we don't really think, "How is this going to affect women who work at home? Women in the workplace with home responsibilities? Women who are single parents?" And I do feel a special responsibility to participate in the public policy process in a way that assures that where something is going to affect women as well as men, that I think through how will this affect women who are at home taking care of children who need to re-enter the work force later on? How does this affect women who didn't get to go beyond high school because their family thought that only boys should go to college, and now they're stuck? I know a lot more about the shape of women's lives and the pattern of women's lives, so I need to look and see how the public policy will affect those patterns, and how it will help or hurt.[82]

Although no woman served as chair of a committee in the 103rd Congress, the report concludes:

> Women members made a difference in the 103rd Congress. The voices, views and votes of the female Representatives and Senators who served from 1993 to 1995 made themselves heard and felt in the legislative debate and in the legislation passed. Even though they were a mere one-tenth of the membership, and slightly more than half of them were freshmen, the Congresswomen found ways to have an impact within an institution in which women's perspectives have seldom been recognized and where more senior and better positioned (almost always male) members often dominate.[83]

NOTES ON WOMEN IN OFFICE

1. Are you surprised that women in Congress believe that if they don't raise issues important to women, no one does? Do you think that this assessment is likely to be accurate? Why or why not?

2. If you are a woman, would you feel a responsibility to represent women if you were in elected office? Why or why not? If you are a man, would you see any need to think particularly about women's needs, interests, and the effect of proposed legislation on women? Why or why not?

3. Would you give an edge to a woman candidate in deciding for whom to vote? For example, if you are pro-choice and consider that a top priority item, would you be more likely to vote for a moderate pro-choice women over a moderate pro-choice man with similar credentials? Why? Do the men and women in your class answer these questions differently?

---

82. Id. at 15–16.

83. Id. at 24.

D. GLOBAL FEMINISM AND EQUALITY

For many American women, the Convention on the Elimination of All Forms of Discrimination Against Women (CEDAW)[84] has been their first introduction to global feminism. Many have worked for adoption of CEDAW by the United States and by various local entities, such as cities and counties within the United States.

CEDAW was adopted by the General Assembly of the United Nations on December 18, 1979, and is the only comprehensive treaty on human rights for women. It defines sex discrimination broadly as "any distinction, exclusion, or restriction, made on the basis of sex which has the effect or purpose of impairing or nullifying the recognition, enjoyment or exercise by women of human rights and fundamental freedoms in the political, economic, social, cultural, civil or any other field."[85] CEDAW requires that States Parties take positive steps to eliminate all forms of discrimination against women. Article 3 provides:

> States Parties shall take in all fields, in particular in the political, social, economic and cultural fields, all appropriate measures, including legislation, to ensure the full development and advancement of women, for the purpose of guaranteeing them the exercise and enjoyment of human rights and fundamental freedoms on a basis of equality with men.[86]

Indeed, States Parties are obligated "[t]o modify the social and cultural patterns of conduct of men and women, with a view to achieving the elimination of prejudices and customary and all other practices which are based on the idea of the inferiority or the superiority of either of the sexes or on stereotyped roles for men and women."[87]

CEDAW has important provisions for working women. It requires a comparable worth standard for pay inequities[88] and paid maternity leave or comparable social benefits.[89] And CEDAW requires States Parties "[t]o encourage the provision of the necessary supporting social services to enable parents to combine family obligations with work responsibilities and participation in public life, in particular through promoting the establishment and development of a network of child-care facilities."[90]

President Carter submitted CEDAW to the Senate for ratification in 1980, but the accompanying report from the State Department indicated that many reservations were necessary and the Senate "took no action."[91]

---

84. Convention on the Elimination of All Forms of Discrimination Against Women, 1249 U.N.T.S. 13 (1981) (hereinafter CEDAW).

85. Id. Art. 1.

86. Id. Art. 3.

87. Id. Art. 5(a).

88. Id. Art. 11, § 1(d).

89. Id. Art. 11, § 2(b).

90. Id. Art. 11, § 2(c).

91. Malvina Halberstam, United States Ratification of the Convention on the Elimination of All Forms of Discrimination Against Women, 31 Geo. Wash. J. Int'l L. & Econ. 49, 54 (1997).

In 1994, President Clinton urged Senate ratification but "with four reservations, three understandings, and two declarations."[92] After hearings, the Senate Foreign Relations Committee recommended ratification of the Convention subject to the reservation, understandings, and declarations suggested by the Clinton Administration together with an additional understanding added by Senator Helms. Again no action was taken by the Senate.[93]

Reservations, understandings, and declarations function as objections to certain treaty provisions or interpretations enabling a signatory nation to bind itself only to those parts of the treaty with which it agrees. Indeed, the United States reservations, declarations, and understandings as specified by the Senate Foreign Relations Committee were designed to ensure that if enacted, CEDAW would have absolutely no effect whatsoever within the United States. In addition, as with most other human rights treaties, the United States would have included a declaration that withheld agreement to jurisdiction of an international tribunal.[94] And the treaty would not have been self-executing, i.e., would not become part of United States law unless separately enacted.[95]

In September of 2000, Saudi Arabia became the 166th nation to bind itself to the treaty.[96] Among the nations that have not ratified CEDAW, in addition to the United States, are Afghanistan, North Korea, Iran, and Sudan. The United States does not, of course, publicly admit opposition to women's rights. Rather, it insists that American law adequately protects women's rights. But, as we have seen, the American approach denies women important rights common elsewhere and needed by American women. For example, throughout Europe, women have the right to paid maternity leave and a right not to be fired during pregnancy or maternity leave for any pregnancy-related reason (such as being unable to work).[97] Women in the United States have only the right, as indicated earlier, to a short unpaid leave and can be fired while pregnant for, e.g., being late for work because of morning sickness.[98]

92. Id. at 55.

93. Id.

94. Id. at 60.

95. Louis Henkin, U.S. Ratification of Human Rights Conventions: The Ghost of Senator Bricker, 89 Am. J. Int'l L. 341, 347–48 (1995).

96. See http:www.un.org/womenwatch/daw/cedaw/states.htm.

97. See Case C–394/96, Brown v. Rentokil, [1998] ECR I–4185 (1998) (under European Union law, an employer cannot fire an employee during pregnancy or maternity leave for any reason connected to pregnancy, such as inability to do the job because of pregnancy-related disability) (excerpt in Chapter 9).

98. See, e.g., In Re Carnegie Center Associates, 129 F.3d 290 (3d Cir. 1997) (holding that it was not pregnancy discrimination for employer to fire the secretary on maternity leave rather than, e.g., the one with least seniority or the lowest job evaluations, when a reduction in force was necessary) (excerpt in Chapter 9); Troupe v. May Department Stores Co., 20 F.3d 734 (7th Cir. 1994) (not pregnancy discrimination for employer to fire pregnant worker on the day before she was to go on maternity leave even though supervisor told her she was being fired because employer thought she would not return to work; employee had been tardy or left early a number of times during pregnancy because of morning sickness) (excerpt in Chapter 9).

Gender Mainstreaming

American notions on women's rights are also quite different from emerging international standards in the political arena. CEDAW Article 7 provides:

> States Parties shall take all appropriate measures to eliminate discrimination against women in the political and public life of the country and, in particular, shall ensure to women, on equal terms with men, the right:
>
> (a) To vote in all elections and public referenda and to be eligible for election to all publicly elected bodies;
>
> (b) To participate in the formulation of government policy and the implementation thereof and to hold public office and perform all public functions at all levels of government;
>
> (c) To participate in non-governmental organizations and associations concerned with the public and political life of the country.

This may sound consistent with American notions that women cannot be formally excluded from political participation, but section b in particular has a much thicker meaning in the context of international women's rights. It is an expression of the political goal of the international women's movement: gender mainstreaming, which means the involvement of women at all levels of governmental policymaking and implementation in appropriate numbers (according to their presence in the population) to ensure that women's interests, needs, and concerns are taken into account consistently and throughout the process of governmental policy making and implementation.[99]

A new international norm for democratic legitimacy is emerging: a democracy is legitimate only if women participate at all levels of government in proportion to their presence in the population. Quotas to ensure women's presence in elected office at appropriate levels are seen as an appropriate means to ensure democratic legitimacy. Thus, electoral quotas for women have become an increasingly important part of the international feminist agenda. The Platform for Action of the Fourth World Conference on Women in Beijing in 1994 included the following explanation of the importance of equality in governmental decisionmaking:

> Equality in political decision-making performs a leverage function without which it is highly unlikely that a real integration of the equality dimension in government policy-making is feasible. In this respect, women's equal participation in political life plays a pivotal role in the general process of the advancement of women. Women's equal participation in decision-making is not only a demand for simple justice or democracy but can also be seen as a necessary condition for women's interests to be taken into account. Without the active participation of women and the incorporation of women's perspectives

99. Fourth World Conference on Women, Platform for Action and the Beijing Declaration at 111 (1996) (Platform for Action Strategic Objective G.189).

at all levels of decision-making, the goals of equality, development and peace cannot be achieved.[100]

The goal, as noted earlier, is "gender-mainstreaming":

> In addressing the inequality between men and women in the sharing of power and decision-making at all levels, Governments and other actors should promote an active and visible policy of mainstreaming a gender perspective in all policies and programs so that before decisions are taken, an analysis is made of the effects on women and men, respectively.[101]

The Beijing platform for action explicitly calls for governments to use "positive measures" to correct the "low proportion of women among economic and political decision makers at the local, national, regional and international levels."[102] Governments are to "[t]ake measures, including, where appropriate, in electoral systems that encourage political parties to integrate women in elective and non-elective public positions in the same proportion and at the same levels as men."[103] When appropriate, electoral systems are to be reformed to increase women's representation,[104] and governments are to "[a]im at gender balance in the lists of national candidates nominated for election."[105]

The Council of Europe, a broader (and looser) organization than the European Union and the organization behind the European Convention on Human Rights, supports gender mainstreaming and stresses the importance of having women in 50% of all governmental decisionmaking positions for democratic legitimacy. For example, at the Fourth European Ministerial Conference of the Council of Europe on Equality between Women and Men in November of 1997, the Ministers of the Council of Europe issued a Declaration on Equality between Women and Men as a Fundamental Criterion of Democracy.[106] It recommends gender balance at all levels of governmental decisionmaking and encourages assessment and reform of electoral systems to facilitate the integration of women in proportional numbers at all levels.

The European Union is also taking actions in support of gender mainstreaming. In July of 2000, the Commission of the European Community submitted a proposal to the Council of the European Union, the European Parliament, the Economic and Social Committee, and the Committee of the Regions laying out a "Community framework strategy on gender equality."[107] This proposal identifies as the goal of equality "an

100. Id. at 109 (Platform for Action Strategic Objective G.181).

101. Id. at 111 (Platform for Action Strategic Objective G.189).

102. Id. (Platform for Action Strategic Objective G.186).

103. Id. at 112 (Platform for Action Strategic Objective G.1.190(b)).

104. Id. (Platform for Action Strategic Objective G.1.190(d)).

105. Id. (Platform for Action Strategic Objective G.1.190(j)).

106. Council of Europe, Declaration on Equality between Women and Men as a Fundamental Criterion of Democracy (1997).

107. Communication from the Commission to the Council, The European Parliament, The Economic and Social Committee and the Committee of the Regions, Towards a Community Framework Strategy on Gender Equality 2001–2005 at 2–3, 7–9 (2000) (2000/0143 (CNS)).

inclusive democracy." Such a political structure "requires that all citizens women and men alike * * * participate and be represented equally in the economy, in decision-making, and in social, cultural and civil life." The goal is gender mainstreaming: to ensure that "[w]omen's concerns, needs, and aspirations be taken into account and assume the same importance as men's concerns in the design and implementation of policies." One of the five areas of focus is "promoting equal participation and political representation" in all areas of decisionmaking. The Commission acknowledges that the "persistent under-representation of women in all areas of decision making marks a fundamental democratic deficit which requires Community level action." Among other things, the Commission suggests an assessment of the influence of electoral systems, legislation, quotas, targets and other measures on gender balance in elected political bodies." The goal of this and other European Commission and Council actions related to political representation of women is to see women participate as 50% of the decisionmakers throughout the Union, whether the decision-making body is a local commission or a major institution of the Union.

The United States does not do well when compared, as Table 11 does, with other countries in terms of the presence of women in the country's highest legislative body. Indeed, with a ranking of 73, there are 72 countries around the world in which women are represented in the highest legislative body in higher numbers.

Table 11: Women in the National Legislatures of the Countries in the European Union, Canada, and the United States

As Ranked by the Inter–Parliamentary Union[108]

Rank	Country	Lower or Single House			Upper House		
		Seats	Women	% Women	Seats	Women	% Women
1	Rwanda (party quotas)	80	45	56.3%	26	9	34.6%
2	Sweden (party quotas)[109]	349	162	46.4%%	—	—	—
3	Costa Rica (party quotas)	57	22	38.6%	—	—	—
8	Norway (party quotas)	169	67	39.6	—	—	—
7	Finland (party quotas)	200	80	40.0%	—	—	—
12	Denmark (party quotas)	179	68	38.0%	—	—	—
6	Netherlands (party quotas)	150	63	42.0	75	26	34.7%

108. Rankings of the Inter–Parliamentary Union were current as of February 28, 2010, and include every country in the world (not all of which are included in the table in text, which includes only the countries of the European Union, Canada, and the United States), available at www.ipu.org/wmn-e/classif.htm.

109. The five leading parties require that women and men alternate on party lists. Liane Hansen (anchor), Women From Around the World Look For Ways to Increase Their Numbers in Elected Positions and Leadership Roles, National Public Radio, Weekend Edition, June 11, 2000 (reporter Margot Adler speaking) (hereinafter NPR, Women Around the World).

		Seats	Women	% Women	Seats	Women	% Women
12	Belgium	150	57	38.0%	71	29	40.8%
27	Austria (quota law)	183	51	27.9%	61	18	29.5%
17	Germany (party quotas)[110]	622	204	32.8	69	15	21.7%
26	Switzerland	200	58	29.0%	46	10	21.7%
59	Luxembourg (party quota in 1997)[111]	60	12	20.0%	—	—	—
30	Portugal (quota law unconstitutional)[112]	230	63	27.4%	—	—	—
49	Canada (party quota or other system)	308	68	22.1 %	93	32	34.4 %
61	United Kingdom[113]	646	126	19.5%	733	147	20.1%
73	United States (party quotas)[114]	435	73	16.8%	100	15	15%
77	Ireland (quota law unconstitutional)[115]	166	22	13.3%	60	10	16.7%
79	Greece (quota law for next election)	300	39	13.0%	—	—	—
85	France[116]	574	70	12.2%	331	56	16.9%

The European countries with highest proportions of women in their parliaments have both proportional representation systems *and* some sort of formal quota system either by law or party rule.

Proportional Representation

Most of the countries of the European Union—indeed, almost all the countries of the world—have some form of proportional representation. All the countries of Europe (including the United Kingdom) elect their representatives to the European Parliament by a proportional representation scheme. It has been obvious for some time that women and minority

110. The Social Democratic Party of Germany requires that 40% of candidates on party lists be women. Id.; Voters Should Count on Women, Toronto Star, Apr. 27, 2000.

111. Each party has either quotas or a system favoring women candidates.

112. NPR, Women Around the World, above note 109 (Jane Kramer, reporter for the New Yorker, speaking).

113. In 1997, Tony Blair set a quota of 50% women for Labor candidates running for open seats in Parliament, and the number of women in the House of Commons increased from 63 to 122, sweeping Blair and the Labor party into office. Alexander MacLeod, After Gains, British Women Frustrated with Politics, The Christian Science Monitor, June 27, 2000, at 7; Voters Should Count on Women, Toronto Star, Apr. 27, 2000.

114. One hundred seventy-six countries are included in the ranking. Other countries above the United States in the ranking are: Iceland, New Zealand, Mozambique, South Africa, Bosnia and Herzegovina, Venezuela, Cuba, Grenada, Argentina, Turkmenistan, Viet Nam, Namibia, Seychelles. Australia, Monaco, China, Lao People's Democratic Republic, Croatia, Democratic People's Republic of Korea, Costa Rica, Guyana, Uganda, Estonia, Lithuania, Rwanda, Botswana, Latvia, United Republic of Tanzania, Dominican Republic, Angola, Bahamas, Czech Republic, Tajikistan, Eritrea, Ecuador, Burundi, Slovakia, Jamaica, Saint Kitts and Nevis, San Marino, and Poland.

115. In Ireland, only three of the six major parties have quotas, some as low as 20%.

116. Id. (host Liane Hansen speaking); Lara Marlowe, Jospin's Wife Beats Her Own Drum, The Irish Times, Oct. 25, 2000, at 12.

groups do better at winning elected office under proportional representation systems than under winner-take-all geographic districts, the most common electoral structure in the United States.

In the simplest proportional representation scheme, votes are cast for parties. Before the election, the party publishes a list of the people who are running for that party in each district. Thus, for example, an electoral district might elect 10 representatives to the legislature, and each voter casts one vote for one party, say the Green, Red, or Orange Party. If the Green Party gets 60% of the vote, then the first 6 candidates on its list go to the legislature. If the Red Party gets 30% of the vote, the first 3 candidates on its list go to the legislature. And if the Orange Party receives 10% of the vote, the first candidate on its list goes to the legislature.

There are many variations on proportional representation, and several allow votes for individual candidates, thus maximizing accountability of those in office, who must win reelection on the basis of their personal record as well as their party's. Cumulative voting in modified at-large schemes is one such system. Under a cumulative voting at-large system, voters vote for particular candidates. But voters, not politicians determine how individuals combine into groups for purposes of representation—provided that each electoral district has at least five seats. In a district with five seats, each voter would receive five votes, which can be cast in any way desired among the candidates: a voter could cast one vote for each of five candidates or five votes for a single candidate. (Empirical studies have shown that as long as districts have at least five seats with this scheme, how the politicians draw district lines has no effect on representation in the legislature. Women do best in districts with seven to ten seats.)[117]

By contrast, winner-take-all systems base representation on geographic units drawn up by politicians. Geographic districting *can* create effective democracies in countries with homogeneous populations.[118] The majoritarian systems of England and the United States may have worked fairly well at the time they were designed. In America, at the time the republic was founded, the franchise was limited to a relatively homogenous population: propertied men of European descent. But winner-take-all single-member districts make it difficult for individuals with views that are in the minority to have any voice in policy. Under a proportional representation scheme, minority views are more likely to be represented in the legislative body. And proportional representation schemes facilitate the election of women of all colors and other members of minority groups. Thus, proportional representation schemes facilitate the representation of

117. Douglas J. Amy, Real Choices/New Voices: The Case for Proportional Representation Elections in the United States 51–53, 110–11 (1993).

118. Lani Guinier, Lift Every Voice: Turning a Civil Rights Setback Into a New Vision of Social Justice 256 (1998); Arend Lijphart, Democracies: Patterns of Majoritarian and Consensus Government in Twenty-One Countries 3–4 (1984).

the entire population, not just the people who form a majority in each district.

In a plurality system, like that in United States, parties can be reluctant to nominate a woman lest she lose to a male competitor. Party leaders may hate to deny the candidacy to a man who has been active in the party and who wants to run. And since there is only one candidate in a district, the party cannot balance the ticket nor appeal to a broader group of voters by backing a diverse set of candidates within the district. In a proportional representation system, a woman runs as part of a group, and this can be perceived by party leaders as a less risky strategy. In addition, the party has an incentive to include diverse candidates on its slate in order to appeal to diverse voters within the district. The list of party candidates can be balanced to represent various interests within the party, including not just women but members of other minority groups or of other identifiable party constituencies. Because it is easier for parties in a proportional representation system to field a diverse set of candidates, parties in such systems are also more susceptible to diversification pressure when other parties diversify their slates.

Not surprisingly, of the four countries with the lowest percentages of women in the lower houses of their national legislative bodies in a study of sixteen Western democracies, three have winner-take-all single-member district electoral systems inherited from feudal England (Canada, Great Britain, and the United States).[119]

Quotas for Women Candidates

Not only did the European countries with the highest proportions of women in their parliaments have proportional representation systems, rather than winner-take-all single-member districts, they also had adopted a quota system ensuring that a certain proportion of those elected would be women. The five countries with the highest proportions of women in their national parliament—Sweden, Denmark, Finland, Norway, and the Netherlands all had party quotas, as did Germany, the country ranked sixteenth. The party rules vary from country to country and, in some countries, from party to party. In Sweden, the five major parties have internal rules requiring that men's and women's names alternate on the party list for proportional representation. In Germany the Social Democratic party has a 40% quota for women on its lists of candidates.

The French Experience

The percentage of women in the French parliament lagged significantly behind the level of representation of women in a number of the other countries in the European Union. French women did not obtain the vote until 1944. In 1945, France changed from a majoritarian electoral system to a proportional representation system, but returned to a majoritarian

119. Amy, above note 117, at 103 (Table 5.1).

scheme in 1958.[120] By the 1990's, France was 71st in terms of representation of women, by 2010, France had dropped to 65th as indicated in Table 11. Women served as only 18.9% of the lower house of the French Parliament and as 21.9% of the upper house. Sweden, ranked first among the European countries, had 46.4% women in its parliament.

Part of the problem for French women is that France has an electoral system much like that in the United States: single-member winner-take-all districts. France adds one variation: to win in one round, a candidate must receive a majority of the votes cast; to advance to the second round (when one is necessary), a candidate must receive at least 12.5% of registered (not actual) voters. The person who gets the most votes on the second round wins.

In France, women responded to the low levels of women in parliament with a movement for "parité," which gained momentum in the late 1980's and 1990's, as the combination of proportional representation and quotas increased the level of women's participation in other European parliaments to levels much, much higher than those in France. The Parité Movement pushed for a quota to be enacted by the overwhelmingly male parliament—and succeeded. The Movement published lists of men against Parité, and women voted against them. Within two to three years, 80% of voters supported Parité.[121]

The French Parité Movement began with a constitutional amendment in 1999 because the Italian and Portuguese Supreme Courts had struck quotas as unconstitutional.[122] In May, 2000, the French legislature passed a statute implementing Parité by requiring that every party's political slate must include as many women as men or lose its government-provided campaign financing. The effectiveness of the French Parité Movement can be seen in Table 12. On *this* list, unlike that in table 11, France ranks sixth in representation of women. This success is also attributable to the fact that elections to the European Parliament, unlike those to the French Parliament, are under a proportional representation scheme.

Table 12: Women in the European Parliament
2009 Election[123]

Country	Seats	Women	% Women
1. Finland	13	8	62%

120. University of Helsinki, Women in the European Union, Chapter 5.2; The Situation of Women in Politics, available at www.helsinki.fi/science/xantippa/wee/weetext/wee252.html. France did use a proportional representation system for the 1986 parliamentary system, and that election returned an all-time high of 24.7% women to parliament.

121. NPR, Women Around the World, above note 109 (Francoise Gaspard, leader of the French Parité Movement, speaking); Marlowe, above note 116.

122. NPR, Women Around the World, above note 109 (Jane Kramer, reporter for The New Yorker, speaking).

123. European Elections 4–7 June, 2009 European Parliament Elections Results 2009: Representation of Women, August 2009, available at http://www.womenlobby.org/SiteResources/data/MediaArchive/Newsflash/NF2009/Women% 20in% 20the% 20new% 20EP% 20July2009_EN.pdf.

Country	Seats	Women	% Women
2. Sweden	18	10	56%
3. Estonia	6	3	50.0%
4. Netherland	25	12	48%
5. Bulgaria	17	8	47%
5. Denmark	13	6	46%
6. France	72	33	44%
6. Austria	17	7	41%
6. Slovakia	13	5	38.0%
7. Latvia	8	3	38.0%
7. Germany	99	37	37%
7. Belgium	22	8	36%
7. Hungary	22	8	36.0%
7. Portugal	22	8	36%
8. Romania	33	12	36%
9. Spain	50	15	36%
10. United Kingdom	72	24	33.0%
11. Cyprus	6	2	33%
12. Greece	22	7	32.0%
13. Slovenia	7	2	29.0%
14. Lithuania	12	3	25%
15. Ireland	12	3	25%
16. Italy	72	18	25%
17. Poland	50	11	22%
18. Czech Republic	22	4	18%
19. Luxembourg	6	1	17%
20. Malta	5	0	0%
Total	736	261	35.5%

NOTES ON GLOBAL FEMINISM

1. Compare the definition of sex discrimination in CEDAW and the notion of sex discrimination in the constitutional cases described in Chapter 2. Would quotas for women in elections violate CEDAW? Would such quotas violate the United States Constitution?

2. What do you think of CEDAW's definition of sex discrimination? Would American women be better off with a similar definition in Title VII (applying to employment) or Title IX (applying to education) or the Constitu-

tion? What new challenges could be brought, under Title VII, Title IX, or the Constitution, were we to adopt the CEDAW definition?

3. Would any of the constitutional sex-discrimination cases you studied in Chapter 2 (see chart at the end of Chapter 2 for a quick review) come out differently under the CEDAW standard? Could a man allege sex discrimination under the CEDAW standard? Are there other possible differences? Which standard do you prefer? Why?

4. Although the United States routinely puts reservations on international treaties and conventions involving human rights, such as CEDAW, to ensure that America's law on human rights is not changed by treaty and cannot be overruled by any international tribunal, the United States has been willing to change American law and bind the United States to jurisdiction of an international tribunal in treaties dealing with free trade. See, e.g., Andrea Knox, The World Trade Organization at a Crossroads, World Trade, Oct. 1, 1999, at 34. What explains this difference?

5. The United States Constitution states that the president has the power to make treaties "with the Advice and Consent of the Senate." Do you think that there is a relationship between women's underrepresentation in the Senate (non-Hispanic white men are 80% of Senators; non-Hispanic white women 14%) and the failure of the United States to ratify CEDAW as well as the United Nations Convention on the Rights of the Child (which, among other things, bans executions of juvenile offenders and has been ratified by all countries except the United States and Somalia)? Why is the United States so unwilling to endorse treaties guaranteeing rights to women and children? Is it really, as the State Department insisted in proposing the enactment of CEDAW with reservations, declarations, and understandings ensuring that it would have no effect, that American law already protects women's rights? Or is it that those in power oppose stronger rights for women, even when such rights are common in other similar parts of the world?

6. Compare the percentages of women in the House and Senate of the United States Congress with the percentages of women in the parliaments of the European nations and the percentages of women in the European parliament. Are you surprised by the fact that the United States ranked 73rd worldwide in terms of women's representation in the national legislature as of 2010? Are you surprised by the high levels of women's representation in the European parliament, where the level is over twice that in the American Congress? What explains this difference?

7. Were you aware, before you took this course, of the use and success of electoral quotas for women in Europe and the broad support for gender mainstreaming by this means in the international feminist movement? Where did you hear about them? Has the mainstream media reported these developments?

8. Why do you think European women responded to the problem of women in elected office with pressure for quotas? Why were they successful? Why have women done so much better in Europe in terms of political equality? Why have American women failed to give the same level of attention to the need for political equality?

9. Do you agree with the Beijing Platform for Action that women's equal participation in governmental decision-making is a demand for simple justice, a demand for (real) democracy, and a necessary prerequisite for women's interests to be taken into account? Would most Americans agree? What do you see as the sticking points either for yourself or for Americans in general? Can you imagine a major American governmental institution conceding, as the European Commission did, that the underrepresentation of women in all levels of governmental decisionmaking "marks a fundamental democratic deficit" requiring immediate action on a national level? What explains these differences?

10. The Recommendation of the European Commission, described above, offers gender mainstreaming as a theoretical basis for the European and international feminist focus on political equality: In order to integrate women's needs, perspectives, interests, and concerns into all levels of governmental decisionmaking, we need to integrate women into governmental decisionmaking bodies in proportion to their numbers in the population. Do you agree or disagree with this analysis of the meaning of equality and how to achieve it? With which feminist theory discussed in Chapter 3 is this vision of equality most consistent?

11. What are the strongest arguments you can make for and against electoral quotas? Do quotas suggest that women are not qualified for public office? What are the qualifications for a good representative in a legislative body? Why might women be better representatives in some respects than men regardless of objective "qualifications"? What are the actual "qualifications" for high elective office in the United States today given how campaigns are conducted and their cost? What are the actual "qualifications" one would look for in an ideal representative, ignoring electability?

12. The Beijing Platform for Action paragraph 181, quoted above, clearly sees gender mainstreaming—equal participation by women in all levels of governmental decisionmaking—as a necessary precondition to equality. Why? What is the reasoning behind this view? What is the platform's vision of equality in this paragraph? Do you agree? Do you think it is possible for women to achieve equality prior to obtaining parity in governmental decisionmaking?

13. Would quotas facilitate the ability of women to combine politics and mothering? Would quotas help overcome women's reluctance to go after highly competitive positions? Are these arguments for quotas? Are the women elected under a quota requirement likely to be women who will *not* push for change because, for example, they are likely to be beholden to party bosses?

14. Are quotas undemocratic? Or do they enhance democracy?

E. A POLITICS OF EQUALITY

Are we are so used to women's underrepresentation in elective office that we do not see it as undermining the legitimacy of our democracy? If women were another historically disadvantaged and still subordinate majority group with similar levels of representation, would the legitimacy of the structure would be suspect? Christine Boyle, a Canadian scholar, poses this question in the form of a hypothetical:

> Imagine a country in which all or most of the women, but not the men, lived in one geographical area—for example, Ontario. One can then examine the laws applying to and the economic position of "Ontarians" from a neutral standpoint. It will be found that the position of Ontarians is not good in Canadian society. They have been systematically discriminated against throughout their history; for example, their property was taken from them without compensation, they had no rights to their children, enfranchisement was ridiculed and bitterly opposed, and they still rarely sit in Parliament or on the bench. They are subjected to assault and sexual abuse by non-Ontarians, and they largely work at menial tasks for which they are paid much less than non-Ontarians, or nothing. In addition, they are depicted ever more widely by various media as being less than human, as objects for the sexual gratification of non-Ontarians. One has only to attempt such an account to realize that there exist two fundamentally different groups in Canada (and, of course, elsewhere). It is submitted that an electoral system which does not reflect any confrontation of that fact is inadequate.[124]

Boyle is suggesting that we would "naturally" respond to such inequity by suggesting separate representation of Ontarians along geographic lines, i.e., that Ontarians would elect their own representatives to the legislature.

The situation of women, of course, is different from that of the hypothetical Ontarians in that women are not in certain geographic areas. The Canadian Advisory Council on the Status of Women argues that there is no good reason to so privilege geographically identifiable groups over other groups with interests that are not always identical. The Canadian Advisory Council points out that women's geographic dispersion

> does not mean * * * that the problem disappears or that we should give up on the task of finding a solution. One of the fundamental underlying assumptions in our constitution is * * * that "Geography is Destiny." This has many consequences. The intense focus on federal-provincial relations, and on territorial representation, are two examples. The federalism model recognizes geographic and some kinds of cultural diversity, but makes invisible other kinds of diversity such as gender.
>
> While women in Canada may have different views about many constitutional issues (and why not?), from a feminist perspective it is important to question the territorial (originally property-based) model that works so well to keep women out of politics.[125]

---

124. Christine Boyle, Home Rule for Women: Power-Sharing Between Men and Women, 7 Dalhousie L.J. 790, 796 (1983).

125. Canadian Advisory Council on the Status of Women, A Feminist Guide to the Canadian Constitution 56–57 (Lynn Smith & Eleanor Wachtel, eds. Aug. 1992).

One could, of course, make similar points about the United States.

Many feminists argue, even many committed to judicially enforced formal equality,[126] that we must primarily look to women for their own creation of equality within the legal system through political participation, rather than to the Supreme Court and the lower federal courts deciding constitutional sex equality cases. The European approach of "gender mainstreaming"—as it is called in the international community—helps ensure such participation. As an approach that focuses on using whatever means is necessary, including quotas, to ensure women's proportional share of governmental decisionmaking at all levels, it gives women themselves authority and allows women to determine how to integrate women's interests and needs into the public agenda, rather than relying on a Supreme Court imposing an abstract notion of formal equality.[127] This is a strategy *not* focused on men.[128] It recognizes both the conflict of interest between women and men, hence the need for women in elective office, and the fact that men are potential political allies.[129] It is consistent with feminist method, especially the emphasis on listening to women.[130] Moreover, the approach stresses not the universality of women's needs, which tends to be the focus in arguing to a court, but rather the need to form coalitions across race and class to address the varying needs of various women.[131]

We close with a discussion of a number of proposed electoral reforms that may facilitate the representation of women of all colors and other minorities in numbers proportional to their presence in the population. Five types of changes are discussed here: (1) campaign reform, particularly campaign finance reform; (2) adoption of policies designed to maximize voter turnout; (3) votes for children, to be exercised by a parent or legal guardian until the child reaches 18; (4) a shift from single-member winner-take-all districts to some form of proportional representation for all elections other than the United States Senate; and (5) proportional representation for the Senate combined with a quota of 50% women (requiring a constitutional amendment).

1. Campaign reform, including reform of campaign financing. Campaigns in the United States are fantastically expensive relative to their cost in other democracies, in part because of the importance of media

126. See, e.g., Ruth Bader Ginsburg & Barbara Flagg, Some Reflections on the Feminist Legal Thought of the 1970s, [1989] U. Chi. Legal F. 9, 18 (excerpt in Chapter 3).

127. A number of feminists have stressed the importance of seeing women as active agents, rather than passive victims. See, e.g., Angela P. Harris, Race and Essentialism in Feminist Legal Theory, 42 Stan. L. Rev. 581 (1990); Martha Mahoney, Whiteness and Women, In Practice and Theory: A Reply to Catharine A. MacKinnon, 5 Yale J. L. & Feminism 217 (1993).

128. See Sarah Hoagland, Lesbian Ethics 57–58 (1988).

129. See Harris, above note 127, at 612.

130. See Catharine A. MacKinnon, Consciousness Raising, in Toward a Feminist Theory of the State 83 (1989) (excerpt in Chapter 5).

131. See Harris, above note 127, at 612–14; Mari Matsuda, Standing Beside, My Sister, Facing the Enemy: Legal Theory Out of Coalition, in Where Is Your Body? 63 (1996) (excerpt in Chapter 7).

advertising and in part because they last so long. Compare, for example, campaigns in Great Britain, where there is a "long history of banning paid political advertising in the broadcast media" (though candidates and parties are allocated free broadcast time) and the formal period for national election campaigns is just over a month.[132] By the time a candidate wins in the United States, she is indebted to many special interests, regardless of what a majority of voters may want, and many points of view may be excluded due to the sheer incapacity to raise sufficient funds to compete.

In order to facilitate women's access to the political system do we need reform of campaigns themselves? What changes, if any, do you think would be most effective: requirements that campaigns be shorter, bans on advertisements in the broadcast media, free media time for candidates, public financing of campaigns, limits on monetary donations and the ability of political action committees to spend money on behalf of candidates?

2. *Maximizing voter turnout.* In the 2008 presidential election, 63% of those eligible voted[133]. In the 2004 presidential election, 64% of those eligible voted, a slight upturn from the 60% of voters who turned out for the 2000 presidential election.[134] Yet, other industrialized nations generate a larger voter turnout when compared to the United States (compare, for example, Belgium (2007) 91.08%, Austria (2008) 81.71%, Australia (2007) 95.17%, Germany (2005) 77.7%, Italy (2008) 80.54%).[135] Current participation rates are also low relative to earlier eras. Between 1840 and 1896, 78% of eligible American voters turned out to vote in presidential elections.[136] Do these non-participation rates suggest that our current political system is failing as a democracy in fundamental ways?

Although women now vote at higher rates than men, poor people (disproportionately women) and racial minorities (many of them women) are less likely than others to vote. Countries with higher voting rates usually have not only some system of proportional representation, so that all votes count and the poor are more likely to be able to vote for a candidate speaking to their interests, but also policies that foster voting. By contrast, the United States "is one of the few if not the only major democracy in the world that requires advance registration as a prerequi-

---

132. Gillian Peele. Governing the UK: British Politics in the 21st Century, 4th ed, Blackwell Publishing, 263 (2004).

133. American University Center for the Study of the American Electorate, 2008 Turnout Report: African Americans, Anger, Fear and Youth Propel Turnout of Highest Level since 1960 (December 17, 2008), available at http://www1.american.edu/ia/cdem/csae/pdfs/2008pdfoffinal edited.pdf.

134. U.S. Census Bureau, U.S. Voter Turnout Up in 2004, Census Bureau Reports (May 26, 2005).

135. International Institute for Democracy and Electoral Assistance (IDEA), Voter Turnout, available at http://www.idea.int/uid/fieldview.cfm?id=221.

136. Daniel Hays Lowenstein, Election Law: Cases and Materials 42 (1995).

site to voting without the government assuming responsibility for seeing to it that all eligible people are registered."[137]

What kinds of changes might increase voter turnout: eliminating the obligation to register in advance, making it easier to register near election day, holding elections less frequently (for example, a maximum of one election day every two years, with *all* local and national elections on the same date) and on a holiday or Sunday with paid time-off for voters who work on those days? Should voting be made an obligation of citizenship? Both Belgium and Australia take this approach: citizens are *required* to vote. Belgium and Australia are two of the three top countries in terms of voter turnout of twenty industrialized democracies, though enforcement is lax and penalties light.[138]

3. Votes for children. In the United States, single-member election districts are drawn so that each district has roughly the same number of people. And it is people, not eligible voters, who are counted almost universally in districting schemes in the United States. Districts with many children or others ineligible to vote have, therefore, the same level of representation but fewer residents who can vote than districts with few such residents. Thus, in a district with many children or other people ineligible to vote, a vote counts for more. But voters who do not live in households with children often have interests that conflict with those of children and their caretakers. For example, those without children at home may be less interested in adequate funding of public education than parents with children at home.

Jane Rutherford has argued that the basic problem with this scheme is vote dilution. The Supreme Court's one person, one vote rule (applicable in all elections except those to the Senate) is designed to guard against vote dilution, which would occur were a state able to give more weight to some citizens' views than to others. Yet without proxies for parents, "that is precisely what happens to parents."[139] In the average congressional district, parents and children are 66% of the people in the district (and are all counted for districting purposes, i.e., in allocating representatives per so many people in the population), but exercise only 54% percent of the votes.[140] People living in households without children comprise 34% of the population in the average congressional district but enjoy 46% of the votes. On a household basis, households without children have 140% "of the voting power of households with children."[141] And part of the voting power enjoyed by households without children is the result of living near households with children, though the interests of the households without children are likely to conflict with the needs of children.[142]

---

137. Lowenstein, above note 136, at 48–49.

138. Id. at 33 n.2, 53.

139. Jane Rutherford, One Child, One Vote: Proxies for Parents, 82 Minn. L. Rev. 1463, 1465, 1512 (1998).

140. Id. at 1466.

141. Id. at 1512.

142. Id. at 1466, 1512, 1512 n.211.

Rutherford points out that a household with two adults has the same amount of political weight—the same amount of representation—as a household with two adults and two children. In the first household, every member of the household has a vote. In the second household, half do not have votes. And the voters, if they are good parents, "will essentially split their votes ... so they represent their needs and the needs of their children." She argues that giving parents proxies to vote for children redresses this problem and evens out political weight on a per capita basis, the goal of the one person, one vote rule.[143]

Do current poverty rates indicate the need such an adjustment in political power? As Rutherford has pointed out, "fifty years ago it was the elderly who were poor."[144] Social Security and Medicare have eliminated most poverty among the elderly. Although these are expensive programs, they have survived because of the political power of the elderly. Today, it is disproportionately children (and their caretakers, particularly in single-mother families) who are poor. Children have no direct political power to use in pressing for effective governmental programs lowering their poverty rates. And their indirect power—through their parents—is diluted because it is folded into the parents' own vote. Yet, as discussed earlier in this chapter, children are a public good. Everyone benefits from having younger generations of taxpayers and workers, particularly as we age.

Are votes for children (to be exercised by their custodial caretakers) especially important for women because almost all mothers live with their children and must think about their needs and the needs of their children when they enter the voting booth? Would votes for children significantly change the political clout of one of the poorest identifiable groups in our society, single mothers with children.

Giving parents proxy votes for children is a novel idea and therefore seems strange. Is it constitutional? There is no constitutional provision banning such an electoral structure and no constitutional case definitively indicating that it would be impermissible. How do you think a court would analyze a challenge to such a law?[145]

4. *Proportional representation for bodies other than the United States Senate.* As noted earlier, winner-take-all systems with geographic districting *can* create effective democracies in countries with homogeneous populations.[146] Voters in this country have not been a homogeneous group for some time, and the results of using a system that works only for homogenous populations is clear from the data in Tables 6 through 9, above, showing the overwhelming overrepresentation of non-Hispanic white men in elective office, particularly at the highest levels. As Douglas Amy puts it in the opening line to his book on proportional representation, "[t]he

143. Id. at 1512. Sylvia Ann Hewlettt and Cornell West have also proposed proxy votes for children. Hewlett and West, The War Against Parents: What We Can Do For America's Beleaguered Moms and Dads 240–41 (1998).

144. Rutherford, above note 139, at 1465.

145. Id. at 1514–17.

146. Guinier, above note 118, at 256; Lijphart, above note 118, at 3–4.

American election system is unfair, outmoded, and undemocratic."[147] Yet few Americans "are even aware of these problems. * * * We assume that this system is the epitome of democracy and a model for the rest of the free world. But nothing could be further from the truth."[148]

Almost all younger democracies have some form of proportional representation. Even England—from which we inherited our voting structure based on the notion of representing geographic units[149]—is reconsidering its use of single-member winner-take-all districts. As noted earlier, there are many forms of proportional representation. And proportional representation schemes could be adopted without constitutional amendment for all elections other than those to the Senate.

Proportional and semiproportional representation schemes are generally believed to have a number of advantages:

1. Electoral systems based on proportional representation facilitate the representation of the entire population, particularly women of all colors and members of other minority groups.
2. Debates on policy issues can be substantively better when more options and interests are brought to the table.
3. Voters are more likely to vote when their vote counts and they have more options than when two parties are both trying to capture the middle.
4. Candidates are less likely to engage in negative campaigning and more likely to actually engage on issues, since they must maximize their own vote, not just defeat one specific opponent.
5. Because candidates can win election by expressing substantive views with which only a minority of voters agree, they are likely to talk about substantive issues rather than merely mouth platitudes while projecting the right image.[150]

The standard concern with proportional and semiproportional representation systems is fear of balkanization and instability, i.e., a fear that there will many small parties, that extremist parties will be therefore have a great deal of power as larger parties attempt to form coalition governments and, as a result, that governments will collapse too often on a parliamentary vote of no confidence.[151] But proportional representation schemes can be structured to avoid this problem. Moreover, since the United States is not a parliamentary system, government will not fall because of shifting coalitions during a president's term.

147. Amy, above note 117, at 1.

148. Id.

149. Lani Guinier, The Tyranny of the Majority: Fundamental Fairness in Representative Democracy 128 (1994).

150. For a more thorough discussion of these and other advantages of proportional representation, see Amy, above note 117, at 1–152; Guinier, above note 118, at 251–311.

151. See Amy, above note 117, at 157–60.

Indeed, including a proportional representation component in an electoral scheme may actually stabilize a democracy. To the extent proportional representation encourages voter turnout, it may contribute to stability: "democracies with lower voter turn-out levels have higher amounts of citizen turmoil and violence."[152] Hitler's rise to power has been attributed to the rapid political mobilization of a large group of new voters who had previously been disengaged.[153] Might proportional representation actually protect democracies from extremist takeovers by keeping more voters engaged in the political system?

In the 1990's, Cynthia McKinney, a former political science professor and a Democratic member of the U.S. House of Representatives, twice "introduced legislation to allow states to adopt proportional and semiproportional voting systems for congressional elections."[154] A proportional or semiproportional representation scheme could be designed for all legislative bodies at the state and federal level other than the United States Senate without constitutional modification. Would you favor a shift to such a system for legislative elections other than the Senate?

5. *Proportional representation for the Senate (requiring a constitutional amendment).* The Constitution requires two Senators, each with one vote, from each state. Currently, each Senator from each state is elected in a winner-take-all single-member-district election.

Without constitutional amendment, Senate elections could be reorganized to allow cumulative voting, though both Senators would be up for election at the same time. Each voter would have two votes and could cast one for each of two candidates or could cast both for a single candidate. Under such a scheme, each state would be a multi-member district of two with cumulative voting. Alternatively, the Constitution could be amended to provide for regional election of Senators with multi-member districts and cumulative voting (as opposed to the current constitutionally required form of representation: two Senators from each state).

A third, and more radical, option would require each state to send at least one woman to the Senate. Given the current constitutional standard for sex discrimination, this would violate the Equal Protection clause of the Fourteenth Amendment as interpreted by the Supreme Court and would therefore require a constitutional amendment. Mary Becker has proposed amending the Constitution with a new ERA:

> Section 1. Neither any state nor the federal government shall deprive any woman or man of life, liberty, or property, without due process of law; nor deny to any woman or man within its jurisdiction the equal protection of the laws.
>
> Section 2. Each state shall have at least one senator who is a woman. Congress shall, through appropriate legislation, establish laws

---

152. Guinier, above note 118, at 251.

153. Id. at 269.

154. Id. at 261.

to enforce this provision and may determine that it become effective only upon the retirement of male incumbents in the Senate.

Section 3. Congress shall have the ultimate power to enforce this Amendment and to determine its scope and meaning.[155]

This amendment would both (1) require that one Senator from each state be a woman, and (2) give ultimate power to determine the meaning of sex equality to the United States Congress (with 50% women in its upper chamber) rather than to the United States Supreme Court.

Any of these three changes in the method of electing Senators would be likely to increase the representation of currently underrepresented groups in the Senate as well as to broaden Senators' perspectives and ideas on substantive and policy issues. Would you favor such changes to Senate elections? What are the downsides to such changes?

NOTES ON EQUALITY IN POLITICS

1. The immediate problem is that even raising electoral reform for discussion in any popular forum seems impossible. Recall the furor over Lani Guinier's nomination early in the Clinton administration to head the Civil Rights Division of the Justice Department, a position requiring Senate confirmation. Guinier had advocated proportional representation as a remedy for some violations of the Voting Rights Act and had suggested that minorities might not always be treated fairly by the majority. For suggesting that American democracy might be flawed and that proportional or semiproportional representation—methods used in most of the world's democracies—might better integrate the views of those traditionally underrepresented, the Wall Street Journal castigated her as a "Quota Queen" and "out of the mainstream." Newsweek titled a story "Crowning a Quota Queen." Others used "Loony Lani," the "Czarina of Czeparatism," the "Princess of Proportionality," and "Real America's Madwoman." In the end, as a result of the media frenzy (and the administration's failure to launch any defense), Guinier's name was withdrawn by the President. See Guinier, Lift Every Voice: Turning A Civil Rights Setback into A New Vision of Social Justice 36–56. (1998). Given this background, the initial problem with moving to a proportional or semiproportional representation system like those in place in most of the world is the difficulty of even raising the issue in the United States. Guinier did not in fact advocate quotas—only proportional representation. Do you think Americans have become more receptive to proportional representation * * * in the years since Guinier's nomination? What would the reaction be to a proposal for quotas for women along the lines of Parité in France?

2. In addition to the Voting Rights Act of 1965 (which has sometimes been interpreted by the Supreme Court as requiring racial balance as a remedy for violations), quotas do exist today in various forms in our governmental system and in the party structure. For example, the Federal Election Commission has six members, and no more than three are to be "affiliated

155. Mary Becker, The Sixties Shift to Formal Equality and the Courts: An Argument for Pragmatism and Politics, 40 Wm. & Mary L. Rev. 209, 264 (1998).

with the same political party." 2 U.S.C.A. § 437c(a)(1). The Securities and Exchange Commission (15 U.S.C.A. § 78d(a)), the Federal Trade Commission (15 U.S.C.A. § 41), and the Commodity Futures Trading Commission (7 U.S.C.A. § 4a(a)(1)) each consist of five members, no more than three to be "members of the same political party." Similar rules apply to the Board of Directors of the Federal Deposit Insurance Corporation (12 U.S.C.A. § 1812(a)(2)) and the Federal Housing Finance Board (12 U.S.C.A. § 1422a(b)(2)). Both major parties have National Committees consisting of one man and one woman from each state.

Several states have enacted gender balance legislation, providing that boards, commissions, committees, and councils of all kinds appointed by elected officials be gender balanced. Two states have enacted such legislation as binding law: North Dakota and Iowa. Iowa Code Ann. § 69.16A; N.D. Cent. Code § 54–06–19. Montana has a nonbinding gender balance resolution. Mont. Code Ann. § 2–15–108. Iowa has mandatory quotas for *elected* Judicial Nominating Commissioners, one man and one woman to be elected from each district. Iowa Code Ann. § 373.2.

How would the case for quotas for women in elective office be similar to, and different from, the case for quotas in these settings? Are these quotas constitutional? Why or why not? See Bachur v. Democratic National Party, 836 F.2d 837 (4th Cir. 1987) (holding constitutional Maryland rules implementing policies of the national party requiring voters to cast an equal number of votes for women and men as delegates to the Democratic convention). Would quotas for women be constitutional in light of Congress's power under the Nineteenth Amendment to enforce women's right to vote "by appropriate legislation"? U.S. Const. Amend. XIX.

If you think that such quotas would be unconstitutional (recall that the supreme courts of Italy and Portugal struck gender quotas similar to France's as unconstitutional), is this another example of the conservative nature of binding judicial review? Constitutional law aside, what do you see as the major problems with quotas as a means of ensuring that women in elected office are proportional to the numbers of women in the population?

3. Should women begin by pressing for internal party quotas, such as the quota now in place in both parties with respect to membership on National Committees? European women in a number of countries, as noted above, have been quite successful in increasing levels of representation as a result of internal party quotas for "winnable" or "safe" seats. Supporters of internal party quotas could publish lists of men in elected office who refused to support the internal quota, and women and other supporters of internal quotas could then vote against them at the next election. (Recall that this tactic was used in France with respect to elected officials' support of Parité, the proposed law requiring that 50% of those elected be women). Would these tactics work here? Assume, as may well be true, that women will not achieve equality in any arena until they have first achieved political equality. What strategies would you adopt to achieve political equality in the United States?

4. Would you support Becker's proposed ERA? What do you like about it? What do you dislike about it?

5. How important would various feminist theorists described in Chapter 3 consider women's presence in elective office, and what means would they see as appropriate to this end? How important do you consider the analysis of the political representation issue in your assessment of the overall strengths and weaknesses of these various feminist approaches? Does each feminist approach have strengths and weaknesses? What are they? Which has influenced most the way you look at the world or approach legal issues? Which do you expect to use in the future in thinking about how to resolve specific legal issues?

6. Are women focusing on political power just when real power is shifting from governments to the huge multinational corporations? Are men in Europe allowing women into political power just when—as is often the case—power is shifting elsewhere? As one commentator on Parité recently observed, "[R]eal power is no longer political. It's financial." Liane Hansen (anchor), Women From Around the World Look For Ways to Increase Their Numbers in Elected Positions and Leadership Roles, National Public Radio, Weekend Edition, June 11, 2000 (Jane Kramer, reporter for The New Yorker, speaking). As of 2005, women held 16.4% of corporate officer positions in Fortune 500 companies, 5.2% of top-earning corporate officer positions in Fortune 500 companies, and only eight Fortune 500 CEO positions, available at http://www.catalyst.org/file/207/2005% 20cote.pdf. How would you begin thinking about ensuring that women exercise their fair share of economic decision making?

INDEX

References are to Pages

References are to Pages

References are to Pages

References are to Pages

References are to Pages

References are to Pages

References are to Pages

References are to Pages

References are to Pages

†